Yearbook
of Tourism Statistics

Data 2008–2012

2014 Edition

World Tourism Organization (UNWTO)
Calle Capitán Haya 42 · 28020 Madrid · Spain

Yearbook of Tourism Statistics, Data 2008 – 2012, 2014 Edition
ISBN (printed version):   978-92-844-1590-8
ISBN (electronic version): 978-92-844-1591-5

Published by the World Tourism Organization (UNWTO), Madrid, Spain.
First printing: 2014
All rights reserved.

Printed in Spain.

The designations employed and the presentation of material in this publication do not imply the expression of any opinions whatsoever on the part of the Secretariat of the World Tourism Organization concerning the legal status of any country, territory, city or area, or of its authorities or concerning the delimitation of its frontiers or boundaries.

World Tourism Organization (UNWTO)   Tel.: (+34) 915 678 100
Calle Capitán Haya, 42   Fax: (+34) 915 713 733
28020 Madrid   Website: www.unwto.org
Spain   E-mail: omt@unwto.org

Foreword

Decision making requires reliable information to guide adequate policies and development strategies. To support countries monitor and better understand the impact and evolution of tourism across their economies, the World Tourism Organization (UNWTO) systematically gathers tourism statistics from countries and territories around the world into a vast database that, each year, gives way to two key statistical publications: the *Compendium of Tourism Statistics* and the *Yearbook of Tourism Statistics.* Together, these two publications constitute the most comprehensive statistical information available on the tourism sector.

The UNWTO *Compendium of Tourism Statistics* provides data and indicators on inbound, outbound and domestic tourism, as well as on the number and types of tourism industries, the number of employees by tourism industries, and macroeconomic indicators related to international tourism. This data is complemented by the *Yearbook of Tourism Statistics* which focuses specifically on inbound tourism related data (total arrivals and overnight stays), broken down by country of origin.

The statistics presented in the 2014 Editions of the *Compendium* and the *Yearbook* give an insight into tourism's multiple facets and its ever growing importance and are an indispensible reference guide for all tourism stakeholders. Above all, they provide decision makers with the evidence for more informed policy-making and, as a result, more sustainable tourism development.

Taleb Rifai
UNWTO Secretary-General

Avant-propos

La prise de décision doit pouvoir s'appuyer sur des informations fiables permettant de définir des politiques et des stratégies de développement adéquates. Pour aider les pays à assurer le suivi de l'impact et de l'évolution du tourisme dans leurs économies et à en avoir une meilleure compréhension, l'Organisation mondiale du tourisme (OMT) procède à une collecte systématique de statistiques du tourisme auprès de pays et de territoires du monde entier. Ces statistiques sont rassemblées dans une vaste base de données qui permet, chaque année, de faire paraître deux publications statistiques clés : le *Compendium des statistiques du tourisme* et l'*Annuaire des statistiques du tourisme.* À elles deux, ces publications offrent les informations statistiques les plus complètes sur le secteur touristique.

Le *Compendium des statistiques du tourisme* préparé par l'OMT contient des données et des indicateurs sur le tourisme récepteur, émetteur et interne, sur le nombre et les types d'industries touristiques et le nombre de salariés par industrie touristique, ainsi que des indicateurs macroéconomiques liés au tourisme international. Ces données sont complétées par l'*Annuaire des statistiques du tourisme* qui se concentre spécifiquement sur les données liées au tourisme récepteur (nombre total d'arrivées et de nuitées), avec une ventilation par pays d'origine.

Les statistiques présentées dans les éditions 2014 du *Compendium* et de l'*Annuaire* apportent un éclairage sur les multiples facettes du tourisme et sur son importance croissante. Elles constituent un guide de référence incontournable pour toutes les parties prenantes du secteur touristique. Et par-dessus tout, elles fournissent aux décideurs les éléments d'appréciation dont ils ont besoin pour formuler des politiques en connaissance de cause et, partant, assurer un développement plus durable du tourisme.

Taleb Rifai
Secrétaire général de l'OMT

Prólogo

La adopción de decisiones requiere información fiable que permita orientar adecuadamente las políticas y las estrategias de desarrollo. Con el fin de ayudar a los países a supervisar y entender mejor la incidencia y la evolución del turismo en su economía, la Organización Mundial del Turismo (OMT) compila sistemáticamente estadísticas de turismo de países y territorios de todo el mundo en una extensa base de datos que cada año da lugar a dos publicaciones estadísticas clave: el *Compendio de estadísticas de turismo* y el *Anuario de estadísticas de turismo.* Juntas, estas dos publicaciones constituyen la más completa información estadística disponible sobre el sector turístico.

El *Compendio de estadísticas de turismo* de la OMT proporciona datos e indicadores sobre turismo receptor, emisor e interno, sobre el número y los tipos de industrias turísticas, sobre el número de asalariados por industria turística y sobre aspectos macroeconómicos relacionados con el turismo internacional. Estos datos se complementan con el *Anuario de estadísticas de turismo* que se centra específicamente en los datos relacionados con el turismo receptor (totales de llegadas y de pernoctaciones) desglosados por país de origen.

Las estadísticas presentadas en las ediciones de 2014 del *Compendio* y del *Anuario* permiten explorar las múltiples facetas del turismo y su creciente importancia y son una guía de referencia indispensable para todos los agentes del turismo. Sobre todo, proporcionan datos fehacientes a los responsables públicos para que sus políticas tengan mayor fundamento y, como resultado, promuevan el desarrollo de un turismo más sostenible.

Taleb Rifai
Secretario General de la OMT

TABLE OF CONTENTS

Pages

FOREWORD / AVANT-PROPOS /
   PRÓLOGO iii

INTRODUCTION / INTRODUCCIÓN xiii

COUNTRY TABLES 1

Notes to tables
English.. 833
French 847
Spanish... 861
Data sources 875

COUNTRY TABLES BY ALPHABETICAL ORDER

Albania/Albanie... 3
Algeria/Algérie/Argelia 5
American Samoa/Samoa américaines/Samoa
   Americana 7
Andorra/Andorre 9
Angola 10
Anguilla/Anguila 14
Antigua and Barbuda/Antigua-et-Barbuda/
   Antigua y Barbuda 16
Argentina/Argentine..................................... 18
Armenia/Arménie 19
Aruba 22
Australia/Australie....................................... 26
Austria/Autriche 31
Azerbaijan/Azerbaïdjan/Azerbaiyán 39

Bahamas 45
Bahrain/Bahreïn/Bahrein 55
Barbados/Barbade....................................... 59
Belarus/Bélarus/Belarús 63
Belgium/Belgique/Bélgica.............................. 66
Belize/Belice 82
Benin/Bénin 84
Bermuda/Bermudes...................................... 87
Bhutan/Bhoutan/Bhután 88
Bolivia/Bolivie 94
Bosnia and Herzegovina/Bosnie-Herzégovine/
   Bosnia y Herzegovina................................ 97
Brazil/Brésil/Brasil...................................... 101
British Virgin Islands/Îles Vierges
   Britanniques/Islas Vírgenes Británicas 103
Brunei Darussalam/Brunéi Darussalam 105
Bulgaria/Bulgarie 107
Burkina Faso 115
Burundi 117

Cambodia/Cambodge/Camboya 118
Canada/Canadá 121
Cape Verde/Cap-Vert/Cabo Verde.................. 130
Cayman Islands/Îles Caïmanes/Islas Caimán . 132
Central African Republic/République
   centrafricaine/República Centroafricana 136
Chad/Tchad 138
Chile/Chili 141

China/Chine 145
Colombia/Colombie... 149
Comoros/Comores/Comoras 154
Congo... 155
Cook Islands/Îles Cook/Islas Cook................... 162
Costa Rica... 163
Croatia/Croatie/Croacia................................... 165
Cuba... 171
Curaçao.. 175
Cyprus/Chypre/Chipre..................................... 178
Czech Republic/République tchèque/
   República Checa... 184

Democratic Republic of the Congo/
   République démocratique du Congo/
   República Democrática del Congo................. 192
Denmark/Danemark/Dinamarca....................... 194
Dominica/Dominique 198
Dominican Republic/République
   dominicaine/República Dominicana 200

Ecuador/Équateur 202
Egypt/Égypte/Egipto....................................... 207
El Salvador.. 215
Eritrea/Érythrée 221
Estonia/Estonie 223
Ethiopia/Éthiopie/Etiopía 231

Fiji/Fidji 233
Finland/Finlande/Finlandia 235
France/Francia 252
French Polynesia/Polynésie française/
   Polinesia Francesa...................................... 258

Gambia/Gambie 266
Georgia/Géorgie... 267
Germany/Allemagne/Alemania 274
Greece/Grèce/Grecia...................................... 282
Grenada/Grenade/Granada 292
Guadeloupe/Guadalupe 297
Guam 298
Guatemala... 299
Guyana/Guyane 301

Haiti/Haïti/Haití 302
Honduras... 303
Hong Kong, China/Hong-Kong (Chine)/
   Hong Kong (China) 306
Hungary/Hongrie/Hungría 313

Iceland/Islande/Islandia.................................. 319
India/Inde 324
Indonesia/Indonésie 329
Iran, Islamic Republic of/Iran (République
   islamique d')/Irán (República Islámica del)..... 335
Iraq 338
Ireland/Irlande/Irlanda 339
Israel/Israël... 341
Italy/Italie/Italia 353

TABLE OF CONTENTS

Pages
Pages

Jamaica/Jamaïque 367
Japan/Japon/Japón 370
Jordan/Jordanie/Jordania 372

Kazakhstan/Kazajstán 378
Kenya 381
Kiribati... 383
Korea, Republic of/Corée (République de)/
   Corea (República de) 384
Kuwait/Koweït... 389
Kyrgyzstan/Kirghizistan/Kirguistán 394

Lao People's Democratic Republic/
   République démocratique populaire lao/
   República Democrática Popular Lao 396
Latvia/Lettonie/Letonia 398
Lebanon/Liban/Líbano.............................. 407
Lesotho... 411
Liechtenstein 412
Lithuania/Lituanie/Lituania.......................... 420
Luxembourg/Luxemburgo.......................... 428

Macao, China/Macao (Chine)/Macao (China). 436
Madagascar.. 444
Malawi 446
Malaysia/Malaisie/Malasia.......................... 448
Maldives/Maldivas 453
Mali/Malí 457
Malta/Malte.. 460
Marshall Islands/Îles Marshall/Islas Marshall .. 463
Martinique/Martinica 466
Mauritius/Maurice/Mauricio.......................... 471
Mexico/Mexique/México 477
Monaco/Mónaco 479
Mongolia/Mongolie 481
Montenegro/Monténégro 489
Montserrat 497
Morocco/Maroc/Marruecos......................... 499
Mozambique 505
Myanmar... 506

Namibia/Namibie 510
Nepal/Népal... 512
Netherlands/Pays-Bas/Países Bajos.............. 518
New Caledonia/Nouvelle-Calédonie/
   Nueva Caledonia 524
New Zealand/Nouvelle-Zélande/
   Nueva Zelandia 528
Nicaragua 533
Niger/Níger 537
Nigeria/Nigéria.. 538
Niue/Nioué... 542
Northern Mariana Islands/Îles Mariannes
   septentrionales/Islas Marianas
   Septentrionales..................................... 543
Norway/Norvège/Noruega 544

Oman/Omán... 549

Pakistan/Pakistán.................................... 553
Palau/Palaos 557
Palestine/Palestina.................................. 558
Panama/Panamá 560
Papua New Guinea/Papouasie-Nouvelle-
   Guinée/Papua Nueva Guinea 565
Paraguay... 566
Peru/Pérou/Perú 570
Philippines/Filipinas.................................. 574
Poland/Pologne/Polonia 578
Portugal... 600
Puerto Rico/Porto Rico.............................. 604

Qatar 607

Republic of Moldova/République de Moldova/
   República de Moldova............................... 609
Reunion/Réunion/Reunión 616
Romania/Roumanie/Rumania 617
Russian Federation/Fédération de Russie/
   Federación de Rusia 629
Rwanda 634

Saint Kitts and Nevis/Saint-Kitts-et-Nevis/
   Saint Kitts y Nevis 637
Saint Lucia/Sainte-Lucie/Santa Lucía 638
Saint Vincent and the Grenadines/
   Saint-Vincent-et-les Grenadines/
   San Vicente y las Granadinas...................... 640
Samoa.. 642
San Marino/Saint-Marin 643
Sao Tome and Principe/Sao Tomé-et-
   Principe/Santo Tomé y Príncipe................... 646
Saudi Arabia/Arabie saoudite/Arabia Saudita .. 648
Senegal/Sénégal...................................... 652
Serbia/Serbie 654
Seychelles 658
Sierra Leone/Sierra Leona 661
Singapore/Singapour/Singapur 666
Sint Maarten/Saint-Martin/San Martín............. 670
Slovakia/Slovaquie/Eslovaquia 671
Slovenia/Slovénie/Eslovenia 675
Solomon Islands/Îles Salomon/
   Islas Salomón 683
South Africa/Afrique du Sud/Sudáfrica............ 684
Spain/Espagne/España.............................. 694
Sri Lanka 703
Sudan/Soudan/Sudán 709
Suriname 710
Swaziland/Swazilandia............................... 711
Sweden/Suède/Suecia 714
Switzerland/Suisse/Suiza 721
Syrian Arab Republic/République arabe
   syrienne/República Arabe Siria 725

Taiwan, Province of China/Taiwan (Province
   de Chine)/Taiwán (Provincia de China) 735
Tajikistan/Tadjikistan/Tayikistán...................... 741
Thailand/Thaïlande/Tailandia........................ 743

Yearbook of Tourism Statistics, Data 2008 – 2012, 2014 Edition

TABLE OF CONTENTS

Pages | Pages

The former Yugoslav Republic of Macedonia/
Ex-République yougoslave de Macédoine/
Ex República Yugoslava de Macedonia 752
Timor-Leste 760
Togo 761
Tonga 763
Trinidad and Tobago/Trinité-et-Tobago/
Trinidad y Tabago..................................... 764
Tunisia/Tunisie/Túnez 769
Turkey/Turquie/Turquía 775
Turks and Caicos Islands/Îles Turques et
Caïques/Islas Turcas y Caicos 793
Tuvalu... 794

Uganda/Ouganda 795
Ukraine/Ucrania.. 797
United Kingdom/Royaume-Uni/Reino Unido ... 802
United Republic of Tanzania/République-
Unie de Tanzanie/República Unida
de Tanzanía.. 808
United States of America/États-Unis
d'Amérique/Estados Unidos de América 812
United States Virgin Islands/Îles Vierges
américaines/Islas Vírgenes Americanas 817
Uruguay 819
Uzbekistan/Ouzbékistan/Uzbekistán 820

Vanuatu 821
Venezuela.. 822
Viet Nam... 824

Yemen/Yémen 825

Zambia/Zambie.. 829
Zimbabwe 830

COUNTRY TABLES BY GEOGRAPHICAL ORDER

AFRICA – AFRIQUE – ÁFRICA

East Africa – Afrique orientale – África
Oriental
Burundi 117
Comoros 154
Djibouti... n.a.
Eritrea.. 221
Ethiopia.. 231
Kenya 381
Madagascar... 444
Malawi 446
Mauritius... 471
Mozambique 505
Reunion 616
Rwanda 634
Seychelles 658
Somalia... n.a.
Uganda 795
United Republic of Tanzania 808

Zambia 829
Zimbabwe.. 830

Central Africa – Afrique centrale –
África Central
Angola 10
Cameroon .... n.a.
Central African Republic 136
Chad.. 138
Congo.. 155
Democratic Republic of the Congo 192
Equatorial Guinea .... n.a.
Gabon .... n.a.
Sao Tome and Principe................................. 646

North Africa – Afrique du Nord –
África del Norte
Algeria 5
Morocco 499
South Sudan .... n.a.
Sudan 709
Tunisia 769

Southern Africa – Afrique australe –
África Austral
Botswana .... n.a.
Lesotho 411
Namibia 510
South Africa... 684
Swaziland.. 711

West Africa – Afrique occidentale –
África Occidental
Benin 84
Burkina Faso 115
Cape Verde... 130
Côte d'Ivoire .... n.a.
Gambia... 266
Ghana .... n.a.
Guinea.. n.a.
Guinea-Bissau.. n.a.
Liberia .... n.a.
Mali 457
Mauritania .... n.a.
Niger.. 537
Nigeria 538
Saint Helena.. n.a.
Senegal 652
Sierra Leone.. 661
Togo 761

AMERICAS – AMÉRIQUES – AMÉRICAS

Caribbean – Caraïbes – El Caribe
Anguilla 14
Antigua and Barbuda 16
Aruba... 22
Bahamas... 45
Barbados... 59

Yearbook of Tourism Statistics, Data 2008 – 2012, 2014 Edition

TABLE OF CONTENTS

Pages   Pages

	Pages
Bermuda	87
British Virgin Islands	103
Cayman Islands	132
Cuba	171
Curaçao	175
Dominica	198
Dominican Republic	200
Grenada	292
Guadeloupe	297
Haiti	302
Jamaica	367
Martinique	466
Montserrat	497
Puerto Rico	604
Saint Kitts and Nevis	637
Saint Lucia	638
Saint Vincent and the Grenadines	640
Sint Maarten	670
Trinidad and Tobago	764
Turks and Caicos Islands	793
United States Virgin Islands	817

Central America – Amérique centrale – América Central

	Pages
Belize	82
Costa Rica	163
El Salvador	215
Guatemala	299
Honduras	303
Nicaragua	533
Panama	560

North America – Amérique du nord – América del Norte

	Pages
Canada	121
Greenland	n.a.
Mexico	477
Saint Pierre and Miquelon	n.a.
United States of America	812

South America – Amérique du Sud – América del Sur

	Pages
Argentina	18
Bolivia	94
Brazil	101
Chile	141
Colombia	149
Ecuador	202
Falkland Islands	n.a.
French Guiana	n.a.
Guyana	301
Paraguay	566
Peru	570
Suriname	710
Uruguay	819
Venezuela	822

EAST ASIA AND THE PACIFIC – ASIE DE L'EST ET LE PACIFIQUE – ASIA ORIENTAL Y EL PACÍFICO

North-East Asia – Asie du Nord-Est – Asia del Nordeste

	Pages
China	145
Hong Kong, China	306
Japan	370
Korea, Democratic People's Republic of	n.a.
Korea, Republic of	384
Macao, China	436
Mongolia	481
Taiwan, Province of China	735

South-East Asia – Asie du Sud-Est – Asia del Sudeste

	Pages
Brunei Darussalam	105
Cambodia	118
Indonesia	329
Lao People's Democratic Republic	396
Malaysia	448
Myanmar	506
Philippines	574
Singapore	666
Thailand	743
Timor-Leste	760
Viet Nam	824

Australasia – Australasie

	Pages
Australia	26
New Zealand	528

Melanesia – Mélanésie

	Pages
Fiji	233
New Caledonia	524
Papua New Guinea	565
Solomon Islands	683
Vanuatu	821

Micronesia – Micronésie

	Pages
Guam	298
Kiribati	383
Marshall Islands	463
Micronesia, Federated States of	n.a.
Nauru	n.a.
Northern Mariana Islands	543
Palau	557

Polynesia – Polynésie – Polinesia

	Pages
American Samoa	7
Cook Islands	162
French Polynesia	258
Niue	542
Pitcairn	n.a.
Samoa	642
Tokelau	n.a.
Tonga	763
Tuvalu	794
Wallis and Futuna Islands	n.a.

TABLE OF CONTENTS

Pages

Pages

**SOUTH ASIA – ASIE DU SUD –
ASIA MERIDIONAL**

Afghanistan .... n.a.
Bangladesh .... n.a.
Bhutan 88
India 324
Iran, Islamic Republic of 335
Maldives 453
Nepal 512
Pakistan 553
Sri Lanka 703

EUROPE – EUROPA

**Central/Eastern Europe –
Europe Centrale/orientale –
Europa Central/Oriental**

Armenia 19
Azerbaijan 39
Belarus 63
Bulgaria 107
Czech Republic 184
Estonia 223
Georgia 267
Hungary 313
Kazakhstan 378
Kyrgyzstan 394
Latvia 398
Lithuania 420
Poland 578
Republic of Moldova 609
Romania 617
Russian Federation 629
Slovakia 671
Tajikistan 741
Turkmenistan .... n.a.
Ukraine 797
Uzbekistan 820

**Northern Europe – Europe du Nord –
Europa del Norte**

Denmark 194
Finland 235
Iceland 319
Ireland 339
Norway 544
Sweden 714
United Kingdom 802

**Southern Europe – Europe du Sud –
Europa meridional**

Albania 3
Andorra 9
Bosnia and Herzegovina 97
Croatia 165
Greece 282

Holy See .... n.a.
Italy 353
Malta 460
Montenegro 489
Portugal 600
San Marino 643
Serbia 654
Slovenia 675
Spain 694
The Former Yugoslav Republic of Macedonia . 752

**Western Europe – Europe occidentale –
Europa occidental**

Austria 31
Belgium 66
France 252
Germany 274
Liechtenstein 412
Luxembourg 428
Monaco 479
Netherlands 518
Switzerland 721

**East Mediterranean Europe – Europe
méditerranéenne orientale –
Europa Mediterránea Oriental**

Cyprus 178
Israel 341
Turkey 775

**MIDDLE EAST – MOYEN-ORIENT –
ORIENTE MEDIO**

Bahrain 55
Egypt 207
Iraq 338
Jordan 372
Kuwait 389
Lebanon 407
Libya .... n.a.
Oman 549
Palestine 558
Qatar 607
Saudi Arabia 648
Syrian Arab Republic 725
United Arab Emirates .... n.a.
Yemen 825

n.a. Not available

INTRODUCTION

The *Yearbook of Tourism Statistics 2014 Edition* presents inbound tourism data for 197 countries and territories, broken down by country of origin. It is the 66th edition in a series initiated in 1947. It constitutes, together with the *Compendium of Tourism Statistics*, the World Tourism Organization's (UNWTO) main dataset and publications on annual tourism statistics, both under the responsibility of the Statistics and Tourism Satellite Account Programme.

The *Yearbook* contains data on total arrivals and overnight stays of international inbound tourism, broken down by country of origin for both arrivals and overnight stays.

> **Arrivals**

    A.   Border statistics
- Table 1.   Arrivals of non-resident tourists at national borders
- Table 2.   Arrivals of non-resident visitors at national borders

    B.   Statistics on accommodation establishments
- Table 3.   Arrivals of non-resident tourists in hotels and similar establishments
- Table 4.   Arrivals of non-resident tourists in all types of accommodation establishments.

When a person visits the same country several times a year, each visit is counted as one arrival. If a person visits several countries during the course of a single trip, his/her arrival in each country is also recorded separately. Consequently, *arrivals* are not necessarily equal to the number of persons travelling, as one person can generate several arrivals.

Arrivals data correspond to international visitors to the economic territory of the country of reference and include both tourists and same-day, non-resident visitors.

Data may be obtained from different sources: border statistics derived from administrative records (police, immigration, traffic counts, and other types of controls), border surveys and registrations at accommodation establishments.

> **Overnight stays**

- Table 5.   Overnight stays of non-resident tourists in hotels and similar establishments
- Table 6.   Overnight stays of non-resident tourists in all types of accommodation establishments.

Overnight stays refers to the number of nights spent by non-resident tourists in accommodation establishments (*guests*). If one person travels to a country and spends five nights there, that makes five tourist overnight stays (or person-nights).

In the 2014 hardcover edition of the *Yearbook*, the titles of the tables, names of countries, regions and sub-regions as well as the classification included in the tables are provided in English only, with notes in English, French and Spanish. Countries are classified according to the English alphabetical order. Data published originates from official sources and has undergone various checks by UNWTO's Statistics and Tourism Satellite Account Programme, which consults the reporting entity in the event that discrepancies are detected.

The 2014 Edition of the *Yearbook* reflects official data as entered in the UNWTO database as of 9 December 2013. Any corrections or changes in the tables received after this date will be included in the next edition of the *Yearbook*. Due to the rounding in the partial figures, the totals shown in the different tables of the *Yearbook* may not coincide with the totals shown in the basic indicators of the *Compendium of Tourism Statistics*.

UNWTO wishes to express its gratitude to the national tourism administrations and national statistical offices for their valuable support, recognizing especially the crucial role of all contributing countries and territories for their continued commitment to the development and improvement of tourism statistics.

Madrid, January 2014

INTRODUCTION

L'édition 2014 de l'*Annuaire des statistiques du tourisme* présente des données sur le tourisme récepteur de 197 pays et territoires, ventilées par pays d'origine. C'est la 66ème édition d'une série lancée en 1947. L'Annuaire et le *Compendium des statistiques du tourisme* constituent à eux deux les principales réalisations de l'Organisation mondiale du tourisme (OMT) en termes de bases de données et de publications sur les statistiques annuelles du tourisme. Tous deux sont préparés sous la direction du programme Statistiques et compte satellite du tourisme.

L'*Annuaire* contient des données sur le nombre total d'arrivées et de nuitées du tourisme récepteur international, ventilées par pays d'origine pour les arrivées comme pour les nuitées.

> **Arrivées**

    A.   Statistiques aux frontières
- Tableau 1. Arrivées de touristes non résidents aux frontières nationales
- Tableau 2. Arrivées de visiteurs non résidents aux frontières nationales

    B.   Statistiques sur les établissements d'hébergement
- Tableau 3. Nuitées de touristes non résidents dans les hôtels et établissements assimilés
- Tableau 4. Nuitées de touristes non résidents dans tous les types d'établissements d'hébergement.

Lorsqu'une personne visite le même pays plusieurs fois dans l'année, chacune de ses visites est comptée séparément comme une arrivée. Si une personne visite plusieurs pays au cours d'un seul et même voyage, son arrivée dans chaque pays est elle aussi enregistrée séparément. Par conséquent, le nombre d'*arrivées* n'est pas forcément égal au nombre de personnes qui voyagent, étant donné qu'une personne peut donner lieu à plusieurs arrivées.

Les données des arrivées correspondent aux visiteurs internationaux sur le territoire économique du pays dont il s'agit, visiteurs qui comprennent à la fois les touristes et les visiteurs de la journée (excursionnistes) non résidents.

Ces données peuvent être obtenues de différentes sources : statistiques aux frontières tirées des registres administratifs (police, immigration, comptages de véhicules et autres types de contrôle), enquêtes aux frontières et registres des établissements d'hébergement.

> **Nuitées**

- Tableau 5.   Nuitées de touristes non résidents dans les hôtels et établissements assimilés
- Tableau 6.   Nuitées de touristes non résidents dans tous les types d'établissements d'hébergement.

Les *nuitées* correspondent au nombre de nuits que les touristes non résidents ont passées dans les établissements d'hébergement (en qualité de *clients*). Si une personne se rend dans un pays et y passe cinq nuits, on enregistre cinq nuitées de touriste (ou nuits-personne).

Dans l'édition 2014 reliée de l'*Annuaire*, les titres des tableaux, les noms des pays, des régions et des sous-régions ainsi que la classification incluse dans les tableaux apparaissent uniquement en anglais, tandis que les notes sont en anglais, espagnol et français. Les pays sont classés selon l'ordre alphabétique anglais. Les données publiées proviennent de sources officielles et ont fait l'objet de différentes vérifications de la part du programme de l'OMT Statistiques et compte satellite du tourisme, qui contacte l'entité déclarante si elle repère des divergences.

L'édition 2014 de l'*Annuaire* reflète les données officielles telles qu'elles ont été saisies dans la base de données de l'OMT au 9 décembre 2013. Toutes les corrections ou modifications ayant été reçues après cette date apparaîtront dans l'édition suivante de l'*Annuaire*. En raison de l'arrondissement des données partielles, les totaux figurant dans les différents tableaux de l'*Annuaire* peuvent ne pas correspondre aux totaux des indicateurs de base du *Compendium des statistiques du tourisme*.

INTRODUCTION

L'OMT exprime sa gratitude, pour leur aide précieuse, aux administrations nationales du tourisme et aux bureaux nationaux de statistique. Elle tient à saluer plus spécialement le rôle crucial joué par tous les pays et territoires ayant apporté leur contribution, témoignant de leur engagement constant à l'appui du développement et de l'amélioration des statistiques du tourisme.

Madrid, janvier 2014

INTRODUCCIÓN

La edición de 2014 del *Anuario de estadísticas de turismo* presenta datos sobre turismo receptor para 197 países y territorios, desglosados por país de origen. Constituye la 66ª edición de una serie que comenzó en 1947. El *Anuario* y el *Compendio de estadísticas de turismo* son los conjuntos de datos y publicaciones más importantes de la Organización Mundial del Turismo (OMT) sobre estadísticas anuales de turismo, siendo ambos responsabilidad del Programa de Estadísticas y Cuenta Satélite del Turismo.

El *Anuario* contiene datos sobre totales de llegadas y pernoctaciones del turismo receptor internacional, desglosados en ambos casos por país de origen.

> **Llegadas**

  A. Estadísticas de fronteras
- Tabla 1. Llegadas de turistas no residentes a las fronteras nacionales
- Tabla 2. Llegadas de visitantes no residentes a las fronteras nacionales

  B. Estadísticas en establecimientos de alojamiento
- Tabla 3. Llegadas de turistas no residentes a los hoteles y establecimientos asimilados
- Tabla 4. Llegadas de turistas no residentes a todo tipo de establecimientos de alojamiento

Cuando una persona visita un mismo país varias veces en un año, cada una de esas visitas se cuenta como una llegada. Si una persona visita varios países en el transcurso de un mismo viaje, cada llegada a uno de esos países se registra también por separado. Por lo tanto, el número de *llegadas* no coincide necesariamente con el número de personas que viajan, ya que una persona puede generar varias llegadas.

Los datos de llegadas se refieren a los visitantes internacionales que llegan al territorio económico del país de referencia, sean turistas o visitantes del día no residentes.

Los datos pueden proceder de diversas fuentes: estadísticas de fronteras basadas en registros administrativos (policía, inmigración, recuentos de circulación y otros tipos de controles), encuestas en las fronteras y registros en establecimientos de alojamiento.

> **Pernoctaciones**

- Tabla 5. Pernoctaciones de turistas no residentes en hoteles y establecimientos asimilados
- Tabla 6. Pernoctaciones de turistas no residentes en todo tipo de establecimientos de alojamiento

Las *pernoctaciones* se refieren al número de noches que pasan los turistas no residentes en establecimientos de alojamiento (*huéspedes*). Si una persona viaja a un país y pasa en él cinco noches, se contarán cinco pernoctaciones turísticas (o pernoctaciones/persona).

En la edición impresa de 2014 del *Anuario,* los títulos de las tablas, los nombres de los países, las regiones y las subregiones, así como la clasificación incluida en las tablas, figuran únicamente en inglés, mientras que las notas aparecen en español, francés e inglés. Los países aparecen siguiendo el orden alfabético en inglés. Los datos publicados proceden de fuentes oficiales y han sido comprobados por el Programa de Estadísticas y Cuenta Satélite de Turismo de la OMT, que consulta a la entidad en caso de que se detecten discrepancias.

La edición de 2014 del *Anuario* muestra los datos oficiales introducidos en la base de datos estadística de la OMT a 9 de diciembre de 2013. Por lo tanto, cualquier corrección o cambio en las tablas recibido después de esta fecha aparecerá en la siguiente edición del *Anuario*. Debido al redondeo de las cifras parciales, los totales que figuran en las distintas tablas del *Anuario* pueden no coincidir con los totales que aparecen en los indicadores básicos del *Compendio de estadísticas de turismo*.

INTRODUCCIÓN

La Organización Mundial del Turismo desea expresar su agradecimiento por su valioso apoyo a las administraciones nacionales de turismo y a las oficinas nacionales de estadística, y reconocer especialmente el papel crucial de todos los países y territorios que contribuyen con sus datos y mantienen su compromiso de desarrollar y mejorar las estadísticas de turismo.

Madrid, enero de 2014

Country tables
2008-2012

➢ <u>Arrivals</u>

   A.   Border statistics

- Table 1.   Arrivals of non-resident tourists at national borders

- Table 2.   Arrivals of non-resident visitors at national borders

   B.   Statistics on accommodation establishments

- Table 3.   Arrivals of non-resident tourists in hotels and similar establishments

- Table 4.   Arrivals of non-resident tourists in all types of accommodation establishments

➢ <u>Overnight stays</u>

- Table 5.   Overnight stays of non-resident tourists in hotels and similar establishments

- Table 6.   Overnight stays of non-resident tourists in all types of accommodation establishments

ALBANIA

2. Arrivals of non-resident visitors at national borders, by nationality

	2008	2009	2010	2011	2012	Market share 2012	% Change 2012-2011
TOTAL (*)	1,419,191	1,855,634	2,417,337	2,932,132	3,513,666	100.00	19.83
AFRICA	317	211	3,193	432	1,057	0.03	144.68
Central Africa	56	23	12	12	175	0.00	1,358.33
Democratic Republic of the Congo	56	23	12	12	175	0.00	1,358.33
North Africa	133	164	3,041	252	535	0.02	112.30
Morocco	68	78	2,924	139	184	0.01	32.37
Sudan	22	33	54	39	266	0.01	582.05
Tunisia	43	53	63	74	85	0.00	14.86
Southern Africa	128	24	140	168	347	0.01	106.55
South Africa	128	24	140	168	347	0.01	106.55
AMERICAS	60,978	59,945	61,878	70,291	73,810	2.10	5.01
Caribbean	28	50	782	263	627	0.02	138.40
Dominican Republic	8	18	59	20	28	0.00	40.00
Saint Lucia	20	32	723	243	599	0.02	146.50
Central America	42	60	25	59	78	0.00	32.20
El Salvador	27	26	11	18	20	0.00	11.11
Honduras	7	24	13	32	52	0.00	62.50
Nicaragua	8	10	1	9	6	0.00	-33.33
North America	59,996	57,875	59,941	67,529	71,454	2.03	5.81
Canada	9,511	9,243	10,301	11,468	12,761	0.36	11.27
Mexico	131	33	103	111	72	0.00	-35.14
United States of America	50,354	48,599	49,537	55,950	58,621	1.67	4.77
South America	912	1,960	1,130	2,440	1,651	0.05	-32.34
Argentina	192	140	294	293	310	0.01	5.80
Brazil	566	1,660	609	1,871	1,084	0.03	-42.06
Colombia	35	66	60	97	100	0.00	3.09
Peru	66	51	101	108	84	0.00	-22.22
Uruguay	16	11	22	22	23	0.00	4.55
Venezuela	37	32	44	49	50	0.00	2.04
EAST ASIA AND THE PACIFIC	15,419	28,433	11,361	17,418	19,689	0.56	13.04
North-East Asia	5,972	19,991	4,303	7,170	9,126	0.26	27.28
China	1,267	1,346	1,718	1,967	3,129	0.09	59.07
Japan	1,067	1,116	1,529	2,713	2,475	0.07	-8.77
Korea, Republic of	3,638	17,529	1,056	2,490	3,522	0.10	41.45
South-East Asia	777	835	759	2,220	923	0.03	-58.42
Malaysia	224	238	243	1,423	286	0.01	-79.90
Philippines	207	439	397	547	443	0.01	-19.01
Singapore	175	115	62	110	126	0.00	14.55
Thailand	171	43	57	140	68	0.00	-51.43
Australasia	8,670	7,607	6,299	8,028	9,640	0.27	20.08
Australia	7,523	6,435	5,429	6,753	8,337	0.24	23.46
New Zealand	1,147	1,172	870	1,275	1,303	0.04	2.20
EUROPE	1,335,227	1,512,734	2,238,958	2,738,846	3,214,111	91.47	17.35
Central/Eastern Europe	60,038	60,880	63,722	82,418	90,643	2.58	9.98
Bulgaria	13,210	14,327	13,760	16,117	18,759	0.53	16.39
Czech Republic	7,029	7,000	7,006	8,165	9,350	0.27	14.51
Estonia	1,073	1,143	510	640	1,068	0.03	66.88
Hungary	5,709	4,697	5,939	6,319	6,580	0.19	4.13
Lithuania	793	984	889	1,312	1,733	0.05	32.09
Poland	14,427	17,037	17,350	23,869	26,528	0.75	11.14
Republic of Moldova	5	243	365	491	454	0.01	-7.54
Romania	6,086	7,242	8,705	10,399	10,278	0.29	-1.16
Russian Federation	7,331	4,555	5,657	9,752	10,074	0.29	3.30
Slovakia	2,348	2,456	2,133	2,861	2,928	0.08	2.34

3

Yearbook of Tourism Statistics, Data 2008 – 2012, 2014 Edition

ALBANIA

2. Arrivals of non-resident visitors at national borders, by nationality

	2008	2009	2010	2011	2012	Market share 2012	% Change 2012-2011
Ukraine	2,027	1,196	1,408	2,493	2,891	0.08	15.96
Northern Europe	**79,553**	**79,931**	**85,463**	**109,924**	**117,434**	**3.34**	**6.83**
Denmark	2,408	2,831	3,186	4,068	4,893	0.14	20.28
Finland	3,146	3,094	3,299	4,671	4,154	0.12	-11.07
Iceland	94	233	383	236	317	0.01	34.32
Ireland	2,648	2,910	2,425	2,701	2,677	0.08	-0.89
Norway	4,294	3,654	5,315	7,556	9,519	0.27	25.98
Sweden	6,920	6,073	8,604	14,673	17,335	0.49	18.14
United Kingdom	60,043	61,136	62,251	76,019	78,539	2.24	3.31
Southern Europe	**1,058,063**	**1,220,254**	**1,912,383**	**2,320,746**	**2,759,374**	**78.53**	**18.90**
Bosnia and Herzegovina	3,636	3,833	8,646	9,094	11,334	0.32	24.63
Croatia	10,237	11,824	26,438	20,734	22,524	0.64	8.63
Greece	85,505	106,227	113,008	155,086	225,175	6.41	45.19
Holy See	17	8	14		14	0.00	
Italy	98,573	109,702	125,036	135,389	147,018	4.18	8.59
Malta	2,877	781	1,586	735	3,852	0.11	424.08
Montenegro	120,125	128,547	123,833	159,838	186,536	5.31	16.70
Portugal	581	780	640	1,167	2,003	0.06	71.64
Serbia	59,557	40,873	43,940	48,029	38,156	1.09	-20.56
Slovenia	7,513	9,745	9,834	11,283	10,554	0.30	-6.46
Spain	2,870	3,573	3,813	4,288	4,184	0.12	-2.43
TFYR of Macedonia	341,801	330,939	276,268	335,380	399,281	11.36	19.05
Other countries of Southern Europe (*)	324,771	473,422	1,179,327	1,439,723	1,708,743	48.63	18.69
Western Europe	**101,616**	**116,030**	**141,187**	**186,531**	**200,462**	**5.71**	**7.47**
Austria	12,292	11,809	15,659	21,149	22,562	0.64	6.68
Belgium	8,197	9,609	11,094	14,973	16,189	0.46	8.12
France	18,369	20,165	25,651	30,410	30,128	0.86	-0.93
Germany	38,428	48,408	55,919	73,102	70,060	1.99	-4.16
Luxembourg	243	388	540	690	798	0.02	15.65
Netherlands	8,427	9,691	10,055	15,333	18,179	0.52	18.56
Switzerland	15,660	15,960	22,269	30,874	42,546	1.21	37.81
East Mediterranean Europe	**35,957**	**35,639**	**36,203**	**39,227**	**46,198**	**1.31**	**17.77**
Cyprus	1,140	733	850	890	1,082	0.03	21.57
Israel	2,242	4,337	1,809	2,121	2,292	0.07	8.06
Turkey	32,575	30,569	33,544	36,216	42,824	1.22	18.25
MIDDLE EAST	**1,115**	**1,313**	**1,247**	**1,178**	**1,524**	**0.04**	**29.37**
Egypt	579	675	724	616	567	0.02	-7.95
Iraq	19	26	24	17	31	0.00	82.35
Jordan	88	82	72	83	154	0.00	85.54
Kuwait	75	94	41	29	195	0.01	572.41
Libya	47	37	65	36	62	0.00	72.22
Palestine	53	26	32	39	55	0.00	41.03
Saudi Arabia	107	202	151	206	318	0.01	54.37
Syrian Arab Republic	147	171	138	152	142	0.00	-6.58
SOUTH ASIA	**484**	**661**	**764**	**909**	**1,135**	**0.03**	**24.86**
Bangladesh	14	30	31	42	45	0.00	7.14
India	262	393	423	514	565	0.02	9.92
Iran, Islamic Republic of	161	150	196	265	408	0.01	53.96
Nepal	5	7	10	7	2	0.00	-71.43
Pakistan	42	81	104	81	115	0.00	41.98
NOT SPECIFIED	**5,651**	**252,337**	**99,936**	**103,058**	**202,340**	**5.76**	**96.34**
Other countries of the World	5,651	252,337	99,936	103,058	202,340	5.76	96.34

Yearbook of Tourism Statistics, Data 2008 – 2012, 2014 Edition

ALGERIA

2. Arrivals of non-resident visitors at national borders, by nationality

		2008	2009	2010	2011	2012	Market share 2012	% Change 2012-2011
TOTAL	(*)	1,771,749	1,911,506	2,070,496	2,394,887	2,634,056	100.00	9.99
AFRICA		194,403	257,936	310,684	554,380	635,237	24.12	14.59
North Africa		163,009	215,211	262,337	502,251	552,721	20.98	10.05
Morocco		14,852	17,300	17,115	17,218	21,125	0.80	22.69
Tunisia		148,157	197,911	245,222	485,033	531,596	20.18	9.60
West Africa		23,127	29,277	35,429	38,991	42,387	1.61	8.71
Mali		18,100	23,907	30,648	34,478	35,752	1.36	3.70
Mauritania		4,043	4,450	4,318	3,445	4,435	0.17	28.74
Niger		984	920	463	1,068	2,200	0.08	105.99
Other Africa		8,267	13,448	12,918	13,138	40,129	1.52	205.44
Other countries of Africa		8,267	13,448	12,918	13,138	40,129	1.52	205.44
AMERICAS		10,939	13,120	10,495	12,265	11,844	0.45	-3.43
North America		8,328	10,085	7,442	9,155	9,383	0.36	2.49
Canada		3,919	5,010	3,151	4,063	3,844	0.15	-5.39
Mexico		282	380	370	393	525	0.02	33.59
United States of America		4,127	4,695	3,921	4,699	5,014	0.19	6.70
South America		878	857	898	733	708	0.03	-3.41
Argentina		377	273	376	275	256	0.01	-6.91
Brazil		501	584	522	458	452	0.02	-1.31
Other Americas		1,733	2,178	2,155	2,377	1,753	0.07	-26.25
Other countries of the Americas		1,733	2,178	2,155	2,377	1,753	0.07	-26.25
EAST ASIA AND THE PACIFIC		39,227	46,613	42,171	55,246	54,978	2.09	-0.49
North-East Asia		4,208	4,468	3,325	23,725	28,951	1.10	22.03
China					20,153	25,383	0.96	25.95
Japan		4,208	4,468	3,325	3,572	3,568	0.14	-0.11
Australasia		683	662	775	832	571	0.02	-31.37
Australia		585	560	667	687	474	0.02	-31.00
New Zealand		98	102	108	145	97	0.00	-33.10
Other East Asia and the Pacific		34,336	41,483	38,071	30,689	25,456	0.97	-17.05
Other countries of Asia		34,336	41,483	38,071	30,689	25,456	0.97	-17.05
EUROPE		267,552	283,843	241,637	218,629	239,578	9.10	9.58
Northern Europe		11,757	12,968	10,688	11,023	10,207	0.39	-7.40
Denmark		638	668	441	450	462	0.02	2.67
Finland		277	461	336	389	361	0.01	-7.20
Norway		846	884	660	935	687	0.03	-26.52
Sweden		1,293	1,580	1,227	1,257	1,285	0.05	2.23
United Kingdom		8,703	9,375	8,024	7,992	7,412	0.28	-7.26
Southern Europe		41,028	49,634	49,183	53,310	64,336	2.44	20.68
Greece		584	581	525	548	960	0.04	75.18
Italy		15,477	18,824	16,886	19,127	23,070	0.88	20.61
Portugal		4,967	6,483	6,139	5,584	7,257	0.28	29.96
Spain		20,000	23,746	25,633	28,051	33,049	1.25	17.82
Western Europe		194,291	197,546	161,654	133,199	141,767	5.38	6.43
Austria		1,095	1,253	1,037	1,121	1,292	0.05	15.25
Belgium		6,051	6,843	6,414	5,889	6,319	0.24	7.30
France		170,538	171,314	140,129	112,241	119,518	4.54	6.48
Germany		10,961	12,148	9,244	9,492	9,937	0.38	4.69
Luxembourg		134	176	193	93	136	0.01	46.24
Netherlands		1,818	2,217	1,764	1,541	1,490	0.06	-3.31
Switzerland		3,694	3,595	2,873	2,822	3,075	0.12	8.97
East Mediterranean Europe		11,323	12,140	9,783	9,653	10,369	0.39	7.42
Turkey		11,323	12,140	9,783	9,653	10,369	0.39	7.42
Other Europe		9,153	11,555	10,329	11,444	12,899	0.49	12.71
Other countries of Europe		9,153	11,555	10,329	11,444	12,899	0.49	12.71

Yearbook of Tourism Statistics, Data 2008 – 2012, 2014 Edition

ALGERIA

2. Arrivals of non-resident visitors at national borders, by nationality

	2008	2009	2010	2011	2012	Market share 2012	% Change 2012-2011
MIDDLE EAST	44,576	54,298	50,000	61,122	40,318	1.53	-34.04
Libya	13,940	16,359	19,313	28,615	25,850	0.98	-9.66
Syrian Arab Republic				12,444			
Other countries of Middle East	30,636	37,939	30,687	20,063	14,468	0.55	-27.89
NOT SPECIFIED	1,215,052	1,255,696	1,415,509	1,493,245	1,652,101	62.72	10.64
Nationals Residing Abroad	1,215,052	1,255,696	1,415,509	1,493,245	1,652,101	62.72	10.64

Yearbook of Tourism Statistics, Data 2008 – 2012, 2014 Edition

AMERICAN SAMOA

1. Arrivals of non-resident tourists at national borders, by nationality

	2008	2009	2010	2011	2012	Market share 2012	% Change 2012-2011
TOTAL	24,283	23,544	22,629	21,929	21,612	100.00	-1.45
AFRICA	26	25	15	9	40	0.19	344.44
Southern Africa					10	0.05	
South Africa					10	0.05	
Other Africa	26	25	15	9	30	0.14	233.33
Other countries of Africa					30	0.14	
All countries of Africa	26	25	15	9			
AMERICAS	7,638	7,876	7,727	6,717	6,618	30.62	-1.47
Central America	28	20	28	19	238	1.10	1,152.63
All countries of Central America	28	20	28	19	238	1.10	1,152.63
North America	7,580	7,819	7,672	6,662	6,311	29.20	-5.27
Canada	121	85	132	97	128	0.59	31.96
Mexico	5	10	17	17	24	0.11	41.18
United States of America	7,454	7,724	7,523	6,548	6,159	28.50	-5.94
South America	30	37	27	36	69	0.32	91.67
All countries of South America	30	37	27	36	69	0.32	91.67
EAST ASIA AND THE PACIFIC	16,148	15,165	14,465	14,751	14,487	67.03	-1.79
North-East Asia	505	570	430	577	649	3.00	12.48
China	229	325	257	401	400	1.85	-0.25
Japan	87	74	40	58	64	0.30	10.34
Korea, Republic of	84	69	83	55	116	0.54	110.91
Taiwan, Province of China	105	102	50	63	69	0.32	9.52
South-East Asia	488	408	342	377	509	2.36	35.01
Indonesia	51	61	38	43	68	0.31	58.14
Malaysia	7	5	3	10	14	0.06	40.00
Philippines	407	323	289	307	383	1.77	24.76
Singapore	15	15	10	15	27	0.12	80.00
Thailand	8	4	2	2	3	0.01	50.00
Viet Nam					13	0.06	
Other countries of South-East Asia					1	0.00	
Australasia	4,027	4,116	3,565	3,717	3,636	16.82	-2.18
Australia	957	933	812	910	892	4.13	-1.98
New Zealand	3,070	3,183	2,753	2,807	2,744	12.70	-2.24
Melanesia	401	415	387	367	462	2.14	25.89
Fiji	351	312	355	332	352	1.63	6.02
Papua New Guinea	26	19	15	9	32	0.15	255.56
Solomon Islands	18	24	9	18	56	0.26	211.11
Vanuatu	6	60	8	8	22	0.10	175.00
Micronesia	63	30	28	24	29	0.13	20.83
Kiribati	4	11	8	6	11	0.05	83.33
Micronesia, Federated States of	59	19	20	18	12	0.06	-33.33
Palau					6	0.03	
Polynesia	10,546	9,572	9,669	9,646	9,157	42.37	-5.07
Samoa	10,281	9,244	9,301	9,439	8,909	41.22	-5.62
Tonga	265	328	368	207	248	1.15	19.81
Other East Asia and the Pacific	118	54	44	43	45	0.21	4.65
Other countries of Oceania	118	54	44	43	45	0.21	4.65
EUROPE	387	410	367	380	373	1.73	-1.84
Central/Eastern Europe	2	3	3	7	12	0.06	71.43
Russian Federation	2	3	3	7	12	0.06	71.43
Northern Europe	153	205	165	143	163	0.75	13.99
Denmark	9	7	6	7	4	0.02	-42.86
Finland	4	4	5	3	1	0.00	-66.67
Norway	5	26	8	5	16	0.07	220.00

7

AMERICAN SAMOA

1. Arrivals of non-resident tourists at national borders, by nationality

	2008	2009	2010	2011	2012	Market share 2012	% Change 2012-2011
Sweden	6	11	5	7	15	0.07	114.29
United Kingdom	129	157	141	121	127	0.59	4.96
Southern Europe	**60**	**68**	**45**	**50**	**74**	**0.34**	**48.00**
Italy	15	34	9	19	29	0.13	52.63
Portugal	22	16	18	14	27	0.12	92.86
Spain	23	18	18	17	18	0.08	5.88
Western Europe	**155**	**113**	**131**	**126**	**110**	**0.51**	**-12.70**
Austria	12	6	3	4	4	0.02	0.00
Belgium	12	2	4	1	1	0.00	0.00
France	50	38	36	53	40	0.19	-24.53
Germany	52	40	63	39	41	0.19	5.13
Netherlands	21	20	18	18	20	0.09	11.11
Switzerland	8	7	7	11	4	0.02	-63.64
Other Europe	**17**	**21**	**23**	**54**	**14**	**0.06**	**-74.07**
Other countries of Europe	17	21	23	54	14	0.06	-74.07
MIDDLE EAST	**3**	**2**	**2**	**5**	**1**	**0.00**	**-80.00**
All countries of Middle East	3	2	2	5	1	0.00	-80.00
SOUTH ASIA	**37**	**35**	**26**	**44**	**70**	**0.32**	**59.09**
Bangladesh	1				5	0.02	
India	35	32	18	18	50	0.23	177.78
Nepal					7	0.03	
Pakistan			1	1	1	0.00	0.00
Sri Lanka	1	3	7	25	7	0.03	-72.00
NOT SPECIFIED	**44**	**31**	**27**	**23**	**23**	**0.11**	**0.00**
Other countries of the World	44	31	27	23	23	0.11	0.00

8

ANDORRA

1. Arrivals of non-resident tourists at national borders, by country of residence

		2008	2009	2010	2011	2012	Market share 2012	% Change 2012-2011
TOTAL	(*)	**2,059,451**	**1,829,869**	**1,808,001**	**2,241,559**	**2,237,939**	**100.00**	**-0.16**
EUROPE		**2,059,451**	**1,829,869**	**1,808,001**	**2,241,559**	**2,237,939**	**100.00**	**-0.16**
Southern Europe		**1,555,475**	**1,409,868**	**1,414,298**	**1,588,907**	**1,570,604**	**70.18**	**-1.15**
Spain		1,555,475	1,409,868	1,414,298	1,588,907	1,570,604	70.18	-1.15
Western Europe		**402,299**	**332,783**	**310,800**	**341,484**	**345,898**	**15.46**	**1.29**
France		402,299	332,783	310,800	341,484	345,898	15.46	1.29
Other Europe		**101,677**	**87,218**	**82,903**	**311,168**	**321,437**	**14.36**	**3.30**
Other countries of Europe		101,677	87,218	82,903	311,168	321,437	14.36	3.30

Yearbook of Tourism Statistics, Data 2008 – 2012, 2014 Edition

ANGOLA

1. Arrivals of non-resident tourists at national borders, by country of residence

	2008	2009	2010	2011	2012	Market share 2012	% Change 2012-2011
TOTAL	294,131	365,533	424,754	480,965	526,238	100.00	9.41
AFRICA	37,219	46,476	72,519	147,903	173,297	32.93	17.17
East Africa	4,053	4,271	7,418	15,740	16,847	3.20	7.03
Burundi	58	21	34	37	40	0.01	8.11
Comoros	6	5					
Djibouti	2	1	6	6	2	0.00	-66.67
Eritrea	146	366	351	467	645	0.12	38.12
Ethiopia	258	252	383	300	345	0.07	15.00
Kenya	249	326	411	516	465	0.09	-9.88
Madagascar	31	48	91	77	138	0.03	79.22
Malawi	129	98	96	113	92	0.02	-18.58
Mauritius	83	104	43	63	214	0.04	239.68
Mozambique	1,400	1,550	3,089	1,577	1,720	0.33	9.07
Rwanda	112	75	71	60	71	0.01	18.33
Seychelles	1	9	7	3	17	0.00	466.67
Somalia	5	10	16	120	254	0.05	111.67
Uganda	57	67	70	157	84	0.02	-46.50
United Republic of Tanzania	191	140	120	174	380	0.07	118.39
Zambia	752	601	1,313	10,894	10,976	2.09	0.75
Zimbabwe	573	598	1,317	1,176	1,404	0.27	19.39
Central Africa	6,429	5,414	9,387	23,203	11,202	2.13	-51.72
Cameroon	658	633	3,405	556	470	0.09	-15.47
Central African Republic	44	22	21	18	161	0.03	794.44
Chad	56	79	69	61	104	0.02	70.49
Congo	954	728	568	9,436	660	0.13	-93.01
Democratic Republic of the Congo	1,108	890	446	10,241	6,958	1.32	-32.06
Equatorial Guinea	129	72	85	101	91	0.02	-9.90
Gabon	437	294	956	142	229	0.04	61.27
Sao Tome and Principe	3,043	2,696	3,837	2,648	2,529	0.48	-4.49
North Africa	693	2,956	9,364	967	998	0.19	3.21
Algeria	262	2,589	3,460	327	406	0.08	24.16
Morocco	123	115	2,762	295	150	0.03	-49.15
Sudan	81	72	30	96	46	0.01	-52.08
Tunisia	227	180	3,112	249	396	0.08	59.04
Southern Africa	17,306	27,238	32,872	100,467	136,504	25.94	35.87
Botswana	469	130	88	145	179	0.03	23.45
Lesotho	67	19	20	40	27	0.01	-32.50
Namibia	1,174	1,225	3,506	37,834	54,219	10.30	43.31
South Africa	15,476	25,803	29,217	62,380	82,021	15.59	31.49
Swaziland	120	61	41	68	58	0.01	-14.71
West Africa	8,738	6,597	13,478	6,321	7,746	1.47	22.54
Benin	111	90	1,134	47	58	0.01	23.40
Burkina Faso	81	68	101	46	49	0.01	6.52
Cape Verde	2,049	1,085	821	957	1,070	0.20	11.81
Côte d'Ivoire	230	571	1,495	309	228	0.04	-26.21
Gambia	597	327	230	303	393	0.07	29.70
Ghana	217	289	1,483	325	321	0.06	-1.23
Guinea	1,201	280	32	27	128	0.02	374.07
Guinea-Bissau	459	353	974	495	452	0.09	-8.69
Liberia	31	31	39	18	29	0.01	61.11
Mali	514	532	1,839	392	736	0.14	87.76
Mauritania	570	426	449	471	1,425	0.27	202.55
Niger	72	18	131	48	112	0.02	133.33
Nigeria	2,205	2,038	2,996	2,528	2,337	0.44	-7.56
Senegal	240	341	1,635	215	254	0.05	18.14
Sierra Leone	111	91	56	70	111	0.02	58.57

ANGOLA

1. Arrivals of non-resident tourists at national borders, by country of residence

	2008	2009	2010	2011	2012	Market share 2012	% Change 2012-2011
Togo	50	57	63	70	43	0.01	-38.57
Other Africa				1,205			
Other countries of Africa				1,205			
AMERICAS	59,358	76,321	82,835	58,233	67,639	12.85	16.15
Caribbean	3,236	5,674	4,811	4,454	5,309	1.01	19.20
Antigua and Barbuda	1		1		20	0.00	
Aruba	2	4	1				
Bahamas	1	7	4		2	0.00	
Barbados			8				
Cuba	2,754	5,045	4,113	4,058	4,563	0.87	12.44
Dominica	3			6	46	0.01	666.67
Dominican Republic	24	40	167	7	2	0.00	-71.43
Grenada		2					
Guadeloupe		1					
Haiti	4	8	3	2	16	0.00	700.00
Jamaica	7	8	12		43	0.01	
Martinique	2		1		103	0.02	
Puerto Rico	2	3	4				
Trinidad and Tobago	436	556	497	381	514	0.10	34.91
Central America	320	407	554	273	4,888	0.93	1,690.48
Belize		5	4	7	15	0.00	114.29
Costa Rica	11	30	77	30	34	0.01	13.33
El Salvador	5	33	15	9	5	0.00	-44.44
Guatemala	17	22	27	49	167	0.03	240.82
Honduras	248	225	154	162	206	0.04	27.16
Nicaragua	18	15	181	3	13	0.00	333.33
Panama	21	77	96	13	4,448	0.85	34,115.38
North America	17,595	18,055	25,826	19,782	22,492	4.27	13.70
Canada	2,978	2,583	3,024	2,223	2,434	0.46	9.49
Mexico	298	332	2,489	389	1,825	0.35	369.15
United States of America	14,319	15,140	20,313	17,170	18,233	3.46	6.19
South America	38,207	52,185	51,644	33,683	34,950	6.64	3.76
Argentina	598	1,492	1,849	789	1,870	0.36	137.01
Bolivia	102	126	133	134	140	0.03	4.48
Brazil	35,231	46,866	45,848	29,738	29,336	5.57	-1.35
Chile	469	326	471	167	184	0.03	10.18
Colombia	548	665	779	602	621	0.12	3.16
Ecuador	75	230	498	144	144	0.03	0.00
Guyana	49	688	818	843	1,175	0.22	39.38
Paraguay	62	118	66	50	130	0.02	160.00
Peru	223	595	353	388	437	0.08	12.63
Uruguay	142	193	149	141	116	0.02	-17.73
Venezuela	708	886	680	687	797	0.15	16.01
Other Americas				41			
Other countries of the Americas				41			
EAST ASIA AND THE PACIFIC	59,051	66,492	80,515	87,626	94,326	17.92	7.65
North-East Asia	46,126	54,056	62,336	71,241	71,079	13.51	-0.23
China	43,035	51,900	60,577	69,907	69,334	13.18	-0.82
Japan	580	759	904	800	856	0.16	7.00
Korea, Dem. People's Republic of	476	461	246	135	175	0.03	29.63
Korea, Republic of	1,953	821	504	279	531	0.10	90.32
Macao, China	4	11	7	1	6	0.00	500.00
Mongolia	20	1					
Taiwan, Province of China	58	103	98	119	177	0.03	48.74
South-East Asia	11,534	11,021	15,538	15,210	22,021	4.18	44.78
Cambodia	9	2	5	1	2	0.00	100.00

11

ANGOLA

1. Arrivals of non-resident tourists at national borders, by country of residence

	2008	2009	2010	2011	2012	Market share 2012	% Change 2012-2011
Indonesia	977	1,536	1,336	948	1,155	0.22	21.84
Malaysia	598	844	836	789	737	0.14	-6.59
Myanmar		3			44	0.01	
Philippines	7,043	6,096	8,414	7,452	8,553	1.63	14.77
Singapore	125	295	299	225	1,617	0.31	618.67
Thailand	121	180	288	313	157	0.03	-49.84
Timor-Leste	4	3	9	33	17	0.00	-48.48
Viet Nam	2,657	2,062	4,351	5,449	9,739	1.85	78.73
Australasia	**1,391**	**1,415**	**2,638**	**1,175**	**1,226**	**0.23**	**4.34**
Australia	1,120	1,197	1,473	944	913	0.17	-3.28
New Zealand	271	218	1,165	231	313	0.06	35.50
Melanesia			**3**				
Solomon Islands			3				
EUROPE	**129,711**	**160,918**	**170,216**	**170,246**	**174,768**	**33.21**	**2.66**
Central/Eastern Europe	**8,031**	**9,294**	**10,247**	**7,595**	**10,196**	**1.94**	**34.25**
Armenia	66	57	22	36	22	0.00	-38.89
Azerbaijan	155	167	144	152	217	0.04	42.76
Bulgaria	364	322	229	262	396	0.08	51.15
Czech Republic	191	168	846	127	110	0.02	-13.39
Estonia	33	21	28	14	30	0.01	114.29
Georgia	50	20	23	28	72	0.01	157.14
Hungary	89	146	77	56	88	0.02	57.14
Kazakhstan	118	129	95	86	230	0.04	167.44
Kyrgyzstan	28	31	2				
Latvia		46	36	85	75	0.01	-11.76
Lithuania	249	242	186	249	295	0.06	18.47
Poland	1,772	1,395	1,949	1,803	2,033	0.39	12.76
Republic of Moldova	51	837	1,381		1,101	0.21	
Romania	786	814	1,934	975	1,154	0.22	18.36
Russian Federation	2,477	2,694	1,484	1,737	1,849	0.35	6.45
Slovakia	43	51	53	62	50	0.01	-19.35
Tajikistan		14	2	4			
Turkmenistan	3	20	6	18	87	0.02	383.33
Ukraine	1,500	1,994	1,670	1,794	2,264	0.43	26.20
Uzbekistan	56	126	80	107	123	0.02	14.95
Northern Europe	**24,869**	**20,613**	**22,586**	**36,398**	**34,687**	**6.59**	**-4.70**
Denmark	720	1,332	957	939	1,150	0.22	22.47
Finland	151	71	90	712	106	0.02	-85.11
Iceland	51	14	24	10	51	0.01	410.00
Ireland	493	544	485	555	911	0.17	64.14
Norway	2,282	2,269	1,728	1,836	1,953	0.37	6.37
Sweden	747	513	536	414	480	0.09	15.94
United Kingdom	20,425	15,870	18,766	31,932	30,036	5.71	-5.94
Southern Europe	**61,115**	**97,328**	**109,916**	**94,454**	**102,906**	**19.56**	**8.95**
Albania	41	11	8	7	7	0.00	0.00
Andorra		180	4	2			
Bosnia and Herzegovina		24	34	23	28	0.01	21.74
Croatia	1,103	1,119	947	1,147	1,237	0.24	7.85
Greece	121	105	116	109	122	0.02	11.93
Italy	3,324	4,259	3,854	4,133	4,137	0.79	0.10
Malta	83	77	69	54	85	0.02	57.41
Portugal	53,658	86,330	100,645	84,755	92,204	17.52	8.79
Serbia		12	40	16			
Serbia and Montenegro	120	68	13				
Slovenia	56	115	88	70	429	0.08	512.86
Spain	2,593	5,007	4,052	4,138	4,657	0.88	12.54
TFYR of Macedonia	16	21	46				

12

ANGOLA

1. Arrivals of non-resident tourists at national borders, by country of residence

	2008	2009	2010	2011	2012	Market share 2012	% Change 2012-2011
Western Europe	**33,682**	**30,343**	**25,003**	**27,801**	**24,257**	**4.61**	**-12.75**
Austria	141	246	234	201	231	0.04	14.93
Belgium	1,654	1,650	1,472	1,458	1,258	0.24	-13.72
France	26,649	21,760	18,243	20,884	17,297	3.29	-17.18
Germany	2,551	3,361	2,334	2,254	2,486	0.47	10.29
Luxembourg	6	9	17	5	81	0.02	1,520.00
Monaco			1				
Netherlands	2,180	2,910	2,098	2,324	2,219	0.42	-4.52
Switzerland	501	407	604	675	685	0.13	1.48
East Mediterranean Europe	**2,014**	**3,340**	**2,464**	**2,454**	**2,722**	**0.52**	**10.92**
Cyprus		8	7	15	30	0.01	100.00
Israel	1,899	3,081	2,183	2,036	2,190	0.42	7.56
Turkey	115	251	274	403	502	0.10	24.57
Other Europe				**1,544**			
Other countries of Europe				1,544			
MIDDLE EAST	**2,682**	**4,404**	**8,639**	**2,946**	**5,681**	**1.08**	**92.84**
Egypt	784	1,634	3,177	1,181	1,506	0.29	27.52
Iraq	3	8	138	7	235	0.04	3,257.14
Jordan	116	129	147	152	147	0.03	-3.29
Kuwait	2	6	6	2			
Lebanon	1,530	2,291	2,701	1,315	2,342	0.45	78.10
Libya	56	17	972	24	38	0.01	58.33
Oman	6	19			1	0.00	
Palestine	3	40	43	31	207	0.04	567.74
Qatar		17	3	1			
Saudi Arabia	8	8	274	2	11	0.00	450.00
Syrian Arab Republic	154	168	1,147	184	19	0.00	-89.67
United Arab Emirates	12	49	2	10	11	0.00	10.00
Yemen	7	15	14	37	746	0.14	1,916.22
Other countries of Middle East	1	3	15		418	0.08	
SOUTH ASIA	**6,110**	**10,922**	**10,030**	**14,011**	**10,527**	**2.00**	**-24.87**
Afghanistan	3	13	3	9	4	0.00	-55.56
Bangladesh	103	308	211	231	271	0.05	17.32
India	5,262	9,517	8,831	12,741	9,231	1.75	-27.55
Iran, Islamic Republic of	18	70	51	38	94	0.02	147.37
Maldives			12	8	36	0.01	350.00
Nepal	106	125	224	84	101	0.02	20.24
Pakistan	573	814	628	827	696	0.13	-15.84
Sri Lanka	45	75	70	73	94	0.02	28.77

Yearbook of Tourism Statistics, Data 2008 – 2012, 2014 Edition

ANGUILLA

1. Arrivals of non-resident tourists at national borders, by country of residence

		2008	2009	2010	2011	2012	Market share 2012	% Change 2012-2011
TOTAL	(*)	68,284	57,891	61,998	65,783	64,698	100.00	-1.65
AMERICAS		57,024	49,029	53,136	56,606	55,267	85.42	-2.37
Caribbean		14,748	12,924	11,851	10,954	10,181	15.74	-7.06
Puerto Rico		838	724	346	286	484	0.75	69.23
Other countries of the Caribbean		13,910	12,200	11,505	10,668	9,697	14.99	-9.10
North America		42,276	36,105	41,285	45,652	45,086	69.69	-1.24
Canada		2,074	2,032	2,403	2,823	3,291	5.09	16.58
United States of America		40,202	34,073	38,882	42,829	41,795	64.60	-2.41
EUROPE		8,943	7,457	7,544	7,523	7,223	11.16	-3.99
Northern Europe		3,816	2,947	2,914	3,118	2,599	4.02	-16.65
United Kingdom		3,816	2,947	2,914	3,118	2,599	4.02	-16.65
Southern Europe		1,583	1,312	1,449	1,226	1,065	1.65	-13.13
Italy		1,583	1,312	1,449	1,226	1,065	1.65	-13.13
Western Europe		2,237	2,083	2,215	1,994	2,303	3.56	15.50
Austria		105	69	82	105	109	0.17	3.81
Belgium		77	83	86	71	139	0.21	95.77
France		1,410	1,404	1,425	1,321	1,507	2.33	14.08
Germany		449	425	478	372	419	0.65	12.63
Luxembourg		8	1	2		6	0.01	
Switzerland		188	101	142	125	123	0.19	-1.60
Other Europe		1,307	1,115	966	1,185	1,256	1.94	5.99
Other countries of Europe		1,307	1,115	966	1,185	1,256	1.94	5.99
NOT SPECIFIED		2,317	1,405	1,318	1,654	2,208	3.41	33.49
Other countries of the World		2,317	1,405	1,318	1,654	2,208	3.41	33.49

14

ANGUILLA

2. Arrivals of non-resident visitors at national borders, by country of residence

	2008	2009	2010	2011	2012	Market share 2012	% Change 2012-2011
TOTAL	127,861	112,115	118,411	123,558	129,391	100.00	4.72
AMERICAS	99,785	88,459	93,584	97,166	101,803	78.68	4.77
Caribbean	29,087	25,976	25,103	23,626	23,619	18.25	-0.03
Puerto Rico	1,016	909	559	403	655	0.51	62.53
Other countries of the Caribbean	28,071	25,067	24,544	23,223	22,964	17.75	-1.12
North America	70,698	62,483	68,481	73,540	78,184	60.42	6.31
Canada	4,970	5,110	5,982	7,141	7,994	6.18	11.95
United States of America	65,728	57,373	62,499	66,399	70,190	54.25	5.71
EUROPE	23,584	20,412	20,260	20,451	21,417	16.55	4.72
Northern Europe	5,730	4,667	4,471	4,557	4,251	3.29	-6.71
United Kingdom	5,730	4,667	4,471	4,557	4,251	3.29	-6.71
Southern Europe	2,552	2,385	2,278	2,139	2,431	1.88	13.65
Italy	2,552	2,385	2,278	2,139	2,431	1.88	13.65
Western Europe	10,942	9,831	10,369	10,267	10,758	8.31	4.78
Austria	214	157	213	205	232	0.18	13.17
Belgium	476	195	381	373	426	0.33	14.21
France	8,864	8,220	8,148	8,336	8,665	6.70	3.95
Germany	1,001	931	1,239	1,024	1,091	0.84	6.54
Luxembourg	27	13	22	11	14	0.01	27.27
Switzerland	360	315	366	318	330	0.26	3.77
Other Europe	4,360	3,529	3,142	3,488	3,977	3.07	14.02
Other countries of Europe	4,360	3,529	3,142	3,488	3,977	3.07	14.02
NOT SPECIFIED	4,492	3,244	4,567	5,941	6,171	4.77	3.87
Other countries of the World	4,492	3,244	4,567	5,941	6,171	4.77	3.87

ANTIGUA AND BARBUDA

1. Arrivals of non-resident tourists at national borders, by country of residence

		2008	2009	2010	2011	2012	Market share 2012	% Change 2012-2011
TOTAL	(*)	265,844	234,410	229,943	241,331			
AMERICAS		151,785	138,489	137,254	145,556			
Caribbean		48,954	41,546	37,505	37,887			
Anguilla		1,014						
Aruba		66						
Bahamas		262						
Barbados		4,455						
Bermuda		362						
Bonaire		6						
British Virgin Islands		1,827						
Cayman Islands		123						
Cuba		277						
Curaçao		116						
Dominica		5,890						
Dominican Republic		1,174						
Grenada		898						
Guadeloupe		1,149						
Haiti		98						
Jamaica		5,832						
Martinique		296						
Montserrat		3,527						
Puerto Rico		955						
Saint Kitts and Nevis		4,150						
Saint Lucia		2,831						
Saint Vincent and the Grenadines		1,444						
Sint Maarten		1,480						
Trinidad and Tobago		7,019						
Turks and Caicos Islands		78						
United States Virgin Islands		3,446						
Other countries of the Caribbean		179						
All countries of the Caribbean			41,546	37,505	37,887			
Central America		491	488	333	434			
Belize		75						
Other countries of Central America		416	488	333	434			
North America		97,221	95,015	99,416	107,235			
Canada		13,189	12,947	17,818	22,403			
United States of America		84,032	82,068	81,598	84,832			
South America		5,119	1,440					
Argentina		222						
Brazil		245						
Colombia		136						
Guyana		3,740						
Suriname		185						
Venezuela		361						
Other countries of South America		230	1,440					
EUROPE		110,266	93,442	88,945	92,097			
Northern Europe		93,150	73,251	66,623	69,184			
Denmark		346						
Ireland		1,949						
Norway		511						
Sweden		830						
United Kingdom		89,514	73,251	66,623	69,184			
Southern Europe		8,027	7,726	10,180	11,048			
Greece		90						
Italy		7,212	7,726	10,180	11,048			
Portugal		121						

Yearbook of Tourism Statistics, Data 2008 – 2012, 2014 Edition

ANTIGUA AND BARBUDA

1. Arrivals of non-resident tourists at national borders, by country of residence

	2008	2009	2010	2011	2012	Market share 2012	% Change 2012-2011
Spain	604						
Western Europe	**7,558**	**5,319**	**5,000**	**4,646**			
Austria	301						
Belgium	313						
France	1,710	1,567	1,661	1,747			
Germany	3,597	3,752	3,339	2,899			
Luxembourg	27						
Netherlands	589						
Switzerland	1,021						
Other Europe	**1,531**	**7,146**	**7,142**	**7,219**			
Other countries of Europe	1,531	7,146	7,142	7,219			
NOT SPECIFIED	**3,793**	**2,479**	**3,744**	**3,678**			
Other countries of the World	3,793	2,479	3,744	3,678			

Yearbook of Tourism Statistics, Data 2008 – 2012, 2014 Edition

ARGENTINA

1. Arrivals of non-resident tourists at national borders, by nationality

	2008	2009	2010	2011	2012	Market share 2012	% Change 2012-2011
TOTAL	4,700,492	4,307,666	5,325,130	5,704,650	5,585,062	100.00	-2.10
AMERICAS	3,710,497	3,392,017	4,367,985	4,760,388	4,671,362	83.64	-1.87
North America	445,407	395,376	404,770	360,616	355,253	6.36	-1.49
Canada, United States	445,407	395,376	404,770	360,616	355,253	6.36	-1.49
South America	2,800,113	2,580,176	3,544,037	3,898,602	3,813,858	68.29	-2.17
Bolivia	147,846	164,406	184,697	231,636	251,508	4.50	8.58
Brazil	873,794	718,203	1,196,832	1,282,374	1,217,144	21.79	-5.09
Chile	940,496	820,128	1,076,372	1,101,337	1,135,197	20.33	3.07
Paraguay	391,217	389,619	432,200	627,620	602,614	10.79	-3.98
Uruguay	446,760	487,820	653,936	655,635	607,395	10.88	-7.36
Other Americas	464,977	416,465	419,178	501,170	502,251	8.99	0.22
Other countries of the Americas	464,977	416,465	419,178	501,170	502,251	8.99	0.22
EUROPE	765,962	721,622	751,331	738,778	706,335	12.65	-4.39
Other Europe	765,962	721,622	751,331	738,778	706,335	12.65	-4.39
All countries of Europe	765,962	721,622	751,331	738,778	706,335	12.65	-4.39
NOT SPECIFIED	224,033	194,027	205,814	205,484	207,365	3.71	0.92
Other countries of the World	224,033	194,027	205,814	205,484	207,365	3.71	0.92

Yearbook of Tourism Statistics, Data 2008 – 2012, 2014 Edition

ARMENIA

1. Arrivals of non-resident tourists at national borders, by country of residence

	2008	2009	2010	2011	2012	Market share 2012	% Change 2012-2011
TOTAL	558,443	575,284	683,979	757,935	843,330	100.00	11.27
AFRICA	643	443	215	603	648	0.08	7.46
East Africa	98	83		19	31	0.00	63.16
Ethiopia	70	65		14	21	0.00	50.00
Zambia				2	6	0.00	200.00
Zimbabwe	28	18		3	4	0.00	33.33
Central Africa	60	30		29	13	0.00	-55.17
Cameroon	60	30		29	13	0.00	-55.17
North Africa	430	330	215	365	382	0.05	4.66
Algeria	250	180	215	211	215	0.03	1.90
Morocco	180	150		154	167	0.02	8.44
Southern Africa	30			182	187	0.02	2.75
All countries of Southern Africa	30			182	187	0.02	2.75
West Africa	25			8	35	0.00	337.50
Liberia	25			8	35	0.00	337.50
AMERICAS	135,550	134,940	135,673	144,632	112,188	13.30	-22.43
Caribbean	50		31	22	43	0.01	95.45
Cuba	50		30	22	43	0.01	95.45
Puerto Rico			1				
Central America	110		60	70	22	0.00	-68.57
El Salvador			4	3	3	0.00	0.00
Guatemala	40		1	9	12	0.00	33.33
Honduras	15			2	2	0.00	0.00
Nicaragua	55		55	56	5	0.00	-91.07
North America	95,860	95,000	97,760	103,715	72,432	8.59	-30.16
Canada	32,110	30,200	30,350	32,807	3,127	0.37	-90.47
Mexico	1,500	1,700	1,650	1,992	90	0.01	-95.48
United States of America	62,250	63,100	65,760	68,916	69,215	8.21	0.43
South America	39,530	39,940	37,822	40,825	39,691	4.71	-2.78
Argentina	26,450	26,600	24,350	26,414	25,088	2.97	-5.02
Brazil	10,110	10,500	10,490	11,203	11,394	1.35	1.70
Chile	190		180	178	139	0.02	-21.91
Colombia			25	27	25	0.00	-7.41
Ecuador			18	10	20	0.00	100.00
Guyana			2	2	1	0.00	-50.00
Peru	260	200	217	218	219	0.03	0.46
Uruguay	2,140	2,240	2,170	2,411	2,460	0.29	2.03
Venezuela	380	400	370	362	345	0.04	-4.70
EAST ASIA AND THE PACIFIC	24,365	24,600	25,584	29,222	29,685	3.52	1.58
North-East Asia	19,925	20,300	21,008	23,510	23,551	2.79	0.17
China	8,100	8,400	8,450	9,713	9,738	1.15	0.26
Japan	11,110	11,900	11,730	12,973	12,968	1.54	-0.04
Korea, Republic of	350		733	591	706	0.08	19.46
Mongolia	210		41	42	37	0.00	-11.90
Taiwan, Province of China	155		54	191	102	0.01	-46.60
South-East Asia	220		236	357	538	0.06	50.70
Cambodia				13	6	0.00	-53.85
Indonesia			21	49	126	0.01	157.14
Malaysia			50	98	77	0.01	-21.43
Philippines	140		127	128	227	0.03	77.34
Thailand	80		36	55	94	0.01	70.91
Viet Nam			2	14	8	0.00	-42.86

Yearbook of Tourism Statistics, Data 2008 – 2012, 2014 Edition

ARMENIA

1. Arrivals of non-resident tourists at national borders, by country of residence

	2008	2009	2010	2011	2012	Market share 2012	% Change 2012-2011
Australasia	**4,220**	**4,300**	**4,340**	**5,355**	**5,596**	**0.66**	**4.50**
Australia	4,200	4,300	4,340	5,224	5,414	0.64	3.64
New Zealand	20			131	182	0.02	38.93
EUROPE	**308,266**	**311,268**	**350,926**	**375,195**	**490,076**	**58.11**	**30.62**
Central/Eastern Europe	**212,479**	**215,198**	**240,223**	**253,639**	**366,514**	**43.46**	**44.50**
Bulgaria	3,780	3,950	3,915	4,506	4,506	0.53	0.00
Commonwealth Independent States	202,650	208,328	228,810	239,978	350,241	41.53	45.95
Czech Republic	1,540	1,720	1,745	1,825	3,015	0.36	65.21
Estonia	250				585	0.07	
Hungary	660		489	572	515	0.06	-9.97
Latvia	640		761	970	985	0.12	1.55
Lithuania	250		750	919	1,506	0.18	63.87
Poland	1,340	1,200	2,350	3,351	3,758	0.45	12.15
Romania	850		890	899	815	0.10	-9.34
Slovakia	519		513	619	588	0.07	-5.01
Northern Europe	**12,880**	**11,900**	**14,013**	**14,308**	**15,012**	**1.78**	**4.92**
Denmark	890	990	1,071	1,263	1,417	0.17	12.19
Finland	590	710	826	826	1,108	0.13	34.14
Iceland			16	31	39	0.00	25.81
Ireland	170	250	765	416	473	0.06	13.70
Norway	890	940	975	917	712	0.08	-22.36
Sweden	890	910	1,640	1,727	1,919	0.23	11.12
United Kingdom	9,450	8,100	8,720	9,128	9,344	1.11	2.37
Southern Europe	**21,540**	**20,600**	**21,415**	**25,151**	**27,256**	**3.23**	**8.37**
Albania			55	48	80	0.01	66.67
Bosnia and Herzegovina	1,110	950	985	1,034	160	0.02	-84.53
Croatia	50		235	270	211	0.03	-21.85
Greece	9,940	8,700	8,930	11,765	13,092	1.55	11.28
Italy	7,580	7,900	7,945	8,722	9,684	1.15	11.03
Malta			95	48	30	0.00	-37.50
Portugal			730	729	395	0.05	-45.82
Serbia	70				355	0.04	
Serbia and Montenegro	650	700			411	0.05	
Slovenia	550	700	760	762	315	0.04	-58.66
Spain	1,590	1,650	1,680	1,773	2,523	0.30	42.30
Western Europe	**55,967**	**57,070**	**58,854**	**65,013**	**67,312**	**7.98**	**3.54**
Austria	5,120	5,200	5,270	6,137	6,336	0.75	3.24
Belgium	4,680	4,800	4,830	5,122	5,974	0.71	16.63
France	23,500	24,100	24,250	24,735	25,209	2.99	1.92
Germany	18,780	18,970	19,120	22,193	22,627	2.68	1.96
Netherlands	2,297	2,300	3,604	4,814	5,260	0.62	9.26
Switzerland	1,590	1,700	1,780	2,012	1,906	0.23	-5.27
East Mediterranean Europe	**5,400**	**6,500**	**16,421**	**17,084**	**13,982**	**1.66**	**-18.16**
Cyprus	1,250	1,800	1,930	2,143	283	0.03	-86.79
Israel	2,250	2,500	2,834	3,124	4,070	0.48	30.28
Turkey	1,900	2,200	11,657	11,817	9,629	1.14	-18.52
MIDDLE EAST	**43,800**	**44,690**	**46,470**	**49,598**	**50,680**	**6.01**	**2.18**
Egypt	550	590	615	597	500	0.06	-16.25
Iraq	290		398	911	1,062	0.13	16.58
Jordan			358	363	329	0.04	-9.37
Kuwait			44	97	174	0.02	79.38
Lebanon	22,200	23,100	23,330	24,171	24,109	2.86	-0.26
Libya				18	3	0.00	-83.33
Qatar	110		120	121	16	0.00	-86.78
Saudi Arabia	50		80	73	22	0.00	-69.86
Syrian Arab Republic	20,210	21,000	21,340	23,001	24,188	2.87	5.16
United Arab Emirates	390		185	246	277	0.03	12.60

20

ARMENIA

1. Arrivals of non-resident tourists at national borders, by country of residence

	2008	2009	2010	2011	2012	Market share 2012	% Change 2012-2011
SOUTH ASIA	**45,819**	**59,343**	**125,111**	**158,685**	**160,053**	**18.98**	**0.86**
Afghanistan	750			4	33	0.00	725.00
Bangladesh	150			6	14	0.00	133.33
India	3,970	4,100	4,180	4,311	4,881	0.58	13.22
Iran, Islamic Republic of	40,699	55,243	120,863	154,278	155,028	18.38	0.49
Nepal			15	23	24	0.00	4.35
Pakistan	250		38	36	34	0.00	-5.56
Sri Lanka			15	27	39	0.00	44.44

Yearbook of Tourism Statistics, Data 2008 – 2012, 2014 Edition

ARUBA

1. Arrivals of non-resident tourists at national borders, by country of residence

	2008	2009	2010	2011	2012	Market share 2012	% Change 2012-2011
TOTAL	**826,677**	**812,623**	**824,330**	**868,973**	**903,934**	**100.00**	**4.02**
AMERICAS	**748,922**	**735,339**	**745,723**	**784,980**	**820,484**	**90.77**	**4.52**
Caribbean	**26,939**	**24,554**	**26,457**	**29,481**	**32,126**	**3.55**	**8.97**
Dominican Republic	931	839	1,028	1,161	1,497	0.17	28.94
Netherlands Antilles	21,992	21,536	23,363	25,773	27,361	3.03	6.16
Puerto Rico	1,660	119	86	19	74	0.01	289.47
Trinidad and Tobago	1,175	873	953	1,268	1,817	0.20	43.30
Other countries of the Caribbean	1,181	1,187	1,027	1,260	1,377	0.15	9.29
North America	**572,310**	**563,308**	**574,533**	**572,891**	**578,090**	**63.95**	**0.91**
Canada	32,530	33,856	37,643	40,487	45,887	5.08	13.34
Mexico	1,407	1,348	1,223	1,293	1,328	0.15	2.71
United States of America	538,373	528,104	535,667	531,111	530,875	58.73	-0.04
South America	**149,673**	**147,477**	**144,733**	**182,608**	**210,268**	**23.26**	**15.15**
Argentina	4,195	5,486	6,365	10,326	12,865	1.42	24.59
Brazil	8,745	10,594	20,235	22,413	21,070	2.33	-5.99
Chile	1,689	1,345	1,840	2,431	3,163	0.35	30.11
Colombia	13,439	15,685	15,004	16,703	18,127	2.01	8.53
Ecuador	2,316	1,186	2,532	3,520	1,659	0.18	-52.87
Peru	1,181	1,092	1,372	1,377	1,007	0.11	-26.87
Suriname	2,376	3,651	3,556	4,220	5,117	0.57	21.26
Venezuela	112,986	105,063	90,709	117,838	143,201	15.84	21.52
Other countries of South America	2,746	3,375	3,120	3,780	4,059	0.45	7.38
EAST ASIA AND THE PACIFIC	**157**	**158**	**152**	**118**	**176**	**0.02**	**49.15**
North-East Asia	**157**	**158**	**152**	**118**	**176**	**0.02**	**49.15**
Japan	157	158	152	118	176	0.02	49.15
EUROPE	**73,772**	**75,000**	**76,077**	**80,874**	**79,570**	**8.80**	**-1.61**
Central/Eastern Europe	**247**	**272**	**285**	**444**	**441**	**0.05**	**-0.68**
Russian Federation	247	272	285	444	441	0.05	-0.68
Northern Europe	**13,719**	**16,018**	**21,477**	**21,836**	**22,168**	**2.45**	**1.52**
Denmark	349	305	166	350	293	0.03	-16.29
Finland	996	826	766	963	648	0.07	-32.71
Norway	593	613	617	808	1,230	0.14	52.23
Sweden	2,810	2,762	5,398	5,845	6,285	0.70	7.53
United Kingdom	8,971	11,512	14,530	13,870	13,712	1.52	-1.14
Southern Europe	**6,231**	**8,148**	**4,065**	**7,911**	**5,333**	**0.59**	**-32.59**
Italy	3,885	6,369	2,869	6,514	3,963	0.44	-39.16
Portugal	316	200	165	244	181	0.02	-25.82
Spain	2,030	1,579	1,031	1,153	1,189	0.13	3.12
Western Europe	**50,163**	**47,885**	**47,573**	**47,441**	**48,376**	**5.35**	**1.97**
Austria	325	347	407	368	351	0.04	-4.62
Belgium	2,016	2,161	2,377	2,424	2,803	0.31	15.64
Germany	5,125	3,357	3,568	3,493	4,054	0.45	16.06
Netherlands	41,874	41,211	40,294	40,068	39,973	4.42	-0.24
Switzerland	823	809	927	1,088	1,195	0.13	9.83
Other Europe	**3,412**	**2,677**	**2,677**	**3,242**	**3,252**	**0.36**	**0.31**
Other countries of Europe	3,412	2,677	2,677	3,242	3,252	0.36	0.31
NOT SPECIFIED	**3,826**	**2,126**	**2,378**	**3,001**	**3,704**	**0.41**	**23.43**
Other countries of the World	3,826	2,126	2,378	3,001	3,704	0.41	23.43

Yearbook of Tourism Statistics, Data 2008 – 2012, 2014 Edition

ARUBA

3. Arrivals of non-resident tourists in hotels and similar establishments, by country of residence

	2008	2009	2010	2011	2012	Market share 2012	% Change 2012-2011
TOTAL	728,119	719,347	727,590	735,677	764,104	100.00	3.86
AMERICAS	675,830	664,735	672,653	679,373	709,269	92.82	4.40
Caribbean	13,769	13,273	15,068	12,707	14,320	1.87	12.69
Dominican Republic	308	328	387	266	402	0.05	51.13
Netherlands Antilles	10,578	11,502	13,284	10,966	11,840	1.55	7.97
Trinidad and Tobago	802	642	748	954	1,476	0.19	54.72
Other countries of the Caribbean	2,081	801	649	521	602	0.08	15.55
North America	542,489	534,620	542,173	529,139	534,708	69.98	1.05
Canada	29,995	31,274	34,496	36,224	40,678	5.32	12.30
Mexico	1,043	1,050	1,026	953	1,001	0.13	5.04
United States of America	511,451	502,296	506,651	491,962	493,029	64.52	0.22
South America	119,572	116,842	115,412	137,527	160,241	20.97	16.52
Argentina	3,972	5,283	6,167	9,820	12,209	1.60	24.33
Brazil	8,328	10,115	19,558	21,027	19,513	2.55	-7.20
Chile	1,612	1,288	1,778	2,317	3,039	0.40	31.16
Colombia	10,269	11,470	11,804	12,569	13,748	1.80	9.38
Ecuador	2,001	805	2,236	3,171	1,279	0.17	-59.67
Peru	884	797	1,086	1,103	795	0.10	-27.92
Suriname	1,032	1,627	1,728	1,443	1,902	0.25	31.81
Venezuela	89,333	81,467	67,455	81,943	103,437	13.54	26.23
Other countries of South America	2,141	3,990	3,600	4,134	4,319	0.57	4.48
EAST ASIA AND THE PACIFIC	136	126	108	95	93	0.01	-2.11
North-East Asia	136	126	108	95	93	0.01	-2.11
Japan	136	126	108	95	93	0.01	-2.11
EUROPE	50,708	52,819	54,415	55,841	53,757	7.04	-3.73
Central/Eastern Europe	112	140	187	230	299	0.04	30.00
Russian Federation	112	140	187	230	299	0.04	30.00
Northern Europe	12,838	14,895	20,381	19,910	20,378	2.67	2.35
Denmark	272	215	126	218	202	0.03	-7.34
Finland	911	756	699	781	543	0.07	-30.47
Norway	422	495	483	672	997	0.13	48.36
Sweden	2,646	2,641	5,172	5,463	5,773	0.76	5.67
United Kingdom	8,587	10,788	13,901	12,776	12,863	1.68	0.68
Southern Europe	5,230	7,236	3,252	6,705	4,168	0.55	-37.84
Italy	3,889	5,972	2,383	5,721	3,238	0.42	-43.40
Portugal	179	158	134	186	146	0.02	-21.51
Spain	1,162	1,106	735	798	784	0.10	-1.75
Western Europe	29,872	28,493	28,583	26,855	26,783	3.51	-0.27
Austria	265	294	321	274	298	0.04	8.76
Belgium	1,590	1,641	1,869	1,841	2,123	0.28	15.32
Germany	3,508	2,877	2,952	2,673	3,059	0.40	14.44
Netherlands	23,867	23,017	22,718	21,266	20,374	2.67	-4.19
Switzerland	642	664	723	801	929	0.12	15.98
Other Europe	2,656	2,055	2,012	2,141	2,129	0.28	-0.56
Other countries of Europe	2,656	2,055	2,012	2,141	2,129	0.28	-0.56
NOT SPECIFIED	1,445	1,667	414	368	985	0.13	167.66
Other countries of the World	1,445	1,667	414	368	985	0.13	167.66

Yearbook of Tourism Statistics, Data 2008 – 2012, 2014 Edition

ARUBA

5. Overnight stays of non-resident tourists in hotels and similar establishments, by country of residence

	2008	2009	2010	2011	2012	Market share 2012	% Change 2012-2011
TOTAL	5,169,616	5,138,557	5,272,565	5,254,913	5,433,271	100.00	3.39
AMERICAS	4,647,484	4,595,415	4,697,020	4,695,165	4,880,490	89.83	3.95
Caribbean	54,633	51,214	56,565	46,313	53,664	0.99	15.87
Dominican Republic	1,219	1,538	1,785	1,376	2,109	0.04	53.27
Netherlands Antilles	37,629	41,718	47,684	38,499	41,514	0.76	7.83
Trinidad and Tobago	4,605	3,588	3,794	4,078	7,026	0.13	72.29
Other countries of the Caribbean	11,180	4,370	3,302	2,360	3,015	0.06	27.75
North America	3,946,339	3,894,317	3,956,611	3,863,749	3,900,405	71.79	0.95
Canada	248,060	261,918	285,358	294,698	327,457	6.03	11.12
United States of America	3,698,279	3,632,399	3,671,253	3,569,051	3,572,948	65.76	0.11
South America	646,512	649,884	683,844	785,103	926,421	17.05	18.00
Argentina	32,797	43,811	50,572	80,994	104,302	1.92	28.78
Brazil	52,664	63,805	120,697	131,284	122,155	2.25	-6.95
Chile	11,216	8,842	12,752	16,176	21,734	0.40	34.36
Colombia	63,853	72,056	73,261	72,547	78,147	1.44	7.72
Ecuador	9,015	5,329	11,778	14,851	7,435	0.14	-49.94
Peru	6,100	6,354	7,556	6,663	5,577	0.10	-16.30
Suriname	5,234	8,090	7,658	7,036	9,437	0.17	34.12
Venezuela	448,485	421,498	378,816	432,287	553,592	10.19	28.06
Other countries of South America	17,148	20,099	20,754	23,265	24,042	0.44	3.34
EAST ASIA AND THE PACIFIC	584	586	381	329	396	0.01	20.36
North-East Asia	584	586	381	329	396	0.01	20.36
Japan	584	586	381	329	396	0.01	20.36
EUROPE	499,879	533,300	567,032	550,733	539,457	9.93	-2.05
Central/Eastern Europe	1,062	1,327	1,983	2,174	2,940	0.05	35.23
Russian Federation	1,062	1,327	1,983	2,174	2,940	0.05	35.23
Northern Europe	147,437	180,769	251,231	233,408	239,047	4.40	2.42
Denmark	2,616	2,063	952	1,654	1,473	0.03	-10.94
Finland	7,864	7,325	7,410	7,976	5,299	0.10	-33.56
Norway	4,357	5,108	4,863	6,876	11,169	0.21	62.43
Sweden	26,507	30,218	63,992	66,937	70,568	1.30	5.42
United Kingdom	106,093	136,055	174,014	149,965	150,538	2.77	0.38
Southern Europe	36,748	57,499	25,447	54,250	33,291	0.61	-38.63
Italy	28,312	47,652	19,028	47,313	25,895	0.48	-45.27
Portugal	1,383	1,335	855	1,281	917	0.02	-28.42
Spain	7,053	8,512	5,564	5,656	6,479	0.12	14.55
Western Europe	288,406	275,891	270,810	243,460	245,373	4.52	0.79
Austria	2,528	3,033	3,471	2,971	3,084	0.06	3.80
Belgium	14,899	15,785	17,094	15,542	18,730	0.34	20.51
Germany	34,662	32,206	29,323	28,161	30,733	0.57	9.13
Netherlands	230,003	218,619	214,323	189,557	184,378	3.39	-2.73
Switzerland	6,314	6,248	6,599	7,229	8,448	0.16	16.86
Other Europe	26,226	17,814	17,561	17,441	18,806	0.35	7.83
Other countries of Europe	26,226	17,814	17,561	17,441	18,806	0.35	7.83
NOT SPECIFIED	21,669	9,256	8,132	8,686	12,928	0.24	48.84
Other countries of the World	21,669	9,256	8,132	8,686	12,928	0.24	48.84

Yearbook of Tourism Statistics, Data 2008 – 2012, 2014 Edition

ARUBA

6. Overnight stays of non-resident tourists in all types of accommodation establishments, by country of residence

	2008	2009	2010	2011	2012	Market share 2012	% Change 2012-2011
TOTAL	6,268,072	6,172,913	6,466,217	6,685,807	6,907,143	100.00	3.31
AMERICAS	5,383,932	5,270,446	5,539,453	5,742,183	5,954,445	86.21	3.70
Caribbean	167,815	141,274	157,940	184,875	203,436	2.95	10.04
Dominican Republic	11,764	9,363	18,508	29,922	31,938	0.46	6.74
Netherlands Antilles	125,845	113,347	120,034	125,284	139,658	2.02	11.47
Puerto Rico	10,357	609	617	95	345	0.00	263.16
Trinidad and Tobago	9,972	6,876	6,883	8,545	11,379	0.16	33.17
Other countries of the Caribbean	9,877	11,079	11,898	21,029	20,116	0.29	-4.34
North America	4,251,499	4,191,931	4,286,388	4,274,388	4,314,691	62.47	0.94
Canada	280,012	295,177	325,361	345,578	390,284	5.65	12.94
Mexico	11,499	8,498	9,058	8,776	9,415	0.14	7.28
United States of America	3,959,988	3,888,256	3,951,969	3,920,034	3,914,992	56.68	-0.13
South America	964,618	937,241	1,095,125	1,282,920	1,436,318	20.79	11.96
Argentina	35,923	46,072	53,291	86,820	111,984	1.62	28.98
Brazil	56,279	67,939	127,293	141,571	133,560	1.93	-5.66
Chile	11,886	9,341	13,530	17,240	22,911	0.33	32.89
Colombia	130,998	128,743	145,143	169,478	172,653	2.50	1.87
Ecuador	13,682	10,236	18,022	21,632	14,902	0.22	-31.11
Peru	11,475	11,348	14,233	13,499	10,807	0.16	-19.94
Suriname	23,566	32,114	29,295	36,174	39,558	0.57	9.35
Venezuela	655,480	612,030	670,662	772,863	903,545	13.08	16.91
Other countries of South America	25,329	19,418	23,656	23,643	26,398	0.38	11.65
EAST ASIA AND THE PACIFIC	702	739	562	540	640	0.01	18.52
North-East Asia	702	739	562	540	640	0.01	18.52
Japan	702	739	562	540	640	0.01	18.52
EUROPE	847,336	884,079	906,628	909,099	914,934	13.25	0.64
Central/Eastern Europe	2,171	2,282	2,654	3,093	4,172	0.06	34.89
Russian Federation	2,171	2,282	2,654	3,093	4,172	0.06	34.89
Northern Europe	160,821	195,808	267,813	258,940	261,432	3.78	0.96
Denmark	3,410	2,987	1,343	2,682	1,998	0.03	-25.50
Finland	9,814	8,320	8,487	12,502	6,375	0.09	-49.01
Norway	7,339	7,377	6,906	8,941	14,497	0.21	62.14
Sweden	28,648	31,780	67,185	72,012	76,991	1.11	6.91
United Kingdom	111,610	145,344	183,892	162,803	161,571	2.34	-0.76
Southern Europe	48,154	68,960	38,159	69,172	49,238	0.71	-28.82
Italy	34,024	52,893	25,680	56,166	34,580	0.50	-38.43
Portugal	1,808	1,997	1,259	1,772	1,242	0.02	-29.91
Spain	12,322	14,070	11,220	11,234	13,416	0.19	19.42
Western Europe	605,296	591,452	571,025	546,676	567,249	8.21	3.76
Austria	3,221	3,922	4,242	3,719	3,480	0.05	-6.43
Belgium	20,945	23,548	25,045	23,199	27,649	0.40	19.18
Germany	49,172	39,523	37,778	37,818	41,489	0.60	9.71
Netherlands	522,524	515,662	494,926	472,198	482,881	6.99	2.26
Switzerland	9,434	8,797	9,034	9,742	11,750	0.17	20.61
Other Europe	30,894	25,577	26,977	31,218	32,843	0.48	5.21
Other countries of Europe	30,894	25,577	26,977	31,218	32,843	0.48	5.21
NOT SPECIFIED	36,102	17,649	19,574	33,985	37,124	0.54	9.24
Other countries of the World	36,102	17,649	19,574	33,985	37,124	0.54	9.24

 Yearbook of Tourism Statistics, Data 2008 – 2012, 2014 Edition

AUSTRALIA

2. Arrivals of non-resident visitors at national borders, by country of residence

		2008	2009	2010	2011	2012	Market share 2012	% Change 2012-2011
TOTAL	(*)	5,585,824	5,584,075	5,885,091	5,875,065	6,145,593	100.00	4.60
AFRICA		93,239	84,107	89,271	91,642	84,465	1.37	-7.83
East Africa		19,962	18,867	21,707	21,271	20,098	0.33	-5.51
Burundi		37	41	8	36	38	0.00	5.56
Comoros		19			15	13	0.00	-13.33
Djibouti		18			17	20	0.00	17.65
Eritrea		35	28	22	18	26	0.00	44.44
Ethiopia		264	235	338	248	227	0.00	-8.47
Kenya		2,504	2,790	2,966	2,956	2,903	0.05	-1.79
Madagascar		144	98	168	99	214	0.00	116.16
Malawi		217	177	155	202	251	0.00	24.26
Mauritius		6,976	6,304	7,270	7,378	7,085	0.12	-3.97
Mozambique		287	201	299	344	251	0.00	-27.03
Reunion		3,391	3,855	4,941	3,802	3,284	0.05	-13.62
Rwanda		45	51	98	145	113	0.00	-22.07
Seychelles		458	371	531	398	297	0.00	-25.38
Somalia		60	21	73	89	95	0.00	6.74
Uganda		442	333	556	633	592	0.01	-6.48
United Republic of Tanzania		798	869	781	1,040	816	0.01	-21.54
Zambia		1,017	874	938	1,341	1,229	0.02	-8.35
Zimbabwe		3,250	2,619	2,563	2,510	2,644	0.04	5.34
Central Africa		687	394	494	700	863	0.01	23.29
Angola		273	108	352	170	261	0.00	53.53
Cameroon		45	105	32	123	78	0.00	-36.59
Central African Republic		3			3	5	0.00	66.67
Chad		31	56	10	146	157	0.00	7.53
Congo		254	73	64	109	108	0.00	-0.92
Democratic Republic of the Congo		36	13	21	15	38	0.00	153.33
Equatorial Guinea		3	35	3	3	58	0.00	1,833.33
Gabon		39	4	12	126	155	0.00	23.02
Sao Tome and Principe		3			5	3	0.00	-40.00
North Africa		559	719	1,120	1,005	1,034	0.02	2.89
Algeria		143	213	256	357	272	0.00	-23.81
Morocco		132	275	416	317	308	0.01	-2.84
Sudan		200	162	263	100	300	0.00	200.00
Tunisia		84	69	185	231	154	0.00	-33.33
Southern Africa		69,816	61,584	63,608	65,817	59,230	0.96	-10.01
Botswana		557	625	726	719	730	0.01	1.53
Lesotho		27	60	77	47	67	0.00	42.55
Namibia		673	435	446	520	567	0.01	9.04
South Africa		68,460	60,291	62,198	64,370	57,739	0.94	-10.30
Swaziland		99	173	161	161	127	0.00	-21.12
West Africa		2,171	2,435	2,231	2,761	3,119	0.05	12.97
Benin		8	5	10	5	27	0.00	440.00
Burkina Faso		16	6	18	32	50	0.00	56.25
Cape Verde		4		3	4	9	0.00	125.00
Côte d'Ivoire		55	57	61	24	47	0.00	95.83
Gambia		25	14	12	30	26	0.00	-13.33
Ghana		431	513	523	590	718	0.01	21.69
Guinea		121	31	175	114	151	0.00	32.46
Guinea-Bissau		3						
Liberia		111	46	44	78	134	0.00	71.79
Mali		19	114	43	44	54	0.00	22.73
Mauritania		287	309	193	108	102	0.00	-5.56
Niger		21	80	26	192	35	0.00	-81.77
Nigeria		958	1,169	1,006	1,294	1,604	0.03	23.96

Yearbook of Tourism Statistics, Data 2008 – 2012, 2014 Edition

AUSTRALIA

2. Arrivals of non-resident visitors at national borders, by country of residence

	2008	2009	2010	2011	2012	Market share 2012	% Change 2012-2011
Senegal	63	53	74	77	78	0.00	1.30
Sierra Leone	33	31	37	136	62	0.00	-54.41
Togo	16	7	6	33	22	0.00	-33.33
Other Africa	**44**	**108**	**111**	**88**	**121**	**0.00**	**37.50**
Other countries of Africa	44	108	111	88	121	0.00	37.50
AMERICAS	**644,163**	**670,055**	**661,819**	**645,833**	**683,454**	**11.12**	**5.83**
Caribbean	**2,977**	**2,992**	**3,193**	**2,690**	**2,727**	**0.04**	**1.38**
Anguilla	6	19		3			
Antigua and Barbuda	13	11	13	13	11	0.00	-15.38
Aruba	9	56		38	45	0.00	18.42
Bahamas	148	290	162	236	214	0.00	-9.32
Barbados	96	225	270	144	173	0.00	20.14
Bermuda	474	604	511	545	270	0.00	-50.46
British Virgin Islands	7		44		112	0.00	
Cayman Islands	319	428	626	337	413	0.01	22.55
Cuba	90	161	239	224	98	0.00	-56.25
Dominica	101	47	18	47	197	0.00	319.15
Dominican Republic	115	43	86	54	81	0.00	50.00
Grenada	43	66	57	153	166	0.00	8.50
Guadeloupe	34	69	22	30	14	0.00	-53.33
Haiti	52	15	62	73	10	0.00	-86.30
Jamaica	359	324	298	255	224	0.00	-12.16
Martinique	54	46	77	12			
Montserrat	12	5	28	4			
Netherlands Antilles		19		9			
Puerto Rico	570	192	273	48	226	0.00	370.83
Saint Kitts and Nevis	38	7	12	19	8	0.00	-57.89
Saint Lucia	25	22	27	26	30	0.00	15.38
Saint Vincent and the Grenadines	14	12	12	18	28	0.00	55.56
Trinidad and Tobago	322	328	356	360	407	0.01	13.06
Turks and Caicos Islands	43	3		42			
United States Virgin Islands	33						
Central America	**1,417**	**1,129**	**1,134**	**954**	**1,213**	**0.02**	**27.15**
Belize	82	34	15	10	32	0.00	220.00
Costa Rica	458	430	341	311	314	0.01	0.96
El Salvador	271	163	184	113	190	0.00	68.14
Guatemala	282	128	254	119	140	0.00	17.65
Honduras	122	71	98	89	65	0.00	-26.97
Nicaragua	63	27	28	124	126	0.00	1.61
Panama	139	264	210	185	317	0.01	71.35
Other countries of Central America		12	4	3	29	0.00	866.67
North America	**586,622**	**609,770**	**600,570**	**580,188**	**604,982**	**9.84**	**4.27**
Canada	124,637	123,330	121,870	117,636	119,848	1.95	1.88
Mexico	7,477	6,685	6,578	6,384	6,144	0.10	-3.76
Saint Pierre and Miquelon		11					
United States of America	454,444	479,744	472,122	456,156	478,990	7.79	5.01
Other countries of North America	64			12			
South America	**53,147**	**56,164**	**56,922**	**62,001**	**74,532**	**1.21**	**20.21**
Argentina	5,832	8,607	8,611	9,389	13,632	0.22	45.19
Bolivia	264	178	221	207	266	0.00	28.50
Brazil	25,010	25,846	26,904	29,203	30,916	0.50	5.87
Chile	10,268	10,156	9,538	10,483	14,076	0.23	34.27
Colombia	5,799	6,197	6,140	6,552	8,060	0.13	23.02
Ecuador	513	423	430	733	657	0.01	-10.37
Falkland Islands, Malvinas	76		26		23	0.00	
French Guiana	30	22					
Guyana	35	39	59	68	36	0.00	-47.06

27

Yearbook of Tourism Statistics, Data 2008 – 2012, 2014 Edition

AUSTRALIA

2. Arrivals of non-resident visitors at national borders, by country of residence

	2008	2009	2010	2011	2012	Market share 2012	% Change 2012-2011
Paraguay	303	103	198	175	165	0.00	-5.71
Peru	2,378	2,325	2,255	2,564	2,726	0.04	6.32
Suriname	36	23	17	36	59	0.00	63.89
Uruguay	1,122	877	1,042	1,080	1,961	0.03	81.57
Venezuela	1,440	1,357	1,469	1,508	1,955	0.03	29.64
Other countries of South America	41	11	12	3			
EAST ASIA AND THE PACIFIC	**3,244,422**	**3,226,010**	**3,515,746**	**3,568,832**	**3,777,897**	**61.47**	**5.86**
North-East Asia	**1,257,717**	**1,162,638**	**1,321,624**	**1,328,607**	**1,454,237**	**23.66**	**9.46**
China	356,428	366,362	453,738	542,123	626,457	10.19	15.56
Hong Kong, China	143,956	156,892	163,930	166,400	176,701	2.88	6.19
Japan	457,257	355,421	398,151	332,573	353,993	5.76	6.44
Korea, Dem. People's Republic of	10	52	3	3	9	0.00	200.00
Korea, Republic of	218,311	180,878	214,118	197,825	196,674	3.20	-0.58
Macao, China	3,478	3,784	3,448	3,830	4,246	0.07	10.86
Mongolia	631	711	1,100	1,395	1,568	0.03	12.40
Taiwan, Province of China	77,646	98,538	87,136	84,458	94,589	1.54	12.00
South-East Asia	**714,565**	**789,968**	**861,954**	**896,909**	**951,919**	**15.49**	**6.13**
Brunei Darussalam	7,942	7,832	7,783	8,142	6,989	0.11	-14.16
Cambodia	4,300	5,443	5,277	5,089	5,030	0.08	-1.16
Indonesia	94,265	108,738	123,890	140,372	145,577	2.37	3.71
Lao People's Democratic Republic	1,907	2,025	1,660	1,684	1,682	0.03	-0.12
Malaysia	171,019	211,545	237,018	241,181	262,591	4.27	8.88
Myanmar	1,390	1,627	1,626	2,068	2,070	0.03	0.10
Philippines	46,898	47,418	51,440	56,667	58,965	0.96	4.06
Singapore	270,900	285,342	307,994	318,546	343,662	5.59	7.88
Thailand	79,539	81,804	84,147	85,421	83,869	1.36	-1.82
Timor-Leste	3,225	3,243	3,892	3,826	3,951	0.06	3.27
Viet Nam	33,180	34,937	37,227	33,913	37,533	0.61	10.67
Other countries of South-East Asia		14					
Australasia	**1,113,313**	**1,110,456**	**1,161,658**	**1,172,726**	**1,201,199**	**19.55**	**2.43**
New Zealand	1,113,313	1,110,456	1,161,658	1,172,726	1,201,199	19.55	2.43
Melanesia	**133,824**	**141,680**	**148,332**	**146,897**	**147,409**	**2.40**	**0.35**
Fiji	29,732	32,462	33,370	32,352	32,658	0.53	0.95
New Caledonia	45,817	45,669	45,808	41,677	38,741	0.63	-7.04
Norfolk Island	2,895	2,551	2,349	2,737	2,049	0.03	-25.14
Papua New Guinea	38,751	43,629	48,855	51,798	56,620	0.92	9.31
Solomon Islands	8,282	7,389	8,212	7,917	7,511	0.12	-5.13
Vanuatu	8,347	9,980	9,738	10,416	9,830	0.16	-5.63
Micronesia	**5,518**	**5,369**	**4,477**	**4,582**	**5,040**	**0.08**	**10.00**
Guam	1,797	1,744	1,671	1,124	855	0.01	-23.93
Kiribati	1,301	1,345	943	1,148	1,214	0.02	5.75
Marshall Islands	141	215	177	154	234	0.00	51.95
Micronesia, Federated States of	304	267	258	290	384	0.01	32.41
Nauru	1,666	1,524	1,233	1,614	2,196	0.04	36.06
Northern Mariana Islands	76	17	11	3			
Palau	233	257	184	249	157	0.00	-36.95
Polynesia	**19,114**	**15,653**	**17,592**	**18,574**	**17,572**	**0.29**	**-5.39**
American Samoa	42	122	100	75	39	0.00	-48.00
Cook Islands	1,814	1,473	1,859	1,799	1,726	0.03	-4.06
French Polynesia	5,754	4,438	3,777	3,522	2,945	0.05	-16.38
Niue	371	209	180	62	301	0.00	385.48
Samoa	5,009	4,241	5,249	4,941	5,447	0.09	10.24
Tokelau	86	84	4	41	179	0.00	336.59
Tonga	5,460	4,507	5,969	7,587	6,382	0.10	-15.88
Tuvalu	204	250	213	171	254	0.00	48.54
Wallis and Futuna Islands	374	329	241	376	299	0.00	-20.48

Yearbook of Tourism Statistics, Data 2008 – 2012, 2014 Edition

AUSTRALIA

2. Arrivals of non-resident visitors at national borders, by country of residence

	2008	2009	2010	2011	2012	Market share 2012	% Change 2012-2011
Other East Asia and the Pacific	371	246	109	537	521	0.01	-2.98
Other countries of Oceania	371	246	109	537	521	0.01	-2.98
EUROPE	1,381,169	1,362,172	1,347,469	1,291,218	1,300,414	21.16	0.71
Central/Eastern Europe	46,982	45,277	46,061	47,057	54,533	0.89	15.89
Armenia	109	73	87	142	178	0.00	25.35
Azerbaijan	178	94	110	155	125	0.00	-19.35
Belarus	210	269	353	256	419	0.01	63.67
Bulgaria	1,011	1,255	1,033	963	1,293	0.02	34.27
Czech Republic	2,488	1,740	4,921	4,947	6,494	0.11	31.27
Czech Republic/Slovakia	4,063	5,368	1,879	1,681	1,378	0.02	-18.02
Estonia	1,867	2,238	2,190	2,388	2,930	0.05	22.70
Georgia	30	112	40	78	100	0.00	28.21
Hungary	4,014	4,055	3,718	3,752	4,330	0.07	15.41
Kazakhstan	667	647	904	897	1,012	0.02	12.82
Kyrgyzstan	83	102	90	73	120	0.00	64.38
Latvia	968	1,005	785	798	964	0.02	20.80
Lithuania	973	753	760	843	1,080	0.02	28.11
Poland	10,517	8,393	8,752	8,745	9,507	0.15	8.71
Republic of Moldova	71	85	135	86	123	0.00	43.02
Romania	1,579	1,493	1,452	1,112	1,604	0.03	44.24
Russian Federation	12,795	12,436	13,631	14,494	16,839	0.27	16.18
Slovakia	2,150	2,237	2,343	2,368	2,457	0.04	3.76
Tajikistan	72	37	28	20	26	0.00	30.00
Turkmenistan	9	20	4	9	8	0.00	-11.11
Ukraine	2,739	2,533	2,597	3,052	3,237	0.05	6.06
USSR (former)	178	68	14		13	0.00	
Uzbekistan	211	264	235	198	296	0.00	49.49
Northern Europe	828,369	813,499	788,626	753,727	746,740	12.15	-0.93
Channel Islands	623	1,513	1,085	872	1,282	0.02	47.02
Denmark	24,036	24,118	23,047	22,079	22,712	0.37	2.87
Faeroe Islands	96	42	94	21	24	0.00	14.29
Finland	11,336	11,935	11,929	11,979	13,197	0.21	10.17
Iceland	905	627	442	518	458	0.01	-11.58
Ireland	68,155	62,546	52,961	58,711	61,193	1.00	4.23
Isle of Man	584	809	434	453	656	0.01	44.81
Norway	17,353	17,615	19,125	17,884	19,046	0.31	6.50
Sweden	34,352	32,816	34,354	34,264	36,243	0.59	5.78
United Kingdom	670,919	661,442	645,155	606,926	591,903	9.63	-2.48
Other countries of Northern Europe	10	36		20	26	0.00	30.00
Southern Europe	109,820	99,319	103,642	100,656	109,556	1.78	8.84
Albania	261	259	183	190	211	0.00	11.05
Andorra	196	139	107	100	139	0.00	39.00
Bosnia and Herzegovina	631	638	713	689	666	0.01	-3.34
Croatia	3,296	2,187	2,118	2,085	2,401	0.04	15.16
Gibraltar	98	96	221	125	110	0.00	-12.00
Greece	6,944	6,813	8,094	7,452	8,604	0.14	15.46
Holy See	16						
Italy	58,730	55,106	56,399	54,956	60,939	0.99	10.89
Malta	2,730	2,659	2,773	2,748	2,394	0.04	-12.88
Portugal	4,388	3,673	3,748	3,498	4,137	0.07	18.27
San Marino	43	25	45	24	14	0.00	-41.67
Serbia and Montenegro	2,274	1,918	2,437	2,436	2,356	0.04	-3.28
Slovenia	2,494	2,369	2,315	2,388	2,221	0.04	-6.99
Spain	26,243	22,054	23,007	22,654	23,808	0.39	5.09
TFYR of Macedonia	1,476	1,383	1,482	1,311	1,556	0.03	18.69
Western Europe	373,558	382,470	386,273	369,012	371,455	6.04	0.66
Austria	17,083	16,704	16,244	14,080	14,218	0.23	0.98

29

AUSTRALIA

2. Arrivals of non-resident visitors at national borders, by country of residence

	2008	2009	2010	2011	2012	Market share 2012	% Change 2012-2011
Belgium	13,762	14,646	16,240	15,588	15,616	0.25	0.18
France	85,650	93,290	97,280	93,951	97,465	1.59	3.74
Germany	160,717	161,334	160,350	153,839	154,888	2.52	0.68
Liechtenstein	135	89	87	23	54	0.00	134.78
Luxembourg	1,109	1,276	1,056	926	842	0.01	-9.07
Monaco	431	495	517	532	706	0.01	32.71
Netherlands	54,643	51,462	49,989	47,593	44,084	0.72	-7.37
Switzerland	40,028	43,174	44,510	42,480	43,582	0.71	2.59
East Mediterranean Europe	**22,297**	**21,574**	**22,836**	**20,724**	**18,119**	**0.29**	**-12.57**
Cyprus	1,933	2,150	2,095	1,990	2,073	0.03	4.17
Israel	15,500	14,249	14,485	12,283	10,272	0.17	-16.37
Turkey	4,864	5,175	6,256	6,451	5,774	0.09	-10.49
Other Europe	**143**	**33**	**31**	**42**	**11**	**0.00**	**-73.81**
Other countries of Europe	143	33	31	42	11	0.00	-73.81
MIDDLE EAST	**74,695**	**79,610**	**87,140**	**81,594**	**86,939**	**1.41**	**6.55**
Bahrain	2,142	2,462	2,373	1,674	1,407	0.02	-15.95
Egypt	2,676	2,654	3,026	2,634	2,786	0.05	5.77
Iraq	566	843	1,143	1,088	951	0.02	-12.59
Jordan	1,285	1,270	1,108	1,177	1,187	0.02	0.85
Kuwait	3,053	2,343	3,017	2,936	3,360	0.05	14.44
Lebanon	6,097	5,779	5,276	5,245	5,234	0.09	-0.21
Libya	170	258	660	237	202	0.00	-14.77
Oman	2,701	2,237	2,616	2,353	2,081	0.03	-11.56
Qatar	3,032	3,664	4,646	5,151	5,526	0.09	7.28
Saudi Arabia	10,883	13,015	13,663	13,575	13,409	0.22	-1.22
Syrian Arab Republic	860	751	600	368	166	0.00	-54.89
United Arab Emirates	41,132	44,130	48,774	45,001	50,535	0.82	12.30
Yemen	30	116	184	37	8	0.00	-78.38
Other countries of Middle East	68	88	54	118	87	0.00	-26.27
SOUTH ASIA	**148,089**	**162,022**	**183,526**	**195,896**	**212,392**	**3.46**	**8.42**
Afghanistan	176	312	293	301	568	0.01	88.70
Bangladesh	4,230	5,495	6,457	7,351	7,429	0.12	1.06
Bhutan	178	194	262	263	319	0.01	21.29
India	116,001	124,888	138,705	148,191	159,279	2.59	7.48
Iran, Islamic Republic of	4,625	4,890	7,481	8,538	9,183	0.15	7.55
Maldives	486	460	574	460	412	0.01	-10.43
Nepal	3,840	5,090	5,192	4,767	6,125	0.10	28.49
Pakistan	5,244	6,776	7,910	8,877	9,699	0.16	9.26
Sri Lanka	13,309	13,917	16,652	17,148	19,378	0.32	13.00
NOT SPECIFIED	**47**	**99**	**120**	**50**	**32**	**0.00**	**-36.00**
Other countries of the World	47	99	120	50	32	0.00	-36.00

Yearbook of Tourism Statistics, Data 2008 – 2012, 2014 Edition

AUSTRIA

3. Arrivals of non-resident tourists in hotels and similar establishments, by country of residence

	2008	2009	2010	2011	2012	Market share 2012	% Change 2012-2011
TOTAL (*)	16,091,160	15,520,385	16,169,935	16,972,001	17,727,876	100.00	4.45
AFRICA	35,565	34,631	40,676	47,141	51,561	0.29	9.38
Southern Africa	16,376	12,764	17,099	17,533	18,528	0.10	5.68
South Africa	16,376	12,764	17,099	17,533	18,528	0.10	5.68
Other Africa	19,189	21,867	23,577	29,608	33,033	0.19	11.57
Other countries of Africa	19,189	21,867	23,577	29,608	33,033	0.19	11.57
AMERICAS	599,728	546,539	638,867	664,935	717,953	4.05	7.97
North America	518,240	468,770	543,442	536,997	566,318	3.19	5.46
Canada	75,940	69,227	77,923	84,364	84,154	0.47	-0.25
United States of America	442,300	399,543	465,519	452,633	482,164	2.72	6.52
South America			3,407	43,453	57,897	0.33	33.24
Brazil			3,407	43,453	57,897	0.33	33.24
Other Americas	81,488	77,769	92,018	84,485	93,738	0.53	10.95
Other countries of the Americas	81,488	77,769	92,018	84,485	93,738	0.53	10.95
EAST ASIA AND THE PACIFIC	642,244	582,651	668,022	820,794	1,004,065	5.66	22.33
North-East Asia	445,074	418,173	477,455	603,608	756,265	4.27	25.29
China	147,364	147,417	173,116	245,340	338,064	1.91	37.79
Japan	200,791	191,321	206,217	220,691	253,019	1.43	14.65
Korea, Republic of	68,360	50,103	62,534	83,011	108,458	0.61	30.65
Taiwan, Province of China	28,559	29,332	35,588	54,566	56,724	0.32	3.95
South-East Asia	42,826	39,072	47,799	67,930	83,706	0.47	23.22
All countries of South-East Asia	42,826	39,072	47,799	67,930	83,706	0.47	23.22
Australasia	111,997	89,781	99,269	107,836	117,214	0.66	8.70
Australia	97,768	78,521	87,742	96,316	104,646	0.59	8.65
New Zealand	14,229	11,260	11,527	11,520	12,568	0.07	9.10
Other East Asia and the Pacific	42,347	35,625	43,499	41,420	46,880	0.26	13.18
Other countries of Asia	42,347	35,625	43,499	41,420	46,880	0.26	13.18
EUROPE	14,350,098	13,964,009	14,405,592	15,009,616	15,446,474	87.13	2.91
Central/Eastern Europe	1,634,118	1,516,356	1,635,813	1,832,305	1,918,559	10.82	4.71
Bulgaria	54,015	50,093	50,052	56,949	59,797	0.34	5.00
Czech Republic	302,131	318,086	332,214	360,611	366,885	2.07	1.74
Estonia	15,760	12,805	15,805	13,293	15,291	0.09	15.03
Hungary	311,619	283,542	291,622	310,792	319,381	1.80	2.76
Latvia	18,848	11,640	11,322	12,844	14,890	0.08	15.93
Lithuania	20,578	13,937	14,383	15,722	16,675	0.09	6.06
Poland	220,801	206,416	228,861	247,051	239,135	1.35	-3.20
Romania	280,007	238,325	223,919	236,469	224,779	1.27	-4.94
Russian Federation	243,778	208,613	275,932	359,348	422,243	2.38	17.50
Slovakia	85,157	89,048	97,499	106,142	108,670	0.61	2.38
Ukraine	53,711	56,623	60,041	75,288	90,152	0.51	19.74
Other countries Central/East Europe	27,713	27,228	34,163	37,796	40,661	0.23	7.58
Northern Europe	1,281,341	1,117,272	1,182,644	1,152,609	1,184,028	6.68	2.73
Denmark	206,458	199,532	205,901	200,370	201,446	1.14	0.54
Finland	63,153	68,630	68,690	73,418	74,046	0.42	0.86
Iceland	7,793	5,441	6,525	6,823	6,927	0.04	1.52
Ireland	66,085	52,473	48,052	42,994	43,115	0.24	0.28
Norway	62,511	57,437	68,649	73,605	75,079	0.42	2.00
Sweden	169,067	139,883	164,721	158,229	165,285	0.93	4.46
United Kingdom	706,274	593,876	620,106	597,170	618,130	3.49	3.51
Southern Europe	1,477,196	1,434,049	1,483,900	1,561,455	1,500,368	8.46	-3.91
Croatia	99,228	83,348	79,825	80,470	81,092	0.46	0.77
Greece	90,445	83,145	73,029	59,856	49,980	0.28	-16.50
Italy	882,436	895,285	907,257	918,414	880,136	4.96	-4.17
Malta	5,309	3,632	5,048	5,172	5,391	0.03	4.23
Portugal	27,864	26,231	28,212	30,014	25,580	0.14	-14.77

31

AUSTRIA

3. Arrivals of non-resident tourists in hotels and similar establishments, by country of residence

	2008	2009	2010	2011	2012	Market share 2012	% Change 2012-2011
Serbia and Montenegro	48,917	49,721	70,662	92,072	93,490	0.53	1.54
Slovenia	71,314	70,358	73,650	81,001	82,522	0.47	1.88
Spain	251,683	222,329	246,217	294,456	282,177	1.59	-4.17
Western Europe	**9,854,942**	**9,792,268**	**9,978,470**	**10,315,335**	**10,672,792**	**60.20**	**3.47**
Belgium	354,566	353,483	353,391	373,709	372,756	2.10	-0.26
France	395,148	397,979	414,677	434,953	431,308	2.43	-0.84
Germany	7,341,427	7,258,959	7,394,154	7,547,259	7,826,949	44.15	3.71
Luxembourg	43,338	44,468	46,863	49,262	50,143	0.28	1.79
Netherlands	888,748	875,811	853,187	864,401	886,240	5.00	2.53
Switzerland	831,715	861,568	916,198	1,045,751	1,105,396	6.24	5.70
East Mediterranean Europe	**102,501**	**104,064**	**124,765**	**147,912**	**170,727**	**0.96**	**15.42**
Cyprus	8,790	8,310	9,029	7,677	7,635	0.04	-0.55
Israel	53,445	58,826	65,551	73,296	84,939	0.48	15.88
Turkey	40,266	36,928	50,185	66,939	78,153	0.44	16.75
MIDDLE EAST	**95,226**	**89,519**	**109,523**	**142,173**	**189,193**	**1.07**	**33.07**
All countries of Middle East	95,226	89,519	109,523	142,173	189,193	1.07	33.07
SOUTH ASIA	**44,840**	**45,482**	**57,368**	**79,891**	**84,574**	**0.48**	**5.86**
All countries of South Asia	44,840	45,482	57,368	79,891	84,574	0.48	5.86
NOT SPECIFIED	**323,459**	**257,554**	**249,887**	**207,451**	**234,056**	**1.32**	**12.82**
Other countries of the World	323,459	257,554	249,887	207,451	234,056	1.32	12.82

Yearbook of Tourism Statistics, Data 2008 – 2012, 2014 Edition

AUSTRIA

4. Arrivals of non-resident tourists in all types of accommodation establishments, by country of residence

	2008	2009	2010	2011	2012	Market share 2012	% Change 2012-2011
TOTAL (*)	21,935,409	21,355,439	22,004,266	23,011,956	24,150,776	100.00	4.95
AFRICA	39,957	38,794	44,965	52,345	58,087	0.24	10.97
Southern Africa	19,418	15,699	19,874	20,479	21,737	0.09	6.14
South Africa	19,418	15,699	19,874	20,479	21,737	0.09	6.14
Other Africa	20,539	23,095	25,091	31,866	36,350	0.15	14.07
Other countries of Africa	20,539	23,095	25,091	31,866	36,350	0.15	14.07
AMERICAS	672,610	616,730	708,515	742,821	805,619	3.34	8.45
North America	572,513	523,314	596,125	594,679	629,280	2.61	5.82
Canada	88,955	81,466	90,684	98,545	97,807	0.40	-0.75
United States of America	483,558	441,848	505,441	496,134	531,473	2.20	7.12
South America			3,918	50,796	68,257	0.28	34.37
Brazil			3,918	50,796	68,257	0.28	34.37
Other Americas	100,097	93,416	108,472	97,346	108,082	0.45	11.03
Other countries of the Americas	100,097	93,416	108,472	97,346	108,082	0.45	11.03
EAST ASIA AND THE PACIFIC	705,701	645,203	741,244	914,840	1,105,297	4.58	20.82
North-East Asia	475,655	445,635	512,054	654,442	812,653	3.36	24.17
China	156,190	155,179	182,282	259,944	354,657	1.47	36.44
Japan	208,150	198,751	213,581	228,559	261,261	1.08	14.31
Korea, Republic of	79,928	59,351	77,560	106,359	134,856	0.56	26.79
Taiwan, Province of China	31,387	32,354	38,631	59,580	61,879	0.26	3.86
South-East Asia	46,276	43,269	53,425	74,242	90,866	0.38	22.39
All countries of South-East Asia	46,276	43,269	53,425	74,242	90,866	0.38	22.39
Australasia	139,384	118,112	129,818	142,258	151,922	0.63	6.79
Australia	121,314	103,063	114,457	126,169	134,800	0.56	6.84
New Zealand	18,070	15,049	15,361	16,089	17,122	0.07	6.42
Other East Asia and the Pacific	44,386	38,187	45,947	43,898	49,856	0.21	13.57
Other countries of Asia	44,386	38,187	45,947	43,898	49,856	0.21	13.57
EUROPE	19,993,474	19,613,283	20,042,806	20,818,964	21,599,410	89.44	3.75
Central/Eastern Europe	2,242,687	2,131,821	2,279,602	2,519,532	2,633,952	10.91	4.54
Bulgaria	59,439	56,305	55,947	63,992	68,238	0.28	6.64
Czech Republic	522,680	556,073	569,279	603,581	619,287	2.56	2.60
Estonia	20,549	16,551	19,670	16,759	21,179	0.09	26.37
Hungary	462,627	426,498	442,245	466,860	472,793	1.96	1.27
Latvia	25,252	15,634	15,766	18,371	21,058	0.09	14.63
Lithuania	31,075	23,766	23,007	25,417	26,757	0.11	5.27
Poland	335,141	317,222	346,582	372,924	362,870	1.50	-2.70
Romania	316,235	273,225	261,439	275,722	265,774	1.10	-3.61
Russian Federation	264,115	230,598	305,714	400,399	476,397	1.97	18.98
Slovakia	117,183	123,164	135,332	148,080	152,960	0.63	3.30
Ukraine	58,994	63,929	68,264	86,649	102,720	0.43	18.55
Other countries Central/East Europe	29,397	28,856	36,357	40,778	43,919	0.18	7.70
Northern Europe	1,595,397	1,403,027	1,478,706	1,447,011	1,500,402	6.21	3.69
Denmark	318,612	312,734	321,642	313,013	316,890	1.31	1.24
Finland	73,678	79,189	80,922	87,105	91,363	0.38	4.89
Iceland	8,788	6,198	7,613	7,912	8,440	0.03	6.67
Ireland	79,982	64,110	59,152	53,416	53,210	0.22	-0.39
Norway	73,703	67,775	79,838	84,951	87,230	0.36	2.68
Sweden	215,321	171,774	198,122	191,405	202,297	0.84	5.69
United Kingdom	825,313	701,247	731,417	709,209	740,972	3.07	4.48
Southern Europe	1,733,501	1,694,882	1,748,616	1,842,030	1,794,186	7.43	-2.60
Croatia	129,338	109,903	105,712	105,184	106,129	0.44	0.90
Greece	95,381	88,208	77,587	64,210	53,689	0.22	-16.39
Italy	1,033,306	1,056,491	1,067,721	1,086,957	1,060,105	4.39	-2.47
Malta	5,732	4,086	5,424	5,877	5,884	0.02	0.12
Portugal	31,514	30,082	32,051	33,846	29,617	0.12	-12.49

33

AUSTRIA

4. Arrivals of non-resident tourists in all types of accommodation establishments, by country of residence

	2008	2009	2010	2011	2012	Market share 2012	% Change 2012-2011
Serbia and Montenegro	53,015	54,602	78,950	102,125	104,145	0.43	1.98
Slovenia	101,944	102,126	106,520	117,740	122,677	0.51	4.19
Spain	283,271	249,384	274,651	326,091	311,940	1.29	-4.34
Western Europe	**14,306,248**	**14,263,593**	**14,392,893**	**14,841,017**	**15,473,410**	**64.07**	**4.26**
Belgium	462,822	461,299	461,784	488,810	494,014	2.05	1.06
France	473,235	478,747	499,894	521,955	519,519	2.15	-0.47
Germany	10,709,251	10,622,835	10,706,153	10,929,670	11,411,557	47.25	4.41
Luxembourg	50,444	51,164	53,804	57,004	58,229	0.24	2.15
Netherlands	1,650,134	1,654,959	1,617,692	1,644,620	1,714,513	7.10	4.25
Switzerland	960,362	994,589	1,053,566	1,198,958	1,275,578	5.28	6.39
East Mediterranean Europe	**115,641**	**119,960**	**142,989**	**169,374**	**197,460**	**0.82**	**16.58**
Cyprus	9,475	8,951	9,624	8,218	8,244	0.03	0.32
Israel	63,587	71,678	80,296	89,834	105,317	0.44	17.24
Turkey	42,579	39,331	53,069	71,322	83,899	0.35	17.63
MIDDLE EAST	**102,099**	**97,053**	**120,055**	**160,005**	**218,070**	**0.90**	**36.29**
All countries of Middle East	102,099	97,053	120,055	160,005	218,070	0.90	36.29
SOUTH ASIA	**46,990**	**47,604**	**59,780**	**83,911**	**88,864**	**0.37**	**5.90**
All countries of South Asia	46,990	47,604	59,780	83,911	88,864	0.37	5.90
NOT SPECIFIED	**374,578**	**296,772**	**286,901**	**239,070**	**275,429**	**1.14**	**15.21**
Other countries of the World	374,578	296,772	286,901	239,070	275,429	1.14	15.21

Yearbook of Tourism Statistics, Data 2008 – 2012, 2014 Edition

AUSTRIA

5. Overnight stays of non-resident tourists in hotels and similar establishments, by country of residence

		2008	2009	2010	2011	2012	Market share 2012	% Change 2012-2011
TOTAL	(*)	60,468,710	57,798,255	58,314,787	59,146,607	61,359,896	100.00	3.74
AFRICA		123,372	108,776	128,883	149,633	160,143	0.26	7.02
Southern Africa		66,071	50,416	59,254	62,914	64,044	0.10	1.80
South Africa		66,071	50,416	59,254	62,914	64,044	0.10	1.80
Other Africa		57,301	58,360	69,629	86,719	96,099	0.16	10.82
Other countries of Africa		57,301	58,360	69,629	86,719	96,099	0.16	10.82
AMERICAS		1,448,208	1,342,812	1,524,758	1,568,231	1,680,026	2.74	7.13
North America		1,262,868	1,159,958	1,313,600	1,283,178	1,334,351	2.17	3.99
Canada		185,771	170,513	190,823	205,616	202,047	0.33	-1.74
United States of America		1,077,097	989,445	1,122,777	1,077,562	1,132,304	1.85	5.08
South America				7,924	96,380	131,874	0.21	36.83
Brazil				7,924	96,380	131,874	0.21	36.83
Other Americas		185,340	182,854	203,234	188,673	213,801	0.35	13.32
Other countries of the Americas		185,340	182,854	203,234	188,673	213,801	0.35	13.32
EAST ASIA AND THE PACIFIC		1,183,238	1,096,782	1,214,144	1,418,535	1,718,206	2.80	21.13
North-East Asia		752,997	727,575	795,424	955,351	1,193,440	1.94	24.92
China		217,115	206,576	249,334	340,655	471,430	0.77	38.39
Japan		390,347	387,987	393,431	417,538	484,679	0.79	16.08
Korea, Republic of		101,163	82,138	91,387	116,888	154,567	0.25	32.24
Taiwan, Province of China		44,372	50,874	61,272	80,270	82,764	0.13	3.11
South-East Asia		79,496	74,191	89,710	122,214	145,245	0.24	18.84
All countries of South-East Asia		79,496	74,191	89,710	122,214	145,245	0.24	18.84
Australasia		256,457	212,390	235,320	251,823	282,412	0.46	12.15
Australia		226,153	187,649	208,685	225,447	252,215	0.41	11.87
New Zealand		30,304	24,741	26,635	26,376	30,197	0.05	14.49
Other East Asia and the Pacific		94,288	82,626	93,690	89,147	97,109	0.16	8.93
Other countries of Asia		94,288	82,626	93,690	89,147	97,109	0.16	8.93
EUROPE		56,567,773	54,267,191	54,438,114	54,939,775	56,512,270	92.10	2.86
Central/Eastern Europe		5,146,585	4,817,482	5,050,336	5,547,838	5,811,896	9.47	4.76
Bulgaria		128,090	119,747	123,252	137,444	147,078	0.24	7.01
Czech Republic		890,714	970,092	992,854	1,066,545	1,085,607	1.77	1.79
Estonia		55,108	43,394	51,130	42,431	45,658	0.07	7.61
Hungary		986,308	878,544	873,197	918,744	941,573	1.53	2.48
Latvia		60,416	37,803	34,040	37,172	42,946	0.07	15.53
Lithuania		72,457	51,068	45,664	47,798	52,933	0.09	10.74
Poland		748,703	729,691	752,794	801,360	774,235	1.26	-3.38
Romania		736,540	662,774	627,184	645,438	615,389	1.00	-4.66
Russian Federation		954,639	802,394	981,242	1,217,496	1,420,315	2.31	16.66
Slovakia		262,316	281,003	295,712	313,888	322,289	0.53	2.68
Ukraine		172,307	166,819	178,530	217,819	253,422	0.41	16.35
Other countries Central/East Europe		78,987	74,153	94,737	101,703	110,451	0.18	8.60
Northern Europe		5,578,304	4,772,415	4,803,177	4,615,983	4,688,301	7.64	1.57
Denmark		924,429	884,510	888,454	849,192	832,941	1.36	-1.91
Finland		213,363	233,717	225,430	241,533	246,732	0.40	2.15
Iceland		34,498	19,335	21,327	24,939	25,179	0.04	0.96
Ireland		319,568	250,742	211,253	182,739	183,218	0.30	0.26
Norway		204,430	191,839	223,083	234,757	254,205	0.41	8.28
Sweden		619,118	523,827	584,509	579,911	606,415	0.99	4.57
United Kingdom		3,262,898	2,668,445	2,649,121	2,502,912	2,539,611	4.14	1.47
Southern Europe		3,897,326	3,751,722	3,805,545	3,867,234	3,681,034	6.00	-4.81
Croatia		271,907	241,935	219,400	209,847	210,857	0.34	0.48
Greece		260,044	231,312	201,413	163,446	134,926	0.22	-17.45
Italy		2,375,772	2,367,675	2,372,913	2,352,970	2,224,264	3.62	-5.47
Malta		20,911	15,008	19,697	18,590	20,265	0.03	9.01
Portugal		72,799	73,430	74,792	76,836	69,508	0.11	-9.54

35

AUSTRIA

5. Overnight stays of non-resident tourists in hotels and similar establishments, by country of residence

	2008	2009	2010	2011	2012	Market share 2012	% Change 2012-2011
Serbia and Montenegro	113,528	116,137	161,867	202,324	201,663	0.33	-0.33
Slovenia	171,512	177,879	182,082	201,087	206,430	0.34	2.66
Spain	610,853	528,346	573,381	642,134	613,121	1.00	-4.52
Western Europe	**41,627,063**	**40,605,574**	**40,398,966**	**40,466,734**	**41,853,848**	**68.21**	**3.43**
Belgium	1,874,394	1,848,562	1,793,325	1,860,265	1,847,697	3.01	-0.68
France	1,413,693	1,414,698	1,445,896	1,484,696	1,470,441	2.40	-0.96
Germany	30,740,151	29,851,032	29,701,628	29,328,739	30,460,997	49.64	3.86
Luxembourg	232,320	232,605	240,851	254,089	246,205	0.40	-3.10
Netherlands	4,448,949	4,276,323	4,091,901	3,999,146	4,088,591	6.66	2.24
Switzerland	2,917,556	2,982,354	3,125,365	3,539,799	3,739,917	6.10	5.65
East Mediterranean Europe	**318,495**	**319,998**	**380,090**	**441,986**	**477,191**	**0.78**	**7.97**
Cyprus	25,561	24,770	27,261	22,238	21,135	0.03	-4.96
Israel	187,735	199,474	227,075	256,823	268,538	0.44	4.56
Turkey	105,199	95,754	125,754	162,925	187,518	0.31	15.09
MIDDLE EAST	**303,292**	**270,280**	**327,847**	**409,365**	**538,580**	**0.88**	**31.56**
All countries of Middle East	303,292	270,280	327,847	409,365	538,580	0.88	31.56
SOUTH ASIA	**90,224**	**90,103**	**103,892**	**145,647**	**148,667**	**0.24**	**2.07**
All countries of South Asia	90,224	90,103	103,892	145,647	148,667	0.24	2.07
NOT SPECIFIED	**752,603**	**622,311**	**577,149**	**515,421**	**602,004**	**0.98**	**16.80**
Other countries of the World	752,603	622,311	577,149	515,421	602,004	0.98	16.80

Yearbook of Tourism Statistics, Data 2008 – 2012, 2014 Edition

AUSTRIA

6. Overnight stays of non-resident tourists in all types of accommodation establishments, by country of residence

	2008	2009	2010	2011	2012	Market share 2012	% Change 2012-2011
TOTAL (*)	92,839,547	89,864,164	89,857,167	90,705,554	95,051,917	100.00	4.79
AFRICA	147,641	130,413	152,378	177,467	194,232	0.20	9.45
Southern Africa	84,317	66,412	74,114	79,954	81,604	0.09	2.06
South Africa	84,317	66,412	74,114	79,954	81,604	0.09	2.06
Other Africa	63,324	64,001	78,264	97,513	112,628	0.12	15.50
Other countries of Africa	63,324	64,001	78,264	97,513	112,628	0.12	15.50
AMERICAS	1,642,552	1,531,406	1,723,910	1,788,074	1,940,897	2.04	8.55
North America	1,423,529	1,317,648	1,472,085	1,449,928	1,530,172	1.61	5.53
Canada	224,884	207,190	229,015	246,821	244,467	0.26	-0.95
United States of America	1,198,645	1,110,458	1,243,070	1,203,107	1,285,705	1.35	6.87
South America			9,371	113,007	156,943	0.17	38.88
Brazil			9,371	113,007	156,943	0.17	38.88
Other Americas	219,023	213,758	242,454	225,139	253,782	0.27	12.72
Other countries of the Americas	219,023	213,758	242,454	225,139	253,782	0.27	12.72
EAST ASIA AND THE PACIFIC	1,337,593	1,244,356	1,382,262	1,634,091	1,961,328	2.06	20.03
North-East Asia	816,142	784,816	863,947	1,057,035	1,314,322	1.38	24.34
China	236,433	222,225	267,483	369,718	506,618	0.53	37.03
Japan	409,001	407,112	412,494	437,949	508,292	0.53	16.06
Korea, Republic of	120,650	97,859	116,720	158,835	205,918	0.22	29.64
Taiwan, Province of China	50,058	57,620	67,250	90,533	93,494	0.10	3.27
South-East Asia	88,129	84,200	101,781	136,251	161,903	0.17	18.83
All countries of South-East Asia	88,129	84,200	101,781	136,251	161,903	0.17	18.83
Australasia	332,893	285,489	315,130	343,338	379,139	0.40	10.43
Australia	292,188	250,998	279,417	304,430	335,554	0.35	10.22
New Zealand	40,705	34,491	35,713	38,908	43,585	0.05	12.02
Other East Asia and the Pacific	100,429	89,851	101,404	97,467	105,964	0.11	8.72
Other countries of Asia	100,429	89,851	101,404	97,467	105,964	0.11	8.72
EUROPE	88,336,909	85,776,665	85,388,146	85,806,605	89,290,120	93.94	4.06
Central/Eastern Europe	7,937,810	7,745,592	8,091,969	8,838,267	9,265,872	9.75	4.84
Bulgaria	147,606	145,774	150,509	168,678	185,793	0.20	10.15
Czech Republic	1,778,581	1,955,027	1,972,457	2,078,822	2,123,891	2.23	2.17
Estonia	74,626	60,901	68,219	59,150	70,231	0.07	18.73
Hungary	1,641,621	1,499,474	1,510,379	1,597,850	1,624,206	1.71	1.65
Latvia	88,530	59,085	55,052	62,767	73,406	0.08	16.95
Lithuania	128,062	105,013	93,384	97,039	110,189	0.12	13.55
Poland	1,389,296	1,385,970	1,422,764	1,518,525	1,478,694	1.56	-2.62
Romania	898,885	841,457	822,928	853,549	831,278	0.87	-2.61
Russian Federation	1,105,921	969,166	1,195,360	1,501,355	1,785,754	1.88	18.94
Slovakia	388,827	424,182	464,825	499,057	525,192	0.55	5.24
Ukraine	203,501	209,856	226,260	282,264	326,274	0.34	15.59
Other countries Central/East Europe	92,354	89,687	109,832	119,211	130,964	0.14	9.86
Northern Europe	7,226,117	6,306,276	6,369,751	6,166,919	6,325,512	6.65	2.57
Denmark	1,523,212	1,501,450	1,514,888	1,464,303	1,447,258	1.52	-1.16
Finland	257,353	279,429	280,480	303,829	336,601	0.35	10.79
Iceland	40,122	23,427	26,001	30,121	32,657	0.03	8.42
Ireland	386,959	308,291	269,442	235,490	234,778	0.25	-0.30
Norway	253,482	240,005	271,184	282,148	307,116	0.32	8.85
Sweden	846,633	689,808	754,680	746,684	786,586	0.83	5.34
United Kingdom	3,918,356	3,263,866	3,253,076	3,104,344	3,180,516	3.35	2.45
Southern Europe	4,952,813	4,837,856	4,903,684	4,995,293	4,853,145	5.11	-2.85
Croatia	424,858	387,895	351,491	333,806	334,594	0.35	0.24
Greece	284,383	255,116	221,551	183,410	151,809	0.16	-17.23
Italy	2,979,137	3,015,873	3,020,992	3,013,847	2,917,854	3.07	-3.19
Malta	23,011	17,177	21,815	21,891	22,418	0.02	2.41
Portugal	85,427	90,141	94,320	90,226	86,515	0.09	-4.11

37

AUSTRIA

6. Overnight stays of non-resident tourists in all types of accommodation establishments, by country of residence

	2008	2009	2010	2011	2012	Market share 2012	% Change 2012-2011
Serbia and Montenegro	139,210	144,902	210,582	256,448	257,491	0.27	0.41
Slovenia	306,447	310,055	317,008	354,656	374,446	0.39	5.58
Spain	710,340	616,697	665,925	741,009	708,018	0.74	-4.45
Western Europe	**67,846,928**	**66,494,567**	**65,559,316**	**65,267,644**	**68,250,456**	**71.80**	**4.57**
Belgium	2,563,793	2,530,232	2,464,985	2,565,423	2,583,143	2.72	0.69
France	1,733,339	1,739,002	1,785,956	1,834,629	1,818,852	1.91	-0.86
Germany	50,144,306	48,856,862	48,155,743	47,389,531	49,606,383	52.19	4.68
Luxembourg	280,882	274,864	284,358	301,951	295,170	0.31	-2.25
Netherlands	9,562,516	9,451,747	9,071,437	8,899,263	9,389,082	9.88	5.50
Switzerland	3,562,092	3,641,860	3,796,837	4,276,847	4,557,826	4.80	6.57
East Mediterranean Europe	**373,241**	**392,374**	**463,426**	**538,482**	**595,135**	**0.63**	**10.52**
Cyprus	29,085	28,388	30,235	24,764	24,458	0.03	-1.24
Israel	230,032	257,619	295,279	337,004	364,306	0.38	8.10
Turkey	114,124	106,367	137,912	176,714	206,371	0.22	16.78
MIDDLE EAST	**365,598**	**331,139**	**410,128**	**527,108**	**712,514**	**0.75**	**35.17**
All countries of Middle East	365,598	331,139	410,128	527,108	712,514	0.75	35.17
SOUTH ASIA	**98,688**	**96,857**	**110,442**	**158,686**	**164,226**	**0.17**	**3.49**
All countries of South Asia	98,688	96,857	110,442	158,686	164,226	0.17	3.49
NOT SPECIFIED	**910,566**	**753,328**	**689,901**	**613,523**	**788,600**	**0.83**	**28.54**
Other countries of the World	910,566	753,328	689,901	613,523	788,600	0.83	28.54

Yearbook of Tourism Statistics, Data 2008 – 2012, 2014 Edition

AZERBAIJAN

2. Arrivals of non-resident visitors at national borders, by country of residence

	2008	2009	2010	2011	2012	Market share 2012	% Change 2012-2011
TOTAL	1,898,936	1,830,367	1,962,906	2,239,141	2,484,048	100.00	10.94
AFRICA	1,630	1,732	2,056	1,781	1,504	0.06	-15.55
East Africa	247	140	165	189	30	0.00	-84.13
British Indian Ocean Territory	6	2					
Burundi	4	3	2	5			
Comoros	2	1	9	12			
Djibouti	3	2	6	4			
Eritrea	1	2	1	4			
Ethiopia	30	36	30	22	30	0.00	36.36
Kenya	34	12	37	22			
Madagascar	2	3	1	4			
Malawi	6	3	3	4			
Mauritius	37	19	15	32			
Mozambique	7	6	7	6			
Reunion	52	15					
Rwanda	10	2	6	15			
Somalia	2	1	3	1			
Uganda	27	12	13	21			
United Republic of Tanzania	9	8	15	13			
Zambia	7		9	7			
Zimbabwe	8	13	8	17			
Central Africa	181	142	63	109	40	0.00	-63.30
Angola	47	24	9	14			
Cameroon	42	47	40	55	40	0.00	-27.27
Central African Republic	1			1			
Congo	12	6	1	11			
Democratic Republic of the Congo	10	5	9	9			
Equatorial Guinea	1						
Gabon	28	28	4	19			
Sao Tome and Principe	40	32					
North Africa	405	557	634	506	293	0.01	-42.09
Algeria	137	213	229	180	135	0.01	-25.00
Morocco	123	196	155	183	158	0.01	-13.66
Sudan	63	50	98	47			
Tunisia	82	98	152	96			
Southern Africa	464	553	728	567	878	0.04	54.85
Botswana	1	2	9	4			
Lesotho	3			4			
Namibia	6		2	8			
South Africa	453	549	716	550	878	0.04	59.64
Swaziland	1	2	1	1			
West Africa	333	340	466	410	263	0.01	-35.85
Benin	2	2	6	7			
Burkina Faso	4	7	6	7			
Côte d'Ivoire	24	10	12	29			
Gambia	6	3	17	9			
Ghana	13	37	38	64			
Guinea	15	7	16	7			
Guinea-Bissau	1	4	3	1			
Liberia	6	7	7				
Mali	9	3	12	19			
Mauritania	6	9	53	4			
Niger	3	6	5	7			
Nigeria	209	218	223	178	263	0.01	47.75
Senegal	28	25	45	43			
Sierra Leone	4	1	12	33			

39

AZERBAIJAN

2. Arrivals of non-resident visitors at national borders, by country of residence

	2008	2009	2010	2011	2012	Market share 2012	% Change 2012-2011
Togo	3	1	11	2			
AMERICAS	**17,329**	**15,445**	**15,789**	**15,532**	**17,771**	**0.72**	**14.42**
Caribbean	**261**	**346**	**386**	**484**	**350**	**0.01**	**-27.69**
Anguilla	3						
Aruba	22	13					
Bahamas	1	2	3	4			
Barbados	6	3	3	4			
Cayman Islands	1			2			
Cuba	26	32	88	81	74	0.00	-8.64
Dominica	1	2	2	8			
Dominican Republic	2	12	13	33			
Grenada	6	9	1	3			
Haiti	1	1		1			
Jamaica	3	3	2	8			
Montserrat	1						
Trinidad and Tobago	168	253	274	336	276	0.01	-17.86
Turks and Caicos Islands	20	16		4			
Central America	**40**	**25**	**56**	**92**			
Belize	5	1	6	3			
Costa Rica	6	6	11	18			
El Salvador	9	2	4	7			
Guatemala	5	7	6	15			
Honduras	7	5	15	20			
Nicaragua	1	1	7	14			
Panama	7	3	7	15			
North America	**15,780**	**13,833**	**14,134**	**13,465**	**16,253**	**0.65**	**20.71**
Canada	2,356	2,036	2,050	1,851	2,566	0.10	38.63
Mexico	110	134	98	171			
United States of America	13,314	11,663	11,986	11,443	13,687	0.55	19.61
South America	**1,248**	**1,241**	**1,213**	**1,491**	**1,168**	**0.05**	**-21.66**
Argentina	140	97	71	159			
Bolivia	62	27	53	36	34	0.00	-5.56
Brazil	255	399	434	500	516	0.02	3.20
Chile	35	13	28	35	66	0.00	88.57
Colombia	364	349	332	417	427	0.02	2.40
Ecuador	63	44	37	89			
Guyana	1	1	1	2			
Paraguay	35	12	11	7			
Peru	47	43	31	54			
Suriname	1		2				
Uruguay	95	47	26	18			
Venezuela	150	209	187	174	125	0.01	-28.16
EAST ASIA AND THE PACIFIC	**16,190**	**13,839**	**14,730**	**15,092**	**15,620**	**0.63**	**3.50**
North-East Asia	**11,180**	**9,680**	**10,405**	**11,060**	**10,161**	**0.41**	**-8.13**
China	7,138	6,322	5,846	6,224	5,060	0.20	-18.70
Hong Kong, China	2	1					
Japan	1,434	1,076	1,809	2,098	2,230	0.09	6.29
Korea, Dem. People's Republic of	5	4	15	3	42	0.00	1,300.00
Korea, Republic of	2,446	2,082	2,647	2,461	2,829	0.11	14.95
Macao, China	6	3		1			
Mongolia	71	84	59	87			
Taiwan, Province of China	78	108	29	186			
South-East Asia	**3,345**	**2,763**	**2,898**	**2,539**	**3,714**	**0.15**	**46.28**
Brunei Darussalam	14	6	9	4			
Cambodia	15	14		7			
Indonesia	378	314	353	440	577	0.02	31.14
Lao People's Democratic Republic			2	8			

40

AZERBAIJAN

2. Arrivals of non-resident visitors at national borders, by country of residence

	2008	2009	2010	2011	2012	Market share 2012	% Change 2012-2011
Malaysia	802	603	550	402	805	0.03	100.25
Myanmar	15	24	39	13			
Philippines	1,505	1,216	1,153	1,003	1,322	0.05	31.80
Singapore	254	246	316	203	315	0.01	55.17
Thailand	309	245	298	207	386	0.02	86.47
Viet Nam	53	95	178	252	309	0.01	22.62
Australasia	**1,656**	**1,390**	**1,419**	**1,485**	**1,745**	**0.07**	**17.51**
Australia	1,276	1,109	1,122	1,129	1,296	0.05	14.79
New Zealand	380	281	297	356	449	0.02	26.12
Melanesia	**2**	**1**		**1**			
Fiji	1	1		1			
Solomon Islands	1						
Micronesia	**4**	**2**	**1**	**1**			
Kiribati	2		1				
Palau	2	2		1			
Polynesia	**3**	**3**	**7**	**6**			
Samoa	1	1	3	2			
Tuvalu	2	2	4	4			
EUROPE	**1,541,306**	**1,454,046**	**1,568,063**	**1,786,769**	**2,147,027**	**86.43**	**20.16**
Central/Eastern Europe	**1,313,235**	**1,205,273**	**1,282,747**	**1,470,964**	**1,760,149**	**70.86**	**19.66**
Belarus	4,660	5,308	5,479	5,724	7,038	0.28	22.96
Bulgaria	1,193	1,351	1,638	1,984	2,231	0.09	12.45
Czech Republic	784	948	1,013	1,025	1,279	0.05	24.78
Estonia	794	606	566	559	791	0.03	41.50
Georgia	607,875	529,613	491,942	573,063	763,251	30.73	33.19
Hungary	510	597	737	910	950	0.04	4.40
Kazakhstan	15,335	16,048	19,209	28,225	25,295	1.02	-10.38
Kyrgyzstan	1,850	1,921	2,279	2,337	2,905	0.12	24.30
Latvia	1,101	1,281	1,295	1,536	1,875	0.08	22.07
Lithuania	1,063	1,133	1,372	1,557	1,698	0.07	9.06
Poland	1,830	1,699	2,455	2,224	3,168	0.13	42.45
Republic of Moldova	1,705	4,289	3,645	3,753	4,375	0.18	16.57
Romania	885	1,039	1,296	1,417	1,678	0.07	18.42
Russian Federation	630,860	598,894	701,110	786,684	876,013	35.27	11.36
Slovakia	405	511	518	445	622	0.03	39.78
Tajikistan	703	675	742	1,009	1,264	0.05	25.27
Turkmenistan	5,155	3,687	4,072	3,969	4,906	0.20	23.61
Ukraine	28,420	28,606	31,500	40,030	42,393	1.71	5.90
Uzbekistan	8,107	7,067	11,879	14,513	18,417	0.74	26.90
Northern Europe	**35,604**	**31,508**	**30,488**	**30,666**	**36,739**	**1.48**	**19.80**
Denmark	682	688	745	870	1,099	0.04	26.32
Finland	973	1,098	1,041	699	902	0.04	29.04
Iceland	64	219	170	384	651	0.03	69.53
Ireland	838	757	961	919	969	0.04	5.44
Norway	2,300	1,921	2,054	1,874	1,981	0.08	5.71
Sweden	1,385	1,126	1,357	1,274	2,012	0.08	57.93
United Kingdom	29,362	25,699	24,160	24,646	29,125	1.17	18.17
Southern Europe	**8,885**	**9,851**	**10,025**	**10,072**	**14,015**	**0.56**	**39.15**
Albania	116	159	136	177			
Andorra	2	1	6	5			
Bosnia and Herzegovina	901	1,301	276	179	278	0.01	55.31
Croatia	519	415	497	730	1,092	0.04	49.59
Greece	680	736	729	832	1,213	0.05	45.79
Holy See	9	14	17	13			
Italy	3,762	4,066	4,732	4,857	6,767	0.27	39.32
Malta	37	30	61	68	84	0.00	23.53
Portugal	867	976	948	414	512	0.02	23.67

Yearbook of Tourism Statistics, Data 2008 – 2012, 2014 Edition

AZERBAIJAN

2. Arrivals of non-resident visitors at national borders, by country of residence

	2008	2009	2010	2011	2012	Market share 2012	% Change 2012-2011
San Marino	1	3	1	2			
Serbia			655	907	1,589	0.06	75.19
Slovenia	247	254	237	265	491	0.02	85.28
Spain	697	936	1,074	1,388	1,685	0.07	21.40
TFYR of Macedonia	254	175	292	221	301	0.01	36.20
Other countries of Southern Europe	793	785	364	14	3	0.00	-78.57
Western Europe	**19,341**	**23,431**	**23,781**	**26,643**	**34,206**	**1.38**	**28.39**
Austria	1,392	1,801	2,513	3,021	3,499	0.14	15.82
Belgium	1,980	2,389	2,233	2,299	2,255	0.09	-1.91
France	3,833	3,994	4,128	4,799	5,870	0.24	22.32
Germany	8,740	10,695	10,602	11,927	16,445	0.66	37.88
Liechtenstein	39	1	3	4			
Luxembourg	154	527	378	316	460	0.02	45.57
Monaco	1		8	5			
Netherlands	2,180	2,595	2,689	3,026	3,970	0.16	31.20
Switzerland	1,022	1,429	1,227	1,246	1,707	0.07	37.00
East Mediterranean Europe	**164,241**	**183,983**	**221,022**	**248,424**	**301,918**	**12.15**	**21.53**
Cyprus	181	159	82	147			
Israel	6,233	6,516	6,346	5,671	6,369	0.26	12.31
Turkey	157,827	177,308	214,594	242,606	295,549	11.90	21.82
MIDDLE EAST	**3,716**	**3,095**	**3,581**	**3,932**	**4,414**	**0.18**	**12.26**
Bahrain	78	80	87	97	107	0.00	10.31
Egypt	541	407	559	663	955	0.04	44.04
Iraq	677	476	549	679	917	0.04	35.05
Jordan	576	299	392	379	387	0.02	2.11
Kuwait	158	149	322	324	233	0.01	-28.09
Lebanon	239	282	270	308	363	0.01	17.86
Libya	45	38	36	27	54	0.00	100.00
Oman	48	67	63	26			
Palestine	34	42	25	68	53	0.00	-22.06
Qatar	89	131	83	123			
Saudi Arabia	416	290	312	284	380	0.02	33.80
Syrian Arab Republic	375	492	390	426	414	0.02	-2.82
United Arab Emirates	346	270	412	469	551	0.02	17.48
Yemen	94	72	81	59			
SOUTH ASIA	**316,514**	**339,949**	**356,590**	**414,045**	**292,006**	**11.76**	**-29.47**
Afghanistan	443	303	194	270	393	0.02	45.56
Bangladesh	294	453	576	439	1,151	0.05	162.19
Bhutan	2			3			
India	4,236	3,721	3,755	3,715	5,048	0.20	35.88
Iran, Islamic Republic of	308,650	329,913	349,960	407,576	283,739	11.42	-30.38
Maldives	1	5	4	5			
Nepal	48	52	56	79			
Pakistan	2,738	5,416	1,949	1,743	1,675	0.07	-3.90
Sri Lanka	102	86	96	215			
NOT SPECIFIED	**2,251**	**2,261**	**2,097**	**1,990**	**5,706**	**0.23**	**186.73**
Other countries of the World	2,251	2,261	2,097	1,990	5,706	0.23	186.73

42

AZERBAIJAN

3. Arrivals of non-resident tourists in hotels and similar establishments, by country of residence

	2008	2009	2010	2011	2012	Market share 2012	% Change 2012-2011
TOTAL	224,112	208,868	212,356	257,987	372,117	100.00	44.24
AMERICAS	13,357	11,622	15,013	7,947	22,807	6.13	186.99
North America	13,357	11,622	15,013	7,947	22,807	6.13	186.99
Canada	570	272	548	630	3,229	0.87	412.54
United States of America	12,787	11,350	14,465	7,317	19,578	5.26	167.57
EAST ASIA AND THE PACIFIC	6,762	5,087	6,913	4,448	5,648	1.52	26.98
North-East Asia	5,406	4,499	6,167	4,448	5,648	1.52	26.98
China	4,285	3,545	5,037	3,671	4,329	1.16	17.92
Japan	696	950	782	777	1,319	0.35	69.76
Korea, Dem. People's Republic of	425	4	348				
South-East Asia	951	275	431				
Malaysia	597	56	269				
Philippines	354	219	162				
Australasia	405	313	315				
Australia	405	313	315				
EUROPE	141,327	138,817	139,139	167,342	243,784	65.51	45.68
Central/Eastern Europe	50,542	39,420	43,052	54,662	71,400	19.19	30.62
Belarus	510	523	1,181				
Georgia	7,677	8,210	2,435	3,701	6,516	1.75	76.06
Kazakhstan	2,366	1,841	2,070	3,856	5,464	1.47	41.70
Latvia	63	108	394	424	792	0.21	86.79
Poland	444	80	500	946	1,220	0.33	28.96
Romania	120	67	195	495	700	0.19	41.41
Russian Federation	34,253	23,261	29,570	36,503	45,404	12.20	24.38
Ukraine	5,109	5,330	6,707	8,737	11,304	3.04	29.38
Northern Europe	55,342	26,823	17,077	29,904	68,793	18.49	130.05
Finland	589	123	227	225	591	0.16	162.67
Norway	2,660	1,451	2,209	3,285	4,304	1.16	31.02
Sweden	1,179	522	448	880	2,270	0.61	157.95
United Kingdom	50,914	24,727	14,193	25,514	61,628	16.56	141.55
Southern Europe	2,514	4,534	4,914	5,248	9,075	2.44	72.92
Greece	166	87	161				
Italy	1,695	4,021	4,005	3,706	7,390	1.99	99.41
Spain	653	426	748	1,542	1,685	0.45	9.27
Western Europe	9,121	11,729	12,508	16,229	37,494	10.08	131.03
Austria	726	1,195	912				
Belgium	626	269	840	651	1,613	0.43	147.77
France	2,759	3,512	3,696	4,767	7,320	1.97	53.56
Germany	3,842	5,903	6,115	9,903	20,358	5.47	105.57
Netherlands	1,168	850	945	908	8,203	2.20	803.41
East Mediterranean Europe	23,808	56,311	61,588	61,299	57,022	15.32	-6.98
Israel	1,969	2,935	3,305	1,431	7,438	2.00	419.78
Turkey	21,839	53,376	58,283	59,868	49,584	13.32	-17.18
MIDDLE EAST	57	2	387				
United Arab Emirates	57	2	387				
SOUTH ASIA	12,073	31,255	19,423	23,158	25,250	6.79	9.03
India	560	1,162	485	743	4,713	1.27	534.32
Iran, Islamic Republic of	10,657	29,798	18,775	21,779	20,009	5.38	-8.13
Pakistan	856	295	163	636	528	0.14	-16.98
NOT SPECIFIED	50,536	22,085	31,481	55,092	74,628	20.05	35.46
Other countries of the World	50,536	22,085	31,481	55,092	74,628	20.05	35.46

Yearbook of Tourism Statistics, Data 2008 – 2012, 2014 Edition

AZERBAIJAN

5. Overnight stays of non-resident tourists in hotels and similar establishments, by country of residence

	2008	2009	2010	2011	2012	Market share 2012	% Change 2012-2011
TOTAL	636,678	561,343	568,056	673,811	803,089	100.00	19.19
AMERICAS	37,316	25,071	25,627	15,560	51,978	6.47	234.05
North America	37,316	25,071	25,627	15,560	51,978	6.47	234.05
Canada	2,020	458	937	1,148	4,165	0.52	262.80
United States of America	35,296	24,613	24,690	14,412	47,813	5.95	231.76
EAST ASIA AND THE PACIFIC	11,677	12,013	16,198	9,085	11,420	1.42	25.70
North-East Asia	7,907	10,388	12,457	9,085	11,420	1.42	25.70
China	5,668	8,424	10,205	6,694	9,300	1.16	38.93
Japan	1,211	1,952	1,874	2,391	2,120	0.26	-11.33
Korea, Dem. People's Republic of	1,028	12	378				
South-East Asia	2,750	1,172	3,263				
Malaysia	336	104	2,833				
Philippines	2,414	1,068	430				
Australasia	1,020	453	478				
Australia	1,020	453	478				
EUROPE	249,279	292,247	421,195	489,685	555,199	69.13	13.38
Central/Eastern Europe	74,242	87,195	94,923	133,824	157,586	19.62	17.76
Georgia	10,773	13,301	4,748	6,465	9,875	1.23	52.75
Kazakhstan	4,699	8,726	5,787	12,719	12,381	1.54	-2.66
Latvia	258	380	745	597	1,405	0.17	135.34
Poland	1,886	794	763	1,685	1,775	0.22	5.34
Romania	403	302	786	605	891	0.11	47.27
Russian Federation	43,660	51,411	66,894	84,323	102,399	12.75	21.44
Ukraine	12,563	12,281	15,200	27,430	28,860	3.59	5.21
Northern Europe	78,396	69,477	43,292	72,962	148,264	18.46	103.21
Finland	1,180	781	374	270	691	0.09	155.93
Norway	6,055	2,649	2,624	3,736	4,857	0.60	30.01
Sweden	2,085	686	588	2,144	2,737	0.34	27.66
United Kingdom	69,076	65,361	39,706	66,812	139,979	17.43	109.51
Southern Europe	6,572	6,683	8,310	9,172	11,417	1.42	24.48
Greece	283	287	332				
Italy	5,580	5,770	6,639	6,798	9,115	1.13	34.08
Spain	709	626	1,339	2,374	2,302	0.29	-3.03
Western Europe	21,832	24,145	21,645	25,200	62,592	7.79	148.38
Austria	1,019	1,499	1,508				
Belgium	2,910	479	1,084	800	2,697	0.34	237.13
France	6,674	7,253	5,808	6,218	9,968	1.24	60.31
Germany	9,170	12,496	11,959	16,906	41,054	5.11	142.84
Netherlands	2,059	2,418	1,286	1,276	8,873	1.10	595.38
East Mediterranean Europe	68,237	104,747	253,025	248,527	175,340	21.83	-29.45
Israel	2,545	3,622	4,133	1,969	8,209	1.02	316.91
Turkey	65,692	101,125	248,892	246,558	167,131	20.81	-32.21
MIDDLE EAST	151	22	535				
United Arab Emirates	151	22	535				
SOUTH ASIA	23,843	52,079	48,079	49,322	40,176	5.00	-18.54
India	1,153	1,767	1,289	2,960	6,169	0.77	108.41
Iran, Islamic Republic of	20,922	49,733	46,509	44,819	33,384	4.16	-25.51
Pakistan	1,768	579	281	1,543	623	0.08	-59.62
NOT SPECIFIED	314,412	179,911	56,422	110,159	144,316	17.97	31.01
Other countries of the World	314,412	179,911	56,422	110,159	144,316	17.97	31.01

Yearbook of Tourism Statistics, Data 2008 – 2012, 2014 Edition

BAHAMAS

1. Arrivals of non-resident tourists at national borders, by country of residence

	2008	2009	2010	2011	2012	Market share 2012	% Change 2012-2011
TOTAL	1,462,993	1,326,996	1,370,159	1,346,359	1,421,548	100.00	5.58
AFRICA	1,785	1,778	1,654	1,733	2,245	0.16	29.54
East Africa	142	179	145	136	187	0.01	37.50
Burundi		1	1				
Comoros		2					
Djibouti		1	1		1	0.00	
Eritrea		3	2		1	0.00	
Ethiopia	8	14	16	14	9	0.00	-35.71
Kenya	25	19	36	27	40	0.00	48.15
Madagascar	2	11	1	1	5	0.00	400.00
Malawi	3	6	2	1	10	0.00	900.00
Mauritius	14	25	12	20	25	0.00	25.00
Mozambique	7	9	3	4	14	0.00	250.00
Rwanda	18	3	2				
Seychelles	8	8	8	4	1	0.00	-75.00
Somalia		2					
Uganda	11	22	21	8	21	0.00	162.50
United Republic of Tanzania	15	23	8	9	6	0.00	-33.33
Zambia	16	17	7	22	20	0.00	-9.09
Zimbabwe	15	13	25	26	34	0.00	30.77
Central Africa	42	57	35	88	104	0.01	18.18
Angola	10	16	6	31	27	0.00	-12.90
Cameroon	9	17	1	6	7	0.00	16.67
Central African Republic	1	2		2			
Chad	2	7	13	15	21	0.00	40.00
Congo	10	13	7	9	23	0.00	155.56
Equatorial Guinea				13	4	0.00	-69.23
Gabon	10	2	8	12	22	0.00	83.33
North Africa	86	138	82	76	101	0.01	32.89
Algeria	22	1	2	10	5	0.00	-50.00
Morocco	51	58	68	42	80	0.01	90.48
Sudan	1	5		2	1	0.00	-50.00
Tunisia	12	74	12	22	15	0.00	-31.82
Southern Africa	1,250	1,175	1,226	1,222	1,629	0.11	33.31
Botswana	9	23	36	24	27	0.00	12.50
Lesotho	1	7	8	1			
Namibia	10	21	16	11	19	0.00	72.73
South Africa	1,213	1,090	1,127	1,169	1,561	0.11	33.53
Swaziland	17	34	39	17	22	0.00	29.41
West Africa	265	229	166	211	224	0.02	6.16
Benin	2	1					
Burkina Faso		2	1	4	1	0.00	-75.00
Cape Verde	1	3	1	7	1	0.00	-85.71
Côte d'Ivoire	12	6	8	18	10	0.00	-44.44
Gambia	2	8	1	1	2	0.00	100.00
Ghana	33	38	27	30	37	0.00	23.33
Guinea	19	10	3	7	1	0.00	-85.71
Liberia		3	1	2	2	0.00	0.00
Mali	1	1	5	1			
Mauritania	2	3	2	1	1	0.00	0.00
Niger		4		1			
Nigeria	173	128	95	121	133	0.01	9.92
Senegal	8	15	18	12	20	0.00	66.67
Sierra Leone	10	6	3	6	9	0.00	50.00
Togo	2	1	1		7	0.00	

Yearbook of Tourism Statistics, Data 2008 – 2012, 2014 Edition

BAHAMAS

1. Arrivals of non-resident tourists at national borders, by country of residence

	2008	2009	2010	2011	2012	Market share 2012	% Change 2012-2011
AMERICAS	1,331,016	1,213,297	1,255,738	1,230,531	1,302,696	91.64	5.86
Caribbean	22,060	18,451	18,046	17,456	16,763	1.18	-3.97
Anguilla	58	29	50	23	28	0.00	21.74
Antigua and Barbuda	157	122	131	169	158	0.01	-6.51
Aruba	94	106	78	117	142	0.01	21.37
Barbados	1,129	852	1,052	943	977	0.07	3.61
Bermuda	958	1,009	857	805	987	0.07	22.61
British Virgin Islands	155	99	119	91	125	0.01	37.36
Cayman Islands	2,279	1,964	1,699	1,458	1,393	0.10	-4.46
Cuba	252	365	365	455	412	0.03	-9.45
Curaçao	164	137	153	164	209	0.01	27.44
Dominica	137	166	117	138	117	0.01	-15.22
Dominican Republic	547	578	493	540	548	0.04	1.48
Grenada	100	76	55	74	80	0.01	8.11
Haiti	3,243	1,318	556	491	343	0.02	-30.14
Jamaica	6,966	6,207	6,831	6,888	6,441	0.45	-6.49
Martinique	31	57	41	50	70	0.00	40.00
Montserrat	13	19	16	9	8	0.00	-11.11
Netherlands Antilles	53	23	33	22	5	0.00	-77.27
Puerto Rico	227	226	252	270	283	0.02	4.81
Saint Kitts and Nevis	124	144	127	100	73	0.01	-27.00
Saint Lucia	238	197	199	199	209	0.01	5.03
Saint Vincent and the Grenadines	88	74	72	85	71	0.00	-16.47
Sint Eustatius	5	4	4	6	3	0.00	-50.00
Sint Maarten	145	75	68	114	112	0.01	-1.75
Trinidad and Tobago	1,752	1,453	1,693	1,759	1,725	0.12	-1.93
Turks and Caicos Islands	3,031	3,080	2,946	2,433	2,178	0.15	-10.48
United States Virgin Islands	26	18	20	14	21	0.00	50.00
Other countries of the Caribbean	88	53	19	39	45	0.00	15.38
Central America	1,770	1,987	1,851	2,819	3,599	0.25	27.67
Belize	120	123	117	122	122	0.01	0.00
Costa Rica	401	372	334	490	579	0.04	18.16
El Salvador	214	257	126	209	127	0.01	-39.23
Guatemala	228	312	295	356	603	0.04	69.38
Honduras	179	194	196	254	188	0.01	-25.98
Nicaragua	82	90	97	79	133	0.01	68.35
Panama	546	639	686	1,309	1,847	0.13	41.10
North America	1,295,824	1,179,664	1,220,032	1,187,547	1,256,376	88.38	5.80
Canada	114,960	107,041	119,321	124,166	131,045	9.22	5.54
Greenland	3	2	3	1	4	0.00	300.00
Mexico	3,590	3,895	3,524	4,698	3,873	0.27	-17.56
United States of America	1,177,271	1,068,726	1,097,184	1,058,682	1,121,454	78.89	5.93
South America	11,362	13,195	15,809	22,709	25,958	1.83	14.31
Argentina	2,050	2,579	3,167	4,992	5,339	0.38	6.95
Bolivia	83	158	113	141	228	0.02	61.70
Brazil	3,863	4,309	5,310	6,595	7,475	0.53	13.34
Chile	537	548	637	1,106	1,113	0.08	0.63
Colombia	809	1,281	1,720	4,155	4,822	0.34	16.05
Ecuador	544	487	529	547	1,163	0.08	112.61
Guyana	366	306	373	433	378	0.03	-12.70
Paraguay	194	250	620	838	922	0.06	10.02
Peru	800	807	879	1,027	1,189	0.08	15.77
Suriname	96	87	97	88	81	0.01	-7.95
Uruguay	194	230	323	405	509	0.04	25.68
Venezuela	1,826	2,153	2,041	2,382	2,739	0.19	14.99

Yearbook of Tourism Statistics, Data 2008 – 2012, 2014 Edition

BAHAMAS

1. Arrivals of non-resident tourists at national borders, by country of residence

	2008	2009	2010	2011	2012	Market share 2012	% Change 2012-2011
EAST ASIA AND THE PACIFIC	6,902	6,232	7,143	6,707	8,126	0.57	21.16
North-East Asia	2,544	2,081	2,527	2,045	2,877	0.20	40.68
China	265	486	384	682	890	0.06	30.50
Hong Kong, China	358	205	283	277	369	0.03	33.21
Japan	1,424	1,018	874	776	1,012	0.07	30.41
Korea, Dem. People's Republic of	1		1	2	5	0.00	150.00
Korea, Republic of	323	298	514	228	426	0.03	86.84
Mongolia	2	8	1	2	4	0.00	100.00
Taiwan, Province of China	171	66	470	78	171	0.01	119.23
South-East Asia	887	760	947	764	892	0.06	16.75
Brunei Darussalam	5	2	5	2	3	0.00	50.00
Cambodia	1	4	3	6	5	0.00	-16.67
Indonesia	55	65	73	58	103	0.01	77.59
Lao People's Democratic Republic		3			2	0.00	
Malaysia	100	59	165	99	106	0.01	7.07
Myanmar		4	2	3	10	0.00	233.33
Philippines	347	315	297	232	235	0.02	1.29
Singapore	251	201	293	280	292	0.02	4.29
Thailand	118	86	84	67	122	0.01	82.09
Viet Nam	10	21	25	17	14	0.00	-17.65
Australasia	3,390	3,328	3,634	3,871	4,307	0.30	11.26
Australia	2,778	2,758	3,075	3,267	3,608	0.25	10.44
New Zealand	612	570	559	604	699	0.05	15.73
Melanesia	58	30	12	16	29	0.00	81.25
Fiji	9	17	7	8	12	0.00	50.00
Papua New Guinea	2	4	2	4	13	0.00	225.00
Solomon Islands	45	3	2	3	2	0.00	-33.33
Vanuatu	2	6	1	1	2	0.00	100.00
Micronesia	7	11	5	3	6	0.00	100.00
Kiribati		5		1			
Marshall Islands		2	1				
Micronesia, Federated States of	3	4	4	2	4	0.00	100.00
Nauru	3						
Palau	1				2	0.00	
Polynesia	16	22	18	8	15	0.00	87.50
French Polynesia	12	13	13	5	8	0.00	60.00
Samoa	2	6	5	3	5	0.00	66.67
Tonga	2	3			2	0.00	
EUROPE	94,547	79,637	78,885	78,916	79,505	5.59	0.75
Central/Eastern Europe	2,346	2,923	4,141	4,334	4,705	0.33	8.56
Armenia	4	11	7	3	5	0.00	66.67
Azerbaijan	4	15	4	19	23	0.00	21.05
Bulgaria	81	113	166	144	131	0.01	-9.03
Czech Republic	197	303	407	330	354	0.02	7.27
Estonia	31	120	96	85	145	0.01	70.59
Georgia	24	19	21	21	39	0.00	85.71
Hungary	278	289	369	334	325	0.02	-2.69
Kazakhstan	26	12	52	18	92	0.01	411.11
Kyrgyzstan		6	8				
Latvia	31	55	76	59	70	0.00	18.64
Lithuania	47	33	74	85	105	0.01	23.53
Poland	674	574	785	924	863	0.06	-6.60
Republic of Moldova	3	5	19	7	21	0.00	200.00
Romania	261	253	398	334	297	0.02	-11.08
Russian Federation	414	822	1,203	1,582	1,893	0.13	19.66

BAHAMAS

1. Arrivals of non-resident tourists at national borders, by country of residence

	2008	2009	2010	2011	2012	Market share 2012	% Change 2012-2011
Slovakia	128	166	276	235	190	0.01	-19.15
Tajikistan		3			5	0.00	
Turkmenistan	1	3	4		5	0.00	
Ukraine	142	112	173	149	139	0.01	-6.71
Uzbekistan		9	3	5	3	0.00	-40.00
Northern Europe	**41,106**	**32,057**	**28,791**	**28,679**	**30,022**	**2.11**	**4.68**
Denmark	1,039	1,007	933	921	938	0.07	1.85
Faeroe Islands	5	4	2	14	9	0.00	-35.71
Finland	725	751	696	584	650	0.05	11.30
Iceland	149	70	75	100	61	0.00	-39.00
Ireland	1,501	1,184	970	638	684	0.05	7.21
Norway	1,358	1,088	1,337	1,228	1,182	0.08	-3.75
Sweden	1,762	1,552	1,599	1,698	1,789	0.13	5.36
United Kingdom	34,567	26,401	23,179	23,496	24,709	1.74	5.16
Southern Europe	**14,341**	**12,421**	**13,899**	**13,589**	**12,180**	**0.86**	**-10.37**
Albania	4	16	10	10	11	0.00	10.00
Andorra	25	30	20	9	40	0.00	344.44
Bosnia and Herzegovina	4	8	18	6	23	0.00	283.33
Croatia	98	98	124	119	113	0.01	-5.04
Greece	444	392	450	472	368	0.03	-22.03
Italy	10,866	9,269	10,228	9,853	8,710	0.61	-11.60
Malta	54	55	52	77	57	0.00	-25.97
Montenegro	1	5	3	6	3	0.00	-50.00
Portugal	531	402	629	505	468	0.03	-7.33
San Marino	18	15	7	21	1	0.00	-95.24
Serbia	69	66	61	80	88	0.01	10.00
Serbia and Montenegro	8	2	1				
Slovenia	89	67	99	111	96	0.01	-13.51
Spain	2,122	1,979	2,180	2,295	2,175	0.15	-5.23
TFYR of Macedonia	8	17	17	25	27	0.00	8.00
Western Europe	**35,570**	**31,033**	**30,747**	**31,158**	**31,252**	**2.20**	**0.30**
Austria	1,657	1,533	1,461	1,439	1,555	0.11	8.06
Belgium	1,752	1,436	1,466	1,355	1,216	0.09	-10.26
France	14,423	13,667	12,495	13,190	12,857	0.90	-2.52
Germany	10,526	8,236	8,632	7,973	8,556	0.60	7.31
Liechtenstein	30	40	22	54	41	0.00	-24.07
Luxembourg	183	202	207	178	206	0.01	15.73
Monaco	173	184	133	154	132	0.01	-14.29
Netherlands	2,657	1,924	2,075	1,835	1,677	0.12	-8.61
Switzerland	4,169	3,811	4,256	4,980	5,012	0.35	0.64
East Mediterranean Europe	**1,184**	**1,203**	**1,307**	**1,153**	**1,346**	**0.09**	**16.74**
Cyprus	115	109	93	114	97	0.01	-14.91
Israel	725	774	742	684	771	0.05	12.72
Turkey	344	320	472	355	478	0.03	34.65
Other Europe					**3**		
Other countries of Europe					3		
MIDDLE EAST	**670**	**708**	**593**	**708**	**833**	**0.06**	**17.66**
Bahrain	52	31	52	22	31	0.00	40.91
Egypt	66	74	76	66	71	0.00	7.58
Iraq	1	3	4		2	0.00	
Jordan	27	28	15	16	16	0.00	0.00
Kuwait	55	77	65	93	122	0.01	31.18
Lebanon	43	28	22	37	32	0.00	-13.51
Libya			2				
Oman	7	13	8	9	14	0.00	55.56

48

BAHAMAS

1. Arrivals of non-resident tourists at national borders, by country of residence

	2008	2009	2010	2011	2012	Market share 2012	% Change 2012-2011
Palestine	1	2	2				
Qatar	44	38	25	31	30	0.00	-3.23
Saudi Arabia	156	155	113	214	226	0.02	5.61
Syrian Arab Republic	9	10	7	6	2	0.00	-66.67
United Arab Emirates	207	249	202	211	287	0.02	36.02
Yemen	2			3			
SOUTH ASIA	**696**	**526**	**666**	**494**	**715**	**0.05**	**44.74**
Afghanistan		5	2	2	3	0.00	50.00
Bangladesh	12	6	18	15	13	0.00	-13.33
Bhutan	1	3	2	1			
India	605	435	561	398	596	0.04	49.75
Iran, Islamic Republic of	6	7	9	6	15	0.00	150.00
Maldives	1	3		1	4	0.00	300.00
Nepal	15	16	15	13	11	0.00	-15.38
Pakistan	25	12	20	17	25	0.00	47.06
Sri Lanka	31	39	39	41	48	0.00	17.07
NOT SPECIFIED	**27,377**	**24,818**	**25,480**	**27,270**	**27,428**	**1.93**	**0.58**
Other countries of the World	27,377	24,818	25,480	27,270	27,428	1.93	0.58

Yearbook of Tourism Statistics, Data 2008 – 2012, 2014 Edition

BAHAMAS

6. Overnight stays of non-resident tourists in all types of accommodation establishments, by country of residence

	2008	2009	2010	2011	2012	Market share 2012	% Change 2012-2011
TOTAL (*)	9,678,609	9,039,234	9,128,113	9,123,171	9,626,984	100.00	5.52
AFRICA	23,455	21,000	22,515	22,988	36,207	0.38	57.50
East Africa	1,674	2,124	1,444	1,182	2,716	0.03	129.78
Burundi		4	30				
Comoros		9					
Djibouti		5	3		2	0.00	
Eritrea		12	16		6	0.00	
Ethiopia	46	114	122	147	95	0.00	-35.37
Kenya	226	123	362	145	397	0.00	173.79
Madagascar	33	54	3	7	20	0.00	185.71
Malawi	16	36	10	5	59	0.00	1,080.00
Mauritius	502	652	124	332	525	0.01	58.13
Mozambique	98	31	15	22	58	0.00	163.64
Rwanda	103	12	6				
Seychelles	64	104	87	45	7	0.00	-84.44
Somalia		7					
Uganda	119	397	317	71	168	0.00	136.62
United Republic of Tanzania	54	286	128	71	57	0.00	-19.72
Zambia	237	184	37	138	202	0.00	46.38
Zimbabwe	176	94	184	199	1,120	0.01	462.81
Central Africa	258	277	213	580	612	0.01	5.52
Angola	70	44	44	105	156	0.00	48.57
Cameroon	69	81	5	193	58	0.00	-69.95
Central African Republic	2	10		15			
Chad	16	34	91	111	147	0.00	32.43
Congo	71	96	20	28	127	0.00	353.57
Equatorial Guinea				56	15	0.00	-73.21
Gabon	30	12	53	72	109	0.00	51.39
North Africa	484	817	513	671	543	0.01	-19.08
Algeria	39	2	4	132	37	0.00	-71.97
Morocco	330	297	469	335	442	0.00	31.94
Sudan	4	21		6	10	0.00	66.67
Tunisia	111	497	40	198	54	0.00	-72.73
Southern Africa	19,471	16,192	19,163	18,327	30,365	0.32	65.68
Botswana	115	530	237	286	205	0.00	-28.32
Lesotho	5	39	29	7			
Namibia	118	185	122	66	245	0.00	271.21
South Africa	19,041	15,183	18,587	17,706	29,760	0.31	68.08
Swaziland	192	255	188	262	155	0.00	-40.84
West Africa	1,568	1,590	1,182	2,228	1,971	0.02	-11.54
Benin	8	4					
Burkina Faso		8	25	18	22	0.00	22.22
Cape Verde	2	34	14	102	1	0.00	-99.02
Côte d'Ivoire	43	29	46	95	59	0.00	-37.89
Gambia	7	43	4	2	29	0.00	1,350.00
Ghana	166	421	268	688	463	0.00	-32.70
Guinea	58	67	13	39	5	0.00	-87.18
Liberia		13	2	14	7	0.00	-50.00
Mali	2	4	25	7			
Mauritania	4	37	4	28	5	0.00	-82.14
Niger		22		3			
Nigeria	1,144	804	631	1,115	975	0.01	-12.56
Saint Helena					3	0.00	
Senegal	59	70	127	89	175	0.00	96.63
Sierra Leone	67	31	21	28	145	0.00	417.86
Togo	8	3	2		82	0.00	

Yearbook of Tourism Statistics, Data 2008 – 2012, 2014 Edition

BAHAMAS

6. Overnight stays of non-resident tourists in all types of accommodation establishments, by country of residence

	2008	2009	2010	2011	2012	Market share 2012	% Change 2012-2011
AMERICAS	8,409,420	7,900,946	8,027,668	8,011,185	8,479,309	88.08	5.84
Caribbean	190,161	158,798	152,196	152,018	153,828	1.60	1.19
Anguilla	264	171	252	106	145	0.00	36.79
Antigua and Barbuda	971	1,283	865	1,393	1,341	0.01	-3.73
Aruba	560	586	404	940	798	0.01	-15.11
Barbados	6,757	4,956	6,811	5,620	5,938	0.06	5.66
Bermuda	7,902	8,069	6,170	5,306	7,227	0.08	36.20
British Virgin Islands	919	1,123	1,288	765	1,093	0.01	42.88
Cayman Islands	9,093	8,774	8,244	7,005	6,920	0.07	-1.21
Cuba	5,921	5,695	6,109	7,572	8,674	0.09	14.55
Curaçao	794	798	837	798	1,017	0.01	27.44
Dominica	1,226	1,063	657	1,291	842	0.01	-34.78
Dominican Republic	2,964	4,958	3,078	3,519	3,725	0.04	5.85
Grenada	557	565	386	728	410	0.00	-43.68
Haiti	49,281	20,919	7,817	5,670	4,599	0.05	-18.89
Jamaica	70,133	66,985	75,673	79,694	80,296	0.83	0.76
Martinique	133	288	212	370	412	0.00	11.35
Montserrat	95	153	179	64	36	0.00	-43.75
Netherlands Antilles	263	194	166	303	28	0.00	-90.76
Puerto Rico	1,149	982	1,207	1,263	1,316	0.01	4.20
Saint Kitts and Nevis	692	981	976	903	434	0.00	-51.94
Saint Lucia	1,778	1,534	1,771	1,845	2,637	0.03	42.93
Saint Vincent and the Grenadines	946	973	606	847	548	0.01	-35.30
Sint Eustatius	23	11	23	55	68	0.00	23.64
Sint Maarten	962	562	374	697	778	0.01	11.62
Trinidad and Tobago	12,304	10,684	12,101	11,750	11,808	0.12	0.49
Turks and Caicos Islands	13,916	15,758	15,725	12,887	12,283	0.13	-4.69
United States Virgin Islands	143	71	144	74	133	0.00	79.73
Other countries of the Caribbean	415	662	121	553	322	0.00	-41.77
Central America	11,322	13,297	14,136	19,125	24,260	0.25	26.85
Belize	825	759	741	891	889	0.01	-0.22
Costa Rica	3,343	2,373	2,983	3,058	3,975	0.04	29.99
El Salvador	1,145	2,123	1,247	1,726	1,234	0.01	-28.51
Guatemala	1,610	1,928	2,509	2,921	4,854	0.05	66.18
Honduras	1,014	1,336	1,592	2,466	1,812	0.02	-26.52
Nicaragua	378	761	489	401	798	0.01	99.00
Panama	3,007	4,017	4,575	7,662	10,698	0.11	39.62
North America	8,140,131	7,650,947	7,770,613	7,706,085	8,138,642	84.54	5.61
Canada	913,157	897,050	957,193	980,819	1,031,243	10.71	5.14
Greenland	42	6	27	4	44	0.00	1,000.00
Mexico	21,594	26,254	21,607	27,329	32,425	0.34	18.65
United States of America	7,205,338	6,727,637	6,791,786	6,697,933	7,074,930	73.49	5.63
South America	67,806	77,904	90,723	133,957	162,579	1.69	21.37
Argentina	11,860	14,351	17,534	30,298	34,381	0.36	13.48
Bolivia	392	793	637	866	1,167	0.01	34.76
Brazil	20,256	22,125	27,723	36,658	44,741	0.46	22.05
Chile	3,027	3,787	3,683	7,262	7,478	0.08	2.97
Colombia	5,501	8,547	10,242	23,209	29,240	0.30	25.99
Ecuador	3,264	3,265	3,589	3,819	6,195	0.06	62.22
Guyana	5,217	4,904	4,953	5,664	6,255	0.06	10.43
Paraguay	667	860	2,082	2,690	3,009	0.03	11.86
Peru	4,382	4,716	6,441	7,049	9,247	0.10	31.18
Suriname	468	1,374	452	491	494	0.01	0.61
Uruguay	3,233	1,805	2,596	3,173	4,129	0.04	30.13
Venezuela	9,539	11,377	10,791	12,778	16,243	0.17	27.12

Yearbook of Tourism Statistics, Data 2008 – 2012, 2014 Edition

BAHAMAS

6. Overnight stays of non-resident tourists in all types of accommodation establishments, by country of residence

	2008	2009	2010	2011	2012	Market share 2012	% Change 2012-2011
EAST ASIA AND THE PACIFIC	66,453	67,705	68,944	67,681	77,319	0.80	14.24
North-East Asia	13,571	11,890	13,645	11,882	16,165	0.17	36.05
China	1,457	3,207	2,881	4,364	5,506	0.06	26.17
Hong Kong, China	2,636	1,045	1,698	1,606	2,296	0.02	42.96
Japan	7,135	5,895	4,406	4,165	5,730	0.06	37.58
Korea, Dem. People's Republic of	6		6	38	22	0.00	-42.11
Korea, Republic of	1,649	1,354	2,448	1,256	2,017	0.02	60.59
Mongolia	5	35	7	92	32	0.00	-65.22
Taiwan, Province of China	683	354	2,199	361	562	0.01	55.68
South-East Asia	9,304	7,965	10,822	8,705	8,738	0.09	0.38
Brunei Darussalam	18	8	17	14	15	0.00	7.14
Cambodia	3	14	21	23	13	0.00	-43.48
Indonesia	600	568	485	321	533	0.01	66.04
Lao People's Democratic Republic		12			13	0.00	
Malaysia	1,134	414	975	731	548	0.01	-25.03
Myanmar		13	5	14	125	0.00	792.86
Philippines	4,803	4,514	6,102	3,899	4,652	0.05	19.31
Singapore	1,790	1,138	2,261	2,626	1,685	0.02	-35.83
Thailand	916	1,076	737	897	1,000	0.01	11.48
Viet Nam	40	208	219	180	154	0.00	-14.44
Australasia	43,058	47,292	44,069	46,933	51,970	0.54	10.73
Australia	32,120	36,009	33,712	35,512	37,250	0.39	4.89
New Zealand	10,938	11,283	10,357	11,421	14,720	0.15	28.89
Melanesia	269	259	138	55	223	0.00	305.45
Fiji	55	198	67	42	116	0.00	176.19
Papua New Guinea	28	22	33	8	90	0.00	1,025.00
Solomon Islands	162	15	22	3	13	0.00	333.33
Vanuatu	24	24	16	2	4	0.00	100.00
Micronesia	94	161	116	15	55	0.00	266.67
Kiribati		26		5			
Marshall Islands		120	90				
Micronesia, Federated States of	74	15	26	10	49	0.00	390.00
Nauru	6						
Palau	14				6	0.00	
Polynesia	157	138	154	91	168	0.00	84.62
French Polynesia	120	100	113	74	124	0.00	67.57
Samoa	13	26	41	17	27	0.00	58.82
Tonga	24	12			17	0.00	
EUROPE	911,736	811,786	776,920	773,421	784,104	8.14	1.38
Central/Eastern Europe	20,151	27,387	33,442	38,564	42,308	0.44	9.71
Armenia	68	83	28	7	46	0.00	557.14
Azerbaijan	16	85	13	140	132	0.00	-5.71
Belarus	151	60	98	142	355	0.00	150.00
Bulgaria	828	1,168	1,813	1,530	1,727	0.02	12.88
Czech Republic	2,018	2,535	2,295	2,737	3,173	0.03	15.93
Estonia	361	1,504	908	1,599	2,180	0.02	36.34
Georgia	176	129	138	222	239	0.00	7.66
Hungary	2,077	1,949	2,525	3,090	2,838	0.03	-8.16
Kazakhstan	188	189	377	144	683	0.01	374.31
Kyrgyzstan		199	42				
Latvia	363	385	439	442	618	0.01	39.82
Lithuania	509	339	562	672	978	0.01	45.54
Poland	5,567	5,823	7,226	8,257	7,421	0.08	-10.12
Republic of Moldova	28	20	119	31	165	0.00	432.26
Romania	2,571	2,566	3,863	3,763	4,794	0.05	27.40

Yearbook of Tourism Statistics, Data 2008 – 2012, 2014 Edition

BAHAMAS

6. Overnight stays of non-resident tourists in all types of accommodation establishments, by country of residence

	2008	2009	2010	2011	2012	Market share 2012	% Change 2012-2011
Russian Federation	3,273	6,756	8,805	12,330	14,645	0.15	18.78
Slovakia	837	1,766	2,250	1,705	1,187	0.01	-30.38
Tajikistan		15			22	0.00	
Turkmenistan	4	12	14		15	0.00	
Ukraine	1,116	1,768	1,911	1,735	1,080	0.01	-37.75
Uzbekistan		36	16	18	10	0.00	-44.44
Northern Europe	**457,128**	**381,216**	**342,081**	**337,559**	**345,812**	**3.59**	**2.44**
Denmark	9,050	10,017	8,099	8,836	9,352	0.10	5.84
Faeroe Islands	38	13	28	230	115	0.00	-50.00
Finland	4,869	5,439	4,534	4,965	5,303	0.06	6.81
Iceland	2,094	1,474	1,114	1,503	838	0.01	-44.24
Ireland	12,980	12,679	9,641	7,619	6,854	0.07	-10.04
Norway	11,055	9,685	12,561	11,939	11,049	0.11	-7.45
Sweden	14,853	15,051	14,620	14,772	16,758	0.17	13.44
United Kingdom	402,189	326,858	291,484	287,695	295,543	3.07	2.73
Southern Europe	**108,907**	**98,237**	**102,583**	**103,360**	**96,225**	**1.00**	**-6.90**
Albania	26	192	63	71	78	0.00	9.86
Andorra	345	708	301	59	731	0.01	1,138.98
Bosnia and Herzegovina	34	46	105	65	250	0.00	284.62
Croatia	814	969	1,051	1,387	1,144	0.01	-17.52
Greece	3,210	2,789	3,467	3,860	3,089	0.03	-19.97
Italy	82,947	72,381	73,854	73,297	67,198	0.70	-8.32
Malta	395	487	541	643	673	0.01	4.67
Montenegro	3	95	33	28	43	0.00	53.57
Portugal	3,827	3,375	5,524	4,608	4,202	0.04	-8.81
San Marino	76	66	42	189	6	0.00	-96.83
Serbia	794	802	1,042	1,425	2,042	0.02	43.30
Serbia and Montenegro	158	35	14				
Slovenia	701	438	788	813	761	0.01	-6.40
Spain	15,525	15,745	15,439	16,573	15,775	0.16	-4.82
TFYR of Macedonia	52	109	319	342	233	0.00	-31.87
Western Europe	**318,315**	**296,150**	**289,175**	**285,620**	**289,454**	**3.01**	**1.34**
Austria	15,682	17,033	15,378	14,033	14,554	0.15	3.71
Belgium	14,355	12,957	13,883	13,482	10,680	0.11	-20.78
France	121,517	118,382	106,397	110,396	110,220	1.14	-0.16
Germany	103,234	90,467	90,165	81,903	89,793	0.93	9.63
Liechtenstein	240	230	251	412	227	0.00	-44.90
Luxembourg	1,708	1,869	1,761	2,267	2,062	0.02	-9.04
Monaco	1,654	2,141	1,487	1,376	1,431	0.01	4.00
Netherlands	22,085	17,599	18,206	16,899	15,064	0.16	-10.86
Switzerland	37,840	35,472	41,647	44,852	45,423	0.47	1.27
East Mediterranean Europe	**7,235**	**8,796**	**9,639**	**8,318**	**10,305**	**0.11**	**23.89**
Cyprus	714	625	463	582	970	0.01	66.67
Israel	5,022	6,538	6,636	6,057	7,021	0.07	15.92
Turkey	1,499	1,633	2,540	1,679	2,314	0.02	37.82
MIDDLE EAST	**4,481**	**4,562**	**4,098**	**5,676**	**5,107**	**0.05**	**-10.02**
Bahrain	255	188	314	147	164	0.00	11.56
Egypt	362	461	513	366	538	0.01	46.99
Iraq	10	15	28		16	0.00	
Jordan	130	127	110	99	92	0.00	-7.07
Kuwait	285	441	452	463	643	0.01	38.88
Lebanon	341	167	119	243	169	0.00	-30.45
Libya		8	12				
Oman	38	81	75	51	58	0.00	13.73
Palestine	2	7	11				

Yearbook of Tourism Statistics, Data 2008 – 2012, 2014 Edition

BAHAMAS

6. Overnight stays of non-resident tourists in all types of accommodation establishments, by country of residence

	2008	2009	2010	2011	2012	Market share 2012	% Change 2012-2011
Qatar	331	223	112	183	156	0.00	-14.75
Saudi Arabia	1,587	1,310	865	2,871	1,374	0.01	-52.14
Syrian Arab Republic	57	50	56	67	15	0.00	-77.61
United Arab Emirates	1,072	1,484	1,431	1,172	1,882	0.02	60.58
Yemen	11			14			
SOUTH ASIA	**6,617**	**5,302**	**4,532**	**4,957**	**5,907**	**0.06**	**19.16**
Afghanistan		23	12	18	21	0.00	16.67
Bangladesh	41	25	57	128	43	0.00	-66.41
Bhutan	3	9	5	5			
India	5,739	4,367	3,771	3,691	4,277	0.04	15.88
Iran, Islamic Republic of	34	126	79	43	102	0.00	137.21
Maldives	21	22		4	26	0.00	550.00
Nepal	138	432	164	175	55	0.00	-68.57
Pakistan	168	49	74	188	117	0.00	-37.77
Sri Lanka	473	249	370	705	1,266	0.01	79.57
NOT SPECIFIED	**256,447**	**227,933**	**223,436**	**237,263**	**239,031**	**2.48**	**0.75**
Other countries of the World	256,447	227,933	223,436	237,263	239,031	2.48	0.75

Yearbook of Tourism Statistics, Data 2008 – 2012, 2014 Edition

BAHRAIN

2. Arrivals of non-resident visitors at national borders, by nationality

		2008	2009	2010	2011	2012	Market share 2012	% Change 2012-2011
TOTAL	(*)				6,731,974			
AFRICA					99,545			
East Africa					15,626			
Burundi					1			
Comoros					18			
Djibouti					132			
Eritrea					2,155			
Ethiopia					7,017			
Kenya					2,824			
Madagascar					20			
Malawi					60			
Mauritius					268			
Mozambique					13			
Seychelles					478			
Somalia					1,505			
Uganda					139			
United Republic of Tanzania					330			
Zambia					27			
Zimbabwe					639			
Central Africa					604			
Angola					9			
Cameroon					171			
Chad					173			
Congo					213			
Equatorial Guinea					2			
Gabon					35			
Sao Tome and Principe					1			
North Africa					57,013			
Algeria					4,392			
Morocco					8,657			
Sudan					38,733			
Tunisia					5,231			
Southern Africa					22,026			
Botswana					27			
Namibia					20			
South Africa					21,976			
Swaziland					3			
West Africa					4,215			
Benin					123			
Burkina Faso					29			
Cape Verde					1			
Côte d'Ivoire					64			
Gambia					12			
Ghana					786			
Guinea					61			
Guinea-Bissau					13			
Liberia					5			
Mali					101			
Mauritania					103			
Niger					99			
Nigeria					2,674			
Senegal					123			
Sierra Leone					17			
Togo					4			

Yearbook of Tourism Statistics, Data 2008 – 2012, 2014 Edition

BAHRAIN

2. Arrivals of non-resident visitors at national borders, by nationality

	2008	2009	2010	2011	2012	Market share 2012	% Change 2012-2011
Other Africa				61			
Other countries of Africa				61			
AMERICAS				291,253			
Caribbean				2,340			
Antigua and Barbuda				6			
Bahamas				44			
Barbados				9			
Cayman Islands				3			
Cuba				58			
Dominica				16			
Dominican Republic				29			
Grenada				4			
Jamaica				84			
Netherlands Antilles				4			
Saint Lucia				2			
Saint Vincent and the Grenadines				12			
Trinidad and Tobago				2,069			
Central America				612			
Belize				29			
Costa Rica				141			
El Salvador				37			
Guatemala				69			
Honduras				26			
Nicaragua				37			
Panama				273			
North America				272,186			
Canada				64,019			
Mexico				1,546			
United States of America				206,354			
Other countries of North America				267			
South America				16,115			
Argentina				1,633			
Bolivia				234			
Brazil				2,252			
Chile				167			
Colombia				3,701			
Ecuador				243			
Guyana				6			
Paraguay				2			
Peru				564			
Uruguay				90			
Venezuela				7,223			
EAST ASIA AND THE PACIFIC				338,724			
North-East Asia				69,352			
China				22,418			
Hong Kong, China				3,711			
Japan				17,129			
Korea, Dem. People's Republic of				107			
Korea, Republic of				25,908			
Macao, China				1			
Mongolia				78			
South-East Asia				234,081			
Brunei Darussalam				88			
Cambodia				14			
Indonesia				25,597			
Lao People's Democratic Republic				18			
Malaysia				20,218			

Yearbook of Tourism Statistics, Data 2008 – 2012, 2014 Edition

BAHRAIN

2. Arrivals of non-resident visitors at national borders, by nationality

	2008	2009	2010	2011	2012	Market share 2012	% Change 2012-2011
Myanmar				730			
Philippines				175,775			
Singapore				3,915			
Thailand				7,247			
Viet Nam				479			
Australasia				**35,220**			
Australia				27,315			
New Zealand				7,905			
Melanesia				**46**			
Fiji				42			
Papua New Guinea				4			
Micronesia				**3**			
Marshall Islands				1			
Nauru				1			
Palau				1			
Polynesia				**22**			
Tonga				10			
Tuvalu				12			
EUROPE				**513,232**			
Central/Eastern Europe				**27,396**			
Armenia				79			
Azerbaijan				992			
Belarus				805			
Bulgaria				1,064			
Czech Republic				1,552			
Czech Republic/Slovakia				8			
Estonia				198			
Georgia				213			
Hungary				1,062			
Kazakhstan				498			
Kyrgyzstan				108			
Latvia				234			
Lithuania				123			
Poland				1,866			
Republic of Moldova				154			
Romania				5,102			
Russian Federation				10,630			
Slovakia				633			
Tajikistan				26			
Turkmenistan				272			
Ukraine				1,322			
Uzbekistan				455			
Northern Europe				**281,029**			
Denmark				4,507			
Finland				2,447			
Iceland				147			
Ireland				17,190			
Norway				2,697			
Sweden				3,490			
United Kingdom				250,551			
Southern Europe				**48,638**			
Albania				34			
Bosnia and Herzegovina				345			
Croatia				877			
Greece				6,320			
Italy				28,197			
Malta				235			

57

BAHRAIN

2. Arrivals of non-resident visitors at national borders, by nationality

	2008	2009	2010	2011	2012	Market share 2012	% Change 2012-2011
Montenegro				10			
Portugal				1,897			
San Marino				7			
Serbia				645			
Serbia and Montenegro				688			
Slovenia				101			
Spain				9,205			
TFYR of Macedonia				77			
Western Europe				**128,733**			
Austria				6,196			
Belgium				7,079			
France				38,742			
Germany				55,329			
Liechtenstein				11			
Luxembourg				150			
Monaco				7			
Netherlands				17,715			
Switzerland				3,504			
East Mediterranean Europe				**27,436**			
Cyprus				2,917			
Turkey				24,519			
MIDDLE EAST				**4,276,021**			
Egypt				130,916			
Iraq				7,122			
Jordan				132,041			
Kuwait				275,897			
Lebanon				61,128			
Libya				1,100			
Oman				39,452			
Palestine				34,004			
Qatar				96,214			
Saudi Arabia				3,320,188			
Syrian Arab Republic				74,078			
United Arab Emirates				42,789			
Yemen				61,092			
SOUTH ASIA				**1,213,199**			
Afghanistan				1,649			
Bangladesh				70,858			
Bhutan				16			
India				837,514			
Iran, Islamic Republic of				3,158			
Maldives				54			
Nepal				51,985			
Pakistan				214,952			
Sri Lanka				33,013			

Yearbook of Tourism Statistics, Data 2008 – 2012, 2014 Edition

BARBADOS

1. Arrivals of non-resident tourists at national borders, by country of residence

	2008	2009	2010	2011	2012	Market share 2012	% Change 2012-2011
TOTAL	567,639	518,549	532,150	567,683	536,262	100.00	-5.53
AFRICA	1,389	954	1,284	1,175	1,011	0.19	-13.96
East Africa	187	108	175	193	171	0.03	-11.40
Ethiopia	7	4	2	4	5	0.00	25.00
Kenya	71	38	72	61	63	0.01	3.28
Malawi	11	2	1	3	8	0.00	166.67
Mauritius	24	10	9	22	12	0.00	-45.45
Rwanda	3	1	3	4	2	0.00	-50.00
Seychelles	5		2	10	5	0.00	-50.00
Uganda	23	13	16	16	19	0.00	18.75
United Republic of Tanzania	19	17	15	13	15	0.00	15.38
Zambia	11	8	11	32	16	0.00	-50.00
Zimbabwe	13	15	44	28	26	0.00	-7.14
Central Africa	15	4	19	15	20	0.00	33.33
Angola	4	2	3	6	4	0.00	-33.33
Cameroon	7	2	9	5	7	0.00	40.00
Congo	4		7	4	9	0.00	125.00
North Africa	17	20	24	31	46	0.01	48.39
Morocco	4	13	9	14	13	0.00	-7.14
Sudan	5	1	3		5	0.00	
Tunisia	8	6	12	17	28	0.01	64.71
Southern Africa	554	446	690	420	416	0.08	-0.95
Botswana	33	13	18	22	9	0.00	-59.09
Lesotho	8	5	2	1	4	0.00	300.00
Namibia	9	7	11	8	6	0.00	-25.00
South Africa	501	413	652	366	393	0.07	7.38
Swaziland	3	8	7	23	4	0.00	-82.61
West Africa	616	376	376	516	358	0.07	-30.62
Gambia	10		5	2	6	0.00	200.00
Ghana	168	35	34	41	26	0.00	-36.59
Guinea	4	1	4	2	1	0.00	-50.00
Liberia	1			3	1	0.00	-66.67
Mali		6	1	1			
Nigeria	423	329	326	462	324	0.06	-29.87
Sierra Leone	10	5	6	5			
AMERICAS	309,043	292,435	312,551	336,920	318,381	59.37	-5.50
Caribbean	96,777	88,302	85,573	94,722	90,562	16.89	-4.39
Anguilla	844	797	658	498	456	0.09	-8.43
Antigua and Barbuda	5,519	5,345	4,518	4,287	4,004	0.75	-6.60
Aruba	89	76	98	118	84	0.02	-28.81
Bahamas	1,092	916	921	971	807	0.15	-16.89
Bermuda	1,496	1,482	1,424	1,220	990	0.18	-18.85
British Virgin Islands	2,316	2,132	1,800	1,630	1,410	0.26	-13.50
Cayman Islands	985	886	769	727	514	0.10	-29.30
Cuba	209	185	160	143	123	0.02	-13.99
Curaçao	221	206	212	228	178	0.03	-21.93
Dominica	5,404	5,251	5,185	5,146	4,472	0.83	-13.10
Dominican Republic	298	322	360	391	412	0.08	5.37
Grenada	5,586	5,231	4,941	5,035	4,413	0.82	-12.35
Guadeloupe	1,027	846	1,168	1,010	982	0.18	-2.77
Haiti	152	202	194	212	213	0.04	0.47
Jamaica	10,991	8,078	7,948	8,862	8,423	1.57	-4.95
Martinique	2,612	2,692	2,975	2,844	2,462	0.46	-13.43
Montserrat	351	279	244	250	181	0.03	-27.60
Netherlands Antilles	1,548	1,489	1,317	915	856	0.16	-6.45
Puerto Rico	1,218	898	742	683	587	0.11	-14.06

59

BARBADOS

1. Arrivals of non-resident tourists at national borders, by country of residence

	2008	2009	2010	2011	2012	Market share 2012	% Change 2012-2011
Saint Kitts and Nevis	3,532	3,928	3,589	3,000	2,714	0.51	-9.53
Saint Lucia	10,539	9,421	8,451	8,199	7,479	1.39	-8.78
Saint Vincent and the Grenadines	11,432	10,410	9,900	10,596	10,344	1.93	-2.38
Sint Maarten				238	1	0.00	-99.58
Trinidad and Tobago	28,451	26,510	27,292	36,825	38,005	7.09	3.20
Turks and Caicos Islands	275	200	243	238	130	0.02	-45.38
United States Virgin Islands	590	520	464	456	322	0.06	-29.39
Central America	**1,547**	**1,270**	**1,461**	**1,535**	**1,562**	**0.29**	**1.76**
Belize	574	502	508	573	540	0.10	-5.76
Costa Rica	195	224	318	259	272	0.05	5.02
El Salvador	61	35	41	45	62	0.01	37.78
Guatemala	161	86	136	131	141	0.03	7.63
Honduras	55	31	36	46	68	0.01	47.83
Nicaragua	39	22	17	32	48	0.01	50.00
Panama	462	370	405	449	431	0.08	-4.01
North America	**189,894**	**186,965**	**208,368**	**214,975**	**203,442**	**37.94**	**-5.36**
Canada	57,398	63,826	72,434	71,953	72,020	13.43	0.09
Greenland			1	1			
Mexico	512	434	444	607	660	0.12	8.73
United States of America	131,984	122,705	135,489	142,414	130,762	24.38	-8.18
South America	**20,825**	**15,898**	**17,149**	**25,688**	**22,815**	**4.25**	**-11.18**
Argentina	411	375	317	656	522	0.10	-20.43
Bolivia	50	45	26	30	85	0.02	183.33
Brazil	523	504	2,354	4,842	4,633	0.86	-4.32
Chile	139	116	86	131	116	0.02	-11.45
Colombia	377	333	373	399	509	0.09	27.57
Ecuador	100	35	46	39	65	0.01	66.67
French Guiana	170	58	96	97	126	0.02	29.90
Guyana	16,528	12,010	11,673	16,524	14,167	2.64	-14.26
Paraguay	9	3	2	15	41	0.01	173.33
Peru	106	103	131	92	263	0.05	185.87
Suriname	559	532	518	681	557	0.10	-18.21
Uruguay	43	16	20	49	47	0.01	-4.08
Venezuela	1,810	1,768	1,507	2,133	1,684	0.31	-21.05
EAST ASIA AND THE PACIFIC	**4,147**	**3,325**	**4,107**	**3,723**	**4,498**	**0.84**	**20.82**
North-East Asia	**752**	**891**	**728**	**799**	**923**	**0.17**	**15.52**
China	399	531	397	403	499	0.09	23.82
Hong Kong, China	77	103	82	71	92	0.02	29.58
Japan	208	231	214	310	315	0.06	1.61
Korea, Republic of	14	5	15	6	7	0.00	16.67
Taiwan, Province of China	54	21	20	9	10	0.00	11.11
South-East Asia	**890**	**990**	**970**	**768**	**671**	**0.13**	**-12.63**
Brunei Darussalam	3		3	5	2	0.00	-60.00
Indonesia	80	65	69	76	36	0.01	-52.63
Malaysia	115	91	85	58	89	0.02	53.45
Philippines	514	644	633	506	403	0.08	-20.36
Singapore	126	117	112	86	99	0.02	15.12
Thailand	48	64	61	34	39	0.01	14.71
Viet Nam	4	9	7	3	3	0.00	0.00
Australasia	**2,486**	**1,431**	**2,390**	**2,139**	**2,874**	**0.54**	**34.36**
Australia	2,102	1,169	1,971	1,765	2,512	0.47	42.32
New Zealand	384	262	419	374	362	0.07	-3.21
Melanesia	**16**	**12**	**13**	**13**	**14**	**0.00**	**7.69**
Fiji	11	4	8	11	14	0.00	27.27
Papua New Guinea	4	7	4	2			
Vanuatu	1	1	1				

60

BARBADOS

1. Arrivals of non-resident tourists at national borders, by country of residence

	2008	2009	2010	2011	2012	Market share 2012	% Change 2012-2011
Polynesia	3	1	6	4	16	0.00	300.00
Cook Islands				2	2	0.00	0.00
Samoa	1	1	2	1	8	0.00	700.00
Tonga	2		4	1	6	0.00	500.00
EUROPE	**249,994**	**218,755**	**210,696**	**223,923**	**209,563**	**39.08**	**-6.41**
Central/Eastern Europe	**2,935**	**2,482**	**3,064**	**4,163**	**3,727**	**0.69**	**-10.47**
Azerbaijan	6	1	8	2	15	0.00	650.00
Bulgaria	96	84	59	126	59	0.01	-53.17
Czech Republic	286	278	257	345	318	0.06	-7.83
Czech Republic/Slovakia			2	2			
Estonia	104	98	168	514	70	0.01	-86.38
Georgia	3	3	6	11	12	0.00	9.09
Hungary	162	163	195	196	187	0.03	-4.59
Kazakhstan	31	12	49	41	59	0.01	43.90
Latvia	105	31	52	71	66	0.01	-7.04
Lithuania	29	14	47	68	87	0.02	27.94
Poland	485	343	407	491	405	0.08	-17.52
Romania	150	128	149	144	140	0.03	-2.78
Russian Federation	1,116	1,024	1,217	1,718	1,844	0.34	7.33
Slovakia	141	97	133	161	179	0.03	11.18
Ukraine	221	206	315	273	286	0.05	4.76
Northern Europe	**228,288**	**196,987**	**188,079**	**197,814**	**183,767**	**34.27**	**-7.10**
Denmark	1,010	806	947	938	844	0.16	-10.02
Finland	318	381	426	612	1,353	0.25	121.08
Iceland	98	18	22	21	33	0.01	57.14
Ireland	5,371	4,105	3,852	3,738	3,519	0.66	-5.86
Norway	877	694	1,016	1,056	1,218	0.23	15.34
Sweden	1,519	1,270	1,526	2,299	3,281	0.61	42.71
United Kingdom	219,095	189,713	180,290	189,150	173,519	32.36	-8.26
Southern Europe	**5,914**	**5,940**	**5,507**	**5,972**	**5,204**	**0.97**	**-12.86**
Albania	1	6	8	8	14	0.00	75.00
Andorra	2	7	1	5	1	0.00	-80.00
Bosnia and Herzegovina	4	1	4	5	6	0.00	20.00
Croatia	101	92	63	72	149	0.03	106.94
Gibraltar	37	39	49	29	38	0.01	31.03
Greece	135	72	168	149	136	0.03	-8.72
Italy	4,004	4,421	3,944	4,426	3,710	0.69	-16.18
Malta	58	60	54	37	46	0.01	24.32
Montenegro		4	1	3	2	0.00	-33.33
Portugal	228	157	222	161	187	0.03	16.15
San Marino	27	7	12	25	4	0.00	-84.00
Serbia		39	36	33	37	0.01	12.12
Serbia and Montenegro		4					
Slovenia	150	78	82	95	61	0.01	-35.79
Spain	1,167	953	863	924	813	0.15	-12.01
Western Europe	**12,508**	**13,045**	**13,725**	**15,676**	**16,566**	**3.09**	**5.68**
Austria	529	710	857	916	994	0.19	8.52
Belgium	763	647	624	550	593	0.11	7.82
France	2,875	2,416	2,524	3,167	3,252	0.61	2.68
Germany	6,111	7,038	7,300	8,401	9,182	1.71	9.30
Liechtenstein	14	12	26	22	10	0.00	-54.55
Luxembourg	177	105	155	172	137	0.03	-20.35
Monaco	119	108	108	97	138	0.03	42.27
Netherlands	510	412	310	357	281	0.05	-21.29
Switzerland	1,410	1,597	1,821	1,994	1,979	0.37	-0.75

Yearbook of Tourism Statistics, Data 2008 – 2012, 2014 Edition

BARBADOS

1. Arrivals of non-resident tourists at national borders, by country of residence

	2008	2009	2010	2011	2012	Market share 2012	% Change 2012-2011
East Mediterranean Europe	**349**	**301**	**321**	**298**	**299**	**0.06**	**0.34**
Cyprus	86	92	54	57	35	0.01	-38.60
Israel	166	141	172	179	209	0.04	16.76
Turkey	97	68	95	62	55	0.01	-11.29
MIDDLE EAST	**337**	**299**	**344**	**305**	**233**	**0.04**	**-23.61**
Bahrain	27	15	14	13	7	0.00	-46.15
Egypt	8	13	24	19	14	0.00	-26.32
Jordan	59	9	6	19	16	0.00	-15.79
Kuwait	9	9	6	11	2	0.00	-81.82
Lebanon	16	10	9	28	10	0.00	-64.29
Oman	9	12	4	7	5	0.00	-28.57
Saudi Arabia	61	35	18	55	20	0.00	-63.64
Syrian Arab Republic	6	6	3				
United Arab Emirates	139	188	260	152	158	0.03	3.95
Yemen	3	2		1	1	0.00	0.00
SOUTH ASIA	**1,113**	**1,082**	**1,634**	**1,440**	**886**	**0.17**	**-38.47**
Afghanistan	2	2	26				
Bangladesh	33	30	58	8	3	0.00	-62.50
India	963	959	1,317	1,230	758	0.14	-38.37
Iran, Islamic Republic of	8	2	3	6	5	0.00	-16.67
Maldives	2		1		2	0.00	
Nepal	10	9	8	16	13	0.00	-18.75
Pakistan	60	50	122	119	62	0.01	-47.90
Sri Lanka	35	30	99	61	43	0.01	-29.51
NOT SPECIFIED	**1,616**	**1,699**	**1,534**	**197**	**1,690**	**0.32**	**757.87**
Other countries of the World	1,616	1,699	1,534	197	1,690	0.32	757.87

Yearbook of Tourism Statistics, Data 2008 – 2012, 2014 Edition

BELARUS

1. Arrivals of non-resident tourists at national borders, by nationality

		2008	2009	2010	2011	2012	Market share 2012	% Change 2012-2011
TOTAL	(*)	91,232	94,719	119,370	116,049	118,749	100.00	2.33
AFRICA		73	138	101	44	16	0.01	-63.64
East Africa			2	8				
Ethiopia				8				
Zimbabwe			2					
Central Africa			3	4	1			
Angola			2	4				
Cameroon					1			
Congo			1					
North Africa		10	11	11	8	1	0.00	-87.50
Algeria		2	3	7	3	1	0.00	-66.67
Morocco		3	5	1	5			
Sudan		1		3				
Tunisia		4	3					
Southern Africa		11	67	24	21	8	0.01	-61.90
Lesotho					2			
Namibia			5	4	2			
South Africa		11	62	20	17	8	0.01	-52.94
West Africa		52	55	54	14	7	0.01	-50.00
Côte d'Ivoire					2			
Ghana		17	26	1		3	0.00	
Guinea		1						
Nigeria		34	28	52	12	4	0.00	-66.67
Sierra Leone				1				
Togo			1					
AMERICAS		1,401	1,075	974	657	1,179	0.99	79.45
Caribbean		2	4	1	35			
Anguilla					4			
Cayman Islands					9			
Cuba		2	4					
Dominican Republic					2			
Jamaica				1				
Saint Lucia					20			
Central America		6		2	1	1	0.00	0.00
Costa Rica						1	0.00	
Guatemala					1			
Nicaragua				2				
Panama		6						
North America		1,292	963	820	567	1,114	0.94	96.47
Canada		115	79	129	33	74	0.06	124.24
Mexico		9	20	8	7	23	0.02	228.57
United States of America		1,168	864	683	527	1,017	0.86	92.98
South America		101	108	151	54	64	0.05	18.52
Argentina		11	13	10	11	5	0.00	-54.55
Bolivia			4					
Brazil		37	22	43	29	31	0.03	6.90
Chile		16	12	5	3	4	0.00	33.33
Colombia		6	6		1	4	0.00	300.00
Ecuador					2			
Paraguay				1				
Peru		5	14	9	5	4	0.00	-20.00
Uruguay				1				
Venezuela		26	37	82	3	16	0.01	433.33

Yearbook of Tourism Statistics, Data 2008 – 2012, 2014 Edition

BELARUS

1. Arrivals of non-resident tourists at national borders, by nationality

	2008	2009	2010	2011	2012	Market share 2012	% Change 2012-2011
EAST ASIA AND THE PACIFIC	1,054	963	1,040	4,251	1,015	0.85	-76.12
North-East Asia	924	811	839	1,053	870	0.73	-17.38
China	376	391	603	364	314	0.26	-13.74
Hong Kong, China			1	37	105	0.09	183.78
Japan	393	235	197	269	385	0.32	43.12
Korea, Dem. People's Republic of	1	34	1	2			
Korea, Republic of	76	55	14	50	43	0.04	-14.00
Mongolia		10	3	79	1	0.00	-98.73
Taiwan, Province of China	78	86	20	252	22	0.02	-91.27
South-East Asia	52	57	52	48	11	0.01	-77.08
Indonesia	14	3	4	4			
Malaysia	6	7	5		4	0.00	
Myanmar				2			
Philippines	5	21	5		1	0.00	
Singapore	7	5	1		1	0.00	
Thailand	3	1	8		3	0.00	
Viet Nam	17	20	29	42	2	0.00	-95.24
Australasia	78	95	149	3,150	134	0.11	-95.75
Australia	68	57	132	65	124	0.10	90.77
New Zealand	10	38	17	3,085	10	0.01	-99.68
EUROPE	87,752	91,778	116,342	110,232	116,001	97.69	5.23
Central/Eastern Europe	61,514	69,271	94,218	95,054	102,307	86.15	7.63
Armenia				30	23	0.02	-23.33
Azerbaijan	70	290	194	251	64	0.05	-74.50
Bulgaria	173	143	50	63	24	0.02	-61.90
Czech Republic	464	421	350	334	198	0.17	-40.72
Estonia	1,166	690	595	464	738	0.62	59.05
Georgia				36	149	0.13	313.89
Hungary	96	119	136	105	62	0.05	-40.95
Kazakhstan				165	180	0.15	9.09
Kyrgyzstan	7	29	8	12	8	0.01	-33.33
Latvia	1,425	1,550	1,409	1,550	1,107	0.93	-28.58
Lithuania	2,600	2,979	4,357	3,170	1,688	1.42	-46.75
Poland	2,832	3,729	4,006	2,983	2,027	1.71	-32.05
Republic of Moldova	148	158	104	40	87	0.07	117.50
Romania	66	69	91	99	160	0.13	61.62
Russian Federation	50,444	56,547	80,881	83,843	94,187	79.32	12.34
Slovakia	125	124	118	144	108	0.09	-25.00
Tajikistan				5	5	0.00	0.00
Turkmenistan				26	31	0.03	19.23
Ukraine	1,898	2,423	1,919	1,693	1,441	1.21	-14.88
Uzbekistan				41	20	0.02	-51.22
Northern Europe	9,877	6,701	8,172	4,233	3,832	3.23	-9.47
Denmark	164	185	230	267	100	0.08	-62.55
Finland	962	610	770	560	358	0.30	-36.07
Iceland	37	6	59	476	20	0.02	-95.80
Ireland	144	178	57	39	50	0.04	28.21
Norway	302	156	192	133	51	0.04	-61.65
Sweden	594	604	644	346	220	0.19	-36.42
United Kingdom	7,674	4,962	6,220	2,412	3,033	2.55	25.75
Southern Europe	3,583	3,868	3,428	2,627	2,421	2.04	-7.84
Albania	14	1	49				
Bosnia and Herzegovina	1	5	20	137	12	0.01	-91.24
Croatia	227	195	89	108	97	0.08	-10.19
Greece	41	162	83	49	46	0.04	-6.12
Italy	2,672	2,531	2,275	1,816	1,535	1.29	-15.47
Malta	5	8		5	2	0.00	-60.00

64

BELARUS

1. Arrivals of non-resident tourists at national borders, by nationality

	2008	2009	2010	2011	2012	Market share 2012	% Change 2012-2011
Montenegro		32		17			
Portugal	22	118	72	16	78	0.07	387.50
Serbia	65	277	63	44	162	0.14	268.18
Slovenia	156	238	136	38	23	0.02	-39.47
Spain	372	274	582	349	366	0.31	4.87
TFYR of Macedonia	8	27	59	48	100	0.08	108.33
Western Europe	**5,994**	**5,988**	**4,432**	**4,111**	**3,948**	**3.32**	**-3.96**
Austria	586	471	295	250	220	0.19	-12.00
Belgium	239	155	249	120	247	0.21	105.83
France	1,257	1,114	808	754	749	0.63	-0.66
Germany	3,027	2,568	2,245	2,191	2,071	1.74	-5.48
Liechtenstein			2				
Luxembourg	19	19	12	53	2	0.00	-96.23
Netherlands	386	475	552	327	229	0.19	-29.97
Switzerland	480	1,186	269	416	430	0.36	3.37
East Mediterranean Europe	**6,784**	**5,950**	**6,092**	**4,207**	**3,493**	**2.94**	**-16.97**
Cyprus	206	314	460	272	141	0.12	-48.16
Israel	491	956	925	339	584	0.49	72.27
Turkey	6,087	4,680	4,707	3,596	2,768	2.33	-23.03
MIDDLE EAST	**473**	**331**	**522**	**395**	**270**	**0.23**	**-31.65**
Bahrain				37	8	0.01	-78.38
Egypt	24	26	53	30	47	0.04	56.67
Iraq	30	16	16	22	25	0.02	13.64
Jordan	25	15	14	6	1	0.00	-83.33
Kuwait	12	6	10		2	0.00	
Lebanon	102	83	225	245	117	0.10	-52.24
Libya	27	11	2	6	22	0.02	266.67
Oman				8	13	0.01	62.50
Palestine					13	0.01	
Qatar				6			
Saudi Arabia	19	19	50	9	7	0.01	-22.22
Syrian Arab Republic	103	21	8	3	11	0.01	266.67
United Arab Emirates	131	130	137	23	2	0.00	-91.30
Yemen		4	7		2	0.00	
SOUTH ASIA	**479**	**434**	**391**	**470**	**268**	**0.23**	**-42.98**
Afghanistan	7	1	7	2			
Bangladesh	1	1	1		3	0.00	
India	221	154	73	97	18	0.02	-81.44
Iran, Islamic Republic of	210	255	298	368	235	0.20	-36.14
Maldives				1			
Nepal		5	5		5	0.00	
Pakistan	25	7		1	1	0.00	0.00
Sri Lanka	15	11	7	1	6	0.01	500.00

Yearbook of Tourism Statistics, Data 2008 – 2012, 2014 Edition

BELGIUM

3. Arrivals of non-resident tourists in hotels and similar establishments, by country of residence

	2008	2009	2010	2011	2012	Market share 2012	% Change 2012-2011
TOTAL	5,819,853	5,451,600	5,771,650	6,076,926	6,134,070	100.00	0.94
AFRICA	58,943	59,410	57,194	57,570	56,767	0.93	-1.39
East Africa	**7,630**	**9,575**	**8,734**	**8,573**	**6,464**	**0.11**	**-24.60**
Burundi	513	430	450	530	712	0.01	34.34
Comoros	14	14	58	28	32	0.00	14.29
Djibouti	79	148	138	93	116	0.00	24.73
Eritrea	86	38	66	92	99	0.00	7.61
Ethiopia	3,009	4,474	3,717	3,439	1,077	0.02	-68.68
Kenya	807	931	799	874	1,050	0.02	20.14
Madagascar	270	323	313	283	334	0.01	18.02
Malawi	75	63	69	76	86	0.00	13.16
Mauritius	216	251	227	314	363	0.01	15.61
Mozambique	155	158	132	186	169	0.00	-9.14
Rwanda	708	687	819	735	826	0.01	12.38
Seychelles	314	245	219	337	242	0.00	-28.19
Somalia	109	166	111	175	87	0.00	-50.29
Uganda	387	555	424	358	314	0.01	-12.29
United Republic of Tanzania	357	530	483	417	285	0.00	-31.65
Zambia	73	111	136	127	136	0.00	7.09
Zimbabwe	458	451	573	509	536	0.01	5.30
Central Africa	**11,015**	**10,953**	**10,231**	**10,443**	**10,983**	**0.18**	**5.17**
Angola	1,159	1,144	1,070	1,096	1,237	0.02	12.86
Cameroon	2,048	2,590	2,236	2,078	2,012	0.03	-3.18
Central African Republic	275	234	303	326	438	0.01	34.36
Chad	284	190	171	158	83	0.00	-47.47
Congo	2,339	2,730	2,713	2,494	3,053	0.05	22.41
Democratic Republic of the Congo	3,485	2,975	2,795	3,220	3,331	0.05	3.45
Equatorial Guinea	37	29	126	79	91	0.00	15.19
Gabon	1,342	1,012	775	950	683	0.01	-28.11
Sao Tome and Principe	46	49	42	42	55	0.00	30.95
North Africa	**19,460**	**19,620**	**18,602**	**18,006**	**17,598**	**0.29**	**-2.27**
Algeria	3,160	3,225	3,032	3,116	2,883	0.05	-7.48
Morocco	13,038	13,295	12,218	11,239	11,374	0.19	1.20
Sudan	299	282	389	396	300	0.00	-24.24
Tunisia	2,963	2,818	2,963	3,255	3,041	0.05	-6.57
Southern Africa	**8,824**	**7,441**	**7,735**	**8,481**	**8,770**	**0.14**	**3.41**
Botswana	96	94	125	145	421	0.01	190.34
Lesotho	39	44	56	47	75	0.00	59.57
Namibia	1,298	736	561	402	292	0.00	-27.36
South Africa	6,362	5,657	6,036	7,090	7,145	0.12	0.78
Swaziland	1,029	910	957	797	837	0.01	5.02
West Africa	**12,014**	**11,821**	**11,892**	**12,067**	**12,952**	**0.21**	**7.33**
Benin	541	380	322	489	438	0.01	-10.43
Burkina Faso	382	498	470	678	653	0.01	-3.69
Cape Verde	65	71	152	213	152	0.00	-28.64
Côte d'Ivoire	1,032	1,107	1,155	1,186	1,457	0.02	22.85
Gambia	236	235	265	250	167	0.00	-33.20
Ghana	455	493	648	674	659	0.01	-2.23
Guinea	551	729	694	769	1,199	0.02	55.92
Guinea-Bissau	65	38	85	98	74	0.00	-24.49
Liberia	274	232	257	221	153	0.00	-30.77
Mali	632	628	702	622	908	0.01	45.98
Mauritania	484	423	597	384	412	0.01	7.29
Niger	2,389	2,213	1,198	1,269	1,431	0.02	12.77
Nigeria	1,792	1,841	1,870	2,041	2,170	0.04	6.32
Senegal	1,031	1,338	1,662	1,402	1,598	0.03	13.98

66

BELGIUM

3. Arrivals of non-resident tourists in hotels and similar establishments, by country of residence

	2008	2009	2010	2011	2012	Market share 2012	% Change 2012-2011
Sierra Leone	1,762	1,339	1,573	1,481	1,194	0.02	-19.38
Togo	323	256	242	290	287	0.00	-1.03
AMERICAS	**357,017**	**333,104**	**388,039**	**442,620**	**457,322**	**7.46**	**3.32**
Caribbean	**6,060**	**2,620**	**2,665**	**2,543**	**2,420**	**0.04**	**-4.84**
Antigua and Barbuda	754	249	317	233	173	0.00	-25.75
Bahamas	575	105	374	131	101	0.00	-22.90
Barbados	3,188	579	242	201	133	0.00	-33.83
Cuba	498	240	298	276	399	0.01	44.57
Dominica	94	159	113	175	91	0.00	-48.00
Dominican Republic	295	306	429	418	560	0.01	33.97
Grenada	104	208	108	109	48	0.00	-55.96
Haiti	134	130	180	173	266	0.00	53.76
Jamaica	238	308	369	569	411	0.01	-27.77
Saint Kitts and Nevis	28	35	20	33	71	0.00	115.15
Saint Lucia	19	17	33	24	21	0.00	-12.50
Saint Vincent and the Grenadines	16	70	20	84	23	0.00	-72.62
Trinidad and Tobago	117	214	162	117	123	0.00	5.13
Central America	**3,641**	**3,127**	**3,860**	**4,529**	**4,168**	**0.07**	**-7.97**
Belize	170	167	255	303	522	0.01	72.28
Costa Rica	1,280	1,215	1,475	1,330	1,346	0.02	1.20
El Salvador	619	476	551	849	738	0.01	-13.07
Guatemala	353	342	437	511	419	0.01	-18.00
Honduras	338	247	230	475	300	0.00	-36.84
Nicaragua	426	295	374	398	268	0.00	-32.66
Panama	455	385	538	663	575	0.01	-13.27
North America	**308,767**	**289,411**	**330,889**	**369,894**	**375,574**	**6.12**	**1.54**
Canada	37,752	33,353	40,746	47,127	48,799	0.80	3.55
Mexico	12,773	10,449	13,807	15,978	18,549	0.30	16.09
United States of America	258,242	245,609	276,336	306,789	308,226	5.02	0.47
South America	**38,549**	**37,946**	**50,625**	**65,654**	**75,160**	**1.23**	**14.48**
Argentina	5,405	6,768	8,968	11,944	15,128	0.25	26.66
Bolivia	364	488	353	445	349	0.01	-21.57
Brazil	22,425	19,681	29,135	38,511	42,866	0.70	11.31
Chile	2,257	2,373	2,638	3,566	4,434	0.07	24.34
Colombia	3,169	3,007	3,732	3,865	4,258	0.07	10.17
Ecuador	832	1,052	891	1,083	1,183	0.02	9.23
Guyana	41	64	65	76	67	0.00	-11.84
Paraguay	115	143	182	315	319	0.01	1.27
Peru	1,108	1,100	1,312	1,446	1,706	0.03	17.98
Suriname	214	209	285	450	428	0.01	-4.89
Uruguay	696	1,100	1,317	1,668	1,241	0.02	-25.60
Venezuela	1,923	1,961	1,747	2,285	3,181	0.05	39.21
EAST ASIA AND THE PACIFIC	**239,011**	**208,563**	**226,179**	**275,432**	**334,313**	**5.45**	**21.38**
North-East Asia	**185,352**	**160,141**	**168,188**	**208,499**	**254,427**	**4.15**	**22.03**
China	71,734	71,547	75,201	95,880	115,614	1.88	20.58
Japan	94,948	74,509	75,976	86,778	107,086	1.75	23.40
Korea, Dem. People's Republic of	2,371	1,540	1,687	2,167	2,114	0.03	-2.45
Korea, Republic of	9,623	6,272	10,094	11,930	13,191	0.22	10.57
Mongolia	127	181	137	275	338	0.01	22.91
Taiwan, Province of China	6,549	6,092	5,093	11,469	16,084	0.26	40.24
South-East Asia	**20,014**	**18,317**	**22,282**	**27,101**	**37,732**	**0.62**	**39.23**
Brunei Darussalam	106	90	171	182	208	0.00	14.29
Cambodia	64	134	122	123	176	0.00	43.09
Indonesia	2,039	2,353	2,699	3,250	5,089	0.08	56.58
Lao People's Democratic Republic	245	151	247	252	254	0.00	0.79
Malaysia	3,176	2,565	3,232	4,289	5,067	0.08	18.14
Myanmar	75	104	123	123	104	0.00	-15.45

BELGIUM

3. Arrivals of non-resident tourists in hotels and similar establishments, by country of residence

	2008	2009	2010	2011	2012	Market share 2012	% Change 2012-2011
Philippines	4,711	4,614	4,537	5,330	5,001	0.08	-6.17
Singapore	4,744	3,488	4,333	4,941	6,126	0.10	23.98
Thailand	3,526	3,406	4,909	6,639	13,292	0.22	100.21
Timor-Leste	39	5	26	16	18	0.00	12.50
Viet Nam	1,289	1,407	1,883	1,956	2,397	0.04	22.55
Australasia	**32,506**	**29,307**	**34,778**	**38,805**	**41,338**	**0.67**	**6.53**
Australia	26,858	25,458	30,250	34,238	36,133	0.59	5.53
New Zealand	5,648	3,849	4,528	4,567	5,205	0.08	13.97
Melanesia	**322**	**316**	**374**	**439**	**374**	**0.01**	**-14.81**
Fiji	85	102	150	171	117	0.00	-31.58
Papua New Guinea	92	83	73	75	75	0.00	0.00
Solomon Islands	102	93	128	114	94	0.00	-17.54
Vanuatu	43	38	23	79	88	0.00	11.39
Micronesia	**490**	**263**	**454**	**355**	**330**	**0.01**	**-7.04**
Kiribati	58	27	48	48	26	0.00	-45.83
Marshall Islands	11	2	7	4	9	0.00	125.00
Micronesia, Federated States of	132	54	161	78	145	0.00	85.90
Nauru	176	129	197	191	111	0.00	-41.88
Palau	113	51	41	34	39	0.00	14.71
Polynesia	**327**	**219**	**103**	**233**	**112**	**0.00**	**-51.93**
Samoa	35	28	13	135	60	0.00	-55.56
Tonga	200	86	79	72	34	0.00	-52.78
Tuvalu	92	105	11	26	18	0.00	-30.77
EUROPE	**4,923,917**	**4,675,581**	**4,974,321**	**5,192,869**	**5,170,348**	**84.29**	**-0.43**
Central/Eastern Europe	**297,157**	**265,228**	**301,414**	**340,657**	**358,180**	**5.84**	**5.14**
Armenia	1,033	1,040	1,028	1,192	966	0.02	-18.96
Azerbaijan	696	527	655	1,018	1,167	0.02	14.64
Belarus	1,555	2,490	2,373	2,629	3,092	0.05	17.61
Bulgaria	15,348	14,063	15,205	15,905	16,044	0.26	0.87
Czech Republic	25,197	26,154	28,363	28,356	29,718	0.48	4.80
Estonia	6,156	5,221	6,291	6,791	7,338	0.12	8.05
Georgia	3,233	3,060	2,744	2,245	2,247	0.04	0.09
Hungary	24,327	23,071	24,221	27,746	30,266	0.49	9.08
Kazakhstan	814	835	940	1,147	1,404	0.02	22.41
Kyrgyzstan	161	137	133	212	166	0.00	-21.70
Latvia	6,128	5,529	8,297	9,487	9,917	0.16	4.53
Lithuania	13,933	10,967	13,938	14,805	14,838	0.24	0.22
Poland	83,881	70,407	74,955	78,955	78,088	1.27	-1.10
Republic of Moldova	429	527	590	666	752	0.01	12.91
Romania	32,439	30,999	35,709	39,726	37,782	0.62	-4.89
Russian Federation	60,914	50,435	66,511	87,055	99,321	1.62	14.09
Slovakia	10,099	9,816	10,314	11,539	12,010	0.20	4.08
Tajikistan	109	103	74	152	150	0.00	-1.32
Turkmenistan	122	107	72	117	85	0.00	-27.35
Ukraine	10,053	9,391	8,716	10,555	12,600	0.21	19.37
Uzbekistan	530	349	285	359	229	0.00	-36.21
Northern Europe	**1,184,708**	**997,273**	**1,026,628**	**1,034,371**	**1,060,182**	**17.28**	**2.50**
Denmark	51,332	49,684	51,261	54,763	55,430	0.90	1.22
Finland	31,780	29,445	32,290	34,801	35,535	0.58	2.11
Iceland	5,253	3,678	6,311	5,715	5,469	0.09	-4.30
Ireland	41,087	38,497	38,810	40,749	44,867	0.73	10.11
Norway	32,489	29,322	33,407	36,869	37,617	0.61	2.03
Sweden	69,202	62,365	68,827	68,451	69,535	1.13	1.58
United Kingdom	953,565	784,282	795,722	793,023	811,729	13.23	2.36
Southern Europe	**589,889**	**575,843**	**646,412**	**703,119**	**671,754**	**10.95**	**-4.46**
Albania	2,764	3,547	3,021	4,249	4,576	0.07	7.70
Andorra	1,501	476	479	509	545	0.01	7.07

Yearbook of Tourism Statistics, Data 2008 – 2012, 2014 Edition

BELGIUM

3. Arrivals of non-resident tourists in hotels and similar establishments, by country of residence

	2008	2009	2010	2011	2012	Market share 2012	% Change 2012-2011
Bosnia and Herzegovina	1,862	1,903	1,675	1,971	1,487	0.02	-24.56
Croatia	5,358	5,393	5,972	6,455	7,681	0.13	18.99
Greece	31,647	28,622	28,367	30,952	26,056	0.42	-15.82
Holy See	84	74	89	45	118	0.00	162.22
Italy	222,647	220,777	242,079	262,177	255,623	4.17	-2.50
Malta	4,621	5,030	5,605	6,062	6,001	0.10	-1.01
Montenegro	1,139	478	594	1,031	1,394	0.02	35.21
Portugal	37,552	35,810	37,418	36,588	38,502	0.63	5.23
San Marino	99	179	68	128	703	0.01	449.22
Serbia	6,163	5,906	3,936	6,020	5,256	0.09	-12.69
Slovenia	8,963	7,031	7,992	8,235	7,610	0.12	-7.59
Spain	264,189	259,442	307,875	337,147	314,765	5.13	-6.64
TFYR of Macedonia	1,300	1,175	1,242	1,550	1,437	0.02	-7.29
Western Europe	**2,792,491**	**2,787,372**	**2,942,795**	**3,046,946**	**3,001,592**	**48.93**	**-1.49**
Austria	32,886	32,368	34,259	36,789	39,579	0.65	7.58
France	903,081	921,253	963,845	1,008,316	982,547	16.02	-2.56
Germany	621,934	607,863	640,451	664,550	635,645	10.36	-4.35
Liechtenstein	2,790	2,302	2,000	1,236	777	0.01	-37.14
Luxembourg	65,182	68,150	72,813	80,702	80,691	1.32	-0.01
Monaco	750	934	945	1,041	1,325	0.02	27.28
Netherlands	1,102,665	1,089,867	1,154,451	1,170,608	1,172,463	19.11	0.16
Switzerland	63,203	64,635	74,031	83,704	88,565	1.44	5.81
East Mediterranean Europe	**59,672**	**49,865**	**57,072**	**67,776**	**78,640**	**1.28**	**16.03**
Cyprus	4,741	4,739	5,284	6,722	8,547	0.14	27.15
Israel	29,237	22,224	25,603	28,224	34,218	0.56	21.24
Turkey	25,694	22,902	26,185	32,830	35,875	0.58	9.28
MIDDLE EAST	**21,624**	**19,519**	**24,981**	**30,100**	**35,595**	**0.58**	**18.26**
Bahrain	741	382	393	529	548	0.01	3.59
Egypt	4,232	4,155	5,536	5,444	6,146	0.10	12.89
Iraq	532	494	577	654	500	0.01	-23.55
Jordan	1,225	1,673	1,441	1,364	1,163	0.02	-14.74
Kuwait	1,302	1,186	1,201	1,835	2,257	0.04	23.00
Lebanon	2,153	2,081	2,066	2,918	3,485	0.06	19.43
Libya	578	616	811	420	1,169	0.02	178.33
Oman	328	324	447	559	722	0.01	29.16
Palestine	89	47	63	108	95	0.00	-12.04
Qatar	797	535	780	1,042	1,738	0.03	66.79
Saudi Arabia	3,300	2,827	3,997	4,057	5,466	0.09	34.73
Syrian Arab Republic	708	814	739	632	523	0.01	-17.25
United Arab Emirates	5,404	4,180	6,823	10,299	11,618	0.19	12.81
Yemen	235	205	107	239	165	0.00	-30.96
SOUTH ASIA	**63,047**	**45,221**	**49,912**	**52,356**	**50,199**	**0.82**	**-4.12**
Afghanistan	1,295	2,111	1,078	1,001	1,329	0.02	32.77
Bangladesh	358	396	566	525	538	0.01	2.48
Bhutan	34	80	22	61	159	0.00	160.66
India	53,951	34,711	40,447	42,709	41,297	0.67	-3.31
Iran, Islamic Republic of	5,018	6,029	5,506	5,683	4,754	0.08	-16.35
Maldives	39	49	28	58	33	0.00	-43.10
Nepal	150	196	214	261	249	0.00	-4.60
Pakistan	1,846	1,415	1,764	1,708	1,468	0.02	-14.05
Sri Lanka	356	234	287	350	372	0.01	6.29
NOT SPECIFIED	**156,294**	**110,202**	**51,024**	**25,979**	**29,526**	**0.48**	**13.65**
Other countries of the World	156,294	110,202	51,024	25,979	29,526	0.48	13.65

Yearbook of Tourism Statistics, Data 2008 – 2012, 2014 Edition

BELGIUM

4. Arrivals of non-resident tourists in all types of accommodation establishments, by country of residence

		2008	2009	2010	2011	2012	Market share 2012	% Change 2012-2011
TOTAL	(*)	7,164,765	6,815,141	7,186,419	7,494,141	7,591,393	100.00	1.30
AFRICA		63,250	63,444	61,332	61,949	60,408	0.80	-2.49
East Africa		7,921	9,778	9,171	8,912	6,882	0.09	-22.78
Burundi		630	456	469	545	729	0.01	33.76
Comoros		16	14	60	30	32	0.00	6.67
Djibouti		83	149	142	116	116	0.00	0.00
Eritrea		89	43	76	97	108	0.00	11.34
Ethiopia		3,015	4,491	3,737	3,484	1,101	0.01	-68.40
Kenya		835	946	813	890	1,108	0.01	24.49
Madagascar		292	328	338	315	356	0.00	13.02
Malawi		77	63	75	84	95	0.00	13.10
Mauritius		229	265	257	331	380	0.01	14.80
Mozambique		157	173	132	186	176	0.00	-5.38
Rwanda		745	700	942	762	934	0.01	22.57
Seychelles		314	268	237	341	262	0.00	-23.17
Somalia		114	172	123	178	100	0.00	-43.82
Uganda		396	560	437	372	333	0.00	-10.48
United Republic of Tanzania		366	533	498	458	311	0.00	-32.10
Zambia		78	118	137	130	141	0.00	8.46
Zimbabwe		485	499	698	593	600	0.01	1.18
Central Africa		11,515	11,377	10,569	10,944	11,368	0.15	3.87
Angola		1,194	1,162	1,130	1,326	1,262	0.02	-4.83
Cameroon		2,124	2,664	2,306	2,175	2,077	0.03	-4.51
Central African Republic		277	240	304	328	441	0.01	34.45
Chad		292	193	175	161	85	0.00	-47.20
Congo		2,404	2,763	2,747	2,533	3,075	0.04	21.40
Democratic Republic of the Congo		3,786	3,245	2,940	3,323	3,579	0.05	7.70
Equatorial Guinea		41	29	135	84	93	0.00	10.71
Gabon		1,349	1,022	789	970	693	0.01	-28.56
Sao Tome and Principe		48	59	43	44	63	0.00	43.18
North Africa		20,318	21,058	19,512	19,261	18,632	0.25	-3.27
Algeria		3,587	3,789	3,272	3,543	3,132	0.04	-11.60
Morocco		13,373	13,993	12,780	11,944	11,998	0.16	0.45
Sudan		306	292	398	407	305	0.00	-25.06
Tunisia		3,052	2,984	3,062	3,367	3,197	0.04	-5.05
Southern Africa		10,328	8,790	9,267	9,786	9,551	0.13	-2.40
Botswana		100	96	125	145	423	0.01	191.72
Lesotho		39	44	56	47	76	0.00	61.70
Namibia		1,302	755	599	411	312	0.00	-24.09
South Africa		7,837	6,951	7,508	8,344	7,899	0.10	-5.33
Swaziland		1,050	944	979	839	841	0.01	0.24
West Africa		13,168	12,441	12,813	13,046	13,975	0.18	7.12
Benin		568	394	326	500	479	0.01	-4.20
Burkina Faso		392	508	479	746	697	0.01	-6.57
Cape Verde		70	72	152	214	157	0.00	-26.64
Côte d'Ivoire		1,082	1,134	1,205	1,224	1,489	0.02	21.65
Gambia		239	236	265	255	170	0.00	-33.33
Ghana		465	502	708	737	699	0.01	-5.16
Guinea		555	740	700	785	1,216	0.02	54.90
Guinea-Bissau		66	41	87	98	76	0.00	-22.45
Liberia		276	233	269	228	162	0.00	-28.95
Mali		870	803	939	773	1,051	0.01	35.96
Mauritania		496	428	598	391	418	0.01	6.91
Niger		2,839	2,327	1,506	1,605	1,776	0.02	10.65
Nigeria		2,015	1,928	1,949	2,152	2,245	0.03	4.32
Senegal		1,108	1,374	1,711	1,480	1,693	0.02	14.39

Yearbook of Tourism Statistics, Data 2008 – 2012, 2014 Edition

BELGIUM

4. Arrivals of non-resident tourists in all types of accommodation establishments, by country of residence

	2008	2009	2010	2011	2012	Market share 2012	% Change 2012-2011
Sierra Leone	1,788	1,448	1,674	1,553	1,345	0.02	-13.39
Togo	339	273	245	305	302	0.00	-0.98
AMERICAS	**399,047**	**374,791**	**429,439**	**488,577**	**503,489**	**6.63**	**3.05**
Caribbean	**6,225**	**2,840**	**2,898**	**2,833**	**2,590**	**0.03**	**-8.58**
Antigua and Barbuda	757	310	368	335	188	0.00	-43.88
Bahamas	598	124	429	204	140	0.00	-31.37
Barbados	3,254	638	274	228	104	0.00	-54.39
Cuba	521	255	306	282	427	0.01	51.42
Dominica	101	165	122	180	109	0.00	-39.44
Dominican Republic	321	340	462	470	608	0.01	29.36
Grenada	104	209	109	109	60	0.00	-44.95
Haiti	136	136	186	179	281	0.00	56.98
Jamaica	241	327	399	582	422	0.01	-27.49
Saint Kitts and Nevis	29	35	20	33	80	0.00	142.42
Saint Lucia	19	17	34	26	21	0.00	-19.23
Saint Vincent and the Grenadines	16	70	20	84	23	0.00	-72.62
Trinidad and Tobago	128	214	169	121	127	0.00	4.96
Central America	**3,888**	**3,479**	**4,329**	**5,008**	**4,661**	**0.06**	**-6.93**
Belize	188	210	262	310	573	0.01	84.84
Costa Rica	1,396	1,344	1,664	1,567	1,552	0.02	-0.96
El Salvador	629	489	632	911	798	0.01	-12.40
Guatemala	410	425	536	600	491	0.01	-18.17
Honduras	355	273	250	501	342	0.00	-31.74
Nicaragua	429	327	389	417	295	0.00	-29.26
Panama	481	411	596	702	610	0.01	-13.11
North America	**339,011**	**320,035**	**359,199**	**401,180**	**406,778**	**5.36**	**1.40**
Canada	46,616	41,905	48,517	55,159	56,620	0.75	2.65
Mexico	17,277	13,965	17,679	20,781	23,090	0.30	11.11
United States of America	275,118	264,165	293,003	325,240	327,068	4.31	0.56
South America	**49,923**	**48,437**	**63,013**	**79,556**	**89,460**	**1.18**	**12.45**
Argentina	7,804	9,334	12,106	15,259	18,774	0.25	23.04
Bolivia	480	556	424	565	425	0.01	-24.78
Brazil	28,355	24,770	35,052	45,160	49,547	0.65	9.71
Chile	3,166	3,038	3,467	4,669	5,505	0.07	17.91
Colombia	4,098	3,932	4,855	5,181	5,598	0.07	8.05
Ecuador	1,120	1,255	1,160	1,394	1,448	0.02	3.87
Guyana	41	84	77	81	70	0.00	-13.58
Paraguay	147	164	214	362	372	0.00	2.76
Peru	1,402	1,415	1,714	1,780	2,029	0.03	13.99
Suriname	216	226	310	510	508	0.01	-0.39
Uruguay	873	1,334	1,601	2,091	1,710	0.02	-18.22
Venezuela	2,221	2,329	2,033	2,504	3,474	0.05	38.74
EAST ASIA AND THE PACIFIC	**267,943**	**237,535**	**255,712**	**307,495**	**365,089**	**4.81**	**18.73**
North-East Asia	**201,018**	**173,728**	**183,800**	**225,765**	**271,663**	**3.58**	**20.33**
China	74,959	75,219	79,908	101,448	121,648	1.60	19.91
Japan	100,712	80,093	81,026	91,414	111,690	1.47	22.18
Korea, Dem. People's Republic of	4,321	3,441	4,009	5,363	4,006	0.05	-25.30
Korea, Republic of	13,550	7,853	12,788	14,658	16,542	0.22	12.85
Mongolia	134	183	147	325	348	0.00	7.08
Taiwan, Province of China	7,342	6,939	5,922	12,557	17,429	0.23	38.80
South-East Asia	**21,250**	**20,633**	**24,436**	**29,397**	**40,270**	**0.53**	**36.99**
Brunei Darussalam	106	102	227	198	234	0.00	18.18
Cambodia	68	136	132	136	197	0.00	44.85
Indonesia	2,124	2,483	2,928	3,493	5,352	0.07	53.22
Lao People's Democratic Republic	248	159	251	256	268	0.00	4.69
Malaysia	3,405	2,982	3,712	4,732	5,574	0.07	17.79
Myanmar	76	105	130	127	105	0.00	-17.32

71

BELGIUM

4. Arrivals of non-resident tourists in all types of accommodation establishments, by country of residence

	2008	2009	2010	2011	2012	Market share 2012	% Change 2012-2011
Philippines	4,793	4,731	4,643	5,481	5,145	0.07	-6.13
Singapore	5,039	3,924	4,824	5,488	6,770	0.09	23.36
Thailand	3,893	4,370	5,478	7,254	13,905	0.18	91.69
Timor-Leste	40	6	27	25	18	0.00	-28.00
Viet Nam	1,458	1,635	2,084	2,207	2,702	0.04	22.43
Australasia	**44,519**	**42,352**	**46,502**	**51,217**	**52,244**	**0.69**	**2.01**
Australia	37,084	36,684	40,480	45,026	45,343	0.60	0.70
New Zealand	7,435	5,668	6,022	6,191	6,901	0.09	11.47
Melanesia	**328**	**321**	**381**	**456**	**398**	**0.01**	**-12.72**
Fiji	87	105	154	178	122	0.00	-31.46
Papua New Guinea	94	84	74	76	75	0.00	-1.32
Solomon Islands	103	94	130	122	113	0.00	-7.38
Vanuatu	44	38	23	80	88	0.00	10.00
Micronesia	**499**	**280**	**487**	**374**	**366**	**0.00**	**-2.14**
Kiribati	58	27	48	49	27	0.00	-44.90
Marshall Islands	11	2	12	4	12	0.00	200.00
Micronesia, Federated States of	136	54	161	79	145	0.00	83.54
Nauru	181	132	225	208	143	0.00	-31.25
Palau	113	65	41	34	39	0.00	14.71
Polynesia	**329**	**221**	**106**	**286**	**148**	**0.00**	**-48.25**
Samoa	37	28	13	171	94	0.00	-45.03
Tonga	200	87	81	77	34	0.00	-55.84
Tuvalu	92	106	12	38	20	0.00	-47.37
EUROPE	**6,187,002**	**5,956,385**	**6,310,386**	**6,522,652**	**6,542,882**	**86.19**	**0.31**
Central/Eastern Europe	**317,011**	**285,636**	**323,683**	**363,437**	**384,234**	**5.06**	**5.72**
Armenia	1,052	1,138	1,172	1,299	1,017	0.01	-21.71
Azerbaijan	716	547	694	1,068	1,211	0.02	13.39
Belarus	1,631	2,584	2,505	2,774	3,268	0.04	17.81
Bulgaria	15,980	14,623	15,874	16,221	16,698	0.22	2.94
Czech Republic	27,834	29,339	31,311	31,368	33,270	0.44	6.06
Estonia	6,286	5,461	6,566	7,041	7,718	0.10	9.62
Georgia	3,252	3,158	2,803	2,261	2,341	0.03	3.54
Hungary	27,259	24,985	26,633	30,643	32,312	0.43	5.45
Kazakhstan	822	866	961	1,197	1,436	0.02	19.97
Kyrgyzstan	170	143	147	218	176	0.00	-19.27
Latvia	6,524	5,854	8,762	10,104	10,518	0.14	4.10
Lithuania	15,123	11,946	14,834	15,429	15,495	0.20	0.43
Poland	90,916	78,976	84,115	87,733	87,800	1.16	0.08
Republic of Moldova	463	539	601	684	788	0.01	15.20
Romania	34,113	32,291	37,186	41,399	40,051	0.53	-3.26
Russian Federation	62,490	52,031	68,609	89,942	103,338	1.36	14.89
Slovakia	11,238	10,957	11,197	12,500	13,155	0.17	5.24
Tajikistan	114	106	82	174	183	0.00	5.17
Turkmenistan	160	115	108	118	89	0.00	-24.58
Ukraine	10,333	9,605	9,234	10,879	13,131	0.17	20.70
Uzbekistan	535	372	289	385	239	0.00	-37.92
Northern Europe	**1,285,095**	**1,089,227**	**1,117,879**	**1,135,286**	**1,176,327**	**15.50**	**3.62**
Denmark	58,914	57,206	58,283	62,073	63,231	0.83	1.87
Finland	34,042	31,312	34,238	36,665	38,168	0.50	4.10
Iceland	5,455	3,897	6,489	6,021	5,857	0.08	-2.72
Ireland	44,149	41,648	41,581	44,072	48,556	0.64	10.17
Norway	33,808	30,745	35,122	38,463	39,505	0.52	2.71
Sweden	72,722	65,776	72,647	72,161	73,780	0.97	2.24
United Kingdom	1,036,005	858,643	869,519	875,831	907,230	11.95	3.59
Southern Europe	**642,122**	**633,603**	**702,088**	**756,201**	**722,500**	**9.52**	**-4.46**
Albania	2,855	3,696	3,245	4,624	4,892	0.06	5.80
Andorra	1,520	546	523	637	634	0.01	-0.47

72

BELGIUM

4. Arrivals of non-resident tourists in all types of accommodation establishments, by country of residence

	2008	2009	2010	2011	2012	Market share 2012	% Change 2012-2011
Bosnia and Herzegovina	1,895	2,009	1,729	2,048	1,583	0.02	-22.71
Croatia	5,768	5,729	6,830	6,787	8,433	0.11	24.25
Greece	32,376	29,848	29,176	31,851	27,083	0.36	-14.97
Holy See	85	81	91	46	118	0.00	156.52
Italy	236,405	236,806	258,163	278,908	274,010	3.61	-1.76
Malta	4,719	5,120	5,642	6,246	6,100	0.08	-2.34
Montenegro	1,183	484	611	1,047	1,421	0.02	35.72
Portugal	39,705	38,170	39,429	39,065	40,931	0.54	4.78
San Marino	100	185	68	129	709	0.01	449.61
Serbia	6,255	6,034	4,071	6,269	5,468	0.07	-12.78
Slovenia	9,901	7,922	9,177	9,719	9,165	0.12	-5.70
Spain	298,019	295,764	342,025	367,236	340,396	4.48	-7.31
TFYR of Macedonia	1,336	1,209	1,308	1,589	1,557	0.02	-2.01
Western Europe	**3,880,799**	**3,895,618**	**4,107,209**	**4,197,026**	**4,177,462**	**55.03**	**-0.47**
Austria	35,959	36,272	37,623	40,897	44,167	0.58	8.00
France	1,079,638	1,096,341	1,153,949	1,211,281	1,205,415	15.88	-0.48
Germany	775,172	770,258	814,684	838,287	812,595	10.70	-3.06
Liechtenstein	2,804	2,321	2,025	1,270	847	0.01	-33.31
Luxembourg	78,012	80,116	83,906	93,689	94,147	1.24	0.49
Monaco	754	948	954	1,068	1,374	0.02	28.65
Netherlands	1,838,987	1,838,549	1,933,579	1,920,003	1,921,901	25.32	0.10
Switzerland	69,473	70,813	80,489	90,531	97,016	1.28	7.16
East Mediterranean Europe	**61,975**	**52,301**	**59,527**	**70,702**	**82,359**	**1.08**	**16.49**
Cyprus	4,778	4,848	5,358	6,797	8,697	0.11	27.95
Israel	30,421	23,389	26,507	29,410	35,851	0.47	21.90
Turkey	26,776	24,064	27,662	34,495	37,811	0.50	9.61
MIDDLE EAST	**22,067**	**19,976**	**25,599**	**30,602**	**36,340**	**0.48**	**18.75**
Bahrain	785	389	422	565	548	0.01	-3.01
Egypt	4,333	4,296	5,611	5,553	6,331	0.08	14.01
Iraq	585	561	669	753	563	0.01	-25.23
Jordan	1,229	1,695	1,518	1,388	1,198	0.02	-13.69
Kuwait	1,342	1,211	1,232	1,850	2,304	0.03	24.54
Lebanon	2,181	2,116	2,148	2,962	3,529	0.05	19.14
Libya	583	628	818	432	1,183	0.02	173.84
Oman	337	328	449	569	723	0.01	27.07
Palestine	154	68	108	116	147	0.00	26.72
Qatar	806	539	780	1,052	1,791	0.02	70.25
Saudi Arabia	3,320	2,857	4,047	4,111	5,613	0.07	36.54
Syrian Arab Republic	710	841	780	659	531	0.01	-19.42
United Arab Emirates	5,467	4,240	6,910	10,350	11,714	0.15	13.18
Yemen	235	207	107	242	165	0.00	-31.82
SOUTH ASIA	**64,480**	**46,950**	**51,726**	**54,726**	**52,420**	**0.69**	**-4.21**
Afghanistan	1,439	2,184	1,337	1,417	1,431	0.02	0.99
Bangladesh	436	412	614	570	573	0.01	0.53
Bhutan	35	80	23	79	167	0.00	111.39
India	54,838	35,730	41,554	44,195	42,771	0.56	-3.22
Iran, Islamic Republic of	5,233	6,560	5,780	5,941	5,185	0.07	-12.73
Maldives	40	51	28	71	52	0.00	-26.76
Nepal	161	206	238	285	278	0.00	-2.46
Pakistan	1,912	1,473	1,844	1,803	1,579	0.02	-12.42
Sri Lanka	386	254	308	365	384	0.01	5.21
NOT SPECIFIED	**160,976**	**116,060**	**52,225**	**28,140**	**30,765**	**0.41**	**9.33**
Other countries of the World	160,976	116,060	52,225	28,140	30,765	0.41	9.33

Yearbook of Tourism Statistics, Data 2008 – 2012, 2014 Edition

BELGIUM

5. Overnight stays of non-resident tourists in hotels and similar establishments, by country of residence

	2008	2009	2010	2011	2012	Market share 2012	% Change 2012-2011
TOTAL	11,119,811	10,336,598	10,854,245	11,436,408	11,525,660	100.00	0.78
AFRICA	134,136	134,559	140,428	137,706	138,419	1.20	0.52
East Africa	17,287	21,708	20,959	20,423	18,218	0.16	-10.80
Burundi	1,546	1,598	1,348	1,773	1,910	0.02	7.73
Comoros	88	35	99	55	70	0.00	27.27
Djibouti	220	460	274	199	298	0.00	49.75
Eritrea	187	73	172	206	171	0.00	-16.99
Ethiopia	4,149	6,413	6,651	5,349	2,357	0.02	-55.94
Kenya	2,749	2,665	2,528	2,337	3,145	0.03	34.57
Madagascar	768	824	685	672	745	0.01	10.86
Malawi	209	201	218	205	301	0.00	46.83
Mauritius	591	648	593	1,885	2,023	0.02	7.32
Mozambique	619	544	524	480	470	0.00	-2.08
Rwanda	1,566	1,768	2,331	2,127	2,455	0.02	15.42
Seychelles	622	730	403	891	522	0.00	-41.41
Somalia	198	482	425	297	153	0.00	-48.48
Uganda	1,396	1,595	1,270	898	893	0.01	-0.56
United Republic of Tanzania	935	2,317	1,628	1,303	910	0.01	-30.16
Zambia	209	346	479	446	595	0.01	33.41
Zimbabwe	1,235	1,009	1,331	1,300	1,200	0.01	-7.69
Central Africa	24,728	23,486	25,971	26,088	26,050	0.23	-0.15
Angola	2,142	2,391	2,911	3,038	3,346	0.03	10.14
Cameroon	4,229	4,679	5,228	4,841	4,300	0.04	-11.18
Central African Republic	829	680	1,040	785	976	0.01	24.33
Chad	836	625	412	340	224	0.00	-34.12
Congo	5,093	6,378	6,772	6,171	7,032	0.06	13.95
Democratic Republic of the Congo	8,356	6,500	7,616	8,562	8,128	0.07	-5.07
Equatorial Guinea	274	92	264	156	209	0.00	33.97
Gabon	2,815	2,030	1,626	2,099	1,706	0.01	-18.72
Sao Tome and Principe	154	111	102	96	129	0.00	34.38
North Africa	41,665	43,688	39,269	39,280	40,315	0.35	2.63
Algeria	10,373	9,904	8,473	7,711	7,186	0.06	-6.81
Morocco	23,921	25,863	22,978	23,036	25,041	0.22	8.70
Sudan	953	788	1,065	909	786	0.01	-13.53
Tunisia	6,418	7,133	6,753	7,624	7,302	0.06	-4.22
Southern Africa	22,561	18,431	20,259	21,955	23,679	0.21	7.85
Botswana	329	232	412	352	708	0.01	101.14
Lesotho	125	116	126	104	219	0.00	110.58
Namibia	1,743	1,212	1,472	698	1,121	0.01	60.60
South Africa	18,430	15,010	16,397	19,226	19,906	0.17	3.54
Swaziland	1,934	1,861	1,852	1,575	1,725	0.01	9.52
West Africa	27,895	27,246	33,970	29,960	30,157	0.26	0.66
Benin	1,313	1,180	1,095	1,324	1,435	0.01	8.38
Burkina Faso	914	1,301	1,743	2,270	2,033	0.02	-10.44
Cape Verde	217	189	376	468	252	0.00	-46.15
Côte d'Ivoire	2,495	2,579	2,847	2,786	3,242	0.03	16.37
Gambia	606	703	1,125	653	335	0.00	-48.70
Ghana	1,364	1,231	2,237	1,958	1,689	0.01	-13.74
Guinea	1,141	2,619	2,675	1,682	2,264	0.02	34.60
Guinea-Bissau	218	67	283	236	328	0.00	38.98
Liberia	566	427	573	514	302	0.00	-41.25
Mali	1,236	1,437	1,756	1,695	1,763	0.02	4.01
Mauritania	1,218	1,044	1,486	934	1,038	0.01	11.13
Niger	4,835	3,870	2,316	2,416	3,745	0.03	55.01
Nigeria	4,513	3,909	5,456	5,414	4,803	0.04	-11.29
Senegal	2,693	3,347	4,753	3,430	3,722	0.03	8.51

74

BELGIUM

5. Overnight stays of non-resident tourists in hotels and similar establishments, by country of residence

	2008	2009	2010	2011	2012	Market share 2012	% Change 2012-2011
Sierra Leone	3,752	2,676	3,552	3,464	2,454	0.02	-29.16
Togo	814	667	1,697	716	752	0.01	5.03
AMERICAS	**791,552**	**727,655**	**840,134**	**955,148**	**974,996**	**8.46**	**2.08**
Caribbean	**11,378**	**5,388**	**5,857**	**5,649**	**5,393**	**0.05**	**-4.53**
Antigua and Barbuda	1,130	469	634	505	454	0.00	-10.10
Bahamas	761	188	552	265	175	0.00	-33.96
Barbados	5,839	938	589	442	304	0.00	-31.22
Cuba	1,212	613	556	722	869	0.01	20.36
Dominica	167	378	291	342	164	0.00	-52.05
Dominican Republic	689	771	1,127	957	1,150	0.01	20.17
Grenada	211	281	356	219	108	0.00	-50.68
Haiti	408	334	537	423	653	0.01	54.37
Jamaica	516	658	648	1,075	929	0.01	-13.58
Saint Kitts and Nevis	51	66	53	143	197	0.00	37.76
Saint Lucia	50	83	174	109	41	0.00	-62.39
Saint Vincent and the Grenadines	38	145	37	146	39	0.00	-73.29
Trinidad and Tobago	306	464	303	301	310	0.00	2.99
Central America	**9,095**	**7,511**	**8,800**	**9,244**	**8,890**	**0.08**	**-3.83**
Belize	281	291	449	507	1,018	0.01	100.79
Costa Rica	3,235	2,934	3,260	2,766	2,658	0.02	-3.90
El Salvador	1,328	1,098	1,214	1,607	1,514	0.01	-5.79
Guatemala	871	870	1,118	1,037	1,028	0.01	-0.87
Honduras	1,223	703	675	1,048	649	0.01	-38.07
Nicaragua	1,097	759	962	747	655	0.01	-12.32
Panama	1,060	856	1,122	1,532	1,368	0.01	-10.70
North America	**687,833**	**638,070**	**724,173**	**805,749**	**812,364**	**7.05**	**0.82**
Canada	89,467	79,201	95,307	110,521	113,500	0.98	2.70
Mexico	24,085	18,833	25,267	29,144	32,300	0.28	10.83
United States of America	574,281	540,036	603,599	666,084	666,564	5.78	0.07
South America	**83,246**	**76,686**	**101,304**	**134,506**	**148,349**	**1.29**	**10.29**
Argentina	10,662	12,771	17,415	23,443	28,320	0.25	20.80
Bolivia	1,154	1,258	920	1,080	680	0.01	-37.04
Brazil	47,729	39,403	57,118	79,664	85,582	0.74	7.43
Chile	5,176	4,893	5,580	7,493	9,447	0.08	26.08
Colombia	6,400	5,832	7,647	6,768	7,560	0.07	11.70
Ecuador	1,727	2,395	1,851	2,148	2,475	0.02	15.22
Guyana	106	189	184	273	173	0.00	-36.63
Paraguay	416	401	487	793	618	0.01	-22.07
Peru	2,565	2,437	2,759	3,149	3,589	0.03	13.97
Suriname	721	774	706	1,409	1,040	0.01	-26.19
Uruguay	1,604	2,401	3,037	3,382	2,533	0.02	-25.10
Venezuela	4,986	3,932	3,600	4,904	6,332	0.05	29.12
EAST ASIA AND THE PACIFIC	**434,716**	**382,073**	**416,187**	**499,647**	**588,684**	**5.11**	**17.82**
North-East Asia	**324,118**	**282,435**	**296,213**	**357,350**	**425,982**	**3.70**	**19.21**
China	109,815	112,941	115,428	141,839	166,841	1.45	17.63
Japan	183,631	144,168	150,866	172,833	209,728	1.82	21.35
Korea, Dem. People's Republic of	5,118	3,023	3,801	5,192	4,212	0.04	-18.88
Korea, Republic of	15,896	12,768	17,813	21,782	22,800	0.20	4.67
Mongolia	280	285	283	573	511	0.00	-10.82
Taiwan, Province of China	9,378	9,250	8,022	15,131	21,890	0.19	44.67
South-East Asia	**42,293**	**36,588**	**46,355**	**55,553**	**71,003**	**0.62**	**27.81**
Brunei Darussalam	218	180	381	515	524	0.00	1.75
Cambodia	292	329	367	379	422	0.00	11.35
Indonesia	4,330	4,736	6,554	6,546	8,722	0.08	33.24
Lao People's Democratic Republic	492	295	459	504	430	0.00	-14.68
Malaysia	7,075	5,380	6,436	8,500	10,187	0.09	19.85
Myanmar	139	144	261	194	239	0.00	23.20

75

BELGIUM

5. Overnight stays of non-resident tourists in hotels and similar establishments, by country of residence

	2008	2009	2010	2011	2012	Market share 2012	% Change 2012-2011
Philippines	8,182	6,965	7,359	9,716	8,190	0.07	-15.71
Singapore	10,932	8,451	10,797	12,165	23,731	0.21	95.08
Thailand	7,708	7,475	9,538	12,699	13,822	0.12	8.84
Timor-Leste	122	11	89	20	62	0.00	210.00
Viet Nam	2,803	2,622	4,114	4,315	4,674	0.04	8.32
Australasia	**65,685**	**61,278**	**71,725**	**84,466**	**89,730**	**0.78**	**6.23**
Australia	53,499	53,178	62,640	73,046	78,157	0.68	7.00
New Zealand	12,186	8,100	9,085	11,420	11,573	0.10	1.34
Melanesia	**889**	**826**	**849**	**1,135**	**1,058**	**0.01**	**-6.78**
Fiji	388	253	294	414	397	0.00	-4.11
Papua New Guinea	194	332	227	213	209	0.00	-1.88
Solomon Islands	222	167	265	316	274	0.00	-13.29
Vanuatu	85	74	63	192	178	0.00	-7.29
Micronesia	**1,009**	**459**	**852**	**670**	**635**	**0.01**	**-5.22**
Kiribati	142	42	122	101	69	0.00	-31.68
Marshall Islands	15	4	7	8	20	0.00	150.00
Micronesia, Federated States of	171	68	334	120	217	0.00	80.83
Nauru	322	221	307	371	190	0.00	-48.79
Palau	359	124	82	70	139	0.00	98.57
Polynesia	**722**	**487**	**193**	**473**	**276**	**0.00**	**-41.65**
Samoa	108	54	19	255	127	0.00	-50.20
Tonga	381	240	156	168	105	0.00	-37.50
Tuvalu	233	193	18	50	44	0.00	-12.00
EUROPE	**9,261,233**	**8,728,486**	**9,182,019**	**9,593,960**	**9,554,215**	**82.90**	**-0.41**
Central/Eastern Europe	**638,463**	**558,868**	**631,326**	**737,367**	**754,250**	**6.54**	**2.29**
Armenia	2,570	2,545	4,768	2,786	2,335	0.02	-16.19
Azerbaijan	1,905	1,713	1,847	2,761	3,115	0.03	12.82
Belarus	2,714	4,238	3,853	4,918	5,240	0.05	6.55
Bulgaria	31,032	29,080	32,118	35,099	32,908	0.29	-6.24
Czech Republic	50,321	52,577	58,653	61,253	61,357	0.53	0.17
Estonia	11,214	9,919	11,334	12,026	13,187	0.11	9.65
Georgia	6,458	6,446	5,775	4,670	4,996	0.04	6.98
Hungary	63,006	53,123	50,629	58,694	69,178	0.60	17.86
Kazakhstan	3,039	2,401	2,476	3,233	3,722	0.03	15.13
Kyrgyzstan	479	258	326	399	381	0.00	-4.51
Latvia	11,421	9,534	14,080	15,971	16,341	0.14	2.32
Lithuania	25,942	21,231	25,782	27,571	28,039	0.24	1.70
Poland	183,166	149,135	162,008	183,088	172,926	1.50	-5.55
Republic of Moldova	1,086	1,461	1,640	1,823	2,207	0.02	21.06
Romania	74,558	71,879	81,096	100,182	85,466	0.74	-14.69
Russian Federation	119,895	102,914	133,000	172,752	198,101	1.72	14.67
Slovakia	28,043	21,453	22,510	26,688	27,620	0.24	3.49
Tajikistan	302	312	196	371	441	0.00	18.87
Turkmenistan	326	263	266	187	193	0.00	3.21
Ukraine	19,496	17,425	18,140	21,994	25,859	0.22	17.57
Uzbekistan	1,490	961	829	901	638	0.01	-29.19
Northern Europe	**2,364,275**	**1,962,570**	**1,992,823**	**2,003,730**	**2,049,666**	**17.78**	**2.29**
Denmark	94,834	92,088	95,219	101,083	102,410	0.89	1.31
Finland	60,837	54,459	61,678	68,671	67,793	0.59	-1.28
Iceland	12,775	8,496	13,885	13,609	13,045	0.11	-4.14
Ireland	79,786	77,600	72,457	77,673	88,257	0.77	13.63
Norway	62,904	57,588	65,957	74,393	75,264	0.65	1.17
Sweden	128,929	113,129	127,844	127,462	130,399	1.13	2.30
United Kingdom	1,924,210	1,559,210	1,555,783	1,540,839	1,572,498	13.64	2.05
Southern Europe	**1,197,317**	**1,194,579**	**1,309,535**	**1,423,395**	**1,411,717**	**12.25**	**-0.82**
Albania	5,481	13,770	7,244	8,139	8,432	0.07	3.60
Andorra	4,862	2,292	925	1,084	1,000	0.01	-7.75

76

BELGIUM

5. Overnight stays of non-resident tourists in hotels and similar establishments, by country of residence

	2008	2009	2010	2011	2012	Market share 2012	% Change 2012-2011
Bosnia and Herzegovina	4,171	3,698	3,773	4,147	3,052	0.03	-26.40
Croatia	12,316	13,019	13,540	13,416	15,253	0.13	13.69
Greece	70,789	65,140	62,938	66,501	55,631	0.48	-16.35
Holy See	175	155	166	104	280	0.00	169.23
Italy	441,199	447,082	486,592	522,022	517,997	4.49	-0.77
Malta	10,806	10,954	11,669	12,982	13,172	0.11	1.46
Montenegro	2,279	1,404	1,361	2,368	3,655	0.03	54.35
Portugal	86,935	76,679	79,399	77,053	122,635	1.06	59.16
San Marino	149	508	141	219	1,578	0.01	620.55
Serbia	13,055	13,660	10,403	14,438	13,071	0.11	-9.47
Slovenia	17,891	15,314	16,236	16,951	16,634	0.14	-1.87
Spain	524,277	528,284	612,194	680,499	635,975	5.52	-6.54
TFYR of Macedonia	2,932	2,620	2,954	3,472	3,352	0.03	-3.46
Western Europe	**4,930,806**	**4,902,867**	**5,126,293**	**5,285,997**	**5,176,282**	**44.91**	**-2.08**
Austria	67,402	68,778	72,122	80,125	87,165	0.76	8.79
France	1,475,516	1,511,377	1,566,510	1,652,525	1,618,189	14.04	-2.08
Germany	1,243,047	1,219,512	1,285,781	1,316,049	1,260,399	10.94	-4.23
Liechtenstein	6,056	4,979	3,884	2,407	1,531	0.01	-36.39
Luxembourg	128,926	132,001	139,409	149,036	145,481	1.26	-2.39
Monaco	1,466	1,810	1,895	1,951	2,509	0.02	28.60
Netherlands	1,884,428	1,838,111	1,919,062	1,924,846	1,890,974	16.41	-1.76
Switzerland	123,965	126,299	137,630	159,058	170,034	1.48	6.90
East Mediterranean Europe	**130,372**	**109,602**	**122,042**	**143,471**	**162,300**	**1.41**	**13.12**
Cyprus	12,034	11,633	12,397	15,458	19,898	0.17	28.72
Israel	59,132	46,341	51,490	58,242	66,008	0.57	13.33
Turkey	59,206	51,628	58,155	69,771	76,394	0.66	9.49
MIDDLE EAST	**77,666**	**58,297**	**74,513**	**84,545**	**109,126**	**0.95**	**29.07**
Bahrain	1,577	1,081	1,202	1,684	1,470	0.01	-12.71
Egypt	11,561	10,919	13,274	12,505	13,950	0.12	11.56
Iraq	1,533	1,771	2,077	1,713	1,426	0.01	-16.75
Jordan	3,234	4,084	3,752	3,535	3,201	0.03	-9.45
Kuwait	4,399	3,878	3,999	6,080	7,479	0.06	23.01
Lebanon	5,880	5,516	5,571	6,932	8,415	0.07	21.39
Libya	1,877	1,474	1,799	1,144	5,776	0.05	404.90
Oman	1,161	1,057	1,587	1,980	2,433	0.02	22.88
Palestine	358	101	152	233	273	0.00	17.17
Qatar	4,085	1,927	2,965	3,294	6,411	0.06	94.63
Saudi Arabia	10,149	8,731	11,118	12,755	17,593	0.15	37.93
Syrian Arab Republic	1,827	2,695	1,973	1,646	1,343	0.01	-18.41
United Arab Emirates	29,440	14,518	24,723	30,508	38,642	0.34	26.66
Yemen	585	545	321	536	714	0.01	33.21
SOUTH ASIA	**127,831**	**94,671**	**104,830**	**116,850**	**108,091**	**0.94**	**-7.50**
Afghanistan	2,452	4,037	3,237	3,137	3,360	0.03	7.11
Bangladesh	621	870	1,240	1,377	1,253	0.01	-9.01
Bhutan	74	263	44	96	226	0.00	135.42
India	107,704	71,101	82,881	94,665	88,619	0.77	-6.39
Iran, Islamic Republic of	11,349	14,087	12,287	12,434	10,010	0.09	-19.49
Maldives	85	89	80	109	68	0.00	-37.61
Nepal	291	401	401	519	604	0.01	16.38
Pakistan	4,310	3,200	3,970	3,582	3,089	0.03	-13.76
Sri Lanka	945	623	690	931	862	0.01	-7.41
NOT SPECIFIED	**292,677**	**210,857**	**96,134**	**48,552**	**52,129**	**0.45**	**7.37**
Other countries of the World	292,677	210,857	96,134	48,552	52,129	0.45	7.37

Yearbook of Tourism Statistics, Data 2008 – 2012, 2014 Edition

BELGIUM

6. Overnight stays of non-resident tourists in all types of accommodation establishments, by country of residence

		2008	2009	2010	2011	2012	Market share 2012	% Change 2012-2011
TOTAL	(*)	16,360,702	15,452,987	16,169,676	16,723,867	16,644,416	100.00	-0.48
AFRICA		143,531	144,605	151,982	150,181	149,900	0.90	-0.19
East Africa		17,938	22,257	22,281	21,175	19,227	0.12	-9.20
Burundi		1,808	1,686	1,401	1,798	1,993	0.01	10.85
Comoros		90	35	103	59	70	0.00	18.64
Djibouti		228	461	278	258	298	0.00	15.50
Eritrea		192	83	191	212	182	0.00	-14.15
Ethiopia		4,159	6,457	6,696	5,476	2,423	0.01	-55.75
Kenya		2,816	2,701	2,564	2,368	3,285	0.02	38.72
Madagascar		822	832	730	758	834	0.01	10.03
Malawi		222	201	228	215	314	0.00	46.05
Mauritius		607	673	646	1,909	2,113	0.01	10.69
Mozambique		626	619	524	480	500	0.00	4.17
Rwanda		1,649	1,803	2,808	2,165	2,584	0.02	19.35
Seychelles		622	770	437	904	554	0.00	-38.72
Somalia		203	500	458	317	186	0.00	-41.32
Uganda		1,432	1,608	1,338	934	926	0.01	-0.86
United Republic of Tanzania		966	2,348	1,667	1,409	958	0.01	-32.01
Zambia		215	358	480	449	604	0.00	34.52
Zimbabwe		1,281	1,122	1,732	1,464	1,403	0.01	-4.17
Central Africa		25,818	25,049	27,000	27,333	27,520	0.17	0.68
Angola		2,211	2,453	2,989	3,327	3,393	0.02	1.98
Cameroon		4,499	5,217	5,446	5,041	4,464	0.03	-11.45
Central African Republic		832	694	1,041	788	986	0.01	25.13
Chad		846	637	427	349	226	0.00	-35.24
Congo		5,322	6,481	6,864	6,294	7,166	0.04	13.85
Democratic Republic of the Congo		8,838	7,290	8,203	9,137	9,192	0.06	0.60
Equatorial Guinea		280	92	275	161	213	0.00	32.30
Gabon		2,830	2,044	1,648	2,138	1,737	0.01	-18.76
Sao Tome and Principe		160	141	107	98	143	0.00	45.92
North Africa		44,057	47,528	41,706	42,375	43,029	0.26	1.54
Algeria		11,094	10,942	8,929	8,519	7,898	0.05	-7.29
Morocco		25,279	27,927	24,688	24,737	26,566	0.16	7.39
Sudan		982	824	1,096	923	794	0.00	-13.98
Tunisia		6,702	7,835	6,993	8,196	7,771	0.05	-5.19
Southern Africa		24,711	21,181	24,338	26,624	25,897	0.16	-2.73
Botswana		333	234	412	352	713	0.00	102.56
Lesotho		125	116	126	104	221	0.00	112.50
Namibia		1,756	1,290	1,580	710	1,234	0.01	73.80
South Africa		20,533	17,636	20,280	23,563	21,998	0.13	-6.64
Swaziland		1,964	1,905	1,940	1,895	1,731	0.01	-8.65
West Africa		31,007	28,590	36,657	32,674	34,227	0.21	4.75
Benin		1,479	1,228	1,120	1,386	1,664	0.01	20.06
Burkina Faso		947	1,333	1,772	2,765	2,162	0.01	-21.81
Cape Verde		223	190	376	470	257	0.00	-45.32
Côte d'Ivoire		2,557	2,618	2,972	2,872	3,417	0.02	18.98
Gambia		610	705	1,125	662	339	0.00	-48.79
Ghana		1,417	1,266	2,485	2,123	1,848	0.01	-12.95
Guinea		1,147	2,640	2,683	1,712	2,295	0.01	34.05
Guinea-Bissau		220	72	286	236	330	0.00	39.83
Liberia		568	429	593	522	313	0.00	-40.04
Mali		1,507	1,648	2,060	1,927	1,980	0.01	2.75
Mauritania		1,237	1,049	1,487	946	1,053	0.01	11.31
Niger		6,441	4,157	3,488	3,288	5,677	0.03	72.66
Nigeria		5,133	4,249	5,835	5,760	5,043	0.03	-12.45
Senegal		2,863	3,414	4,886	3,636	4,048	0.02	11.33

78

BELGIUM

6. Overnight stays of non-resident tourists in all types of accommodation establishments, by country of residence

	2008	2009	2010	2011	2012	Market share 2012	% Change 2012-2011
Sierra Leone	3,810	2,852	3,789	3,598	3,014	0.02	-16.23
Togo	848	740	1,700	771	787	0.00	2.08
AMERICAS	**852,482**	**791,281**	**907,808**	**1,031,301**	**1,060,104**	**6.37**	**2.79**
Caribbean	**11,754**	**5,786**	**6,318**	**6,152**	**5,684**	**0.03**	**-7.61**
Antigua and Barbuda	1,133	597	712	633	471	0.00	-25.59
Bahamas	799	207	689	414	326	0.00	-21.26
Barbados	5,937	1,029	626	478	179	0.00	-62.55
Cuba	1,301	659	566	734	909	0.01	23.84
Dominica	175	392	302	351	184	0.00	-47.58
Dominican Republic	733	823	1,178	1,042	1,228	0.01	17.85
Grenada	211	283	359	219	122	0.00	-44.29
Haiti	424	344	560	460	698	0.00	51.74
Jamaica	525	694	728	1,111	945	0.01	-14.94
Saint Kitts and Nevis	53	66	53	143	210	0.00	46.85
Saint Lucia	50	83	178	111	41	0.00	-63.06
Saint Vincent and the Grenadines	38	145	37	146	39	0.00	-73.29
Trinidad and Tobago	375	464	330	310	332	0.00	7.10
Central America	**9,602**	**8,271**	**9,581**	**10,095**	**9,648**	**0.06**	**-4.43**
Belize	320	380	466	531	1,118	0.01	110.55
Costa Rica	3,410	3,243	3,588	3,138	2,956	0.02	-5.80
El Salvador	1,339	1,115	1,368	1,727	1,605	0.01	-7.06
Guatemala	946	996	1,244	1,195	1,138	0.01	-4.77
Honduras	1,262	777	710	1,102	714	0.00	-35.21
Nicaragua	1,102	868	990	809	696	0.00	-13.97
Panama	1,223	892	1,215	1,593	1,421	0.01	-10.80
North America	**731,882**	**685,622**	**771,286**	**858,657**	**872,371**	**5.24**	**1.60**
Canada	103,266	92,726	108,803	125,031	128,972	0.77	3.15
Mexico	29,424	23,473	30,545	35,751	38,894	0.23	8.79
United States of America	599,192	569,423	631,938	697,875	704,505	4.23	0.95
South America	**99,244**	**91,602**	**120,623**	**156,397**	**172,401**	**1.04**	**10.23**
Argentina	13,655	16,303	22,270	28,268	33,624	0.20	18.95
Bolivia	1,296	1,359	1,042	1,250	837	0.01	-33.04
Brazil	56,454	46,531	66,453	90,458	97,658	0.59	7.96
Chile	6,498	5,812	6,797	9,468	11,121	0.07	17.46
Colombia	7,631	7,075	9,213	8,692	9,831	0.06	13.10
Ecuador	2,118	2,741	2,371	2,581	2,925	0.02	13.33
Guyana	106	269	196	278	176	0.00	-36.69
Paraguay	467	457	541	855	757	0.00	-11.46
Peru	2,970	2,884	3,379	3,649	4,189	0.03	14.80
Suriname	724	812	754	1,575	1,189	0.01	-24.51
Uruguay	1,840	2,732	3,480	4,020	3,250	0.02	-19.15
Venezuela	5,485	4,627	4,127	5,303	6,844	0.04	29.06
EAST ASIA AND THE PACIFIC	**475,517**	**425,803**	**462,634**	**552,824**	**643,212**	**3.86**	**16.35**
North-East Asia	**346,108**	**302,506**	**318,948**	**383,230**	**453,342**	**2.72**	**18.30**
China	114,587	118,001	122,462	150,047	176,335	1.06	17.52
Japan	192,322	152,694	158,383	180,330	217,775	1.31	20.76
Korea, Dem. People's Republic of	7,631	5,737	7,057	9,671	7,146	0.04	-26.11
Korea, Republic of	20,611	15,135	21,393	25,411	27,507	0.17	8.25
Mongolia	288	288	295	780	528	0.00	-32.31
Taiwan, Province of China	10,669	10,651	9,358	16,991	24,051	0.14	41.55
South-East Asia	**44,066**	**41,388**	**49,866**	**59,317**	**75,882**	**0.46**	**27.93**
Brunei Darussalam	218	208	455	537	567	0.00	5.59
Cambodia	296	338	383	396	460	0.00	16.16
Indonesia	4,442	4,974	6,979	6,863	9,118	0.05	32.86
Lao People's Democratic Republic	501	308	463	508	453	0.00	-10.83
Malaysia	7,427	6,028	7,215	9,096	10,925	0.07	20.11
Myanmar	145	146	274	202	240	0.00	18.81

79

BELGIUM

6. Overnight stays of non-resident tourists in all types of accommodation establishments, by country of residence

	2008	2009	2010	2011	2012	Market share 2012	% Change 2012-2011
Philippines	8,366	7,112	7,601	10,162	8,795	0.05	-13.45
Singapore	11,328	9,098	11,518	13,092	15,116	0.09	15.46
Thailand	8,170	10,199	10,456	13,760	24,938	0.15	81.24
Timor-Leste	124	12	90	34	62	0.00	82.35
Viet Nam	3,049	2,965	4,432	4,667	5,208	0.03	11.59
Australasia	**82,618**	**80,027**	**91,847**	**107,831**	**111,834**	**0.67**	**3.71**
Australia	67,745	69,087	80,066	93,539	96,566	0.58	3.24
New Zealand	14,873	10,940	11,781	14,292	15,268	0.09	6.83
Melanesia	**925**	**844**	**861**	**1,176**	**1,124**	**0.01**	**-4.42**
Fiji	390	267	301	434	411	0.00	-5.30
Papua New Guinea	225	334	230	218	209	0.00	-4.13
Solomon Islands	223	169	267	330	326	0.00	-1.21
Vanuatu	87	74	63	194	178	0.00	-8.25
Micronesia	**1,076**	**549**	**915**	**706**	**711**	**0.00**	**0.71**
Kiribati	142	42	122	106	70	0.00	-33.96
Marshall Islands	15	4	14	8	26	0.00	225.00
Micronesia, Federated States of	175	68	334	121	217	0.00	79.34
Nauru	385	284	363	401	259	0.00	-35.41
Palau	359	151	82	70	139	0.00	98.57
Polynesia	**724**	**489**	**197**	**564**	**319**	**0.00**	**-43.44**
Samoa	110	54	19	327	166	0.00	-49.24
Tonga	381	241	158	174	105	0.00	-39.66
Tuvalu	233	194	20	63	48	0.00	-23.81
EUROPE	**14,375,789**	**13,703,740**	**14,362,734**	**14,728,013**	**14,503,733**	**87.14**	**-1.52**
Central/Eastern Europe	**721,375**	**639,908**	**746,507**	**868,655**	**894,999**	**5.38**	**3.03**
Armenia	2,636	2,854	5,243	3,004	2,429	0.01	-19.14
Azerbaijan	1,947	1,749	1,969	2,825	3,246	0.02	14.90
Belarus	2,909	4,487	4,130	5,155	5,524	0.03	7.16
Bulgaria	32,074	30,578	33,550	35,785	35,661	0.21	-0.35
Czech Republic	59,104	59,920	65,544	70,373	74,586	0.45	5.99
Estonia	11,574	10,401	11,953	12,490	14,202	0.09	13.71
Georgia	6,581	6,658	5,870	4,697	5,161	0.03	9.88
Hungary	70,385	59,506	58,050	67,498	77,030	0.46	14.12
Kazakhstan	3,054	2,496	2,536	3,368	3,802	0.02	12.89
Kyrgyzstan	497	265	343	409	403	0.00	-1.47
Latvia	12,160	10,122	15,004	17,328	19,075	0.11	10.08
Lithuania	29,020	23,512	27,420	29,032	29,912	0.18	3.03
Poland	223,246	197,467	238,986	272,693	252,372	1.52	-7.45
Republic of Moldova	1,655	1,502	1,663	1,859	2,296	0.01	23.51
Romania	77,977	76,319	87,254	107,076	97,126	0.58	-9.29
Russian Federation	125,937	107,530	138,376	179,392	206,265	1.24	14.98
Slovakia	37,969	25,032	28,062	31,420	37,477	0.23	19.28
Tajikistan	319	315	205	393	536	0.00	36.39
Turkmenistan	474	273	357	188	197	0.00	4.79
Ukraine	20,355	17,894	19,158	22,615	27,038	0.16	19.56
Uzbekistan	1,502	1,028	834	1,055	661	0.00	-37.35
Northern Europe	**2,654,036**	**2,217,800**	**2,247,665**	**2,286,958**	**2,374,752**	**14.27**	**3.84**
Denmark	117,574	114,196	116,335	123,655	124,455	0.75	0.65
Finland	68,878	59,134	66,162	73,064	74,824	0.45	2.41
Iceland	13,831	9,370	14,536	14,488	14,346	0.09	-0.98
Ireland	87,580	87,497	78,751	87,665	106,463	0.64	21.44
Norway	66,079	61,051	69,907	78,252	81,869	0.49	4.62
Sweden	137,572	121,646	138,103	138,595	142,090	0.85	2.52
United Kingdom	2,162,522	1,764,906	1,763,871	1,771,239	1,830,705	11.00	3.36
Southern Europe	**1,306,469**	**1,315,923**	**1,425,684**	**1,537,009**	**1,530,626**	**9.20**	**-0.42**
Albania	5,919	14,131	7,683	8,889	9,226	0.06	3.79
Andorra	4,885	2,424	979	1,307	1,142	0.01	-12.62

Yearbook of Tourism Statistics, Data 2008 – 2012, 2014 Edition

BELGIUM

6. Overnight stays of non-resident tourists in all types of accommodation establishments, by country of residence

	2008	2009	2010	2011	2012	Market share 2012	% Change 2012-2011
Bosnia and Herzegovina	4,299	3,869	4,067	5,195	3,475	0.02	-33.11
Croatia	13,237	13,691	23,165	14,384	16,745	0.10	16.41
Greece	73,080	82,302	65,158	69,084	60,479	0.36	-12.46
Holy See	186	169	170	105	280	0.00	166.67
Italy	471,865	477,343	517,006	555,628	558,412	3.35	0.50
Malta	11,077	11,183	11,774	13,536	13,422	0.08	-0.84
Montenegro	2,356	1,417	1,404	2,422	3,709	0.02	53.14
Portugal	95,452	85,378	83,964	84,060	130,880	0.79	55.70
San Marino	151	534	141	222	1,590	0.01	616.22
Serbia	13,291	13,816	10,731	14,994	13,629	0.08	-9.10
Slovenia	20,980	17,336	20,768	27,785	23,006	0.14	-17.20
Spain	586,498	589,606	675,582	735,857	691,068	4.15	-6.09
TFYR of Macedonia	3,193	2,724	3,092	3,541	3,563	0.02	0.62
Western Europe	**9,557,507**	**9,414,937**	**9,814,878**	**9,884,862**	**9,531,386**	**57.26**	**-3.58**
Austria	75,200	77,851	80,752	90,910	99,529	0.60	9.48
France	2,071,472	2,089,571	2,173,874	2,301,498	2,297,067	13.80	-0.19
Germany	1,901,580	1,879,846	1,992,544	2,027,052	1,933,004	11.61	-4.64
Liechtenstein	6,094	5,012	3,924	2,536	1,639	0.01	-35.37
Luxembourg	185,554	184,544	189,479	203,259	199,877	1.20	-1.66
Monaco	1,470	1,933	1,910	2,039	2,603	0.02	27.66
Netherlands	5,175,164	5,035,124	5,220,042	5,081,035	4,804,043	28.86	-5.45
Switzerland	140,973	141,056	152,353	176,533	193,624	1.16	9.68
East Mediterranean Europe	**136,402**	**115,172**	**128,000**	**150,529**	**171,970**	**1.03**	**14.24**
Cyprus	12,166	11,888	12,580	15,788	20,687	0.12	31.03
Israel	62,858	49,272	54,224	62,349	70,843	0.43	13.62
Turkey	61,378	54,012	61,196	72,392	80,440	0.48	11.12
MIDDLE EAST	**79,053**	**59,874**	**77,266**	**85,920**	**112,878**	**0.68**	**31.38**
Bahrain	1,624	1,107	1,243	1,771	1,470	0.01	-17.00
Egypt	11,724	11,207	13,553	12,730	15,513	0.09	21.86
Iraq	1,638	1,987	2,451	1,972	1,753	0.01	-11.11
Jordan	3,247	4,176	4,283	3,617	3,337	0.02	-7.74
Kuwait	4,783	4,024	4,177	6,118	7,711	0.05	26.04
Lebanon	5,941	5,573	5,724	7,034	8,520	0.05	21.13
Libya	1,883	1,508	1,817	1,163	5,803	0.03	398.97
Oman	1,188	1,085	1,589	2,008	2,436	0.01	21.31
Palestine	626	242	696	246	384	0.00	56.10
Qatar	4,108	1,971	2,965	3,306	6,661	0.04	101.48
Saudi Arabia	10,188	8,812	11,291	12,966	17,959	0.11	38.51
Syrian Arab Republic	1,831	2,922	2,064	1,693	1,360	0.01	-19.67
United Arab Emirates	29,687	14,713	25,092	30,757	39,257	0.24	27.64
Yemen	585	547	321	539	714	0.00	32.47
SOUTH ASIA	**130,228**	**98,108**	**108,265**	**121,261**	**113,125**	**0.68**	**-6.71**
Afghanistan	2,616	4,150	3,625	4,020	3,480	0.02	-13.43
Bangladesh	716	908	1,303	1,441	1,299	0.01	-9.85
Bhutan	76	263	46	118	234	0.00	98.31
India	109,055	72,852	85,089	97,323	91,440	0.55	-6.04
Iran, Islamic Republic of	11,945	15,502	12,859	12,983	11,675	0.07	-10.07
Maldives	101	91	80	122	114	0.00	-6.56
Nepal	311	417	447	564	643	0.00	14.01
Pakistan	4,398	3,281	4,095	3,733	3,353	0.02	-10.18
Sri Lanka	1,010	644	721	957	887	0.01	-7.31
NOT SPECIFIED	**304,102**	**229,576**	**98,987**	**54,367**	**61,464**	**0.37**	**13.05**
Other countries of the World	304,102	229,576	98,987	54,367	61,464	0.37	13.05

Yearbook of Tourism Statistics, Data 2008 – 2012, 2014 Edition

BELIZE

1. Arrivals of non-resident tourists at national borders, by nationality

	2008	2009	2010	2011	2012	Market share 2012	% Change 2012-2011
TOTAL	245,026	232,249	241,919	250,263	277,135	100.00	10.74
AFRICA	512	668	577	472	453	0.16	-4.01
Other Africa	512	668	577	472	453	0.16	-4.01
All countries of Africa	512	668	577	472	453	0.16	-4.01
AMERICAS	195,645	188,240	195,568	203,128	226,961	81.90	11.73
Caribbean	2,307	2,388	2,505	2,049	2,288	0.83	11.64
Jamaica	584	669	663	599	644	0.23	7.54
Other countries of the Caribbean	1,723	1,719	1,842	1,451	1,644	0.59	13.33
Central America	20,207	22,208	21,908	16,834	16,112	5.81	-4.29
Guatemala	11,674	12,957	12,448	7,423	7,048	2.54	-5.05
Honduras	3,105	3,506	3,680	3,731	3,892	1.40	4.30
Other countries of Central America	5,428	5,745	5,780	5,679	5,172	1.87	-8.93
North America	171,112	161,555	168,958	181,984	206,029	74.34	13.21
Canada	17,695	17,211	18,246	20,093	24,223	8.74	20.55
Mexico	5,763	4,783	4,840	5,598	5,164	1.86	-7.74
United States of America	147,654	139,561	145,872	156,293	176,642	63.74	13.02
South America	2,019	2,089	2,197	2,261	2,532	0.91	11.97
All countries of South America	2,019	2,089	2,197	2,261	2,532	0.91	11.97
EAST ASIA AND THE PACIFIC	5,234	4,973	6,069	5,737	6,933	2.50	20.85
Other East Asia and the Pacific	5,234	4,973	6,069	5,737	6,933	2.50	20.85
All countries of Asia	2,774	2,459	2,937	2,995	3,443	1.24	14.94
All countries of Oceania	2,460	2,514	3,133	2,741	3,490	1.26	27.31
EUROPE	34,269	29,603	30,025	30,142	29,362	10.59	-2.59
Northern Europe	11,230	9,334	10,142	9,046	8,999	3.25	-0.52
Sweden	1,130	800	841	847	1,018	0.37	20.17
United Kingdom	10,100	8,534	9,301	8,199	7,981	2.88	-2.66
Southern Europe	3,998	3,151	3,412	3,657	3,018	1.09	-17.48
Italy	2,371	1,679	1,877	2,218	1,774	0.64	-20.01
Spain	1,627	1,472	1,535	1,440	1,244	0.45	-13.60
Western Europe	12,047	9,994	9,856	10,254	10,122	3.65	-1.29
France	3,258	3,269	2,916	3,101	3,308	1.19	6.66
Germany	4,161	3,376	3,438	3,262	3,525	1.27	8.06
Netherlands	3,915	2,607	2,461	2,869	2,384	0.86	-16.92
Switzerland	713	742	1,041	1,021	905	0.33	-11.39
Other Europe	6,994	7,124	6,615	7,184	7,223	2.61	0.54
Other countries of Europe	6,994	7,124	6,615	7,184	7,223	2.61	0.54
MIDDLE EAST	588	400	863	628	1,324	0.48	110.93
All countries of Middle East	588	400	863	628	1,324	0.48	110.93
NOT SPECIFIED	8,778	8,365	8,817	10,157	12,102	4.37	19.15
Nationals Residing Abroad	8,778	8,365	8,817	10,157	12,102	4.37	19.15

Yearbook of Tourism Statistics, Data 2008 – 2012, 2014 Edition

BELIZE

2. Arrivals of non-resident visitors at national borders, by nationality

		2008	2009	2010	2011	2012	Market share 2012	% Change 2012-2011
TOTAL	(*)	**990,757**	**1,091,406**	**1,197,326**	**1,177,462**	**1,051,907**	**100.00**	**-10.66**
AMERICAS		**881,904**	**989,821**	**1,105,499**	**1,077,276**	**958,330**	**91.10**	**-11.04**
Caribbean		**7,906**	**9,067**	**7,823**	**7,646**	**7,617**	**0.72**	**-0.38**
Cuba		904	1,170	1,165	1,121	1,081	0.10	-3.57
Jamaica		1,173	1,292	1,213	1,184	1,266	0.12	6.93
Other countries of the Caribbean		5,829	6,605	5,445	5,341	5,270	0.50	-1.33
Central America		**114,525**	**129,308**	**154,968**	**168,044**	**171,256**	**16.28**	**1.91**
Costa Rica		1,210	1,230	1,235	1,056	1,350	0.13	27.84
El Salvador		4,533	4,792	5,182	5,069	5,961	0.57	17.60
Guatemala		102,090	116,123	141,083	154,954	155,745	14.81	0.51
Honduras		4,324	4,824	5,283	5,070	6,068	0.58	19.68
Other countries of Central America		2,368	2,339	2,185	1,895	2,132	0.20	12.51
North America		**753,015**	**840,771**	**933,035**	**892,230**	**769,176**	**73.12**	**-13.79**
Canada		53,102	60,503	63,971	67,257	68,331	6.50	1.60
Mexico		29,432	26,259	26,101	33,864	36,652	3.48	8.23
United States of America		670,481	754,009	842,963	791,109	664,193	63.14	-16.04
South America		**6,458**	**10,675**	**9,673**	**9,356**	**10,281**	**0.98**	**9.89**
All countries of South America		6,458	10,675	9,673	9,356	10,281	0.98	9.89
EAST ASIA AND THE PACIFIC		**5,742**	**5,925**	**6,424**	**7,862**	**10,361**	**0.98**	**31.79**
Other East Asia and the Pacific		**5,742**	**5,925**	**6,424**	**7,862**	**10,361**	**0.98**	**31.79**
All countries of Asia		5,742	5,925	6,424	7,862	10,361	0.98	31.79
EUROPE		**95,572**	**86,247**	**75,690**	**84,038**	**73,446**	**6.98**	**-12.60**
Northern Europe		**33,468**	**19,885**	**18,500**	**20,474**	**16,263**	**1.55**	**-20.57**
United Kingdom		33,468	19,885	18,500	20,474	16,263	1.55	-20.57
Other Europe		**62,104**	**66,362**	**57,190**	**63,564**	**57,183**	**5.44**	**-10.04**
Other countries of Europe		62,104	66,362	57,190	63,564	57,183	5.44	-10.04
NOT SPECIFIED		**7,539**	**9,413**	**9,713**	**8,286**	**9,770**	**0.93**	**17.91**
Other countries of the World		7,539	9,413	9,713	8,286	9,770	0.93	17.91

Yearbook of Tourism Statistics, Data 2008 – 2012, 2014 Edition

BENIN

1. Arrivals of non-resident tourists at national borders, by country of residence

	2008	2009	2010	2011	2012	Market share 2012	% Change 2012-2011
TOTAL	**188,000**	**190,000**	**199,491**	**209,475**	**219,949**	**100.00**	**5.00**
AFRICA	**117,929**	**90,757**	**138,000**	**125,685**	**135,347**	**61.54**	**7.69**
East Africa	**3,713**	**2,634**	**5,914**	**5,027**	**5,397**	**2.45**	**7.36**
Burundi	74	31	1,035	611	512	0.23	-16.20
Comoros	72	106	515	498	566	0.26	13.65
Djibouti	46	30	120	200	105	0.05	-47.50
Eritrea			9		11	0.01	
Ethiopia	126	47	110	118	88	0.04	-25.42
Kenya	332	142	76	120	315	0.14	162.50
Madagascar	332	239	980	612	714	0.32	16.67
Malawi	12	35	1,100	940	669	0.30	-28.83
Mauritius	42	1	33		15	0.01	
Mozambique	115	26	500	610	380	0.17	-37.70
Rwanda	1,081	1,061	845	900	810	0.37	-10.00
Seychelles	18	20	11	5	21	0.01	320.00
Somalia	397	717	300	187	481	0.22	157.22
Uganda	66	60	54	47	200	0.09	325.53
United Republic of Tanzania	715	78	88	150	33	0.02	-78.00
Zambia	218	11	121	18	300	0.14	1,566.67
Zimbabwe	67	30	17	11	177	0.08	1,509.09
Central Africa	**38,570**	**24,163**	**58,494**	**50,263**	**33,762**	**15.35**	**-32.83**
Angola	3,504	609	11,410	9,872	473	0.22	-95.21
Cameroon	7,244	5,357	10,620	12,500	13,879	6.31	11.03
Central African Republic	1,445	840	800	700	600	0.27	-14.29
Chad	1,481	1,900	2,007	1,800	2,200	1.00	22.22
Congo	12,468	6,839	25,953	22,897	9,633	4.38	-57.93
Democratic Republic of the Congo	370	47	915	600	456	0.21	-24.00
Equatorial Guinea	1,740	253	200	87	820	0.37	842.53
Gabon	10,287	8,313	6,589	1,807	5,699	2.59	215.38
Sao Tome and Principe	31	5			2	0.00	
North Africa	**3,361**	**2,526**	**2,697**	**2,500**	**6,534**	**2.97**	**161.36**
Algeria	750	966	850	740	1,600	0.73	116.22
Morocco	869	416	600	700	1,053	0.48	50.43
Sudan	400	227	320	350	600	0.27	71.43
Tunisia	1,342	917	927	710	3,281	1.49	362.11
Southern Africa	**2,099**	**1,160**	**977**	**512**	**983**	**0.45**	**91.99**
Botswana	153	135	200	99	80	0.04	-19.19
Lesotho	22	47	55	36	60	0.03	66.67
Namibia	74	63	57	20	55	0.03	175.00
South Africa	1,850	915	663	346	780	0.35	125.43
Swaziland			2	11	8	0.00	-27.27
West Africa	**70,186**	**60,274**	**69,918**	**67,383**	**88,671**	**40.31**	**31.59**
Burkina Faso	10,600	9,700	9,122	6,980	9,891	4.50	41.70
Cape Verde	440	700	540	410	610	0.28	48.78
Côte d'Ivoire	12,940	7,550	18,937	15,813	19,500	8.87	23.32
Gambia	234	545	180	200	858	0.39	329.00
Ghana	4,196	5,126	4,400	5,500	6,008	2.73	9.24
Guinea	1,740	422	1,800	918	1,799	0.82	95.97
Guinea-Bissau	177	116	200	325	500	0.23	53.85
Liberia	291	178	300	340	660	0.30	94.12
Mali	1,729	1,273	1,945	2,600	3,012	1.37	15.85
Mauritania	446	445	333	260	366	0.17	40.77
Niger	5,240	5,900	6,000	5,500	8,100	3.68	47.27
Nigeria	21,150	13,184	15,975	17,614	20,200	9.18	14.68
Senegal	4,111	3,059	4,600	3,100	5,877	2.67	89.58
Sierra Leone	225	525	186	223	300	0.14	34.53

Yearbook of Tourism Statistics, Data 2008 – 2012, 2014 Edition

BENIN

1. Arrivals of non-resident tourists at national borders, by country of residence

	2008	2009	2010	2011	2012	Market share 2012	% Change 2012-2011
Togo	6,667	11,551	5,400	7,600	10,990	5.00	44.61
AMERICAS	**3,926**	**5,104**	**3,173**	**3,066**	**4,558**	**2.07**	**48.66**
Caribbean	**556**	**336**	**266**	**189**	**92**	**0.04**	**-51.32**
Cuba	97	117	57	28	12	0.01	-57.14
Dominican Republic		91	19	11	15	0.01	36.36
Guadeloupe	67		7	10	4	0.00	-60.00
Haiti	145	120	152	129	33	0.02	-74.42
Jamaica	165	8	11	6	21	0.01	250.00
Netherlands Antilles	82		20	5	7	0.00	40.00
Central America	**1**			**11**	**25**	**0.01**	**127.27**
Honduras				3	7	0.00	133.33
Nicaragua	1			8	18	0.01	125.00
North America	**2,175**	**3,756**	**1,974**	**2,150**	**3,439**	**1.56**	**59.95**
Canada	652	952	612	840	1,093	0.50	30.12
Mexico	75	120	375	420	350	0.16	-16.67
United States of America	1,448	2,684	987	890	1,996	0.91	124.27
South America	**1,194**	**1,012**	**933**	**716**	**1,002**	**0.46**	**39.94**
Argentina	344	604	500	422	577	0.26	36.73
Bolivia			9	12	20	0.01	66.67
Brazil	850	360	407	120	360	0.16	200.00
Chile			2	20	7	0.00	-65.00
Colombia		48	11	89	11	0.01	-87.64
Uruguay			3	13	4	0.00	-69.23
Venezuela			1	40	23	0.01	-42.50
EAST ASIA AND THE PACIFIC	**1,633**	**860**	**800**	**1,126**	**2,726**	**1.24**	**142.10**
North-East Asia	**1,468**	**603**	**679**	**972**	**2,533**	**1.15**	**160.60**
China	1,073	410	371	580	1,877	0.85	223.62
Japan	196	174	200	240	557	0.25	132.08
Korea, Dem. People's Republic of	199	19	108	152	99	0.05	-34.87
South-East Asia	**165**	**113**	**88**	**97**	**157**	**0.07**	**61.86**
Indonesia	101	45	13	25	99	0.05	296.00
Malaysia	9	19	6	2	12	0.01	500.00
Philippines	22	12	7	5	7	0.00	40.00
Singapore	33	1	12	12	9	0.00	-25.00
Thailand		22	41	34	19	0.01	-44.12
Viet Nam		14	9	19	11	0.01	-42.11
Australasia		**144**	**33**	**55**	**36**	**0.02**	**-34.55**
Australia		144	30	19	21	0.01	10.53
New Zealand			3	36	15	0.01	-58.33
Melanesia				**2**			
Fiji				2			
EUROPE	**50,706**	**35,448**	**32,886**	**57,081**	**54,339**	**24.71**	**-4.80**
Northern Europe	**1,554**	**3,856**	**610**	**2,903**	**1,482**	**0.67**	**-48.95**
Denmark	23	1,538	291	300	445	0.20	48.33
Finland	6	578	22	30	13	0.01	-56.67
Ireland	11	34	33	987	87	0.04	-91.19
Norway	639	358	45	800	360	0.16	-55.00
Sweden	875	1,348	219	786	577	0.26	-26.59
Southern Europe	**5,820**	**6,224**	**2,897**	**4,855**	**4,646**	**2.11**	**-4.30**
Bosnia and Herzegovina				2			
Greece	100	314	300	206	100	0.05	-51.46
Italy	3,066	3,237	1,438	3,074	2,996	1.36	-2.54
Montenegro			1	7			
Portugal	630	466	346	600	500	0.23	-16.67
Serbia and Montenegro				1			
Slovenia			5	15			

Yearbook of Tourism Statistics, Data 2008 – 2012, 2014 Edition

BENIN

1. Arrivals of non-resident tourists at national borders, by country of residence

	2008	2009	2010	2011	2012	Market share 2012	% Change 2012-2011
Spain	2,024	2,207	807	950	1,050	0.48	10.53
Western Europe	**34,244**	**17,616**	**22,641**	**41,132**	**41,011**	**18.65**	**-0.29**
Austria	295	222	600	200	180	0.08	-10.00
Belgium	1,910	2,162	4,670	3,600	4,000	1.82	11.11
France	15,846	2,519	13,206	20,386	19,783	8.99	-2.96
Germany	2,718	1,992	1,950	2,317	2,210	1.00	-4.62
Luxembourg	182	30	81	229	144	0.07	-37.12
Netherlands	4,127	4,120	900	8,900	7,056	3.21	-20.72
Switzerland	9,166	6,571	1,234	5,500	7,638	3.47	38.87
East Mediterranean Europe	**252**	**142**	**108**	**202**	**120**	**0.05**	**-40.59**
Israel	252	142	88	135	99	0.05	-26.67
Turkey			20	67	21	0.01	-68.66
Other Europe	**8,836**	**7,610**	**6,630**	**7,989**	**7,080**	**3.22**	**-11.38**
Other countries of Europe	8,836	7,610	6,630	7,989	7,080	3.22	-11.38
MIDDLE EAST	**291**	**367**	**2,388**	**2,670**	**2,916**	**1.33**	**9.21**
Egypt			45	41	33	0.02	-19.51
Iraq	13	30	19	11	7	0.00	-36.36
Jordan	5	20	33	7			
Kuwait	1		15	25	19	0.01	-24.00
Lebanon	97	290	1,300	1,659	1,897	0.86	14.35
Libya			940	889	797	0.36	-10.35
Palestine	55		20	17	10	0.00	-41.18
Qatar		18	11	12	144	0.07	1,100.00
Saudi Arabia	120	9	3	5			
Syrian Arab Republic			2	4	9	0.00	125.00
SOUTH ASIA	**691**	**453**	**845**	**1,147**	**1,063**	**0.48**	**-7.32**
Afghanistan	20	181	81	58	100	0.05	72.41
Bangladesh				2			
India	634	212	707	1,037	900	0.41	-13.21
Iran, Islamic Republic of	17	9	22	19	45	0.02	136.84
Nepal	3	1	5	11	6	0.00	-45.45
Pakistan	17	50	30	15	12	0.01	-20.00
Sri Lanka				5			
NOT SPECIFIED	**12,824**	**57,011**	**21,399**	**18,700**	**19,000**	**8.64**	**1.60**
Other countries of the World	12,824	57,011	21,399	18,700	19,000	8.64	1.60

Yearbook of Tourism Statistics, Data 2008 – 2012, 2014 Edition

BERMUDA

1. Arrivals of non-resident tourists at national borders, by country of residence

	2008	2009	2010	2011	2012	Market share 2012	% Change 2012-2011
TOTAL (*)	**263,613**	**235,860**	**232,262**	**236,038**	**232,063**	**100.00**	**-1.68**
AMERICAS	**216,595**	**197,515**	**196,418**	**202,107**	**198,743**	**85.64**	**-1.66**
North America	**216,595**	**197,515**	**196,418**	**202,107**	**198,743**	**85.64**	**-1.66**
Canada	27,207	24,867	30,402	29,217	30,565	13.17	4.61
United States of America	189,388	172,648	166,016	172,890	168,178	72.47	-2.73
EAST ASIA AND THE PACIFIC	**795**	**811**	**1,088**	**1,058**	**868**	**0.37**	**-17.96**
North-East Asia	**386**	**336**	**385**	**367**	**331**	**0.14**	**-9.81**
Japan	386	336	385	367	331	0.14	-9.81
Australasia	**409**	**475**	**703**	**691**	**537**	**0.23**	**-22.29**
Australia	409	475	703	691	537	0.23	-22.29
EUROPE	**35,003**	**28,949**	**28,498**	**26,940**	**25,766**	**11.10**	**-4.36**
Northern Europe	**29,584**	**24,218**	**23,501**	**21,797**	**21,226**	**9.15**	**-2.62**
Sweden	329	313	261	273	197	0.08	-27.84
United Kingdom	29,255	23,905	23,240	21,524	21,029	9.06	-2.30
Southern Europe	**1,544**	**1,253**	**1,244**	**1,184**	**906**	**0.39**	**-23.48**
Italy	1,544	1,253	1,244	1,184	906	0.39	-23.48
Western Europe	**2,963**	**2,516**	**2,760**	**2,870**	**2,532**	**1.09**	**-11.78**
Austria	171	135	168	176	122	0.05	-30.68
France	954	754	711	698	572	0.25	-18.05
Germany	1,293	1,032	994	1,116	990	0.43	-11.29
Switzerland	545	595	887	880	848	0.37	-3.64
Other Europe	**912**	**962**	**993**	**1,089**	**1,102**	**0.47**	**1.19**
Other countries of Europe	912	962	993	1,089	1,102	0.47	1.19
NOT SPECIFIED	**11,220**	**8,585**	**6,258**	**5,933**	**6,686**	**2.88**	**12.69**
Other countries of the World	11,220	8,585	6,258	5,933	6,686	2.88	12.69

Yearbook of Tourism Statistics, Data 2008 – 2012, 2014 Edition

BHUTAN

1. Arrivals of non-resident tourists at national borders, by nationality

		2008	2009	2010	2011	2012	Market share 2012	% Change 2012-2011
TOTAL	(*)	27,642	23,480	27,210	37,479	43,931	100.00	17.21
AFRICA		77	48	102	92	93	0.21	1.09
East Africa		5	7	6	21	4	0.01	-80.95
Kenya		1	2	4	6	2	0.00	-66.67
Mauritius		3	5	1	14			
Seychelles						1	0.00	
Somalia		1						
Uganda					1			
United Republic of Tanzania					1			
Zambia						1	0.00	
Central Africa					3	2	0.00	-33.33
Chad					3	2	0.00	-33.33
North Africa			5		1	1	0.00	0.00
Morocco			4			1	0.00	
Sudan					1			
Tunisia			1					
Southern Africa		71	36	74	63	82	0.19	30.16
Namibia		5		1	1	5	0.01	400.00
South Africa		65	32	70	62	77	0.18	24.19
Swaziland		1	4	3				
West Africa		1			4	4	0.01	0.00
Benin					1			
Liberia		1						
Nigeria					3	4	0.01	33.33
Other Africa				22				
Other countries of Africa				22				
AMERICAS		8,240	5,743	6,506	8,056	7,879	17.93	-2.20
Caribbean		1			8	3	0.01	-62.50
Antigua and Barbuda					1			
Cuba		1			1			
Dominican Republic						2	0.00	
Grenada					1			
Haiti					1			
Jamaica					1			
Trinidad and Tobago					3	1	0.00	-66.67
Central America		1	2	13	17	13	0.03	-23.53
Belize				1	1			
Costa Rica				10	1	5	0.01	400.00
El Salvador					2			
Guatemala			2		11			
Honduras		1		2				
Panama					2	8	0.02	300.00
North America		7,931	5,467	6,141	7,511	7,199	16.39	-4.15
Canada		852	556	786	1,061	999	2.27	-5.84
Mexico		138	125	166	224	193	0.44	-13.84
United States of America		6,941	4,786	5,189	6,226	6,007	13.67	-3.52
South America		307	274	338	520	664	1.51	27.69
Argentina		21	59	40	80	88	0.20	10.00
Bolivia						2	0.00	
Brazil		249	178	229	304	462	1.05	51.97
Chile		15	8	18	45	40	0.09	-11.11
Colombia		5	14	27	45	40	0.09	-11.11
Ecuador					1	4	0.01	
Peru		7	6	19	12	6	0.01	-50.00
Uruguay			1	1		7	0.02	

88

BHUTAN

1. Arrivals of non-resident tourists at national borders, by nationality

	2008	2009	2010	2011	2012	Market share 2012	% Change 2012-2011
Venezuela	10	8	3	34	15	0.03	-55.88
Other Americas			14				
Other countries of the Americas			14				
EAST ASIA AND THE PACIFIC	**7,412**	**7,743**	**8,599**	**14,949**	**21,329**	**48.55**	**42.68**
North-East Asia	**4,072**	**4,412**	**4,827**	**8,147**	**12,178**	**27.72**	**49.48**
China	1,069	1,143	1,494	2,896	3,766	8.57	30.04
Japan	2,749	3,136	2,963	3,943	6,967	15.86	76.69
Korea, Dem. People's Republic of	43			3	11	0.03	266.67
Korea, Republic of	97	49	182	407	630	1.43	54.79
Macao, China		1	3				
Mongolia			1	7	3	0.01	-57.14
Taiwan, Province of China	114	83	184	891	801	1.82	-10.10
South-East Asia	**1,636**	**2,239**	**2,277**	**4,885**	**7,033**	**16.01**	**43.97**
Brunei Darussalam				3	1	0.00	-66.67
Cambodia	1	2			3	0.01	
Indonesia	36	98	110	295	202	0.46	-31.53
Lao People's Democratic Republic				4	2	0.00	-50.00
Malaysia	221	367	356	788	1,307	2.98	65.86
Myanmar	5	5	1	3	12	0.03	300.00
Philippines	72	59	119	128	243	0.55	89.84
Singapore	667	708	785	1,349	1,605	3.65	18.98
Thailand	627	975	875	2,235	3,573	8.13	59.87
Viet Nam	7	25	31	80	85	0.19	6.25
Australasia	**1,704**	**1,092**	**1,423**	**1,917**	**2,118**	**4.82**	**10.49**
Australia	1,524	970	1,318	1,773	1,926	4.38	8.63
New Zealand	180	122	105	144	192	0.44	33.33
Other East Asia and the Pacific			72				
Other countries of Asia			72				
EUROPE	**11,778**	**9,861**	**11,883**	**14,181**	**14,412**	**32.81**	**1.63**
Central/Eastern Europe	**820**	**720**	**857**	**1,065**	**1,007**	**2.29**	**-5.45**
Armenia				10	1	0.00	-90.00
Azerbaijan				1			
Belarus	2	2	2	1	11	0.03	1,000.00
Bulgaria	13	12	11	11	14	0.03	27.27
Czech Republic	65	77	71	135	148	0.34	9.63
Estonia	54	14	31	2	12	0.03	500.00
Georgia					5	0.01	
Hungary	54	49	65	45	69	0.16	53.33
Kazakhstan	1	5		15	3	0.01	-80.00
Kyrgyzstan				1	1	0.00	0.00
Latvia	9	3	9	44	32	0.07	-27.27
Lithuania	32	4	13	44	3	0.01	-93.18
Poland	233	184	268	311	240	0.55	-22.83
Republic of Moldova					2	0.00	
Romania	12	19	52	35	19	0.04	-45.71
Russian Federation	245	270	275	291	365	0.83	25.43
Slovakia	55	53	32	38	36	0.08	-5.26
Ukraine	44	28	27	81	44	0.10	-45.68
Uzbekistan	1		1		2	0.00	
Northern Europe	**3,473**	**2,521**	**2,690**	**4,025**	**3,370**	**7.67**	**-16.27**
Denmark	127	153	412	430	332	0.76	-22.79
Finland	191	161	174	245	112	0.25	-54.29
Iceland	13			7	5	0.01	-28.57
Ireland	98	59	59	78	72	0.16	-7.69
Norway	109	92	136	214	142	0.32	-33.64
Sweden	177	88	137	256	241	0.55	-5.86
United Kingdom	2,758	1,968	1,772	2,795	2,466	5.61	-11.77

Yearbook of Tourism Statistics, Data 2008 – 2012, 2014 Edition

BHUTAN

1. Arrivals of non-resident tourists at national borders, by nationality

	2008	2009	2010	2011	2012	Market share 2012	% Change 2012-2011
Southern Europe	1,761	1,506	1,826	2,054	1,831	4.17	-10.86
Albania				2			
Andorra		3	1	1	6	0.01	500.00
Bosnia and Herzegovina		1		2	1	0.00	-50.00
Croatia	8	4	1	6	15	0.03	150.00
Greece	45	107	88	70	60	0.14	-14.29
Italy	751	759	1,028	1,014	786	1.79	-22.49
Malta				4	9	0.02	125.00
Montenegro				1	1	0.00	0.00
Portugal	91	116	116	214	118	0.27	-44.86
Serbia				2	5	0.01	150.00
Slovenia	63	30	64	11	41	0.09	272.73
Spain	803	485	528	727	789	1.80	8.53
Yugoslavia, SFR (former)		1					
Western Europe	5,549	4,899	6,272	6,689	7,817	17.79	16.86
Austria	472	420	505	528	611	1.39	15.72
Belgium	432	364	404	539	505	1.15	-6.31
France	1,402	1,189	1,454	1,585	1,847	4.20	16.53
Germany	1,717	1,587	2,250	2,287	2,880	6.56	25.93
Liechtenstein				3	5	0.01	66.67
Luxembourg	14	16	23	33	38	0.09	15.15
Monaco					6	0.01	
Netherlands	915	780	847	933	993	2.26	6.43
Switzerland	597	543	789	781	932	2.12	19.33
East Mediterranean Europe	175	215	232	348	387	0.88	11.21
Cyprus	6	5	5	4	7	0.02	75.00
Israel	78	159	127	278	172	0.39	-38.13
Turkey	91	51	100	66	208	0.47	215.15
Other Europe				6			
Other countries of Europe				6			
MIDDLE EAST	29	31	27	44	36	0.08	-18.18
Bahrain				1			
Egypt		18	10				
Jordan	2		1	21	3	0.01	-85.71
Kuwait	5		2	8	8	0.02	0.00
Lebanon	9		5	4	5	0.01	25.00
Oman	4		1	2	5	0.01	150.00
Saudi Arabia	2			2	12	0.03	500.00
United Arab Emirates	7		8	5	3	0.01	-40.00
Yemen				1			
Other countries of Middle East		13					
SOUTH ASIA	106	52	93	157	182	0.41	15.92
Afghanistan					2	0.00	
Bangladesh	1						
Iran, Islamic Republic of			1	4	1	0.00	-75.00
Nepal	78	41	60	145	150	0.34	3.45
Pakistan	1	5	2	2	12	0.03	500.00
Sri Lanka	26	6	30	6	17	0.04	183.33
NOT SPECIFIED			2				
Other countries of the World			2				

Yearbook of Tourism Statistics, Data 2008 – 2012, 2014 Edition

BHUTAN

5. Overnight stays of non-resident tourists in hotels and similar establishments, by nationality

	2008	2009	2010	2011	2012	Market share 2012	% Change 2012-2011
TOTAL				276,880	303,319	100.00	9.55
AFRICA					687	0.23	
East Africa					25	0.01	
Kenya					12	0.00	
Seychelles					10	0.00	
Zambia					3	0.00	
Central Africa					8	0.00	
Chad					8	0.00	
North Africa					8	0.00	
Morocco					8	0.00	
Southern Africa					610	0.20	
Namibia					30	0.01	
South Africa					580	0.19	
West Africa					36	0.01	
Nigeria					36	0.01	
AMERICAS				59,791	60,999	20.11	2.02
Caribbean					12	0.00	
Dominican Republic					6	0.00	
Trinidad and Tobago					6	0.00	
Central America					72	0.02	
Costa Rica					20	0.01	
Panama					52	0.02	
North America				59,791	57,268	18.88	-4.22
Canada				9,503	8,118	2.68	-14.57
Mexico					1,113	0.37	
United States of America				50,288	48,037	15.84	-4.48
South America					3,647	1.20	
Argentina					476	0.16	
Bolivia					8	0.00	
Brazil					2,487	0.82	
Chile					327	0.11	
Colombia					195	0.06	
Ecuador					27	0.01	
Peru					27	0.01	
Uruguay					27	0.01	
Venezuela					73	0.02	
EAST ASIA AND THE PACIFIC				71,882	116,845	38.52	62.55
North-East Asia				35,991	60,587	19.97	68.34
China				14,694	18,666	6.15	27.03
Japan				21,297	34,013	11.21	59.71
Korea, Dem. People's Republic of					44	0.01	
Korea, Republic of					2,880	0.95	
Mongolia					13	0.00	
Taiwan, Province of China					4,971	1.64	
South-East Asia				19,364	36,727	12.11	89.67
Brunei Darussalam					3	0.00	
Cambodia					9	0.00	
Indonesia					1,237	0.41	
Lao People's Democratic Republic					13	0.00	
Malaysia					7,215	2.38	
Myanmar					50	0.02	
Philippines					1,500	0.49	
Singapore				9,591	11,101	3.66	15.74
Thailand				9,773	15,059	4.96	54.09
Viet Nam					540	0.18	

Yearbook of Tourism Statistics, Data 2008 – 2012, 2014 Edition

BHUTAN

5. Overnight stays of non-resident tourists in hotels and similar establishments, by nationality

	2008	2009	2010	2011	2012	Market share 2012	% Change 2012-2011
Australasia				16,527	19,531	6.44	18.18
Australia				16,527	17,666	5.82	6.89
New Zealand					1,865	0.61	
EUROPE				59,888	123,585	40.74	106.36
Central/Eastern Europe					6,236	2.06	
Armenia					4	0.00	
Belarus					71	0.02	
Bulgaria					66	0.02	
Czech Republic					1,208	0.40	
Estonia					76	0.03	
Georgia					29	0.01	
Hungary					328	0.11	
Kazakhstan					16	0.01	
Kyrgyzstan					7	0.00	
Latvia					266	0.09	
Lithuania					28	0.01	
Poland					1,243	0.41	
Republic of Moldova					12	0.00	
Romania					103	0.03	
Russian Federation					2,217	0.73	
Slovakia					280	0.09	
Ukraine					268	0.09	
Uzbekistan					14	0.00	
Northern Europe				24,549	27,886	9.19	13.59
Denmark					3,015	0.99	
Finland					797	0.26	
Iceland					42	0.01	
Ireland					511	0.17	
Norway					985	0.32	
Sweden					1,607	0.53	
United Kingdom				24,549	20,929	6.90	-14.75
Southern Europe					12,996	4.28	
Andorra					48	0.02	
Bosnia and Herzegovina					8	0.00	
Croatia					97	0.03	
Greece					367	0.12	
Italy					6,162	2.03	
Malta					100	0.03	
Montenegro					4	0.00	
Portugal					702	0.23	
Serbia					29	0.01	
Slovenia					287	0.09	
Spain					5,192	1.71	
Western Europe				35,339	74,069	24.42	109.60
Austria					5,378	1.77	
Belgium					4,656	1.54	
France				14,065	16,946	5.59	20.48
Germany				21,274	26,350	8.69	23.86
Liechtenstein					54	0.02	
Luxembourg					313	0.10	
Monaco					54	0.02	
Netherlands					10,154	3.35	
Switzerland					10,164	3.35	
East Mediterranean Europe					2,398	0.79	
Cyprus					41	0.01	
Israel					1,229	0.41	
Turkey					1,128	0.37	

BHUTAN

5. Overnight stays of non-resident tourists in hotels and similar establishments, by nationality

	2008	2009	2010	2011	2012	Market share 2012	% Change 2012-2011
MIDDLE EAST					227	0.07	
Jordan					32	0.01	
Kuwait					43	0.01	
Lebanon					30	0.01	
Oman					15	0.00	
Saudi Arabia					97	0.03	
United Arab Emirates					10	0.00	
SOUTH ASIA					976	0.32	
Afghanistan					14	0.00	
Iran, Islamic Republic of					10	0.00	
Nepal					859	0.28	
Pakistan					33	0.01	
Sri Lanka					60	0.02	
NOT SPECIFIED				85,319			
Other countries of the World				85,319			

Yearbook of Tourism Statistics, Data 2008 – 2012, 2014 Edition

BOLIVIA

1. Arrivals of non-resident tourists at national borders, by nationality

	2008	2009	2010	2011	2012	Market share 2012	% Change 2012-2011
TOTAL (*)	**593,727**	**671,227**	**807,136**	**952,571**	**1,114,467**	**100.00**	**17.00**
AFRICA	**1,028**	**1,115**	**1,336**	**646**	**3,176**	**0.28**	**391.64**
Other Africa	**1,028**	**1,115**	**1,336**	**646**	**3,176**	**0.28**	**391.64**
All countries of Africa	1,028	1,115	1,336	646	3,176	0.28	391.64
AMERICAS	**406,709**	**473,364**	**595,471**	**739,071**	**895,002**	**80.31**	**21.10**
North America	**56,442**	**51,850**	**67,826**	**66,417**	**64,574**	**5.79**	**-2.77**
Canada	10,981	11,682	15,434	14,257	12,910	1.16	-9.45
Mexico	36,316	30,577	40,923	10,304	11,184	1.00	8.54
United States of America	9,145	9,591	11,469	41,856	40,480	3.63	-3.29
South America	**337,968**	**403,336**	**503,903**	**652,301**	**810,709**	**72.74**	**24.28**
Argentina	81,204	109,935	134,184	192,509	226,881	20.36	17.85
Brazil	38,361	57,880	63,579	64,209	73,786	6.62	14.92
Chile	46,337	50,819	64,382	72,844	102,962	9.24	41.35
Colombia	11,643	14,477	18,372	16,764	23,168	2.08	38.20
Ecuador	5,598	6,682	11,178	7,342	9,885	0.89	34.64
Paraguay	16,821	19,803	19,060	19,527	20,731	1.86	6.17
Peru	127,317	130,521	170,935	260,783	333,561	29.93	27.91
Uruguay	5,082	5,527	9,467	8,183	8,613	0.77	5.25
Venezuela	5,605	7,692	12,746	10,140	11,122	1.00	9.68
Other Americas	**12,299**	**18,178**	**23,742**	**20,353**	**19,719**	**1.77**	**-3.12**
Other countries of the Americas	12,299	18,178	23,742	20,353	19,719	1.77	-3.12
EAST ASIA AND THE PACIFIC	**38,610**	**39,730**	**46,248**	**42,045**	**48,631**	**4.36**	**15.66**
North-East Asia	**8,631**	**8,035**	**6,683**	**7,813**	**11,873**	**1.07**	**51.96**
Japan	8,631	8,035	6,683	7,813	11,873	1.07	51.96
Other East Asia and the Pacific	**29,979**	**31,695**	**39,565**	**34,232**	**36,758**	**3.30**	**7.38**
Other countries of Asia	12,502	13,961	17,774	16,664	18,952	1.70	13.73
All countries of Oceania	17,477	17,734	21,791	17,568	17,806	1.60	1.35
EUROPE	**147,380**	**157,018**	**164,081**	**170,809**	**167,658**	**15.04**	**-1.84**
Northern Europe	**23,679**	**25,245**	**24,404**	**22,729**	**22,365**	**2.01**	**-1.60**
Sweden	3,685	4,498	5,185	6,403	4,616	0.41	-27.91
United Kingdom	19,994	20,747	19,219	16,326	17,749	1.59	8.72
Southern Europe	**29,300**	**30,587**	**27,621**	**41,205**	**42,865**	**3.85**	**4.03**
Italy	10,915	10,379	11,310	14,263	12,327	1.11	-13.57
Spain	18,385	20,208	16,311	26,942	30,538	2.74	13.35
Western Europe	**64,096**	**69,284**	**70,996**	**73,334**	**68,532**	**6.15**	**-6.55**
France	26,331	28,165	32,364	29,587	29,815	2.68	0.77
Germany	22,575	25,691	24,036	26,869	23,043	2.07	-14.24
Netherlands	7,379	7,574	6,906	6,651	6,724	0.60	1.10
Switzerland	7,811	7,854	7,690	10,227	8,950	0.80	-12.49
Other Europe	**30,305**	**31,902**	**41,060**	**33,541**	**33,896**	**3.04**	**1.06**
Other countries of Europe	30,305	31,902	41,060	33,541	33,896	3.04	1.06

94

BOLIVIA

3. Arrivals of non-resident tourists in hotels and similar establishments, by nationality

		2008	2009	2010	2011	2012	Market share 2012	% Change 2012-2011
TOTAL	(*)	490,783	499,811	527,200	560,325	563,486	100.00	0.56
AFRICA		1,467	1,501	1,583	1,635	1,644	0.29	0.55
Other Africa		1,467	1,501	1,583	1,635	1,644	0.29	0.55
All countries of Africa		1,467	1,501	1,583	1,635	1,644	0.29	0.55
AMERICAS		297,443	303,935	320,592	348,185	350,149	62.14	0.56
North America		57,944	59,500	62,762	70,448	70,845	12.57	0.56
Canada		10,622	10,634	11,217	12,951	13,024	2.31	0.56
Mexico		6,420	6,621	6,984	7,335	7,376	1.31	0.56
United States of America		40,902	42,245	44,561	50,162	50,445	8.95	0.56
South America		229,214	234,337	247,179	268,185	269,698	47.86	0.56
Argentina		53,994	55,316	58,347	62,816	63,170	11.21	0.56
Brazil		34,674	35,748	37,707	40,908	41,139	7.30	0.56
Chile		26,218	25,647	27,052	30,947	31,122	5.52	0.57
Colombia		10,239	10,651	11,235	12,813	12,885	2.29	0.56
Ecuador		6,022	6,335	6,682	7,021	7,061	1.25	0.57
Paraguay		5,239	5,418	5,715	5,934	5,967	1.06	0.56
Peru		83,892	85,639	90,332	96,582	97,127	17.24	0.56
Uruguay		3,397	3,815	4,024	4,078	4,101	0.73	0.56
Venezuela		5,539	5,768	6,085	7,086	7,126	1.26	0.56
Other Americas		10,285	10,098	10,651	9,552	9,606	1.70	0.57
Other countries of the Americas		10,285	10,098	10,651	9,552	9,606	1.70	0.57
EAST ASIA AND THE PACIFIC		26,689	27,071	28,554	27,978	28,136	4.99	0.56
North-East Asia		7,419	7,435	7,842	7,536	7,579	1.35	0.57
Japan		7,419	7,435	7,842	7,536	7,579	1.35	0.57
Other East Asia and the Pacific		19,270	19,636	20,712	20,442	20,557	3.65	0.56
Other countries of Asia		7,103	7,121	7,511	7,067	7,107	1.26	0.57
All countries of Oceania		12,167	12,515	13,201	13,375	13,450	2.39	0.56
EUROPE		165,184	167,304	176,471	182,527	183,557	32.58	0.56
Northern Europe		25,725	25,506	26,903	28,082	28,241	5.01	0.57
Sweden		3,335	3,437	3,625	3,657	3,678	0.65	0.57
United Kingdom		22,390	22,069	23,278	24,425	24,563	4.36	0.56
Southern Europe		26,962	27,181	28,670	29,936	30,105	5.34	0.56
Italy		9,632	9,325	9,836	10,935	10,997	1.95	0.57
Spain		17,330	17,856	18,834	19,001	19,108	3.39	0.56
Western Europe		69,805	70,637	74,508	79,650	80,099	14.21	0.56
France		26,990	27,011	28,491	30,697	30,870	5.48	0.56
Germany		23,435	23,847	25,154	26,406	26,555	4.71	0.56
Netherlands		9,540	9,630	10,158	11,924	11,991	2.13	0.56
Switzerland		9,840	10,149	10,705	10,623	10,683	1.90	0.56
East Mediterranean Europe		12,031	12,387	13,066	12,847	12,919	2.29	0.56
Israel		12,031	12,387	13,066	12,847	12,919	2.29	0.56
Other Europe		30,661	31,593	33,324	32,012	32,193	5.71	0.57
Other countries of Europe		30,661	31,593	33,324	32,012	32,193	5.71	0.57

Yearbook of Tourism Statistics, Data 2008 – 2012, 2014 Edition

BOLIVIA

5. Overnight stays of non-resident tourists in hotels and similar establishments, by nationality

		2008	2009	2010	2011	2012	Market share 2012	% Change 2012-2011
TOTAL	(*)	848,486	850,351	864,868	896,294	852,445	100.00	-4.89
AFRICA		4,033	4,079	4,152	4,175	3,971	0.47	-4.89
Other Africa		4,033	4,079	4,152	4,175	3,971	0.47	-4.89
All countries of Africa		4,033	4,079	4,152	4,175	3,971	0.47	-4.89
AMERICAS		531,624	533,163	542,263	564,443	536,829	62.98	-4.89
North America		103,916	104,432	106,213	112,502	106,998	12.55	-4.89
Canada		17,104	16,521	16,802	19,420	18,470	2.17	-4.89
Mexico		11,785	11,842	12,044	13,876	13,197	1.55	-4.89
United States of America		75,027	76,069	77,367	79,206	75,331	8.84	-4.89
South America		392,285	394,018	400,744	415,728	395,390	46.38	-4.89
Argentina		94,231	94,464	96,101	98,214	93,409	10.96	-4.89
Brazil		70,571	71,037	72,349	74,727	71,071	8.34	-4.89
Chile		36,661	36,867	37,496	39,042	37,132	4.36	-4.89
Colombia		27,096	27,460	27,829	28,351	26,964	3.16	-4.89
Ecuador		12,791	12,985	13,207	14,785	14,062	1.65	-4.89
Paraguay		12,552	12,826	13,023	15,956	15,175	1.78	-4.89
Peru		114,404	114,868	116,827	119,423	113,581	13.32	-4.89
Uruguay		6,999	7,096	7,217	7,692	7,316	0.86	-4.89
Venezuela		16,980	16,415	16,695	17,538	16,680	1.96	-4.89
Other Americas		35,423	34,713	35,306	36,213	34,441	4.04	-4.89
Other countries of the Americas		35,423	34,713	35,306	36,213	34,441	4.04	-4.89
EAST ASIA AND THE PACIFIC		44,850	45,356	46,130	48,539	46,165	5.42	-4.89
North-East Asia		16,122	16,245	16,522	17,211	16,369	1.92	-4.89
Japan		16,122	16,245	16,522	17,211	16,369	1.92	-4.89
Other East Asia and the Pacific		28,728	29,111	29,608	31,328	29,796	3.50	-4.89
Other countries of Asia		11,939	12,016	12,221	13,701	13,031	1.53	-4.89
All countries of Oceania		16,789	17,095	17,387	17,627	16,765	1.97	-4.89
EUROPE		267,979	267,753	272,323	279,137	265,480	31.14	-4.89
Northern Europe		38,819	39,081	39,748	41,553	39,519	4.64	-4.89
Sweden		6,619	6,735	6,850	7,967	7,576	0.89	-4.91
United Kingdom		32,200	32,346	32,898	33,586	31,943	3.75	-4.89
Southern Europe		51,217	50,630	51,494	53,010	50,417	5.91	-4.89
Italy		16,550	16,478	16,759	17,298	16,452	1.93	-4.89
Spain		34,667	34,152	34,735	35,712	33,965	3.98	-4.89
Western Europe		99,526	99,740	101,443	104,762	99,637	11.69	-4.89
France		36,511	36,065	36,681	38,005	36,146	4.24	-4.89
Germany		32,800	33,153	33,719	34,576	32,884	3.86	-4.89
Netherlands		14,140	14,335	14,580	15,967	15,186	1.78	-4.89
Switzerland		16,075	16,187	16,463	16,214	15,421	1.81	-4.89
East Mediterranean Europe		29,811	29,424	29,926	30,529	29,035	3.41	-4.89
Israel		29,811	29,424	29,926	30,529	29,035	3.41	-4.89
Other Europe		48,606	48,878	49,712	49,283	46,872	5.50	-4.89
Other countries of Europe		48,606	48,878	49,712	49,283	46,872	5.50	-4.89

Yearbook of Tourism Statistics, Data 2008 – 2012, 2014 Edition

BOSNIA AND HERZEGOVINA

4. Arrivals of non-resident tourists in all types of accommodation establishments, by country of residence

	2008	2009	2010	2011	2012	Market share 2012	% Change 2012-2011
TOTAL	321,511	310,942	365,454	391,945	438,585	100.00	11.90
AMERICAS	8,862	8,126	10,389	10,411	11,947	2.72	14.75
North America	8,862	8,126	10,389	10,411	11,947	2.72	14.75
Canada	1,473	1,462	2,150	1,874	2,204	0.50	17.61
United States of America	7,389	6,664	8,239	8,537	9,743	2.22	14.13
EAST ASIA AND THE PACIFIC	5,348	4,496	7,092	9,464	11,549	2.63	22.03
North-East Asia	2,842	2,379	3,741	5,445	6,795	1.55	24.79
China	534	478	770	2,244	3,369	0.77	50.13
Japan	2,308	1,901	2,971	3,201	3,426	0.78	7.03
Australasia	2,506	2,117	3,351	4,019	4,754	1.08	18.29
Australia	2,238	1,853	2,951	3,601	4,165	0.95	15.66
New Zealand	268	264	400	418	589	0.13	40.91
EUROPE	300,672	291,903	338,500	355,718	384,067	87.57	7.97
Central/Eastern Europe	26,311	27,370	34,236	41,324	48,113	10.97	16.43
Bulgaria	1,632	1,654	1,632	2,133	2,573	0.59	20.63
Czech Republic	3,472	3,171	3,366	3,557	3,913	0.89	10.01
Hungary	4,193	5,124	4,906	5,415	5,920	1.35	9.33
Poland	12,041	12,616	17,888	22,633	27,017	6.16	19.37
Romania	1,433	1,830	2,748	3,048	3,641	0.83	19.46
Russian Federation	1,549	1,526	2,140	2,567	3,061	0.70	19.24
Slovakia	1,991	1,449	1,556	1,971	1,988	0.45	0.86
Northern Europe	15,975	14,406	17,318	17,456	18,056	4.12	3.44
Denmark	1,992	1,637	1,776	1,507	1,611	0.37	6.90
Finland	943	873	1,030	1,027	981	0.22	-4.48
Iceland	103	155	97	82	188	0.04	129.27
Ireland	1,229	983	2,638	1,897	1,428	0.33	-24.72
Norway	2,311	2,332	2,493	2,438	2,259	0.52	-7.34
Sweden	3,804	3,349	3,608	4,551	4,940	1.13	8.55
United Kingdom	5,593	5,077	5,676	5,954	6,649	1.52	11.67
Southern Europe	190,234	179,763	202,443	210,812	220,001	50.16	4.36
Albania	958	1,916	3,996	1,732	2,064	0.47	19.17
Croatia	53,512	50,838	56,100	64,028	72,587	16.55	13.37
Greece	1,459	2,214	2,824	3,623	3,190	0.73	-11.95
Italy	16,090	15,443	23,749	26,379	26,137	5.96	-0.92
Montenegro	8,129	7,848	8,392	7,679	7,474	1.70	-2.67
Portugal	840	840	961	1,119	795	0.18	-28.95
Serbia	60,481	56,221	56,370	54,169	57,380	13.08	5.93
Slovenia	36,596	34,580	40,246	41,267	39,949	9.11	-3.19
Spain	7,618	5,053	5,155	5,662	5,656	1.29	-0.11
TFYR of Macedonia	4,551	4,810	4,650	5,154	4,769	1.09	-7.47
Western Europe	49,526	50,840	53,532	53,830	57,473	13.10	6.77
Austria	12,163	13,005	14,344	14,786	15,990	3.65	8.14
Belgium	2,419	2,401	2,110	1,835	2,138	0.49	16.51
France	9,576	9,291	10,734	9,609	10,141	2.31	5.54
Germany	17,201	17,813	17,281	18,220	19,581	4.46	7.47
Luxembourg	467	343	192	254	224	0.05	-11.81
Netherlands	4,703	5,124	5,567	5,465	5,141	1.17	-5.93
Switzerland	2,997	2,863	3,304	3,661	4,258	0.97	16.31
East Mediterranean Europe	14,369	15,397	25,834	27,724	35,397	8.07	27.68
Israel	2,278	1,737	1,810	1,831	2,895	0.66	58.11
Turkey	12,091	13,660	24,024	25,893	32,502	7.41	25.52
Other Europe	4,257	4,127	5,137	4,572	5,027	1.15	9.95
Other countries of Europe	4,257	4,127	5,137	4,572	5,027	1.15	9.95

Yearbook of Tourism Statistics, Data 2008 – 2012, 2014 Edition

BOSNIA AND HERZEGOVINA

4. Arrivals of non-resident tourists in all types of accommodation establishments, by country of residence

	2008	2009	2010	2011	2012	Market share 2012	% Change 2012-2011
MIDDLE EAST	330	313	624	937	1,754	0.40	87.19
Egypt	145	134	160	286	324	0.07	13.29
Saudi Arabia	185	179	464	651	1,430	0.33	119.66
SOUTH ASIA	151	206	253	167	163	0.04	-2.40
Iran, Islamic Republic of	151	206	253	167	163	0.04	-2.40
NOT SPECIFIED	6,148	5,898	8,596	15,248	29,105	6.64	90.88
Other countries of the World	6,148	5,898	8,596	15,248	29,105	6.64	90.88

Yearbook of Tourism Statistics, Data 2008 – 2012, 2014 Edition

BOSNIA AND HERZEGOVINA

6. Overnight stays of non-resident tourists in all types of accommodation establishments, by country of residence

	2008	2009	2010	2011	2012	Market share 2012	% Change 2012-2011
TOTAL	718,750	671,128	772,754	836,005	931,081	100.00	11.37
AMERICAS	23,321	23,040	26,540	24,145	25,425	2.73	5.30
North America	23,321	23,040	26,540	24,145	25,425	2.73	5.30
Canada	3,475	3,496	4,159	3,599	4,538	0.49	26.09
United States of America	19,846	19,544	22,381	20,546	20,887	2.24	1.66
EAST ASIA AND THE PACIFIC	9,418	7,817	10,869	14,789	17,755	1.91	20.06
North-East Asia	5,298	4,210	5,523	8,438	10,000	1.07	18.51
China	1,322	934	1,255	3,874	4,880	0.52	25.97
Japan	3,976	3,276	4,268	4,564	5,120	0.55	12.18
Australasia	4,120	3,607	5,346	6,351	7,755	0.83	22.11
Australia	3,674	3,143	4,815	5,744	6,918	0.74	20.44
New Zealand	446	464	531	607	837	0.09	37.89
EUROPE	669,347	620,832	708,598	758,494	807,045	86.68	6.40
Central/Eastern Europe	73,837	71,731	95,613	116,052	127,820	13.73	10.14
Bulgaria	3,784	4,077	3,845	4,591	5,146	0.55	12.09
Czech Republic	11,414	9,744	10,387	11,015	9,757	1.05	-11.42
Hungary	7,293	11,404	9,996	12,833	11,310	1.21	-11.87
Poland	36,776	33,467	54,989	65,853	75,009	8.06	13.90
Romania	3,490	4,576	6,545	9,253	9,709	1.04	4.93
Russian Federation	4,526	4,889	6,300	7,699	12,549	1.35	63.00
Slovakia	6,554	3,574	3,551	4,808	4,340	0.47	-9.73
Northern Europe	38,461	34,974	45,787	42,146	41,632	4.47	-1.22
Denmark	4,789	4,117	4,359	3,670	3,692	0.40	0.60
Finland	1,895	1,984	2,046	2,428	1,872	0.20	-22.90
Iceland	174	774	208	351	544	0.06	54.99
Ireland	2,974	2,667	13,440	8,296	5,152	0.55	-37.90
Norway	4,914	4,612	5,125	5,278	5,238	0.56	-0.76
Sweden	10,179	8,943	9,185	9,939	12,221	1.31	22.96
United Kingdom	13,536	11,877	11,424	12,184	12,913	1.39	5.98
Southern Europe	405,861	358,304	392,490	421,745	447,594	48.07	6.13
Albania	1,943	3,183	7,236	3,201	3,926	0.42	22.65
Croatia	108,233	93,601	104,863	130,326	150,814	16.20	15.72
Greece	3,916	4,718	8,128	6,625	6,094	0.65	-8.02
Italy	31,826	32,685	49,113	54,485	56,001	6.01	2.78
Montenegro	21,123	19,506	22,830	19,174	18,384	1.97	-4.12
Portugal	1,713	2,129	2,132	2,325	1,885	0.20	-18.92
Serbia	142,811	120,850	113,840	114,424	121,639	13.06	6.31
Slovenia	68,493	60,762	64,959	69,960	69,183	7.43	-1.11
Spain	16,547	11,337	10,398	10,429	9,497	1.02	-8.94
TFYR of Macedonia	9,256	9,533	8,991	10,796	10,171	1.09	-5.79
Western Europe	106,682	112,843	115,270	115,108	115,325	12.39	0.19
Austria	21,920	22,734	25,229	27,885	28,620	3.07	2.64
Belgium	5,636	5,751	5,180	4,426	4,377	0.47	-1.11
France	25,881	24,835	28,476	24,882	22,399	2.41	-9.98
Germany	35,493	40,944	36,925	37,627	38,968	4.19	3.56
Luxembourg	1,221	693	396	810	610	0.07	-24.69
Netherlands	10,607	11,840	12,531	12,142	11,190	1.20	-7.84
Switzerland	5,924	6,046	6,533	7,336	9,161	0.98	24.88
East Mediterranean Europe	34,580	34,837	48,795	53,893	63,791	6.85	18.37
Israel	3,499	2,900	3,446	3,483	4,823	0.52	38.47
Turkey	31,081	31,937	45,349	50,410	58,968	6.33	16.98
Other Europe	9,926	8,143	10,643	9,550	10,883	1.17	13.96
Other countries of Europe	9,926	8,143	10,643	9,550	10,883	1.17	13.96

Yearbook of Tourism Statistics, Data 2008 – 2012, 2014 Edition

BOSNIA AND HERZEGOVINA

6. Overnight stays of non-resident tourists in all types of accommodation establishments, by country of residence

	2008	2009	2010	2011	2012	Market share 2012	% Change 2012-2011
MIDDLE EAST	**1,358**	**1,048**	**1,689**	**2,762**	**5,081**	**0.55**	**83.96**
Egypt	682	381	545	763	986	0.11	29.23
Saudi Arabia	676	667	1,144	1,999	4,095	0.44	104.85
SOUTH ASIA	**425**	**580**	**577**	**526**	**514**	**0.06**	**-2.28**
Iran, Islamic Republic of	425	580	577	526	514	0.06	-2.28
NOT SPECIFIED	**14,881**	**17,811**	**24,481**	**35,289**	**75,261**	**8.08**	**113.27**
Other countries of the World	14,881	17,811	24,481	35,289	75,261	8.08	113.27

Yearbook of Tourism Statistics, Data 2008 – 2012, 2014 Edition

BRAZIL

1. Arrivals of non-resident tourists at national borders, by country of residence

	2008	2009	2010	2011	2012	Market share 2012	% Change 2012-2011
TOTAL	5,050,099	4,802,217	5,161,379	5,433,354	5,676,843	100.00	4.48
AFRICA	75,824	78,110	83,688	86,511	92,349	1.63	6.75
Central Africa	25,307	36,123	38,051	37,221	37,779	0.67	1.50
Angola	25,307	36,123	38,051	37,221	37,779	0.67	1.50
Southern Africa	29,429	23,132	21,311	22,754	23,047	0.41	1.29
South Africa	29,429	23,132	21,311	22,754	23,047	0.41	1.29
West Africa	7,540	6,108	5,391	5,993	6,898	0.12	15.10
Cape Verde	4,781	4,233	2,664	2,736	3,235	0.06	18.24
Nigeria	2,759	1,875	2,727	3,257	3,663	0.06	12.47
Other Africa	13,548	12,747	18,935	20,543	24,625	0.43	19.87
Other countries of Africa	13,548	12,747	18,935	20,543	24,625	0.43	19.87
AMERICAS	2,883,839	2,862,171	3,196,300	3,401,592	3,582,256	63.10	5.31
Caribbean	6,268	3,550	4,004	4,246	4,292	0.08	1.08
Cuba	6,268	3,550	4,004	4,246	4,292	0.08	1.08
Central America	41,800	28,271	34,929	38,633	38,862	0.68	0.59
Costa Rica	10,548	8,539	9,792	10,125	10,284	0.18	1.57
Guatemala	6,294	3,725	5,136	5,453	5,294	0.09	-2.92
Panama	8,148	5,153	6,424	7,344	7,496	0.13	2.07
Other countries of Central America	16,810	10,854	13,577	15,711	15,788	0.28	0.49
North America	765,380	734,998	773,181	729,756	716,583	12.62	-1.81
Canada	62,681	63,296	64,188	70,358	68,462	1.21	-2.69
Mexico	77,193	68,028	67,616	64,451	61,658	1.09	-4.33
United States of America	625,506	603,674	641,377	594,947	586,463	10.33	-1.43
South America	2,070,391	2,095,352	2,384,186	2,628,957	2,822,519	49.72	7.36
Argentina	1,017,675	1,211,159	1,399,592	1,593,775	1,671,604	29.45	4.88
Bolivia	84,072	83,454	99,359	85,429	112,639	1.98	31.85
Chile	240,087	170,491	200,724	217,200	250,586	4.41	15.37
Colombia	96,846	78,010	85,567	91,345	100,324	1.77	9.83
Ecuador	32,018	26,220	23,095	25,495	26,462	0.47	3.79
French Guiana	15,275	15,152	12,592	9,457	9,278	0.16	-1.89
Guyana	6,292	4,594	5,236	4,314	3,400	0.06	-21.19
Paraguay	217,709	180,373	194,340	192,730	246,401	4.34	27.85
Peru	93,693	78,975	81,020	86,795	91,996	1.62	5.99
Suriname	4,699	3,626	2,930	3,952	4,859	0.09	22.95
Uruguay	199,403	189,412	228,545	261,204	253,864	4.47	-2.81
Venezuela	62,622	53,886	51,186	57,261	51,106	0.90	-10.75
EAST ASIA AND THE PACIFIC	256,271	208,379	210,582	260,642	294,228	5.18	12.89
North-East Asia	163,149	119,025	128,450	163,855	189,036	3.33	15.37
China	39,514	28,230	37,849	55,978	65,945	1.16	17.81
Japan	81,270	66,655	59,742	63,247	73,102	1.29	15.58
Korea, Republic of	42,365	24,140	30,859	44,630	49,989	0.88	12.01
Australasia	46,349	48,186	45,982	44,451	52,503	0.92	18.11
Australia	37,034	38,756	36,846	35,642	43,161	0.76	21.10
New Zealand	9,315	9,430	9,136	8,809	9,342	0.16	6.05
Other East Asia and the Pacific	46,773	41,168	36,150	52,336	52,689	0.93	0.67
Other countries of Asia	46,122	41,059	35,830	52,130	52,377	0.92	0.47
Other countries of Oceania	651	109	320	206	312	0.01	51.46
EUROPE	1,814,146	1,642,070	1,651,840	1,662,829	1,685,728	29.69	1.38
Central/Eastern Europe	46,666	35,913	40,224	50,601	56,170	0.99	11.01
Czech Republic	7,162	5,258	5,732	6,774	7,657	0.13	13.04
Hungary	6,989	5,525	4,854	5,045	5,240	0.09	3.87
Poland	18,665	15,092	13,775	16,427	18,132	0.32	10.38
Russian Federation	13,850	10,038	15,863	22,355	25,141	0.44	12.46

101

BRAZIL

1. Arrivals of non-resident tourists at national borders, by country of residence

	2008	2009	2010	2011	2012	Market share 2012	% Change 2012-2011
Northern Europe	321,566	297,534	280,480	267,938	274,391	4.83	2.41
Denmark	25,539	25,645	21,460	22,208	22,780	0.40	2.58
Finland	17,826	15,873	13,251	13,049	11,994	0.21	-8.08
Ireland	21,999	17,620	16,475	16,871	18,457	0.33	9.40
Norway	31,429	29,339	27,793	30,462	30,319	0.53	-0.47
Sweden	43,594	36,414	34,146	35,784	35,293	0.62	-1.37
United Kingdom	181,179	172,643	167,355	149,564	155,548	2.74	4.00
Southern Europe	701,274	619,318	621,433	610,027	585,512	10.31	-4.02
Greece	10,368	7,550	7,537	6,423	6,343	0.11	-1.25
Italy	265,724	253,545	245,491	229,484	230,114	4.05	0.27
Portugal	222,558	183,697	189,065	183,728	168,649	2.97	-8.21
Spain	202,624	174,526	179,340	190,392	180,406	3.18	-5.24
Western Europe	670,255	625,420	633,388	647,075	681,971	12.01	5.39
Austria	26,506	24,185	26,603	26,560	28,035	0.49	5.55
Belgium	31,940	31,526	34,030	32,773	34,169	0.60	4.26
France	214,440	205,860	199,719	207,890	218,626	3.85	5.16
Germany	254,264	215,595	226,630	241,739	258,437	4.55	6.91
Netherlands	81,936	75,518	76,411	72,162	73,133	1.29	1.35
Switzerland	61,169	72,736	69,995	65,951	69,571	1.23	5.49
East Mediterranean Europe	37,813	29,405	36,976	41,646	33,523	0.59	-19.50
Israel	37,813	29,405	36,976	41,646	33,523	0.59	-19.50
Other Europe	36,572	34,480	39,339	45,542	54,161	0.95	18.93
Other countries of Europe	36,572	34,480	39,339	45,542	54,161	0.95	18.93
SOUTH ASIA	19,456	11,361	18,829	21,530	22,096	0.39	2.63
India	19,456	11,361	18,829	21,530	22,096	0.39	2.63
NOT SPECIFIED	563	126	140	250	186	0.00	-25.60
Other countries of the World	563	126	140	250	186	0.00	-25.60

102

BRITISH VIRGIN ISLANDS

1. Arrivals of non-resident tourists at national borders, by country of residence

	2008	2009	2010	2011	2012	Market share 2012	% Change 2012-2011
TOTAL	346,035	308,792	330,343				
AMERICAS	296,230	263,466	280,233				
Caribbean	44,982	41,148	44,963				
Antigua and Barbuda	1,563	1,375	1,440				
Barbados	1,038	923	971				
Dominica	1,814	1,653	1,777				
Dominican Republic	945	830	880				
Grenada	564	503	532				
Haiti	52	80	64				
Jamaica	1,611	1,448	1,574				
Puerto Rico	16,764	14,890	15,628				
Saint Kitts and Nevis	3,326	2,950	3,107				
Saint Lucia	799	715	764				
Saint Vincent and the Grenadines	1,992	1,758	1,884				
Trinidad and Tobago	1,604	1,420	1,484				
Other countries of the Caribbean	12,910	12,603	14,858				
North America	248,057	219,510	232,221				
Canada	8,675	7,741	8,408				
United States of America	239,382	211,769	223,813				
South America	918	824	858				
Guyana	918	824	858				
Other Americas	2,273	1,984	2,191				
Other countries of the Americas	2,273	1,984	2,191				
EUROPE	41,728	37,591	41,184				
Northern Europe	20,598	18,417	20,004				
Sweden	667	589	632				
United Kingdom	19,931	17,828	19,372				
Southern Europe	4,840	4,549	5,146				
Italy	3,938	3,729	4,225				
Spain	902	820	921				
Western Europe	11,400	10,270	11,346				
France	5,933	5,347	5,901				
Germany	4,208	3,834	4,275				
Netherlands	1,259	1,089	1,170				
Other Europe	4,890	4,355	4,688				
Other countries of Europe	4,890	4,355	4,688				
NOT SPECIFIED	8,077	7,735	8,926				
Other countries of the World	8,077	7,735	8,926				

Yearbook of Tourism Statistics, Data 2008 – 2012, 2014 Edition

BRITISH VIRGIN ISLANDS

2. Arrivals of non-resident visitors at national borders, by country of residence

	2008	2009	2010	2011	2012	Market share 2012	% Change 2012-2011
TOTAL	934,269	856,865	842,498				
AMERICAS	685,901	628,154	616,341				
Caribbean	32,939	30,691	30,565				
All countries of the Caribbean	32,939	30,691	30,565				
North America	644,458	589,792	578,303				
Canada	33,439	29,928	28,773				
United States of America	611,019	559,864	549,530				
South America	8,504	7,671	7,473				
All countries of South America	8,504	7,671	7,473				
EUROPE	231,849	215,017	212,248				
Other Europe	231,849	215,017	212,248				
All countries of Europe	231,849	215,017	212,248				
NOT SPECIFIED	16,519	13,694	13,909				
Other countries of the World	16,519	13,694	13,909				

Yearbook of Tourism Statistics, Data 2008 – 2012, 2014 Edition

BRUNEI DARUSSALAM

1. Arrivals of non-resident tourists at national borders, by nationality

		2008	2009	2010	2011	2012	Market share 2012	% Change 2012-2011
TOTAL	(*)	225,757	157,474	214,290	242,061	209,108	100.00	-13.61
AMERICAS		5,652	5,108	5,940	6,611	6,304	3.01	-4.64
North America		5,652	5,108	5,940	6,611	6,304	3.01	-4.64
Canada		2,244	1,940	2,199	2,411	2,237	1.07	-7.22
United States of America		3,408	3,168	3,741	4,200	4,067	1.94	-3.17
EAST ASIA AND THE PACIFIC		186,475	121,652	170,555	194,809	169,641	81.13	-12.92
North-East Asia		53,277	23,637	33,055	41,397	40,227	19.24	-2.83
China		27,652	15,800	24,579	32,853	27,490	13.15	-16.32
Hong Kong, China		1,782	1,197	1,210	1,270	1,601	0.77	26.06
Japan		4,489	3,549	3,637	4,140	4,310	2.06	4.11
Korea, Republic of		17,548	1,604	1,712	1,696	4,277	2.05	152.18
Taiwan, Province of China		1,806	1,487	1,917	1,438	2,549	1.22	77.26
South-East Asia		98,039	75,955	109,939	124,186	115,902	55.43	-6.67
Asean countries		98,039						
Cambodia			133	251	227	216	0.10	-4.85
Indonesia			8,576	16,343	20,350	18,245	8.73	-10.34
Lao People's Democratic Republic			44	106	123	165	0.08	34.15
Malaysia			38,193	54,127	61,470	56,214	26.88	-8.55
Myanmar			300	529	522	570	0.27	9.20
Philippines			11,013	14,720	17,446	19,189	9.18	9.99
Singapore			14,221	15,973	16,221	15,933	7.62	-1.78
Thailand			3,390	4,589	4,809	3,997	1.91	-16.89
Viet Nam			85	3,301	3,018	1,373	0.66	-54.51
Australasia		35,159	22,060	27,561	29,226	13,512	6.46	-53.77
Australia		25,732	13,824	17,237	18,845	11,877	5.68	-36.98
New Zealand		9,427	8,236	10,324	10,381	1,635	0.78	-84.25
EUROPE		22,765	21,553	26,199	28,581	20,837	9.96	-27.09
Central/Eastern Europe		290	705	989	1,009	934	0.45	-7.43
Czech Republic			355	305	228	104	0.05	-54.39
Poland			155	297	352	351	0.17	-0.28
Russian Federation		290	195	387	429	479	0.23	11.66
Northern Europe		17,386	15,687	18,834	20,203	12,960	6.20	-35.85
Denmark		327	276	343	363	256	0.12	-29.48
Finland			129	145	151	234	0.11	54.97
Ireland		427	322	379	699	376	0.18	-46.21
Norway			261	250	400	339	0.16	-15.25
Sweden		440	313	301	368	354	0.17	-3.80
United Kingdom		16,192	14,386	17,416	18,222	11,401	5.45	-37.43
Southern Europe		674	847	1,162	1,293	1,080	0.52	-16.47
Greece			40	91	81	91	0.04	12.35
Italy		674	467	524	676	561	0.27	-17.01
Portugal			107	184	218	128	0.06	-41.28
Spain			233	363	318	300	0.14	-5.66
Western Europe		4,415	4,314	5,214	6,076	5,863	2.80	-3.51
Austria			89	88	86	128	0.06	48.84
Belgium			192	219	219	197	0.09	-10.05
France		1,350	1,195	1,315	2,301	1,780	0.85	-22.64
Germany		1,693	1,520	1,713	1,819	1,706	0.82	-6.21
Netherlands		1,035	1,081	1,127	1,332	1,437	0.69	7.88
Switzerland		337	237	752	319	615	0.29	92.79
MIDDLE EAST			711	1,571	1,527	819	0.39	-46.37
Bahrain			42	51	34	36	0.02	5.88
Kuwait			48	58	53	67	0.03	26.42

Yearbook of Tourism Statistics, Data 2008 – 2012, 2014 Edition

BRUNEI DARUSSALAM

1. Arrivals of non-resident tourists at national borders, by nationality

	2008	2009	2010	2011	2012	Market share 2012	% Change 2012-2011
Oman		160	174	266	242	0.12	-9.02
Qatar		14	19	20	94	0.04	370.00
Saudi Arabia		261	1,021	837	180	0.09	-78.49
United Arab Emirates		186	248	317	200	0.10	-36.91
SOUTH ASIA	**5,317**	**4,451**	**7,241**	**7,573**	**7,782**	**3.72**	**2.76**
Bangladesh	430	387	844	1,004	996	0.48	-0.80
India	3,540	2,879	4,904	4,616	5,104	2.44	10.57
Nepal	801	483	597	986	677	0.32	-31.34
Pakistan	546	474	607	579	509	0.24	-12.09
Sri Lanka		228	289	388	496	0.24	27.84
NOT SPECIFIED	**5,548**	**3,999**	**2,784**	**2,960**	**3,725**	**1.78**	**25.84**
Other countries of the World	5,548	3,999	2,784	2,960	3,725	1.78	25.84

Yearbook of Tourism Statistics, Data 2008 – 2012, 2014 Edition

BULGARIA

2. Arrivals of non-resident visitors at national borders, by country of residence

	2008	2009	2010	2011	2012	Market share 2012	% Change 2012-2011
TOTAL	8,532,972	7,872,805	8,374,034	8,712,821	8,866,552	100.00	1.76
AFRICA	2,178	2,242	2,452	2,323	2,608	0.03	12.27
East Africa	38	25	54	39	80	0.00	105.13
Ethiopia	38	25	54	39	80	0.00	105.13
North Africa	1,635	1,695	1,921	1,876	1,931	0.02	2.93
Algeria	434	425	499	457	506	0.01	10.72
Morocco	582	686	617	614	841	0.01	36.97
Sudan	123	126	130	346	147	0.00	-57.51
Tunisia	496	458	675	459	437	0.00	-4.79
West Africa	505	522	477	408	597	0.01	46.32
Ghana	98	107	116	66	83	0.00	25.76
Nigeria	407	415	361	342	514	0.01	50.29
AMERICAS	91,956	82,101	83,617	87,722	93,603	1.06	6.70
Caribbean	322	402	334	279	357	0.00	27.96
Cuba	322	402	334	279	357	0.00	27.96
North America	87,642	77,406	78,787	82,095	87,596	0.99	6.70
Canada	14,228	13,262	14,260	14,849	16,061	0.18	8.16
Mexico	1,919	1,438	1,745	1,763	2,212	0.02	25.47
United States of America	71,495	62,706	62,782	65,483	69,323	0.78	5.86
South America	3,992	4,293	4,496	5,348	5,650	0.06	5.65
Argentina	1,004	1,155	980	995	1,216	0.01	22.21
Brazil	2,486	2,666	2,954	3,744	3,849	0.04	2.80
Venezuela	502	472	562	609	585	0.01	-3.94
EAST ASIA AND THE PACIFIC	48,049	41,773	43,772	51,145	56,053	0.63	9.60
North-East Asia	24,810	22,571	25,604	30,257	33,858	0.38	11.90
China	6,207	6,165	6,438	6,638	8,685	0.10	30.84
Japan	9,830	8,458	9,969	10,236	11,148	0.13	8.91
Korea, Republic of	8,445	7,582	8,834	12,940	13,508	0.15	4.39
Mongolia	328	366	363	443	517	0.01	16.70
South-East Asia	5,693	4,593	4,116	3,869	5,207	0.06	34.58
Indonesia	2,960	2,034	1,674	1,667	2,438	0.03	46.25
Viet Nam	2,733	2,559	2,442	2,202	2,769	0.03	25.75
Australasia	17,546	14,609	14,052	17,019	16,988	0.19	-0.18
Australia	14,294	11,941	11,461	14,267	14,207	0.16	-0.42
New Zealand	3,252	2,668	2,591	2,752	2,781	0.03	1.05
EUROPE	8,260,649	7,602,264	8,080,924	8,389,436	8,525,443	96.15	1.62
Central/Eastern Europe	3,042,840	2,705,690	2,875,306	3,058,269	3,273,290	36.92	7.03
Belarus	28,034	36,882	49,163	43,450	84,684	0.96	94.90
Czech Republic	167,738	197,863	184,440	176,135	173,739	1.96	-1.36
Hungary	151,237	137,195	124,438	123,735	120,883	1.36	-2.30
Poland	257,713	304,659	294,131	289,742	286,267	3.23	-1.20
Republic of Moldova	59,567	75,740	93,468	109,862	113,888	1.28	3.66
Romania	1,769,194	1,398,694	1,445,342	1,499,415	1,468,179	16.56	-2.08
Russian Federation	296,918	295,713	389,864	469,772	609,630	6.88	29.77
Slovakia	161,621	104,243	95,380	94,355	90,076	1.02	-4.54
Ukraine	150,818	154,701	199,080	251,803	325,944	3.68	29.44
Northern Europe	850,305	639,799	578,807	562,614	494,720	5.58	-12.07
Denmark	122,364	90,672	84,172	81,860	72,216	0.81	-11.78
Finland	77,021	57,057	45,527	43,620	38,926	0.44	-10.76
Iceland	6,647	4,294	2,131	2,055	1,845	0.02	-10.22
Ireland	67,090	46,102	33,089	29,941	26,722	0.30	-10.75
Norway	87,362	59,598	55,414	48,707	28,993	0.33	-40.47
Sweden	118,913	65,148	48,992	49,492	43,942	0.50	-11.21
United Kingdom	370,908	316,928	309,482	306,939	282,076	3.18	-8.10

Yearbook of Tourism Statistics, Data 2008 – 2012, 2014 Edition

BULGARIA

2. Arrivals of non-resident visitors at national borders, by country of residence

	2008	2009	2010	2011	2012	Market share 2012	% Change 2012-2011
Southern Europe	1,763,094	1,732,575	2,022,288	2,257,849	2,237,346	25.23	-0.91
Albania	10,415	12,993	14,241	26,512	27,966	0.32	5.48
Bosnia and Herzegovina	20,140	18,626	16,972	38,551	41,882	0.47	8.64
Croatia	26,036	22,802	21,355	26,520	23,781	0.27	-10.33
Greece	881,458	924,220	1,017,914	1,120,640	1,087,260	12.26	-2.98
Italy	104,931	126,108	125,683	130,259	128,851	1.45	-1.08
Malta	10,757	7,479	6,370	4,178	4,369	0.05	4.57
Montenegro	1,831	5,237	11,515	14,401	13,501	0.15	-6.25
Portugal	11,536	9,339	9,381	9,099	7,325	0.08	-19.50
Serbia	311,666	217,940	307,838	365,644	396,448	4.47	8.42
Slovenia	20,055	22,871	22,550	22,340	22,459	0.25	0.53
Spain	40,869	54,847	58,499	60,026	59,322	0.67	-1.17
TFYR of Macedonia	323,400	310,113	409,970	439,679	424,182	4.78	-3.52
Western Europe	1,357,524	1,578,158	1,508,192	1,489,738	1,421,600	16.03	-4.57
Austria	157,027	182,075	181,577	186,438	185,242	2.09	-0.64
Belgium	93,269	96,334	91,183	91,947	95,678	1.08	4.06
France	148,417	196,174	181,317	182,407	180,060	2.03	-1.29
Germany	759,660	898,352	853,430	836,845	784,678	8.85	-6.23
Luxembourg	5,159	6,408	4,681	4,432	4,232	0.05	-4.51
Netherlands	165,231	157,485	156,436	149,193	144,382	1.63	-3.22
Switzerland	28,761	41,330	39,568	38,476	27,328	0.31	-28.97
East Mediterranean Europe	1,246,886	946,042	1,096,331	1,020,966	1,098,487	12.39	7.59
Cyprus	24,324	22,557	22,050	21,361	18,689	0.21	-12.51
Israel	105,882	106,825	131,144	138,951	95,586	1.08	-31.21
Turkey	1,116,680	816,660	943,137	860,654	984,212	11.10	14.36
MIDDLE EAST	21,875	21,352	25,413	23,972	29,646	0.33	23.67
Egypt	1,865	1,848	1,633	1,902	2,545	0.03	33.81
Iraq	1,392	2,551	2,849	2,633	4,300	0.05	63.31
Jordan	2,038	1,606	1,941	1,573	1,376	0.02	-12.52
Kuwait	1,352	998	1,685	2,977	3,412	0.04	14.61
Lebanon	5,056	4,794	5,543	4,997	5,776	0.07	15.59
Libya	414	390	390	169	372	0.00	120.12
Saudi Arabia	244	156	214	217	233	0.00	7.37
Syrian Arab Republic	9,286	8,837	10,962	9,368	11,375	0.13	21.42
United Arab Emirates	228	172	196	136	257	0.00	88.97
SOUTH ASIA	21,294	23,025	24,105	27,129	25,911	0.29	-4.49
Afghanistan	367	441	353	424	620	0.01	46.23
Bangladesh	120	178	180	128	162	0.00	26.56
India	4,605	4,106	3,696	3,849	4,722	0.05	22.68
Iran, Islamic Republic of	15,714	17,782	19,299	22,026	19,459	0.22	-11.65
Pakistan	488	518	577	702	948	0.01	35.04
NOT SPECIFIED	86,971	100,048	113,751	131,094	133,288	1.50	1.67
Other countries of the World	86,971	100,048	113,751	131,094	133,288	1.50	1.67

Yearbook of Tourism Statistics, Data 2008 – 2012, 2014 Edition

BULGARIA

3. Arrivals of non-resident tourists in hotels and similar establishments, by country of residence

	2008	2009	2010	2011	2012	Market share 2012	% Change 2012-2011
TOTAL	2,204,650	1,931,258	2,064,167	2,387,427	2,579,134	100.00	8.03
AFRICA	1,379	796	674	808	1,445	0.06	78.84
Southern Africa	1,379	796	674	808	1,445	0.06	78.84
South Africa	1,379	796	674	808	1,445	0.06	78.84
AMERICAS	50,655	37,648	41,281	42,687	48,428	1.88	13.45
North America	36,309	30,668	34,935	39,646	45,349	1.76	14.38
Canada	7,247	4,197	5,076	5,936	6,754	0.26	13.78
United States of America	29,062	26,471	29,859	33,710	38,595	1.50	14.49
South America	14,346	6,980	6,346	3,041	3,079	0.12	1.25
Brazil	14,346	6,980	6,346	3,041	3,079	0.12	1.25
EAST ASIA AND THE PACIFIC	114,984	117,952	130,119	150,226	38,021	1.47	-74.69
North-East Asia	17,301	16,007	21,335	24,928	29,352	1.14	17.75
China	2,574	3,851	3,847	5,439	9,095	0.35	67.22
Japan	12,185	9,942	13,332	12,749	13,501	0.52	5.90
Korea, Republic of	2,542	2,214	4,156	6,740	6,756	0.26	0.24
Australasia	7,251	4,659	5,467	7,846	8,669	0.34	10.49
Australia	7,251	4,659	5,467	7,846	8,669	0.34	10.49
Other East Asia and the Pacific	90,432	97,286	103,317	117,452			
Other countries of Asia	90,432	97,286	103,317	117,452			
EUROPE	1,931,433	1,686,025	1,770,522	2,054,116	2,321,070	89.99	13.00
Central/Eastern Europe	576,504	589,654	667,050	872,086	1,022,723	39.65	17.27
Czech Republic	33,589	34,565	36,261	44,259	58,249	2.26	31.61
Estonia	7,902	5,193	5,004	6,172	7,684	0.30	24.50
Hungary	25,629	20,661	24,991	31,994	31,239	1.21	-2.36
Latvia	6,055	4,423	3,677	4,868	7,080	0.27	45.44
Lithuania	5,590	4,890	4,044	7,014	11,180	0.43	59.40
Poland	56,772	61,427	83,997	110,661	127,214	4.93	14.96
Romania	192,585	243,253	259,225	332,740	332,022	12.87	-0.22
Russian Federation	198,466	175,695	196,211	246,464	323,731	12.55	31.35
Slovakia	20,938	15,276	17,186	28,032	31,203	1.21	11.31
Ukraine	28,978	24,271	36,454	59,882	93,121	3.61	55.51
Northern Europe	383,487	281,152	274,242	283,446	288,708	11.19	1.86
Denmark	46,478	30,706	31,701	28,976	27,601	1.07	-4.75
Finland	37,190	26,434	25,262	25,463	20,280	0.79	-20.36
Iceland	2,066	3,141	1,153	1,647	1,014	0.04	-38.43
Ireland	24,983	15,386	11,349	11,527	9,922	0.38	-13.92
Norway	39,325	31,011	31,602	40,778	40,859	1.58	0.20
Sweden	47,798	30,425	25,828	26,789	24,644	0.96	-8.01
United Kingdom	185,647	144,049	147,347	148,266	164,388	6.37	10.87
Southern Europe	254,869	226,491	234,003	225,396	206,895	8.02	-8.21
Greece	144,685	123,084	139,868	126,586	108,371	4.20	-14.39
Italy	53,756	52,337	48,282	54,312	55,524	2.15	2.23
Malta	9,015	4,196	1,516	1,999	2,893	0.11	44.72
Portugal	9,177	6,889	7,870	5,903	5,587	0.22	-5.35
Slovenia	8,927	11,698	9,727	11,390	10,767	0.42	-5.47
Spain	29,309	28,287	26,740	25,206	23,753	0.92	-5.76
Western Europe	613,024	495,853	484,213	544,773	569,262	22.07	4.50
Austria	34,818	28,912	30,900	35,206	39,078	1.52	11.00
Belgium	49,889	34,394	33,096	35,482	34,728	1.35	-2.13
France	89,890	83,457	68,062	70,223	72,855	2.82	3.75
Germany	377,322	299,031	305,048	352,518	370,588	14.37	5.13
Luxembourg	3,293	2,902	1,975	2,655	2,389	0.09	-10.02
Netherlands	42,124	35,658	34,110	34,259	33,925	1.32	-0.97
Switzerland	15,688	11,499	11,022	14,430	15,699	0.61	8.79

Yearbook of Tourism Statistics, Data 2008 – 2012, 2014 Edition

BULGARIA

3. Arrivals of non-resident tourists in hotels and similar establishments, by country of residence

	2008	2009	2010	2011	2012	Market share 2012	% Change 2012-2011
East Mediterranean Europe	**55,806**	**48,803**	**54,148**	**56,215**	**149,514**	**5.80**	**165.97**
Cyprus	10,775	8,198	6,486	6,484	5,553	0.22	-14.36
Israel					77,094	2.99	
Turkey	45,031	40,605	47,662	49,731	66,867	2.59	34.46
Other Europe	**47,743**	**44,072**	**56,866**	**72,200**	**83,968**	**3.26**	**16.30**
Other countries of Europe	47,743	44,072	56,866	72,200	83,968	3.26	16.30
NOT SPECIFIED	**106,199**	**88,837**	**121,571**	**139,590**	**170,170**	**6.60**	**21.91**
Other countries of the World	106,199	88,837	121,571	139,590	170,170	6.60	21.91

Yearbook of Tourism Statistics, Data 2008 – 2012, 2014 Edition

BULGARIA

4. Arrivals of non-resident tourists in all types of accommodation establishments, by country of residence

	2008	2009	2010	2011	2012	Market share 2012	% Change 2012-2011
TOTAL	2,226,185	1,948,000	2,084,300	2,422,524	2,632,062	100.00	8.65
AMERICAS	31,576	26,767	30,182	34,076	39,581	1.50	16.16
North America	31,576	26,767	30,182	34,076	39,581	1.50	16.16
United States of America	31,576	26,767	30,182	34,076	39,581	1.50	16.16
EAST ASIA AND THE PACIFIC	12,191	9,952	13,381	12,823	13,969	0.53	8.94
North-East Asia	12,191	9,952	13,381	12,823	13,969	0.53	8.94
Japan	12,191	9,952	13,381	12,823	13,969	0.53	8.94
EUROPE	2,032,421	1,788,994	1,884,543	2,191,202	2,355,534	89.49	7.50
Central/Eastern Europe	583,538	595,205	674,367	887,229	1,048,139	39.82	18.14
Czech Republic	34,845	34,951	36,856	45,027	59,772	2.27	32.75
Estonia	7,921	5,207	5,027	6,224	7,758	0.29	24.65
Hungary	25,947	20,946	25,232	32,613	31,950	1.21	-2.03
Latvia	6,119	4,435	3,707	4,935	7,234	0.27	46.59
Lithuania	5,623	4,904	4,082	7,055	11,355	0.43	60.95
Poland	57,786	62,207	84,953	111,637	129,411	4.92	15.92
Romania	193,306	243,902	261,118	336,177	336,135	12.77	-0.01
Russian Federation	201,530	178,158	199,046	253,232	336,326	12.78	32.81
Slovakia	21,147	15,628	17,372	28,206	31,421	1.19	11.40
Ukraine	29,314	24,867	36,974	62,123	96,777	3.68	55.78
Northern Europe	385,232	280,534	275,400	285,440	291,209	11.06	2.02
Denmark	46,650	30,759	31,803	29,149	27,861	1.06	-4.42
Finland	37,222	26,467	25,301	25,738	20,418	0.78	-20.67
Ireland	25,313	15,575	11,427	11,602	10,051	0.38	-13.37
Norway	39,410	31,194	31,834	40,992	41,196	1.57	0.50
Sweden	48,097	30,741	26,005	27,069	24,839	0.94	-8.24
United Kingdom	188,540	145,798	149,030	150,890	166,844	6.34	10.57
Southern Europe	298,362	266,724	288,174	292,260	287,170	10.91	-1.74
Greece	145,133	123,856	140,804	127,800	109,539	4.16	-14.29
Italy	54,094	52,622	48,686	55,028	56,329	2.14	2.36
Malta	9,041	4,230	1,560	2,004	2,905	0.11	44.96
Portugal	9,197	6,946	7,985	6,005	5,729	0.22	-4.60
Serbia	17,451	15,592	22,725	26,054	27,360	1.04	5.01
Slovenia	9,099	11,763	9,790	11,548	10,937	0.42	-5.29
Spain	29,449	28,589	27,096	25,774	24,663	0.94	-4.31
TFYR of Macedonia	24,898	23,126	29,528	38,047	49,708	1.89	30.65
Western Europe	618,474	499,804	488,291	551,242	577,555	21.94	4.77
Austria	35,121	29,120	31,117	35,542	39,521	1.50	11.20
Belgium	50,122	34,635	33,374	35,817	35,327	1.34	-1.37
France	91,421	84,644	69,446	72,370	75,492	2.87	4.31
Germany	380,077	300,340	306,687	354,957	373,133	14.18	5.12
Luxembourg	3,301	2,933	1,980	2,659	2,442	0.09	-8.16
Netherlands	42,665	36,549	34,613	35,293	35,692	1.36	1.13
Switzerland	15,767	11,583	11,074	14,604	15,948	0.61	9.20
East Mediterranean Europe	146,815	146,727	158,311	175,031	151,461	5.75	-13.47
Cyprus	10,788	8,213	6,511	6,555	5,617	0.21	-14.31
Israel	90,566	97,462	103,671	117,797	77,934	2.96	-33.84
Turkey	45,461	41,052	48,129	50,679	67,910	2.58	34.00
NOT SPECIFIED	149,997	122,287	156,194	184,423	222,978	8.47	20.91
Other countries of the World	149,997	122,287	156,194	184,423	222,978	8.47	20.91

Yearbook of Tourism Statistics, Data 2008 – 2012, 2014 Edition

BULGARIA

5. Overnight stays of non-resident tourists in hotels and similar establishments, by country of residence

	2008	2009	2010	2011	2012	Market share 2012	% Change 2012-2011
TOTAL	11,640,780	9,377,995	10,454,674	12,286,819	13,151,707	100.00	7.04
AFRICA	4,403	2,240	1,899	2,927	7,176	0.05	145.17
Southern Africa	4,403	2,240	1,899	2,927	7,176	0.05	145.17
South Africa	4,403	2,240	1,899	2,927	7,176	0.05	145.17
AMERICAS	225,467	146,207	142,309	110,531	128,583	0.98	16.33
North America	112,212	95,580	96,701	99,095	117,554	0.89	18.63
Canada	13,047	10,157	13,462	14,338	15,738	0.12	9.76
United States of America	99,165	85,423	83,239	84,757	101,816	0.77	20.13
South America	113,255	50,627	45,608	11,436	11,029	0.08	-3.56
Brazil	113,255	50,627	45,608	11,436	11,029	0.08	-3.56
EAST ASIA AND THE PACIFIC	61,500	41,903	48,889	64,030	77,039	0.59	20.32
North-East Asia	41,086	30,141	37,105	45,360	55,459	0.42	22.26
China	6,739	7,719	8,205	13,582	20,562	0.16	51.39
Japan	26,686	18,757	21,953	20,644	23,538	0.18	14.02
Korea, Republic of	7,661	3,665	6,947	11,134	11,359	0.09	2.02
Australasia	20,414	11,762	11,784	18,670	21,580	0.16	15.59
Australia	20,414	11,762	11,784	18,670	21,580	0.16	15.59
EUROPE	10,914,006	8,805,328	9,712,792	11,486,671	12,101,170	92.01	5.35
Central/Eastern Europe	3,312,419	3,058,719	4,001,282	5,220,334	5,968,116	45.38	14.32
Czech Republic	196,841	194,018	206,265	271,504	338,316	2.57	24.61
Estonia	44,544	29,559	29,930	35,373	42,794	0.33	20.98
Hungary	123,083	92,049	102,379	153,830	139,896	1.06	-9.06
Latvia	35,224	26,241	18,112	27,151	37,627	0.29	38.58
Lithuania	29,524	40,233	23,196	39,481	61,315	0.47	55.30
Poland	394,354	422,449	552,650	738,158	785,551	5.97	6.42
Romania	693,671	814,994	1,024,323	1,344,116	1,336,926	10.17	-0.53
Russian Federation	1,458,427	1,182,012	1,689,907	2,021,541	2,430,560	18.48	20.23
Slovakia	143,694	109,154	122,474	197,160	208,857	1.59	5.93
Ukraine	193,057	148,010	232,046	392,020	586,274	4.46	49.55
Northern Europe	2,459,141	1,679,111	1,636,183	1,725,908	1,666,401	12.67	-3.45
Denmark	287,714	187,559	190,379	180,737	167,529	1.27	-7.31
Finland	241,346	166,021	151,093	157,388	112,015	0.85	-28.83
Iceland	11,549	5,991	2,273	5,669	2,892	0.02	-48.99
Ireland	152,610	74,184	54,060	59,664	44,600	0.34	-25.25
Norway	292,151	218,108	221,828	300,114	282,728	2.15	-5.79
Sweden	303,427	185,943	143,934	157,623	133,213	1.01	-15.49
United Kingdom	1,170,344	841,305	872,616	864,713	923,424	7.02	6.79
Southern Europe	562,584	508,133	519,154	496,042	476,058	3.62	-4.03
Greece	275,165	227,528	272,585	241,627	210,235	1.60	-12.99
Italy	126,511	122,537	113,966	129,987	141,744	1.08	9.04
Malta	26,200	25,812	4,372	6,192	8,409	0.06	35.80
Portugal	35,308	26,635	26,188	18,740	18,093	0.14	-3.45
Slovenia	37,374	41,025	39,732	47,811	47,214	0.36	-1.25
Spain	62,026	64,596	62,311	51,685	50,363	0.38	-2.56
Western Europe	4,006,406	2,986,215	2,905,168	3,289,394	3,292,096	25.03	0.08
Austria	117,140	88,377	99,926	116,028	133,636	1.02	15.18
Belgium	312,633	183,207	177,382	186,123	165,979	1.26	-10.82
France	349,777	296,842	231,324	219,726	237,470	1.81	8.08
Germany	2,902,130	2,158,649	2,161,331	2,512,804	2,507,244	19.06	-0.22
Luxembourg	21,182	16,994	10,795	15,222	13,349	0.10	-12.30
Netherlands	232,628	200,092	187,193	191,668	179,958	1.37	-6.11
Switzerland	70,916	42,054	37,217	47,823	54,460	0.41	13.88

Yearbook of Tourism Statistics, Data 2008 – 2012, 2014 Edition

BULGARIA

5. Overnight stays of non-resident tourists in hotels and similar establishments, by country of residence

	2008	2009	2010	2011	2012	Market share 2012	% Change 2012-2011
East Mediterranean Europe	**408,594**	**429,142**	**474,545**	**532,993**	**443,511**	**3.37**	**-16.79**
Cyprus	29,357	20,557	16,886	16,566	14,677	0.11	-11.40
Israel	269,838	322,539	367,271	414,753	301,176	2.29	-27.38
Turkey	109,399	86,046	90,388	101,674	127,658	0.97	25.56
Other Europe	**164,862**	**144,008**	**176,460**	**222,000**	**254,988**	**1.94**	**14.86**
Other countries of Europe	164,862	144,008	176,460	222,000	254,988	1.94	14.86
NOT SPECIFIED	**435,404**	**382,317**	**548,785**	**622,660**	**837,739**	**6.37**	**34.54**
Other countries of the World	435,404	382,317	548,785	622,660	837,739	6.37	34.54

Yearbook of Tourism Statistics, Data 2008 – 2012, 2014 Edition

BULGARIA

6. Overnight stays of non-resident tourists in all types of accommodation establishments, by country of residence

	2008	2009	2010	2011	2012	Market share 2012	% Change 2012-2011
TOTAL	11,802,017	9,472,345	10,565,210	12,461,275	13,451,440	100.00	7.95
AMERICAS	99,850	96,816	97,390	85,575	104,127	0.77	21.68
North America	99,850	96,816	97,390	85,575	104,127	0.77	21.68
Canada		10,220	13,567				
United States of America	99,850	86,596	83,823	85,575	104,127	0.77	21.68
EAST ASIA AND THE PACIFIC	26,692	18,767	22,011	20,743	24,493	0.18	18.08
North-East Asia	26,692	18,767	22,011	20,743	24,493	0.18	18.08
Japan	26,692	18,767	22,011	20,743	24,493	0.18	18.08
EUROPE	11,028,841	8,867,048	9,792,302	11,616,363	12,333,431	91.69	6.17
Central/Eastern Europe	3,383,139	3,099,171	4,050,728	5,314,646	6,160,384	45.80	15.91
Czech Republic	202,321	195,421	207,897	275,231	343,170	2.55	24.68
Estonia	44,581	29,575	30,022	35,653	43,249	0.32	21.31
Hungary	125,209	92,831	103,146	155,692	142,886	1.06	-8.23
Latvia	35,789	26,285	18,179	27,395	38,302	0.28	39.81
Lithuania	29,587	40,261	23,504	39,563	62,027	0.46	56.78
Poland	400,590	426,285	557,115	742,170	796,880	5.92	7.37
Romania	696,816	817,729	1,030,997	1,352,372	1,349,832	10.03	-0.19
Russian Federation	1,504,039	1,206,505	1,719,881	2,083,019	2,564,743	19.07	23.13
Slovakia	145,895	111,339	123,773	197,981	210,004	1.56	6.07
Ukraine	198,312	152,940	236,214	405,570	609,291	4.53	50.23
Northern Europe	2,477,804	1,690,235	1,652,523	1,738,579	1,676,837	12.47	-3.55
Denmark	288,709	187,739	190,953	181,296	168,452	1.25	-7.08
Finland	241,438	166,156	151,252	158,391	112,451	0.84	-29.00
Ireland	155,677	75,310	54,550	59,827	44,971	0.33	-24.83
Norway	292,918	219,266	223,309	301,560	284,142	2.11	-5.78
Sweden	305,329	187,713	144,705	158,568	133,664	0.99	-15.71
United Kingdom	1,193,733	854,051	887,754	878,937	933,157	6.94	6.17
Southern Europe	716,164	639,827	691,398	707,583	726,597	5.40	2.69
Greece	275,937	229,429	274,294	243,808	212,745	1.58	-12.74
Italy	127,169	123,179	114,744	131,836	144,100	1.07	9.30
Malta	26,244	26,135	4,476	6,202	8,425	0.06	35.84
Portugal	35,331	26,859	26,569	19,213	18,870	0.14	-1.79
Serbia	72,979	60,121	86,581	98,667	99,352	0.74	0.69
Slovenia	37,694	41,154	39,819	48,258	47,862	0.36	-0.82
Spain	62,286	65,670	63,518	53,598	52,058	0.39	-2.87
TFYR of Macedonia	78,524	67,280	81,397	106,001	143,185	1.06	35.08
Western Europe	4,041,316	3,006,838	2,921,514	3,319,203	3,321,979	24.70	0.08
Austria	118,346	88,934	100,933	117,062	134,874	1.00	15.22
Belgium	313,316	183,610	178,003	187,027	167,228	1.24	-10.59
France	353,227	299,004	233,878	224,861	244,828	1.82	8.88
Germany	2,926,449	2,166,644	2,171,123	2,528,594	2,516,335	18.71	-0.48
Luxembourg	21,196	17,189	10,800	15,226	13,463	0.10	-11.58
Netherlands	237,391	209,180	189,461	197,970	190,147	1.41	-3.95
Switzerland	71,391	42,277	37,316	48,463	55,104	0.41	13.70
East Mediterranean Europe	410,418	430,977	476,139	536,352	447,634	3.33	-16.54
Cyprus	29,376	20,598	16,984	16,713	14,808	0.11	-11.40
Israel	270,098	322,842	367,885	415,573	302,855	2.25	-27.12
Turkey	110,944	87,537	91,270	104,066	129,971	0.97	24.89
NOT SPECIFIED	646,634	489,714	653,507	738,594	989,389	7.36	33.96
Other countries of the World	646,634	489,714	653,507	738,594	989,389	7.36	33.96

Yearbook of Tourism Statistics, Data 2008 – 2012, 2014 Edition

BURKINA FASO

3. Arrivals of non-resident tourists in hotels and similar establishments, by nationality

	2008	2009	2010	2011	2012	Market share 2012	% Change 2012-2011
TOTAL	271,796	269,227	274,330	237,725			
AFRICA	112,702	119,243	128,237	117,337			
West Africa	92,608	98,238	102,591	96,848			
Benin	11,005	11,138	11,754	10,032			
Côte d'Ivoire	18,176	18,090	19,251	18,276			
Ghana	7,996	8,412	8,402	10,152			
Guinea	4,046	4,747	4,922	5,103			
Mali	12,258	14,474	15,643	14,846			
Mauritania	2,213	1,943	2,217	2,501			
Niger	11,811	14,888	14,342	12,486			
Nigeria	5,079	5,561	4,297	4,045			
Senegal	10,481	9,875	10,638	9,570			
Togo	9,543	9,110	11,125	9,837			
Other Africa	20,094	21,005	25,646	20,489			
Other countries of Africa	20,094	21,005	25,646	20,489			
AMERICAS	18,016	17,509	20,154	17,333			
North America	16,129	15,026	17,927	14,697			
Canada	6,695	6,434	8,833	7,442			
United States of America	9,434	8,592	9,094	7,255			
Other Americas	1,887	2,483	2,227	2,636			
Other countries of the Americas	1,887	2,483	2,227	2,636			
EAST ASIA AND THE PACIFIC	6,045	7,253	7,313	8,180			
North-East Asia	1,460	1,591	1,898	1,587			
China	1,460	1,591	1,898	1,587			
Other East Asia and the Pacific	4,585	5,662	5,415	6,593			
Other countries of Asia	4,585	5,662	5,415	6,593			
EUROPE	124,426	116,180	107,098	85,535			
Northern Europe	5,253	4,712	4,523	4,749			
United Kingdom	5,253	4,712	4,523	4,749			
Southern Europe	7,260	6,726	5,892	4,875			
Italy	7,260	6,726	5,892	4,875			
Western Europe	100,571	92,592	85,784	64,898			
Belgium	7,889	7,806	7,344	6,491			
France	75,528	67,866	63,715	42,296			
Germany	7,524	7,193	6,855	6,420			
Netherlands	4,656	4,536	3,645	5,545			
Switzerland	4,974	5,191	4,225	4,146			
Other Europe	11,342	12,150	10,899	11,013			
Other countries of Europe	11,342	12,150	10,899	11,013			
MIDDLE EAST	2,015	1,572	1,355	1,795			
Lebanon	2,015	1,572	1,355	1,795			
NOT SPECIFIED	8,592	7,470	10,173	7,545			
Nationals Residing Abroad	8,592	7,470	10,173	7,545			

Yearbook of Tourism Statistics, Data 2008 – 2012, 2014 Edition

BURKINA FASO

5. Overnight stays of non-resident tourists in hotels and similar establishments, by nationality

	2008	2009	2010	2011	2012	Market share 2012	% Change 2012-2011
TOTAL	814,217	792,843	815,196	707,944			
AFRICA	360,498	375,082	392,274	334,706			
West Africa	282,510	293,719	305,845	269,016			
Benin	32,984	34,132	36,638	29,374			
Côte d'Ivoire	58,436	57,028	58,043	55,124			
Ghana	21,401	21,263	21,589	23,036			
Guinea	12,636	14,229	15,755	12,467			
Mali	37,389	44,645	46,189	40,983			
Mauritania	5,824	5,231	6,801	5,824			
Niger	34,363	42,360	38,899	31,823			
Nigeria	12,982	14,887	13,187	10,450			
Senegal	37,537	32,468	38,229	33,137			
Togo	28,958	27,476	30,515	26,798			
Other Africa	77,988	81,363	86,429	65,690			
Other countries of Africa	77,988	81,363	86,429	65,690			
AMERICAS	67,766	58,773	74,409	57,519			
North America	62,382	52,178	67,600	49,563			
Canada	23,542	20,890	29,056	24,562			
United States of America	38,840	31,288	38,544	25,001			
Other Americas	5,384	6,595	6,809	7,956			
Other countries of the Americas	5,384	6,595	6,809	7,956			
EAST ASIA AND THE PACIFIC	19,370	24,640	28,062	30,555			
North-East Asia	5,534	4,978	8,001	6,391			
China	5,534	4,978	8,001	6,391			
Other East Asia and the Pacific	13,836	19,662	20,061	24,164			
Other countries of Asia	13,836	19,662	20,061	24,164			
EUROPE	340,751	312,750	293,932	266,094			
Northern Europe	13,453	12,476	11,020	10,988			
United Kingdom	13,453	12,476	11,020	10,988			
Southern Europe	21,483	20,810	16,702	15,447			
Italy	21,483	20,810	16,702	15,447			
Western Europe	273,482	244,159	234,284	204,979			
Belgium	35,630	22,330	22,515	20,794			
France	188,714	176,285	169,317	141,106			
Germany	23,158	20,374	19,612	20,619			
Netherlands	11,959	11,032	10,064	9,875			
Switzerland	14,021	14,138	12,776	12,585			
Other Europe	32,333	35,305	31,926	34,680			
Other countries of Europe	32,333	35,305	31,926	34,680			
MIDDLE EAST	4,933	3,623	3,596	4,449			
Lebanon	4,933	3,623	3,596	4,449			
NOT SPECIFIED	20,899	17,975	22,923	14,621			
Nationals Residing Abroad	20,899	17,975	22,923	14,621			

Yearbook of Tourism Statistics, Data 2008 – 2012, 2014 Edition

BURUNDI

1. Arrivals of non-resident tourists at national borders, by nationality

		2008	2009	2010	2011	2012	Market share 2012	% Change 2012-2011
TOTAL	(*)	**201,795**	**211,884**	**142,311**				
AFRICA		**177,579**	**186,457**	**122,045**				
Other Africa		**177,579**	**186,457**	**122,045**				
All countries of Africa		177,579	186,457	122,045				
AMERICAS		**5,044**	**5,297**	**3,883**				
Other Americas		**5,044**	**5,297**	**3,883**				
All countries of the Americas		5,044	5,297	3,883				
EAST ASIA AND THE PACIFIC		**4,237**	**4,449**	**2,912**				
Other East Asia and the Pacific		**4,237**	**4,449**	**2,912**				
All countries of Asia		4,237	4,449	2,912				
EUROPE		**12,107**	**12,713**	**9,985**				
Other Europe		**12,107**	**12,713**	**9,985**				
All countries of Europe		12,107	12,713	9,985				
NOT SPECIFIED		**2,828**	**2,968**	**3,486**				
Other countries of the World		2,828	2,968	3,486				

Yearbook of Tourism Statistics, Data 2008 – 2012, 2014 Edition

CAMBODIA

1. Arrivals of non-resident tourists at national borders, by country of residence

	2008	2009	2010	2011	2012	Market share 2012	% Change 2012-2011
TOTAL	**2,125,465**	**2,161,577**	**2,508,289**	**2,881,862**	**3,584,307**	**100.00**	**24.37**
AFRICA	**4,040**	**5,403**	**4,627**	**5,993**	**5,626**	**0.16**	**-6.12**
East Africa				582	346	0.01	-40.55
Kenya				283	266	0.01	-6.01
Uganda				299	80	0.00	-73.24
Central Africa	340	1,051	493	545	291	0.01	-46.61
Cameroon	340	1,051	493	388	225	0.01	-42.01
Congo				157	66	0.00	-57.96
North Africa	38	32	37	48	52	0.00	8.33
Sudan	38	32	37	48	52	0.00	8.33
Southern Africa	2,180	2,104	2,459	3,216	3,530	0.10	9.76
South Africa	2,180	2,104	2,459	3,216	3,530	0.10	9.76
West Africa	1,131	1,724	1,272	1,278	813	0.02	-36.38
Ghana	132	624	503	415	149	0.00	-64.10
Liberia				335	94	0.00	-71.94
Nigeria	999	1,100	769	528	570	0.02	7.95
Other Africa	351	492	366	324	594	0.02	83.33
Other countries of Africa	351	492	366	324	594	0.02	83.33
AMERICAS	**204,878**	**201,130**	**199,089**	**217,500**	**244,291**	**6.82**	**12.32**
Central America				201	245	0.01	21.89
Costa Rica				201	245	0.01	21.89
North America	185,349	187,544	187,880	199,901	225,069	6.28	12.59
Canada	36,891	36,340	38,718	42,462	47,829	1.33	12.64
Mexico	3,379	2,722	3,157	3,486	4,164	0.12	19.45
United States of America	145,079	148,482	146,005	153,953	173,076	4.83	12.42
South America	6,682	7,541	8,803	14,711	15,351	0.43	4.35
Argentina	1,645	1,717	2,212	5,223	4,500	0.13	-13.84
Brazil	2,058	2,204	2,490	3,616	5,110	0.14	41.32
Chile	1,639	1,943	2,240	2,633	2,973	0.08	12.91
Colombia	785	942	1,060	2,060	1,497	0.04	-27.33
Ecuador				184	191	0.01	3.80
Peru	388	422	468	483	576	0.02	19.25
Uruguay	167	313	333	512	504	0.01	-1.56
Other Americas	12,847	6,045	2,406	2,687	3,626	0.10	34.95
Other countries of the Americas	12,847	6,045	2,406	2,687	3,626	0.10	34.95
EAST ASIA AND THE PACIFIC	**1,436,249**	**1,467,406**	**1,788,814**	**2,084,540**	**2,685,192**	**74.92**	**28.81**
North-East Asia	**646,432**	**548,422**	**715,045**	**855,697**	**1,026,152**	**28.63**	**19.92**
China	129,626	128,210	177,636	247,197	333,894	9.32	35.07
Hong Kong, China	3,320	3,888	4,378	5,266	8,282	0.23	57.27
Japan	163,806	146,286	151,795	161,804	179,327	5.00	10.83
Korea, Republic of	266,525	197,725	289,702	342,810	411,491	11.48	20.03
Mongolia	155	194	305	257	347	0.01	35.02
Taiwan, Province of China	83,000	72,119	91,229	98,363	92,811	2.59	-5.64
South-East Asia	**676,492**	**808,661**	**962,570**	**1,101,111**	**1,514,267**	**42.25**	**37.52**
Brunei Darussalam	356	406	460	481	964	0.03	100.42
Indonesia	9,198	9,585	12,636	15,817	22,544	0.63	42.53
Lao People's Democratic Republic	60,933	94,181	92,276	128,525	254,022	7.09	97.64
Malaysia	80,738	77,759	89,952	102,929	116,764	3.26	13.44
Myanmar	2,461	2,316	2,614	4,199	4,744	0.13	12.98
Philippines	39,294	49,079	56,156	70,718	97,487	2.72	37.85
Singapore	40,945	41,273	45,079	47,594	53,184	1.48	11.75
Thailand	109,020	102,018	149,108	116,758	201,422	5.62	72.51
Viet Nam	209,516	316,202	514,289	614,090	763,136	21.29	24.27
Other countries of South-East Asia	124,031	115,842					

118

CAMBODIA

1. Arrivals of non-resident tourists at national borders, by country of residence

	2008	2009	2010	2011	2012	Market share 2012	% Change 2012-2011
Australasia	99,087	98,678	107,306	121,485	136,773	3.82	12.58
Australia	84,957	84,581	93,598	105,010	117,729	3.28	12.11
New Zealand	14,130	14,097	13,708	16,475	19,044	0.53	15.59
Melanesia				117	106	0.00	-9.40
Fiji				117	106	0.00	-9.40
Other East Asia and the Pacific	14,238	11,645	3,893	6,130	7,894	0.22	28.78
Other countries East Asia/Pacific	14,238	11,645	3,893	6,130	7,894	0.22	28.78
EUROPE	463,602	470,181	495,586	551,452	621,700	17.35	12.74
Central/Eastern Europe	30,219	34,457	54,401	93,538	129,591	3.62	38.54
Bulgaria	322	384	445	470	696	0.02	48.09
Czech Republic	2,147	2,649	3,113	3,310	4,064	0.11	22.78
Estonia				954	1,022	0.03	7.13
Hungary	2,193	2,184	2,740	2,585	2,537	0.07	-1.86
Kazakhstan				1,224	1,842	0.05	50.49
Lithuania				1,238	1,089	0.03	-12.04
Poland	5,630	6,319	8,712	9,151	9,994	0.28	9.21
Romania	569	774	1,171	1,081	1,327	0.04	22.76
Russian Federation	16,927	19,395	34,170	67,747	99,750	2.78	47.24
Slovakia	762	895	1,286	1,269	1,693	0.05	33.41
Ukraine	1,669	1,857	2,764	3,788	4,999	0.14	31.97
Uzbekistan				721	578	0.02	-19.83
Northern Europe	153,376	153,311	145,767	151,600	160,447	4.48	5.84
Denmark	9,371	8,937	7,810	9,352	10,013	0.28	7.07
Finland	6,833	6,559	5,244	6,410	6,343	0.18	-1.05
Iceland	274	183	229	355	578	0.02	62.82
Ireland	11,255	9,037	8,567	8,541	8,865	0.25	3.79
Norway	7,875	7,017	7,774	8,128	8,251	0.23	1.51
Sweden	19,675	14,741	13,076	14,762	16,215	0.45	9.84
United Kingdom	98,093	106,837	103,067	104,052	110,182	3.07	5.89
Southern Europe	42,831	38,405	44,082	49,023	54,163	1.51	10.48
Croatia	355	313	470	532	705	0.02	32.52
Greece	1,441	1,406	1,395	1,168	1,073	0.03	-8.13
Italy	19,516	17,154	19,808	20,837	22,625	0.63	8.58
Portugal	2,284	2,481	2,554	3,081	3,061	0.09	-0.65
Serbia				408	411	0.01	0.74
Slovenia	891	740	692	874	939	0.03	7.44
Spain	18,344	16,311	19,163	22,123	25,349	0.71	14.58
Western Europe	215,227	226,057	238,812	242,011	259,499	7.24	7.23
Austria	7,276	8,681	8,547	7,601	8,148	0.23	7.20
Belgium	13,179	12,980	14,295	13,905	14,762	0.41	6.16
France	97,517	105,437	113,285	117,408	121,175	3.38	3.21
Germany	59,903	59,916	62,864	63,398	72,537	2.02	14.42
Luxembourg	486	472	639	497	474	0.01	-4.63
Monaco				82	55	0.00	-32.93
Netherlands	22,408	22,058	23,537	22,725	24,559	0.69	8.07
Switzerland	14,458	16,513	15,645	16,395	17,789	0.50	8.50
East Mediterranean Europe	8,095	7,179	9,238	9,929	11,329	0.32	14.10
Israel	6,131	5,439	6,186	6,644	7,921	0.22	19.22
Turkey	1,964	1,740	3,052	3,285	3,408	0.10	3.74
Other Europe	13,854	10,772	3,286	5,351	6,671	0.19	24.67
Other countries of Europe	13,854	10,772	3,286	5,351	6,671	0.19	24.67
MIDDLE EAST	947	1,144	1,071	1,565	2,148	0.06	37.25
Egypt	155	173	220	196	219	0.01	11.73
Iraq				91	83	0.00	-8.79
Kuwait	472	633	543	530	712	0.02	34.34
Oman				107	150	0.00	40.19

Yearbook of Tourism Statistics, Data 2008 – 2012, 2014 Edition

CAMBODIA

1. Arrivals of non-resident tourists at national borders, by country of residence

	2008	2009	2010	2011	2012	Market share 2012	% Change 2012-2011
Palestine				34	51	0.00	50.00
Qatar				62	70	0.00	12.90
Saudi Arabia	52	48	64	78	87	0.00	11.54
United Arab Emirates				155	243	0.01	56.77
Yemen				98	156	0.00	59.18
Other countries of Middle East	268	290	244	214	377	0.01	76.17
SOUTH ASIA	**15,749**	**16,313**	**19,102**	**20,812**	**25,350**	**0.71**	**21.80**
Afghanistan	40	126	180	113	154	0.00	36.28
Bangladesh	708	925	1,658	1,316	1,367	0.04	3.88
Bhutan				81	134	0.00	65.43
India	12,467	12,461	13,542	15,240	18,999	0.53	24.67
Iran, Islamic Republic of	297	338	518	696	646	0.02	-7.18
Nepal	929	908	1,081	1,156	1,478	0.04	27.85
Pakistan	577	798	1,092	1,113	1,168	0.03	4.94
Sri Lanka	731	757	1,031	1,097	1,404	0.04	27.99

Yearbook of Tourism Statistics, Data 2008 – 2012, 2014 Edition

CANADA

1. Arrivals of non-resident tourists at national borders, by country of residence

		2008	2009	2010	2011	2012	Market share 2012	% Change 2012-2011
TOTAL	(*)	17,140,559	15,735,613	16,217,938	16,013,160	16,342,699	100.00	2.06
AFRICA		79,927	75,717	81,277	85,902	91,858	0.56	6.93
East Africa		15,004	14,219	14,956	15,137	17,530	0.11	15.81
Burundi		235	254	269	318	441	0.00	38.68
Comoros		39	54	61	110	74	0.00	-32.73
Djibouti		117	66	195	112	151	0.00	34.82
Eritrea		264	198	241	218	248	0.00	13.76
Ethiopia		1,265	1,182	1,296	1,284	2,019	0.01	57.24
Kenya		3,494	3,430	3,441	3,509	3,788	0.02	7.95
Madagascar		674	600	662	693	657	0.00	-5.19
Malawi		229	228	304	319	255	0.00	-20.06
Mauritius		1,846	1,738	2,103	1,953	2,066	0.01	5.79
Mozambique		257	255	265	330	327	0.00	-0.91
Reunion		1,799	1,257	1,226	1,523	1,753	0.01	15.10
Rwanda		394	386	451	436	560	0.00	28.44
Seychelles		91	63	70	42	62	0.00	47.62
Somalia		75	195	215	217	210	0.00	-3.23
Uganda		1,209	1,120	1,375	1,228	1,620	0.01	31.92
United Republic of Tanzania		1,675	1,742	1,542	1,450	1,799	0.01	24.07
Zambia		635	701	502	583	660	0.00	13.21
Zimbabwe		706	750	738	812	840	0.01	3.45
Central Africa		3,784	3,695	3,888	3,798	4,508	0.03	18.69
Angola		459	307	395	382	355	0.00	-7.07
Cameroon		1,451	1,711	1,758	1,743	2,178	0.01	24.96
Central African Republic		34	22	16	28	30	0.00	7.14
Chad		114	163	111	111	193	0.00	73.87
Congo		123	85	84	176	155	0.00	-11.93
Democratic Republic of the Congo		1,039	897	1,003	859	1,175	0.01	36.79
Equatorial Guinea		26	37	22	11	7	0.00	-36.36
Gabon		538	473	495	488	413	0.00	-15.37
Sao Tome and Principe				4		2	0.00	
North Africa		20,881	21,666	22,909	24,919	27,330	0.17	9.68
Algeria		5,896	6,446	6,954	8,216	9,707	0.06	18.15
Morocco		10,907	10,832	11,471	11,760	12,676	0.08	7.79
Sudan		432	390	550	519	489	0.00	-5.78
Tunisia		3,646	3,998	3,932	4,424	4,458	0.03	0.77
Western Sahara				2				
Southern Africa		24,998	19,957	20,473	22,791	22,032	0.13	-3.33
Botswana		605	571	598	558	619	0.00	10.93
Lesotho		74	114	71	87	71	0.00	-18.39
Namibia		441	420	707	1,193	415	0.00	-65.21
South Africa		23,774	18,715	18,916	20,826	20,706	0.13	-0.58
Swaziland		104	137	181	127	221	0.00	74.02
West Africa		15,193	16,111	19,003	19,240	20,454	0.13	6.31
Benin		767	795	735	795	601	0.00	-24.40
Burkina Faso		855	698	758	772	1,048	0.01	35.75
Cape Verde		45	10	21	13	16	0.00	23.08
Côte d'Ivoire		1,181	1,087	1,093	715	1,286	0.01	79.86
Gambia		70	164	138	148	128	0.00	-13.51
Ghana		2,079	2,008	2,138	2,264	2,581	0.02	14.00
Guinea		633	495	540	657	757	0.00	15.22
Guinea-Bissau		2	10	27	2			
Liberia		109	107	137	202	143	0.00	-29.21
Mali		733	883	744	953	847	0.01	-11.12
Mauritania		217	199	158	236	244	0.00	3.39
Niger		274	243	195	233	237	0.00	1.72

Yearbook of Tourism Statistics, Data 2008 – 2012, 2014 Edition

CANADA

1. Arrivals of non-resident tourists at national borders, by country of residence

		2008	2009	2010	2011	2012	Market share 2012	% Change 2012-2011
Nigeria		5,952	7,371	10,195	9,821	10,239	0.06	4.26
Saint Helena					13			
Senegal		1,855	1,667	1,711	1,896	1,861	0.01	-1.85
Sierra Leone		111	117	142	142	140	0.00	-1.41
Togo		310	257	271	378	326	0.00	-13.76
Other Africa		**67**	**69**	**48**	**17**	**4**	**0.00**	**-76.47**
Other countries of Africa	(*)	67	69	48	17	4	0.00	-76.47
AMERICAS		**13,111,691**	**12,150,425**	**12,336,321**	**12,079,843**	**12,395,137**	**75.85**	**2.61**
Caribbean		**136,707**	**128,036**	**134,944**	**134,975**	**133,385**	**0.82**	**-1.18**
Anguilla		162	140	213	159	216	0.00	35.85
Antigua and Barbuda		1,768	1,373	1,408	1,605	1,771	0.01	10.34
Bahamas		9,446	9,284	9,139	8,932	9,040	0.06	1.21
Barbados		11,192	10,822	11,897	11,462	11,448	0.07	-0.12
Bermuda		20,461	19,234	21,604	20,800	19,077	0.12	-8.28
British Virgin Islands		489	570	476	504	477	0.00	-5.36
Cayman Islands		5,958	5,636	5,379	6,281	5,883	0.04	-6.34
Cuba		5,860	5,554	5,281	5,172	5,512	0.03	6.57
Dominica		480	513	641	706	518	0.00	-26.63
Dominican Republic		4,319	4,114	5,330	5,087	5,478	0.03	7.69
Grenada		1,174	965	944	894	1,053	0.01	17.79
Guadeloupe		3,672	3,152	3,984	4,264	3,696	0.02	-13.32
Haiti		6,481	6,659	6,230	6,725	7,377	0.05	9.70
Jamaica		25,413	24,323	26,077	25,147	25,197	0.15	0.20
Martinique		2,587	2,394	2,806	2,921	3,215	0.02	10.07
Montserrat		32	33	59	19	26	0.00	36.84
Netherlands Antilles		1,128	1,269	1,503	1,838	1,832	0.01	-0.33
Puerto Rico		1,517	1,103	995	1,005	939	0.01	-6.57
Saint Kitts and Nevis		786	863	832	872	811	0.00	-7.00
Saint Lucia		3,381	2,934	3,668	3,937	3,130	0.02	-20.50
Saint Vincent and the Grenadines		3,839	2,898	3,351	3,257	2,398	0.01	-26.37
Trinidad and Tobago		24,883	22,779	21,778	22,004	22,815	0.14	3.69
Turks and Caicos Islands		1,629	1,349	1,281	1,337	1,418	0.01	6.06
United States Virgin Islands		50	75	68	47	58	0.00	23.40
Central America		**19,813**	**19,045**	**19,926**	**19,448**	**21,439**	**0.13**	**10.24**
Belize		1,048	825	946	1,017	1,246	0.01	22.52
Costa Rica		4,782	4,647	4,682	4,438	4,868	0.03	9.69
El Salvador		2,770	2,326	2,160	1,770	2,019	0.01	14.07
Guatemala		5,863	6,598	6,938	6,443	7,266	0.04	12.77
Honduras		1,589	1,167	1,248	1,487	1,463	0.01	-1.61
Nicaragua		896	894	949	896	960	0.01	7.14
Panama	(*)	2,865	2,588	3,003	3,397	3,617	0.02	6.48
North America		**12,792,893**	**11,856,529**	**12,009,757**	**11,743,918**	**12,046,445**	**73.71**	**2.58**
Greenland		335	213	406	267	247	0.00	-7.49
Mexico		266,295	168,724	120,499	132,217	141,921	0.87	7.34
Saint Pierre and Miquelon		22,383	20,359	18,008	16,071	17,327	0.11	7.82
United States of America		12,503,880	11,667,233	11,870,844	11,595,363	11,886,950	72.74	2.51
South America		**162,278**	**146,815**	**171,694**	**181,502**	**193,868**	**1.19**	**6.81**
Argentina		18,094	15,013	16,744	17,737	16,619	0.10	-6.30
Bolivia		962	831	853	976	1,078	0.01	10.45
Brazil		71,619	61,829	80,188	87,904	93,570	0.57	6.45
Chile		14,336	13,602	18,255	17,336	20,399	0.12	17.67
Colombia		17,397	16,568	16,267	18,762	20,074	0.12	6.99
Ecuador		4,115	3,716	3,792	3,633	3,558	0.02	-2.06
Falkland Islands, Malvinas		4	12	8	5	23	0.00	360.00
French Guiana		195	182	185	238	259	0.00	8.82
Guyana		4,106	3,947	3,267	3,803	4,484	0.03	17.91
Paraguay		1,169	1,074	1,202	1,312	1,207	0.01	-8.00

122

CANADA

1. Arrivals of non-resident tourists at national borders, by country of residence

	2008	2009	2010	2011	2012	Market share 2012	% Change 2012-2011
Peru	9,460	8,016	10,119	9,470	10,577	0.06	11.69
Suriname	339	262	283	262	357	0.00	36.26
Uruguay	1,963	1,638	1,921	2,180	1,930	0.01	-11.47
Venezuela	18,519	20,125	18,610	17,884	19,733	0.12	10.34
EAST ASIA AND THE PACIFIC	**1,230,626**	**1,025,526**	**1,170,281**	**1,222,621**	**1,285,606**	**7.87**	**5.15**
North-East Asia	**810,261**	**654,969**	**763,735**	**787,524**	**828,960**	**5.07**	**5.26**
China	159,927	160,833	194,979	243,692	288,279	1.76	18.30
Hong Kong, China	128,139	107,410	114,973	123,060	120,022	0.73	-2.47
Japan	276,091	197,752	235,510	211,062	226,215	1.38	7.18
Korea, Dem. People's Republic of	4	2	8				
Korea, Republic of	183,895	138,150	164,282	151,101	139,999	0.86	-7.35
Macao, China	107	151	181	157	301	0.00	91.72
Mongolia	553	671	989	769	969	0.01	26.01
Taiwan, Province of China	61,545	50,000	52,813	57,683	53,175	0.33	-7.82
South-East Asia	**130,776**	**121,165**	**124,704**	**146,489**	**149,227**	**0.91**	**1.87**
Brunei Darussalam	515	450	527	548	509	0.00	-7.12
Cambodia	571	566	502	762	837	0.01	9.84
Indonesia	10,814	11,117	12,428	15,142	16,864	0.10	11.37
Lao People's Democratic Republic	223	180	176	223	268	0.00	20.18
Malaysia	12,892	8,754	11,255	11,867	12,077	0.07	1.77
Myanmar	396	487	318	262	179	0.00	-31.68
Philippines	61,758	61,473	54,946	59,674	63,141	0.39	5.81
Singapore	24,904	21,043	24,770	29,254	30,492	0.19	4.23
Thailand	13,248	11,419	13,197	21,449	16,952	0.10	-20.97
Viet Nam	5,455	5,676	6,585	7,308	7,908	0.05	8.21
Australasia	**285,252**	**245,971**	**278,280**	**285,114**	**303,818**	**1.86**	**6.56**
Australia	238,802	204,383	232,855	242,430	258,115	1.58	6.47
New Zealand	46,450	41,588	45,425	42,684	45,703	0.28	7.07
Melanesia	**2,756**	**2,122**	**2,122**	**1,940**	**2,295**	**0.01**	**18.30**
Fiji	1,607	1,216	1,091	903	879	0.01	-2.66
New Caledonia	845	690	749	819	1,072	0.01	30.89
Papua New Guinea	225	140	185	138	269	0.00	94.93
Solomon Islands	21	24	28	31	18	0.00	-41.94
Vanuatu	58	52	69	49	57	0.00	16.33
Micronesia	**106**	**150**	**112**	**109**	**90**	**0.00**	**-17.43**
Guam	11	35	22	18	13	0.00	-27.78
Kiribati	4	13	18	26	14	0.00	-46.15
Marshall Islands	17	36	9	14	12	0.00	-14.29
Micronesia, Federated States of	65	62	47	41	47	0.00	14.63
Nauru			12	4	4	0.00	0.00
Northern Mariana Islands	9	4	4	6			
Polynesia	**1,459**	**1,135**	**1,312**	**1,437**	**1,210**	**0.01**	**-15.80**
American Samoa	31	28	53	23	18	0.00	-21.74
Cook Islands	28	12	26	6	20	0.00	233.33
French Polynesia	1,353	1,046	1,201	1,371	1,139	0.01	-16.92
Samoa	26	10	14	12	18	0.00	50.00
Tonga	19	31	12	22	15	0.00	-31.82
Tuvalu			2	3			
Wallis and Futuna Islands	2	8	4				
Other East Asia and the Pacific	**16**	**14**	**16**	**8**	**6**	**0.00**	**-25.00**
Other countries East Asia/Pacific	12	10	2		2	0.00	
Other countries of Oceania (*)	4	4	14	8	4	0.00	-50.00
EUROPE	**2,495,966**	**2,260,592**	**2,374,057**	**2,354,532**	**2,297,574**	**14.06**	**-2.42**
Central/Eastern Europe	**135,297**	**121,203**	**126,917**	**126,371**	**128,561**	**0.79**	**1.73**
Armenia	451	341	480	604	477	0.00	-21.03
Azerbaijan	364	408	455	476	627	0.00	31.72
Bulgaria	3,646	3,278	3,210	3,128	2,999	0.02	-4.12

Yearbook of Tourism Statistics, Data 2008 – 2012, 2014 Edition

CANADA

1. Arrivals of non-resident tourists at national borders, by country of residence

	2008	2009	2010	2011	2012	Market share 2012	% Change 2012-2011
Czech Republic	15,599	16,068	11,864	11,112	11,492	0.07	3.42
Estonia	2,024	1,675	1,540	1,577	1,723	0.01	9.26
Georgia	201	214	378	283	282	0.00	-0.35
Hungary	11,131	11,752	12,284	12,878	11,228	0.07	-12.81
Kazakhstan	1,938	2,004	2,116	2,158	2,382	0.01	10.38
Kyrgyzstan	244	283	245	261	304	0.00	16.48
Latvia	3,046	2,398	2,488	2,027	2,281	0.01	12.53
Lithuania	1,886	1,461	1,715	1,871	2,154	0.01	15.13
Poland	34,354	28,352	29,295	29,536	31,677	0.19	7.25
Republic of Moldova	1,067	1,480	1,783	1,910	2,130	0.01	11.52
Romania	17,784	15,408	15,633	15,416	13,832	0.08	-10.28
Russian Federation	24,422	19,389	25,027	23,796	25,220	0.15	5.98
Slovakia	6,228	6,516	7,567	7,320	7,107	0.04	-2.91
Tajikistan	60	65	80	64	50	0.00	-21.88
Turkmenistan	34	78	75	70	70	0.00	0.00
Ukraine	10,599	9,755	10,406	11,675	12,214	0.07	4.62
Uzbekistan	219	278	276	209	312	0.00	49.28
Northern Europe	**1,017,039**	**850,301**	**874,143**	**846,280**	**818,070**	**5.01**	**-3.33**
Denmark	30,866	26,654	33,085	38,179	37,656	0.23	-1.37
Faeroe Islands	69	83	151	97	108	0.00	11.34
Finland	17,400	14,742	16,791	14,706	14,215	0.09	-3.34
Iceland	6,613	3,450	4,244	5,087	3,449	0.02	-32.20
Ireland	49,593	43,664	46,273	42,638	43,382	0.27	1.74
Norway	23,147	20,329	24,723	24,691	25,657	0.16	3.91
Sweden	34,947	30,866	37,187	41,054	39,682	0.24	-3.34
United Kingdom	854,404	710,513	711,689	679,828	653,921	4.00	-3.81
Southern Europe	**218,802**	**208,326**	**219,305**	**215,140**	**200,227**	**1.23**	**-6.93**
Albania	1,504	1,349	1,330	1,156	1,174	0.01	1.56
Andorra	273	327	364	281	224	0.00	-20.28
Bosnia and Herzegovina	1,748	1,487	1,529	1,389	1,127	0.01	-18.86
Croatia	4,084	4,569	5,248	5,273	5,851	0.04	10.96
Gibraltar	248	238	261	324	211	0.00	-34.88
Greece	13,681	12,058	12,799	12,482	12,795	0.08	2.51
Holy See	9	1	4	6	19	0.00	216.67
Italy	96,050	92,393	101,738	98,191	93,127	0.57	-5.16
Malta	1,958	2,090	1,892	1,875	1,742	0.01	-7.09
Portugal	20,955	18,108	19,556	20,879	21,019	0.13	0.67
San Marino	38	30	64	48	24	0.00	-50.00
Serbia and Montenegro	5,887	4,949	5,467	5,270	4,863	0.03	-7.72
Slovenia	3,611	2,979	3,702	3,212	2,881	0.02	-10.31
Spain	67,811	66,733	64,383	63,858	54,413	0.33	-14.79
TFYR of Macedonia	945	1,015	968	896	757	0.00	-15.51
Western Europe	**1,047,629**	**1,012,096**	**1,078,818**	**1,089,427**	**1,073,600**	**6.57**	**-1.45**
Austria	33,032	32,949	38,086	36,925	35,646	0.22	-3.46
Belgium	49,798	48,057	52,600	54,848	54,174	0.33	-1.23
France	420,895	407,653	435,465	459,140	455,300	2.79	-0.84
Germany	319,895	309,684	332,086	315,901	311,692	1.91	-1.33
Liechtenstein	291	462	483	473	395	0.00	-16.49
Luxembourg	4,081	3,497	4,179	4,260	4,599	0.03	7.96
Monaco	1,152	1,204	1,286	1,315	1,199	0.01	-8.82
Netherlands	121,050	109,133	109,208	105,842	100,644	0.62	-4.91
Switzerland	97,435	99,457	105,425	110,723	109,951	0.67	-0.70
East Mediterranean Europe	**77,199**	**68,666**	**74,874**	**77,314**	**77,116**	**0.47**	**-0.26**
Cyprus	2,002	1,535	1,853	1,712	1,845	0.01	7.77
Israel	66,236	57,704	60,681	63,322	62,935	0.39	-0.61
Turkey	8,961	9,427	12,340	12,280	12,336	0.08	0.46

Yearbook of Tourism Statistics, Data 2008 – 2012, 2014 Edition

CANADA

1. Arrivals of non-resident tourists at national borders, by country of residence

	2008	2009	2010	2011	2012	Market share 2012	% Change 2012-2011
MIDDLE EAST	77,272	77,602	83,668	85,069	85,464	0.52	0.46
Bahrain	1,454	1,553	1,671	1,696	1,397	0.01	-17.63
Egypt	9,387	9,009	10,434	8,942	9,852	0.06	10.18
Iraq	775	1,190	1,576	1,554	1,343	0.01	-13.58
Jordan	3,887	3,443	3,422	3,787	3,662	0.02	-3.30
Kuwait	3,268	3,197	3,385	3,615	3,872	0.02	7.11
Lebanon	8,990	8,300	8,372	9,925	9,245	0.06	-6.85
Libya	1,575	1,504	1,558	441	1,091	0.01	147.39
Oman	1,285	1,300	1,536	1,387	1,423	0.01	2.60
Qatar	3,563	3,740	4,072	4,803	4,896	0.03	1.94
Saudi Arabia	16,710	17,799	20,124	18,756	19,603	0.12	4.52
Syrian Arab Republic	2,045	2,277	2,209	2,506	1,830	0.01	-26.98
United Arab Emirates	23,837	23,904	25,000	27,378	27,026	0.17	-1.29
Yemen	496	386	309	279	224	0.00	-19.71
SOUTH ASIA	145,077	145,751	172,334	185,193	187,060	1.14	1.01
Afghanistan	591	656	680	812	1,077	0.01	32.64
Bangladesh	4,213	4,120	5,455	5,138	4,886	0.03	-4.90
Bhutan	52	97	299	372	392	0.00	5.38
India	110,890	107,959	127,619	139,213	146,652	0.90	5.34
Iran, Islamic Republic of	8,201	11,830	15,616	14,329	11,962	0.07	-16.52
Maldives	37	53	44	73	63	0.00	-13.70
Nepal	915	1,164	1,435	1,445	1,485	0.01	2.77
Pakistan	14,847	16,804	17,574	19,685	16,298	0.10	-17.21
Sri Lanka	5,331	3,068	3,612	4,126	4,245	0.03	2.88

Yearbook of Tourism Statistics, Data 2008 – 2012, 2014 Edition

CANADA

2. Arrivals of non-resident visitors at national borders, by country of residence

		2008	2009	2010	2011	2012	Market share 2012	% Change 2012-2011
TOTAL	(*)	27,370,200	24,695,500	25,621,300	25,066,500	25,300,800	100.00	0.93
AFRICA		80,400	76,300	81,800	86,500	76,600	0.30	-11.45
Southern Africa		24,100	19,100	19,200	21,100	21,200	0.08	0.47
South Africa		24,100	19,100	19,200	21,100	21,200	0.08	0.47
Other Africa		56,300	57,200	62,600	65,400	55,400	0.22	-15.29
Other countries of Africa		56,300	57,200	62,600	65,400	55,400	0.22	-15.29
AMERICAS		23,220,000	21,014,000	21,636,800	21,035,300	21,236,600	83.94	0.96
Caribbean		137,300	128,700	135,700	135,900	134,400	0.53	-1.10
Bermuda		20,500	19,200	21,600	20,800	19,100	0.08	-8.17
Jamaica		25,500	24,500	26,200	25,400	25,600	0.10	0.79
Trinidad and Tobago		25,000	22,900	21,900	22,100	22,900	0.09	3.62
Other countries of the Caribbean		66,300	62,100	66,000	67,600	66,800	0.26	-1.18
North America		22,899,100	20,718,200	21,307,800	20,696,800	20,884,400	82.54	0.91
Greenland		300	200	400	300	300	0.00	0.00
Mexico		270,800	172,000	123,800	136,900	147,700	0.58	7.89
Saint Pierre and Miquelon		22,400	20,400	18,000	16,100	17,300	0.07	7.45
United States of America		22,605,600	20,525,600	21,165,600	20,543,500	20,719,100	81.89	0.85
South America		163,600	147,900	173,200	182,900	196,000	0.77	7.16
Argentina		18,300	15,100	16,800	17,900	16,800	0.07	-6.15
Brazil		72,100	62,200	80,800	88,500	94,600	0.37	6.89
Colombia		17,600	16,800	16,500	19,000	20,400	0.08	7.37
Venezuela		18,700	20,300	18,800	18,000	19,900	0.08	10.56
Other countries of South America		36,900	33,500	40,300	39,500	44,300	0.18	12.15
Other Americas		20,000	19,200	20,100	19,700	21,800	0.09	10.66
Other countries of the Americas		20,000	19,200	20,100	19,700	21,800	0.09	10.66
EAST ASIA AND THE PACIFIC		1,280,200	1,064,200	1,211,300	1,262,300	1,346,800	5.32	6.69
North-East Asia		846,100	680,000	787,800	809,500	867,500	3.43	7.16
China	(*)	166,400	166,900	201,000	249,700	299,000	1.18	19.74
Hong Kong, China		132,400	111,800	119,400	126,800	123,900	0.49	-2.29
Japan		287,200	205,600	243,000	218,800	240,000	0.95	9.69
Korea, Republic of		196,600	144,100	170,000	155,700	150,600	0.60	-3.28
Taiwan, Province of China		63,500	51,600	54,400	58,500	54,000	0.21	-7.69
South-East Asia		125,600	116,800	120,100	142,700	145,900	0.58	2.24
Indonesia		11,000	11,500	12,900	15,800	17,800	0.07	12.66
Malaysia		13,200	9,000	11,500	12,200	12,700	0.05	4.10
Philippines		62,300	62,700	56,600	61,200	64,700	0.26	5.72
Singapore		25,600	21,900	25,600	30,800	32,800	0.13	6.49
Thailand		13,500	11,700	13,500	22,700	17,900	0.07	-21.15
Australasia		296,800	256,400	291,400	297,300	319,700	1.26	7.53
Australia		248,700	213,700	244,200	253,300	272,200	1.08	7.46
New Zealand		48,100	42,700	47,200	44,000	47,500	0.19	7.95
Other East Asia and the Pacific		11,700	11,000	12,000	12,800	13,700	0.05	7.03
Other countries of Asia		7,300	7,600	8,400	9,300	10,100	0.04	8.60
Other countries of Oceania		4,400	3,400	3,600	3,500	3,600	0.01	2.86
EUROPE		2,560,200	2,310,900	2,427,400	2,403,400	2,359,400	9.33	-1.83
Central/Eastern Europe		142,000	127,000	133,300	132,200	134,300	0.53	1.59
Commonwealth Independent States		41,300	36,000	43,100	43,100	45,700	0.18	6.03
Czech Republic/Slovakia		22,200	23,000	19,600	18,700	18,800	0.07	0.53
Estonia	(*)	7,000	5,600	5,800	5,500	6,300	0.02	14.55
Hungary	(*)	36,700	33,800	35,200	35,100	31,300	0.12	-10.83
Poland		34,800	28,600	29,600	29,800	32,200	0.13	8.05
Northern Europe		1,036,700	867,400	893,900	864,400	839,100	3.32	-2.93
Denmark	(*)	32,200	27,400	33,900	38,900	38,600	0.15	-0.77
Finland		17,700	15,000	17,000	15,000	14,500	0.06	-3.33

CANADA

2. Arrivals of non-resident visitors at national borders, by country of residence

		2008	2009	2010	2011	2012	Market share 2012	% Change 2012-2011
Iceland		6,600	3,500	4,300	5,200	3,500	0.01	-32.69
Ireland		50,600	44,600	48,000	43,900	44,600	0.18	1.59
Norway		23,600	20,600	25,200	25,000	26,000	0.10	4.00
Sweden		35,800	31,600	37,700	41,500	40,200	0.16	-3.13
United Kingdom	(*)	870,200	724,700	727,800	694,900	671,700	2.65	-3.34
Southern Europe		**234,200**	**218,700**	**226,700**	**223,000**	**211,800**	**0.84**	**-5.02**
Greece		14,000	12,300	13,100	12,800	13,300	0.05	3.91
Italy	(*)	108,500	101,500	110,400	106,500	103,800	0.41	-2.54
Portugal		21,500	18,500	19,900	21,300	21,500	0.08	0.94
Spain		75,900	72,900	68,600	68,100	59,100	0.23	-13.22
Yugoslavia, SFR (former)	(*)	14,300	13,500	14,700	14,300	14,100	0.06	-1.40
Western Europe		**1,070,400**	**1,029,500**	**1,099,300**	**1,106,900**	**1,096,700**	**4.33**	**-0.92**
Austria		33,600	33,400	38,800	37,300	36,200	0.14	-2.95
Belgium / Luxembourg		54,500	52,100	57,400	59,600	59,700	0.24	0.17
France	(*)	426,800	413,300	442,400	466,200	463,300	1.83	-0.62
Germany		332,000	318,800	342,000	324,000	322,400	1.27	-0.49
Netherlands		123,900	110,700	111,000	107,100	102,900	0.41	-3.92
Switzerland	(*)	99,600	101,200	107,700	112,700	112,200	0.44	-0.44
East Mediterranean Europe		**76,900**	**68,300**	**74,200**	**76,900**	**77,500**	**0.31**	**0.78**
Israel		67,900	58,800	61,800	64,400	65,000	0.26	0.93
Turkey		9,000	9,500	12,400	12,500	12,500	0.05	0.00
MIDDLE EAST		**88,400**	**92,100**	**102,200**	**102,400**	**99,800**	**0.39**	**-2.54**
All countries of Middle East		88,400	92,100	102,200	102,400	99,800	0.39	-2.54
SOUTH ASIA		**141,000**	**138,000**	**161,800**	**176,600**	**181,600**	**0.72**	**2.83**
All countries of South Asia		141,000	138,000	161,800	176,600	181,600	0.72	2.83

Yearbook of Tourism Statistics, Data 2008 – 2012, 2014 Edition

CANADA

6. Overnight stays of non-resident tourists in all types of accommodation establishments, by country of residence

		2008	2009	2010	2011	2012	Market share 2012	% Change 2012-2011
TOTAL	(*)	126,067,400	114,888,500	120,102,200	124,395,700	129,164,700	100.00	3.83
AFRICA		1,888,100	1,689,300	1,952,400	2,489,000	2,295,000	1.78	-7.79
Southern Africa		401,800	331,100	352,100	405,900	300,000	0.23	-26.09
South Africa		401,800	331,100	352,100	405,900	300,000	0.23	-26.09
Other Africa		1,486,300	1,358,200	1,600,300	2,083,100	1,995,000	1.54	-4.23
Other countries of Africa		1,486,300	1,358,200	1,600,300	2,083,100	1,995,000	1.54	-4.23
AMERICAS		60,777,100	55,439,100	55,583,800	56,223,100	60,472,400	46.82	7.56
Caribbean		1,890,900	1,610,500	2,167,400	2,206,000	2,786,900	2.16	26.33
Bermuda		291,900	156,200	207,600	197,700	276,900	0.21	40.06
Jamaica		377,200	357,000	603,600	651,800	763,400	0.59	17.12
Trinidad and Tobago		463,400	370,000	462,800	466,200	657,100	0.51	40.95
Other countries of the Caribbean		758,400	727,300	893,400	890,300	1,089,500	0.84	22.37
North America		55,897,600	51,071,600	50,263,600	50,417,100	54,167,200	41.94	7.44
Greenland		2,500	2,200	2,900	2,000	2,300	0.00	15.00
Mexico		5,105,400	3,622,000	2,584,400	2,907,700	3,195,600	2.47	9.90
Saint Pierre and Miquelon		147,000	82,500	71,900	81,200	120,400	0.09	48.28
United States of America		50,642,700	47,364,900	47,604,400	47,426,200	50,848,900	39.37	7.22
South America		2,739,600	2,397,400	2,911,000	3,325,800	3,240,200	2.51	-2.57
Argentina		247,200	200,500	250,600	302,100	210,100	0.16	-30.45
Brazil		1,344,500	979,600	1,381,800	1,464,400	1,530,700	1.19	4.53
Colombia		321,300	313,900	415,200	541,000	526,000	0.41	-2.77
Venezuela		265,500	350,600	275,400	319,100	296,400	0.23	-7.11
Other countries of South America		561,100	552,800	588,000	699,200	677,000	0.52	-3.18
Other Americas		249,000	359,600	241,800	274,200	278,100	0.22	1.42
Other countries of the Americas		249,000	359,600	241,800	274,200	278,100	0.22	1.42
EAST ASIA AND THE PACIFIC		21,494,200	19,924,400	22,529,200	25,110,400	26,469,100	20.49	5.41
North-East Asia		14,766,900	13,027,800	15,588,000	17,026,200	18,127,100	14.03	6.47
China	(*)	4,439,300	4,470,800	5,401,000	6,903,700	8,136,200	6.30	17.85
Hong Kong, China		2,022,400	1,780,000	1,958,100	2,131,700	2,237,400	1.73	4.96
Japan		3,103,500	2,468,500	3,045,800	2,754,300	2,800,000	2.17	1.66
Korea, Republic of		4,172,100	3,450,500	4,232,400	4,007,600	4,012,100	3.11	0.11
Taiwan, Province of China		1,029,600	858,000	950,700	1,228,900	941,400	0.73	-23.39
South-East Asia		2,952,700	3,189,400	3,108,700	4,082,800	3,936,700	3.05	-3.58
Indonesia		190,600	180,200	128,000	216,800	214,400	0.17	-1.11
Malaysia		129,000	185,200	234,500	122,100	123,700	0.10	1.31
Philippines		2,138,700	2,384,800	2,043,400	3,098,400	3,018,700	2.34	-2.57
Singapore		308,900	234,700	293,700	347,700	336,600	0.26	-3.19
Thailand		185,500	204,500	409,100	297,800	243,300	0.19	-18.30
Australasia		3,605,200	3,546,600	3,606,400	3,808,800	4,168,700	3.23	9.45
Australia		2,935,200	2,644,200	3,023,600	3,293,300	3,424,500	2.65	3.98
New Zealand		670,000	902,400	582,800	515,500	744,200	0.58	44.36
Other East Asia and the Pacific		169,400	160,600	226,100	192,600	236,600	0.18	22.85
Other countries of Asia		99,500	103,200	162,200	133,500	172,700	0.13	29.36
Other countries of Oceania		69,900	57,400	63,900	59,100	63,900	0.05	8.12
EUROPE		37,283,600	33,197,600	34,504,500	34,400,300	33,552,600	25.98	-2.46
Central/Eastern Europe		2,924,000	2,304,100	3,124,200	3,510,300	3,048,400	2.36	-13.16
Commonwealth Independent States		961,800	632,300	1,258,800	1,071,300	1,136,300	0.88	6.07
Czech Republic/Slovakia		509,800	425,200	377,100	619,800	374,800	0.29	-39.53
Estonia	(*)	198,400	63,500	111,200	49,900	61,700	0.05	23.65
Hungary	(*)	612,700	680,900	782,500	976,800	747,600	0.58	-23.46
Poland		641,300	502,200	594,600	792,500	728,000	0.56	-8.14
Northern Europe		13,336,900	11,085,100	10,796,400	10,564,700	10,611,200	8.22	0.44
Denmark	(*)	443,600	332,700	363,800	381,600	484,000	0.37	26.83
Finland		164,200	215,500	262,200	152,800	152,100	0.12	-0.46

128

CANADA

6. Overnight stays of non-resident tourists in all types of accommodation establishments, by country of residence

		2008	2009	2010	2011	2012	Market share 2012	% Change 2012-2011
Iceland		84,200	28,700	40,700	46,500	45,800	0.04	-1.51
Ireland		570,900	453,400	559,900	636,100	780,500	0.60	22.70
Norway		229,000	230,800	280,700	358,500	336,900	0.26	-6.03
Sweden		482,100	463,800	379,800	537,800	488,400	0.38	-9.19
United Kingdom	(*)	11,362,900	9,360,200	8,909,300	8,451,400	8,323,500	6.44	-1.51
Southern Europe		**3,357,200**	**3,112,900**	**2,926,800**	**2,814,900**	**2,643,700**	**2.05**	**-6.08**
Greece		141,500	188,400	185,600	122,500	226,500	0.18	84.90
Italy	(*)	1,343,600	1,196,600	1,270,800	1,213,300	1,264,200	0.98	4.20
Portugal		358,200	347,600	243,800	223,000	312,700	0.24	40.22
Spain		966,600	898,500	821,100	750,500	529,300	0.41	-29.47
Yugoslavia, SFR (former)	(*)	547,300	481,800	405,500	505,600	311,000	0.24	-38.49
Western Europe		**16,790,300**	**15,845,000**	**16,872,700**	**16,554,700**	**16,203,900**	**12.55**	**-2.12**
Austria		455,900	530,000	601,400	397,000	376,300	0.29	-5.21
Belgium / Luxembourg		786,900	661,400	925,100	858,200	671,100	0.52	-21.80
France	(*)	7,014,600	6,351,000	6,657,200	6,939,200	7,026,200	5.44	1.25
Germany		5,249,400	5,160,900	5,515,100	5,082,700	4,804,600	3.72	-5.47
Netherlands		1,847,400	1,579,400	1,565,500	1,497,800	1,499,500	1.16	0.11
Switzerland	(*)	1,436,100	1,562,300	1,608,400	1,779,800	1,826,200	1.41	2.61
East Mediterranean Europe		**875,200**	**850,500**	**784,400**	**955,700**	**1,045,400**	**0.81**	**9.39**
Israel		716,000	604,300	646,200	757,700	818,000	0.63	7.96
Turkey		159,200	246,200	138,200	198,000	227,400	0.18	14.85
MIDDLE EAST		**1,832,700**	**1,961,100**	**2,282,300**	**2,427,000**	**2,383,800**	**1.85**	**-1.78**
All countries of Middle East		1,832,700	1,961,100	2,282,300	2,427,000	2,383,800	1.85	-1.78
SOUTH ASIA		**2,791,700**	**2,677,000**	**3,250,000**	**3,745,900**	**3,991,800**	**3.09**	**6.56**
All countries of South Asia		2,791,700	2,677,000	3,250,000	3,745,900	3,991,800	3.09	6.56

Yearbook of Tourism Statistics, Data 2008 – 2012, 2014 Edition

CAPE VERDE

3. Arrivals of non-resident tourists in hotels and similar establishments, by country of residence

		2008	2009	2010	2011	2012	Market share 2012	% Change 2012-2011
TOTAL		285,141	287,183	336,086	428,273	482,267	100.00	12.61
AFRICA		193	175	218	2,819	278	0.06	-90.14
Southern Africa		193	175	218	2,819	278	0.06	-90.14
South Africa		193	175	218	2,819	278	0.06	-90.14
AMERICAS		4,004	3,935	3,188	3,711	4,906	1.02	32.20
North America		4,004	3,935	3,188	3,711	4,906	1.02	32.20
United States of America		4,004	3,935	3,188	3,711	4,906	1.02	32.20
EUROPE		234,309	244,060	297,614	385,424	402,932	83.55	4.54
Northern Europe		51,680	57,011	72,019	90,481	115,238	23.90	27.36
United Kingdom		51,680	57,011	72,019	90,481	115,238	23.90	27.36
Southern Europe		116,690	98,891	108,508	135,858	110,849	22.98	-18.41
Italy		48,956	42,628	40,717	56,378	30,345	6.29	-46.18
Portugal		57,854	50,617	60,277	65,693	67,790	14.06	3.19
Spain		9,880	5,646	7,514	13,787	12,714	2.64	-7.78
Western Europe		65,939	88,158	117,087	159,085	176,845	36.67	11.16
Austria		876	977	962	1,772	1,571	0.33	-11.34
Belgium	(*)	8,632	22,091	21,655	24,169	34,608	7.18	43.19
France		21,057	22,675	43,496	66,641	69,593	14.43	4.43
Germany		32,705	40,138	48,920	60,495	67,306	13.96	11.26
Switzerland		2,669	2,277	2,054	6,008	3,767	0.78	-37.30
NOT SPECIFIED		46,635	39,013	35,066	36,319	74,151	15.38	104.17
Other countries of the World		46,635	39,013	35,066	36,319	74,151	15.38	104.17

Yearbook of Tourism Statistics, Data 2008 – 2012, 2014 Edition

CAPE VERDE

5. Overnight stays of non-resident tourists in hotels and similar establishments, by country of residence

		2008	2009	2010	2011	2012	Market share 2012	% Change 2012-2011
TOTAL		1,711,875	1,897,573	2,217,563	2,703,909	3,184,524	100.00	17.77
AFRICA		543	606	663	14,540	851	0.03	-94.15
Southern Africa		543	606	663	14,540	851	0.03	-94.15
South Africa		543	606	663	14,540	851	0.03	-94.15
AMERICAS		12,521	10,632	10,162	12,988	12,286	0.39	-5.40
North America		12,521	10,632	10,162	12,988	12,286	0.39	-5.40
United States of America		12,521	10,632	10,162	12,988	12,286	0.39	-5.40
EUROPE		1,448,975	1,663,042	2,006,352	2,507,979	2,723,056	85.51	8.58
Northern Europe		423,350	517,655	610,465	766,740	1,057,852	33.22	37.97
United Kingdom		423,350	517,655	610,465	766,740	1,057,852	33.22	37.97
Southern Europe		651,021	556,055	609,939	794,378	596,085	18.72	-24.96
Italy		339,693	290,662	278,261	397,473	215,113	6.75	-45.88
Portugal		271,595	242,905	299,228	335,688	318,099	9.99	-5.24
Spain		39,733	22,488	32,450	61,217	62,873	1.97	2.71
Western Europe		374,604	589,332	785,948	946,861	1,069,119	33.57	12.91
Austria		4,841	5,541	5,397	13,208	9,282	0.29	-29.72
Belgium	(*)	51,305	161,667	159,061	171,851	245,814	7.72	43.04
France		68,612	102,015	241,527	293,334	300,622	9.44	2.48
Germany		236,739	307,861	370,359	426,532	495,341	15.55	16.13
Switzerland		13,107	12,248	9,604	41,936	18,060	0.57	-56.93
NOT SPECIFIED		249,836	223,293	200,386	168,402	448,331	14.08	166.23
Other countries of the World		249,836	223,293	200,386	168,402	448,331	14.08	166.23

Yearbook of Tourism Statistics, Data 2008 – 2012, 2014 Edition

CAYMAN ISLANDS

1. Arrivals of non-resident tourists at national borders, by country of residence

		2008	2009	2010	2011	2012	Market share 2012	% Change 2012-2011
TOTAL	(*)	302,879	271,949	288,190	309,091	321,647	100.00	4.06
AFRICA		538	518	673	615	665	0.21	8.13
East Africa		43	48	76	67	41	0.01	-38.81
Comoros		2	3	2	1			
Eritrea					1			
Ethiopia		1		5				
Kenya		16	26	34	31	12	0.00	-61.29
Madagascar			1	1	1	4	0.00	300.00
Malawi		1	3	1		4	0.00	
Mauritius		6	1	7	4	3	0.00	-25.00
Reunion					1			
Rwanda					3			
Seychelles					1	2	0.00	100.00
Somalia					1			
Uganda		1	1		2			
United Republic of Tanzania				1	5	1	0.00	-80.00
Zambia		3	5	4	7	2	0.00	-71.43
Zimbabwe		13	8	18	12	13	0.00	8.33
Central Africa		7	9	20	28	29	0.01	3.57
Angola		1				4	0.00	
Cameroon			2			1	0.00	
Chad		1		1		1	0.00	
Congo				1				
Gabon		1		1				
Sao Tome and Principe		4	7	17	28	23	0.01	-17.86
North Africa		9	2	6	6	10	0.00	66.67
Algeria			1		1			
Morocco		3		4	4	9	0.00	125.00
Sudan		1	1	2	1	1	0.00	0.00
Tunisia		5						
Southern Africa		452	420	547	464	549	0.17	18.32
Botswana		10	7	8	10	5	0.00	-50.00
Lesotho						1	0.00	
Namibia		4	5		1	2	0.00	100.00
South Africa		397	364	487	386	478	0.15	23.83
Swaziland		41	44	52	67	63	0.02	-5.97
West Africa		27	39	24	50	36	0.01	-28.00
Cape Verde		1	3	1				
Côte d'Ivoire		4				1	0.00	
Gambia		1		1	1			
Ghana		6	8	6	6	3	0.00	-50.00
Liberia			1	1	1	1	0.00	0.00
Mauritania			1		1			
Nigeria		11	19	10	35	28	0.01	-20.00
Saint Helena			3					
Senegal		1		1	1	2	0.00	100.00
Sierra Leone		1		1	2			
Togo		2	4	3	3	1	0.00	-66.67
AMERICAS		278,584	249,692	264,999	284,543	296,355	92.14	4.15
Caribbean		15,171	12,985	13,000	12,531	14,071	4.37	12.29
Anguilla		32	10	37	16	12	0.00	-25.00
Antigua and Barbuda		98	27	72	64	66	0.02	3.13
Bahamas		732	717	1,048	830	772	0.24	-6.99
Barbados		541	446	478	460	636	0.20	38.26
Bermuda		731	570	788	526	553	0.17	5.13
British Virgin Islands		126	72	97	98	97	0.03	-1.02

132

CAYMAN ISLANDS

1. Arrivals of non-resident tourists at national borders, by country of residence

	2008	2009	2010	2011	2012	Market share 2012	% Change 2012-2011
Cuba	428	340	1,328	1,815	2,451	0.76	35.04
Dominica	39	14	23	19	28	0.01	47.37
Dominican Republic	220	243	247	292	254	0.08	-13.01
Grenada	37	24	37	22	30	0.01	36.36
Guadeloupe	1	1	10	9	1	0.00	-88.89
Haiti	14	26	13	15	16	0.00	6.67
Jamaica	10,470	9,527	7,609	7,378	8,070	2.51	9.38
Martinique			17	2			
Montserrat	17	6	11	7	9	0.00	28.57
Netherlands Antilles	2	8	12	9	3	0.00	-66.67
Puerto Rico	83	67	76	58	72	0.02	24.14
Saint Kitts and Nevis	27	26	47	39	45	0.01	15.38
Saint Lucia	115	80	81	73	71	0.02	-2.74
Saint Vincent and the Grenadines	40	35	47	38	48	0.01	26.32
Sint Maarten	22	10	9	10	5	0.00	-50.00
Trinidad and Tobago	876	609	758	632	700	0.22	10.76
Turks and Caicos Islands	469	96	111	66	62	0.02	-6.06
United States Virgin Islands	51	31	44	53	70	0.02	32.08
Central America	**2,059**	**2,200**	**1,839**	**1,910**	**2,354**	**0.73**	**23.25**
Belize		107	99	107	108	0.03	0.93
Costa Rica	112	170	131	118	90	0.03	-23.73
El Salvador	187	18	21	55	19	0.01	-65.45
Guatemala	12	56	66	48	73	0.02	52.08
Honduras	1,392	1,418	1,277	1,310	1,621	0.50	23.74
Nicaragua	208	284	118	106	133	0.04	25.47
Panama	148	147	127	166	310	0.10	86.75
North America	**259,446**	**232,705**	**248,343**	**268,035**	**277,759**	**86.36**	**3.63**
Canada	18,544	17,254	19,499	24,629	24,092	7.49	-2.18
Mexico	440	409	383	477	458	0.14	-3.98
United States of America	240,462	215,042	228,461	242,929	253,209	78.72	4.23
South America	**1,908**	**1,802**	**1,817**	**2,067**	**2,171**	**0.67**	**5.03**
Argentina	173	274	296	377	515	0.16	36.60
Bolivia	18	1	11	4	3	0.00	-25.00
Brazil	401	438	536	681	662	0.21	-2.79
Chile	71	100	97	117	116	0.04	-0.85
Colombia	543	421	355	286	307	0.10	7.34
Ecuador	70	67	57	68	69	0.02	1.47
Falkland Islands, Malvinas	1	1	1				
French Guiana		1		1			
Guyana	312	244	194	194	170	0.05	-12.37
Paraguay	3		2	4	1	0.00	-75.00
Peru	132	84	80	109	125	0.04	14.68
Suriname	6	6	6	36	40	0.01	11.11
Uruguay	6	19	28	19	14	0.00	-26.32
Venezuela	172	146	154	171	149	0.05	-12.87
EAST ASIA AND THE PACIFIC	**1,626**	**1,816**	**1,872**	**1,981**	**2,288**	**0.71**	**15.50**
North-East Asia	**197**	**312**	**280**	**490**	**540**	**0.17**	**10.20**
China	71	51	47	119	193	0.06	62.18
Hong Kong, China	58	50	51	81	70	0.02	-13.58
Japan	24	193	153	261	225	0.07	-13.79
Korea, Republic of	28	9	25	24	34	0.01	41.67
Mongolia					2	0.00	
Taiwan, Province of China	16	9	4	5	16	0.00	220.00
South-East Asia	**220**	**276**	**212**	**154**	**119**	**0.04**	**-22.73**
Brunei Darussalam		4	1	2			
Cambodia	1	2	2	1	4	0.00	300.00
Indonesia	15	16	19	15	10	0.00	-33.33

Yearbook of Tourism Statistics, Data 2008 – 2012, 2014 Edition

CAYMAN ISLANDS

1. Arrivals of non-resident tourists at national borders, by country of residence

	2008	2009	2010	2011	2012	Market share 2012	% Change 2012-2011
Malaysia		42	35	34	26	0.01	-23.53
Myanmar		3					
Philippines	134	147	85	32			
Singapore	59	46	66	61	66	0.02	8.20
Thailand	11	10	4	7	12	0.00	71.43
Timor-Leste				1			
Viet Nam		6		1	1	0.00	0.00
Australasia	**1,206**	**1,223**	**1,369**	**1,332**	**1,620**	**0.50**	**21.62**
Australia	922	942	1,118	1,069	1,267	0.39	18.52
New Zealand	284	281	251	263	353	0.11	34.22
Melanesia	**1**		**5**	**1**	**1**	**0.00**	**0.00**
Fiji			1	1			
New Caledonia			1				
Norfolk Island					1	0.00	
Papua New Guinea				1			
Solomon Islands			2				
Vanuatu	1						
Micronesia	**1**	**5**	**5**	**3**	**6**	**0.00**	**100.00**
Cocos (Keeling) Islands			1	1	2	0.00	100.00
Guam		2		1	3	0.00	200.00
Kiribati	1		2		1	0.00	
Marshall Islands			1				
Micronesia, Federated States of		2					
Nauru		1		1			
Palau				1			
Polynesia	**1**		**1**	**1**	**2**	**0.00**	**100.00**
Niue			1		2	0.00	
Samoa				1			
Tonga	1						
EUROPE	**21,419**	**19,262**	**19,999**	**21,313**	**21,582**	**6.71**	**1.26**
Central/Eastern Europe	**367**	**470**	**464**	**664**	**638**	**0.20**	**-3.92**
Armenia					2		
Bulgaria	14	24	27	43	23	0.01	-46.51
Czech Republic	72	129	79	120	98	0.03	-18.33
Estonia	1	13	6	31	8	0.00	-74.19
Georgia		1		1			
Hungary	43	82	95	95	100	0.03	5.26
Kazakhstan		1		4	3	0.00	-25.00
Latvia	8	7	6	11	12	0.00	9.09
Lithuania	6	1	18	17	6	0.00	-64.71
Poland	68	70	71	136	121	0.04	-11.03
Republic of Moldova				1	1	0.00	0.00
Romania	43	63	65	88	89	0.03	1.14
Russian Federation	87	45	81	85	92	0.03	8.24
Slovakia		21		22	50	0.02	127.27
Ukraine	25	13	16	8	34	0.01	325.00
Uzbekistan					1	0.00	
Northern Europe	**16,296**	**14,605**	**14,215**	**14,539**	**14,321**	**4.45**	**-1.50**
Denmark	209	124	138	200	172	0.05	-14.00
Faeroe Islands	1						
Finland	81	48	69	113	106	0.03	-6.19
Iceland	24	2	9	13	10	0.00	-23.08
Ireland	1,161	965	946	1,085	956	0.30	-11.89
Isle of Man		7	8	7	7	0.00	0.00
Norway	225	137	243	224	255	0.08	13.84
Svalbard and Jan Mayen Islands				1			
Sweden	318	222	299	362	381	0.12	5.25

Yearbook of Tourism Statistics, Data 2008 – 2012, 2014 Edition

CAYMAN ISLANDS

1. Arrivals of non-resident tourists at national borders, by country of residence

	2008	2009	2010	2011	2012	Market share 2012	% Change 2012-2011
United Kingdom	14,277	13,100	12,503	12,534	12,434	3.87	-0.80
Southern Europe	**1,524**	**1,514**	**2,152**	**2,688**	**3,098**	**0.96**	**15.25**
Albania	2	1	1		1	0.00	
Andorra	122	61	82	67	31	0.01	-53.73
Bosnia and Herzegovina		4	1	3			
Croatia	13	12	11	12	6	0.00	-50.00
Gibraltar	16	20	10	4	8	0.00	100.00
Greece	60	53	73	67	58	0.02	-13.43
Holy See	1		1				
Italy	879	960	935	1,104	1,143	0.36	3.53
Malta	7	3	2	7	2	0.00	-71.43
Portugal	78	62	115	114	160	0.05	40.35
San Marino		2	1		3	0.00	
Serbia		15	13	11	7	0.00	-36.36
Serbia and Montenegro		4					
Slovenia	21	19	36	32	48	0.01	50.00
Spain	324	298	870	1,264	1,631	0.51	29.03
TFYR of Macedonia	1		1	3			
Western Europe	**3,074**	**2,577**	**3,038**	**3,290**	**3,397**	**1.06**	**3.25**
Austria	235	187	248	245	237	0.07	-3.27
Belgium	162	106	131	155	138	0.04	-10.97
France	623	501	603	639	739	0.23	15.65
Germany	991	913	1,106	1,174	1,219	0.38	3.83
Liechtenstein	2	2	1	7	6	0.00	-14.29
Luxembourg	14	9	13	21	9	0.00	-57.14
Monaco	5	5	5	13	8	0.00	-38.46
Netherlands	500	404	440	490	441	0.14	-10.00
Switzerland	542	450	491	546	600	0.19	9.89
East Mediterranean Europe	**158**	**96**	**130**	**132**	**128**	**0.04**	**-3.03**
Cyprus	15	9	15	8	9	0.00	12.50
Israel	102	60	99	105	100	0.03	-4.76
Turkey	41	27	16	19	19	0.01	0.00
MIDDLE EAST	**99**	**88**	**98**	**118**	**136**	**0.04**	**15.25**
Bahrain	2	3	2	8	6	0.00	-25.00
Egypt	15	12	5	13	13	0.00	0.00
Iraq		1					
Jordan			4	2	1	0.00	-50.00
Kuwait	3	6	4	4	6	0.00	50.00
Lebanon	12	4	4	2	6	0.00	200.00
Libya					1	0.00	
Oman	2	3	8	1	3	0.00	200.00
Qatar	8		16	31	35	0.01	12.90
Saudi Arabia	50	44	41	42	39	0.01	-7.14
Syrian Arab Republic	1			1			
United Arab Emirates	6	14	13	14	26	0.01	85.71
Yemen		1	1				
SOUTH ASIA	**214**	**202**	**187**	**179**	**198**	**0.06**	**10.61**
Afghanistan	2	1	1				
Bangladesh	2	1	1	1	1	0.00	0.00
India	190	171	157	149	161	0.05	8.05
Iran, Islamic Republic of	1		5	2	3	0.00	50.00
Nepal	2	11	7	4	14	0.00	250.00
Pakistan	8	2	5	5	2	0.00	-60.00
Sri Lanka	9	16	11	18	17	0.01	-5.56
NOT SPECIFIED	**399**	**371**	**362**	**342**	**423**	**0.13**	**23.68**
Other countries of the World	399	371	362	342	423	0.13	23.68

Yearbook of Tourism Statistics, Data 2008 – 2012, 2014 Edition

CENTRAL AFRICAN REPUBLIC

1. Arrivals of non-resident tourists at national borders, by nationality

	2008	2009	2010	2011	2012	Market share 2012	% Change 2012-2011
TOTAL (*)	**30,611**	**52,429**	**53,821**				
AFRICA	**16,038**	**26,984**	**26,684**				
East Africa	**498**	**2,052**	**2,284**				
Rwanda	190	566	674				
Other countries of East Africa	308	1,486	1,610				
Central Africa	**7,230**	**9,964**	**10,926**				
Cameroon	2,895	4,125	2,861				
Chad	1,275	3,221	2,732				
Congo	1,107	734	1,845				
Democratic Republic of the Congo	795	588	1,124				
Gabon	912	695	762				
Other countries of Central Africa	246	601	1,602				
North Africa	**604**	**1,884**	**2,184**				
Sudan	154	886	577				
Other countries of North Africa	450	998	1,607				
Southern Africa	**580**	**2,898**	**1,587**				
South Africa	386	1,553	709				
Other countries of Southern Africa	194	1,345	878				
West Africa	**5,826**	**8,795**	**8,737**				
Benin	692	1,386	1,088				
Côte d'Ivoire	1,024	1,116	1,236				
Mali	276	1,052	924				
Nigeria	811	1,133	1,350				
Senegal	1,127	1,662	1,577				
Togo	298	1,124	736				
Other countries of West Africa	1,598	1,322	1,826				
Other Africa	**1,300**	**1,391**	**966**				
Other countries of Africa	1,300	1,391	966				
AMERICAS	**1,300**	**3,171**	**5,074**				
North America	**984**	**2,443**	**3,287**				
Canada	209	1,076	1,130				
United States of America	775	1,367	2,157				
Other Americas	**316**	**728**	**1,787**				
Other countries of the Americas	316	728	1,787				
EAST ASIA AND THE PACIFIC	**2,174**	**3,888**	**5,035**				
North-East Asia	**400**	**2,656**	**3,319**				
China	292	1,748	1,997				
Japan	108	908	1,322				
Other East Asia and the Pacific	**1,774**	**1,232**	**1,716**				
Other countries of Asia	1,774	1,232	1,716				
EUROPE	**10,559**	**16,612**	**13,141**				
Northern Europe	**212**	**2,028**	**868**				
United Kingdom	212	2,028	868				
Southern Europe	**788**	**2,017**	**1,229**				
Italy	788	2,017	1,229				
Western Europe	**8,256**	**8,263**	**9,899**				
Belgium	476	1,407	803				
France	6,975	4,431	7,661				
Germany	433	1,276	672				
Switzerland	372	1,149	763				
Other Europe	**1,303**	**4,304**	**1,145**				
Other countries of Europe	1,303	4,304	1,145				

Yearbook of Tourism Statistics, Data 2008 – 2012, 2014 Edition

CENTRAL AFRICAN REPUBLIC

1. Arrivals of non-resident tourists at national borders, by nationality

	2008	2009	2010	2011	2012	Market share 2012	% Change 2012-2011
MIDDLE EAST	**448**	**1,257**	**2,747**				
Lebanon	387	712	1,484				
Other countries of Middle East	61	545	1,263				
NOT SPECIFIED	**92**	**517**	**1,140**				
Other countries of the World	92	517	1,140				

Yearbook of Tourism Statistics, Data 2008 – 2012, 2014 Edition

CHAD

1. Arrivals of non-resident tourists at national borders, by nationality

	2008	2009	2010	2011	2012	Market share 2012	% Change 2012-2011
TOTAL	**61,000**	**70,000**	**71,000**				
AFRICA	**41,000**	**16,000**	**34,000**				
Other Africa	**41,000**	**16,000**	**34,000**				
All countries of Africa	41,000	16,000	34,000				
AMERICAS	**3,000**	**11,000**	**6,000**				
Other Americas	**3,000**	**11,000**	**6,000**				
All countries of the Americas	3,000	11,000	6,000				
EAST ASIA AND THE PACIFIC	**3,000**	**9,000**	**3,000**				
Other East Asia and the Pacific	**3,000**	**9,000**	**3,000**				
All countries East Asia/Pacific	3,000	9,000	3,000				
EUROPE	**12,000**	**24,000**	**25,000**				
Other Europe	**12,000**	**24,000**	**25,000**				
All countries of Europe	12,000	24,000	25,000				
MIDDLE EAST	**1,000**	**10,000**	**2,000**				
All countries of Middle East	1,000	10,000	2,000				
SOUTH ASIA	**1,000**		**1,000**				
All countries of South Asia	1,000		1,000				

Yearbook of Tourism Statistics, Data 2008 – 2012, 2014 Edition

CHAD

3. Arrivals of non-resident tourists in hotels and similar establishments, by nationality

	2008	2009	2010	2011	2012	Market share 2012	% Change 2012-2011
TOTAL (*)	21,871	31,169	14,298				
AFRICA	5,933	7,890	4,007				
East Africa	288	74	146				
All countries of East Africa	288	74	146				
Central Africa	1,332	2,389	990				
All countries of Central Africa	1,332	2,389	990				
North Africa	627	1,174	208				
All countries of North Africa	627	1,174	208				
West Africa	1,046	3,112	657				
All countries of West Africa	1,046	3,112	657				
Other Africa	2,640	1,141	2,006				
Other countries of Africa	2,640	1,141	2,006				
AMERICAS	2,395	3,553	1,440				
North America	1,741	3,091	1,311				
Canada	42	512	230				
United States of America	1,699	2,579	1,081				
Other Americas	654	462	129				
Other countries of the Americas	654	462	129				
EAST ASIA AND THE PACIFIC	1,039	1,124	457				
North-East Asia	114	536	113				
China	77	536	57				
Japan	33		21				
Korea, Republic of	4		35				
Other East Asia and the Pacific	925	588	344				
Other countries East Asia/Pacific	925	588	344				
EUROPE	12,251	16,348	8,170				
Northern Europe	756	518	281				
United Kingdom	607	518	281				
Scandinavia	149						
Southern Europe	421	484	224				
Italy	421	484	224				
Western Europe	7,294	7,253	6,435				
Belgium	491	335	198				
France	6,142	6,564	5,843				
Germany	298	285	243				
Netherlands	147	33	52				
Switzerland	216	36	99				
Other Europe	3,780	8,093	1,230				
Other countries of Europe	3,780	8,093	1,230				
MIDDLE EAST	253	2,254	224				
Egypt	23	190	30				
Lebanon	8	136	20				
Libya	12	827	7				
Saudi Arabia	1		22				
Syrian Arab Republic	5		4				
Other countries of Middle East	204	1,101	141				

Yearbook of Tourism Statistics, Data 2008 – 2012, 2014 Edition

CHAD

5. Overnight stays of non-resident tourists in hotels and similar establishments, by nationality

		2008	2009	2010	2011	2012	Market share 2012	% Change 2012-2011
TOTAL	(*)			36,916				
AFRICA				13,913				
East Africa				251				
All countries of East Africa				251				
Central Africa				3,214				
All countries of Central Africa				3,214				
North Africa				866				
All countries of North Africa				866				
West Africa				2,184				
All countries of West Africa				2,184				
Other Africa				7,398				
Other countries of Africa				7,398				
AMERICAS				3,494				
North America				2,895				
Canada				670				
United States of America				2,225				
Other Americas				599				
Other countries of the Americas				599				
EAST ASIA AND THE PACIFIC				1,119				
North-East Asia				233				
China				183				
Japan				41				
Korea, Republic of				9				
Other East Asia and the Pacific				886				
Other countries East Asia/Pacific				886				
EUROPE				17,782				
Northern Europe				702				
United Kingdom				702				
Southern Europe				527				
Italy				527				
Western Europe				13,158				
Belgium				493				
France				11,433				
Germany				845				
Netherlands				111				
Switzerland				276				
Other Europe				3,395				
Other countries of Europe				3,395				
MIDDLE EAST				608				
Egypt				29				
Lebanon				38				
Libya				100				
Saudi Arabia				1				
Syrian Arab Republic				12				
Other countries of Middle East				428				

Yearbook of Tourism Statistics, Data 2008 – 2012, 2014 Edition

CHILE

1. Arrivals of non-resident tourists at national borders, by nationality

		2008	2009	2010	2011	2012	Market share 2012	% Change 2012-2011
TOTAL	(*)	2,710,024	2,759,695	2,800,637	3,137,285	3,554,279	100.00	13.29
AFRICA		4,673	3,894	3,967	4,127	4,293	0.12	4.02
East Africa		104	132	121	81	80	0.00	-1.23
Kenya		74	63	53	50	54	0.00	8.00
Somalia					1			
Zimbabwe		30	69	68	30	26	0.00	-13.33
Central Africa		89	59	28	52	44	0.00	-15.38
Angola		89	59	28	52	44	0.00	-15.38
North Africa		439	299	246	198	483	0.01	143.94
Algeria		242	151	76	55	262	0.01	376.36
Morocco		157	121	145	118	149	0.00	26.27
Tunisia		40	27	25	25	72	0.00	188.00
Southern Africa		3,412	2,996	3,016	3,392	3,192	0.09	-5.90
South Africa		3,412	2,996	3,016	3,392	3,192	0.09	-5.90
West Africa		109	75	144	97	143	0.00	47.42
Cape Verde		2	18	8	9	12	0.00	33.33
Ghana		23	17	47	24	39	0.00	62.50
Nigeria		84	40	89	64	92	0.00	43.75
Other Africa		520	333	412	307	351	0.01	14.33
Other countries of Africa		520	333	412	307	351	0.01	14.33
AMERICAS		2,076,345	2,174,166	2,222,002	2,532,750	2,899,056	81.57	14.46
Caribbean		5,415	5,680	6,193	8,023	8,232	0.23	2.61
Bahamas		77	52	19	59	44	0.00	-25.42
Barbados		61	57	48	75	84	0.00	12.00
Cuba		1,439	1,230	1,277	1,066	1,074	0.03	0.75
Dominica		18	26	18	49	67	0.00	36.73
Dominican Republic		2,827	3,260	3,491	4,683	4,878	0.14	4.16
Grenada		11	23	15	32	59	0.00	84.38
Haiti		391	477	820	1,389	1,215	0.03	-12.53
Jamaica		232	166	124	159	184	0.01	15.72
Puerto Rico		44	22	10	110	192	0.01	74.55
Saint Lucia		19	13	10	20	28	0.00	40.00
Saint Vincent and the Grenadines		26	27	7	18	30	0.00	66.67
Trinidad and Tobago		200	253	272	253	222	0.01	-12.25
Other countries of the Caribbean		70	74	82	110	155	0.00	40.91
Central America		13,944	12,677	12,175	13,577	15,530	0.44	14.38
Belize		62	59	37	49	79	0.00	61.22
Costa Rica		4,414	4,121	4,081	4,882	5,635	0.16	15.42
El Salvador		1,866	1,720	1,540	1,715	1,809	0.05	5.48
Guatemala		2,317	2,140	1,952	2,158	2,420	0.07	12.14
Honduras		1,107	841	926	1,096	1,272	0.04	16.06
Nicaragua		781	707	696	641	731	0.02	14.04
Panama		3,397	3,089	2,943	3,036	3,584	0.10	18.05
North America		239,060	226,002	204,346	221,706	229,948	6.47	3.72
Canada		36,981	34,574	32,389	34,297	35,250	0.99	2.78
Mexico		33,494	28,711	29,007	34,947	36,196	1.02	3.57
United States of America		168,548	162,693	142,937	152,446	158,493	4.46	3.97
Other countries of North America		37	24	13	16	9	0.00	-43.75
South America		1,817,926	1,929,807	1,999,288	2,289,444	2,645,346	74.43	15.55
Argentina		863,897	996,813	1,001,125	1,118,767	1,377,645	38.76	23.14
Bolivia		307,845	309,401	307,475	321,488	355,758	10.01	10.66
Brazil		252,973	209,485	229,337	324,594	373,840	10.52	15.17
Colombia		46,452	47,768	52,477	67,834	81,884	2.30	20.71
Ecuador		23,075	23,097	23,591	27,888	28,596	0.80	2.54
Guyana		34	28	22	29	36	0.00	24.14
Paraguay		22,853	22,349	28,267	30,024	28,979	0.82	-3.48

141

Yearbook of Tourism Statistics, Data 2008 – 2012, 2014 Edition

CHILE

1. Arrivals of non-resident tourists at national borders, by nationality

	2008	2009	2010	2011	2012	Market share 2012	% Change 2012-2011
Peru	252,472	269,534	308,759	338,916	338,026	9.51	-0.26
Suriname	45	68	16	36	62	0.00	72.22
Uruguay	27,010	29,804	30,614	36,888	35,624	1.00	-3.43
Venezuela	21,255	21,460	17,602	22,980	24,790	0.70	7.88
Other countries of South America	15		3		106	0.00	
EAST ASIA AND THE PACIFIC	**79,108**	**73,370**	**71,888**	**77,715**	**97,820**	**2.75**	**25.87**
North-East Asia	**29,724**	**27,399**	**29,052**	**34,215**	**40,272**	**1.13**	**17.70**
China	6,303	6,256	6,787	10,076	12,088	0.34	19.97
Japan	13,728	13,129	14,261	12,693	15,059	0.42	18.64
Korea, Dem. People's Republic of	711	345	333	358	450	0.01	25.70
Korea, Republic of	7,856	6,582	6,541	9,808	11,030	0.31	12.46
Mongolia	44	20	27	23	19	0.00	-17.39
Taiwan, Province of China	1,082	1,067	1,103	1,257	1,626	0.05	29.36
South-East Asia	**3,312**	**3,015**	**3,360**	**3,740**	**4,422**	**0.12**	**18.24**
Brunei Darussalam	9	4	2	20	6	0.00	-70.00
Cambodia	4		9	3	5	0.00	66.67
Indonesia	522	406	627	607	635	0.02	4.61
Lao People's Democratic Republic		2	13		4	0.00	
Malaysia	636	645	625	743	861	0.02	15.88
Myanmar	25	9	16	18	18	0.00	0.00
Philippines	1,193	869	891	1,036	1,280	0.04	23.55
Singapore	544	493	770	810	915	0.03	12.96
Thailand	308	296	304	379	573	0.02	51.19
Viet Nam	71	291	103	124	125	0.00	0.81
Australasia	**45,687**	**42,335**	**39,014**	**38,900**	**52,003**	**1.46**	**33.68**
Australia	36,542	33,601	30,694	31,105	43,341	1.22	39.34
New Zealand	9,145	8,734	8,320	7,795	8,662	0.24	11.12
Polynesia	**19**	**1**	**5**		**5**	**0.00**	
Samoa	6	1	5		5	0.00	
Tuvalu	13						
Other East Asia and the Pacific	**366**	**620**	**457**	**860**	**1,118**	**0.03**	**30.00**
Other countries of Asia	291	386	381	806	1,033	0.03	28.16
Other countries of Oceania	75	234	76	54	85	0.00	57.41
EUROPE	**409,320**	**383,168**	**363,117**	**375,857**	**388,474**	**10.93**	**3.36**
Central/Eastern Europe	**12,966**	**11,585**	**10,742**	**13,161**	**15,596**	**0.44**	**18.50**
Armenia	16	18	23	15	22	0.00	46.67
Azerbaijan	7	6	9	16	12	0.00	-25.00
Bulgaria	431	475	505	548	752	0.02	37.23
Estonia	216	242	187	254	411	0.01	61.81
Georgia	42	8	13	33	22	0.00	-33.33
Hungary	1,261	959	759	749	1,005	0.03	34.18
Kazakhstan	57	34	40	31	43	0.00	38.71
Kyrgyzstan	4	8	10	5	4	0.00	-20.00
Latvia	345	241	222	202	309	0.01	52.97
Lithuania	407	410	243	312	327	0.01	4.81
Poland	4,543	4,291	3,967	3,987	4,030	0.11	1.08
Republic of Moldova	27	8	14	26	19	0.00	-26.92
Romania	1,069	893	867	1,111	1,088	0.03	-2.07
Russian Federation	2,909	2,582	2,629	4,344	5,792	0.16	33.33
Slovakia	919	908	682	830	901	0.03	8.55
Tajikistan	1		4		2	0.00	
Turkmenistan				7			
Ukraine	703	489	560	683	848	0.02	24.16
Uzbekistan	9	13	8	8	9	0.00	12.50
Northern Europe	**89,955**	**78,609**	**71,015**	**73,724**	**73,427**	**2.07**	**-0.40**
Denmark	5,957	5,010	4,667	4,802	4,976	0.14	3.62

142

CHILE

1. Arrivals of non-resident tourists at national borders, by nationality

	2008	2009	2010	2011	2012	Market share 2012	% Change 2012-2011
Finland	3,243	3,035	2,831	3,104	3,071	0.09	-1.06
Iceland	311	230	209	342	354	0.01	3.51
Ireland	6,880	4,879	4,135	3,782	3,556	0.10	-5.98
Norway	6,770	5,561	5,665	5,793	6,176	0.17	6.61
Sweden	13,450	12,289	11,981	12,355	12,873	0.36	4.19
United Kingdom	53,344	47,605	41,527	43,546	42,421	1.19	-2.58
Southern Europe	**97,187**	**88,953**	**85,372**	**90,648**	**99,126**	**2.79**	**9.35**
Albania	84	26	51	60	57	0.00	-5.00
Andorra	84	134	89	100	129	0.00	29.00
Bosnia and Herzegovina	24	13	40	41	60	0.00	46.34
Croatia	640	553	653	642	610	0.02	-4.98
Greece	1,707	1,314	1,185	1,198	961	0.03	-19.78
Holy See	4	3	4	2	6	0.00	200.00
Italy	28,778	27,477	26,603	27,164	28,540	0.80	5.07
Malta	94	137	97	103	162	0.00	57.28
Portugal	4,913	3,566	3,820	4,630	4,913	0.14	6.11
San Marino	29	16	15	13	16	0.00	23.08
Serbia	331	313	264	324	359	0.01	10.80
Slovenia	964	880	646	696	639	0.02	-8.19
Spain	59,512	54,504	51,874	55,643	62,646	1.76	12.59
TFYR of Macedonia	23	17	31	32	28	0.00	-12.50
Western Europe	**178,315**	**174,976**	**167,979**	**170,470**	**174,409**	**4.91**	**2.31**
Austria	6,789	7,508	6,894	6,809	7,180	0.20	5.45
Belgium	9,052	8,748	8,804	9,268	9,659	0.27	4.22
France	59,343	61,130	60,091	60,993	60,220	1.69	-1.27
Germany	64,910	62,006	57,899	58,202	62,891	1.77	8.06
Liechtenstein	50	35	51	40	33	0.00	-17.50
Luxembourg	301	295	288	276	333	0.01	20.65
Monaco	18	36	13	22	20	0.00	-9.09
Netherlands	20,002	18,430	17,072	17,374	16,402	0.46	-5.59
Switzerland	17,850	16,788	16,867	17,486	17,671	0.50	1.06
East Mediterranean Europe	**25,294**	**23,583**	**23,049**	**24,432**	**22,283**	**0.63**	**-8.80**
Cyprus	63	58	80	86	66	0.00	-23.26
Israel	23,827	22,235	21,543	22,777	20,435	0.57	-10.28
Turkey	1,404	1,290	1,426	1,569	1,782	0.05	13.58
Other Europe	**5,603**	**5,462**	**4,960**	**3,422**	**3,633**	**0.10**	**6.17**
Other countries of Europe	5,603	5,462	4,960	3,422	3,633	0.10	6.17
MIDDLE EAST	**464**	**517**	**506**	**478**	**651**	**0.02**	**36.19**
Bahrain	6	5	4	2	11	0.00	450.00
Egypt	98	70	83	117	132	0.00	12.82
Iraq	8	66	8	7	17	0.00	142.86
Jordan	104	61	55	69	76	0.00	10.14
Kuwait	6	2	57	24	16	0.00	-33.33
Lebanon	111	96	76	89	119	0.00	33.71
Libya		5	4	3	12	0.00	300.00
Oman	11	6	2	3	24	0.00	700.00
Qatar	5		28	5	2	0.00	-60.00
Saudi Arabia	10	30	27	60	62	0.00	3.33
Syrian Arab Republic	44	36	32	35	49	0.00	40.00
United Arab Emirates	33	58	104	13	62	0.00	376.92
Yemen	5	4	1	6	3	0.00	-50.00
Other countries of Middle East	23	78	25	45	66	0.00	46.67
SOUTH ASIA	**2,890**	**2,821**	**2,794**	**3,155**	**3,379**	**0.10**	**7.10**
Afghanistan	30	23	11	12	102	0.00	750.00
Bangladesh	27	28	55	25	14	0.00	-44.00
Bhutan	1	1	2	2	4	0.00	100.00

Yearbook of Tourism Statistics, Data 2008 – 2012, 2014 Edition

CHILE

1. Arrivals of non-resident tourists at national borders, by nationality

	2008	2009	2010	2011	2012	Market share 2012	% Change 2012-2011
India	2,451	2,339	2,206	2,671	2,871	0.08	7.49
Iran, Islamic Republic of	69	58	83	83	88	0.00	6.02
Maldives	1		7				
Nepal	35	36	26	27	49	0.00	81.48
Pakistan	230	307	377	295	212	0.01	-28.14
Sri Lanka	46	29	27	40	39	0.00	-2.50
NOT SPECIFIED	**137,224**	**121,759**	**136,363**	**143,203**	**160,606**	**4.52**	**12.15**
Other countries of the World	107	65	57	140	200	0.01	42.86
Nationals Residing Abroad	137,117	121,694	136,306	143,063	160,406	4.51	12.12

144

CHINA

2. Arrivals of non-resident visitors at national borders, by nationality

	2008	2009	2010	2011	2012	Market share 2012	% Change 2012-2011
TOTAL	130,027,393	126,475,923	133,762,239	135,423,453	132,405,325	100.00	-2.23
AFRICA	323,921	340,443	391,475	424,482	439,619	0.33	3.57
East Africa	72,955	77,544	96,882	111,792	120,435	0.09	7.73
Burundi	793	727	934	1,298	1,241	0.00	-4.39
Comoros	418	443	733	781	870	0.00	11.40
Ethiopia	11,292	11,952	14,776	18,561	23,086	0.02	24.38
Kenya	11,656	11,169	13,051	15,158	15,696	0.01	3.55
Madagascar	4,485	6,308	8,377	9,392	9,931	0.01	5.74
Mauritius	14,734	15,084	17,465	18,289	17,454	0.01	-4.57
Mozambique	1,473	1,732	2,280	3,195	3,751	0.00	17.40
Seychelles	1,157	1,145	1,346	1,385	1,467	0.00	5.92
Somalia	489	564	709	951	1,300	0.00	36.70
Uganda	6,464	7,742	10,821	14,456	14,878	0.01	2.92
United Republic of Tanzania	10,898	13,429	15,246	16,441	18,572	0.01	12.96
Zambia	3,079	2,888	4,256	4,813	5,659	0.00	17.58
Zimbabwe	6,017	4,361	6,888	7,072	6,530	0.00	-7.66
Central Africa	19,175	19,971	24,087	26,540	30,203	0.02	13.80
Cameroon	6,265	6,886	6,871	7,052	7,873	0.01	11.64
Central African Republic	256	327	375	426	572	0.00	34.27
Chad	624	685	824	808	945	0.00	16.96
Congo	4,528	4,409	4,408	5,111	5,584	0.00	9.25
Democratic Republic of the Congo	6,484	6,853	10,491	12,080	14,001	0.01	15.90
Gabon	1,018	811	1,118	1,063	1,228	0.00	15.52
North Africa	49,725	55,396	61,910	62,376	63,499	0.05	1.80
Algeria	20,243	24,893	25,776	27,982	27,627	0.02	-1.27
Morocco	11,756	12,434	14,034	13,810	13,973	0.01	1.18
Sudan	9,052	9,928	11,475	11,944	11,766	0.01	-1.49
Tunisia	8,674	8,141	10,625	8,640	10,133	0.01	17.28
Southern Africa	57,042	53,847	68,899	72,201	76,506	0.06	5.96
Botswana	1,357	1,643	2,367	2,545	2,436	0.00	-4.28
Lesotho	422	343	474	555	595	0.00	7.21
Namibia	801	892	1,327	1,438	1,722	0.00	19.75
South Africa	54,251	50,783	64,477	67,354	71,529	0.05	6.20
Swaziland	211	186	254	309	224	0.00	-27.51
West Africa	104,997	108,684	110,067	119,111	111,797	0.08	-6.14
Benin	3,970	3,887	4,694	4,993	4,819	0.00	-3.48
Côte d'Ivoire	2,570	2,445	2,886	2,301	3,697	0.00	60.67
Gambia	1,681	1,874	2,167	2,100	2,169	0.00	3.29
Ghana	17,160	14,657	17,152	19,767	16,918	0.01	-14.41
Guinea	8,030	8,005	9,068	9,868	9,987	0.01	1.21
Mali	14,293	12,230	14,389	15,038	13,806	0.01	-8.19
Niger	5,090	5,457	6,465	6,890	7,945	0.01	15.31
Nigeria	43,515	50,567	41,372	45,440	38,852	0.03	-14.50
Senegal	4,811	5,625	7,484	8,026	8,492	0.01	5.81
Sierra Leone	1,165	1,172	1,279	1,585	1,871	0.00	18.04
Togo	2,712	2,765	3,111	3,103	3,241	0.00	4.45
Other Africa	20,027	25,001	29,630	32,462	37,179	0.03	14.53
Other countries of Africa	20,027	25,001	29,630	32,462	37,179	0.03	14.53
AMERICAS	2,581,855	2,491,190	2,995,397	3,201,031	3,179,516	2.40	-0.67
Caribbean	14,107	12,548	13,805	13,857	15,798	0.01	14.01
Antigua and Barbuda	173	201	268	223	277	0.00	24.22
Bahamas	651	401	586	623	669	0.00	7.38
Cuba	3,632	2,391	2,705	2,433	2,644	0.00	8.67
Dominica	927	890	661	578	701	0.00	21.28
Dominican Republic	2,818	2,593	3,036	2,943	3,301	0.00	12.16

145

CHINA

2. Arrivals of non-resident visitors at national borders, by nationality

	2008	2009	2010	2011	2012	Market share 2012	% Change 2012-2011
Haiti	304	203	270	336	378	0.00	12.50
Jamaica	3,258	3,627	3,978	4,612	5,330	0.00	15.57
Netherlands Antilles	7	3	4	1	3	0.00	200.00
Puerto Rico	7	14	11	8	7	0.00	-12.50
Trinidad and Tobago	2,330	2,225	2,286	2,100	2,488	0.00	18.48
Central America	**19,843**	**18,371**	**21,827**	**22,661**	**23,339**	**0.02**	**2.99**
Belize	4,002	3,474	3,186	3,225	3,053	0.00	-5.33
Costa Rica	4,568	4,111	5,084	5,451	5,748	0.00	5.45
El Salvador	1,074	860	987	1,120	1,218	0.00	8.75
Guatemala	1,924	1,637	2,135	2,350	2,538	0.00	8.00
Honduras	2,648	2,459	2,780	2,709	2,943	0.00	8.64
Panama	5,627	5,830	7,655	7,806	7,839	0.01	0.42
North America	**2,370,080**	**2,292,444**	**2,744,250**	**2,917,845**	**2,884,069**	**2.18**	**-1.16**
Canada	534,712	550,333	685,304	747,981	708,294	0.53	-5.31
Mexico	48,920	32,298	49,351	53,720	57,716	0.04	7.44
United States of America	1,786,448	1,709,813	2,009,595	2,116,144	2,118,059	1.60	0.09
South America	**176,335**	**166,294**	**213,441**	**244,915**	**253,872**	**0.19**	**3.66**
Argentina	19,158	16,767	23,084	25,656	24,883	0.02	-3.01
Bolivia	3,451	4,083	5,252	6,470	6,454	0.00	-0.25
Brazil	74,656	63,676	85,050	97,912	99,445	0.08	1.57
Chile	13,014	12,245	15,927	17,763	19,661	0.01	10.69
Colombia	21,186	20,441	26,870	31,792	34,315	0.03	7.94
Ecuador	5,159	4,893	6,271	7,211	7,965	0.01	10.46
Guyana	715	782	761	837	1,072	0.00	28.08
Paraguay	1,142	1,119	1,673	1,535	1,444	0.00	-5.93
Peru	10,537	10,910	12,798	14,190	15,043	0.01	6.01
Suriname	2,287	2,658	2,637	2,944	3,056	0.00	3.80
Uruguay	2,616	2,641	3,540	3,784	3,886	0.00	2.70
Venezuela	22,414	26,079	29,578	34,821	36,648	0.03	5.25
Other Americas	**1,490**	**1,533**	**2,074**	**1,753**	**2,438**	**0.00**	**39.08**
Other countries of the Americas	1,490	1,533	2,074	1,753	2,438	0.00	39.08
EAST ASIA AND THE PACIFIC	**119,584,350**	**117,588,819**	**122,889,279**	**123,828,043**	**120,801,853**	**91.24**	**-2.44**
North-East Asia	**113,915,659**	**111,734,016**	**116,353,704**	**117,301,530**	**113,992,778**	**86.09**	**-2.82**
Hong Kong, China	78,350,129	77,335,996	79,321,851	79,357,701	78,712,983	59.45	-0.81
Japan	3,446,117	3,317,459	3,731,200	3,658,169	3,518,153	2.66	-3.83
Korea, Dem. People's Republic of	101,824	103,880	116,382	152,300	180,573	0.14	18.56
Korea, Republic of	3,960,392	3,197,538	4,076,392	4,185,398	4,069,868	3.07	-2.76
Macao, China	22,966,336	22,718,406	23,172,939	23,690,767	21,160,557	15.98	-10.68
Mongolia	705,270	576,696	794,386	994,181	1,010,450	0.76	1.64
Taiwan, Province of China	4,385,591	4,484,041	5,140,554	5,263,014	5,340,194	4.03	1.47
South-East Asia	**4,979,513**	**5,182,042**	**5,745,684**	**5,666,788**	**5,893,827**	**4.45**	**4.01**
Brunei Darussalam	7,594	7,538	10,051	9,449	9,409	0.01	-0.42
Cambodia	18,548	20,104	24,265	26,534	29,803	0.02	12.32
Indonesia	426,251	469,044	573,409	608,675	621,970	0.47	2.18
Lao People's Democratic Republic	8,754	9,674	11,927	14,186	16,764	0.01	18.17
Malaysia	1,040,494	1,059,004	1,245,160	1,245,092	1,235,463	0.93	-0.77
Myanmar	508,995	607,737	493,400	191,038	205,936	0.16	7.80
Philippines	795,255	748,943	828,284	894,309	961,975	0.73	7.57
Singapore	875,826	889,538	1,003,658	1,062,993	1,027,745	0.78	-3.32
Thailand	554,275	541,830	635,539	608,044	647,597	0.49	6.50
Viet Nam	743,521	828,630	919,991	1,006,468	1,137,165	0.86	12.99
Australasia	**676,718**	**661,980**	**777,394**	**847,082**	**902,579**	**0.68**	**6.55**
Australia	571,534	561,542	661,342	726,184	774,328	0.58	6.63
New Zealand	105,184	100,438	116,052	120,898	128,251	0.10	6.08
Melanesia	**2,662**	**2,788**	**3,805**	**3,710**	**3,988**	**0.00**	**7.49**
Fiji	2,265	2,398	3,342	3,207	3,462	0.00	7.95
Vanuatu	397	390	463	503	526	0.00	4.57

146

CHINA

2. Arrivals of non-resident visitors at national borders, by nationality

	2008	2009	2010	2011	2012	Market share 2012	% Change 2012-2011
Micronesia	2,908	1,988	2,289	2,652	2,590	0.00	-2.34
Kiribati	2,908	1,988	2,289	2,652	2,590	0.00	-2.34
Polynesia	1,345	1,183	1,139	1,379	1,355	0.00	-1.74
Tonga	1,345	1,183	1,139	1,379	1,355	0.00	-1.74
Other East Asia and the Pacific	5,545	4,822	5,264	4,902	4,736	0.00	-3.39
Other countries of Asia	352	329	560	412	350	0.00	-15.05
Other countries of Oceania	5,193	4,493	4,704	4,490	4,386	0.00	-2.32
EUROPE	6,688,442	5,131,487	6,365,849	6,771,977	6,769,946	5.11	-0.03
Central/Eastern Europe	3,861,098	2,392,709	3,180,919	3,528,537	3,415,649	2.58	-3.20
Armenia	4,364	3,528	4,684	5,347	5,492	0.00	2.71
Azerbaijan	17,453	15,122	18,605	18,202	17,757	0.01	-2.44
Belarus	8,701	7,458	10,914	10,939	14,121	0.01	29.09
Bulgaria	15,856	13,846	16,421	17,556	16,847	0.01	-4.04
Czech Republic	17,345	15,768	19,483	20,285	21,229	0.02	4.65
Georgia	6,308	5,178	5,355	6,719	6,458	0.00	-3.88
Hungary	17,490	13,626	15,791	16,289	16,905	0.01	3.78
Kazakhstan	300,732	279,875	380,312	506,215	491,381	0.37	-2.93
Kyrgyzstan	43,493	32,787	35,444	47,633	48,105	0.04	0.99
Latvia	5,970	5,066	5,708	5,747	7,341	0.01	27.74
Lithuania	6,646	5,821	7,000	7,508	8,730	0.01	16.28
Poland	60,958	53,718	62,109	67,986	68,605	0.05	0.91
Romania	32,168	27,760	33,232	36,290	35,262	0.03	-2.83
Russian Federation	3,123,415	1,742,973	2,370,313	2,536,321	2,426,161	1.83	-4.34
Slovakia	5,386	4,969	9,028	9,183	10,508	0.01	14.43
Tajikistan	22,123	17,480	23,398	26,441	28,739	0.02	8.69
Turkmenistan	9,160	11,647	14,836	15,590	15,629	0.01	0.25
Ukraine	105,556	86,553	105,711	120,248	120,214	0.09	-0.03
Uzbekistan	57,974	49,534	42,575	54,038	56,165	0.04	3.94
Northern Europe	929,552	874,363	978,140	1,007,792	1,041,094	0.79	3.30
Denmark	81,033	77,340	86,718	84,637	84,330	0.06	-0.36
Finland	70,577	60,906	69,226	65,288	67,811	0.05	3.86
Iceland	4,156	2,686	3,056	3,009	3,370	0.00	12.00
Ireland	35,128	31,221	36,164	37,596	42,166	0.03	12.16
Norway	49,449	47,653	53,500	51,428	53,478	0.04	3.99
Sweden	137,686	125,771	154,513	170,137	171,588	0.13	0.85
United Kingdom	551,523	528,786	574,963	595,697	618,351	0.47	3.80
Southern Europe	423,710	415,259	485,354	491,243	508,936	0.38	3.60
Albania	2,883	2,586	2,740	2,638	2,478	0.00	-6.07
Croatia	18,449	16,072	16,159	16,355	16,918	0.01	3.44
Greece	34,445	32,060	34,690	32,652	32,490	0.02	-0.50
Italy	194,362	191,357	229,233	235,041	251,991	0.19	7.21
Malta	1,725	1,563	1,934	1,833	2,015	0.00	9.93
Montenegro	1,665	4,431	6,038	6,584	6,959	0.01	5.70
Portugal	43,917	43,634	47,678	47,033	48,577	0.04	3.28
Serbia	5,738	6,236	8,448	9,231	10,593	0.01	14.75
Serbia and Montenegro	8,302	2,835	179				
Spain	112,224	114,485	138,255	139,876	136,915	0.10	-2.12
Western Europe	1,323,650	1,292,574	1,533,403	1,543,373	1,603,610	1.21	3.90
Austria	56,273	56,223	67,289	66,922	66,079	0.05	-1.26
Belgium	61,398	60,770	76,249	70,400	71,103	0.05	1.00
France	429,967	424,770	512,734	493,132	524,837	0.40	6.43
Germany	528,858	518,533	608,621	637,015	659,627	0.50	3.55
Liechtenstein	256	251	378	300	310	0.00	3.33
Luxembourg	2,451	2,446	4,471	2,692	3,276	0.00	21.69
Monaco	144	118	237	88	118	0.00	34.09
Netherlands	180,891	166,884	189,128	197,530	195,474	0.15	-1.04
Switzerland	63,412	62,579	74,296	75,294	82,786	0.06	9.95

147

CHINA

2. Arrivals of non-resident visitors at national borders, by nationality

	2008	2009	2010	2011	2012	Market share 2012	% Change 2012-2011
East Mediterranean Europe	**131,635**	**140,254**	**171,413**	**184,250**	**181,749**	**0.14**	**-1.36**
Cyprus	2,926	2,884	3,569	3,229	3,148	0.00	-2.51
Israel	68,349	73,008	83,384	82,234	82,548	0.06	0.38
Turkey	60,360	64,362	84,460	98,787	96,053	0.07	-2.77
Other Europe	**18,797**	**16,328**	**16,620**	**16,782**	**18,908**	**0.01**	**12.67**
Other countries of Europe	18,797	16,328	16,620	16,782	18,908	0.01	12.67
MIDDLE EAST	**178,131**	**207,488**	**246,794**	**239,427**	**264,171**	**0.20**	**10.33**
Bahrain	3,959	3,792	3,839	3,222	3,085	0.00	-4.25
Egypt	44,716	49,665	59,119	60,880	72,662	0.05	19.35
Iraq	10,624	19,234	22,246	19,289	20,746	0.02	7.55
Jordan	21,018	22,661	25,343	27,568	27,553	0.02	-0.05
Kuwait	6,215	6,948	7,746	8,303	9,042	0.01	8.90
Lebanon	19,050	20,186	22,251	22,854	22,607	0.02	-1.08
Libya	9,764	11,051	12,956	3,414	12,605	0.01	269.21
Oman	3,423	3,619	4,739	4,630	5,006	0.00	8.12
Palestine	4,146	5,050	6,886	6,336	6,874	0.01	8.49
Qatar	2,086	1,876	2,940	2,431	2,499	0.00	2.80
Saudi Arabia	13,649	19,030	27,223	34,635	35,424	0.03	2.28
Syrian Arab Republic	16,879	19,745	21,029	18,473	15,773	0.01	-14.62
United Arab Emirates	4,936	5,256	8,816	9,041	8,274	0.01	-8.48
Yemen	17,666	19,375	21,661	18,351	22,021	0.02	20.00
SOUTH ASIA	**668,806**	**714,327**	**871,339**	**956,602**	**948,300**	**0.72**	**-0.87**
Afghanistan	12,230	15,519	11,809	11,695	11,651	0.01	-0.38
Bangladesh	31,352	32,281	41,648	47,661	50,855	0.04	6.70
Bhutan	261	282	569	597	619	0.00	3.69
India	436,625	448,942	549,321	606,474	610,194	0.46	0.61
Iran, Islamic Republic of	68,025	87,636	116,999	125,077	90,991	0.07	-27.25
Maldives	1,373	1,330	2,025	2,623	3,589	0.00	36.83
Nepal	21,726	23,272	30,796	31,944	40,949	0.03	28.19
Pakistan	72,854	81,491	87,320	92,518	96,707	0.07	4.53
Sri Lanka	24,360	23,574	30,852	38,013	42,745	0.03	12.45
NOT SPECIFIED	**1,888**	**2,169**	**2,106**	**1,891**	**1,920**	**0.00**	**1.53**
Other countries of the World	1,888	2,169	2,106	1,891	1,920	0.00	1.53

Yearbook of Tourism Statistics, Data 2008 – 2012, 2014 Edition

COLOMBIA

1. Arrivals of non-resident tourists at national borders, by country of residence

		2008	2009	2010	2011	2012	Market share 2012	% Change 2012-2011
TOTAL	(*)	1,222,925	1,353,486	1,404,452	2,042,196	2,174,587	100.00	6.48
AFRICA		1,969	2,014	2,252	2,833	2,561	0.12	-9.60
East Africa		271	374	292	332	413	0.02	24.40
British Indian Ocean Territory				8	7	1	0.00	-85.71
Burundi		1	7	7	4	5	0.00	25.00
Djibouti		3	3	5	9			
Eritrea		24	33	8	12	19	0.00	58.33
Ethiopia		45	51	25	30	43	0.00	43.33
Kenya		93	113	73	124	181	0.01	45.97
Madagascar		5	5	13	9	13	0.00	44.44
Malawi		5	5	8	6	6	0.00	0.00
Mauritius		7	11	15	9	9	0.00	0.00
Mozambique		15	26	11	33	26	0.00	-21.21
Reunion				6	7			
Rwanda		9	14	12	5	9	0.00	80.00
Seychelles				1	2			
Somalia		1				1	0.00	
Uganda		45	40	37	21	35	0.00	66.67
United Republic of Tanzania			27	21	13	16	0.00	23.08
Zambia		8	13	15	16	12	0.00	-25.00
Zimbabwe		10	26	27	25	37	0.00	48.00
Central Africa		171	198	213	274	224	0.01	-18.25
Angola		88	78	53	21	27	0.00	28.57
Cameroon		24	52	42	91	57	0.00	-37.36
Central African Republic		10	10	47	65	31	0.00	-52.31
Chad		2	8	10	5	11	0.00	120.00
Congo		35	37	36	61	82	0.00	34.43
Democratic Republic of the Congo			3					
Equatorial Guinea		6	6	12	9	5	0.00	-44.44
Gabon		5	4	11	18	11	0.00	-38.89
Sao Tome and Principe		1		2	4			
North Africa		158	186	583	575	562	0.03	-2.26
Algeria		31	49	371	362	413	0.02	14.09
Morocco		87	101	89	118	70	0.00	-40.68
Sudan		11	16	7	16	17	0.00	6.25
Tunisia		29	20	115	78	62	0.00	-20.51
Western Sahara				1	1			
Southern Africa		1,063	979	897	1,241	1,114	0.05	-10.23
Botswana			5	6	14	5	0.00	-64.29
Lesotho				1	16	4	0.00	-75.00
Namibia		3	5	8	2	17	0.00	750.00
South Africa		1,060	969	882	1,207	1,088	0.05	-9.86
Swaziland					2			
West Africa		306	277	267	411	248	0.01	-39.66
Benin		9	12	10	6	17	0.00	183.33
Burkina Faso		10	10	19	12	3	0.00	-75.00
Cape Verde		2	6	13	32	23	0.00	-28.13
Côte d'Ivoire		17	17	18	26	20	0.00	-23.08
Gambia		3	6	3	5	3	0.00	-40.00
Ghana		25	50	47	32	55	0.00	71.88
Guinea		37	6	11	16	5	0.00	-68.75
Guinea-Bissau			4	5	4	3	0.00	-25.00
Liberia		3	5	8	2	8	0.00	300.00
Mali		13	7	2	46	1	0.00	-97.83
Mauritania		2	2	4	14	5	0.00	-64.29
Niger		2	5	12	21	5	0.00	-76.19

Yearbook of Tourism Statistics, Data 2008 – 2012, 2014 Edition

COLOMBIA

1. Arrivals of non-resident tourists at national borders, by country of residence

	2008	2009	2010	2011	2012	Market share 2012	% Change 2012-2011
Nigeria	152	101	76	116	83	0.00	-28.45
Saint Helena			2	6	8	0.00	33.33
Senegal	27	23	23	62			
Sierra Leone		7	7	4	6	0.00	50.00
Togo	4	16	7	7	3	0.00	-57.14
AMERICAS	**969,075**	**1,063,828**	**1,140,144**	**1,192,916**	**1,277,598**	**58.75**	**7.10**
Caribbean	**13,631**	**15,802**	**28,705**	**32,047**	**35,123**	**1.62**	**9.60**
Anguilla	2	251	3	1	2	0.00	100.00
Antigua and Barbuda	35		39	31	47	0.00	51.61
Aruba	50	498	5,270	5,272	5,454	0.25	3.45
Bahamas	192	17	170	188	228	0.01	21.28
Barbados	151	2	100	135	126	0.01	-6.67
Bermuda	35	78	57	47	178	0.01	278.72
British Virgin Islands	6	150	3	3	3	0.00	0.00
Cayman Islands	197	122	120	102	145	0.01	42.16
Cuba	4,136	25	2,427	2,325	2,410	0.11	3.66
Curaçao	43		5,705	6,859	7,442	0.34	8.50
Dominica	42	4,074	150	203	198	0.01	-2.46
Dominican Republic	6,991	50	8,682	8,641	9,322	0.43	7.88
Grenada	33	44	25	87			
Guadeloupe	1	51	96	67	44	0.00	-34.33
Haiti	210		243	227	360	0.02	58.59
Jamaica	451	233	426	502	502	0.02	0.00
Martinique	1	149	78	21	25	0.00	19.05
Montserrat		2			2	0.00	
Netherlands Antilles	4	3					
Puerto Rico	135		3,951	6,141	6,885	0.32	12.12
Saint Kitts and Nevis			17	26			
Saint Lucia	40	8,820	41	51	103	0.00	101.96
Saint Vincent and the Grenadines	49	13	30	37	27	0.00	-27.03
Trinidad and Tobago	826	48	1,064	1,081	1,581	0.07	46.25
Turks and Caicos Islands	1	35	3				
Other countries of the Caribbean		1,137	5		39	0.00	
Central America	**65,553**	**68,785**	**80,083**	**85,602**	**88,295**	**4.06**	**3.15**
Belize	138	156	170	176	146	0.01	-17.05
Costa Rica	21,179	20,184	22,589	23,394	24,068	1.11	2.88
El Salvador	3,867	4,512	6,300	9,465	11,965	0.55	26.41
Guatemala	7,020	7,693	7,795	9,823	9,422	0.43	-4.08
Honduras	3,359	3,657	4,078	4,121	4,533	0.21	10.00
Nicaragua	1,611	1,627	1,329	1,457	1,573	0.07	7.96
Panama	28,379	30,956	37,822	37,166	36,588	1.68	-1.56
North America	**351,192**	**400,489**	**452,739**	**439,522**	**451,692**	**20.77**	**2.77**
Canada	27,632	28,157	30,389	35,848	41,878	1.93	16.82
Mexico	59,107	57,474	64,886	75,011	80,865	3.72	7.80
United States of America	264,453	314,858	357,464	328,663	328,949	15.13	0.09
South America	**538,699**	**578,752**	**578,617**	**635,745**	**702,488**	**32.30**	**10.50**
Argentina	51,057	61,358	77,499	86,365	103,370	4.75	19.69
Bolivia	5,945	6,293	6,119	6,280	9,081	0.42	44.60
Brazil	45,506	47,493	63,794	90,646	83,112	3.82	-8.31
Chile	29,716	36,168	42,976	53,732	73,869	3.40	37.48
Ecuador	93,452	101,820	116,359	101,512	107,452	4.94	5.85
French Guiana	26	25	25	25	26	0.00	4.00
Guyana	138	130	112	150	210	0.01	40.00
Paraguay	1,754	1,634	2,102	2,544	2,951	0.14	16.00
Peru	66,313	77,733	74,093	71,488	82,797	3.81	15.82
Suriname	285	409	361	410	404	0.02	-1.46
Uruguay	7,178	7,611	7,558	7,586	9,004	0.41	18.69

Yearbook of Tourism Statistics, Data 2008 – 2012, 2014 Edition

COLOMBIA

1. Arrivals of non-resident tourists at national borders, by country of residence

	2008	2009	2010	2011	2012	Market share 2012	% Change 2012-2011
Venezuela	237,329	238,078	187,619	215,007	230,212	10.59	7.07
EAST ASIA AND THE PACIFIC	**21,228**	**25,784**	**25,225**	**28,807**	**33,533**	**1.54**	**16.41**
North-East Asia	**13,230**	**14,619**	**12,367**	**14,166**	**17,749**	**0.82**	**25.29**
China	3,296	4,264	3,378	4,196	5,604	0.26	33.56
Hong Kong, China	21	14	157	211	294	0.01	39.34
Japan	5,302	4,987	4,312	4,769	5,578	0.26	16.96
Korea, Dem. People's Republic of	2	3	203	178	34	0.00	-80.90
Korea, Republic of	3,415	4,015	3,510	3,973	5,228	0.24	31.59
Mongolia	9	10	13	3			
Taiwan, Province of China	1,185	1,326	794	836	1,011	0.05	20.93
South-East Asia	**1,921**	**2,704**	**2,974**	**3,395**	**3,654**	**0.17**	**7.63**
Brunei Darussalam	3	8	12	7	12	0.00	71.43
Cambodia	4	9	12	4	16	0.00	300.00
Indonesia	277	363	494	485	515	0.02	6.19
Lao People's Democratic Republic	4	209	93	42	6	0.00	-85.71
Malaysia	196	4	281	333	437	0.02	31.23
Myanmar	2	20	3	8	8	0.00	0.00
Philippines	1,153	1,728	1,591	1,994	2,062	0.09	3.41
Singapore	190	210	306	317	363	0.02	14.51
Thailand	86	41	122	118	144	0.01	22.03
Viet Nam	6	112	60	87	91	0.00	4.60
Australasia	**6,060**	**8,440**	**9,694**	**11,042**	**12,013**	**0.55**	**8.79**
Australia	5,039	7,104	8,401	9,569	10,439	0.48	9.09
New Zealand	1,021	1,336	1,293	1,473	1,574	0.07	6.86
Melanesia	**11**	**7**	**101**	**131**	**87**	**0.00**	**-33.59**
Fiji	7	2	5	18	2	0.00	-88.89
New Caledonia	1	1	76	87	70	0.00	-19.54
Papua New Guinea	1	2	8	2	8	0.00	300.00
Solomon Islands	2	1		3	1	0.00	-66.67
Vanuatu		1	12	21	6	0.00	-71.43
Micronesia	**4**	**9**	**23**	**14**	**9**	**0.00**	**-35.71**
Cocos (Keeling) Islands			2				
Guam			3	4			
Kiribati	1	1	4	2			
Micronesia, Federated States of		1	8	5	7	0.00	40.00
Midway Islands	1	1	3	2			
Nauru			1				
Northern Mariana Islands		1		1			
Palau	1	4	2				
Wake Island	1	1			2	0.00	
Polynesia	**2**	**5**	**66**	**57**	**16**	**0.00**	**-71.93**
French Polynesia		1	59	55	16	0.00	-70.91
Tonga	1	4	6	1			
Wallis and Futuna Islands	1		1	1			
Other East Asia and the Pacific				**2**	**5**	**0.00**	**150.00**
Other countries of Asia				1	1	0.00	0.00
Other countries of Oceania				1	4	0.00	300.00
EUROPE	**226,762**	**257,435**	**232,186**	**266,972**	**272,230**	**12.52**	**1.97**
Central/Eastern Europe	**5,821**	**7,809**	**7,129**	**10,379**	**9,564**	**0.44**	**-7.85**
Armenia	13	20	8	18	22	0.00	22.22
Azerbaijan	7	7	28	20	44	0.00	120.00
Bulgaria	196	51	120	125	160	0.01	28.00
Czech Republic	681	609	1,111	814	346	0.02	-57.49
Estonia	62	2,471	116	369	202	0.01	-45.26
Georgia	15	10	28	54	46	0.00	-14.81
Hungary	415	483	420	406	505	0.02	24.38
Kazakhstan	40	43	31	32	42	0.00	31.25

Yearbook of Tourism Statistics, Data 2008 – 2012, 2014 Edition

COLOMBIA

1. Arrivals of non-resident tourists at national borders, by country of residence

	2008	2009	2010	2011	2012	Market share 2012	% Change 2012-2011
Kyrgyzstan	4	3	6	3	5	0.00	66.67
Latvia	77	104	104	158	182	0.01	15.19
Lithuania	203	216	168	325	200	0.01	-38.46
Poland	1,221	1,067	1,499	2,728	2,198	0.10	-19.43
Republic of Moldova	13	1,668	19	38	32	0.00	-15.79
Romania	659		591	884	897	0.04	1.47
Russian Federation	1,572	10	2,079	3,577	3,877	0.18	8.39
Slovakia	287	624	396	490	401	0.02	-18.16
Turkmenistan	3	2	93	30	3	0.00	-90.00
Ukraine	345	396	304	297	399	0.02	34.34
Uzbekistan	8	25	8	11	3	0.00	-72.73
Northern Europe	**31,172**	**35,927**	**33,384**	**37,108**	**37,254**	**1.71**	**0.39**
Denmark	1,744	2,032	1,761	2,080	2,115	0.10	1.68
Finland	1,099	1,251	1,286	1,720	2,122	0.10	23.37
Iceland	95	189	133	156	226	0.01	44.87
Ireland	1,734	2,166	1,754	1,654	2,150	0.10	29.99
Isle of Man	2,978	4,351	1,628	1,052	1,033	0.05	-1.81
Norway	2,032	2,161	2,395	2,603	2,713	0.12	4.23
Sweden	4,378	4,830	4,372	4,741	4,778	0.22	0.78
United Kingdom	17,112	18,947	20,055	23,102	22,117	1.02	-4.26
Southern Europe	**90,595**	**108,281**	**102,636**	**111,049**	**114,240**	**5.25**	**2.87**
Albania	31	34	44	29	26	0.00	-10.34
Andorra	82	87	40	62	51	0.00	-17.74
Bosnia and Herzegovina	20	21	18	10	16	0.00	60.00
Croatia	262	343	286	410	433	0.02	5.61
Greece	893	827	731	869	763	0.04	-12.20
Holy See	7	6	8	4	7	0.00	75.00
Italy	24,320	26,054	22,706	22,699	22,098	1.02	-2.65
Malta	51	67	40	70	40	0.00	-42.86
Montenegro		4					
Portugal	2,094	2,381	1,825	2,585	3,147	0.14	21.74
San Marino	17	4	11	8	13	0.00	62.50
Serbia and Montenegro	29	80	107	117	159	0.01	35.90
Slovenia	498	406	324	420	432	0.02	2.86
Spain	62,176	77,913	76,485	83,761	87,052	4.00	3.93
TFYR of Macedonia	115	54	11	5	3	0.00	-40.00
Western Europe	**83,961**	**96,551**	**81,284**	**100,422**	**103,259**	**4.75**	**2.83**
Austria	2,540	2,849	2,443	3,006	3,469	0.16	15.40
Belgium	3,433	4,115	3,500	4,101	4,708	0.22	14.80
France	27,381	30,366	29,898	33,105	32,948	1.52	-0.47
Germany	22,133	26,138	24,134	36,010	36,568	1.68	1.55
Liechtenstein	24	27	20	22	47	0.00	113.64
Luxembourg	129	154	144	180	202	0.01	12.22
Monaco	14	15	26	39	32	0.00	-17.95
Netherlands	20,576	23,621	12,064	13,721	14,285	0.66	4.11
Switzerland	7,731	9,266	9,055	10,238	11,000	0.51	7.44
East Mediterranean Europe	**7,615**	**8,867**	**7,706**	**7,949**	**7,852**	**0.36**	**-1.22**
Cyprus	53	82	67	45	61	0.00	35.56
Israel	7,016	8,036	6,808	6,729	6,631	0.30	-1.46
Turkey	546	749	831	1,175	1,160	0.05	-1.28
Other Europe	**7,598**		**47**	**65**	**61**	**0.00**	**-6.15**
Other countries of Europe	7,598		47	65	61	0.00	-6.15
MIDDLE EAST	**1,188**	**1,311**	**908**	**1,101**	**1,179**	**0.05**	**7.08**
Bahrain	6	6	20	16	20	0.00	25.00
Egypt	132	179	200	241	227	0.01	-5.81
Iraq	4	7	9	26			
Jordan	57	63	55	69	32	0.00	-53.62

152

COLOMBIA

1. Arrivals of non-resident tourists at national borders, by country of residence

	2008	2009	2010	2011	2012	Market share 2012	% Change 2012-2011
Kuwait	12	27	21	35	31	0.00	-11.43
Lebanon	843	808	359	300	334	0.02	11.33
Libya	8	6	12	5	16	0.00	220.00
Oman	4	5	1	14	13	0.00	-7.14
Palestine	32	27	26	52	100	0.00	92.31
Qatar	3	16	9	12	30	0.00	150.00
Saudi Arabia	27	48	69	165	134	0.01	-18.79
Syrian Arab Republic	39	34	23	13	9	0.00	-30.77
United Arab Emirates	16	81	98	151	229	0.01	51.66
Yemen	5	4	6	2	4	0.00	100.00
SOUTH ASIA	**2,492**	**2,924**	**3,375**	**3,309**	**3,144**	**0.14**	**-4.99**
Afghanistan	30	21	507	378	32	0.00	-91.53
Bangladesh	41	30	29	51	18	0.00	-64.71
Bhutan	1	5	1	4	5	0.00	25.00
India	2,038	2,483	2,533	2,516	2,899	0.13	15.22
Iran, Islamic Republic of	224	206	167	174			
Maldives	3		2	2			
Nepal	22	41	30	57	30	0.00	-47.37
Pakistan	99	102	79	96	138	0.01	43.75
Sri Lanka	34	36	27	31	22	0.00	-29.03
NOT SPECIFIED	**211**	**190**	**362**	**546,258**	**584,342**	**26.87**	**6.97**
Other countries of the World	211	190	362	234	781	0.04	233.76
Nationals Residing Abroad				546,024	583,561	26.84	6.87

Yearbook of Tourism Statistics, Data 2008 – 2012, 2014 Edition

COMOROS

1. Arrivals of non-resident tourists at national borders, by nationality

		2008	2009	2010	2011	2012	Market share 2012	% Change 2012-2011
TOTAL	(*)	**14,753**	**11,306**	**15,251**	**18,765**			
AFRICA		**2,148**	**2,889**	**1,800**	**1,428**			
East Africa		**724**	**1,113**		**1,393**			
Madagascar		210	206		112			
Mauritius					21			
Reunion		514	907		480			
Other countries of East Africa					780			
Other Africa		**1,424**	**1,776**	**1,800**	**35**			
Other countries of Africa		1,424	1,776		35			
All countries of Africa				1,800				
AMERICAS		**258**	**137**	**213**	**846**			
Other Americas		**258**	**137**	**213**	**846**			
All countries of the Americas		258	137	213	846			
EAST ASIA AND THE PACIFIC		**353**	**272**	**167**	**613**			
Other East Asia and the Pacific		**353**	**272**	**167**	**613**			
All countries of Asia		157	183	167	613			
All countries of Oceania		196	89					
EUROPE		**11,021**	**7,484**	**12,498**	**14,543**			
Northern Europe		**213**	**146**	**1,046**	**1,708**			
United Kingdom		213	146	1,046	1,708			
Western Europe		**10,575**	**7,074**	**10,720**	**11,535**			
France		10,509	6,957	10,720	11,535			
Germany		66	117					
Other Europe		**233**	**264**	**732**	**1,300**			
Other countries of Europe		233	264	732	1,300			
NOT SPECIFIED		**973**	**524**	**573**	**1,335**			
Other countries of the World		973	524	573	1,335			

Yearbook of Tourism Statistics, Data 2008 – 2012, 2014 Edition

CONGO

2. Arrivals of non-resident visitors at national borders, by country of residence

	2008	2009	2010	2011	2012	Market share 2012	% Change 2012-2011
TOTAL (*)				224,207	259,026	100.00	15.53
AFRICA				153,356	147,969	57.13	-3.51
East Africa				5,970	3,611	1.39	-39.51
Burundi				443	332	0.13	-25.06
Comoros					350	0.14	
Ethiopia				774	444	0.17	-42.64
Kenya				2,453	857	0.33	-65.06
Madagascar				889	378	0.15	-57.48
Malawi					35	0.01	
Mauritius					35	0.01	
Rwanda				425	698	0.27	64.24
Uganda				387	162	0.06	-58.14
United Republic of Tanzania				406	127	0.05	-68.72
Zambia					12	0.00	
Zimbabwe				193	181	0.07	-6.22
Central Africa				110,296	108,116	41.74	-1.98
Angola				9,661	7,896	3.05	-18.27
Cameroon				10,242	12,531	4.84	22.35
Central African Republic				2,492	3,786	1.46	51.93
Chad				1,682	847	0.33	-49.64
Democratic Republic of the Congo				80,170	78,331	30.24	-2.29
Equatorial Guinea					320	0.12	
Gabon				5,991	4,336	1.67	-27.62
Sao Tome and Principe				58	69	0.03	18.97
North Africa				2,167	7,329	2.83	238.21
Algeria				58	2,895	1.12	4,891.38
Morocco				1,181	2,681	1.04	127.01
Sudan				58	216	0.08	272.41
Tunisia				870	1,537	0.59	76.67
Southern Africa				4,058	2,616	1.01	-35.53
Botswana					12	0.00	
Namibia					127	0.05	
South Africa				4,058	2,477	0.96	-38.96
West Africa				30,865	26,297	10.15	-14.80
Benin				6,397	4,134	1.60	-35.38
Burkina Faso				1,372	1,404	0.54	2.33
Cape Verde					35	0.01	
Côte d'Ivoire				3,730	4,290	1.66	15.01
Gambia				56	177	0.07	216.07
Ghana				251	1,383	0.53	451.00
Guinea				2,165	320	0.12	-85.22
Guinea-Bissau					424	0.16	
Liberia				58	165	0.06	184.48
Mali				7,171	5,615	2.17	-21.70
Mauritania				1,026	1,819	0.70	77.29
Niger				541	316	0.12	-41.59
Nigeria				2,183	2,142	0.83	-1.88
Senegal				5,064	3,067	1.18	-39.44
Sierra Leone					23	0.01	
Togo				851	983	0.38	15.51
AMERICAS				3,767	9,743	3.76	158.64
Caribbean					112	0.04	
Cuba					77	0.03	
Haiti					35	0.01	

155

CONGO

2. Arrivals of non-resident visitors at national borders, by country of residence

	2008	2009	2010	2011	2012	Market share 2012	% Change 2012-2011
Central America					23	0.01	
El Salvador					23	0.01	
North America				3,574	8,845	3.41	147.48
Canada				1,024	1,367	0.53	33.50
Mexico				193	2,126	0.82	1,001.55
United States of America				2,357	5,352	2.07	127.07
South America				193	763	0.29	295.34
Brazil					662	0.26	
Chile					54	0.02	
Colombia				193	23	0.01	-88.08
Guyana					12	0.00	
Peru					12	0.00	
EAST ASIA AND THE PACIFIC				8,814	19,666	7.59	123.12
North-East Asia				7,093	12,156	4.69	71.38
China				6,919	9,641	3.72	39.34
Japan				116	2,376	0.92	1,948.28
Korea, Republic of				58	139	0.05	139.66
South-East Asia				967	7,287	2.81	653.57
Cambodia					12	0.00	
Indonesia					185	0.07	
Malaysia				387	3,856	1.49	896.38
Philippines				387	3,165	1.22	717.83
Singapore				193	69	0.03	-64.25
Australasia				754	223	0.09	-70.42
Australia				696	69	0.03	-90.09
New Zealand				58	154	0.06	165.52
EUROPE				51,524	75,725	29.23	46.97
Central/Eastern Europe				1,525	7,301	2.82	378.75
Bulgaria				56	309	0.12	451.79
Hungary					12	0.00	
Lithuania					58	0.02	
Poland				58	1,541	0.59	2,556.90
Republic of Moldova					12	0.00	
Romania				367	1,311	0.51	257.22
Russian Federation				986	4,023	1.55	308.01
Slovakia				58	23	0.01	-60.34
Ukraine					12	0.00	
Northern Europe				2,223	6,463	2.50	190.73
Denmark					12	0.00	
Finland					35	0.01	
Ireland				541	35	0.01	-93.53
Norway				387	35	0.01	-90.96
Sweden				174	231	0.09	32.76
United Kingdom				1,121	6,115	2.36	445.50
Southern Europe				3,517	11,115	4.29	216.04
Bosnia and Herzegovina					12	0.00	
Croatia					12	0.00	
Italy				2,357	5,984	2.31	153.88
Portugal				425	748	0.29	76.00
Spain				735	4,359	1.68	493.06
Western Europe				44,066	50,484	19.49	14.56
Austria					35	0.01	
Belgium				3,729	4,958	1.91	32.96
France				37,998	40,744	15.73	7.23
Germany				1,875	2,177	0.84	16.11
Luxembourg					23	0.01	
Netherlands				116	1,334	0.52	1,050.00

156

CONGO

2. Arrivals of non-resident visitors at national borders, by country of residence

	2008	2009	2010	2011	2012	Market share 2012	% Change 2012-2011
Switzerland				348	1,213	0.47	248.56
East Mediterranean Europe				**193**	**362**	**0.14**	**87.56**
Cyprus					54	0.02	
Israel				193	285	0.11	47.67
Turkey					23	0.01	
MIDDLE EAST				**4,524**	**3,214**	**1.24**	**-28.96**
Egypt				696	656	0.25	-5.75
Lebanon				1,702	2,007	0.77	17.92
Palestine					12	0.00	
Qatar					46	0.02	
Saudi Arabia					23	0.01	
Syrian Arab Republic				1,933	23	0.01	-98.81
United Arab Emirates				193	424	0.16	119.69
Yemen					23	0.01	
SOUTH ASIA				**2,222**	**2,709**	**1.05**	**21.92**
Bangladesh				425			
India				1,410	2,373	0.92	68.30
Iran, Islamic Republic of					66	0.03	
Pakistan				387	270	0.10	-30.23

Yearbook of Tourism Statistics, Data 2008 – 2012, 2014 Edition

CONGO

3. Arrivals of non-resident tourists in hotels and similar establishments, by country of residence

		2008	2009	2010	2011	2012	Market share 2012	% Change 2012-2011
TOTAL	(*)	**62,106**	**93,797**	**100,691**	**167,587**	**203,978**	**100.00**	**21.71**
AFRICA		**25,780**	**38,327**	**41,122**	**72,822**	**94,697**	**46.43**	**30.04**
Central Africa		**12,760**	**17,113**	**20,420**	**37,893**	**50,609**	**24.81**	**33.56**
Angola		2,134	3,193	3,352	13,386	7,577	3.71	-43.40
Cameroon		2,792	3,182	3,954	6,936	14,288	7.00	106.00
Central African Republic		576	1,114	1,482	1,579	2,037	1.00	29.01
Chad		191	630	625	774	1,044	0.51	34.88
Democratic Republic of the Congo		5,224	7,052	8,712	9,567	10,495	5.15	9.70
Gabon		1,629	1,763	2,116	5,099	14,714	7.21	188.57
Other countries of Central Africa		214	179	179	552	454	0.22	-17.75
North Africa		**2,105**	**9,406**	**6,332**	**7,960**	**10,422**	**5.11**	**30.93**
All countries of North Africa		2,105	9,406	6,332	7,960	10,422	5.11	30.93
West Africa		**6,046**	**8,507**	**10,203**	**19,598**	**25,968**	**12.73**	**32.50**
Benin		129	60	76				
Côte d'Ivoire		1,064	1,873	1,974	3,532	5,253	2.58	48.73
Mali		546	1,265	1,505	2,213	2,362	1.16	6.73
Mauritania					44			
Senegal		845	1,092	1,421	2,034	2,837	1.39	39.48
Togo		392	941	938	1,057	1,293	0.63	22.33
Other countries of West Africa		3,070	3,276	4,289	10,718	14,223	6.97	32.70
Other Africa		**4,869**	**3,301**	**4,167**	**7,371**	**7,698**	**3.77**	**4.44**
Other countries of Africa		4,869	3,301	4,167	7,371	7,698	3.77	4.44
AMERICAS		**2,528**	**4,976**	**4,899**	**10,572**	**11,250**	**5.52**	**6.41**
North America		**1,693**	**2,948**	**2,882**	**4,671**	**6,312**	**3.09**	**35.13**
Canada		322	792	733	1,018	2,417	1.18	137.43
United States of America		1,371	2,156	2,149	3,653	3,895	1.91	6.62
Other Americas		**835**	**2,028**	**2,017**	**5,901**	**4,938**	**2.42**	**-16.32**
Other countries of the Americas		835	2,028	2,017	5,901	4,938	2.42	-16.32
EAST ASIA AND THE PACIFIC		**1,117**	**2,974**	**3,442**	**12,140**	**11,318**	**5.55**	**-6.77**
North-East Asia		**418**	**1,307**	**1,574**	**3,011**	**3,846**	**1.89**	**27.73**
China		349	994	1,351	2,592	3,452	1.69	33.18
Japan		69	313	223	419	394	0.19	-5.97
Other East Asia and the Pacific		**699**	**1,667**	**1,868**	**9,129**	**7,472**	**3.66**	**-18.15**
Other countries of Asia		699	1,667	1,868	9,129	7,472	3.66	-18.15
EUROPE		**30,246**	**43,885**	**46,154**	**68,300**	**82,427**	**40.41**	**20.68**
Central/Eastern Europe		**730**	**953**	**1,269**	**2,328**	**1,937**	**0.95**	**-16.80**
Russian Federation		730	953	1,269	2,328	1,937	0.95	-16.80
Northern Europe		**819**	**2,565**	**3,607**	**6,159**	**12,375**	**6.07**	**100.93**
United Kingdom		819	2,565	3,607	6,159	12,375	6.07	100.93
Southern Europe		**1,617**	**3,097**	**2,945**	**4,570**	**3,674**	**1.80**	**-19.61**
Italy		1,617	3,097	2,945	4,570	3,674	1.80	-19.61
Western Europe		**24,097**	**33,374**	**33,213**	**46,026**	**52,117**	**25.55**	**13.23**
Belgium		1,056	1,149	1,518	2,425	2,572	1.26	6.06
France		22,473	30,343	30,181	40,888	46,915	23.00	14.74
Germany		419	831	762	1,666	1,258	0.62	-24.49
Switzerland		149	1,051	752	1,047	1,372	0.67	31.04
Other Europe		**2,983**	**3,896**	**5,120**	**9,217**	**12,324**	**6.04**	**33.71**
Other countries of Europe		2,983	3,896	5,120	9,217	12,324	6.04	33.71
MIDDLE EAST					**233**			
Lebanon					163			
Other countries of Middle East					70			

158

CONGO

3. Arrivals of non-resident tourists in hotels and similar establishments, by country of residence

	2008	2009	2010	2011	2012	Market share 2012	% Change 2012-2011
SOUTH ASIA				447	186	0.09	-58.39
India				447	186	0.09	-58.39
NOT SPECIFIED	2,435	3,635	5,074	3,073	4,100	2.01	33.42
Other countries of the World	2,435	3,635	5,074	3,073	4,100	2.01	33.42

Yearbook of Tourism Statistics, Data 2008 – 2012, 2014 Edition

CONGO

5. Overnight stays of non-resident tourists in hotels and similar establishments, by country of residence

		2008	2009	2010	2011	2012	Market share 2012	% Change 2012-2011
TOTAL	(*)	196,734	192,886	218,845	364,681	552,929	100.00	51.62
AFRICA		82,142	75,426	94,226	160,181	258,342	46.72	61.28
Central Africa		35,390	35,272	46,652	80,898	137,775	24.92	70.31
Angola		5,719	6,000	9,641	25,361	24,605	4.45	-2.98
Cameroon		8,705	7,439	10,072	18,391	42,395	7.67	130.52
Central African Republic		1,828	2,334	3,353	3,530	4,780	0.86	35.41
Chad		591	1,078	1,116	1,453	2,029	0.37	39.64
Democratic Republic of the Congo		11,416	14,286	16,615	18,454	25,564	4.62	38.53
Gabon		6,317	3,703	5,217	12,211	36,890	6.67	202.10
Other countries of Central Africa		814	432	638	1,498	1,512	0.27	0.93
North Africa		5,740	13,506	10,019	13,137	20,208	3.65	53.83
All countries of North Africa		5,740	13,506	10,019	13,137	20,208	3.65	53.83
West Africa		22,877	17,609	25,544	47,284	78,350	14.17	65.70
Benin		389	236	388				
Côte d'Ivoire		4,012	3,606	4,087	7,974	11,919	2.16	49.47
Mali		1,361	2,390	3,163	4,873	5,242	0.95	7.57
Mauritania					71	10	0.00	-85.92
Senegal		4,159	1,750	3,040	4,366	4,474	0.81	2.47
Togo		1,262	1,625	1,675	1,860	2,209	0.40	18.76
Other countries of West Africa		11,694	8,002	13,191	28,140	54,496	9.86	93.66
Other Africa		18,135	9,039	12,011	18,862	22,009	3.98	16.68
Other countries of Africa		18,135	9,039	12,011	18,862	22,009	3.98	16.68
AMERICAS		7,694	12,345	12,154	26,339	43,632	7.89	65.66
North America		5,648	7,086	6,865	11,163	17,618	3.19	57.82
Canada		1,660	1,717	1,627	2,120	7,005	1.27	230.42
United States of America		3,988	5,369	5,238	9,043	10,613	1.92	17.36
Other Americas		2,046	5,259	5,289	15,176	26,014	4.70	71.42
Other countries of the Americas		2,046	5,259	5,289	15,176	26,014	4.70	71.42
EAST ASIA AND THE PACIFIC		3,096	6,889	6,998	27,600	35,188	6.36	27.49
North-East Asia		1,113	3,361	3,352	7,894	12,272	2.22	55.46
China		941	2,547	2,917	6,735	10,067	1.82	49.47
Japan		172	814	435	1,159	2,205	0.40	90.25
Other East Asia and the Pacific		1,983	3,528	3,646	19,706	22,916	4.14	16.29
Other countries of Asia		1,983	3,528	3,646	19,706	22,916	4.14	16.29
EUROPE		94,903	90,923	94,172	143,911	207,160	37.47	43.95
Central/Eastern Europe		1,411	1,830	2,484	4,780	5,691	1.03	19.06
Russian Federation		1,411	1,830	2,484	4,780	5,691	1.03	19.06
Northern Europe		3,692	7,948	11,785	20,573	45,608	8.25	121.69
United Kingdom		3,692	7,948	11,785	20,573	45,608	8.25	121.69
Southern Europe		7,091	10,287	9,599	13,490	12,703	2.30	-5.83
Italy		7,091	10,287	9,599	13,490	12,703	2.30	-5.83
Western Europe		74,029	60,755	59,272	84,400	115,327	20.86	36.64
Belgium		3,229	2,761	3,999	5,867	6,882	1.24	17.30
France		69,245	54,777	52,536	73,020	102,998	18.63	41.05
Germany		1,037	1,684	1,520	3,697	3,372	0.61	-8.79
Switzerland		518	1,533	1,217	1,816	2,075	0.38	14.26
Other Europe		8,680	10,103	11,032	20,668	27,831	5.03	34.66
Other countries of Europe		8,680	10,103	11,032	20,668	27,831	5.03	34.66
MIDDLE EAST					593			
Lebanon					344			
Other countries of Middle East					249			

160

CONGO

5. Overnight stays of non-resident tourists in hotels and similar establishments, by country of residence

	2008	2009	2010	2011	2012	Market share 2012	% Change 2012-2011
SOUTH ASIA				**1,506**	**1,870**	**0.34**	**24.17**
India				1,506	1,870	0.34	24.17
NOT SPECIFIED	**8,899**	**7,303**	**11,295**	**4,551**	**6,737**	**1.22**	**48.03**
Other countries of the World	8,899	7,303	11,295	4,551	6,737	1.22	48.03

Yearbook of Tourism Statistics, Data 2008 – 2012, 2014 Edition

COOK ISLANDS

1. Arrivals of non-resident tourists at national borders, by country of residence

		2008	2009	2010	2011	2012	Market share 2012	% Change 2012-2011
TOTAL	(*)	94,776	101,229	104,265	113,114	122,384	100.00	8.20
AMERICAS		5,674	6,066	6,995	6,915	6,672	5.45	-3.51
North America		5,674	6,066	6,590	6,499	6,672	5.45	2.66
Canada		2,085	2,069	2,262	2,044	2,082	1.70	1.86
United States of America		3,589	3,997	4,328	4,455	4,590	3.75	3.03
Other Americas				405	416			
Other countries of the Americas				405	416			
EAST ASIA AND THE PACIFIC		75,238	82,066	86,713	95,905	104,696	85.55	9.17
North-East Asia						449	0.37	
China						167	0.14	
Hong Kong, China						43	0.04	
Japan						239	0.20	
South-East Asia						156	0.13	
Indonesia						45	0.04	
Philippines						68	0.06	
Singapore						43	0.04	
Australasia		72,641	78,331	84,328	93,724	103,283	84.39	10.20
Australia		11,229	14,795	16,841	18,538	20,921	17.09	12.85
New Zealand		61,412	63,536	67,487	75,186	82,362	67.30	9.54
Polynesia		1,090	1,120	838	643	622	0.51	-3.27
French Polynesia		1,090	1,120	838	643	622	0.51	-3.27
Other East Asia and the Pacific		1,507	2,615	1,547	1,538	186	0.15	-87.91
All countries of Asia		549	676	780	687	186	0.15	-72.93
Other countries of Oceania		958	1,939	767	851			
EUROPE		13,491	12,448	10,547	10,290	9,466	7.73	-8.01
Central/Eastern Europe						23	0.02	
Poland						23	0.02	
Northern Europe		8,596	7,040	5,126	4,800	3,962	3.24	-17.46
Denmark		315	214	174	157	128	0.10	-18.47
Finland		108	107	169	382	263	0.21	-31.15
Ireland						33	0.03	
Norway		310	303	287	253	205	0.17	-18.97
Sweden		728	518	498	534	528	0.43	-1.12
United Kingdom		7,135	5,898	3,998	3,474	2,805	2.29	-19.26
Southern Europe		728	894	1,088	1,201	1,055	0.86	-12.16
Italy		456	533	711	697	612	0.50	-12.20
Slovenia		98	132	153	286	156	0.13	-45.45
Spain		174	229	224	218	287	0.23	31.65
Western Europe		3,415	3,821	3,663	3,721	4,021	3.29	8.06
Austria		290	389	324	353	305	0.25	-13.60
Belgium		56	80	74	105	91	0.07	-13.33
France		206	236	213	125	257	0.21	105.60
Germany		2,215	2,466	2,296	2,293	2,444	2.00	6.59
Netherlands		130	79	160	105	211	0.17	100.95
Switzerland		518	571	596	740	713	0.58	-3.65
East Mediterranean Europe						10	0.01	
Israel						10	0.01	
Other Europe		752	693	670	568	395	0.32	-30.46
Other countries of Europe		752	693	670	568	395	0.32	-30.46
SOUTH ASIA						32	0.03	
India						32	0.03	
NOT SPECIFIED		373	649	10	4	1,518	1.24	37,850.00
Other countries of the World		373	649	10	4	1,518	1.24	37,850.00

Yearbook of Tourism Statistics, Data 2008 – 2012, 2014 Edition

COSTA RICA

1. Arrivals of non-resident tourists at national borders, by nationality

	2008	2009	2010	2011	2012	Market share 2012	% Change 2012-2011
TOTAL	2,089,174	1,922,579	2,099,829	2,192,059	2,343,213	100.00	6.90
AFRICA	1,852	1,631	1,823	1,898	1,971	0.08	3.85
Other Africa	1,852	1,631	1,823	1,898	1,971	0.08	3.85
All countries of Africa	1,852	1,631	1,823	1,898	1,971	0.08	3.85
AMERICAS	1,754,547	1,634,866	1,781,572	1,856,794	2,009,211	85.75	8.21
Caribbean	15,289	16,184	14,579	13,043	12,052	0.51	-7.60
Cuba	5,888	7,043	5,882	4,399	3,583	0.15	-18.55
Dominican Republic	6,077	5,836	5,094	5,199	4,893	0.21	-5.89
Jamaica	616	725	752	719	698	0.03	-2.92
Puerto Rico	83	47	95	25	35	0.00	40.00
Trinidad and Tobago	772	846	972	976	985	0.04	0.92
Other countries of the Caribbean	1,853	1,687	1,784	1,725	1,858	0.08	7.71
Central America	648,586	588,739	642,517	670,271	721,049	30.77	7.58
Belize	928	975	843	838	846	0.04	0.95
El Salvador	46,837	44,185	53,669	61,257	64,923	2.77	5.98
Guatemala	40,840	40,340	48,682	54,759	55,334	2.36	1.05
Honduras	31,714	31,324	34,043	35,598	35,036	1.50	-1.58
Nicaragua	455,412	413,713	427,362	432,766	474,011	20.23	9.53
Panama	72,855	58,202	77,918	85,053	90,899	3.88	6.87
North America	976,561	920,371	1,005,309	1,044,569	1,139,624	48.64	9.10
Canada	109,854	102,471	119,654	133,033	151,568	6.47	13.93
Mexico	59,545	47,771	54,662	52,707	66,959	2.86	27.04
United States of America	807,162	770,129	830,993	858,829	921,097	39.31	7.25
South America	114,111	109,572	119,167	128,911	136,486	5.82	5.88
Argentina	19,522	18,987	20,080	22,186	24,545	1.05	10.63
Bolivia	2,541	1,788	2,025	2,071	1,826	0.08	-11.83
Brazil	12,340	11,617	13,121	14,449	15,071	0.64	4.30
Chile	9,350	7,682	8,504	9,129	10,000	0.43	9.54
Colombia	33,644	32,014	32,999	33,121	33,712	1.44	1.78
Ecuador	4,883	4,431	5,039	5,637	5,674	0.24	0.66
Paraguay	636	657	786	975	912	0.04	-6.46
Peru	7,692	8,167	9,122	10,076	10,164	0.43	0.87
Uruguay	2,997	3,091	2,905	3,030	3,150	0.13	3.96
Venezuela	20,506	21,138	24,586	28,237	31,432	1.34	11.31
EAST ASIA AND THE PACIFIC	28,197	26,900	29,479	31,432	35,891	1.53	14.19
North-East Asia	13,730	13,256	14,411	14,591	17,178	0.73	17.73
China	2,992	3,346	3,589	4,525	6,573	0.28	45.26
Japan	5,368	4,746	5,026	4,758	5,117	0.22	7.55
Korea, Republic of	2,697	2,724	3,236	3,311	3,437	0.15	3.81
Taiwan, Province of China	2,673	2,440	2,560	1,997	2,051	0.09	2.70
Australasia	8,627	7,995	8,597	9,613	10,277	0.44	6.91
Australia, New Zealand	8,627	7,995	8,597	9,613	10,277	0.44	6.91
Other East Asia and the Pacific	5,840	5,649	6,471	7,228	8,436	0.36	16.71
Other countries of Asia	5,840	5,649	6,471	7,228	8,436	0.36	16.71
EUROPE	299,798	259,126	286,923	301,929	296,091	12.64	-1.93
Central/Eastern Europe	6,727	5,826	6,832	7,342	7,567	0.32	3.06
Czech Republic	1,579	1,466	2,184	1,639	1,618	0.07	-1.28
Poland	2,208	1,926	2,085	2,425	2,405	0.10	-0.82
Russian Federation	2,940	2,434	2,563	3,278	3,544	0.15	8.11
Northern Europe	63,076	47,640	53,744	55,841	51,619	2.20	-7.56
Denmark	4,718	3,823	3,834	4,269	4,002	0.17	-6.25
Finland	1,934	1,930	1,930	1,775	1,667	0.07	-6.08
Ireland	3,367	2,730	2,828	2,557	2,554	0.11	-0.12
Norway	4,081	3,336	3,455	3,709	3,635	0.16	-2.00

Yearbook of Tourism Statistics, Data 2008 – 2012, 2014 Edition

COSTA RICA

1. Arrivals of non-resident tourists at national borders, by nationality

	2008	2009	2010	2011	2012	Market share 2012	% Change 2012-2011
Sweden	8,726	6,939	6,952	7,842	7,831	0.33	-0.14
United Kingdom	40,250	28,882	34,745	35,689	31,930	1.36	-10.53
Southern Europe	**75,822**	**66,761**	**70,513**	**70,141**	**69,856**	**2.98**	**-0.41**
Italy	18,994	18,497	19,658	20,225	20,335	0.87	0.54
Portugal	2,799	1,807	2,363	2,134	2,016	0.09	-5.53
Spain	54,029	46,457	48,492	47,782	47,505	2.03	-0.58
Western Europe	**137,392**	**124,017**	**139,683**	**150,311**	**148,089**	**6.32**	**-1.48**
Austria	6,124	5,504	5,863	6,348	6,150	0.26	-3.12
Belgium	8,368	9,509	13,306	12,508	10,235	0.44	-18.17
France	34,622	30,737	35,266	38,290	38,139	1.63	-0.39
Germany	44,705	40,918	44,539	49,225	50,938	2.17	3.48
Netherlands	30,615	25,006	26,373	27,731	25,758	1.10	-7.11
Switzerland	12,958	12,343	14,336	16,209	16,869	0.72	4.07
East Mediterranean Europe	**10,419**	**8,972**	**9,511**	**11,210**	**11,095**	**0.47**	**-1.03**
Israel	10,419	8,972	9,511	11,210	11,095	0.47	-1.03
Other Europe	**6,362**	**5,910**	**6,640**	**7,084**	**7,865**	**0.34**	**11.02**
Other countries of Europe	6,362	5,910	6,640	7,084	7,865	0.34	11.02
NOT SPECIFIED	**4,780**	**56**	**32**	**6**	**49**	**0.00**	**716.67**
Other countries of the World	4,780	56	32	6	49	0.00	716.67

164

CROATIA

3. Arrivals of non-resident tourists in hotels and similar establishments, by country of residence

		2008	2009	2010	2011	2012	Market share 2012	% Change 2012-2011
TOTAL	(*)	3,919,786	3,684,215	3,955,433	4,308,270	4,521,803	100.00	4.96
AMERICAS		146,835	115,723	133,053	145,742	165,720	3.66	13.71
North America		146,835	115,723	133,053	145,742	165,720	3.66	13.71
Canada		24,813	22,484	27,998	31,663	35,821	0.79	13.13
United States of America		122,022	93,239	105,055	114,079	129,899	2.87	13.87
EAST ASIA AND THE PACIFIC		189,565	180,905	180,589	183,799	211,491	4.68	15.07
North-East Asia		132,974	143,868	132,315	125,263	148,515	3.28	18.56
Japan		132,974	143,868	132,315	125,263	148,515	3.28	18.56
Australasia		56,591	37,037	48,274	58,536	62,976	1.39	7.59
Australia		49,601	31,510	41,439	51,889	53,843	1.19	3.77
New Zealand		6,990	5,527	6,835	6,647	9,133	0.20	37.40
EUROPE		3,521,313	3,321,698	3,542,954	3,813,900	3,898,870	86.22	2.23
Central/Eastern Europe		707,059	611,022	671,586	741,519	781,957	17.29	5.45
Belarus		2,990	1,672	1,524	1,928	2,720	0.06	41.08
Bulgaria		26,316	29,535	25,655	30,098	30,412	0.67	1.04
Czech Republic		140,997	128,366	132,801	143,765	149,281	3.30	3.84
Estonia		5,532	3,731	2,038	2,845	4,525	0.10	59.05
Hungary		112,150	95,719	94,728	103,733	105,071	2.32	1.29
Latvia		7,476	3,995	4,006	4,821	5,798	0.13	20.27
Lithuania		17,842	10,526	8,709	7,874	8,751	0.19	11.14
Poland		103,614	108,591	129,645	144,994	155,353	3.44	7.14
Romania		35,403	33,056	29,946	33,355	33,199	0.73	-0.47
Russian Federation		144,909	95,660	128,827	138,529	141,939	3.14	2.46
Slovakia		84,786	74,309	78,210	90,587	96,161	2.13	6.15
Ukraine		25,044	25,862	35,497	38,990	48,747	1.08	25.02
Northern Europe		339,072	304,474	325,678	344,210	395,081	8.74	14.78
Denmark		24,281	20,992	22,441	21,476	24,558	0.54	14.35
Finland		15,147	14,016	15,218	21,644	24,480	0.54	13.10
Iceland		2,068	1,232	1,134	1,507	1,337	0.03	-11.28
Ireland		23,097	18,338	17,839	17,194	17,326	0.38	0.77
Norway		42,419	38,662	48,956	52,202	56,480	1.25	8.20
Sweden		67,632	59,186	62,838	67,079	73,668	1.63	9.82
United Kingdom		164,428	152,048	157,252	163,108	197,232	4.36	20.92
Southern Europe		1,000,312	938,117	997,684	1,062,707	934,417	20.66	-12.07
Bosnia and Herzegovina		95,516	86,799	89,328	94,267	91,502	2.02	-2.93
Greece		10,542	16,241	30,065	30,491	19,103	0.42	-37.35
Italy		423,672	427,513	417,452	421,637	376,391	8.32	-10.73
Portugal		24,539	20,333	20,986	23,658	18,404	0.41	-22.21
Slovenia		304,948	238,973	267,917	308,612	295,493	6.53	-4.25
Spain		124,196	132,133	158,288	168,357	120,767	2.67	-28.27
TFYR of Macedonia		16,899	16,125	13,648	15,685	12,757	0.28	-18.67
Western Europe		1,358,535	1,359,383	1,415,957	1,517,096	1,637,402	36.21	7.93
Austria		367,003	416,271	440,930	486,521	522,960	11.57	7.49
Belgium		44,342	44,650	50,022	55,812	63,094	1.40	13.05
France		275,476	242,739	231,098	232,885	239,209	5.29	2.72
Germany		527,118	510,558	538,617	583,473	638,838	14.13	9.49
Luxembourg		1,621	2,244	2,353	2,453	2,392	0.05	-2.49
Netherlands		83,237	82,965	82,109	79,597	90,391	2.00	13.56
Switzerland		59,738	59,956	70,828	76,355	80,518	1.78	5.45
East Mediterranean Europe		38,131	38,093	58,292	65,299	67,711	1.50	3.69
Israel		24,991	21,140	25,437	26,539	26,392	0.58	-0.55
Turkey		13,140	16,953	32,855	38,760	41,319	0.91	6.60
Other Europe		78,204	70,609	73,757	83,069	82,302	1.82	-0.92
Other countries of Europe		78,204	70,609	73,757	83,069	82,302	1.82	-0.92
NOT SPECIFIED		62,073	65,889	98,837	164,829	245,722	5.43	49.08
Other countries of the World		62,073	65,889	98,837	164,829	245,722	5.43	49.08

Yearbook of Tourism Statistics, Data 2008 – 2012, 2014 Edition

CROATIA

4. Arrivals of non-resident tourists in all types of accommodation establishments, by country of residence

	2008	2009	2010	2011	2012	Market share 2012	% Change 2012-2011
TOTAL (*)	8,664,581	8,693,796	9,110,742	9,926,674	10,369,226	100.00	4.46
AFRICA	10,801	9,904	11,293	13,399	16,935	0.16	26.39
Southern Africa	5,775	4,790	5,578	6,908	8,460	0.08	22.47
South Africa	5,775	4,790	5,578	6,908	8,460	0.08	22.47
Other Africa	5,026	5,114	5,715	6,491	8,475	0.08	30.57
Other countries of Africa	5,026	5,114	5,715	6,491	8,475	0.08	30.57
AMERICAS	214,128	179,685	208,417	250,418	291,988	2.82	16.60
North America	191,523	155,178	176,614	201,135	230,052	2.22	14.38
Canada	36,824	34,763	41,483	48,877	55,090	0.53	12.71
United States of America	151,346	118,996	132,751	150,831	173,501	1.67	15.03
Other countries of North America	3,353	1,419	2,380	1,427	1,461	0.01	2.38
South America	7,821	9,836	14,015	22,083	30,913	0.30	39.99
Brazil	7,821	9,836	14,015	22,083	30,913	0.30	39.99
Other Americas	14,784	14,671	17,788	27,200	31,023	0.30	14.06
Other countries of the Americas	14,784	14,671	17,788	27,200	31,023	0.30	14.06
EAST ASIA AND THE PACIFIC	274,544	271,067	298,789	360,124	468,856	4.52	30.19
North-East Asia	161,979	181,114	178,797	187,260	245,097	2.36	30.89
China	6,302	7,534	13,195	22,459	43,249	0.42	92.57
Japan	143,608	163,173	147,119	131,630	155,088	1.50	17.82
Korea, Republic of	12,069	10,407	18,483	33,171	46,760	0.45	40.97
Australasia	89,866	62,137	76,690	95,561	104,258	1.01	9.10
Australia	76,670	51,452	64,526	82,729	87,735	0.85	6.05
New Zealand	13,196	10,685	12,164	12,832	16,523	0.16	28.76
Other East Asia and the Pacific	22,699	27,816	43,302	77,303	119,501	1.15	54.59
Other countries of Asia	20,156	24,906	39,916	74,286	116,732	1.13	57.14
Other countries of Oceania	2,543	2,910	3,386	3,017	2,769	0.03	-8.22
EUROPE	8,165,108	8,233,140	8,592,243	9,302,733	9,591,447	92.50	3.10
Central/Eastern Europe	1,936,045	1,886,151	2,005,719	2,173,622	2,249,141	21.69	3.47
Belarus	3,795	3,547	2,605	3,231	4,819	0.05	49.15
Bulgaria	29,961	34,678	29,586	36,699	36,538	0.35	-0.44
Czech Republic	588,911	578,517	605,732	638,036	647,211	6.24	1.44
Estonia	9,297	7,352	5,464	6,128	8,610	0.08	40.50
Hungary	338,007	298,359	297,667	328,106	307,912	2.97	-6.15
Latvia	13,143	7,658	7,142	8,813	10,640	0.10	20.73
Lithuania	33,955	23,514	20,029	20,674	23,684	0.23	14.56
Poland	373,451	417,849	454,445	494,702	544,134	5.25	9.99
Romania	66,649	64,536	57,761	63,526	61,272	0.59	-3.55
Russian Federation	165,569	121,971	164,999	182,203	196,308	1.89	7.74
Slovakia	282,982	292,450	310,031	335,021	337,429	3.25	0.72
Ukraine	30,325	35,720	50,258	56,483	70,584	0.68	24.97
Northern Europe	565,891	539,520	580,086	610,153	699,148	6.74	14.59
Denmark	80,130	76,068	77,412	73,975	85,854	0.83	16.06
Finland	23,203	24,612	27,145	34,583	38,806	0.37	12.21
Iceland	2,537	1,638	1,562	2,317	1,913	0.02	-17.44
Ireland	34,540	29,252	28,933	28,284	28,166	0.27	-0.42
Norway	71,192	66,269	85,135	92,276	102,090	0.98	10.64
Sweden	121,993	112,613	118,682	122,454	135,363	1.31	10.54
United Kingdom	232,296	229,068	241,217	256,264	306,956	2.96	19.78
Southern Europe	2,566,370	2,583,878	2,645,066	2,882,202	2,655,965	25.61	-7.85
Bosnia and Herzegovina	238,549	212,505	217,051	222,978	220,375	2.13	-1.17
Greece	12,840	18,570	32,567	33,068	21,283	0.21	-35.64
Italy	1,008,598	1,057,893	1,018,375	1,150,311	1,050,514	10.13	-8.68
Malta	1,208	1,485	1,265	1,358	1,474	0.01	8.54
Montenegro	9,689	9,089	9,798	12,361	12,353	0.12	-0.06
Portugal	31,759	26,087	28,171	29,319	23,470	0.23	-19.95

166

CROATIA

4. Arrivals of non-resident tourists in all types of accommodation establishments, by country of residence

	2008	2009	2010	2011	2012	Market share 2012	% Change 2012-2011
Serbia	84,256	85,211	86,797	86,582	85,768	0.83	-0.94
Slovenia	984,807	962,604	1,016,572	1,099,919	1,053,553	10.16	-4.22
Spain	165,101	180,013	211,094	220,957	166,176	1.60	-24.79
TFYR of Macedonia	29,563	30,421	23,376	25,349	20,999	0.20	-17.16
Western Europe	**3,021,215**	**3,156,404**	**3,265,719**	**3,521,052**	**3,869,890**	**37.32**	**9.91**
Austria	692,282	776,450	810,340	892,467	945,578	9.12	5.95
Belgium	91,925	93,913	103,341	119,916	137,261	1.32	14.46
France	423,098	393,192	388,320	394,482	418,412	4.04	6.07
Germany	1,404,832	1,463,281	1,525,133	1,661,346	1,852,731	17.87	11.52
Luxembourg	3,138	3,745	4,152	4,344	4,579	0.04	5.41
Netherlands	283,929	296,086	285,257	286,986	335,266	3.23	16.82
Switzerland	122,011	129,737	149,176	161,511	176,063	1.70	9.01
East Mediterranean Europe	**52,921**	**50,209**	**71,539**	**79,945**	**85,537**	**0.82**	**6.99**
Cyprus	2,051	1,194	1,292	1,505	1,299	0.01	-13.69
Israel	33,120	28,421	32,657	34,162	35,541	0.34	4.04
Turkey	17,750	20,594	37,590	44,278	48,697	0.47	9.98
Other Europe	**22,666**	**16,978**	**24,114**	**35,759**	**31,766**	**0.31**	**-11.17**
Other countries of Europe	22,666	16,978	24,114	35,759	31,766	0.31	-11.17

Yearbook of Tourism Statistics, Data 2008 – 2012, 2014 Edition

CROATIA

5. Overnight stays of non-resident tourists in hotels and similar establishments, by country of residence

		2008	2009	2010	2011	2012	Market share 2012	% Change 2012-2011
TOTAL	(*)	17,675,115	16,085,143	17,011,494	18,054,427	18,879,352	100.00	4.57
AMERICAS		336,982	270,297	300,442	339,156	376,508	1.99	11.01
North America		336,982	270,297	300,442	339,156	376,508	1.99	11.01
Canada		58,299	54,242	65,110	73,497	85,968	0.46	16.97
United States of America		278,683	216,055	235,332	265,659	290,540	1.54	9.37
EAST ASIA AND THE PACIFIC		300,531	274,120	285,356	293,168	342,636	1.81	16.87
North-East Asia		184,961	195,926	183,752	172,514	206,548	1.09	19.73
Japan		184,961	195,926	183,752	172,514	206,548	1.09	19.73
Australasia		115,570	78,194	101,604	120,654	136,088	0.72	12.79
Australia		101,933	66,355	88,128	106,993	117,084	0.62	9.43
New Zealand		13,637	11,839	13,476	13,661	19,004	0.10	39.11
EUROPE		16,903,919	15,400,318	16,225,867	17,131,890	17,733,233	93.93	3.51
Central/Eastern Europe		4,250,320	3,493,424	3,879,788	4,186,799	4,360,817	23.10	4.16
Belarus		16,195	8,339	9,819	10,005	15,380	0.08	53.72
Bulgaria		46,098	55,451	46,181	53,035	50,553	0.27	-4.68
Czech Republic		900,781	825,402	840,197	909,239	949,286	5.03	4.40
Estonia		16,737	10,985	7,046	10,865	17,019	0.09	56.64
Hungary		542,739	440,346	427,483	465,975	464,386	2.46	-0.34
Latvia		18,203	11,627	11,741	16,915	15,808	0.08	-6.54
Lithuania		42,925	30,544	24,425	22,512	25,172	0.13	11.82
Poland		557,494	530,160	612,847	650,808	681,650	3.61	4.74
Romania		142,274	128,222	113,154	122,011	115,103	0.61	-5.66
Russian Federation		1,242,375	804,646	1,048,374	1,097,479	1,098,621	5.82	0.10
Slovakia		539,632	473,104	496,353	561,659	599,534	3.18	6.74
Ukraine		184,867	174,598	242,168	266,296	328,305	1.74	23.29
Northern Europe		1,823,299	1,591,319	1,614,129	1,707,353	1,986,602	10.52	16.36
Denmark		141,294	111,402	120,757	113,135	132,082	0.70	16.75
Finland		70,785	49,955	58,124	94,675	106,418	0.56	12.40
Iceland		12,389	3,190	2,762	4,584	4,354	0.02	-5.02
Ireland		113,940	78,599	75,534	74,018	79,628	0.42	7.58
Norway		240,732	210,419	266,199	285,399	312,163	1.65	9.38
Sweden		381,493	319,897	317,539	330,658	363,085	1.92	9.81
United Kingdom		862,666	817,857	773,214	804,884	988,872	5.24	22.86
Southern Europe		3,782,882	3,315,224	3,413,491	3,561,161	3,152,708	16.70	-11.47
Bosnia and Herzegovina		308,155	292,519	288,596	309,914	312,777	1.66	0.92
Greece		20,829	34,463	62,625	55,248	34,864	0.18	-36.90
Italy		1,638,053	1,603,643	1,507,672	1,472,506	1,263,444	6.69	-14.20
Portugal		47,464	41,399	40,586	45,365	37,597	0.20	-17.12
Slovenia		1,474,141	1,043,760	1,176,469	1,324,916	1,244,806	6.59	-6.05
Spain		243,071	255,892	304,662	317,822	227,553	1.21	-28.40
TFYR of Macedonia		51,169	43,548	32,881	35,390	31,667	0.17	-10.52
Western Europe		6,750,876	6,689,689	6,945,842	7,279,935	7,858,864	41.63	7.95
Austria		1,702,116	1,897,595	1,993,975	2,148,567	2,301,769	12.19	7.13
Belgium		207,285	205,373	233,560	249,681	268,480	1.42	7.53
France		1,086,737	969,855	892,091	887,044	894,038	4.74	0.79
Germany		3,076,621	2,954,812	3,142,763	3,313,031	3,640,139	19.28	9.87
Luxembourg		6,072	7,822	8,935	9,469	9,507	0.05	0.40
Netherlands		436,807	425,941	414,685	396,548	448,030	2.37	12.98
Switzerland		235,238	228,291	259,833	275,595	296,901	1.57	7.73
East Mediterranean Europe		88,474	97,484	162,721	177,974	153,627	0.81	-13.68
Israel		53,959	50,704	63,702	68,351	56,847	0.30	-16.83
Turkey		34,515	46,780	99,019	109,623	96,780	0.51	-11.72
Other Europe		208,068	213,178	209,896	218,668	220,615	1.17	0.89
Other countries of Europe		208,068	213,178	209,896	218,668	220,615	1.17	0.89
NOT SPECIFIED		133,683	140,408	199,829	290,213	426,975	2.26	47.12
Other countries of the World		133,683	140,408	199,829	290,213	426,975	2.26	47.12

Yearbook of Tourism Statistics, Data 2008 – 2012, 2014 Edition

CROATIA

6. Overnight stays of non-resident tourists in all types of accommodation establishments, by country of residence

		2008	2009	2010	2011	2012	Market share 2012	% Change 2012-2011
TOTAL	(*)	49,267,686	49,229,508	50,992,321	54,751,305	57,522,137	100.00	5.06
AFRICA		34,449	36,754	37,341	42,304	57,723	0.10	36.45
Southern Africa		13,736	13,938	14,056	16,306	20,298	0.04	24.48
South Africa		13,736	13,938	14,056	16,306	20,298	0.04	24.48
Other Africa		20,713	22,816	23,285	25,998	37,425	0.07	43.95
Other countries of Africa		20,713	22,816	23,285	25,998	37,425	0.07	43.95
AMERICAS		557,894	480,807	545,362	652,142	735,252	1.28	12.74
North America		498,579	417,470	463,931	534,071	588,014	1.02	10.10
Canada		102,831	98,933	114,692	134,288	149,828	0.26	11.57
United States of America		386,971	314,442	341,398	395,084	433,227	0.75	9.65
Other countries of North America		8,777	4,095	7,841	4,699	4,959	0.01	5.53
South America		20,368	25,323	35,740	54,003	70,386	0.12	30.34
Brazil		20,368	25,323	35,740	54,003	70,386	0.12	30.34
Other Americas		38,947	38,014	45,691	64,068	76,852	0.13	19.95
Other countries of the Americas		38,947	38,014	45,691	64,068	76,852	0.13	19.95
EAST ASIA AND THE PACIFIC		505,000	475,070	547,070	643,828	834,331	1.45	29.59
North-East Asia		230,166	251,305	253,351	263,618	347,038	0.60	31.64
China		11,816	15,479	23,143	34,578	64,092	0.11	85.35
Japan		201,097	221,002	204,422	185,740	220,499	0.38	18.71
Korea, Republic of		17,253	14,824	25,786	43,300	62,447	0.11	44.22
Australasia		214,335	155,878	186,405	225,283	257,600	0.45	14.35
Australia		183,851	128,472	157,872	194,777	218,164	0.38	12.01
New Zealand		30,484	27,406	28,533	30,506	39,436	0.07	29.27
Other East Asia and the Pacific		60,499	67,887	107,314	154,927	229,693	0.40	48.26
Other countries of Asia		54,246	61,726	99,967	149,079	223,212	0.39	49.73
Other countries of Oceania		6,253	6,161	7,347	5,848	6,481	0.01	10.82
EUROPE		48,170,343	48,236,877	49,862,548	53,413,031	55,894,831	97.17	4.65
Central/Eastern Europe		12,513,238	12,031,352	12,920,632	13,936,471	14,427,977	25.08	3.53
Belarus		23,579	20,001	17,986	19,210	29,988	0.05	56.11
Bulgaria		58,751	70,899	58,791	75,977	68,210	0.12	-10.22
Czech Republic		4,062,609	3,961,828	4,170,084	4,388,696	4,519,489	7.86	2.98
Estonia		29,946	24,159	19,860	24,141	34,847	0.06	44.35
Hungary		1,871,609	1,594,794	1,604,753	1,746,138	1,629,552	2.83	-6.68
Latvia		40,129	24,460	23,749	31,368	34,379	0.06	9.60
Lithuania		109,128	82,665	70,692	73,438	90,907	0.16	23.79
Poland		2,451,471	2,685,037	2,895,162	3,134,012	3,407,685	5.92	8.73
Romania		309,448	294,486	253,556	270,523	251,242	0.44	-7.13
Russian Federation		1,431,033	1,051,991	1,375,981	1,497,761	1,577,872	2.74	5.35
Slovakia		1,900,977	1,974,402	2,084,013	2,282,066	2,294,100	3.99	0.53
Ukraine		224,558	246,630	346,005	393,141	489,706	0.85	24.56
Northern Europe		3,177,956	2,997,092	3,104,617	3,251,431	3,774,899	6.56	16.10
Denmark		591,756	562,683	567,053	537,679	625,723	1.09	16.37
Finland		105,243	95,110	108,557	151,599	172,298	0.30	13.65
Iceland		14,651	5,245	4,825	7,751	6,971	0.01	-10.06
Ireland		165,238	126,881	124,131	119,384	127,510	0.22	6.81
Norway		419,384	387,475	489,923	545,800	606,801	1.05	11.18
Sweden		704,352	628,127	637,408	652,363	730,219	1.27	11.93
United Kingdom		1,177,332	1,191,571	1,172,720	1,236,855	1,505,377	2.62	21.71
Southern Europe		12,726,630	12,587,745	12,783,262	13,582,233	12,807,391	22.27	-5.70
Bosnia and Herzegovina		1,196,953	1,077,624	1,047,909	1,061,467	1,066,036	1.85	0.43
Greece		28,731	42,522	70,697	63,877	43,232	0.08	-32.32
Italy		4,834,063	4,925,252	4,731,832	4,994,547	4,534,564	7.88	-9.21
Malta		4,212	6,490	5,544	5,702	6,369	0.01	11.70
Montenegro		41,159	31,960	29,917	31,352	31,662	0.06	0.99
Portugal		75,536	58,214	70,060	61,541	54,408	0.09	-11.59

169

CROATIA

6. Overnight stays of non-resident tourists in all types of accommodation establishments, by country of residence

	2008	2009	2010	2011	2012	Market share 2012	% Change 2012-2011
Serbia	380,031	433,445	419,553	433,048	415,313	0.72	-4.10
Slovenia	5,681,930	5,512,808	5,885,315	6,389,183	6,239,493	10.85	-2.34
Spain	336,155	360,003	423,468	437,258	333,766	0.58	-23.67
TFYR of Macedonia	147,860	139,427	98,967	104,258	82,548	0.14	-20.82
Western Europe	**19,564,534**	**20,435,860**	**20,781,204**	**22,314,522**	**24,593,589**	**42.75**	**10.21**
Austria	3,903,820	4,258,338	4,420,058	4,836,232	5,103,762	8.87	5.53
Belgium	502,873	509,980	545,342	604,678	687,426	1.20	13.68
France	1,609,816	1,510,894	1,464,114	1,483,546	1,538,457	2.67	3.70
Germany	10,682,174	11,166,827	11,476,383	12,487,389	13,946,703	24.25	11.69
Luxembourg	13,421	15,630	17,345	18,941	21,156	0.04	11.69
Netherlands	2,313,619	2,424,071	2,244,521	2,223,874	2,565,712	4.46	15.37
Switzerland	538,811	550,120	613,441	659,862	730,373	1.27	10.69
East Mediterranean Europe	**126,289**	**131,065**	**199,690**	**219,204**	**201,135**	**0.35**	**-8.24**
Cyprus	5,512	3,692	3,738	4,471	3,734	0.01	-16.48
Israel	70,782	66,167	80,293	86,284	76,327	0.13	-11.54
Turkey	49,995	61,206	115,659	128,449	121,074	0.21	-5.74
Other Europe	**61,696**	**53,763**	**73,143**	**109,170**	**89,840**	**0.16**	**-17.71**
Other countries of Europe	61,696	53,763	73,143	109,170	89,840	0.16	-17.71

Yearbook of Tourism Statistics, Data 2008 – 2012, 2014 Edition

CUBA

2. Arrivals of non-resident visitors at national borders, by country of residence

	2008	2009	2010	2011	2012	Market share 2012	% Change 2012-2011
TOTAL	**2,348,340**	**2,429,809**	**2,531,745**	**2,716,317**	**2,838,607**	**100.00**	**4.50**
AFRICA	**7,346**	**8,691**	**8,698**	**8,202**	**10,975**	**0.39**	**33.81**
East Africa	**821**	**1,370**	**1,050**	**646**	**675**	**0.02**	**4.49**
All countries of East Africa	821	1,370	1,050	646	675	0.02	4.49
Central Africa	**1,514**	**1,757**	**2,558**	**3,180**	**4,196**	**0.15**	**31.95**
Angola	997	1,440	2,307	2,838	3,793	0.13	33.65
Other countries of Central Africa	517	317	251	342	403	0.01	17.84
North Africa	**1,480**	**1,935**	**1,882**	**1,789**	**1,994**	**0.07**	**11.46**
All countries of North Africa	1,480	1,935	1,882	1,789	1,994	0.07	11.46
Southern Africa	**1,463**	**1,385**	**1,223**	**1,355**	**2,300**	**0.08**	**69.74**
All countries of Southern Africa	1,463	1,385	1,223	1,355	2,300	0.08	69.74
West Africa	**2,068**	**2,244**	**1,985**	**1,232**	**1,810**	**0.06**	**46.92**
All countries of West Africa	2,068	2,244	1,985	1,232	1,810	0.06	46.92
AMERICAS	**1,380,232**	**1,535,853**	**1,664,043**	**1,799,074**	**1,926,601**	**67.87**	**7.09**
Caribbean	**245,741**	**315,039**	**389,766**	**413,409**	**399,756**	**14.08**	**-3.30**
Antigua and Barbuda	178	201	54	76	89	0.00	17.11
Bahamas	3,826	3,456	3,122	2,966	3,007	0.11	1.38
Barbados	337	695	209	165	172	0.01	4.24
Bermuda	109	210	143	99	114	0.00	15.15
Cayman Islands	461	562	480	583	637	0.02	9.26
Dominica	404	521	138	112	91	0.00	-18.75
Dominican Republic	5,102	5,022	4,735	4,969	4,807	0.17	-3.26
Grenada	119	110	93	81	84	0.00	3.70
Guadeloupe	7	6	8				
Haiti	4,061	4,691	2,549	3,839	3,836	0.14	-0.08
Jamaica	2,721	2,173	1,512	1,285	1,309	0.05	1.87
Martinique	17	5	5	3			
Netherlands Antilles	84	49	51	86	37	0.00	-56.98
Puerto Rico	50	64	19	10	4	0.00	-60.00
Saint Lucia	567	188	148	179	104	0.00	-41.90
Saint Vincent and the Grenadines	117	94	141	102	120	0.00	17.65
Trinidad and Tobago	724	811	855	892	1,097	0.04	22.98
Other countries of the Caribbean	226,857	296,181	375,504	397,962	384,248	13.54	-3.45
Central America	**30,356**	**29,801**	**26,695**	**29,075**	**33,425**	**1.18**	**14.96**
Belize	478	800	211	230	300	0.01	30.43
Costa Rica	8,449	7,855	7,319	8,071	8,119	0.29	0.59
El Salvador	4,952	3,496	2,368	2,700	3,817	0.13	41.37
Guatemala	5,042	3,874	3,268	3,689	3,712	0.13	0.62
Honduras	1,793	1,819	1,686	1,950	2,806	0.10	43.90
Nicaragua	1,858	2,280	2,187	2,088	2,373	0.08	13.65
Panama	7,784	9,677	9,656	10,347	12,298	0.43	18.86
North America	**944,202**	**1,028,826**	**1,074,944**	**1,152,210**	**1,248,035**	**43.97**	**8.32**
Canada	818,246	914,884	945,248	1,002,318	1,071,696	37.75	6.92
Mexico	84,052	61,487	66,650	76,326	78,289	2.76	2.57
United States of America	41,904	52,455	63,046	73,566	98,050	3.45	33.28
South America	**159,933**	**162,187**	**172,638**	**204,380**	**245,385**	**8.64**	**20.06**
Argentina	47,405	48,543	58,612	75,968	94,691	3.34	24.65
Bolivia	1,639	2,002	1,600	1,286	2,204	0.08	71.38
Brazil	13,865	13,498	14,367	14,507	16,174	0.57	11.49
Chile	18,895	18,205	17,521	23,527	27,551	0.97	17.10
Colombia	22,178	21,287	20,624	24,873	33,343	1.17	34.05
Ecuador	9,391	9,473	7,011	6,964	6,281	0.22	-9.81
French Guiana	5	5	5		1	0.00	
Guyana	574	617	238	297	294	0.01	-1.01
Paraguay	369	492	412	559	677	0.02	21.11
Peru	9,598	14,708	16,049	15,188	19,737	0.70	29.95

Yearbook of Tourism Statistics, Data 2008 – 2012, 2014 Edition

CUBA

2. Arrivals of non-resident visitors at national borders, by country of residence

	2008	2009	2010	2011	2012	Market share 2012	% Change 2012-2011
Suriname	114	114	106	106	149	0.01	40.57
Uruguay	3,967	4,585	5,128	7,009	7,910	0.28	12.85
Venezuela	31,931	28,657	30,965	34,096	36,373	1.28	6.68
Other countries of South America	2	1					
EAST ASIA AND THE PACIFIC	**44,225**	**40,558**	**41,349**	**48,498**	**53,158**	**1.87**	**9.61**
North-East Asia	**22,270**	**20,887**	**21,811**	**25,403**	**31,790**	**1.12**	**25.14**
China	11,252	12,352	11,247	14,749	18,836	0.66	27.71
Hong Kong, China	14	10	6	10	15	0.00	50.00
Japan	5,550	5,460	6,372	5,420	7,348	0.26	35.57
Korea, Dem. People's Republic of	472	338	202	318	234	0.01	-26.42
Korea, Republic of	4,452	2,382	3,481	4,352	4,568	0.16	4.96
Mongolia	56	36	46	78	98	0.00	25.64
Taiwan, Province of China	469	305	449	468	688	0.02	47.01
Other countries of North-East Asia	5	4	8	8	3	0.00	-62.50
South-East Asia	**12,891**	**11,812**	**11,419**	**14,611**	**11,061**	**0.39**	**-24.30**
Cambodia	27	19	17	19	25	0.00	31.58
Indonesia	766	562	990	1,277	854	0.03	-33.12
Lao People's Democratic Republic	16	15	14	3	8	0.00	166.67
Malaysia	292	253	387	299	404	0.01	35.12
Philippines	10,567	9,478	8,721	11,561	8,289	0.29	-28.30
Singapore	155	233	239	255	261	0.01	2.35
Thailand	196	204	157	159	241	0.01	51.57
Viet Nam	832	1,000	867	1,031	960	0.03	-6.89
Other countries of South-East Asia	40	48	27	7	19	0.00	171.43
Australasia	**8,910**	**7,763**	**8,076**	**8,423**	**10,253**	**0.36**	**21.73**
Australia	7,226	6,410	6,797	7,115	8,719	0.31	22.54
New Zealand	1,684	1,353	1,279	1,308	1,534	0.05	17.28
Melanesia	**16**	**19**	**18**	**41**	**40**	**0.00**	**-2.44**
Fiji	14	7	16	15	25	0.00	66.67
New Caledonia		1	1	20	1	0.00	-95.00
Papua New Guinea	2	11	1	1	4	0.00	300.00
Vanuatu				5	10	0.00	100.00
Micronesia	**20**	**30**	**18**	**13**	**8**	**0.00**	**-38.46**
All countries of Micronesia	20	30	18	13	8	0.00	-38.46
Polynesia		**20**	**7**	**7**	**6**	**0.00**	**-14.29**
All countries of Polynesia		20	7	7	6	0.00	-14.29
Other East Asia and the Pacific	**118**	**27**					
Other countries of Oceania	118	27					
EUROPE	**909,086**	**838,340**	**809,515**	**852,065**	**839,258**	**29.57**	**-1.50**
Central/Eastern Europe	**101,478**	**85,081**	**100,070**	**127,179**	**136,926**	**4.82**	**7.66**
Bulgaria	1,940	1,663	1,517	1,832	1,885	0.07	2.89
Czech Republic	11,214	11,516	8,855	8,927	8,723	0.31	-2.29
Estonia	855	494	383	527	592	0.02	12.33
Hungary	4,135	3,439	3,028	3,512	3,064	0.11	-12.76
Latvia	823	529	607	691	954	0.03	38.06
Lithuania	1,494	866	1,180	1,279	1,185	0.04	-7.35
Poland	21,730	13,501	12,793	13,972	13,035	0.46	-6.71
Romania	3,416	2,693	2,705	3,023	3,336	0.12	10.35
Russian Federation	40,621	37,391	56,245	78,472	86,944	3.06	10.80
Slovakia	4,357	4,387	4,115	4,324	4,679	0.16	8.21
Ukraine	8,637	6,353	5,686	6,771	7,519	0.26	11.05
Uzbekistan	40	49	86	68	117	0.00	72.06
Other countries Central/East Europe	2,216	2,200	2,870	3,781	4,893	0.17	29.41
Northern Europe	**235,441**	**206,188**	**207,119**	**210,758**	**193,677**	**6.82**	**-8.10**
Denmark	10,179	8,782	8,476	8,009	8,031	0.28	0.27
Finland	5,779	5,265	4,935	5,756	6,381	0.22	10.86

Yearbook of Tourism Statistics, Data 2008 – 2012, 2014 Edition

CUBA

2. Arrivals of non-resident visitors at national borders, by country of residence

	2008	2009	2010	2011	2012	Market share 2012	% Change 2012-2011
Iceland	257	190	154	188	242	0.01	28.72
Ireland	8,586	6,592	5,638	5,171	4,972	0.18	-3.85
Norway	9,974	7,202	7,441	8,754	10,743	0.38	22.72
Sweden	6,720	5,837	6,131	7,055	9,571	0.34	35.66
United Kingdom	193,932	172,318	174,343	175,822	153,737	5.42	-12.56
Other countries of Northern Europe	14	2	1	3			
Southern Europe	**289,531**	**285,845**	**247,098**	**235,698**	**203,233**	**7.16**	**-13.77**
Albania	416	376	404	351	378	0.01	7.69
Andorra	111	124	113	113	81	0.00	-28.32
Bosnia and Herzegovina	428	307	299	288	304	0.01	5.56
Croatia	1,817	1,442	1,344	1,383	1,578	0.06	14.10
Greece	7,533	4,769	4,263	3,427	2,551	0.09	-25.56
Italy	126,042	118,347	112,298	110,432	103,290	3.64	-6.47
Malta	136	140	117	125	117	0.00	-6.40
Montenegro	76	96	142	151	165	0.01	9.27
Portugal	25,542	26,055	18,762	13,733	9,148	0.32	-33.39
San Marino	132	145	119	111	94	0.00	-15.32
Serbia			1,683	1,669	2,022	0.07	21.15
Serbia and Montenegro	1,292	1,430					
Slovenia	2,749	2,358	2,130	1,941	1,853	0.07	-4.53
Spain	121,166	129,224	104,948	101,631	81,354	2.87	-19.95
Other countries of Southern Europe	2,091	1,032	476	343	298	0.01	-13.12
Western Europe	**272,255**	**253,812**	**246,704**	**266,923**	**294,292**	**10.37**	**10.25**
Austria	13,450	12,004	11,486	11,803	13,250	0.47	12.26
Belgium	15,681	15,722	13,049	14,266	14,414	0.51	1.04
France	90,731	83,478	80,470	94,370	101,522	3.58	7.58
Germany	100,964	93,437	93,136	95,124	108,712	3.83	14.28
Liechtenstein	61	62	64	85	87	0.00	2.35
Luxembourg	647	613	598	693	724	0.03	4.47
Monaco	33	34	19	37	45	0.00	21.62
Netherlands	33,548	33,123	31,787	32,402	35,284	1.24	8.89
Switzerland	17,140	15,339	16,095	18,143	20,254	0.71	11.64
East Mediterranean Europe	**10,381**	**7,414**	**8,524**	**11,507**	**11,130**	**0.39**	**-3.28**
Cyprus	537	367	282	344	240	0.01	-30.23
Israel	3,945	3,306	3,926	5,327	4,857	0.17	-8.82
Turkey	5,899	3,741	4,316	5,836	6,033	0.21	3.38
MIDDLE EAST	**1,981**	**1,810**	**2,053**	**1,814**	**2,191**	**0.08**	**20.78**
Bahrain	15	17	22	22	22	0.00	0.00
Egypt	324	240	271	292	23	0.00	-92.12
Iraq	63	54	67	78	103	0.00	32.05
Jordan	202	211	172	162	173	0.01	6.79
Kuwait	20	23	153	52	47	0.00	-9.62
Lebanon	655	533	522	574	616	0.02	7.32
Libya	50	80	73	29	12	0.00	-58.62
Oman	26	56	27	19	50	0.00	163.16
Palestine	71	96	71	56	60	0.00	7.14
Qatar	58	17	34	7	36	0.00	414.29
Saudi Arabia	66	115	185	210	300	0.01	42.86
Syrian Arab Republic	355	215	368	266	388	0.01	45.86
Yemen	58	76	52	32	36	0.00	12.50
Other countries of Middle East	18	77	36	15	325	0.01	2,066.67
SOUTH ASIA	**5,156**	**4,467**	**5,832**	**5,841**	**5,901**	**0.21**	**1.03**
Afghanistan	23	49	42	48	61	0.00	27.08
Bangladesh	69	80	118	91	108	0.00	18.68
India	2,730	2,551	3,614	3,574	3,480	0.12	-2.63
Iran, Islamic Republic of	784	940	1,092	1,075	1,048	0.04	-2.51

Yearbook of Tourism Statistics, Data 2008 – 2012, 2014 Edition

CUBA

2. Arrivals of non-resident visitors at national borders, by country of residence

	2008	2009	2010	2011	2012	Market share 2012	% Change 2012-2011
Maldives	53	55	81	1	3	0.00	200.00
Pakistan	867	179	208	185	212	0.01	14.59
Sri Lanka	541	483	487	362	466	0.02	28.73
Other countries of South Asia	89	130	190	505	523	0.02	3.56
NOT SPECIFIED	**314**	**90**	**255**	**823**	**523**	**0.02**	**-36.45**
Other countries of the World	314	90	255	823	523	0.02	-36.45

Yearbook of Tourism Statistics, Data 2008 – 2012, 2014 Edition

CURAÇAO

1. Arrivals of non-resident tourists at national borders, by country of residence

		2008	2009	2010	2011	2012	Market share 2012	% Change 2012-2011
TOTAL	(*)	**408,942**	**366,679**	**341,651**	**390,111**	**419,810**	**100.00**	**7.61**
AMERICAS		**264,986**	**210,790**	**170,818**	**210,093**	**234,912**	**55.96**	**11.81**
Caribbean		**41,154**	**36,637**	**39,107**	**41,573**	**39,999**	**9.53**	**-3.79**
Aruba		16,848	16,756	18,817	20,453	21,641	5.15	5.81
Barbados		754	862	1,144	929	705	0.17	-24.11
Dominican Republic		2,612	2,644	2,927	4,098	4,125	0.98	0.66
Haiti		1,770	1,811	1,914	2,273	2,321	0.55	2.11
Jamaica		9,591	7,064	5,109	5,155	3,888	0.93	-24.58
Puerto Rico		845	756	711	442	360	0.09	-18.55
Trinidad and Tobago		6,499	5,318	6,852	6,438	5,388	1.28	-16.31
Other countries of the Caribbean		2,235	1,426	1,633	1,785	1,571	0.37	-11.99
Central America		**642**	**634**	**734**	**841**	**1,131**	**0.27**	**34.48**
Panama		642	634	734	841	1,131	0.27	34.48
North America		**50,924**	**42,560**	**56,449**	**71,655**	**71,692**	**17.08**	**0.05**
Canada		7,244	6,513	7,628	8,769	9,790	2.33	11.64
United States of America		43,680	36,047	48,821	62,886	61,902	14.75	-1.56
South America		**172,266**	**130,959**	**74,528**	**96,024**	**122,090**	**29.08**	**27.15**
Argentina		762	709	929	1,289	1,843	0.44	42.98
Brazil		4,215	4,466	8,096	8,825	9,255	2.20	4.87
Chile		462	338	357	534	594	0.14	11.24
Colombia		5,359	6,260	6,280	8,181	10,420	2.48	27.37
Ecuador		3,081	1,744	2,319	2,629	2,884	0.69	9.70
Guyana		822	917	1,029	990	1,019	0.24	2.93
Peru		606	288	266	179	213	0.05	18.99
Suriname		6,220	9,218	9,440	9,978	10,773	2.57	7.97
Venezuela		148,890	105,932	44,350	61,567	83,148	19.81	35.05
Other countries of South America		1,849	1,087	1,462	1,852	1,941	0.46	4.81
EUROPE		**136,747**	**149,538**	**163,831**	**169,142**	**174,707**	**41.62**	**3.29**
Northern Europe		**6,908**	**5,316**	**5,448**	**5,730**	**5,010**	**1.19**	**-12.57**
Denmark		501	446	299	464	304	0.07	-34.48
Finland		1,191	887	747	667	582	0.14	-12.74
Norway		655	659	742	835	743	0.18	-11.02
Sweden		1,667	1,236	1,480	1,224	1,248	0.30	1.96
United Kingdom		2,894	2,088	2,180	2,540	2,133	0.51	-16.02
Southern Europe		**2,554**	**1,819**	**2,332**	**2,992**	**2,736**	**0.65**	**-8.56**
Italy		1,024	730	1,131	1,851	1,294	0.31	-30.09
Portugal		502	248	249	229	296	0.07	29.26
Spain		1,028	841	952	912	1,146	0.27	25.66
Western Europe		**123,493**	**139,055**	**152,739**	**156,458**	**161,954**	**38.58**	**3.51**
Austria		350	340	367	474	1,158	0.28	144.30
Belgium		3,156	3,744	4,429	5,114	5,065	1.21	-0.96
Germany		5,516	6,842	6,652	8,065	15,638	3.73	93.90
Netherlands		113,696	127,175	140,161	141,529	138,201	32.92	-2.35
Switzerland		775	954	1,130	1,276	1,892	0.45	48.28
Other Europe		**3,792**	**3,348**	**3,312**	**3,962**	**5,007**	**1.19**	**26.38**
Other countries of Europe		3,792	3,348	3,312	3,962	5,007	1.19	26.38
NOT SPECIFIED		**7,209**	**6,351**	**7,002**	**10,876**	**10,191**	**2.43**	**-6.30**
Other countries of the World		7,209	6,351	7,002	10,876	10,191	2.43	-6.30

Yearbook of Tourism Statistics, Data 2008 – 2012, 2014 Edition

CURAÇAO

3. Arrivals of non-resident tourists in hotels and similar establishments, by country of residence

		2008	2009	2010	2011	2012	Market share 2012	% Change 2012-2011
TOTAL	(*)	224,322	234,070	223,044	248,884	230,499	100.00	-7.39
AMERICAS		171,083	140,072	117,250	144,713	139,416	60.48	-3.66
Caribbean		21,051	18,313	23,834	22,673	19,086	8.28	-15.82
Aruba		7,951	7,072	10,763	11,163	10,535	4.57	-5.63
Barbados		494	672	793	663	453	0.20	-31.67
Dominican Republic		1,082	816	875	953	926	0.40	-2.83
Haiti		203	844	893	1,093	889	0.39	-18.66
Jamaica		4,914	3,344	3,369	2,099	1,353	0.59	-35.54
Puerto Rico		662	469	558	320	238	0.10	-25.63
Trinidad and Tobago		4,638	4,263	5,586	5,140	3,866	1.68	-24.79
Other countries of the Caribbean		1,107	833	997	1,242	826	0.36	-33.49
North America		36,275	32,781	46,925	57,240	48,155	20.89	-15.87
Canada		4,835	5,436	6,567	7,185	6,731	2.92	-6.32
United States of America		31,440	27,345	40,358	50,055	41,424	17.97	-17.24
South America		113,757	88,978	46,491	64,800	72,175	31.31	11.38
Argentina		457	547	797	1,014	1,232	0.53	21.50
Brazil		2,762	3,704	7,413	7,423	6,271	2.72	-15.52
Colombia		2,339	2,685	3,473	4,920	5,595	2.43	13.72
Ecuador		2,703	1,439	2,100	2,404	1,841	0.80	-23.42
Guyana		334	461	581	587	557	0.24	-5.11
Peru		240	142		82	79	0.03	-3.66
Suriname		2,226	3,325	843	4,362	4,095	1.78	-6.12
Venezuela		100,855	75,154	29,349	42,163	50,557	21.93	19.91
Other countries of South America		1,841	1,521	1,935	1,845	1,948	0.85	5.58
EUROPE		51,759	92,603	104,420	102,017	89,158	38.68	-12.60
Northern Europe		4,039	3,739	3,836	3,691	3,021	1.31	-18.15
Denmark		311	317	193	333	130	0.06	-60.96
Finland		736	808	676	541	467	0.20	-13.68
Norway		292	462	489	555	467	0.20	-15.86
Sweden		1,219	962	1,181	977	784	0.34	-19.75
United Kingdom		1,481	1,190	1,297	1,285	1,173	0.51	-8.72
Southern Europe		996	1,029	1,401	1,974	1,303	0.57	-33.99
Italy		406	476	795	1,427	656	0.28	-54.03
Portugal		169	147	150	95	98	0.04	3.16
Spain		421	406	456	452	549	0.24	21.46
Western Europe		45,235	86,277	97,525	94,417	83,163	36.08	-11.92
Austria		139	246	266	338	737	0.32	118.05
Belgium		1,802	2,389	3,094	3,285	2,978	1.29	-9.35
Germany		2,516	4,588	4,443	5,211	9,194	3.99	76.43
Netherlands		40,012	78,385	88,885	84,674	69,097	29.98	-18.40
Switzerland		766	669	837	909	1,157	0.50	27.28
Other Europe		1,489	1,558	1,658	1,935	1,671	0.72	-13.64
Other countries of Europe		1,489	1,558	1,658	1,935	1,671	0.72	-13.64
NOT SPECIFIED		1,480	1,395	1,374	2,154	1,925	0.84	-10.63
Other countries of the World		1,480	1,395	1,374	2,154	1,925	0.84	-10.63

Yearbook of Tourism Statistics, Data 2008 – 2012, 2014 Edition

CURAÇAO

6. Overnight stays of non-resident tourists in all types of accommodation establishments, by country of residence

	2008	2009	2010	2011	2012	Market share 2012	% Change 2012-2011
TOTAL	2,978,363	2,696,798	2,907,435	3,200,356	3,665,520	100.00	14.53
AMERICAS	1,277,791	1,028,550	1,063,734	1,303,411	1,629,643	44.46	25.03
Caribbean	208,523	180,228	213,512	251,473	264,385	7.21	5.13
Aruba	77,766	72,310	83,351	90,905	114,200	3.12	25.63
Barbados	3,089	2,982	5,237	4,042	3,482	0.09	-13.85
Dominican Republic	25,763	24,222	34,200	62,157	59,519	1.62	-4.24
Haiti	14,767	13,383	16,621	20,005	22,481	0.61	12.38
Jamaica	46,078	37,292	32,190	36,021	28,546	0.78	-20.75
Puerto Rico	3,880	3,187	2,930	1,902	2,054	0.06	7.99
Trinidad and Tobago	23,463	19,120	27,823	26,221	23,396	0.64	-10.77
Other countries of the Caribbean	13,717	7,732	11,160	10,220	10,707	0.29	4.77
North America	384,873	300,174	375,576	469,450	505,455	13.79	7.67
Canada	61,406	53,342	62,825	75,057	84,101	2.29	12.05
United States of America	323,467	246,832	312,751	394,393	421,354	11.50	6.84
South America	684,395	548,148	474,646	582,488	859,803	23.46	47.61
Argentina	4,666	3,923	5,730	7,569	12,345	0.34	63.10
Brazil	20,863	22,602	40,540	45,886	56,936	1.55	24.08
Colombia	77,967	81,107	87,177	108,327	102,486	2.80	-5.39
Ecuador	13,486	7,589	12,179	12,244	16,120	0.44	31.66
Guyana	4,823	4,713	5,555	6,182	7,020	0.19	13.56
Peru	5,485			1,501	1,926	0.05	28.31
Suriname	43,713	60,472	60,660	61,025	72,412	1.98	18.66
Venezuela	496,077	353,292	242,654	318,410	567,849	15.49	78.34
Other countries of South America	17,315	14,450	20,151	21,344	22,709	0.62	6.40
EUROPE	1,644,197	1,634,474	1,805,450	1,850,752	1,964,369	53.59	6.14
Northern Europe	66,445	52,081	54,611	51,459	49,951	1.36	-2.93
Denmark	5,153	4,113	2,999	4,213	3,124	0.09	-25.85
Finland	10,765	8,037	6,910	5,153	4,930	0.13	-4.33
Norway	5,611	6,528	6,900	7,781	6,972	0.19	-10.40
Sweden	15,968	11,899	15,023	11,661	11,943	0.33	2.42
United Kingdom	28,948	21,504	22,779	22,651	22,982	0.63	1.46
Southern Europe	20,954	16,812	19,570	25,566	27,101	0.74	6.00
Italy	6,305	5,730	9,103	14,549	10,688	0.29	-26.54
Portugal	5,480	2,886	1,659	2,127	4,030	0.11	89.47
Spain	9,169	8,196	8,808	8,890	12,383	0.34	39.29
Western Europe	1,525,024	1,540,097	1,704,960	1,738,421	1,855,035	50.61	6.71
Austria	3,466	3,769	3,940	5,004	11,515	0.31	130.12
Belgium	38,583	40,101	45,585	50,378	52,512	1.43	4.24
Germany	72,424	81,164	78,149	94,222	168,494	4.60	78.83
Netherlands	1,403,478	1,406,180	1,566,903	1,576,224	1,604,893	43.78	1.82
Switzerland	7,073	8,883	10,383	12,593	17,621	0.48	39.93
Other Europe	31,774	25,484	26,309	35,306	32,282	0.88	-8.57
Other countries of Europe	31,774	25,484	26,309	35,306	32,282	0.88	-8.57
NOT SPECIFIED	56,375	33,774	38,251	46,193	71,508	1.95	54.80
Other countries of the World	56,375	33,774	38,251	46,193	71,508	1.95	54.80

Yearbook of Tourism Statistics, Data 2008 – 2012, 2014 Edition

CYPRUS

1. Arrivals of non-resident tourists at national borders, by country of residence

	2008	2009	2010	2011	2012	Market share 2012	% Change 2012-2011
TOTAL	2,401,625	2,139,007	2,169,491	2,388,857	2,459,687	100.00	2.97
AFRICA	7,535	6,833	6,481	6,615	5,617	0.23	-15.09
Southern Africa	6,249	5,623	4,816	5,793	4,708	0.19	-18.73
South Africa	6,249	5,623	4,816	5,793	4,708	0.19	-18.73
Other Africa	1,286	1,210	1,665	822	909	0.04	10.58
Other countries of Africa	1,286	1,210	1,665	822	909	0.04	10.58
AMERICAS	27,777	23,737	31,357	32,080	25,084	1.02	-21.81
North America	26,629	22,619	29,541	31,012	24,292	0.99	-21.67
Canada	5,512	4,698	6,822	5,180	3,830	0.16	-26.06
United States of America	21,117	17,921	22,719	25,832	20,462	0.83	-20.79
Other Americas	1,148	1,118	1,816	1,068	792	0.03	-25.84
Other countries of the Americas	1,148	1,118	1,816	1,068	792	0.03	-25.84
EAST ASIA AND THE PACIFIC	16,567	15,060	19,093	16,535	15,746	0.64	-4.77
North-East Asia	1,446	1,520	2,377	2,049	2,475	0.10	20.79
China	722	441	655	651	735	0.03	12.90
Japan	354	560	1,194	694	1,249	0.05	79.97
Korea, Republic of		60	144	292	81	0.00	-72.26
Other countries of North-East Asia	370	459	384	412	410	0.02	-0.49
Australasia	12,160	10,996	14,139	13,110	12,218	0.50	-6.80
Australia	11,506	10,523	13,282	12,455	11,681	0.47	-6.21
New Zealand	654	473	857	655	537	0.02	-18.02
Other East Asia and the Pacific	2,961	2,544	2,577	1,376	1,053	0.04	-23.47
Other countries of Asia	2,922	2,511	2,534	1,294	1,025	0.04	-20.79
Other countries of Oceania	39	33	43	82	28	0.00	-65.85
EUROPE	2,297,405	2,037,775	2,051,932	2,275,563	2,351,013	95.58	3.32
Central/Eastern Europe	284,538	243,243	321,554	460,212	599,116	24.36	30.18
Bulgaria	10,675	8,922	8,905	10,247	10,443	0.42	1.91
Czech Republic	20,027	20,477	15,458	20,576	14,741	0.60	-28.36
Estonia	1,884	2,077	970	2,074	1,591	0.06	-23.29
Georgia	95	195	146	141	194	0.01	37.59
Hungary	9,641	9,700	10,721	11,334	12,376	0.50	9.19
Latvia	2,150	1,538	1,825	1,934	2,088	0.08	7.96
Lithuania	2,294	1,423	2,546	2,182	6,766	0.28	210.08
Poland	20,358	17,186	18,439	24,236	30,981	1.26	27.83
Romania	20,346	19,931	19,980	30,601	20,557	0.84	-32.82
Russian Federation	180,926	148,740	223,861	334,083	474,426	19.29	42.01
Slovakia	5,048	3,719	5,061	5,030	3,608	0.15	-28.27
Ukraine	8,847	7,496	11,766	14,274	19,482	0.79	36.49
Other countries Central/East Europe	2,247	1,839	1,876	3,500	1,863	0.08	-46.77
Northern Europe	1,525,535	1,318,879	1,243,031	1,277,048	1,215,250	49.41	-4.84
Denmark	38,216	29,667	30,335	34,064	31,763	1.29	-6.75
Finland	32,333	32,758	32,886	36,289	29,216	1.19	-19.49
Iceland	281	223	144	88	280	0.01	218.18
Ireland	23,632	18,537	10,527	9,662	7,832	0.32	-18.94
Norway	63,470	60,245	63,347	64,024	69,410	2.82	8.41
Sweden	124,948	108,253	109,746	112,212	117,286	4.77	4.52
United Kingdom	1,242,655	1,069,196	996,046	1,020,709	959,463	39.01	-6.00
Southern Europe	162,722	162,546	154,782	172,168	183,784	7.47	6.75
Greece	133,015	131,875	127,667	138,721	132,990	5.41	-4.13
Italy	16,859	15,604	12,992	16,828	34,415	1.40	104.51
Malta	3,421	6,154	4,358	4,511	4,866	0.20	7.87
Montenegro	68	104	168	86			
Portugal	855	1,106	1,161	1,034	925	0.04	-10.54
Serbia	3,322	3,678	3,431	3,986	3,960	0.16	-0.65
Slovenia	1,541	953	1,046	2,245	1,124	0.05	-49.93

178

CYPRUS

1. Arrivals of non-resident tourists at national borders, by country of residence

	2008	2009	2010	2011	2012	Market share 2012	% Change 2012-2011
Spain	3,641	3,072	3,959	4,757	5,504	0.22	15.70
Western Europe	**290,362**	**280,455**	**292,856**	**333,038**	**311,926**	**12.68**	**-6.34**
Austria	26,620	27,463	21,559	23,341	23,166	0.94	-0.75
Belgium	26,368	22,966	24,125	27,346	25,930	1.05	-5.18
France	36,099	26,187	28,749	34,363	35,955	1.46	4.63
Germany	132,058	131,161	139,190	157,890	144,407	5.87	-8.54
Luxembourg	4,355	3,020	3,374	3,154	2,591	0.11	-17.85
Netherlands	26,302	30,996	34,212	41,631	33,024	1.34	-20.67
Switzerland	38,560	38,662	41,647	45,313	46,853	1.90	3.40
East Mediterranean Europe	**32,169**	**31,480**	**38,197**	**32,174**	**39,473**	**1.60**	**22.69**
Israel	32,034	31,364	37,876	31,910	39,420	1.60	23.53
Turkey	135	116	321	264	53	0.00	-79.92
Other Europe	**2,079**	**1,172**	**1,512**	**923**	**1,464**	**0.06**	**58.61**
Other countries of Europe	2,079	1,172	1,512	923	1,464	0.06	58.61
MIDDLE EAST	**48,280**	**49,947**	**51,110**	**50,799**	**56,402**	**2.29**	**11.03**
Bahrain	2,790	2,970	2,184	1,766	1,862	0.08	5.44
Egypt	4,351	5,067	4,324	4,940	5,338	0.22	8.06
Iraq	58	89	358	1,409	2,757	0.11	95.67
Jordan	3,071	4,040	3,575	4,184	3,490	0.14	-16.59
Kuwait	4,049	2,544	1,480	1,268	1,698	0.07	33.91
Lebanon	14,192	15,431	20,664	21,202	25,658	1.04	21.02
Libya	449	408	298	145	169	0.01	16.55
Saudi Arabia	2,978	2,071	2,463	1,445	1,537	0.06	6.37
Syrian Arab Republic	1,392	1,455	1,626	983	1,272	0.05	29.40
United Arab Emirates	12,853	14,197	11,832	11,433	10,664	0.43	-6.73
Other countries of Middle East	2,097	1,675	2,306	2,024	1,957	0.08	-3.31
SOUTH ASIA	**3,751**	**5,020**	**8,406**	**6,963**	**5,666**	**0.23**	**-18.63**
Iran, Islamic Republic of	1,799	3,627	4,336	5,742	4,402	0.18	-23.34
Other countries of South Asia	1,952	1,393	4,070	1,221	1,264	0.05	3.52
NOT SPECIFIED	**310**	**635**	**1,112**	**302**	**159**	**0.01**	**-47.35**
Other countries of the World	310	635	1,112	302	159	0.01	-47.35

Yearbook of Tourism Statistics, Data 2008 – 2012, 2014 Edition

CYPRUS

3. Arrivals of non-resident tourists in hotels and similar establishments, by country of residence

	2008	2009	2010	2011	2012	Market share 2012	% Change 2012-2011
TOTAL	1,753,561	1,646,564	1,788,372	1,921,951	1,996,168	100.00	3.86
AFRICA	1,055	1,529	2,201	2,090	1,793	0.09	-14.21
Southern Africa	1,055	1,529	2,201	2,090	1,793	0.09	-14.21
South Africa	1,055	1,529	2,201	2,090	1,793	0.09	-14.21
AMERICAS	15,799	19,706	23,951	23,828	18,827	0.94	-20.99
North America	15,799	19,706	23,951	23,828	18,827	0.94	-20.99
Canada	6,059	9,155	10,709	9,917	5,846	0.29	-41.05
United States of America	9,740	10,551	13,242	13,911	12,981	0.65	-6.69
EAST ASIA AND THE PACIFIC	7,378	8,535	9,616	8,247	10,529	0.53	27.67
North-East Asia	2,609	3,585	4,339	4,199	6,342	0.32	51.04
China	1,084	1,405	1,631	1,533	3,442	0.17	124.53
Japan	1,525	2,180	2,708	2,666	2,900	0.15	8.78
Australasia	4,769	4,950	5,277	4,048	4,187	0.21	3.43
Australia	4,769	4,950	5,277	4,048	4,187	0.21	3.43
EUROPE	1,637,978	1,517,681	1,642,363	1,768,517	1,842,889	92.32	4.21
Central/Eastern Europe	223,495	187,270	268,914	379,716	485,021	24.30	27.73
Bulgaria	3,734	3,726	3,971	4,357	3,275	0.16	-24.83
Czech Republic	16,566	15,396	16,037	18,965	14,211	0.71	-25.07
Estonia	1,051	1,985	1,381	1,579	1,730	0.09	9.56
Hungary	7,229	6,162	7,934	7,425	7,470	0.37	0.61
Latvia	914	1,016	1,273	953	1,515	0.08	58.97
Lithuania	929	2,043	3,051	1,176	3,521	0.18	199.40
Poland	15,490	15,517	19,388	24,404	23,571	1.18	-3.41
Romania	10,030	9,511	10,109	14,551	9,846	0.49	-32.33
Russian Federation	163,831	128,174	201,250	302,423	415,598	20.82	37.42
Slovakia	3,721	3,740	4,520	3,883	4,284	0.21	10.33
Northern Europe	1,038,101	943,525	941,827	946,180	937,568	46.97	-0.91
Denmark	23,574	22,626	25,714	25,307	26,269	1.32	3.80
Finland	25,532	28,168	30,466	33,941	25,793	1.29	-24.01
Iceland	2,235	4,314	2,583	4,903	4,122	0.21	-15.93
Ireland	13,518	14,293	12,076	10,106	9,983	0.50	-1.22
Norway	51,799	57,228	63,207	69,191	65,107	3.26	-5.90
Sweden	105,019	101,245	104,324	108,476	109,094	5.47	0.57
United Kingdom	816,424	715,651	703,457	694,256	697,200	34.93	0.42
Southern Europe	98,303	100,933	108,677	114,691	109,916	5.51	-4.16
Greece	66,349	68,394	74,281	74,791	60,956	3.05	-18.50
Italy	22,151	18,170	19,472	22,121	32,996	1.65	49.16
Malta	1,406	5,543	4,299	5,013	3,968	0.20	-20.85
Portugal	2,081	2,523	2,514	2,921	3,245	0.16	11.09
Slovenia	1,875	1,533	1,595	2,411	1,938	0.10	-19.62
Spain	4,441	4,770	6,516	7,434	6,813	0.34	-8.35
Western Europe	278,079	285,953	322,945	327,930	310,384	15.55	-5.35
Austria	18,643	20,036	21,459	19,477	18,652	0.93	-4.24
Belgium	19,989	20,850	24,017	25,434	24,522	1.23	-3.59
France	46,227	36,571	47,785	50,169	48,952	2.45	-2.43
Germany	139,640	147,826	159,998	155,843	144,239	7.23	-7.45
Luxembourg	2,505	3,625	3,248	2,654	2,929	0.15	10.36
Netherlands	23,523	27,573	33,077	40,683	31,824	1.59	-21.78
Switzerland	27,552	29,472	33,361	33,670	39,266	1.97	16.62
NOT SPECIFIED	91,351	99,113	110,241	119,269	122,130	6.12	2.40
Other countries of the World	91,351	99,113	110,241	119,269	122,130	6.12	2.40

Yearbook of Tourism Statistics, Data 2008 – 2012, 2014 Edition

CYPRUS

4. Arrivals of non-resident tourists in all types of accommodation establishments, by country of residence

	2008	2009	2010	2011	2012	Market share 2012	% Change 2012-2011
TOTAL	1,761,777	1,671,864	1,814,328	1,947,446	2,021,180	100.00	3.79
AFRICA	1,068	1,655	2,347	2,220	1,901	0.09	-14.37
Southern Africa	1,068	1,655	2,347	2,220	1,901	0.09	-14.37
South Africa	1,068	1,655	2,347	2,220	1,901	0.09	-14.37
AMERICAS	15,816	20,054	24,394	24,223	19,202	0.95	-20.73
North America	15,816	20,054	24,394	24,223	19,202	0.95	-20.73
Canada	6,061	9,289	10,872	10,077	5,976	0.30	-40.70
United States of America	9,755	10,765	13,522	14,146	13,226	0.65	-6.50
EAST ASIA AND THE PACIFIC	7,385	8,900	10,055	8,681	10,960	0.54	26.25
North-East Asia	2,609	3,804	4,616	4,469	6,628	0.33	48.31
China	1,084	1,508	1,760	1,656	3,601	0.18	117.45
Japan	1,525	2,296	2,856	2,813	3,027	0.15	7.61
Australasia	4,776	5,096	5,439	4,212	4,332	0.21	2.85
Australia	4,776	5,096	5,439	4,212	4,332	0.21	2.85
EUROPE	1,645,990	1,540,209	1,665,018	1,791,403	1,864,734	92.26	4.09
Central/Eastern Europe	223,693	189,726	272,261	383,165	488,791	24.18	27.57
Bulgaria	3,744	3,877	4,162	4,533	3,463	0.17	-23.60
Czech Republic	16,599	15,637	16,330	19,240	14,421	0.71	-25.05
Estonia	1,051	2,099	1,500	1,714	1,832	0.09	6.88
Hungary	7,242	6,332	8,139	7,613	7,627	0.38	0.18
Latvia	914	1,117	1,381	1,054	1,613	0.08	53.04
Lithuania	929	2,144	3,179	1,279	3,658	0.18	186.00
Poland	15,510	15,733	19,654	24,667	23,855	1.18	-3.29
Romania	10,049	9,733	10,375	14,857	10,094	0.50	-32.06
Russian Federation	163,920	129,186	202,889	304,189	417,827	20.67	37.36
Slovakia	3,735	3,868	4,652	4,019	4,401	0.22	9.50
Northern Europe	1,044,932	958,753	955,346	959,568	950,389	47.02	-0.96
Denmark	23,915	22,908	26,262	25,739	26,594	1.32	3.32
Finland	25,626	28,524	30,849	34,320	26,148	1.29	-23.81
Iceland	2,237	4,489	2,713	5,066	4,221	0.21	-16.68
Ireland	13,552	14,481	12,276	10,353	10,208	0.51	-1.40
Norway	52,139	57,889	63,828	70,261	66,069	3.27	-5.97
Sweden	105,158	105,194	107,581	111,753	112,104	5.55	0.31
United Kingdom	822,305	725,268	711,837	702,076	705,045	34.88	0.42
Southern Europe	98,416	102,381	110,235	116,239	111,491	5.52	-4.08
Greece	66,396	68,936	74,873	75,314	61,466	3.04	-18.39
Italy	22,212	18,449	19,850	22,487	33,486	1.66	48.91
Malta	1,406	5,709	4,477	5,219	4,117	0.20	-21.12
Portugal	2,083	2,729	2,633	3,057	3,356	0.17	9.78
Slovenia	1,875	1,628	1,706	2,529	2,047	0.10	-19.06
Spain	4,444	4,930	6,696	7,633	7,019	0.35	-8.04
Western Europe	278,949	289,349	327,176	332,431	314,063	15.54	-5.53
Austria	18,703	20,317	21,777	19,806	18,941	0.94	-4.37
Belgium	20,061	21,168	24,351	25,789	24,846	1.23	-3.66
France	46,468	37,104	48,519	50,806	49,644	2.46	-2.29
Germany	139,980	149,064	161,708	157,835	145,490	7.20	-7.82
Luxembourg	2,506	3,786	3,415	2,816	3,051	0.15	8.35
Netherlands	23,647	28,042	33,621	41,286	32,395	1.60	-21.54
Switzerland	27,584	29,868	33,785	34,093	39,696	1.96	16.43
NOT SPECIFIED	91,518	101,046	112,514	120,919	124,383	6.15	2.86
Other countries of the World	91,518	101,046	112,514	120,919	124,383	6.15	2.86

Yearbook of Tourism Statistics, Data 2008 – 2012, 2014 Edition

CYPRUS

5. Overnight stays of non-resident tourists in hotels and similar establishments, by country of residence

	2008	2009	2010	2011	2012	Market share 2012	% Change 2012-2011
TOTAL	13,151,048	11,488,361	12,267,921	12,933,024	13,333,840	100.00	3.10
AFRICA	3,783	5,355	7,581	8,262	6,354	0.05	-23.09
Southern Africa	3,783	5,355	7,581	8,262	6,354	0.05	-23.09
South Africa	3,783	5,355	7,581	8,262	6,354	0.05	-23.09
AMERICAS	66,888	87,796	92,594	99,121	77,523	0.58	-21.79
North America	66,888	87,796	92,594	99,121	77,523	0.58	-21.79
Canada	28,464	47,940	46,115	54,906	29,918	0.22	-45.51
United States of America	38,424	39,856	46,479	44,215	47,605	0.36	7.67
EAST ASIA AND THE PACIFIC	27,613	32,763	31,498	24,997	34,652	0.26	38.62
North-East Asia	8,156	9,652	11,079	10,421	18,097	0.14	73.66
China	4,391	4,388	4,974	4,764	11,165	0.08	134.36
Japan	3,765	5,264	6,105	5,657	6,932	0.05	22.54
Australasia	19,457	23,111	20,419	14,576	16,555	0.12	13.58
Australia	19,457	23,111	20,419	14,576	16,555	0.12	13.58
EUROPE	12,658,846	10,968,124	11,725,629	12,322,509	12,704,386	95.28	3.10
Central/Eastern Europe	1,705,779	1,389,566	2,023,462	2,708,095	3,650,713	27.38	34.81
Bulgaria	21,368	21,800	23,259	21,767	13,096	0.10	-39.84
Czech Republic	123,123	115,004	110,833	126,912	99,858	0.75	-21.32
Estonia	6,876	11,952	7,592	8,054	8,474	0.06	5.21
Hungary	41,018	34,447	40,934	39,560	37,587	0.28	-4.99
Latvia	4,610	4,182	6,302	3,555	6,026	0.05	69.51
Lithuania	5,276	11,251	18,392	4,501	17,905	0.13	297.80
Poland	125,237	114,197	141,083	164,444	143,160	1.07	-12.94
Romania	47,034	42,316	51,588	70,293	47,557	0.36	-32.34
Russian Federation	1,304,608	1,009,963	1,594,304	2,244,688	3,250,651	24.38	44.82
Slovakia	26,629	24,454	29,175	24,321	26,399	0.20	8.54
Northern Europe	8,473,944	7,145,584	7,033,697	6,894,782	6,585,354	49.39	-4.49
Denmark	173,196	166,314	184,340	177,212	188,571	1.41	6.41
Finland	186,566	191,165	215,030	223,188	166,146	1.25	-25.56
Iceland	15,070	33,531	15,771	40,591	18,861	0.14	-53.53
Ireland	98,282	94,174	76,487	51,280	48,603	0.36	-5.22
Norway	511,293	430,975	519,232	530,107	523,524	3.93	-1.24
Sweden	857,287	754,013	803,474	775,120	791,063	5.93	2.06
United Kingdom	6,632,250	5,475,412	5,219,363	5,097,284	4,848,586	36.36	-4.88
Southern Europe	389,444	382,878	395,405	394,850	363,526	2.73	-7.93
Greece	222,743	237,930	234,997	232,519	166,006	1.24	-28.61
Italy	118,840	87,210	91,616	90,120	134,035	1.01	48.73
Malta	6,342	22,334	21,081	22,393	16,680	0.13	-25.51
Portugal	11,942	10,543	13,182	11,605	14,292	0.11	23.15
Slovenia	11,419	8,672	9,115	12,613	9,268	0.07	-26.52
Spain	18,158	16,189	25,414	25,600	23,245	0.17	-9.20
Western Europe	2,089,679	2,050,096	2,273,065	2,324,782	2,104,793	15.79	-9.46
Austria	144,870	142,865	155,367	142,150	122,974	0.92	-13.49
Belgium	144,906	147,207	171,904	166,798	143,024	1.07	-14.25
France	231,656	171,133	218,898	245,568	220,257	1.65	-10.31
Germany	1,170,838	1,149,174	1,219,945	1,216,119	1,093,426	8.20	-10.09
Luxembourg	19,502	23,852	23,025	19,346	18,306	0.14	-5.38
Netherlands	154,421	182,201	221,999	275,127	211,518	1.59	-23.12
Switzerland	223,486	233,664	261,927	259,674	295,288	2.21	13.71
NOT SPECIFIED	393,918	394,323	410,619	478,135	510,925	3.83	6.86
Other countries of the World	393,918	394,323	410,619	478,135	510,925	3.83	6.86

Yearbook of Tourism Statistics, Data 2008 – 2012, 2014 Edition

CYPRUS

6. Overnight stays of non-resident tourists in all types of accommodation establishments, by country of residence

	2008	2009	2010	2011	2012	Market share 2012	% Change 2012-2011
TOTAL	13,208,954	11,666,663	12,448,159	13,112,597	13,488,127	100.00	2.86
AFRICA	3,804	5,827	8,163	8,790	6,693	0.05	-23.86
Southern Africa	3,804	5,827	8,163	8,790	6,693	0.05	-23.86
South Africa	3,804	5,827	8,163	8,790	6,693	0.05	-23.86
AMERICAS	66,974	89,289	94,657	100,766	78,785	0.58	-21.81
North America	66,974	89,289	94,657	100,766	78,785	0.58	-21.81
Canada	28,520	48,525	46,820	55,546	30,354	0.23	-45.35
United States of America	38,454	40,764	47,837	45,220	48,431	0.36	7.10
EAST ASIA AND THE PACIFIC	27,620	34,465	33,151	26,656	35,982	0.27	34.99
North-East Asia	8,156	10,748	12,038	11,369	18,917	0.14	66.39
China	4,391	4,766	5,486	5,262	11,656	0.09	121.51
Japan	3,765	5,982	6,552	6,107	7,261	0.05	18.90
Australasia	19,464	23,717	21,113	15,287	17,065	0.13	11.63
Australia	19,464	23,717	21,113	15,287	17,065	0.13	11.63
EUROPE	12,798,536	11,134,307	11,890,914	12,487,513	12,847,344	95.25	2.88
Central/Eastern Europe	1,789,421	1,405,506	2,046,319	2,729,730	3,670,439	27.21	34.46
Bulgaria	21,383	22,507	24,184	22,549	13,620	0.10	-39.60
Czech Republic	123,302	116,430	112,649	128,604	100,735	0.75	-21.67
Estonia	6,876	12,519	8,199	8,699	8,849	0.07	1.72
Hungary	41,084	35,277	42,361	40,592	38,207	0.28	-5.88
Latvia	4,610	4,592	6,820	3,978	6,357	0.05	59.80
Lithuania	5,276	11,731	18,999	4,908	18,487	0.14	276.67
Poland	125,331	115,410	142,645	165,858	144,369	1.07	-12.96
Romania	129,695	43,424	53,018	71,825	48,508	0.36	-32.46
Russian Federation	1,305,211	1,018,545	1,607,554	2,257,729	3,264,465	24.20	44.59
Slovakia	26,653	25,071	29,890	24,988	26,842	0.20	7.42
Northern Europe	8,525,033	7,268,409	7,141,690	7,000,579	6,685,854	49.57	-4.50
Denmark	175,193	167,784	187,791	179,754	190,022	1.41	5.71
Finland	186,745	193,340	217,471	225,410	167,746	1.24	-25.58
Iceland	15,072	34,385	16,338	41,247	19,718	0.15	-52.20
Ireland	98,531	95,163	77,765	52,862	49,867	0.37	-5.67
Norway	514,070	435,388	523,564	539,137	531,709	3.94	-1.38
Sweden	857,700	786,829	831,000	797,679	818,324	6.07	2.59
United Kingdom	6,677,722	5,555,520	5,287,761	5,164,490	4,908,468	36.39	-4.96
Southern Europe	389,744	389,138	402,525	402,342	368,505	2.73	-8.41
Greece	222,674	240,230	237,444	234,764	167,520	1.24	-28.64
Italy	119,188	88,416	93,534	92,264	135,624	1.01	47.00
Malta	6,342	23,036	21,963	23,309	17,187	0.13	-26.26
Portugal	11,946	11,532	13,747	12,384	14,642	0.11	18.23
Slovenia	11,419	9,126	9,683	13,137	9,606	0.07	-26.88
Spain	18,175	16,798	26,154	26,484	23,926	0.18	-9.66
Western Europe	2,094,338	2,071,254	2,300,380	2,354,862	2,122,546	15.74	-9.87
Austria	145,002	144,525	157,408	144,218	124,448	0.92	-13.71
Belgium	145,214	149,130	173,863	168,537	144,399	1.07	-14.32
France	232,228	173,554	222,107	248,492	222,853	1.65	-10.32
Germany	1,173,741	1,158,271	1,232,561	1,231,935	1,100,343	8.16	-10.68
Luxembourg	19,504	24,734	24,138	20,466	18,784	0.14	-8.22
Netherlands	154,927	184,973	225,595	279,000	214,291	1.59	-23.19
Switzerland	223,722	236,067	264,708	262,214	297,428	2.21	13.43
NOT SPECIFIED	312,020	402,775	421,274	488,872	519,323	3.85	6.23
Other countries of the World	312,020	402,775	421,274	488,872	519,323	3.85	6.23

Yearbook of Tourism Statistics, Data 2008 – 2012, 2014 Edition

CZECH REPUBLIC

3. Arrivals of non-resident tourists in hotels and similar establishments, by nationality

	2008	2009	2010	2011	2012	Market share 2012	% Change 2012-2011
TOTAL	6,134,720	5,609,025	5,974,227	6,376,697	6,796,436	100.00	6.58
AFRICA	21,335	18,592	24,290	28,423	33,412	0.49	17.55
Southern Africa	5,257	4,068	5,163	6,039	8,905	0.13	47.46
South Africa	5,257	4,068	5,163	6,039	8,905	0.13	47.46
Other Africa	16,078	14,524	19,127	22,384	24,507	0.36	9.48
Other countries of Africa	16,078	14,524	19,127	22,384	24,507	0.36	9.48
AMERICAS	412,037	379,615	440,387	465,364	559,948	8.24	20.32
North America	349,305	317,828	367,084	380,253	443,197	6.52	16.55
Canada	43,836	42,793	50,930	54,163	60,753	0.89	12.17
Mexico	15,207	12,806	16,215	20,811	25,025	0.37	20.25
United States of America	290,262	262,229	299,939	305,279	357,419	5.26	17.08
South America	24,890	28,590	36,781	42,360	55,210	0.81	30.34
Brazil	24,890	28,590	36,781	42,360	55,210	0.81	30.34
Other Americas	37,842	33,197	36,522	42,751	61,541	0.91	43.95
Other countries of the Americas	37,842	33,197	36,522	42,751	61,541	0.91	43.95
EAST ASIA AND THE PACIFIC	479,744	465,479	568,741	657,245	729,644	10.74	11.02
North-East Asia	237,659	225,361	283,759	320,947	406,545	5.98	26.67
China	50,664	59,429	76,809	105,878	142,259	2.09	34.36
Japan	120,937	112,814	131,223	119,914	134,855	1.98	12.46
Korea, Republic of	66,058	53,118	75,727	95,155	129,431	1.90	36.02
Australasia	54,376	49,562	62,352	70,335	77,289	1.14	9.89
Australia	48,102	43,906	56,021	63,076	68,880	1.01	9.20
New Zealand	6,274	5,656	6,331	7,259	8,409	0.12	15.84
Other East Asia and the Pacific	187,709	190,556	222,630	265,963	245,810	3.62	-7.58
Other countries of Asia	181,880	185,660	217,234	260,872	240,267	3.54	-7.90
Other countries of Oceania	5,829	4,896	5,396	5,091	5,543	0.08	8.88
EUROPE	5,221,604	4,745,339	4,940,809	5,225,665	5,449,715	80.18	4.29
Central/Eastern Europe	1,300,779	1,137,156	1,304,962	1,535,280	1,716,918	25.26	11.83
Bulgaria	18,805	17,365	19,836	21,551	23,533	0.35	9.20
Estonia	18,422	12,665	11,431	15,523	16,339	0.24	5.26
Hungary	93,706	82,669	96,623	102,198	105,498	1.55	3.23
Latvia	19,720	9,488	8,100	9,383	12,633	0.19	34.64
Lithuania	60,936	41,511	40,552	45,460	40,757	0.60	-10.35
Poland	329,189	299,525	313,918	338,014	336,109	4.95	-0.56
Romania	45,174	46,185	49,199	56,227	56,221	0.83	-0.01
Russian Federation	395,222	310,294	398,438	537,268	666,705	9.81	24.09
Slovakia	250,488	244,896	266,218	303,921	338,167	4.98	11.27
Ukraine	69,117	72,558	100,647	105,735	120,956	1.78	14.40
Northern Europe	827,233	688,439	688,224	626,261	652,705	9.60	4.22
Denmark	96,653	89,481	101,251	89,329	97,031	1.43	8.62
Finland	45,799	40,005	39,078	43,167	45,248	0.67	4.82
Iceland	4,211	3,455	3,398	3,466	3,546	0.05	2.31
Ireland	52,702	32,023	26,738	21,432	25,472	0.37	18.85
Norway	75,150	83,501	75,919	69,917	58,444	0.86	-16.41
Sweden	80,732	77,632	82,417	78,400	84,247	1.24	7.46
United Kingdom	471,986	362,342	359,423	320,550	338,717	4.98	5.67
Southern Europe	781,685	700,884	673,630	717,798	697,468	10.26	-2.83
Croatia	39,886	36,500	39,580	46,977	42,199	0.62	-10.17
Greece	73,316	65,694	50,063	43,496	33,925	0.50	-22.00
Italy	362,496	344,667	323,854	328,612	343,059	5.05	4.40
Malta	2,040	1,766	1,869	2,346	2,865	0.04	22.12
Portugal	25,864	26,419	26,016	23,362	25,751	0.38	10.23
Serbia and Montenegro	12,964	13,371	18,962	27,749	27,025	0.40	-2.61
Slovenia	24,027	24,037	23,007	24,318	25,977	0.38	6.82
Spain	241,092	188,430	190,279	220,938	196,667	2.89	-10.99

184

CZECH REPUBLIC

3. Arrivals of non-resident tourists in hotels and similar establishments, by nationality

	2008	2009	2010	2011	2012	Market share 2012	% Change 2012-2011
Western Europe	2,031,777	1,955,883	1,990,148	2,070,982	2,108,628	31.03	1.82
Austria	162,387	169,803	183,098	177,819	195,828	2.88	10.13
Belgium	79,199	80,144	78,195	80,078	78,468	1.15	-2.01
France	222,388	209,956	240,675	272,209	263,103	3.87	-3.35
Germany	1,337,372	1,278,621	1,258,852	1,303,329	1,332,320	19.60	2.22
Liechtenstein	746	811	896	901	952	0.01	5.66
Luxembourg	3,486	5,332	5,038	4,952	3,724	0.05	-24.80
Netherlands	161,627	146,862	151,359	159,089	155,060	2.28	-2.53
Switzerland	64,572	64,354	72,035	72,605	79,173	1.16	9.05
East Mediterranean Europe	99,320	119,407	135,419	136,255	147,895	2.18	8.54
Cyprus	7,779	7,811	8,154	7,510	4,162	0.06	-44.58
Israel	56,570	78,561	81,980	80,716	88,419	1.30	9.54
Turkey	34,971	33,035	45,285	48,029	55,314	0.81	15.17
Other Europe	180,810	143,570	148,426	139,089	126,101	1.86	-9.34
Other countries of Europe	180,810	143,570	148,426	139,089	126,101	1.86	-9.34
SOUTH ASIA					23,717	0.35	
India					23,717	0.35	

Yearbook of Tourism Statistics, Data 2008 – 2012, 2014 Edition

CZECH REPUBLIC

4. Arrivals of non-resident tourists in all types of accommodation establishments, by nationality

	2008	2009	2010	2011	2012	Market share 2012	% Change 2012-2011
TOTAL	6,649,410	6,032,370	6,333,996	6,715,067	7,164,576	100.00	6.69
AFRICA	22,934	20,191	25,981	29,759	35,231	0.49	18.39
Southern Africa	5,566	4,445	5,365	6,184	9,156	0.13	48.06
South Africa	5,566	4,445	5,365	6,184	9,156	0.13	48.06
Other Africa	17,368	15,746	20,616	23,575	26,075	0.36	10.60
Other countries of Africa	17,368	15,746	20,616	23,575	26,075	0.36	10.60
AMERICAS	434,061	397,586	460,259	480,668	574,951	8.02	19.61
North America	368,699	333,235	384,163	393,061	455,547	6.36	15.90
Canada	47,518	45,549	54,004	56,615	62,823	0.88	10.97
Mexico	16,124	13,375	17,276	21,496	25,814	0.36	20.09
United States of America	305,057	274,311	312,883	314,950	366,910	5.12	16.50
South America	26,106	29,634	37,811	43,248	56,314	0.79	30.21
Brazil	26,106	29,634	37,811	43,248	56,314	0.79	30.21
Other Americas	39,256	34,717	38,285	44,359	63,090	0.88	42.23
Other countries of the Americas	39,256	34,717	38,285	44,359	63,090	0.88	42.23
EAST ASIA AND THE PACIFIC	501,793	484,815	586,903	673,850	746,513	10.42	10.78
North-East Asia	244,861	232,015	289,925	326,897	413,384	5.77	26.46
China	53,108	61,798	79,186	108,629	145,409	2.03	33.86
Japan	123,275	114,777	133,052	121,663	136,557	1.91	12.24
Korea, Republic of	68,478	55,440	77,687	96,605	131,418	1.83	36.04
Australasia	61,772	55,669	67,676	74,787	80,805	1.13	8.05
Australia	54,361	48,715	60,240	66,783	71,760	1.00	7.45
New Zealand	7,411	6,954	7,436	8,004	9,045	0.13	13.01
Other East Asia and the Pacific	195,160	197,131	229,302	272,166	252,324	3.52	-7.29
Other countries of Asia	189,037	192,021	223,236	266,790	246,670	3.44	-7.54
Other countries of Oceania	6,123	5,110	6,066	5,376	5,654	0.08	5.17
EUROPE	5,690,622	5,129,778	5,260,853	5,530,790	5,783,833	80.73	4.58
Central/Eastern Europe	1,451,205	1,258,082	1,417,334	1,646,597	1,842,376	25.72	11.89
Bulgaria	21,394	18,713	20,970	22,613	24,645	0.34	8.99
Estonia	20,689	13,480	12,505	16,288	17,348	0.24	6.51
Hungary	103,826	90,096	103,485	107,689	111,608	1.56	3.64
Latvia	20,501	9,998	8,502	10,098	13,346	0.19	32.16
Lithuania	66,180	45,168	44,550	48,737	44,050	0.61	-9.62
Poland	376,592	341,136	350,637	371,127	370,910	5.18	-0.06
Romania	48,435	48,367	50,762	57,484	57,807	0.81	0.56
Russian Federation	418,184	326,895	414,671	559,021	694,138	9.69	24.17
Slovakia	299,278	287,810	307,192	344,101	382,595	5.34	11.19
Ukraine	76,126	76,419	104,060	109,439	125,929	1.76	15.07
Northern Europe	864,446	716,102	712,788	646,218	673,035	9.39	4.15
Denmark	108,552	99,563	109,292	96,311	103,816	1.45	7.79
Finland	48,270	42,537	40,690	44,599	46,753	0.65	4.83
Iceland	4,940	3,535	3,509	3,518	3,635	0.05	3.33
Ireland	54,447	33,159	28,152	22,366	26,307	0.37	17.62
Norway	79,773	85,001	77,343	70,948	59,402	0.83	-16.27
Sweden	84,185	80,961	85,159	80,525	86,595	1.21	7.54
United Kingdom	484,279	371,346	368,643	327,951	346,527	4.84	5.66
Southern Europe	806,322	726,129	693,609	736,824	718,641	10.03	-2.47
Croatia	41,219	38,268	40,889	48,192	43,756	0.61	-9.20
Greece	74,737	66,648	51,002	44,054	34,737	0.48	-21.15
Italy	374,632	357,492	332,551	337,645	353,165	4.93	4.60
Malta	2,172	1,803	1,916	2,407	2,995	0.04	24.43
Portugal	26,896	27,482	27,088	24,416	26,763	0.37	9.61
Serbia and Montenegro	13,703	14,021	19,672	28,287	27,867	0.39	-1.48
Slovenia	25,723	26,009	24,480	26,045	27,821	0.39	6.82
Spain	247,240	194,406	196,011	225,778	201,537	2.81	-10.74

Yearbook of Tourism Statistics, Data 2008 – 2012, 2014 Edition

CZECH REPUBLIC

4. Arrivals of non-resident tourists in all types of accommodation establishments, by nationality

	2008	2009	2010	2011	2012	Market share 2012	% Change 2012-2011
Western Europe	2,277,650	2,160,024	2,148,046	2,220,718	2,269,154	31.67	2.18
Austria	170,663	177,715	189,886	185,719	203,891	2.85	9.78
Belgium	87,240	87,851	83,404	85,316	83,672	1.17	-1.93
France	235,654	223,901	251,468	283,480	275,449	3.84	-2.83
Germany	1,475,858	1,393,112	1,348,482	1,386,976	1,420,698	19.83	2.43
Liechtenstein	777	911	915	924	996	0.01	7.79
Luxembourg	3,697	5,415	5,323	5,054	3,828	0.05	-24.26
Netherlands	236,193	203,764	194,138	197,975	198,687	2.77	0.36
Switzerland	67,568	67,355	74,430	75,274	81,933	1.14	8.85
East Mediterranean Europe	103,394	122,784	138,512	139,223	151,468	2.11	8.80
Cyprus	8,249	7,987	8,278	7,643	4,387	0.06	-42.60
Israel	59,102	80,634	83,997	82,346	90,582	1.26	10.00
Turkey	36,043	34,163	46,237	49,234	56,499	0.79	14.76
Other Europe	187,605	146,657	150,564	141,210	129,159	1.80	-8.53
Other countries of Europe	187,605	146,657	150,564	141,210	129,159	1.80	-8.53
SOUTH ASIA					24,048	0.34	
India					24,048	0.34	

Yearbook of Tourism Statistics, Data 2008 – 2012, 2014 Edition

CZECH REPUBLIC

5. Overnight stays of non-resident tourists in hotels and similar establishments, by nationality

	2008	2009	2010	2011	2012	Market share 2012	% Change 2012-2011
TOTAL	17,740,781	16,013,046	16,880,869	18,027,007	18,948,721	100.00	5.11
AFRICA	70,029	56,814	71,152	78,046	86,857	0.46	11.29
Southern Africa	13,983	11,496	13,241	15,061	20,878	0.11	38.62
South Africa	13,983	11,496	13,241	15,061	20,878	0.11	38.62
Other Africa	56,046	45,318	57,911	62,985	65,979	0.35	4.75
Other countries of Africa	56,046	45,318	57,911	62,985	65,979	0.35	4.75
AMERICAS	1,115,514	1,010,235	1,155,862	1,216,515	1,404,544	7.41	15.46
North America	951,647	846,664	964,078	992,152	1,107,657	5.85	11.64
Canada	125,195	120,114	143,566	149,447	164,024	0.87	9.75
Mexico	37,196	30,065	39,002	50,339	60,566	0.32	20.32
United States of America	789,256	696,485	781,510	792,366	883,067	4.66	11.45
South America	67,613	74,753	98,668	115,350	144,080	0.76	24.91
Brazil	67,613	74,753	98,668	115,350	144,080	0.76	24.91
Other Americas	96,254	88,818	93,116	109,013	152,807	0.81	40.17
Other countries of the Americas	96,254	88,818	93,116	109,013	152,807	0.81	40.17
EAST ASIA AND THE PACIFIC	1,015,958	966,083	1,161,176	1,316,457	1,450,777	7.66	10.20
North-East Asia	440,710	407,374	494,443	555,377	676,430	3.57	21.80
China	96,850	106,193	132,195	182,071	229,306	1.21	25.94
Japan	244,465	219,406	247,050	230,877	249,039	1.31	7.87
Korea, Republic of	99,395	81,775	115,198	142,429	198,085	1.05	39.08
Australasia	142,470	124,008	155,166	172,989	184,537	0.97	6.68
Australia	126,479	109,769	138,896	154,612	164,991	0.87	6.71
New Zealand	15,991	14,239	16,270	18,377	19,546	0.10	6.36
Other East Asia and the Pacific	432,778	434,701	511,567	588,091	589,810	3.11	0.29
Other countries of Asia	420,073	422,923	499,778	576,267	578,182	3.05	0.33
Other countries of Oceania	12,705	11,778	11,789	11,824	11,628	0.06	-1.66
EUROPE	15,539,280	13,979,914	14,492,679	15,415,989	15,946,392	84.16	3.44
Central/Eastern Europe	3,910,107	3,313,849	3,879,450	4,806,764	5,429,718	28.65	12.96
Bulgaria	45,019	39,862	43,634	49,264	54,818	0.29	11.27
Estonia	40,000	29,788	22,053	31,360	31,241	0.16	-0.38
Hungary	204,991	174,756	213,690	223,134	217,692	1.15	-2.44
Latvia	33,319	18,286	15,558	19,164	25,616	0.14	33.67
Lithuania	88,613	65,956	64,702	71,018	68,428	0.36	-3.65
Poland	662,994	618,352	649,343	693,354	691,766	3.65	-0.23
Romania	109,503	115,283	127,306	143,815	133,413	0.70	-7.23
Russian Federation	1,951,831	1,542,449	1,948,142	2,667,596	3,193,148	16.85	19.70
Slovakia	514,475	473,299	517,688	586,675	647,100	3.42	10.30
Ukraine	259,362	235,818	277,334	321,384	366,496	1.93	14.04
Northern Europe	2,263,129	1,896,006	1,868,866	1,662,426	1,696,440	8.95	2.05
Denmark	311,428	284,961	333,323	278,625	305,368	1.61	9.60
Finland	137,808	120,218	112,361	125,401	126,675	0.67	1.02
Iceland	11,275	8,694	9,062	10,354	9,480	0.05	-8.44
Ireland	148,038	88,341	71,965	55,391	65,420	0.35	18.11
Norway	220,894	250,016	222,229	201,504	157,083	0.83	-22.04
Sweden	211,566	207,307	213,811	203,369	218,905	1.16	7.64
United Kingdom	1,222,120	936,469	906,115	787,782	813,509	4.29	3.27
Southern Europe	2,288,439	2,026,641	1,935,317	2,034,797	1,924,164	10.15	-5.44
Croatia	115,550	104,003	111,694	131,050	116,884	0.62	-10.81
Greece	224,435	199,346	152,926	125,987	100,113	0.53	-20.54
Italy	1,041,743	983,227	926,051	922,535	951,873	5.02	3.18
Malta	6,394	5,219	5,971	8,123	10,808	0.06	33.05
Portugal	75,564	75,679	74,952	70,418	68,756	0.36	-2.36
Serbia and Montenegro	39,582	38,954	55,015	78,396	72,741	0.38	-7.21
Slovenia	46,424	44,993	42,515	48,739	51,509	0.27	5.68
Spain	738,747	575,220	566,193	649,549	551,480	2.91	-15.10

Yearbook of Tourism Statistics, Data 2008 – 2012, 2014 Edition

CZECH REPUBLIC

5. Overnight stays of non-resident tourists in hotels and similar establishments, by nationality

	2008	2009	2010	2011	2012	Market share 2012	% Change 2012-2011
Western Europe	**6,220,823**	**5,928,794**	**5,944,796**	**6,074,507**	**6,069,407**	**32.03**	**-0.08**
Austria	336,649	345,584	373,309	361,679	389,782	2.06	7.77
Belgium	216,547	220,146	210,497	210,354	202,380	1.07	-3.79
France	559,642	538,260	624,549	709,314	676,641	3.57	-4.61
Germany	4,408,594	4,194,151	4,090,860	4,134,975	4,151,206	21.91	0.39
Liechtenstein	1,531	1,537	1,881	1,857	1,872	0.01	0.81
Luxembourg	9,010	13,853	12,654	12,941	10,080	0.05	-22.11
Netherlands	529,213	454,876	452,529	467,587	443,592	2.34	-5.13
Switzerland	159,637	160,387	178,517	175,800	193,854	1.02	10.27
East Mediterranean Europe	**326,382**	**399,090**	**452,152**	**457,672**	**471,728**	**2.49**	**3.07**
Cyprus	23,443	22,980	23,028	22,644	13,218	0.07	-41.63
Israel	211,673	288,901	308,411	306,303	313,945	1.66	2.49
Turkey	91,266	87,209	120,713	128,725	144,565	0.76	12.31
Other Europe	**530,400**	**415,534**	**412,098**	**379,823**	**354,935**	**1.87**	**-6.55**
Other countries of Europe	530,400	415,534	412,098	379,823	354,935	1.87	-6.55
SOUTH ASIA					**60,151**	**0.32**	
India					60,151	0.32	

Yearbook of Tourism Statistics, Data 2008 – 2012, 2014 Edition

CZECH REPUBLIC

6. Overnight stays of non-resident tourists in all types of accommodation establishments, by nationality

	2008	2009	2010	2011	2012	Market share 2012	% Change 2012-2011
TOTAL	19,987,022	17,746,893	18,365,947	19,424,839	20,521,815	100.00	5.65
AFRICA	76,738	64,047	77,616	87,561	96,372	0.47	10.06
Southern Africa	15,013	13,570	13,880	15,564	21,915	0.11	40.81
South Africa	15,013	13,570	13,880	15,564	21,915	0.11	40.81
Other Africa	61,725	50,477	63,736	71,997	74,457	0.36	3.42
Other countries of Africa	61,725	50,477	63,736	71,997	74,457	0.36	3.42
AMERICAS	1,191,156	1,071,563	1,218,499	1,268,806	1,452,847	7.08	14.51
North America	1,020,494	901,250	1,019,997	1,037,527	1,149,843	5.60	10.83
Canada	135,953	127,476	151,646	156,000	170,482	0.83	9.28
Mexico	39,510	31,460	41,762	52,131	62,911	0.31	20.68
United States of America	845,031	742,314	826,589	829,396	916,450	4.47	10.50
South America	70,744	77,968	101,183	117,483	146,619	0.71	24.80
Brazil	70,744	77,968	101,183	117,483	146,619	0.71	24.80
Other Americas	99,918	92,345	97,319	113,796	156,385	0.76	37.43
Other countries of the Americas	99,918	92,345	97,319	113,796	156,385	0.76	37.43
EAST ASIA AND THE PACIFIC	1,119,539	1,057,706	1,240,989	1,387,785	1,541,091	7.51	11.05
North-East Asia	455,652	423,022	507,766	568,386	693,412	3.38	22.00
China	101,712	111,120	136,742	187,380	235,932	1.15	25.91
Japan	249,603	225,308	251,422	234,651	254,611	1.24	8.51
Korea, Republic of	104,337	86,594	119,602	146,355	202,869	0.99	38.61
Australasia	160,029	137,152	166,472	181,900	191,822	0.93	5.45
Australia	141,590	120,030	147,661	161,942	170,717	0.83	5.42
New Zealand	18,439	17,122	18,811	19,958	21,105	0.10	5.75
Other East Asia and the Pacific	503,858	497,532	566,751	637,499	655,857	3.20	2.88
Other countries of Asia	490,598	485,242	553,635	625,233	643,848	3.14	2.98
Other countries of Oceania	13,260	12,290	13,116	12,266	12,009	0.06	-2.10
EUROPE	17,599,589	15,553,577	15,828,843	16,680,687	17,370,103	84.64	4.13
Central/Eastern Europe	4,430,966	3,697,146	4,274,339	5,236,276	5,948,053	28.98	13.59
Bulgaria	53,069	42,744	46,409	52,372	58,117	0.28	10.97
Estonia	45,983	31,590	24,903	32,956	34,371	0.17	4.29
Hungary	230,114	192,150	229,777	237,938	233,990	1.14	-1.66
Latvia	35,818	20,483	17,381	21,128	27,146	0.13	28.48
Lithuania	99,430	73,039	76,616	78,413	75,700	0.37	-3.46
Poland	786,381	718,423	739,425	777,019	778,963	3.80	0.25
Romania	119,011	120,276	131,105	147,744	137,907	0.67	-6.66
Russian Federation	2,111,252	1,662,497	2,092,320	2,864,815	3,448,183	16.80	20.36
Slovakia	655,858	582,305	620,723	683,159	762,346	3.71	11.59
Ukraine	294,050	253,639	295,680	340,732	391,330	1.91	14.85
Northern Europe	2,365,404	1,971,360	1,939,815	1,719,639	1,753,507	8.54	1.97
Denmark	350,938	316,392	361,741	301,254	327,208	1.59	8.62
Finland	143,654	125,916	116,376	129,864	131,531	0.64	1.28
Iceland	13,023	8,906	9,339	10,475	9,688	0.05	-7.51
Ireland	152,875	91,087	75,449	58,009	67,367	0.33	16.13
Norway	231,944	253,652	225,457	204,004	159,379	0.78	-21.87
Sweden	221,040	215,927	220,996	208,897	224,883	1.10	7.65
United Kingdom	1,251,930	959,480	930,457	807,136	833,451	4.06	3.26
Southern Europe	2,354,663	2,087,408	1,986,789	2,087,523	1,979,847	9.65	-5.16
Croatia	119,485	109,733	116,052	134,320	120,791	0.59	-10.07
Greece	228,943	202,184	156,070	128,466	102,742	0.50	-20.02
Italy	1,073,038	1,013,057	947,233	946,206	975,915	4.76	3.14
Malta	6,777	5,360	6,094	8,298	11,280	0.05	35.94
Portugal	79,193	79,484	78,510	73,830	72,044	0.35	-2.42
Serbia and Montenegro	42,286	41,093	57,484	80,647	75,581	0.37	-6.28
Slovenia	50,651	49,304	45,675	52,767	55,619	0.27	5.40
Spain	754,290	587,193	579,671	662,989	565,875	2.76	-14.65

190

CZECH REPUBLIC

6. Overnight stays of non-resident tourists in all types of accommodation establishments, by nationality

	2008	2009	2010	2011	2012	Market share 2012	% Change 2012-2011
Western Europe	**7,536,214**	**6,945,606**	**6,729,373**	**6,768,995**	**6,821,991**	**33.24**	**0.78**
Austria	357,826	364,287	391,722	380,184	408,422	1.99	7.43
Belgium	243,160	241,499	226,078	228,509	220,052	1.07	-3.70
France	593,443	568,151	649,458	739,150	704,820	3.43	-4.64
Germany	5,291,228	4,851,927	4,609,595	4,578,249	4,600,971	22.42	0.50
Liechtenstein	1,636	1,656	1,927	1,907	1,991	0.01	4.40
Luxembourg	9,671	14,152	13,356	13,351	10,466	0.05	-21.61
Netherlands	869,668	736,412	652,844	644,627	673,649	3.28	4.50
Switzerland	169,582	167,522	184,393	183,018	201,620	0.98	10.16
East Mediterranean Europe	**357,445**	**428,188**	**479,140**	**481,548**	**501,568**	**2.44**	**4.16**
Cyprus	24,222	23,486	23,752	23,171	13,995	0.07	-39.60
Israel	239,193	314,341	332,110	325,646	337,676	1.65	3.69
Turkey	94,030	90,361	123,278	132,731	149,897	0.73	12.93
Other Europe	**554,897**	**423,869**	**419,387**	**386,706**	**365,137**	**1.78**	**-5.58**
Other countries of Europe	554,897	423,869	419,387	386,706	365,137	1.78	-5.58
SOUTH ASIA					**61,402**	**0.30**	
India					61,402	0.30	

Yearbook of Tourism Statistics, Data 2008 – 2012, 2014 Edition

DEMOCRATIC REPUBLIC OF THE CONGO

1. Arrivals of non-resident tourists at national borders, by nationality

		2008	2009	2010	2011	2012	Market share 2012	% Change 2012-2011
TOTAL	(*)	**49,971**	**53,402**	**81,117**	**186,000**			
AFRICA		**27,969**	**31,328**	**20,301**	**43,765**			
East Africa					11,926			
Burundi					2,107			
Kenya					2,668			
Rwanda					2,665			
United Republic of Tanzania					2,593			
Zambia					1,893			
Central Africa			1,916	10,219	10,955			
Angola					5,529			
Congo			805	3,995	5,426			
Other countries of Central Africa			1,111	6,224				
North Africa					6,906			
Morocco					1,698			
Tunisia					1,850			
Other countries of North Africa					3,358			
Southern Africa					4,962			
South Africa					4,962			
Other Africa		**27,969**	**29,412**	**10,082**	**9,016**			
Other countries of Africa			29,412	10,082	9,016			
All countries of Africa		27,969						
AMERICAS		**3,665**	**3,433**	**7,184**	**20,507**			
Central America					2,585			
Panama					89			
Other countries of Central America					2,496			
North America					12,386			
Canada					6,694			
Mexico					1,540			
Other countries of North America					4,152			
South America					5,536			
Brazil					1,708			
Paraguay					1,131			
Other countries of South America					2,697			
Other Americas		**3,665**	**3,433**	**7,184**				
All countries of the Americas		3,665	3,433	7,184				
EAST ASIA AND THE PACIFIC		**5,233**	**5,540**	**3,884**	**14,272**			
South-East Asia				85	1,670			
Thailand				85	1,670			
Australasia				178	2,489			
Australia, New Zealand				178	2,489			
Other East Asia and the Pacific		**5,233**	**5,540**	**3,621**	**10,113**			
Other countries of Asia				3,621	10,113			
All countries of Asia		4,969	5,244					
All countries of Oceania		264	296					
EUROPE		**13,104**	**13,101**	**35,012**	**67,895**			
Central/Eastern Europe					7,322			
Russian Federation					1,980			
Ukraine					1,872			
Other countries Central/East Europe					3,470			
Northern Europe					10,925			
Norway					1,826			
United Kingdom					5,997			
Other countries of Northern Europe					3,102			
Southern Europe		**1,102**	**1,182**	**4,153**	**10,975**			

Yearbook of Tourism Statistics, Data 2008 – 2012, 2014 Edition

DEMOCRATIC REPUBLIC OF THE CONGO

1. Arrivals of non-resident tourists at national borders, by nationality

	2008	2009	2010	2011	2012	Market share 2012	% Change 2012-2011
Italy	1,102	1,182	2,012	4,053			
Portugal				2,244			
Spain				2,657			
Other countries of Southern Europe			2,141	2,021			
Western Europe	**8,218**	**8,165**	**25,036**	**36,068**			
Belgium	4,159	4,087	12,047	15,631			
France	2,793	2,654	10,038	14,734			
Germany	1,266	1,424	1,595	3,081			
Other countries of Western Europe			1,356	2,622			
East Mediterranean Europe			**353**	**2,605**			
Israel			353	2,605			
Other Europe	**3,784**	**3,754**	**5,470**				
Other countries of Europe	3,784	3,754	5,470				
MIDDLE EAST			**1,650**	**6,060**			
Lebanon			1,243	3,560			
Other countries of Middle East			407	2,500			
SOUTH ASIA			**2,767**	**5,668**			
India			2,767	5,668			
NOT SPECIFIED			**10,319**	**27,833**			
Other countries of the World				27,833			
Nationals Residing Abroad			10,319				

Yearbook of Tourism Statistics, Data 2008 – 2012, 2014 Edition

DENMARK

3. Arrivals of non-resident tourists in hotels and similar establishments, by country of residence

		2008	2009	2010	2011	2012	Market share 2012	% Change 2012-2011
TOTAL	(*)	2,056,812	1,892,468	2,157,344	1,498,610	1,706,597	100.00	13.88
AMERICAS		136,899	142,854	154,726	120,507	138,777	8.13	15.16
North America		122,035	127,827	136,337	104,894	117,634	6.89	12.15
Canada		12,629	13,665	14,561	11,422	13,937	0.82	22.02
United States of America		109,406	114,162	121,776	93,472	103,697	6.08	10.94
Other Americas		14,864	15,027	18,389	15,613	21,143	1.24	35.42
Other countries of the Americas		14,864	15,027	18,389	15,613	21,143	1.24	35.42
EAST ASIA AND THE PACIFIC		65,946	66,150	73,319	50,637	66,284	3.88	30.90
North-East Asia		27,922	29,584	32,625	19,778	23,388	1.37	18.25
Japan		27,922	29,584	32,625	19,778	23,388	1.37	18.25
South-East Asia		38,024	36,566	40,694	30,859	42,896	2.51	39.01
All countries of South-East Asia		38,024	36,566	40,694	30,859	42,896	2.51	39.01
EUROPE		1,804,329	1,631,994	1,866,553	1,279,511	1,438,402	84.28	12.42
Central/Eastern Europe		17,324	16,418	17,858	17,072	14,530	0.85	-14.89
Poland		17,324	16,418	17,858	17,072	14,530	0.85	-14.89
Northern Europe		1,157,557	1,010,917	1,153,621	764,803	862,597	50.54	12.79
Finland		45,469	45,284	52,872	49,862	43,552	2.55	-12.65
Norway		379,738	361,167	394,494	253,400	304,511	17.84	20.17
Sweden		532,363	425,779	509,385	337,455	377,684	22.13	11.92
United Kingdom		199,987	178,687	196,870	124,086	136,850	8.02	10.29
Southern Europe		94,999	103,179	113,243	74,683	79,448	4.66	6.38
Italy		45,044	49,141	53,314	47,678	48,034	2.81	0.75
Spain		49,955	54,038	59,929	27,005	31,414	1.84	16.33
Western Europe		378,915	377,299	431,231	305,597	328,958	19.28	7.64
Austria		7,276	7,960	13,054	8,864	11,651	0.68	31.44
Belgium / Luxembourg		21,655	22,621	26,035	19,824	18,457	1.08	-6.90
France		39,896	45,773	51,792	43,833	39,286	2.30	-10.37
Germany		214,855	204,221	232,219	146,131	164,812	9.66	12.78
Netherlands		71,601	69,469	78,183	55,365	62,533	3.66	12.95
Switzerland		23,632	27,255	29,948	31,580	32,219	1.89	2.02
Other Europe		155,534	124,181	150,600	117,356	152,869	8.96	30.26
Other countries of Europe		155,534	124,181	150,600	117,356	152,869	8.96	30.26
NOT SPECIFIED		49,638	51,470	62,746	47,955	63,134	3.70	31.65
Other countries of the World		49,638	51,470	62,746	47,955	63,134	3.70	31.65

Yearbook of Tourism Statistics, Data 2008 – 2012, 2014 Editic

DENMARK

4. Arrivals of non-resident tourists in all types of accommodation establishments, by country of residence

		2008	2009	2010	2011	2012	Market share 2012	% Change 2012-2011
TOTAL	(*)	**9,563,857**	**9,264,870**	**9,425,096**	**8,471,236**	**8,676,217**	**100.00**	**2.42**
AMERICAS		**627,050**	**647,752**	**645,508**	**683,949**	**702,014**	**8.09**	**2.64**
North America		**557,398**	**589,593**	**583,730**	**618,952**	**631,300**	**7.28**	**1.99**
Canada		83,025	77,559	77,925	87,697	90,154	1.04	2.80
United States of America		474,373	512,034	505,805	531,255	541,146	6.24	1.86
Other Americas		**69,652**	**58,159**	**61,778**	**64,997**	**70,714**	**0.82**	**8.80**
Other countries of the Americas		69,652	58,159	61,778	64,997	70,714	0.82	8.80
EAST ASIA AND THE PACIFIC		**190,727**	**182,297**	**190,452**	**166,176**	**181,379**	**2.09**	**9.15**
North-East Asia		**33,233**	**30,726**	**33,837**	**20,687**	**24,267**	**0.28**	**17.31**
Japan		33,233	30,726	33,837	20,687	24,267	0.28	17.31
South-East Asia		**157,494**	**151,571**	**156,615**	**145,489**	**157,112**	**1.81**	**7.99**
All countries of South-East Asia		157,494	151,571	156,615	145,489	157,112	1.81	7.99
EUROPE		**8,330,154**	**7,988,695**	**8,128,384**	**7,173,932**	**7,296,241**	**84.09**	**1.70**
Central/Eastern Europe		**98,640**	**91,520**	**92,107**	**88,417**	**86,291**	**0.99**	**-2.40**
Poland		98,640	91,520	92,107	88,417	86,291	0.99	-2.40
Northern Europe		**3,925,567**	**3,639,024**	**3,789,674**	**3,372,219**	**3,502,298**	**40.37**	**3.86**
Finland		57,493	57,483	65,521	62,594	56,623	0.65	-9.54
Norway		1,693,932	1,628,381	1,665,429	1,481,565	1,557,060	17.95	5.10
Sweden		1,433,781	1,241,798	1,336,600	1,176,408	1,221,862	14.08	3.86
United Kingdom		740,361	711,362	722,124	651,652	666,753	7.68	2.32
Southern Europe		**409,408**	**316,881**	**327,122**	**341,657**	**346,464**	**3.99**	**1.41**
Italy		223,456	169,588	173,964	194,519	195,204	2.25	0.35
Spain		185,952	147,293	153,158	147,138	151,260	1.74	2.80
Western Europe		**3,449,058**	**3,337,909**	**3,349,660**	**2,946,599**	**2,939,723**	**33.88**	**-0.23**
Austria		53,532	42,971	48,442	48,827	51,878	0.60	6.25
Belgium / Luxembourg		111,960	110,248	113,754	106,963	105,242	1.21	-1.61
France		243,178	234,620	241,755	243,304	240,664	2.77	-1.09
Germany		2,593,135	2,538,209	2,526,299	2,165,225	2,156,586	24.86	-0.40
Netherlands		344,607	319,267	323,513	280,182	282,062	3.25	0.67
Switzerland		102,646	92,594	95,897	102,098	103,291	1.19	1.17
Other Europe		**447,481**	**603,361**	**569,821**	**425,040**	**421,465**	**4.86**	**-0.84**
Other countries of Europe		447,481	603,361	569,821	425,040	421,465	4.86	-0.84
NOT SPECIFIED		**415,926**	**446,126**	**460,752**	**447,179**	**496,583**	**5.72**	**11.05**
Other countries of the World		415,926	446,126	460,752	447,179	496,583	5.72	11.05

Yearbook of Tourism Statistics, Data 2008 – 2012, 2014 Edition

DENMARK

5. Overnight stays of non-resident tourists in hotels and similar establishments, by country of residence

		2008	2009	2010	2011	2012	Market share 2012	% Change 2012-2011
TOTAL	(*)	4,751,680	4,434,605	5,074,913	5,590,430	5,944,744	100.00	6.34
AMERICAS		413,163	431,758	467,686	601,770	552,067	9.29	-8.26
North America		373,600	391,009	416,958	450,350	468,667	7.88	4.07
Canada		33,785	37,152	40,126	52,960	54,574	0.92	3.05
United States of America		339,815	353,857	376,832	397,390	414,093	6.97	4.20
Other Americas		39,563	40,749	50,728	151,420	83,400	1.40	-44.92
Other countries of the Americas		39,563	40,749	50,728	151,420	83,400	1.40	-44.92
EAST ASIA AND THE PACIFIC		192,926	193,646	214,596	145,150	258,310	4.35	77.96
North-East Asia		77,185	81,651	89,357	89,630	91,459	1.54	2.04
Japan		77,185	81,651	89,357	89,630	91,459	1.54	2.04
South-East Asia		115,741	111,995	125,239	55,520	166,851	2.81	200.52
All countries of South-East Asia		115,741	111,995	125,239	55,520	166,851	2.81	200.52
EUROPE		3,991,500	3,649,142	4,197,280	4,643,770	4,888,049	82.22	5.26
Central/Eastern Europe		48,989	46,443	50,516	63,820	63,109	1.06	-1.11
Poland		48,989	46,443	50,516	63,820	63,109	1.06	-1.11
Northern Europe		2,358,611	2,080,994	2,384,952	2,656,930	2,737,353	46.05	3.03
Finland		108,359	105,718	122,099	151,220	183,732	3.09	21.50
Norway		835,757	795,048	879,665	962,900	989,783	16.65	2.79
Sweden		939,857	751,752	907,694	1,011,340	1,021,330	17.18	0.99
United Kingdom		474,638	428,476	475,494	531,470	542,508	9.13	2.08
Southern Europe		267,201	293,227	327,276	321,710	317,222	5.34	-1.40
Italy		150,933	166,386	184,397	180,240	192,736	3.24	6.93
Spain		116,268	126,841	142,879	141,470	124,486	2.09	-12.01
Western Europe		875,022	875,918	1,006,870	1,112,520	1,158,306	19.48	4.12
Austria		20,714	22,658	37,151	38,470	46,935	0.79	22.00
Belgium / Luxembourg		46,391	49,445	58,000	70,160	74,776	1.26	6.58
France		98,017	113,184	129,445	148,630	156,352	2.63	5.20
Germany		463,858	439,583	501,766	533,910	552,175	9.29	3.42
Netherlands		178,769	173,471	195,282	198,780	196,141	3.30	-1.33
Switzerland		67,273	77,577	85,226	122,570	131,927	2.22	7.63
Other Europe		441,677	352,560	427,666	488,790	612,059	10.30	25.22
Other countries of Europe		441,677	352,560	427,666	488,790	612,059	10.30	25.22
NOT SPECIFIED		154,091	160,059	195,351	199,740	246,318	4.14	23.32
Other countries of the World		154,091	160,059	195,351	199,740	246,318	4.14	23.32

Yearbook of Tourism Statistics, Data 2008 – 2012, 2014 Edition

DENMARK

6. Overnight stays of non-resident tourists in all types of accommodation establishments, by country of residence

	2008	2009	2010	2011	2012	Market share 2012	% Change 2012-2011
TOTAL (*)	45,852,357	43,984,095	44,361,815	45,921,450	45,580,674	100.00	-0.74
AMERICAS	2,701,036	2,673,126	2,696,883	3,039,300	2,983,687	6.55	-1.83
North America	2,263,189	2,245,932	2,258,517	2,366,170	2,384,420	5.23	0.77
Canada	439,161	376,110	379,119	405,660	406,722	0.89	0.26
United States of America	1,824,028	1,869,822	1,879,398	1,960,510	1,977,698	4.34	0.88
Other Americas	437,847	427,194	438,366	673,130	599,267	1.31	-10.97
Other countries of the Americas	437,847	427,194	438,366	673,130	599,267	1.31	-10.97
EAST ASIA AND THE PACIFIC	721,115	712,777	738,729	541,320	661,269	1.45	22.16
North-East Asia	86,850	86,256	94,329	94,570	96,158	0.21	1.68
Japan	86,850	86,256	94,329	94,570	96,158	0.21	1.68
South-East Asia	634,265	626,521	644,400	446,750	565,111	1.24	26.49
All countries of South-East Asia	634,265	626,521	644,400	446,750	565,111	1.24	26.49
EUROPE	39,947,835	38,086,453	38,346,505	40,004,500	39,156,089	85.91	-2.12
Central/Eastern Europe	1,047,295	1,020,454	1,016,069	1,015,060	1,009,731	2.22	-0.52
Poland	1,047,295	1,020,454	1,016,069	1,015,060	1,009,731	2.22	-0.52
Northern Europe	13,622,331	12,559,044	12,927,175	13,417,230	13,461,897	29.53	0.33
Finland	175,960	176,606	197,533	227,250	260,697	0.57	14.72
Norway	6,497,089	6,193,991	6,306,417	6,505,840	6,483,348	14.22	-0.35
Sweden	4,289,861	3,734,035	3,925,394	4,117,910	4,130,696	9.06	0.31
United Kingdom	2,659,421	2,454,412	2,497,831	2,566,230	2,587,156	5.68	0.82
Southern Europe	1,621,764	1,543,969	1,577,749	1,626,530	1,615,457	3.54	-0.68
Italy	938,103	897,200	914,919	938,210	946,448	2.08	0.88
Spain	683,661	646,769	662,830	688,320	669,009	1.47	-2.81
Western Europe	20,864,248	20,152,466	19,940,571	20,824,840	20,188,077	44.29	-3.06
Austria	211,597	203,081	219,006	227,340	235,205	0.52	3.46
Belgium / Luxembourg	380,101	384,806	395,449	414,320	413,324	0.91	-0.24
France	1,303,955	1,306,349	1,329,176	1,365,050	1,372,648	3.01	0.56
Germany	16,788,074	16,237,180	15,976,463	16,798,930	16,255,458	35.66	-3.24
Netherlands	1,811,010	1,676,310	1,664,214	1,614,690	1,500,124	3.29	-7.10
Switzerland	369,511	344,740	356,263	404,510	411,318	0.90	1.68
Other Europe	2,792,197	2,810,520	2,884,941	3,120,840	2,880,927	6.32	-7.69
Other countries of Europe	2,792,197	2,810,520	2,884,941	3,120,840	2,880,927	6.32	-7.69
NOT SPECIFIED	2,482,371	2,511,739	2,579,698	2,336,330	2,779,629	6.10	18.97
Other countries of the World	2,482,371	2,511,739	2,579,698	2,336,330	2,779,629	6.10	18.97

Yearbook of Tourism Statistics, Data 2008 – 2012, 2014 Edition

DOMINICA

1. Arrivals of non-resident tourists at national borders, by country of residence

	2008	2009	2010	2011	2012	Market share 2012	% Change 2012-2011
TOTAL	81,112	74,924	76,518	75,546	78,965	100.00	4.53
AMERICAS	66,645	62,894	64,789	62,901	64,793	82.05	3.01
Caribbean	40,965	40,540	41,536	40,820	41,622	52.71	1.96
Anguilla	545	443	418	334	309	0.39	-7.49
Antigua and Barbuda	4,068	3,763	3,670	3,479	3,454	4.37	-0.72
Aruba	61	34	73	42	44	0.06	4.76
Bahamas	94	106	126	134	107	0.14	-20.15
Barbados	1,956	1,935	1,961	1,897	2,208	2.80	16.39
Bermuda	85	58	48	60	45	0.06	-25.00
Bonaire	8	12	9	3	7	0.01	133.33
British Virgin Islands	979	1,085	1,089	1,079	968	1.23	-10.29
Cayman Islands	48	19	10	22	19	0.02	-13.64
Cuba	105	76	88	73	77	0.10	5.48
Curaçao	109	102	117	107	60	0.08	-43.93
Dominican Republic	154	183	300	224	273	0.35	21.88
Grenada	312	397	325	419	289	0.37	-31.03
Guadeloupe	14,029	15,053	15,707	15,089	16,009	20.27	6.10
Haiti	745	974	831	705	880	1.11	24.82
Jamaica	550	592	526	555	428	0.54	-22.88
Martinique	6,180	5,409	6,096	6,428	7,002	8.87	8.93
Montserrat	112	114	98	131	95	0.12	-27.48
Puerto Rico	187	360	296	246	267	0.34	8.54
Saint Kitts and Nevis	525	478	579	494	463	0.59	-6.28
Saint Lucia	2,081	1,952	1,914	2,080	1,980	2.51	-4.81
Saint Vincent and the Grenadines	501	536	469	548	492	0.62	-10.22
Sint Maarten	2,272	1,993	2,089	1,898	1,869	2.37	-1.53
Trinidad and Tobago	1,325	1,335	1,356	1,621	1,323	1.68	-18.38
Turks and Caicos Islands	18	37	26	24	14	0.02	-41.67
United States Virgin Islands	3,830	3,426	3,230	3,103	2,912	3.69	-6.16
Other countries of the Caribbean	86	68	85	25	28	0.04	12.00
Central America	106	92	99	200	129	0.16	-35.50
Belize	25	38	38	45	31	0.04	-31.11
Other countries of Central America	81	54	61	155	98	0.12	-36.77
North America	23,906	20,847	22,150	20,855	22,097	27.98	5.96
Canada	3,346	2,618	2,859	2,986	3,063	3.88	2.58
Mexico	42	36	25	49	32	0.04	-34.69
United States of America	20,518	18,193	19,266	17,820	19,002	24.06	6.63
South America	1,668	1,415	1,004	1,026	945	1.20	-7.89
Argentina	15	21	24	16	24	0.03	50.00
Brazil	12	17	27	48	45	0.06	-6.25
Colombia	26	40	36	48	54	0.07	12.50
French Guiana	78	81	53	136	126	0.16	-7.35
Guyana	250	279	293	295	276	0.35	-6.44
Suriname	38	30	32	50	28	0.04	-44.00
Venezuela	1,212	909	501	410	345	0.44	-15.85
Other countries of South America	37	38	38	23	47	0.06	104.35
EAST ASIA AND THE PACIFIC	359	360	475	557	805	1.02	44.52
North-East Asia	279	309	368	462	574	0.73	24.24
China	147	178	227	341	360	0.46	5.57
Japan	94	111	115	91	107	0.14	17.58
Taiwan, Province of China	38	20	26	30	107	0.14	256.67
Australasia	80	51	107	95	231	0.29	143.16
Australia	80	51	107	95	231	0.29	143.16

Yearbook of Tourism Statistics, Data 2008 – 2012, 2014 Edition

DOMINICA

1. Arrivals of non-resident tourists at national borders, by country of residence

	2008	2009	2010	2011	2012	Market share 2012	% Change 2012-2011
EUROPE	13,787	11,590	10,725	11,538	12,816	16.23	11.08
Northern Europe	7,748	4,851	5,080	5,138	5,244	6.64	2.06
Denmark	124	106	81	78	100	0.13	28.21
Ireland	67	61	58	63	73	0.09	15.87
Norway	42	39	44	55	78	0.10	41.82
Sweden	304	291	296	320	327	0.41	2.19
United Kingdom	7,211	4,354	4,601	4,622	4,666	5.91	0.95
Southern Europe	234	269	241	259	283	0.36	9.27
Greece	6	20	10	11	23	0.03	109.09
Italy	104	124	107	135	139	0.18	2.96
Portugal	21	28	12	9	15	0.02	66.67
Spain	103	97	112	104	106	0.13	1.92
Western Europe	5,485	6,172	5,092	5,699	6,727	8.52	18.04
Austria	137	127	129	147	176	0.22	19.73
Belgium	173	165	163	187	193	0.24	3.21
France	3,783	4,469	3,323	3,680	4,188	5.30	13.80
Germany	879	966	898	1,011	1,397	1.77	38.18
Luxembourg	9	3	8	11	16	0.02	45.45
Netherlands	220	172	182	185	162	0.21	-12.43
Switzerland	284	270	389	478	595	0.75	24.48
Other Europe	320	298	312	442	562	0.71	27.15
Other countries of Europe	320	298	312	442	562	0.71	27.15
NOT SPECIFIED	321	80	529	550	551	0.70	0.18
Other countries of the World	321	80	529	550	551	0.70	0.18

Yearbook of Tourism Statistics, Data 2008 – 2012, 2014 Edition

DOMINICAN REPUBLIC

1. Arrivals of non-resident tourists at national borders, by country of residence

		2008	2009	2010	2011	2012	Market share 2012	% Change 2012-2011
TOTAL	(*)	3,979,672	3,992,303	4,124,543	4,306,431	4,562,606	100.00	5.95
AMERICAS		2,127,963	2,202,697	2,367,965	2,559,180	2,818,384	61.77	10.13
Caribbean		133,470	138,236	154,201	143,254	151,566	3.32	5.80
Aruba		2,420	1,910	1,873	1,888	1,505	0.03	-20.29
Cuba		3,876	3,295	3,818	3,838	3,996	0.09	4.12
Curaçao		4,183	4,366	4,407	4,382	5,311	0.12	21.20
Guadeloupe		5,157	5,334	5,188	3,436	6,077	0.13	76.86
Haiti		7,120	5,456	9,518	9,717	9,431	0.21	-2.94
Jamaica		1,292	882	1,124	1,027	1,046	0.02	1.85
Martinique		4,639	3,386	4,252	3,833	4,618	0.10	20.48
Puerto Rico		97,592	107,610	118,201	109,505	112,593	2.47	2.82
Sint Maarten		3,012	2,944	2,520	2,654	3,411	0.07	28.52
Trinidad and Tobago		1,467	943	1,438	1,207	1,272	0.03	5.39
Turks and Caicos Islands		1,220	1,041	1,036	918	1,241	0.03	35.19
United States Virgin Islands		1,492	1,069	826	849	1,065	0.02	25.44
Central America		28,512	30,083	29,124	35,033	36,363	0.80	3.80
Costa Rica		8,717	8,110	8,411	9,618	9,879	0.22	2.71
El Salvador		3,760	3,462	3,710	3,870	3,922	0.09	1.34
Guatemala		5,149	5,783	5,420	6,708	6,259	0.14	-6.69
Honduras		2,230	1,759	2,177	2,458	1,997	0.04	-18.76
Panama		8,656	10,969	9,406	12,379	14,306	0.31	15.57
North America		1,771,326	1,819,294	1,902,316	1,988,935	2,195,068	48.11	10.36
Canada		639,796	650,111	662,058	668,290	689,543	15.11	3.18
Mexico		23,632	18,308	20,695	23,467	26,610	0.58	13.39
United States of America		1,107,898	1,150,875	1,219,563	1,297,178	1,478,915	32.41	14.01
South America		188,621	208,580	276,016	383,450	429,778	9.42	12.08
Argentina		35,476	43,130	69,182	97,462	101,321	2.22	3.96
Bolivia		1,137	3,053	5,106	7,621	7,401	0.16	-2.89
Brazil		13,513	19,570	37,153	76,625	79,937	1.75	4.32
Chile		28,541	29,495	40,729	49,862	60,804	1.33	21.94
Colombia		31,137	29,156	31,263	40,982	44,955	0.99	9.69
Ecuador		16,686	15,797	16,597	18,786	13,889	0.30	-26.07
Peru		16,049	19,825	24,636	30,646	38,953	0.85	27.11
Uruguay		2,567	3,865	4,454	5,626	5,870	0.13	4.34
Venezuela		42,384	42,635	45,196	53,079	72,680	1.59	36.93
Other countries of South America		1,131	2,054	1,700	2,761	3,968	0.09	43.72
Other Americas		6,034	6,504	6,308	8,508	5,609	0.12	-34.07
Other countries of the Americas		6,034	6,504	6,308	8,508	5,609	0.12	-34.07
EAST ASIA AND THE PACIFIC		7,624	6,753	8,345	9,773	8,557	0.19	-12.44
North-East Asia		4,350	3,831	4,738	4,989	4,702	0.10	-5.75
China		491	381	646	901	963	0.02	6.88
Japan		2,281	2,036	2,231	2,270	2,036	0.04	-10.31
Korea, Republic of		1,014	937	1,406	1,300	1,216	0.03	-6.46
Taiwan, Province of China		564	477	455	518	487	0.01	-5.98
Australasia		1,874	1,397	1,676	1,361	1,658	0.04	21.82
Australia		1,874	1,397	1,676	1,361	1,658	0.04	21.82
Other East Asia and the Pacific		1,400	1,525	1,931	3,423	2,197	0.05	-35.82
Other countries of Asia		1,400	1,525	1,931	3,423	2,197	0.05	-35.82
EUROPE		1,310,611	1,204,701	1,142,666	1,132,009	1,094,841	24.00	-3.28
Central/Eastern Europe		54,010	63,195	92,670	139,462	180,134	3.95	29.16
Bulgaria		536	499	582	555	613	0.01	10.45
Czech Republic		4,726	5,526	6,112	5,996	5,522	0.12	-7.91
Hungary		768	704	803	780	546	0.01	-30.00
Poland		5,436	3,795	4,934	6,906	6,587	0.14	-4.62
Romania		565	592	748	971	567	0.01	-41.61

200

DOMINICAN REPUBLIC

1. Arrivals of non-resident tourists at national borders, by country of residence

	2008	2009	2010	2011	2012	Market share 2012	% Change 2012-2011
Russian Federation	39,734	49,752	76,059	120,752	163,157	3.58	35.12
Ukraine	2,245	2,327	3,432	3,502	3,142	0.07	-10.28
Northern Europe	**228,822**	**198,892**	**185,826**	**149,997**	**106,755**	**2.34**	**-28.83**
Denmark	2,298	2,061	2,145	1,709	2,299	0.05	34.52
Finland	2,768	4,445	4,245	2,383	2,785	0.06	16.87
Ireland	2,893	1,767	1,564	1,096	840	0.02	-23.36
Norway	2,207	2,575	1,891	1,527	1,617	0.04	5.89
Sweden	5,702	6,153	7,760	5,339	3,603	0.08	-32.52
United Kingdom	212,954	181,891	168,221	137,943	95,611	2.10	-30.69
Southern Europe	**400,067**	**390,347**	**321,994**	**299,872**	**271,826**	**5.96**	**-9.35**
Greece	868	567	495	454	342	0.01	-24.67
Italy	127,383	115,775	94,952	99,822	89,767	1.97	-10.07
Portugal	32,178	42,730	36,941	29,403	25,525	0.56	-13.19
Spain	239,638	231,275	189,606	170,193	156,192	3.42	-8.23
Western Europe	**623,377**	**545,410**	**530,292**	**540,275**	**533,201**	**11.69**	**-1.31**
Austria	9,642	10,049	9,640	8,239	7,914	0.17	-3.94
Belgium	43,176	38,129	38,187	36,955	34,111	0.75	-7.70
France	279,408	247,038	230,975	246,416	245,033	5.37	-0.56
Germany	206,940	178,533	181,318	183,847	183,533	4.02	-0.17
Luxembourg	391	473	495	435	570	0.01	31.03
Netherlands	49,960	41,605	40,100	37,861	34,225	0.75	-9.60
Switzerland	33,860	29,583	29,577	26,522	27,815	0.61	4.88
East Mediterranean Europe	**1,710**	**1,445**	**1,476**	**1,204**	**1,077**	**0.02**	**-10.55**
Israel	1,710	1,445	1,476	1,204	1,077	0.02	-10.55
Other Europe	**2,625**	**5,412**	**10,408**	**1,199**	**1,848**	**0.04**	**54.13**
Other countries of Europe	2,625	5,412	10,408	1,199	1,848	0.04	54.13
SOUTH ASIA	**754**	**806**	**848**	**964**	**941**	**0.02**	**-2.39**
India	754	806	848	964	941	0.02	-2.39
NOT SPECIFIED	**532,720**	**577,346**	**604,719**	**604,505**	**639,883**	**14.02**	**5.85**
Other countries of the World	778	659	1,286	1,071	970	0.02	-9.43
Nationals Residing Abroad	531,942	576,687	603,433	603,434	638,913	14.00	5.88

Yearbook of Tourism Statistics, Data 2008 – 2012, 2014 Edition

ECUADOR

2. Arrivals of non-resident visitors at national borders, by nationality

		2008	2009	2010	2011	2012	Market share 2012	% Change 2012-2011
TOTAL	(*)	1,005,297	968,499	1,047,098	1,141,037	1,271,953	100.00	11.47
AFRICA		1,560	3,254	3,227	2,487	3,892	0.31	56.49
East Africa		163	546	461	189	357	0.03	88.89
Burundi		3	2	3	1	3	0.00	200.00
Comoros		4	1	5	6	12	0.00	100.00
Djibouti		1	4	3	2	4	0.00	100.00
Ethiopia		44	175	188	14	21	0.00	50.00
Kenya		52	267	164	58	66	0.01	13.79
Madagascar		8	10	17	12	23	0.00	91.67
Malawi		3	2	1	2			
Mauritius		3	1	7	9	13	0.00	44.44
Mozambique		8	13	18	16	23	0.00	43.75
Rwanda		2	1	5	3	78	0.01	2,500.00
Seychelles		2	1		1	6	0.00	500.00
Somalia						26	0.00	
Uganda		8	16	14	23	27	0.00	17.39
United Republic of Tanzania		9	29	13	26	37	0.00	42.31
Zambia		6	12	3	2	6	0.00	200.00
Zimbabwe		10	12	20	14	12	0.00	-14.29
Central Africa		86	180	174	153	156	0.01	1.96
Angola		14	30	27	9	26	0.00	188.89
Cameroon		41	85	73	70	65	0.01	-7.14
Central African Republic		2	15	15	10	13	0.00	30.00
Chad		6	6	13	19	18	0.00	-5.26
Congo		15	32	38	37	28	0.00	-24.32
Equatorial Guinea		1	2	2	4	4	0.00	0.00
Gabon		5	4	2	4	1	0.00	-75.00
Sao Tome and Principe		2	6	4		1	0.00	
North Africa		260	534	513	499	829	0.07	66.13
Algeria		65	173	129	183	183	0.01	0.00
Morocco		47	90	82	93	97	0.01	4.30
Sudan		2	10	33	33	444	0.03	1,245.45
Tunisia		18	28	29	30	44	0.00	46.67
Western Sahara		128	233	240	160	61	0.00	-61.88
Southern Africa		630	606	627	989	988	0.08	-0.10
Botswana		2	15	13	1	12	0.00	1,100.00
Lesotho		2	4	3	5	7	0.00	40.00
Namibia		2	25	13	4	17	0.00	325.00
South Africa		621	556	594	976	882	0.07	-9.63
Swaziland		3	6	4	3	70	0.01	2,233.33
West Africa		199	847	675	372	638	0.05	71.51
Benin		13	27	30	24	24	0.00	0.00
Burkina Faso			4	7	8	10	0.00	25.00
Cape Verde		12	15	37	36	40	0.00	11.11
Côte d'Ivoire						40	0.00	
Gambia		1	9	7	2	10	0.00	400.00
Ghana		19	66	49	70	57	0.00	-18.57
Guinea		29	79	67	43	26	0.00	-39.53
Guinea-Bissau						2	0.00	
Liberia		6	9	7	9	6	0.00	-33.33
Mali			3	8	11	14	0.00	27.27
Mauritania		7	31	24	27	13	0.00	-51.85
Nigeria		94	545	359	80	76	0.01	-5.00
Senegal		16	30	32	22	246	0.02	1,018.18
Sierra Leone		2	29	48	40	70	0.01	75.00
Togo						4	0.00	

202

ECUADOR

2. Arrivals of non-resident visitors at national borders, by nationality

	2008	2009	2010	2011	2012	Market share 2012	% Change 2012-2011
Other Africa	222	541	777	285	924	0.07	224.21
Other countries of Africa	222	541	777	285	924	0.07	224.21
AMERICAS	753,266	734,524	810,281	885,383	995,861	78.29	12.48
Caribbean	14,424	31,209	31,707	29,902	27,874	2.19	-6.78
Antigua and Barbuda	3	6	7	5	6	0.00	20.00
Bahamas	29	47	61	60	68	0.01	13.33
Barbados	50	55	33	43	44	0.00	2.33
Bermuda		24	10	10	16	0.00	60.00
Cuba	10,904	27,065	27,001	24,064	21,482	1.69	-10.73
Curaçao	3	13	8	8	6	0.00	-25.00
Dominica	41	44	64	38	42	0.00	10.53
Dominican Republic	2,408	2,480	2,619	2,446	2,648	0.21	8.26
Grenada	13	16	20	11	19	0.00	72.73
Guadeloupe		12	15	14	26	0.00	85.71
Haiti	270	1,257	1,681	2,545	3,020	0.24	18.66
Jamaica	118	137	119	161	170	0.01	5.59
Puerto Rico	21	26	31	39	57	0.00	46.15
Saint Lucia	19	15	8	28	10	0.00	-64.29
Saint Vincent and the Grenadines	2		4	7	8	0.00	14.29
Trinidad and Tobago	182			398	252	0.02	-36.68
Other countries of the Caribbean	361	12	26	25			
Central America	13,649	13,652	15,772	21,021	24,836	1.95	18.15
Belize	64	57	41	37	51	0.00	37.84
Costa Rica	4,045	3,921	4,560	4,833	5,060	0.40	4.70
El Salvador	1,310	1,419	1,994	2,655	3,700	0.29	39.36
Guatemala	1,780	2,048	2,296	2,230	3,101	0.24	39.06
Honduras	1,115	1,072	1,256	1,391	1,581	0.12	13.66
Nicaragua	831	856	985	984	1,253	0.10	27.34
Panama	4,504	4,279	4,640	8,891	10,090	0.79	13.49
North America	280,934	278,280	288,705	285,896	294,687	23.17	3.07
Canada	22,839	22,489	23,867	24,834	26,980	2.12	8.64
Mexico	13,689	13,695	15,757	19,457	19,643	1.54	0.96
United States of America	244,406	242,096	249,081	241,605	248,064	19.50	2.67
South America	444,251	411,381	474,097	548,564	648,464	50.98	18.21
Argentina	21,718	22,675	30,653	37,465	46,203	3.63	23.32
Bolivia	4,797	4,487	5,522	4,964	5,362	0.42	8.02
Brazil	15,052	14,395	15,083	17,543	18,172	1.43	3.59
Chile	24,212	25,195	28,478	34,864	41,647	3.27	19.46
Colombia	200,487	160,116	203,916	265,557	349,457	27.47	31.59
Guyana	36	51	54	45	60	0.00	33.33
Paraguay	884	1,233	1,115	1,375	1,219	0.10	-11.35
Peru	147,420	150,548	154,216	144,905	137,096	10.78	-5.39
Suriname	54	74	87	80	51	0.00	-36.25
Uruguay	2,758	2,967	3,152	3,458	3,493	0.27	1.01
Venezuela	26,771	29,416	31,558	38,308	45,704	3.59	19.31
Other countries of South America	62	224	263				
Other Americas	8	2					
Other countries of the Americas	8	2					
EAST ASIA AND THE PACIFIC	34,134	30,247	31,859	41,587	44,895	3.53	7.95
North-East Asia	21,230	14,888	14,674	18,037	19,060	1.50	5.67
China	14,287	7,844	6,879	9,296	12,241	0.96	31.68
Hong Kong, China	152	143	158	217	259	0.02	19.35
Japan	5,533	4,951	5,106	5,114	5,342	0.42	4.46

Yearbook of Tourism Statistics, Data 2008 – 2012, 2014 Edition

ECUADOR

2. Arrivals of non-resident visitors at national borders, by nationality

	2008	2009	2010	2011	2012	Market share 2012	% Change 2012-2011
Korea, Dem. People's Republic of					10	0.00	
Korea, Republic of	663	1,294	1,810	2,621	419	0.03	-84.01
Mongolia	7	2	3	12	6	0.00	-50.00
Taiwan, Province of China	588	654	718	777	783	0.06	0.77
South-East Asia	**3,190**	**2,939**	**3,499**	**9,627**	**11,931**	**0.94**	**23.93**
Brunei Darussalam	1	2	1		8	0.00	
Cambodia	7	4	2	3	10	0.00	233.33
Indonesia	325	194	262	382	761	0.06	99.21
Malaysia	187	192	251	257	314	0.02	22.18
Myanmar	42	130	158	352	294	0.02	-16.48
Philippines	2,202	2,060	2,330	7,990	9,717	0.76	21.61
Singapore	199	201	292	368	364	0.03	-1.09
Thailand	61	72	148	193	356	0.03	84.46
Viet Nam	166	84	55	82	107	0.01	30.49
Australasia	**9,696**	**9,876**	**10,820**	**11,882**	**13,663**	**1.07**	**14.99**
Australia	7,902	8,241	9,167	10,238	11,781	0.93	15.07
New Zealand	1,794	1,635	1,653	1,644	1,882	0.15	14.48
Melanesia	**3**	**49**	**65**	**33**	**79**	**0.01**	**139.39**
Fiji	2	4	3	5	26	0.00	420.00
New Caledonia		45	62	26	38	0.00	46.15
Papua New Guinea	1			2	15	0.00	650.00
Micronesia	**7**	**5**	**38**	**31**	**125**	**0.01**	**303.23**
Kiribati	2	4	34	30	121	0.01	303.33
Marshall Islands	2		2		1	0.00	
Micronesia, Federated States of	3	1	2	1	3	0.00	200.00
Polynesia	**8**	**9**	**17**	**18**	**10**	**0.00**	**-44.44**
French Polynesia	8	9	17	18	10	0.00	-44.44
Other East Asia and the Pacific		**2,481**	**2,746**	**1,959**	**27**	**0.00**	**-98.62**
Other countries of Asia		2,481	2,613	1,857			
Other countries of Oceania			133	102	27	0.00	-73.53
EUROPE	**198,177**	**197,062**	**197,527**	**206,923**	**212,459**	**16.70**	**2.68**
Central/Eastern Europe	**5,949**	**9,156**	**9,288**	**13,276**	**9,508**	**0.75**	**-28.38**
Armenia	22	11		18	15	0.00	-16.67
Azerbaijan	30	32		37	52	0.00	40.54
Belarus	82	113	113	170	241	0.02	41.76
Bulgaria	221	225	268	277	434	0.03	56.68
Czech Republic	892	919	846	900	1,040	0.08	15.56
Estonia	150	109	103	115	151	0.01	31.30
Georgia	14	23		103	70	0.01	-32.04
Hungary	467	398	360	363	387	0.03	6.61
Kazakhstan	48	60		119	109	0.01	-8.40
Kyrgyzstan	1	6		8	5	0.00	-37.50
Latvia	122	186	132	279	179	0.01	-35.84
Lithuania	287	284	185	324	440	0.03	35.80
Poland	1,783	2,144	1,903	2,458	2,478	0.19	0.81
Republic of Moldova	20		32	47	18	0.00	-61.70
Romania	643	567	617	939	1,013	0.08	7.88
Russian Federation	141	2,768	3,350	4,445	181	0.01	-95.93
Slovakia	41	461	381	315	50	0.00	-84.13
Tajikistan	1	1			9	0.00	
Turkmenistan	1	1		2	2	0.00	0.00
Ukraine	977	840	998	2,348	2,623	0.21	11.71
Uzbekistan	6	8		9	11	0.00	22.22

Yearbook of Tourism Statistics, Data 2008 – 2012, 2014 Edition

ECUADOR

2. Arrivals of non-resident visitors at national borders, by nationality

	2008	2009	2010	2011	2012	Market share 2012	% Change 2012-2011
Northern Europe	**38,504**	**37,536**	**34,880**	**35,044**	**34,377**	**2.70**	**-1.90**
Denmark	3,148	2,867	2,867	2,795	2,526	0.20	-9.62
Finland	1,038	1,047	1,116	1,233	1,163	0.09	-5.68
Iceland	110	104	99	163	192	0.02	17.79
Ireland	2,916	2,871	2,398	2,388	2,920	0.23	22.28
Norway	2,201	1,993	2,026	1,942	1,986	0.16	2.27
Sweden	3,868	3,624	3,777	3,646	4,446	0.35	21.94
United Kingdom	25,223	25,030	22,597	22,877	21,144	1.66	-7.58
Southern Europe	**66,476**	**73,869**	**76,727**	**78,462**	**83,991**	**6.60**	**7.05**
Albania	33	56	71	100	142	0.01	42.00
Andorra	23	15	23	36	33	0.00	-8.33
Bosnia and Herzegovina	24	9	9	11	13	0.00	18.18
Croatia	246	218	248	421	549	0.04	30.40
Greece	535	544	562	486	601	0.05	23.66
Holy See	4	2	4	1			
Italy	13,799	14,759	15,076	14,645	14,775	1.16	0.89
Malta	39	49	51	23	49	0.00	113.04
Portugal	1,405	1,520	1,404	1,781	1,626	0.13	-8.70
San Marino	1	3	4	8	12	0.00	50.00
Serbia and Montenegro	161				178	0.01	
Slovenia	269	294	245	284	248	0.02	-12.68
Spain	49,937	56,400	59,030	60,666	65,765	5.17	8.41
Western Europe	**70,347**	**71,823**	**72,156**	**75,193**	**79,149**	**6.22**	**5.26**
Austria	2,571	2,456	2,522	2,786	3,096	0.24	11.13
Belgium	4,851	5,021	4,945	5,129	5,341	0.42	4.13
France	18,876	19,810	20,272	20,431	19,546	1.54	-4.33
Germany	24,227	24,841	25,011	26,669	29,582	2.33	10.92
Liechtenstein	18	18	23	22	23	0.00	4.55
Luxembourg	136	197	137	154	168	0.01	9.09
Monaco	5	4	8	2	4	0.00	100.00
Netherlands	11,123	10,690	10,354	10,546	12,328	0.97	16.90
Switzerland	8,540	8,786	8,884	9,454	9,061	0.71	-4.16
East Mediterranean Europe	**4,592**	**4,678**	**4,319**	**4,948**	**5,431**	**0.43**	**9.76**
Cyprus	28	22	19	28	38	0.00	35.71
Israel	4,262	4,335	4,300	4,246	4,599	0.36	8.31
Turkey	302	321		674	794	0.06	17.80
Other Europe	**12,309**		**157**		**3**	**0.00**	
Other countries of Europe	12,309		157		3	0.00	
MIDDLE EAST	**443**	**532**	**551**	**575**	**1,036**	**0.08**	**80.17**
Bahrain	14	4	6	3	10	0.00	233.33
Egypt	56	115	133	122	175	0.01	43.44
Iraq	7	13	8	12	17	0.00	41.67
Jordan	83	67	66	70	68	0.01	-2.86
Kuwait	6	13	30	21	19	0.00	-9.52
Lebanon	133	222	228	202	453	0.04	124.26
Libya	6			13	15	0.00	15.38
Oman	2	5	4		11	0.00	
Palestine	2						
Qatar	1	10	11	6	4	0.00	-33.33
Saudi Arabia	25	27	52	49	39	0.00	-20.41
Syrian Arab Republic	26			37	23	0.00	-37.84
United Arab Emirates	2	11	13	16	15	0.00	-6.25
Yemen	78	45		24	23	0.00	-4.17
Other countries of Middle East	2				164	0.01	

Yearbook of Tourism Statistics, Data 2008 – 2012, 2014 Edition

ECUADOR

2. Arrivals of non-resident visitors at national borders, by nationality

	2008	2009	2010	2011	2012	Market share 2012	% Change 2012-2011
SOUTH ASIA	**1,666**	**2,880**	**3,653**	**4,082**	**4,308**	**0.34**	**5.54**
Afghanistan	28	70	62	13	11	0.00	-15.38
Bangladesh	107	321	362	115	36	0.00	-68.70
Bhutan	2	2		4			
India	1,212	1,570	2,060	3,073	3,769	0.30	22.65
Iran, Islamic Republic of	13		232	374	4	0.00	-98.93
Maldives	8	8	5	6	5	0.00	-16.67
Nepal	82	234	159	25	35	0.00	40.00
Pakistan	179	497	518	128	144	0.01	12.50
Sri Lanka	35	178	255	344	304	0.02	-11.63
NOT SPECIFIED	**16,051**				**9,502**	**0.75**	
Other countries of the World	16,051				9,502	0.75	

Yearbook of Tourism Statistics, Data 2008 – 2012, 2014 Edition

EGYPT

2. Arrivals of non-resident visitors at national borders, by nationality

	2008	2009	2010	2011	2012	Market share 2012	% Change 2012-2011
TOTAL (*)	12,835,351	12,535,885	14,730,813	9,845,066	11,531,858	100.00	17.13
AFRICA	400,979	455,262	491,416	434,867	428,168	3.71	-1.54
East Africa	29,624	42,019	48,167	34,970	38,872	0.34	11.16
Burundi	503	574	467	304	312	0.00	2.63
Comoros	1,955	850	877	447	234	0.00	-47.65
Djibouti	1,653	2,131	2,545	1,781	2,000	0.02	12.30
Eritrea	2,986	5,323	6,661	4,743	5,881	0.05	23.99
Ethiopia	4,911	6,409	6,668	4,879	6,880	0.06	41.01
Kenya	7,080	8,233	9,613	8,301	8,123	0.07	-2.14
Malawi	447	429	445	258	267	0.00	3.49
Mauritius	671	1,004	999	529	525	0.00	-0.76
Mozambique	408	343	405	235	255	0.00	8.51
Rwanda	426	510	419	385	411	0.00	6.75
Seychelles	92	85	126	110	82	0.00	-25.45
Somalia	2,805	6,781	6,350	4,414	4,332	0.04	-1.86
Uganda	1,822	2,495	2,533	3,138	3,208	0.03	2.23
United Republic of Tanzania	1,719	4,709	7,567	4,310	5,193	0.05	20.49
Zambia	745	1,097	1,120	509	528	0.00	3.73
Zimbabwe	1,401	1,046	1,372	627	641	0.01	2.23
Central Africa	5,808	5,940	6,030	23,187	4,841	0.04	-79.12
Angola	576	678	547	303	354	0.00	16.83
Cameroon	997	1,264	1,185	936	934	0.01	-0.21
Central African Republic	255	116	188	67	113	0.00	68.66
Chad	2,199	2,292	2,620	20,758	2,314	0.02	-88.85
Congo	928	1,035	686	443	341	0.00	-23.02
Democratic Republic of the Congo	561	242	532	464	633	0.01	36.42
Gabon	290	301	262	216	152	0.00	-29.63
Sao Tome and Principe	2	12	10				
North Africa	271,482	296,555	319,137	282,187	296,964	2.58	5.24
Algeria	37,958	44,585	22,782	20,982	26,955	0.23	28.47
Morocco	39,495	53,663	57,591	37,274	39,417	0.34	5.75
Sudan	159,124	159,588	189,731	200,376	198,018	1.72	-1.18
Tunisia	34,905	38,719	49,033	23,555	32,574	0.28	38.29
Southern Africa	36,142	32,981	38,260	19,604	22,638	0.20	15.48
Botswana	152	166		103			
Lesotho	151	147	107	79	71	0.00	-10.13
Namibia	288	416	389	181	233	0.00	28.73
South Africa	35,414	31,930	37,635	19,164	22,205	0.19	15.87
Swaziland	137	322	129	77	129	0.00	67.53
West Africa	56,789	76,006	77,846	74,271	63,850	0.55	-14.03
Benin	464	543	387	253	376	0.00	48.62
Côte d'Ivoire	1,185	1,056	1,262	702	842	0.01	19.94
Gambia	314	308	348	155	181	0.00	16.77
Ghana	6,161	8,291	10,018	8,366	8,502	0.07	1.63
Guinea	1,447	1,679	1,491	1,520	1,267	0.01	-16.64
Guinea-Bissau	222	62	36	73	16	0.00	-78.08
Liberia	224	185	276	178	259	0.00	45.51
Mali	653	729	739	1,612	643	0.01	-60.11
Mauritania	1,247	1,781	2,008	1,396	1,263	0.01	-9.53
Niger	2,170	1,156	1,343	10,670	2,915	0.03	-72.68
Nigeria	40,636	57,967	57,731	47,889	46,182	0.40	-3.56
Senegal	1,384	1,425	1,432	999	895	0.01	-10.41
Sierra Leone	263	297	248	149	222	0.00	48.99
Togo	419	527	527	309	287	0.00	-7.12
Other Africa	1,134	1,761	1,976	648	1,003	0.01	54.78

Yearbook of Tourism Statistics, Data 2008 – 2012, 2014 Edition

EGYPT

2. Arrivals of non-resident visitors at national borders, by nationality

	2008	2009	2010	2011	2012	Market share 2012	% Change 2012-2011
Other countries of Africa	1,134	1,761	1,976	648	1,003	0.01	54.78
AMERICAS	**486,099**	**488,785**	**563,365**	**287,187**	**285,280**	**2.47**	**-0.66**
Caribbean	**2,622**	**3,259**	**3,393**	**1,715**	**1,682**	**0.01**	**-1.92**
Bahamas	51	83	63	22	39	0.00	77.27
Barbados	82	58	60	32	71	0.00	121.88
Cuba	760	823	742	437	493	0.00	12.81
Dominica	681	801	941	382	413	0.00	8.12
Haiti	70	104	125	67	86	0.00	28.36
Jamaica	394	742	645	192	219	0.00	14.06
Trinidad and Tobago	584	648	817	583	361	0.00	-38.08
Central America	**4,837**	**7,497**	**9,082**	**4,083**	**3,189**	**0.03**	**-21.90**
Costa Rica	1,279	1,360	2,333	663	1,176	0.01	77.38
El Salvador	1,535	1,425	1,125	788	507	0.00	-35.66
Guatemala	660	1,326	1,796	494	615	0.01	24.49
Honduras	1,018	2,577	2,907	387	438	0.00	13.18
Nicaragua	98	448	387	191	296	0.00	54.97
Panama	247	361	534	1,560	157	0.00	-89.94
North America	**420,463**	**421,593**	**476,314**	**240,990**	**238,143**	**2.07**	**-1.18**
Canada	85,052	88,591	96,418	50,687	51,623	0.45	1.85
Mexico	16,299	11,720	18,373	5,695	6,886	0.06	20.91
United States of America	319,112	321,282	361,523	184,608	179,634	1.56	-2.69
South America	**57,699**	**55,869**	**74,027**	**40,184**	**41,916**	**0.36**	**4.31**
Argentina	10,449	9,949	14,341	6,397	7,019	0.06	9.72
Bolivia	453	536	770	422	385	0.00	-8.77
Brazil	22,075	19,695	30,384	17,249	15,554	0.13	-9.83
Chile	4,519	4,263	4,847	2,370	2,764	0.02	16.62
Colombia	9,521	9,731	11,073	7,218	8,529	0.07	18.16
Ecuador	2,653	2,618	3,529	2,124	2,477	0.02	16.62
Guyana	33	33	39	17	20	0.00	17.65
Paraguay	173	226	260	122	197	0.00	61.48
Peru	2,413	3,362	3,691	1,806	2,312	0.02	28.02
Suriname	252	70	85	47	167	0.00	255.32
Uruguay	1,228	1,295	1,549	930	823	0.01	-11.51
Venezuela	3,930	4,091	3,459	1,482	1,669	0.01	12.62
Other Americas	**478**	**567**	**549**	**215**	**350**	**0.00**	**62.79**
Other countries of the Americas	478	567	549	215	350	0.00	62.79
EAST ASIA AND THE PACIFIC	**494,891**	**448,416**	**559,018**	**277,866**	**304,926**	**2.64**	**9.74**
North-East Asia	**252,452**	**208,812**	**288,997**	**109,687**	**135,056**	**1.17**	**23.13**
China	67,714	80,933	106,227	48,620	61,155	0.53	25.78
Japan	108,225	92,409	126,393	27,635	39,008	0.34	41.15
Korea, Republic of	57,857	27,585	45,024	26,437	27,414	0.24	3.70
Mongolia	325	471	311	252	237	0.00	-5.95
Taiwan, Province of China	18,331	7,414	11,042	6,743	7,242	0.06	7.40
South-East Asia	**152,011**	**154,479**	**176,156**	**121,454**	**127,126**	**1.10**	**4.67**
Cambodia	70	107	77	77	88	0.00	14.29
Indonesia	33,303	35,377	44,841	31,236	32,651	0.28	4.53
Malaysia	26,727	29,592	32,564	25,681	30,409	0.26	18.41
Philippines	64,191	62,358	67,477	44,332	45,668	0.40	3.01
Singapore	7,224	6,707	8,889	4,189	4,180	0.04	-0.21
Thailand	18,494	18,578	20,075	13,997	13,171	0.11	-5.90
Viet Nam	2,002	1,760	2,233	1,942	959	0.01	-50.62
Australasia	**78,667**	**74,772**	**84,007**	**43,573**	**39,984**	**0.35**	**-8.24**
Australia	66,653	63,029	71,723	36,676	33,280	0.29	-9.26
New Zealand	12,014	11,743	12,284	6,897	6,704	0.06	-2.80
Polynesia	**19**	**51**	**54**	**5**	**5**	**0.00**	**0.00**
Samoa	19	51	54	5	5	0.00	0.00

Yearbook of Tourism Statistics, Data 2008 – 2012, 2014 Edition

EGYPT

2. Arrivals of non-resident visitors at national borders, by nationality

	2008	2009	2010	2011	2012	Market share 2012	% Change 2012-2011
Other East Asia and the Pacific	11,742	10,302	9,804	3,147	2,755	0.02	-12.46
Other countries of Asia	11,742	10,302	9,804	3,147	2,755	0.02	-12.46
EUROPE	9,621,738	9,416,206	11,176,923	7,211,060	8,415,612	72.98	16.70
Central/Eastern Europe	2,913,014	2,879,908	3,943,193	2,480,873	3,239,061	28.09	30.56
Armenia	7,247	5,834	8,725	3,381	4,618	0.04	36.59
Azerbaijan	2,480	2,870	2,927	1,146	1,539	0.01	34.29
Bulgaria	18,457	15,562	15,513	5,896	5,143	0.04	-12.77
Czech Republic/Slovakia	268,189	216,798	287,617	158,674	134,940	1.17	-14.96
Estonia	50,112	35,353	29,405	18,638	24,095	0.21	29.28
Georgia	3,005	3,049	5,726	3,883	7,023	0.06	80.87
Hungary	65,598	58,528	68,428	48,381	43,001	0.37	-11.12
Kazakhstan	21,867	13,114	17,950	5,512	9,266	0.08	68.11
Poland	598,928	454,567	593,596	378,134	462,721	4.01	22.37
Romania	50,459	38,903	55,649	23,864	27,276	0.24	14.30
Russian Federation	1,825,312	2,035,330	2,855,723	1,832,388	2,518,275	21.84	37.43
Uzbekistan	1,360		1,934	976	1,164	0.01	19.26
Northern Europe	1,607,857	1,801,029	2,023,857	1,371,079	1,407,458	12.20	2.65
Denmark	84,744	100,349	135,051	93,347	126,062	1.09	35.05
Finland	63,763	65,227	93,865	42,191	41,133	0.36	-2.51
Iceland	743	624	879	614	1,360	0.01	121.50
Ireland	36,744	62,458	30,733	18,976	18,375	0.16	-3.17
Norway	66,577	66,948	97,431	64,716	74,483	0.65	15.09
Sweden	153,427	158,699	209,992	116,822	134,270	1.16	14.94
United Kingdom	1,201,859	1,346,724	1,455,906	1,034,413	1,011,775	8.77	-2.19
Southern Europe	1,375,935	1,309,096	1,450,553	671,699	834,608	7.24	24.25
Albania	5,686	5,127	4,034	3,115	2,467	0.02	-20.80
Croatia	10,018	9,407	11,891	5,248	6,068	0.05	15.63
Greece	62,291	45,849	53,236	18,678	19,464	0.17	4.21
Italy	1,073,159	1,047,997	1,144,384	555,246	718,703	6.23	29.44
Malta	1,689	2,081	2,821	4,524	1,739	0.02	-61.56
Portugal	15,878	17,182	20,451	8,607	8,688	0.08	0.94
Serbia and Montenegro	25,620	22,247	37,404	27,100	24,970	0.22	-7.86
Slovenia	25,358	22,979	26,930	14,272	18,317	0.16	28.34
Spain	156,236	136,227	149,402	34,909	34,192	0.30	-2.05
Western Europe	2,669,047	2,603,121	2,860,729	1,985,465	2,212,684	19.19	11.44
Austria	208,547	214,298	240,516	168,298	179,279	1.55	6.52
Belgium	209,007	189,475	195,919	155,793	150,401	1.30	-3.46
France	586,861	551,694	599,363	344,949	318,449	2.76	-7.68
Germany	1,202,509	1,202,339	1,328,960	964,599	1,164,556	10.10	20.73
Luxembourg	7,166	9,056	7,920	4,933	4,917	0.04	-0.32
Monaco	102	182	183	61			
Netherlands	279,765	249,017	291,154	206,684	239,237	2.07	15.75
Switzerland	175,090	187,060	196,714	140,148	155,845	1.35	11.20
East Mediterranean Europe	276,494	258,767	299,024	215,329	194,405	1.69	-9.72
Cyprus	11,215	9,411	9,195	3,566	3,980	0.03	11.61
Israel	213,125	203,275	226,456	177,808	132,217	1.15	-25.64
Turkey	52,154	46,081	63,373	33,955	58,208	0.50	71.43
Other Europe	779,391	564,285	599,567	486,615	527,396	4.57	8.38
Other countries of Europe	779,391	564,285	599,567	486,615	527,396	4.57	8.38
MIDDLE EAST	1,675,960	1,571,212	1,761,245	1,511,401	1,965,492	17.04	30.04
Bahrain	21,035	19,098	20,290	12,587	14,831	0.13	17.83
Iraq	26,170	32,437	38,432	35,137	38,950	0.34	10.85
Jordan	173,913	164,247	171,217	151,835	179,344	1.56	18.12
Kuwait	133,758	138,376	145,402	76,512	95,696	0.83	25.07
Lebanon	68,959	74,822	75,475	52,340	56,958	0.49	8.82
Libya	481,548	410,222	451,068	524,544	583,044	5.06	11.15

209

Yearbook of Tourism Statistics, Data 2008 – 2012, 2014 Edition

EGYPT

2. Arrivals of non-resident visitors at national borders, by nationality

	2008	2009	2010	2011	2012	Market share 2012	% Change 2012-2011
Oman	23,318	19,037	20,435	12,391	13,554	0.12	9.39
Palestine	68,353	104,712	177,333	229,844	326,815	2.83	42.19
Qatar	24,451	21,123	24,787	16,129	24,765	0.21	53.54
Saudi Arabia	402,287	347,971	374,946	198,320	241,635	2.10	21.84
Syrian Arab Republic	112,450	106,864	115,657	102,367	259,639	2.25	153.64
United Arab Emirates	53,552	49,578	53,815	24,661	27,034	0.23	9.62
Yemen	86,166	82,725	92,388	74,734	103,227	0.90	38.13
SOUTH ASIA	**116,199**	**118,004**	**144,192**	**101,718**	**107,602**	**0.93**	**5.78**
Afghanistan	720	894	1,126	732	1,420	0.01	93.99
Bangladesh	3,844	6,965	6,252	12,023	9,073	0.08	-24.54
India	88,811	86,698	114,248	73,443	82,698	0.72	12.60
Iran, Islamic Republic of	943	3,503	849	542	754	0.01	39.11
Maldives	279	230	258	218	153	0.00	-29.82
Nepal	1,191	1,413	1,589	1,558	1,008	0.01	-35.30
Pakistan	15,168	12,887	14,203	10,745	9,090	0.08	-15.40
Sri Lanka	5,243	5,414	5,667	2,457	3,406	0.03	38.62
NOT SPECIFIED	**39,485**	**38,000**	**34,654**	**20,967**	**24,778**	**0.21**	**18.18**
Other countries of the World	39,485	38,000	34,654	20,967	24,778	0.21	18.18

Yearbook of Tourism Statistics, Data 2008 – 2012, 2014 Editic

EGYPT

5. Overnight stays of non-resident tourists in hotels and similar establishments, by nationality

	2008	2009	2010	2011	2012	Market share 2012	% Change 2012-2011
TOTAL	129,233,930	126,533,535	147,385,089	114,213,521	137,818,546	100.00	20.67
AFRICA	5,112,829	5,357,057	5,956,672	6,100,700	5,898,603	4.28	-3.31
East Africa	329,869	450,945	468,586	377,237	398,295	0.29	5.58
Burundi	4,027	7,443	6,302	3,824	4,715	0.00	23.30
Comoros	36,174	22,437	11,993	9,950	2,820	0.00	-71.66
Djibouti	20,493	31,778	34,214	26,808	21,856	0.02	-18.47
Eritrea	32,524	37,741	35,698	38,814	38,497	0.03	-0.82
Ethiopia	90,499	144,588	154,521	114,463	126,755	0.09	10.74
Kenya	62,707	78,238	93,421	90,525	88,825	0.06	-1.88
Malawi	3,913	4,468	6,326	3,131	3,335	0.00	6.52
Mauritius	4,848	6,812	9,787	6,227	6,124	0.00	-1.65
Mozambique	4,033	4,703	4,090	2,943	1,863	0.00	-36.70
Rwanda	5,124	6,977	6,641	4,256	4,413	0.00	3.69
Seychelles	509	628	1,560	873	589	0.00	-32.53
Somalia	21,502	45,404	41,305	19,461	37,949	0.03	95.00
Uganda	14,606	20,981	16,995	21,878	30,876	0.02	41.13
United Republic of Tanzania	15,033	23,913	27,674	23,436	17,641	0.01	-24.73
Zambia	5,944	7,724	10,284	5,956	5,949	0.00	-0.12
Zimbabwe	7,933	7,110	7,775	4,692	6,088	0.00	29.75
Central Africa	93,325	108,539	110,183	416,279	97,551	0.07	-76.57
Angola	8,208	9,769	7,539	5,174	3,442	0.00	-33.48
Cameroon	11,308	18,014	14,996	11,708	21,799	0.02	86.19
Chad	57,429	60,846	65,681	391,786	55,620	0.04	-85.80
Congo	12,338	15,847	18,236	4,510	12,837	0.01	184.63
Gabon	4,042	4,063	3,731	3,101	3,853	0.00	24.25
North Africa	3,918,583	4,094,967	4,706,765	4,607,119	4,856,867	3.52	5.42
Algeria	363,696	447,637	198,863	140,645	220,149	0.16	56.53
Morocco	361,179	419,087	459,692	385,108	322,276	0.23	-16.32
Sudan	2,885,978	2,939,349	3,676,806	3,909,918	3,923,017	2.85	0.34
Tunisia	307,730	288,894	371,404	171,448	391,425	0.28	128.31
Southern Africa	251,161	205,790	227,142	159,839	150,939	0.11	-5.57
Lesotho	1,204	1,174	1,311	669	121	0.00	-81.91
Namibia	2,831	5,617	4,016	2,198	2,875	0.00	30.80
South Africa	245,160	196,939	220,803	156,679	147,498	0.11	-5.86
Swaziland	1,966	2,060	1,012	293	445	0.00	51.88
West Africa	497,436	467,852	428,039	516,223	355,521	0.26	-31.13
Côte d'Ivoire	10,995	12,313	13,540	9,018	15,545	0.01	72.38
Ghana	24,188	29,868	34,278	44,467	22,787	0.02	-48.76
Guinea	13,020	19,692	14,898	13,074	8,478	0.01	-35.15
Liberia	2,828	2,022	2,756	1,664	2,097	0.00	26.02
Mali	7,271	10,482	5,916	14,381	13,867	0.01	-3.57
Mauritania	12,489	17,655	14,735	15,121	11,389	0.01	-24.68
Niger	56,911	15,221	7,269	58,604	11,717	0.01	-80.01
Nigeria	347,168	337,594	316,364	344,069	257,036	0.19	-25.30
Senegal	15,901	16,001	12,304	12,439	10,937	0.01	-12.07
Sierra Leone	2,558	3,604	2,487	1,832	338	0.00	-81.55
Togo	4,107	3,400	3,492	1,554	1,330	0.00	-14.41
Other Africa	22,455	28,964	15,957	24,003	39,430	0.03	64.27
Other countries of Africa	22,455	28,964	15,957	24,003	39,430	0.03	64.27
AMERICAS	5,988,387	5,813,541	6,621,105	4,351,353	4,109,006	2.98	-5.57
Caribbean	24,758	26,897	23,784	17,809	18,863	0.01	5.92
Bahamas	348	742	203	165	114	0.00	-30.91
Barbados	853	534	381	53	340	0.00	541.51
Cuba	7,849	9,139	5,738	4,702	4,080	0.00	-13.23
Dominica	5,128	4,597	4,016	4,197	3,813	0.00	-9.15

211

EGYPT

5. Overnight stays of non-resident tourists in hotels and similar establishments, by nationality

	2008	2009	2010	2011	2012	Market share 2012	% Change 2012-2011
Haiti	557	1,267	471	171	133	0.00	-22.22
Jamaica	1,971	2,272	2,773	2,203	1,185	0.00	-46.21
Trinidad and Tobago	8,052	8,346	10,202	6,318	9,198	0.01	45.58
Central America	**52,640**	**49,037**	**53,795**	**26,650**	**55,229**	**0.04**	**107.24**
Costa Rica	12,538	11,457	13,939	7,405	31,645	0.02	327.35
El Salvador	27,099	16,800	10,811	5,281	13,009	0.01	146.34
Guatemala	5,948	10,198	17,022	6,145	7,790	0.01	26.77
Honduras	3,536	5,644	5,642	5,218	1,129	0.00	-78.36
Nicaragua	1,446	1,574	1,789	726	590	0.00	-18.73
Panama	2,073	3,364	4,592	1,875	1,066	0.00	-43.15
North America	**5,303,908**	**5,201,244**	**5,869,144**	**3,824,276**	**3,503,882**	**2.54**	**-8.38**
Canada	1,101,333	1,133,889	1,255,121	858,008	809,422	0.59	-5.66
Mexico	146,115	110,542	144,387	63,865	89,460	0.06	40.08
United States of America	4,056,460	3,956,813	4,469,636	2,902,403	2,605,000	1.89	-10.25
South America	**603,993**	**533,105**	**670,634**	**480,695**	**530,352**	**0.38**	**10.33**
Argentina	99,677	102,793	134,008	76,337	77,403	0.06	1.40
Bolivia	6,629	5,222	6,350	5,692	3,963	0.00	-30.38
Brazil	212,873	175,243	257,884	186,480	189,994	0.14	1.88
Chile	43,420	42,883	49,486	29,718	34,778	0.03	17.03
Colombia	99,998	99,401	105,020	89,722	109,460	0.08	22.00
Ecuador	26,534	23,561	36,417	26,976	42,221	0.03	56.51
Paraguay	1,487	3,500	2,869	1,744	1,933	0.00	10.84
Peru	21,557	22,449	25,477	19,147	26,415	0.02	37.96
Suriname	918	871	249	81	191	0.00	135.80
Uruguay	16,345	16,524	15,206	14,008	13,915	0.01	-0.66
Venezuela	74,555	40,658	37,668	30,790	30,079	0.02	-2.31
Other Americas	**3,088**	**3,258**	**3,748**	**1,923**	**680**	**0.00**	**-64.64**
Other countries of the Americas	3,088	3,258	3,748	1,923	680	0.00	-64.64
EAST ASIA AND THE PACIFIC	**4,084,051**	**3,818,962**	**5,861,271**	**2,921,263**	**2,951,172**	**2.14**	**1.02**
North-East Asia	**1,737,958**	**1,652,441**	**2,288,906**	**1,228,574**	**1,348,519**	**0.98**	**9.76**
China	540,852	642,331	880,756	555,323	643,130	0.47	15.81
Japan	745,838	707,721	877,508	332,490	308,791	0.22	-7.13
Korea, Republic of	361,697	227,518	347,497	270,570	313,999	0.23	16.05
Mongolia	2,727	8,697	4,008	3,949	2,224	0.00	-43.68
Taiwan, Province of China	86,844	66,174	179,137	66,242	80,375	0.06	21.34
South-East Asia	**1,158,156**	**1,025,127**	**1,161,642**	**946,086**	**944,254**	**0.69**	**-0.19**
Cambodia	310	530	646	204	279	0.00	36.76
Indonesia	423,877	331,638	327,675	259,983	408,271	0.30	57.04
Malaysia	197,960	206,536	245,785	223,029	199,038	0.14	-10.76
Philippines	380,850	324,148	410,095	296,380	231,009	0.17	-22.06
Singapore	77,338	86,415	97,862	69,880	54,169	0.04	-22.48
Thailand	77,821	75,860	79,579	96,610	51,488	0.04	-46.71
Australasia	**1,082,839**	**1,056,791**	**1,122,553**	**702,092**	**621,416**	**0.45**	**-11.49**
Australia	935,995	919,436	977,937	604,408	527,127	0.38	-12.79
New Zealand	146,844	137,355	144,616	97,684	94,289	0.07	-3.48
Polynesia	**18**	**45**	**56**	**4**	**4**	**0.00**	**0.00**
Samoa	18	45	56	4	4	0.00	0.00
Other East Asia and the Pacific	**105,080**	**84,558**	**1,288,114**	**44,507**	**36,979**	**0.03**	**-16.91**
Other countries of Asia	105,080	84,558	1,288,114	44,507	36,979	0.03	-16.91
EUROPE	**90,870,680**	**89,331,393**	**102,969,099**	**73,976,481**	**92,091,887**	**66.82**	**24.49**
Central/Eastern Europe	**22,120,075**	**24,974,882**	**33,738,278**	**20,299,965**	**31,264,097**	**22.68**	**54.01**
Armenia	65,054	64,241	71,008	27,741	45,880	0.03	65.39
Azerbaijan	22,522	27,527	25,061	21,582	19,471	0.01	-9.78
Bulgaria	173,243	138,967	129,931	70,745	56,546	0.04	-20.07
Czech Republic/Slovakia	2,119,978	1,843,756	2,441,086	1,435,309	1,270,117	0.92	-11.51
Estonia	391,799	263,617	223,861	157,134	377,449	0.27	140.21

212

Yearbook of Tourism Statistics, Data 2008 – 2012, 2014 Edition

EGYPT

5. Overnight stays of non-resident tourists in hotels and similar establishments, by nationality

	2008	2009	2010	2011	2012	Market share 2012	% Change 2012-2011
Georgia	24,411	27,762	58,858	35,334	78,229	0.06	121.40
Hungary	589,160	523,747	557,788	477,576	494,559	0.36	3.56
Kazakhstan	260,121	125,919	169,429	65,082	94,170	0.07	44.69
Poland	4,529,071	3,721,789	4,546,312	3,248,698	4,415,632	3.20	35.92
Romania	561,880	319,827	477,899	327,330	380,451	0.28	16.23
Russian Federation	13,382,836	17,917,730	25,037,045	14,433,434	24,031,593	17.44	66.50
Northern Europe	**17,427,199**	**18,306,200**	**21,001,596**	**16,302,687**	**17,645,754**	**12.80**	**8.24**
Denmark	1,119,794	1,129,413	1,469,239	1,266,824	1,586,174	1.15	25.21
Finland	704,038	558,535	914,589	564,362	525,726	0.38	-6.85
Iceland	9,299	6,781	9,396	6,719	5,257	0.00	-21.76
Ireland	413,763	337,774	332,812	258,976	232,368	0.17	-10.27
Norway	778,045	733,639	1,062,004	939,160	1,015,542	0.74	8.13
Sweden	1,948,731	1,746,785	2,315,656	1,809,540	1,733,804	1.26	-4.19
United Kingdom	12,453,529	13,793,273	14,897,900	11,457,106	12,546,883	9.10	9.51
Southern Europe	**13,467,392**	**11,778,286**	**12,945,224**	**7,393,784**	**9,166,151**	**6.65**	**23.97**
Albania	87,621	58,796	49,028	43,332	27,301	0.02	-37.00
Croatia	178,623	127,828	117,065	83,720	103,152	0.07	23.21
Greece	455,660	345,479	400,846	228,658	238,808	0.17	4.44
Italy	10,310,777	9,307,804	9,972,492	6,007,113	7,757,406	5.63	29.14
Malta	15,739	21,774	31,145	16,257	21,325	0.02	31.17
Portugal	153,118	172,143	196,867	112,236	114,527	0.08	2.04
Serbia and Montenegro	356,149	212,665	401,660	310,538	235,324	0.17	-24.22
Slovenia	239,567	202,543	229,338	118,547	228,279	0.17	92.56
Spain	1,670,138	1,329,254	1,546,783	473,383	440,029	0.32	-7.05
Western Europe	**30,584,190**	**28,474,255**	**30,490,671**	**24,299,933**	**27,822,806**	**20.19**	**14.50**
Austria	2,720,936	2,451,865	2,778,529	2,545,486	2,163,113	1.57	-15.02
Belgium	2,114,218	1,951,145	2,005,681	1,665,382	1,788,216	1.30	7.38
France	6,117,383	5,603,877	5,253,060	3,484,272	3,110,938	2.26	-10.71
Germany	14,389,205	13,578,690	14,920,653	11,982,252	15,443,700	11.21	28.89
Luxembourg	75,516	90,078	88,874	44,246	64,211	0.05	45.12
Monaco	1,109	963	1,486	322			
Netherlands	3,214,069	2,930,926	3,471,090	2,921,817	3,422,938	2.48	17.15
Switzerland	1,951,754	1,866,711	1,971,298	1,656,156	1,829,690	1.33	10.48
East Mediterranean Europe	**2,335,736**	**1,564,214**	**1,862,701**	**1,554,914**	**1,720,688**	**1.25**	**10.66**
Cyprus	72,285	72,403	77,869	55,205	47,350	0.03	-14.23
Israel	1,820,323	1,068,808	1,168,750	1,069,937	1,178,908	0.86	10.18
Turkey	443,128	423,003	616,082	429,772	494,430	0.36	15.04
Other Europe	**4,936,088**	**4,233,556**	**2,930,629**	**4,125,198**	**4,472,391**	**3.25**	**8.42**
Other countries of Europe	4,936,088	4,233,556	2,930,629	4,125,198	4,472,391	3.25	8.42
MIDDLE EAST	**21,391,309**	**20,833,755**	**24,313,983**	**25,593,272**	**31,293,260**	**22.71**	**22.27**
Bahrain	338,794	308,319	310,250	191,067	245,897	0.18	28.70
Iraq	468,652	490,934	538,607	750,661	594,621	0.43	-20.79
Jordan	1,705,117	1,669,592	1,936,773	2,535,977	2,693,269	1.95	6.20
Kuwait	2,109,507	2,158,996	2,126,279	1,111,225	1,926,926	1.40	73.41
Lebanon	673,407	685,059	722,037	735,614	1,051,545	0.76	42.95
Libya	5,397,908	5,194,416	6,151,782	8,351,661	8,259,890	5.99	-1.10
Oman	385,979	306,367	320,584	251,165	244,457	0.18	-2.67
Palestine	953,861	1,254,741	2,555,718	3,685,800	3,794,361	2.75	2.95
Qatar	346,585	329,682	369,349	270,589	592,592	0.43	119.00
Saudi Arabia	5,459,214	4,846,004	5,236,041	3,901,955	5,404,566	3.92	38.51
Syrian Arab Republic	1,191,379	1,180,034	1,384,272	1,602,653	3,468,166	2.52	116.40
United Arab Emirates	664,207	751,068	778,397	321,717	377,160	0.27	17.23
Yemen	1,696,699	1,658,543	1,883,894	1,883,188	2,639,810	1.92	40.18
SOUTH ASIA	**1,101,577**	**1,006,483**	**1,248,102**	**1,056,534**	**1,177,490**	**0.85**	**11.45**
Afghanistan	7,598	12,784	14,414	7,718	24,358	0.02	215.60
Bangladesh	29,756	53,998	41,861	128,775	58,214	0.04	-54.79

213

EGYPT

5. Overnight stays of non-resident tourists in hotels and similar establishments, by nationality

	2008	2009	2010	2011	2012	Market share 2012	% Change 2012-2011
India	794,752	698,893	929,390	711,653	892,304	0.65	25.38
Iran, Islamic Republic of	10,674	12,631	14,620	5,672	22,646	0.02	299.26
Maldives	2,122	1,864	1,885	2,033	173	0.00	-91.49
Nepal	16,542	16,489	21,112	17,423	9,953	0.01	-42.87
Pakistan	169,477	145,826	152,900	139,212	126,841	0.09	-8.89
Sri Lanka	70,656	63,998	71,920	44,048	43,001	0.03	-2.38
NOT SPECIFIED	**685,097**	**372,344**	**414,857**	**213,918**	**297,128**	**0.22**	**38.90**
Other countries of the World	685,097	372,344	414,857	213,918	297,128	0.22	38.90

EL SALVADOR

1. Arrivals of non-resident tourists at national borders, by nationality

	2008	2009	2010	2011	2012	Market share 2012	% Change 2012-2011
TOTAL	1,384,773	1,090,926	1,149,562	1,184,497	1,254,724	100.00	5.93
AFRICA	172	91	172	488	883	0.07	80.94
Southern Africa	46	11	156	120	46	0.00	-61.67
South Africa	46	11	156	120	46	0.00	-61.67
Other Africa	126	80	16	368	837	0.07	127.45
Other countries of Africa	126	80	16	368	837	0.07	127.45
AMERICAS	1,342,824	1,066,917	1,122,757	1,139,772	1,219,748	97.21	7.02
Caribbean	3,249	2,452	2,602	3,086	3,078	0.25	-0.26
Cuba	519	596	861	580	594	0.05	2.41
Dominican Republic	2,009	1,321	1,292	1,847	1,475	0.12	-20.14
Haiti	120	95	95	110	87	0.01	-20.91
Jamaica	198	162	119	154	162	0.01	5.19
Trinidad and Tobago	222	66	156	152	239	0.02	57.24
Other countries of the Caribbean	181	212	79	243	521	0.04	114.40
Central America	889,531	673,324	739,843	734,796	740,698	59.03	0.80
Belize	2,342	1,611	2,508	1,317	2,284	0.18	73.42
Costa Rica	27,668	17,714	18,443	20,300	20,306	1.62	0.03
Guatemala	537,578	462,944	518,957	535,245	537,612	42.85	0.44
Honduras	213,075	138,104	145,868	126,446	136,451	10.87	7.91
Nicaragua	96,956	42,844	43,488	40,755	32,566	2.60	-20.09
Panama	11,912	10,107	10,579	10,733	11,479	0.91	6.95
North America	422,907	371,280	356,608	368,641	443,075	35.31	20.19
Canada	32,050	26,333	20,432	28,205	30,216	2.41	7.13
Mexico	28,999	17,633	17,607	19,699	15,950	1.27	-19.03
United States of America	361,858	327,314	318,569	320,737	396,909	31.63	23.75
South America	27,137	19,861	23,704	33,249	32,897	2.62	-1.06
Argentina	4,291	2,673	2,501	3,727	2,524	0.20	-32.28
Bolivia	607	409	401	562	473	0.04	-15.84
Brazil	4,337	3,613	4,180	4,816	4,099	0.33	-14.89
Chile	2,872	1,511	2,090	2,194	1,717	0.14	-21.74
Colombia	6,661	5,957	7,698	12,062	14,913	1.19	23.64
Ecuador	1,503	1,016	1,108	1,706	2,056	0.16	20.52
Paraguay	229	243	322	458	278	0.02	-39.30
Peru	3,292	1,914	2,269	4,334	4,149	0.33	-4.27
Uruguay	838	69	1,183	680	588	0.05	-13.53
Venezuela	2,497	501	1,871	2,656	2,085	0.17	-21.50
Other countries of South America	10	1,955	81	54	15	0.00	-72.22
EAST ASIA AND THE PACIFIC	8,556	5,068	6,750	9,858	8,001	0.64	-18.84
North-East Asia	4,676	1,845	4,011	5,823	4,380	0.35	-24.78
China	1,714	704	2,276	1,527	1,452	0.12	-4.91
Japan	1,882	863	839	3,184	2,354	0.19	-26.07
Korea, Republic of	771	278	896	1,112	574	0.05	-48.38
Taiwan, Province of China	309						
Australasia	1,707	1,803	1,784	2,764	2,337	0.19	-15.45
Australia	1,584	1,706	1,745	2,508	1,989	0.16	-20.69
New Zealand	123	97	39	256	348	0.03	35.94
Other East Asia and the Pacific	2,173	1,420	955	1,271	1,284	0.10	1.02
Other countries of Asia	2,150	1,323	916	1,221	1,144	0.09	-6.31
Other countries of Oceania	23	97	39	50	140	0.01	180.00
EUROPE	33,198	18,842	19,879	34,351	26,068	2.08	-24.11
Central/Eastern Europe	3,566	900	1,004	347	133	0.01	-61.67
Czech Republic/Slovakia	2,994	677	877	250	72	0.01	-71.20
Poland	572	223	127	97	61	0.00	-37.11

Yearbook of Tourism Statistics, Data 2008 – 2012, 2014 Edition

EL SALVADOR

1. Arrivals of non-resident tourists at national borders, by nationality

	2008	2009	2010	2011	2012	Market share 2012	% Change 2012-2011
Northern Europe	**6,215**	**3,145**	**2,238**	**3,921**	**3,498**	**0.28**	**-10.79**
Denmark	1,311	286	284	275	267	0.02	-2.91
Finland	176	105	68	145	139	0.01	-4.14
Iceland	12	539	22	91	18	0.00	-80.22
Ireland	891	421	407	341	274	0.02	-19.65
Norway	270	135	161	197	257	0.02	30.46
Sweden	1,379	632	537	953	904	0.07	-5.14
United Kingdom	2,176	1,027	759	1,919	1,639	0.13	-14.59
Southern Europe	**12,037**	**8,575**	**8,462**	**16,174**	**12,525**	**1.00**	**-22.56**
Greece	172	109	46	61	52	0.00	-14.75
Italy	3,054	2,843	2,475	5,228	3,611	0.29	-30.93
Portugal	232	85	86	265	238	0.02	-10.19
Spain	8,543	5,496	5,843	10,620	8,624	0.69	-18.79
Yugoslavia, SFR (former)	36	42	12				
Western Europe	**9,630**	**5,401**	**5,233**	**11,129**	**7,961**	**0.63**	**-28.47**
Austria	199	185	146	365	207	0.02	-43.29
Belgium	822	260	365	471	392	0.03	-16.77
France	2,063	1,780	1,332	3,023	2,239	0.18	-25.93
Germany	4,128	1,968	2,020	4,993	3,265	0.26	-34.61
Netherlands	1,273	419	589	1,368	1,051	0.08	-23.17
Switzerland	1,145	789	781	909	807	0.06	-11.22
East Mediterranean Europe	**542**	**376**	**477**	**460**	**324**	**0.03**	**-29.57**
Israel	542	376	477	460	324	0.03	-29.57
Other Europe	**1,208**	**445**	**2,465**	**2,320**	**1,627**	**0.13**	**-29.87**
Other countries of Europe	1,208	445	2,465	2,320	1,627	0.13	-29.87
MIDDLE EAST	**23**	**8**	**4**	**28**	**24**	**0.00**	**-14.29**
Egypt	23	8	4	28	24	0.00	-14.29

Yearbook of Tourism Statistics, Data 2008 – 2012, 2014 Edition

EL SALVADOR

3. Arrivals of non-resident tourists in hotels and similar establishments, by nationality

	2008	2009	2010	2011	2012	Market share 2012	% Change 2012-2011
TOTAL	376,170	461,436	595,281	642,280	599,559	100.00	-6.65
AFRICA	2	48	70	202	371	0.06	83.66
Southern Africa		48	70	47	20	0.00	-57.45
South Africa		48	70	47	20	0.00	-57.45
Other Africa	2			155	351	0.06	126.45
Other countries of Africa				155	351	0.06	126.45
All countries of Africa	2						
AMERICAS	361,976	451,021	586,178	624,801	585,268	97.62	-6.33
Caribbean	1,413	1,299	1,057	1,691	1,188	0.20	-29.75
Cuba	5	316	350	318	229	0.04	-27.99
Dominican Republic	1,083	700	525	1,013	569	0.09	-43.83
Jamaica	107	50	39	84	63	0.01	-25.00
Trinidad and Tobago	120	86	48	83	92	0.02	10.84
Other countries of the Caribbean	98	147	95	193	235	0.04	21.76
Central America	288,159	316,414	457,164	504,219	492,983	82.22	-2.23
Belize	792	596	676	722	881	0.15	22.02
Costa Rica	9,352	6,554	4,970	11,132	7,835	1.31	-29.62
Guatemala	176,863	241,194	372,871	416,082	414,588	69.15	-0.36
Honduras	59,022	44,193	48,064	41,991	44,752	7.46	6.58
Nicaragua	38,104	20,137	27,732	28,406	20,498	3.42	-27.84
Panama	4,026	3,740	2,851	5,886	4,429	0.74	-24.75
North America	63,414	119,173	115,975	99,466	70,153	11.70	-29.47
Canada	12,179	8,690	6,835	11,022	12,285	2.05	11.46
Mexico	6,003	2,469	2,579	11,403	4,609	0.77	-59.58
United States of America	45,232	108,014	106,561	77,041	53,259	8.88	-30.87
South America	8,990	7,861	7,248	13,308	15,072	2.51	13.26
Argentina	2,304	1,902	1,264	2,177	1,608	0.27	-26.14
Colombia	3,577	4,240	3,891	7,047	9,494	1.58	34.72
Peru	1,768	1,362	1,147	2,532	2,642	0.44	4.34
Venezuela	1,341	357	946	1,552	1,328	0.22	-14.43
Other Americas		6,274	4,734	6,117	5,872	0.98	-4.01
Other countries of the Americas		6,274	4,734	6,117	5,872	0.98	-4.01
EAST ASIA AND THE PACIFIC	66	2,537	2,379	3,852	3,276	0.55	-14.95
North-East Asia	32	830	1,266	1,841	1,549	0.26	-15.86
China	15	373	925	597	591	0.10	-1.01
Japan	17	457	341	1,244	958	0.16	-22.99
Australasia	15	955	725	1,080	951	0.16	-11.94
Australia	14	904	709	980	809	0.13	-17.45
New Zealand	1	51	16	100	142	0.02	42.00
Other East Asia and the Pacific	19	752	388	931	776	0.13	-16.65
Other countries of Asia	19	701	372	911	716	0.12	-21.41
Other countries of Oceania		51	16	20	60	0.01	200.00
EUROPE	14,112	7,830	6,652	13,423	10,633	1.77	-20.79
Northern Europe	1,813	767	474	883	779	0.13	-11.78
Ireland	527	223	165	133	112	0.02	-15.79
United Kingdom	1,286	544	309	750	667	0.11	-11.07
Southern Europe	6,854	4,420	3,381	6,193	4,977	0.83	-19.64
Italy	1,805	1,507	1,006	2,043	1,469	0.25	-28.10
Spain	5,049	2,913	2,375	4,150	3,508	0.59	-15.47
Western Europe	4,411	2,208	1,601	3,667	2,667	0.44	-27.27
France	1,219	943	541	1,181	911	0.15	-22.86
Germany	2,440	1,043	821	1,951	1,328	0.22	-31.93
Netherlands	752	222	239	535	428	0.07	-20.00

Yearbook of Tourism Statistics, Data 2008 – 2012, 2014 Edition

EL SALVADOR

3. Arrivals of non-resident tourists in hotels and similar establishments, by nationality

	2008	2009	2010	2011	2012	Market share 2012	% Change 2012-2011
East Mediterranean Europe	320	199	194	180	133	0.02	-26.11
Israel	320	199	194	180	133	0.02	-26.11
Other Europe	714	236	1,002	2,500	2,077	0.35	-16.92
Other countries of Europe	714	236	1,002	2,500	2,077	0.35	-16.92
MIDDLE EAST	14		2	2	11	0.00	450.00
Egypt	14		2	2	11	0.00	450.00

Yearbook of Tourism Statistics, Data 2008 – 2012, 2014 Edition

EL SALVADOR

5. Overnight stays of non-resident tourists in hotels and similar establishments, by nationality

	2008	2009	2010	2011	2012	Market share 2012	% Change 2012-2011
TOTAL		2,741,223	2,815,521	2,694,470	2,367,753	100.00	-12.13
AFRICA				1,803	3,650	0.15	102.44
Other Africa				1,803	3,650	0.15	102.44
All countries of Africa				1,803	3,650	0.15	102.44
AMERICAS		2,667,294	2,767,057	2,538,226	2,231,342	94.24	-12.09
Caribbean		6,130	6,505	14,046	12,377	0.52	-11.88
All countries of the Caribbean		6,130	6,505	14,046	12,377	0.52	-11.88
Central America		1,683,310	1,809,771	1,390,387	1,276,372	53.91	-8.20
Belize		4,029	6,270	5,994	9,183	0.39	53.20
Costa Rica		44,285	26,448	92,393	81,637	3.45	-11.64
Guatemala		1,157,361	1,297,393	954,245	892,586	37.70	-6.46
Honduras		345,260	364,670	152,449	139,962	5.91	-8.19
Nicaragua		107,110	108,720	136,456	106,853	4.51	-21.69
Panama		25,265	6,270	48,850	46,151	1.95	-5.53
North America		928,202	891,521	932,237	734,811	31.03	-21.18
Canada		65,834	51,080	98,532	117,258	4.95	19.00
Mexico		44,084	44,018	98,421	43,859	1.85	-55.44
United States of America		818,284	796,423	735,284	573,694	24.23	-21.98
South America		49,652	59,260	201,556	207,782	8.78	3.09
All countries of South America		49,652	59,260	201,556	207,782	8.78	3.09
EAST ASIA AND THE PACIFIC		8,163	10,579	36,045	32,540	1.37	-9.72
Other East Asia and the Pacific		8,163	10,579	36,045	32,540	1.37	-9.72
All countries East Asia/Pacific		8,163	10,579	36,045	32,540	1.37	-9.72
EUROPE		65,766	37,885	118,396	100,221	4.23	-15.35
Southern Europe		13,740	26,294	37,100	33,482	1.41	-9.75
Spain		13,740	26,294	37,100	33,482	1.41	-9.75
Western Europe		4,921	9,090	17,443	12,679	0.54	-27.31
Germany		4,921	9,090	17,443	12,679	0.54	-27.31
Other Europe		47,105	2,501	63,853	54,060	2.28	-15.34
Other countries of Europe		47,105	2,501	63,853	54,060	2.28	-15.34

Yearbook of Tourism Statistics, Data 2008 – 2012, 2014 Edition

EL SALVADOR

6. Overnight stays of non-resident tourists in all types of accommodation establishments, by nationality

	2008	2009	2010	2011	2012	Market share 2012	% Change 2012-2011
TOTAL	9,642,351	5,844,349	6,045,433	6,404,634	7,516,856	100.00	17.37
AFRICA	1,617	683	1,118	4,613	8,651	0.12	87.54
Other Africa	1,617	683	1,118	4,613	8,651	0.12	87.54
All countries of Africa	1,617	683	1,118	4,613	8,651	0.12	87.54
AMERICAS	9,447,888	5,712,853	5,932,413	6,004,796	7,183,025	95.56	19.62
Caribbean	30,541	18,390	16,913	25,614	32,078	0.43	25.24
All countries of the Caribbean	30,541	18,390	16,913	25,614	32,078	0.43	25.24
Central America	3,397,116	2,760,903	3,443,471	2,150,875	2,108,974	28.06	-1.95
Belize	26,699	12,086	16,302	10,931	23,801	0.32	117.74
Costa Rica	315,415	132,856	119,880	168,490	211,588	2.81	25.58
Guatemala	1,774,007	1,481,422	2,335,307	1,227,534	1,157,452	15.40	-5.71
Honduras	767,070	925,889	656,406	459,061	426,756	5.68	-7.04
Nicaragua	378,128	132,856	195,696	195,775	169,763	2.26	-13.29
Panama	135,797	75,794	119,880	89,084	119,614	1.59	34.27
North America	5,748,861	2,784,604	2,317,953	3,483,323	4,715,615	62.73	35.38
Canada	304,475	197,501	132,808	252,150	288,407	3.84	14.38
Mexico	342,188	132,251	114,446	170,025	151,775	2.02	-10.73
United States of America	5,102,198	2,454,852	2,070,699	3,061,148	4,275,433	56.88	39.67
South America	271,370	148,956	154,076	344,984	326,358	4.34	-5.40
All countries of South America	271,370	148,956	154,076	344,984	326,358	4.34	-5.40
EAST ASIA AND THE PACIFIC	80,426	62,038	32,026	92,242	79,461	1.06	-13.86
Other East Asia and the Pacific	80,426	62,038	32,026	92,242	79,461	1.06	-13.86
All countries East Asia/Pacific	80,426	62,038	32,026	92,242	79,461	1.06	-13.86
EUROPE	112,420	68,775	79,876	302,983	245,719	3.27	-18.90
Southern Europe	69,198	41,219	37,980	94,942	82,319	1.10	-13.30
Spain	69,198	41,219	37,980	94,942	82,319	1.10	-13.30
Western Europe	33,437	14,763	30,300	44,637	31,167	0.41	-30.18
Germany	33,437	14,763	30,300	44,637	31,167	0.41	-30.18
Other Europe	9,785	12,793	11,596	163,404	132,233	1.76	-19.08
Other countries of Europe	9,785	12,793	11,596	163,404	132,233	1.76	-19.08

Yearbook of Tourism Statistics, Data 2008 – 2012, 2014 Edition

ERITREA

2. Arrivals of non-resident visitors at national borders, by nationality

	2008	2009	2010	2011	2012	Market share 2012	% Change 2012-2011
TOTAL	69,897	79,334	83,947	107,090			
AFRICA	4,929	6,825	7,854	21,319			
East Africa	677	466	804	662			
Ethiopia	38	32	68	49			
Kenya	312	234	247	343			
Madagascar	1						
Malawi	14	11	15	7			
Mozambique	10	3	3	8			
Somalia	152	44	75	30			
Uganda	29	22	67	35			
United Republic of Tanzania	19	14	14	15			
Zambia	52	68	214	102			
Zimbabwe	50	38	101	73			
North Africa	3,570	5,866	6,220	19,653			
Sudan	3,570	5,866	6,220	19,653			
Southern Africa	168	157	460	471			
Botswana	2	2	6	3			
Namibia	7	2	4	16			
South Africa	159	153	450	452			
Other Africa	514	336	370	533			
Other countries of Africa	514	336	370	533			
AMERICAS	858	775	1,149	1,314			
North America	728	710	1,085	1,269			
Canada	229	199	347	438			
United States of America	499	511	738	831			
Other Americas	130	65	64	45			
Other countries of the Americas	130	65	64	45			
EAST ASIA AND THE PACIFIC	1,824	1,403	1,436	1,698			
North-East Asia	1,322	858	659	1,010			
China	468	671	594	871			
Japan	773	151	60	78			
Korea, Republic of	81	36	5	61			
South-East Asia	95	211	272	179			
Indonesia	12	27	34	48			
Malaysia	35	2	5	12			
Philippines	47	182	233	117			
Singapore	1			2			
Australasia	191	196	215	322			
Australia	165	183	186	291			
New Zealand	26	13	29	31			
Other East Asia and the Pacific	216	138	290	187			
Other countries of Asia	216	138	290	187			
EUROPE	5,182	5,064	4,869	5,169			
Northern Europe	1,040	1,249	1,143	1,324			
United Kingdom	680	843	703	968			
Scandinavia	360	406	440	356			
Southern Europe	2,108	1,944	1,754	1,694			
Italy	2,108	1,944	1,754	1,694			
Western Europe	1,499	1,373	1,609	1,610			
Benelux	58	49	41	47			
France	270	372	381	260			
Germany	742	775	880	1,004			
Netherlands	267	78	151	159			
Switzerland	156	75	104	138			

Yearbook of Tourism Statistics, Data 2008 – 2012, 2014 Edition

ERITREA

2. Arrivals of non-resident visitors at national borders, by nationality

	2008	2009	2010	2011	2012	Market share 2012	% Change 2012-2011
Other countries of Western Europe	6	24	52	2			
East Mediterranean Europe	**52**	**25**	**19**	**35**			
Israel	52	25	19	35			
Other Europe	**483**	**473**	**344**	**506**			
Other countries of Europe	483	473	344	506			
MIDDLE EAST	**1,494**	**1,343**	**1,326**	**1,224**			
Egypt	347	262	282	304			
Saudi Arabia	553	423	261	392			
Yemen	161	275	473	299			
Other countries of Middle East	433	383	310	229			
SOUTH ASIA	**395**	**718**	**730**	**577**			
India	395	718	730	577			
NOT SPECIFIED	**55,215**	**63,206**	**66,583**	**75,789**			
Other countries of the World	44	41					
Nationals Residing Abroad	55,171	63,165	66,583	75,789			

Yearbook of Tourism Statistics, Data 2008 – 2012, 2014 Edition

ESTONIA

3. Arrivals of non-resident tourists in hotels and similar establishments, by country of residence

	2008	2009	2010	2011	2012	Market share 2012	% Change 2012-2011
TOTAL	1,353,034	1,307,548	1,487,497	1,702,592	1,746,733	100.00	2.59
AFRICA	1,087	880	1,155	1,946	1,881	0.11	-3.34
Southern Africa	258	219	230	404	411	0.02	1.73
South Africa	258	219	230	404	411	0.02	1.73
Other Africa	829	661	925	1,542	1,470	0.08	-4.67
Other countries of Africa	829	661	925	1,542	1,470	0.08	-4.67
AMERICAS	22,477	20,387	24,996	29,728	35,682	2.04	20.03
North America	20,259	18,509	21,748	25,918	31,101	1.78	20.00
Canada	2,861	3,876	2,807	3,725	3,801	0.22	2.04
United States of America	17,398	14,633	18,941	22,193	27,300	1.56	23.01
South America	777	1,034	1,833	1,700	2,640	0.15	55.29
Brazil	777	1,034	1,833	1,700	2,640	0.15	55.29
Other Americas	1,441	844	1,415	2,110	1,941	0.11	-8.01
Other countries of the Americas	1,441	844	1,415	2,110	1,941	0.11	-8.01
EAST ASIA AND THE PACIFIC	16,087	18,164	19,943	26,416	32,121	1.84	21.60
North-East Asia	8,843	10,016	11,464	15,534	17,552	1.00	12.99
China	1,701	1,888	2,642	5,185	5,426	0.31	4.65
Japan	6,578	6,973	6,988	8,263	8,138	0.47	-1.51
Korea, Republic of	564	1,155	1,834	2,086	3,988	0.23	91.18
Australasia	3,295	3,046	3,127	4,383	3,917	0.22	-10.63
Australia	3,295	3,046	3,127	4,383	3,917	0.22	-10.63
Other East Asia and the Pacific	3,949	5,102	5,352	6,499	10,652	0.61	63.90
Other countries of Asia	3,110	4,487	4,708	5,696	9,837	0.56	72.70
Other countries of Oceania	839	615	644	803	815	0.05	1.49
EUROPE	1,312,582	1,264,256	1,429,858	1,632,102	1,663,515	95.24	1.92
Central/Eastern Europe	215,800	206,269	261,785	353,824	422,271	24.17	19.34
Bulgaria	925	916	1,501	1,559	1,522	0.09	-2.37
Czech Republic	4,299	4,385	3,855	4,588	5,385	0.31	17.37
Hungary	3,062	2,015	2,447	3,318	3,073	0.18	-7.38
Latvia	67,755	59,849	63,625	74,751	86,502	4.95	15.72
Lithuania	36,285	29,077	29,848	41,543	41,699	2.39	0.38
Poland	18,253	15,001	17,491	24,807	22,921	1.31	-7.60
Romania	1,028	1,128	1,257	2,213	2,140	0.12	-3.30
Russian Federation	78,494	89,429	135,665	192,456	247,975	14.20	28.85
Slovakia	1,154	860	1,393	1,469	2,441	0.14	66.17
Ukraine	4,545	3,609	4,703	7,120	8,613	0.49	20.97
Northern Europe	897,890	889,818	975,315	1,030,368	986,663	56.49	-4.24
Denmark	13,652	11,354	10,341	12,821	13,395	0.77	4.48
Finland	707,477	730,011	810,711	812,998	796,851	45.62	-1.99
Iceland	1,019	546	717	947	825	0.05	-12.88
Ireland	2,810	2,297	1,986	7,185	4,585	0.26	-36.19
Norway	45,838	39,318	39,258	49,984	47,128	2.70	-5.71
Sweden	83,484	74,833	78,696	82,839	75,454	4.32	-8.91
United Kingdom	43,610	31,459	33,606	63,594	48,425	2.77	-23.85
Southern Europe	45,756	37,391	42,780	61,287	56,480	3.23	-7.84
Greece	2,404	2,240	3,319	2,613	2,425	0.14	-7.19
Italy	23,542	17,673	20,851	30,262	27,140	1.55	-10.32
Malta	216	212	258	247	345	0.02	39.68
Portugal	2,376	2,358	2,100	2,703	2,612	0.15	-3.37
Slovenia	1,064	787	1,149	1,126	1,475	0.08	30.99
Spain	16,154	14,121	15,103	24,336	22,483	1.29	-7.61
Western Europe	130,692	110,386	122,082	152,872	160,393	9.18	4.92
Austria	7,646	6,078	4,819	7,131	7,472	0.43	4.78
Belgium	6,130	5,460	5,760	8,502	7,424	0.43	-12.68
France	16,163	14,776	16,694	19,008	20,406	1.17	7.35

ESTONIA

3. Arrivals of non-resident tourists in hotels and similar establishments, by country of residence

	2008	2009	2010	2011	2012	Market share 2012	% Change 2012-2011
Germany	83,034	68,236	77,447	94,082	99,395	5.69	5.65
Luxembourg	722	814	878	964	1,369	0.08	42.01
Netherlands	10,931	9,863	10,100	15,063	15,111	0.87	0.32
Switzerland	6,066	5,159	6,384	8,122	9,216	0.53	13.47
East Mediterranean Europe	**3,286**	**2,834**	**3,567**	**4,861**	**5,420**	**0.31**	**11.50**
Cyprus	569	286	380	470	637	0.04	35.53
Turkey	2,717	2,548	3,187	4,391	4,783	0.27	8.93
Other Europe	**19,158**	**17,558**	**24,329**	**28,890**	**32,288**	**1.85**	**11.76**
Other countries of Europe	19,158	17,558	24,329	28,890	32,288	1.85	11.76
NOT SPECIFIED	**801**	**3,861**	**11,545**	**12,400**	**13,534**	**0.77**	**9.15**
Other countries of the World	801	3,861	11,545	12,400	13,534	0.77	9.15

Yearbook of Tourism Statistics, Data 2008 – 2012, 2014 Editi

ESTONIA

4. Arrivals of non-resident tourists in all types of accommodation establishments, by country of residence

	2008	2009	2010	2011	2012	Market share 2012	% Change 2012-2011
TOTAL	1,433,346	1,380,540	1,563,952	1,807,919	1,873,519	100.00	3.63
AFRICA	1,152	1,031	1,221	2,057	2,039	0.11	-0.88
Southern Africa	268	258	259	433	460	0.02	6.24
South Africa	268	258	259	433	460	0.02	6.24
Other Africa	884	773	962	1,624	1,579	0.08	-2.77
Other countries of Africa	884	773	962	1,624	1,579	0.08	-2.77
AMERICAS	24,990	23,023	27,213	32,454	39,608	2.11	22.04
North America	22,532	20,864	23,742	28,095	34,114	1.82	21.42
Canada	3,347	4,580	3,239	4,271	4,513	0.24	5.67
United States of America	19,185	16,284	20,503	23,824	29,601	1.58	24.25
South America	878	1,162	1,899	1,985	3,167	0.17	59.55
Brazil	878	1,162	1,899	1,985	3,167	0.17	59.55
Other Americas	1,580	997	1,572	2,374	2,327	0.12	-1.98
Other countries of the Americas	1,580	997	1,572	2,374	2,327	0.12	-1.98
EAST ASIA AND THE PACIFIC	18,164	20,210	21,687	29,348	36,364	1.94	23.91
North-East Asia	9,474	10,663	12,063	16,692	19,030	1.02	14.01
China	1,895	2,058	2,823	5,549	5,934	0.32	6.94
Japan	6,862	7,253	7,235	8,732	8,778	0.47	0.53
Korea, Republic of	717	1,352	2,005	2,411	4,318	0.23	79.10
Australasia	4,171	3,849	3,695	5,472	5,516	0.29	0.80
Australia	4,171	3,849	3,695	5,472	5,516	0.29	0.80
Other East Asia and the Pacific	4,519	5,698	5,929	7,184	11,818	0.63	64.50
Other countries of Asia	3,336	4,753	5,063	6,216	10,619	0.57	70.83
Other countries of Oceania	1,183	945	866	968	1,199	0.06	23.86
EUROPE	1,388,201	1,332,335	1,502,008	1,731,493	1,781,861	95.11	2.91
Central/Eastern Europe	241,233	227,474	285,508	385,521	465,921	24.87	20.85
Bulgaria	993	1,005	1,625	1,668	1,640	0.09	-1.68
Czech Republic	5,113	5,232	4,550	5,669	6,474	0.35	14.20
Hungary	3,648	2,306	2,800	3,694	3,540	0.19	-4.17
Latvia	79,527	68,320	72,684	85,229	100,638	5.37	18.08
Lithuania	41,396	33,441	34,107	47,003	47,397	2.53	0.84
Poland	20,859	17,062	19,522	27,093	25,513	1.36	-5.83
Romania	1,136	1,167	1,343	2,295	2,326	0.12	1.35
Russian Federation	82,280	93,947	141,964	203,204	266,192	14.21	31.00
Slovakia	1,362	978	1,643	1,860	2,812	0.15	51.18
Ukraine	4,919	4,016	5,270	7,806	9,389	0.50	20.28
Northern Europe	926,796	917,900	1,004,269	1,071,562	1,030,761	55.02	-3.81
Denmark	14,281	12,036	11,140	13,902	14,091	0.75	1.36
Finland	728,181	750,984	832,874	840,714	829,225	44.26	-1.37
Iceland	1,082	588	761	994	890	0.05	-10.46
Ireland	3,129	2,512	2,192	8,243	5,359	0.29	-34.99
Norway	47,240	40,915	40,414	51,510	48,479	2.59	-5.88
Sweden	86,308	77,470	81,196	86,287	78,412	4.19	-9.13
United Kingdom	46,575	33,395	35,692	69,912	54,305	2.90	-22.32
Southern Europe	51,655	42,462	48,332	69,540	64,727	3.45	-6.92
Albania	159	94	173	198	303	0.02	53.03
Croatia	660	526	719	1,232	1,124	0.06	-8.77
Greece	2,535	2,337	3,447	2,711	2,586	0.14	-4.61
Italy	26,280	19,959	23,017	33,618	30,574	1.63	-9.05
Malta	271	248	315	314	403	0.02	28.34
Portugal	2,644	2,617	2,471	3,026	3,010	0.16	-0.53
Slovenia	1,262	974	1,330	1,335	1,724	0.09	29.14
Spain	17,844	15,707	16,860	27,106	25,003	1.33	-7.76
Western Europe	145,850	124,060	135,403	170,941	182,058	9.72	6.50
Austria	8,561	6,859	5,473	7,841	8,293	0.44	5.76

225

ESTONIA

4. Arrivals of non-resident tourists in all types of accommodation establishments, by country of residence

	2008	2009	2010	2011	2012	Market share 2012	% Change 2012-2011
Belgium	6,860	6,077	6,418	9,197	8,312	0.44	-9.62
France	18,522	16,864	19,319	22,301	24,089	1.29	8.02
Germany	91,915	75,966	84,454	103,559	111,251	5.94	7.43
Luxembourg	779	890	902	992	1,469	0.08	48.08
Netherlands	12,533	11,595	11,713	17,968	18,279	0.98	1.73
Switzerland	6,680	5,809	7,124	9,083	10,365	0.55	14.11
East Mediterranean Europe	**3,441**	**3,071**	**3,974**	**5,208**	**5,820**	**0.31**	**11.75**
Cyprus	580	326	414	479	661	0.04	38.00
Turkey	2,861	2,745	3,560	4,729	5,159	0.28	9.09
Other Europe	**19,226**	**17,368**	**24,522**	**28,721**	**32,574**	**1.74**	**13.42**
Other countries of Europe	19,226	17,368	24,522	28,721	32,574	1.74	13.42
NOT SPECIFIED	**839**	**3,941**	**11,823**	**12,567**	**13,647**	**0.73**	**8.59**
Other countries of the World	839	3,941	11,823	12,567	13,647	0.73	8.59

Yearbook of Tourism Statistics, Data 2008 – 2012, 2014 Editio

ESTONIA

5. Overnight stays of non-resident tourists in hotels and similar establishments, by country of residence

	2008	2009	2010	2011	2012	Market share 2012	% Change 2012-2011
TOTAL	2,727,007	2,555,011	3,002,781	3,478,042	3,498,683	100.00	0.59
AFRICA	2,524	1,944	2,787	3,816	3,732	0.11	-2.20
Southern Africa	475	455	539	657	762	0.02	15.98
South Africa	475	455	539	657	762	0.02	15.98
Other Africa	2,049	1,489	2,248	3,159	2,970	0.08	-5.98
Other countries of Africa	2,049	1,489	2,248	3,159	2,970	0.08	-5.98
AMERICAS	51,585	46,958	53,996	64,839	77,584	2.22	19.66
North America	46,640	43,039	46,752	56,528	68,670	1.96	21.48
Canada	6,575	9,409	6,110	8,747	8,616	0.25	-1.50
United States of America	40,065	33,630	40,642	47,781	60,054	1.72	25.69
South America	1,830	2,148	3,996	3,797	4,977	0.14	31.08
Brazil	1,830	2,148	3,996	3,797	4,977	0.14	31.08
Other Americas	3,115	1,771	3,248	4,514	3,937	0.11	-12.78
Other countries of the Americas	3,115	1,771	3,248	4,514	3,937	0.11	-12.78
EAST ASIA AND THE PACIFIC	30,248	33,695	38,152	48,752	55,430	1.58	13.70
North-East Asia	15,657	17,464	20,238	26,527	27,823	0.80	4.89
China	3,204	3,548	4,665	8,469	8,694	0.25	2.66
Japan	11,495	12,363	12,677	14,855	14,169	0.40	-4.62
Korea, Republic of	958	1,553	2,896	3,203	4,960	0.14	54.85
Australasia	6,963	6,310	6,962	9,277	8,282	0.24	-10.73
Australia	6,963	6,310	6,962	9,277	8,282	0.24	-10.73
Other East Asia and the Pacific	7,628	9,921	10,952	12,948	19,325	0.55	49.25
Other countries of Asia	6,048	8,682	9,276	11,136	17,708	0.51	59.02
Other countries of Oceania	1,580	1,239	1,676	1,812	1,617	0.05	-10.76
EUROPE	2,640,897	2,464,562	2,888,022	3,335,568	3,335,327	95.33	-0.01
Central/Eastern Europe	419,591	394,986	522,252	715,840	832,558	23.80	16.31
Bulgaria	2,126	3,658	5,449	4,710	3,810	0.11	-19.11
Czech Republic	8,596	7,774	7,610	9,696	10,545	0.30	8.76
Hungary	7,535	4,605	6,864	8,762	6,182	0.18	-29.45
Latvia	102,682	88,626	97,436	111,767	126,751	3.62	13.41
Lithuania	58,425	45,612	45,987	65,522	66,625	1.90	1.68
Poland	39,395	26,625	30,640	43,913	42,329	1.21	-3.61
Romania	2,380	2,496	3,484	4,934	5,065	0.14	2.66
Russian Federation	182,900	205,037	310,840	446,742	547,408	15.65	22.53
Slovakia	3,520	2,014	3,089	3,277	5,394	0.15	64.60
Ukraine	12,032	8,539	10,853	16,517	18,449	0.53	11.70
Northern Europe	1,809,929	1,727,616	1,978,864	2,107,122	1,997,289	57.09	-5.21
Denmark	29,749	23,626	21,523	25,159	25,620	0.73	1.83
Finland	1,367,177	1,367,795	1,612,483	1,617,598	1,584,126	45.28	-2.07
Iceland	2,428	1,355	1,985	2,357	1,942	0.06	-17.61
Ireland	7,339	5,565	5,332	17,440	11,220	0.32	-35.67
Norway	121,855	104,416	99,161	118,550	107,236	3.07	-9.54
Sweden	177,469	152,235	162,442	171,475	153,484	4.39	-10.49
United Kingdom	103,912	72,624	75,938	154,543	113,661	3.25	-26.45
Southern Europe	100,649	80,023	95,793	134,896	119,365	3.41	-11.51
Greece	5,606	4,955	7,424	5,511	5,197	0.15	-5.70
Italy	52,514	39,458	47,414	68,573	58,965	1.69	-14.01
Malta	794	570	491	591	734	0.02	24.20
Portugal	5,311	5,269	5,809	5,631	5,568	0.16	-1.12
Slovenia	2,344	2,137	2,277	2,473	3,136	0.09	26.81
Spain	34,080	27,634	32,378	52,117	45,765	1.31	-12.19
Western Europe	265,008	221,861	240,615	313,537	315,767	9.03	0.71
Austria	16,468	12,980	9,954	14,880	14,947	0.43	0.45
Belgium	12,513	12,224	12,619	18,650	15,908	0.45	-14.70
France	32,721	30,104	34,230	37,789	39,885	1.14	5.55

227

ESTONIA

5. Overnight stays of non-resident tourists in hotels and similar establishments, by country of residence

	2008	2009	2010	2011	2012	Market share 2012	% Change 2012-2011
Germany	166,278	133,783	148,813	191,846	193,904	5.54	1.07
Luxembourg	1,571	1,533	1,703	1,868	2,631	0.08	40.85
Netherlands	24,038	21,130	21,167	32,482	31,359	0.90	-3.46
Switzerland	11,419	10,107	12,129	16,022	17,133	0.49	6.93
East Mediterranean Europe	**6,777**	**5,834**	**8,294**	**10,154**	**11,079**	**0.32**	**9.11**
Cyprus	1,453	602	1,064	1,338	1,384	0.04	3.44
Turkey	5,324	5,232	7,230	8,816	9,695	0.28	9.97
Other Europe	**38,943**	**34,242**	**42,204**	**54,019**	**59,269**	**1.69**	**9.72**
Other countries of Europe	38,943	34,242	42,204	54,019	59,269	1.69	9.72
NOT SPECIFIED	**1,753**	**7,852**	**19,824**	**25,067**	**26,610**	**0.76**	**6.16**
Other countries of the World	1,753	7,852	19,824	25,067	26,610	0.76	6.16

Yearbook of Tourism Statistics, Data 2008 – 2012, 2014 Edition

ESTONIA

6. Overnight stays of non-resident tourists in all types of accommodation establishments, by country of residence

	2008	2009	2010	2011	2012	Market share 2012	% Change 2012-2011
TOTAL	2,932,662	2,740,696	3,203,721	3,748,865	3,823,039	100.00	1.98
AFRICA	2,761	2,309	2,910	4,214	4,622	0.12	9.68
Southern Africa	498	544	596	761	946	0.02	24.31
South Africa	498	544	596	761	946	0.02	24.31
Other Africa	2,263	1,765	2,314	3,453	3,676	0.10	6.46
Other countries of Africa	2,263	1,765	2,314	3,453	3,676	0.10	6.46
AMERICAS	59,445	55,624	61,255	72,277	87,711	2.29	21.35
North America	53,863	51,103	53,582	62,703	77,177	2.02	23.08
Canada	7,849	11,493	7,277	10,316	10,452	0.27	1.32
United States of America	46,014	39,610	46,305	52,387	66,725	1.75	27.37
South America	2,168	2,495	4,122	4,326	5,924	0.15	36.94
Brazil	2,168	2,495	4,122	4,326	5,924	0.15	36.94
Other Americas	3,414	2,026	3,551	5,248	4,610	0.12	-12.16
Other countries of the Americas	3,414	2,026	3,551	5,248	4,610	0.12	-12.16
EAST ASIA AND THE PACIFIC	36,629	39,571	43,893	57,269	66,701	1.74	16.47
North-East Asia	17,726	19,174	21,520	29,129	31,870	0.83	9.41
China	4,344	4,268	5,057	9,429	10,337	0.27	9.63
Japan	12,143	12,998	13,303	15,967	15,723	0.41	-1.53
Korea, Republic of	1,239	1,908	3,160	3,733	5,810	0.15	55.64
Australasia	9,495	8,643	8,390	11,982	12,100	0.32	0.98
Australia	9,495	8,643	8,390	11,982	12,100	0.32	0.98
Other East Asia and the Pacific	9,408	11,754	13,983	16,158	22,731	0.59	40.68
Other countries of Asia	7,184	9,620	11,886	13,969	20,343	0.53	45.63
Other countries of Oceania	2,224	2,134	2,097	2,189	2,388	0.06	9.09
EUROPE	2,831,975	2,634,927	3,074,832	3,589,403	3,637,093	95.14	1.33
Central/Eastern Europe	482,436	446,534	578,495	793,482	942,192	24.65	18.74
Bulgaria	2,399	4,578	5,856	5,470	4,552	0.12	-16.78
Czech Republic	11,223	10,008	9,768	12,488	20,886	0.55	67.25
Hungary	9,205	5,426	8,079	10,136	8,429	0.22	-16.84
Latvia	123,299	103,091	112,122	130,154	152,491	3.99	17.16
Lithuania	69,555	55,465	55,535	77,428	77,585	2.03	0.20
Poland	48,254	31,878	36,442	52,153	50,351	1.32	-3.46
Romania	2,801	2,700	3,719	5,304	5,633	0.15	6.20
Russian Federation	198,319	220,945	330,276	475,905	593,783	15.53	24.77
Slovakia	4,020	2,499	4,143	5,172	6,985	0.18	35.05
Ukraine	13,361	9,944	12,555	19,272	21,497	0.56	11.55
Northern Europe	1,882,155	1,794,481	2,047,552	2,201,059	2,095,755	54.82	-4.78
Denmark	31,684	25,725	23,489	27,928	27,887	0.73	-0.15
Finland	1,415,884	1,416,113	1,664,139	1,677,119	1,651,965	43.21	-1.50
Iceland	2,547	1,452	2,056	2,478	2,166	0.06	-12.59
Ireland	8,342	6,170	5,893	19,820	13,177	0.34	-33.52
Norway	125,683	108,207	102,019	122,443	111,131	2.91	-9.24
Sweden	185,592	158,492	168,165	179,523	161,460	4.22	-10.06
United Kingdom	112,423	78,322	81,791	171,748	127,969	3.35	-25.49
Southern Europe	117,321	94,629	112,817	159,106	144,082	3.77	-9.44
Albania	413	299	370	666	578	0.02	-13.21
Croatia	1,500	1,420	1,667	2,346	2,140	0.06	-8.78
Greece	6,027	5,293	7,876	5,761	6,081	0.16	5.55
Italy	60,692	46,856	54,451	79,455	70,070	1.83	-11.81
Malta	948	637	621	710	853	0.02	20.14
Portugal	6,487	6,549	7,610	7,408	7,254	0.19	-2.08
Slovenia	2,744	2,486	2,853	3,233	3,962	0.10	22.55
Spain	38,510	31,089	37,369	59,527	53,144	1.39	-10.72
Western Europe	301,476	257,020	278,869	366,843	379,876	9.94	3.55
Austria	19,219	14,684	12,862	17,612	17,672	0.46	0.34

Yearbook of Tourism Statistics, Data 2008 – 2012, 2014 Edition

ESTONIA

6. Overnight stays of non-resident tourists in all types of accommodation establishments, by country of residence

	2008	2009	2010	2011	2012	Market share 2012	% Change 2012-2011
Belgium	14,237	14,258	14,678	20,445	18,162	0.48	-11.17
France	38,416	35,908	44,236	51,223	54,790	1.43	6.96
Germany	187,665	154,260	167,508	218,698	227,959	5.96	4.23
Luxembourg	1,670	1,680	1,758	1,923	2,897	0.08	50.65
Netherlands	27,662	24,876	24,227	38,930	38,906	1.02	-0.06
Switzerland	12,607	11,354	13,600	18,012	19,490	0.51	8.21
East Mediterranean Europe	**7,427**	**7,233**	**11,599**	**11,986**	**13,144**	**0.34**	**9.66**
Cyprus	1,550	901	1,331	1,384	1,648	0.04	19.08
Turkey	5,877	6,332	10,268	10,602	11,496	0.30	8.43
Other Europe	**41,160**	**35,030**	**45,500**	**56,927**	**62,044**	**1.62**	**8.99**
Other countries of Europe	41,160	35,030	45,500	56,927	62,044	1.62	8.99
NOT SPECIFIED	**1,852**	**8,265**	**20,831**	**25,702**	**26,912**	**0.70**	**4.71**
Other countries of the World	1,852	8,265	20,831	25,702	26,912	0.70	4.71

Yearbook of Tourism Statistics, Data 2008 – 2012, 2014 Edition

ETHIOPIA

1. Arrivals of non-resident tourists at national borders, by country of residence

		2008	2009	2010	2011	2012	Market share 2012	% Change 2012-2011
TOTAL	(*)	330,157	427,286	468,305	523,438	596,341	100.00	13.93
AFRICA		115,999	150,102	140,076	160,311	168,609	28.27	5.18
East Africa		39,137	49,143	53,291	52,087	57,540	9.65	10.47
Djibouti		5,038	7,276	8,140	5,962	8,944	1.50	50.02
Eritrea		362	628	686	340	601	0.10	76.76
Kenya		10,417	15,532	15,322	19,904	20,279	3.40	1.88
Malawi		1,926	2,657	3,878	3,625	4,175	0.70	15.17
Rwanda		2,994	3,306	4,123	2,542	3,581	0.60	40.87
Somalia		6,275	4,020	4,543	1,842	2,388	0.40	29.64
Uganda		4,527	6,330	7,151	7,148	7,154	1.20	0.08
United Republic of Tanzania		4,387	5,797	5,756	5,464	5,965	1.00	9.17
Zimbabwe		3,211	3,597	3,692	5,260	4,453	0.75	-15.34
Central Africa		4,794	5,423	5,190	3,966	3,587	0.60	-9.56
Chad		4,794	5,423	5,190	3,966	3,587	0.60	-9.56
North Africa		9,792	12,515	12,979	17,922	16,814	2.82	-6.18
Sudan		9,792	12,515	12,979	17,922	16,814	2.82	-6.18
Southern Africa		6,402	8,427	10,541	13,433	11,470	1.92	-14.61
South Africa		6,402	8,427	10,541	13,433	11,470	1.92	-14.61
West Africa		17,036	18,811	17,938	23,034	23,859	4.00	3.58
Ghana		3,728	3,255	4,407	4,764	5,129	0.86	7.66
Mali		3,564	3,651	3,097	1,833	2,029	0.34	10.69
Nigeria		9,744	11,905	10,434	16,437	16,701	2.80	1.61
Other Africa		38,838	55,783	40,137	49,869	55,339	9.28	10.97
Other countries of Africa		38,838	55,783	40,137	49,869	55,339	9.28	10.97
AMERICAS		59,240	77,826	95,203	96,246	121,210	20.33	25.94
North America		58,252	76,647	88,601	93,933	114,648	19.23	22.05
Canada		8,574	9,490	11,871	12,889	15,007	2.52	16.43
United States of America		49,678	67,157	76,730	81,044	99,641	16.71	22.95
Other Americas		988	1,179	6,602	2,313	6,562	1.10	183.70
Other countries of the Americas		988	1,179	6,602	2,313	6,562	1.10	183.70
EAST ASIA AND THE PACIFIC		23,141	30,837	38,669	35,768	52,392	8.79	46.48
North-East Asia		16,986	23,210	27,892	26,424	40,219	6.74	52.21
China		13,791	18,968	22,722	20,197	35,383	5.93	75.19
Japan		2,012	2,770	3,377	3,283	2,986	0.50	-9.05
Korea, Republic of		1,183	1,472	1,793	2,944	1,850	0.31	-37.16
South-East Asia		835	1,213	2,045	1,406	1,553	0.26	10.46
Philippines		835	1,213	2,045	1,406	1,553	0.26	10.46
Australasia		3,664	4,340	5,221	5,874	5,252	0.88	-10.59
Australia		3,120	3,835	4,655	4,914	4,479	0.75	-8.85
New Zealand		544	505	566	960	773	0.13	-19.48
Other East Asia and the Pacific		1,656	2,074	3,511	2,064	5,368	0.90	160.08
Other countries of Asia		1,656	2,065	3,456	1,054	4,174	0.70	296.02
Other countries of Oceania			9	55	1,010	1,194	0.20	18.22
EUROPE		95,354	118,689	136,690	162,784	181,309	30.40	11.38
Central/Eastern Europe		933	1,296	1,269	1,740	1,849	0.31	6.26
Russian Federation		933	1,296	1,269	1,740	1,849	0.31	6.26
Northern Europe		29,400	37,504	43,295	49,252	52,841	8.86	7.29
Denmark		1,470	2,121	2,313	2,622	2,805	0.47	6.98
Finland		1,062	1,346	2,028	2,213	2,567	0.43	16.00
Norway		2,824	3,307	4,521	5,068	5,248	0.88	3.55
Sweden		5,761	7,576	9,343	10,404	10,616	1.78	2.04
United Kingdom		18,283	23,154	25,090	28,945	31,605	5.30	9.19
Southern Europe		12,225	15,393	17,641	20,129	23,696	3.97	17.72
Greece		990	925	1,113	965	1,075	0.18	11.40

Yearbook of Tourism Statistics, Data 2008 – 2012, 2014 Edition

ETHIOPIA

1. Arrivals of non-resident tourists at national borders, by country of residence

	2008	2009	2010	2011	2012	Market share 2012	% Change 2012-2011
Italy	11,235	14,468	16,528	19,164	22,621	3.79	18.04
Western Europe	**35,153**	**46,580**	**51,377**	**69,490**	**78,376**	**13.14**	**12.79**
Austria	1,473	2,194	2,172	3,772	2,859	0.48	-24.20
Belgium	2,805	4,073	4,506	6,998	5,366	0.90	-23.32
France	8,965	12,000	12,635	16,517	20,970	3.52	26.96
Germany	12,643	16,695	18,777	24,780	29,917	5.02	20.73
Netherlands	6,372	7,864	8,863	9,052	10,613	1.78	17.24
Switzerland	2,895	3,754	4,424	8,371	8,651	1.45	3.34
East Mediterranean Europe	**8,755**	**8,885**	**10,448**	**9,165**	**10,732**	**1.80**	**17.10**
Israel	7,249	6,608	7,484	6,369	7,754	1.30	21.75
Turkey	1,506	2,277	2,964	2,796	2,978	0.50	6.51
Other Europe	**8,888**	**9,031**	**12,660**	**13,008**	**13,815**	**2.32**	**6.20**
Other countries of Europe	8,888	9,031	12,660	13,008	13,815	2.32	6.20
MIDDLE EAST	**25,228**	**37,428**	**42,301**	**47,583**	**51,282**	**8.60**	**7.77**
Egypt	2,422	4,123	3,671	2,956	2,983	0.50	0.91
Kuwait	1,101	1,854	1,194	2,158	1,977	0.33	-8.39
Saudi Arabia	7,160	10,456	14,019	18,891	18,435	3.09	-2.41
United Arab Emirates	6,650	9,271	11,077	8,255	9,368	1.57	13.48
Yemen	5,641	6,918	6,847	5,340	6,172	1.03	15.58
Other countries of Middle East	2,254	4,806	5,493	9,983	12,347	2.07	23.68
SOUTH ASIA	**11,195**	**12,404**	**15,366**	**20,746**	**21,539**	**3.61**	**3.82**
India	10,560	11,525	14,607	19,667	19,211	3.22	-2.32
Pakistan	635	879	759	1,079	2,328	0.39	115.76

FIJI

1. Arrivals of non-resident tourists at national borders, by country of residence

		2008	2009	2010	2011	2012	Market share 2012	% Change 2012-2011
TOTAL	(*)	585,031	542,186	631,868	675,050	660,590	100.00	-2.14
AMERICAS		81,538	65,044	66,092	69,188	69,904	10.58	1.03
North America		81,538	65,044	66,092	69,188	69,904	10.58	1.03
Canada		17,871	13,452	12,970	14,099	13,426	2.03	-4.77
United States of America		63,667	51,592	53,122	55,089	56,478	8.55	2.52
EAST ASIA AND THE PACIFIC		430,808	415,414	503,660	542,354	535,252	81.03	-1.31
North-East Asia		30,316	25,052	39,943	40,812	39,377	5.96	-3.52
China			4,087	18,147	24,389	26,395	4.00	8.23
Hong Kong, China				1,748	1,706	1,509	0.23	-11.55
Japan		21,918	14,975	12,011	9,616	7,069	1.07	-26.49
Korea, Republic of		7,421	4,904	6,327	5,101	4,404	0.67	-13.66
Taiwan, Province of China		977	1,086	1,710				
South-East Asia		566						
Malaysia		566						
Australasia		347,626	339,487	416,042	448,010	443,413	67.12	-1.03
Australia		247,608	248,589	318,185	344,829	337,291	51.06	-2.19
New Zealand		100,018	90,898	97,857	103,181	106,122	16.06	2.85
Other East Asia and the Pacific		52,300	50,875	47,675	53,532	52,462	7.94	-2.00
Other countries of Asia		16,364	15,797	8,477	14,709	13,576	2.06	-7.70
Other countries East Asia/Pacific		35,936	35,078	39,198	38,823	38,886	5.89	0.16
EUROPE		63,447	55,139	53,901	56,408	46,403	7.02	-17.74
Northern Europe		39,515	31,055	27,995	29,333	21,585	3.27	-26.41
Denmark		1,351	1,345	1,025	1,139	1,065	0.16	-6.50
Finland		570	523	498	629	579	0.09	-7.95
Norway		1,626	1,509	1,126	1,599	1,442	0.22	-9.82
Sweden		2,033	1,465	1,533	1,912	1,423	0.22	-25.58
United Kingdom		33,935	26,213	23,813	24,054	17,076	2.58	-29.01
Southern Europe		3,950	4,374	4,834	4,600	4,315	0.65	-6.20
Italy		2,879	3,255	3,582	3,252	2,994	0.45	-7.93
Spain		1,071	1,119	1,252	1,348	1,321	0.20	-2.00
Western Europe		16,904	17,188	18,014	18,736	16,715	2.53	-10.79
Austria		1,065	1,012	1,102	1,065	1,031	0.16	-3.19
Belgium		348	343	403				
France		4,507	4,683	4,603	4,995	4,375	0.66	-12.41
Germany		6,983	7,223	7,710	8,319	7,841	1.19	-5.75
Netherlands		2,230	2,077	2,010	2,017	1,590	0.24	-21.17
Switzerland		1,771	1,850	2,186	2,340	1,878	0.28	-19.74
Other Europe		3,078	2,522	3,058	3,739	3,788	0.57	1.31
Other countries of Europe		3,078	2,522	3,058	3,739	3,788	0.57	1.31
SOUTH ASIA				1,836	2,188	2,507	0.38	14.58
India				1,836	2,188	2,507	0.38	14.58
NOT SPECIFIED		9,238	6,589	6,379	4,912	6,524	0.99	32.82
Other countries of the World		9,238	6,589	6,379	4,912	6,524	0.99	32.82

233

FIJI

5. Overnight stays of non-resident tourists in hotels and similar establishments, by country of residence

	2008	2009	2010	2011	2012	Market share 2012	% Change 2012-2011
TOTAL	2,489,146	2,356,903	2,889,509	3,102,536	3,126,620	100.00	0.78
AMERICAS	288,707	240,957	264,710	271,405	278,336	8.90	2.55
North America	288,707	240,957	264,710	271,405	278,336	8.90	2.55
Canada	42,722	34,132	37,961	39,296	38,056	1.22	-3.16
United States of America	245,985	206,825	226,749	232,109	240,280	7.68	3.52
EAST ASIA AND THE PACIFIC	1,852,541	1,732,209	2,171,475	2,324,761	2,334,928	74.68	0.44
North-East Asia	77,042	65,078	50,842	40,851	32,518	1.04	-20.40
Japan	77,042	65,078	50,842	40,851	32,518	1.04	-20.40
Australasia	1,709,860	1,604,548	2,050,037	2,198,908	2,197,219	70.27	-0.08
Australia	1,300,673	1,264,015	1,698,625	1,835,563	1,820,317	58.22	-0.83
New Zealand	409,187	340,533	351,412	363,345	376,902	12.05	3.73
Other East Asia and the Pacific	65,639	62,583	70,596	85,002	105,191	3.36	23.75
Other countries of Oceania	65,639	62,583	70,596	85,002	105,191	3.36	23.75
EUROPE	221,948	237,444	253,374	258,621	225,762	7.22	-12.71
Northern Europe	132,717	143,592	134,985	124,693	104,186	3.33	-16.45
United Kingdom	132,717	143,592	134,985	124,693	104,186	3.33	-16.45
Other Europe	89,231	93,852	118,389	133,928	121,576	3.89	-9.22
Other countries of Europe	89,231	93,852	118,389	133,928	121,576	3.89	-9.22
NOT SPECIFIED	125,950	146,293	199,950	247,749	287,594	9.20	16.08
Other countries of the World	125,950	146,293	199,950	247,749	287,594	9.20	16.08

Yearbook of Tourism Statistics, Data 2008 – 2012, 2014 Edition

FINLAND

2. Arrivals of non-resident visitors at national borders, by country of residence

		2008	2009	2010	2011	2012	Market share 2012	% Change 2012-2011
TOTAL	(*)	**6,072,000**	**5,695,000**	**6,182,000**	**7,260,000**	**7,636,000**	**100.00**	**5.18**
AFRICA		**11,000**	**7,000**	**14,000**	**11,000**	**16,000**	**0.21**	**45.45**
Other Africa		**11,000**	**7,000**	**14,000**	**11,000**	**16,000**	**0.21**	**45.45**
All countries of Africa		11,000	7,000	14,000	11,000	16,000	0.21	45.45
AMERICAS		**163,000**	**151,000**	**150,000**	**181,000**	**223,000**	**2.92**	**23.20**
North America		**137,000**	**127,000**	**121,000**	**145,000**	**199,000**	**2.61**	**37.24**
Canada		21,000	23,000	32,000	24,000	25,000	0.33	4.17
Mexico		2,000						
United States of America		114,000	104,000	89,000	121,000	174,000	2.28	43.80
South America		**26,000**	**24,000**	**29,000**	**35,000**	**24,000**	**0.31**	**-31.43**
All countries of South America		26,000	24,000	29,000	35,000	24,000	0.31	-31.43
Other Americas					**1,000**			
Other countries of the Americas					1,000			
EAST ASIA AND THE PACIFIC		**314,000**	**310,000**	**347,000**	**427,000**	**474,000**	**6.21**	**11.01**
North-East Asia		**202,000**	**203,000**	**220,000**	**270,000**	**307,000**	**4.02**	**13.70**
China		66,000	61,000	73,000	74,000	116,000	1.52	56.76
Hong Kong, China		3,000						
Japan		105,000	142,000	109,000	150,000	143,000	1.87	-4.67
Korea, Republic of		22,000		38,000	46,000	48,000	0.63	4.35
Taiwan, Province of China		6,000						
South-East Asia		**9,000**						
Singapore		3,000						
Thailand		6,000						
Australasia		**53,000**		**43,000**	**23,000**	**33,000**	**0.43**	**43.48**
Australia		51,000		43,000	23,000	33,000	0.43	43.48
New Zealand		2,000						
Other East Asia and the Pacific		**50,000**	**107,000**	**84,000**	**134,000**	**134,000**	**1.75**	**0.00**
Other countries of Asia		50,000	107,000	84,000	132,000	131,000	1.72	-0.76
Other countries of Oceania					2,000	3,000	0.04	50.00
EUROPE		**5,540,000**	**5,182,000**	**5,646,000**	**6,641,000**	**6,923,000**	**90.66**	**4.25**
Central/Eastern Europe		**3,061,000**	**2,889,000**	**3,302,000**	**4,134,000**	**4,562,000**	**59.74**	**10.35**
Czech Republic		21,000		22,000	26,000	31,000	0.41	19.23
Estonia		522,000	583,000	561,000	708,000	758,000	9.93	7.06
Hungary		25,000		20,000		13,000	0.17	
Latvia		59,000	54,000	37,000	39,000	36,000	0.47	-7.69
Lithuania		33,000	16,000	29,000	38,000	41,000	0.54	7.89
Poland		40,000	44,000	55,000	62,000	77,000	1.01	24.19
Romania		6,000				12,000	0.16	
Russian Federation		2,331,000	2,192,000	2,561,000	3,261,000	3,578,000	46.86	9.72
Slovakia		3,000						
Ukraine		21,000		17,000		16,000	0.21	
Northern Europe		**1,397,000**	**1,278,000**	**1,272,000**	**1,291,000**	**1,324,000**	**17.34**	**2.56**
Denmark		89,000	98,000	102,000	116,000	114,000	1.49	-1.72
Iceland		4,000						
Ireland		36,000						
Norway		187,000	160,000	195,000	216,000	235,000	3.08	8.80
Sweden		765,000	753,000	712,000	681,000	702,000	9.19	3.08
United Kingdom		316,000	267,000	263,000	278,000	273,000	3.58	-1.80
Southern Europe		**262,000**	**202,000**	**213,000**	**228,000**	**183,000**	**2.40**	**-19.74**
Greece		21,000						
Italy		102,000	79,000	85,000	108,000	94,000	1.23	-12.96
Portugal		20,000		18,000				
Slovenia		3,000						
Spain		116,000	123,000	110,000	120,000	89,000	1.17	-25.83

Yearbook of Tourism Statistics, Data 2008 – 2012, 2014 Edition

FINLAND

2. Arrivals of non-resident visitors at national borders, by country of residence

	2008	2009	2010	2011	2012	Market share 2012	% Change 2012-2011
Western Europe	769,000	667,000	747,000	821,000	752,000	9.85	-8.40
Austria	50,000	44,000	47,000	35,000	48,000	0.63	37.14
Belgium	57,000	64,000	57,000	48,000	53,000	0.69	10.42
France	120,000	94,000	132,000	145,000	127,000	1.66	-12.41
Germany	376,000	332,000	363,000	399,000	342,000	4.48	-14.29
Luxembourg	2,000						
Netherlands	93,000	80,000	86,000	101,000	92,000	1.20	-8.91
Switzerland	71,000	53,000	62,000	93,000	90,000	1.18	-3.23
East Mediterranean Europe	17,000						
Cyprus	1,000						
Israel	10,000						
Turkey	6,000						
Other Europe	34,000	146,000	112,000	167,000	102,000	1.34	-38.92
Other countries of Europe	34,000	146,000	112,000	167,000	102,000	1.34	-38.92
MIDDLE EAST	12,000	9,000					
All countries of Middle East	12,000	9,000					
SOUTH ASIA	32,000	23,000	25,000				
India	32,000	23,000	25,000				
NOT SPECIFIED		13,000					
Other countries of the World		13,000					

Yearbook of Tourism Statistics, Data 2008 – 2012, 2014 Edition

FINLAND

4. Arrivals of non-resident tourists in all types of accommodation establishments, by country of residence

	2008	2009	2010	2011	2012	Market share 2012	% Change 2012-2011
TOTAL	2,494,334	2,220,267	2,318,712	2,622,586	2,778,464	100.00	5.94
AFRICA	4,988	5,904	6,666	7,233	7,871	0.28	8.82
East Africa	826	1,002	1,446	1,506	1,657	0.06	10.03
British Indian Ocean Territory	4		5	2	30	0.00	1,400.00
Burundi			13	7	5	0.00	-28.57
Djibouti			9	27	11	0.00	-59.26
Eritrea	5	10	23	31	11	0.00	-64.52
Ethiopia	94	125	190	209	215	0.01	2.87
Kenya	194	276	435	388	425	0.02	9.54
Madagascar		4	9	2	7	0.00	250.00
Malawi	9	8	33	16	58	0.00	262.50
Mauritius	38	15	39	25	72	0.00	188.00
Mozambique	36	46	26	90	73	0.00	-18.89
Reunion		3	16	34	39	0.00	14.71
Rwanda	14	11	26	32	63	0.00	96.88
Seychelles	9	43	18	29	48	0.00	65.52
Somalia	73	54	72	84	37	0.00	-55.95
Uganda	22	51	49	102	112	0.00	9.80
United Republic of Tanzania	200	252	330	296	259	0.01	-12.50
Zambia	74	76	99	77	147	0.01	90.91
Zimbabwe	54	28	54	55	45	0.00	-18.18
Central Africa	224	221	597	458	523	0.02	14.19
Angola	22	27	430	159	277	0.01	74.21
Cameroon	34	56	72	62	63	0.00	1.61
Central African Republic	17	22	7	18	24	0.00	33.33
Chad			5	4	6	0.00	50.00
Congo	48	45	33	116	103	0.00	-11.21
Democratic Republic of the Congo	97	59	24	67	24	0.00	-64.18
Gabon	6	12	23	32	24	0.00	-25.00
Sao Tome and Principe			3		2	0.00	
North Africa	1,000	994	796	785	964	0.03	22.80
Algeria	499	362	259	200	266	0.01	33.00
Morocco	274	310	259	334	381	0.01	14.07
Sudan	46	90	94	65	62	0.00	-4.62
Tunisia	181	232	184	186	255	0.01	37.10
Southern Africa	2,358	2,198	2,264	2,686	2,896	0.10	7.82
Botswana	13	10	102	43	36	0.00	-16.28
Namibia	62	112	77	119	198	0.01	66.39
South Africa	2,231	2,022	1,975	2,389	2,532	0.09	5.99
Swaziland	52	54	110	135	130	0.00	-3.70
West Africa	580	1,489	1,563	1,798	1,831	0.07	1.84
Benin	16	25	26	22	17	0.00	-22.73
Burkina Faso		5	4	4	11	0.00	175.00
Côte d'Ivoire	30	8	24	47	56	0.00	19.15
Gambia	16	43	30	43	76	0.00	76.74
Ghana	54	139	115	256	246	0.01	-3.91
Guinea			30	30	12	0.00	-60.00
Guinea-Bissau				7			
Liberia	5	17	22	8	9	0.00	12.50
Mali	8	42	42	89	101	0.00	13.48
Mauritania		9	12	14	20	0.00	42.86
Niger	114	151	206	184	196	0.01	6.52
Nigeria	186	470	505	651	621	0.02	-4.61
Saint Helena		47	42	3	7	0.00	133.33
Senegal	29	111	150	94	101	0.00	7.45
Sierra Leone	117	417	346	326	347	0.01	6.44

237

FINLAND

4. Arrivals of non-resident tourists in all types of accommodation establishments, by country of residence

	2008	2009	2010	2011	2012	Market share 2012	% Change 2012-2011
Togo	5	5	9	20	11	0.00	-45.00
AMERICAS	**107,107**	**90,882**	**97,324**	**119,984**	**123,138**	**4.43**	**2.63**
Caribbean	**466**	**841**	**531**	**730**	**779**	**0.03**	**6.71**
Anguilla		10	17	11	12	0.00	9.09
Antigua and Barbuda	13	8	12	13	5	0.00	-61.54
Bahamas	124	243	16	14	44	0.00	214.29
Barbados		10	5	22	13	0.00	-40.91
Bermuda	6	122	11	16	19	0.00	18.75
Cayman Islands	7	28	6	7	10	0.00	42.86
Cuba	125	145	99	261	289	0.01	10.73
Dominica		7	31	20	23	0.00	15.00
Dominican Republic	24	22	30	43	70	0.00	62.79
Grenada		9	30	9	18	0.00	100.00
Guadeloupe		4	16	30	1	0.00	-96.67
Haiti	4	10	44	27	35	0.00	29.63
Jamaica	39	63	86	103	112	0.00	8.74
Netherlands Antilles	29	38	30	26	40	0.00	53.85
Puerto Rico	31	71	57	50	29	0.00	-42.00
Saint Kitts and Nevis			10	1	4	0.00	300.00
Saint Vincent and the Grenadines		8	6	2	2	0.00	0.00
Trinidad and Tobago	51	19	18	21	28	0.00	33.33
Turks and Caicos Islands	5	14		11	19	0.00	72.73
United States Virgin Islands	8	10	7	43	6	0.00	-86.05
Central America	**236**	**422**	**658**	**737**	**555**	**0.02**	**-24.69**
Belize	29	30	24	27	7	0.00	-74.07
Costa Rica	63	177	185	271	179	0.01	-33.95
El Salvador	57	31	206	239	205	0.01	-14.23
Guatemala	22	59	99	27	65	0.00	140.74
Honduras	11	18	37	44	28	0.00	-36.36
Nicaragua	30	55	40	60	47	0.00	-21.67
Panama	24	52	67	69	24	0.00	-65.22
North America	**99,112**	**82,478**	**87,500**	**106,724**	**108,678**	**3.91**	**1.83**
Canada	12,832	11,805	11,308	14,291	15,075	0.54	5.49
Greenland	25	55	39	71	66	0.00	-7.04
Mexico	1,948	1,765	1,983	2,634	2,356	0.08	-10.55
United States of America	84,307	68,853	74,170	89,728	91,181	3.28	1.62
South America	**7,293**	**7,141**	**8,635**	**11,793**	**13,126**	**0.47**	**11.30**
Argentina	826	820	1,061	1,514	1,444	0.05	-4.62
Bolivia	73	34	60	85	50	0.00	-41.18
Brazil	4,213	4,239	5,277	6,563	8,123	0.29	23.77
Chile	636	540	834	1,002	1,218	0.04	21.56
Colombia	265	495	485	566	798	0.03	40.99
Ecuador	57	71	132	147	228	0.01	55.10
Falkland Islands, Malvinas		8	14	17	8	0.00	-52.94
French Guiana			7		11	0.00	
Guyana			16	11	2	0.00	-81.82
Paraguay	13	12	11	24	6	0.00	-75.00
Peru	210	211	195	307	307	0.01	0.00
Suriname		24	26	29	31	0.00	6.90
Uruguay	344	398	272	1,140	509	0.02	-55.35
Venezuela	656	289	245	388	391	0.01	0.77
EAST ASIA AND THE PACIFIC	**177,552**	**144,300**	**159,050**	**192,810**	**228,488**	**8.22**	**18.50**
North-East Asia	**140,801**	**114,836**	**126,618**	**152,385**	**182,810**	**6.58**	**19.97**
China	39,866	32,603	39,217	50,280	59,491	2.14	18.32
Hong Kong, China	3,149	3,610	3,285	6,107	8,202	0.30	34.30
Japan	80,180	65,949	68,747	75,680	91,783	3.30	21.28
Korea, Dem. People's Republic of	1,039	1,123	1,358	850	1,927	0.07	126.71

Yearbook of Tourism Statistics, Data 2008 – 2012, 2014 Edition

FINLAND

4. Arrivals of non-resident tourists in all types of accommodation establishments, by country of residence

	2008	2009	2010	2011	2012	Market share 2012	% Change 2012-2011
Korea, Republic of	10,602	7,450	9,578	12,446	13,609	0.49	9.34
Macao, China	8	22	60	63	92	0.00	46.03
Mongolia	44	58	137	96	128	0.00	33.33
Taiwan, Province of China	5,913	4,021	4,236	6,863	7,578	0.27	10.42
South-East Asia	**11,149**	**10,186**	**13,184**	**19,016**	**21,942**	**0.79**	**15.39**
Brunei Darussalam		13	2	8	17	0.00	112.50
Cambodia	6	14	8	14	7	0.00	-50.00
Indonesia	990	869	1,293	2,276	2,721	0.10	19.55
Lao People's Democratic Republic	59	75	62	69	45	0.00	-34.78
Malaysia	1,287	1,143	1,168	1,420	2,054	0.07	44.65
Myanmar	48	34	87	43	72	0.00	67.44
Philippines	722	967	1,221	1,327	1,202	0.04	-9.42
Singapore	3,079	2,427	2,356	5,244	6,729	0.24	28.32
Thailand	4,620	4,139	6,486	8,095	8,387	0.30	3.61
Viet Nam	338	505	501	520	708	0.03	36.15
Australasia	**25,404**	**19,135**	**18,988**	**20,984**	**23,417**	**0.84**	**11.59**
Australia	23,159	17,684	17,547	19,337	21,553	0.78	11.46
New Zealand	2,245	1,451	1,441	1,647	1,864	0.07	13.18
Melanesia	**58**	**56**	**143**	**134**	**97**	**0.00**	**-27.61**
Fiji	21		92	64	32	0.00	-50.00
New Caledonia	15	31	23	34	44	0.00	29.41
Papua New Guinea	13	10	8	26	10	0.00	-61.54
Solomon Islands	9	15	20	10	11	0.00	10.00
Micronesia	**20**	**14**	**36**	**33**	**14**	**0.00**	**-57.58**
Guam	20	14	17	14	2	0.00	-85.71
Kiribati			19	17	11	0.00	-35.29
Nauru				2	1	0.00	-50.00
Polynesia	**120**	**73**	**81**	**258**	**208**	**0.01**	**-19.38**
American Samoa	97	55	27	207	145	0.01	-29.95
Cook Islands				11	2	0.00	-81.82
French Polynesia			7	20	16	0.00	-20.00
Tokelau	10	18	42	13	35	0.00	169.23
Tonga	13		5	5			
Tuvalu				2	10	0.00	400.00
EUROPE	**2,056,016**	**1,846,249**	**1,921,558**	**2,150,835**	**2,238,356**	**80.56**	**4.07**
Central/Eastern Europe	**670,201**	**623,189**	**691,669**	**831,157**	**937,617**	**33.75**	**12.81**
Armenia	189	203	143	203	256	0.01	26.11
Azerbaijan	90	218	153	234	399	0.01	70.51
Belarus	1,080	1,280	2,097	2,040	2,359	0.08	15.64
Bulgaria	2,191	2,586	2,099	2,633	1,979	0.07	-24.84
Czech Republic	12,316	11,748	11,999	13,924	14,262	0.51	2.43
Estonia	92,182	73,071	82,448	91,814	94,800	3.41	3.25
Georgia	1,117	976	924	1,176	1,385	0.05	17.77
Hungary	8,684	9,731	9,408	10,612	8,224	0.30	-22.50
Kazakhstan	658	775	776	704	1,416	0.05	101.14
Kyrgyzstan	37	34	48	36	207	0.01	475.00
Latvia	21,060	17,227	20,163	21,189	20,256	0.73	-4.40
Lithuania	13,377	10,931	11,337	12,091	13,697	0.49	13.28
Poland	26,817	24,418	26,331	28,395	28,451	1.02	0.20
Republic of Moldova	109	114	94	204	263	0.01	28.92
Romania	5,700	6,306	5,983	6,042	6,396	0.23	5.86
Russian Federation	476,635	456,388	509,237	630,064	731,261	26.32	16.06
Slovakia	3,123	2,914	3,707	3,768	4,570	0.16	21.28
Tajikistan	41		28	22	75	0.00	240.91
Turkmenistan	21	7	6	17	32	0.00	88.24
Ukraine	4,700	4,179	4,606	5,895	7,246	0.26	22.92
Uzbekistan	74	83	82	94	83	0.00	-11.70

239

Yearbook of Tourism Statistics, Data 2008 – 2012, 2014 Edition

FINLAND

4. Arrivals of non-resident tourists in all types of accommodation establishments, by country of residence

	2008	2009	2010	2011	2012	Market share 2012	% Change 2012-2011
Northern Europe	668,832	574,800	584,252	617,437	617,828	22.24	0.06
Denmark	59,140	48,591	48,569	55,968	50,618	1.82	-9.56
Faeroe Islands	99	378	139	195	275	0.01	41.03
Iceland	4,048	3,266	3,384	4,332	4,197	0.15	-3.12
Ireland	10,887	7,754	6,894	7,235	7,610	0.27	5.18
Norway	90,223	74,967	80,403	87,851	92,478	3.33	5.27
Sweden	312,858	278,169	290,922	307,045	301,651	10.86	-1.76
United Kingdom	191,577	161,675	153,941	154,811	160,999	5.79	4.00
Southern Europe	158,965	137,558	133,855	153,120	124,883	4.49	-18.44
Albania	540	505	360	268	332	0.01	23.88
Andorra	123	116	157	82	141	0.01	71.95
Bosnia and Herzegovina	245	227	210	287	237	0.01	-17.42
Croatia	1,803	1,418	1,450	2,001	1,503	0.05	-24.89
Gibraltar	8		50	40	48	0.00	20.00
Greece	10,777	9,088	7,588	7,825	5,828	0.21	-25.52
Holy See			5	1	6	0.00	500.00
Italy	75,325	65,270	61,656	72,412	60,000	2.16	-17.14
Malta	283	380	377	413	390	0.01	-5.57
Montenegro		9	50	7	22	0.00	214.29
Portugal	7,213	7,365	8,212	7,330	7,027	0.25	-4.13
San Marino	15	64	39	58	103	0.00	77.59
Serbia		369	623	759	828	0.03	9.09
Slovenia	3,293	2,511	3,055	3,071	2,995	0.11	-2.47
Spain	59,200	50,077	50,023	58,320	45,206	1.63	-22.49
TFYR of Macedonia	140	159		246	217	0.01	-11.79
Western Europe	545,935	498,518	495,406	534,613	542,197	19.51	1.42
Austria	22,705	23,572	24,892	29,413	30,705	1.11	4.39
Belgium	23,115	21,181	21,713	23,112	24,927	0.90	7.85
France	87,881	79,877	82,813	83,460	83,217	3.00	-0.29
Germany	283,051	249,277	246,137	270,897	268,810	9.67	-0.77
Liechtenstein	553	605	195	273	240	0.01	-12.09
Luxembourg	1,792	1,721	1,675	1,892	2,136	0.08	12.90
Monaco	181	226	178	199	293	0.01	47.24
Netherlands	77,449	74,867	68,907	71,922	72,961	2.63	1.44
Switzerland	49,208	47,192	48,896	53,445	58,908	2.12	10.22
East Mediterranean Europe	12,083	12,184	16,376	14,508	15,831	0.57	9.12
Cyprus	657	754	687	619	666	0.02	7.59
Israel	5,862	5,364	8,023	6,294	6,830	0.25	8.52
Turkey	5,564	6,066	7,666	7,595	8,335	0.30	9.74
MIDDLE EAST	3,866	4,008	3,793	4,278	4,687	0.17	9.56
Bahrain	605	230	99	107	97	0.00	-9.35
Egypt	646	690	720	1,016	839	0.03	-17.42
Iraq	148	164	167	161	158	0.01	-1.86
Jordan	149	121	128	167	155	0.01	-7.19
Kuwait	244	178	168	226	196	0.01	-13.27
Lebanon	176	296	214	168	275	0.01	63.69
Libya	60	64	68	25	66	0.00	164.00
Oman	21	101	232	119	146	0.01	22.69
Qatar	83	119	157	136	170	0.01	25.00
Saudi Arabia	1,160	1,184	811	761	983	0.04	29.17
Syrian Arab Republic	65	81	85	112	102	0.00	-8.93
United Arab Emirates	490	726	912	1,260	1,476	0.05	17.14
Yemen	19	54	32	20	24	0.00	20.00
SOUTH ASIA	18,910	15,625	16,849	18,604	17,152	0.62	-7.80
Afghanistan	946	948	781	538	323	0.01	-39.96
Bangladesh	54	132	97	125	180	0.01	44.00

240

FINLAND

4. Arrivals of non-resident tourists in all types of accommodation establishments, by country of residence

	2008	2009	2010	2011	2012	Market share 2012	% Change 2012-2011
Bhutan		6		7	4	0.00	-42.86
India	16,079	12,941	14,100	15,827	14,432	0.52	-8.81
Iran, Islamic Republic of	1,201	913	1,165	1,249	1,260	0.05	0.88
Maldives		5	9	7	2	0.00	-71.43
Nepal	83	155	170	185	271	0.01	46.49
Pakistan	490	436	473	542	528	0.02	-2.58
Sri Lanka	57	89	54	124	152	0.01	22.58
NOT SPECIFIED	**125,895**	**113,299**	**113,472**	**128,842**	**158,772**	**5.71**	**23.23**
Other countries of the World	125,895	113,299	113,472	128,842	158,772	5.71	23.23

Yearbook of Tourism Statistics, Data 2008 – 2012, 2014 Edition

FINLAND

5. Overnight stays of non-resident tourists in hotels and similar establishments, by country of residence

	2008	2009	2010	2011	2012	Market share 2012	% Change 2012-2011
TOTAL	4,767,662	4,197,575	4,296,915	4,711,041	4,948,446	100.00	5.04
AFRICA	17,178	19,267	18,612	18,790	21,352	0.43	13.63
East Africa	2,251	3,479	3,639	4,115	4,741	0.10	15.21
British Indian Ocean Territory	5		8	4	36	0.00	800.00
Burundi			26	18	27	0.00	50.00
Djibouti			28	33	15	0.00	-54.55
Eritrea	6	15	41	43	13	0.00	-69.77
Ethiopia	221	439	547	487	522	0.01	7.19
Kenya	629	1,243	1,087	1,070	1,366	0.03	27.66
Madagascar	9	17	21	3	19	0.00	533.33
Malawi	13	40	113	39	144	0.00	269.23
Mauritius	69	54	54	82	248	0.01	202.44
Mozambique	117	184	76	211	273	0.01	29.38
Reunion		9	40	31	62	0.00	100.00
Rwanda	30	33	47	42	121	0.00	188.10
Seychelles	19	90	58	68	98	0.00	44.12
Somalia	156	69	108	82	54	0.00	-34.15
Uganda	79	220	126	346	271	0.01	-21.68
United Republic of Tanzania	505	710	802	1,038	700	0.01	-32.56
Zambia	283	299	391	382	604	0.01	58.12
Zimbabwe	110	57	66	136	168	0.00	23.53
Central Africa	385	410	1,448	839	1,272	0.03	51.61
Angola	44	41	1,090	259	747	0.02	188.42
Cameroon	65	110	189	121	178	0.00	47.11
Central African Republic	26	51	18	23	39	0.00	69.57
Chad			12	6	25	0.00	316.67
Congo	43	67	47	188	200	0.00	6.38
Democratic Republic of the Congo	191	104	26	149	29	0.00	-80.54
Gabon	16	37	60	86	49	0.00	-43.02
Sao Tome and Principe			6	7	5	0.00	-28.57
North Africa	2,616	2,672	2,449	1,764	2,140	0.04	21.32
Algeria	1,426	842	901	424	776	0.02	83.02
Morocco	575	731	593	735	743	0.02	1.09
Sudan	124	358	369	153	118	0.00	-22.88
Tunisia	491	741	586	452	503	0.01	11.28
Southern Africa	7,791	6,270	6,624	8,114	8,915	0.18	9.87
Botswana	21	40	128	107	205	0.00	91.59
Namibia	316	325	271	328	681	0.01	107.62
South Africa	7,331	5,756	5,983	7,357	7,616	0.15	3.52
Swaziland	123	149	242	322	413	0.01	28.26
West Africa	1,532	4,003	4,447	3,958	4,284	0.09	8.24
Benin	49	85	86	36	39	0.00	8.33
Burkina Faso		40	24	8	59	0.00	637.50
Côte d'Ivoire	59	22	88	101	144	0.00	42.57
Gambia	30	55	82	53	92	0.00	73.58
Ghana	429	725	564	1,128	674	0.01	-40.25
Guinea			84	52	25	0.00	-51.92
Guinea-Bissau				24			
Liberia	16	43	42	13	87	0.00	569.23
Mali		78	100	131	267	0.01	103.82
Mauritania	10	56	54	51	51	0.00	0.00
Niger	255	295	483	357	388	0.01	8.68
Nigeria	353	1,256	1,339	1,104	1,140	0.02	3.26
Saint Helena		198	207	5	18	0.00	260.00
Senegal	45	281	357	207	339	0.01	63.77
Sierra Leone	274	857	901	654	907	0.02	38.69

242

FINLAND

5. Overnight stays of non-resident tourists in hotels and similar establishments, by country of residence

	2008	2009	2010	2011	2012	Market share 2012	% Change 2012-2011
Togo	12	12	36	34	54	0.00	58.82
Other Africa	**2,603**	**2,433**	**5**				
Other countries of Africa	2,603	2,433	5				
AMERICAS	**256,922**	**220,461**	**231,342**	**263,612**	**265,357**	**5.36**	**0.66**
Caribbean	**1,248**	**3,124**	**1,382**	**1,576**	**2,055**	**0.04**	**30.39**
Anguilla		86	57	27	12	0.00	-55.56
Antigua and Barbuda	32	17	23	21	10	0.00	-52.38
Aruba				41	23	0.00	-43.90
Bahamas	230	371	24	39	269	0.01	589.74
Barbados	5	22	22	66	62	0.00	-6.06
Bermuda	24	903	39	23	32	0.00	39.13
Cayman Islands	21	267	7	28	23	0.00	-17.86
Cuba	275	312	165	472	714	0.01	51.27
Dominica		11	92	34	47	0.00	38.24
Dominican Republic	49	34	68	156	181	0.00	16.03
Grenada		11	72	12	30	0.00	150.00
Guadeloupe		9	53	74	1	0.00	-98.65
Haiti	15	34	83	50	56	0.00	12.00
Jamaica	67	187	243	161	291	0.01	80.75
Netherlands Antilles	62	105	69	46	24	0.00	-47.83
Puerto Rico	63	444	148	86	74	0.00	-13.95
Saint Kitts and Nevis			38	1	10	0.00	900.00
Saint Vincent and the Grenadines		88	76	3	2	0.00	-33.33
Trinidad and Tobago	386	153	78	60	108	0.00	80.00
Turks and Caicos Islands	11	47	8	18	71	0.00	294.44
United States Virgin Islands	8	23	17	158	15	0.00	-90.51
Central America	**687**	**1,343**	**1,433**	**1,354**	**1,275**	**0.03**	**-5.83**
Belize	137	95	71	48	7	0.00	-85.42
Costa Rica	144	530	514	538	395	0.01	-26.58
El Salvador	81	63	292	358	457	0.01	27.65
Guatemala	42	153	192	47	159	0.00	238.30
Honduras	18	48	63	47	55	0.00	17.02
Nicaragua	209	246	141	145	120	0.00	-17.24
Panama	56	208	160	171	82	0.00	-52.05
North America	**235,587**	**198,154**	**207,918**	**234,361**	**232,652**	**4.70**	**-0.73**
Canada	31,747	30,326	29,277	32,595	34,318	0.69	5.29
Greenland	51	307	95	169	111	0.00	-34.32
Mexico	4,579	4,603	4,959	5,118	4,857	0.10	-5.10
United States of America	199,210	162,918	173,587	196,479	193,366	3.91	-1.58
South America	**19,371**	**17,812**	**20,601**	**26,321**	**29,375**	**0.59**	**11.60**
Argentina	1,928	2,265	2,405	3,433	2,860	0.06	-16.69
Bolivia	104	70	83	165	129	0.00	-21.82
Brazil	11,308	11,365	13,039	15,605	19,411	0.39	24.39
Chile	1,815	1,237	1,791	2,002	2,446	0.05	22.18
Colombia	595	1,236	1,263	1,183	1,590	0.03	34.40
Ecuador	94	146	262	302	474	0.01	56.95
Falkland Islands, Malvinas		56	20	29	10	0.00	-65.52
Guyana		10	44	16	8	0.00	-50.00
Paraguay	89	19	16	113	43	0.00	-61.95
Peru	722	479	377	758	583	0.01	-23.09
Suriname		75	58	135	147	0.00	8.89
Uruguay	412	205	598	1,773	729	0.01	-58.88
Venezuela	2,304	649	645	807	945	0.02	17.10
Other Americas	**29**	**28**	**8**				
Other countries of the Americas	29	28	8				

243

FINLAND

5. Overnight stays of non-resident tourists in hotels and similar establishments, by country of residence

	2008	2009	2010	2011	2012	Market share 2012	% Change 2012-2011
EAST ASIA AND THE PACIFIC	345,776	290,970	310,617	352,656	406,923	8.22	15.39
North-East Asia	272,532	228,043	243,179	274,949	320,477	6.48	16.56
China	84,891	65,950	75,332	89,244	96,781	1.96	8.45
Hong Kong, China	4,531	6,015	5,303	9,385	11,932	0.24	27.14
Japan	149,294	130,171	132,540	141,527	171,590	3.47	21.24
Korea, Dem. People's Republic of	2,124	2,827	2,722	1,531	4,722	0.10	208.43
Korea, Republic of	22,041	16,074	18,931	22,236	24,115	0.49	8.45
Macao, China	13	78	141	123	174	0.00	41.46
Mongolia	222	149	334	334	342	0.01	2.40
Taiwan, Province of China	9,416	6,779	7,876	10,569	10,821	0.22	2.38
South-East Asia	24,871	23,211	27,736	32,118	37,178	0.75	15.75
Brunei Darussalam		31	10	16	24	0.00	50.00
Cambodia	7	106	14	29	101	0.00	248.28
Indonesia	1,987	1,814	2,374	3,588	4,462	0.09	24.36
Lao People's Democratic Republic	92	123	109	156	98	0.00	-37.18
Malaysia	2,814	3,083	3,235	3,079	3,984	0.08	29.39
Myanmar	128	36	175	82	80	0.00	-2.44
Philippines	1,565	3,356	3,364	2,237	2,527	0.05	12.96
Singapore	7,239	6,496	5,763	12,310	12,543	0.25	1.89
Thailand	10,052	7,054	11,608	9,500	11,865	0.24	24.89
Viet Nam	987	1,112	1,084	1,121	1,494	0.03	33.27
Australasia	48,002	39,448	39,147	44,828	48,777	0.99	8.81
Australia	43,738	36,309	36,410	41,371	44,904	0.91	8.54
New Zealand	4,264	3,139	2,737	3,457	3,873	0.08	12.03
Melanesia	126	195	279	279	171	0.00	-38.71
Fiji	25		156	114	47	0.00	-58.77
New Caledonia	46	57	40	70	88	0.00	25.71
Papua New Guinea	29	36	16	61	17	0.00	-72.13
Solomon Islands	26	71	46	34	16	0.00	-52.94
Vanuatu		31	21		3	0.00	
Micronesia	31	33	87	70	36	0.00	-48.57
Guam	31	33	32	35	3	0.00	-91.43
Kiribati			48	32	21	0.00	-34.38
Micronesia, Federated States of			7		11	0.00	
Nauru				3	1	0.00	-66.67
Polynesia	214	40	189	412	284	0.01	-31.07
American Samoa	161		34	286	185	0.00	-35.31
French Polynesia		8	15	72	17	0.00	-76.39
Tokelau	26	32	124	43	68	0.00	58.14
Tonga	27		16	6			
Wallis and Futuna Islands				5	14	0.00	180.00
EUROPE	3,838,340	3,415,728	3,484,840	3,810,834	3,957,343	79.97	3.84
Central/Eastern Europe	1,279,908	1,160,003	1,268,560	1,502,726	1,671,194	33.77	11.21
Armenia	678	699	577	406	702	0.01	72.91
Azerbaijan	242	517	372	606	993	0.02	63.86
Belarus	3,188	3,502	8,040	6,484	6,613	0.13	1.99
Bulgaria	5,835	6,449	5,931	5,914	4,806	0.10	-18.74
Czech Republic	23,819	23,304	23,373	26,909	29,421	0.59	9.34
Estonia	154,392	125,169	152,605	171,737	179,349	3.62	4.43
Georgia	2,091	2,015	1,793	2,319	2,960	0.06	27.64
Hungary	20,609	20,572	19,432	22,448	18,021	0.36	-19.72
Kazakhstan	2,635	3,634	3,142	2,338	5,659	0.11	142.04
Kyrgyzstan	124	95	187	123	385	0.01	213.01
Latvia	30,222	25,131	30,237	28,712	31,974	0.65	11.36
Lithuania	20,539	16,588	17,526	19,427	24,048	0.49	23.79
Poland	58,836	52,615	56,075	61,322	65,585	1.33	6.95
Republic of Moldova	293	371	276	412	762	0.02	84.95
Romania	14,185	14,082	14,553	15,573	14,703	0.30	-5.59

Yearbook of Tourism Statistics, Data 2008 – 2012, 2014 Edition

FINLAND

5. Overnight stays of non-resident tourists in hotels and similar establishments, by country of residence

	2008	2009	2010	2011	2012	Market share 2012	% Change 2012-2011
Russian Federation	919,045	843,842	909,186	1,110,551	1,251,335	25.29	12.68
Slovakia	8,518	6,750	10,190	9,417	11,336	0.23	20.38
Tajikistan	59	11	52	46	234	0.00	408.70
Turkmenistan	62		10	52	104	0.00	100.00
Ukraine	14,308	14,422	14,786	17,748	21,925	0.44	23.54
Uzbekistan	228	235	217	182	279	0.01	53.30
Northern Europe	**1,192,942**	**1,008,357**	**988,580**	**1,014,509**	**1,031,452**	**20.84**	**1.67**
Denmark	101,702	79,848	79,708	88,542	80,257	1.62	-9.36
Faeroe Islands	272	1,758	454	309	542	0.01	75.40
Iceland	9,237	7,387	7,984	10,129	8,952	0.18	-11.62
Ireland	26,978	16,974	15,567	14,145	14,885	0.30	5.23
Norway	137,522	112,556	119,062	130,089	143,211	2.89	10.09
Sweden	436,835	384,158	404,164	427,838	419,890	8.49	-1.86
United Kingdom	480,396	405,676	361,641	343,457	363,715	7.35	5.90
Southern Europe	**316,375**	**291,042**	**281,281**	**304,738**	**248,670**	**5.03**	**-18.40**
Albania	1,276	1,364	912	647	688	0.01	6.34
Andorra	232	214	295	145	491	0.01	238.62
Bosnia and Herzegovina	489	623	664	776	528	0.01	-31.96
Croatia	5,686	3,774	3,609	4,950	4,728	0.10	-4.48
Gibraltar	19	1,379	105	89	87	0.00	-2.25
Greece	23,619	23,054	18,015	17,077	13,201	0.27	-22.70
Holy See			10	2	8	0.00	300.00
Italy	148,868	137,134	127,207	138,225	116,293	2.35	-15.87
Malta	819	1,086	946	1,033	912	0.02	-11.71
Montenegro		25	107	16	81	0.00	406.25
Portugal	15,270	18,148	19,129	16,711	16,423	0.33	-1.72
San Marino	38	122	89	161	354	0.01	119.88
Serbia		844	1,908	1,870	1,772	0.04	-5.24
Slovenia	7,020	5,524	6,167	5,821	6,670	0.13	14.59
Spain	113,039	97,363	101,576	116,727	85,865	1.74	-26.44
TFYR of Macedonia		388	542	488	569	0.01	16.60
Western Europe	**1,017,122**	**925,766**	**910,614**	**955,502**	**970,587**	**19.61**	**1.58**
Austria	41,215	41,249	42,519	49,857	49,864	1.01	0.01
Belgium	46,096	41,836	42,319	44,824	47,901	0.97	6.86
France	203,978	184,659	185,221	186,464	190,892	3.86	2.37
Germany	490,084	437,459	424,910	450,681	444,459	8.98	-1.38
Liechtenstein	1,156	1,378	497	407	434	0.01	6.63
Luxembourg	3,622	3,801	3,662	3,517	4,034	0.08	14.70
Monaco	343	441	355	323	568	0.01	75.85
Netherlands	146,405	132,727	129,637	130,465	130,037	2.63	-0.33
Switzerland	84,223	82,216	81,494	88,964	102,398	2.07	15.10
East Mediterranean Europe	**31,993**	**30,560**	**35,805**	**33,359**	**35,440**	**0.72**	**6.24**
Cyprus	1,778	1,843	1,841	1,952	1,704	0.03	-12.70
Israel	15,917	14,210	17,345	15,321	16,430	0.33	7.24
Turkey	14,298	14,507	16,619	16,086	17,306	0.35	7.58
MIDDLE EAST	**14,330**	**13,008**	**11,266**	**11,410**	**12,447**	**0.25**	**9.09**
Bahrain	1,149	623	220	227	266	0.01	17.18
Egypt	2,196	2,238	2,169	2,603	2,051	0.04	-21.21
Iraq	374	326	425	722	416	0.01	-42.38
Jordan	440	427	131	419	340	0.01	-18.85
Kuwait	1,043	510	653	568	559	0.01	-1.58
Lebanon	751	726	729	429	610	0.01	42.19
Libya	396	143	195	65	195	0.00	200.00
Oman	72	312	400	301	854	0.02	183.72
Qatar	507	603	569	273	541	0.01	98.17
Saudi Arabia	5,814	4,704	3,038	2,344	2,950	0.06	25.85
Syrian Arab Republic	93	201	323	285	450	0.01	57.89

245

FINLAND

5. Overnight stays of non-resident tourists in hotels and similar establishments, by country of residence

	2008	2009	2010	2011	2012	Market share 2012	% Change 2012-2011
United Arab Emirates	1,368	1,807	2,283	3,103	3,111	0.06	0.26
Yemen	127	388	131	71	104	0.00	46.48
SOUTH ASIA	**73,093**	**60,290**	**66,698**	**58,961**	**48,230**	**0.97**	**-18.20**
Afghanistan	2,183	2,393	2,242	1,576	545	0.01	-65.42
Bangladesh	100	294	222	351	601	0.01	71.23
Bhutan		20		10	13	0.00	30.00
India	63,393	51,406	57,589	52,196	42,128	0.85	-19.29
Iran, Islamic Republic of	3,610	2,418	2,767	2,866	2,739	0.06	-4.43
Maldives	19	26	33	35	2	0.00	-94.29
Nepal	136	546	474	410	586	0.01	42.93
Pakistan	3,378	2,892	3,224	1,267	1,086	0.02	-14.29
Sri Lanka	274	295	147	250	530	0.01	112.00
NOT SPECIFIED	**222,023**	**177,851**	**173,540**	**194,778**	**236,794**	**4.79**	**21.57**
Other countries of the World	222,023	177,851	173,540	194,778	236,794	4.79	21.57

Yearbook of Tourism Statistics, Data 2008 – 2012, 2014 Edition

FINLAND

6. Overnight stays of non-resident tourists in all types of accommodation establishments, by country of residence

	2008	2009	2010	2011	2012	Market share 2012	% Change 2012-2011
TOTAL	5,502,542	4,890,006	5,005,068	5,507,468	5,802,959	100.00	5.37
AFRICA	15,620	17,475	19,572	20,115	22,609	0.39	12.40
East Africa	2,397	3,569	3,900	4,435	4,937	0.09	11.32
British Indian Ocean Territory	5		8	4	36	0.00	800.00
Burundi			27	18	29	0.00	61.11
Djibouti	4		28	33	15	0.00	-54.55
Eritrea	8	19	41	51	18	0.00	-64.71
Ethiopia	258	445	565	509	564	0.01	10.81
Kenya	656	1,266	1,131	1,092	1,405	0.02	28.66
Madagascar	10	18	25	3	19	0.00	533.33
Malawi	13	40	125	39	144	0.00	269.23
Mauritius	86	54	132	82	256	0.00	212.20
Mozambique	118	188	76	211	273	0.00	29.38
Reunion		9	40	49	63	0.00	28.57
Rwanda	30	33	52	46	121	0.00	163.04
Seychelles	19	90	62	70	98	0.00	40.00
Somalia	175	87	128	251	57	0.00	-77.29
Uganda	81	220	135	371	293	0.01	-21.02
United Republic of Tanzania	524	733	842	1,083	741	0.01	-31.58
Zambia	291	302	391	382	619	0.01	62.04
Zimbabwe	119	65	92	141	186	0.00	31.91
Central Africa	468	384	1,525	869	1,353	0.02	55.70
Angola	47	41	1,091	259	765	0.01	195.37
Cameroon	72		236	134	191	0.00	42.54
Central African Republic	26	69	18	33	41	0.00	24.24
Chad			16	6	27	0.00	350.00
Congo	92	91	47	191	211	0.00	10.47
Democratic Republic of the Congo	215	140	51	153	59	0.00	-61.44
Gabon	12	43	60	86	54	0.00	-37.21
Sao Tome and Principe	4		6	7	5	0.00	-28.57
North Africa	2,813	2,872	2,568	1,939	2,309	0.04	19.08
Algeria	1,472	909	922	465	794	0.01	70.75
Morocco	676	832	667	841	857	0.01	1.90
Sudan	166	363	370	158	121	0.00	-23.42
Tunisia	499	768	609	475	537	0.01	13.05
Southern Africa	8,160	6,379	6,861	8,498	9,117	0.16	7.28
Botswana	21	44	128	107	205	0.00	91.59
Lesotho			9	22	32	0.00	45.45
Namibia	320	327	273	367	709	0.01	93.19
South Africa	7,696	6,008	6,209	7,644	7,743	0.13	1.30
Swaziland	123		242	358	428	0.01	19.55
West Africa	1,782	4,271	4,718	4,374	4,893	0.08	11.87
Benin	49	103	39	40	50	0.00	25.00
Burkina Faso		43	24	9	59	0.00	555.56
Côte d'Ivoire	57	24	109	105	144	0.00	37.14
Gambia	36	77	82	79	165	0.00	108.86
Ghana	457	781	582	1,179	738	0.01	-37.40
Guinea	14		110	59	27	0.00	-54.24
Guinea-Bissau				24			
Liberia	20	56	45	13	87	0.00	569.23
Mali	13	79	102	131	267	0.00	103.82
Mauritania	6	57	56	51	51	0.00	0.00
Niger	255	305	556	374	400	0.01	6.95
Nigeria	522	1,349	1,500	1,353	1,558	0.03	15.15
Saint Helena		207	207	5	18	0.00	260.00
Senegal	57	315	360	257	361	0.01	40.47

247

FINLAND

6. Overnight stays of non-resident tourists in all types of accommodation establishments, by country of residence

	2008	2009	2010	2011	2012	Market share 2012	% Change 2012-2011
Sierra Leone	284	860	910	658	911	0.02	38.45
Togo	12	15	36	37	57	0.00	54.05
AMERICAS	**265,941**	**228,274**	**239,089**	**276,012**	**275,824**	**4.75**	**-0.07**
Caribbean	**1,339**	**3,170**	**1,335**	**1,590**	**2,165**	**0.04**	**36.16**
Anguilla		86	57	27	12	0.00	-55.56
Antigua and Barbuda	32	17	23	21	10	0.00	-52.38
Bahamas	230	371	30	39	269	0.00	589.74
Barbados		22	22	66	63	0.00	-4.55
Bermuda	29	991	39	23	32	0.00	39.13
Cayman Islands	21	267	7	28	23	0.00	-17.86
Cuba	330	334	175	509	725	0.01	42.44
Dominica		11	92	34	49	0.00	44.12
Dominican Republic	73	38	68	156	183	0.00	17.31
Grenada		11	72	13	30	0.00	130.77
Guadeloupe		9	53	74	1	0.00	-98.65
Haiti	16	34	85	50	59	0.00	18.00
Jamaica	74	199	243	161	291	0.01	80.75
Netherlands Antilles	62	105	69	46	69	0.00	50.00
Puerto Rico	63	442	149	86	74	0.00	-13.95
Saint Kitts and Nevis			38	1	10	0.00	900.00
Saint Lucia			10	20	69	0.00	245.00
Trinidad and Tobago	390	163	78	60	108	0.00	80.00
Turks and Caicos Islands	11	47	8	18	73	0.00	305.56
United States Virgin Islands	8	23	17	158	15	0.00	-90.51
Central America	**722**	**1,374**	**1,524**	**1,444**	**1,335**	**0.02**	**-7.55**
Belize	137	95	71	48	7	0.00	-85.42
Costa Rica	159	533	546	576	424	0.01	-26.39
El Salvador	83	63	304	358	470	0.01	31.28
Guatemala	45	165	200	47	163	0.00	246.81
Honduras	24	49	63	63	61	0.00	-3.17
Nicaragua	217	254	151	178	126	0.00	-29.21
Panama	57	215	189	174	84	0.00	-51.72
North America	**243,122**	**204,630**	**214,566**	**242,508**	**241,117**	**4.16**	**-0.57**
Canada	33,680	32,295	30,455	34,754	36,792	0.63	5.86
Greenland	55	307	95	169	111	0.00	-34.32
Mexico	5,000	5,134	5,534	5,731	5,489	0.09	-4.22
United States of America	204,387	166,894	178,482	201,854	198,725	3.42	-1.55
South America	**20,758**	**19,100**	**21,664**	**30,470**	**31,207**	**0.54**	**2.42**
Argentina	2,041	2,368	2,538	3,660	3,121	0.05	-14.73
Bolivia	138	79	104	175	136	0.00	-22.29
Brazil	11,875	11,877	13,489	16,339	20,207	0.35	23.67
Chile	1,939	1,326	1,925	2,180	2,564	0.04	17.61
Colombia	636	1,257	1,324	1,618	1,763	0.03	8.96
Ecuador	106	151	267	341	538	0.01	57.77
Falkland Islands, Malvinas		56	21	29	10	0.00	-65.52
French Guiana			16		24	0.00	
Guyana		10	44	16	8	0.00	-50.00
Paraguay	97	20	16	116	44	0.00	-62.07
Peru	802	519	446	851	638	0.01	-25.03
Suriname	5	75	58	135	147	0.00	8.89
Uruguay	790	612	672	4,129	1,054	0.02	-74.47
Venezuela	2,329	750	744	881	953	0.02	8.17
EAST ASIA AND THE PACIFIC	**363,579**	**306,455**	**327,557**	**396,783**	**447,094**	**7.70**	**12.68**
North-East Asia	**281,330**	**235,910**	**252,112**	**285,874**	**332,109**	**5.72**	**16.17**
China	87,074	67,542	77,540	92,099	100,057	1.72	8.64
Hong Kong, China	4,819	6,159	5,497	9,792	12,534	0.22	28.00
Japan	154,020	134,363	136,804	146,433	176,919	3.05	20.82

248

FINLAND

6. Overnight stays of non-resident tourists in all types of accommodation establishments, by country of residence

	2008	2009	2010	2011	2012	Market share 2012	% Change 2012-2011
Korea, Dem. People's Republic of	2,147	2,921	2,777	1,541	4,786	0.08	210.58
Korea, Republic of	23,149	17,419	20,730	24,385	26,013	0.45	6.68
Macao, China	22	78	141	123	177	0.00	43.90
Mongolia	224	160	351	365	342	0.01	-6.30
Taiwan, Province of China	9,875	7,268	8,272	11,136	11,281	0.19	1.30
South-East Asia	**28,646**	**26,904**	**31,932**	**61,397**	**62,129**	**1.07**	**1.19**
Brunei Darussalam		31	10	18	41	0.00	127.78
Cambodia	11	106	14	30	108	0.00	260.00
Indonesia	2,021	1,837	2,421	3,668	4,900	0.08	33.59
Lao People's Democratic Republic	101	123	113	156	98	0.00	-37.18
Malaysia	2,957	3,151	3,470	3,214	4,130	0.07	28.50
Myanmar	130	49	176	84	96	0.00	14.29
Philippines	1,605	3,357	3,453	2,289	2,562	0.04	11.93
Singapore	7,350	6,652	6,028	12,757	13,047	0.22	2.27
Thailand	13,448	10,162	15,120	37,922	35,575	0.61	-6.19
Viet Nam	1,023	1,436	1,127	1,259	1,572	0.03	24.86
Australasia	**53,212**	**43,265**	**42,957**	**48,752**	**52,317**	**0.90**	**7.31**
Australia	48,237	39,767	39,677	44,875	48,035	0.83	7.04
New Zealand	4,975	3,498	3,280	3,877	4,282	0.07	10.45
Melanesia	**148**	**172**	**280**	**279**	**175**	**0.00**	**-37.28**
Fiji	46		157	114	48	0.00	-57.89
New Caledonia	47	62	40	70	94	0.00	34.29
Papua New Guinea	29	39	16	61	17	0.00	-72.13
Solomon Islands	26	71	46	34	16	0.00	-52.94
All countries of Melanesia			21				
Micronesia	**31**	**33**	**87**	**71**	**36**	**0.00**	**-49.30**
Guam	31	33	32	35	3	0.00	-91.43
Kiribati			48	33	21	0.00	-36.36
Micronesia, Federated States of			7		11	0.00	
Nauru				3	1	0.00	-66.67
Polynesia	**212**	**171**	**189**	**410**	**328**	**0.01**	**-20.00**
American Samoa	162	129	34	286	185	0.00	-35.31
French Polynesia		12	15	72	17	0.00	-76.39
Tokelau	23	30	124	43	68	0.00	58.14
Tonga	27		16	6			
Tuvalu				3	58	0.00	1,833.33
EUROPE	**4,540,859**	**4,074,071**	**4,157,709**	**4,543,390**	**4,753,805**	**81.92**	**4.63**
Central/Eastern Europe	**1,494,168**	**1,380,370**	**1,512,867**	**1,782,115**	**2,032,730**	**35.03**	**14.06**
Armenia	733	709	587	432	716	0.01	65.74
Azerbaijan	250	527	439	642	1,053	0.02	64.02
Belarus	6,616	6,753	10,683	9,621	10,688	0.18	11.09
Bulgaria	6,292	6,836	6,400	6,207	5,166	0.09	-16.77
Czech Republic	30,380	28,175	27,936	32,474	35,273	0.61	8.62
Estonia	205,627	167,816	205,429	228,187	235,482	4.06	3.20
Georgia	2,167	2,090	1,856	2,369	3,046	0.05	28.58
Hungary	22,478	22,719	22,214	25,388	20,157	0.35	-20.60
Kazakhstan	2,841	3,760	3,295	2,391	5,980	0.10	150.10
Kyrgyzstan	124	99	191	134	385	0.01	187.31
Latvia	45,428	33,446	39,002	38,528	42,368	0.73	9.97
Lithuania	27,444	21,747	24,037	25,277	31,998	0.55	26.59
Poland	68,915	63,935	67,902	74,860	76,385	1.32	2.04
Republic of Moldova	304	432	293	434	785	0.01	80.88
Romania	18,609	16,758	18,204	17,360	17,391	0.30	0.18
Russian Federation	1,030,345	979,526	1,056,424	1,286,598	1,506,900	25.97	17.12
Slovakia	9,717	8,866	11,424	10,934	12,391	0.21	13.33
Tajikistan	66	9	56	47	238	0.00	406.38
Turkmenistan	62	6	17	53	104	0.00	96.23
Ukraine	15,532	15,903	16,255	19,893	25,920	0.45	30.30

Yearbook of Tourism Statistics, Data 2008 – 2012, 2014 Edition

FINLAND

6. Overnight stays of non-resident tourists in all types of accommodation establishments, by country of residence

	2008	2009	2010	2011	2012	Market share 2012	% Change 2012-2011
Uzbekistan	238	258	223	286	304	0.01	6.29
Northern Europe	**1,451,556**	**1,223,492**	**1,194,777**	**1,236,933**	**1,238,948**	**21.35**	**0.16**
Denmark	110,173	87,449	85,609	94,823	86,676	1.49	-8.59
Faeroe Islands	283	1,841	483	346	666	0.01	92.49
Iceland	9,728	7,707	8,360	10,572	9,485	0.16	-10.28
Ireland	29,218	18,922	16,827	16,772	16,939	0.29	1.00
Norway	182,531	149,279	159,377	173,254	182,639	3.15	5.42
Sweden	571,904	494,002	517,849	552,129	537,002	9.25	-2.74
United Kingdom	547,719	464,292	406,272	389,037	405,541	6.99	4.24
Southern Europe	**353,806**	**320,967**	**311,941**	**340,072**	**277,532**	**4.78**	**-18.39**
Albania	1,300	1,409	952	748	751	0.01	0.40
Andorra	256	221	295	153	495	0.01	223.53
Bosnia and Herzegovina	553	634	671	798	535	0.01	-32.96
Croatia	6,127	3,911	3,838	5,152	4,858	0.08	-5.71
Gibraltar	19	1,379	105	89	87	0.00	-2.25
Greece	24,703	24,277	18,924	17,810	13,879	0.24	-22.07
Holy See		5	10	2	26	0.00	1,200.00
Italy	167,418	151,658	142,389	156,509	130,847	2.25	-16.40
Malta	859	1,172	989	1,118	962	0.02	-13.95
Montenegro		26	107	16	81	0.00	406.25
Portugal	17,193	18,912	19,875	17,606	17,411	0.30	-1.11
San Marino	38	122	109	173	391	0.01	126.01
Serbia		971	2,063	2,131	1,894	0.03	-11.12
Slovenia	8,247	6,590	7,248	7,191	7,923	0.14	10.18
Spain	126,508	109,240	113,804	130,046	96,820	1.67	-25.55
TFYR of Macedonia	585	440	562	530	572	0.01	7.92
Western Europe	**1,207,465**	**1,116,337**	**1,099,502**	**1,148,255**	**1,166,539**	**20.10**	**1.59**
Austria	49,899	48,921	50,836	57,325	57,494	0.99	0.29
Belgium	50,419	45,909	46,521	49,021	53,449	0.92	9.03
France	230,448	212,887	213,414	213,588	217,886	3.75	2.01
Germany	579,970	525,880	510,280	541,031	534,239	9.21	-1.26
Liechtenstein	1,156	1,410	524	471	470	0.01	-0.21
Luxembourg	3,906	4,046	3,934	3,891	4,575	0.08	17.58
Monaco	343	450	355	326	608	0.01	86.50
Netherlands	182,077	169,213	165,779	164,593	164,918	2.84	0.20
Switzerland	109,247	107,621	107,859	118,009	132,900	2.29	12.62
East Mediterranean Europe	**33,864**	**32,905**	**38,622**	**36,015**	**38,056**	**0.66**	**5.67**
Cyprus	1,831	1,889	1,875	1,992	1,747	0.03	-12.30
Israel	17,203	15,701	19,370	17,320	18,317	0.32	5.76
Turkey	14,830	15,315	17,377	16,703	17,992	0.31	7.72
MIDDLE EAST	**14,573**	**13,231**	**11,749**	**11,647**	**12,658**	**0.22**	**8.68**
Bahrain	1,149	629	220	227	266	0.00	17.18
Egypt	2,304	2,312	2,297	2,687	2,094	0.04	-22.07
Iraq	383	376	444	752	446	0.01	-40.69
Jordan	451	434	345	435	364	0.01	-16.32
Kuwait	1,085	511	664	571	560	0.01	-1.93
Lebanon	759	767	745	462	620	0.01	34.20
Libya	398	146	215	69	196	0.00	184.06
Oman	72	313	400	301	854	0.01	183.72
Qatar	509	607	581	273	543	0.01	98.90
Saudi Arabia	5,840	4,714	3,064	2,376	2,954	0.05	24.33
Syrian Arab Republic	110	204	325	306	450	0.01	47.06
United Arab Emirates	1,386	1,830	2,304	3,105	3,207	0.06	3.29
Yemen	127	388	145	83	104	0.00	25.30

Yearbook of Tourism Statistics, Data 2008 – 2012, 2014 Edition

FINLAND

6. Overnight stays of non-resident tourists in all types of accommodation establishments, by country of residence

	2008	2009	2010	2011	2012	Market share 2012	% Change 2012-2011
SOUTH ASIA	**73,977**	**61,207**	**68,094**	**60,849**	**49,788**	**0.86**	**-18.18**
Afghanistan	2,189	2,404	2,266	1,616	576	0.01	-64.36
Bangladesh	122	328	259	364	631	0.01	73.35
Bhutan		20		10	13	0.00	30.00
India	63,997	52,138	58,657	53,672	42,756	0.74	-20.34
Iran, Islamic Republic of	3,736	2,484	2,924	3,032	2,862	0.05	-5.61
Maldives	19	26	33	35	2	0.00	-94.29
Nepal	163	556	523	470	651	0.01	38.51
Pakistan	3,452	2,927	3,285	1,386	1,722	0.03	24.24
Sri Lanka	299	324	147	264	575	0.01	117.80
NOT SPECIFIED	**227,993**	**189,293**	**181,298**	**198,672**	**241,181**	**4.16**	**21.40**
Other countries of the World	227,993	189,293	181,298	198,672	241,181	4.16	21.40

Yearbook of Tourism Statistics, Data 2008 – 2012, 2014 Edition

FRANCE

1. Arrivals of non-resident tourists at national borders, by country of residence

		2008	2009	2010	2011	2012	Market share 2012	% Change 2012-2011
TOTAL	(*)	79,219,000	76,766,000	77,648,325	81,550,308	83,012,679	100.00	1.79
AFRICA		1,765,000	1,823,000	1,720,086	2,129,199	2,075,669	2.50	-2.51
North Africa		1,125,000	1,268,000	1,191,148	1,387,011	1,398,897	1.69	0.86
All countries of North Africa	(*)	1,125,000	1,268,000	1,191,148	1,387,011	1,398,897	1.69	0.86
Other Africa		640,000	555,000	528,938	742,188	676,772	0.82	-8.81
Other countries of Africa		640,000	555,000	528,938	742,188	676,772	0.82	-8.81
AMERICAS		5,963,000	5,491,000	5,679,079	6,674,810	6,461,701	7.78	-3.19
North America		4,609,000	4,288,000	4,192,314	4,796,433	4,323,631	5.21	-9.86
Canada		896,000	873,000	961,804	937,963	931,232	1.12	-0.72
Mexico		385,000	354,000	321,363	506,553	363,798	0.44	-28.18
United States of America		3,328,000	3,061,000	2,909,147	3,351,917	3,028,601	3.65	-9.65
Other Americas		1,354,000	1,203,000	1,486,765	1,878,377	2,138,070	2.58	13.83
Other countries of the Americas		1,354,000	1,203,000	1,486,765	1,878,377	2,138,070	2.58	13.83
EAST ASIA AND THE PACIFIC		3,484,000	3,371,000	3,583,594	4,120,568	4,393,071	5.29	6.61
North-East Asia		1,452,000	1,437,000	1,505,608	1,742,131	2,125,798	2.56	22.02
China	(*)	778,000	740,000	909,631	1,129,872	1,393,515	1.68	23.33
Japan		674,000	697,000	595,977	612,259	732,283	0.88	19.60
Other East Asia and the Pacific		2,032,000	1,934,000	2,077,986	2,378,437	2,267,273	2.73	-4.67
Other countries of Asia		948,000	842,000	909,414	1,107,263	1,042,885	1.26	-5.81
All countries of Oceania		1,084,000	1,092,000	1,168,572	1,271,174	1,224,388	1.47	-3.68
EUROPE		67,304,000	65,246,000	65,776,196	67,846,133	69,262,259	83.44	2.09
Central/Eastern Europe		1,811,000	1,278,000	1,187,584	1,561,971	1,329,472	1.60	-14.88
Poland		481,000	365,000	370,308	433,714	433,761	0.52	0.01
Other countries Central/East Europe		1,330,000	913,000	817,276	1,128,257	895,711	1.08	-20.61
Northern Europe		16,043,000	14,362,000	14,411,002	14,433,476	14,121,654	17.01	-2.16
Denmark		658,000	696,000	614,136	654,986	535,860	0.65	-18.19
Finland		278,000	182,000	285,953	262,485	235,788	0.28	-10.17
Sweden		732,000	603,000	614,269	682,859	617,964	0.74	-9.50
United Kingdom/Ireland		14,375,000	12,881,000	12,896,644	12,833,146	12,732,042	15.34	-0.79
Southern Europe		15,026,000	13,447,000	13,359,596	14,676,259	15,306,857	18.44	4.30
Greece		270,000	357,000	244,151	169,005	164,400	0.20	-2.72
Italy		8,233,000	7,250,000	7,178,166	8,067,905	8,025,096	9.67	-0.53
Portugal		883,000	966,000	998,223	1,005,365	1,069,331	1.29	6.36
Spain		5,640,000	4,874,000	4,939,056	5,433,984	6,048,030	7.29	11.30
Western Europe		33,109,000	34,900,000	35,368,819	35,537,734	36,831,875	44.37	3.64
Austria		747,000	646,000	765,220	992,343	1,054,287	1.27	6.24
Belgium / Luxembourg		9,408,000	10,900,000	10,741,692	10,768,892	11,126,814	13.40	3.32
Germany		11,645,000	10,692,000	11,409,526	11,622,256	12,225,972	14.73	5.19
Netherlands		6,244,000	7,224,000	7,002,184	6,493,126	6,355,369	7.66	-2.12
Switzerland	(*)	5,065,000	5,438,000	5,450,197	5,661,117	6,069,433	7.31	7.21
Other Europe		1,315,000	1,259,000	1,449,195	1,636,693	1,672,401	2.01	2.18
Other countries of Europe		1,315,000	1,259,000	1,449,195	1,636,693	1,672,401	2.01	2.18
MIDDLE EAST		703,000	835,000	889,370	779,598	819,979	0.99	5.18
All countries of Middle East		703,000	835,000	889,370	779,598	819,979	0.99	5.18

252

FRANCE

3. Arrivals of non-resident tourists in hotels and similar establishments, by country of residence

	2008	2009	2010	2011	2012	Market share 2012	% Change 2012-2011
TOTAL (*)	32,137,170	28,765,875	29,500,638	30,262,220	30,931,015	100.00	2.21
AFRICA	416,939	416,147	433,959	454,676	512,617	1.66	12.74
North Africa	179,030	182,986	206,040	202,725	218,752	0.71	7.91
All countries of North Africa	179,030	182,986	206,040	202,725	218,752	0.71	7.91
Other Africa	237,909	233,161	227,919	251,951	293,865	0.95	16.64
Other countries of Africa	237,909	233,161	227,919	251,951	293,865	0.95	16.64
AMERICAS	3,605,956	3,297,733	3,573,000	3,807,590	4,123,624	13.33	8.30
North America	2,912,108	2,644,740	2,750,429	2,865,287	3,148,538	10.18	9.89
Canada	423,298	371,351	403,184	428,512	453,026	1.46	5.72
United States of America	2,488,810	2,273,389	2,347,245	2,436,775	2,695,512	8.71	10.62
Other Americas	693,848	652,993	822,571	942,303	975,086	3.15	3.48
Other countries of the Americas	693,848	652,993	822,571	942,303	975,086	3.15	3.48
EAST ASIA AND THE PACIFIC	2,528,215	2,459,439	2,802,070	3,150,363	3,406,057	11.01	8.12
North-East Asia	1,556,281	1,507,798	1,696,261	1,838,287	1,962,173	6.34	6.74
China	416,525	395,210	567,294	728,996	810,857	2.62	11.23
Japan	1,139,756	1,112,588	1,128,967	1,109,291	1,151,316	3.72	3.79
Australasia	285,173	253,192	319,151	369,033	426,023	1.38	15.44
Australia	285,173	253,192	319,151	369,033	426,023	1.38	15.44
Other East Asia and the Pacific	686,761	698,449	786,658	943,043	1,017,861	3.29	7.93
Other countries East Asia/Pacific	686,761	698,449	786,658	943,043	1,017,861	3.29	7.93
EUROPE	25,180,344	22,203,552	22,203,237	22,318,562	22,274,552	72.01	-0.20
Central/Eastern Europe	1,152,584	932,590	1,125,930	1,330,744	1,521,360	4.92	14.32
Bulgaria	32,168	23,876	25,763	26,264	29,663	0.10	12.94
Czech Republic	82,827	66,121	91,993	110,075	119,299	0.39	8.38
Estonia	7,902	5,709	6,623	10,078	19,061	0.06	89.13
Hungary	54,986	56,438	56,670	68,135	70,557	0.23	3.55
Latvia	5,989	5,643	8,098	9,966	11,321	0.04	13.60
Lithuania	16,710	12,407	18,058	20,535	32,963	0.11	60.52
Poland	216,715	194,398	206,571	233,215	266,746	0.86	14.38
Romania	110,182	88,998	103,163	126,943	134,469	0.43	5.93
Russian Federation	593,695	452,463	581,221	695,762	799,977	2.59	14.98
Slovakia	31,410	26,537	27,770	29,771	37,304	0.12	25.30
Northern Europe	7,958,339	6,423,132	6,220,033	6,042,173	6,173,428	19.96	2.17
Denmark	218,432	202,401	214,811	216,016	226,004	0.73	4.62
Finland	94,610	95,532	102,261	116,116	108,270	0.35	-6.76
Iceland	18,144	14,393	14,407	21,337	17,772	0.06	-16.71
Ireland	267,763	230,997	218,994	212,715	205,542	0.66	-3.37
Norway	150,442	136,376	153,949	166,002	189,829	0.61	14.35
Sweden	247,177	200,340	225,477	260,138	266,440	0.86	2.42
United Kingdom	6,961,771	5,543,093	5,290,134	5,049,849	5,159,571	16.68	2.17
Southern Europe	6,034,807	5,338,970	5,402,525	5,150,548	4,632,424	14.98	-10.06
Croatia	26,765	18,274	16,019	19,308	20,738	0.07	7.41
Greece	152,550	146,790	128,429	109,358	95,051	0.31	-13.08
Italy	3,108,112	2,790,805	2,753,302	2,547,150	2,324,181	7.51	-8.75
Malta	13,967	7,584	12,465	11,733	14,913	0.05	27.10
Portugal	279,888	258,253	285,639	269,944	279,783	0.90	3.64
Slovenia	19,199	18,267	17,689	18,084	16,619	0.05	-8.10
Spain	2,434,326	2,098,997	2,188,982	2,174,971	1,881,139	6.08	-13.51
Western Europe	9,386,149	8,989,714	8,832,428	9,186,330	9,300,684	30.07	1.24
Austria	188,392	168,817	176,899	180,566	192,488	0.62	6.60
Belgium	2,732,157	2,780,830	2,703,367	2,776,012	2,757,888	8.92	-0.65
Germany	3,230,890	2,915,293	2,961,428	3,044,555	3,072,482	9.93	0.92
Luxembourg	105,667	109,364	120,975	132,090	145,387	0.47	10.07
Netherlands	1,947,591	1,845,505	1,708,485	1,740,397	1,712,944	5.54	-1.58

Yearbook of Tourism Statistics, Data 2008 – 2012, 2014 Edition

FRANCE

3. Arrivals of non-resident tourists in hotels and similar establishments, by country of residence

	2008	2009	2010	2011	2012	Market share 2012	% Change 2012-2011
Switzerland	1,181,452	1,169,905	1,161,274	1,312,710	1,419,495	4.59	8.13
East Mediterranean Europe	**94,899**	**78,054**	**110,862**	**127,120**	**130,655**	**0.42**	**2.78**
Cyprus	12,747	9,822	14,050	14,201	12,186	0.04	-14.19
Turkey	82,152	68,232	96,812	112,919	118,469	0.38	4.92
Other Europe	**553,566**	**441,092**	**511,459**	**481,647**	**516,001**	**1.67**	**7.13**
Other countries of Europe	553,566	441,092	511,459	481,647	516,001	1.67	7.13
MIDDLE EAST	**405,716**	**389,004**	**488,372**	**531,029**	**614,165**	**1.99**	**15.66**
All countries of Middle East	405,716	389,004	488,372	531,029	614,165	1.99	15.66

254

FRANCE

5. Overnight stays of non-resident tourists in hotels and similar establishments, by country of residence

	2008	2009	2010	2011	2012	Market share 2012	% Change 2012-2011
TOTAL (*)	71,064,602	63,203,046	64,920,009	66,531,774	68,373,288	100.00	2.77
AFRICA	1,003,129	1,014,682	1,084,530	1,125,192	1,261,256	1.84	12.09
North Africa	422,420	433,374	492,705	490,290	521,853	0.76	6.44
All countries of North Africa	422,420	433,374	492,705	490,290	521,853	0.76	6.44
Other Africa	580,709	581,308	591,825	634,902	739,403	1.08	16.46
Other countries of Africa	580,709	581,308	591,825	634,902	739,403	1.08	16.46
AMERICAS	8,673,036	8,177,377	8,927,903	9,554,010	10,436,552	15.26	9.24
North America	6,873,893	6,428,335	6,670,289	6,970,489	7,722,072	11.29	10.78
Canada	996,645	912,536	972,684	1,040,536	1,088,186	1.59	4.58
United States of America	5,877,248	5,515,799	5,697,605	5,929,953	6,633,886	9.70	11.87
Other Americas	1,799,143	1,749,042	2,257,614	2,583,521	2,714,480	3.97	5.07
Other countries of the Americas	1,799,143	1,749,042	2,257,614	2,583,521	2,714,480	3.97	5.07
EAST ASIA AND THE PACIFIC	5,480,219	5,311,596	6,054,390	6,709,726	7,320,193	10.71	9.10
North-East Asia	3,308,083	3,185,836	3,601,998	3,825,222	4,106,471	6.01	7.35
China	827,163	787,259	1,135,802	1,425,143	1,587,843	2.32	11.42
Japan	2,480,920	2,398,577	2,466,196	2,400,079	2,518,628	3.68	4.94
Australasia	675,563	620,935	773,935	905,152	1,059,022	1.55	17.00
Australia	675,563	620,935	773,935	905,152	1,059,022	1.55	17.00
Other East Asia and the Pacific	1,496,573	1,504,825	1,678,457	1,979,352	2,154,700	3.15	8.86
Other countries East Asia/Pacific	1,496,573	1,504,825	1,678,457	1,979,352	2,154,700	3.15	8.86
EUROPE	54,757,802	47,584,765	47,487,562	47,703,196	47,689,066	69.75	-0.03
Central/Eastern Europe	2,879,278	2,306,107	2,811,538	3,360,381	3,788,506	5.54	12.74
Bulgaria	78,875	56,735	61,434	63,159	70,311	0.10	11.32
Czech Republic	172,060	137,018	184,850	228,132	252,174	0.37	10.54
Estonia	18,312	14,096	16,278	25,037	44,828	0.07	79.05
Hungary	120,345	122,960	123,711	149,052	154,834	0.23	3.88
Latvia	15,746	13,357	20,150	23,810	27,209	0.04	14.28
Lithuania	35,577	27,637	38,988	44,207	65,891	0.10	49.05
Poland	461,908	394,792	437,865	507,607	565,277	0.83	11.36
Romania	258,848	215,504	250,006	302,306	310,791	0.45	2.81
Russian Federation	1,646,336	1,264,371	1,618,949	1,947,541	2,212,210	3.24	13.59
Slovakia	71,271	59,637	59,307	69,530	84,981	0.12	22.22
Northern Europe	17,210,125	13,784,180	13,114,328	12,940,552	13,348,953	19.52	3.16
Denmark	500,678	480,447	507,530	513,918	530,778	0.78	3.28
Finland	224,072	237,551	254,255	290,536	267,951	0.39	-7.77
Iceland	44,778	37,553	32,195	45,955	39,913	0.06	-13.15
Ireland	779,330	640,646	594,492	556,262	544,210	0.80	-2.17
Norway	370,605	334,715	389,393	417,336	477,837	0.70	14.50
Sweden	582,414	491,988	550,374	647,723	643,655	0.94	-0.63
United Kingdom	14,708,248	11,561,280	10,786,089	10,468,822	10,844,609	15.86	3.59
Southern Europe	14,174,075	12,510,498	12,553,739	11,807,781	10,598,909	15.50	-10.24
Croatia	62,393	43,236	36,735	44,517	47,238	0.07	6.11
Greece	426,942	422,277	359,587	294,792	246,065	0.36	-16.53
Italy	7,227,364	6,479,711	6,358,381	5,823,314	5,349,181	7.82	-8.14
Malta	48,033	25,150	41,378	35,601	45,107	0.07	26.70
Portugal	620,543	582,836	640,313	587,338	596,644	0.87	1.58
Slovenia	43,120	36,386	39,107	40,102	36,114	0.05	-9.94
Spain	5,745,680	4,920,902	5,078,238	4,982,117	4,278,560	6.26	-14.12
Western Europe	18,989,572	17,767,289	17,552,574	18,155,607	18,493,490	27.05	1.86
Austria	428,958	386,168	409,640	412,709	444,052	0.65	7.59
Belgium	5,460,783	5,347,716	5,253,448	5,327,365	5,292,230	7.74	-0.66
Germany	6,652,298	5,914,513	6,023,998	6,187,813	6,298,651	9.21	1.79
Luxembourg	217,081	222,704	248,607	264,340	287,645	0.42	8.82
Netherlands	3,749,982	3,483,710	3,235,647	3,289,240	3,237,801	4.74	-1.56

FRANCE

5. Overnight stays of non-resident tourists in hotels and similar establishments, by country of residence

	2008	2009	2010	2011	2012	Market share 2012	% Change 2012-2011
Switzerland	2,480,470	2,412,478	2,381,234	2,674,140	2,933,111	4.29	9.68
East Mediterranean Europe	**246,380**	**209,409**	**300,426**	**331,430**	**336,658**	**0.49**	**1.58**
Cyprus	37,971	28,988	42,144	40,481	34,567	0.05	-14.61
Turkey	208,409	180,421	258,282	290,949	302,091	0.44	3.83
Other Europe	**1,258,372**	**1,007,282**	**1,154,957**	**1,107,445**	**1,122,550**	**1.64**	**1.36**
Other countries of Europe	1,258,372	1,007,282	1,154,957	1,107,445	1,122,550	1.64	1.36
MIDDLE EAST	**1,150,416**	**1,114,626**	**1,365,624**	**1,439,650**	**1,666,221**	**2.44**	**15.74**
All countries of Middle East	1,150,416	1,114,626	1,365,624	1,439,650	1,666,221	2.44	15.74

Yearbook of Tourism Statistics, Data 2008 – 2012, 2014 Editi

FRANCE

6. Overnight stays of non-resident tourists in all types of accommodation establishments, by country of residence

		2008	2009	2010	2011	2012	Market share 2012	% Change 2012-2011
TOTAL	(*)	**526,159,000**	**512,189,000**	**525,290,805**	**564,312,694**	**577,662,738**	**100.00**	**2.37**
AFRICA		**23,532,000**	**25,232,000**	**25,281,135**	**30,215,144**	**30,420,702**	**5.27**	**0.68**
North Africa		**15,296,000**	**17,852,000**	**18,129,051**	**20,159,578**	**20,326,901**	**3.52**	**0.83**
All countries of North Africa	(*)	15,296,000	17,852,000	18,129,051	20,159,578	20,326,901	3.52	0.83
Other Africa		**8,236,000**	**7,380,000**	**7,152,084**	**10,055,566**	**10,093,801**	**1.75**	**0.38**
Other countries of Africa		8,236,000	7,380,000	7,152,084	10,055,566	10,093,801	1.75	0.38
AMERICAS		**52,017,000**	**48,277,000**	**50,257,940**	**58,829,765**	**57,558,279**	**9.96**	**-2.16**
North America		**40,758,000**	**37,506,000**	**38,059,369**	**43,780,507**	**40,153,413**	**6.95**	**-8.28**
Canada		8,732,000	8,676,000	9,877,596	9,925,792	10,118,750	1.75	1.94
Mexico		3,638,000	2,929,000	2,582,545	3,514,368	2,958,690	0.51	-15.81
United States of America		28,388,000	25,901,000	25,599,228	30,340,347	27,075,973	4.69	-10.76
Other Americas		**11,259,000**	**10,771,000**	**12,198,571**	**15,049,258**	**17,404,866**	**3.01**	**15.65**
Other countries of the Americas		11,259,000	10,771,000	12,198,571	15,049,258	17,404,866	3.01	15.65
EAST ASIA AND THE PACIFIC		**25,390,000**	**25,746,000**	**27,596,504**	**31,431,319**	**34,308,406**	**5.94**	**9.15**
North-East Asia		**9,132,000**	**9,555,000**	**10,171,242**	**11,999,862**	**15,158,093**	**2.62**	**26.32**
China	(*)	5,021,000	5,383,000	6,567,036	8,101,469	10,534,088	1.82	30.03
Japan		4,111,000	4,172,000	3,604,206	3,898,393	4,624,005	0.80	18.61
Other East Asia and the Pacific		**16,258,000**	**16,191,000**	**17,425,262**	**19,431,457**	**19,150,313**	**3.32**	**-1.45**
Other countries of Asia		7,381,000	7,233,000	7,760,752	9,168,629	9,060,448	1.57	-1.18
All countries of Oceania		8,877,000	8,958,000	9,664,510	10,262,828	10,089,865	1.75	-1.69
EUROPE		**418,746,000**	**405,119,000**	**413,343,054**	**436,080,496**	**447,360,507**	**77.44**	**2.59**
Central/Eastern Europe		**15,258,000**	**10,774,000**	**11,055,047**	**15,255,542**	**11,517,280**	**1.99**	**-24.50**
Poland		4,218,000	3,059,000	3,289,252	3,729,750	3,327,491	0.58	-10.79
Other countries Central/East Europe		11,040,000	7,715,000	7,765,795	11,525,792	8,189,789	1.42	-28.94
Northern Europe		**100,209,000**	**91,146,000**	**93,648,852**	**98,065,797**	**97,961,473**	**16.96**	**-0.11**
Denmark		4,290,000	4,652,000	4,080,089	4,758,150	3,935,740	0.68	-17.28
Finland		1,965,000	1,269,000	1,706,775	1,763,746	1,466,494	0.25	-16.85
Sweden		4,882,000	3,469,000	3,623,595	4,456,088	4,050,852	0.70	-9.09
United Kingdom/Ireland		89,072,000	81,756,000	84,238,393	87,087,813	88,508,387	15.32	1.63
Southern Europe		**82,355,000**	**74,855,000**	**72,619,935**	**80,861,842**	**85,959,118**	**14.88**	**6.30**
Greece		2,264,000	2,512,000	1,736,860	1,191,442	1,094,147	0.19	-8.17
Italy		44,674,000	40,657,000	40,487,586	45,189,492	45,216,995	7.83	0.06
Portugal		7,481,000	6,948,000	6,716,569	6,965,789	8,723,512	1.51	25.23
Spain		27,936,000	24,738,000	23,678,920	27,515,119	30,924,464	5.35	12.39
Western Europe		**210,598,000**	**218,447,000**	**224,807,827**	**228,144,158**	**238,417,905**	**41.27**	**4.50**
Austria		6,579,000	5,471,000	7,044,550	9,743,991	9,462,527	1.64	-2.89
Belgium / Luxembourg		51,622,000	59,506,000	58,598,440	59,421,145	62,526,863	10.82	5.23
Germany		78,482,000	70,768,000	76,798,195	80,290,768	84,213,182	14.58	4.89
Netherlands		46,981,000	54,196,000	54,288,511	49,606,579	49,470,321	8.56	-0.27
Switzerland	(*)	26,934,000	28,506,000	28,078,131	29,081,675	32,745,012	5.67	12.60
Other Europe		**10,326,000**	**9,897,000**	**11,211,393**	**13,753,157**	**13,504,731**	**2.34**	**-1.81**
Other countries of Europe		10,326,000	9,897,000	11,211,393	13,753,157	13,504,731	2.34	-1.81
MIDDLE EAST		**6,474,000**	**7,815,000**	**8,812,172**	**7,755,970**	**8,014,844**	**1.39**	**3.34**
All countries of Middle East		6,474,000	7,815,000	8,812,172	7,755,970	8,014,844	1.39	3.34

FRENCH POLYNESIA

1. Arrivals of non-resident tourists at national borders, by country of residence

		2008	2009	2010	2011	2012	Market share 2012	% Change 2012-2011
TOTAL	(*)	196,496	160,447	153,919	162,776	168,978	100.00	3.81
AFRICA		338	278	275	272	288	0.17	5.88
Other Africa		338	278	275	272	288	0.17	5.88
All countries of Africa		338	278	275	272	288	0.17	5.88
AMERICAS		70,506	51,716	53,338	63,547	67,212	39.78	5.77
Central America		108	135	134	137	175	0.10	27.74
All countries of Central America		108	135	134	137	175	0.10	27.74
North America		63,833	45,790	47,302	57,876	60,959	36.08	5.33
Canada		7,271	4,265	5,468	7,458	7,034	4.16	-5.69
Hawaii, USA		367	377	285	288	331	0.20	14.93
Mexico		1,200	745	814	1,033	1,067	0.63	3.29
United States of America		54,995	40,403	40,735	49,097	52,527	31.09	6.99
South America		6,565	5,791	5,902	5,534	6,078	3.60	9.83
Argentina		1,951	1,433	1,253	1,098	1,264	0.75	15.12
Brazil		2,455	2,047	2,360	2,530	2,787	1.65	10.16
Chile		1,585	1,706	1,849	1,328	1,328	0.79	0.00
Other countries of South America		574	605	440	578	699	0.41	20.93
EAST ASIA AND THE PACIFIC		42,386	35,106	33,196	34,052	38,089	22.54	11.86
North-East Asia		20,261	17,948	15,682	14,846	15,394	9.11	3.69
China		388	543	1,143	978	1,183	0.70	20.96
Hong Kong, China		259	99	1	214	301	0.18	40.65
Japan		18,769	16,353	13,761	12,990	12,989	7.69	-0.01
Korea, Republic of		650	765	686	506	682	0.40	34.78
Taiwan, Province of China		195	188	91	158	239	0.14	51.27
South-East Asia		668	674	659	616	614	0.36	-0.32
Indonesia		83	128	98	86	65	0.04	-24.42
Malaysia		70	62	104	72	134	0.08	86.11
Philippines		202	187	176	121	91	0.05	-24.79
Singapore		202	191	200	200	244	0.14	22.00
Thailand		111	106	81	137	80	0.05	-41.61
Australasia		16,773	11,471	12,073	13,720	17,390	10.29	26.75
Australia		10,228	6,557	6,945	8,236	10,224	6.05	24.14
New Zealand		6,545	4,914	5,128	5,484	7,166	4.24	30.67
Melanesia		3,911	4,006	4,048	4,085	4,114	2.43	0.71
Fiji		96	131	108	139	92	0.05	-33.81
New Caledonia		3,815	3,875	3,940	3,946	4,022	2.38	1.93
Polynesia		373	379	342	361	251	0.15	-30.47
Cook Islands		309	268	265	284	215	0.13	-24.30
Samoa	(*)	46	75	72	54	24	0.01	-55.56
Tonga		18	36	5	23	12	0.01	-47.83
Other East Asia and the Pacific		400	628	392	424	326	0.19	-23.11
Other countries of Asia		51	79	56	77	37	0.02	-51.95
Other countries of Oceania		349	549	336	347	289	0.17	-16.71
EUROPE		82,838	72,857	66,561	64,272	62,661	37.08	-2.51
Central/Eastern Europe		805	601	519	699	587	0.35	-16.02
Russian Federation		805	601	519	699	587	0.35	-16.02
Northern Europe		6,337	4,523	3,790	3,522	3,538	2.09	0.45
Denmark		259	228	236	162	197	0.12	21.60
Finland		301	234	232	205	194	0.11	-5.37
Norway		272	168	158	201	244	0.14	21.39
Sweden		528	411	324	283	286	0.17	1.06
United Kingdom		4,977	3,482	2,840	2,671	2,617	1.55	-2.02
Southern Europe		20,232	16,835	15,623	14,320	12,664	7.49	-11.56
Italy		13,802	11,944	11,208	10,471	9,409	5.57	-10.14
Portugal		470	337	311	374	251	0.15	-32.89

258

FRENCH POLYNESIA

1. Arrivals of non-resident tourists at national borders, by country of residence

	2008	2009	2010	2011	2012	Market share 2012	% Change 2012-2011
Spain	5,960	4,554	4,104	3,475	3,004	1.78	-13.55
Western Europe	**53,042**	**48,551**	**44,976**	**43,817**	**44,077**	**26.08**	**0.59**
Austria	998	999	757	688	619	0.37	-10.03
Belgium	2,025	995	796	852	882	0.52	3.52
France	42,374	39,256	36,544	35,835	35,898	21.24	0.18
Germany	4,511	4,346	4,256	3,604	3,552	2.10	-1.44
Luxembourg	168	143	198	109	135	0.08	23.85
Netherlands	726	676	565	487	432	0.26	-11.29
Switzerland	2,240	2,136	1,860	2,242	2,559	1.51	14.14
Other Europe	**2,422**	**2,347**	**1,653**	**1,914**	**1,795**	**1.06**	**-6.22**
Other countries of Europe	2,422	2,347	1,653	1,914	1,795	1.06	-6.22
MIDDLE EAST	**182**	**201**	**231**	**201**	**268**	**0.16**	**33.33**
All countries of Middle East	182	201	231	201	268	0.16	33.33
SOUTH ASIA	**246**	**289**	**318**	**432**	**460**	**0.27**	**6.48**
India	246	289	318	432	460	0.27	6.48

Yearbook of Tourism Statistics, Data 2008 – 2012, 2014 Edition

FRENCH POLYNESIA

3. Arrivals of non-resident tourists in hotels and similar establishments, by country of residence

	2008	2009	2010	2011	2012	Market share 2012	% Change 2012-2011
TOTAL	172,827	138,151	133,032	142,056	148,443	100.00	4.50
AFRICA	271	213	219	206	237	0.16	15.05
Other Africa	271	213	219	206	237	0.16	15.05
All countries of Africa	271	213	219	206	237	0.16	15.05
AMERICAS	67,364	48,539	50,606	60,773	64,156	43.22	5.57
Central America	92	128	129	126	171	0.12	35.71
All countries of Central America	92	128	129	126	171	0.12	35.71
North America	61,108	43,089	45,015	55,422	58,359	39.31	5.30
Canada	7,047	4,067	5,303	7,241	6,771	4.56	-6.49
Hawaii, USA	133	137	122	127	148	0.10	16.54
Mexico	1,166	710	783	1,005	1,014	0.68	0.90
United States of America	52,762	38,175	38,807	47,049	50,426	33.97	7.18
South America	6,164	5,322	5,462	5,225	5,626	3.79	7.67
Argentina	1,939	1,402	1,213	1,088	1,206	0.81	10.85
Brazil	2,360	1,966	2,252	2,469	2,678	1.80	8.46
Chile	1,314	1,387	1,581	1,111	1,077	0.73	-3.06
Other countries of South America	551	567	416	557	665	0.45	19.39
EAST ASIA AND THE PACIFIC	37,931	31,156	29,146	29,949	34,019	22.92	13.59
North-East Asia	19,864	17,740	15,496	14,610	15,207	10.24	4.09
China	334	503	1,081	923	1,159	0.78	25.57
Hong Kong, China	235	97	1	197	274	0.18	39.09
Japan	18,494	16,209	13,657	12,859	12,892	8.68	0.26
Korea, Republic of	635	756	672	491	669	0.45	36.25
Taiwan, Province of China	166	175	85	140	213	0.14	52.14
South-East Asia	576	584	566	544	524	0.35	-3.68
Indonesia	72	108	71	71	47	0.03	-33.80
Malaysia	57	50	88	64	122	0.08	90.63
Philippines	180	168	165	114	78	0.05	-31.58
Singapore	187	174	176	185	223	0.15	20.54
Thailand	80	84	66	110	54	0.04	-50.91
Australasia	15,311	10,113	10,832	12,489	16,034	10.80	28.38
Australia	9,668	6,055	6,483	7,680	9,699	6.53	26.29
New Zealand	5,643	4,058	4,349	4,809	6,335	4.27	31.73
Melanesia	1,832	2,117	1,913	1,949	1,991	1.34	2.15
Fiji	57	123	75	100	66	0.04	-34.00
New Caledonia	1,775	1,994	1,838	1,849	1,925	1.30	4.11
Polynesia	129	185	133	130	109	0.07	-16.15
Cook Islands	88	81	99	70	81	0.05	15.71
Samoa	29	70	31	42	18	0.01	-57.14
Tonga	12	34	3	18	10	0.01	-44.44
Other East Asia and the Pacific	219	417	206	227	154	0.10	-32.16
Other countries of Asia	40	63	45	64	24	0.02	-62.50
Other countries of Oceania	179	354	161	163	130	0.09	-20.25
EUROPE	66,862	57,781	52,551	50,518	49,335	33.23	-2.34
Central/Eastern Europe	795	581	515	689	581	0.39	-15.67
Russian Federation	795	581	515	689	581	0.39	-15.67
Northern Europe	6,148	4,344	3,641	3,388	3,395	2.29	0.21
Denmark	240	217	221	155	188	0.13	21.29
Finland	289	230	225	198	192	0.13	-3.03
Norway	257	154	144	192	232	0.16	20.83
Sweden	518	388	310	269	277	0.19	2.97
United Kingdom	4,844	3,355	2,741	2,574	2,506	1.69	-2.64
Southern Europe	19,978	16,543	15,409	14,062	12,469	8.40	-11.33
Italy	13,676	11,828	11,083	10,332	9,322	6.28	-9.78
Portugal	464	328	307	361	241	0.16	-33.24

260

FRENCH POLYNESIA

3. Arrivals of non-resident tourists in hotels and similar establishments, by country of residence

	2008	2009	2010	2011	2012	Market share 2012	% Change 2012-2011
Spain	5,838	4,387	4,019	3,369	2,906	1.96	-13.74
Western Europe	**37,602**	**34,033**	**31,398**	**30,552**	**31,180**	**21.00**	**2.06**
Austria	986	982	740	683	598	0.40	-12.45
Belgium	1,888	873	693	725	756	0.51	4.28
France	27,379	25,187	23,364	22,958	23,489	15.82	2.31
Germany	4,406	4,230	4,148	3,514	3,420	2.30	-2.68
Luxembourg	155	130	191	101	130	0.09	28.71
Netherlands	713	655	540	475	420	0.28	-11.58
Switzerland	2,075	1,976	1,722	2,096	2,367	1.59	12.93
Other Europe	**2,339**	**2,280**	**1,588**	**1,827**	**1,710**	**1.15**	**-6.40**
Other countries of Europe	2,339	2,280	1,588	1,827	1,710	1.15	-6.40
MIDDLE EAST	**159**	**185**	**202**	**180**	**242**	**0.16**	**34.44**
All countries of Middle East	159	185	202	180	242	0.16	34.44
SOUTH ASIA	**240**	**277**	**308**	**430**	**454**	**0.31**	**5.58**
India	240	277	308	430	454	0.31	5.58

Yearbook of Tourism Statistics, Data 2008 – 2012, 2014 Edition

FRENCH POLYNESIA

5. Overnight stays of non-resident tourists in hotels and similar establishments, by country of residence

	2008	2009	2010	2011	2012	Market share 2012	% Change 2012-2011
TOTAL	1,967,581	1,601,188	1,569,826	1,657,407	1,733,039	100.00	4.56
AFRICA	3,794	2,911	2,833	2,833	3,430	0.20	21.07
Other Africa	3,794	2,911	2,833	2,833	3,430	0.20	21.07
All countries of Africa	3,794	2,911	2,833	2,833	3,430	0.20	21.07
AMERICAS	688,873	482,246	506,164	590,195	630,817	36.40	6.88
Central America	933	1,364	1,498	1,122	1,875	0.11	67.11
All countries of Central America	933	1,364	1,498	1,122	1,875	0.11	67.11
North America	621,563	425,814	445,653	534,201	567,611	32.75	6.25
Canada	82,885	48,205	62,979	82,105	77,126	4.45	-6.06
Hawaii, USA	1,435	1,360	1,608	1,408	1,583	0.09	12.43
Mexico	11,401	6,711	7,383	8,459	9,185	0.53	8.58
United States of America	525,842	369,538	373,683	442,229	479,717	27.68	8.48
South America	66,377	55,068	59,013	54,872	61,331	3.54	11.77
Argentina	21,684	16,434	14,010	13,529	15,518	0.90	14.70
Brazil	26,744	21,016	24,908	24,896	27,820	1.61	11.74
Chile	12,227	12,101	15,410	10,828	10,931	0.63	0.95
Other countries of South America	5,722	5,517	4,685	5,619	7,062	0.41	25.68
EAST ASIA AND THE PACIFIC	281,295	238,941	231,803	251,157	291,060	16.79	15.89
North-East Asia	123,804	111,427	98,496	98,263	104,957	6.06	6.81
China	2,999	4,356	9,465	8,052	10,461	0.60	29.92
Hong Kong, China	2,180	865	1	1,891	2,740	0.16	44.90
Japan	112,938	100,200	84,081	83,243	84,871	4.90	1.96
Korea, Republic of	4,255	4,587	4,245	3,755	4,932	0.28	31.34
Taiwan, Province of China	1,432	1,419	704	1,322	1,953	0.11	47.73
South-East Asia	5,800	6,923	5,561	5,234	6,654	0.38	27.13
Indonesia	874	1,315	853	721	1,505	0.09	108.74
Malaysia	610	605	937	821	1,629	0.09	98.42
Philippines	1,775	1,709	1,227	984	795	0.05	-19.21
Singapore	1,652	1,765	1,839	1,491	2,123	0.12	42.39
Thailand	889	1,529	705	1,217	602	0.03	-50.53
Australasia	129,723	90,083	102,763	119,934	152,149	8.78	26.86
Australia	85,543	56,383	65,594	77,965	97,926	5.65	25.60
New Zealand	44,180	33,700	37,169	41,969	54,223	3.13	29.20
Melanesia	18,853	24,425	21,392	24,071	24,036	1.39	-0.15
Fiji	390	1,138	709	1,010	522	0.03	-48.32
New Caledonia	18,463	23,287	20,683	23,061	23,514	1.36	1.96
Polynesia	946	1,629	1,242	1,377	1,172	0.07	-14.89
Cook Islands	593	659	913	601	906	0.05	50.75
Samoa	84	288	307	645	156	0.01	-75.81
Tonga	269	682	22	131	110	0.01	-16.03
Other East Asia and the Pacific	2,169	4,454	2,349	2,278	2,092	0.12	-8.17
Other countries of Asia	406	736	764	626	515	0.03	-17.73
Other countries of Oceania	1,763	3,718	1,585	1,652	1,577	0.09	-4.54
EUROPE	989,760	873,019	824,401	808,104	801,656	46.26	-0.80
Central/Eastern Europe	10,103	7,250	6,008	8,607	7,329	0.42	-14.85
Russian Federation	10,103	7,250	6,008	8,607	7,329	0.42	-14.85
Northern Europe	65,264	45,831	40,233	35,964	38,613	2.23	7.37
Denmark	3,718	3,338	3,416	2,215	3,238	0.19	46.19
Finland	3,395	2,201	2,684	2,167	1,839	0.11	-15.14
Norway	3,154	1,895	1,976	2,319	3,880	0.22	67.31
Sweden	6,310	4,262	3,885	3,513	3,371	0.19	-4.04
United Kingdom	48,687	34,135	28,272	25,750	26,285	1.52	2.08
Southern Europe	213,802	178,393	162,466	148,594	130,506	7.53	-12.17
Italy	156,028	135,168	123,124	113,602	101,171	5.84	-10.94
Portugal	5,443	3,171	3,053	3,797	2,937	0.17	-22.65

262

FRENCH POLYNESIA

5. Overnight stays of non-resident tourists in hotels and similar establishments, by country of residence

	2008	2009	2010	2011	2012	Market share 2012	% Change 2012-2011
Spain	52,331	40,054	36,289	31,195	26,398	1.52	-15.38
Western Europe	**674,044**	**615,218**	**596,736**	**593,303**	**605,400**	**34.93**	**2.04**
Austria	12,778	12,471	10,600	9,440	8,849	0.51	-6.26
Belgium	23,953	14,739	11,837	12,265	13,315	0.77	8.56
France	533,401	488,396	481,901	482,488	484,981	27.98	0.52
Germany	58,785	57,548	53,935	46,516	49,156	2.84	5.68
Luxembourg	2,300	1,835	2,915	1,718	1,985	0.11	15.54
Netherlands	8,715	7,704	6,964	6,060	5,812	0.34	-4.09
Switzerland	34,112	32,525	28,584	34,816	41,302	2.38	18.63
Other Europe	**26,547**	**26,327**	**18,958**	**21,636**	**19,808**	**1.14**	**-8.45**
Other countries of Europe	26,547	26,327	18,958	21,636	19,808	1.14	-8.45
MIDDLE EAST	**1,761**	**1,978**	**2,347**	**2,037**	**2,636**	**0.15**	**29.41**
All countries of Middle East	1,761	1,978	2,347	2,037	2,636	0.15	29.41
SOUTH ASIA	**2,098**	**2,093**	**2,278**	**3,081**	**3,440**	**0.20**	**11.65**
India	2,098	2,093	2,278	3,081	3,440	0.20	11.65

Yearbook of Tourism Statistics, Data 2008 – 2012, 2014 Edition

FRENCH POLYNESIA

6. Overnight stays of non-resident tourists in all types of accommodation establishments, by country of residence

	2008	2009	2010	2011	2012	Market share 2012	% Change 2012-2011
TOTAL	2,602,805	2,204,955	2,166,994	2,281,874	2,379,851	100.00	4.29
AFRICA	5,424	4,321	5,868	5,171	5,238	0.22	1.30
Other Africa	5,424	4,321	5,868	5,171	5,238	0.22	1.30
All countries of Africa	5,424	4,321	5,868	5,171	5,238	0.22	1.30
AMERICAS	748,884	539,282	559,071	640,922	692,322	29.09	8.02
Central America	1,487	1,650	1,582	1,385	1,920	0.08	38.63
All countries of Central America	1,487	1,650	1,582	1,385	1,920	0.08	38.63
North America	673,094	474,378	491,536	578,347	620,961	26.09	7.37
Canada	88,554	52,840	67,846	88,141	86,936	3.65	-1.37
Hawaii, USA	5,358	4,858	3,983	4,523	4,928	0.21	8.95
Mexico	12,164	7,439	8,992	9,206	10,642	0.45	15.60
United States of America	567,018	409,241	410,715	476,477	518,455	21.79	8.81
South America	74,303	63,254	65,953	61,190	69,441	2.92	13.48
Argentina	22,090	16,997	14,430	13,683	16,649	0.70	21.68
Brazil	29,420	23,186	27,606	26,337	30,054	1.26	14.11
Chile	16,435	16,704	18,556	14,967	14,937	0.63	-0.20
Other countries of South America	6,358	6,367	5,361	6,203	7,801	0.33	25.76
EAST ASIA AND THE PACIFIC	357,036	311,768	306,380	330,019	370,639	15.57	12.31
North-East Asia	129,712	114,526	102,025	103,762	109,219	4.59	5.26
China	3,792	5,021	10,923	9,164	10,978	0.46	19.79
Hong Kong, China	2,795	881	1	2,451	3,478	0.15	41.90
Japan	116,798	102,346	85,818	85,537	86,552	3.64	1.19
Korea, Republic of	4,432	4,680	4,459	4,667	5,696	0.24	22.05
Taiwan, Province of China	1,895	1,598	824	1,943	2,515	0.11	29.44
South-East Asia	8,530	11,067	7,879	7,662	9,712	0.41	26.76
Indonesia	1,489	2,450	1,696	1,171	2,171	0.09	85.40
Malaysia	1,045	1,005	1,180	1,083	2,030	0.09	87.44
Philippines	2,145	2,029	1,414	1,206	1,293	0.05	7.21
Singapore	1,894	2,121	2,320	1,898	2,468	0.10	30.03
Thailand	1,957	3,462	1,269	2,304	1,750	0.07	-24.05
Australasia	153,218	113,636	123,910	142,081	176,519	7.42	24.24
Australia	95,417	66,511	74,142	88,400	108,364	4.55	22.58
New Zealand	57,801	47,125	49,768	53,681	68,155	2.86	26.96
Melanesia	55,869	58,579	61,370	64,715	65,400	2.75	1.06
Fiji	1,124	1,220	1,312	1,777	1,005	0.04	-43.44
New Caledonia	54,745	57,359	60,058	62,938	64,395	2.71	2.31
Polynesia	4,107	3,891	4,555	4,402	3,181	0.13	-27.74
Cook Islands	2,761	2,741	2,999	3,183	2,715	0.11	-14.70
Samoa	1,002	802	1,503	1,029	326	0.01	-68.32
Tonga	344	348	53	190	140	0.01	-26.32
Other East Asia and the Pacific	5,600	10,069	6,641	7,397	6,608	0.28	-10.67
Other countries of Asia	635	1,200	1,169	2,019	971	0.04	-51.91
Other countries of Oceania	4,965	8,869	5,472	5,378	5,637	0.24	4.82
EUROPE	1,487,016	1,344,929	1,289,821	1,299,966	1,304,206	54.80	0.33
Central/Eastern Europe	10,545	7,811	6,133	8,762	7,499	0.32	-14.41
Russian Federation	10,545	7,811	6,133	8,762	7,499	0.32	-14.41
Northern Europe	69,349	49,853	44,092	39,706	43,315	1.82	9.09
Denmark	4,222	3,955	3,748	2,314	3,449	0.14	49.05
Finland	3,809	2,245	2,807	2,341	1,850	0.08	-20.97
Norway	3,521	2,159	2,308	2,779	4,155	0.17	49.51
Sweden	6,425	4,863	4,195	3,854	3,573	0.15	-7.29
United Kingdom	51,372	36,631	31,034	28,418	30,288	1.27	6.58
Southern Europe	220,274	185,035	169,435	156,422	136,455	5.73	-12.76
Italy	159,250	137,994	126,849	117,760	103,466	4.35	-12.14
Portugal	5,551	3,292	3,139	4,164	3,120	0.13	-25.07

264

FRENCH POLYNESIA

6. Overnight stays of non-resident tourists in all types of accommodation establishments, by country of residence

	2008	2009	2010	2011	2012	Market share 2012	% Change 2012-2011
Spain	55,473	43,749	39,447	34,498	29,869	1.26	-13.42
Western Europe	**1,158,114**	**1,074,293**	**1,048,989**	**1,070,680**	**1,094,502**	**45.99**	**2.22**
Austria	13,032	12,730	10,872	9,604	9,294	0.39	-3.23
Belgium	27,862	17,870	15,682	15,898	17,845	0.75	12.25
France	1,005,332	936,340	921,390	948,470	959,467	40.32	1.16
Germany	60,993	60,118	57,119	49,204	52,577	2.21	6.86
Luxembourg	2,610	2,065	3,071	1,958	2,060	0.09	5.21
Netherlands	9,083	8,127	7,656	6,340	6,159	0.26	-2.85
Switzerland	39,202	37,043	33,199	39,206	47,100	1.98	20.13
Other Europe	**28,734**	**27,937**	**21,172**	**24,396**	**22,435**	**0.94**	**-8.04**
Other countries of Europe	28,734	27,937	21,172	24,396	22,435	0.94	-8.04
MIDDLE EAST	**2,260**	**2,364**	**3,353**	**2,691**	**3,477**	**0.15**	**29.21**
All countries of Middle East	2,260	2,364	3,353	2,691	3,477	0.15	29.21
SOUTH ASIA	**2,185**	**2,291**	**2,501**	**3,105**	**3,969**	**0.17**	**27.83**
India	2,185	2,291	2,501	3,105	3,969	0.17	27.83

Yearbook of Tourism Statistics, Data 2008 – 2012, 2014 Edition

GAMBIA

1. Arrivals of non-resident tourists at national borders, by nationality

		2008	2009	2010	2011	2012	Market share 2012	% Change 2012-2011
TOTAL	(*)	146,759	141,569	91,099	106,393	157,323	100.00	47.87
AFRICA		2,568	3,111	2,274	15,306	16,191	10.29	5.78
Other Africa		2,568	3,111	2,274	15,306	16,191	10.29	5.78
All countries of Africa		2,568	3,111	2,274	15,306	16,191	10.29	5.78
AMERICAS		1,786	2,342	1,504	2,236	3,149	2.00	40.83
North America		1,786	2,342	1,504	2,236	3,149	2.00	40.83
Canada		392	412	241	200			
United States of America		1,394	1,930	1,263	2,036	3,149	2.00	54.67
EAST ASIA AND THE PACIFIC		74	151	77	66			
North-East Asia		74	151	77	66			
Taiwan, Province of China		74	151	77	66			
EUROPE		123,313	115,260	72,984	86,692	108,633	69.05	25.31
Central/Eastern Europe		406	425	489	261	465	0.30	78.16
Czech Republic		106	71	219	27	193	0.12	614.81
Estonia		90	56	43	11			
Poland		210	298	227	223	272	0.17	21.97
Northern Europe		87,117	85,814	53,891	61,571	73,266	46.57	18.99
Denmark		4,540	4,547	2,627	1,316	1,660	1.06	26.14
Finland		5,844	3,586	1,598	2,904	1,896	1.21	-34.71
Iceland		38	42	23	67			
Ireland		893	1,277	1,530	2,662	2,084	1.32	-21.71
Norway		5,324	4,123	1,370	1,253	1,540	0.98	22.91
Sweden		8,370	8,302	6,493	6,387	8,057	5.12	26.15
United Kingdom		62,108	63,937	40,250	46,982	58,029	36.89	23.51
Southern Europe		6,630	6,211	4,147	5,206	3,982	2.53	-23.51
Greece		8	43	24	9			
Italy		941	1,200	245	234	412	0.26	76.07
Spain		5,681	4,968	3,878	4,963	3,570	2.27	-28.07
Western Europe		29,160	22,810	14,457	19,654	30,920	19.65	57.32
Austria		409	351	254	489	402	0.26	-17.79
Belgium		3,192	3,118	1,983	2,234	5,322	3.38	138.23
France		833	1,130	834	812	1,147	0.73	41.26
Germany		5,289	3,539	2,290	3,020	5,350	3.40	77.15
Netherlands		18,920	14,246	8,870	12,906	18,699	11.89	44.89
Switzerland		517	426	226	193			
NOT SPECIFIED		19,018	20,705	14,260	2,093	29,350	18.66	1,302.29
Other countries of the World		2,933	3,757	3,079	2,093	6,098	3.88	191.35
Nationals Residing Abroad		16,085	16,948	11,181		23,252	14.78	

266

GEORGIA

2. Arrivals of non-resident visitors at national borders, by country of residence

	2008	2009	2010	2011	2012	Market share 2012	% Change 2012-2011
TOTAL	1,290,108	1,500,049	2,031,717	2,822,363	4,428,221	100.00	56.90
AFRICA	677	1,090	3,397	4,229	7,110	0.16	68.12
East Africa	114	210	2,242	1,878	3,789	0.09	101.76
Burundi	1	3			5	0.00	
Comoros	2			2	8	0.00	300.00
Djibouti			2	1	7	0.00	600.00
Eritrea		4		1	9	0.00	800.00
Ethiopia	11	17	32	17	36	0.00	111.76
Kenya	23	16	26	18	53	0.00	194.44
Madagascar	15	16	41	18	36	0.00	100.00
Malawi	1	2	4	6	7	0.00	16.67
Mauritius	13	14	19	4	28	0.00	600.00
Mozambique	7	4	1		8	0.00	
Reunion		12	55	18	15	0.00	-16.67
Rwanda	5	14	9	9	17	0.00	88.89
Seychelles	6	2	445	403	546	0.01	35.48
Somalia	10	15	56	47	48	0.00	2.13
Uganda	6	12	21	25	31	0.00	24.00
United Republic of Tanzania	5	7	12	13	13	0.00	0.00
Zambia	2	8	252	173	274	0.01	58.38
Zimbabwe	6	61	1,263	1,122	2,647	0.06	135.92
Other countries of East Africa	1	3	4	1	1	0.00	0.00
Central Africa	95	175	70	89	89	0.00	0.00
Angola	1	2	4	1	4	0.00	300.00
Cameroon	34	130	38	63	60	0.00	-4.76
Central African Republic	10	1	4	2	3	0.00	50.00
Chad			1	1	2	0.00	100.00
Congo	14	12	8	13	14	0.00	7.69
Gabon	32	19	15	9	6	0.00	-33.33
Sao Tome and Principe	4	11					
North Africa	81	114	213	358	582	0.01	62.57
Algeria	26	13	44	34	58	0.00	70.59
Morocco	16	46	96	262	342	0.01	30.53
Sudan	14	28	37	28	49	0.00	75.00
Tunisia	25	27	36	34	133	0.00	291.18
Southern Africa	130	197	248	536	990	0.02	84.70
Botswana		6	4		2	0.00	
Lesotho				1			
Namibia		1	16	7	15	0.00	114.29
South Africa	130	179	228	525	973	0.02	85.33
Swaziland		11		3			
West Africa	257	394	624	1,368	1,660	0.04	21.35
Benin	2		4	2	15	0.00	650.00
Burkina Faso		8	1	2	3	0.00	50.00
Cape Verde	18	7	80	23	10	0.00	-56.52
Côte d'Ivoire	55	200	87	49	68	0.00	38.78
Gambia	3	7	1		13	0.00	
Ghana	27	68	17	62	84	0.00	35.48
Guinea	10	16	1	11	11	0.00	0.00
Guinea-Bissau				1	5	0.00	400.00
Liberia	48	9	295	822	389	0.01	-52.68
Mali	5	9	1	10	11	0.00	10.00
Mauritania	3			4	6	0.00	50.00
Niger			2	5	11	0.00	120.00
Nigeria	71	60	67	325	958	0.02	194.77
Senegal	7	4	59	43	63	0.00	46.51

Yearbook of Tourism Statistics, Data 2008 – 2012, 2014 Edition

GEORGIA

2. Arrivals of non-resident visitors at national borders, by country of residence

	2008	2009	2010	2011	2012	Market share 2012	% Change 2012-2011
Sierra Leone	8	4	3	7	10	0.00	42.86
Togo		2	6	2	3	0.00	50.00
AMERICAS	**17,552**	**19,659**	**24,656**	**29,286**	**33,898**	**0.77**	**15.75**
Caribbean	**141**	**177**	**1,291**	**1,028**	**497**	**0.01**	**-51.65**
Anguilla				1	1	0.00	0.00
Antigua and Barbuda	63	67	1,046	682	173	0.00	-74.63
Bahamas		31	44	147	24	0.00	-83.67
Barbados	2	2	1	1	4	0.00	300.00
Bermuda		1					
British Virgin Islands			22	26	26	0.00	0.00
Cuba	26	15	30	37	57	0.00	54.05
Dominica			2		6	0.00	
Dominican Republic	1	9	1	11	15	0.00	36.36
Grenada		1			2	0.00	
Guadeloupe		1	1				
Haiti	1	1	11	3	6	0.00	100.00
Jamaica	7	7	26	6	30	0.00	400.00
Netherlands Antilles					1	0.00	
Puerto Rico		2	2	9	1	0.00	-88.89
Saint Kitts and Nevis		1	2	6	52	0.00	766.67
Saint Lucia			1		9	0.00	
Saint Vincent and the Grenadines	1		9	12	11	0.00	-8.33
Trinidad and Tobago	40	39	56	58	44	0.00	-24.14
Turks and Caicos Islands			18	15	21	0.00	40.00
United States Virgin Islands			19	14	14	0.00	0.00
Central America	**121**	**48**	**284**	**321**	**314**	**0.01**	**-2.18**
Belize		2	5	4	4	0.00	0.00
Costa Rica	11	5	8	21	58	0.00	176.19
El Salvador	48	7	26	9	36	0.00	300.00
Guatemala	3	6	2	22	30	0.00	36.36
Honduras	21	15	34	27	37	0.00	37.04
Nicaragua	1	1	2	3	5	0.00	66.67
Panama	37	12	207	235	144	0.00	-38.72
North America	**16,982**	**18,924**	**22,232**	**26,716**	**31,697**	**0.72**	**18.64**
Canada	1,276	1,913	2,052	2,345	2,951	0.07	25.84
Mexico	54	77	99	135	233	0.01	72.59
United States of America	15,652	16,934	20,081	24,236	28,513	0.64	17.65
South America	**308**	**510**	**849**	**1,221**	**1,390**	**0.03**	**13.84**
Argentina	79	158	97	164	203	0.00	23.78
Bolivia	11	9	15	10	35	0.00	250.00
Brazil	102	169	257	311	428	0.01	37.62
Chile	10	13	31	48	70	0.00	45.83
Colombia	21	37	72	70	103	0.00	47.14
Ecuador	20	50	33	135	62	0.00	-54.07
French Guiana			155	332	305	0.01	-8.13
Guyana	2	2		3	2	0.00	-33.33
Paraguay		1	13	12	14	0.00	16.67
Peru	20	29	72	65	71	0.00	9.23
Suriname			2		13	0.00	
Uruguay	34	7	9	40	18	0.00	-55.00
Venezuela	9	35	93	31	66	0.00	112.90
EAST ASIA AND THE PACIFIC	**9,747**	**11,373**	**14,492**	**19,613**	**26,062**	**0.59**	**32.88**
North-East Asia	**3,620**	**4,152**	**5,807**	**10,862**	**15,929**	**0.36**	**46.65**
China	1,771	2,013	2,725	6,522	9,995	0.23	53.25
Hong Kong, China	3	5	21	14	34	0.00	142.86
Japan	1,209	919	1,798	2,419	3,447	0.08	42.50
Korea, Dem. People's Republic of			8	1	3	0.00	200.00

Yearbook of Tourism Statistics, Data 2008 – 2012, 2014 Edition

GEORGIA

2. Arrivals of non-resident visitors at national borders, by country of residence

	2008	2009	2010	2011	2012	Market share 2012	% Change 2012-2011
Korea, Republic of	536	662	935	1,419	1,763	0.04	24.24
Mongolia	46	106	86	128	167	0.00	30.47
Taiwan, Province of China	55	447	234	359	520	0.01	44.85
South-East Asia	**5,245**	**6,024**	**7,334**	**6,894**	**7,904**	**0.18**	**14.65**
Brunei Darussalam			3	6			
Cambodia	25	6	7	11	8	0.00	-27.27
Indonesia	152	188	600	311	389	0.01	25.08
Lao People's Democratic Republic	4	4	5	1	7	0.00	600.00
Malaysia	81	58	67	112	281	0.01	150.89
Myanmar	398	202	92	84	74	0.00	-11.90
Philippines	4,465	5,386	6,342	6,114	6,310	0.14	3.21
Singapore	68	53	115	84	237	0.01	182.14
Thailand	45	92	45	110	252	0.01	129.09
Viet Nam	7	35	58	61	346	0.01	467.21
Australasia	**846**	**1,153**	**1,193**	**1,618**	**2,094**	**0.05**	**29.42**
Australia	644	949	956	1,319	1,658	0.04	25.70
New Zealand	202	204	237	299	436	0.01	45.82
Melanesia	**5**	**8**	**62**	**23**	**54**	**0.00**	**134.78**
Fiji	2	3	2		41	0.00	
Papua New Guinea			1	4	1	0.00	-75.00
Solomon Islands	2	3	9	8	5	0.00	-37.50
Vanuatu	1	2	50	11	7	0.00	-36.36
Micronesia	**5**	**1**	**71**	**164**	**50**	**0.00**	**-69.51**
Kiribati	5		1				
Marshall Islands		1	68	164	48	0.00	-70.73
Nauru			2				
Palau					2	0.00	
Polynesia	**26**	**35**	**25**	**52**	**31**	**0.00**	**-40.38**
American Samoa		7	9	6	9	0.00	50.00
French Polynesia				3	2	0.00	-33.33
Samoa	1	1	5	31	5	0.00	-83.87
Tonga		5	1	2	1	0.00	-50.00
Tuvalu	24	21	2	10	3	0.00	-70.00
Wallis and Futuna Islands	1	1	8		11	0.00	
EUROPE	**1,243,408**	**1,447,516**	**1,956,552**	**2,695,235**	**4,225,635**	**95.43**	**56.78**
Central/Eastern Europe	**811,766**	**974,871**	**1,317,444**	**1,830,148**	**2,541,032**	**57.38**	**38.84**
Armenia	281,463	351,049	547,510	699,382	921,929	20.82	31.82
Azerbaijan	344,936	418,992	497,969	714,418	931,933	21.05	30.45
Belarus	1,981	2,503	5,016	5,344	7,972	0.18	49.18
Bulgaria	8,547	7,123	8,738	10,309	10,668	0.24	3.48
Czech Republic	1,947	2,290	3,060	3,897	4,984	0.11	27.89
Estonia	2,482	1,754	2,207	2,749	4,366	0.10	58.82
Hungary	826	808	836	1,130	1,337	0.03	18.32
Kazakhstan	4,523	5,531	8,411	18,565	15,115	0.34	-18.58
Kyrgyzstan	787	1,107	2,222	3,183	2,626	0.06	-17.50
Latvia	3,643	2,588	3,525	4,802	5,693	0.13	18.55
Lithuania	3,029	2,448	2,916	4,081	5,319	0.12	30.34
Poland	4,479	4,634	7,105	12,082	20,563	0.46	70.20
Republic of Moldova	1,261	1,880	2,390	2,737	4,001	0.09	46.18
Romania	1,782	1,614	1,933	2,347	3,597	0.08	53.26
Russian Federation	114,459	127,937	170,584	278,458	513,930	11.61	84.56
Slovakia	520	861	976	1,085	1,300	0.03	19.82
Tajikistan	194	237	333	540	687	0.02	27.22
Turkmenistan	468	375	1,287	1,126	2,550	0.06	126.47
Ukraine	32,988	39,339	47,596	58,966	76,610	1.73	29.92
Uzbekistan	1,451	1,801	2,830	4,947	5,852	0.13	18.29
Northern Europe	**13,947**	**16,523**	**18,168**	**21,130**	**26,211**	**0.59**	**24.05**

Yearbook of Tourism Statistics, Data 2008 – 2012, 2014 Edition

GEORGIA

2. Arrivals of non-resident visitors at national borders, by country of residence

	2008	2009	2010	2011	2012	Market share 2012	% Change 2012-2011
Denmark	859	1,036	1,370	1,452	2,130	0.05	46.69
Finland	774	944	1,227	1,460	2,236	0.05	53.15
Iceland	37	45	47	161	102	0.00	-36.65
Ireland	663	804	884	970	1,330	0.03	37.11
Norway	942	894	1,184	1,483	1,894	0.04	27.71
Sweden	1,721	2,167	2,471	2,991	3,714	0.08	24.17
United Kingdom	8,951	10,633	10,985	12,613	14,805	0.33	17.38
Southern Europe	**19,544**	**23,190**	**27,710**	**32,188**	**37,286**	**0.84**	**15.84**
Albania	113	161	329	258	403	0.01	56.20
Andorra	2	2	6	9	13	0.00	44.44
Bosnia and Herzegovina	151	203	206	340	503	0.01	47.94
Croatia	408	533	623	1,307	839	0.02	-35.81
Greece	12,914	14,300	16,424	17,664	19,777	0.45	11.96
Holy See	36	35	36	35	38	0.00	8.57
Italy	3,920	4,994	5,886	6,873	8,438	0.19	22.77
Malta	61	86	167	91	102	0.00	12.09
Montenegro	53	406	574	194	136	0.00	-29.90
Portugal	210	283	448	559	863	0.02	54.38
San Marino	5	15	74	35	41	0.00	17.14
Serbia		12	3	593	1,223	0.03	106.24
Slovenia	284	410	528	833	777	0.02	-6.72
Spain	1,322	1,585	2,229	3,156	3,758	0.08	19.07
TFYR of Macedonia	65	165	177	241	375	0.01	55.60
Western Europe	**29,061**	**31,491**	**37,878**	**47,839**	**56,617**	**1.28**	**18.35**
Austria	2,614	1,794	2,488	3,144	4,737	0.11	50.67
Belgium	1,309	1,622	1,991	2,391	2,795	0.06	16.90
France	6,186	6,941	8,486	10,695	12,004	0.27	12.24
Germany	13,267	15,351	17,619	22,204	26,448	0.60	19.11
Liechtenstein	19	9	7	11	21	0.00	90.91
Luxembourg	72	65	111	126	165	0.00	30.95
Monaco	5	6	2	7	1	0.00	-85.71
Netherlands	4,054	4,145	5,198	6,883	7,437	0.17	8.05
Switzerland	1,535	1,558	1,976	2,378	3,009	0.07	26.53
East Mediterranean Europe	**369,090**	**401,441**	**555,352**	**763,930**	**1,564,489**	**35.33**	**104.79**
Cyprus	267	202	312	407	402	0.01	-1.23
Israel	17,413	16,757	19,447	25,438	30,851	0.70	21.28
Turkey	351,410	384,482	535,593	738,085	1,533,236	34.62	107.73
MIDDLE EAST	**3,247**	**3,308**	**3,427**	**5,663**	**17,141**	**0.39**	**202.68**
Bahrain	3	8	5	19	110	0.00	478.95
Egypt	602	391	431	733	2,596	0.06	254.16
Iraq	76	157	126	599	6,947	0.16	1,059.77
Jordan	208	155	172	216	318	0.01	47.22
Kuwait	66	46	59	110	374	0.01	240.00
Lebanon	175	249	272	481	742	0.02	54.26
Libya	21	13	24	26	70	0.00	169.23
Oman	4	13	21	14	154	0.00	1,000.00
Palestine	2	10	14	7	18	0.00	157.14
Qatar	2	4	22	21	72	0.00	242.86
Saudi Arabia	39	19	189	166	1,169	0.03	604.22
Syrian Arab Republic	1,970	2,135	2,021	3,115	4,020	0.09	29.05
United Arab Emirates	58	72	60	147	498	0.01	238.78
Yemen	21	36	11	9	53	0.00	488.89
SOUTH ASIA	**13,457**	**14,572**	**27,810**	**66,073**	**97,925**	**2.21**	**48.21**
Afghanistan	34	55	45	63	111	0.00	76.19
Bangladesh	140	130	77	495	135	0.00	-72.73
Bhutan					1	0.00	

270

GEORGIA

2. Arrivals of non-resident visitors at national borders, by country of residence

	2008	2009	2010	2011	2012	Market share 2012	% Change 2012-2011
India	2,712	3,674	5,653	4,578	6,833	0.15	49.26
Iran, Islamic Republic of	10,038	9,848	21,313	60,191	89,697	2.03	49.02
Maldives	11	10	9	5	12	0.00	140.00
Nepal	38	244	284	145	178	0.00	22.76
Pakistan	414	329	220	316	401	0.01	26.90
Sri Lanka	70	282	209	280	557	0.01	98.93
NOT SPECIFIED	**2,020**	**2,531**	**1,383**	**2,264**	**20,450**	**0.46**	**803.27**
Other countries of the World	2,020	2,531	1,383	2,264	20,450	0.46	803.27

Yearbook of Tourism Statistics, Data 2008 – 2012, 2014 Edition

GEORGIA

3. Arrivals of non-resident tourists in hotels and similar establishments, by country of residence

	2008	2009	2010	2011	2012	Market share 2012	% Change 2012-2011
TOTAL	103,698	150,898	306,547	438,477	625,558	100.00	42.67
AFRICA	112	434	337	1,436	4,433	0.71	208.70
Other Africa	112	434	337	1,436	4,433	0.71	208.70
All countries of Africa	112	434	337	1,436	4,433	0.71	208.70
AMERICAS	13,696	21,500	29,338	27,340	39,297	6.28	43.73
North America	13,158	21,049	28,942	26,444	38,097	6.09	44.07
Canada	193	504	3,414	543	1,746	0.28	221.55
Mexico	15	14	6	6	51	0.01	750.00
United States of America	12,950	20,531	25,522	25,895	36,300	5.80	40.18
South America	449	431	366	495	991	0.16	100.20
Argentina	15	80	138	340	564	0.09	65.88
Brazil	21	63	227	125	410	0.07	228.00
Chile	136	131	1	12	13	0.00	8.33
Uruguay	277	157		18	4	0.00	-77.78
Other Americas	89	20	30	401	209	0.03	-47.88
Other countries of the Americas	89	20	30	401	209	0.03	-47.88
EAST ASIA AND THE PACIFIC	2,077	2,881	4,787	9,627	15,475	2.47	60.75
North-East Asia	1,444	1,598	2,309	5,398	6,245	1.00	15.69
China	542	920	582	4,099	4,439	0.71	8.29
Japan	902	678	1,727	1,299	1,806	0.29	39.03
Australasia	299	301	954	356	933	0.15	162.08
Australia	299	301	954	356	933	0.15	162.08
Other East Asia and the Pacific	334	982	1,524	3,873	8,297	1.33	114.23
Other countries of Asia	334	982	1,524	3,873	8,297	1.33	114.23
EUROPE	86,664	124,849	250,977	347,543	498,471	79.68	43.43
Central/Eastern Europe	36,572	63,079	124,288	171,029	253,041	40.45	47.95
Armenia	5,938	16,239	27,715	32,947	42,630	6.81	29.39
Azerbaijan	7,575	14,465	30,501	48,124	67,064	10.72	39.36
Belarus	392	445	1,374	1,528	4,674	0.75	205.89
Bulgaria	482	1,581	1,269	1,254	2,489	0.40	98.48
Czech Republic	975	856	1,619	3,926	4,519	0.72	15.10
Hungary	265	339	1,002	692	1,372	0.22	98.27
Kazakhstan	1,600	1,496	3,481	6,383	7,155	1.14	12.09
Kyrgyzstan	1,069	1,203	602	787	839	0.13	6.61
Poland	1,562	3,026	4,671	6,549	17,075	2.73	160.73
Republic of Moldova	502	264	740	1,035	1,480	0.24	43.00
Romania	752	550	1,568	1,133	1,993	0.32	75.90
Russian Federation	4,679	7,479	11,436	17,379	40,683	6.50	134.09
Slovakia	181	370	560	528	576	0.09	9.09
Tajikistan	384	285	735	668	631	0.10	-5.54
Turkmenistan	347	970	8,336	10,191	975	0.16	-90.43
Ukraine	6,114	9,096	18,537	25,542	45,288	7.24	77.31
Uzbekistan	903	453	1,046	1,489	1,564	0.25	5.04
Other countries Central/East Europe	2,852	3,962	9,096	10,874	12,034	1.92	10.67
Northern Europe	9,495	10,625	16,342	25,409	27,217	4.35	7.12
Denmark	362	561	1,084	1,720	2,034	0.33	18.26
Finland	343	488	762	1,006	1,436	0.23	42.74
Iceland	136	50	81	516	262	0.04	-49.22
Ireland	172	87	662	834	1,367	0.22	63.91
Norway	248	390	329	520	1,355	0.22	160.58
Sweden	1,632	939	1,835	2,349	3,305	0.53	40.70
United Kingdom	6,602	8,110	11,589	18,464	17,458	2.79	-5.45
Southern Europe	4,191	6,090	9,424	17,149	17,749	2.84	3.50
Greece	1,335	1,324	2,598	5,164	5,339	0.85	3.39
Italy	1,857	3,145	4,167	6,519	7,052	1.13	8.18

Yearbook of Tourism Statistics, Data 2008 – 2012, 2014 Edition

GEORGIA

3. Arrivals of non-resident tourists in hotels and similar establishments, by country of residence

	2008	2009	2010	2011	2012	Market share 2012	% Change 2012-2011
Portugal	173	125	280	818	765	0.12	-6.48
Serbia and Montenegro	24	84	233	50	131	0.02	162.00
Spain	802	1,412	2,146	4,598	4,462	0.71	-2.96
Western Europe	**14,409**	**16,055**	**27,823**	**38,079**	**46,076**	**7.37**	**21.00**
Austria	2,919	1,159	2,438	3,081	3,777	0.60	22.59
Belgium	730	819	1,115	1,643	2,372	0.38	44.37
France	2,169	3,537	6,520	8,275	10,763	1.72	30.07
Germany	5,997	8,348	11,837	18,571	20,893	3.34	12.50
Luxembourg	168	157	1,113	229	223	0.04	-2.62
Netherlands	2,090	1,920	4,327	5,400	6,110	0.98	13.15
Switzerland	336	115	473	880	1,938	0.31	120.23
East Mediterranean Europe	**21,814**	**28,599**	**72,087**	**95,419**	**151,528**	**24.22**	**58.80**
Israel	6,854	10,667	26,367	27,359	32,765	5.24	19.76
Turkey	14,960	17,932	45,720	68,060	118,763	18.99	74.50
Other Europe	**183**	**401**	**1,013**	**458**	**2,860**	**0.46**	**524.45**
Other countries of Europe	183	401	1,013	458	2,860	0.46	524.45
SOUTH ASIA	**503**	**1,234**	**17,413**	**23,990**	**41,678**	**6.66**	**73.73**
India	282	688	1,355	1,415	2,681	0.43	89.47
Iran, Islamic Republic of	221	546	16,058	22,575	38,997	6.23	72.74
NOT SPECIFIED	**646**		**3,695**	**28,541**	**26,204**	**4.19**	**-8.19**
Other countries of the World	646		3,695	28,541	26,204	4.19	-8.19

Yearbook of Tourism Statistics, Data 2008 – 2012, 2014 Edition

GERMANY

3. Arrivals of non-resident tourists in hotels and similar establishments, by country of residence

		2008	2009	2010	2011	2012	Market share 2012	% Change 2012-2011
TOTAL		22,131,203	21,467,043	23,896,638	25,310,793	27,076,452	100.00	6.98
AFRICA		144,895	144,609	180,743	181,422	212,239	0.78	16.99
Southern Africa		48,409	46,865	61,996	64,399	70,126	0.26	8.89
South Africa		48,409	46,865	61,996	64,399	70,126	0.26	8.89
Other Africa		96,486	97,744	118,747	117,023	142,113	0.52	21.44
Other countries of Africa		96,486	97,744	118,747	117,023	142,113	0.52	21.44
AMERICAS		2,418,916	2,322,295	2,720,333	2,754,473	2,972,331	10.98	7.91
North America		2,166,892	2,098,850	2,421,642	2,400,339	2,555,439	9.44	6.46
Canada		232,011	208,940	251,173	259,836	271,944	1.00	4.66
Mexico		53,678	43,720	59,394	64,206	71,881	0.27	11.95
United States of America		1,881,203	1,846,190	2,111,075	2,076,297	2,211,614	8.17	6.52
South America		145,834	121,725	176,576	216,933	255,679	0.94	17.86
Brazil		145,834	121,725	176,576	216,933	255,679	0.94	17.86
Other Americas		106,190	101,720	122,115	137,201	161,213	0.60	17.50
Other countries of the Americas		106,190	101,720	122,115	137,201	161,213	0.60	17.50
EAST ASIA AND THE PACIFIC		1,847,568	1,656,636	2,037,023	2,312,695	2,663,265	9.84	15.16
North-East Asia		1,177,131	1,059,437	1,278,733	1,493,324	1,744,687	6.44	16.83
China	(*)	402,972	367,819	491,112	615,346	729,438	2.69	18.54
Japan		573,974	517,842	586,012	624,970	714,938	2.64	14.40
Korea, Republic of		125,916	111,194	130,590	158,848	194,582	0.72	22.50
Taiwan, Province of China		74,269	62,582	71,019	94,160	105,729	0.39	12.29
Australasia		217,490	197,796	252,881	267,027	289,316	1.07	8.35
Australia, New Zealand		217,490	197,796	252,881	267,027	289,316	1.07	8.35
Other East Asia and the Pacific		452,947	399,403	505,409	552,344	629,262	2.32	13.93
Other countries East Asia/Pacific	(*)	452,947	399,403	505,409	552,344	629,262	2.32	13.93
EUROPE		16,698,473	16,363,802	17,995,732	19,163,324	20,215,986	74.66	5.49
Central/Eastern Europe		1,573,727	1,412,665	1,697,777	1,978,456	2,249,185	8.31	13.68
Baltic countries		136,211	114,029	132,348	149,817	165,403	0.61	10.40
Czech Republic		273,907	246,627	283,448	320,627	345,274	1.28	7.69
Hungary		188,306	163,796	187,158	206,567	215,338	0.80	4.25
Poland		504,073	453,899	536,123	602,766	650,150	2.40	7.86
Russian Federation		471,230	434,314	558,700	698,679	873,020	3.22	24.95
Northern Europe		4,188,625	3,895,275	4,347,998	4,447,148	4,690,113	17.32	5.46
Denmark		932,048	955,600	1,021,525	1,048,335	1,147,029	4.24	9.41
Finland		229,930	220,830	250,488	265,213	263,784	0.97	-0.54
Iceland		37,131	33,278	30,926	33,560	30,055	0.11	-10.44
Ireland		127,465	120,070	123,081	119,797	117,375	0.43	-2.02
Norway		309,952	296,674	349,394	349,537	374,112	1.38	7.03
Sweden		781,316	696,742	784,273	775,409	815,093	3.01	5.12
United Kingdom		1,770,783	1,572,081	1,788,311	1,855,297	1,942,665	7.17	4.71
Southern Europe		2,324,051	2,284,089	2,429,673	2,493,084	2,497,597	9.22	0.18
Greece		174,927	179,664	157,339	152,300	119,296	0.44	-21.67
Italy		1,297,414	1,311,616	1,392,917	1,411,844	1,447,877	5.35	2.55
Portugal		117,938	102,422	111,561	113,138	108,543	0.40	-4.06
Spain		733,772	690,387	767,856	815,802	821,881	3.04	0.75
Western Europe		7,613,710	7,862,667	8,472,059	9,069,147	9,482,412	35.02	4.56
Austria		1,112,266	1,156,134	1,284,219	1,393,422	1,454,911	5.37	4.41
Belgium		922,531	956,360	1,006,397	1,057,611	1,094,003	4.04	3.44
France		1,086,649	1,107,476	1,207,179	1,299,743	1,356,161	5.01	4.34
Luxembourg		172,587	186,184	198,047	202,295	213,252	0.79	5.42
Netherlands		2,720,042	2,793,164	2,960,893	3,055,443	3,140,309	11.60	2.78
Switzerland		1,599,635	1,663,349	1,815,324	2,060,633	2,223,776	8.21	7.92
East Mediterranean Europe		300,620	298,532	357,075	400,916	454,145	1.68	13.28
Israel		130,529	142,953	171,942	185,951	219,360	0.81	17.97

274

GERMANY

3. Arrivals of non-resident tourists in hotels and similar establishments, by country of residence

	2008	2009	2010	2011	2012	Market share 2012	% Change 2012-2011
Turkey	170,091	155,579	185,133	214,965	234,785	0.87	9.22
Other Europe	**697,740**	**610,574**	**691,150**	**774,573**	**842,534**	**3.11**	**8.77**
Other countries of Europe	697,740	610,574	691,150	774,573	842,534	3.11	8.77
MIDDLE EAST	**234,951**	**254,820**	**331,426**	**337,139**	**439,607**	**1.62**	**30.39**
All countries of Middle East	234,951	254,820	331,426	337,139	439,607	1.62	30.39
NOT SPECIFIED	**786,400**	**724,881**	**631,381**	**561,740**	**573,024**	**2.12**	**2.01**
Other countries of the World	786,400	724,881	631,381	561,740	573,024	2.12	2.01

Yearbook of Tourism Statistics, Data 2008 – 2012, 2014 Edition

GERMANY

4. Arrivals of non-resident tourists in all types of accommodation establishments, by country of residence

		2008	2009	2010	2011	2012	Market share 2012	% Change 2012-2011
TOTAL		24,884,017	24,219,634	26,875,288	28,374,101	30,410,491	100.00	7.18
AFRICA		159,670	158,458	192,895	193,193	226,767	0.75	17.38
Southern Africa		53,077	50,675	66,512	68,100	74,459	0.24	9.34
South Africa		53,077	50,675	66,512	68,100	74,459	0.24	9.34
Other Africa		106,593	107,783	126,383	125,093	152,308	0.50	21.76
Other countries of Africa		106,593	107,783	126,383	125,093	152,308	0.50	21.76
AMERICAS		2,572,554	2,475,506	2,882,982	2,914,184	3,155,152	10.38	8.27
North America		2,290,649	2,221,644	2,547,859	2,517,136	2,689,183	8.84	6.84
Canada		256,243	233,526	275,413	281,876	295,234	0.97	4.74
Mexico		60,720	49,280	66,107	71,501	79,996	0.26	11.88
United States of America		1,973,686	1,938,838	2,206,339	2,163,759	2,313,953	7.61	6.94
South America		160,284	136,274	194,960	237,125	279,092	0.92	17.70
Brazil		160,284	136,274	194,960	237,125	279,092	0.92	17.70
Other Americas		121,621	117,588	140,163	159,923	186,877	0.61	16.85
Other countries of the Americas		121,621	117,588	140,163	159,923	186,877	0.61	16.85
EAST ASIA AND THE PACIFIC		1,990,945	1,790,469	2,046,055	2,296,515	2,665,861	8.77	16.08
North-East Asia		1,242,796	1,113,479	1,336,237	1,552,033	1,815,214	5.97	16.96
China	(*)	421,452	384,576	510,611	637,362	757,290	2.49	18.82
Japan		597,655	537,984	605,231	642,542	734,475	2.42	14.31
Korea, Republic of		144,093	123,937	144,306	172,839	210,983	0.69	22.07
Taiwan, Province of China		79,596	66,982	76,089	99,290	112,466	0.37	13.27
Australasia		270,660	255,069	276,097	282,278	313,123	1.03	10.93
Australia				276,097	282,278	313,123	1.03	10.93
Australia, New Zealand		270,660	255,069					
Other East Asia and the Pacific		477,489	421,921	433,721	462,204	537,524	1.77	16.30
Other countries of Asia				389,075	420,164	489,743	1.61	16.56
Other countries East Asia/Pacific	(*)	477,489	421,921					
Other countries of Oceania				44,646	42,040	47,781	0.16	13.66
EUROPE		19,095,571	18,781,861	20,609,923	21,860,790	23,121,212	76.03	5.77
Central/Eastern Europe		1,746,202	1,565,423	2,229,922	2,589,652	2,936,102	9.65	13.38
Baltic countries		156,514	129,138					
Bulgaria				56,077	68,444	71,995	0.24	5.19
Czech Republic		308,982	281,313	320,868	358,908	391,964	1.29	9.21
Estonia				37,503	42,326	46,142	0.15	9.02
Hungary		207,056	180,562	203,445	224,933	235,645	0.77	4.76
Latvia				42,191	50,044	55,318	0.18	10.54
Lithuania				68,474	73,470	82,775	0.27	12.67
Poland		575,228	514,561	604,274	684,193	737,327	2.42	7.77
Romania				153,693	170,581	188,517	0.62	10.51
Russian Federation		498,422	459,849	590,092	737,105	918,226	3.02	24.57
Slovakia				78,113	86,773	95,712	0.31	10.30
Ukraine				75,192	92,875	112,481	0.37	21.11
Northern Europe		4,724,999	4,403,474	4,906,426	4,999,834	5,294,118	17.41	5.89
Denmark		1,110,376	1,138,910	1,214,319	1,242,806	1,356,666	4.46	9.16
Finland		257,951	249,252	281,263	293,948	291,788	0.96	-0.73
Iceland		41,422	36,862	36,488	37,910	34,261	0.11	-9.63
Ireland		143,606	137,629	140,736	134,820	135,039	0.44	0.16
Norway		349,331	328,479	387,468	388,896	416,842	1.37	7.19
Sweden		853,836	762,679	859,261	846,615	897,033	2.95	5.96
United Kingdom		1,968,477	1,749,663	1,986,891	2,054,839	2,162,489	7.11	5.24
Southern Europe		2,540,423	2,502,734	2,735,986	2,796,957	2,809,878	9.24	0.46
Greece		183,522	188,030	166,319	160,856	126,920	0.42	-21.10
Italy		1,421,505	1,444,144	1,524,134	1,538,369	1,581,041	5.20	2.77
Malta				11,697	11,871	13,650	0.04	14.99
Portugal		125,988	109,462	120,824	120,859	118,063	0.39	-2.31

276

GERMANY

4. Arrivals of non-resident tourists in all types of accommodation establishments, by country of residence

	2008	2009	2010	2011	2012	Market share 2012	% Change 2012-2011
Slovenia			70,227	75,496	80,549	0.26	6.69
Spain	809,408	761,098	842,785	889,506	889,655	2.93	0.02
Western Europe	**8,996,810**	**9,321,918**	**10,047,229**	**10,706,647**	**11,231,799**	**36.93**	**4.90**
Austria	1,204,752	1,252,439	1,387,683	1,494,688	1,567,483	5.15	4.87
Belgium	1,026,367	1,070,316	1,131,887	1,192,592	1,238,094	4.07	3.82
France	1,220,138	1,249,522	1,366,153	1,462,096	1,535,077	5.05	4.99
Luxembourg	186,893	200,690	215,443	220,006	232,117	0.76	5.50
Netherlands	3,584,865	3,692,084	3,917,640	4,035,783	4,169,435	13.71	3.31
Switzerland	1,773,795	1,856,867	2,028,423	2,301,482	2,489,593	8.19	8.17
East Mediterranean Europe	**319,713**	**317,864**	**395,106**	**442,339**	**500,423**	**1.65**	**13.13**
Cyprus			13,891	14,434	17,837	0.06	23.58
Israel	141,914	155,231	187,818	203,595	237,822	0.78	16.81
Turkey	177,799	162,633	193,397	224,310	244,764	0.80	9.12
Other Europe	**767,424**	**670,448**	**295,254**	**325,361**	**348,892**	**1.15**	**7.23**
Other countries of Europe	767,424	670,448	295,254	325,361	348,892	1.15	7.23
MIDDLE EAST	**241,786**	**258,883**	**336,193**	**343,263**	**449,249**	**1.48**	**30.88**
All countries of Middle East	241,786	258,883	336,193	343,263	449,249	1.48	30.88
SOUTH ASIA			**141,524**	**160,599**	**171,738**	**0.56**	**6.94**
India			141,524	160,599	171,738	0.56	6.94
NOT SPECIFIED	**823,491**	**754,457**	**665,716**	**605,557**	**620,512**	**2.04**	**2.47**
Other countries of the World	823,491	754,457	665,716	605,557	620,512	2.04	2.47

Yearbook of Tourism Statistics, Data 2008 – 2012, 2014 Edition

GERMANY

5. Overnight stays of non-resident tourists in hotels and similar establishments, by country of residence

		2008	2009	2010	2011	2012	Market share 2012	% Change 2012-2011
TOTAL		47,561,639	45,843,407	50,772,948	53,792,524	58,095,898	100.00	8.00
AFRICA		393,134	376,662	453,711	443,677	543,734	0.94	22.55
Southern Africa		123,825	108,501	134,544	144,314	160,232	0.28	11.03
South Africa		123,825	108,501	134,544	144,314	160,232	0.28	11.03
Other Africa		269,309	268,161	319,167	299,363	383,502	0.66	28.11
Other countries of Africa		269,309	268,161	319,167	299,363	383,502	0.66	28.11
AMERICAS		5,395,749	5,090,630	5,863,967	5,923,716	6,271,629	10.80	5.87
North America		4,766,670	4,548,764	5,142,578	5,067,656	5,261,067	9.06	3.82
Canada		488,265	432,096	512,524	530,166	550,539	0.95	3.84
Mexico		133,646	107,071	141,119	153,911	170,805	0.29	10.98
United States of America		4,144,759	4,009,597	4,488,935	4,383,579	4,539,723	7.81	3.56
South America		362,163	296,142	429,256	525,484	623,076	1.07	18.57
Brazil		362,163	296,142	429,256	525,484	623,076	1.07	18.57
Other Americas		266,916	245,724	292,133	330,576	387,486	0.67	17.22
Other countries of the Americas		266,916	245,724	292,133	330,576	387,486	0.67	17.22
EAST ASIA AND THE PACIFIC		3,980,855	3,462,566	4,310,627	4,878,163	5,610,292	9.66	15.01
North-East Asia		2,364,904	2,030,661	2,481,330	2,870,391	3,337,189	5.74	16.26
China	(*)	876,020	766,508	1,032,983	1,241,960	1,475,819	2.54	18.83
Japan		1,060,190	906,759	1,036,699	1,138,115	1,270,967	2.19	11.67
Korea, Republic of		273,786	233,316	262,273	315,924	385,548	0.66	22.04
Taiwan, Province of China		154,908	124,078	149,375	174,392	204,855	0.35	17.47
Australasia		463,236	423,949	546,152	577,128	631,090	1.09	9.35
Australia, New Zealand		463,236	423,949	546,152	577,128	631,090	1.09	9.35
Other East Asia and the Pacific		1,152,715	1,007,956	1,283,145	1,430,644	1,642,013	2.83	14.77
Other countries East Asia/Pacific	(*)	1,152,715	1,007,956	1,283,145	1,430,644	1,642,013	2.83	14.77
EUROPE		35,554,880	34,783,705	38,033,826	40,519,845	43,373,658	74.66	7.04
Central/Eastern Europe		3,472,457	3,110,431	3,707,247	4,457,679	5,322,121	9.16	19.39
Baltic countries		250,235	204,589	238,022	275,443	317,108	0.55	15.13
Czech Republic		547,995	499,256	565,906	651,421	718,082	1.24	10.23
Hungary		417,541	377,999	440,823	535,195	598,861	1.03	11.90
Poland		1,081,222	956,111	1,118,897	1,356,513	1,618,221	2.79	19.29
Russian Federation		1,175,464	1,072,476	1,343,599	1,639,107	2,069,849	3.56	26.28
Northern Europe		8,221,560	7,650,809	8,503,790	8,698,831	9,330,906	16.06	7.27
Denmark		1,847,358	1,895,593	2,027,862	2,062,665	2,306,836	3.97	11.84
Finland		444,312	438,008	499,570	533,981	546,510	0.94	2.35
Iceland		81,681	74,762	73,615	76,905	69,975	0.12	-9.01
Ireland		293,949	270,026	276,716	266,560	255,655	0.44	-4.09
Norway		562,358	551,187	645,967	656,572	733,928	1.26	11.78
Sweden		1,342,166	1,216,781	1,357,009	1,367,349	1,477,351	2.54	8.04
United Kingdom		3,649,736	3,204,452	3,623,051	3,734,799	3,940,651	6.78	5.51
Southern Europe		5,078,958	4,975,509	5,309,414	5,386,074	5,471,023	9.42	1.58
Greece		452,341	459,479	402,810	380,303	297,418	0.51	-21.79
Italy		2,743,350	2,747,124	2,947,684	2,931,157	3,107,427	5.35	6.01
Portugal		274,457	233,117	256,445	262,877	252,969	0.44	-3.77
Spain		1,608,810	1,535,789	1,702,475	1,811,737	1,813,209	3.12	0.08
Western Europe		16,445,603	16,920,139	18,027,338	19,152,028	20,062,636	34.53	4.75
Austria		2,195,499	2,277,439	2,527,378	2,732,558	2,896,779	4.99	6.01
Belgium		2,128,818	2,174,456	2,251,265	2,341,702	2,435,610	4.19	4.01
France		2,046,944	2,094,192	2,295,164	2,475,242	2,560,627	4.41	3.45
Luxembourg		382,314	411,155	430,286	435,570	453,163	0.78	4.04
Netherlands		6,552,553	6,701,012	6,977,366	7,122,264	7,305,258	12.57	2.57
Switzerland		3,139,475	3,261,885	3,545,879	4,044,692	4,411,199	7.59	9.06
East Mediterranean Europe		743,205	709,786	872,018	970,018	1,115,737	1.92	15.02
Israel		335,658	368,306	444,757	485,488	578,518	1.00	19.16

278

Yearbook of Tourism Statistics, Data 2008 – 2012, 2014 Edition

GERMANY

5. Overnight stays of non-resident tourists in hotels and similar establishments, by country of residence

	2008	2009	2010	2011	2012	Market share 2012	% Change 2012-2011
Turkey	407,547	341,480	427,261	484,530	537,219	0.92	10.87
Other Europe	**1,593,097**	**1,417,031**	**1,614,019**	**1,855,215**	**2,071,235**	**3.57**	**11.64**
Other countries of Europe	1,593,097	1,417,031	1,614,019	1,855,215	2,071,235	3.57	11.64
MIDDLE EAST	**726,775**	**734,450**	**926,413**	**960,767**	**1,218,746**	**2.10**	**26.85**
All countries of Middle East	726,775	734,450	926,413	960,767	1,218,746	2.10	26.85
NOT SPECIFIED	**1,510,246**	**1,395,394**	**1,184,404**	**1,066,356**	**1,077,839**	**1.86**	**1.08**
Other countries of the World	1,510,246	1,395,394	1,184,404	1,066,356	1,077,839	1.86	1.08

Yearbook of Tourism Statistics, Data 2008 – 2012, 2014 Edition

GERMANY

6. Overnight stays of non-resident tourists in all types of accommodation establishments, by country of residence

		2008	2009	2010	2011	2012	Market share 2012	% Change 2012-2011
TOTAL		56,536,906	54,823,716	60,310,448	63,746,372	68,827,658	100.00	7.97
AFRICA		463,399	448,260	513,985	504,517	621,727	0.90	23.23
Southern Africa		141,343	123,220	149,026	156,752	174,892	0.25	11.57
South Africa		141,343	123,220	149,026	156,752	174,892	0.25	11.57
Other Africa		322,056	325,040	364,959	347,765	446,835	0.65	28.49
Other countries of Africa		322,056	325,040	364,959	347,765	446,835	0.65	28.49
AMERICAS		5,880,884	5,562,598	6,350,191	6,429,114	6,842,839	9.94	6.44
North America		5,157,891	4,918,084	5,515,227	5,439,369	5,676,268	8.25	4.36
Canada		556,503	499,531	579,401	597,579	623,867	0.91	4.40
Mexico		155,948	127,248	166,453	180,193	197,625	0.29	9.67
United States of America		4,445,440	4,291,305	4,769,373	4,661,597	4,854,776	7.05	4.14
South America		404,608	339,588	482,310	586,590	694,440	1.01	18.39
Brazil		404,608	339,588	482,310	586,590	694,440	1.01	18.39
Other Americas		318,385	304,926	352,654	403,155	472,131	0.69	17.11
Other countries of the Americas		318,385	304,926	352,654	403,155	472,131	0.69	17.11
EAST ASIA AND THE PACIFIC		4,417,449	3,851,425	4,267,183	4,770,515	5,519,403	8.02	15.70
North-East Asia		2,559,379	2,182,324	2,632,462	3,041,171	3,532,984	5.13	16.17
China	(*)	942,988	820,187	1,092,470	1,322,564	1,563,298	2.27	18.20
Japan		1,130,328	959,969	1,084,285	1,185,279	1,325,544	1.93	11.83
Korea, Republic of		318,330	267,428	294,829	346,856	423,530	0.62	22.11
Taiwan, Province of China		167,733	134,740	160,878	186,472	220,612	0.32	18.31
Australasia		596,610	562,589	613,212	637,644	701,601	1.02	10.03
Australia				613,212	637,644	701,601	1.02	10.03
Australia, New Zealand		596,610	562,589					
Other East Asia and the Pacific		1,261,460	1,106,512	1,021,509	1,091,700	1,284,818	1.87	17.69
Other countries of Asia				923,769	997,508	1,179,009	1.71	18.20
Other countries East Asia/Pacific	(*)	1,261,460	1,106,512					
Other countries of Oceania				97,740	94,192	105,809	0.15	12.33
EUROPE		43,328,769	42,624,382	46,456,990	49,268,358	52,746,984	76.64	7.06
Central/Eastern Europe		4,102,134	3,683,872	5,269,138	6,320,231	7,520,207	10.93	18.99
Baltic countries		295,321	239,775					
Bulgaria				142,014	173,845	196,009	0.28	12.75
Czech Republic		656,259	606,507	672,257	765,879	858,798	1.25	12.13
Estonia				68,751	80,347	89,411	0.13	11.28
Hungary		495,179	445,567	510,219	618,408	714,635	1.04	15.56
Latvia				84,129	99,889	116,914	0.17	17.04
Lithuania				125,968	139,190	164,942	0.24	18.50
Poland		1,346,876	1,192,951	1,380,549	1,716,479	2,013,267	2.93	17.29
Romania				401,726	465,393	557,124	0.81	19.71
Russian Federation		1,308,499	1,199,072	1,486,471	1,786,603	2,247,281	3.27	25.79
Slovakia				220,444	267,996	301,061	0.44	12.34
Ukraine				176,610	206,202	260,765	0.38	26.46
Northern Europe		9,614,770	8,963,273	9,952,349	10,155,974	10,892,993	15.83	7.26
Denmark		2,296,078	2,360,550	2,528,220	2,583,749	2,855,677	4.15	10.52
Finland		509,257	502,844	574,818	600,392	612,339	0.89	1.99
Iceland		94,171	87,199	89,025	88,452	82,401	0.12	-6.84
Ireland		345,736	329,938	331,405	312,169	302,591	0.44	-3.07
Norway		652,915	623,853	733,407	749,284	843,686	1.23	12.60
Sweden		1,494,198	1,359,645	1,514,850	1,525,431	1,659,463	2.41	8.79
United Kingdom		4,222,415	3,699,244	4,180,624	4,296,497	4,536,836	6.59	5.59
Southern Europe		5,712,163	5,607,912	6,145,142	6,226,372	6,371,819	9.26	2.34
Greece		491,863	499,064	438,501	414,230	329,824	0.48	-20.38
Italy		3,070,813	3,101,720	3,295,849	3,262,617	3,468,347	5.04	6.31
Malta				29,642	30,830	35,038	0.05	13.65
Portugal		306,961	256,603	292,773	290,202	289,827	0.42	-0.13

280

GERMANY

6. Overnight stays of non-resident tourists in all types of accommodation establishments, by country of residence

	2008	2009	2010	2011	2012	Market share 2012	% Change 2012-2011
Slovenia			158,871	183,319	220,981	0.32	20.54
Spain	1,842,526	1,750,525	1,929,506	2,045,174	2,027,802	2.95	-0.85
Western Europe	**21,212,870**	**21,927,960**	**23,391,115**	**24,655,304**	**25,847,274**	**37.55**	**4.83**
Austria	2,482,052	2,573,826	2,838,779	3,030,904	3,221,467	4.68	6.29
Belgium	2,473,257	2,540,634	2,639,425	2,755,820	2,870,823	4.17	4.17
France	2,431,320	2,509,231	2,735,869	2,933,315	3,064,548	4.45	4.47
Luxembourg	455,023	486,020	507,506	517,564	539,748	0.78	4.29
Netherlands	9,689,240	9,962,061	10,483,114	10,653,148	10,939,882	15.89	2.69
Switzerland	3,681,978	3,856,188	4,186,422	4,764,553	5,210,806	7.57	9.37
East Mediterranean Europe	**822,049**	**786,909**	**998,998**	**1,111,834**	**1,282,607**	**1.86**	**15.36**
Cyprus			35,692	36,982	45,690	0.07	23.55
Israel	382,439	416,107	505,206	554,795	660,936	0.96	19.13
Turkey	439,610	370,802	458,100	520,057	575,981	0.84	10.75
Other Europe	**1,864,783**	**1,654,456**	**700,248**	**798,643**	**832,084**	**1.21**	**4.19**
Other countries of Europe	1,864,783	1,654,456	700,248	798,643	832,084	1.21	4.19
MIDDLE EAST	**776,550**	**770,980**	**968,336**	**1,006,856**	**1,284,583**	**1.87**	**27.58**
All countries of Middle East	776,550	770,980	968,336	1,006,856	1,284,583	1.87	27.58
SOUTH ASIA			**455,655**	**547,480**	**584,508**	**0.85**	**6.76**
India			455,655	547,480	584,508	0.85	6.76
NOT SPECIFIED	**1,669,855**	**1,566,071**	**1,298,108**	**1,219,532**	**1,227,614**	**1.78**	**0.66**
Other countries of the World	1,669,855	1,566,071	1,298,108	1,219,532	1,227,614	1.78	0.66

Yearbook of Tourism Statistics, Data 2008 – 2012, 2014 Edition

GREECE

1. Arrivals of non-resident tourists at national borders, by country of residence

		2008	2009	2010	2011	2012	Market share 2012	% Change 2012-2011
TOTAL	(*)	15,938,806	14,914,534	15,007,490	16,427,248	15,517,625	100.00	-5.54
AFRICA		44,569	25,576	28,314	33,775	32,688	0.21	-3.22
Southern Africa		35,689	20,539	19,985	21,981	19,686	0.13	-10.44
South Africa		35,689	20,539	19,985	21,981	19,686	0.13	-10.44
Other Africa		8,880	5,037	8,329	11,794	13,002	0.08	10.24
Other countries of Africa		8,880	5,037	8,329	11,794	13,002	0.08	10.24
AMERICAS		849,014	729,446	691,379	719,661	558,729	3.60	-22.36
North America		780,149	675,168	622,129	632,527	484,592	3.12	-23.39
Canada		158,447	134,983	113,358	142,287	102,694	0.66	-27.83
Mexico		8,877	8,909	10,470	5,532	8,067	0.05	45.82
United States of America		612,825	531,276	498,301	484,708	373,831	2.41	-22.88
South America		41,783	38,418	51,787	65,952	51,332	0.33	-22.17
Argentina		14,298	13,878	17,772	13,834	20,207	0.13	46.07
Brazil		27,485	24,540	34,015	52,118	31,125	0.20	-40.28
Other Americas		27,082	15,860	17,463	21,182	22,805	0.15	7.66
Other countries of the Americas		27,082	15,860	17,463	21,182	22,805	0.15	7.66
EAST ASIA AND THE PACIFIC		217,999	206,209	199,452	207,360	215,864	1.39	4.10
North-East Asia		21,258	19,681	31,264	27,809	27,145	0.17	-2.39
China		5,941	7,793	13,620	15,838	12,203	0.08	-22.95
Japan		10,926	6,765	10,021	10,125	8,841	0.06	-12.68
Korea, Republic of		4,391	5,123	7,623	1,846	6,101	0.04	230.50
Australasia		136,086	133,869	108,088	115,902	117,852	0.76	1.68
Australia		136,086	133,869	108,088	115,902	117,852	0.76	1.68
Other East Asia and the Pacific		60,655	52,659	60,100	63,649	70,867	0.46	11.34
Other countries of Asia		36,819	25,016	42,015	44,572	55,351	0.36	24.18
Other countries of Oceania		23,836	27,643	18,085	19,077	15,516	0.10	-18.67
EUROPE		14,766,811	13,884,208	14,034,319	15,429,714	14,661,081	94.48	-4.98
Central/Eastern Europe		2,133,018	1,902,280	2,281,324	2,551,433	2,404,238	15.49	-5.77
Bulgaria		623,476	657,130	664,389	686,209	599,110	3.86	-12.69
Czech Republic		267,596	267,833	294,936	309,062	289,034	1.86	-6.48
Estonia		26,018	21,242	13,842	9,862	4,757	0.03	-51.76
Hungary		180,914	70,894	109,160	69,756	69,789	0.45	0.05
Latvia		31,010	12,027	21,948	7,846	15,300	0.10	95.00
Lithuania		34,537	37,501	16,295	13,666	21,601	0.14	58.06
Poland		270,039	203,487	402,170	450,618	254,682	1.64	-43.48
Romania		327,261	307,596	257,939	223,699	230,396	1.48	2.99
Russian Federation		309,071	276,021	451,239	738,927	874,787	5.64	18.39
Slovakia		63,096	48,549	49,406	41,788	44,782	0.29	7.16
Northern Europe		3,429,941	3,294,786	2,782,059	2,790,183	2,928,408	18.87	4.95
Denmark		245,946	264,040	240,563	244,986	205,194	1.32	-16.24
Finland		147,746	170,341	205,282	167,632	154,134	0.99	-8.05
Iceland		4,476	3,340			2,059	0.01	
Ireland		93,534	73,167	65,623	58,939	32,357	0.21	-45.10
Norway		277,303	315,595	187,319	226,627	294,114	1.90	29.78
Sweden		382,922	356,154	281,069	333,906	319,756	2.06	-4.24
United Kingdom		2,278,014	2,112,149	1,802,203	1,758,093	1,920,794	12.38	9.25
Southern Europe		2,361,460	1,895,695	2,016,863	2,263,450	2,151,868	13.87	-4.93
Albania		242,999	234,276	242,083	411,245	469,213	3.02	14.10
Italy		1,099,983	935,011	843,613	938,232	848,073	5.47	-9.61
Malta		11,702	4,367	9,651	1,368	2,206	0.01	61.26
Portugal		24,678	13,300	19,497	34,642	20,483	0.13	-40.87
Serbia and Montenegro		686,996	498,356	706,635	692,059	620,450	4.00	-10.35
Slovenia		75,185	45,924	40,082	31,130	35,721	0.23	14.75
Spain		219,917	164,461	155,302	154,774	155,722	1.00	0.61
Western Europe		5,276,551	5,040,130	4,406,588	5,083,455	4,442,810	28.63	-12.60

282

GREECE

1. Arrivals of non-resident tourists at national borders, by country of residence

		2008	2009	2010	2011	2012	Market share 2012	% Change 2012-2011
Austria		354,748	352,223	338,367	310,358	236,416	1.52	-23.82
Belgium		420,748	334,240	339,836	432,625	326,937	2.11	-24.43
France		910,021	962,435	868,346	1,149,388	977,376	6.30	-14.97
Germany		2,469,151	2,364,486	2,038,871	2,240,481	2,108,787	13.59	-5.88
Luxembourg		25,135	22,792	18,593	28,475	15,192	0.10	-46.65
Netherlands		756,940	651,440	528,157	560,723	478,483	3.08	-14.67
Switzerland		339,808	352,514	274,418	361,405	299,619	1.93	-17.10
East Mediterranean Europe		**766,771**	**717,537**	**1,333,121**	**1,217,957**	**1,234,844**	**7.96**	**1.39**
Cyprus		474,941	434,746	574,764	439,757	424,827	2.74	-3.40
Israel		84,221	82,443	197,159	226,110	207,711	1.34	-8.14
Turkey		207,609	200,348	561,198	552,090	602,306	3.88	9.10
Other Europe		**799,070**	**1,033,780**	**1,214,364**	**1,523,236**	**1,498,913**	**9.66**	**-1.60**
Other countries of Europe		799,070	1,033,780	1,214,364	1,523,236	1,498,913	9.66	-1.60
MIDDLE EAST		**47,702**	**55,844**	**44,837**	**27,990**	**35,632**	**0.23**	**27.30**
Egypt	(*)	13,556	12,610	15,925	4,675	4,724	0.03	1.05
Lebanon	(*)	11,457	14,753	4,639	4,916	12,846	0.08	161.31
Other countries of Middle East		22,689	28,481	24,273	18,399	18,062	0.12	-1.83
SOUTH ASIA		**847**	**1,647**	**9,189**	**8,748**	**13,631**	**0.09**	**55.82**
Iran, Islamic Republic of		847	1,647	9,189	8,748	13,631	0.09	55.82
NOT SPECIFIED		**11,864**	**11,604**					
Other countries of the World		11,864	11,604					

283

GREECE

3. Arrivals of non-resident tourists in hotels and similar establishments, by country of residence

	2008	2009	2010	2011	2012	Market share 2012	% Change 2012-2011
TOTAL	8,657,775	8,542,307	8,964,224	10,041,765	9,243,952	100.00	-7.94
AFRICA	38,640	37,283	45,813	55,596	90,691	0.98	63.13
Southern Africa	1,437	1,516	1,615	1,901	1,784	0.02	-6.15
South Africa	1,437	1,516	1,615	1,901	1,784	0.02	-6.15
Other Africa	37,203	35,767	44,198	53,695	88,907	0.96	65.58
Other countries of Africa	37,203	35,767	44,198	53,695	88,907	0.96	65.58
AMERICAS	835,832	784,527	811,559	847,173	639,022	6.91	-24.57
North America	751,449	698,606	713,437	725,429	536,429	5.80	-26.05
Canada	118,213	110,149	110,993	119,584	85,464	0.92	-28.53
United States of America	633,236	588,457	602,444	605,845	450,965	4.88	-25.56
South America	37,533	34,549	41,974	57,899	43,878	0.47	-24.22
Brazil	37,533	34,549	41,974	57,899	43,878	0.47	-24.22
Other Americas	46,850	51,372	56,148	63,845	58,715	0.64	-8.04
Other countries of the Americas	46,850	51,372	56,148	63,845	58,715	0.64	-8.04
EAST ASIA AND THE PACIFIC	505,147	496,523	622,797	722,597	661,396	7.15	-8.47
North-East Asia	146,249	145,023	139,789	165,597	137,077	1.48	-17.22
China	49,883	48,033	59,268	87,323	88,450	0.96	1.29
Japan	95,429	96,075	79,228	74,971	45,711	0.49	-39.03
Korea, Republic of	937	915	1,293	3,303	2,916	0.03	-11.72
Australasia	133,547	114,951	149,887	167,884	152,208	1.65	-9.34
Australia	133,547	114,951	149,887	167,884	152,208	1.65	-9.34
Other East Asia and the Pacific	225,351	236,549	333,121	389,116	372,111	4.03	-4.37
Other countries of Asia	216,232	229,008	324,059	377,419	362,471	3.92	-3.96
Other countries of Oceania	9,119	7,541	9,062	11,697	9,640	0.10	-17.59
EUROPE	7,277,317	7,219,060	7,476,544	8,409,601	7,847,647	84.89	-6.68
Central/Eastern Europe	1,336,587	1,264,196	1,322,434	1,644,773	1,744,185	18.87	6.04
Bulgaria	165,667	152,479	126,122	146,586	145,347	1.57	-0.85
Czech Republic	149,116	164,347	151,759	164,349	155,605	1.68	-5.32
Estonia	16,805	14,294	15,353	14,063	13,644	0.15	-2.98
Hungary	61,060	47,746	43,399	45,950	41,161	0.45	-10.42
Latvia	14,497	11,208	9,080	10,585	10,094	0.11	-4.64
Lithuania	24,189	17,461	15,703	18,618	17,341	0.19	-6.86
Poland	210,658	231,087	234,075	288,028	245,554	2.66	-14.75
Romania	193,630	181,291	153,496	172,575	185,920	2.01	7.73
Russian Federation	426,843	376,138	494,020	686,717	820,618	8.88	19.50
Slovakia	43,760	39,336	35,849	40,370	32,551	0.35	-19.37
Ukraine	30,362	28,809	43,578	56,932	76,350	0.83	34.11
Northern Europe	1,789,628	1,822,281	1,938,724	2,158,294	2,102,141	22.74	-2.60
Denmark	158,872	158,482	164,095	183,434	171,736	1.86	-6.38
Finland	112,433	126,025	129,759	160,140	144,970	1.57	-9.47
Iceland	6,097	3,970	3,082	4,419	4,668	0.05	5.63
Ireland	44,893	42,870	40,344	40,411	30,984	0.34	-23.33
Norway	173,053	181,891	207,069	236,119	245,972	2.66	4.17
Sweden	234,614	242,262	284,355	322,286	316,719	3.43	-1.73
United Kingdom	1,059,666	1,066,781	1,110,020	1,211,485	1,187,092	12.84	-2.01
Southern Europe	857,197	844,945	867,639	934,303	733,694	7.94	-21.47
Italy	624,161	600,955	656,834	701,056	564,754	6.11	-19.44
Malta	3,682	5,131	4,017	4,375	3,729	0.04	-14.77
Portugal	21,220	21,765	20,153	18,784	13,853	0.15	-26.25
Slovenia	39,350	35,465	30,576	30,612	25,361	0.27	-17.15
Spain	168,784	181,629	156,059	179,476	125,997	1.36	-29.80
Western Europe	2,813,695	2,822,129	2,824,398	3,079,658	2,670,366	28.89	-13.29
Austria	192,185	191,743	175,593	171,512	149,786	1.62	-12.67
Belgium	233,136	225,718	232,627	265,696	229,144	2.48	-13.76
France	678,145	749,442	737,178	826,929	714,749	7.73	-13.57

284

GREECE

3. Arrivals of non-resident tourists in hotels and similar establishments, by country of residence

	2008	2009	2010	2011	2012	Market share 2012	% Change 2012-2011
Germany	1,162,613	1,136,774	1,163,238	1,244,474	1,082,024	11.71	-13.05
Luxembourg	15,550	12,814	11,229	13,282	12,066	0.13	-9.16
Netherlands	386,567	360,959	360,747	395,221	333,474	3.61	-15.62
Switzerland	145,499	144,679	143,786	162,544	149,123	1.61	-8.26
East Mediterranean Europe	**247,310**	**230,711**	**253,482**	**274,331**	**293,118**	**3.17**	**6.85**
Cyprus	185,930	169,978	177,129	168,104	164,877	1.78	-1.92
Turkey	61,380	60,733	76,353	106,227	128,241	1.39	20.72
Other Europe	**232,900**	**234,798**	**269,867**	**318,242**	**304,143**	**3.29**	**-4.43**
Other countries of Europe	232,900	234,798	269,867	318,242	304,143	3.29	-4.43
NOT SPECIFIED	**839**	**4,914**	**7,511**	**6,798**	**5,196**	**0.06**	**-23.57**
Other countries of the World	839	4,914	7,511	6,798	5,196	0.06	-23.57

Yearbook of Tourism Statistics, Data 2008 – 2012, 2014 Edition

GREECE

4. Arrivals of non-resident tourists in all types of accommodation establishments, by country of residence

	2008	2009	2010	2011	2012	Market share 2012	% Change 2012-2011
TOTAL	8,886,342	8,781,095	9,196,924	10,266,462			
AFRICA	38,810	37,504	46,093	55,790			
Southern Africa	1,485	1,550	1,663	1,960			
South Africa	1,485	1,550	1,663	1,960			
Other Africa	37,325	35,954	44,430	53,830			
Other countries of Africa	37,325	35,954	44,430	53,830			
AMERICAS	843,700	787,843	815,038	850,413			
North America	758,699	701,449	716,216	728,131			
Canada	120,997	111,296	112,313	120,967			
United States of America	637,702	590,153	603,903	607,164			
South America	37,679	34,749	42,140	58,097			
Brazil	37,679	34,749	42,140	58,097			
Other Americas	47,322	51,645	56,682	64,185			
Other countries of the Americas	47,322	51,645	56,682	64,185			
EAST ASIA AND THE PACIFIC	514,340	503,190	630,840	730,454			
North-East Asia	146,424	145,123	139,913	165,745			
China	49,944	48,096	59,342	87,390			
Japan	95,520	96,106	79,270	75,036			
Korea, Republic of	960	921	1,301	3,319			
Australasia	140,035	120,243	155,742	173,662			
Australia	140,035	120,243	155,742	173,662			
Other East Asia and the Pacific	227,881	237,824	335,185	391,047			
Other countries of Asia	216,719	229,498	324,825	378,168			
Other countries of Oceania	11,162	8,326	10,360	12,879			
EUROPE	7,488,603	7,447,642	7,697,419	8,622,981			
Central/Eastern Europe	1,354,223	1,285,292	1,342,227	1,665,235			
Bulgaria	168,519	157,747	132,129	153,847			
Czech Republic	152,101	167,117	154,061	166,828			
Estonia	17,023	14,491	15,540	14,175			
Hungary	63,770	50,562	45,989	48,158			
Latvia	14,647	11,310	9,183	10,669			
Lithuania	24,336	17,653	15,813	18,798			
Poland	215,763	237,055	239,536	293,197			
Romania	196,307	183,934	155,393	174,554			
Russian Federation	427,171	376,589	494,555	687,161			
Slovakia	44,133	39,898	36,317	40,780			
Ukraine	30,453	28,936	43,711	57,068			
Northern Europe	1,800,865	1,832,848	1,948,282	2,167,087			
Denmark	161,027	160,463	166,271	185,139			
Finland	112,737	126,309	129,971	160,329			
Iceland	6,109	3,984	3,096	4,442			
Ireland	45,814	43,501	40,842	40,905			
Norway	173,359	182,179	207,416	236,425			
Sweden	235,321	242,848	284,998	322,822			
United Kingdom	1,066,498	1,073,564	1,115,688	1,217,025			
Southern Europe	898,783	889,395	909,213	973,552			
Italy	660,103	639,105	692,595	734,806			
Malta	3,734	5,451	4,049	4,404			
Portugal	21,421	22,170	20,444	19,049			
Slovenia	41,627	38,150	33,079	33,083			
Spain	171,898	184,519	159,046	182,210			
Western Europe	2,951,000	2,970,561	2,968,753	3,218,628			
Austria	202,789	203,996	187,287	182,204			
Belgium	236,879	230,155	236,960	270,132			
France	717,225	790,787	777,158	867,489			

286

GREECE

4. Arrivals of non-resident tourists in all types of accommodation establishments, by country of residence

	2008	2009	2010	2011	2012	Market share 2012	% Change 2012-2011
Germany	1,215,964	1,195,325	1,217,220	1,295,676			
Luxembourg	15,607	12,880	11,289	13,347			
Netherlands	410,899	385,918	387,692	420,422			
Switzerland	151,637	151,500	151,147	169,358			
East Mediterranean Europe	**247,958**	**231,367**	**254,288**	**275,060**			
Cyprus	186,332	170,404	177,493	168,433			
Turkey	61,626	60,963	76,795	106,627			
Other Europe	**235,774**	**238,179**	**274,656**	**323,419**			
Other countries of Europe	235,774	238,179	274,656	323,419			
NOT SPECIFIED	**889**	**4,916**	**7,534**	**6,824**			
Other countries of the World	889	4,916	7,534	6,824			

Yearbook of Tourism Statistics, Data 2008 – 2012, 2014 Edition

GREECE

5. Overnight stays of non-resident tourists in hotels and similar establishments, by country of residence

	2008	2009	2010	2011	2012	Market share 2012	% Change 2012-2011
TOTAL	47,233,616	45,925,585	48,243,634	53,768,033	50,445,674	100.00	-6.18
AFRICA	118,897	113,352	120,683	170,882	467,720	0.93	173.71
Southern Africa	4,085	5,004	5,054	6,147	6,165	0.01	0.29
South Africa	4,085	5,004	5,054	6,147	6,165	0.01	0.29
Other Africa	114,812	108,348	115,629	164,735	461,555	0.91	180.18
Other countries of Africa	114,812	108,348	115,629	164,735	461,555	0.91	180.18
AMERICAS	1,752,995	1,664,877	1,715,269	1,894,781	1,436,308	2.85	-24.20
North America	1,545,520	1,460,114	1,487,159	1,617,227	1,201,979	2.38	-25.68
Canada	263,894	253,912	253,154	278,404	202,817	0.40	-27.15
United States of America	1,281,626	1,206,202	1,234,005	1,338,823	999,162	1.98	-25.37
South America	92,487	81,156	98,118	132,134	100,911	0.20	-23.63
Brazil	92,487	81,156	98,118	132,134	100,911	0.20	-23.63
Other Americas	114,988	123,607	129,992	145,420	133,418	0.26	-8.25
Other countries of the Americas	114,988	123,607	129,992	145,420	133,418	0.26	-8.25
EAST ASIA AND THE PACIFIC	1,163,160	1,215,251	1,580,516	1,847,533	1,726,496	3.42	-6.55
North-East Asia	263,328	249,525	241,942	297,335	240,444	0.48	-19.13
China	98,890	92,937	108,841	160,404	153,134	0.30	-4.53
Japan	162,963	155,058	131,185	132,566	83,257	0.17	-37.20
Korea, Republic of	1,475	1,530	1,916	4,365	4,053	0.01	-7.15
Australasia	311,999	271,811	346,096	392,709	347,382	0.69	-11.54
Australia	311,999	271,811	346,096	392,709	347,382	0.69	-11.54
Other East Asia and the Pacific	587,833	693,915	992,478	1,157,489	1,138,670	2.26	-1.63
Other countries of Asia	567,537	676,359	971,473	1,127,023	1,114,669	2.21	-1.10
Other countries of Oceania	20,296	17,556	21,005	30,466	24,001	0.05	-21.22
EUROPE	44,195,194	42,915,120	44,805,322	49,830,236	46,798,727	92.77	-6.08
Central/Eastern Europe	8,069,453	7,733,283	8,514,530	10,510,562	11,207,349	22.22	6.63
Bulgaria	451,791	453,389	391,898	476,494	486,278	0.96	2.05
Czech Republic	1,187,155	1,296,205	1,200,054	1,294,741	1,185,447	2.35	-8.44
Estonia	104,340	86,759	89,982	85,492	77,818	0.15	-8.98
Hungary	372,708	278,030	261,180	279,339	248,954	0.49	-10.88
Latvia	86,343	67,982	53,634	63,135	60,578	0.12	-4.05
Lithuania	152,967	120,061	102,320	114,394	102,788	0.20	-10.15
Poland	1,357,097	1,466,042	1,497,626	1,834,435	1,568,013	3.11	-14.52
Romania	856,111	806,581	711,191	808,992	863,531	1.71	6.74
Russian Federation	2,991,588	2,713,015	3,655,568	4,905,157	5,920,404	11.74	20.70
Slovakia	328,504	290,110	282,382	317,825	242,744	0.48	-23.62
Ukraine	180,849	155,109	268,695	330,558	450,794	0.89	36.37
Northern Europe	12,043,035	12,025,104	12,927,181	14,035,613	13,706,472	27.17	-2.35
Denmark	1,056,943	1,031,557	1,091,539	1,195,555	1,128,720	2.24	-5.59
Finland	767,725	851,657	881,678	1,036,516	942,163	1.87	-9.10
Iceland	37,323	19,612	13,119	18,871	18,792	0.04	-0.42
Ireland	253,048	236,494	212,770	197,548	146,855	0.29	-25.66
Norway	1,303,311	1,310,086	1,517,015	1,626,310	1,679,782	3.33	3.29
Sweden	1,529,135	1,570,400	1,851,611	2,072,624	2,021,860	4.01	-2.45
United Kingdom	7,095,550	7,005,298	7,359,449	7,888,189	7,768,300	15.40	-1.52
Southern Europe	3,841,162	3,515,676	3,405,767	3,729,433	2,969,793	5.89	-20.37
Italy	3,159,042	2,806,170	2,789,213	3,062,246	2,468,756	4.89	-19.38
Malta	14,563	22,252	17,271	17,736	16,214	0.03	-8.58
Portugal	67,295	69,801	66,021	60,984	43,232	0.09	-29.11
Slovenia	219,516	208,494	177,661	174,292	145,296	0.29	-16.64
Spain	380,746	408,959	355,601	414,175	296,295	0.59	-28.46
Western Europe	18,531,304	17,987,125	18,014,357	19,324,593	16,676,775	33.06	-13.70
Austria	1,350,641	1,211,417	1,175,892	1,139,149	985,309	1.95	-13.50
Belgium	1,523,693	1,452,533	1,471,804	1,597,661	1,369,807	2.72	-14.26
France	3,182,160	3,480,867	3,404,558	3,833,788	3,325,641	6.59	-13.25

288

GREECE

5. Overnight stays of non-resident tourists in hotels and similar establishments, by country of residence

	2008	2009	2010	2011	2012	Market share 2012	% Change 2012-2011
Germany	8,756,063	8,332,465	8,509,308	9,073,654	7,789,309	15.44	-14.15
Luxembourg	108,665	90,724	81,101	85,895	70,625	0.14	-17.78
Netherlands	2,727,542	2,552,027	2,513,056	2,623,056	2,251,146	4.46	-14.18
Switzerland	882,540	867,092	858,638	971,390	884,938	1.75	-8.90
East Mediterranean Europe	**675,152**	**614,701**	**677,384**	**703,330**	**725,549**	**1.44**	**3.16**
Cyprus	548,944	495,477	525,704	502,203	482,097	0.96	-4.00
Turkey	126,208	119,224	151,680	201,127	243,452	0.48	21.04
Other Europe	**1,035,088**	**1,039,231**	**1,266,103**	**1,526,705**	**1,512,789**	**3.00**	**-0.91**
Other countries of Europe	1,035,088	1,039,231	1,266,103	1,526,705	1,512,789	3.00	-0.91
NOT SPECIFIED	**3,370**	**16,985**	**21,844**	**24,601**	**16,423**	**0.03**	**-33.24**
Other countries of the World	3,370	16,985	21,844	24,601	16,423	0.03	-33.24

Yearbook of Tourism Statistics, Data 2008 – 2012, 2014 Edition

GREECE

6. Overnight stays of non-resident tourists in all types of accommodation establishments, by country of residence

	2008	2009	2010	2011	2012	Market share 2012	% Change 2012-2011
TOTAL	47,973,949	46,676,987	48,986,136	54,518,196			
AFRICA	119,353	114,011	121,483	171,446			
Southern Africa	4,202	5,083	5,203	6,277			
South Africa	4,202	5,083	5,203	6,277			
Other Africa	115,151	108,928	116,280	165,169			
Other countries of Africa	115,151	108,928	116,280	165,169			
AMERICAS	1,771,301	1,672,432	1,723,589	1,902,383			
North America	1,561,762	1,466,392	1,493,714	1,623,500			
Canada	270,703	256,506	256,299	281,707			
United States of America	1,291,059	1,209,886	1,237,415	1,341,793			
South America	92,914	81,628	98,540	132,597			
Brazil	92,914	81,628	98,540	132,597			
Other Americas	116,625	124,412	131,335	146,286			
Other countries of the Americas	116,625	124,412	131,335	146,286			
EAST ASIA AND THE PACIFIC	1,185,829	1,230,135	1,600,396	1,866,523			
North-East Asia	263,683	249,763	242,152	297,557			
China	99,006	93,087	108,966	160,512			
Japan	163,172	155,139	131,261	132,663			
Korea, Republic of	1,505	1,537	1,925	4,382			
Australasia	328,405	283,840	361,433	407,396			
Australia	328,405	283,840	361,433	407,396			
Other East Asia and the Pacific	593,741	696,532	996,811	1,161,570			
Other countries of Asia	569,083	677,278	972,699	1,128,399			
Other countries of Oceania	24,658	19,254	24,112	33,171			
EUROPE	44,893,896	43,643,422	45,518,776	50,553,177			
Central/Eastern Europe	8,128,401	7,803,121	8,583,404	10,590,489			
Bulgaria	462,741	472,060	415,843	509,675			
Czech Republic	1,196,075	1,304,435	1,207,537	1,303,131			
Estonia	104,710	87,233	90,412	85,711			
Hungary	381,234	286,772	268,718	286,207			
Latvia	86,675	68,168	53,813	63,266			
Lithuania	153,257	120,520	102,656	114,743			
Poland	1,373,192	1,483,854	1,515,522	1,853,481			
Romania	867,150	817,749	718,749	817,306			
Russian Federation	2,992,321	2,714,642	3,656,772	4,906,374			
Slovakia	329,942	292,305	284,424	319,732			
Ukraine	181,104	155,383	268,958	330,863			
Northern Europe	12,079,205	12,058,253	12,960,034	14,067,363			
Denmark	1,066,901	1,040,490	1,101,202	1,203,989			
Finland	768,473	852,338	882,435	1,037,072			
Iceland	37,336	19,645	13,170	18,910			
Ireland	255,863	238,108	214,181	199,068			
Norway	1,304,017	1,310,892	1,518,004	1,627,143			
Sweden	1,531,684	1,573,083	1,854,258	2,075,562			
United Kingdom	7,114,931	7,023,697	7,376,784	7,905,619			
Southern Europe	3,965,365	3,642,299	3,528,191	3,851,303			
Italy	3,270,159	2,918,214	2,897,992	3,171,276			
Malta	14,660	23,237	17,325	17,796			
Portugal	67,802	70,628	66,687	61,553			
Slovenia	225,087	215,373	184,148	181,300			
Spain	387,657	414,847	362,039	419,378			
Western Europe	18,984,303	18,456,065	18,460,432	19,768,501			
Austria	1,395,337	1,257,525	1,222,500	1,185,220			
Belgium	1,534,085	1,464,392	1,484,285	1,610,084			
France	3,270,879	3,574,165	3,497,512	3,926,078			

290

GREECE

6. Overnight stays of non-resident tourists in all types of accommodation establishments, by country of residence

	2008	2009	2010	2011	2012	Market share 2012	% Change 2012-2011
Germany	8,972,596	8,554,859	8,702,157	9,272,121			
Luxembourg	108,822	90,907	81,305	86,102			
Netherlands	2,801,166	2,626,203	2,592,614	2,697,669			
Switzerland	901,418	888,014	880,059	991,227			
East Mediterranean Europe	**677,643**	**616,451**	**678,925**	**704,890**			
Cyprus	549,902	496,687	526,562	503,119			
Turkey	127,741	119,764	152,363	201,771			
Other Europe	**1,058,979**	**1,067,233**	**1,307,790**	**1,570,631**			
Other countries of Europe	1,058,979	1,067,233	1,307,790	1,570,631			
NOT SPECIFIED	**3,570**	**16,987**	**21,892**	**24,667**			
Other countries of the World	3,570	16,987	21,892	24,667			

Yearbook of Tourism Statistics, Data 2008 – 2012, 2014 Edition

GRENADA

1. Arrivals of non-resident tourists at national borders, by nationality

	2008	2009	2010	2011	2012	Market share 2012	% Change 2012-2011
TOTAL	130,363	113,894	110,419	118,295	116,242	100.00	-1.74
AFRICA	644	725	667	617	517	0.44	-16.21
East Africa	79	103	83	62	59	0.05	-4.84
Ethiopia			1		2	0.00	
Kenya	30	42	20	19	28	0.02	47.37
Mauritius	3	7	12	5	4	0.00	-20.00
Uganda	17	12	11	9	14	0.01	55.56
Zambia	16	13	8	21	8	0.01	-61.90
Zimbabwe	13	29	31	8	3	0.00	-62.50
Central Africa	3	6	6	4	1	0.00	-75.00
Cameroon	1	6	6	3	1	0.00	-66.67
Democratic Republic of the Congo	2			1			
North Africa	3	3	7	4	11	0.01	175.00
Algeria	3	1	2	1	1	0.00	0.00
Morocco		2	4	3	2	0.00	-33.33
Sudan			1		8	0.01	
Southern Africa	228	288	223	286	207	0.18	-27.62
Botswana	87	107	64	110	50	0.04	-54.55
South Africa	141	181	159	176	157	0.14	-10.80
West Africa	249	307	314	243	221	0.19	-9.05
Ghana	15	18	24	26	20	0.02	-23.08
Liberia	6	2	1		1	0.00	
Nigeria	228	286	287	217	199	0.17	-8.29
Senegal		1	2		1	0.00	
Other Africa	82	18	34	18	18	0.02	0.00
Other countries of Africa	82	18	34	18	18	0.02	0.00
AMERICAS	66,159	61,648	59,175	64,855	66,828	57.49	3.04
Caribbean	29,039	25,205	22,784	25,877	24,188	20.81	-6.53
Anguilla	71	71	41	44	58	0.05	31.82
Antigua and Barbuda	652	831	534	510	383	0.33	-24.90
Bahamas	119	124	109	94	61	0.05	-35.11
Barbados	4,791	4,027	3,579	3,526	3,124	2.69	-11.40
Cayman Islands	45	39	44	38	28	0.02	-26.32
Cuba	143	119	89	71	82	0.07	15.49
Dominica	510	425	476	472	581	0.50	23.09
Dominican Republic	30	64	35	29	44	0.04	51.72
Guadeloupe	60	26	100	64	29	0.02	-54.69
Haiti	26	27	26	26	39	0.03	50.00
Jamaica	1,724	1,212	966	987	955	0.82	-3.24
Montserrat	50	52	50	35	39	0.03	11.43
Saint Kitts and Nevis	277	333	305	300	226	0.19	-24.67
Saint Lucia	1,650	1,485	1,505	1,275	1,328	1.14	4.16
Saint Vincent and the Grenadines	2,146	1,930	1,712	1,922	1,452	1.25	-24.45
Sint Maarten	102	103	123	95	108	0.09	13.68
Trinidad and Tobago	15,548	13,277	12,283	15,715	15,086	12.98	-4.00
Other countries of the Caribbean	1,095	1,060	807	674	565	0.49	-16.17
Central America	282	201	187	172	114	0.10	-33.72
Belize	61	65	69	60	43	0.04	-28.33
Costa Rica	159	32	20	18	12	0.01	-33.33
Honduras	5	6	6	6	4	0.00	-33.33
Nicaragua	5	13	10	8	8	0.01	0.00
Panama	25	52	48	34	35	0.03	2.94
Other countries of Central America	27	33	34	46	12	0.01	-73.91
North America	33,715	33,268	33,446	36,240	39,773	34.22	9.75
Canada	7,100	7,194	7,322	7,490	8,065	6.94	7.68

Yearbook of Tourism Statistics, Data 2008 – 2012, 2014 Edition

GRENADA

1. Arrivals of non-resident tourists at national borders, by nationality

	2008	2009	2010	2011	2012	Market share 2012	% Change 2012-2011
Mexico	80	91	69	36	47	0.04	30.56
United States of America	26,535	25,983	26,055	28,714	31,661	27.24	10.26
South America	**3,123**	**2,974**	**2,758**	**2,566**	**2,753**	**2.37**	**7.29**
Argentina	127	120	120	116	89	0.08	-23.28
Bolivia	15	12	28	9	36	0.03	300.00
Brazil	202	284	365	354	385	0.33	8.76
Chile	31	73	39	37	51	0.04	37.84
Colombia	70	97	64	50	73	0.06	46.00
Ecuador	12	10	8	9	14	0.01	55.56
Guyana	1,205	1,122	1,113	1,073	1,176	1.01	9.60
Paraguay			21	30	31	0.03	3.33
Peru	14	28	21	36	22	0.02	-38.89
Suriname	72	82	114	103	78	0.07	-24.27
Uruguay	5	13	10	13	14	0.01	7.69
Venezuela	1,368	1,131	850	736	776	0.67	5.43
Other countries of South America	2	2	5		8	0.01	
EAST ASIA AND THE PACIFIC	**1,129**	**1,442**	**1,527**	**1,432**	**849**	**0.73**	**-40.71**
North-East Asia	**77**	**81**	**94**	**101**	**84**	**0.07**	**-16.83**
Japan	77	81	94	101	84	0.07	-16.83
Australasia	**477**	**304**	**355**	**361**	**325**	**0.28**	**-9.97**
Australia	411	248	313	306	251	0.22	-17.97
New Zealand	66	56	42	55	74	0.06	34.55
Melanesia		**4**	**3**	**2**	**1**	**0.00**	**-50.00**
Fiji		4	3	2	1	0.00	-50.00
Other East Asia and the Pacific	**575**	**1,053**	**1,075**	**968**	**439**	**0.38**	**-54.65**
Other countries of Asia	575	1,053	1,075	968	439	0.38	-54.65
EUROPE	**44,676**	**36,096**	**35,361**	**36,277**	**32,826**	**28.24**	**-9.51**
Central/Eastern Europe	**549**	**384**	**547**	**490**	**416**	**0.36**	**-15.10**
Bulgaria	9	25	7	11	7	0.01	-36.36
Czech Republic/Slovakia	115	67	144	141	111	0.10	-21.28
Hungary	43	5	38	50	21	0.02	-58.00
Poland	125	87	97	115	88	0.08	-23.48
Romania	26	26	16	26	17	0.01	-34.62
Ukraine	2	4	34	2	6	0.01	200.00
USSR (former)	227	170	211	145	162	0.14	11.72
Other countries Central/East Europe	2				4	0.00	
Northern Europe	**37,103**	**29,335**	**28,073**	**29,489**	**26,239**	**22.57**	**-11.02**
Denmark	327	282	231	188	143	0.12	-23.94
Finland	80	85	56	129	94	0.08	-27.13
Ireland	445	502	370	367	220	0.19	-40.05
Norway	370	365	344	339	286	0.25	-15.63
Sweden	442	386	481	638	538	0.46	-15.67
United Kingdom	35,439	27,715	26,591	27,828	24,958	21.47	-10.31
Southern Europe	**897**	**825**	**986**	**754**	**717**	**0.62**	**-4.91**
Greece	27	28	52	44	36	0.03	-18.18
Italy	612	578	697	512	533	0.46	4.10
Malta	15	7	3	3	4	0.00	33.33
Portugal	42	44	38	41	24	0.02	-41.46
Serbia and Montenegro	7	3	1				
Spain	194	165	195	154	120	0.10	-22.08
Western Europe	**6,024**	**5,457**	**5,686**	**5,429**	**3,783**	**3.25**	**-30.32**
Austria	520	545	512	500	255	0.22	-49.00
Belgium	175	134	175	171	134	0.12	-21.64
France	1,063	1,105	1,229	1,332	1,110	0.95	-16.67
Germany	3,183	2,698	2,613	2,347	1,497	1.29	-36.22
Liechtenstein			2		1	0.00	

Yearbook of Tourism Statistics, Data 2008 – 2012, 2014 Edition

GRENADA

1. Arrivals of non-resident tourists at national borders, by nationality

	2008	2009	2010	2011	2012	Market share 2012	% Change 2012-2011
Luxembourg	17	18	24	17	9	0.01	-47.06
Netherlands	403	340	486	357	186	0.16	-47.90
Switzerland	663	617	645	705	591	0.51	-16.17
East Mediterranean Europe	**58**	**69**	**50**	**59**	**31**	**0.03**	**-47.46**
Cyprus	4	1	8	5	4	0.00	-20.00
Israel	32	25	33	42	19	0.02	-54.76
Turkey	22	43	9	12	8	0.01	-33.33
Other Europe	**45**	**26**	**19**	**56**	**1,640**	**1.41**	**2,828.57**
Other countries of Europe	45	26	19	56	1,640	1.41	2,828.57
MIDDLE EAST	**97**	**64**	**59**	**52**	**45**	**0.04**	**-13.46**
Egypt	4	2	4	4	4	0.00	0.00
Iraq	1						
Jordan	4	2	1	3	2	0.00	-33.33
Lebanon	37	32	11	7	8	0.01	14.29
Saudi Arabia			6	5	2	0.00	-60.00
Syrian Arab Republic	28	23	21	26	9	0.01	-65.38
Other countries of Middle East	23	5	16	7	20	0.02	185.71
NOT SPECIFIED	**17,658**	**13,919**	**13,630**	**15,062**	**15,177**	**13.06**	**0.76**
Other countries of the World	554	34	133	171	403	0.35	135.67
Nationals Residing Abroad	17,104	13,885	13,497	14,891	14,774	12.71	-0.79

GRENADA

3. Arrivals of non-resident tourists in hotels and similar establishments, by nationality

	2008	2009	2010	2011	2012	Market share 2012	% Change 2012-2011
TOTAL	61,882	51,098	49,530	58,077	60,063	100.00	3.42
AMERICAS	29,751	26,914	25,419	32,612	35,685	59.41	9.42
Caribbean	14,847	13,356	11,437	14,006	14,185	23.62	1.28
All countries of the Caribbean	14,847	13,356	11,437	14,006	14,185	23.62	1.28
North America	14,072	12,931	13,542	18,220	21,017	34.99	15.35
Canada	2,784	2,974	3,152	3,671	4,247	7.07	15.69
United States of America	11,288	9,957	10,390	14,549	16,770	27.92	15.27
South America	832	627	440	386	483	0.80	25.13
Venezuela	832	627	440	386	483	0.80	25.13
EUROPE	29,208	22,182	21,626	23,222	21,886	36.44	-5.75
Northern Europe	24,374	18,352	17,518	19,158	18,162	30.24	-5.20
Sweden	253	229	256	337	334	0.56	-0.89
United Kingdom	24,121	18,123	17,262	18,821	17,828	29.68	-5.28
Southern Europe	316	271	319	280	207	0.34	-26.07
Italy	316	271	319	280	207	0.34	-26.07
Western Europe	2,669	2,091	2,200	2,276	1,627	2.71	-28.51
France	336	305	373	497	459	0.76	-7.65
Germany	1,995	1,537	1,485	1,405	911	1.52	-35.16
Switzerland	338	249	342	374	257	0.43	-31.28
Other Europe	1,849	1,468	1,589	1,508	1,890	3.15	25.33
Other countries of Europe	1,849	1,468	1,589	1,508	1,890	3.15	25.33
NOT SPECIFIED	2,923	2,002	2,485	2,243	2,492	4.15	11.10
Other countries of the World	2,133	1,408	2,105	1,984	2,230	3.71	12.40
Nationals Residing Abroad	790	594	380	259	262	0.44	1.16

Yearbook of Tourism Statistics, Data 2008 – 2012, 2014 Edition

GRENADA

4. Arrivals of non-resident tourists in all types of accommodation establishments, by nationality

	2008	2009	2010	2011	2012	Market share 2012	% Change 2012-2011
TOTAL	130,363	113,894	110,419	118,295	116,242	100.00	-1.74
AMERICAS	64,042	60,782	57,129	64,224	64,690	55.65	0.73
Caribbean	29,039	26,474	22,902	27,284	24,188	20.81	-11.35
All countries of the Caribbean	29,039	26,474	22,902	27,284	24,188	20.81	-11.35
North America	33,635	33,177	33,377	36,204	39,726	34.18	9.73
Canada	7,100	7,194	7,322	7,490	8,065	6.94	7.68
United States of America	26,535	25,983	26,055	28,714	31,661	27.24	10.26
South America	1,368	1,131	850	736	776	0.67	5.43
Venezuela	1,368	1,131	850	736	776	0.67	5.43
EUROPE	44,676	36,086	35,350	36,235	32,826	28.24	-9.41
Northern Europe	35,881	28,101	27,072	28,466	25,496	21.93	-10.43
Sweden	442	386	481	638	538	0.46	-15.67
United Kingdom	35,439	27,715	26,591	27,828	24,958	21.47	-10.31
Southern Europe	612	578	697	512	533	0.46	4.10
Italy	612	578	697	512	533	0.46	4.10
Western Europe	4,909	4,420	4,487	4,384	3,198	2.75	-27.05
France	1,063	1,105	1,229	1,332	1,110	0.95	-16.67
Germany	3,183	2,698	2,613	2,347	1,497	1.29	-36.22
Switzerland	663	617	645	705	591	0.51	-16.17
Other Europe	3,274	2,987	3,094	2,873	3,599	3.10	25.27
Other countries of Europe	3,274	2,987	3,094	2,873	3,599	3.10	25.27
NOT SPECIFIED	21,645	17,026	17,940	17,836	18,726	16.11	4.99
Other countries of the World	4,541	3,141	4,443	2,945	3,952	3.40	34.19
Nationals Residing Abroad	17,104	13,885	13,497	14,891	14,774	12.71	-0.79

Yearbook of Tourism Statistics, Data 2008 – 2012, 2014 Edition

GUADELOUPE

1. Arrivals of non-resident tourists at national borders, by country of residence

		2008	2009	2010	2011	2012	Market share 2012	% Change 2012-2011
TOTAL	(*)		346,507	392,282				
AFRICA			187					
North Africa			187					
Morocco			187					
AMERICAS			1,919	1,354				
Caribbean			1,170	709				
Dominica			94					
Haiti			140					
Martinique			936	709				
North America			281					
United States of America			281					
South America			468	645				
Guyana			468	645				
EUROPE			343,465	384,801				
Northern Europe			842					
Norway			281					
United Kingdom			561					
Southern Europe			2,666					
Italy			2,105					
Spain			561					
Western Europe			337,291	370,482				
Austria			281					
Belgium			4,631					
France			329,011	370,482				
Germany			1,403					
Luxembourg			187					
Switzerland			1,778					
Other Europe			2,666	14,319				
Other countries of Europe			2,666	14,319				
NOT SPECIFIED			936	6,127				
Other countries of the World			936	6,127				

Yearbook of Tourism Statistics, Data 2008 – 2012, 2014 Edition

GUAM

1. Arrivals of non-resident tourists at national borders, by country of residence

	2008	2009	2010	2011	2012	Market share 2012	% Change 2012-2011
TOTAL	1,141,779	1,052,871	1,196,295	1,159,778	1,283,296	100.00	10.65
AMERICAS	53,848	56,192	61,887	62,102	50,850	3.96	-18.12
North America	53,848	56,192	61,887	62,102	50,850	3.96	-18.12
Canada	773	667	661	757	814	0.06	7.53
United States of America	53,075	55,525	61,226	61,345	50,036	3.90	-18.44
EAST ASIA AND THE PACIFIC	1,033,798	982,625	1,119,681	1,081,873	1,217,480	94.87	12.53
North-East Asia	989,456	936,353	1,071,331	1,034,138	1,172,263	91.35	13.36
China	1,951	3,286	4,765	7,068	8,845	0.69	25.14
Hong Kong, China	4,276	2,872	6,890	8,903	8,609	0.67	-3.30
Japan	850,034	825,129	893,667	824,005	923,124	71.93	12.03
Korea, Republic of	110,590	82,978	134,689	149,076	182,541	14.22	22.45
Taiwan, Province of China	22,605	22,088	31,320	45,086	49,144	3.83	9.00
South-East Asia	11,189	11,927	12,736	10,681	10,835	0.84	1.44
Philippines	10,902	11,581	12,340	10,097	10,418	0.81	3.18
Thailand	226	293	318	488	302	0.02	-38.11
Viet Nam	61	53	78	96	115	0.01	19.79
Australasia	2,437	2,418	3,093	3,867	3,097	0.24	-19.91
Australia	2,437	2,418	3,093	3,867	3,097	0.24	-19.91
Micronesia	30,716	31,927	32,521	33,187	31,285	2.44	-5.73
Marshall Islands	965	1,022	1,247	1,192	1,152	0.09	-3.36
Micronesia, Federated States of	8,602	9,683	9,537	10,222	10,067	0.78	-1.52
Nauru	13						
Northern Mariana Islands	17,607	17,811	18,301	18,062	16,648	1.30	-7.83
Palau	3,529	3,411	3,436	3,711	3,418	0.27	-7.90
EUROPE	1,710	2,005	1,948	2,117	5,702	0.44	169.34
Central/Eastern Europe	122	339	422	632	4,037	0.31	538.77
Russian Federation	122	339	422	632	4,037	0.31	538.77
Other Europe	1,588	1,666	1,526	1,485	1,665	0.13	12.12
Other countries of Europe	1,588	1,666	1,526	1,485	1,665	0.13	12.12
NOT SPECIFIED	52,423	12,049	12,779	13,686	9,264	0.72	-32.31
Other countries of the World	52,423	12,049	12,779	13,686	9,264	0.72	-32.31

Yearbook of Tourism Statistics, Data 2008 – 2012, 2014 Editio

GUATEMALA

2. Arrivals of non-resident visitors at national borders, by nationality

	2008	2009	2010	2011	2012	Market share 2012	% Change 2012-2011
TOTAL (*)	1,715,426	1,776,868	1,875,777	1,822,663	1,951,173	100.00	7.05
AMERICAS	1,517,540	1,563,934	1,644,754	1,599,430	1,711,075	87.69	6.98
Caribbean	6,731	7,936	7,733	5,906	6,023	0.31	1.98
Cuba	2,769	2,398	1,847	1,717	1,940	0.10	12.99
Dominican Republic	3,021	4,612	4,688	3,038	2,720	0.14	-10.47
Other countries of the Caribbean	941	926	1,198	1,151	1,363	0.07	18.42
Central America	935,604	892,696	933,817	930,258	1,010,753	51.80	8.65
Belize	31,803	37,191	43,816	35,960	35,481	1.82	-1.33
Costa Rica	41,545	46,504	48,088	42,039	44,984	2.31	7.01
El Salvador	647,568	507,802	485,888	542,316	604,871	31.00	11.53
Honduras	155,063	211,456	258,765	223,010	235,680	12.08	5.68
Nicaragua	47,171	77,688	83,819	74,362	77,238	3.96	3.87
Panama	12,454	12,055	13,441	12,571	12,499	0.64	-0.57
North America	515,905	604,813	645,521	604,596	631,947	32.39	4.52
Canada	36,079	47,675	46,774	42,719	53,696	2.75	25.70
Mexico	92,905	105,456	127,691	132,661	144,076	7.38	8.60
United States of America	386,921	451,682	471,056	429,216	434,175	22.25	1.16
South America	59,300	58,489	57,683	58,670	62,352	3.20	6.28
Argentina	10,933	10,973	11,519	12,178	12,165	0.62	-0.11
Brazil	7,689	7,444	7,640	7,313	7,382	0.38	0.94
Chile	6,532	6,605	6,262	6,390	6,514	0.33	1.94
Colombia	16,289	16,930	15,710	15,520	16,478	0.84	6.17
Ecuador	2,634	2,413	2,581	2,470	3,175	0.16	28.54
Peru	4,819	4,095	3,524	3,819	3,898	0.20	2.07
Venezuela	6,681	6,267	6,759	7,425	9,066	0.46	22.10
Other countries of South America	3,723	3,762	3,688	3,555	3,674	0.19	3.35
EAST ASIA AND THE PACIFIC	30,480	29,811	39,128	36,601	41,013	2.10	12.05
North-East Asia	21,707	17,898	20,098	20,602	22,234	1.14	7.92
China	635	594	809	1,385	1,853	0.09	33.79
Japan	6,521	5,110	7,081	6,956	8,853	0.45	27.27
Korea, Dem. People's Republic of	64	16	16	622	63	0.00	-89.87
Korea, Republic of	10,373	9,361	8,810	9,288	8,257	0.42	-11.10
Taiwan, Province of China	4,114	2,817	3,382	2,351	3,208	0.16	36.45
Australasia	7,011	9,567	12,591	10,866	15,401	0.79	41.74
Australia	5,664	7,931	10,520	9,048	13,221	0.68	46.12
New Zealand	1,347	1,636	2,071	1,818	2,180	0.11	19.91
Other East Asia and the Pacific	1,762	2,346	6,439	5,133	3,378	0.17	-34.19
Other countries of Asia	1,728	2,124	6,314	5,034	3,224	0.17	-35.96
Other countries of Oceania	34	222	125	99	154	0.01	55.56
EUROPE	165,025	180,387	189,586	184,356	196,590	10.08	6.64
Central/Eastern Europe	6,333	12,066	10,718	10,834	11,046	0.57	1.96
Armenia	10	14	9	19	17	0.00	-10.53
Azerbaijan	1	1	2	5	9	0.00	80.00
Belarus	17	30	38	18	10	0.00	-44.44
Bulgaria	212	234	261	235	268	0.01	14.04
Czech Republic	1,047	4,475	3,160	1,551	1,930	0.10	24.44
Estonia	255	275	255	245	275	0.01	12.24
Georgia	138	17	15	184	16	0.00	-91.30
Hungary	483	531	777	482	579	0.03	20.12
Kazakhstan	3	6	17	15	38	0.00	153.33
Kyrgyzstan	1	4	3	6	2	0.00	-66.67
Lithuania	152	258	339	263	582	0.03	121.29
Poland	2,256	3,498	2,591	3,071	3,166	0.16	3.09
Republic of Moldova	60	17	15	11	16	0.00	45.45
Romania	223	180	665	515	366	0.02	-28.93

GUATEMALA

2. Arrivals of non-resident visitors at national borders, by nationality

	2008	2009	2010	2011	2012	Market share 2012	% Change 2012-2011
Russian Federation	958	1,312	1,687	2,653	2,574	0.13	-2.98
Slovakia	332	879	564	1,000	487	0.02	-51.30
Tajikistan			3	3	13	0.00	333.33
Turkmenistan	1	2	2	2	8	0.00	300.00
Ukraine	178	314	309	548	685	0.04	25.00
Uzbekistan	6	19	6	8	5	0.00	-37.50
Northern Europe	**37,502**	**42,163**	**42,900**	**39,615**	**46,530**	**2.38**	**17.46**
Denmark	4,396	4,621	4,373	4,076	4,521	0.23	10.92
Finland	1,114	1,353	1,378	1,327	1,182	0.06	-10.93
Iceland	125	97	173	144	135	0.01	-6.25
Ireland	2,168	2,776	2,904	2,835	2,989	0.15	5.43
Norway	3,076	3,073	3,342	2,922	2,490	0.13	-14.78
Sweden	4,392	5,020	4,169	3,770	3,927	0.20	4.16
United Kingdom	22,231	25,223	26,561	24,541	31,286	1.60	27.48
Southern Europe	**41,678**	**41,014**	**44,889**	**45,695**	**46,264**	**2.37**	**1.25**
Albania	12	51	31	39	47	0.00	20.51
Andorra	30	15	31	60	41	0.00	-31.67
Bosnia and Herzegovina	1	5	12	16	1	0.00	-93.75
Croatia	133	113	148	151	204	0.01	35.10
Gibraltar			5	12	1	0.00	-91.67
Greece	502	615	682	576	713	0.04	23.78
Holy See	4	8	12	6	9	0.00	50.00
Italy	14,746	12,630	14,582	16,819	17,577	0.90	4.51
Malta	73	141	58	96	83	0.00	-13.54
Montenegro	1	9	3	13	2	0.00	-84.62
Portugal	968	971	1,040	942	1,197	0.06	27.07
San Marino	6	12	10	8	5	0.00	-37.50
Serbia	1	6	5	3	11	0.00	266.67
Slovenia	364	540	448	518	567	0.03	9.46
Spain	24,806	25,863	27,788	26,426	25,774	1.32	-2.47
TFYR of Macedonia	31	35	34	10	32	0.00	220.00
Western Europe	**70,902**	**77,235**	**80,445**	**76,160**	**80,968**	**4.15**	**6.31**
Austria	2,912	3,109	3,244	3,090	3,525	0.18	14.08
Belgium	5,476	5,866	6,868	6,127	5,456	0.28	-10.95
France	21,539	28,022	26,503	24,874	27,870	1.43	12.04
Germany	19,630	21,334	20,979	20,516	22,835	1.17	11.30
Liechtenstein	42	18	65	23	18	0.00	-21.74
Luxembourg	107	93	67	99	72	0.00	-27.27
Monaco	8	5	2	6	5	0.00	-16.67
Netherlands	15,781	12,818	16,661	15,093	14,840	0.76	-1.68
Switzerland	5,407	5,970	6,056	6,332	6,347	0.33	0.24
East Mediterranean Europe	**8,416**	**7,723**	**10,466**	**11,895**	**11,509**	**0.59**	**-3.25**
Cyprus	18	37	31	52	89	0.00	71.15
Israel	8,047	7,330	9,762	11,282	10,719	0.55	-4.99
Turkey	351	356	673	561	701	0.04	24.96
Other Europe	**194**	**186**	**168**	**157**	**273**	**0.01**	**73.89**
Other countries of Europe	194	186	168	157	273	0.01	73.89
MIDDLE EAST	**281**	**467**	**431**	**537**	**578**	**0.03**	**7.64**
All countries of Middle East	281	467	431	537	578	0.03	7.64
NOT SPECIFIED	**2,100**	**2,269**	**1,878**	**1,739**	**1,917**	**0.10**	**10.24**
Other countries of the World	2,100	2,269	1,878	1,739	1,917	0.10	10.24

300

GUYANA

1. Arrivals of non-resident tourists at national borders, by country of residence

		2008	2009	2010	2011	2012	Market share 2012	% Change 2012-2011
TOTAL	(*)	**129,595**	**141,281**	**151,926**	**156,871**	**176,642**	**100.00**	**12.60**
AMERICAS		**118,364**	**130,979**	**141,200**	**107,247**	**124,602**	**70.54**	**16.18**
Caribbean		**27,860**	**28,026**	**29,487**				
All countries of the Caribbean		27,860	28,026	29,487				
North America		**87,820**	**100,767**	**108,347**	**107,247**	**124,602**	**70.54**	**16.18**
Canada		21,470	23,812	25,381	23,965	25,977	14.71	8.40
United States of America		66,350	76,955	82,966	83,282	98,625	55.83	18.42
Other Americas		**2,684**	**2,186**	**3,366**				
Other countries of the Americas		2,684	2,186	3,366				
EUROPE		**8,937**	**8,277**	**8,357**	**8,284**	**8,877**	**5.03**	**7.16**
Other Europe		**8,937**	**8,277**	**8,357**	**8,284**	**8,877**	**5.03**	**7.16**
All countries of Europe		8,937	8,277	8,357	8,284	8,877	5.03	7.16
NOT SPECIFIED		**2,294**	**2,025**	**2,369**	**41,340**	**43,163**	**24.44**	**4.41**
Other countries of the World		2,294	2,025	2,369	41,340	43,163	24.44	4.41

Yearbook of Tourism Statistics, Data 2008 – 2012, 2014 Edition

HAITI

1. Arrivals of non-resident tourists at national borders, by country of residence

		2008	2009	2010	2011	2012	Market share 2012	% Change 2012-2011
TOTAL	(*)	**258,070**	**387,218**	**254,732**	**348,755**			
AMERICAS		**199,333**	**335,135**	**220,791**	**309,024**			
Caribbean		**6,148**	**24,989**	**9,954**	**11,552**			
Dominican Republic		2,638	9,910	3,168	4,487			
Jamaica		451	6,050	689	819			
Other countries of the Caribbean		3,059	9,029	6,097	6,246			
North America		**186,190**	**300,288**	**204,485**	**288,014**			
Canada		19,963	31,017	20,119	19,568			
Mexico		619	1,047	1,123	1,024			
United States of America		165,608	268,224	183,243	267,422			
Other Americas		**6,995**	**9,858**	**6,352**	**9,458**			
Other countries of the Americas		6,995	9,858	6,352	9,458			
EUROPE		**21,262**	**24,573**	**26,755**	**31,437**			
Western Europe		**14,653**	**12,508**	**14,261**	**18,432**			
France		14,653	12,508	14,261	18,432			
Other Europe		**6,609**	**12,065**	**12,494**	**13,005**			
Other countries of Europe		6,609	12,065	12,494	13,005			
NOT SPECIFIED		**37,475**	**27,510**	**7,186**	**8,294**			
Other countries of the World		37,475	27,510	7,186	8,294			

Yearbook of Tourism Statistics, Data 2008 – 2012, 2014 Editic

HONDURAS

1. Arrivals of non-resident tourists at national borders, by nationality

	2008	2009	2010	2011	2012	Market share 2012	% Change 2012-2011
TOTAL (*)	868,535	835,531	862,548	871,468	894,677	100.00	2.66
AFRICA	218	303	409	431	730	0.08	69.37
East Africa	22	36	46	49	80	0.01	63.27
Ethiopia	6	8	10	12	20	0.00	66.67
Kenya	11	20	25	26	42	0.00	61.54
Zimbabwe	5	8	11	11	18	0.00	63.64
Central Africa	8	12	15	16	25	0.00	56.25
Cameroon	5	7	10	10	15	0.00	50.00
Congo	1	2	2	2	4	0.00	100.00
Gabon	2	3	3	4	6	0.00	50.00
North Africa	9	13	16	17	30	0.00	76.47
Algeria	1	1	1	2	2	0.00	0.00
Morocco	7	10	13	13	24	0.00	84.62
Tunisia	1	2	2	2	4	0.00	100.00
Southern Africa	142	195	266	279	482	0.05	72.76
South Africa	142	195	266	279	482	0.05	72.76
West Africa	25	30	42	46	73	0.01	58.70
Côte d'Ivoire	3	4	6	6	10	0.00	66.67
Ghana	3	3	5	5	8	0.00	60.00
Nigeria	19	23	31	35	55	0.01	57.14
Other Africa	12	17	24	24	40	0.00	66.67
Other countries of Africa	12	17	24	24	40	0.00	66.67
AMERICAS	789,779	744,218	753,154	758,751	734,399	82.09	-3.21
Caribbean	3,203	5,226	7,060	6,479	9,935	1.11	53.34
Antigua and Barbuda	5	8	10	9	15	0.00	66.67
Bahamas	29	46	64	59	90	0.01	52.54
Barbados	13	19	26	23	34	0.00	47.83
Bermuda	1	1	2	1	2	0.00	100.00
Cayman Islands	961	1,544	2,058	1,912	2,867	0.32	49.95
Cuba	838	1,381	1,874	1,731	2,653	0.30	53.26
Dominica	11	17	24	19	33	0.00	73.68
Dominican Republic	833	1,382	1,846	1,694	2,622	0.29	54.78
Haiti	140	220	321	283	441	0.05	55.83
Jamaica	151	251	333	308	477	0.05	54.87
Puerto Rico	73	114	155	143	219	0.02	53.15
Saint Vincent and the Grenadines	8	12	14	12	19	0.00	58.33
Trinidad and Tobago	45	72	97	86	134	0.01	55.81
Other countries of the Caribbean	95	159	236	199	329	0.04	65.33
Central America	453,076	394,717	434,800	409,642	389,570	43.54	-4.90
Belize	2,303	1,986	2,179	2,057	1,969	0.22	-4.28
Costa Rica	25,157	21,831	24,073	22,825	21,629	2.42	-5.24
El Salvador	167,427	145,157	159,755	150,343	142,961	15.98	-4.91
Guatemala	127,484	111,220	122,641	115,768	110,230	12.32	-4.78
Nicaragua	121,583	106,598	117,342	110,299	104,904	11.73	-4.89
Panama	9,122	7,925	8,810	8,350	7,877	0.88	-5.66
North America	320,423	325,248	285,593	316,620	292,022	32.64	-7.77
Canada	18,606	19,062	16,838	18,530	17,086	1.91	-7.79
Mexico	23,379	23,513	20,613	22,968	21,045	2.35	-8.37
Saint Pierre and Miquelon	6	6	5	5	4	0.00	-20.00
United States of America	278,432	282,667	248,137	275,117	253,887	28.38	-7.72
South America	13,077	19,027	25,701	26,010	42,872	4.79	64.83
Argentina	2,515	3,690	4,990	5,046	8,404	0.94	66.55
Bolivia	491	697	936	960	1,567	0.18	63.23
Brazil	1,344	1,957	2,658	2,684	4,418	0.49	64.61
Chile	1,634	2,381	3,209	3,257	5,346	0.60	64.14

303

HONDURAS

1. Arrivals of non-resident tourists at national borders, by nationality

	2008	2009	2010	2011	2012	Market share 2012	% Change 2012-2011
Colombia	3,114	4,545	6,143	6,210	10,239	1.14	64.88
Ecuador	930	1,341	1,803	1,817	2,981	0.33	64.06
French Guiana	11	15	21	21	34	0.00	61.90
Guyana	32	46	58	57	101	0.01	77.19
Paraguay	162	229	306	307	506	0.06	64.82
Peru	1,118	1,625	2,190	2,220	3,653	0.41	64.55
Suriname	7	10	13	12	22	0.00	83.33
Uruguay	420	605	823	829	1,358	0.15	63.81
Venezuela	1,299	1,886	2,551	2,590	4,243	0.47	63.82
EAST ASIA AND THE PACIFIC	**8,453**	**10,475**	**14,143**	**16,346**	**29,860**	**3.34**	**82.67**
North-East Asia	**6,146**	**7,642**	**10,337**	**11,933**	**21,828**	**2.44**	**82.92**
China	1,489	1,831	2,539	2,865	5,280	0.59	84.29
Hong Kong, China	10	12	19	20	35	0.00	75.00
Japan	2,319	2,873	3,889	4,466	8,158	0.91	82.67
Korea, Dem. People's Republic of	1,347	1,670	2,280	2,660	4,762	0.53	79.02
Korea, Republic of	919	1,180	1,523	1,792	3,390	0.38	89.17
Taiwan, Province of China	62	76	87	130	203	0.02	56.15
South-East Asia	**468**	**560**	**767**	**881**	**1,588**	**0.18**	**80.25**
Indonesia	63	68	90	101	178	0.02	76.24
Malaysia	63	77	104	122	219	0.02	79.51
Philippines	329	398	549	633	1,146	0.13	81.04
Thailand	13	17	24	25	45	0.01	80.00
Australasia	**1,661**	**2,054**	**2,740**	**3,191**	**5,815**	**0.65**	**82.23**
Australia	1,331	1,650	2,206	2,569	4,683	0.52	82.29
New Zealand	330	404	534	622	1,132	0.13	81.99
Other East Asia and the Pacific	**178**	**219**	**299**	**341**	**629**	**0.07**	**84.46**
Other countries of Asia	178	219	299	341	629	0.07	84.46
EUROPE	**69,160**	**79,375**	**93,268**	**94,099**	**126,379**	**14.13**	**34.30**
Central/Eastern Europe	**1,637**	**1,890**	**2,172**	**2,235**	**2,952**	**0.33**	**32.08**
Bulgaria	430	491	544	582	747	0.08	28.35
Czech Republic/Slovakia	269	316	371	373	501	0.06	34.32
Hungary	68	78	90	94	121	0.01	28.72
Poland	349	400	486	488	651	0.07	33.40
Romania	86	100	119	121	159	0.02	31.40
Russian Federation	331	382	421	433	584	0.07	34.87
Ukraine	104	123	141	144	189	0.02	31.25
Northern Europe	**14,995**	**17,289**	**20,073**	**20,255**	**27,395**	**3.06**	**35.25**
Denmark	1,573	1,798	2,120	2,146	2,860	0.32	33.27
Finland	569	651	757	763	1,013	0.11	32.77
Iceland	93	107	124	125	168	0.02	34.40
Ireland	756	875	1,004	1,027	1,392	0.16	35.54
Norway	1,114	1,297	1,489	1,494	2,064	0.23	38.15
Sweden	2,261	2,580	2,969	2,958	4,009	0.45	35.53
United Kingdom	8,629	9,981	11,610	11,742	15,889	1.78	35.32
Southern Europe	**27,034**	**30,919**	**36,738**	**37,149**	**49,546**	**5.54**	**33.37**
Andorra	9	11	13	13	16	0.00	23.08
Croatia	36	43	52	48	69	0.01	43.75
Greece	206	239	286	274	383	0.04	39.78
Italy	15,285	17,392	20,773	20,977	27,739	3.10	32.24
Malta	11	12	14	13	18	0.00	38.46
Portugal	270	309	371	365	500	0.06	36.99
Spain	11,217	12,913	15,229	15,459	20,821	2.33	34.69
Western Europe	**24,119**	**27,707**	**32,446**	**32,577**	**43,970**	**4.91**	**34.97**
Austria	727	829	971	981	1,310	0.15	33.54
Belgium	1,693	1,966	2,315	2,351	3,193	0.36	35.81
France	5,103	5,878	6,853	6,872	9,282	1.04	35.07

304

HONDURAS

1. Arrivals of non-resident tourists at national borders, by nationality

	2008	2009	2010	2011	2012	Market share 2012	% Change 2012-2011
Germany	9,067	10,459	12,183	12,219	16,583	1.85	35.71
Luxembourg	19	24	26	26	37	0.00	42.31
Netherlands	4,715	5,359	6,381	6,393	8,538	0.95	33.55
Switzerland	2,795	3,192	3,717	3,735	5,027	0.56	34.59
East Mediterranean Europe	**1,343**	**1,532**	**1,797**	**1,840**	**2,458**	**0.27**	**33.59**
Cyprus	6	8	8	8	11	0.00	37.50
Israel	1,277	1,457	1,713	1,756	2,344	0.26	33.49
Turkey	60	67	76	76	103	0.01	35.53
Other Europe	**32**	**38**	**42**	**43**	**58**	**0.01**	**34.88**
Other countries of Europe	32	38	42	43	58	0.01	34.88
MIDDLE EAST	**119**	**156**	**210**	**245**	**450**	**0.05**	**83.67**
Egypt	32	40	57	65	119	0.01	83.08
Jordan	21	27	36	41	77	0.01	87.80
Kuwait	6	8	9	14	22	0.00	57.14
Lebanon	12	16	21	23	47	0.01	104.35
Libya	1	2	2	3	4	0.00	33.33
Palestine	43	58	77	90	166	0.02	84.44
Syrian Arab Republic	4	5	8	9	15	0.00	66.67
SOUTH ASIA	**302**	**376**	**513**	**598**	**1,071**	**0.12**	**79.10**
Bangladesh	6	8	12	12	24	0.00	100.00
India	242	297	408	479	852	0.10	77.87
Iran, Islamic Republic of	11	17	22	25	45	0.01	80.00
Pakistan	28	35	46	53	97	0.01	83.02
Sri Lanka	15	19	25	29	53	0.01	82.76
NOT SPECIFIED	**504**	**628**	**851**	**998**	**1,788**	**0.20**	**79.16**
Other countries of the World	504	628	851	998	1,788	0.20	79.16

Yearbook of Tourism Statistics, Data 2008 – 2012, 2014 Edition

HONG KONG, CHINA

1. Arrivals of non-resident tourists at national borders, by country of residence

	2008	2009	2010	2011	2012	Market share 2012	% Change 2012-2011
TOTAL	17,319,400	16,926,100	20,085,155	22,316,073	23,770,195	100.00	6.52
AFRICA	119,000	101,700	105,322	98,132	89,548	0.38	-8.75
Southern Africa	33,900	32,100	36,993	38,550	34,485	0.15	-10.54
South Africa	33,900	32,100	36,993	38,550	34,485	0.15	-10.54
Other Africa	85,100	69,600	68,329	59,582	55,063	0.23	-7.58
Other countries of Africa	85,100	69,600	68,329	59,582	55,063	0.23	-7.58
AMERICAS	1,231,800	1,107,600	1,245,553	1,279,072	1,247,581	5.25	-2.46
Central America					13,049	0.05	
Honduras					819	0.00	
Other countries of Central America					12,230	0.05	
North America	1,119,500	1,016,500	1,129,579	1,152,460	1,142,545	4.81	-0.86
Canada	281,900	260,700	290,827	291,454	278,028	1.17	-4.61
Mexico					22,887	0.10	
United States of America	837,600	755,800	838,752	861,006	841,630	3.54	-2.25
South America					91,987	0.39	
Argentina					10,278	0.04	
Brazil					33,174	0.14	
Venezuela					12,754	0.05	
Other countries of South America					35,781	0.15	
Other Americas	112,300	91,100	115,974	126,612			
Other countries of the Americas	112,300	91,100	115,974	126,612			
EAST ASIA AND THE PACIFIC	14,311,900	14,169,300	16,966,228	19,178,636	20,671,911	86.97	7.79
North-East Asia	11,739,900	11,708,400	14,088,673	16,118,154	17,655,990	74.28	9.54
China	9,379,700	9,663,600	11,678,055	13,599,768	15,110,372	63.57	11.11
Japan	816,800	779,600	823,575	787,220	774,426	3.26	-1.63
Korea, Republic of	637,800	401,600	587,866	670,835	725,783	3.05	8.19
Macao, China	256,200	249,800	274,616	281,678	291,219	1.23	3.39
Taiwan, Province of China	649,400	613,800	724,561	778,653	754,190	3.17	-3.14
South-East Asia	1,939,100	1,890,100	2,254,040	2,438,931	2,397,188	10.08	-1.71
Indonesia	261,900	263,900	340,147	379,915	370,161	1.56	-2.57
Malaysia	372,300	326,300	424,491	452,172	434,212	1.83	-3.97
Philippines	451,500	455,800	493,092	542,967	585,760	2.46	7.88
Singapore	479,500	456,700	527,560	585,727	530,561	2.23	-9.42
Thailand	298,600	303,200	356,060	380,647	388,681	1.64	2.11
Viet Nam					63,596	0.27	
Other countries of South-East Asia	75,300	84,200	112,690	97,503	24,217	0.10	-75.16
Australasia	596,100	535,400	585,199	575,332	567,838	2.39	-1.30
Australia	509,900	462,600	505,907	500,225	495,441	2.08	-0.96
New Zealand	86,200	72,800	79,292	75,107	72,397	0.30	-3.61
Other East Asia and the Pacific	36,800	35,400	38,316	46,219	50,895	0.21	10.12
Other countries of Asia	33,000	31,400	32,222	39,945	44,906	0.19	12.42
Other countries of Oceania	3,800	4,000	6,094	6,274	5,989	0.03	-4.54
EUROPE	1,325,700	1,217,500	1,317,418	1,335,876	1,440,964	6.06	7.87
Central/Eastern Europe					125,919	0.53	
Russian Federation					125,919	0.53	
Northern Europe	572,500	515,500	525,472	515,207	534,913	2.25	3.82
Denmark					20,770	0.09	
Finland					19,861	0.08	
Norway					15,404	0.06	
Sweden					42,486	0.18	
United Kingdom	467,200	415,400	421,566	413,156	436,392	1.84	5.62
Scandinavia	105,300	100,100	103,906	102,051			
Southern Europe	127,900	119,300	130,783	131,718	128,324	0.54	-2.58
Italy	75,300	69,100	76,918	75,509	74,431	0.31	-1.43

Yearbook of Tourism Statistics, Data 2008 – 2012, 2014 Edit

HONG KONG, CHINA

1. Arrivals of non-resident tourists at national borders, by country of residence

	2008	2009	2010	2011	2012	Market share 2012	% Change 2012-2011
Portugal					12,530	0.05	
Spain					41,363	0.17	
Spain,Portugal	52,600	50,200	53,865	56,209			
Western Europe	**496,600**	**465,500**	**507,015**	**496,148**	**483,982**	**2.04**	**-2.45**
Austria	18,600	18,400	20,310	19,156	19,057	0.08	-0.52
Belgium	23,100	23,500	24,977	24,145	23,554	0.10	-2.45
France	168,600	156,300	173,604	168,653	163,210	0.69	-3.23
Germany	170,800	156,500	170,170	163,975	161,970	0.68	-1.22
Netherlands	78,700	73,800	77,895	78,543	73,616	0.31	-6.27
Switzerland	36,800	37,000	40,059	41,676	42,575	0.18	2.16
East Mediterranean Europe					**57,285**	**0.24**	
Israel					38,187	0.16	
Turkey					19,098	0.08	
Other Europe	**128,700**	**117,200**	**154,148**	**192,803**	**110,541**	**0.47**	**-42.67**
Other countries of Europe	128,700	117,200	154,148	192,803	110,541	0.47	-42.67
MIDDLE EAST	**99,500**	**98,600**	**114,601**	**112,259**	**51,152**	**0.22**	**-54.43**
Bahrain					1,487	0.01	
Egypt					5,275	0.02	
Jordan					3,433	0.01	
Kuwait					4,839	0.02	
Saudi Arabia					14,731	0.06	
United Arab Emirates					12,616	0.05	
Other countries of Middle East					8,771	0.04	
All countries of Middle East	99,500	98,600	114,601	112,259			
SOUTH ASIA	**231,500**	**231,400**	**336,033**	**312,098**	**269,039**	**1.13**	**-13.80**
India	231,500	231,400	336,033	312,098	269,039	1.13	-13.80

Yearbook of Tourism Statistics, Data 2008 – 2012, 2014 Edition

HONG KONG, CHINA

2. Arrivals of non-resident visitors at national borders, by country of residence

	2008	2009	2010	2011	2012	Market share 2012	% Change 2012-2011
TOTAL	29,506,575	29,590,654	36,030,331	41,921,310	48,615,113	100.00	15.97
AFRICA	210,251	182,384	204,105	192,854	173,355	0.36	-10.11
East Africa	62,182	52,958	58,583	54,292	48,267	0.10	-11.10
Burundi	22	20	27	12	15	0.00	25.00
Comoros	22	29	52	71	56	0.00	-21.13
Djibouti	50	61	42	88	43	0.00	-51.14
Eritrea	39	20	30	19	20	0.00	5.26
Ethiopia	978	905	902	637	1,007	0.00	58.08
Kenya	6,529	4,941	4,839	4,955	4,180	0.01	-15.64
Madagascar	4,292	4,645	4,277	4,005	3,322	0.01	-17.05
Malawi	853	1,014	1,200	1,205	1,128	0.00	-6.39
Mauritius	22,373	18,421	23,217	21,914	18,382	0.04	-16.12
Mozambique	1,238	1,558	2,100	2,344	1,962	0.00	-16.30
Rwanda	220	352	432	298	383	0.00	28.52
Seychelles	479	446	572	565	522	0.00	-7.61
Somalia	20	9	6	4	1	0.00	-75.00
Uganda	6,062	4,936	4,338	3,991	3,004	0.01	-24.73
United Republic of Tanzania	14,331	11,260	10,745	8,334	8,842	0.02	6.10
Zambia	3,583	2,849	3,553	3,577	3,396	0.01	-5.06
Zimbabwe	1,091	1,492	2,251	2,273	2,004	0.00	-11.83
Central Africa	5,025	4,093	3,638	3,142	3,168	0.01	0.83
Angola	688	522	538	748	660	0.00	-11.76
Cameroon	1,635	1,228	706	597	426	0.00	-28.64
Central African Republic	58	86	96	54	57	0.00	5.56
Chad	314	315	218	135	136	0.00	0.74
Congo	515	372	270	209	235	0.00	12.44
Democratic Republic of the Congo	1,293	1,165	1,393	1,014	1,198	0.00	18.15
Equatorial Guinea	75	74	78	114	128	0.00	12.28
Gabon	422	330	331	253	312	0.00	23.32
Sao Tome and Principe	25	1	8	18	16	0.00	-11.11
North Africa	22,875	18,861	20,947	17,841	17,491	0.04	-1.96
Algeria	12,537	10,833	10,943	9,700	8,770	0.02	-9.59
Morocco	6,047	4,854	5,737	4,972	4,828	0.01	-2.90
South Sudan					3	0.00	
Sudan	136	147	102	90	81	0.00	-10.00
Tunisia	4,155	3,027	4,165	3,079	3,809	0.01	23.71
Southern Africa	67,748	65,484	81,785	84,364	74,045	0.15	-12.23
Botswana	1,803	2,252	2,838	2,594	1,774	0.00	-31.61
Lesotho	198	143	274	302	275	0.00	-8.94
Namibia	445	546	637	995	1,102	0.00	10.75
South Africa	65,024	62,246	77,658	79,989	70,660	0.15	-11.66
Swaziland	278	297	378	484	234	0.00	-51.65
West Africa	52,421	40,988	39,152	33,209	30,384	0.06	-8.51
Benin	3,074	2,244	2,135	2,217	1,777	0.00	-19.85
Burkina Faso	2,817	2,356	2,562	1,667	2,832	0.01	69.89
Cape Verde	446	296	294	238	243	0.00	2.10
Côte d'Ivoire	759	450	390	262	365	0.00	39.31
Gambia	2,327	2,465	2,575	2,412	2,354	0.00	-2.40
Ghana	3,457	873	681	748	532	0.00	-28.88
Guinea	7,094	6,143	6,056	4,896	4,315	0.01	-11.87
Guinea-Bissau	953	1,489	876	486	327	0.00	-32.72
Liberia	362	252	286	279	150	0.00	-46.24
Mali	11,010	8,613	8,559	7,759	6,455	0.01	-16.81
Mauritania	445	417	464	368	393	0.00	6.79
Niger	4,209	3,446	3,150	2,708	2,577	0.01	-4.84
Nigeria	12,535	9,870	9,189	7,584	6,509	0.01	-14.17

308

HONG KONG, CHINA

2. Arrivals of non-resident visitors at national borders, by country of residence

	2008	2009	2010	2011	2012	Market share 2012	% Change 2012-2011
Senegal	1,777	1,154	962	724	831	0.00	14.78
Sierra Leone	309	195	283	256	166	0.00	-35.16
Togo	847	725	690	605	558	0.00	-7.77
Other Africa				6			
Other countries of Africa				6			
AMERICAS	1,684,734	1,567,807	1,749,558	1,821,096	1,777,842	3.66	-2.38
Caribbean	7,763	7,941	8,436	8,872	8,492	0.02	-4.28
Antigua and Barbuda	100	105	156	127	151	0.00	18.90
Bahamas	515	392	481	513	393	0.00	-23.39
Barbados	250	191	215	152	191	0.00	25.66
Cuba	329	252	349	422	507	0.00	20.14
Dominica	429	416	359	325	325	0.00	0.00
Dominican Republic	1,905	1,874	2,088	2,138	1,872	0.00	-12.44
Grenada	20	31	44	51	52	0.00	1.96
Haiti	92	98	115	126	133	0.00	5.56
Jamaica	2,501	2,932	2,869	3,268	2,959	0.01	-9.46
Saint Kitts and Nevis	159	181	264	361	528	0.00	46.26
Saint Lucia	55	68	90	51	69	0.00	35.29
Saint Vincent and the Grenadines	62	53	40	25	38	0.00	52.00
Trinidad and Tobago	1,346	1,348	1,366	1,313	1,274	0.00	-2.97
Central America	13,456	11,258	12,560	12,706	12,034	0.02	-5.29
Belize	3,036	2,631	2,529	2,638	2,287	0.00	-13.31
Costa Rica	3,248	2,365	3,018	3,237	2,841	0.01	-12.23
El Salvador	612	431	477	522	535	0.00	2.49
Guatemala	1,551	1,279	1,393	1,419	1,623	0.00	14.38
Honduras	1,423	944	1,113	1,147	1,271	0.00	10.81
Nicaragua	93	60	90	101	99	0.00	-1.98
Panama	3,493	3,548	3,940	3,642	3,378	0.01	-7.25
North America	1,556,843	1,452,058	1,604,013	1,652,971	1,608,263	3.31	-2.70
Canada	379,046	361,922	404,252	410,591	392,519	0.81	-4.40
Mexico	31,433	20,063	28,342	30,044	30,987	0.06	3.14
United States of America (*)	1,146,364	1,070,073	1,171,419	1,212,336	1,184,757	2.44	-2.27
South America	106,672	96,547	124,549	146,547	149,053	0.31	1.71
Argentina	10,715	9,570	13,281	13,892	13,642	0.03	-1.80
Bolivia	1,804	1,750	2,063	2,670	2,794	0.01	4.64
Brazil	43,130	33,730	47,821	60,672	58,799	0.12	-3.09
Chile	8,964	8,452	10,215	11,812	12,657	0.03	7.15
Colombia	15,753	15,079	19,760	20,826	22,419	0.05	7.65
Ecuador	3,190	2,742	3,237	3,992	4,020	0.01	0.70
French Guiana		8	2	7	1	0.00	-85.71
Guyana	470	432	460	463	399	0.00	-13.82
Paraguay	1,003	838	865	905	784	0.00	-13.37
Peru	5,643	5,708	6,308	6,717	7,315	0.02	8.90
Suriname	2,283	2,873	2,782	3,050	3,188	0.01	4.52
Uruguay	1,527	1,685	2,273	2,402	2,249	0.00	-6.37
Venezuela	12,190	13,680	15,482	19,139	20,786	0.04	8.61
Other Americas			3				
Other countries of the Americas			3				
EAST ASIA AND THE PACIFIC	25,348,204	25,659,422	31,548,245	37,378,369	44,166,015	90.85	18.16
North-East Asia	22,043,717	22,474,913	27,852,166	33,418,532	40,245,889	82.78	20.43
China	16,862,003	17,956,731	22,684,388	28,100,129	34,911,395	71.81	24.24
Japan	1,324,797	1,204,490	1,316,618	1,283,687	1,254,602	2.58	-2.27
Korea, Dem. People's Republic of	144	174	69	46	103	0.00	123.91
Korea, Republic of	904,320	618,694	891,024	1,020,996	1,078,458	2.22	5.63
Macao, China	696,719	671,276	780,293	843,221	883,479	1.82	4.77
Mongolia	15,253	13,904	15,024	21,720	29,107	0.06	34.01

Yearbook of Tourism Statistics, Data 2008 – 2012, 2014 Edition

HONG KONG, CHINA

2. Arrivals of non-resident visitors at national borders, by country of residence

	2008	2009	2010	2011	2012	Market share 2012	% Change 2012-2011
Taiwan, Province of China	2,240,481	2,009,644	2,164,750	2,148,733	2,088,745	4.30	-2.79
South-East Asia	**2,541,281**	**2,476,546**	**2,927,555**	**3,201,966**	**3,179,331**	**6.54**	**-0.71**
Brunei Darussalam	9,979	11,675	11,031	10,904	10,789	0.02	-1.05
Cambodia	12,225	10,588	12,273	12,120	11,914	0.02	-1.70
Indonesia	348,938	353,631	453,235	520,795	511,893	1.05	-1.71
Lao People's Democratic Republic	1,015	1,229	1,309	2,441	2,456	0.01	0.61
Malaysia	490,561	441,698	578,877	632,858	624,859	1.29	-1.26
Myanmar	4,909	5,459	5,821	8,387	8,558	0.02	2.04
Philippines	568,540	563,750	603,030	659,829	709,753	1.46	7.57
Singapore	632,637	623,730	709,777	793,887	728,224	1.50	-8.27
Thailand	403,301	387,728	449,812	480,497	501,759	1.03	4.43
Timor-Leste	268	243	173	135	129	0.00	-4.44
Viet Nam	68,908	76,815	102,217	80,113	68,997	0.14	-13.88
Australasia	**757,522**	**701,668**	**758,837**	**747,687**	**730,832**	**1.50**	**-2.25**
Australia	643,538	600,085	650,681	644,596	632,462	1.30	-1.88
New Zealand (*)	113,984	101,583	108,156	103,091	98,370	0.20	-4.58
Melanesia	**3,297**	**4,439**	**7,697**	**7,738**	**7,584**	**0.02**	**-1.99**
Fiji	2,009	2,498	5,955	5,631	5,359	0.01	-4.83
Papua New Guinea	889	1,567	1,269	1,595	1,641	0.00	2.88
Solomon Islands	149	129	121	200	251	0.00	25.50
Vanuatu	250	245	352	312	333	0.00	6.73
Micronesia	**1,411**	**1,070**	**1,116**	**1,396**	**1,331**	**0.00**	**-4.66**
Kiribati	198	96	246	593	611	0.00	3.04
Marshall Islands	340	273	276	387	464	0.00	19.90
Micronesia, Federated States of	117	77	100	76	32	0.00	-57.89
Nauru	756	624	494	340	224	0.00	-34.12
Polynesia	**915**	**739**	**834**	**1,008**	**993**	**0.00**	**-1.49**
Samoa	142	141	199	246	268	0.00	8.94
Tonga	595	473	532	651	590	0.00	-9.37
Tuvalu	178	125	103	111	135	0.00	21.62
Other East Asia and the Pacific	**61**	**47**	**40**	**42**	**55**	**0.00**	**30.95**
Other countries of Oceania	61	47	40	42	55	0.00	30.95
EUROPE	**1,810,251**	**1,709,478**	**1,876,192**	**1,912,917**	**1,973,211**	**4.06**	**3.15**
Central/Eastern Europe	**114,342**	**113,476**	**171,974**	**232,052**	**294,979**	**0.61**	**27.12**
Armenia	143	131	213	380	290	0.00	-23.68
Azerbaijan	257	349	543	558	851	0.00	52.51
Belarus	750	722	1,115	1,354	1,518	0.00	12.11
Bulgaria	4,792	3,760	4,465	4,673	5,304	0.01	13.50
Czech Republic	9,838	10,185	10,176	11,445	10,683	0.02	-6.66
Estonia	3,537	3,619	3,993	3,766	4,325	0.01	14.84
Georgia	177	271	262	444	351	0.00	-20.95
Hungary	8,513	7,748	10,170	9,459	8,968	0.02	-5.19
Kazakhstan	1,619	2,018	2,658	3,207	8,580	0.02	167.54
Kyrgyzstan	276	209	317	428	478	0.00	11.68
Latvia	2,072	2,247	2,190	2,280	2,783	0.01	22.06
Lithuania	2,464	2,526	2,673	3,161	3,702	0.01	17.11
Poland	24,590	21,477	24,641	26,889	23,896	0.05	-11.13
Republic of Moldova	261	176	219	322	220	0.00	-31.68
Romania	8,372	7,102	9,363	10,162	10,175	0.02	0.13
Russian Federation	37,153	42,980	86,800	131,537	186,461	0.38	41.76
Slovakia	3,353	3,462	4,085	4,351	4,907	0.01	12.78
Tajikistan	51	57	105	137	90	0.00	-34.31
Turkmenistan	15	16	16	124	42	0.00	-66.13
Ukraine	5,413	3,859	7,321	16,617	20,718	0.04	24.68
Uzbekistan	670	533	649	758	614	0.00	-19.00
Other countries Central/East Europe	26	29			23	0.00	
Northern Europe	**730,933**	**672,389**	**682,010**	**673,278**	**694,849**	**1.43**	**3.20**

Yearbook of Tourism Statistics, Data 2008 – 2012, 2014 Edition

HONG KONG, CHINA

2. Arrivals of non-resident visitors at national borders, by country of residence

	2008	2009	2010	2011	2012	Market share 2012	% Change 2012-2011
Denmark	30,618	27,688	29,156	28,781	26,941	0.06	-6.39
Finland	30,162	34,359	33,559	31,356	30,079	0.06	-4.07
Iceland	1,758	1,295	1,415	1,431	1,426	0.00	-0.35
Ireland	33,178	26,876	26,657	28,169	27,108	0.06	-3.77
Norway	19,673	19,377	20,940	19,870	20,326	0.04	2.29
Sweden	51,560	48,810	54,590	57,114	55,731	0.11	-2.42
United Kingdom	563,984	513,984	515,693	506,557	533,238	1.10	5.27
Southern Europe	**206,034**	**191,060**	**212,677**	**217,394**	**215,778**	**0.44**	**-0.74**
Albania	171	309	238	230	377	0.00	63.91
Andorra	83	136	104	108	93	0.00	-13.89
Bosnia and Herzegovina	619	441	498	446	442	0.00	-0.90
Croatia	3,423	2,610	2,824	2,962	3,262	0.01	10.13
Greece	10,380	8,397	8,784	8,346	8,189	0.02	-1.88
Holy See	6	11	5	5	5	0.00	0.00
Italy	110,583	103,315	118,915	117,199	115,610	0.24	-1.36
Malta	830	707	949	798	861	0.00	7.89
Montenegro					497	0.00	
Portugal	16,984	15,122	13,623	19,094	21,708	0.04	13.69
San Marino	141	94	152	111	92	0.00	-17.12
Serbia					2,963	0.01	
Serbia and Montenegro	1,684	980	1,320	2,174			
Slovenia	2,464	2,253	2,327	2,544	2,751	0.01	8.14
Spain	58,149	56,108	62,350	62,787	58,301	0.12	-7.14
TFYR of Macedonia	517	577	588	590	627	0.00	6.27
Western Europe	**657,985**	**631,970**	**689,383**	**676,699**	**660,833**	**1.36**	**-2.34**
Austria	24,084	24,116	26,944	25,638	25,819	0.05	0.71
Belgium	30,489	31,560	33,398	32,783	31,937	0.07	-2.58
France (*)	229,349	217,568	239,964	233,880	226,118	0.47	-3.32
Germany	224,665	210,828	230,436	223,544	222,820	0.46	-0.32
Liechtenstein	183	230	282	311	335	0.00	7.72
Luxembourg	1,516	1,744	1,941	1,674	1,432	0.00	-14.46
Monaco	229	376	204	135	163	0.00	20.74
Netherlands	102,310	99,450	106,544	107,564	100,068	0.21	-6.97
Switzerland	45,160	46,098	49,670	51,170	52,141	0.11	1.90
East Mediterranean Europe	**100,957**	**100,583**	**120,148**	**113,494**	**106,772**	**0.22**	**-5.92**
Cyprus	2,140	1,626	1,777	1,920	1,276	0.00	-33.54
Israel	62,106	65,266	72,914	69,525	66,807	0.14	-3.91
Turkey	36,711	33,691	45,457	42,049	38,689	0.08	-7.99
MIDDLE EAST	**71,180**	**74,536**	**90,813**	**84,564**	**78,023**	**0.16**	**-7.73**
Bahrain	2,250	1,664	2,466	2,094	1,860	0.00	-11.17
Egypt	11,579	9,505	11,777	10,764	10,839	0.02	0.70
Iraq	122	117	175	183	192	0.00	4.92
Jordan	12,238	11,588	14,806	17,647	14,362	0.03	-18.62
Kuwait	3,510	4,155	5,916	6,878	5,912	0.01	-14.04
Lebanon	1,412	1,257	1,349	1,332	1,303	0.00	-2.18
Libya	51	64	81	11	25	0.00	127.27
Oman	1,217	986	1,387	1,364	1,227	0.00	-10.04
Qatar	2,131	2,087	1,876	2,109	2,264	0.00	7.35
Saudi Arabia	15,693	19,035	28,401	21,192	19,107	0.04	-9.84
Syrian Arab Republic	665	596	741	651	618	0.00	-5.07
United Arab Emirates	12,787	16,195	13,624	14,549	14,410	0.03	-0.96
Yemen	7,525	7,218	8,111	5,735	5,857	0.01	2.13
Other countries of Middle East		69	103	55	47	0.00	-14.55
SOUTH ASIA	**381,797**	**396,914**	**561,323**	**531,401**	**446,667**	**0.92**	**-15.95**
Afghanistan	57	57	80	135	147	0.00	8.89
Bangladesh	6,556	6,040	4,968	4,848	4,917	0.01	1.42

311

HONG KONG, CHINA

2. Arrivals of non-resident visitors at national borders, by country of residence

	2008	2009	2010	2011	2012	Market share 2012	% Change 2012-2011
Bhutan	678	696	767	980	945	0.00	-3.57
India	350,674	366,646	530,910	498,063	414,158	0.85	-16.85
Iran, Islamic Republic of	1,936	2,035	2,650	3,218	2,858	0.01	-11.19
Maldives	332	348	439	766	547	0.00	-28.59
Nepal	4,413	5,060	5,454	6,476	6,906	0.01	6.64
Pakistan	10,496	9,992	9,713	9,958	9,592	0.02	-3.68
Sri Lanka	6,655	6,040	6,342	6,957	6,597	0.01	-5.17
NOT SPECIFIED	**158**	**113**	**95**	**109**			
Other countries of the World	158	113	95	109			

HUNGARY

1. Arrivals of non-resident tourists at national borders, by nationality

	2008	2009	2010	2011	2012	Market share 2012	% Change 2012-2011
TOTAL	8,813,000	9,058,000	9,511,000	10,250,000	10,353,000	100.00	1.00
AFRICA	20,000	22,000	23,000	26,000	26,000	0.25	0.00
Other Africa	20,000	22,000	23,000	26,000	26,000	0.25	0.00
All countries of Africa	20,000	22,000	23,000	26,000	26,000	0.25	0.00
AMERICAS	541,000	548,000	536,000	606,000	567,000	5.48	-6.44
North America	390,000	393,000	390,000	442,000	402,000	3.88	-9.05
United States of America	390,000	393,000	390,000	442,000	402,000	3.88	-9.05
Other Americas	151,000	155,000	146,000	164,000	165,000	1.59	0.61
Other countries of the Americas	151,000	155,000	146,000	164,000	165,000	1.59	0.61
EAST ASIA AND THE PACIFIC	385,000	389,000	381,000	411,000	404,000	3.90	-1.70
Australasia	63,000	63,000	65,000	68,000	69,000	0.67	1.47
Australia	63,000	63,000	65,000	68,000	69,000	0.67	1.47
Other East Asia and the Pacific	322,000	326,000	316,000	343,000	335,000	3.24	-2.33
All countries of Asia	322,000	326,000	316,000	343,000	335,000	3.24	-2.33
EUROPE	7,867,000	8,099,000	8,571,000	9,207,000	9,356,000	90.37	1.62
Central/Eastern Europe	2,423,000	2,421,000	2,657,000	2,806,000	3,145,000	30.38	12.08
Bulgaria	76,000	51,000	134,000	116,000	125,000	1.21	7.76
Czech Republic	230,000	250,000	271,000	315,000	334,000	3.23	6.03
Poland	537,000	612,000	556,000	422,000	694,000	6.70	64.45
Romania	718,000	721,000	912,000	1,153,000	1,092,000	10.55	-5.29
Russian Federation		70,000					
Slovakia	657,000	510,000	586,000	600,000	679,000	6.56	13.17
Ukraine	205,000	207,000	198,000	200,000	221,000	2.13	10.50
Northern Europe	304,000	310,000	319,000	338,000	304,000	2.94	-10.06
United Kingdom	304,000	310,000	319,000	338,000	304,000	2.94	-10.06
Southern Europe	633,000	645,000	689,000	821,000	822,000	7.94	0.12
Croatia	41,000	53,000	32,000	54,000	48,000	0.46	-11.11
Italy	357,000	373,000	330,000	428,000	387,000	3.74	-9.58
Serbia and Montenegro	219,000	211,000	313,000	333,000	381,000	3.68	14.41
Slovenia	16,000	8,000	14,000	6,000	6,000	0.06	0.00
Western Europe	3,582,000	3,714,000	3,850,000	4,016,000	4,037,000	38.99	0.52
Austria	918,000	922,000	935,000	965,000	1,005,000	9.71	4.15
France	231,000	232,000	250,000	283,000	257,000	2.48	-9.19
Germany	2,087,000	2,182,000	2,266,000	2,287,000	2,399,000	23.17	4.90
Netherlands	187,000	203,000	224,000	262,000	196,000	1.89	-25.19
Switzerland	159,000	175,000	175,000	219,000	180,000	1.74	-17.81
Other Europe	925,000	1,009,000	1,056,000	1,226,000	1,048,000	10.12	-14.52
Other countries of Europe	925,000	1,009,000	1,056,000	1,226,000	1,048,000	10.12	-14.52

Yearbook of Tourism Statistics, Data 2008 – 2012, 2014 Edition

HUNGARY

2. Arrivals of non-resident visitors at national borders, by nationality

	2008	2009	2010	2011	2012	Market share 2012	% Change 2012-2011
TOTAL	39,554,000	40,624,000	39,905,000	41,304,000	43,565,000	100.00	5.47
AFRICA	21,000	22,000	23,000	26,000	26,000	0.06	0.00
Other Africa	21,000	22,000	23,000	26,000	26,000	0.06	0.00
All countries of Africa	21,000	22,000	23,000	26,000	26,000	0.06	0.00
AMERICAS	548,000	557,000	547,000	615,000	577,000	1.32	-6.18
North America	396,000	397,000	391,000	443,000	412,000	0.95	-7.00
United States of America	396,000	397,000	391,000	443,000	412,000	0.95	-7.00
Other Americas	152,000	160,000	156,000	172,000	165,000	0.38	-4.07
Other countries of the Americas	152,000	160,000	156,000	172,000	165,000	0.38	-4.07
EAST ASIA AND THE PACIFIC	433,000	439,000	448,000	515,000	459,000	1.05	-10.87
Australasia	64,000	63,000	65,000	68,000	69,000	0.16	1.47
Australia	64,000	63,000	65,000	68,000	69,000	0.16	1.47
Other East Asia and the Pacific	369,000	376,000	383,000	447,000	390,000	0.90	-12.75
All countries of Asia	369,000	376,000	383,000	447,000	390,000	0.90	-12.75
EUROPE	38,552,000	39,606,000	38,887,000	40,148,000	42,503,000	97.56	5.87
Central/Eastern Europe	21,447,000	22,546,000	21,571,000	21,858,000	23,822,000	54.68	8.99
Bulgaria	1,243,000	1,234,000	1,191,000	1,380,000	1,443,000	3.31	4.57
Czech Republic	1,086,000	1,077,000	1,003,000	916,000	1,041,000	2.39	13.65
Poland	1,526,000	1,566,000	1,540,000	1,331,000	1,603,000	3.68	20.44
Romania	8,079,000	7,783,000	7,614,000	7,575,000	7,901,000	18.14	4.30
Russian Federation		106,000					
Slovakia	8,142,000	9,095,000	8,404,000	8,825,000	9,971,000	22.89	12.99
Ukraine	1,371,000	1,685,000	1,819,000	1,831,000	1,863,000	4.28	1.75
Northern Europe	345,000	359,000	356,000	395,000	357,000	0.82	-9.62
United Kingdom	345,000	359,000	356,000	395,000	357,000	0.82	-9.62
Southern Europe	4,354,000	4,217,000	4,153,000	4,952,000	4,301,000	9.87	-13.15
Croatia	990,000	971,000	868,000	934,000	756,000	1.74	-19.06
Italy	616,000	625,000	581,000	663,000	577,000	1.32	-12.97
Serbia and Montenegro	2,279,000	2,203,000	2,329,000	2,964,000	2,658,000	6.10	-10.32
Slovenia	469,000	418,000	375,000	391,000	310,000	0.71	-20.72
Western Europe	10,401,000	10,490,000	10,724,000	10,665,000	11,255,000	25.83	5.53
Austria	6,397,000	6,437,000	6,696,000	6,649,000	7,233,000	16.60	8.78
France	350,000	364,000	351,000	391,000	346,000	0.79	-11.51
Germany	3,103,000	3,130,000	3,135,000	3,026,000	3,188,000	7.32	5.35
Netherlands	307,000	306,000	320,000	326,000	274,000	0.63	-15.95
Switzerland	244,000	253,000	222,000	273,000	214,000	0.49	-21.61
Other Europe	2,005,000	1,994,000	2,083,000	2,278,000	2,768,000	6.35	21.51
Other countries of Europe	2,005,000	1,994,000	2,083,000	2,278,000	2,768,000	6.35	21.51

Yearbook of Tourism Statistics, Data 2008 – 2012, 2014 Edition

HUNGARY

3. Arrivals of non-resident tourists in hotels and similar establishments, by nationality

	2008	2009	2010	2011	2012	Market share 2012	% Change 2012-2011
TOTAL	3,196,784	2,914,328	3,183,753	3,518,363	3,825,319	100.00	8.72
AFRICA	8,772	9,571	9,947	11,400	14,011	0.37	22.90
Other Africa	8,772	9,571	9,947	11,400	14,011	0.37	22.90
All countries of Africa	8,772	9,571	9,947	11,400	14,011	0.37	22.90
AMERICAS	231,431	182,413	214,547	242,138	246,436	6.44	1.78
North America	201,119	155,707	184,479	199,950	196,353	5.13	-1.80
Canada	20,193	17,665	21,039	24,128	23,878	0.62	-1.04
United States of America	180,926	138,042	163,440	175,822	172,475	4.51	-1.90
Other Americas	30,312	26,706	30,068	42,188	50,083	1.31	18.71
Other countries of the Americas	30,312	26,706	30,068	42,188	50,083	1.31	18.71
EAST ASIA AND THE PACIFIC	99,409	89,195	98,067	96,087	103,996	2.72	8.23
North-East Asia	74,520	70,422	76,317	69,154	76,180	1.99	10.16
Japan	74,520	70,422	76,317	69,154	76,180	1.99	10.16
Other East Asia and the Pacific	24,889	18,773	21,750	26,933	27,816	0.73	3.28
All countries of Oceania	24,889	18,773	21,750	26,933	27,816	0.73	3.28
EUROPE	2,733,794	2,511,491	2,656,958	2,931,505	3,195,555	83.54	9.01
Central/Eastern Europe	667,003	647,068	725,302	839,953	931,518	24.35	10.90
Bulgaria	24,958	22,690	24,805	28,742	33,238	0.87	15.64
Czech Republic	94,129	115,168	127,431	154,907	161,940	4.23	4.54
Poland	111,685	103,917	115,761	133,278	145,919	3.81	9.48
Romania	231,051	191,318	195,544	201,579	202,283	5.29	0.35
Russian Federation	87,287	81,794	102,043	120,917	156,083	4.08	29.08
Slovakia	47,473	61,563	67,047	86,011	97,083	2.54	12.87
Ukraine	70,420	70,618	92,671	114,519	134,972	3.53	17.86
Northern Europe	412,275	341,800	353,109	382,369	431,987	11.29	12.98
Denmark	29,590	28,550	30,214	30,465	32,139	0.84	5.49
Finland	38,978	40,683	36,612	37,703	41,423	1.08	9.87
Norway	37,505	32,237	29,730	34,856	43,929	1.15	26.03
Sweden	59,733	55,833	56,182	65,785	81,495	2.13	23.88
United Kingdom	246,469	184,497	200,371	213,560	233,001	6.09	9.10
Southern Europe	425,258	384,787	412,039	471,352	509,075	13.31	8.00
Croatia	30,988	26,210	29,419	31,846	33,959	0.89	6.64
Greece	37,675	35,427	35,040	40,796	33,931	0.89	-16.83
Italy	166,283	165,085	175,412	187,503	218,026	5.70	16.28
Serbia		28,484	43,824	54,456	59,743	1.56	9.71
Serbia and Montenegro	31,629						
Slovenia	19,449	18,629	21,286	25,083	24,025	0.63	-4.22
Spain	139,234	110,952	107,058	131,668	139,391	3.64	5.87
Western Europe	990,537	954,389	1,044,024	1,073,518	1,126,580	29.45	4.94
Austria	221,061	234,358	248,742	269,049	270,337	7.07	0.48
Belgium	41,352	39,585	44,673	51,203	63,012	1.65	23.06
France	127,195	125,694	127,364	138,902	134,176	3.51	-3.40
Germany	489,984	446,624	466,939	479,212	505,284	13.21	5.44
Netherlands	65,893	59,651	89,565	80,569	99,002	2.59	22.88
Switzerland	45,052	48,477	66,741	54,583	54,769	1.43	0.34
East Mediterranean Europe	68,517	63,489	85,204	90,116	100,054	2.62	11.03
Israel	41,525	42,027	50,956	50,970	50,638	1.32	-0.65
Turkey	26,992	21,462	34,248	39,146	49,416	1.29	26.24
Other Europe	170,204	119,958	37,280	74,197	96,341	2.52	29.84
Other countries of Europe	170,204	119,958	37,280	74,197	96,341	2.52	29.84
NOT SPECIFIED	123,378	121,658	204,234	237,233	265,321	6.94	11.84
Other countries of the World	123,378	121,658	204,234	237,233	265,321	6.94	11.84

Yearbook of Tourism Statistics, Data 2008 – 2012, 2014 Edition

HUNGARY

4. Arrivals of non-resident tourists in all types of accommodation establishments, by nationality

	2008	2009	2010	2011	2012	Market share 2012	% Change 2012-2011
TOTAL (*)	3,516,030	3,227,942	3,462,021	3,821,751	4,163,641	100.00	8.95
AFRICA	9,091	9,925	10,096	11,775	14,512	0.35	23.24
Other Africa	9,091	9,925	10,096	11,775	14,512	0.35	23.24
All countries of Africa	9,091	9,925	10,096	11,775	14,512	0.35	23.24
AMERICAS	238,414	187,101	218,240	242,920	254,759	6.12	4.87
North America	206,129	158,738	187,007	202,767	200,746	4.82	-1.00
Canada	21,375	18,403	21,796	24,786	25,001	0.60	0.87
United States of America	184,754	140,335	165,211	177,981	175,745	4.22	-1.26
Other Americas	32,285	28,363	31,233	40,153	54,013	1.30	34.52
Other countries of the Americas	32,285	28,363	31,233	40,153	54,013	1.30	34.52
EAST ASIA AND THE PACIFIC	102,804	91,807	100,527	98,532	107,739	2.59	9.34
North-East Asia	75,261	71,124	76,862	69,724	77,093	1.85	10.57
Japan	75,261	71,124	76,862	69,724	77,093	1.85	10.57
Other East Asia and the Pacific	27,543	20,683	23,665	28,808	30,646	0.74	6.38
All countries of Oceania	27,543	20,683	23,665	28,808	30,646	0.74	6.38
EUROPE	3,040,128	2,815,773	2,927,419	3,225,209	3,516,155	84.45	9.02
Central/Eastern Europe	767,006	753,458	821,967	948,785	1,050,912	25.24	10.76
Bulgaria	25,620	23,500	25,407	29,351	34,196	0.82	16.51
Czech Republic	111,104	135,715	148,623	178,585	187,513	4.50	5.00
Poland	155,688	151,674	155,983	178,607	194,035	4.66	8.64
Romania	245,521	204,436	207,974	216,164	217,631	5.23	0.68
Russian Federation	90,816	82,982	103,766	123,394	159,014	3.82	28.87
Slovakia	64,894	82,773	85,558	105,495	119,872	2.88	13.63
Ukraine	73,363	72,378	94,656	117,189	138,651	3.33	18.31
Northern Europe	443,329	366,885	374,116	405,568	454,118	10.91	11.97
Denmark	44,151	39,001	38,473	40,233	40,121	0.96	-0.28
Finland	41,269	42,827	38,747	40,320	43,569	1.05	8.06
Norway	38,815	33,018	30,560	35,523	44,916	1.08	26.44
Sweden	62,426	58,359	58,212	68,067	83,993	2.02	23.40
United Kingdom	256,668	193,680	208,124	221,425	241,519	5.80	9.07
Southern Europe	441,439	401,260	427,578	490,656	532,569	12.79	8.54
Croatia	32,946	27,714	30,615	33,190	36,028	0.87	8.55
Greece	38,290	35,849	35,422	41,901	34,478	0.83	-17.72
Italy	172,959	173,161	183,259	197,495	229,022	5.50	15.96
Serbia		29,721	45,639	56,506	62,266	1.50	10.19
Serbia and Montenegro	33,360						
Slovenia	21,468	21,134	23,378	27,571	27,171	0.65	-1.45
Spain	142,416	113,681	109,265	133,993	143,604	3.45	7.17
Western Europe	1,139,689	1,103,623	1,136,390	1,208,229	1,275,531	30.63	5.57
Austria	246,108	259,108	272,579	294,931	297,053	7.13	0.72
Belgium	49,525	46,522	51,199	57,920	71,257	1.71	23.03
France	137,408	138,554	139,851	150,733	144,723	3.48	-3.99
Germany	564,876	520,280	528,753	542,333	570,147	13.69	5.13
Netherlands	93,084	86,927	89,565	103,947	133,537	3.21	28.47
Switzerland	48,688	52,232	54,443	58,365	58,814	1.41	0.77
East Mediterranean Europe	69,606	64,415	86,057	91,679	101,527	2.44	10.74
Israel	41,804	42,405	51,220	51,644	50,972	1.22	-1.30
Turkey	27,802	22,010	34,837	40,035	50,555	1.21	26.28
Other Europe	179,059	126,132	81,311	80,292	101,498	2.44	26.41
Other countries of Europe	179,059	126,132	81,311	80,292	101,498	2.44	26.41
NOT SPECIFIED	125,593	123,336	205,739	243,315	270,476	6.50	11.16
Other countries of the World	125,593	123,336	205,739	243,315	270,476	6.50	11.16

Yearbook of Tourism Statistics, Data 2008 – 2012, 2014 Edition

HUNGARY

5. Overnight stays of non-resident tourists in hotels and similar establishments, by nationality

	2008	2009	2010	2011	2012	Market share 2012	% Change 2012-2011
TOTAL	8,488,504	7,773,329	8,316,706	9,049,109	9,938,268	100.00	9.83
AFRICA	26,807	28,315	28,972	32,381	38,352	0.39	18.44
Other Africa	26,807	28,315	28,972	32,381	38,352	0.39	18.44
All countries of Africa	26,807	28,315	28,972	32,381	38,352	0.39	18.44
AMERICAS	604,528	485,368	550,633	606,830	636,912	6.41	4.96
North America	527,444	412,744	472,962	481,637	506,926	5.10	5.25
Canada	58,052	50,865	61,184	38,887	65,583	0.66	68.65
United States of America	469,392	361,879	411,778	442,750	441,343	4.44	-0.32
Other Americas	77,084	72,624	77,671	125,193	129,986	1.31	3.83
Other countries of the Americas	77,084	72,624	77,671	125,193	129,986	1.31	3.83
EAST ASIA AND THE PACIFIC	212,242	185,957	202,183	197,889	220,355	2.22	11.35
North-East Asia	152,507	139,650	145,782	133,383	151,366	1.52	13.48
Japan	152,507	139,650	145,782	133,383	151,366	1.52	13.48
Other East Asia and the Pacific	59,735	46,307	56,401	64,506	68,989	0.69	6.95
All countries of Oceania	59,735	46,307	56,401	64,506	68,989	0.69	6.95
EUROPE	7,399,314	6,835,685	7,069,678	7,675,611	8,469,994	85.23	10.35
Central/Eastern Europe	1,525,927	1,464,910	1,677,433	1,988,959	2,260,108	22.74	13.63
Bulgaria	40,884	36,692	40,363	46,792	56,899	0.57	21.60
Czech Republic	256,796	318,781	365,528	436,830	455,921	4.59	4.37
Poland	279,632	240,593	262,951	303,445	330,566	3.33	8.94
Romania	392,477	329,784	336,707	371,405	373,292	3.76	0.51
Russian Federation	301,884	273,503	366,850	451,762	600,829	6.05	33.00
Slovakia	98,318	129,017	143,945	190,760	213,295	2.15	11.81
Ukraine	155,936	136,540	161,089	187,965	229,306	2.31	21.99
Northern Europe	1,110,204	957,323	952,168	1,016,500	1,189,080	11.96	16.98
Denmark	98,742	92,387	95,861	93,296	103,323	1.04	10.75
Finland	113,326	121,467	110,951	112,380	128,643	1.29	14.47
Norway	122,038	105,990	98,273	111,958	139,836	1.41	24.90
Sweden	173,148	162,166	162,052	185,170	235,276	2.37	27.06
United Kingdom	602,950	475,313	485,031	513,696	582,002	5.86	13.30
Southern Europe	1,066,075	966,244	1,019,444	1,139,061	1,280,332	12.88	12.40
Croatia	85,781	58,010	52,425	58,672	67,575	0.68	15.17
Greece	96,520	92,239	89,828	103,515	91,646	0.92	-11.47
Italy	431,355	439,644	473,325	497,632	594,475	5.98	19.46
Serbia		57,158	85,099	104,301	116,684	1.17	11.87
Serbia and Montenegro	66,973						
Slovenia	36,179	34,888	44,575	49,089	54,652	0.55	11.33
Spain	349,267	284,305	274,192	325,852	355,300	3.58	9.04
Western Europe	3,086,532	2,966,372	3,057,326	3,154,810	3,309,743	33.30	4.91
Austria	568,410	612,313	642,781	687,892	682,035	6.86	-0.85
Belgium	114,204	109,171	121,516	130,676	173,812	1.75	33.01
France	309,650	316,279	325,358	347,309	347,765	3.50	0.13
Germany	1,776,486	1,618,558	1,631,723	1,624,048	1,690,581	17.01	4.10
Netherlands	174,605	158,134	173,896	202,135	256,165	2.58	26.73
Switzerland	143,177	151,917	162,052	162,750	159,385	1.60	-2.07
East Mediterranean Europe	192,008	185,442	326,027	253,624	279,846	2.82	10.34
Israel	127,361	135,885	164,938	165,843	176,147	1.77	6.21
Turkey	64,647	49,557	161,089	87,781	103,699	1.04	18.13
Other Europe	418,568	295,394	37,280	122,657	150,885	1.52	23.01
Other countries of Europe	418,568	295,394	37,280	122,657	150,885	1.52	23.01
NOT SPECIFIED	245,613	238,004	465,240	536,398	572,655	5.76	6.76
Other countries of the World	245,613	238,004	465,240	536,398	572,655	5.76	6.76

Yearbook of Tourism Statistics, Data 2008 – 2012, 2014 Edition

HUNGARY

6. Overnight stays of non-resident tourists in all types of accommodation establishments, by nationality

	2008	2009	2010	2011	2012	Market share 2012	% Change 2012-2011
TOTAL (*)	10,009,531	9,220,148	9,613,728	10,410,774	11,392,183	100.00	9.43
AFRICA	27,545	29,759	29,377	33,368	40,085	0.35	20.13
Other Africa	27,545	29,759	29,377	33,368	40,085	0.35	20.13
All countries of Africa	27,545	29,759	29,377	33,368	40,085	0.35	20.13
AMERICAS	621,618	496,724	562,147	619,267	658,983	5.78	6.41
North America	540,543	420,976	481,793	520,328	519,585	4.56	-0.14
Canada	60,902	52,405	63,528	70,394	69,012	0.61	-1.96
United States of America	479,641	368,571	418,265	449,934	450,573	3.96	0.14
Other Americas	81,075	75,748	80,354	98,939	139,398	1.22	40.89
Other countries of the Americas	81,075	75,748	80,354	98,939	139,398	1.22	40.89
EAST ASIA AND THE PACIFIC	219,363	192,130	208,421	203,628	229,573	2.02	12.74
North-East Asia	154,248	141,170	147,423	134,717	153,447	1.35	13.90
Japan	154,248	141,170	147,423	134,717	153,447	1.35	13.90
Other East Asia and the Pacific	65,115	50,960	60,998	68,911	76,126	0.67	10.47
All countries of Oceania	65,115	50,960	60,998	68,911	76,126	0.67	10.47
EUROPE	8,887,841	8,259,704	8,514,590	9,010,668	9,878,386	86.71	9.63
Central/Eastern Europe	1,827,441	1,790,603	1,969,392	2,321,340	2,623,178	23.03	13.00
Bulgaria	42,157	38,316	42,150	48,308	59,165	0.52	22.47
Czech Republic	311,430	385,272	436,071	514,308	538,591	4.73	4.72
Poland	422,017	393,422	393,513	448,060	485,062	4.26	8.26
Romania	430,524	369,782	370,014	415,493	419,030	3.68	0.85
Russian Federation	316,202	278,833	374,026	461,953	614,077	5.39	32.93
Slovakia	141,029	182,950	186,946	236,311	266,985	2.34	12.98
Ukraine	164,082	142,028	166,672	196,907	240,268	2.11	22.02
Northern Europe	1,263,418	1,076,805	1,056,682	1,131,776	1,290,491	11.33	14.02
Denmark	208,677	169,644	158,707	162,864	159,645	1.40	-1.98
Finland	118,923	127,176	117,858	121,890	135,265	1.19	10.97
Norway	127,065	108,534	101,356	114,464	143,481	1.26	25.35
Sweden	181,660	169,936	169,013	193,588	243,988	2.14	26.03
United Kingdom	627,093	501,515	509,748	538,970	608,112	5.34	12.83
Southern Europe	1,107,126	1,010,473	1,064,731	1,201,761	1,340,741	11.77	11.56
Croatia	90,907	62,147	55,614	62,242	73,346	0.64	17.84
Greece	100,206	93,787	91,650	114,119	93,202	0.82	-18.33
Italy	447,644	463,921	497,806	528,785	624,459	5.48	18.09
Serbia		59,828	90,006	109,055	122,810	1.08	12.61
Serbia and Montenegro	71,014						
Slovenia	40,763	40,408	49,267	55,451	61,453	0.54	10.82
Spain	356,592	290,382	280,388	332,109	365,471	3.21	10.05
Western Europe	4,056,148	3,881,897	3,863,997	3,957,699	4,177,086	36.67	5.54
Austria	690,111	734,195	755,553	809,500	804,268	7.06	-0.65
Belgium	160,801	144,167	154,686	164,605	210,014	1.84	27.59
France	335,813	355,875	364,106	387,038	380,943	3.34	-1.57
Germany	2,355,963	2,155,746	2,102,987	2,082,681	2,146,491	18.84	3.06
Netherlands	355,593	324,521	318,099	336,532	459,543	4.03	36.55
Switzerland	157,867	167,393	168,566	177,343	175,827	1.54	-0.85
East Mediterranean Europe	195,211	187,581	243,826	258,765	283,906	2.49	9.72
Israel	128,002	136,872	166,009	168,081	176,939	1.55	5.27
Turkey	67,209	50,709	77,817	90,684	106,967	0.94	17.96
Other Europe	438,497	312,345	315,962	139,327	162,984	1.43	16.98
Other countries of Europe	438,497	312,345	315,962	139,327	162,984	1.43	16.98
NOT SPECIFIED	253,164	241,831	299,193	543,843	585,156	5.14	7.60
Other countries of the World	253,164	241,831	299,193	543,843	585,156	5.14	7.60

Yearbook of Tourism Statistics, Data 2008 – 2012, 2014 Edition

ICELAND

1. Arrivals of non-resident tourists at national borders, by nationality

		2008	2009	2010	2011	2012	Market share 2012	% Change 2012-2011
TOTAL	(*)	**502,000**	**493,941**	**488,623**	**565,611**	**646,921**	**100.00**	**14.38**
AMERICAS		**51,101**	**54,998**	**64,652**	**95,547**	**113,786**	**17.59**	**19.09**
North America		**51,101**	**54,998**	**64,652**	**95,547**	**113,786**	**17.59**	**19.09**
Canada		10,580	11,074	13,461	17,946	18,760	2.90	4.54
United States of America		40,521	43,924	51,191	77,601	95,026	14.69	22.45
EAST ASIA AND THE PACIFIC		**12,492**	**12,416**	**10,774**	**15,686**	**24,379**	**3.77**	**55.42**
North-East Asia		**12,492**	**12,416**	**10,774**	**15,686**	**24,379**	**3.77**	**55.42**
China		5,760	5,368	5,194	8,784	14,036	2.17	59.79
Japan		6,732	7,048	5,580	6,902	10,343	1.60	49.86
EUROPE		**319,139**	**328,176**	**318,157**	**354,949**	**406,335**	**62.81**	**14.48**
Northern Europe		**194,378**	**185,460**	**178,132**	**198,470**	**236,324**	**36.53**	**19.07**
Denmark		43,595	43,782	42,593	43,765	40,906	6.32	-6.53
Finland		10,858	11,610	11,054	12,057	13,684	2.12	13.49
Norway		36,925	36,703	35,868	41,944	51,534	7.97	22.86
Sweden		32,507	31,585	28,109	32,959	35,601	5.50	8.02
United Kingdom		70,493	61,780	60,508	67,745	94,599	14.62	39.64
Southern Europe		**21,384**	**27,105**	**22,378**	**26,824**	**29,119**	**4.50**	**8.56**
Italy		10,842	13,224	10,068	12,792	13,841	2.14	8.20
Spain		10,542	13,881	12,310	14,032	15,278	2.36	8.88
Western Europe		**103,377**	**115,611**	**117,647**	**129,655**	**140,892**	**21.78**	**8.67**
France		27,313	29,786	30,204	36,747	41,570	6.43	13.12
Germany		48,976	56,467	59,453	61,372	65,179	10.08	6.20
Netherlands		19,644	20,217	18,111	20,757	21,305	3.29	2.64
Switzerland		7,444	9,141	9,879	10,779	12,838	1.98	19.10
NOT SPECIFIED		**119,268**	**98,351**	**95,040**	**99,429**	**102,421**	**15.83**	**3.01**
Other countries of the World		119,268	98,351	95,040	99,429	102,421	15.83	3.01

Yearbook of Tourism Statistics, Data 2008 – 2012, 2014 Edition

ICELAND

3. Arrivals of non-resident tourists in hotels and similar establishments, by nationality

	2008	2009	2010	2011	2012	Market share 2012	% Change 2012-2011
TOTAL	806,163	881,889	874,647	1,017,556	1,185,379	100.00	16.49
AFRICA	1,895	1,852	1,936	1,949	3,737	0.32	91.74
Other Africa	1,895	1,852	1,936	1,949	3,737	0.32	91.74
All countries of Africa	1,895	1,852	1,936	1,949	3,737	0.32	91.74
AMERICAS	73,526	77,548	85,912	133,195	167,975	14.17	26.11
North America	71,567	75,686	83,866	130,162	164,613	13.89	26.47
Canada	12,561	14,068	15,825	21,999	23,496	1.98	6.80
United States of America	59,006	61,618	68,041	108,163	141,117	11.90	30.47
Other Americas	1,959	1,862	2,046	3,033	3,362	0.28	10.85
Other countries of the Americas	1,959	1,862	2,046	3,033	3,362	0.28	10.85
EAST ASIA AND THE PACIFIC	25,578	30,845	27,907	40,478	67,786	5.72	67.46
North-East Asia	14,971	16,133	12,421	17,346	31,092	2.62	79.25
China	4,678	4,922	3,773	6,082	11,212	0.95	84.35
Japan	10,293	11,211	8,648	11,264	19,880	1.68	76.49
Australasia	4,065	4,386	4,782	5,905	8,357	0.71	41.52
Australia	4,065	4,386	4,782	5,905	8,357	0.71	41.52
Other East Asia and the Pacific	6,542	10,326	10,704	17,227	28,337	2.39	64.49
Other countries of Asia	6,542	10,326	10,704	17,227	28,337	2.39	64.49
EUROPE	647,016	718,135	713,506	791,506	905,270	76.37	14.37
Northern Europe	237,244	245,847	235,889	264,682	315,890	26.65	19.35
Denmark	46,333	48,550	50,885	47,790	50,927	4.30	6.56
Finland	10,241	12,372	11,104	12,820	14,922	1.26	16.40
Ireland	4,470	4,346	3,654	4,011	4,181	0.35	4.24
Norway	33,311	34,644	37,569	43,634	53,177	4.49	21.87
Sweden	36,087	34,967	30,515	37,819	39,618	3.34	4.76
United Kingdom	106,802	110,968	102,162	118,608	153,065	12.91	29.05
Southern Europe	74,735	92,236	66,976	90,229	90,977	7.67	0.83
Italy	39,739	50,370	35,469	47,689	45,260	3.82	-5.09
Spain	34,996	41,866	31,507	42,540	45,717	3.86	7.47
Western Europe	297,403	340,182	370,345	383,618	441,926	37.28	15.20
Austria	13,294	18,678	18,443	13,323	14,617	1.23	9.71
Belgium	10,757	13,580	17,476	16,927	16,478	1.39	-2.65
France	67,544	72,938	76,903	93,683	111,550	9.41	19.07
Germany	132,704	159,073	185,066	179,779	206,246	17.40	14.72
Netherlands	49,381	48,647	43,407	49,800	52,742	4.45	5.91
Switzerland	23,723	27,266	29,050	30,106	40,293	3.40	33.84
Other Europe	37,634	39,870	40,296	52,977	56,477	4.76	6.61
Other countries of Europe	37,634	39,870	40,296	52,977	56,477	4.76	6.61
NOT SPECIFIED	58,148	53,509	45,386	50,428	40,611	3.43	-19.47
Other countries of the World	58,148	53,509	45,386	50,428	40,611	3.43	-19.47

Yearbook of Tourism Statistics, Data 2008 – 2012, 2014 Editi

ICELAND

4. Arrivals of non-resident tourists in all types of accommodation establishments, by nationality

	2008	2009	2010	2011	2012	Market share 2012	% Change 2012-2011
TOTAL	1,106,017	1,280,640	1,224,156	1,419,367	1,631,937	100.00	14.98
AFRICA	2,219	1,960	2,086	2,322	4,164	0.26	79.33
Other Africa	2,219	1,960	2,086	2,322	4,164	0.26	79.33
All countries of Africa	2,219	1,960	2,086	2,322	4,164	0.26	79.33
AMERICAS	86,773	97,617	104,346	164,155	202,449	12.41	23.33
North America	84,357	95,274	101,919	160,613	197,838	12.12	23.18
Canada	17,603	21,934	22,671	32,807	34,609	2.12	5.49
United States of America	66,754	73,340	79,248	127,806	163,229	10.00	27.72
Other Americas	2,416	2,343	2,427	3,542	4,611	0.28	30.18
Other countries of the Americas	2,416	2,343	2,427	3,542	4,611	0.28	30.18
EAST ASIA AND THE PACIFIC	30,275	38,174	34,330	49,070	77,894	4.77	58.74
North-East Asia	16,557	18,909	14,782	20,519	35,213	2.16	71.61
China	5,352	6,455	4,940	7,836	13,642	0.84	74.09
Japan	11,205	12,454	9,842	12,683	21,571	1.32	70.08
Australasia	5,978	6,588	6,831	8,580	11,533	0.71	34.42
Australia	5,978	6,588	6,831	8,580	11,533	0.71	34.42
Other East Asia and the Pacific	7,740	12,677	12,717	19,971	31,148	1.91	55.97
Other countries of Asia	7,740	12,677	12,717	19,971	31,148	1.91	55.97
EUROPE	918,025	1,067,217	1,026,184	1,129,461	1,281,276	78.51	13.44
Northern Europe	292,510	301,702	281,319	315,978	376,021	23.04	19.00
Denmark	60,813	64,988	65,146	61,551	64,379	3.94	4.59
Finland	12,552	15,207	13,513	15,191	18,162	1.11	19.56
Ireland	6,701	6,013	5,054	5,153	6,943	0.43	34.74
Norway	38,121	40,569	42,069	50,303	60,113	3.68	19.50
Sweden	42,551	42,928	36,488	44,137	47,690	2.92	8.05
United Kingdom	131,772	131,997	119,049	139,643	178,734	10.95	27.99
Southern Europe	106,637	134,522	99,601	131,285	138,722	8.50	5.66
Italy	55,172	69,344	50,313	65,762	66,088	4.05	0.50
Spain	51,465	65,178	49,288	65,523	72,634	4.45	10.85
Western Europe	465,943	567,214	577,632	600,241	678,764	41.59	13.08
Austria	20,614	29,295	29,092	22,251	25,495	1.56	14.58
Belgium	19,034	26,400	31,181	30,239	31,018	1.90	2.58
France	110,803	134,946	131,002	157,746	183,767	11.26	16.50
Germany	204,591	253,958	270,291	264,121	294,920	18.07	11.66
Netherlands	74,832	77,210	68,529	77,143	81,731	5.01	5.95
Switzerland	36,069	45,405	47,537	48,741	61,833	3.79	26.86
Other Europe	52,935	63,779	67,632	81,957	87,769	5.38	7.09
Other countries of Europe	52,935	63,779	67,632	81,957	87,769	5.38	7.09
NOT SPECIFIED	68,725	75,672	57,210	74,359	66,154	4.05	-11.03
Other countries of the World	68,725	75,672	57,210	74,359	66,154	4.05	-11.03

Yearbook of Tourism Statistics, Data 2008 – 2012, 2014 Edition

ICELAND

5. Overnight stays of non-resident tourists in hotels and similar establishments, by nationality

	2008	2009	2010	2011	2012	Market share 2012	% Change 2012-2011
TOTAL	1,517,102	1,606,424	1,635,742	1,875,116	2,231,963	100.00	19.03
AFRICA	4,622	4,041	3,513	4,105	6,847	0.31	66.80
Other Africa	4,622	4,041	3,513	4,105	6,847	0.31	66.80
All countries of Africa	4,622	4,041	3,513	4,105	6,847	0.31	66.80
AMERICAS	152,376	156,918	177,406	282,096	360,483	16.15	27.79
North America	148,174	152,952	173,606	276,576	353,913	15.86	27.96
Canada	23,999	25,031	30,469	44,758	44,685	2.00	-0.16
United States of America	124,175	127,921	143,137	231,818	309,228	13.85	33.39
Other Americas	4,202	3,966	3,800	5,520	6,570	0.29	19.02
Other countries of the Americas	4,202	3,966	3,800	5,520	6,570	0.29	19.02
EAST ASIA AND THE PACIFIC	48,910	55,974	50,385	70,312	113,205	5.07	61.00
North-East Asia	28,787	30,093	24,672	32,458	55,575	2.49	71.22
China	9,194	9,167	7,761	11,469	19,997	0.90	74.36
Japan	19,593	20,926	16,911	20,989	35,578	1.59	69.51
Australasia	7,360	8,865	8,646	11,263	16,166	0.72	43.53
Australia	7,360	8,865	8,646	11,263	16,166	0.72	43.53
Other East Asia and the Pacific	12,763	17,016	17,067	26,591	41,464	1.86	55.93
Other countries of Asia	12,763	17,016	17,067	26,591	41,464	1.86	55.93
EUROPE	1,198,979	1,286,862	1,301,605	1,431,126	1,683,832	75.44	17.66
Northern Europe	528,210	553,612	540,167	597,458	732,185	32.80	22.55
Denmark	90,735	96,350	102,848	97,359	105,911	4.75	8.78
Finland	26,753	30,057	29,858	33,843	37,730	1.69	11.49
Ireland	9,558	8,763	8,186	8,309	8,709	0.39	4.81
Norway	78,530	83,317	88,105	103,081	124,981	5.60	21.25
Sweden	89,793	87,597	79,018	93,250	103,639	4.64	11.14
United Kingdom	232,841	247,528	232,152	261,616	351,215	15.74	34.25
Southern Europe	105,360	122,309	93,460	126,267	125,878	5.64	-0.31
Italy	54,723	65,506	47,556	65,053	59,736	2.68	-8.17
Spain	50,637	56,803	45,904	61,214	66,142	2.96	8.05
Western Europe	479,644	534,510	586,510	607,959	712,338	31.92	17.17
Austria	20,860	26,662	27,214	21,236	21,842	0.98	2.85
Belgium	17,252	20,464	27,523	26,497	27,147	1.22	2.45
France	95,341	101,777	110,135	134,165	161,597	7.24	20.45
Germany	226,576	265,686	301,285	296,411	349,603	15.66	17.95
Netherlands	81,546	79,869	77,437	84,984	92,181	4.13	8.47
Switzerland	38,069	40,052	42,916	44,666	59,968	2.69	34.26
Other Europe	85,765	76,431	81,468	99,442	113,431	5.08	14.07
Other countries of Europe	85,765	76,431	81,468	99,442	113,431	5.08	14.07
NOT SPECIFIED	112,215	102,629	102,833	87,477	67,596	3.03	-22.73
Other countries of the World	112,215	102,629	102,833	87,477	67,596	3.03	-22.73

Yearbook of Tourism Statistics, Data 2008 – 2012, 2014 Edition

ICELAND

6. Overnight stays of non-resident tourists in all types of accommodation establishments, by nationality

	2008	2009	2010	2011	2012	Market share 2012	% Change 2012-2011
TOTAL	1,942,698	2,134,245	2,144,318	2,444,245	2,888,951	100.00	18.19
AFRICA	4,994	4,159	3,714	4,734	7,539	0.26	59.25
Other Africa	4,994	4,159	3,714	4,734	7,539	0.26	59.25
All countries of Africa	4,994	4,159	3,714	4,734	7,539	0.26	59.25
AMERICAS	171,158	184,803	205,654	329,923	414,870	14.36	25.75
North America	166,352	180,045	201,158	323,594	406,397	14.07	25.59
Canada	30,627	35,608	40,681	60,922	61,904	2.14	1.61
United States of America	135,725	144,437	160,477	262,672	344,493	11.92	31.15
Other Americas	4,806	4,758	4,496	6,329	8,473	0.29	33.88
Other countries of the Americas	4,806	4,758	4,496	6,329	8,473	0.29	33.88
EAST ASIA AND THE PACIFIC	55,466	66,561	60,974	83,344	129,388	4.48	55.25
North-East Asia	31,029	34,216	28,781	37,314	62,037	2.15	66.26
China	10,094	11,118	9,453	13,725	23,631	0.82	72.17
Japan	20,935	23,098	19,328	23,589	38,406	1.33	62.81
Australasia	10,152	12,125	12,146	15,776	21,954	0.76	39.16
Australia	10,152	12,125	12,146	15,776	21,954	0.76	39.16
Other East Asia and the Pacific	14,285	20,220	20,047	30,254	45,397	1.57	50.05
Other countries of Asia	14,285	20,220	20,047	30,254	45,397	1.57	50.05
EUROPE	1,583,712	1,747,898	1,754,128	1,908,585	2,227,247	77.10	16.70
Northern Europe	615,857	637,363	619,523	685,291	829,831	28.72	21.09
Denmark	113,930	122,266	129,359	122,978	129,030	4.47	4.92
Finland	30,658	34,029	33,238	37,677	42,363	1.47	12.44
Ireland	12,601	11,081	10,460	10,078	12,631	0.44	25.33
Norway	87,504	92,493	96,642	114,924	137,268	4.75	19.44
Sweden	98,815	98,890	88,720	103,055	115,631	4.00	12.20
United Kingdom	272,349	278,604	261,104	296,579	392,908	13.60	32.48
Southern Europe	144,534	172,655	134,618	175,958	184,734	6.39	4.99
Italy	73,835	88,020	66,523	86,562	85,306	2.95	-1.45
Spain	70,699	84,635	68,095	89,396	99,428	3.44	11.22
Western Europe	716,843	831,728	882,440	909,221	1,057,213	36.60	16.28
Austria	30,615	40,215	41,476	32,476	35,997	1.25	10.84
Belgium	27,657	35,518	44,855	43,093	46,531	1.61	7.98
France	150,923	175,153	180,137	213,706	259,867	9.00	21.60
Germany	334,841	399,311	430,900	422,704	487,345	16.87	15.29
Netherlands	118,054	119,007	117,328	128,032	139,140	4.82	8.68
Switzerland	54,753	62,524	67,744	69,210	88,333	3.06	27.63
Other Europe	106,478	106,152	117,547	138,115	155,469	5.38	12.56
Other countries of Europe	106,478	106,152	117,547	138,115	155,469	5.38	12.56
NOT SPECIFIED	127,368	130,824	119,848	117,659	109,907	3.80	-6.59
Other countries of the World	127,368	130,824	119,848	117,659	109,907	3.80	-6.59

INDIA

1. Arrivals of non-resident tourists at national borders, by nationality

		2008	2009	2010	2011	2012	Market share 2012	% Change 2012-2011
TOTAL	(*)	5,282,603	5,167,699	5,775,692	6,309,222	6,577,745	100.00	4.26
AFRICA		136,424	158,605	197,090	224,292	251,187	3.82	11.99
East Africa		63,665	75,618	91,544	99,385	125,772	1.91	26.55
Burundi		338	559	703	857	704	0.01	-17.85
Comoros		85	39	133	231	419	0.01	81.39
Djibouti				561	602	835	0.01	38.70
Eritrea		369	523	638	616	639	0.01	3.73
Ethiopia		3,306	3,936	3,797	6,411	11,795	0.18	83.98
Kenya		14,941	22,704	29,223	30,045	34,037	0.52	13.29
Madagascar		686	883	2,377	1,509	1,497	0.02	-0.80
Malawi		731	799	1,250	1,132	10,406	0.16	819.26
Mauritius		19,713	18,866	21,672	22,091	25,013	0.38	13.23
Mozambique		884	1,790	2,442	3,118	3,766	0.06	20.78
Reunion		75	59	102	29	21	0.00	-27.59
Rwanda		651	849	1,344	1,580	1,907	0.03	20.70
Seychelles		1,386	1,339	1,672	2,330	2,220	0.03	-4.72
Somalia		637	525	555	753	701	0.01	-6.91
Uganda		2,285	2,425	3,011	3,615	3,841	0.06	6.25
United Republic of Tanzania		14,872	17,020	17,645	19,470	21,862	0.33	12.29
Zambia		1,995	2,249	2,621	2,944	3,428	0.05	16.44
Zimbabwe		711	1,053	1,798	2,052	2,681	0.04	30.65
Central Africa		3,305	3,389	4,810	7,914	8,811	0.13	11.33
Angola		1,851	1,248	1,620	1,891	2,263	0.03	19.67
Cameroon		467	671	877	912	1,014	0.02	11.18
Central African Republic		59	9	15	37	62	0.00	67.57
Chad		105	154	212	1,198	194	0.00	-83.81
Congo		670	1,100	1,930	3,623	5,093	0.08	40.57
Equatorial Guinea		15	8	11	10	7	0.00	-30.00
Gabon		120	188	134	226	170	0.00	-24.78
Sao Tome and Principe		18	11	11	17	8	0.00	-52.94
North Africa		6,843	8,768	11,766	14,529	17,174	0.26	18.20
Algeria		1,043	1,217	1,203	1,635	1,750	0.03	7.03
Morocco		1,207	1,429	1,724	2,328	3,203	0.05	37.59
Sudan		3,473	4,987	7,418	8,414	9,626	0.15	14.40
Tunisia		1,120	1,135	1,421	2,152	2,595	0.04	20.59
Southern Africa		43,795	47,179	58,271	60,815	53,830	0.82	-11.49
Botswana		385	491	1,050	837	919	0.01	9.80
Lesotho		282	290	523	421	365	0.01	-13.30
Namibia		477	558	613	593	757	0.01	27.66
South Africa		42,337	44,308	55,688	58,430	50,161	0.76	-14.15
Swaziland		314	1,532	397	534	1,628	0.02	204.87
West Africa		18,779	23,550	30,699	41,649	45,565	0.69	9.40
Benin				209	304	189	0.00	-37.83
Burkina Faso		199	259	282	262	300	0.00	14.50
Cape Verde		23	22	42	21	30	0.00	42.86
Côte d'Ivoire		348	639	680	637	873	0.01	37.05
Gambia		105	161	281	380	297	0.00	-21.84
Ghana		1,269	1,381	1,773	2,129	2,390	0.04	12.26
Guinea		211	280	310	341	317	0.00	-7.04
Guinea-Bissau		17	12	18	34	68	0.00	100.00
Liberia		171	144	177	164	245	0.00	49.39
Mali		232	273	495	815	845	0.01	3.68
Mauritania		363	190	131	559	869	0.01	55.46
Niger		338	316	475	600	497	0.01	-17.17
Nigeria		13,997	18,338	23,893	33,537	36,762	0.56	9.62
Saint Helena				53	51	41	0.00	-19.61

Yearbook of Tourism Statistics, Data 2008 – 2012, 2014 Editi

INDIA

1. Arrivals of non-resident tourists at national borders, by nationality

	2008	2009	2010	2011	2012	Market share 2012	% Change 2012-2011
Senegal	919	1,077	1,212	1,234	1,202	0.02	-2.59
Sierra Leone	416	301	371	289	357	0.01	23.53
Togo	171	157	297	292	283	0.00	-3.08
Other Africa	**37**	**101**			**35**	**0.00**	
Other countries of Africa	37	101			35	0.00	
AMERICAS	**1,070,802**	**1,097,813**	**1,236,695**	**1,300,911**	**1,360,373**	**20.68**	**4.57**
Caribbean	**3,280**	**3,563**	**5,135**	**4,644**	**4,489**	**0.07**	**-3.34**
Anguilla			14	8	1	0.00	-87.50
Antigua and Barbuda	31	25	65	35	54	0.00	54.29
Bahamas	169	142	179	212	281	0.00	32.55
Barbados	290	326	451	428	488	0.01	14.02
Bermuda			29	31	6	0.00	-80.65
British Virgin Islands			15	1			
Cayman Islands			12	6	1	0.00	-83.33
Cuba	283	259	338	279	231	0.00	-17.20
Dominica			48	17	26	0.00	52.94
Dominican Republic	235	255	353	459	337	0.01	-26.58
Grenada	108	100	92	107	93	0.00	-13.08
Guadeloupe	4	7	5	2			
Haiti	93	119	89	89	72	0.00	-19.10
Jamaica	463	561	892	768	795	0.01	3.52
Martinique	28	8	12	12	31	0.00	158.33
Montserrat			21	32	81	0.00	153.13
Netherlands Antilles	60	56	75	55	64	0.00	16.36
Puerto Rico			3	7	4	0.00	-42.86
Saint Kitts and Nevis			91	82	76	0.00	-7.32
Saint Lucia	104	50	88	91	118	0.00	29.67
Saint Vincent and the Grenadines			47	24	18	0.00	-25.00
Trinidad and Tobago	1,412	1,655	2,193	1,888	1,708	0.03	-9.53
Turks and Caicos Islands			19	10	4	0.00	-60.00
United States Virgin Islands			4	1			
Central America	**2,834**	**2,670**	**2,616**	**3,351**	**3,152**	**0.05**	**-5.94**
Belize	349	223	356	351	362	0.01	3.13
Costa Rica	537	561	568	1,042	763	0.01	-26.78
El Salvador	309	213	204	215	255	0.00	18.60
Guatemala	515	495	411	429	527	0.01	22.84
Honduras	234	256	195	283	256	0.00	-9.54
Nicaragua	97	109	92	85	81	0.00	-4.71
Panama	793	813	790	946	908	0.01	-4.02
North America	**1,036,569**	**1,059,394**	**1,184,122**	**1,250,581**	**1,307,222**	**19.87**	**4.53**
Canada	222,364	224,069	242,372	259,017	256,021	3.89	-1.16
Mexico	9,272	8,185	10,458	10,876	11,254	0.17	3.48
United States of America	804,933	827,140	931,292	980,688	1,039,947	15.81	6.04
South America	**28,119**	**32,186**	**44,822**	**42,335**	**45,021**	**0.68**	**6.34**
Argentina	5,087	6,011	7,626	9,391	9,831	0.15	4.69
Bolivia	176	280	290	313	334	0.01	6.71
Brazil	11,530	13,964	15,219	17,268	18,440	0.28	6.79
Chile	2,916	2,961	11,340	3,975	4,640	0.07	16.73
Colombia	2,762	2,945	3,663	4,085	4,381	0.07	7.25
Ecuador	549	606	794	1,208	911	0.01	-24.59
Guyana	288	387	601	438	359	0.01	-18.04
Paraguay	242	116	228	221	266	0.00	20.36
Peru	1,261	1,214	1,326	1,592	1,932	0.03	21.36
Suriname	512	514	493	558	539	0.01	-3.41
Uruguay	917	1,068	1,387	1,199	1,249	0.02	4.17
Venezuela	1,879	2,120	1,855	2,087	2,139	0.03	2.49
Other Americas					**489**	**0.01**	

325

INDIA

1. Arrivals of non-resident tourists at national borders, by nationality

	2008	2009	2010	2011	2012	Market share 2012	% Change 2012-2011
Other countries of the Americas					489	0.01	
EAST ASIA AND THE PACIFIC	**866,463**	**865,439**	**1,062,536**	**1,229,632**	**1,321,643**	**20.09**	**7.48**
North-East Asia	**355,230**	**322,797**	**411,947**	**475,951**	**535,622**	**8.14**	**12.54**
China	98,093	100,209	119,530	142,218	168,952	2.57	18.80
Hong Kong, China	519	1,396	1,507	1,712	1,743	0.03	1.81
Japan	145,352	124,756	168,019	193,525	220,015	3.34	13.69
Korea, Dem. People's Republic of	22	4	25	20	181	0.00	805.00
Korea, Republic of	79,802	70,485	95,587	108,680	109,469	1.66	0.73
Macao, China	211	251	669	573	205	0.00	-64.22
Mongolia	2,292	2,232	2,695	3,307	3,418	0.05	3.36
Taiwan, Province of China	28,939	23,464	23,915	25,916	31,639	0.48	22.08
South-East Asia	**332,925**	**360,191**	**439,043**	**520,787**	**540,914**	**8.22**	**3.86**
Brunei Darussalam	5,442	303	456	556	665	0.01	19.60
Cambodia	1,596	1,133	1,715	2,076	2,028	0.03	-2.31
Indonesia	19,609	20,068	26,171	32,530	29,559	0.45	-9.13
Lao People's Democratic Republic	322	294	809		973	0.01	
Malaysia	115,794	135,343	179,077	208,196	195,853	2.98	-5.93
Myanmar	12,147	12,849	14,719	25,043	30,588	0.47	22.14
Philippines	17,222	21,987	24,534	31,151	33,323	0.51	6.97
Singapore	97,851	95,328	107,487	119,022	131,452	2.00	10.44
Thailand	58,065	67,309	76,617	92,404	105,141	1.60	13.78
Viet Nam	4,877	5,577	7,458	9,809	11,332	0.17	15.53
Australasia	**175,470**	**179,950**	**206,671**	**229,431**	**241,022**	**3.66**	**5.05**
Australia	146,209	149,074	169,647	192,592	202,105	3.07	4.94
New Zealand	29,261	30,876	37,024	36,839	38,917	0.59	5.64
Melanesia	**2,349**	**2,248**	**2,971**	**2,997**	**3,105**	**0.05**	**3.60**
Fiji	2,129	2,031	2,508	2,705	2,793	0.04	3.25
New Caledonia			4	2	5	0.00	150.00
Norfolk Island			7	5	3	0.00	-40.00
Papua New Guinea	189	177	356	242	265	0.00	9.50
Solomon Islands	31	40					
Vanuatu			96	43	39	0.00	-9.30
Micronesia	**300**	**207**	**463**	**369**	**311**	**0.00**	**-15.72**
Christmas Island, Australia			2	1			
Guam				2	1	0.00	-50.00
Kiribati	66	30	143	83	74	0.00	-10.84
Nauru	234	177	318	283	236	0.00	-16.61
Polynesia	**189**	**46**	**1,441**	**97**	**669**	**0.01**	**589.69**
American Samoa			1,077	41	278	0.00	578.05
Cook Islands			2				
French Polynesia			25	33	15	0.00	-54.55
Niue	78			4			
Samoa	30	31			43	0.00	
Tonga			297		283	0.00	
Tuvalu	81	15	40	19	50	0.00	163.16
EUROPE	**1,955,824**	**1,869,115**	**2,034,709**	**2,173,422**	**2,236,970**	**34.01**	**2.92**
Central/Eastern Europe	**188,178**	**179,088**	**223,327**	**269,414**	**311,380**	**4.73**	**15.58**
Armenia	1,123	452	641	686	595	0.01	-13.27
Azerbaijan	8,908	859	800	1,058	1,263	0.02	19.38
Belarus	2,155	2,536	3,493	4,567	6,239	0.09	36.61
Bulgaria	2,224	2,370	2,900	2,890	3,621	0.06	25.29
Czech Republic	8,549	8,328	9,918	11,256	11,129	0.17	-1.13
Estonia	4,205	3,496	2,594	2,754	3,005	0.05	9.11
Georgia	669	687	655	4,179	1,029	0.02	-75.38
Hungary	5,263	4,980	6,022	6,900	6,507	0.10	-5.70
Kazakhstan	7,534	6,848	8,786	9,810	11,653	0.18	18.79
Kyrgyzstan	1,036	1,208	1,181	1,340	1,348	0.02	0.60

326

Yearbook of Tourism Statistics, Data 2008 – 2012, 2014 Edition

INDIA

1. Arrivals of non-resident tourists at national borders, by nationality

	2008	2009	2010	2011	2012	Market share 2012	% Change 2012-2011
Latvia	2,611	2,498	3,052	2,968	3,029	0.05	2.06
Lithuania	3,442	2,365	2,598	3,619	3,408	0.05	-5.83
Poland	23,517	19,656	25,424	28,499	25,030	0.38	-12.17
Republic of Moldova	286	1,502	424	470	541	0.01	15.11
Romania	4,689	4,808	5,380	5,988	6,338	0.10	5.85
Russian Federation	91,095	94,945	122,048	144,312	177,526	2.70	23.02
Slovakia	2,833	3,092	3,571	4,061	3,850	0.06	-5.20
Tajikistan	861	749	963	1,359	1,564	0.02	15.08
Turkmenistan	1,316	1,631	1,509	1,946	2,364	0.04	21.48
Ukraine	12,344	12,436	16,462	23,467	29,033	0.44	23.72
Uzbekistan	2,756	3,642	4,906	7,285	9,808	0.15	34.63
Other countries Central/East Europe	762				2,500	0.04	
Northern Europe	**947,202**	**915,655**	**908,900**	**954,614**	**946,520**	**14.39**	**-0.85**
Denmark	34,253	30,857	35,541	34,683	33,084	0.50	-4.61
Faeroe Islands			7	6	5	0.00	-16.67
Finland	29,223	24,874	24,089	23,730	22,416	0.34	-5.54
Iceland	2,013	1,821	2,183	2,589	1,673	0.03	-35.38
Ireland	18,924	19,223	20,329	22,089	24,546	0.37	11.12
Norway	22,369	22,092	22,229	24,578	23,569	0.36	-4.11
Sweden	58,961	43,327	45,028	48,690	51,058	0.78	4.86
United Kingdom	776,530	769,251	759,494	798,249	788,170	11.98	-1.26
Other countries of Northern Europe	4,929	4,210			1,999	0.03	
Southern Europe	**176,892**	**168,155**	**203,898**	**211,408**	**205,663**	**3.13**	**-2.72**
Albania	219	279	330	394	234	0.00	-40.61
Andorra	155	173	157	181	134	0.00	-25.97
Bosnia and Herzegovina			305	329	293	0.00	-10.94
Croatia	2,932	2,990	3,080	3,375	3,158	0.05	-6.43
Gibraltar			5	10	1	0.00	-90.00
Greece	6,672	6,664	7,441	7,253	7,493	0.11	3.31
Italy	85,766	77,873	94,100	100,889	98,743	1.50	-2.13
Malta	665	499	540	516	614	0.01	18.99
Portugal	15,415	17,184	21,038	24,061	24,670	0.38	2.53
San Marino			46	57	130	0.00	128.07
Slovenia	1,771	2,049	3,022	2,938	2,794	0.04	-4.90
Spain	62,535	59,047	72,591	71,405	67,044	1.02	-6.11
Yugoslavia, SFR (former)	762	1,397	1,243		355	0.01	
Western Europe	**589,088**	**554,595**	**638,637**	**671,642**	**701,386**	**10.66**	**4.43**
Austria	25,900	27,930	32,620	36,483	38,585	0.59	5.76
Belgium	36,277	34,759	37,709	40,478	42,604	0.65	5.25
France	207,802	196,462	225,232	231,423	240,674	3.66	4.00
Germany	204,344	191,616	227,720	240,235	254,783	3.87	6.06
Liechtenstein			182	174	136	0.00	-21.84
Luxembourg	1,053	958	1,200	1,256	1,334	0.02	6.21
Monaco			84	108	82	0.00	-24.07
Netherlands	71,605	64,580	70,756	75,153	74,800	1.14	-0.47
Switzerland	42,107	38,290	43,134	46,332	48,388	0.74	4.44
East Mediterranean Europe	**54,464**	**51,622**	**59,947**	**66,344**	**71,520**	**1.09**	**7.80**
Cyprus	810	759	1,008	896	885	0.01	-1.23
Israel	42,720	40,581	43,456	48,089	47,649	0.72	-0.91
Turkey	10,934	10,282	15,483	17,359	22,986	0.35	32.42
Other Europe					**501**	**0.01**	
Other countries of Europe					501	0.01	
MIDDLE EAST	**166,404**	**159,090**	**183,387**	**221,220**	**231,062**	**3.51**	**4.45**
Bahrain	7,224	7,901	7,766	9,587	10,045	0.15	4.78
Egypt	5,326	5,869	8,017	8,791	10,571	0.16	20.25
Iraq	7,789	16,400	28,221	30,808	38,826	0.59	26.03
Jordan	4,154	4,301	4,640	5,061	7,356	0.11	45.35

327

Yearbook of Tourism Statistics, Data 2008 – 2012, 2014 Edition

INDIA

1. Arrivals of non-resident tourists at national borders, by nationality

	2008	2009	2010	2011	2012	Market share 2012	% Change 2012-2011
Kuwait	5,302	5,208	4,764	5,370	5,256	0.08	-2.12
Lebanon	3,418	3,320	3,730	4,296	4,842	0.07	12.71
Libya	494	693	1,280	465	1,620	0.02	248.39
Oman	34,042	32,971	35,485	40,577	49,759	0.76	22.63
Palestine	770	966	1,151	1,241	1,224	0.02	-1.37
Qatar	2,934	2,765	2,735	3,266	4,132	0.06	26.52
Saudi Arabia	16,983	15,552	21,599	26,268	32,127	0.49	22.30
Syrian Arab Republic	2,883	3,215	3,586	4,152	3,971	0.06	-4.36
United Arab Emirates	63,502	47,234	45,482	66,383	41,664	0.63	-37.24
Yemen	11,583	12,695	14,931	14,955	18,654	0.28	24.73
Other countries of Middle East					1,015	0.02	
SOUTH ASIA	**1,051,846**	**1,001,401**	**1,047,444**	**1,139,659**	**1,171,499**	**17.81**	**2.79**
Afghanistan	32,438	50,446	73,389	89,605	95,231	1.45	6.28
Bangladesh	541,884	468,899	431,962	463,543	487,397	7.41	5.15
Bhutan	9,952	10,328	12,048	15,489	15,266	0.23	-1.44
Iran, Islamic Republic of	30,149	34,652	49,265	43,399	40,973	0.62	-5.59
Maldives	54,956	55,159	58,152	53,999	50,428	0.77	-6.61
Nepal	78,133	88,785	104,374	119,131	125,375	1.91	5.24
Pakistan	85,529	53,137	51,739	48,640	59,846	0.91	23.04
Sri Lanka	218,805	239,995	266,515	305,853	296,983	4.51	-2.90
NOT SPECIFIED	**34,840**	**16,236**	**13,831**	**20,086**	**5,011**	**0.08**	**-75.05**
Other countries of the World	34,840	16,236	13,831	20,086	5,011	0.08	-75.05

Yearbook of Tourism Statistics, Data 2008 – 2012, 2014 Editic

INDONESIA

1. Arrivals of non-resident tourists at national borders, by nationality

	2008	2009	2010	2011	2012	Market share 2012	% Change 2012-2011
TOTAL	6,234,497	6,323,730	7,002,944	7,649,731	8,044,462	100.00	5.16
AFRICA	33,081	26,637	28,592	31,651	37,306	0.46	17.87
Southern Africa	14,958	12,999	14,287	16,282	17,433	0.22	7.07
South Africa	14,958	12,999	14,287	16,282	17,433	0.22	7.07
Other Africa	18,123	13,638	14,305	15,369	19,873	0.25	29.31
Other countries of Africa	18,123	13,638	14,305	15,369	19,873	0.25	29.31
AMERICAS	249,968	237,670	255,465	293,306	312,526	3.88	6.55
Central America	9,618	4,587	881	1,044	1,800	0.02	72.41
All countries of Central America	9,618	4,587	881	1,044	1,800	0.02	72.41
North America	219,955	209,046	226,026	260,334	275,844	3.43	5.96
Canada	45,408	43,948	48,349	57,129	58,245	0.72	1.95
United States of America	174,547	165,098	177,677	203,205	217,599	2.70	7.08
South America	20,395	24,037	21,364	26,193	28,155	0.35	7.49
All countries of South America	20,395	24,037	21,364	26,193	28,155	0.35	7.49
Other Americas			7,194	5,735	6,727	0.08	17.30
Other countries of the Americas			7,194	5,735	6,727	0.08	17.30
EAST ASIA AND THE PACIFIC	4,712,610	4,741,596	5,350,445	5,848,604	6,159,068	76.56	5.31
North-East Asia	1,522,344	1,461,827	1,511,249	1,652,613	1,818,053	22.60	10.01
China	354,641	444,598	511,188	594,997	726,088	9.03	22.03
Hong Kong, China	58,260	63,801	73,658	84,985	81,782	1.02	-3.77
Japan	559,888	488,320	416,151	423,113	463,486	5.76	9.54
Korea, Republic of	331,409	260,314	296,060	320,596	328,989	4.09	2.62
Taiwan, Province of China	218,146	204,794	214,192	228,922	217,708	2.71	-4.90
South-East Asia	2,677,990	2,637,066	2,958,976	3,131,818	3,246,001	40.35	3.65
Brunei Darussalam	10,536	13,668	35,874	38,679	16,423	0.20	-57.54
Cambodia	1,959	1,975	5,265	4,628	5,058	0.06	9.29
Lao People's Democratic Republic	786	969	1,932	1,914	2,000	0.02	4.49
Malaysia	1,009,722	1,041,053	1,171,737	1,173,351	1,269,089	15.78	8.16
Myanmar	17,487	18,128	15,582	22,304	29,718	0.37	33.24
Philippines	195,675	196,429	171,181	210,029	236,866	2.94	12.78
Singapore	1,197,267	1,138,071	1,206,360	1,324,839	1,324,706	16.47	-0.01
Thailand	66,012	93,381	111,645	115,036	114,867	1.43	-0.15
Viet Nam	19,710	20,785	24,929	31,106	33,598	0.42	8.01
Other countries of South-East Asia	158,836	112,607	214,471	209,932	213,676	2.66	1.78
Australasia	455,190	609,245	814,920	985,834	1,012,323	12.58	2.69
Australia	418,899	571,541	769,585	933,376	952,717	11.84	2.07
New Zealand	36,291	37,704	45,335	52,458	59,606	0.74	13.63
Other East Asia and the Pacific	57,086	33,458	65,300	78,339	82,691	1.03	5.56
Other countries of Asia	43,972	30,344	60,410	71,742	77,529	0.96	8.07
Other countries of Oceania	13,114	3,114	4,890	6,597	5,162	0.06	-21.75
EUROPE	989,854	1,028,405	1,048,543	1,110,871	1,174,079	14.59	5.69
Central/Eastern Europe	146,967	144,951	145,817	164,358	175,827	2.19	6.98
USSR (former)	74,483	77,018	83,836	96,438	99,448	1.24	3.12
Other countries Central/East Europe	72,484	67,933	61,981	67,920	76,379	0.95	12.45
Northern Europe	251,131	257,342	262,295	278,615	299,144	3.72	7.37
Denmark	18,434	20,062	17,565	19,950	21,168	0.26	6.11
Finland	9,819	15,591	11,566	13,137	15,035	0.19	14.45
Norway	16,468	16,261	16,226	17,803	17,118	0.21	-3.85
Sweden	21,806	22,166	24,603	26,504	26,097	0.32	-1.54
United Kingdom	184,604	183,262	192,335	201,221	219,726	2.73	9.20
Southern Europe	81,652	77,559	81,414	86,574	97,048	1.21	12.10
Italy	40,006	38,028	39,211	42,256	46,651	0.58	10.40
Portugal	11,368	11,331	11,629	13,661	15,406	0.19	12.77
Spain	30,278	28,200	30,574	30,657	34,991	0.43	14.14
Western Europe	487,148	536,310	540,997	564,771	580,353	7.21	2.76

Yearbook of Tourism Statistics, Data 2008 – 2012, 2014 Edition

INDONESIA

1. Arrivals of non-resident tourists at national borders, by nationality

	2008	2009	2010	2011	2012	Market share 2012	% Change 2012-2011
Austria	16,855	17,399	16,889	17,374	19,120	0.24	10.05
Belgium	22,854	25,781	24,493	24,579	28,243	0.35	14.91
France	129,446	165,656	160,913	171,736	184,273	2.29	7.30
Germany	142,767	133,032	144,411	149,110	158,212	1.97	6.10
Netherlands	141,202	154,932	158,957	163,268	152,749	1.90	-6.44
Switzerland	34,024	39,510	35,334	38,704	37,756	0.47	-2.45
Other Europe	**22,956**	**12,243**	**18,020**	**16,553**	**21,707**	**0.27**	**31.14**
Other countries of Europe	22,956	12,243	18,020	16,553	21,707	0.27	31.14
MIDDLE EAST	**73,391**	**113,935**	**143,002**	**163,497**	**144,386**	**1.79**	**-11.69**
Bahrain	891	746	832	879	981	0.01	11.60
Egypt	3,744	3,316	3,650	4,469	6,115	0.08	36.83
Kuwait	2,160	5,875	2,729	4,164	4,738	0.06	13.78
Qatar	1,155	6,579	5,076	4,501	1,265	0.02	-71.90
Saudi Arabia	42,647	73,000	94,440	110,908	92,667	1.15	-16.45
United Arab Emirates	2,960	3,871	4,970	4,720	6,154	0.08	30.38
Yemen	3,831	3,522	5,597	6,729	5,025	0.06	-25.32
Other countries of Middle East	16,003	17,026	25,708	27,127	27,441	0.34	1.16
SOUTH ASIA	**175,593**	**175,487**	**176,897**	**201,802**	**217,097**	**2.70**	**7.58**
Bangladesh	6,155	6,347	5,557	6,394	5,998	0.07	-6.19
India	155,391	156,545	159,373	181,791	196,983	2.45	8.36
Pakistan	7,273	5,880	5,772	6,598	5,330	0.07	-19.22
Sri Lanka	6,774	6,715	6,195	7,019	8,786	0.11	25.17

Yearbook of Tourism Statistics, Data 2008 – 2012, 2014 Edition

INDONESIA

1. Arrivals of non-resident tourists at national borders, by country of residence

	2008	2009	2010	2011	2012	Market share 2012	% Change 2012-2011
TOTAL	6,234,497	6,323,730	7,002,944	7,649,731	8,044,462	100.00	5.16
AFRICA	29,753	28,375	27,200	31,640	41,583	0.52	31.43
Southern Africa	15,012	15,831	12,691	15,579	17,228	0.21	10.58
South Africa	15,012	15,831	12,691	15,579	17,228	0.21	10.58
Other Africa	14,741	12,544	14,509	16,061	24,355	0.30	51.64
Other countries of Africa	14,741	12,544	14,509	16,061	24,355	0.30	51.64
AMERICAS	239,678	229,824	258,584	297,061	312,209	3.88	5.10
Central America	12,116	5,923	1,491	2,315	2,951	0.04	27.47
All countries of Central America	12,116	5,923	1,491	2,315	2,951	0.04	27.47
North America	214,115	205,631	223,520	258,562	269,352	3.35	4.17
Canada	39,784	35,400	43,159	54,287	56,501	0.70	4.08
United States of America	174,331	170,231	180,361	204,275	212,851	2.65	4.20
South America	13,447	18,270	23,288	26,566	27,165	0.34	2.25
All countries of South America	13,447	18,270	23,288	26,566	27,165	0.34	2.25
Other Americas			10,285	9,618	12,741	0.16	32.47
Other countries of the Americas			10,285	9,618	12,741	0.16	32.47
EAST ASIA AND THE PACIFIC	4,848,796	4,834,790	5,375,990	5,923,760	6,236,626	77.53	5.28
North-East Asia	1,509,870	1,398,507	1,455,116	1,601,386	1,756,179	21.83	9.67
China	337,082	395,013	469,365	574,179	686,779	8.54	19.61
Hong Kong, China	81,073	67,967	78,339	86,646	90,560	1.13	4.52
Japan	546,713	475,766	418,971	412,623	450,687	5.60	9.22
Korea, Republic of	320,808	256,522	274,999	306,061	311,618	3.87	1.82
Taiwan, Province of China	224,194	203,239	213,442	221,877	216,535	2.69	-2.41
South-East Asia	2,794,607	2,772,684	3,052,285	3,284,664	3,375,291	41.96	2.76
Brunei Darussalam	12,134	15,709	39,063	48,193	27,734	0.34	-42.45
Malaysia	1,117,454	1,179,366	1,277,476	1,302,237	1,335,531	16.60	2.56
Philippines	159,003	162,463	189,486	223,779	229,806	2.86	2.69
Singapore	1,397,056	1,272,862	1,373,126	1,505,588	1,565,478	19.46	3.98
Thailand	76,842	109,547	123,825	141,771	149,760	1.86	5.64
Viet Nam	12,215	14,456	28,196	36,917	40,084	0.50	8.58
Other countries of South-East Asia	19,903	18,281	21,113	26,179	26,898	0.33	2.75
Australasia	472,811	616,030	803,905	967,792	1,017,452	12.65	5.13
Australia	450,178	584,437	771,792	931,109	961,595	11.95	3.27
New Zealand	22,633	31,593	32,113	36,683	55,857	0.69	52.27
Other East Asia and the Pacific	71,508	47,569	64,684	69,918	87,704	1.09	25.44
Other countries of Asia	62,605	41,115	58,783	62,761	80,490	1.00	28.25
Other countries of Oceania	8,903	6,454	5,901	7,157	7,214	0.09	0.80
EUROPE	924,745	978,369	1,038,420	1,045,865	1,108,521	13.78	5.99
Central/Eastern Europe	126,342	129,969	139,426	152,801	165,786	2.06	8.50
USSR (former)	69,628	72,829	79,398	87,426	95,731	1.19	9.50
Other countries Central/East Europe	56,714	57,140	60,028	65,375	70,055	0.87	7.16
Northern Europe	218,955	244,143	264,815	268,722	289,594	3.60	7.77
Denmark	17,507	19,010	16,755	17,817	22,814	0.28	28.05
Finland	10,535	18,688	13,740	14,117	14,828	0.18	5.04
Norway	17,434	16,141	17,482	16,578	17,562	0.22	5.94
Sweden	23,067	21,033	24,579	27,525	22,303	0.28	-18.97
United Kingdom	150,412	169,271	192,259	192,685	212,087	2.64	10.07
Southern Europe	79,130	81,623	81,716	82,811	94,562	1.18	14.19
Italy	33,300	40,448	38,908	46,145	48,382	0.60	4.85
Portugal	33,407	29,119	13,165	11,070	16,785	0.21	51.63
Spain	12,423	12,056	29,643	25,596	29,395	0.37	14.84
Western Europe	475,195	508,052	533,918	525,671	541,484	6.73	3.01
Austria	17,696	16,771	16,472	15,041	17,226	0.21	14.53
Belgium	21,996	23,836	22,328	22,551	24,129	0.30	7.00
France	125,216	159,924	163,110	148,381	170,046	2.11	14.60

Yearbook of Tourism Statistics, Data 2008 – 2012, 2014 Edition

INDONESIA

1. Arrivals of non-resident tourists at national borders, by country of residence

	2008	2009	2010	2011	2012	Market share 2012	% Change 2012-2011
Germany	137,854	128,649	145,244	145,160	148,146	1.84	2.06
Netherlands	140,771	143,485	151,836	159,063	146,591	1.82	-7.84
Switzerland	31,662	35,387	34,928	35,475	35,346	0.44	-0.36
Other Europe	**25,123**	**14,582**	**18,545**	**15,860**	**17,095**	**0.21**	**7.79**
Other countries of Europe	25,123	14,582	18,545	15,860	17,095	0.21	7.79
MIDDLE EAST	**67,271**	**122,069**	**144,661**	**175,885**	**148,788**	**1.85**	**-15.41**
Bahrain	1,000	740	1,889	1,675	1,910	0.02	14.03
Egypt	2,747	3,031	3,235	2,942	5,160	0.06	75.39
Kuwait	2,083	7,606	5,819	5,014	5,959	0.07	18.85
Saudi Arabia	47,480	92,032	105,549	128,784	95,213	1.18	-26.07
Other countries of Middle East	13,961	18,660	28,169	37,470	40,546	0.50	8.21
SOUTH ASIA	**124,254**	**130,303**	**158,089**	**175,520**	**196,735**	**2.45**	**12.09**
Bangladesh	7,549	6,324	8,724	8,991	12,050	0.15	34.02
India	102,179	110,658	137,027	154,237	168,187	2.09	9.04
Pakistan	7,786	7,580	6,314	6,085	6,028	0.07	-0.94
Sri Lanka	6,740	5,741	6,024	6,207	10,470	0.13	68.68

INDONESIA

3. Arrivals of non-resident tourists in hotels and similar establishments, by country of residence

	2008	2009	2010	2011	2012	Market share 2012	% Change 2012-2011
TOTAL	4,804,838	5,359,218	5,588,783	6,045,250	6,350,697	100.00	5.05
AFRICA	23,061	21,174	23,120	24,603	33,288	0.52	35.30
Other Africa	23,061	21,174	23,120	24,603	33,288	0.52	35.30
All countries of Africa	23,061	21,174	23,120	24,603	33,288	0.52	35.30
AMERICAS	183,714	185,259	210,438	170,264	238,521	3.76	40.09
Central America	11,186	5,201	1,260	1,987	2,258	0.04	13.64
All countries of Central America	11,186	5,201	1,260	1,987	2,258	0.04	13.64
North America	160,964	163,674	181,180	139,925	203,774	3.21	45.63
Canada	30,673	27,711	33,200	41,964	43,424	0.68	3.48
United States of America	130,291	135,963	147,980	97,961	160,350	2.52	63.69
South America	11,564	16,384	20,416	21,223	23,047	0.36	8.59
All countries of South America	11,564	16,384	20,416	21,223	23,047	0.36	8.59
Other Americas			7,582	7,129	9,442	0.15	32.44
Other countries of the Americas			7,582	7,129	9,442	0.15	32.44
EAST ASIA AND THE PACIFIC	3,704,980	4,161,852	4,259,161	4,705,662	4,899,415	77.15	4.12
North-East Asia	1,305,950	1,239,025	1,120,241	1,248,584	1,407,692	22.17	12.74
China	264,960	339,804	365,297	447,912	565,707	8.91	26.30
Hong Kong, China	71,190	59,967	61,860	64,945	74,318	1.17	14.43
Japan	518,876	444,071	280,671	282,152	316,617	4.99	12.22
Korea, Republic of	258,150	217,456	231,063	266,138	262,952	4.14	-1.20
Taiwan, Province of China	192,774	177,727	181,350	187,437	188,098	2.96	0.35
South-East Asia	2,000,520	2,463,107	2,428,002	2,612,808	2,609,396	41.09	-0.13
Brunei Darussalam	8,381	10,904	26,856	37,230	20,761	0.33	-44.24
Malaysia	861,171	1,058,092	1,075,004	1,090,476	1,094,949	17.24	0.41
Philippines	98,647	125,899	117,348	144,464	144,836	2.28	0.26
Singapore	952,200	1,159,110	1,077,207	1,179,577	1,179,670	18.58	0.01
Thailand	59,098	87,299	102,440	120,196	124,632	1.96	3.69
Other countries of South-East Asia	21,023	21,803	29,147	40,865	44,548	0.70	9.01
Australasia	347,487	431,052	666,043	791,269	814,709	12.83	2.96
Australia	329,147	405,082	639,636	766,025	773,598	12.18	0.99
New Zealand	18,340	25,970	26,407	25,244	41,111	0.65	62.85
Other East Asia and the Pacific	51,023	28,668	44,875	53,001	67,618	1.06	27.58
Other countries of Asia	44,282	23,949	40,685	47,894	62,687	0.99	30.89
Other countries of Oceania	6,741	4,719	4,190	5,107	4,931	0.08	-3.45
EUROPE	764,444	805,587	880,989	867,694	917,623	14.45	5.75
Central/Eastern Europe	110,787	111,354	123,035	131,738	136,386	2.15	3.53
USSR (former)	64,304	63,973	71,879	77,827	78,362	1.23	0.69
Other countries Central/East Europe	46,483	47,381	51,156	53,911	58,024	0.91	7.63
Northern Europe	177,635	196,578	221,313	219,603	239,932	3.78	9.26
Denmark	14,767	16,158	14,769	16,277	19,673	0.31	20.86
Finland	8,621	16,093	11,971	12,166	12,551	0.20	3.16
Norway	15,197	13,683	15,777	14,876	14,440	0.23	-2.93
Sweden	20,281	18,348	21,540	22,976	19,489	0.31	-15.18
United Kingdom	118,769	132,296	157,256	153,308	173,779	2.74	13.35
Southern Europe	66,325	65,710	66,474	67,842	77,372	1.22	14.05
Italy	25,778	29,551	31,208	37,494	38,857	0.61	3.64
Portugal				9,255	13,789	0.22	48.99
Spain				21,093	24,726	0.39	17.22
Spain,Portugal	40,547	36,159	35,266				
Western Europe	389,086	419,673	454,452	435,532	450,877	7.10	3.52
Austria	14,272	12,646	13,850	12,245	14,699	0.23	20.04
Belgium	18,082	19,523	19,476	18,293	19,969	0.31	9.16
France	105,384	135,691	141,744	123,323	143,067	2.25	16.01
Germany	116,374	105,490	122,015	119,879	124,138	1.95	3.55
Netherlands	107,955	116,644	126,671	132,048	119,160	1.88	-9.76

333

INDONESIA

3. Arrivals of non-resident tourists in hotels and similar establishments, by country of residence

	2008	2009	2010	2011	2012	Market share 2012	% Change 2012-2011
Switzerland	27,019	29,679	30,696	29,744	29,844	0.47	0.34
Other Europe	**20,611**	**12,272**	**15,715**	**12,979**	**13,056**	**0.21**	**0.59**
Other countries of Europe	20,611	12,272	15,715	12,979	13,056	0.21	0.59
MIDDLE EAST	**44,082**	**96,208**	**115,263**	**156,974**	**131,488**	**2.07**	**-16.24**
Bahrain	694	525	1,379	1,490	1,548	0.02	3.89
Egypt	1,905	2,302	2,263	1,941	3,701	0.06	90.67
Kuwait				3,303	4,461	0.07	35.06
Saudi Arabia	32,231	77,738	85,665	119,521	89,466	1.41	-25.15
Other countries of Middle East	9,252	15,643	25,956	30,719	32,312	0.51	5.19
SOUTH ASIA	**84,557**	**89,138**	**99,812**	**120,053**	**130,362**	**2.05**	**8.59**
Bangladesh	5,485	4,550	5,551	7,203	9,471	0.15	31.49
India	69,222	75,499	85,142	104,373	109,464	1.72	4.88
Pakistan	5,454	5,459	4,928	4,308	4,245	0.07	-1.46
Sri Lanka	4,396	3,630	4,191	4,169	7,182	0.11	72.27

Yearbook of Tourism Statistics, Data 2008 – 2012, 2014 Edition

IRAN, ISLAMIC REPUBLIC OF

2. Arrivals of non-resident visitors at national borders, by nationality

	2008	2009	2010	2011	2012	Market share 2012	% Change 2012-2011
TOTAL		2,116,244	2,938,054	3,353,713	3,833,577	100.00	14.31
AFRICA		4,079	5,568	6,831	11,938	0.31	74.76
East Africa		785	946	1,979	2,991	0.08	51.14
Ethiopia		182	349	479	1,117	0.03	133.19
Kenya		349	309	352	426	0.01	21.02
Somalia		41	74	204	156	0.00	-23.53
Uganda		196	91	79	249	0.01	215.19
United Republic of Tanzania				795	867	0.02	9.06
Zimbabwe		17	123	70	176	0.00	151.43
North Africa		1,326	1,437	1,482	4,281	0.11	188.87
Algeria		247	422	280	662	0.02	136.43
Morocco		241	198	173	1,249	0.03	621.97
Sudan		584	530	608	1,358	0.04	123.36
Tunisia		254	287	421	1,012	0.03	140.38
West Africa		813	868	349	2,065	0.05	491.69
Gambia		33	17	6	27	0.00	350.00
Ghana		86	114	86	367	0.01	326.74
Guinea		67	76	67	40	0.00	-40.30
Mali		51	53	70	124	0.00	77.14
Mauritania		19	52	21	89	0.00	323.81
Nigeria		365	383	38	1,298	0.03	3,315.79
Senegal		192	173	61	120	0.00	96.72
Other Africa		1,155	2,317	3,021	2,601	0.07	-13.90
Other countries of Africa		1,155	2,317	3,021	2,601	0.07	-13.90
AMERICAS		6,151	7,146	6,463	5,913	0.15	-8.51
Caribbean		141	53	94	133	0.00	41.49
Bahamas		1	1		3	0.00	
Cuba		121	26	74	83	0.00	12.16
Dominican Republic		19	26	20	47	0.00	135.00
Central America		13	17	20	32	0.00	60.00
Guatemala		3	1	15	10	0.00	-33.33
Panama		10	16	5	22	0.00	340.00
North America		3,766	4,336	4,287	2,529	0.07	-41.01
Canada		1,826	2,540	2,506	2,150	0.06	-14.21
Mexico		196	187	202	176	0.00	-12.87
United States of America		1,744	1,609	1,579	203	0.01	-87.14
South America		1,323	1,686	1,538	1,979	0.05	28.67
Argentina		188	193	214	344	0.01	60.75
Brazil		588	835	735	727	0.02	-1.09
Chile		89	67	84	98	0.00	16.67
Colombia		111	116	109	162	0.00	48.62
Ecuador		56	92	97	186	0.00	91.75
Peru		42	43	41	56	0.00	36.59
Uruguay		40	35	40	27	0.00	-32.50
Venezuela		209	305	218	379	0.01	73.85
Other Americas		908	1,054	524	1,240	0.03	136.64
Other countries of the Americas		908	1,054	524	1,240	0.03	136.64
EAST ASIA AND THE PACIFIC		27,831	33,624	52,596	92,218	2.41	75.33
North-East Asia		18,960	22,088	37,497	40,817	1.06	8.85
China		4,378	7,648	22,728	26,160	0.68	15.10
Japan		5,647	5,592	4,937	5,143	0.13	4.17
Korea, Dem. People's Republic of		96	77	108	328	0.01	203.70
Korea, Republic of		7,270	7,017	8,075	8,117	0.21	0.52
Mongolia		21	42	52	67	0.00	28.85
Taiwan, Province of China		1,548	1,712	1,597	1,002	0.03	-37.26

335

IRAN, ISLAMIC REPUBLIC OF

2. Arrivals of non-resident visitors at national borders, by nationality

	2008	2009	2010	2011	2012	Market share 2012	% Change 2012-2011
South-East Asia		6,018	8,122	10,533	46,609	1.22	342.50
Indonesia		1,510	1,916	2,725	3,738	0.10	37.17
Malaysia		187	1,748	3,157	3,779	0.10	19.70
Philippines		2,046	2,399	2,286	36,420	0.95	1,493.18
Singapore		26	178	883	612	0.02	-30.69
Thailand		2,094	1,689	1,348	1,647	0.04	22.18
Viet Nam		155	192	134	413	0.01	208.21
Australasia		2,853	3,414	4,399	4,222	0.11	-4.02
Australia		2,853	3,414	3,849	4,218	0.11	9.59
New Zealand				550	4	0.00	-99.27
Other East Asia and the Pacific				167	570	0.01	241.32
Other countries East Asia/Pacific				167	570	0.01	241.32
EUROPE		1,187,149	1,738,398	2,000,785	1,705,799	44.50	-14.74
Central/Eastern Europe		813,256	1,379,203	1,434,739	1,249,238	32.59	-12.93
Armenia		331,868	566,932	533,820	385,164	10.05	-27.85
Azerbaijan		383,588	690,333	732,201	677,457	17.67	-7.48
Bulgaria		489	1,431	1,158	1,020	0.03	-11.92
Czech Republic		554	821	845	724	0.02	-14.32
Georgia		323	194	3,203	3,359	0.09	4.87
Hungary		483	525	606	818	0.02	34.98
Kazakhstan		613	1,222	1,794	1,904	0.05	6.13
Kyrgyzstan		188	402	560	821	0.02	46.61
Lithuania		81	133	212	171	0.00	-19.34
Poland		821	1,052	1,066	7,718	0.20	624.02
Romania		1,368	1,340	1,194	1,088	0.03	-8.88
Russian Federation		6,155	11,281	13,413	14,146	0.37	5.46
Tajikistan		2,327	3,222	3,754	4,953	0.13	31.94
Turkmenistan		80,533	95,000	135,683	141,533	3.69	4.31
Ukraine		2,853	3,819	2,614	5,393	0.14	106.31
Uzbekistan		1,012	1,496	2,616	2,969	0.08	13.49
Northern Europe		16,026	17,195	16,482	16,897	0.44	2.52
Denmark		2,142	2,158	2,016	2,184	0.06	8.33
Finland		673	578	680	679	0.02	-0.15
Iceland		100	30	71	49	0.00	-30.99
Ireland		638	701	730	689	0.02	-5.62
Norway		1,806	1,655	1,840	1,836	0.05	-0.22
Sweden		3,941	4,257	4,594	7,618	0.20	65.82
United Kingdom		6,726	7,816	6,551	3,842	0.10	-41.35
Southern Europe		16,073	14,117	15,149	15,012	0.39	-0.90
Albania		88	72	87	101	0.00	16.09
Bosnia and Herzegovina		124	189	223	233	0.01	4.48
Greece		945	758	702	1,163	0.03	65.67
Italy		10,982	9,167	10,010	9,576	0.25	-4.34
Montenegro			18	35	24	0.00	-31.43
Portugal		502	505	504	623	0.02	23.61
Serbia		183	341	427	431	0.01	0.94
Slovenia		713	544	489	588	0.02	20.25
Spain		2,536	2,523	2,672	2,273	0.06	-14.93
Western Europe		38,882	37,790	35,327	31,117	0.81	-11.92
Austria		4,200	3,480	3,292	2,692	0.07	-18.23
Belgium		489	1,431	1,444	1,284	0.03	-11.08
France		8,037	6,057	5,993	5,863	0.15	-2.17
Germany		18,072	18,488	16,851	17,981	0.47	6.71
Luxembourg		41	44	41	42	0.00	2.44
Netherlands		5,739	6,240	5,466	1,268	0.03	-76.80
Switzerland		2,304	2,050	2,240	1,987	0.05	-11.29
East Mediterranean Europe		300,015	288,165	419,973	392,757	10.25	-6.48

336

Yearbook of Tourism Statistics, Data 2008 – 2012, 2014 Edition

IRAN, ISLAMIC REPUBLIC OF

2. Arrivals of non-resident visitors at national borders, by nationality

	2008	2009	2010	2011	2012	Market share 2012	% Change 2012-2011
Cyprus		187	134	120	142	0.00	18.33
Turkey		299,828	288,031	419,853	392,615	10.24	-6.49
Other Europe		**2,897**	**1,928**	**79,115**	**778**	**0.02**	**-99.02**
Other countries of Europe		2,897	1,928	79,115	778	0.02	-99.02
MIDDLE EAST		**518,819**	**740,004**	**782,096**	**1,332,984**	**34.77**	**70.44**
Bahrain		14,689	36,837	13,362	44,249	1.15	231.16
Egypt		857	975	1,415	3,199	0.08	126.08
Iraq		440,989	548,008	589,074	1,055,447	27.53	79.17
Jordan		850	860	786	1,091	0.03	38.80
Kuwait		16,302	49,572	54,641	68,454	1.79	25.28
Lebanon		11,947	17,416	20,484	18,586	0.48	-9.27
Libya		103	128	261	478	0.01	83.14
Oman		7,707	10,816	9,798	12,120	0.32	23.70
Palestine		167	96	197	419	0.01	112.69
Qatar		1,300	2,568	2,417	2,921	0.08	20.85
Saudi Arabia		14,601	60,107	74,275	111,049	2.90	49.51
Syrian Arab Republic		4,117	2,891	8,442	8,886	0.23	5.26
United Arab Emirates		5,022	9,607	6,719	5,506	0.14	-18.05
Yemen		168	123	225	579	0.02	157.33
SOUTH ASIA		**314,314**	**413,180**	**426,896**	**537,825**	**14.03**	**25.99**
Afghanistan		175,155	214,649	202,369	308,183	8.04	52.29
Bangladesh		655	653	819	1,891	0.05	130.89
India		22,277	23,903	34,770	54,263	1.42	56.06
Maldives		46	44	49	28	0.00	-42.86
Nepal		187	208	235	829	0.02	252.77
Pakistan		115,459	173,068	187,920	170,754	4.45	-9.13
Sri Lanka		535	655	734	1,877	0.05	155.72
NOT SPECIFIED		**57,901**	**134**	**78,046**	**146,900**	**3.83**	**88.22**
Other countries of the World		57,901	134	78,046	62	0.00	-99.92
Nationals Residing Abroad					146,838	3.83	

Yearbook of Tourism Statistics, Data 2008 – 2012, 2014 Edition

IRAQ

2. Arrivals of non-resident visitors at national borders, by nationality

	2008	2009	2010	2011	2012	Market share 2012	% Change 2012-2011
TOTAL	863,657	1,261,921	1,517,766				
AFRICA		24	44				
East Africa		5	44				
Madagascar		3					
Mauritius			44				
United Republic of Tanzania		2					
West Africa		19					
Nigeria		19					
AMERICAS		42	30				
North America		42	30				
Canada			6				
United States of America		42	24				
EAST ASIA AND THE PACIFIC			35				
North-East Asia			1				
Japan			1				
South-East Asia			34				
Indonesia			34				
EUROPE	776	8,564	3,483				
Central/Eastern Europe	749	7,775	2,246				
Azerbaijan	739	7,717	2,246				
Russian Federation		58					
Ukraine	10						
Northern Europe			28				
Ireland			1				
United Kingdom			27				
Western Europe		27					
France		27					
East Mediterranean Europe	27	762	1,209				
Turkey	27	762	1,209				
MIDDLE EAST	4,355	10,752	15,076				
Bahrain	2,959	6,258	7,021				
Jordan			130				
Kuwait	192	94	820				
Lebanon	129	1,916	4,466				
Saudi Arabia	1,075	2,423	2,490				
Syrian Arab Republic			104				
United Arab Emirates		35	45				
Yemen		26					
SOUTH ASIA	852,405	1,194,149	1,443,151				
Afghanistan	234	382	1,673				
Bangladesh		346	11				
India	6,031	13,876	13,860				
Iran, Islamic Republic of	840,362	1,161,541	1,413,792				
Pakistan	5,771	18,004	13,815				
Sri Lanka	7						
NOT SPECIFIED	6,121	48,390	55,947				
Other countries of the World	6,121	48,390	55,947				

Yearbook of Tourism Statistics, Data 2008 – 2012, 2014 Editi

IRELAND

1. Arrivals of non-resident tourists at national borders, by country of residence

		2008	2009	2010	2011	2012	Market share 2012	% Change 2012-2011
TOTAL		8,026,000	7,189,000	7,134,000	7,630,000	7,550,000	100.00	-1.05
AFRICA		54,000	43,000					
Other Africa		54,000	43,000					
All countries of Africa		54,000	43,000					
AMERICAS		985,000	921,000	864,000	917,000	940,000	12.45	2.51
North America		952,000	891,000	864,000	917,000	940,000	12.45	2.51
Canada		103,000	82,000	86,000	99,000	107,000	1.42	8.08
United States of America		849,000	809,000	778,000	818,000	833,000	11.03	1.83
Other Americas		33,000	30,000					
Other countries of the Americas		33,000	30,000					
EAST ASIA AND THE PACIFIC		256,000	233,000	135,000	141,000	158,000	2.09	12.06
North-East Asia		14,000	11,000					
Japan		14,000	11,000					
Australasia		157,000	132,000	135,000	141,000	158,000	2.09	12.06
Australia		134,000	113,000					
New Zealand		23,000	19,000					
Australia, New Zealand				135,000	141,000	158,000	2.09	12.06
Other East Asia and the Pacific		85,000	90,000					
Other countries East Asia/Pacific		85,000	90,000					
EUROPE		6,731,000	5,992,000	5,959,000	6,361,000	6,233,000	82.56	-2.01
Central/Eastern Europe		332,000	258,000					
Czech Republic		45,000	35,000					
Poland		287,000	223,000					
Northern Europe		4,307,000	3,769,000	3,948,000	4,129,000	3,986,000	52.79	-3.46
Denmark		57,000	45,000					
Sweden		80,000	59,000					
United Kingdom	(*)	4,170,000	3,665,000	3,948,000	4,129,000	3,986,000	52.79	-3.46
Southern Europe		475,000	532,000	428,000	450,000	479,000	6.34	6.44
Italy		232,000	276,000	214,000	213,000	240,000	3.18	12.68
Spain		243,000	256,000	214,000	237,000	239,000	3.17	0.84
Western Europe		1,213,000	1,128,000	725,000	820,000	821,000	10.87	0.12
Austria		51,000	45,000					
Belgium		85,000	93,000					
France		412,000	390,000	344,000	400,000	384,000	5.09	-4.00
Germany		456,000	408,000	381,000	420,000	437,000	5.79	4.05
Netherlands		151,000	134,000					
Switzerland		58,000	58,000					
Other Europe		404,000	305,000	858,000	962,000	947,000	12.54	-1.56
Other countries of Europe		404,000	305,000	858,000	962,000	947,000	12.54	-1.56
NOT SPECIFIED				176,000	211,000	219,000	2.90	3.79
Other countries of the World				176,000	211,000	219,000	2.90	3.79

Yearbook of Tourism Statistics, Data 2008 – 2012, 2014 Edition

IRELAND

6. Overnight stays of non-resident tourists in all types of accommodation establishments, by country of residence

		2008	2009	2010	2011	2012	Market share 2012	% Change 2012-2011
TOTAL	(*)	60,057,000	52,917,000	53,045,000	55,248,000	52,075,000	100.00	-5.74
AMERICAS		8,715,000	8,252,000	8,780,000	8,904,000	8,775,000	16.85	-1.45
North America		8,715,000	8,252,000	8,780,000	8,904,000	8,775,000	16.85	-1.45
Canada		1,016,000	1,019,000	1,064,000	1,055,000			
United States of America		7,699,000	7,233,000	7,716,000	7,849,000			
All countries of North America						8,775,000	16.85	
EAST ASIA AND THE PACIFIC		1,685,000	1,565,000			1,835,000	3.52	
Australasia		1,685,000	1,565,000			1,835,000	3.52	
Australia		1,685,000	1,565,000			1,835,000	3.52	
EUROPE		46,167,000	39,935,000	39,662,000	41,374,000	38,409,000	73.76	-7.17
Northern Europe		17,301,000	15,438,000	18,624,000	18,217,000	17,102,000	32.84	-6.12
United Kingdom	(*)	17,301,000	15,438,000	18,624,000	18,217,000	17,102,000	32.84	-6.12
Southern Europe		5,810,000	5,667,000	4,648,000	5,740,000	2,353,000	4.52	-59.01
Italy		2,851,000	2,624,000	2,049,000	2,608,000	2,353,000	4.52	-9.78
Spain		2,959,000	3,043,000	2,599,000	3,132,000			
Western Europe		12,629,000	11,412,000	7,247,000	8,353,000	7,553,000	14.50	-9.58
Belgium		653,000	754,000					
France		5,092,000	5,049,000	3,531,000	4,491,000	3,615,000	6.94	-19.51
Germany		5,222,000	4,044,000	3,716,000	3,862,000	3,938,000	7.56	1.97
Netherlands		1,127,000	954,000					
Switzerland		535,000	611,000					
Other Europe		10,427,000	7,418,000	9,143,000	9,064,000	11,401,000	21.89	25.78
Other countries of Europe		10,427,000	7,418,000	9,143,000	9,064,000	11,401,000	21.89	25.78
NOT SPECIFIED		3,490,000	3,165,000	4,603,000	4,970,000	3,056,000	5.87	-38.51
Other countries of the World		3,490,000	3,165,000	4,603,000	4,970,000	3,056,000	5.87	-38.51

340

ISRAEL

1. Arrivals of non-resident tourists at national borders, by country of residence

		2008	2009	2010	2011	2012	Market share 2012	% Change 2012-2011
TOTAL	(*)	2,560,479	2,311,612	2,791,705	2,808,418	2,871,599	100.00	2.25
AFRICA		73,866	75,615	72,080	85,389	71,106	2.48	-16.73
East Africa		7,639	5,627	8,773	9,276	8,924	0.31	-3.79
Burundi		71	57	108	53	76	0.00	43.40
Comoros		2			5	1	0.00	-80.00
Eritrea		75	59	291	319	369	0.01	15.67
Ethiopia		3,128	1,852	3,191	3,445	2,780	0.10	-19.30
Kenya		1,539	1,318	2,428	2,744	2,297	0.08	-16.29
Madagascar		54	79	53	65	79	0.00	21.54
Malawi		78	83	110	107	106	0.00	-0.93
Mauritius		255	291	286	248	376	0.01	51.61
Mozambique		81	50	55	52	170	0.01	226.92
Rwanda		200	158	158	155	187	0.01	20.65
Seychelles		39	13	18	22	29	0.00	31.82
Somalia					2	1	0.00	-50.00
Uganda		736	596	658	671	882	0.03	31.45
United Republic of Tanzania		850	584	744	705	683	0.02	-3.12
Zambia		180	130	181	165	174	0.01	5.45
Zimbabwe		351	357	492	518	714	0.02	37.84
Central Africa		1,849	1,439	1,425	1,696	2,223	0.08	31.07
Angola		815	433	598	689	734	0.03	6.53
Cameroon		289	400	492	475	491	0.02	3.37
Central African Republic		40	34	57	113	99	0.00	-12.39
Chad		28	19	8	27	32	0.00	18.52
Congo		566	358	152	178	170	0.01	-4.49
Democratic Republic of the Congo			64			446	0.02	
Equatorial Guinea		26		36	92	32	0.00	-65.22
Gabon		85	131	82	122	219	0.01	79.51
North Africa		3,799	3,395	3,462	3,568	3,235	0.11	-9.33
Algeria		10	15	4	12	18	0.00	50.00
Morocco		2,566	2,305	2,473	2,409	2,289	0.08	-4.98
Sudan		9	1	3	24	14	0.00	-41.67
Tunisia		1,214	1,074	982	1,123	914	0.03	-18.61
Southern Africa		22,825	18,210	23,694	22,320	24,341	0.85	9.05
Botswana		100						
Lesotho		37	21	16	18	32	0.00	77.78
Namibia		62	93	2,473	90	233	0.01	158.89
South Africa		22,574	18,055	21,130	22,094	23,975	0.83	8.51
Swaziland		52	41	75	118	101	0.00	-14.41
West Africa		37,640	46,772	34,296	48,072	32,265	1.12	-32.88
Benin		113	88	114	169	183	0.01	8.28
Burkina Faso		212	141	118	152	206	0.01	35.53
Cape Verde		23	59	18	14	35	0.00	150.00
Côte d'Ivoire		1,433	938	1,054	798	611	0.02	-23.43
Gambia		23	13	55	17	59	0.00	247.06
Ghana		810	488	708	1,146	1,186	0.04	3.49
Guinea		31	64	185	34	52	0.00	52.94
Guinea-Bissau			8	5	1	8	0.00	700.00
Liberia		45	45	67	63	40	0.00	-36.51
Mali		45	32	67	26	41	0.00	57.69
Mauritania			5		2	1	0.00	-50.00
Niger		357	353	29	33	44	0.00	33.33
Nigeria		34,300	43,866	31,616	44,972	29,437	1.03	-34.54
Senegal		119	486	110	510	126	0.00	-75.29
Sierra Leone		56	40	58	57	44	0.00	-22.81
Togo		73	146	92	78	192	0.01	146.15

341

ISRAEL

1. Arrivals of non-resident tourists at national borders, by country of residence

	2008	2009	2010	2011	2012	Market share 2012	% Change 2012-2011
Other Africa	114	172	430	457	118	0.00	-74.18
Other countries of Africa	114	172	430	457	118	0.00	-74.18
AMERICAS	783,253	686,651	809,400	776,156	790,983	27.55	1.91
Caribbean	2,409	1,895	2,419	2,366	2,095	0.07	-11.45
Antigua and Barbuda	35	9	22	12	23	0.00	91.67
Bahamas	141	275	59	95	60	0.00	-36.84
Barbados	233	65	42	129	108	0.00	-16.28
Bermuda	9	4	3	17	6	0.00	-64.71
Cayman Islands	4	17	30	3	34	0.00	1,033.33
Cuba	177	146	145	161	159	0.01	-1.24
Dominica	28	26	43	34	17	0.00	-50.00
Dominican Republic	760	646	1,020	847	659	0.02	-22.20
Grenada	17	16	24	24	11	0.00	-54.17
Haiti	148	131	118	207	154	0.01	-25.60
Jamaica	284	173	237	193	291	0.01	50.78
Montserrat			1				
Puerto Rico		1	1				
Saint Kitts and Nevis	6	15	16	16	19	0.00	18.75
Saint Lucia	27	6	71	13	17	0.00	30.77
Saint Vincent and the Grenadines	7	5	10	14	10	0.00	-28.57
Trinidad and Tobago	525	359	575	595	526	0.02	-11.60
Turks and Caicos Islands	6	1	2	5	1	0.00	-80.00
United States Virgin Islands	2			1			
Central America	6,587	5,293	7,793	6,665	8,047	0.28	20.74
Belize	31	18	30	34	38	0.00	11.76
Costa Rica	2,282	1,525	2,260	1,995	2,503	0.09	25.46
El Salvador	966	672	1,123	743	879	0.03	18.30
Guatemala	971	915	1,323	1,125	1,369	0.05	21.69
Honduras	418	394	672	672	699	0.02	4.02
Nicaragua	154	142	172	220	292	0.01	32.73
Panama	1,765	1,627	2,213	1,876	2,267	0.08	20.84
North America	696,263	612,419	697,981	664,145	670,101	23.34	0.90
Canada	68,860	59,492	70,172	64,388	64,964	2.26	0.89
Mexico	22,260	14,952	22,694	18,711	21,532	0.75	15.08
United States of America	605,143	537,975	605,115	581,046	583,605	20.32	0.44
South America	77,994	67,044	101,207	102,980	110,740	3.86	7.54
Argentina	19,666	16,003	22,286	21,628	23,249	0.81	7.49
Bolivia	559	512	607	686	804	0.03	17.20
Brazil	31,216	27,891	48,778	53,054	56,637	1.97	6.75
Chile	5,514	4,244	5,832	5,687	5,470	0.19	-3.82
Colombia	9,027	7,896	10,933	9,506	10,984	0.38	15.55
Ecuador	3,069	2,701	3,495	3,352	3,084	0.11	-8.00
Guyana	27	28	41	67	32	0.00	-52.24
Paraguay	308	332	524	481	459	0.02	-4.57
Peru	2,146	2,336	3,276	2,811	3,622	0.13	28.85
Suriname	17	31	48	42	49	0.00	16.67
Uruguay	2,564	2,275	2,615	2,556	2,465	0.09	-3.56
Venezuela	3,879	2,794	2,768	3,108	3,885	0.14	25.00
Other countries of South America	2	1	4	2			
EAST ASIA AND THE PACIFIC	130,005	94,765	142,345	147,149	171,826	5.98	16.77
North-East Asia	61,458	39,503	64,219	66,233	73,429	2.56	10.86
China	8,923	7,570	12,890	16,806	19,276	0.67	14.70
Hong Kong, China	3,414	2,186	4,052	3,258	4,223	0.15	29.62
Japan	14,506	9,768	13,165	13,444	16,011	0.56	19.09
Korea, Dem. People's Republic of	47		16		24	0.00	
Korea, Republic of	30,712	17,299	29,953	28,005	28,606	1.00	2.15

Yearbook of Tourism Statistics, Data 2008 – 2012, 2014 Editi

ISRAEL

1. Arrivals of non-resident tourists at national borders, by country of residence

	2008	2009	2010	2011	2012	Market share 2012	% Change 2012-2011
Macao, China	46	59	53	49	140	0.00	185.71
Mongolia	153	107	197	193	178	0.01	-7.77
Taiwan, Province of China	3,657	2,514	3,893	4,478	4,971	0.17	11.01
South-East Asia	**37,671**	**28,553**	**43,071**	**48,071**	**63,874**	**2.22**	**32.87**
Brunei Darussalam	15	1	2	12	2	0.00	-83.33
Cambodia	31	24	48	69	113	0.00	63.77
Indonesia	14,336	9,587	17,742	21,946	27,752	0.97	26.46
Lao People's Democratic Republic	39	67	150	240	319	0.01	32.92
Malaysia	2,293	634	1,583	2,943	6,502	0.23	120.93
Myanmar			372	343	595	0.02	73.47
Philippines	8,970	7,321	10,241	9,376	12,187	0.42	29.98
Singapore	8,574	6,468	8,659	8,270	10,246	0.36	23.89
Thailand	2,756	3,397	2,958	3,227	4,273	0.15	32.41
Timor-Leste			1	42	47	0.00	11.90
Viet Nam	657	1,054	1,315	1,603	1,838	0.06	14.66
Australasia	**29,599**	**26,215**	**34,622**	**32,273**	**33,677**	**1.17**	**4.35**
Australia	26,443	23,543	30,738	28,889	30,082	1.05	4.13
New Zealand	3,156	2,672	3,884	3,384	3,595	0.13	6.24
Melanesia	**224**	**210**	**398**	**530**	**787**	**0.03**	**48.49**
Fiji	140	116	194	358	439	0.02	22.63
Papua New Guinea	63	76	178	146	311	0.01	113.01
Solomon Islands	3	6	10	9	16	0.00	77.78
Vanuatu	18	12	16	17	21	0.00	23.53
Micronesia	**24**	**4**	**11**	**16**	**7**	**0.00**	**-56.25**
Kiribati	17		2	3	3	0.00	0.00
Micronesia, Federated States of		3	8	3	4	0.00	33.33
Palau	7	1	1	10			
Polynesia	**12**	**6**	**18**	**26**	**22**	**0.00**	**-15.38**
American Samoa	12	6	1	1	5	0.00	400.00
Samoa			7	5	17	0.00	240.00
Tonga			10	20			
Other East Asia and the Pacific	**1,017**	**274**	**6**		**30**	**0.00**	
Other countries of Asia	996	259			6	0.00	
Other countries of Oceania	21	15	6		24	0.00	
EUROPE	**1,509,426**	**1,397,275**	**1,692,925**	**1,718,382**	**1,746,895**	**60.83**	**1.66**
Central/Eastern Europe	**483,632**	**425,963**	**565,164**	**640,960**	**672,498**	**23.42**	**4.92**
Armenia	891	811	1,503	1,404	1,867	0.07	32.98
Azerbaijan	2,873	2,695	2,912	2,851	3,139	0.11	10.10
Bulgaria	8,620	6,148	7,165	7,489	7,135	0.25	-4.73
Czech Republic	16,385	10,943	13,709	13,028	13,807	0.48	5.98
Estonia	2,620	3,057	5,252	3,555	3,254	0.11	-8.47
Georgia	6,015	4,555	4,477	4,312	4,349	0.15	0.86
Hungary	13,793	9,433	11,787	11,418	9,316	0.32	-18.41
Kazakhstan	6,149	4,534	6,501	9,603	10,914	0.38	13.65
Kyrgyzstan	465	411	496	634	698	0.02	10.09
Latvia	5,863	4,168	4,749	5,370	5,573	0.19	3.78
Lithuania	7,355	4,153	5,124	5,093	5,580	0.19	9.56
Poland	86,900	53,840	69,435	60,410	58,860	2.05	-2.57
Republic of Moldova	4,411	3,121	4,434	3,630	3,968	0.14	9.31
Romania	37,322	28,881	38,475	37,790	39,631	1.38	4.87
Russian Federation	205,570	231,366	318,472	353,419	380,737	13.26	7.73
Slovakia	8,872	8,143	11,595	10,194	10,119	0.35	-0.74
Tajikistan	179	181	251	319	367	0.01	15.05
Turkmenistan	122	165	122	125	232	0.01	85.60
Ukraine	64,298	46,455	55,296	106,807	109,156	3.80	2.20
USSR (former)	23	13	7	4	3	0.00	-25.00
Uzbekistan	4,906	2,890	3,402	3,505	3,793	0.13	8.22

343

ISRAEL

1. Arrivals of non-resident tourists at national borders, by country of residence

	2008	2009	2010	2011	2012	Market share 2012	% Change 2012-2011
Northern Europe	239,563	230,856	247,409	251,117	246,755	8.59	-1.74
Denmark	12,226	12,740	15,182	18,934	18,604	0.65	-1.74
Finland	12,268	17,776	19,503	18,255	17,476	0.61	-4.27
Iceland	393	234	355	320	315	0.01	-1.56
Ireland	9,065	7,490	9,145	8,864	7,564	0.26	-14.67
Norway	13,449	12,050	14,209	15,993	15,485	0.54	-3.18
Sweden	16,806	17,029	20,246	20,739	22,211	0.77	7.10
United Kingdom	175,356	163,537	168,769	168,012	165,100	5.75	-1.73
Southern Europe	239,414	204,631	264,267	206,805	220,733	7.69	6.73
Albania	1,033	659	473	545	497	0.02	-8.81
Andorra	62	50	66	54	57	0.00	5.56
Bosnia and Herzegovina	556	345	418	643	396	0.01	-38.41
Croatia	5,199	5,291	6,097	5,124	5,317	0.19	3.77
Greece	28,822	18,408	24,200	18,979	20,419	0.71	7.59
Holy See	240	289	270	250	263	0.01	5.20
Italy	120,901	116,489	150,176	113,307	126,245	4.40	11.42
Malta	1,448	1,514	2,209	1,215	1,960	0.07	61.32
Montenegro			394	322	469	0.02	45.65
Portugal	11,616	6,886	13,557	8,458	8,352	0.29	-1.25
San Marino	291	98	104	64	99	0.00	54.69
Serbia	1,099	1,397	2,964	4,063	3,725	0.13	-8.32
Serbia and Montenegro		98	60	113			
Slovenia	2,420	2,189	2,560	1,965	2,228	0.08	13.38
Spain	61,232	48,994	59,737	51,033	50,106	1.74	-1.82
TFYR of Macedonia	882	580	621	563	598	0.02	6.22
Yugoslavia, SFR (former)	3,613	1,344	361	107	2	0.00	-98.13
Western Europe	518,645	512,922	591,976	595,797	581,388	20.25	-2.42
Austria	23,822	23,574	28,805	27,738	27,936	0.97	0.71
Belgium	23,419	23,732	31,192	31,769	31,310	1.09	-1.44
France	257,168	253,969	274,114	269,454	263,629	9.18	-2.16
Germany	137,722	139,806	171,487	170,987	158,463	5.52	-7.32
Liechtenstein	86	56	76	80	105	0.00	31.25
Luxembourg	644	639	728	776	777	0.03	0.13
Monaco	15	24	87	44	49	0.00	11.36
Netherlands	48,413	44,511	53,377	58,668	61,981	2.16	5.65
Switzerland	27,356	26,611	32,110	36,281	37,138	1.29	2.36
East Mediterranean Europe	28,172	22,862	24,109	23,703	25,415	0.89	7.22
Cyprus	11,906	9,428	10,432	10,206	9,165	0.32	-10.20
Turkey	16,266	13,434	13,677	13,497	16,250	0.57	20.40
Other Europe		41			106	0.00	
Other countries of Europe		41			106	0.00	
MIDDLE EAST	17,912	18,069	20,928	23,230	27,693	0.96	19.21
Bahrain	3		3	1			
Egypt	1,688	2,263	2,586	2,449	3,797	0.13	55.04
Iraq	144	123	158	157	167	0.01	6.37
Jordan	15,646	15,039	17,824	20,263	23,369	0.81	15.33
Kuwait	3	31	5	8	4	0.00	-50.00
Lebanon	242	398	224	239	252	0.01	5.44
Libya		8	3	3	1	0.00	-66.67
Oman	2	1	1	4	3	0.00	-25.00
Qatar	20	10	9	8	2	0.00	-75.00
Saudi Arabia	7		4				
Syrian Arab Republic	90	125	84	67	61	0.00	-8.96
United Arab Emirates	41		15	8			
Yemen	26	71	12	23	37	0.00	60.87
SOUTH ASIA	33,209	25,746	43,080	41,425	46,795	1.63	12.96

Yearbook of Tourism Statistics, Data 2008 – 2012, 2014 Editic

ISRAEL

1. Arrivals of non-resident tourists at national borders, by country of residence

	2008	2009	2010	2011	2012	Market share 2012	% Change 2012-2011
Afghanistan	6	1	6	2	2	0.00	0.00
Bangladesh	41	10	16	9	16	0.00	77.78
Bhutan	27		4	25	30	0.00	20.00
India	29,413	23,058	40,109	38,481	42,992	1.50	11.72
Iran, Islamic Republic of	700	400	474	409	304	0.01	-25.67
Maldives	19	9	30	64	103	0.00	60.94
Nepal	895	894	493	471	433	0.02	-8.07
Pakistan	22	11	5	9	6	0.00	-33.33
Sri Lanka	2,086	1,363	1,943	1,955	2,909	0.10	48.80
NOT SPECIFIED	**12,808**	**13,491**	**10,947**	**16,687**	**16,301**	**0.57**	**-2.31**
Other countries of the World	12,808	13,491	10,947	16,687	16,301	0.57	-2.31

Yearbook of Tourism Statistics, Data 2008 – 2012, 2014 Edition

ISRAEL

2. Arrivals of non-resident visitors at national borders, by country of residence

		2008	2009	2010	2011	2012	Market share 2012	% Change 2012-2011
TOTAL	(*)	3,034,064	2,739,737	3,443,988	3,362,073	3,520,347	100.00	4.71
AFRICA		77,039	78,496	72,692	88,429	74,859	2.13	-15.35
East Africa		9,767	7,795	10,777	11,258	11,469	0.33	1.87
Burundi		71	57	109	53	76	0.00	43.40
Comoros		2			5	1	0.00	-80.00
Eritrea		75	59	291	324	369	0.01	13.89
Ethiopia		5,224	3,965	5,118	5,341	5,201	0.15	-2.62
Kenya		1,548	1,358	2,434	2,771	2,308	0.07	-16.71
Madagascar		54	79	54	67	83	0.00	23.88
Malawi		83	86	111	107	107	0.00	0.00
Mauritius		255	293	293	279	461	0.01	65.23
Mozambique		89	50	57	55	170	0.00	209.09
Rwanda		200	158	160	155	187	0.01	20.65
Seychelles		39	13	63	22	32	0.00	45.45
Somalia					2	1	0.00	-50.00
Uganda		737	598	659	680	883	0.03	29.85
United Republic of Tanzania		853	587	745	705	684	0.02	-2.98
Zambia		182	130	181	167	176	0.00	5.39
Zimbabwe		355	362	502	525	730	0.02	39.05
Central Africa		1,867	1,453	1,455	1,703	2,331	0.07	36.88
Angola		818	435	608	765	796	0.02	4.05
Cameroon		298	404	494	498	501	0.01	0.60
Central African Republic		43	37	65	115	103	0.00	-10.43
Chad		28	19	9	27	40	0.00	48.15
Congo		568	361	157	182	174	0.00	-4.40
Democratic Republic of the Congo			64			456	0.01	
Equatorial Guinea		26		36	92	34	0.00	-63.04
Gabon		86	133	86	24	227	0.01	845.83
North Africa		3,825	3,408	3,514	3,624	3,295	0.09	-9.08
Algeria		10	15	5	14	18	0.00	28.57
Morocco		2,572	2,313	2,516	2,449	2,332	0.07	-4.78
Sudan		9	1	3	24	20	0.00	-16.67
Tunisia		1,234	1,079	990	1,137	925	0.03	-18.65
Southern Africa		23,302	18,706	22,053	23,134	25,091	0.71	8.46
Botswana		100						
Lesotho		38	22	19	20	32	0.00	60.00
Namibia		62	93	105	90	241	0.01	167.78
South Africa		23,047	18,550	21,826	22,886	24,713	0.70	7.98
Swaziland		55	41	103	138	105	0.00	-23.91
West Africa		38,150	46,908	34,451	48,248	32,546	0.92	-32.54
Benin		115	88	118	193	226	0.01	17.10
Burkina Faso		213	142	118	154	208	0.01	35.06
Cape Verde		24	59	19	14	36	0.00	157.14
Côte d'Ivoire		1,515	969	1,087	802	640	0.02	-20.20
Gambia		23	13	55	17	59	0.00	247.06
Ghana		821	516	716	1,155	1,227	0.03	6.23
Guinea		31	68	185	36	52	0.00	44.44
Liberia		45	45	68	63	40	0.00	-36.51
Mali		45	32	67	26	41	0.00	57.69
Mauritania			5		6	1	0.00	-83.33
Niger		357	353	29	38	44	0.00	15.79
Nigeria		34,713	43,942	31,723	45,093	29,602	0.84	-34.35
Senegal		119	486	111	515	132	0.00	-74.37
Sierra Leone		56	40	58	57	46	0.00	-19.30
Togo		73	150	97	79	192	0.01	143.04

346

ISRAEL

2. Arrivals of non-resident visitors at national borders, by country of residence

	2008	2009	2010	2011	2012	Market share 2012	% Change 2012-2011
Other Africa	128	226	442	462	127	0.00	-72.51
Other countries of Africa	128	226	442	462	127	0.00	-72.51
AMERICAS	814,544	734,596	879,191	855,218	844,992	24.00	-1.20
Caribbean	2,492	1,989	2,622	4,625	2,414	0.07	-47.81
Antigua and Barbuda	37	11	25	15	27	0.00	80.00
Bahamas	147	276	78	156	67	0.00	-57.05
Barbados	236	66	55	138	141	0.00	2.17
Bermuda	9	4	4	19	10	0.00	-47.37
Cayman Islands	4	17	30	3	34	0.00	1,033.33
Cuba	180	148	148	172	164	0.00	-4.65
Dominica	29	26	45	76	18	0.00	-76.32
Dominican Republic	813	655	1,099	1,000	743	0.02	-25.70
Grenada	17	16	25	26	11	0.00	-57.69
Haiti	150	131	128	209	214	0.01	2.39
Jamaica	289	179	259	2,110	311	0.01	-85.26
Puerto Rico		1	3	2			
Saint Kitts and Nevis	6	15	19	16	19	0.00	18.75
Saint Lucia	27	6	71	17	18	0.00	5.88
Saint Vincent and the Grenadines	7	6	10	17	10	0.00	-41.18
Trinidad and Tobago	531	431	621	643	626	0.02	-2.64
Turks and Caicos Islands	8	1	2	5	1	0.00	-80.00
United States Virgin Islands	2			1			
Central America	6,767	5,511	8,737	7,126	8,764	0.25	22.99
Belize	31	18	30	35	38	0.00	8.57
Costa Rica	2,372	1,632	2,747	2,401	2,902	0.08	20.87
El Salvador	982	688	1,176	768	926	0.03	20.57
Guatemala	988	982	1,562	1,221	1,431	0.04	17.20
Honduras	461	400	725	722	727	0.02	0.69
Nicaragua	158	143	200		302	0.01	
Panama	1,775	1,648	2,297	1,979	2,438	0.07	23.19
North America	725,122	656,313	758,790	731,744	714,214	20.29	-2.40
Canada	73,779	67,183	79,716	76,637	72,105	2.05	-5.91
Mexico	23,227	16,327	27,015	21,236	24,176	0.69	13.84
United States of America	628,116	572,803	652,059	633,871	617,933	17.55	-2.51
South America	79,977	70,113	109,037	111,719	119,595	3.40	7.05
Argentina	20,201	16,409	23,364	23,129	24,728	0.70	6.91
Bolivia	571	533	749	711	847	0.02	19.13
Brazil	31,767	28,945	51,983	56,889	59,403	1.69	4.42
Chile	5,787	4,700	6,377	6,381	6,032	0.17	-5.47
Colombia	9,368	8,291	12,197	11,033	13,232	0.38	19.93
Ecuador	3,227	2,907	4,206	3,820	3,822	0.11	0.05
Guyana	27	28	42	71	33	0.00	-53.52
Paraguay	315	337	544	515	491	0.01	-4.66
Peru	2,190	2,401	3,508	2,950	3,876	0.11	31.39
Suriname	17	31	50	45	54	0.00	20.00
Uruguay	2,587	2,419	2,857	2,774	2,718	0.08	-2.02
Venezuela	3,920	3,112	3,160	3,401	4,359	0.12	28.17
Other Americas	186	670	5	4	5	0.00	25.00
Other countries of the Americas	186	670	5	4	5	0.00	25.00
EAST ASIA AND THE PACIFIC	140,446	102,996	159,938	161,588	184,839	5.25	14.39
North-East Asia	69,017	44,021	75,592	73,032	79,344	2.25	8.64
China	9,083	7,714	13,258	17,418	19,633	0.56	12.72
Hong Kong, China	3,679	2,335	4,499	3,723	4,830	0.14	29.73
Japan	14,735	10,031	13,866	14,112	16,481	0.47	16.79
Korea, Dem. People's Republic of			16	16	29	0.00	81.25
Korea, Republic of	37,540	21,113	39,644	32,718	32,724	0.93	0.02
Macao, China	46	59	53	52	156	0.00	200.00

347

ISRAEL

2. Arrivals of non-resident visitors at national borders, by country of residence

	2008	2009	2010	2011	2012	Market share 2012	% Change 2012-2011
Mongolia	156	109	207	204	185	0.01	-9.31
Taiwan, Province of China	3,778	2,660	4,049	4,789	5,306	0.15	10.80
South-East Asia	**38,205**	**29,428**	**43,953**	**49,478**	**66,126**	**1.88**	**33.65**
Brunei Darussalam	15	1	2	12	2	0.00	-83.33
Cambodia	31	24	48	70	114	0.00	62.86
Indonesia	14,357	9,595	17,823	22,019	27,869	0.79	26.57
Lao People's Democratic Republic	39	67	150	240	319	0.01	32.92
Malaysia	2,316	640	1,611	3,276	6,881	0.20	110.04
Myanmar			373	345	599	0.02	73.62
Philippines	9,347	8,077	10,659	9,999	13,560	0.39	35.61
Singapore	8,637	6,520	8,901	8,487	10,476	0.30	23.44
Thailand	2,800	3,450	3,051	3,378	4,398	0.12	30.20
Timor-Leste			7	42	47	0.00	11.90
Viet Nam	663	1,054	1,328	1,610	1,861	0.05	15.59
Australasia	**31,585**	**28,627**	**39,950**	**38,481**	**38,492**	**1.09**	**0.03**
Australia	28,039	25,465	35,188	34,203	34,071	0.97	-0.39
New Zealand	3,546	3,162	4,762	4,278	4,421	0.13	3.34
Melanesia	**226**	**223**	**404**	**554**	**818**	**0.02**	**47.65**
Fiji	142	129	200	380	441	0.01	16.05
Papua New Guinea	63	76	178	148	340	0.01	129.73
Solomon Islands	3	6	10	9	16	0.00	77.78
Vanuatu	18	12	16	17	21	0.00	23.53
Micronesia	**24**	**4**	**12**	**16**	**7**	**0.00**	**-56.25**
Kiribati	17		2	3	3	0.00	0.00
Micronesia, Federated States of		3	9	3	4	0.00	33.33
Palau	7	1	1	10			
Polynesia	**22**	**6**	**21**	**27**	**46**	**0.00**	**70.37**
American Samoa		6	1	1	5	0.00	400.00
Cook Islands			1				
French Polynesia			2				
Samoa	12		7	6	17	0.00	183.33
Tonga	10		10	20	24	0.00	20.00
Other East Asia and the Pacific	**1,367**	**687**	**6**		**6**	**0.00**	
Other countries of Asia	1,356	669			6	0.00	
Other countries of Oceania	11	18	6				
EUROPE	**1,936,303**	**1,764,666**	**2,253,137**	**2,175,690**	**2,323,587**	**66.00**	**6.80**
Central/Eastern Europe	**849,887**	**723,680**	**952,844**	**884,454**	**997,758**	**28.34**	**12.81**
Armenia	1,487	1,170	2,283	1,878	2,587	0.07	37.75
Azerbaijan	3,186	2,991	3,142	2,994	3,335	0.09	11.39
Belarus	17,934	14,442	17,760	15,187	20,342	0.58	33.94
Bulgaria	10,148	7,016	8,135	8,304	8,080	0.23	-2.70
Czech Republic	38,328	23,540	25,184	19,037	17,324	0.49	-9.00
Estonia	3,986	4,023	7,695	4,015	3,755	0.11	-6.48
Georgia	6,351	4,675	4,546	4,345	4,443	0.13	2.26
Hungary	18,000	11,825	15,339	13,745	11,852	0.34	-13.77
Kazakhstan	13,549	10,736	12,224	14,607	19,394	0.55	32.77
Kyrgyzstan	655	659	709	750	954	0.03	27.20
Latvia	7,693	5,094	5,722	5,910	6,411	0.18	8.48
Lithuania	13,352	7,229	9,134	6,969	7,579	0.22	8.75
Poland	156,252	96,880	128,961	95,958	101,912	2.89	6.20
Republic of Moldova	5,509	3,823	4,619	3,867	4,136	0.12	6.96
Romania	38,689	30,494	41,306	40,255	42,898	1.22	6.57
Russian Federation	367,423	408,304	554,364	491,418	587,743	16.70	19.60
Slovakia	15,949	12,909	16,815	13,495	11,523	0.33	-14.61
Tajikistan	313	260	283	402	514	0.01	27.86
Turkmenistan	149	236	191	171	321	0.01	87.72
Ukraine	125,477	73,924	90,711	137,266	138,313	3.93	0.76

348

ISRAEL

2. Arrivals of non-resident visitors at national borders, by country of residence

	2008	2009	2010	2011	2012	Market share 2012	% Change 2012-2011
USSR (former)	82	13	7	4	3	0.00	-25.00
Uzbekistan	5,162	3,437	3,714	3,877	4,339	0.12	11.92
Other countries Central/East Europe	213						
Northern Europe	**257,954**	**251,791**	**283,555**	**311,362**	**296,384**	**8.42**	**-4.81**
Denmark	12,540	13,150	15,949	20,688	20,978	0.60	1.40
Finland	12,447	17,952	19,783	18,640	18,320	0.52	-1.72
Iceland	404	238	384	389	361	0.01	-7.20
Ireland	9,746	8,580	10,427	10,713	8,972	0.25	-16.25
Norway	13,756	12,764	15,288	17,981	17,676	0.50	-1.70
Sweden	17,266	17,793	21,374	21,857	23,665	0.67	8.27
United Kingdom	191,795	181,314	200,350	221,094	206,412	5.86	-6.64
Southern Europe	**255,712**	**223,946**	**325,218**	**255,735**	**277,204**	**7.87**	**8.40**
Albania	1,090	715	591	625	551	0.02	-11.84
Andorra	64	52	87	60	62	0.00	3.33
Bosnia and Herzegovina	625	360	511	690	485	0.01	-29.71
Croatia	5,348	5,398	6,833	6,791	6,587	0.19	-3.00
Greece	33,056	20,642	28,957	19,791	22,050	0.63	11.41
Holy See	247	292	274	256	271	0.01	5.86
Italy	125,649	125,704	185,383	151,245	170,033	4.83	12.42
Malta	1,455	1,517	2,342	1,437	2,354	0.07	63.81
Montenegro			485	401	557	0.02	38.90
Portugal	11,986	7,208	15,341	9,569	9,522	0.27	-0.49
San Marino	291	102	140	82	123	0.00	50.00
Serbia		877	4,720	5,062	4,773	0.14	-5.71
Serbia and Montenegro	1,118	1,556	72	113			
Slovenia	2,862	2,348	3,332	2,682	3,142	0.09	17.15
Spain	65,504	54,144	74,967	56,210	56,040	1.59	-0.30
TFYR of Macedonia	1,166	694	699	596	652	0.02	9.40
Yugoslavia, SFR (former)	5,251	2,337	484	125	2	0.00	-98.40
Western Europe	**538,867**	**539,160**	**663,771**	**698,564**	**723,552**	**20.55**	**3.58**
Austria	24,571	24,924	32,388	35,164	34,764	0.99	-1.14
Belgium	24,782	26,127	35,255	37,040	36,337	1.03	-1.90
France	264,306	263,885	302,695	300,567	300,573	8.54	0.00
Germany	143,209	148,322	199,942	220,688	239,758	6.81	8.64
Liechtenstein	89	59	86	97	124	0.00	27.84
Luxembourg	667	663	837	989	1,025	0.03	3.64
Monaco	16	26	104	60	66	0.00	10.00
Netherlands	53,267	47,587	57,962	63,047	67,850	1.93	7.62
Switzerland	27,960	27,567	34,502	40,912	43,055	1.22	5.24
East Mediterranean Europe	**33,883**	**25,735**	**27,749**	**25,575**	**28,583**	**0.81**	**11.76**
Cyprus	16,299	11,521	12,699	11,552	11,422	0.32	-1.13
Turkey	17,584	14,214	15,050	14,023	17,161	0.49	22.38
Other Europe		**354**			**106**	**0.00**	
Other countries of Europe		354			106	0.00	
MIDDLE EAST	**19,241**	**19,085**	**21,645**	**23,891**	**28,292**	**0.80**	**18.42**
Bahrain	3		3	1			
Egypt	1,846	2,431	2,810	2,663	3,928	0.11	47.50
Iraq	146	123	158	157	168	0.00	7.01
Jordan	16,807	15,885	18,310	20,708	23,834	0.68	15.10
Kuwait	3	31	7	9	4	0.00	-55.56
Lebanon	243	400	228	239	253	0.01	5.86
Libya		8	3	3	1	0.00	-66.67
Oman	2	1	1	4	3	0.00	-25.00
Qatar	24	10	10	8	2	0.00	-75.00
Saudi Arabia	7		4				
Syrian Arab Republic	90	125	84	67	62	0.00	-7.46
United Arab Emirates	44		15	9			

Yearbook of Tourism Statistics, Data 2008 – 2012, 2014 Edition

ISRAEL

2. Arrivals of non-resident visitors at national borders, by country of residence

	2008	2009	2010	2011	2012	Market share 2012	% Change 2012-2011
Yemen	26	71	12	23	37	0.00	60.87
SOUTH ASIA	**33,461**	**26,078**	**43,381**	**41,780**	**47,196**	**1.34**	**12.96**
Afghanistan	6	1	6	2	2	0.00	0.00
Bangladesh	41	10	17	14	16	0.00	14.29
Bhutan	27		4	25	30	0.00	20.00
India	29,652	23,374	40,394	38,870	43,360	1.23	11.55
Iran, Islamic Republic of	701	401	476	411	304	0.01	-26.03
Maldives	19	9	30		103	0.00	
Nepal	903	899	493	477	437	0.01	-8.39
Pakistan	23	11	5	15	6	0.00	-60.00
Sri Lanka	2,089	1,373	1,956	1,966	2,938	0.08	49.44
NOT SPECIFIED	**13,030**	**13,820**	**14,004**	**15,477**	**16,582**	**0.47**	**7.14**
Other countries of the World	13,030	13,820	14,004	15,477	16,582	0.47	7.14

350

ISRAEL

3. Arrivals of non-resident tourists in hotels and similar establishments, by country of residence

		2008	2009	2010	2011	2012	Market share 2012	% Change 2012-2011
TOTAL	(*)	**3,373,000**	**2,620,800**	**3,237,000**	**3,231,900**	**3,170,500**	**100.00**	**-1.90**
AMERICAS		**1,205,600**	**883,500**	**1,133,000**	**1,103,900**	**1,099,100**	**34.67**	**-0.43**
North America		**1,100,600**	**814,700**	**1,010,900**	**973,100**	**954,700**	**30.11**	**-1.89**
All countries of North America		1,100,600	814,700	1,010,900	973,100	954,700	30.11	-1.89
South America		**105,000**	**68,800**	**122,100**	**130,800**	**144,400**	**4.55**	**10.40**
All countries of South America	(*)	105,000	68,800	122,100	130,800	144,400	4.55	10.40
EUROPE		**1,565,100**	**1,255,300**	**1,547,700**	**1,522,600**	**1,425,800**	**44.97**	**-6.36**
Other Europe		**1,565,100**	**1,255,300**	**1,547,700**	**1,522,600**	**1,425,800**	**44.97**	**-6.36**
All countries of Europe		1,565,100	1,255,300	1,547,700	1,522,600	1,425,800	44.97	-6.36
NOT SPECIFIED		**602,300**	**482,000**	**556,300**	**605,400**	**645,600**	**20.36**	**6.64**
Other countries of the World		602,300	482,000	556,300	605,400	645,600	20.36	6.64

Yearbook of Tourism Statistics, Data 2008 – 2012, 2014 Edition

ISRAEL

5. Overnight stays of non-resident tourists in hotels and similar establishments, by country of residence

		2008	2009	2010	2011	2012	Market share 2012	% Change 2012-2011
TOTAL	(*)	10,187,500	8,108,800	9,933,100	9,949,200	9,750,400	100.00	-2.00
AMERICAS		3,488,000	2,628,200	3,313,900	3,212,000	3,179,100	32.60	-1.02
North America		3,181,500	2,421,800	2,958,300	2,828,700	2,785,700	28.57	-1.52
All countries of North America		3,181,500	2,421,800	2,958,300	2,828,700	2,785,700	28.57	-1.52
South America		306,500	206,400	355,600	383,300	393,400	4.03	2.64
All countries of South America	(*)	306,500	206,400	355,600	383,300	393,400	4.03	2.64
EUROPE		5,073,300	4,173,300	5,149,700	5,119,000	4,848,700	49.73	-5.28
Other Europe		5,073,300	4,173,300	5,149,700	5,119,000	4,848,700	49.73	-5.28
All countries of Europe		5,073,300	4,173,300	5,149,700	5,119,000	4,848,700	49.73	-5.28
NOT SPECIFIED		1,626,200	1,307,300	1,469,500	1,618,200	1,722,600	17.67	6.45
Other countries of the World		1,626,200	1,307,300	1,469,500	1,618,200	1,722,600	17.67	6.45

Yearbook of Tourism Statistics, Data 2008 – 2012, 2014 Edition

ITALY

1. Arrivals of non-resident tourists at national borders, by nationality

		2008	2009	2010	2011	2012	Market share 2012	% Change 2012-2011
TOTAL	(*)	42,733,685	43,238,919	43,626,118	46,118,848	46,359,908	100.00	0.52
AFRICA		300,031	248,441	318,179	280,199	225,208	0.49	-19.63
East Africa		33,021	34,856	28,227	32,911	29,643	0.06	-9.93
All countries of East Africa		33,021	34,856	28,227	32,911	29,643	0.06	-9.93
Central Africa		12,304	10,830	10,973	13,033	10,561	0.02	-18.97
All countries of Central Africa		12,304	10,830	10,973	13,033	10,561	0.02	-18.97
North Africa		127,636	105,245	189,253	124,915	84,161	0.18	-32.63
Algeria		22,992	12,664	7,560	11,303	10,548	0.02	-6.68
Morocco		73,857	62,194	145,241	72,468	40,884	0.09	-43.58
Tunisia		25,934	27,363	34,166	34,921	30,398	0.07	-12.95
Other countries of North Africa		4,853	3,024	2,286	6,223	2,331	0.01	-62.54
Southern Africa		82,443	64,956	55,431	67,232	54,903	0.12	-18.34
South Africa		80,504	64,124	55,431	66,054	53,574	0.12	-18.89
Other countries of Southern Africa		1,939	832		1,178	1,329	0.00	12.82
West Africa		44,627	32,554	34,295	42,108	45,940	0.10	9.10
All countries of West Africa		44,627	32,554	34,295	42,108	45,940	0.10	9.10
AMERICAS		3,394,811	3,390,307	3,501,730	4,067,153	3,910,295	8.43	-3.86
Caribbean		23,934	20,044	15,363	28,884	24,454	0.05	-15.34
All countries of the Caribbean		23,934	20,044	15,363	28,884	24,454	0.05	-15.34
Central America		23,319	19,114	20,173	28,114	31,114	0.07	10.67
Costa Rica		7,479	7,969	8,613	14,904	14,851	0.03	-0.36
Panama		5,020	2,336	2,149	2,663	3,238	0.01	21.59
Other countries of Central America		10,820	8,809	9,411	10,547	13,025	0.03	23.49
North America		2,815,658	2,862,090	2,963,977	3,400,653	3,204,846	6.91	-5.76
Canada		425,998	512,890	561,294	574,527	513,885	1.11	-10.56
Mexico		119,798	87,465	74,338	111,543	100,218	0.22	-10.15
United States of America		2,269,448	2,261,735	2,327,342	2,714,583	2,590,359	5.59	-4.58
Other countries of North America		414		1,003		384	0.00	
South America		531,900	489,059	502,217	609,502	649,881	1.40	6.62
Argentina		115,257	138,165	127,537	130,821	159,624	0.34	22.02
Brazil		252,193	188,892	234,199	293,309	310,575	0.67	5.89
Chile		39,219	31,657	47,787	51,437	50,736	0.11	-1.36
Colombia		15,812	18,572	15,683	18,433	28,728	0.06	55.85
Peru		20,213	28,052	21,395	23,732	19,159	0.04	-19.27
Venezuela		52,941	45,467	36,215	60,891	43,113	0.09	-29.20
Other countries of South America		36,265	38,254	19,401	30,879	37,946	0.08	22.89
EAST ASIA AND THE PACIFIC		1,253,482	1,299,901	1,324,474	1,512,096	1,528,003	3.30	1.05
North-East Asia		538,025	565,451	573,999	640,954	681,887	1.47	6.39
China		158,226	138,210	136,780	209,651	231,022	0.50	10.19
Hong Kong, China		19,132	26,748	26,199	40,524	31,200	0.07	-23.01
Japan		283,819	320,591	340,210	314,239	353,547	0.76	12.51
Korea, Republic of		51,645	59,972	59,996	58,490	48,351	0.10	-17.33
Taiwan, Province of China		17,178	10,138	8,124	15,946	15,445	0.03	-3.14
Other countries of North-East Asia		8,025	9,792	2,690	2,104	2,322	0.01	10.36
South-East Asia		89,339	132,965	119,679	94,826	133,296	0.29	40.57
Indonesia		7,121	12,474	14,938	9,573	22,823	0.05	138.41
Malaysia		14,914	16,729	26,154	21,905	23,358	0.05	6.63
Philippines		15,769	19,154	21,682	14,217	25,627	0.06	80.26
Singapore		31,156	28,743	20,146	28,623	34,124	0.07	19.22
Thailand		14,189	51,196	33,206	18,444	25,561	0.06	38.59
Other countries of South-East Asia		6,190	4,669	3,553	2,064	1,803	0.00	-12.65
Australasia		615,660	597,408	624,205	769,764	709,743	1.53	-7.80
Australia		518,897	526,755	548,288	693,265	644,285	1.39	-7.07
New Zealand		96,763	70,653	75,917	76,499	65,458	0.14	-14.43
Melanesia		1,203		1,555	2,449	1,316	0.00	-46.26

Yearbook of Tourism Statistics, Data 2008 – 2012, 2014 Edition

ITALY

1. Arrivals of non-resident tourists at national borders, by nationality

	2008	2009	2010	2011	2012	Market share 2012	% Change 2012-2011
All countries of Melanesia	1,203		1,555	2,449	1,316	0.00	-46.26
Micronesia	**52**		**1,293**	**384**	**882**	**0.00**	**129.69**
All countries of Micronesia	52		1,293	384	882	0.00	129.69
Polynesia	**9,203**	**4,077**	**3,743**	**3,719**	**879**	**0.00**	**-76.36**
American Samoa	8,285	1,668	3,743	2,945			
Samoa	593	776					
Other countries of Polynesia	325	1,633		774	879	0.00	13.57
EUROPE	**37,342,336**	**37,853,912**	**37,921,219**	**39,743,414**	**40,062,889**	**86.42**	**0.80**
Central/Eastern Europe	**4,584,706**	**4,366,233**	**4,894,033**	**5,246,233**	**5,867,085**	**12.66**	**11.83**
Czech Republic	802,406	772,544	816,161	953,555	857,473	1.85	-10.08
Hungary	919,012	620,833	525,595	504,221	498,110	1.07	-1.21
Poland	986,576	1,033,409	1,124,044	1,182,758	1,327,821	2.86	12.26
Romania	663,014	672,205	672,377	644,841	681,349	1.47	5.66
Russian Federation	397,221	431,470	595,275	745,453	950,061	2.05	27.45
Slovakia	382,223	360,843	411,974	388,003	494,401	1.07	27.42
Other countries Central/East Europe	434,254	474,929	748,607	827,402	1,057,870	2.28	27.85
Northern Europe	**5,553,558**	**5,062,988**	**4,920,559**	**5,045,420**	**5,262,553**	**11.35**	**4.30**
Denmark	428,867	451,417	470,812	443,135	534,175	1.15	20.54
Finland	257,948	216,965	217,226	259,229	251,079	0.54	-3.14
Ireland	300,213	336,040	348,638	279,313	306,675	0.66	9.80
Norway	324,067	261,533	264,516	235,290	312,886	0.67	32.98
Sweden	465,579	429,538	444,826	625,500	474,650	1.02	-24.12
United Kingdom	3,761,619	3,361,357	3,163,036	3,195,408	3,377,115	7.28	5.69
Other countries of Northern Europe	15,265	6,138	11,505	7,545	5,973	0.01	-20.83
Southern Europe	**3,527,019**	**4,023,658**	**4,621,045**	**4,595,039**	**4,167,115**	**8.99**	**-9.31**
Albania	72,564	86,930	88,965	139,383	113,873	0.25	-18.30
Bosnia and Herzegovina	23,228	107,867	265,236	257,321	381,674	0.82	48.33
Croatia	153,794	261,155	390,919	359,940	273,025	0.59	-24.15
Greece	428,961	438,965	473,474	369,346	307,458	0.66	-16.76
Malta	77,509	40,835	58,598	72,553	59,666	0.13	-17.76
Portugal	210,496	223,691	284,028	273,900	166,428	0.36	-39.24
Serbia	48,842	121,695	267,995	248,613	354,271	0.76	42.50
Slovenia	208,134	245,459	255,651	170,561	191,132	0.41	12.06
Spain	2,286,773	2,463,309	2,484,724	2,610,373	2,268,144	4.89	-13.11
Other countries of Southern Europe	16,718	33,752	51,455	93,049	51,444	0.11	-44.71
Western Europe	**23,461,407**	**24,135,839**	**23,217,166**	**24,602,584**	**24,478,179**	**52.80**	**-0.51**
Austria	3,098,816	3,403,807	3,361,695	3,205,214	3,083,283	6.65	-3.80
Belgium	1,104,889	1,112,551	1,104,115	1,397,291	1,253,301	2.70	-10.30
France	4,820,493	4,935,031	4,843,586	4,982,877	4,977,292	10.74	-0.11
Germany	9,803,190	9,546,257	8,960,697	9,874,509	10,169,734	21.94	2.99
Luxembourg	97,500	108,020	89,597	101,609	101,379	0.22	-0.23
Netherlands	1,927,042	1,922,473	1,592,483	1,758,978	1,710,635	3.69	-2.75
Switzerland	2,537,807	2,952,608	3,183,639	3,235,773	3,135,368	6.76	-3.10
Other countries of Western Europe	71,670	155,092	81,354	46,333	47,187	0.10	1.84
East Mediterranean Europe	**190,389**	**239,402**	**242,408**	**231,327**	**252,056**	**0.54**	**8.96**
Israel	51,932	72,915	105,578	79,291	71,834	0.15	-9.40
Turkey	138,457	166,487	136,830	152,036	180,222	0.39	18.54
Other Europe	**25,257**	**25,792**	**26,008**	**22,811**	**35,901**	**0.08**	**57.38**
Other countries of Europe	25,257	25,792	26,008	22,811	35,901	0.08	57.38
MIDDLE EAST	**235,614**	**222,200**	**289,353**	**246,530**	**275,989**	**0.60**	**11.95**
Egypt	54,712	46,559	47,639	42,623	37,676	0.08	-11.61
Jordan	16,647	15,429	16,158	27,599	21,114	0.05	-23.50
Lebanon	14,646	17,277	16,875	9,708	19,245	0.04	98.24
Libya	22,924	12,695	14,841	8,687	11,920	0.03	37.22
Saudi Arabia	26,049	15,687	47,494	40,126	50,654	0.11	26.24
United Arab Emirates	71,516	80,049	95,716	62,256	73,776	0.16	18.50
Other countries of Middle East	29,120	34,504	50,630	55,531	61,604	0.13	10.94

Yearbook of Tourism Statistics, Data 2008 – 2012, 2014 Edition

ITALY

1. Arrivals of non-resident tourists at national borders, by nationality

	2008	2009	2010	2011	2012	Market share 2012	% Change 2012-2011
SOUTH ASIA	**207,411**	**224,158**	**270,007**	**269,061**	**357,196**	**0.77**	**32.76**
India	135,517	139,094	182,552	188,408	251,361	0.54	33.41
Iran, Islamic Republic of	27,872	31,173	16,912	33,441	31,843	0.07	-4.78
Pakistan	25,175	29,359	33,383	17,669	28,973	0.06	63.98
Other countries of South Asia	18,847	24,532	37,160	29,543	45,019	0.10	52.38
NOT SPECIFIED			**1,156**	**395**	**328**	**0.00**	**-16.96**
Other countries of the World			1,156	395	328	0.00	-16.96

ITALY

2. Arrivals of non-resident visitors at national borders, by nationality

		2008	2009	2010	2011	2012	Market share 2012	% Change 2012-2011
TOTAL	(*)	70,718,862	71,692,233	73,225,219	75,866,005	76,292,846	100.00	0.56
AFRICA		359,968	287,673	377,484	360,837	275,380	0.36	-23.68
East Africa		35,773	35,510	31,368	37,040	32,521	0.04	-12.20
All countries of East Africa		35,773	35,510	31,368	37,040	32,521	0.04	-12.20
Central Africa		14,086	11,826	11,347	14,197	11,523	0.02	-18.83
Sao Tome and Principe				74		341	0.00	
Other countries of Central Africa				11,273		11,182	0.01	
All countries of Central Africa		14,086	11,826		14,197			
North Africa		168,115	131,023	231,918	182,336	109,294	0.14	-40.06
Algeria		36,144	19,538	17,896	25,264	18,091	0.02	-28.39
Morocco		83,854	66,324	150,887	86,979	42,734	0.06	-50.87
Tunisia		43,083	41,266	60,849	63,231	44,214	0.06	-30.08
Other countries of North Africa		5,034	3,895	2,286	6,862	4,255	0.01	-37.99
Southern Africa		85,792	71,258	60,088	69,011	57,567	0.08	-16.58
South Africa		83,853	70,426	60,088	67,833	56,238	0.07	-17.09
Other countries of Southern Africa		1,939	832		1,178	1,329	0.00	12.82
West Africa		56,202	38,056	42,763	58,253	64,475	0.08	10.68
All countries of West Africa		56,202	38,056	42,763	58,253	64,475	0.08	10.68
AMERICAS		3,922,420	3,760,644	3,968,611	4,828,460	4,757,349	6.24	-1.47
Caribbean		27,942	20,674	16,603	36,015	27,358	0.04	-24.04
All countries of the Caribbean		27,942	20,674	16,603	36,015	27,358	0.04	-24.04
Central America		27,997	21,139	23,661	34,393	37,392	0.05	8.72
Costa Rica		8,990	8,053	9,827	14,904	14,851	0.02	-0.36
Panama		5,020	3,055	2,619	3,170	3,238	0.00	2.15
Other countries of Central America		13,987	10,031	11,215	16,319	19,303	0.03	18.29
North America		3,196,349	3,143,205	3,311,017	3,957,155	3,789,802	4.97	-4.23
Canada		510,157	547,752	604,640	636,858	612,174	0.80	-3.88
Mexico		122,520	89,316	77,019	118,782	105,897	0.14	-10.85
United States of America		2,563,258	2,506,137	2,621,863	3,201,515	3,071,347	4.03	-4.07
Other countries of North America		414		7,495		384	0.00	
South America		670,132	575,626	617,330	800,897	902,797	1.18	12.72
Argentina		145,087	162,298	155,949	162,180	205,764	0.27	26.87
Brazil		299,295	221,802	274,543	398,721	424,831	0.56	6.55
Chile		46,769	32,032	52,491	53,247	56,281	0.07	5.70
Colombia		16,945	20,317	16,472	20,690	29,125	0.04	40.77
Peru		25,470	28,905	23,924	26,154	23,280	0.03	-10.99
Venezuela		78,798	59,717	56,189	97,105	83,285	0.11	-14.23
Other countries of South America		57,768	50,555	37,762	42,800	80,231	0.11	87.46
EAST ASIA AND THE PACIFIC		1,362,724	1,396,924	1,416,478	1,646,410	1,656,647	2.17	0.62
North-East Asia		591,953	610,831	608,046	680,841	722,802	0.95	6.16
China		163,796	145,995	145,991	223,815	251,699	0.33	12.46
Hong Kong, China		19,330	27,466	29,269	50,484	36,787	0.05	-27.13
Japan		318,699	349,710	359,855	326,895	365,304	0.48	11.75
Korea, Republic of		52,915	60,222	60,955	58,836	50,873	0.07	-13.53
Taiwan, Province of China		17,399	12,727	8,817	17,598	15,583	0.02	-11.45
Other countries of North-East Asia		19,814	14,711	3,159	3,213	2,556	0.00	-20.45
South-East Asia		105,746	143,730	132,132	111,828	149,125	0.20	33.35
Indonesia		7,793	15,012	17,037	11,008	23,290	0.03	111.57
Malaysia		16,719	17,734	27,654	22,075	23,915	0.03	8.34
Philippines		18,785	21,933	25,757	19,567	34,958	0.05	78.66
Singapore		40,348	31,075	21,699	34,512	35,471	0.05	2.78
Thailand		15,476	52,307	34,993	22,370	29,112	0.04	30.14
Other countries of South-East Asia		6,625	5,669	4,992	2,296	2,379	0.00	3.61
Australasia		642,087	631,827	665,008	846,988	781,643	1.02	-7.71
Australia		541,146	555,249	584,401	765,527	710,073	0.93	-7.24

356

ITALY

2. Arrivals of non-resident visitors at national borders, by nationality

	2008	2009	2010	2011	2012	Market share 2012	% Change 2012-2011
New Zealand	100,941	76,578	80,607	81,461	71,570	0.09	-12.14
Melanesia	**1,203**	**160**	**1,555**	**2,449**	**1,316**	**0.00**	**-46.26**
All countries of Melanesia	1,203	160	1,555	2,449	1,316	0.00	-46.26
Micronesia	**52**		**1,293**	**384**	**882**	**0.00**	**129.69**
All countries of Micronesia	52		1,293	384	882	0.00	129.69
Polynesia	**21,683**	**10,376**	**8,444**	**3,920**	**879**	**0.00**	**-77.58**
American Samoa	19,351	7,077	5,011	3,146			
Samoa	593	776					
Other countries of Polynesia	1,739	2,523	3,433	774	879	0.00	13.57
EUROPE	**64,492,957**	**65,745,321**	**66,821,317**	**68,359,168**	**68,800,401**	**90.18**	**0.65**
Central/Eastern Europe	**5,307,274**	**5,143,307**	**5,749,328**	**6,211,261**	**7,153,591**	**9.38**	**15.17**
Czech Republic	912,557	897,923	915,028	1,101,088	1,051,130	1.38	-4.54
Hungary	1,089,036	734,637	655,307	658,379	604,932	0.79	-8.12
Poland	1,100,451	1,164,908	1,257,219	1,287,725	1,524,685	2.00	18.40
Romania	827,773	859,744	863,342	982,513	1,059,922	1.39	7.88
Russian Federation	435,814	457,208	645,416	792,560	1,045,379	1.37	31.90
Slovakia	413,197	410,843	475,148	431,024	606,097	0.79	40.62
Other countries Central/East Europe	528,446	618,044	937,868	957,972	1,261,446	1.65	31.68
Northern Europe	**6,046,031**	**5,438,643**	**5,239,507**	**5,436,515**	**5,694,281**	**7.46**	**4.74**
Denmark	479,604	493,788	516,566	464,582	591,348	0.78	27.29
Finland	278,651	235,631	237,220	279,397	281,792	0.37	0.86
Ireland	315,842	349,829	361,657	287,609	318,109	0.42	10.60
Norway	344,315	281,075	282,464	248,948	328,391	0.43	31.91
Sweden	503,434	455,663	481,502	668,911	518,951	0.68	-22.42
United Kingdom	4,108,223	3,615,588	3,348,204	3,479,523	3,646,810	4.78	4.81
Other countries of Northern Europe	15,962	7,069	11,894	7,545	8,880	0.01	17.69
Southern Europe	**8,697,207**	**9,746,658**	**10,250,804**	**10,322,189**	**9,743,174**	**12.77**	**-5.61**
Albania	83,866	97,835	99,047	150,063	147,474	0.19	-1.73
Bosnia and Herzegovina	24,731	152,527	293,249	260,725	410,179	0.54	57.32
Croatia	866,387	1,133,295	1,239,545	1,146,611	1,274,320	1.67	11.14
Greece	611,364	552,039	598,570	467,671	399,267	0.52	-14.63
Malta	115,980	87,304	91,671	100,367	77,356	0.10	-22.93
Portugal	249,007	274,309	380,725	340,350	247,763	0.32	-27.20
Serbia	76,477	159,160	303,033	284,991	404,160	0.53	41.82
Slovenia	3,899,696	4,225,605	4,116,591	4,394,410	4,070,720	5.34	-7.37
Spain	2,741,560	3,005,610	3,045,843	3,061,249	2,631,346	3.45	-14.04
Other countries of Southern Europe	28,139	58,974	82,530	115,752	80,589	0.11	-30.38
Western Europe	**44,172,375**	**45,105,222**	**45,248,161**	**46,052,599**	**45,828,924**	**60.07**	**-0.49**
Austria	6,573,010	7,317,666	7,660,061	6,502,564	6,929,749	9.08	6.57
Belgium	1,265,137	1,288,870	1,248,305	1,672,460	1,441,271	1.89	-13.82
France	10,107,314	10,168,307	9,975,720	10,165,234	10,245,551	13.43	0.79
Germany	11,516,663	11,422,068	10,856,813	11,681,707	11,679,304	15.31	-0.02
Luxembourg	120,841	129,698	114,445	119,621	114,109	0.15	-4.61
Netherlands	2,237,507	2,148,031	1,806,616	2,079,358	1,923,531	2.52	-7.49
Switzerland	12,007,628	12,234,105	13,297,391	13,565,237	13,145,021	17.23	-3.10
Other countries of Western Europe	344,275	396,477	288,810	266,418	350,388	0.46	31.52
East Mediterranean Europe	**240,027**	**283,176**	**303,813**	**310,597**	**341,851**	**0.45**	**10.06**
Israel	75,291	90,331	142,026	134,292	145,055	0.19	8.01
Turkey	164,736	192,845	161,787	176,305	196,796	0.26	11.62
Other Europe	**30,043**	**28,315**	**29,704**	**26,007**	**38,580**	**0.05**	**48.34**
Other countries of Europe	30,043	28,315	29,704	26,007	38,580	0.05	48.34
MIDDLE EAST	**311,533**	**260,945**	**349,821**	**362,070**	**380,597**	**0.50**	**5.12**
Egypt	85,022	54,427	54,849	70,402	55,029	0.07	-21.84
Jordan	17,865	16,431	18,212	29,050	23,595	0.03	-18.78
Lebanon	28,694	20,146	26,459	36,590	45,976	0.06	25.65
Libya	34,232	18,294	26,463	22,568	33,377	0.04	47.90
Saudi Arabia	27,487	18,841	53,503	43,982	58,149	0.08	32.21

Yearbook of Tourism Statistics, Data 2008 – 2012, 2014 Edition

ITALY

2. Arrivals of non-resident visitors at national borders, by nationality

	2008	2009	2010	2011	2012	Market share 2012	% Change 2012-2011
United Arab Emirates	81,832	86,828	112,934	80,829	87,354	0.11	8.07
Other countries of Middle East	36,401	45,978	57,401	78,649	77,117	0.10	-1.95
SOUTH ASIA	**269,260**	**240,726**	**290,352**	**308,665**	**422,144**	**0.55**	**36.76**
India	175,576	144,105	189,629	208,132	280,902	0.37	34.96
Iran, Islamic Republic of	44,726	35,824	24,932	38,683	45,311	0.06	17.13
Pakistan	28,020	31,719	35,924	23,852	47,849	0.06	100.61
Other countries of South Asia	20,938	29,078	39,867	37,998	48,082	0.06	26.54
NOT SPECIFIED			**1,156**	**395**	**328**	**0.00**	**-16.96**
Other countries of the World			1,156	395	328	0.00	-16.96

Yearbook of Tourism Statistics, Data 2008 – 2012, 2014 Editic

ITALY

3. Arrivals of non-resident tourists in hotels and similar establishments, by nationality

		2008	2009	2010	2011	2012	Market share 2012	% Change 2012-2011
TOTAL	(*)	33,666,586	32,632,696	35,020,415	37,983,634			
AFRICA		253,731	250,004	261,939	287,903			
Southern Africa		58,618	52,763	61,542	70,950			
South Africa		58,618	52,763	61,542	70,950			
Other Africa		195,113	197,241	200,397	216,953			
Other countries of Africa		195,113	197,241	200,397	216,953			
AMERICAS		5,339,344	4,949,563	5,503,571	6,002,579			
North America		4,497,745	4,134,823	4,503,592	4,740,665			
Canada		543,382	501,488	574,369	601,077			
Mexico		163,932	135,467	165,582	187,990			
United States of America		3,790,431	3,497,868	3,763,641	3,951,598			
South America		841,599	814,740	999,979	1,261,914			
Argentina		154,827	168,435	205,447	262,304			
Brazil		437,967	399,018	533,471	695,086			
Venezuela		52,294	52,114	49,766	59,860			
Other countries of South America		196,511	195,173	211,295	244,664			
EAST ASIA AND THE PACIFIC		3,179,241	3,006,496	3,612,759	4,218,725			
North-East Asia		2,230,156	2,141,170	2,525,936	2,966,141			
China		686,391	696,778	929,308	1,291,762			
Japan		1,247,846	1,238,474	1,304,394	1,345,981			
Korea, Republic of		295,919	205,918	292,234	328,398			
Australasia		648,667	573,459	674,490	736,905			
Australia		565,384	501,313	595,227	656,600			
New Zealand		83,283	72,146	79,263	80,305			
Other East Asia and the Pacific		300,418	291,867	412,333	515,679			
Other countries of Asia		300,418	291,867	412,333	515,679			
EUROPE		24,066,750	23,545,983	24,711,162	26,419,114			
Central/Eastern Europe		2,433,953	2,181,461	2,524,728	2,978,424			
Czech Republic		299,767	312,073	342,037	357,376			
Estonia		40,125	26,268	25,906	36,008			
Hungary		249,859	230,371	242,192	256,357			
Latvia		34,912	25,918	27,219	35,794			
Lithuania		82,375	52,508	54,384	69,716			
Poland		657,423	621,581	682,019	761,582			
Russian Federation		994,898	838,921	1,069,232	1,372,237			
Slovakia		74,594	73,821	81,739	89,354			
Northern Europe		4,387,004	3,902,653	3,941,823	4,032,572			
Denmark		350,290	335,233	344,390	335,989			
Finland		220,552	213,831	214,958	228,490			
Iceland		26,354	20,599	19,747	19,094			
Ireland		372,535	335,319	304,677	293,654			
Norway		301,872	271,662	294,226	308,167			
Sweden		464,884	428,173	480,807	512,006			
United Kingdom		2,650,517	2,297,836	2,283,018	2,335,172			
Southern Europe		2,518,924	2,419,587	2,520,293	2,585,925			
Croatia		161,178	151,649	142,111	143,113			
Greece		349,115	328,778	319,467	315,987			
Malta		45,086	46,700	51,279	56,031			
Portugal		194,812	197,166	214,588	217,714			
Slovenia		154,382	147,442	150,015	161,765			
Spain		1,614,351	1,547,852	1,642,833	1,691,315			
Western Europe		13,079,387	13,540,694	13,996,316	14,845,638			
Austria		1,341,066	1,463,284	1,524,404	1,593,639			
Belgium		754,249	783,832	800,229	852,979			

Yearbook of Tourism Statistics, Data 2008 – 2012, 2014 Edition

ITALY

3. Arrivals of non-resident tourists in hotels and similar establishments, by nationality

	2008	2009	2010	2011	2012	Market share 2012	% Change 2012-2011
France	2,662,764	2,732,413	2,838,922	3,025,404			
Germany	6,138,269	6,289,216	6,456,004	6,809,122			
Luxembourg	51,796	54,839	54,209	56,938			
Netherlands	882,252	892,568	918,543	956,303			
Switzerland	1,248,991	1,324,542	1,404,005	1,551,253			
East Mediterranean Europe	**424,572**	**390,511**	**468,123**	**511,461**			
Cyprus	19,970	16,285	19,031	18,516			
Israel	234,508	222,325	252,876	264,895			
Turkey	170,094	151,901	196,216	228,050			
Other Europe	**1,222,910**	**1,111,077**	**1,259,879**	**1,465,094**			
Other countries of Europe	1,222,910	1,111,077	1,259,879	1,465,094			
MIDDLE EAST	**190,184**	**212,806**	**246,834**	**289,156**			
Egypt	35,489	37,951	39,664	38,335			
Other countries of Middle East	154,695	174,855	207,170	250,821			
SOUTH ASIA	**150,137**	**147,569**	**184,676**	**236,277**			
India	150,137	147,569	184,676	236,277			
NOT SPECIFIED	**487,199**	**520,275**	**499,474**	**529,880**			
Other countries of the World	487,199	520,275	499,474	529,880			

Yearbook of Tourism Statistics, Data 2008 – 2012, 2014 Edition

ITALY

4. Arrivals of non-resident tourists in all types of accommodation establishments, by nationality

	2008	2009	2010	2011	2012	Market share 2012	% Change 2012-2011
TOTAL	41,796,724	41,124,722	43,794,338	47,460,809			
AFRICA	281,938	277,994	289,502	323,857			
Southern Africa	68,960	63,038	71,950	84,255			
South Africa	68,960	63,038	71,950	84,255			
Other Africa	212,978	214,956	217,552	239,602			
Other countries of Africa	212,978	214,956	217,552	239,602			
AMERICAS	5,982,827	5,571,671	6,195,100	6,785,181			
North America	5,052,001	4,670,934	5,090,819	5,387,397			
Canada	635,182	588,776	670,055	708,380			
Mexico	183,172	153,481	185,244	212,345			
United States of America	4,233,647	3,928,677	4,235,520	4,466,672			
South America	930,826	900,737	1,104,281	1,397,784			
Argentina	175,907	190,837	231,503	297,233			
Brazil	478,562	436,377	580,610	757,691			
Venezuela	57,678	57,583	55,240	66,316			
Other countries of South America	218,679	215,940	236,928	276,544			
EAST ASIA AND THE PACIFIC	3,461,486	3,278,798	3,921,679	4,574,445			
North-East Asia	2,343,791	2,250,841	2,643,095	3,111,195			
China	716,545	727,570	965,857	1,342,518			
Japan	1,307,729	1,298,068	1,363,444	1,410,677			
Korea, Republic of	319,517	225,203	313,794	358,000			
Australasia	796,315	713,880	836,382	910,092			
Australia	683,627	613,799	729,960	803,884			
New Zealand	112,688	100,081	106,422	106,208			
Other East Asia and the Pacific	321,380	314,077	442,202	553,158			
Other countries of Asia	321,380	314,077	442,202	553,158			
EUROPE	31,167,898	31,044,562	32,383,435	34,630,439			
Central/Eastern Europe	3,092,554	2,833,442	3,234,612	3,766,341			
Czech Republic	522,719	540,417	584,478	612,930			
Estonia	46,646	31,158	31,398	41,453			
Hungary	375,956	335,402	350,577	367,577			
Latvia	40,231	30,731	32,855	43,591			
Lithuania	91,582	60,105	63,081	81,269			
Poland	840,259	811,024	888,472	989,436			
Russian Federation	1,046,199	894,659	1,140,432	1,474,137			
Slovakia	128,962	129,946	143,319	155,948			
Northern Europe	5,334,666	4,780,832	4,842,851	4,948,929			
Denmark	606,809	582,009	601,085	579,740			
Finland	255,242	249,324	251,453	269,455			
Iceland	31,506	24,337	23,868	22,552			
Ireland	443,657	402,495	365,193	351,383			
Norway	355,664	324,784	350,400	369,221			
Sweden	556,467	513,491	574,731	609,826			
United Kingdom	3,085,321	2,684,392	2,676,121	2,746,752			
Southern Europe	2,855,207	2,769,729	2,879,943	2,967,086			
Croatia	184,453	175,431	163,619	166,120			
Greece	375,660	355,853	344,641	342,634			
Malta	50,580	52,995	58,543	64,817			
Portugal	219,931	220,538	239,012	242,831			
Slovenia	204,729	203,988	206,354	220,852			
Spain	1,819,854	1,760,924	1,867,774	1,929,832			
Western Europe	18,063,820	18,980,303	19,502,832	20,753,343			
Austria	1,774,887	1,948,791	2,011,317	2,115,524			
Belgium	943,350	994,999	1,013,042	1,079,541			

Yearbook of Tourism Statistics, Data 2008 – 2012, 2014 Edition

ITALY

4. Arrivals of non-resident tourists in all types of accommodation establishments, by nationality

	2008	2009	2010	2011	2012	Market share 2012	% Change 2012-2011
France	3,215,689	3,332,807	3,449,866	3,689,634			
Germany	8,674,799	9,085,679	9,302,743	9,873,213			
Luxembourg	60,985	64,037	64,329	67,008			
Netherlands	1,792,595	1,836,907	1,851,034	1,933,447			
Switzerland	1,601,515	1,717,083	1,810,501	1,994,976			
East Mediterranean Europe	**465,390**	**434,714**	**520,028**	**568,428**			
Cyprus	21,178	17,388	20,569	19,958			
Israel	261,783	252,455	289,049	302,765			
Turkey	182,429	164,871	210,410	245,705			
Other Europe	**1,356,261**	**1,245,542**	**1,403,169**	**1,626,312**			
Other countries of Europe	1,356,261	1,245,542	1,403,169	1,626,312			
MIDDLE EAST	**203,093**	**226,341**	**261,281**	**306,390**			
Egypt	38,836	41,295	43,160	41,998			
Other countries of Middle East	164,257	185,046	218,121	264,392			
SOUTH ASIA	**160,055**	**157,708**	**197,152**	**251,631**			
India	160,055	157,708	197,152	251,631			
NOT SPECIFIED	**539,427**	**567,648**	**546,189**	**588,866**			
Other countries of the World	539,427	567,648	546,189	588,866			

Yearbook of Tourism Statistics, Data 2008 – 2012, 2014 Editic

ITALY

5. Overnight stays of non-resident tourists in hotels and similar establishments, by nationality

		2008	2009	2010	2011	2012	Market share 2012	% Change 2012-2011
TOTAL	(*)	110,491,709	106,828,579	111,551,526	120,014,027			
AFRICA		839,069	781,987	782,638	1,127,921			
Southern Africa		188,665	155,501	170,553	206,296			
South Africa		188,665	155,501	170,553	206,296			
Other Africa		650,404	626,486	612,085	921,625			
Other countries of Africa		650,404	626,486	612,085	921,625			
AMERICAS		13,194,994	12,259,124	13,412,419	14,774,746			
North America		11,065,913	10,195,123	10,979,562	11,795,941			
Canada		1,415,268	1,301,640	1,459,085	1,656,449			
Mexico		387,110	329,798	380,543	425,837			
United States of America		9,263,535	8,563,685	9,139,934	9,713,655			
South America		2,129,081	2,064,001	2,432,857	2,978,805			
Argentina		422,665	433,805	516,089	641,449			
Brazil		1,059,437	976,487	1,247,397	1,582,610			
Venezuela		149,331	153,638	141,684	165,396			
Other countries of South America		497,648	500,071	527,687	589,350			
EAST ASIA AND THE PACIFIC		6,390,073	6,033,692	6,925,435	7,924,700			
North-East Asia		4,020,243	3,868,385	4,323,597	4,939,757			
China		1,101,656	1,120,082	1,404,270	1,895,228			
Japan		2,395,971	2,341,372	2,414,679	2,471,480			
Korea, Republic of		522,616	406,931	504,648	573,049			
Australasia		1,616,225	1,434,028	1,662,709	1,838,566			
Australia		1,399,710	1,243,145	1,451,206	1,624,804			
New Zealand		216,515	190,883	211,503	213,762			
Other East Asia and the Pacific		753,605	731,279	939,129	1,146,377			
Other countries of Asia		753,605	731,279	939,129	1,146,377			
EUROPE		87,809,408	85,394,447	87,994,204	93,501,667			
Central/Eastern Europe		8,594,328	7,928,309	9,119,265	10,368,002			
Czech Republic		1,268,887	1,375,188	1,478,895	1,542,005			
Estonia		110,717	80,156	87,842	115,715			
Hungary		833,480	748,646	765,236	804,953			
Latvia		106,741	86,140	85,843	102,640			
Lithuania		191,189	142,040	148,652	185,029			
Poland		2,312,769	2,216,059	2,412,767	2,487,718			
Russian Federation		3,440,569	2,965,533	3,801,556	4,752,783			
Slovakia		329,976	314,547	338,474	377,159			
Northern Europe		16,454,468	14,317,327	14,231,652	14,809,878			
Denmark		1,321,890	1,269,074	1,287,186	1,268,999			
Finland		783,467	740,426	733,575	779,682			
Iceland		103,585	80,874	71,863	70,991			
Ireland		1,512,182	1,300,099	1,165,921	1,119,810			
Norway		1,060,651	949,952	992,868	1,039,100			
Sweden		1,682,418	1,537,476	1,703,565	1,825,339			
United Kingdom		9,990,275	8,439,426	8,276,674	8,705,957			
Southern Europe		6,811,042	6,556,123	6,710,662	6,885,335			
Croatia		482,137	453,271	412,143	393,114			
Greece		957,336	891,998	853,639	829,791			
Malta		156,082	148,209	171,231	175,554			
Portugal		582,830	560,775	568,408	581,631			
Slovenia		442,693	421,663	427,894	456,855			
Spain		4,189,964	4,080,207	4,277,347	4,448,390			
Western Europe		50,812,758	52,011,396	52,891,926	55,747,098			
Austria		4,711,025	5,085,735	5,273,070	5,584,362			
Belgium		3,008,502	3,094,207	3,088,377	3,229,371			

Yearbook of Tourism Statistics, Data 2008 – 2012, 2014 Edition

ITALY

5. Overnight stays of non-resident tourists in hotels and similar establishments, by nationality

	2008	2009	2010	2011	2012	Market share 2012	% Change 2012-2011
France	7,663,227	7,780,100	7,956,900	8,621,882			
Germany	27,361,414	27,768,674	28,091,376	29,306,486			
Luxembourg	238,942	253,555	249,711	264,721			
Netherlands	3,129,654	3,160,459	3,193,313	3,267,142			
Switzerland	4,699,994	4,868,666	5,039,179	5,473,134			
East Mediterranean Europe	**1,159,326**	**1,075,768**	**1,270,977**	**1,408,162**			
Cyprus	61,420	52,742	61,417	58,012			
Israel	624,896	605,880	716,764	779,624			
Turkey	473,010	417,146	492,796	570,526			
Other Europe	**3,977,486**	**3,505,524**	**3,769,722**	**4,283,192**			
Other countries of Europe	3,977,486	3,505,524	3,769,722	4,283,192			
MIDDLE EAST	**664,245**	**708,535**	**773,622**	**886,737**			
Egypt	132,421	135,776	140,341	146,560			
Other countries of Middle East	531,824	572,759	633,281	740,177			
SOUTH ASIA	**332,124**	**337,851**	**387,672**	**479,236**			
India	332,124	337,851	387,672	479,236			
NOT SPECIFIED	**1,261,796**	**1,312,943**	**1,275,536**	**1,319,020**			
Other countries of the World	1,261,796	1,312,943	1,275,536	1,319,020			

Yearbook of Tourism Statistics, Data 2008 – 2012, 2014 Edition

ITALY

6. Overnight stays of non-resident tourists in all types of accommodation establishments, by nationality

	2008	2009	2010	2011	2012	Market share 2012	% Change 2012-2011
TOTAL	161,797,434	159,493,866	165,202,498	176,474,062			
AFRICA	1,104,421	1,028,095	1,027,597	1,501,871			
Southern Africa	229,829	191,669	210,938	255,991			
South Africa	229,829	191,669	210,938	255,991			
Other Africa	874,592	836,426	816,659	1,245,880			
Other countries of Africa	874,592	836,426	816,659	1,245,880			
AMERICAS	15,551,410	14,513,549	15,883,627	17,500,991			
North America	13,056,361	12,080,237	13,046,664	14,038,324			
Canada	1,739,697	1,612,960	1,798,679	2,024,178			
Mexico	450,830	387,160	440,692	498,265			
United States of America	10,865,834	10,080,117	10,807,293	11,515,881			
South America	2,495,049	2,433,312	2,836,963	3,462,667			
Argentina	501,713	519,315	609,771	757,589			
Brazil	1,226,481	1,137,182	1,427,733	1,809,011			
Venezuela	174,117	178,425	163,986	191,695			
Other countries of South America	592,738	598,390	635,473	704,372			
EAST ASIA AND THE PACIFIC	7,382,734	6,970,551	7,961,682	9,088,145			
North-East Asia	4,440,341	4,287,190	4,733,489	5,416,203			
China	1,221,174	1,254,039	1,564,035	2,089,115			
Japan	2,595,488	2,534,836	2,593,846	2,665,424			
Korea, Republic of	623,679	498,315	575,608	661,664			
Australasia	2,086,210	1,846,456	2,147,422	2,367,349			
Australia	1,764,169	1,572,543	1,861,752	2,081,771			
New Zealand	322,041	273,913	285,670	285,578			
Other East Asia and the Pacific	856,183	836,905	1,080,771	1,304,593			
Other countries of Asia	856,183	836,905	1,080,771	1,304,593			
EUROPE	135,071,788	134,234,320	137,485,494	145,229,651			
Central/Eastern Europe	12,814,604	11,995,567	13,662,293	15,195,030			
Czech Republic	2,737,307	2,841,017	3,077,661	3,168,776			
Estonia	132,794	100,553	108,633	134,152			
Hungary	1,610,168	1,366,001	1,453,372	1,482,498			
Latvia	130,006	109,296	111,807	135,326			
Lithuania	229,048	174,487	186,380	231,275			
Poland	3,519,711	3,400,700	3,736,189	3,883,908			
Russian Federation	3,730,458	3,294,957	4,208,604	5,318,880			
Slovakia	725,112	708,556	779,647	840,215			
Northern Europe	22,369,491	19,652,109	19,686,308	20,103,858			
Denmark	3,374,085	3,208,729	3,311,712	3,139,703			
Finland	948,638	901,719	903,041	958,010			
Iceland	131,455	96,917	89,837	84,211			
Ireland	1,952,516	1,706,869	1,533,856	1,448,777			
Norway	1,393,464	1,255,530	1,316,970	1,366,480			
Sweden	2,211,562	2,013,300	2,193,686	2,311,576			
United Kingdom	12,357,771	10,469,045	10,337,206	10,795,101			
Southern Europe	8,213,873	7,989,916	8,146,446	8,350,266			
Croatia	657,415	640,887	559,823	526,812			
Greece	1,077,392	1,022,691	971,217	952,829			
Malta	183,753	177,540	202,203	207,217			
Portugal	698,721	651,567	671,622	680,305			
Slovenia	668,601	664,166	678,568	718,615			
Spain	4,927,991	4,833,065	5,063,013	5,264,488			
Western Europe	85,253,357	88,733,229	89,590,427	94,427,763			
Austria	7,482,993	8,078,701	8,226,147	8,670,900			
Belgium	4,258,189	4,434,026	4,425,339	4,614,934			

Copyright © 2014, World Tourism Organization (UNWTO)

Yearbook of Tourism Statistics, Data 2008 – 2012, 2014 Edition

ITALY

6. Overnight stays of non-resident tourists in all types of accommodation establishments, by nationality

	2008	2009	2010	2011	2012	Market share 2012	% Change 2012-2011
France	10,158,629	10,447,586	10,623,637	11,432,007			
Germany	45,401,981	47,278,488	47,801,927	50,199,797			
Luxembourg	293,531	309,707	308,829	320,997			
Netherlands	10,675,969	10,875,329	10,674,451	11,043,799			
Switzerland	6,982,065	7,309,392	7,530,097	8,145,329			
East Mediterranean Europe	**1,340,620**	**1,267,778**	**1,491,744**	**1,648,181**			
Cyprus	66,864	57,348	67,900	63,995			
Israel	741,852	734,500	871,404	936,832			
Turkey	531,904	475,930	552,440	647,354			
Other Europe	**5,079,843**	**4,595,721**	**4,908,276**	**5,504,553**			
Other countries of Europe	5,079,843	4,595,721	4,908,276	5,504,553			
MIDDLE EAST	**777,548**	**818,238**	**874,432**	**1,001,851**			
Egypt	170,608	170,842	170,056	181,312			
Other countries of Middle East	606,940	647,396	704,376	820,539			
SOUTH ASIA	**389,659**	**394,709**	**461,311**	**554,886**			
India	389,659	394,709	461,311	554,886			
NOT SPECIFIED	**1,519,874**	**1,534,404**	**1,508,355**	**1,596,667**			
Other countries of the World	1,519,874	1,534,404	1,508,355	1,596,667			

Yearbook of Tourism Statistics, Data 2008 – 2012, 2014 Edition

JAMAICA

1. Arrivals of non-resident tourists at national borders, by country of residence

		2008	2009	2010	2011	2012	Market share 2012	% Change 2012-2011
TOTAL	(*)	1,767,271	1,831,097	1,921,678	1,951,752	1,986,085	100.00	1.76
AFRICA		1,213	1,237	1,169	1,200	1,651	0.08	37.58
Other Africa		1,213	1,237	1,169	1,200	1,651	0.08	37.58
All countries of Africa		1,213	1,237	1,169	1,200	1,651	0.08	37.58
AMERICAS		1,470,488	1,542,976	1,639,875	1,687,308	1,750,890	88.16	3.77
Caribbean		64,467	62,823	56,031	63,360	62,196	3.13	-1.84
Antigua and Barbuda		2,799	2,554	2,235	2,290	2,457	0.12	7.29
Aruba		508	400	398	409	496	0.02	21.27
Bahamas		4,378	5,031	4,884	5,999	5,481	0.28	-8.63
Barbados		6,107	5,027	4,469	5,422	5,315	0.27	-1.97
Bermuda		3,393	3,369	3,112	2,710	2,683	0.14	-1.00
Bonaire		1						
British Virgin Islands		966	1,025	1,054	1,031	1,205	0.06	16.88
Cayman Islands		20,287	23,384	18,409	18,035	16,536	0.83	-8.31
Cuba		839	1,067	562	646	748	0.04	15.79
Curaçao		1,910	1,279	778	893	886	0.04	-0.78
Dominica		584	543	387	418	434	0.02	3.83
Dominican Republic		1,595	1,111	1,038	1,293	1,298	0.07	0.39
Grenada		1,010	640	450	527	518	0.03	-1.71
Guadeloupe		194	121	185	322	448	0.02	39.13
Haiti		273	288	447	392	511	0.03	30.36
Montserrat		146	154	149	143	181	0.01	26.57
Puerto Rico		1,693	1,346	1,447	1,486	1,559	0.08	4.91
Saint Kitts and Nevis		1,068	1,103	950	913	981	0.05	7.45
Saint Lucia		1,712	1,308	990	1,055	1,157	0.06	9.67
Saint Vincent and the Grenadines		841	595	445	676	612	0.03	-9.47
Sint Maarten		950	789	941	1,079	1,352	0.07	25.30
Trinidad and Tobago		10,621	9,622	10,330	15,513	14,947	0.75	-3.65
Turks and Caicos Islands		1,815	1,445	1,545	1,522	1,804	0.09	18.53
Other countries of the Caribbean		777	622	826	586	587	0.03	0.17
Central America		3,609	3,441	3,251	3,655	4,635	0.23	26.81
Belize		582	592	481	612	670	0.03	9.48
Costa Rica		812	799	758	846	1,328	0.07	56.97
El Salvador		299	177	142	174	180	0.01	3.45
Guatemala		284	348	527	501	628	0.03	25.35
Honduras		361	156	131	203	159	0.01	-21.67
Nicaragua		90	85	76	102	60	0.00	-41.18
Panama		1,181	1,284	1,136	1,217	1,610	0.08	32.29
North America		1,390,737	1,465,338	1,570,118	1,606,627	1,663,208	83.74	3.52
Canada		236,193	290,307	325,191	378,938	403,200	20.30	6.40
Mexico		3,602	2,187	1,984	2,124	2,339	0.12	10.12
United States of America		1,150,942	1,172,844	1,242,943	1,225,565	1,257,669	63.32	2.62
South America		11,675	11,374	10,475	13,666	20,851	1.05	52.58
Argentina		1,762	1,695	1,779	2,168	3,739	0.19	72.46
Bolivia		52	34	51	56	28	0.00	-50.00
Brazil		1,865	1,550	1,683	1,597	2,071	0.10	29.68
Chile		812	893	741	1,023	3,654	0.18	257.18
Colombia		1,045	1,001	1,110	1,489	4,062	0.20	172.80
Ecuador		1,865	1,844	1,481	2,979	2,464	0.12	-17.29
Guyana		2,295	2,079	1,827	2,376	2,288	0.12	-3.70
Paraguay		17	30	22	58	40	0.00	-31.03
Peru		482	465	393	485	791	0.04	63.09
Suriname		469	431	441	480	500	0.03	4.17
Uruguay		148	190	139	168	381	0.02	126.79
Venezuela		852	1,145	786	759	750	0.04	-1.19

Yearbook of Tourism Statistics, Data 2008 – 2012, 2014 Edition

JAMAICA

1. Arrivals of non-resident tourists at national borders, by country of residence

	2008	2009	2010	2011	2012	Market share 2012	% Change 2012-2011
Other countries of South America	11	17	22	28	83	0.00	196.43
EAST ASIA AND THE PACIFIC	**7,863**	**7,138**	**6,760**	**7,429**	**8,220**	**0.41**	**10.65**
North-East Asia	**4,110**	**4,013**	**3,703**	**4,281**	**4,681**	**0.24**	**9.34**
China	935	1,142	1,302	1,703	2,102	0.11	23.43
Japan	2,846	2,511	1,950	2,027	2,092	0.11	3.21
Korea, Republic of	211	291	375	477	350	0.02	-26.62
Taiwan, Province of China	118	69	76	74	137	0.01	85.14
South-East Asia	**559**	**450**	**587**	**424**	**481**	**0.02**	**13.44**
Philippines	441	322	479	323	364	0.02	12.69
Singapore	118	128	108	101	117	0.01	15.84
Australasia	**2,783**	**2,218**	**2,121**	**2,269**	**2,597**	**0.13**	**14.46**
Australia	2,439	1,903	1,869	2,040	2,254	0.11	10.49
New Zealand	344	315	252	229	343	0.02	49.78
Other East Asia and the Pacific	**411**	**457**	**349**	**455**	**461**	**0.02**	**1.32**
Other countries of Asia	411	457	349	455	461	0.02	1.32
EUROPE	**286,142**	**277,931**	**272,139**	**253,749**	**223,268**	**11.24**	**-12.01**
Central/Eastern Europe	**5,041**	**4,336**	**4,533**	**4,893**	**4,350**	**0.22**	**-11.10**
Czech Republic/Slovakia	680	578	473	772	615	0.03	-20.34
Hungary	722	276	389	286	317	0.02	10.84
Poland	1,326	1,294	1,299	1,443	1,199	0.06	-16.91
Russian Federation	1,881	1,744	1,945	1,976	1,701	0.09	-13.92
Ukraine	432	444	427	416	518	0.03	24.52
Northern Europe	**195,986**	**191,225**	**190,825**	**179,726**	**151,433**	**7.62**	**-15.74**
Denmark	851	794	772	648	615	0.03	-5.09
Finland	404	526	427	451	427	0.02	-5.32
Ireland	3,431	2,838	2,737	2,459	2,071	0.10	-15.78
Norway	1,061	958	915	1,054	1,030	0.05	-2.28
Sweden	1,803	1,597	1,619	1,607	2,059	0.10	28.13
United Kingdom	188,436	184,512	184,355	173,507	145,231	7.31	-16.30
Southern Europe	**40,112**	**36,703**	**34,107**	**23,492**	**18,136**	**0.91**	**-22.80**
Greece	390	291	249	273	208	0.01	-23.81
Italy	14,563	14,588	13,700	11,700	9,672	0.49	-17.33
Portugal	9,649	9,056	10,076	4,686	3,906	0.20	-16.65
Spain	15,510	12,768	10,082	6,833	4,350	0.22	-36.34
Western Europe	**41,168**	**42,848**	**40,233**	**43,079**	**46,763**	**2.35**	**8.55**
Austria	2,252	2,623	2,641	2,545	2,377	0.12	-6.60
Belgium	6,187	6,610	5,228	5,276	4,882	0.25	-7.47
France	3,916	3,779	3,762	4,748	9,253	0.47	94.88
Germany	18,962	20,220	18,857	19,939	20,236	1.02	1.49
Luxembourg	210	248	207	212	202	0.01	-4.72
Netherlands	7,541	7,023	6,677	7,200	6,714	0.34	-6.75
Switzerland	2,100	2,345	2,861	3,159	3,099	0.16	-1.90
East Mediterranean Europe	**1,442**	**1,132**	**824**	**704**	**840**	**0.04**	**19.32**
Israel	1,135	879	683	597	639	0.03	7.04
Turkey	307	253	141	107	201	0.01	87.85
Other Europe	**2,393**	**1,687**	**1,617**	**1,855**	**1,746**	**0.09**	**-5.88**
Other countries of Europe	2,393	1,687	1,617	1,855	1,746	0.09	-5.88
MIDDLE EAST	**577**	**532**	**542**	**649**	**608**	**0.03**	**-6.32**
Saudi Arabia	28	19	16	36	31	0.00	-13.89
Other countries of Middle East	549	513	526	613	577	0.03	-5.87
SOUTH ASIA	**923**	**1,248**	**1,152**	**1,362**	**1,397**	**0.07**	**2.57**
India	904	1,232	1,127	1,330	1,375	0.07	3.38
Pakistan	19	16	25	32	22	0.00	-31.25
NOT SPECIFIED	**65**	**35**	**41**	**55**	**51**	**0.00**	**-7.27**
Other countries of the World	65	35	41	55	51	0.00	-7.27

JAMAICA

6. Overnight stays of non-resident tourists in all types of accommodation establishments, by country of residence

		2008	2009	2010	2011	2012	Market share 2012	% Change 2012-2011
TOTAL	(*)	15,014,185	15,535,167	15,903,420	15,932,132	15,218,824	100.00	-4.48
AMERICAS		11,074,891	11,655,659	12,155,998	12,430,885	12,910,392	84.83	3.86
Caribbean		435,559	426,111	395,983	410,946	421,481	2.77	2.56
All countries of the Caribbean		435,559	426,111	395,983	410,946	421,481	2.77	2.56
North America		10,510,569	11,110,489	11,641,691	11,885,744	12,299,504	80.82	3.48
Canada, United States		10,510,569	11,110,489	11,641,691	11,885,744	12,299,504	80.82	3.48
Other Americas		128,763	119,059	118,324	134,195	189,407	1.24	41.14
Other countries of the Americas	(*)	128,763	119,059	118,324	134,195	189,407	1.24	41.14
EUROPE		3,808,593	3,740,515	3,608,147	3,344,357	2,151,890	14.14	-35.66
Other Europe		3,808,593	3,740,515	3,608,147	3,344,357	2,151,890	14.14	-35.66
All countries of Europe	(*)	3,808,593	3,740,515	3,608,147	3,344,357	2,151,890	14.14	-35.66
NOT SPECIFIED		130,701	138,993	139,275	156,890	156,542	1.03	-0.22
Other countries of the World		130,701	138,993	139,275	156,890	156,542	1.03	-0.22

Yearbook of Tourism Statistics, Data 2008 – 2012, 2014 Edition

JAPAN

2. Arrivals of non-resident visitors at national borders, by nationality

		2008	2009	2010	2011	2012	Market share 2012	% Change 2012-2011
TOTAL	(*)	8,350,835	6,789,658	8,611,175	6,218,752	8,358,105	100.00	34.40
AFRICA		20,542	17,219	19,076	16,777	21,074	0.25	25.61
Southern Africa		5,610	4,290	4,635	3,942	5,708	0.07	44.80
South Africa		5,610	4,290	4,635	3,942	5,708	0.07	44.80
West Africa		2,272	2,090	2,333	1,834	2,541	0.03	38.55
Ghana		859	792	957	799	1,095	0.01	37.05
Nigeria		1,413	1,298	1,376	1,035	1,446	0.02	39.71
Other Africa		12,660	10,839	12,108	11,001	12,825	0.15	16.58
Other countries of Africa		12,660	10,839	12,108	11,001	12,825	0.15	16.58
AMERICAS		1,005,692	908,098	945,377	716,808	927,552	11.10	29.40
Central America				357	291	346	0.00	18.90
El Salvador				357	291	346	0.00	18.90
North America		960,846	869,129	899,785	680,266	870,566	10.42	27.97
Canada		168,307	152,756	153,303	101,299	135,355	1.62	33.62
Mexico		24,194	16,454	19,248	13,080	18,502	0.22	41.45
United States of America		768,345	699,919	727,234	565,887	716,709	8.58	26.65
South America		37,369	32,398	38,137	31,038	49,870	0.60	60.67
Argentina		4,358	4,379	4,896	3,768	5,239	0.06	39.04
Bolivia		459	459	518	384	477	0.01	24.22
Brazil		20,981	16,899	21,393	18,470	32,111	0.38	73.85
Chile		2,764	2,667	3,053	2,579	3,538	0.04	37.18
Colombia		3,181	2,973	3,052	2,238	3,308	0.04	47.81
Ecuador		890	683	845	480	754	0.01	57.08
Peru		2,370	2,164	2,452	1,857	2,306	0.03	24.18
Venezuela		2,366	2,174	1,928	1,262	2,137	0.03	69.33
Other Americas		7,477	6,571	7,098	5,213	6,770	0.08	29.87
Other countries of the Americas		7,477	6,571	7,098	5,213	6,770	0.08	29.87
EAST ASIA AND THE PACIFIC		6,306,921	4,940,971	6,653,648	4,796,321	6,488,700	77.63	35.28
North-East Asia		5,333,609	4,092,862	5,660,930	4,083,956	5,447,709	65.18	33.39
China		1,000,416	1,006,085	1,412,875	1,043,246	1,425,100	17.05	36.60
Hong Kong, China		550,190	449,568	508,691	364,865	481,665	5.76	32.01
Korea, Republic of		2,382,397	1,586,772	2,439,816	1,658,073	2,042,775	24.44	23.20
Macao, China			17,199	21,330	13,292	19,040	0.23	43.24
Mongolia		10,378	8,946	9,940	10,506	13,376	0.16	27.32
Taiwan, Province of China		1,390,228	1,024,292	1,268,278	993,974	1,465,753	17.54	47.46
South-East Asia		660,119	592,793	722,112	515,154	789,317	9.44	53.22
Brunei Darussalam		1,150	1,138	1,388	971	1,378	0.02	41.92
Cambodia		2,701	3,008	3,189	3,069	3,662	0.04	19.32
Indonesia		66,593	63,617	80,632	61,911	101,460	1.21	63.88
Lao People's Democratic Republic		2,160	2,145	2,209	2,111	2,676	0.03	26.76
Malaysia		105,663	89,509	114,519	81,516	130,183	1.56	59.70
Myanmar		5,106	4,905	5,095	5,106	6,924	0.08	35.61
Philippines		82,177	71,485	77,377	63,099	85,037	1.02	34.77
Singapore		167,894	145,224	180,960	111,354	142,201	1.70	27.70
Thailand		191,881	177,541	214,881	144,969	260,640	3.12	79.79
Viet Nam		34,794	34,221	41,862	41,048	55,156	0.66	34.37
Australasia		275,713	243,226	257,812	186,574	238,257	2.85	27.70
Australia		242,031	211,659	225,751	162,578	206,404	2.47	26.96
New Zealand		33,682	31,567	32,061	23,996	31,853	0.38	32.74
Other East Asia and the Pacific		37,480	12,090	12,794	10,637	13,417	0.16	26.14
Other countries of Asia		34,205	9,103	9,734	8,061	10,161	0.12	26.05
Other countries of Oceania		3,275	2,987	3,060	2,576	3,256	0.04	26.40
EUROPE		909,626	820,128	877,284	582,787	796,761	9.53	36.72
Central/Eastern Europe		100,186	76,200	84,204	58,191	84,353	1.01	44.96

370

JAPAN

2. Arrivals of non-resident visitors at national borders, by nationality

	2008	2009	2010	2011	2012	Market share 2012	% Change 2012-2011
Bulgaria	2,742	2,434	2,238	1,783	2,345	0.03	31.52
Czech Republic	5,792	4,943	5,319	4,525	5,485	0.07	21.22
Hungary	4,821	4,455	4,371	3,182	4,531	0.05	42.39
Poland	10,265	8,638	10,253	7,451	10,668	0.13	43.18
Romania	3,698	3,550	4,664	3,227	4,797	0.06	48.65
Russian Federation	66,270	46,952	51,457	33,793	50,176	0.60	48.48
Slovakia	2,285	1,786	2,192	1,356	2,161	0.03	59.37
Ukraine	4,313	3,442	3,710	2,874	4,190	0.05	45.79
Northern Europe	**294,565**	**259,062**	**266,428**	**200,414**	**256,112**	**3.06**	**27.79**
Denmark	14,486	13,116	14,606	10,821	13,594	0.16	25.63
Finland	20,025	17,797	16,960	10,943	15,529	0.19	41.91
Iceland			589	546	732	0.01	34.07
Ireland	12,513	10,450	10,738	8,294	10,358	0.12	24.89
Norway	10,848	9,855	10,302	7,905	11,447	0.14	44.81
Sweden	30,129	26,384	29,188	21,806	30,458	0.36	39.68
United Kingdom	206,564	181,460	184,045	140,099	173,994	2.08	24.19
Southern Europe	**113,569**	**116,229**	**123,728**	**65,312**	**101,075**	**1.21**	**54.76**
Croatia	1,700	1,325	1,402	918	1,335	0.02	45.42
Greece	4,494	4,350	4,363	2,459	3,074	0.04	25.01
Italy	56,243	59,607	62,394	34,035	51,801	0.62	52.20
Montenegro			70	41	65	0.00	58.54
Portugal	10,280	8,463	10,313	6,227	8,408	0.10	35.02
Serbia			973	754	1,185	0.01	57.16
Serbia and Montenegro			137	64			
Spain	40,852	42,484	44,076	20,814	35,207	0.42	69.15
Western Europe	**361,864**	**333,803**	**365,507**	**235,749**	**320,558**	**3.84**	**35.97**
Austria	13,453	13,684	14,440	8,539	11,633	0.14	36.23
Belgium	15,773	13,899	15,981	10,708	14,608	0.17	36.42
France	147,580	141,251	151,011	95,438	130,142	1.56	36.36
Germany	126,207	110,692	124,360	80,772	108,898	1.30	34.82
Luxembourg			873	432	682	0.01	57.87
Netherlands	34,487	31,186	32,837	23,450	30,266	0.36	29.07
Switzerland	24,364	23,091	26,005	16,410	24,329	0.29	48.26
East Mediterranean Europe	**22,903**	**20,043**	**24,118**	**13,508**	**20,921**	**0.25**	**54.88**
Israel	13,173	12,205	14,189	6,931	10,413	0.12	50.24
Turkey	9,730	7,838	9,929	6,577	10,508	0.13	59.77
Other Europe	**16,539**	**14,791**	**13,299**	**9,613**	**13,742**	**0.16**	**42.95**
Other countries of Europe	16,539	14,791	13,299	9,613	13,742	0.16	42.95
MIDDLE EAST	**3,956**	**7,332**	**10,448**	**7,106**	**10,706**	**0.13**	**50.66**
Egypt	3,956	3,402	3,589	2,584	3,651	0.04	41.29
Lebanon			935	611	820	0.01	34.21
Saudi Arabia		2,750	3,749	2,866	4,208	0.05	46.82
United Arab Emirates		1,180	2,175	1,045	2,027	0.02	93.97
SOUTH ASIA	**102,991**	**95,270**	**104,679**	**98,460**	**112,814**	**1.35**	**14.58**
Bangladesh	6,168	6,360	6,213	6,118	6,310	0.08	3.14
India	67,323	58,918	66,819	59,354	68,914	0.82	16.11
Iran, Islamic Republic of	4,384	4,898	4,831	3,787	4,187	0.05	10.56
Nepal	8,253	9,221	9,484	11,041	13,082	0.16	18.49
Pakistan	7,328	7,335	7,762	8,120	9,196	0.11	13.25
Sri Lanka	9,535	8,538	9,570	10,040	11,125	0.13	10.81
NOT SPECIFIED	**1,107**	**640**	**663**	**493**	**498**	**0.01**	**1.01**
Other countries of the World	1,107	640	663	493	498	0.01	1.01

JORDAN

1. Arrivals of non-resident tourists at national borders, by nationality

	2008	2009	2010	2011	2012	Market share 2012	% Change 2012-2011
TOTAL	3,728,726	3,788,890	4,207,408	3,959,654	4,162,367	100.00	5.12
AFRICA	49,884	46,387	49,762	49,947	55,002	1.32	10.12
East Africa	3,019	3,587	4,666	4,342	6,913	0.17	59.21
Djibouti	35	49	26	25	42	0.00	68.00
Eritrea	373	358	407	367	346	0.01	-5.72
Ethiopia	1,454	2,113	3,106	2,264	4,581	0.11	102.34
Kenya	465	486	599	1,191	1,253	0.03	5.21
Mauritius	160	234	296	299	431	0.01	44.15
Somalia	532	347	232	196	260	0.01	32.65
Central Africa	122	92	164	363	620	0.01	70.80
Chad	122	92	164	363	620	0.01	70.80
North Africa	35,207	32,490	34,354	32,072	32,931	0.79	2.68
Algeria	6,854	6,166	6,270	7,400	9,330	0.22	26.08
Morocco	4,850	4,782	4,293	3,337	4,024	0.10	20.59
Sudan	18,330	17,589	19,511	17,843	15,589	0.37	-12.63
Tunisia	5,173	3,953	4,280	3,492	3,988	0.10	14.20
Southern Africa	9,435	8,072	8,193	9,792	10,595	0.25	8.20
South Africa	9,435	8,072	8,193	9,792	10,595	0.25	8.20
West Africa	908	739	449	581	695	0.02	19.62
Mauritania	312	229	10	16	15	0.00	-6.25
Nigeria	353	448	364	478	584	0.01	22.18
Senegal	243	62	75	87	96	0.00	10.34
Other Africa	1,193	1,407	1,936	2,797	3,248	0.08	16.12
Other countries of Africa	1,193	1,407	1,936	2,797	3,248	0.08	16.12
AMERICAS	200,371	189,776	215,121	189,283	198,631	4.77	4.94
North America	186,163	177,563	194,439	168,862	174,639	4.20	3.42
Canada	19,422	18,682	34,960	27,785	28,512	0.68	2.62
Mexico	4,863	2,944	5,373	3,565	4,703	0.11	31.92
United States of America	161,878	155,937	154,106	137,512	141,424	3.40	2.84
South America	9,774	8,691	16,222	15,582	18,681	0.45	19.89
Argentina	2,565	2,111	3,172	2,446	3,507	0.08	43.38
Brazil	4,561	4,495	8,215	8,317	9,133	0.22	9.81
Chile	105	75	1,952	1,794	1,862	0.04	3.79
Colombia	1,660	1,244	1,510	1,835	2,810	0.07	53.13
Venezuela	883	766	1,373	1,190	1,369	0.03	15.04
Other Americas	4,434	3,522	4,460	4,839	5,311	0.13	9.75
Other countries of the Americas	4,434	3,522	4,460	4,839	5,311	0.13	9.75
EAST ASIA AND THE PACIFIC	146,029	138,404	148,981	154,149	174,733	4.20	13.35
North-East Asia	42,127	35,239	49,738	46,348	50,881	1.22	9.78
China	13,007	12,594	13,882	12,118	12,389	0.30	2.24
Hong Kong, China	82	200	436	1,931	2,151	0.05	11.39
Japan	13,233	12,506	18,779	12,480	14,823	0.36	18.77
Korea, Dem. People's Republic of	58	25	14	52	10	0.00	-80.77
Korea, Republic of	13,221	8,297	14,307	17,678	18,101	0.43	2.39
Taiwan, Province of China	2,526	1,617	2,320	2,089	3,407	0.08	63.09
South-East Asia	77,810	76,496	64,716	78,892	95,221	2.29	20.70
Brunei Darussalam			247	312	399	0.01	27.88
Indonesia	41,626	39,165	32,282	39,551	41,149	0.99	4.04
Malaysia	7,207	6,922	11,890	15,585	22,855	0.55	46.65
Philippines	22,641	25,249	11,893	13,058	15,745	0.38	20.58
Singapore	3,841	2,373	4,544	5,410	7,647	0.18	41.35
Thailand	2,082	2,651	3,860	4,976	7,393	0.18	48.57
Viet Nam	413	136			33	0.00	
Australasia	25,539	25,952	33,716	28,120	27,114	0.65	-3.58
Australia	21,311	21,620	28,420	23,926	23,178	0.56	-3.13

372

JORDAN

1. Arrivals of non-resident tourists at national borders, by nationality

	2008	2009	2010	2011	2012	Market share 2012	% Change 2012-2011
New Zealand	4,228	4,332	5,296	4,194	3,936	0.09	-6.15
Melanesia	**193**	**347**	**418**	**268**	**261**	**0.01**	**-2.61**
Fiji	193	347	418	268	261	0.01	-2.61
Other East Asia and the Pacific	**360**	**370**	**393**	**521**	**1,256**	**0.03**	**141.07**
Other countries of Asia	360	370	393	521	1,256	0.03	141.07
EUROPE	**657,628**	**602,394**	**744,992**	**626,886**	**590,204**	**14.18**	**-5.85**
Central/Eastern Europe	**65,433**	**48,230**	**69,403**	**64,738**	**66,191**	**1.59**	**2.24**
Belarus			1,096	1,091	1,216	0.03	11.46
Bulgaria	2,755	2,151	2,051	1,855	1,815	0.04	-2.16
Czech Republic	3,798	2,802	2,738	2,592	2,356	0.06	-9.10
Hungary	2,794	1,978	5,857	4,360	4,121	0.10	-5.48
Poland	16,288	9,073	9,944	10,513	11,904	0.29	13.23
Romania	3,732	3,428	4,437	4,536	4,195	0.10	-7.52
Russian Federation	24,833	20,777	29,292	25,173	25,724	0.62	2.19
Slovakia	2,035	1,749	1,087	1,672	1,126	0.03	-32.66
Ukraine	7,878	5,302	7,608	7,780	8,647	0.21	11.14
Other countries Central/East Europe	1,320	970	5,293	5,166	5,087	0.12	-1.53
Northern Europe	**90,871**	**101,601**	**109,933**	**113,995**	**110,311**	**2.65**	**-3.23**
Denmark	4,635	6,057	8,730	11,840	8,944	0.21	-24.46
Finland	5,160	6,498	4,808	3,189	3,147	0.08	-1.32
Iceland	188	186	210	261	294	0.01	12.64
Ireland	3,750	3,715	4,816	3,950	4,262	0.10	7.90
Norway	4,752	7,072	7,815	12,182	8,838	0.21	-27.45
Sweden	11,062	14,902	16,373	15,066	14,981	0.36	-0.56
United Kingdom	61,324	63,171	67,181	67,507	69,845	1.68	3.46
Southern Europe	**99,827**	**84,909**	**115,546**	**68,713**	**76,725**	**1.84**	**11.66**
Bosnia and Herzegovina	868	708	801	612	639	0.02	4.41
Croatia	1,355	864	1,420	1,155	973	0.02	-15.76
Greece	5,970	4,768	5,222	3,351	3,368	0.08	0.51
Holy See	86	136					
Italy	41,832	43,529	57,747	36,484	39,631	0.95	8.63
Malta	244	229	306	264	384	0.01	45.45
Portugal	4,540	3,528	5,203	2,573	2,697	0.06	4.82
Serbia					1,370	0.03	
Serbia and Montenegro	3,150	573	86				
Slovenia	2,020	1,318	1,688	983	1,195	0.03	21.57
Spain	39,762	29,256	42,657	22,944	25,764	0.62	12.29
TFYR of Macedonia			304	201	416	0.01	106.97
Other countries of Southern Europe			112	146	288	0.01	97.26
Western Europe	**129,457**	**141,501**	**196,284**	**156,370**	**139,488**	**3.35**	**-10.80**
Austria	5,505	6,522	9,581	8,874	6,457	0.16	-27.24
Belgium	11,078	12,296	16,983	15,942	14,375	0.35	-9.83
France	46,501	53,637	74,893	51,956	41,812	1.00	-19.52
Germany	39,555	41,622	61,080	52,245	47,274	1.14	-9.51
Luxembourg	319	341	490	326	360	0.01	10.43
Netherlands	18,278	18,545	23,604	19,561	22,586	0.54	15.46
Switzerland	8,221	8,538	9,653	7,466	6,624	0.16	-11.28
East Mediterranean Europe	**262,676**	**220,704**	**234,853**	**205,682**	**182,133**	**4.38**	**-11.45**
Cyprus	1,879	1,563	1,768	1,567	1,785	0.04	13.91
Israel	228,601	185,489	197,276	172,465	162,789	3.91	-5.61
Turkey	32,196	33,652	35,809	31,650	17,559	0.42	-44.52
Other Europe	**9,364**	**5,449**	**18,973**	**17,388**	**15,356**	**0.37**	**-11.69**
Other countries of Europe	9,364	5,449	18,973	17,388	15,356	0.37	-11.69
MIDDLE EAST	**1,777,094**	**1,867,473**	**2,054,551**	**1,892,950**	**2,007,452**	**48.23**	**6.05**
Bahrain	48,403	44,983	28,475	19,473	20,072	0.48	3.08
Egypt	50,791	39,885	55,978	53,673	61,251	1.47	14.12
Iraq	180,800	212,670	235,121	286,031	367,476	8.83	28.47

373

JORDAN

1. Arrivals of non-resident tourists at national borders, by nationality

	2008	2009	2010	2011	2012	Market share 2012	% Change 2012-2011
Kuwait	88,146	89,682	57,767	46,450	49,647	1.19	6.88
Lebanon	104,723	96,064	104,168	69,020	53,638	1.29	-22.29
Libya	31,230	34,261	45,898	22,168	97,906	2.35	341.65
Oman	19,722	16,192	15,633	12,154	13,729	0.33	12.96
Palestine	266,845	285,610	324,116	348,257	367,574	8.83	5.55
Qatar	13,692	13,310	9,146	7,234	8,721	0.21	20.56
Saudi Arabia	606,711	644,360	541,401	516,608	582,037	13.98	12.67
Syrian Arab Republic	304,707	310,471	571,824	455,595	316,303	7.60	-30.57
United Arab Emirates	29,745	27,565	22,682	15,894	16,513	0.40	3.89
Yemen	31,579	52,420	42,342	40,393	52,585	1.26	30.18
SOUTH ASIA	**73,571**	**71,778**	**65,243**	**77,078**	**77,759**	**1.87**	**0.88**
Afghanistan	1,064	1,786	1,133	1,056	566	0.01	-46.40
Bangladesh	6,118	7,239	2,948	3,224	2,778	0.07	-13.83
India	36,663	29,760	40,342	51,550	54,202	1.30	5.14
Iran, Islamic Republic of	1,298	1,216	866	960	855	0.02	-10.94
Nepal	2,335	4,021	1,159	917	662	0.02	-27.81
Pakistan	10,768	12,396	8,643	8,945	7,426	0.18	-16.98
Sri Lanka	15,325	15,360	10,152	10,426	11,270	0.27	8.10
NOT SPECIFIED	**824,149**	**872,678**	**928,758**	**969,361**	**1,058,586**	**25.43**	**9.20**
Other countries of the World	5,124	11,260					
Nationals Residing Abroad	819,025	861,418	928,758	969,361	1,058,586	25.43	9.20

Yearbook of Tourism Statistics, Data 2008 – 2012, 2014 Editi

JORDAN

2. Arrivals of non-resident visitors at national borders, by nationality

	2008	2009	2010	2011	2012	Market share 2012	% Change 2012-2011
TOTAL	7,100,478	7,084,552	8,078,380	6,812,436	6,314,250	100.00	-7.31
AFRICA	68,659	63,584	68,722	58,144	59,239	0.94	1.88
East Africa	4,304	4,867	5,179	4,879	7,460	0.12	52.90
Djibouti	38	53	49	44	79	0.00	79.55
Eritrea	472	453	407	367	347	0.01	-5.45
Ethiopia	1,841	2,675	3,106	2,264	4,581	0.07	102.34
Kenya	634	662	629	1,313	1,400	0.02	6.63
Mauritius	202	296	336	332	484	0.01	45.78
Somalia	1,117	728	652	559	569	0.01	1.79
Central Africa	154	116	164	363	620	0.01	70.80
Chad	154	116	164	363	620	0.01	70.80
North Africa	51,661	47,418	52,083	38,983	35,769	0.57	-8.24
Algeria	13,626	12,258	18,453	11,494	10,250	0.16	-10.82
Morocco	5,407	5,331	4,417	3,423	4,101	0.06	19.81
Sudan	25,060	24,047	22,769	20,109	16,898	0.27	-15.97
Tunisia	7,568	5,782	6,444	3,957	4,520	0.07	14.23
Southern Africa	9,930	8,496	8,860	10,493	11,339	0.18	8.06
South Africa	9,930	8,496	8,860	10,493	11,339	0.18	8.06
West Africa	1,090	892	455	588	702	0.01	19.39
Mauritania	336	246	10	16	15	0.00	-6.25
Nigeria	447	567	370	485	590	0.01	21.65
Senegal	307	79	75	87	97	0.00	11.49
Other Africa	1,520	1,795	1,981	2,838	3,349	0.05	18.01
Other countries of Africa	1,520	1,795	1,981	2,838	3,349	0.05	18.01
AMERICAS	244,245	230,436	250,246	216,890	226,374	3.59	4.37
North America	223,475	212,871	224,556	192,123	197,389	3.13	2.74
Canada	35,284	33,939	39,048	30,970	31,940	0.51	3.13
Mexico	6,571	3,978	6,843	4,506	6,060	0.10	34.49
United States of America	181,620	174,954	178,665	156,647	159,389	2.52	1.75
South America	15,262	13,191	20,279	19,253	22,671	0.36	17.75
Argentina	3,995	3,289	4,698	3,579	4,728	0.07	32.10
Brazil	5,770	5,686	9,939	10,110	11,064	0.18	9.44
Chile	2,250	1,607	2,338	2,167	2,129	0.03	-1.75
Colombia	1,753	1,314	1,817	2,109	3,251	0.05	54.15
Venezuela	1,494	1,295	1,487	1,288	1,499	0.02	16.38
Other Americas	5,508	4,374	5,411	5,514	6,314	0.10	14.51
Other countries of the Americas	5,508	4,374	5,411	5,514	6,314	0.10	14.51
EAST ASIA AND THE PACIFIC	166,153	157,281	173,664	169,649	186,976	2.96	10.21
North-East Asia	47,313	39,219	50,541	47,169	51,895	0.82	10.02
China	14,437	13,979	13,976	12,208	12,491	0.20	2.32
Hong Kong, China	110	268	439	1,975	2,186	0.03	10.68
Japan	13,810	13,052	19,052	12,829	15,321	0.24	19.42
Korea, Dem. People's Republic of	64	27	14	52	10	0.00	-80.77
Korea, Republic of	16,002	10,043	14,559	17,859	18,225	0.29	2.05
Taiwan, Province of China	2,890	1,850	2,501	2,246	3,662	0.06	63.05
South-East Asia	87,647	86,178	84,780	90,155	102,889	1.63	14.12
Indonesia	46,979	44,202	40,729	42,792	43,604	0.69	1.90
Malaysia	8,143	7,822	12,600	15,977	23,209	0.37	45.27
Philippines	25,510	28,448	22,315	20,572	20,697	0.33	0.61
Singapore	4,267	2,636	5,078	5,546	7,746	0.12	39.67
Thailand	2,293	2,920	3,860	4,976	7,393	0.12	48.57
Viet Nam	455	150	198	292	240	0.00	-17.81
Australasia	30,375	30,866	37,095	31,065	29,972	0.47	-3.52
Australia	25,347	25,714	31,025	26,175	25,300	0.40	-3.34
New Zealand	5,028	5,152	6,070	4,890	4,672	0.07	-4.46

375

JORDAN

2. Arrivals of non-resident visitors at national borders, by nationality

	2008	2009	2010	2011	2012	Market share 2012	% Change 2012-2011
Melanesia	229	413	536	353	371	0.01	5.10
Fiji	229	413	536	353	371	0.01	5.10
Other East Asia and the Pacific	589	605	712	907	1,849	0.03	103.86
Other countries of Asia	589	605	712	907	1,849	0.03	103.86
EUROPE	1,020,139	930,747	1,117,010	897,386	767,148	12.15	-14.51
Central/Eastern Europe	174,403	128,805	156,416	112,894	112,991	1.79	0.09
Belarus		1,420	1,545	1,345	1,660	0.03	23.42
Bulgaria	3,446	2,690	2,906	2,398	2,169	0.03	-9.55
Czech Republic	11,748	8,668	8,303	4,786	3,292	0.05	-31.22
Hungary	4,771	3,377	7,518	5,016	4,614	0.07	-8.01
Poland	35,805	19,946	24,563	15,266	15,492	0.25	1.48
Romania	5,412	4,972	5,444	5,357	6,055	0.10	13.03
Russian Federation	83,822	70,132	79,142	56,624	60,252	0.95	6.41
Slovakia	3,633	3,122	3,678	2,629	1,653	0.03	-37.12
Ukraine	16,419	11,051	12,509	10,685	11,236	0.18	5.16
Other countries Central/East Europe	9,347	3,427	10,808	8,788	6,568	0.10	-25.26
Northern Europe	122,297	135,048	152,623	141,555	135,840	2.15	-4.04
Denmark	5,694	7,441	9,490	13,044	10,088	0.16	-22.66
Finland	5,651	7,116	7,727	6,197	7,888	0.12	27.29
Iceland	188	186	210	261	294	0.00	12.64
Ireland	4,358	4,317	5,386	4,210	4,550	0.07	8.08
Norway	5,560	8,275	9,327	14,293	10,381	0.16	-27.37
Sweden	12,081	16,274	17,505	15,877	15,800	0.25	-0.48
United Kingdom	88,765	91,439	102,978	87,673	86,839	1.38	-0.95
Southern Europe	112,652	97,477	129,596	75,403	85,178	1.35	12.96
Bosnia and Herzegovina	2,855	2,328	2,213	1,227	916	0.01	-25.35
Croatia	1,749	1,115	1,599	1,247	1,160	0.02	-6.98
Greece	6,447	5,138	5,458	3,505	3,493	0.06	-0.34
Holy See	101	160					
Italy	47,478	49,403	65,756	40,861	45,180	0.72	10.57
Malta	286	269	306	264	384	0.01	45.45
Portugal	4,962	3,856	5,565	2,717	2,867	0.05	5.52
Serbia					1,697	0.03	
Serbia and Montenegro	3,387	627	96				
Slovenia	2,334	1,522	1,749	1,006	1,233	0.02	22.56
Spain	41,215	30,325	44,190	23,875	27,101	0.43	13.51
TFYR of Macedonia	1,838	2,734	2,556	552	835	0.01	51.27
Other countries of Southern Europe			108	149	312	0.00	109.40
Western Europe	161,674	176,800	240,861	179,792	165,592	2.62	-7.90
Austria	6,195	7,340	9,881	9,103	6,773	0.11	-25.60
Belgium	16,092	17,862	21,375	18,578	16,053	0.25	-13.59
France	57,118	65,884	102,890	63,076	50,601	0.80	-19.78
Germany	53,323	56,110	69,460	59,074	59,549	0.94	0.80
Luxembourg	319	341	552	364	406	0.01	11.54
Netherlands	19,589	19,876	25,842	21,114	24,527	0.39	16.16
Switzerland	9,038	9,387	10,861	8,483	7,683	0.12	-9.43
East Mediterranean Europe	428,305	381,926	416,741	369,643	251,852	3.99	-31.87
Cyprus	1,900	1,580	1,987	1,761	2,005	0.03	13.86
Israel	279,463	226,759	243,975	211,889	203,740	3.23	-3.85
Turkey	146,942	153,587	170,779	155,993	46,107	0.73	-70.44
Other Europe	20,808	10,691	20,773	18,099	15,695	0.25	-13.28
Other countries of Europe	20,808	10,691	20,773	18,099	15,695	0.25	-13.28
MIDDLE EAST	5,123,967	5,133,608	5,418,565	4,366,252	3,897,092	61.72	-10.75
Bahrain	92,636	86,092	100,221	43,645	35,941	0.57	-17.65
Egypt	697,921	548,068	383,168	326,511	353,827	5.60	8.37
Iraq	240,985	283,464	241,482	292,129	373,107	5.91	27.72

376

JORDAN

2. Arrivals of non-resident visitors at national borders, by nationality

	2008	2009	2010	2011	2012	Market share 2012	% Change 2012-2011
Kuwait	138,229	140,638	142,110	69,420	66,690	1.06	-3.93
Lebanon	193,893	177,860	189,612	108,638	65,859	1.04	-39.38
Libya	35,536	38,985	48,685	23,264	101,938	1.61	338.18
Oman	22,530	18,497	21,440	13,730	14,333	0.23	4.39
Palestine	361,174	386,573	408,383	441,574	470,241	7.45	6.49
Qatar	18,297	17,787	15,725	9,127	9,688	0.15	6.15
Saudi Arabia	1,123,453	1,193,168	1,332,680	1,074,190	1,144,118	18.12	6.51
Syrian Arab Republic	2,125,439	2,165,646	2,451,995	1,903,749	1,190,201	18.85	-37.48
United Arab Emirates	37,965	35,182	36,932	18,045	17,530	0.28	-2.85
Yemen	35,909	41,648	46,132	42,230	53,619	0.85	26.97
SOUTH ASIA	**84,177**	**82,169**	**101,060**	**114,361**	**97,247**	**1.54**	**-14.96**
Afghanistan	1,272	2,135	2,826	2,518	1,069	0.02	-57.55
Bangladesh	6,850	8,105	5,387	5,428	3,784	0.06	-30.29
India	41,962	34,061	51,461	64,971	60,913	0.96	-6.25
Iran, Islamic Republic of	1,456	1,364	1,037	1,132	897	0.01	-20.76
Nepal	2,572	4,428	5,445	4,807	2,732	0.04	-43.17
Pakistan	13,042	15,014	21,489	23,339	14,774	0.23	-36.70
Sri Lanka	17,023	17,062	13,415	12,166	13,078	0.21	7.50
NOT SPECIFIED	**393,138**	**486,727**	**949,113**	**989,754**	**1,080,174**	**17.11**	**9.14**
Other countries of the World	6,964	15,303					
Nationals Residing Abroad	386,174	471,424	949,113	989,754	1,080,174	17.11	9.14

Yearbook of Tourism Statistics, Data 2008 – 2012, 2014 Edition

KAZAKHSTAN

2. Arrivals of non-resident visitors at national borders, by country of residence

	2008	2009	2010	2011	2012	Market share 2012	% Change 2012-2011
TOTAL	4,117,242	3,774,352	4,097,387	5,685,132	6,163,204	100.00	8.41
AFRICA	2,276	2,530	3,315	2,195	11,470	0.19	422.55
East Africa	187	106	1,677	141	8,572	0.14	5,979.43
Ethiopia	15	11	17	21	22	0.00	4.76
Kenya	52	52	56	51	130	0.00	154.90
Madagascar	2	1	8	3	10	0.00	233.33
Uganda	86	6	1,567	30	8,361	0.14	27,770.00
United Republic of Tanzania	5	16	1	7	12	0.00	71.43
Zambia	8	5	2	8	17	0.00	112.50
Zimbabwe	19	15	26	21	20	0.00	-4.76
Central Africa	39	859	15	43	46	0.00	6.98
Angola	13	7	5	2	11	0.00	450.00
Chad	2	831	2	5	6	0.00	20.00
Congo	24	21	8	36	29	0.00	-19.44
North Africa	299	346	418	506	699	0.01	38.14
Algeria	106	150	138	130	165	0.00	26.92
Morocco	74	86	140	183	404	0.01	120.77
Sudan	47	41	45	50	44	0.00	-12.00
Tunisia	72	69	95	143	86	0.00	-39.86
Southern Africa	1,408	969	958	1,114	1,497	0.02	34.38
South Africa	1,408	969	958	1,114	1,497	0.02	34.38
West Africa	343	250	247	391	656	0.01	67.77
Burkina Faso	4	3	5	8	13	0.00	62.50
Côte d'Ivoire	12	6	15	11	13	0.00	18.18
Ghana	48	41	40	43	42	0.00	-2.33
Guinea-Bissau	1	1	1				
Liberia	6	2	4	2	11	0.00	450.00
Mali	15	2	3	19	17	0.00	-10.53
Mauritania	7	6	6	16	9	0.00	-43.75
Niger	5	11	2	7	27	0.00	285.71
Nigeria	234	152	156	249	493	0.01	97.99
Senegal	11	26	15	36	31	0.00	-13.89
AMERICAS	30,230	27,563	27,715	29,308	34,241	0.56	16.83
Caribbean	256	264	329	498	349	0.01	-29.92
Anguilla	3	1	2				
Barbados		1	3	5	11	0.00	120.00
Cuba	184	201	233	293	288	0.00	-1.71
Dominica	3		6	6			
Jamaica	4	6	3		8	0.00	
Saint Lucia		5	48	171	14	0.00	-91.81
Trinidad and Tobago	62	50	34	23	28	0.00	21.74
Central America	50	83	132	54	120	0.00	122.22
Costa Rica	10	14	17	12	51	0.00	325.00
El Salvador	12	31	68	22	40	0.00	81.82
Guatemala	5	4	12	3	2	0.00	-33.33
Honduras	12	21	15	8	9	0.00	12.50
Panama	11	13	20	9	18	0.00	100.00
North America	28,507	25,731	25,794	27,054	31,909	0.52	17.95
Canada	5,434	4,944	5,155	5,393	6,024	0.10	11.70
Mexico	129	130	178	198	279	0.00	40.91
United States of America	22,944	20,657	20,461	21,463	25,606	0.42	19.30
South America	1,417	1,485	1,460	1,702	1,863	0.03	9.46
Argentina	289	308	258	255	274	0.00	7.45
Brazil	368	546	425	608	727	0.01	19.57
Chile	51	59	178	158	167	0.00	5.70

378

KAZAKHSTAN

2. Arrivals of non-resident visitors at national borders, by country of residence

	2008	2009	2010	2011	2012	Market share 2012	% Change 2012-2011
Colombia	324	266	255	239	212	0.00	-11.30
Ecuador	64	59	49	47	51	0.00	8.51
Peru	45	33	61	62	71	0.00	14.52
Uruguay	49	6	32	5	13	0.00	160.00
Venezuela	227	208	202	328	348	0.01	6.10
EAST ASIA AND THE PACIFIC	**197,880**	**170,560**	**148,951**	**177,944**	**200,012**	**3.25**	**12.40**
North-East Asia	**186,743**	**159,471**	**137,670**	**166,583**	**187,142**	**3.04**	**12.34**
China	154,220	134,251	108,630	128,312	154,226	2.50	20.20
Hong Kong, China	22	13	49	71	426	0.01	500.00
Japan	5,237	4,271	4,428	4,720	6,049	0.10	28.16
Korea, Dem. People's Republic of	118	106	182	125	49	0.00	-60.80
Korea, Republic of	16,999	12,627	13,740	16,589	16,963	0.28	2.25
Macao, China	1				1		
Mongolia	9,513	7,944	10,419	11,305	9,077	0.15	-19.71
Taiwan, Province of China	633	259	222	5,460	352	0.01	-93.55
South-East Asia	**6,823**	**7,226**	**7,535**	**7,748**	**8,488**	**0.14**	**9.55**
Cambodia	14	20	21	4	19	0.00	375.00
Indonesia	531	622	504	692	723	0.01	4.48
Lao People's Democratic Republic	22	31	17	10	25	0.00	150.00
Malaysia	1,352	1,223	1,488	2,194	2,179	0.04	-0.68
Myanmar	18	5	19	42	39	0.00	-7.14
Philippines	2,998	3,366	3,708	3,215	3,035	0.05	-5.60
Singapore	659	483	437	491	736	0.01	49.90
Thailand	1,086	1,122	1,153	908	984	0.02	8.37
Viet Nam	143	354	188	192	748	0.01	289.58
Australasia	**4,308**	**3,856**	**3,737**	**3,596**	**4,347**	**0.07**	**20.88**
Australia	3,589	3,224	3,158	2,980	3,628	0.06	21.74
New Zealand	719	632	579	616	719	0.01	16.72
Melanesia	**6**	**6**	**4**	**17**	**27**	**0.00**	**58.82**
Papua New Guinea	6	6	4	17	27	0.00	58.82
Polynesia		**1**	**5**		**8**	**0.00**	
Samoa		1	5		8	0.00	
EUROPE	**3,853,180**	**3,539,975**	**3,875,397**	**5,436,269**	**5,874,175**	**95.31**	**8.06**
Central/Eastern Europe	**3,623,495**	**3,337,708**	**3,668,845**	**5,227,740**	**5,585,175**	**90.62**	**6.84**
Armenia	11,007	12,659	18,121	26,093	37,337	0.61	43.09
Azerbaijan	32,621	39,750	54,386	63,849	83,811	1.36	31.26
Belarus	10,574	11,218	12,411	13,302	20,399	0.33	53.35
Bulgaria	1,524	1,368	1,539	1,591	2,194	0.04	37.90
Czech Republic	2,189	2,097	2,141	2,531	3,645	0.06	44.01
Estonia	635	639	600	715	1,074	0.02	50.21
Georgia	8,977	7,081	7,661	10,536	11,686	0.19	10.91
Hungary	2,970	2,832	2,846	3,455	4,452	0.07	28.86
Kyrgyzstan	935,769	864,912	930,493	1,539,885	1,454,124	23.59	-5.57
Latvia	1,753	1,238	1,638	1,614	2,785	0.05	72.55
Lithuania	2,207	2,553	2,541	3,194	4,824	0.08	51.03
Poland	5,136	4,172	4,400	5,157	7,405	0.12	43.59
Republic of Moldova	8,122	7,379	8,483	9,425	12,028	0.20	27.62
Romania	3,312	2,071	2,110	2,820	3,139	0.05	11.31
Russian Federation	953,632	934,972	1,041,978	1,346,594	1,371,306	22.25	1.84
Slovakia	1,051	826	1,058	1,084	1,524	0.02	40.59
Tajikistan	205,366	193,518	162,387	187,956	176,212	2.86	-6.25
Turkmenistan	23,927	24,119	22,537	26,369	40,185	0.65	52.39
Ukraine	48,248	65,210	50,074	49,272	58,428	0.95	18.58
Uzbekistan	1,364,475	1,159,094	1,341,441	1,932,298	2,288,617	37.13	18.44
Northern Europe	**31,907**	**32,691**	**33,425**	**33,727**	**36,176**	**0.59**	**7.26**
Denmark	1,078	918	976	969	1,206	0.02	24.46
Finland	1,246	1,225	1,292	1,152	1,825	0.03	58.42

Yearbook of Tourism Statistics, Data 2008 – 2012, 2014 Edition

KAZAKHSTAN

2. Arrivals of non-resident visitors at national borders, by country of residence

	2008	2009	2010	2011	2012	Market share 2012	% Change 2012-2011
Iceland	54	71	68	35	109	0.00	211.43
Ireland	1,131	1,053	1,213	1,469	2,125	0.03	44.66
Norway	1,251	1,739	2,458	2,218	1,482	0.02	-33.18
Sweden	1,219	1,155	1,507	1,554	1,947	0.03	25.29
United Kingdom	25,928	26,530	25,911	26,330	27,482	0.45	4.38
Southern Europe	**18,526**	**19,702**	**21,323**	**21,162**	**28,310**	**0.46**	**33.78**
Albania	135	87	106	125	441	0.01	252.80
Bosnia and Herzegovina	222	122	165	207	321	0.01	55.07
Croatia	909	977	999	1,102	1,506	0.02	36.66
Greece	1,352	1,205	1,518	1,211	1,523	0.02	25.76
Italy	12,837	13,920	14,223	15,161	18,445	0.30	21.66
Malta	46	25	46	48	87	0.00	81.25
Portugal	472	428	465	517	676	0.01	30.75
Serbia		449	953	23	1,424	0.02	6,091.30
Slovenia	481	444	477	511	694	0.01	35.81
Spain	2,072	2,045	2,371	2,257	3,193	0.05	41.47
Western Europe	**105,268**	**92,572**	**95,202**	**88,217**	**132,467**	**2.15**	**50.16**
Austria	2,608	2,234	2,566	2,395	8,447	0.14	252.69
Belgium	1,988	2,100	2,325	1,886	2,275	0.04	20.63
France	8,172	7,788	8,606	9,141	12,394	0.20	35.59
Germany	85,199	73,891	74,311	67,725	100,911	1.64	49.00
Liechtenstein	7	11	13	27	3	0.00	-88.89
Luxembourg	111	73	94	82	103	0.00	25.61
Monaco	15	10	8	1	21	0.00	2,000.00
Netherlands	5,378	4,857	5,372	5,035	5,983	0.10	18.83
Switzerland	1,790	1,608	1,907	1,925	2,330	0.04	21.04
East Mediterranean Europe	**73,984**	**57,302**	**56,602**	**65,423**	**92,047**	**1.49**	**40.70**
Cyprus	47	74	114	81	148	0.00	82.72
Israel	5,660	4,572	4,212	4,614	6,042	0.10	30.95
Turkey	68,277	52,656	52,276	60,728	85,857	1.39	41.38
MIDDLE EAST	**4,526**	**4,808**	**5,164**	**5,103**	**5,391**	**0.09**	**5.64**
Bahrain	99	30	26	60	67	0.00	11.67
Egypt	897	1,114	1,112	1,024	1,038	0.02	1.37
Iraq	84	110	153	191	275	0.00	43.98
Jordan	545	528	731	672	785	0.01	16.82
Kuwait	71	130	104	102	53	0.00	-48.04
Lebanon	614	693	779	799	724	0.01	-9.39
Libya	35	72	59	44	36	0.00	-18.18
Oman	111	82	130	122	155	0.00	27.05
Palestine	101	164	152	192	185	0.00	-3.65
Qatar	193	121	99	173	284	0.00	64.16
Saudi Arabia	383	478	381	329	378	0.01	14.89
Syrian Arab Republic	490	517	594	541	569	0.01	5.18
United Arab Emirates	903	769	844	854	842	0.01	-1.41
SOUTH ASIA	**23,779**	**22,232**	**20,671**	**22,894**	**24,624**	**0.40**	**7.56**
Afghanistan	4,764	4,366	2,362	2,236	2,525	0.04	12.92
Bangladesh	331	511	360	284	217	0.00	-23.59
Bhutan	4	6	7	10	8	0.00	-20.00
India	11,658	11,734	11,904	13,778	14,716	0.24	6.81
Iran, Islamic Republic of	4,017	3,071	3,714	3,876	4,265	0.07	10.04
Nepal	138	110	95	124	116	0.00	-6.45
Pakistan	2,758	2,324	2,069	2,437	2,236	0.04	-8.25
Sri Lanka	109	110	160	149	541	0.01	263.09
NOT SPECIFIED	**5,371**	**6,684**	**16,174**	**11,419**	**13,291**	**0.22**	**16.39**
Other countries of the World	5,371	6,684	16,174	11,419	13,291	0.22	16.39

KENYA

2. Arrivals of non-resident visitors at national borders, by country of residence

	2008	2009	2010	2011	2012	Market share 2012	% Change 2012-2011
TOTAL	1,203,000	1,490,000	1,609,000				
AFRICA	136,000	158,000	279,000				
Other Africa	136,000	158,000	279,000				
All countries of Africa	136,000	158,000	279,000				
AMERICAS	89,000	111,000	131,000				
Other Americas	89,000	111,000	131,000				
All countries of the Americas	89,000	111,000	131,000				
EAST ASIA AND THE PACIFIC	111,000	122,000	162,000				
Other East Asia and the Pacific	111,000	122,000	162,000				
All countries of Asia	111,000	122,000	162,000				
EUROPE	819,000	1,040,000	932,000				
Other Europe	819,000	1,040,000	932,000				
All countries of Europe	819,000	1,040,000	932,000				
NOT SPECIFIED	48,000	59,000	105,000				
Other countries of the World	48,000	59,000	105,000				

Yearbook of Tourism Statistics, Data 2008 – 2012, 2014 Edition

KENYA

5. Overnight stays of non-resident tourists in hotels and similar establishments, by country of residence

	2008	2009	2010	2011	2012	Market share 2012	% Change 2012-2011
TOTAL	2,080,100	4,062,400	4,260,100				
AFRICA	283,600	485,700	451,700				
East Africa	86,300	174,100	129,400				
Uganda	43,200	103,000	67,900				
United Republic of Tanzania	43,100	71,100	61,500				
North Africa	17,000	25,400	28,300				
All countries of North Africa	17,000	25,400	28,300				
Southern Africa	52,600	87,800	88,100				
All countries of Southern Africa	52,600	87,800	88,100				
West Africa	26,300	45,400	55,100				
All countries of West Africa	26,300	45,400	55,100				
Other Africa	101,400	153,000	150,800				
Other countries of Africa	101,400	153,000	150,800				
AMERICAS	197,000	325,700	347,100				
North America	180,300	292,300	314,000				
Canada	32,200	58,500	59,800				
United States of America	148,100	233,800	254,200				
Other Americas	16,700	33,400	33,100				
Other countries of the Americas	16,700	33,400	33,100				
EAST ASIA AND THE PACIFIC	107,600	166,900	194,600				
North-East Asia	38,900	71,000	91,500				
China	20,700	33,200	50,700				
Japan	18,200	37,800	40,800				
Australasia	42,300	54,900	60,200				
Australia, New Zealand	42,300	54,900	60,200				
Other East Asia and the Pacific	26,400	41,000	42,900				
Other countries of Asia	26,400	41,000	42,900				
EUROPE	1,323,600	2,798,100	2,933,400				
Northern Europe	535,300	1,007,000	1,048,800				
United Kingdom	486,600	909,700	964,700				
Scandinavia	48,700	97,300	84,100				
Southern Europe	158,200	383,200	651,000				
Italy	158,200	383,200	651,000				
Western Europe	470,100	1,044,900	869,000				
France	63,800	231,800	222,700				
Germany	339,500	685,600	563,200				
Switzerland	66,800	127,500	83,100				
Other Europe	160,000	363,000	364,600				
Other countries of Europe	160,000	363,000	364,600				
MIDDLE EAST	20,000	37,500	36,600				
All countries of Middle East	20,000	37,500	36,600				
SOUTH ASIA	51,200	83,300	91,100				
India	51,200	83,300	91,100				
NOT SPECIFIED	97,100	165,200	205,600				
Other countries of the World	97,100	165,200	205,600				

Yearbook of Tourism Statistics, Data 2008 – 2012, 2014 Editic

KIRIBATI

1. Arrivals of non-resident tourists at national borders, by nationality

		2008	2009	2010	2011	2012	Market share 2012	% Change 2012-2011
TOTAL	(*)	3,871	3,944	4,701	5,264	4,907	100.00	-6.78
AMERICAS		928	699	827	1,063	682	13.90	-35.84
North America		928	699	827	1,063	682	13.90	-35.84
Canada		41	47	51	67			
United States of America		887	652	776	996	682	13.90	-31.53
EAST ASIA AND THE PACIFIC		2,481	2,695	3,240	2,887	2,514	51.23	-12.92
North-East Asia		190	288	429	298	200	4.08	-32.89
Japan		190	234	244	236	200	4.08	-15.25
Taiwan, Province of China			54	185	62			
Australasia		1,152	1,286	1,383	1,432	1,343	27.37	-6.22
Australia		868	934	913	809	857	17.46	5.93
New Zealand		284	352	470	623	486	9.90	-21.99
Other East Asia and the Pacific		1,139	1,121	1,428	1,157	971	19.79	-16.08
Other countries of Asia		370	379	387				
Other countries of Oceania		769	742	1,041	1,157	971	19.79	-16.08
EUROPE		304	382	368	412	328	6.68	-20.39
Northern Europe		129	135	153	226	109	2.22	-51.77
United Kingdom		129	135	153	226	109	2.22	-51.77
Southern Europe		10	11	14				
Italy		10	11	14				
Western Europe		114	185	144	112	219	4.46	95.54
France		71	120	72	43			
Germany		40	50	55	69	219	4.46	217.39
Switzerland		3	15	17				
Other Europe		51	51	57	74			
Other countries of Europe		51	51	57	74			
NOT SPECIFIED		158	168	266	902	1,383	28.18	53.33
Other countries of the World		158	168	266	902	1,383	28.18	53.33

Yearbook of Tourism Statistics, Data 2008 – 2012, 2014 Edition

KOREA, REPUBLIC OF

2. Arrivals of non-resident visitors at national borders, by nationality

		2008	2009	2010	2011	2012	Market share 2012	% Change 2012-2011
TOTAL	(*)	6,890,841	7,817,533	8,797,658	9,794,796	11,140,028	100.00	13.73
AFRICA		20,720	22,487	26,892	30,334	32,237	0.29	6.27
East Africa		3,259	4,874	5,949	7,438	7,836	0.07	5.35
Burundi		15	14	27	70	49	0.00	-30.00
Comoros		2	6		13	38	0.00	192.31
Djibouti		6	12	13	14	10	0.00	-28.57
Eritrea		10	11	18	29	39	0.00	34.48
Ethiopia		464	439	599	915	967	0.01	5.68
Kenya		686	816	1,017	1,312	1,528	0.01	16.46
Madagascar		70	107	88	109	161	0.00	47.71
Malawi		26	28	94	101	102	0.00	0.99
Mauritius		264	495	567	502	558	0.01	11.16
Mozambique		89	83	90	174	198	0.00	13.79
Reunion					3	3	0.00	0.00
Rwanda		106	109	121	229	258	0.00	12.66
Seychelles		60	43	83	71	84	0.00	18.31
Somalia		7	11	9	16	23	0.00	43.75
Uganda		244	246	295	402	475	0.00	18.16
United Republic of Tanzania		930	2,175	2,534	3,060	2,807	0.03	-8.27
Zambia		97	93	124	160	251	0.00	56.88
Zimbabwe		183	186	270	258	285	0.00	10.47
Central Africa		917	1,028	1,440	1,674	2,233	0.02	33.39
Angola		195	314	438	476	850	0.01	78.57
Cameroon		310	318	386	444	564	0.01	27.03
Central African Republic		10	6	25	35	41	0.00	17.14
Chad		8	4	21	36	28	0.00	-22.22
Congo		100	90	63	103	103	0.00	0.00
Democratic Republic of the Congo		188	157	328	327	298	0.00	-8.87
Equatorial Guinea		14	6	34	40	48	0.00	20.00
Gabon		92	127	140	204	294	0.00	44.12
Sao Tome and Principe			6	5	9	7	0.00	-22.22
North Africa		3,063	3,198	3,536	4,168	4,675	0.04	12.16
Algeria		700	667	804	1,000	1,209	0.01	20.90
Morocco		849	943	887	1,280	1,242	0.01	-2.97
South Sudan					4	82	0.00	1,950.00
Sudan		903	965	1,085	978	1,053	0.01	7.67
Tunisia		611	623	760	905	1,088	0.01	20.22
Western Sahara					1	1	0.00	0.00
Southern Africa		7,162	7,768	9,869	10,172	10,674	0.10	4.94
Botswana		27	23	27	57	96	0.00	68.42
Lesotho		32	13	20	31	30	0.00	-3.23
Namibia		151	163	154	183	172	0.00	-6.01
South Africa		6,910	7,530	9,633	9,833	10,298	0.09	4.73
Swaziland		42	39	35	68	78	0.00	14.71
West Africa		6,319	5,619	6,098	6,882	6,817	0.06	-0.94
Benin		64	73	52	77	78	0.00	1.30
Burkina Faso		56	26	46	80	92	0.00	15.00
Cape Verde		26	20	29	23	34	0.00	47.83
Côte d'Ivoire		253	180	206	142	181	0.00	27.46
Gambia		18	34	27	41	71	0.00	73.17
Ghana		1,891	1,673	2,062	2,214	2,024	0.02	-8.58
Guinea		72	87	45	110	109	0.00	-0.91
Guinea-Bissau		9	3	6	14	16	0.00	14.29
Liberia		107	89	105	158	138	0.00	-12.66
Mali		60	75	53	96	82	0.00	-14.58
Mauritania		13	8	14	43	84	0.00	95.35

384

KOREA, REPUBLIC OF

2. Arrivals of non-resident visitors at national borders, by nationality

	2008	2009	2010	2011	2012	Market share 2012	% Change 2012-2011
Niger	27	28	38	63	43	0.00	-31.75
Nigeria	3,471	3,024	3,032	3,390	3,453	0.03	1.86
Saint Helena	7	5	9	14	6	0.00	-57.14
Senegal	181	228	274	330	314	0.00	-4.85
Sierra Leone	19	29	45	35	33	0.00	-5.71
Togo	45	37	55	52	59	0.00	13.46
Other Africa					2	0.00	
Other countries of Africa					2	0.00	
AMERICAS	**744,615**	**751,697**	**813,860**	**827,383**	**876,149**	**7.86**	**5.89**
Caribbean	**1,444**	**1,292**	**1,731**	**2,058**	**2,612**	**0.02**	**26.92**
Antigua and Barbuda	12	16	28	22	33	0.00	50.00
Bahamas	47	33	75	83	72	0.00	-13.25
Barbados	34	36	58	79	56	0.00	-29.11
Bermuda	3		4	2	1	0.00	-50.00
British Virgin Islands	75	50	109	112	50	0.00	-55.36
Cuba	227	132	85	221	80	0.00	-63.80
Dominica	41	38	37	40	54	0.00	35.00
Dominican Republic	274	344	343	451	517	0.00	14.63
Grenada	17	8	12	28	31	0.00	10.71
Haiti	48	42	66	86	133	0.00	54.65
Jamaica	286	312	442	500	811	0.01	62.20
Montserrat		4	4				
Netherlands Antilles	10		16	10	42	0.00	320.00
Puerto Rico	1	4	4	7	22	0.00	214.29
Saint Kitts and Nevis	6	19	24	54	88	0.00	62.96
Saint Lucia	26	30	11	22	39	0.00	77.27
Saint Vincent and the Grenadines	85	44	91	34	205	0.00	502.94
Trinidad and Tobago	252	180	322	271	378	0.00	39.48
Turks and Caicos Islands				36			
Central America	**2,429**	**2,994**	**3,873**	**3,734**	**4,342**	**0.04**	**16.28**
Belize	80	70	53	39	61	0.00	56.41
Costa Rica	336	548	669	757	968	0.01	27.87
El Salvador	569	639	694	685	574	0.01	-16.20
Guatemala	623	581	680	742	753	0.01	1.48
Honduras	297	620	918	762	903	0.01	18.50
Nicaragua	135	133	316	191	314	0.00	64.40
Panama	389	403	543	558	769	0.01	37.81
North America	**720,357**	**726,048**	**782,037**	**792,085**	**836,323**	**7.51**	**5.59**
Canada	104,022	109,249	121,214	122,223	128,431	1.15	5.08
Mexico	6,252	5,472	7,934	8,359	10,026	0.09	19.94
United States of America	610,083	611,327	652,889	661,503	697,866	6.26	5.50
South America	**20,374**	**21,356**	**26,206**	**29,503**	**32,865**	**0.30**	**11.40**
Argentina	2,194	2,350	3,196	2,984	3,316	0.03	11.13
Bolivia	438	451	534	572	648	0.01	13.29
Brazil	9,844	10,145	12,747	14,639	15,761	0.14	7.66
Chile	1,842	1,735	2,109	2,828	3,245	0.03	14.75
Colombia	1,840	2,376	2,303	2,674	3,233	0.03	20.91
Ecuador	495	546	815	868	944	0.01	8.76
Guyana	35	77	58	50	214	0.00	328.00
Paraguay	326	377	451	445	510	0.00	14.61
Peru	1,525	1,690	2,127	2,424	2,687	0.02	10.85
Suriname	41	38	40	54	93	0.00	72.22
Uruguay	188	150	206	280	357	0.00	27.50
Venezuela	1,606	1,421	1,620	1,685	1,857	0.02	10.21
Other Americas	**11**	**7**	**13**	**3**	**7**	**0.00**	**133.33**
Other countries of the Americas	11	7	13	3	7	0.00	133.33
EAST ASIA AND THE PACIFIC	**5,035,806**	**6,029,612**	**6,769,195**	**7,678,884**	**8,913,347**	**80.01**	**16.08**

Yearbook of Tourism Statistics, Data 2008 – 2012, 2014 Edition

KOREA, REPUBLIC OF

2. Arrivals of non-resident visitors at national borders, by nationality

	2008	2009	2010	2011	2012	Market share 2012	% Change 2012-2011
North-East Asia	**4,073,601**	**5,037,628**	**5,583,188**	**6,277,955**	**7,346,617**	**65.95**	**17.02**
China	1,167,891	1,342,317	1,875,157	2,220,196	2,836,892	25.47	27.78
Hong Kong, China	160,325	215,769	228,582	280,849	360,027	3.23	28.19
Japan	2,378,102	3,053,311	3,023,009	3,289,051	3,518,792	31.59	6.99
Macao, China	4,462	7,157	8,130	11,647	21,557	0.19	85.09
Mongolia	42,577	38,446	41,958	48,004	61,116	0.55	27.31
Taiwan, Province of China	320,244	380,628	406,352	428,208	548,233	4.92	28.03
South-East Asia	**834,036**	**860,971**	**1,039,112**	**1,244,309**	**1,399,359**	**12.56**	**12.46**
Brunei Darussalam	924	925	1,268	1,434	2,070	0.02	44.35
Cambodia	6,895	6,041	7,194	12,438	18,567	0.17	49.28
Indonesia	81,001	80,988	95,239	124,474	149,247	1.34	19.90
Lao People's Democratic Republic	930	1,104	1,999	2,477	3,294	0.03	32.98
Malaysia	83,754	80,105	113,675	156,281	178,082	1.60	13.95
Myanmar	50,636	56,044	57,916	70,168	67,917	0.61	-3.21
Philippines	276,710	271,962	297,452	337,268	331,346	2.97	-1.76
Singapore	95,960	96,622	112,855	124,565	154,073	1.38	23.69
Thailand	160,687	190,972	260,718	309,143	387,441	3.48	25.33
Timor-Leste	137	230	583	530	815	0.01	53.77
Viet Nam	76,402	75,978	90,213	105,531	106,507	0.96	0.92
Australasia	**120,573**	**123,106**	**139,382**	**149,102**	**158,358**	**1.42**	**6.21**
Australia	96,138	99,153	112,409	122,494	128,812	1.16	5.16
New Zealand	24,435	23,953	26,973	26,608	29,546	0.27	11.04
Melanesia	**4,033**	**4,517**	**4,827**	**4,299**	**4,739**	**0.04**	**10.23**
Fiji	3,678	4,127	4,486	3,856	4,224	0.04	9.54
New Caledonia				3			
Papua New Guinea	261	251	214	261	256	0.00	-1.92
Solomon Islands	78	109	94	130	174	0.00	33.85
Vanuatu	16	30	33	49	85	0.00	73.47
Micronesia	**2,363**	**2,119**	**1,423**	**1,834**	**2,481**	**0.02**	**35.28**
Kiribati	2,170	1,909	1,254	1,605	2,019	0.02	25.79
Marshall Islands	58	45	67	55	148	0.00	169.09
Micronesia, Federated States of	52	77	66	86	72	0.00	-16.28
Nauru	31	11	9	25	53	0.00	112.00
Palau	52	77	27	63	189	0.00	200.00
Polynesia	**596**	**700**	**457**	**419**	**719**	**0.01**	**71.60**
American Samoa		8	9	4	3	0.00	-25.00
French Polynesia	3	4	6	69	2	0.00	-97.10
Samoa	116	137	172	92	174	0.00	89.13
Tonga	77	111	139	112	193	0.00	72.32
Tuvalu	400	440	131	142	347	0.00	144.37
Other East Asia and the Pacific	**604**	**571**	**806**	**966**	**1,074**	**0.01**	**11.18**
Other countries of Asia	604	567	806	966	1,067	0.01	10.46
Other countries of Oceania		4			7	0.00	
EUROPE	**645,748**	**645,624**	**708,948**	**752,961**	**807,244**	**7.25**	**7.21**
Central/Eastern Europe	**236,986**	**224,765**	**256,329**	**279,822**	**305,854**	**2.75**	**9.30**
Armenia	188	207	195	283	323	0.00	14.13
Azerbaijan	488	506	679	706	761	0.01	7.79
Belarus	862	813	772	859	968	0.01	12.69
Bulgaria	6,171	6,220	7,525	8,103	7,186	0.06	-11.32
Czech Republic	6,455	6,307	6,589	7,103	8,353	0.07	17.60
Estonia	740	771	759	905	944	0.01	4.31
Georgia	778	677	687	842	803	0.01	-4.63
Hungary	1,889	2,144	2,365	2,384	2,703	0.02	13.38
Kazakhstan	5,831	5,699	7,417	8,421	11,039	0.10	31.09
Kyrgyzstan	2,632	2,652	2,424	2,109	2,783	0.02	31.96
Latvia	2,159	1,958	2,559	2,111	2,259	0.02	7.01
Lithuania	1,052	1,142	1,366	1,572	1,827	0.02	16.22

Yearbook of Tourism Statistics, Data 2008 – 2012, 2014 Editi

KOREA, REPUBLIC OF

2. Arrivals of non-resident visitors at national borders, by nationality

	2008	2009	2010	2011	2012	Market share 2012	% Change 2012-2011
Poland	11,054	10,598	11,555	13,451	13,656	0.12	1.52
Republic of Moldova	198	178	191	218	221	0.00	1.38
Romania	6,618	6,601	8,699	9,780	10,650	0.10	8.90
Russian Federation	136,342	137,054	150,730	154,835	166,721	1.50	7.68
Slovakia	1,623	1,682	1,841	2,558	2,833	0.03	10.75
Tajikistan	564	410	696	1,171	1,433	0.01	22.37
Turkmenistan	262	196	196	199	363	0.00	82.41
Ukraine	27,326	22,597	25,373	31,162	27,782	0.25	-10.85
Uzbekistan	23,754	16,353	23,711	31,050	42,246	0.38	36.06
Northern Europe	**137,016**	**137,223**	**147,564**	**158,582**	**166,003**	**1.49**	**4.68**
Denmark	8,764	7,813	7,978	8,435	8,952	0.08	6.13
Faeroe Islands				1			
Finland	9,625	9,131	9,339	10,320	9,973	0.09	-3.36
Iceland	278	214	308	384	418	0.00	8.85
Ireland	6,589	5,991	6,257	7,199	7,035	0.06	-2.28
Norway	12,323	10,968	12,821	13,371	13,958	0.13	4.39
Sweden	12,423	11,941	13,351	14,228	15,495	0.14	8.90
United Kingdom	87,014	91,165	97,510	104,644	110,172	0.99	5.28
Southern Europe	**52,916**	**56,433**	**61,626**	**65,085**	**72,490**	**0.65**	**11.38**
Albania	95	101	122	143	164	0.00	14.69
Andorra	13	23	26	17	36	0.00	111.76
Bosnia and Herzegovina	34	42	75	52	69	0.00	32.69
Croatia	6,455	6,001	5,755	6,117	5,780	0.05	-5.51
Greece	7,080	7,885	7,975	8,802	8,600	0.08	-2.29
Holy See	9	8	12	5	8	0.00	60.00
Italy	21,156	22,894	25,686	26,442	28,941	0.26	9.45
Malta	164	148	212	240	206	0.00	-14.17
Montenegro	44	347	1,287	1,522	1,434	0.01	-5.78
Portugal	3,830	5,003	5,574	6,397	8,702	0.08	36.03
San Marino	10	30	5	27	5	0.00	-81.48
Serbia	42	503	1,047	1,304	1,498	0.01	14.88
Serbia and Montenegro	2,202	1,684	81	51	18	0.00	-64.71
Slovenia	1,103	974	973	924	1,080	0.01	16.88
Spain	10,623	10,691	12,590	12,884	15,833	0.14	22.89
TFYR of Macedonia	56	99	206	158	116	0.00	-26.58
Western Europe	**197,751**	**204,308**	**214,440**	**220,186**	**230,570**	**2.07**	**4.72**
Austria	7,621	8,017	8,956	9,227	9,750	0.09	5.67
Belgium	6,913	6,828	7,803	7,793	8,894	0.08	14.13
France	59,789	61,426	66,192	69,459	71,140	0.64	2.42
Germany	91,555	97,691	98,119	99,468	102,262	0.92	2.81
Liechtenstein	25	34	26	49	41	0.00	-16.33
Luxembourg	347	451	465	480	437	0.00	-8.96
Monaco	12	11	12	17	60	0.00	252.94
Netherlands	21,875	20,358	22,669	23,279	25,886	0.23	11.20
Switzerland	9,614	9,492	10,198	10,414	12,100	0.11	16.19
East Mediterranean Europe	**20,402**	**22,552**	**28,751**	**28,986**	**32,065**	**0.29**	**10.62**
Cyprus	241	359	438	472	531	0.00	12.50
Israel	7,587	9,784	11,993	11,216	12,244	0.11	9.17
Turkey	12,574	12,409	16,320	17,298	19,290	0.17	11.52
Other Europe	**677**	**343**	**238**	**300**	**262**	**0.00**	**-12.67**
Other countries of Europe	677	343	238	300	262	0.00	-12.67
MIDDLE EAST	**18,208**	**19,759**	**24,574**	**29,340**	**34,693**	**0.31**	**18.24**
Bahrain	202	296	261	328	367	0.00	11.89
Egypt	4,162	3,852	5,138	5,845	5,753	0.05	-1.57
Iraq	1,674	1,975	2,210	2,090	2,695	0.02	28.95
Jordan	2,509	3,007	3,137	3,520	3,521	0.03	0.03
Kuwait	702	463	870	1,047	1,116	0.01	6.59

Yearbook of Tourism Statistics, Data 2008 – 2012, 2014 Edition

KOREA, REPUBLIC OF

2. Arrivals of non-resident visitors at national borders, by nationality

	2008	2009	2010	2011	2012	Market share 2012	% Change 2012-2011
Lebanon	853	824	1,198	1,335	1,172	0.01	-12.21
Libya	1,327	2,162	1,726	800	3,246	0.03	305.75
Oman	435	366	721	873	1,001	0.01	14.66
Palestine	148	207	257	253	266	0.00	5.14
Qatar	345	318	311	506	676	0.01	33.60
Saudi Arabia	2,664	3,040	3,875	6,904	7,970	0.07	15.44
Syrian Arab Republic	1,706	1,829	1,853	2,263	2,024	0.02	-10.56
United Arab Emirates	1,010	887	2,433	2,958	3,866	0.03	30.70
Yemen	471	533	584	618	1,020	0.01	65.05
SOUTH ASIA	**118,036**	**113,740**	**134,503**	**148,431**	**146,655**	**1.32**	**-1.20**
Afghanistan	528	611	780	1,028	972	0.01	-5.45
Bangladesh	7,202	6,718	8,899	9,302	9,243	0.08	-0.63
Bhutan	158	180	250	278	311	0.00	11.87
India	73,130	72,779	86,547	92,047	91,700	0.82	-0.38
Iran, Islamic Republic of	8,054	7,854	8,387	9,532	6,568	0.06	-31.10
Maldives	208	263	279	354	324	0.00	-8.47
Nepal	5,107	6,994	7,574	10,095	13,698	0.12	35.69
Pakistan	9,690	8,935	9,270	10,121	9,691	0.09	-4.25
Sri Lanka	13,959	9,406	12,517	15,674	14,148	0.13	-9.74
NOT SPECIFIED	**307,708**	**234,614**	**319,686**	**327,463**	**329,703**	**2.96**	**0.68**
Other countries of the World	157	194	192	203	145	0.00	-28.57
Nationals Residing Abroad	307,551	234,420	319,494	327,260	329,558	2.96	0.70

Yearbook of Tourism Statistics, Data 2008 – 2012, 2014 Edit

KUWAIT

2. Arrivals of non-resident visitors at national borders, by nationality

	2008	2009	2010	2011	2012	Market share 2012	% Change 2012-2011
TOTAL	4,735,910	5,087,781	5,207,785	5,574,302	5,728,697	100.00	2.77
AFRICA	64,768	73,260	95,080	113,314	113,437	1.98	0.11
East Africa	22,801	28,071	50,575	69,836	65,704	1.15	-5.92
Burundi	26	14	11	22	15	0.00	-31.82
Comoros	92	166	425	303	411	0.01	35.64
Djibouti	74	95	92	82	116	0.00	41.46
Eritrea	985	1,207	1,044	969	976	0.02	0.72
Ethiopia	17,039	21,109	43,611	63,866	57,541	1.00	-9.90
Kenya	875	1,293	1,622	1,416	1,396	0.02	-1.41
Madagascar	244	600	705	458	1,978	0.03	331.88
Malawi	50	40	50	92	102	0.00	10.87
Mauritius	108	124	143	86	103	0.00	19.77
Mozambique	22	31	17	32	37	0.00	15.63
Rwanda	3	1	3	15	18	0.00	20.00
Seychelles	40	35	24	34	32	0.00	-5.88
Somalia	2,647	2,674	2,170	1,935	1,948	0.03	0.67
Uganda	189	203	131	117	574	0.01	390.60
United Republic of Tanzania	202	169	211	212	235	0.00	10.85
Zambia	58	39	75	10	23	0.00	130.00
Zimbabwe	147	271	241	187	199	0.00	6.42
Central Africa	1,727	1,465	1,219	949	745	0.01	-21.50
Angola	24	21	12	20	34	0.00	70.00
Cameroon	140	82	108	50	60	0.00	20.00
Central African Republic	32	101	32	34	37	0.00	8.82
Chad	1,471	1,216	1,032	794	571	0.01	-28.09
Congo	1	2		7	5	0.00	-28.57
Democratic Republic of the Congo	52	35	30	36	26	0.00	-27.78
Gabon	7	8	5	8	12	0.00	50.00
North Africa	27,428	29,498	31,462	31,973	36,551	0.64	14.32
Algeria	3,041	3,201	3,694	3,566	4,116	0.07	15.42
Morocco	10,474	11,086	11,808	11,451	13,006	0.23	13.58
Sudan	8,318	8,302	8,043	9,049	10,420	0.18	15.15
Tunisia	5,595	6,909	7,917	7,907	9,009	0.16	13.94
Southern Africa	4,892	5,568	5,337	4,550	4,494	0.08	-1.23
Botswana		5	6	29	37	0.00	27.59
Lesotho	1	1	62	13	23	0.00	76.92
Namibia	22	4	15	13	9	0.00	-30.77
South Africa	4,764	5,350	5,023	4,424	4,312	0.08	-2.53
Swaziland	105	208	231	71	113	0.00	59.15
West Africa	7,918	8,657	6,485	5,960	5,937	0.10	-0.39
Benin	185	172	203	226	260	0.00	15.04
Burkina Faso	72	60	70	101	97	0.00	-3.96
Cape Verde	1	4	2		6	0.00	
Côte d'Ivoire	158	84	58	89	71	0.00	-20.22
Gambia	33	37	54	66	72	0.00	9.09
Ghana	4,681	5,045	3,084	2,662	2,331	0.04	-12.43
Guinea	132	108	97	70	78	0.00	11.43
Guinea-Bissau	3		21	6	13	0.00	116.67
Liberia	293	263	288	224	221	0.00	-1.34
Mali	109	101	120	143	238	0.00	66.43
Mauritania	269	294	266	293	387	0.01	32.08
Niger	118	147	173	189	189	0.00	0.00
Nigeria	1,168	1,615	1,281	1,173	1,170	0.02	-0.26
Saint Helena	10	1		1	3	0.00	200.00
Senegal	371	410	336	385	443	0.01	15.06
Sierra Leone	123	121	133	158	247	0.00	56.33

389

KUWAIT

2. Arrivals of non-resident visitors at national borders, by nationality

	2008	2009	2010	2011	2012	Market share 2012	% Change 2012-2011
Togo	192	195	299	174	111	0.00	-36.21
Other Africa	**2**	**1**	**2**	**46**	**6**	**0.00**	**-86.96**
Other countries of Africa	2	1	2	46	6	0.00	-86.96
AMERICAS	**219,039**	**229,288**	**226,943**	**222,973**	**184,619**	**3.22**	**-17.20**
Caribbean	**471**	**516**	**478**	**578**	**671**	**0.01**	**16.09**
Aruba	1	1	6	4			
Bahamas	9	4	17	15	11	0.00	-26.67
Barbados	17	21	12	11	10	0.00	-9.09
Bermuda		1	4	8	31	0.00	287.50
Cuba	39	44	18	33	65	0.00	96.97
Curaçao				1			
Dominican Republic	205	177	165	196	248	0.00	26.53
Grenada	22	24	30	13	17	0.00	30.77
Guadeloupe	3						
Haiti	45	41	31	72	84	0.00	16.67
Jamaica	41	59	61	88	93	0.00	5.68
Martinique	1						
Saint Kitts and Nevis	3		4	2	7	0.00	250.00
Saint Lucia	4	4	7	7	5	0.00	-28.57
Saint Vincent and the Grenadines				3	1	0.00	-66.67
Trinidad and Tobago	81	140	123	125	99	0.00	-20.80
Central America	**300**	**423**	**399**	**290**	**290**	**0.01**	**0.00**
Belize	151	162	175	153	127	0.00	-16.99
Costa Rica	10	27	21	24	19	0.00	-20.83
El Salvador	41	127	159	50	39	0.00	-22.00
Guatemala	11	26	10	20	36	0.00	80.00
Honduras	27	40	4	21	10	0.00	-52.38
Nicaragua	7	8	4	2	4	0.00	100.00
Panama	53	33	26	20	55	0.00	175.00
North America	**215,147**	**224,756**	**222,270**	**218,016**	**179,569**	**3.13**	**-17.63**
Canada	36,867	40,440	41,156	39,130	39,060	0.68	-0.18
Mexico	374	374	276	369	385	0.01	4.34
United States of America	177,906	183,942	180,838	178,517	140,124	2.45	-21.51
South America	**3,114**	**3,588**	**3,789**	**4,081**	**4,081**	**0.07**	**0.00**
Argentina	438	514	441	609	532	0.01	-12.64
Bolivia	85	66	99	86	80	0.00	-6.98
Brazil	1,082	1,143	1,374	1,252	1,209	0.02	-3.43
Chile	84	103	99	72	91	0.00	26.39
Colombia	440	542	420	410	469	0.01	14.39
Ecuador	89	130	166	138	197	0.00	42.75
French Guiana	1	6	20		2	0.00	
Guyana	9	8	20	17	23	0.00	35.29
Paraguay	7	14	6	9	7	0.00	-22.22
Peru	89	77	42	52	149	0.00	186.54
Suriname	9	19	9	12	26	0.00	116.67
Uruguay	12	33	29	51	48	0.00	-5.88
Venezuela	769	933	1,064	1,373	1,248	0.02	-9.10
Other Americas	**7**	**5**	**7**	**8**	**8**	**0.00**	**0.00**
Other countries of the Americas	7	5	7	8	8	0.00	0.00
EAST ASIA AND THE PACIFIC	**244,241**	**249,653**	**229,734**	**226,602**	**230,571**	**4.02**	**1.75**
North-East Asia	**25,951**	**20,855**	**25,571**	**31,941**	**32,188**	**0.56**	**0.77**
China	9,546	8,207	10,925	14,208	13,283	0.23	-6.51
Hong Kong, China	273	212	244	211	218	0.00	3.32
Japan	6,215	4,606	4,959	4,798	5,291	0.09	10.28
Korea, Dem. People's Republic of	831	728		442	354	0.01	-19.91
Korea, Republic of	8,795	6,838	9,111	11,677	12,731	0.22	9.03

Yearbook of Tourism Statistics, Data 2008 – 2012, 2014 Editic

KUWAIT

2. Arrivals of non-resident visitors at national borders, by nationality

	2008	2009	2010	2011	2012	Market share 2012	% Change 2012-2011
Macao, China	2	3	4	10	4	0.00	-60.00
Mongolia	191	106	170	399	197	0.00	-50.63
Taiwan, Province of China	98	155	158	196	110	0.00	-43.88
South-East Asia	**199,097**	**207,446**	**184,929**	**179,100**	**184,353**	**3.22**	**2.93**
Brunei Darussalam	4	31	37	14	21	0.00	50.00
Cambodia	55	100	64	70	113	0.00	61.43
Indonesia	65,391	63,419	35,664	25,793	17,693	0.31	-31.40
Lao People's Democratic Republic	4	72	20	14	34	0.00	142.86
Malaysia	4,067	3,495	4,105	4,320	4,294	0.07	-0.60
Myanmar	211	332	188	376	297	0.01	-21.01
Philippines	117,812	130,417	135,182	139,988	154,389	2.70	10.29
Singapore	1,535	1,275	1,457	1,323	1,174	0.02	-11.26
Thailand	8,852	7,561	7,631	6,670	5,544	0.10	-16.88
Timor-Leste	19	7	8	6	7	0.00	16.67
Viet Nam	1,147	737	573	526	787	0.01	49.62
Australasia	**17,841**	**20,293**	**18,557**	**15,293**	**13,821**	**0.24**	**-9.63**
Australia	14,915	16,990	15,306	12,543	11,180	0.20	-10.87
New Zealand	2,926	3,303	3,251	2,750	2,641	0.05	-3.96
Melanesia	**1,241**	**941**	**565**	**147**	**92**	**0.00**	**-37.41**
Fiji	1,241	941	565	147	92	0.00	-37.41
Micronesia	**39**	**33**	**45**	**22**	**16**	**0.00**	**-27.27**
Kiribati	2						
Marshall Islands	4	4	7	5	3	0.00	-40.00
Palau	33	29	38	17	13	0.00	-23.53
Polynesia	**55**	**19**	**16**	**15**	**13**	**0.00**	**-13.33**
Cook Islands	7	12	8	9	7	0.00	-22.22
Samoa	4	3	1		1	0.00	
Tonga	44	4	7	6	5	0.00	-16.67
Other East Asia and the Pacific	**17**	**66**	**51**	**84**	**88**	**0.00**	**4.76**
Other countries of Asia	17	66	51	84	88	0.00	4.76
EUROPE	**181,162**	**184,248**	**191,455**	**188,306**	**185,227**	**3.23**	**-1.64**
Central/Eastern Europe	**26,413**	**21,729**	**25,211**	**20,218**	**19,788**	**0.35**	**-2.13**
Armenia	440	464	526	586	643	0.01	9.73
Azerbaijan	202	289	290	340	410	0.01	20.59
Belarus	604	602	454	376	287	0.01	-23.67
Bulgaria	4,177	3,301	3,490	3,223	3,365	0.06	4.41
Czech Republic	884	686	1,353	779	617	0.01	-20.80
Czech Republic/Slovakia	2				1	0.00	
Estonia	103	29	38	33	51	0.00	54.55
Georgia	3,659	2,731	1,832	1,135	551	0.01	-51.45
Hungary	1,166	1,197	1,380	1,345	1,497	0.03	11.30
Kazakhstan	313	197	238	277	218	0.00	-21.30
Kyrgyzstan	257	512	634	696	649	0.01	-6.75
Latvia	48	63	85	98	152	0.00	55.10
Lithuania	132	108	107	120	209	0.00	74.17
Poland	1,810	1,593	1,955	1,806	1,781	0.03	-1.38
Republic of Moldova	65	60	54	52	86	0.00	65.38
Romania	2,392	3,688	5,609	3,499	3,480	0.06	-0.54
Russian Federation	7,466	3,969	2,579	3,190	3,119	0.05	-2.23
Slovakia	606	576	2,772	915	693	0.01	-24.26
Tajikistan	106	69	118	129	208	0.00	61.24
Turkmenistan	18	36	48	12	33	0.00	175.00
Ukraine	1,371	981	1,050	1,051	1,141	0.02	8.56
Uzbekistan	592	578	599	556	597	0.01	7.37
Northern Europe	**81,349**	**83,734**	**83,947**	**87,000**	**86,222**	**1.51**	**-0.89**
Denmark	2,990	3,367	3,206	3,063	3,279	0.06	7.05
Finland	1,308	1,094	1,025	1,097	930	0.02	-15.22

Yearbook of Tourism Statistics, Data 2008 – 2012, 2014 Edition

KUWAIT

2. Arrivals of non-resident visitors at national borders, by nationality

	2008	2009	2010	2011	2012	Market share 2012	% Change 2012-2011
Iceland	91	139	81	110	105	0.00	-4.55
Ireland	2,935	2,936	3,000	3,174	3,424	0.06	7.88
Norway	2,187	2,566	2,659	2,433	1,962	0.03	-19.36
Sweden	6,298	6,512	6,614	6,826	6,820	0.12	-0.09
United Kingdom	65,540	67,120	67,362	70,297	69,702	1.22	-0.85
Southern Europe	**19,253**	**24,125**	**25,325**	**24,199**	**24,349**	**0.43**	**0.62**
Albania	224	98	199	205	224	0.00	9.27
Andorra		2	2	7	8	0.00	14.29
Bosnia and Herzegovina	1,575	1,509	1,124	1,327	904	0.02	-31.88
Croatia	481	615	806	774	658	0.01	-14.99
Greece	1,869	1,887	2,416	2,759	2,510	0.04	-9.03
Holy See	17	11					
Italy	8,806	11,222	10,925	10,021	11,002	0.19	9.79
Malta	124	116	222	169	223	0.00	31.95
Montenegro			11	33	48	0.00	45.45
Portugal	1,043	867	1,141	989	1,449	0.03	46.51
San Marino	3	10	3	7	8	0.00	14.29
Serbia	25	235	628	923	942	0.02	2.06
Serbia and Montenegro	1,475	1,430					
Slovenia	173	153	286	231	296	0.01	28.14
Spain	2,762	5,118	6,771	6,382	5,691	0.10	-10.83
TFYR of Macedonia	676	852	791	372	386	0.01	3.76
Western Europe	**41,601**	**42,666**	**44,451**	**44,669**	**43,486**	**0.76**	**-2.65**
Austria	1,814	1,984	1,997	1,914	1,690	0.03	-11.70
Belgium	1,745	2,374	2,755	2,407	2,035	0.04	-15.45
France	14,345	14,907	15,084	15,209	15,844	0.28	4.18
Germany	14,579	14,159	15,283	14,962	14,455	0.25	-3.39
Liechtenstein	22	18	13	23	70	0.00	204.35
Luxembourg	115	111	97	87	104	0.00	19.54
Monaco	9	3	6		3	0.00	
Netherlands	6,589	7,070	7,101	7,869	7,243	0.13	-7.96
Switzerland	2,383	2,040	2,115	2,198	2,042	0.04	-7.10
East Mediterranean Europe	**12,534**	**11,893**	**11,764**	**11,653**	**10,868**	**0.19**	**-6.74**
Cyprus	368	323	286	380	614	0.01	61.58
Turkey	12,166	11,570	11,478	11,273	10,254	0.18	-9.04
Other Europe	**12**	**101**	**757**	**567**	**514**	**0.01**	**-9.35**
Other countries of Europe	12	101	757	567	514	0.01	-9.35
MIDDLE EAST	**2,778,066**	**2,996,469**	**3,103,394**	**3,434,185**	**3,609,287**	**63.00**	**5.10**
Bahrain	112,910	125,962	122,192	121,482	163,783	2.86	34.82
Egypt	532,753	540,708	569,452	594,099	646,093	11.28	8.75
Iraq	100,872	89,908	69,080	70,058	76,757	1.34	9.56
Jordan	85,356	90,023	94,480	97,267	103,020	1.80	5.91
Lebanon	117,055	119,998	117,686	104,739	108,277	1.89	3.38
Libya	551	535	677	455	773	0.01	69.89
Oman	16,645	16,711	18,035	17,865	19,782	0.35	10.73
Palestine	7,170	7,480	7,622	6,640	6,775	0.12	2.03
Qatar	29,236	32,170	30,873	33,023	35,861	0.63	8.59
Saudi Arabia	1,425,049	1,613,460	1,708,661	2,063,815	2,160,291	37.71	4.67
Syrian Arab Republic	304,605	306,561	307,949	269,013	227,429	3.97	-15.46
United Arab Emirates	36,355	41,763	45,957	45,659	49,458	0.86	8.32
Yemen	9,509	11,190	10,730	10,070	10,988	0.19	9.12
SOUTH ASIA	**1,224,937**	**1,316,151**	**1,327,607**	**1,351,987**	**1,355,377**	**23.66**	**0.25**
Afghanistan	23,534	20,045	12,607	12,457	12,467	0.22	0.08
Bangladesh	93,585	104,757	102,390	107,817	105,983	1.85	-1.70
Bhutan	24	36	72	123	77	0.00	-37.40
India	673,671	733,117	751,059	789,694	826,526	14.43	4.66
Iran, Islamic Republic of	90,839	89,219	81,136	72,067	72,432	1.26	0.51

392

Yearbook of Tourism Statistics, Data 2008 – 2012, 2014 Editic

KUWAIT

2. Arrivals of non-resident visitors at national borders, by nationality

	2008	2009	2010	2011	2012	Market share 2012	% Change 2012-2011
Maldives	22	16	14	41	49	0.00	19.51
Nepal	37,939	54,209	52,971	53,812	47,546	0.83	-11.64
Pakistan	214,427	219,502	228,028	215,194	200,037	3.49	-7.04
Sri Lanka	90,896	95,250	99,330	100,782	90,260	1.58	-10.44
NOT SPECIFIED	**23,697**	**38,712**	**33,572**	**36,935**	**50,179**	**0.88**	**35.86**
Other countries of the World	23,697	38,712	33,572	36,935	50,179	0.88	35.86

Yearbook of Tourism Statistics, Data 2008 – 2012, 2014 Edition

KYRGYZSTAN

2. Arrivals of non-resident visitors at national borders, by country of residence

	2008	2009	2010	2011	2012	Market share 2012	% Change 2012-2011
TOTAL	1,844,396	1,394,175	854,900	2,277,554	2,405,954	100.00	5.64
AMERICAS	15,086	12,986	8,753	17,739	18,947	0.79	6.81
North America	15,086	12,986	8,753	17,739	18,947	0.79	6.81
Canada	1,705	1,976	1,706	1,917	2,240	0.09	16.85
United States of America	13,381	11,010	7,047	15,822	16,707	0.69	5.59
EAST ASIA AND THE PACIFIC	31,157	32,366	23,898	33,247	34,263	1.42	3.06
North-East Asia	29,172	29,950	22,432	31,498	32,096	1.33	1.90
China	22,487	22,919	18,384	25,315	24,115	1.00	-4.74
Japan	2,026	2,119	988	2,487	2,324	0.10	-6.55
Korea, Republic of	4,659	4,912	3,060	3,696	5,657	0.24	53.06
South-East Asia	159	267	86	127	249	0.01	96.06
Malaysia	159	267	86	127	249	0.01	96.06
Australasia	1,826	2,149	1,380	1,622	1,918	0.08	18.25
Australia	1,568	1,810	1,196	1,389	1,680	0.07	20.95
New Zealand	258	339	184	233	238	0.01	2.15
EUROPE	1,783,601	1,332,286	804,293	2,208,239	2,333,206	96.98	5.66
Central/Eastern Europe	1,740,147	1,291,048	775,438	2,168,520	2,284,717	94.96	5.36
Armenia	576	425	307	1,001	889	0.04	-11.19
Azerbaijan	1,330	1,244	1,315	4,005	3,618	0.15	-9.66
Belarus	1,064	1,038	548	1,703	1,337	0.06	-21.49
Czech Republic	156	339	141	81	130	0.01	60.49
Georgia	720	910	624	910	1,008	0.04	10.77
Hungary	279	447	222	369	456	0.02	23.58
Kazakhstan	737,460	687,326	541,710	864,963	1,675,644	69.65	93.72
Lithuania	491	296	175	422	588	0.02	39.34
Poland	1,046	813	453	702	991	0.04	41.17
Republic of Moldova	933	880	472	1,224	821	0.03	-32.92
Russian Federation	204,794	158,820	134,436	1,020,575	364,591	15.15	-64.28
Tajikistan	218,727	239,342	68,311	50,946	72,087	3.00	41.50
Turkmenistan	3,834	5,430	5,002	310	431	0.02	39.03
Ukraine	3,160	4,287	1,582	9,102	3,538	0.15	-61.13
Uzbekistan	565,577	189,451	20,140	212,207	158,588	6.59	-25.27
Northern Europe	4,614	5,760	6,970	4,543	6,387	0.27	40.59
Denmark	126	89	77	137	274	0.01	100.00
Finland	266	303	180	174	280	0.01	60.92
Ireland	261	631	349	276	300	0.01	8.70
Norway	420	545	383	518	962	0.04	85.71
Sweden	186	316	221	240	363	0.02	51.25
United Kingdom	3,355	3,876	5,760	3,198	4,208	0.17	31.58
Southern Europe	3,139	2,824	1,374	2,124	2,053	0.09	-3.34
Italy	1,145	1,321	914	1,477	1,131	0.05	-23.43
Spain	1,994	1,503	460	647	922	0.04	42.50
Western Europe	18,546	18,290	11,788	16,572	20,554	0.85	24.03
Austria	782	1,072	558	525	868	0.04	65.33
Belgium	792	968	430	596	741	0.03	24.33
France	3,563	3,209	1,818	3,743	3,935	0.16	5.13
Germany	10,271	9,850	7,278	8,607	11,734	0.49	36.33
Netherlands	1,269	1,220	709	852	1,222	0.05	43.43
Switzerland	1,869	1,971	995	2,249	2,054	0.09	-8.67
East Mediterranean Europe	17,155	14,364	8,723	16,480	19,495	0.81	18.29
Israel	999	988	591	745	1,106	0.05	48.46
Turkey	16,156	13,376	8,132	15,735	18,389	0.76	16.87
MIDDLE EAST	213	205	93	126	271	0.01	115.08
Saudi Arabia	213	205	93	126	271	0.01	115.08

394

KYRGYZSTAN

2. Arrivals of non-resident visitors at national borders, by country of residence

	2008	2009	2010	2011	2012	Market share 2012	% Change 2012-2011
SOUTH ASIA	**7,159**	**7,134**	**4,996**	**7,351**	**7,321**	**0.30**	**-0.41**
Afghanistan	568	474	420	551	610	0.03	10.71
India	1,120	1,744	1,788	2,029	2,801	0.12	38.05
Iran, Islamic Republic of	3,703	2,987	1,497	2,696	1,935	0.08	-28.23
Pakistan	1,768	1,929	1,291	2,075	1,975	0.08	-4.82
NOT SPECIFIED	**7,180**	**9,198**	**12,867**	**10,852**	**11,946**	**0.50**	**10.08**
Other countries of the World	7,180	9,198	12,867	10,852	11,946	0.50	10.08

Yearbook of Tourism Statistics, Data 2008 – 2012, 2014 Edition

LAO PEOPLE´S DEMOCRATIC REPUBLIC

2. Arrivals of non-resident visitors at national borders, by nationality

	2008	2009	2010	2011	2012	Market share 2012	% Change 2012-2011
TOTAL	1,736,787	2,008,363	2,513,028	2,723,564	3,330,089	100.00	22.27
AMERICAS	75,266	53,348	67,291	69,990	75,851	2.28	8.37
North America	69,412	50,294	63,419	64,514	70,124	2.11	8.70
Canada	14,695	10,955	13,637	14,422	16,744	0.50	16.10
United States of America	54,717	39,339	49,782	50,092	53,380	1.60	6.56
Other Americas	5,854	3,054	3,872	5,476	5,727	0.17	4.58
Other countries of the Americas	5,854	3,054	3,872	5,476	5,727	0.17	4.58
EAST ASIA AND THE PACIFIC	1,479,847	1,818,291	2,256,705	2,461,424	3,057,857	91.83	24.23
North-East Asia	158,151	176,702	226,588	228,410	299,708	9.00	31.21
China	105,852	128,226	161,854	150,791	199,857	6.00	32.54
Japan	31,569	28,081	34,076	37,883	42,026	1.26	10.94
Korea, Republic of	18,065	17,876	27,312	34,707	53,829	1.62	55.10
Taiwan, Province of China	2,665	2,519	3,346	5,029	3,996	0.12	-20.54
South-East Asia	1,285,531	1,611,009	1,990,932	2,191,224	2,712,478	81.45	23.79
Brunei Darussalam	338	267	197	354	533	0.02	50.56
Cambodia	5,482	7,530	6,908	7,561	15,140	0.45	100.24
Indonesia	2,043	3,158	2,245	3,338	4,256	0.13	27.50
Malaysia	15,625	13,816	15,427	17,702	22,785	0.68	28.71
Myanmar	1,698	1,794	1,652	1,765	1,730	0.05	-1.98
Philippines	12,647	8,331	10,341	11,847	14,281	0.43	20.55
Singapore	4,866	5,286	6,087	7,130	10,545	0.32	47.90
Thailand	891,448	1,274,064	1,517,064	1,579,941	1,937,612	58.18	22.64
Viet Nam	351,384	296,763	431,011	561,586	705,596	21.19	25.64
Australasia	32,544	27,688	34,931	36,759	39,296	1.18	6.90
Australia	28,180	24,209	30,538	31,874	33,878	1.02	6.29
New Zealand	4,364	3,479	4,393	4,885	5,418	0.16	10.91
Other East Asia and the Pacific	3,621	2,892	4,254	5,031	6,375	0.19	26.71
Other countries East Asia/Pacific	3,621	2,892	4,254	5,031	6,375	0.19	26.71
EUROPE	172,846	132,412	181,840	185,771	189,043	5.68	1.76
Central/Eastern Europe	3,206	2,861	4,835	7,019	8,642	0.26	23.12
Russian Federation	3,206	2,861	4,835	7,019	8,642	0.26	23.12
Northern Europe	52,160	38,377	54,207	52,237	53,693	1.61	2.79
Denmark	3,657	2,977	5,359	4,769	5,054	0.15	5.98
Finland	2,729	1,985	2,470	2,742	2,962	0.09	8.02
Norway	2,909	2,221	2,845	3,178	3,307	0.10	4.06
Sweden	6,827	4,150	6,261	5,926	6,676	0.20	12.66
United Kingdom	36,038	27,044	37,272	35,622	35,694	1.07	0.20
Southern Europe	10,153	8,980	11,848	12,080	10,863	0.33	-10.07
Greece	569	537	578	451	366	0.01	-18.85
Italy	6,467	5,481	7,075	6,977	6,289	0.19	-9.86
Spain	3,117	2,962	4,195	4,652	4,208	0.13	-9.54
Western Europe	89,860	70,134	93,658	93,595	98,843	2.97	5.61
Austria	2,843	2,450	2,565	3,801	2,860	0.09	-24.76
Belgium	4,908	3,868	5,012	5,241	6,284	0.19	19.90
France	39,077	31,775	44,844	44,399	46,903	1.41	5.64
Germany	25,191	17,710	22,583	21,280	23,417	0.70	10.04
Netherlands	11,315	8,504	10,032	9,164	9,283	0.28	1.30
Switzerland	6,526	5,827	8,622	9,710	10,096	0.30	3.98
East Mediterranean Europe	4,090	2,236	3,700	4,232	3,241	0.10	-23.42
Israel	4,090	2,236	3,700	4,232	3,241	0.10	-23.42
Other Europe	13,377	9,824	13,592	16,608	13,761	0.41	-17.14
Other countries of Europe	13,377	9,824	13,592	16,608	13,761	0.41	-17.14

Yearbook of Tourism Statistics, Data 2008 – 2012, 2014 Editi

LAO PEOPLE´S DEMOCRATIC REPUBLIC

2. Arrivals of non-resident visitors at national borders, by nationality

	2008	2009	2010	2011	2012	Market share 2012	% Change 2012-2011
SOUTH ASIA	**2,652**	**2,280**	**3,321**	**3,227**	**3,275**	**0.10**	**1.49**
India	2,652	2,280	3,321	3,227	3,275	0.10	1.49
NOT SPECIFIED	**6,176**	**2,032**	**3,871**	**3,152**	**4,063**	**0.12**	**28.90**
Other countries of the World	6,176	2,032	3,871	3,152	4,063	0.12	28.90

Yearbook of Tourism Statistics, Data 2008 – 2012, 2014 Edition

LATVIA

2. Arrivals of non-resident visitors at national borders, by country of residence

		2008	2009	2010	2011	2012	Market share 2012	% Change 2012-2011
TOTAL	(*)	5,496,205	4,726,585	5,042,260	5,538,393			
AFRICA			5,059	7,422	4,345			
East Africa			317	144	656			
United Republic of Tanzania			317	144	656			
Central Africa					143			
Congo					143			
North Africa			3,671	5,190	1,135			
Algeria			660	583	188			
Morocco			1,877	3,509	947			
Tunisia			1,134	1,098				
Southern Africa			460	146	1,081			
South Africa			460	146	1,081			
West Africa			611	1,942	1,330			
Gambia					286			
Ghana				343				
Liberia				175				
Niger			611		279			
Nigeria				1,424	765			
AMERICAS		37,615	60,256	62,408	76,550			
Caribbean			472	808	383			
Cuba			292	808	383			
Jamaica			180					
North America		37,615	55,904	54,772	70,354			
Canada		6,064	9,099	10,417	9,074			
Mexico			1,273	2,553	1,704			
United States of America		31,551	45,532	41,802	59,576			
South America			3,880	6,828	5,813			
Argentina			460	1,291	764			
Brazil			1,438	3,148	1,970			
Chile			493	1,729	1,756			
Peru				197	143			
Suriname				144				
Uruguay			1,163	319	711			
Venezuela			326		469			
EAST ASIA AND THE PACIFIC		21,911	35,405	47,040	49,521			
North-East Asia		13,881	17,030	27,595	26,769			
China		5,973	5,042	13,131	13,500			
Hong Kong, China			652		596			
Japan		6,347	7,937	10,483	10,072			
Korea, Republic of		1,561	1,973	2,402	1,323			
Mongolia			1,426	1,291	1,278			
Taiwan, Province of China				288				
South-East Asia		1,343	9,513	8,786	9,142			
Indonesia			4,166	3,170	2,120			
Malaysia			1,134	2,336	711			
Philippines		1,343	1,736	2,233	2,093			
Singapore			360					
Thailand			2,117	726	3,081			
Viet Nam				321	1,137			
Australasia		6,687	8,862	10,659	13,610			
Australia		4,719	5,040	5,738	9,340			
New Zealand		1,968	3,822	4,921	4,270			
EUROPE		5,410,212	4,611,254	4,901,853	5,386,291			
Central/Eastern Europe		4,169,827	3,450,735	3,537,615	3,879,175			
Armenia		2,497	2,029	9,441	8,045			

Yearbook of Tourism Statistics, Data 2008 – 2012, 2014 Edition

LATVIA

2. Arrivals of non-resident visitors at national borders, by country of residence

	2008	2009	2010	2011	2012	Market share 2012	% Change 2012-2011
Azerbaijan		4,305	4,376	3,115			
Belarus	111,528	113,276	101,469	125,854			
Bulgaria	3,233	5,708	10,733	11,860			
Czech Republic	32,056	28,881	31,279	42,145			
Estonia	1,384,561	946,292	957,038	1,040,672			
Georgia	5,241	17,266	23,885	16,882			
Hungary	8,810	10,517	15,821	14,339			
Kazakhstan	30,712	19,380	19,036	23,005			
Kyrgyzstan		1,991	1,127	3,854			
Lithuania	1,958,709	1,731,017	1,707,920	1,788,940			
Poland	207,524	201,811	210,457	234,118			
Republic of Moldova	6,548	9,467	10,239	8,548			
Romania	3,451	3,827	8,713	7,070			
Russian Federation	356,888	297,328	348,070	449,797			
Slovakia	8,454	8,267	11,759	12,381			
Tajikistan		1,798	4,063	3,879			
Turkmenistan		116	736	188			
Ukraine	40,196	37,462	46,528	62,322			
Uzbekistan	9,419	9,997	14,925	22,161			
Northern Europe	**763,417**	**704,111**	**857,075**	**908,149**			
Denmark	42,515	51,798	65,418	63,997			
Finland	198,102	172,919	202,644	188,915			
Iceland	3,604	4,986	6,130	16,418			
Ireland	22,249	21,539	22,282	25,593			
Norway	80,309	87,446	121,438	150,077			
Sweden	323,456	271,840	352,486	351,185			
United Kingdom	93,182	93,583	86,677	111,964			
Southern Europe	**94,040**	**85,709**	**113,331**	**138,023**			
Albania		180	146				
Andorra				379			
Bosnia and Herzegovina		163	144				
Croatia	3,713	3,544	4,007	8,692			
Greece	5,241	4,065	6,666	6,581			
Italy	55,357	41,392	53,482	71,540			
Malta	1,683	3,814	4,285	3,964			
Montenegro			197				
Portugal	7,067	9,164	12,927	13,956			
Serbia			2,355	523			
Slovenia	2,480	2,728	4,709	4,818			
Spain	18,499	18,145	22,108	26,100			
TFYR of Macedonia		2,514	2,305	1,470			
Western Europe	**373,334**	**348,770**	**360,688**	**431,176**			
Austria	15,695	9,918	16,045	21,419			
Belgium	21,548	23,802	41,150	48,766			
France	40,312	35,513	35,490	49,204			
Germany	261,778	226,461	218,449	249,112			
Liechtenstein		681	806	1,422			
Luxembourg	2,231	2,699	5,837	7,129			
Monaco		940	351	848			
Netherlands	19,903	31,053	28,833	32,048			
Switzerland	11,867	17,703	13,727	21,228			
East Mediterranean Europe	**9,594**	**21,929**	**33,144**	**29,768**			
Cyprus		2,711	5,511	3,015			
Israel	4,228	9,601	15,699	18,464			
Turkey	5,366	9,617	11,934	8,289			
MIDDLE EAST		**1,924**	**7,514**	**1,858**			
Bahrain			175	191			

399

LATVIA

2. Arrivals of non-resident visitors at national borders, by country of residence

	2008	2009	2010	2011	2012	Market share 2012	% Change 2012-2011
Egypt		635	1,027	140			
Iraq			146	383			
Jordan		158	197	188			
Kuwait			1,303	765			
Lebanon		455	2,949				
Qatar			1,055				
Saudi Arabia		180	144				
Syrian Arab Republic			518				
United Arab Emirates		496		191			
SOUTH ASIA	**4,329**	**7,790**	**11,283**	**11,063**			
Afghanistan			526				
Bangladesh		180	197				
India	4,329	3,737	7,147	7,790			
Iran, Islamic Republic of		2,305	1,467	188			
Nepal				564			
Pakistan		1,568	1,946	2,333			
Sri Lanka				188			
NOT SPECIFIED	**22,138**	**4,897**	**4,740**	**8,765**			
Other countries of the World	22,138	4,897	4,740	8,765			

Yearbook of Tourism Statistics, Data 2008 – 2012, 2014 Editic

LATVIA

4. Arrivals of non-resident tourists in all types of accommodation establishments, by country of residence

	2008	2009	2010	2011	2012	Market share 2012	% Change 2012-2011
TOTAL	944,690	753,875	877,774	1,063,294	1,096,274	100.00	3.10
AFRICA	389	347	428	786			
East Africa	7	15	19	59			
Kenya	4	7	12	44			
Uganda		3		10			
United Republic of Tanzania	2	4	5	2			
Zimbabwe	1	1	2	3			
Central Africa	25	28	32	54			
Angola	8	2	2	11			
Cameroon	11	15	11	21			
Central African Republic	6	6	15	21			
Congo			3	1			
Democratic Republic of the Congo		5	1				
North Africa	65	56	97	167			
Algeria	12	16	18	15			
Morocco	28	26	64	54			
Tunisia	25	14	15	98			
Southern Africa	229	165	182	353			
Namibia	2		11	6			
South Africa	116	126	132	151			
Swaziland	111	39	39	196			
West Africa	63	83	98	153			
Benin	2						
Gambia	1			1			
Ghana	2	7	1	14			
Liberia			2	2			
Mauritania		2	2	9			
Niger	4	3	15	18			
Nigeria	27	30	29	46			
Senegal		1	11	2			
Sierra Leone	27	40	38	61			
AMERICAS	24,690	19,027	22,589	24,820	27,061	2.47	9.03
Caribbean	8	26	29	25			
Antigua and Barbuda		1	1	5			
Barbados		9					
Cuba	7	7	13	19			
Dominican Republic	1	7					
Jamaica		2	15	1			
Central America	40	53	70	94			
Belize	1	2	1				
Costa Rica	19	43	33	57			
Guatemala	9		21	17			
Panama	11	8	15	20			
North America	23,583	17,737	21,001	22,212	25,484	2.32	14.73
Canada	2,889	2,418	2,703	3,587	3,298	0.30	-8.06
Greenland	20	4	11	3			
Mexico	334	486	424	507			
United States of America	20,340	14,829	17,863	18,115	22,186	2.02	22.47
South America	1,059	1,211	1,489	2,489	1,577	0.14	-36.64
Argentina	345	165	320	362			
Bolivia	42	10	11	1			
Brazil	523	801	848	1,647	1,577	0.14	-4.25
Chile	34	86	85	173			
Colombia	18	73	68	87			
Ecuador	16	6	8	13			
Peru	48	15	40	54			

Yearbook of Tourism Statistics, Data 2008 – 2012, 2014 Edition

LATVIA

4. Arrivals of non-resident tourists in all types of accommodation establishments, by country of residence

	2008	2009	2010	2011	2012	Market share 2012	% Change 2012-2011
Suriname				22			
Uruguay	7	8	66	38			
Venezuela	26	47	43	92			
EAST ASIA AND THE PACIFIC	**13,464**	**14,389**	**15,482**	**18,426**	**15,667**	**1.43**	**-14.97**
North-East Asia	**8,668**	**9,684**	**9,991**	**11,802**	**10,988**	**1.00**	**-6.90**
China	936	1,593	1,963	2,893	3,666	0.33	26.72
Hong Kong, China	55	97	144	435			
Japan	6,043	6,690	5,428	5,843	7,322	0.67	25.31
Korea, Dem. People's Republic of	51	447	397	383			
Korea, Republic of	1,212	332	1,562	1,475			
Mongolia	15	30	19	20			
Taiwan, Province of China	356	495	478	753			
South-East Asia	**541**	**979**	**1,395**	**1,421**			
Indonesia	44	159	123	104			
Lao People's Democratic Republic	1	2	116	19			
Malaysia	82	137	51	117			
Philippines	92	108	125	277			
Singapore	83	103	171	328			
Thailand	156	448	777	487			
Viet Nam	83	22	32	89			
Australasia	**4,255**	**3,726**	**4,096**	**5,203**	**4,679**	**0.43**	**-10.07**
Australia	3,934	3,395	3,636	4,616	4,679	0.43	1.36
New Zealand	321	331	460	587			
EUROPE	**897,356**	**713,375**	**827,934**	**1,007,215**	**1,021,867**	**93.21**	**1.45**
Central/Eastern Europe	**339,513**	**265,867**	**338,473**	**447,263**	**503,666**	**45.94**	**12.61**
Armenia	131	171	290	669			
Azerbaijan	430	487	738	1,434	1,388	0.13	-3.21
Belarus	14,992	14,901	15,247	16,682	21,545	1.97	29.15
Bulgaria	1,844	1,318	1,467	1,785	1,835	0.17	2.80
Czech Republic	8,861	5,948	5,226	5,600	6,434	0.59	14.89
Estonia	82,296	58,762	62,906	81,979	87,026	7.94	6.16
Georgia	909	1,169	1,172	1,491	1,481	0.14	-0.67
Hungary	2,731	2,122	2,873	4,375	2,823	0.26	-35.47
Kazakhstan	830	484	1,157	1,665			
Kyrgyzstan	42	51	151	184			
Lithuania	107,173	71,811	84,509	100,561	93,270	8.51	-7.25
Poland	30,701	24,038	27,447	35,309	32,103	2.93	-9.08
Republic of Moldova	452	338	425	560			
Romania	3,391	1,982	2,699	2,771	3,006	0.27	8.48
Russian Federation	70,778	72,227	119,007	174,343	232,552	21.21	33.39
Slovakia	2,007	1,332	1,602	2,587	3,125	0.29	20.80
Tajikistan	55	94	132	100			
Turkmenistan	17	40	22	52			
Ukraine	11,314	7,667	9,479	12,746	13,015	1.19	2.11
Uzbekistan	559	925	1,924	2,370	4,063	0.37	71.43
Northern Europe	**304,402**	**231,602**	**262,686**	**290,767**	**253,113**	**23.09**	**-12.95**
Denmark	17,100	12,686	12,859	15,075	16,871	1.54	11.91
Finland	93,025	72,024	79,655	90,991	74,172	6.77	-18.48
Iceland	688	485	840	1,108	910	0.08	-17.87
Ireland	12,120	6,012	4,380	4,190	4,099	0.37	-2.17
Norway	61,261	49,190	64,273	72,309	67,643	6.17	-6.45
Sweden	62,830	55,609	61,155	63,135	51,458	4.69	-18.50
United Kingdom	57,378	35,596	39,524	43,959	37,960	3.46	-13.65
Southern Europe	**54,175**	**47,724**	**52,053**	**68,429**	**60,401**	**5.51**	**-11.73**
Albania	60	76	118	286			
Andorra	14	32	31	69			
Bosnia and Herzegovina	22	99	87	134			

402

LATVIA

4. Arrivals of non-resident tourists in all types of accommodation establishments, by country of residence

	2008	2009	2010	2011	2012	Market share 2012	% Change 2012-2011
Croatia	556	626	815	529	881	0.08	66.54
Gibraltar	4		2	13			
Greece	3,357	2,836	3,216	3,431	2,884	0.26	-15.94
Italy	31,372	27,303	27,510	37,963	33,205	3.03	-12.53
Malta	101	184	160	251	399	0.04	58.96
Montenegro		14	10	37			
Portugal	2,440	2,638	2,958	3,212	2,393	0.22	-25.50
San Marino	4	13	3	32			
Serbia	51	221	236	515			
Slovenia	1,273	1,048	1,144	1,222	1,400	0.13	14.57
Spain	14,837	12,551	15,706	20,680	19,239	1.75	-6.97
TFYR of Macedonia	84	83	57	55			
Western Europe	**191,083**	**159,010**	**162,488**	**184,053**	**188,604**	**17.20**	**2.47**
Austria	11,364	8,543	6,554	8,515	8,197	0.75	-3.73
Belgium	7,562	8,811	11,005	13,092	11,140	1.02	-14.91
France	20,123	18,296	19,032	19,635	20,912	1.91	6.50
Germany	122,682	93,739	98,305	113,064	120,447	10.99	6.53
Liechtenstein	17	18	14	107			
Luxembourg	909	925	826	857	948	0.09	10.62
Monaco	31	77	118	127			
Netherlands	19,060	18,893	18,113	18,358	17,682	1.61	-3.68
Switzerland	9,335	9,708	8,521	10,298	9,278	0.85	-9.90
East Mediterranean Europe	**8,183**	**9,172**	**12,234**	**16,703**	**16,083**	**1.47**	**-3.71**
Cyprus	670	780	408	632	575	0.05	-9.02
Israel	4,351	3,586	4,328	6,216	6,045	0.55	-2.75
Turkey	3,162	4,806	7,498	9,855	9,463	0.86	-3.98
MIDDLE EAST	**368**	**478**	**648**	**972**			
Bahrain	6	12	16	10			
Egypt	241	196	208	282			
Iraq	19	67	91	62			
Jordan	1	11	22	17			
Kuwait	17	41	30	85			
Lebanon	21	22	87	80			
Libya	14	8	57	55			
Qatar			4	8			
Saudi Arabia	13	24	27	130			
Syrian Arab Republic	12	20	29	49			
United Arab Emirates	24	77	75	192			
Yemen			2	2			
SOUTH ASIA	**969**	**1,081**	**1,418**	**2,029**	**1,422**	**0.13**	**-29.92**
Afghanistan	63	19	87	109			
Bangladesh	17	28	22	11			
India	719	867	913	1,411	1,422	0.13	0.78
Iran, Islamic Republic of	97	94	159	210			
Nepal	2	1	19	57			
Pakistan	64	51	174	190			
Sri Lanka	7	21	44	41			
NOT SPECIFIED	**7,454**	**5,178**	**9,275**	**9,046**	**30,257**	**2.76**	**234.48**
Other countries of the World	7,454	5,178	9,275	9,046	30,257	2.76	234.48

Yearbook of Tourism Statistics, Data 2008 – 2012, 2014 Edition

LATVIA

6. Overnight stays of non-resident tourists in all types of accommodation establishments, by country of residence

	2008	2009	2010	2011	2012	Market share 2012	% Change 2012-2011
TOTAL	2,115,618	1,699,562	1,912,336	2,257,021	2,429,093	100.00	7.62
AFRICA	767	555	1,019	1,762			
East Africa	23	35	105	278			
Kenya	17	13	53	262			
Uganda		14		11			
United Republic of Tanzania	2	4	34	2			
Zimbabwe	4	4	18	3			
Central Africa	86	43	126	135			
Angola	37	2	4	14			
Cameroon	25	19	56	46			
Central African Republic	24	15	60	74			
Congo		7	5	1			
Democratic Republic of the Congo			1				
North Africa	151	104	187	348			
Algeria	28	20	51	43			
Morocco	44	42	91	100			
Tunisia	79	42	45	205			
Southern Africa	406	235	378	758			
Namibia	4		27	8			
South Africa	224	235	293	352			
Swaziland	178		58	398			
West Africa	101	138	223	243			
Benin	6						
Gambia	2			1			
Ghana	6	12	5	24			
Liberia			8	2			
Mauritania		12	28	15			
Niger	4	8	15	31			
Nigeria	55	58	60	86			
Senegal		1	21	4			
Sierra Leone	28	47	86	80			
AMERICAS	56,356	47,030	58,740	60,081	61,195	2.52	1.85
Caribbean	17	68	64	47			
Antigua and Barbuda		1	1	5			
Barbados		28					
Cuba	13	20	32	40			
Dominican Republic	4	12					
Jamaica		7	31	2			
Central America	62	79	90	180			
Belize	1	5	2				
Costa Rica	29	61	41	74			
Guatemala	19		24	43			
Panama	13	13	23	63			
North America	54,069	44,268	55,451	54,514	58,058	2.39	6.50
Canada	7,159	5,212	6,306	8,575	7,517	0.31	-12.34
Greenland	31	12	28	9			
Mexico	574	764	886	1,065			
United States of America	46,305	38,280	48,231	44,865	50,541	2.08	12.65
South America	2,208	2,615	3,135	5,340	3,137	0.13	-41.25
Argentina	653	405	683	912			
Bolivia	56	60	23	4			
Brazil	1,175	1,650	1,841	3,495	3,137	0.13	-10.24
Chile	93	163	156	402			
Colombia	24	139	151	163			
Ecuador	37	11	10	19			
Peru	82	38	83	84			

404

LATVIA

6. Overnight stays of non-resident tourists in all types of accommodation establishments, by country of residence

	2008	2009	2010	2011	2012	Market share 2012	% Change 2012-2011
Suriname				25			
Uruguay	17	43	123	69			
Venezuela	71	106	65	167			
EAST ASIA AND THE PACIFIC	**24,776**	**27,824**	**29,406**	**36,012**	**30,823**	**1.27**	**-14.41**
North-East Asia	**14,809**	**17,912**	**17,792**	**21,506**	**20,298**	**0.84**	**-5.62**
China	2,150	3,231	3,804	5,521	7,533	0.31	36.44
Hong Kong, China	122	174	306	764			
Japan	10,521	11,967	9,680	9,924	12,765	0.53	28.63
Korea, Dem. People's Republic of	92	607	691	995			
Korea, Republic of	1,267	1,026	2,555	2,903			
Mongolia	24	119	35	27			
Taiwan, Province of China	633	788	721	1,372			
South-East Asia	**1,017**	**2,221**	**2,602**	**2,748**			
Indonesia	82	380	231	189			
Lao People's Democratic Republic	1	3	124	19			
Malaysia	120	267	114	189			
Philippines	167	360	257	561			
Singapore	178	290	448	856			
Thailand	311	863	1,345	762			
Viet Nam	158	58	83	172			
Australasia	**8,950**	**7,691**	**9,012**	**11,758**	**10,525**	**0.43**	**-10.49**
Australia	8,367	7,004	8,063	10,581	10,525	0.43	-0.53
New Zealand	583	687	949	1,177			
EUROPE	**1,989,715**	**1,609,225**	**1,785,749**	**2,132,688**	**2,267,221**	**93.34**	**6.31**
Central/Eastern Europe	**785,869**	**649,913**	**740,745**	**973,489**	**1,149,532**	**47.32**	**18.08**
Armenia	453	480	724	1,225			
Azerbaijan	1,331	1,242	1,956	3,790	5,849	0.24	54.33
Belarus	102,435	131,484	82,616	83,329	91,620	3.77	9.95
Bulgaria	5,331	2,542	3,757	3,492	5,678	0.23	62.60
Czech Republic	17,268	10,749	10,946	11,265	15,099	0.62	34.03
Estonia	129,936	90,246	95,985	127,749	136,610	5.62	6.94
Georgia	2,432	2,808	2,403	5,385	8,273	0.34	53.63
Hungary	5,346	4,443	5,051	7,877	5,572	0.23	-29.26
Kazakhstan	2,229	1,314	2,692	4,139			
Kyrgyzstan	265	247	607	1,273			
Lithuania	196,461	120,457	128,760	180,541	162,918	6.71	-9.76
Poland	64,194	42,185	45,193	57,819	58,108	2.39	0.50
Republic of Moldova	985	1,061	1,437	1,069			
Romania	8,585	4,417	6,220	6,445	7,431	0.31	15.30
Russian Federation	194,999	196,582	320,130	433,560	587,953	24.20	35.61
Slovakia	4,971	2,893	3,685	5,554	9,804	0.40	76.52
Tajikistan	234	535	729	589			
Turkmenistan	32	75	44	174			
Ukraine	46,422	33,855	22,303	29,562	38,613	1.59	30.62
Uzbekistan	1,960	2,298	5,507	8,652	16,004	0.66	84.97
Northern Europe	**649,407**	**493,328**	**556,115**	**603,010**	**551,047**	**22.69**	**-8.62**
Denmark	34,299	25,518	26,245	31,180	37,565	1.55	20.48
Finland	184,841	153,309	160,956	181,742	154,407	6.36	-15.04
Iceland	1,479	992	2,341	2,720	2,055	0.08	-24.45
Ireland	28,701	13,878	10,192	9,291	9,119	0.38	-1.85
Norway	139,703	118,591	159,181	172,330	162,957	6.71	-5.44
Sweden	120,101	102,788	105,615	111,434	102,058	4.20	-8.41
United Kingdom	140,283	78,252	91,585	94,313	82,886	3.41	-12.12
Southern Europe	**128,198**	**106,701**	**110,926**	**141,046**	**129,437**	**5.33**	**-8.23**
Albania	121	196	203	357			
Andorra	27	106	64	146			
Bosnia and Herzegovina	59	169	146	324			

405

LATVIA

6. Overnight stays of non-resident tourists in all types of accommodation establishments, by country of residence

	2008	2009	2010	2011	2012	Market share 2012	% Change 2012-2011
Croatia	1,673	1,310	2,193	1,202	2,411	0.10	100.58
Gibraltar	7		5	41			
Greece	8,504	6,696	7,019	8,080	6,436	0.26	-20.35
Italy	71,373	60,433	59,453	78,070	71,760	2.95	-8.08
Malta	238	358	312	461	899	0.04	95.01
Montenegro		15	12	141			
Portugal	7,453	5,945	6,747	7,180	6,059	0.25	-15.61
San Marino	17	25	10	156			
Serbia	174	522	569	1,141			
Slovenia	2,435	2,166	2,590	2,397	3,147	0.13	31.29
Spain	35,973	28,518	31,442	41,256	38,725	1.59	-6.13
TFYR of Macedonia	144	242	161	94			
Western Europe	**402,997**	**334,139**	**346,917**	**377,006**	**399,570**	**16.45**	**5.99**
Austria	23,491	17,078	13,441	16,638	17,162	0.71	3.15
Belgium	15,120	19,468	25,151	28,577	23,519	0.97	-17.70
France	42,626	39,470	38,734	40,432	43,736	1.80	8.17
Germany	264,728	197,465	209,921	225,812	252,943	10.41	12.01
Liechtenstein	26	36	23	178			
Luxembourg	2,242	2,052	1,794	1,867	2,110	0.09	13.02
Monaco	60	121	152	208			
Netherlands	35,800	38,297	39,743	42,179	40,303	1.66	-4.45
Switzerland	18,904	20,152	17,958	21,115	19,797	0.81	-6.24
East Mediterranean Europe	**23,244**	**25,144**	**31,046**	**38,137**	**37,635**	**1.55**	**-1.32**
Cyprus	1,700	1,722	1,191	1,927	1,694	0.07	-12.09
Israel	12,642	10,417	13,519	15,036	14,815	0.61	-1.47
Turkey	8,902	13,005	16,336	21,174	21,126	0.87	-0.23
MIDDLE EAST	**947**	**1,389**	**1,817**	**2,096**			
Bahrain	21	24	51	18			
Egypt	664	499	692	776			
Iraq	54	386	156	118			
Jordan	2	64	90	46			
Kuwait	43	73	37	123			
Lebanon	37	73	228	177			
Libya	41	13	160	99			
Qatar			4	12			
Saudi Arabia	21	73	80	278			
Syrian Arab Republic	21	38	122	104			
United Arab Emirates	43	146	195	341			
Yemen			2	4			
SOUTH ASIA	**2,375**	**2,360**	**5,410**	**4,457**	**3,951**	**0.16**	**-11.35**
Afghanistan	157	34	191	229			
Bangladesh	42	46	49	28			
India	1,735	1,941	4,521	3,302	3,951	0.16	19.65
Iran, Islamic Republic of	174	203	282	344			
Nepal	3	1	48	97			
Pakistan	257	75	262	408			
Sri Lanka	7	60	57	49			
NOT SPECIFIED	**40,682**	**11,179**	**30,195**	**19,925**	**65,903**	**2.71**	**230.76**
Other countries of the World	40,682	11,179	30,195	19,925	65,903	2.71	230.76

Yearbook of Tourism Statistics, Data 2008 – 2012, 2014 Editic

LEBANON

1. Arrivals of non-resident tourists at national borders, by nationality

		2008	2009	2010	2011	2012	Market share 2012	% Change 2012-2011
TOTAL	(*)	**1,332,533**	**1,844,106**	**2,167,989**	**1,655,051**	**1,365,845**	**100.00**	**-17.47**
AFRICA		**50,732**	**66,140**	**66,225**	**82,643**	**82,368**	**6.03**	**-0.33**
East Africa		**19,010**	**24,536**	**21,616**	**43,095**	**43,484**	**3.18**	**0.90**
Burundi		13	26	2	18	20	0.00	11.11
Comoros		15	60	95	186	171	0.01	-8.06
Djibouti		35	64	54	42	68	0.00	61.90
Eritrea		578	709	616	468	305	0.02	-34.83
Ethiopia		15,198	18,031	18,676	39,158	39,321	2.88	0.42
Kenya		320	431	635	1,687	1,763	0.13	4.51
Madagascar		1,818	4,085	375	280	389	0.03	38.93
Malawi		86	87	93	93	113	0.01	21.51
Mauritius		51	133	87	128	104	0.01	-18.75
Mozambique		54	39	61	97	110	0.01	13.40
Rwanda		22	87	31	35	53	0.00	51.43
Seychelles		28	62	48	35	37	0.00	5.71
Somalia		245	223	402	308	424	0.03	37.66
Uganda		95	89	106	106	100	0.01	-5.66
United Republic of Tanzania		248	245	179	289	315	0.02	9.00
Zambia		76	73	76	91	96	0.01	5.49
Zimbabwe		128	92	80	74	95	0.01	28.38
Central Africa		**1,613**	**1,997**	**1,583**	**1,848**	**2,012**	**0.15**	**8.87**
Angola		91	78	75	96	89	0.01	-7.29
Cameroon		276	450	402	560	882	0.06	57.50
Central African Republic		96	102	81	66	55	0.00	-16.67
Chad		40	107	59	58	41	0.00	-29.31
Congo		280	500	319	415	441	0.03	6.27
Equatorial Guinea		15	21	22	16	8	0.00	-50.00
Gabon		815	737	625	633	488	0.04	-22.91
Sao Tome and Principe			2		4	8	0.00	100.00
North Africa		**15,538**	**22,904**	**25,572**	**20,327**	**20,087**	**1.47**	**-1.18**
Algeria		3,203	4,648	5,377	4,223	4,005	0.29	-5.16
Morocco		5,281	7,503	7,830	6,318	6,219	0.46	-1.57
Sudan		3,163	4,377	4,723	3,813	3,720	0.27	-2.44
Tunisia		3,891	6,376	7,642	5,973	6,143	0.45	2.85
Southern Africa		**1,794**	**2,382**	**2,451**	**2,026**	**2,162**	**0.16**	**6.71**
Botswana			5	2	1	2	0.00	100.00
Lesotho			7	4	3	2	0.00	-33.33
Namibia		20	44	22	22	19	0.00	-13.64
South Africa		1,774	2,326	2,418	2,000	2,139	0.16	6.95
Swaziland				5				
West Africa		**12,777**	**14,321**	**15,003**	**15,347**	**14,623**	**1.07**	**-4.72**
Benin		357	406	412	515	422	0.03	-18.06
Burkina Faso		372	494	491	613	566	0.04	-7.67
Cape Verde		1	13	7	7	4	0.00	-42.86
Côte d'Ivoire		2,358	2,618	2,851	2,055	1,847	0.14	-10.12
Gambia		225	231	293	317	358	0.03	12.93
Ghana		2,910	3,187	3,435	4,115	3,940	0.29	-4.25
Guinea		663	529	574	627	516	0.04	-17.70
Guinea-Bissau		112	89	62	67	43	0.00	-35.82
Liberia		194	258	225	213	224	0.02	5.16
Mali		224	184	247	255	291	0.02	14.12
Mauritania		196	233	182	179	221	0.02	23.46
Niger		126	183	140	122	107	0.01	-12.30
Nigeria		2,037	2,475	2,828	2,703	2,628	0.19	-2.77
Senegal		1,695	1,997	1,796	1,809	1,502	0.11	-16.97
Sierra Leone		1,033	1,073	1,071	1,163	1,181	0.09	1.55

407

LEBANON

1. Arrivals of non-resident tourists at national borders, by nationality

	2008	2009	2010	2011	2012	Market share 2012	% Change 2012-2011
Togo	274	351	389	587	773	0.06	31.69
AMERICAS	**176,647**	**232,694**	**248,725**	**222,671**	**221,174**	**16.19**	**-0.67**
Caribbean	**647**	**815**	**895**	**842**	**858**	**0.06**	**1.90**
Antigua and Barbuda	15	61	60	41	27	0.00	-34.15
Bahamas		3	3	6	5	0.00	-16.67
Barbados	14	10	10	4	12	0.00	200.00
Cuba	204	209	167	133	138	0.01	3.76
Dominican Republic	151	236	335	414	354	0.03	-14.49
Grenada	2	27	18	14	17	0.00	21.43
Haiti	50	63	55	31	36	0.00	16.13
Jamaica	53	69	57	37	57	0.00	54.05
Puerto Rico	1		1		1	0.00	
Saint Kitts and Nevis	7	9	22	58	82	0.01	41.38
Saint Lucia	3	4	7	1	4	0.00	300.00
Saint Vincent and the Grenadines	34	34	37	29	41	0.00	41.38
Trinidad and Tobago	113	90	123	74	84	0.01	13.51
Central America	**822**	**1,286**	**1,400**	**1,095**	**1,064**	**0.08**	**-2.83**
Belize	176	218	261	219	217	0.02	-0.91
Costa Rica	76	119	247	93	93	0.01	0.00
El Salvador	31	132	109	62	64	0.00	3.23
Guatemala	69	129	150	72	60	0.00	-16.67
Honduras	38	31	59	42	36	0.00	-14.29
Nicaragua	21	32	21	25	16	0.00	-36.00
Panama	411	625	553	582	578	0.04	-0.69
North America	**152,419**	**201,377**	**214,607**	**192,243**	**188,365**	**13.79**	**-2.02**
Canada	66,780	87,144	88,002	79,978	75,751	5.55	-5.29
Mexico	1,796	2,332	3,303	2,100	2,075	0.15	-1.19
United States of America	83,843	111,901	123,302	110,165	110,539	8.09	0.34
South America	**22,759**	**29,216**	**31,823**	**28,491**	**30,887**	**2.26**	**8.41**
Argentina	916	1,542	2,114	1,397	1,432	0.10	2.51
Bolivia	73	82	105	94	103	0.01	9.57
Brazil	9,932	13,332	15,371	13,431	13,383	0.98	-0.36
Chile	695	642	822	740	604	0.04	-18.38
Colombia	1,155	1,440	1,370	1,202	1,203	0.09	0.08
Ecuador	300	290	399	355	296	0.02	-16.62
Paraguay	473	574	584	556	577	0.04	3.78
Peru	176	178	287	233	238	0.02	2.15
Suriname	49	71	93	38	48	0.00	26.32
Uruguay	92	143	143	135	136	0.01	0.74
Venezuela	8,898	10,922	10,535	10,310	12,867	0.94	24.80
EAST ASIA AND THE PACIFIC	**89,452**	**128,919**	**133,451**	**112,163**	**101,518**	**7.43**	**-9.49**
North-East Asia	**7,928**	**10,088**	**14,782**	**11,164**	**8,019**	**0.59**	**-28.17**
China	2,472	3,895	5,938	4,862	3,564	0.26	-26.70
Hong Kong, China	65	136	215	126	88	0.01	-30.16
Japan	1,934	2,562	3,906	2,186	1,541	0.11	-29.51
Korea, Dem. People's Republic of	38	35	84	63	72	0.01	14.29
Korea, Republic of	2,987	3,168	4,200	3,606	2,571	0.19	-28.70
Mongolia	5	18	25	31	42	0.00	35.48
Taiwan, Province of China	427	274	414	290	141	0.01	-51.38
South-East Asia	**39,233**	**54,772**	**58,236**	**44,615**	**41,623**	**3.05**	**-6.71**
Brunei Darussalam	2	40	24	83	56	0.00	-32.53
Cambodia	6	11	229	240	251	0.02	4.58
Indonesia	7,451	10,567	10,525	8,446	9,218	0.67	9.14
Lao People's Democratic Republic		3	1	14			
Malaysia	2,875	3,587	4,901	4,580	3,598	0.26	-21.44
Myanmar	78	48	47	65	37	0.00	-43.08

408

LEBANON

1. Arrivals of non-resident tourists at national borders, by nationality

	2008	2009	2010	2011	2012	Market share 2012	% Change 2012-2011
Philippines	28,042	39,384	41,174	30,172	27,620	2.02	-8.46
Singapore	392	626	828	517	432	0.03	-16.44
Thailand	184	288	308	355	307	0.02	-13.52
Viet Nam	203	218	199	143	104	0.01	-27.27
Australasia	**42,193**	**63,899**	**60,302**	**56,249**	**51,734**	**3.79**	**-8.03**
Australia	40,884	62,140	58,150	54,522	50,261	3.68	-7.82
New Zealand	1,309	1,759	2,152	1,727	1,473	0.11	-14.71
Melanesia	**98**	**160**	**130**	**134**	**142**	**0.01**	**5.97**
Fiji	98	158	129	133	140	0.01	5.26
Papua New Guinea		1	1	1			
Vanuatu		1			2	0.00	
Polynesia			**1**	**1**			
Tonga			1	1			
EUROPE	**348,262**	**454,742**	**550,866**	**487,150**	**445,758**	**32.64**	**-8.50**
Central/Eastern Europe	**32,371**	**39,616**	**47,248**	**43,164**	**39,565**	**2.90**	**-8.34**
Armenia	1,511	1,810	2,123	1,889	1,617	0.12	-14.40
Azerbaijan	114	222	255	261	306	0.02	17.24
Belarus	1,572	1,972	2,379	2,279	2,383	0.17	4.56
Bulgaria	1,537	1,842	2,591	2,167	2,020	0.15	-6.78
Czech Republic	1,724	2,140	2,780	1,838	1,820	0.13	-0.98
Estonia	162	186	380	416	132	0.01	-68.27
Georgia	147	223	344	393	422	0.03	7.38
Hungary	1,433	1,657	1,886	1,411	1,168	0.09	-17.22
Kazakhstan	289	497	555	567	598	0.04	5.47
Kyrgyzstan	79	143	161	225	157	0.01	-30.22
Latvia	391	400	614	597	353	0.03	-40.87
Lithuania	358	453	725	709	512	0.04	-27.79
Poland	3,694	4,397	4,906	3,837	3,118	0.23	-18.74
Republic of Moldova	1,082	1,275	1,439	1,461	1,366	0.10	-6.50
Romania	3,157	3,933	4,639	4,190	4,272	0.31	1.96
Russian Federation	8,333	9,838	12,175	11,121	9,954	0.73	-10.49
Slovakia	841	1,024	1,143	1,014	738	0.05	-27.22
Tajikistan	63	66	92	80	91	0.01	13.75
Turkmenistan	46	54	57	72	88	0.01	22.22
Ukraine	5,546	7,024	7,484	8,140	8,450	0.62	3.81
Uzbekistan	292	460	520	497			
Northern Europe	**81,478**	**104,587**	**121,219**	**108,408**	**100,284**	**7.34**	**-7.49**
Denmark	14,510	18,078	19,332	16,830	13,937	1.02	-17.19
Finland	1,352	1,661	2,391	1,810	2,392	0.18	32.15
Iceland	126	153	211	143	81	0.01	-43.36
Ireland	2,283	3,222	4,050	4,953	5,232	0.38	5.63
Norway	3,498	4,552	5,484	4,697	4,088	0.30	-12.97
Sweden	21,624	26,894	29,512	26,752	24,340	1.78	-9.02
United Kingdom	38,085	50,027	60,239	53,223	50,214	3.68	-5.65
Southern Europe	**42,726**	**58,699**	**66,961**	**52,268**	**49,020**	**3.59**	**-6.21**
Albania	49	95	98	87	99	0.01	13.79
Andorra		9	14	3	4	0.00	33.33
Bosnia and Herzegovina	235	306	361	251	286	0.02	13.94
Croatia	517	679	779	641	729	0.05	13.73
Greece	6,071	8,041	9,328	7,695	7,532	0.55	-2.12
Holy See	65	68	79	109	155	0.01	42.20
Italy	23,085	32,619	36,625	28,808	25,539	1.87	-11.35
Malta	141	252	300	258	216	0.02	-16.28
Portugal	1,309	1,707	2,091	1,701	1,475	0.11	-13.29
San Marino	20	13	17	10	3	0.00	-70.00
Serbia	312	678	1,212	1,091	1,055	0.08	-3.30
Serbia and Montenegro	626	390	70		13	0.00	

409

LEBANON

1. Arrivals of non-resident tourists at national borders, by nationality

	2008	2009	2010	2011	2012	Market share 2012	% Change 2012-2011
Slovenia	197	314	385	292	290	0.02	-0.68
Spain	9,987	13,343	15,417	11,301	11,472	0.84	1.51
TFYR of Macedonia	112	185	185	21	152	0.01	623.81
Western Europe	**175,177**	**230,620**	**263,433**	**239,734**	**220,810**	**16.17**	**-7.89**
Austria	3,235	4,252	5,823	5,002	4,665	0.34	-6.74
Belgium	10,924	13,661	15,379	13,497	12,873	0.94	-4.62
France	91,071	120,408	139,534	128,999	120,134	8.80	-6.87
Germany	53,851	69,847	76,854	68,401	62,160	4.55	-9.12
Liechtenstein	13	17	13	20	20	0.00	0.00
Luxembourg	227	378	406	357	232	0.02	-35.01
Monaco	31	55	60	85	26	0.00	-69.41
Netherlands	7,357	10,268	11,824	10,281	9,298	0.68	-9.56
Switzerland	8,468	11,734	13,540	12,935	11,402	0.83	-11.85
Other countries of Western Europe				157			
East Mediterranean Europe	**16,510**	**21,220**	**52,005**	**43,576**	**36,079**	**2.64**	**-17.20**
Cyprus	7,181	8,241	9,325	7,932	7,229	0.53	-8.86
Turkey	9,329	12,979	42,680	35,644	28,850	2.11	-19.06
MIDDLE EAST	**532,871**	**761,852**	**867,898**	**560,273**	**436,964**	**31.99**	**-22.01**
Bahrain	17,424	25,218	25,096	9,493	7,365	0.54	-22.42
Egypt	41,657	57,379	67,773	62,825	64,017	4.69	1.90
Iraq	72,805	101,561	129,847	129,294	126,982	9.30	-1.79
Jordan	180,887	223,793	274,615	129,640	89,100	6.52	-31.27
Kuwait	68,936	102,537	95,824	61,756	40,121	2.94	-35.03
Libya	2,964	3,913	4,570	2,484	5,094	0.37	105.07
Oman	4,012	5,717	6,639	4,494	3,128	0.23	-30.40
Qatar	14,093	19,358	18,436	11,171	5,124	0.38	-54.13
Saudi Arabia	101,749	173,294	191,066	111,701	72,658	5.32	-34.95
United Arab Emirates	24,673	42,974	46,923	32,058	17,742	1.30	-44.66
Yemen	3,671	6,108	7,109	5,357	5,633	0.41	5.15
SOUTH ASIA	**133,067**	**197,941**	**299,087**	**188,242**	**76,157**	**5.58**	**-59.54**
Afghanistan	306	450	420	383	432	0.03	12.79
Bangladesh	9,430	16,047	19,980	23,730	20,557	1.51	-13.37
Bhutan	13	19	7	4	13	0.00	225.00
India	10,668	13,946	16,117	15,378	13,513	0.99	-12.13
Iran, Islamic Republic of	92,547	145,706	241,514	131,870	28,134	2.06	-78.67
Maldives	4	5	7	5	36	0.00	620.00
Nepal	8,705	8,435	6,975	4,560	3,803	0.28	-16.60
Pakistan	2,491	3,336	3,729	3,448	2,992	0.22	-13.23
Sri Lanka	8,903	9,997	10,338	8,864	6,677	0.49	-24.67
NOT SPECIFIED	**1,502**	**1,818**	**1,737**	**1,909**	**1,906**	**0.14**	**-0.16**
Other countries of the World	1,502	1,818	1,737	1,909	1,906	0.14	-0.16

Yearbook of Tourism Statistics, Data 2008 – 2012, 2014 Editi

LESOTHO

2. Arrivals of non-resident visitors at national borders, by country of residence

	2008	2009	2010	2011	2012	Market share 2012	% Change 2012-2011
TOTAL	293,073	343,743	425,870	398,149	422,597	100.00	6.14
AFRICA	259,407	314,218	400,823	379,507	403,763	95.54	6.39
East Africa	8,145	6,905	6,135	4,550	5,911	1.40	29.91
Kenya	253	301	386	261	246	0.06	-5.75
Malawi	404	430	333	295	309	0.07	4.75
Mauritius	198	136	112	97	125	0.03	28.87
Mozambique	140	210	302	359	610	0.14	69.92
Uganda	1,294	269	268	205	204	0.05	-0.49
United Republic of Tanzania	1,038	240	208	144	204	0.05	41.67
Zambia	669	806	707	570	662	0.16	16.14
Zimbabwe	4,149	4,513	3,819	2,619	3,551	0.84	35.59
Southern Africa	249,043	306,121	393,645	374,161	397,159	93.98	6.15
Botswana	1,796	2,060	1,922	1,419	1,752	0.41	23.47
South Africa	246,014	302,655	390,849	371,867	394,336	93.31	6.04
Swaziland	1,233	1,406	874	875	1,071	0.25	22.40
West Africa	209	206	233	154	132	0.03	-14.29
Ghana	103	84	61	59	42	0.01	-28.81
Nigeria	106	122	172	95	90	0.02	-5.26
Other Africa	2,010	986	810	642	561	0.13	-12.62
Other countries of Africa	2,010	986	810	642	561	0.13	-12.62
AMERICAS	4,556	4,122	3,907	3,180	3,059	0.72	-3.81
North America	3,078	4,017	3,739	3,080	2,940	0.70	-4.55
Canada	1,767	805	662	502	718	0.17	43.03
United States of America	1,311	3,212	3,077	2,578	2,222	0.53	-13.81
Other Americas	1,478	105	168	100	119	0.03	19.00
Other countries of the Americas	1,478	105	168	100	119	0.03	19.00
EAST ASIA AND THE PACIFIC	5,566	5,150	3,938	2,407	2,783	0.66	15.62
North-East Asia	2,446	2,378	1,728	860	1,159	0.27	34.77
China	1,136	2,233	1,596	724	998	0.24	37.85
Taiwan, Province of China	1,310	145	132	136	161	0.04	18.38
Australasia	1,813	770	871	621	609	0.14	-1.93
Australia	1,813	770	871	621	609	0.14	-1.93
Other East Asia and the Pacific	1,307	2,002	1,339	926	1,015	0.24	9.61
Other countries of Asia	1,307	2,002	1,339	926	1,015	0.24	9.61
EUROPE	22,717	19,726	16,719	12,751	12,672	3.00	-0.62
Northern Europe	6,444	5,552	4,723	3,201	2,398	0.57	-25.09
Denmark	1,711	248	232	117	152	0.04	29.91
Ireland	2,106	397	349	189	230	0.05	21.69
Sweden	382	288	316	310	205	0.05	-33.87
United Kingdom	2,245	4,619	3,826	2,585	1,811	0.43	-29.94
Southern Europe	371	422	213	291	310	0.07	6.53
Italy	371	422	213	291	310	0.07	6.53
Western Europe	6,933	10,862	9,653	7,485	7,906	1.87	5.62
France	659	1,592	1,342	668	566	0.13	-15.27
Germany	3,349	5,015	4,425	3,927	3,746	0.89	-4.61
Netherlands	2,925	4,255	3,886	2,890	3,594	0.85	24.36
Other Europe	8,969	2,890	2,130	1,774	2,058	0.49	16.01
Other countries of Europe	8,969	2,890	2,130	1,774	2,058	0.49	16.01
MIDDLE EAST	385	177	70	13	13	0.00	0.00
All countries of Middle East	385	177	70	13	13	0.00	0.00
SOUTH ASIA	404	256	285	261	212	0.05	-18.77
India	404	256	285	261	212	0.05	-18.77
NOT SPECIFIED	38	94	128	30	95	0.02	216.67
Other countries of the World	38	94	128	30	95	0.02	216.67

Yearbook of Tourism Statistics, Data 2008 – 2012, 2014 Edition

LIECHTENSTEIN

3. Arrivals of non-resident tourists in hotels and similar establishments, by country of residence

	2008	2009	2010	2011	2012	Market share 2012	% Change 2012-2011
TOTAL	58,454	52,285	49,804	53,326	53,598	100.00	0.51
AFRICA	177	171	132	138	382	0.71	176.81
Southern Africa	57	75	57	73	72	0.13	-1.37
South Africa	57	75	57	73	72	0.13	-1.37
Other Africa	120	96	75	65	310	0.58	376.92
Other countries of Africa	120	96	75	65	310	0.58	376.92
AMERICAS	2,439	2,260	2,397	2,714	3,293	6.14	21.33
North America	1,971	1,941	2,088	2,323	2,507	4.68	7.92
Canada	248	222	255	343	291	0.54	-15.16
Mexico	52	28	23	47	60	0.11	27.66
United States of America	1,671	1,691	1,810	1,933	2,156	4.02	11.54
South America	173	154	176	230	394	0.74	71.30
Brazil	173	154	176	230	394	0.74	71.30
Other Americas	295	165	133	161	392	0.73	143.48
Other countries of the Americas	295	165	133	161	392	0.73	143.48
EAST ASIA AND THE PACIFIC	1,679	1,330	1,656	1,858	2,220	4.14	19.48
North-East Asia	806	637	752	994	1,147	2.14	15.39
China	171	147	272	399	498	0.93	24.81
Hong Kong, China	39	31	43	45	70	0.13	55.56
Japan	435	361	316	400	445	0.83	11.25
Korea, Republic of	95	49	71	87	83	0.15	-4.60
Taiwan, Province of China	66	49	50	63	51	0.10	-19.05
Australasia	303	219	289	280	354	0.66	26.43
Australia	303	219	289	280	354	0.66	26.43
Other East Asia and the Pacific	570	474	615	584	719	1.34	23.12
Other countries of Asia	570	474	615	554	659	1.23	18.95
Other countries of Oceania				30	60	0.11	100.00
EUROPE	54,067	48,210	45,393	48,252	46,154	86.11	-4.35
Central/Eastern Europe	2,673	2,531	2,453	3,016	3,131	5.84	3.81
Bulgaria	135	93	93	95	69	0.13	-27.37
Czech Republic	493	511	550	650	625	1.17	-3.85
Estonia	57	63	15	32	46	0.09	43.75
Hungary	772	624	521	548	442	0.82	-19.34
Latvia	36	44	51	37	84	0.16	127.03
Lithuania	51	38	49	85	42	0.08	-50.59
Poland	345	282	323	352	329	0.61	-6.53
Romania	190	122	119	163	199	0.37	22.09
Russian Federation	460	593	572	911	962	1.79	5.60
Slovakia	134	161	160	143	218	0.41	52.45
Ukraine					115	0.21	
Northern Europe	4,174	3,808	3,404	4,143	3,813	7.11	-7.97
Denmark	545	428	504	508	571	1.07	12.40
Finland	299	278	173	287	349	0.65	21.60
Iceland	41	45	39	67	50	0.09	-25.37
Ireland	167	117	128	133	149	0.28	12.03
Norway	281	282	357	424	398	0.74	-6.13
Sweden	389	444	362	457	443	0.83	-3.06
United Kingdom	2,452	2,214	1,841	2,267	1,853	3.46	-18.26
Southern Europe	3,376	2,879	2,912	2,970	3,099	5.78	4.34
Croatia	102	83	60	56	55	0.10	-1.79
Greece	195	235	231	192	150	0.28	-21.88
Italy	2,231	1,775	1,844	1,973	2,151	4.01	9.02
Malta	9	20	17	38	58	0.11	52.63
Portugal	165	180	153	164	146	0.27	-10.98
Slovenia	135	125	86	78	126	0.24	61.54

412

Yearbook of Tourism Statistics, Data 2008 – 2012, 2014 Editic

LIECHTENSTEIN

3. Arrivals of non-resident tourists in hotels and similar establishments, by country of residence

	2008	2009	2010	2011	2012	Market share 2012	% Change 2012-2011
Spain	539	461	521	469	413	0.77	-11.94
Western Europe	**43,490**	**38,656**	**36,177**	**37,451**	**35,746**	**66.69**	**-4.55**
Austria	2,964	2,525	2,355	2,447	2,294	4.28	-6.25
Belgium	1,108	1,063	811	1,071	1,029	1.92	-3.92
France	1,302	1,121	1,163	1,270	1,138	2.12	-10.39
Germany	19,510	16,697	15,518	14,341	13,284	24.78	-7.37
Luxembourg	636	630	605	564	412	0.77	-26.95
Netherlands	1,175	1,086	1,112	1,167	1,156	2.16	-0.94
Switzerland	16,795	15,534	14,613	16,591	16,433	30.66	-0.95
East Mediterranean Europe	**107**	**68**	**131**	**129**	**152**	**0.28**	**17.83**
Cyprus	10	3	16	15	19	0.04	26.67
Turkey	97	65	115	114	133	0.25	16.67
Other Europe	**247**	**268**	**316**	**543**	**213**	**0.40**	**-60.77**
Other countries of Europe	247	268	316	543	213	0.40	-60.77
SOUTH ASIA	**73**	**84**	**70**	**96**	**65**	**0.12**	**-32.29**
India	73	84	70	96	65	0.12	-32.29
NOT SPECIFIED	**19**	**230**	**156**	**268**	**1,484**	**2.77**	**453.73**
Other countries of the World	19	230	156	268	1,484	2.77	453.73

Yearbook of Tourism Statistics, Data 2008 – 2012, 2014 Edition

LIECHTENSTEIN

4. Arrivals of non-resident tourists in all types of accommodation establishments, by country of residence

	2008	2009	2010	2011	2012	Market share 2012	% Change 2012-2011
TOTAL					62,382	100.00	
AFRICA					391	0.63	
Southern Africa					73	0.12	
South Africa					73	0.12	
Other Africa					318	0.51	
Other countries of Africa					318	0.51	
AMERICAS					3,545	5.68	
North America					2,729	4.37	
Canada					361	0.58	
Mexico					61	0.10	
United States of America					2,307	3.70	
South America					401	0.64	
Brazil					401	0.64	
Other Americas					415	0.67	
Other countries of the Americas					415	0.67	
EAST ASIA AND THE PACIFIC					2,452	3.93	
North-East Asia					1,263	2.02	
China					542	0.87	
Hong Kong, China					75	0.12	
Japan					481	0.77	
Korea, Republic of					102	0.16	
Taiwan, Province of China					63	0.10	
Australasia					407	0.65	
Australia					407	0.65	
Other East Asia and the Pacific					782	1.25	
Other countries of Asia					700	1.12	
Other countries of Oceania					82	0.13	
EUROPE					54,440	87.27	
Central/Eastern Europe					3,416	5.48	
Bulgaria					73	0.12	
Czech Republic					714	1.14	
Estonia					55	0.09	
Hungary					469	0.75	
Latvia					85	0.14	
Lithuania					42	0.07	
Poland					410	0.66	
Romania					211	0.34	
Russian Federation					997	1.60	
Slovakia					234	0.38	
Ukraine					126	0.20	
Northern Europe					4,345	6.97	
Denmark					651	1.04	
Finland					373	0.60	
Iceland					53	0.08	
Ireland					184	0.29	
Norway					456	0.73	
Sweden					483	0.77	
United Kingdom					2,145	3.44	
Southern Europe					3,348	5.37	
Croatia					63	0.10	
Greece					153	0.25	
Italy					2,307	3.70	
Malta					58	0.09	
Portugal					154	0.25	
Slovenia					137	0.22	

414

Yearbook of Tourism Statistics, Data 2008 – 2012, 2014 Edition

LIECHTENSTEIN

4. Arrivals of non-resident tourists in all types of accommodation establishments, by country of residence

	2008	2009	2010	2011	2012	Market share 2012	% Change 2012-2011
Spain					476	0.76	
Western Europe					**42,954**	**68.86**	
Austria					2,585	4.14	
Belgium					1,154	1.85	
France					1,301	2.09	
Germany					16,728	26.82	
Luxembourg					419	0.67	
Netherlands					1,529	2.45	
Switzerland					19,238	30.84	
East Mediterranean Europe					**158**	**0.25**	
Cyprus					19	0.03	
Turkey					139	0.22	
Other Europe					**219**	**0.35**	
Other countries of Europe					219	0.35	
SOUTH ASIA					**70**	**0.11**	
India					70	0.11	
NOT SPECIFIED					**1,484**	**2.38**	
Other countries of the World					1,484	2.38	

Yearbook of Tourism Statistics, Data 2008 – 2012, 2014 Edition

LIECHTENSTEIN

5. Overnight stays of non-resident tourists in hotels and similar establishments, by country of residence

	2008	2009	2010	2011	2012	Market share 2012	% Change 2012-2011
TOTAL	131,095	117,806	111,458	112,459	111,345	100.00	-0.99
AFRICA	592	556	326	357	605	0.54	69.47
Southern Africa	121	135	115	185	178	0.16	-3.78
South Africa	121	135	115	185	178	0.16	-3.78
Other Africa	471	421	211	172	427	0.38	148.26
Other countries of Africa	471	421	211	172	427	0.38	148.26
AMERICAS	5,498	4,452	4,679	5,463	6,781	6.09	24.13
North America	4,453	3,934	4,117	4,729	5,086	4.57	7.55
Canada	504	519	524	503	450	0.40	-10.54
Mexico	97	102	62	109	206	0.19	88.99
United States of America	3,852	3,313	3,531	4,117	4,430	3.98	7.60
South America	395	213	226	360	645	0.58	79.17
Brazil	395	213	226	360	645	0.58	79.17
Other Americas	650	305	336	374	1,050	0.94	180.75
Other countries of the Americas	650	305	336	374	1,050	0.94	180.75
EAST ASIA AND THE PACIFIC	4,396	3,155	3,682	3,837	4,793	4.30	24.92
North-East Asia	2,491	1,575	1,829	2,161	2,721	2.44	25.91
China	780	383	593	864	1,205	1.08	39.47
Hong Kong, China	176	54	58	96	101	0.09	5.21
Japan	1,071	836	719	764	1,038	0.93	35.86
Korea, Republic of	291	169	261	231	266	0.24	15.15
Taiwan, Province of China	173	133	198	206	111	0.10	-46.12
Australasia	529	333	432	420	593	0.53	41.19
Australia	529	333	432	420	593	0.53	41.19
Other East Asia and the Pacific	1,376	1,247	1,421	1,256	1,479	1.33	17.75
Other countries of Asia	1,376	1,247	1,421	1,195	1,379	1.24	15.40
Other countries of Oceania				61	100	0.09	63.93
EUROPE	120,354	109,141	102,267	101,780	95,938	86.16	-5.74
Central/Eastern Europe	5,290	4,295	4,219	5,029	5,707	5.13	13.48
Bulgaria	302	194	174	151	115	0.10	-23.84
Czech Republic	807	801	757	940	914	0.82	-2.77
Estonia	110	131	21	62	52	0.05	-16.13
Hungary	1,094	877	970	851	950	0.85	11.63
Latvia	59	112	284	49	129	0.12	163.27
Lithuania	130	55	78	98	77	0.07	-21.43
Poland	629	502	557	675	579	0.52	-14.22
Romania	501	220	220	280	483	0.43	72.50
Russian Federation	1,366	1,025	846	1,587	1,763	1.58	11.09
Slovakia	292	378	312	336	439	0.39	30.65
Ukraine					206	0.19	
Northern Europe	7,799	8,263	6,678	7,302	6,190	5.56	-15.23
Denmark	880	822	856	967	990	0.89	2.38
Finland	477	493	294	395	509	0.46	28.86
Iceland	87	151	70	217	112	0.10	-48.39
Ireland	475	243	342	280	217	0.19	-22.50
Norway	353	381	490	629	498	0.45	-20.83
Sweden	672	1,046	673	771	661	0.59	-14.27
United Kingdom	4,855	5,127	3,953	4,043	3,203	2.88	-20.78
Southern Europe	6,657	5,076	6,147	5,439	4,879	4.38	-10.30
Croatia	250	129	135	100	96	0.09	-4.00
Greece	599	532	854	434	303	0.27	-30.18
Italy	3,825	3,146	3,216	3,644	3,242	2.91	-11.03
Malta	24	29	46	124	148	0.13	19.35
Portugal	424	288	438	239	219	0.20	-8.37
Slovenia	216	149	139	141	196	0.18	39.01

416

LIECHTENSTEIN

5. Overnight stays of non-resident tourists in hotels and similar establishments, by country of residence

	2008	2009	2010	2011	2012	Market share 2012	% Change 2012-2011
Spain	1,319	803	1,319	757	675	0.61	-10.83
Western Europe	**99,611**	**90,965**	**84,219**	**81,884**	**78,440**	**70.45**	**-4.21**
Austria	5,476	4,705	4,217	4,273	3,923	3.52	-8.19
Belgium	4,474	4,174	3,176	3,890	3,783	3.40	-2.75
France	2,444	2,002	2,119	2,238	1,937	1.74	-13.45
Germany	45,786	39,996	37,337	32,454	28,464	25.56	-12.29
Luxembourg	2,727	2,591	2,833	2,178	1,463	1.31	-32.83
Netherlands	2,339	2,404	2,090	2,130	2,221	1.99	4.27
Switzerland	36,365	35,093	32,447	34,721	36,649	32.91	5.55
East Mediterranean Europe	**407**	**144**	**449**	**290**	**300**	**0.27**	**3.45**
Cyprus	19	6	26	31	38	0.03	22.58
Turkey	388	138	423	259	262	0.24	1.16
Other Europe	**590**	**398**	**555**	**1,836**	**422**	**0.38**	**-77.02**
Other countries of Europe	590	398	555	1,836	422	0.38	-77.02
SOUTH ASIA	**230**	**148**	**166**	**205**	**239**	**0.21**	**16.59**
India	230	148	166	205	239	0.21	16.59
NOT SPECIFIED	**25**	**354**	**338**	**817**	**2,989**	**2.68**	**265.85**
Other countries of the World	25	354	338	817	2,989	2.68	265.85

Yearbook of Tourism Statistics, Data 2008 – 2012, 2014 Edition

LIECHTENSTEIN

6. Overnight stays of non-resident tourists in all types of accommodation establishments, by country of residence

	2008	2009	2010	2011	2012	Market share 2012	% Change 2012-2011
TOTAL					136,276	100.00	
AFRICA					619	0.45	
Southern Africa					181	0.13	
South Africa					181	0.13	
Other Africa					438	0.32	
Other countries of Africa					438	0.32	
AMERICAS					7,705	5.65	
North America					5,942	4.36	
Canada					808	0.59	
Mexico					209	0.15	
United States of America					4,925	3.61	
South America					658	0.48	
Brazil					658	0.48	
Other Americas					1,105	0.81	
Other countries of the Americas					1,105	0.81	
EAST ASIA AND THE PACIFIC					5,447	4.00	
North-East Asia					3,048	2.24	
China					1,345	0.99	
Hong Kong, China					113	0.08	
Japan					1,119	0.82	
Korea, Republic of					340	0.25	
Taiwan, Province of China					131	0.10	
Australasia					722	0.53	
Australia					722	0.53	
Other East Asia and the Pacific					1,677	1.23	
Other countries of Asia					1,503	1.10	
Other countries of Oceania					174	0.13	
EUROPE					119,267	87.52	
Central/Eastern Europe					6,521	4.79	
Bulgaria					123	0.09	
Czech Republic					1,149	0.84	
Estonia					61	0.04	
Hungary					1,012	0.74	
Latvia					130	0.10	
Lithuania					77	0.06	
Poland					910	0.67	
Romania					504	0.37	
Russian Federation					1,855	1.36	
Slovakia					478	0.35	
Ukraine					222	0.16	
Northern Europe					7,274	5.34	
Denmark					1,162	0.85	
Finland					556	0.41	
Iceland					140	0.10	
Ireland					270	0.20	
Norway					626	0.46	
Sweden					763	0.56	
United Kingdom					3,757	2.76	
Southern Europe					5,327	3.91	
Croatia					125	0.09	
Greece					315	0.23	
Italy					3,465	2.54	
Malta					148	0.11	
Portugal					239	0.18	
Slovenia					216	0.16	

Yearbook of Tourism Statistics, Data 2008 – 2012, 2014 Editic

LIECHTENSTEIN

6. Overnight stays of non-resident tourists in all types of accommodation establishments, by country of residence

	2008	2009	2010	2011	2012	Market share 2012	% Change 2012-2011
Spain					819	0.60	
Western Europe					**99,363**	**72.91**	
Austria					4,442	3.26	
Belgium					4,240	3.11	
France					2,395	1.76	
Germany					39,238	28.79	
Luxembourg					1,490	1.09	
Netherlands					3,153	2.31	
Switzerland					44,405	32.58	
East Mediterranean Europe					**345**	**0.25**	
Cyprus					38	0.03	
Turkey					307	0.23	
Other Europe					**437**	**0.32**	
Other countries of Europe					437	0.32	
SOUTH ASIA					**249**	**0.18**	
India					249	0.18	
NOT SPECIFIED					**2,989**	**2.19**	
Other countries of the World					2,989	2.19	

419

LITHUANIA

3. Arrivals of non-resident tourists in hotels and similar establishments, by country of residence

	2008	2009	2010	2011	2012	Market share 2012	% Change 2012-2011
TOTAL	824,860	684,471	760,885	909,274	1,008,138	100.00	10.87
AFRICA	1,222	1,151	1,493	3,009	1,697	0.17	-43.60
Other Africa	1,222	1,151	1,493	3,009	1,697	0.17	-43.60
All countries of Africa	1,222	1,151	1,493	3,009	1,697	0.17	-43.60
AMERICAS	23,968	18,760	24,209	30,879	33,984	3.37	10.06
North America	21,677	17,066	21,713	27,445	26,725	2.65	-2.62
Canada	2,700	1,698	2,858	3,705	2,714	0.27	-26.75
United States of America	18,977	15,368	18,855	23,740	24,011	2.38	1.14
Other Americas	2,291	1,694	2,496	3,434	7,259	0.72	111.39
Other countries of the Americas	2,291	1,694	2,496	3,434	7,259	0.72	111.39
EAST ASIA AND THE PACIFIC	18,534	17,873	20,555	29,574	37,716	3.74	27.53
North-East Asia	11,007	9,779	10,779	13,613	14,926	1.48	9.65
China	1,785	2,298	3,236	5,278	5,877	0.58	11.35
Japan	9,222	7,481	7,543	8,335	9,049	0.90	8.57
Other East Asia and the Pacific	7,527	8,094	9,776	15,961	22,790	2.26	42.79
Other countries of Asia	4,364	4,603	6,523	12,087	18,552	1.84	53.49
All countries of Oceania	3,163	3,491	3,253	3,874	4,238	0.42	9.40
EUROPE	781,136	646,687	714,628	845,812	934,741	92.72	10.51
Central/Eastern Europe	395,846	336,708	391,181	464,477	540,191	53.58	16.30
Belarus	32,901	39,861	56,786	77,431	98,302	9.75	26.95
Bulgaria	1,386	1,409	1,131	1,694	1,525	0.15	-9.98
Czech Republic	8,624	9,270	6,564	6,779	7,555	0.75	11.45
Estonia	37,164	27,348	29,986	35,188	36,919	3.66	4.92
Hungary	2,648	2,073	2,941	3,462	3,569	0.35	3.09
Latvia	75,537	55,832	60,460	59,764	67,121	6.66	12.31
Poland	139,471	115,661	125,988	130,426	117,280	11.63	-10.08
Romania	2,102	2,377	2,074	3,892	2,923	0.29	-24.90
Russian Federation	81,112	70,707	93,907	128,874	183,651	18.22	42.50
Slovakia	1,875	1,635	1,732	2,557	2,050	0.20	-19.83
Ukraine	10,037	7,055	8,413	12,270	17,680	1.75	44.09
Other countries Central/East Europe	2,989	3,480	1,199	2,140	1,616	0.16	-24.49
Northern Europe	147,383	105,808	122,044	131,045	144,588	14.34	10.33
Denmark	15,652	12,007	15,026	16,581	19,751	1.96	19.12
Finland	39,730	29,055	33,093	34,502	35,845	3.56	3.89
Iceland	1,707	1,718	823	907	1,668	0.17	83.90
Ireland	7,342	4,481	3,513	4,075	5,111	0.51	25.42
Norway	22,195	15,342	16,141	19,177	25,824	2.56	34.66
Sweden	21,719	18,463	19,265	24,472	21,120	2.09	-13.70
United Kingdom	39,038	24,742	34,183	31,331	35,269	3.50	12.57
Southern Europe	45,404	37,093	39,664	56,579	51,394	5.10	-9.16
Greece	2,550	2,942	2,646	3,254	2,402	0.24	-26.18
Italy	26,435	19,926	21,180	29,151	27,697	2.75	-4.99
Portugal	2,445	2,065	2,030	2,660	2,121	0.21	-20.26
Spain	13,974	12,160	13,808	21,514	19,174	1.90	-10.88
Western Europe	168,728	144,525	137,348	163,603	181,886	18.04	11.18
Austria	7,795	6,478	5,902	6,484	7,882	0.78	21.56
Belgium	7,099	6,889	7,066	7,088	8,201	0.81	15.70
France	23,172	20,287	21,367	23,223	23,470	2.33	1.06
Germany	115,200	97,486	90,207	109,439	126,297	12.53	15.40
Luxembourg	785	816	523	694	686	0.07	-1.15
Netherlands	10,357	8,255	8,573	11,773	10,642	1.06	-9.61
Switzerland	4,320	4,314	3,710	4,902	4,708	0.47	-3.96

Yearbook of Tourism Statistics, Data 2008 – 2012, 2014 Edit

LITHUANIA

3. Arrivals of non-resident tourists in hotels and similar establishments, by country of residence

	2008	2009	2010	2011	2012	Market share 2012	% Change 2012-2011
East Mediterranean Europe	**7,849**	**7,346**	**8,028**	**12,140**	**12,326**	**1.22**	**1.53**
Israel	5,179	4,521	5,045	6,679	7,652	0.76	14.57
Turkey	2,670	2,825	2,983	5,461	4,674	0.46	-14.41
Other Europe	**15,926**	**15,207**	**16,363**	**17,968**	**4,356**	**0.43**	**-75.76**
Other countries of Europe	15,926	15,207	16,363	17,968	4,356	0.43	-75.76

Yearbook of Tourism Statistics, Data 2008 – 2012, 2014 Edition

LITHUANIA

4. Arrivals of non-resident tourists in all types of accommodation establishments, by country of residence

	2008	2009	2010	2011	2012	Market share 2012	% Change 2012-2011
TOTAL	909,983	752,389	840,368	1,003,843	1,125,338	100.00	12.10
AFRICA	1,253	1,177	1,523	3,034	1,762	0.16	-41.92
Other Africa	1,253	1,177	1,523	3,034	1,762	0.16	-41.92
All countries of Africa	1,253	1,177	1,523	3,034	1,762	0.16	-41.92
AMERICAS	26,402	20,489	25,247	32,302	36,132	3.21	11.86
North America	23,565	18,756	22,665	28,727	27,955	2.48	-2.69
Canada	2,890	1,795	2,999	3,877	2,876	0.26	-25.82
United States of America	20,675	16,961	19,666	24,850	25,079	2.23	0.92
South America	1,150	1,020	1,282	1,543	1,889	0.17	22.42
Brazil	1,150	1,020	1,282	1,543	1,889	0.17	22.42
Other Americas	1,687	713	1,300	2,032	6,288	0.56	209.45
Other countries of the Americas	1,687	713	1,300	2,032	6,288	0.56	209.45
EAST ASIA AND THE PACIFIC	19,215	18,470	21,283	30,829	39,502	3.51	28.13
North-East Asia	11,884	11,015	12,283	16,547	18,083	1.61	9.28
China	1,898	2,515	3,309	5,522	6,124	0.54	10.90
Japan	9,349	7,599	7,654	8,528	9,465	0.84	10.99
Korea, Republic of	637	901	1,320	2,497	2,494	0.22	-0.12
Australasia	3,501	3,686	3,702	4,130	4,532	0.40	9.73
Australia	3,501	3,686	3,702	4,130	4,532	0.40	9.73
Other East Asia and the Pacific	3,830	3,769	5,298	10,152	16,887	1.50	66.34
Other countries of Asia	3,830	3,769	5,298	10,152	16,887	1.50	66.34
EUROPE	863,113	712,253	792,315	937,678	1,047,942	93.12	11.76
Central/Eastern Europe	449,754	376,163	438,864	517,221	613,300	54.50	18.58
Belarus	45,694	52,193	71,436	92,248	117,037	10.40	26.87
Bulgaria	1,452	1,522	1,189	1,764	1,657	0.15	-6.07
Czech Republic	9,348	10,066	8,618	7,852	8,522	0.76	8.53
Estonia	41,058	30,340	32,527	37,409	39,712	3.53	6.16
Hungary	2,851	2,159	3,587	3,670	3,740	0.33	1.91
Latvia	84,722	62,815	66,519	66,145	76,431	6.79	15.55
Poland	156,283	125,662	135,856	139,632	127,033	11.29	-9.02
Romania	2,434	2,554	2,275	4,192	3,211	0.29	-23.40
Russian Federation	91,992	78,690	105,869	148,267	214,337	19.05	44.56
Slovakia	1,987	1,753	1,888	2,768	2,254	0.20	-18.57
Ukraine	11,933	8,409	9,100	13,274	19,366	1.72	45.89
Northern Europe	150,699	109,537	127,264	136,906	150,961	13.41	10.27
Denmark	16,042	12,338	15,416	16,925	20,149	1.79	19.05
Finland	40,639	30,211	35,137	36,483	37,545	3.34	2.91
Iceland	1,715	1,742	845	929	1,687	0.15	81.59
Ireland	7,701	4,577	3,875	4,317	5,673	0.50	31.41
Norway	22,569	15,657	16,846	20,092	26,461	2.35	31.70
Sweden	22,158	19,101	19,747	25,303	21,694	1.93	-14.26
United Kingdom	39,875	25,911	35,398	32,857	37,752	3.35	14.90
Southern Europe	48,192	39,869	43,487	63,057	58,258	5.18	-7.61
Greece	2,620	2,964	2,680	3,326	2,474	0.22	-25.62
Italy	27,081	20,689	22,547	31,490	30,137	2.68	-4.30
Malta	323	205	217	293	471	0.04	60.75
Portugal	2,537	2,175	2,238	2,809	2,308	0.21	-17.84
Slovenia	1,358	1,124	1,254	2,404	1,713	0.15	-28.74
Spain	14,273	12,712	14,551	22,735	21,155	1.88	-6.95
Western Europe	187,943	161,068	157,463	189,695	207,914	18.48	9.60
Austria	8,086	6,833	6,249	6,948	8,257	0.73	18.84
Belgium	7,351	7,104	7,585	7,852	8,800	0.78	12.07
France	24,456	21,641	23,248	25,684	26,423	2.35	2.88
Germany	130,327	110,163	105,832	128,930	144,975	12.88	12.44
Luxembourg	803	816	544	724	953	0.08	31.63

Yearbook of Tourism Statistics, Data 2008 – 2012, 2014 Edition

LITHUANIA

4. Arrivals of non-resident tourists in all types of accommodation establishments, by country of residence

	2008	2009	2010	2011	2012	Market share 2012	% Change 2012-2011
Netherlands	12,437	9,876	9,997	14,137	13,322	1.18	-5.77
Switzerland	4,483	4,635	4,008	5,420	5,184	0.46	-4.35
East Mediterranean Europe	**9,118**	**8,142**	**9,015**	**13,180**	**13,452**	**1.20**	**2.06**
Cyprus	681	401	500	374	403	0.04	7.75
Israel	5,655	4,830	5,413	7,151	8,159	0.73	14.10
Turkey	2,782	2,911	3,102	5,655	4,890	0.43	-13.53
Other Europe	**17,407**	**17,474**	**16,222**	**17,619**	**4,057**	**0.36**	**-76.97**
Other countries of Europe	17,407	17,474	16,222	17,619	4,057	0.36	-76.97

Yearbook of Tourism Statistics, Data 2008 – 2012, 2014 Edition

LITHUANIA

5. Overnight stays of non-resident tourists in hotels and similar establishments, by country of residence

	2008	2009	2010	2011	2012	Market share 2012	% Change 2012-2011
TOTAL	1,544,487	1,322,983	1,509,883	1,818,031	2,001,745	100.00	10.11
AFRICA	2,327	2,715	3,157	6,812	4,350	0.22	-36.14
Other Africa	2,327	2,715	3,157	6,812	4,350	0.22	-36.14
All countries of Africa	2,327	2,715	3,157	6,812	4,350	0.22	-36.14
AMERICAS	58,037	40,088	59,025	61,071	73,610	3.68	20.53
North America	53,128	36,248	54,101	54,552	56,683	2.83	3.91
Canada	4,611	3,745	5,732	6,829	5,946	0.30	-12.93
United States of America	48,517	32,503	48,369	47,723	50,737	2.53	6.32
Other Americas	4,909	3,840	4,924	6,519	16,927	0.85	159.66
Other countries of the Americas	4,909	3,840	4,924	6,519	16,927	0.85	159.66
EAST ASIA AND THE PACIFIC	36,872	35,196	37,487	56,241	75,291	3.76	33.87
North-East Asia	20,394	16,887	17,161	20,261	24,383	1.22	20.34
China	4,835	4,418	5,238	8,497	10,363	0.52	21.96
Japan	15,559	12,469	11,923	11,764	14,020	0.70	19.18
Other East Asia and the Pacific	16,478	18,309	20,326	35,980	50,908	2.54	41.49
Other countries of Asia	9,755	10,847	13,905	28,007	41,863	2.09	49.47
All countries of Oceania	6,723	7,462	6,421	7,973	9,045	0.45	13.45
EUROPE	1,447,251	1,244,984	1,410,214	1,693,907	1,848,494	92.34	9.13
Central/Eastern Europe	718,303	624,685	753,271	881,220	1,053,051	52.61	19.50
Belarus	55,346	73,816	108,583	129,163	163,837	8.18	26.85
Bulgaria	2,835	2,854	2,420	3,528	3,160	0.16	-10.43
Czech Republic	13,663	24,506	11,032	13,326	23,299	1.16	74.84
Estonia	59,328	44,169	46,544	54,845	56,726	2.83	3.43
Hungary	5,652	5,159	6,435	7,348	6,887	0.34	-6.27
Latvia	114,677	84,599	92,477	93,217	104,194	5.21	11.78
Poland	251,433	204,378	246,085	249,892	249,640	12.47	-0.10
Romania	4,481	5,462	4,652	8,091	5,416	0.27	-33.06
Russian Federation	170,122	146,956	203,133	285,646	397,950	19.88	39.32
Slovakia	3,478	3,085	3,451	5,063	3,820	0.19	-24.55
Ukraine	31,074	21,360	16,152	25,799	34,606	1.73	34.14
Other countries Central/East Europe	6,214	8,341	12,307	5,302	3,516	0.18	-33.69
Northern Europe	281,598	207,753	231,042	263,691	282,594	14.12	7.17
Denmark	27,382	26,270	27,659	34,651	33,219	1.66	-4.13
Finland	74,050	53,112	63,220	68,419	68,497	3.42	0.11
Iceland	4,028	2,801	1,662	1,945	3,526	0.18	81.29
Ireland	13,856	9,414	6,973	8,300	10,589	0.53	27.58
Norway	51,468	34,846	34,285	44,958	57,954	2.90	28.91
Sweden	39,076	32,824	33,684	44,739	39,081	1.95	-12.65
United Kingdom	71,738	48,486	63,559	60,679	69,728	3.48	14.91
Southern Europe	89,737	78,652	94,657	135,791	112,408	5.62	-17.22
Greece	5,797	6,330	6,983	7,987	6,594	0.33	-17.44
Italy	52,263	41,795	46,442	62,312	58,525	2.92	-6.08
Portugal	5,038	5,670	6,366	8,207	4,963	0.25	-39.53
Spain	26,639	24,857	34,866	57,285	42,326	2.11	-26.11
Western Europe	310,217	282,261	283,045	339,932	355,547	17.76	4.59
Austria	13,670	12,625	10,587	12,548	13,762	0.69	9.67
Belgium	13,620	15,180	14,489	15,229	16,721	0.84	9.80
France	39,166	39,308	55,419	58,285	44,354	2.22	-23.90
Germany	214,697	189,777	178,337	218,073	244,118	12.20	11.94
Luxembourg	1,282	1,355	914	1,171	1,156	0.06	-1.28
Netherlands	20,101	15,792	16,313	25,667	26,725	1.34	4.12
Switzerland	7,681	8,224	6,986	8,959	8,711	0.44	-2.77

Yearbook of Tourism Statistics, Data 2008 – 2012, 2014 Editic

LITHUANIA

5. Overnight stays of non-resident tourists in hotels and similar establishments, by country of residence

	2008	2009	2010	2011	2012	Market share 2012	% Change 2012-2011
East Mediterranean Europe	**18,414**	**21,266**	**24,039**	**34,704**	**36,231**	**1.81**	**4.40**
Israel	12,773	12,060	14,643	19,530	23,186	1.16	18.72
Turkey	5,641	9,206	9,396	15,174	13,045	0.65	-14.03
Other Europe	**28,982**	**30,367**	**24,160**	**38,569**	**8,663**	**0.43**	**-77.54**
Other countries of Europe	28,982	30,367	24,160	38,569	8,663	0.43	-77.54

Yearbook of Tourism Statistics, Data 2008 – 2012, 2014 Edition

LITHUANIA

6. Overnight stays of non-resident tourists in all types of accommodation establishments, by country of residence

	2008	2009	2010	2011	2012	Market share 2012	% Change 2012-2011
TOTAL	2,055,953	1,758,447	1,999,251	2,377,346	2,622,298	100.00	10.30
AFRICA	2,398	2,827	3,224	6,866	4,548	0.17	-33.76
Other Africa	2,398	2,827	3,224	6,866	4,548	0.17	-33.76
All countries of Africa	2,398	2,827	3,224	6,866	4,548	0.17	-33.76
AMERICAS	63,488	46,043	61,964	65,530	80,172	3.06	22.34
North America	57,958	42,022	56,913	58,767	61,331	2.34	4.36
Canada	5,030	4,103	6,027	7,507	6,533	0.25	-12.97
United States of America	52,928	37,919	50,886	51,260	54,798	2.09	6.90
South America	2,443	2,508	2,486	3,068	3,815	0.15	24.35
Brazil	2,443	2,508	2,486	3,068	3,815	0.15	24.35
Other Americas	3,087	1,513	2,565	3,695	15,026	0.57	306.66
Other countries of the Americas	3,087	1,513	2,565	3,695	15,026	0.57	306.66
EAST ASIA AND THE PACIFIC	39,213	41,574	39,360	59,084	82,555	3.15	39.72
North-East Asia	23,426	24,785	20,276	25,505	29,684	1.13	16.39
China	6,028	9,896	5,350	8,920	10,807	0.41	21.15
Japan	15,790	12,686	12,140	12,101	14,902	0.57	23.15
Korea, Republic of	1,608	2,203	2,786	4,484	3,975	0.15	-11.35
Australasia	7,391	7,837	7,416	8,507	9,577	0.37	12.58
Australia	7,391	7,837	7,416	8,507	9,577	0.37	12.58
Other East Asia and the Pacific	8,396	8,952	11,668	25,072	43,294	1.65	72.68
Other countries of Asia	8,396	8,952	11,668	25,072	43,294	1.65	72.68
EUROPE	1,950,854	1,668,003	1,894,703	2,245,866	2,455,023	93.62	9.31
Central/Eastern Europe	1,055,553	912,678	1,076,511	1,244,497	1,475,705	56.28	18.58
Belarus	229,790	250,314	293,417	312,565	353,382	13.48	13.06
Bulgaria	3,033	3,021	2,535	3,769	3,727	0.14	-1.11
Czech Republic	14,933	25,897	13,466	14,892	25,140	0.96	68.82
Estonia	67,566	49,918	51,342	60,523	63,621	2.43	5.12
Hungary	6,057	5,527	12,226	7,682	7,255	0.28	-5.56
Latvia	140,435	100,225	109,891	112,104	127,773	4.87	13.98
Poland	312,498	239,067	281,286	277,979	277,327	10.58	-0.23
Romania	10,259	7,995	5,119	8,885	6,087	0.23	-31.49
Russian Federation	224,966	195,401	282,318	412,645	568,669	21.69	37.81
Slovakia	3,696	3,342	3,769	5,446	4,588	0.17	-15.75
Ukraine	42,320	31,971	21,142	28,007	38,136	1.45	36.17
Northern Europe	291,018	217,638	242,990	278,985	297,733	11.35	6.72
Denmark	28,300	27,026	28,433	35,615	34,531	1.32	-3.04
Finland	75,964	55,508	67,439	73,608	72,116	2.75	-2.03
Iceland	4,037	2,878	1,699	1,980	3,594	0.14	81.52
Ireland	14,657	9,640	7,900	8,848	12,096	0.46	36.71
Norway	53,053	36,123	36,180	47,301	59,667	2.28	26.14
Sweden	40,488	34,507	34,916	46,967	40,871	1.56	-12.98
United Kingdom	74,519	51,956	66,423	64,666	74,858	2.85	15.76
Southern Europe	95,432	84,565	102,852	151,723	127,869	4.88	-15.72
Greece	5,979	6,377	7,109	8,224	6,721	0.26	-18.28
Italy	53,597	43,550	49,094	67,187	63,756	2.43	-5.11
Malta	578	508	609	990	936	0.04	-5.45
Portugal	5,360	6,002	6,780	8,544	5,339	0.20	-37.51
Slovenia	2,501	2,129	2,541	5,802	3,703	0.14	-36.18
Spain	27,417	25,999	36,719	60,976	47,414	1.81	-22.24
Western Europe	449,211	389,675	407,441	491,336	502,212	19.15	2.21
Austria	14,233	13,225	11,104	13,435	14,336	0.55	6.71
Belgium	14,110	15,675	15,546	16,494	17,815	0.68	8.01
France	43,129	42,650	59,466	62,955	50,824	1.94	-19.27
Germany	343,494	288,365	293,747	356,978	374,229	14.27	4.83
Luxembourg	1,304	1,355	958	1,224	1,795	0.07	46.65

LITHUANIA

6. Overnight stays of non-resident tourists in all types of accommodation establishments, by country of residence

	2008	2009	2010	2011	2012	Market share 2012	% Change 2012-2011
Netherlands	24,973	19,214	19,133	30,454	33,649	1.28	10.49
Switzerland	7,968	9,191	7,487	9,796	9,564	0.36	-2.37
East Mediterranean Europe	**25,462**	**26,648**	**30,720**	**41,852**	**43,535**	**1.66**	**4.02**
Cyprus	1,301	868	1,041	800	1,009	0.04	26.13
Israel	17,687	16,133	19,988	25,394	29,028	1.11	14.31
Turkey	6,474	9,647	9,691	15,658	13,498	0.51	-13.79
Other Europe	**34,178**	**36,799**	**34,189**	**37,473**	**7,969**	**0.30**	**-78.73**
Other countries of Europe	34,178	36,799	34,189	37,473	7,969	0.30	-78.73

Yearbook of Tourism Statistics, Data 2008 – 2012, 2014 Edition

LUXEMBOURG

3. Arrivals of non-resident tourists in hotels and similar establishments, by country of residence

		2008	2009	2010	2011	2012	Market share 2012	% Change 2012-2011
TOTAL	(*)	675,209	651,273	651,532	682,361	746,619	100.00	9.42
AFRICA		4,087	3,021	2,775	9,792	13,841	1.85	41.35
Southern Africa		1,024	476	832	926	1,088	0.15	17.49
South Africa		1,024	476	832	926	1,088	0.15	17.49
Other Africa		3,063	2,545	1,943	8,866	12,753	1.71	43.84
Other countries of Africa		3,063	2,545	1,943	8,866	12,753	1.71	43.84
AMERICAS		29,253	25,816	27,426	35,094	34,875	4.67	-0.62
North America		23,407	21,146	21,485	20,173	22,062	2.95	9.36
Canada		4,284	3,564	3,485	3,277	4,223	0.57	28.87
United States of America		19,123	17,582	18,000	16,896	17,839	2.39	5.58
South America		2,997	2,167	2,473	2,265	3,466	0.46	53.02
Brazil		2,997	2,167	2,473	2,265	3,466	0.46	53.02
Other Americas		2,849	2,503	3,468	12,656	9,347	1.25	-26.15
Other countries of the Americas		2,849	2,503	3,468	12,656	9,347	1.25	-26.15
EAST ASIA AND THE PACIFIC		26,952	28,792	32,969	52,195	71,124	9.53	36.27
North-East Asia		16,707	17,628	20,400	32,165	48,837	6.54	51.83
China		11,739	13,608	15,529	25,708	40,954	5.49	59.30
Japan		4,195	3,308	3,431	5,280	6,875	0.92	30.21
Korea, Republic of		773	712	1,440	1,177	1,008	0.14	-14.36
Australasia		2,339	1,838	2,102	2,132	2,554	0.34	19.79
Australia		2,339	1,838	2,102	2,132	2,554	0.34	19.79
Other East Asia and the Pacific		7,906	9,326	10,467	17,898	19,733	2.64	10.25
Other countries of Asia		7,906	9,326	10,467	17,898	19,733	2.64	10.25
EUROPE		611,781	591,200	586,879	585,280	626,779	83.95	7.09
Central/Eastern Europe		22,920	20,936	23,506	24,429	28,351	3.80	16.05
Bulgaria		1,332	1,229	1,008	1,177	1,129	0.15	-4.08
Czech Republic		2,437	2,397	2,719	1,931	2,787	0.37	44.33
Estonia		595	481	518	520	566	0.08	8.85
Hungary		1,777	1,754	1,628	1,639	2,211	0.30	34.90
Latvia		379	463	531	485	564	0.08	16.29
Lithuania		1,116	796	679	726	1,032	0.14	42.15
Poland		4,554	4,002	5,267	4,946	5,080	0.68	2.71
Romania		2,453	2,222	2,637	2,625	2,873	0.38	9.45
Russian Federation		7,109	6,470	7,125	8,919	9,895	1.33	10.94
Slovakia		555	678	859	804	981	0.13	22.01
Ukraine		613	444	535	657	1,233	0.17	87.67
Northern Europe		74,339	65,478	64,742	56,368	64,551	8.65	14.52
Denmark		9,223	7,550	6,681	3,982	4,118	0.55	3.42
Finland		2,484	2,423	2,442	2,150	2,405	0.32	11.86
Iceland		614	463	712	770	659	0.09	-14.42
Ireland		3,019	2,423	2,505	2,374	2,671	0.36	12.51
Norway		2,680	2,243	2,219	2,055	2,109	0.28	2.63
Sweden		6,107	5,441	5,847	4,704	4,541	0.61	-3.47
United Kingdom		50,212	44,935	44,336	40,333	48,048	6.44	19.13
Southern Europe		47,458	42,553	42,723	41,109	43,327	5.80	5.40
Greece		2,799	2,207	2,263	1,934	2,027	0.27	4.81
Italy		20,895	18,672	17,738	17,593	17,675	2.37	0.47
Malta		574	569	470	455	478	0.06	5.05
Portugal		7,354	7,106	7,702	8,140	8,542	1.14	4.94
Slovenia		1,440	908	1,042	742	883	0.12	19.00
Spain		14,396	13,091	13,508	12,245	13,722	1.84	12.06
Western Europe		452,381	451,308	445,137	446,814	471,159	63.11	5.45
Austria		4,878	4,995	5,484	5,549	5,457	0.73	-1.66
Belgium		149,285	146,911	147,935	150,740	156,353	20.94	3.72
France		100,183	104,923	112,343	115,643	117,829	15.78	1.89

428

LUXEMBOURG

3. Arrivals of non-resident tourists in hotels and similar establishments, by country of residence

	2008	2009	2010	2011	2012	Market share 2012	% Change 2012-2011
Germany	100,161	95,866	92,209	96,766	103,501	13.86	6.96
Netherlands	80,559	79,588	70,048	61,769	69,406	9.30	12.36
Switzerland	17,315	19,025	17,118	16,347	18,613	2.49	13.86
East Mediterranean Europe	**2,971**	**2,991**	**3,485**	**3,926**	**6,552**	**0.88**	**66.89**
Cyprus	379	444	422	366	405	0.05	10.66
Turkey	2,592	2,547	3,063	3,560	6,147	0.82	72.67
Other Europe	**11,712**	**7,934**	**7,286**	**12,634**	**12,839**	**1.72**	**1.62**
Other countries of Europe	11,712	7,934	7,286	12,634	12,839	1.72	1.62
NOT SPECIFIED	**3,136**	**2,444**	**1,483**				
Other countries of the World	3,136	2,444	1,483				

Yearbook of Tourism Statistics, Data 2008 – 2012, 2014 Edition

LUXEMBOURG

4. Arrivals of non-resident tourists in all types of accommodation establishments, by country of residence

	2008	2009	2010	2011	2012	Market share 2012	% Change 2012-2011
TOTAL	876,551	846,685	805,472	873,952	905,042	100.00	3.56
AFRICA	4,300	3,296	2,886	10,115	14,025	1.55	38.66
Southern Africa	1,066	519	870	1,007	1,135	0.13	12.71
South Africa	1,066	519	870	1,007	1,135	0.13	12.71
Other Africa	3,234	2,777	2,016	9,108	12,890	1.42	41.52
Other countries of Africa	3,234	2,777	2,016	9,108	12,890	1.42	41.52
AMERICAS	32,445	28,720	28,975	37,658	36,087	3.99	-4.17
North America	25,792	23,289	22,565	21,836	22,887	2.53	4.81
Canada	5,101	4,211	3,736	3,768	4,477	0.49	18.82
United States of America	20,691	19,078	18,829	18,068	18,410	2.03	1.89
South America	3,300	2,514	2,622	2,547	3,635	0.40	42.72
Brazil	3,300	2,514	2,622	2,547	3,635	0.40	42.72
Other Americas	3,353	2,917	3,788	13,275	9,565	1.06	-27.95
Other countries of the Americas	3,353	2,917	3,788	13,275	9,565	1.06	-27.95
EAST ASIA AND THE PACIFIC	30,513	32,039	34,879	55,682	72,661	8.03	30.49
North-East Asia	18,476	19,221	21,262	34,163	49,299	5.45	44.31
China	12,329	14,271	15,933	26,555	41,118	4.54	54.84
Japan	4,648	3,706	3,575	5,633	7,033	0.78	24.85
Korea, Republic of	1,499	1,244	1,754	1,975	1,148	0.13	-41.87
Australasia	3,292	2,616	2,594	2,767	2,974	0.33	7.48
Australia	3,292	2,616	2,594	2,767	2,974	0.33	7.48
Other East Asia and the Pacific	8,745	10,202	11,023	18,752	20,388	2.25	8.72
Other countries of Asia	8,745	10,202	11,023	18,752	20,388	2.25	8.72
EUROPE	805,482	779,128	737,093	770,497	782,269	86.43	1.53
Central/Eastern Europe	26,376	23,708	25,079	27,673	30,049	3.32	8.59
Bulgaria	1,390	1,369	1,080	1,306	1,172	0.13	-10.26
Czech Republic	2,900	2,986	3,090	2,450	3,045	0.34	24.29
Estonia	614	507	531	595	610	0.07	2.52
Hungary	2,128	2,096	1,836	1,869	2,359	0.26	26.22
Latvia	392	473	570	1,002	584	0.06	-41.72
Lithuania	1,163	828	731	773	1,094	0.12	41.53
Poland	6,263	5,033	5,810	5,952	5,716	0.63	-3.97
Romania	2,826	2,336	2,750	2,831	3,049	0.34	7.70
Russian Federation	7,425	6,852	7,248	9,280	10,079	1.11	8.61
Slovakia	650	778	895	936	1,087	0.12	16.13
Ukraine	625	450	538	679	1,254	0.14	84.68
Northern Europe	88,174	77,291	75,161	67,483	72,520	8.01	7.46
Denmark	11,377	9,452	7,866	5,568	5,375	0.59	-3.47
Finland	3,207	3,131	2,817	2,773	2,741	0.30	-1.15
Iceland	655	504	737	834	674	0.07	-19.18
Ireland	3,402	2,858	2,993	2,790	2,923	0.32	4.77
Norway	3,234	2,818	2,535	2,324	2,451	0.27	5.46
Sweden	6,831	6,092	6,291	5,345	5,001	0.55	-6.44
United Kingdom	59,468	52,436	51,922	47,849	53,355	5.90	11.51
Southern Europe	51,887	47,003	45,351	45,098	46,032	5.09	2.07
Greece	2,898	2,310	2,369	2,019	2,065	0.23	2.28
Italy	22,514	20,345	18,691	19,026	18,838	2.08	-0.99
Malta	579	571	472	459	484	0.05	5.45
Portugal	7,888	7,650	8,023	8,772	8,998	0.99	2.58
Slovenia	1,623	1,215	1,304	966	1,010	0.11	4.55
Spain	16,385	14,912	14,492	13,856	14,637	1.62	5.64
Western Europe	623,981	619,886	580,404	611,323	614,021	67.84	0.44
Austria	5,453	5,567	5,967	6,093	5,975	0.66	-1.94
Belgium	176,591	172,251	167,501	176,091	177,175	19.58	0.62
France	109,660	114,001	118,447	124,511	123,878	13.69	-0.51

430

LUXEMBOURG

4. Arrivals of non-resident tourists in all types of accommodation establishments, by country of residence

	2008	2009	2010	2011	2012	Market share 2012	% Change 2012-2011
Germany	123,985	118,334	108,927	119,188	122,524	13.54	2.80
Netherlands	189,516	189,081	161,150	167,227	164,609	18.19	-1.57
Switzerland	18,776	20,652	18,412	18,213	19,860	2.19	9.04
East Mediterranean Europe	**3,052**	**3,043**	**3,508**	**3,971**	**6,597**	**0.73**	**66.13**
Cyprus	383	449	424	339	406	0.04	19.76
Turkey	2,669	2,594	3,084	3,632	6,191	0.68	70.46
Other Europe	**12,012**	**8,197**	**7,590**	**14,949**	**13,050**	**1.44**	**-12.70**
Other countries of Europe	12,012	8,197	7,590	14,949	13,050	1.44	-12.70
NOT SPECIFIED	**3,811**	**3,502**	**1,639**				
Other countries of the World	3,811	3,502	1,639				

Yearbook of Tourism Statistics, Data 2008 – 2012, 2014 Edition

LUXEMBOURG

5. Overnight stays of non-resident tourists in hotels and similar establishments, by country of residence

		2008	2009	2010	2011	2012	Market share 2012	% Change 2012-2011
TOTAL	(*)	1,307,286	1,191,576	1,163,204	1,282,014	1,347,537	100.00	5.11
AFRICA		11,885	8,016	7,856	22,064	29,034	2.15	31.59
Southern Africa		2,834	1,337	2,656	3,127	3,361	0.25	7.48
South Africa		2,834	1,337	2,656	3,127	3,361	0.25	7.48
Other Africa		9,051	6,679	5,200	18,937	25,673	1.91	35.57
Other countries of Africa		9,051	6,679	5,200	18,937	25,673	1.91	35.57
AMERICAS		74,322	58,393	64,060	74,810	41,752	3.10	-44.19
North America		59,749	48,641	50,618	46,404	15,003	1.11	-67.67
Canada		12,432	8,780	7,928	8,071	10,789	0.80	33.68
United States of America		47,317	39,861	42,690	38,333	4,214	0.31	-89.01
South America		7,543	4,750	5,527	5,095	6,673	0.50	30.97
Brazil		7,543	4,750	5,527	5,095	6,673	0.50	30.97
Other Americas		7,030	5,002	7,915	23,311	20,076	1.49	-13.88
Other countries of the Americas		7,030	5,002	7,915	23,311	20,076	1.49	-13.88
EAST ASIA AND THE PACIFIC		55,699	56,218	61,246	93,898	115,369	8.56	22.87
North-East Asia		27,342	27,369	28,401	42,191	59,778	4.44	41.68
China		18,831	19,863	19,392	32,403	48,195	3.58	48.74
Japan		7,130	6,280	5,770	7,864	9,779	0.73	24.35
Korea, Republic of		1,381	1,226	3,239	1,924	1,804	0.13	-6.24
Australasia		4,719	3,687	3,991	4,207	4,994	0.37	18.71
Australia		4,719	3,687	3,991	4,207	4,994	0.37	18.71
Other East Asia and the Pacific		23,638	25,162	28,854	47,500	50,597	3.75	6.52
Other countries of Asia		23,638	25,162	28,854	47,500	50,597	3.75	6.52
EUROPE		1,159,367	1,064,704	1,026,366	1,091,242	1,161,382	86.19	6.43
Central/Eastern Europe		60,677	49,797	54,477	53,114	63,224	4.69	19.03
Bulgaria		4,117	3,296	2,943	2,758	2,982	0.22	8.12
Czech Republic		7,199	7,541	6,567	4,626	6,977	0.52	50.82
Estonia		1,708	1,105	1,103	1,162	1,133	0.08	-2.50
Hungary		4,646	5,207	4,936	4,350	5,604	0.42	28.83
Latvia		1,013	1,206	1,141	974	1,285	0.10	31.93
Lithuania		2,555	1,481	1,511	1,471	2,436	0.18	65.60
Poland		17,208	10,196	12,786	13,101	14,563	1.08	11.16
Romania		6,478	5,655	6,795	7,038	7,222	0.54	2.61
Russian Federation		12,941	11,545	12,820	14,430	16,673	1.24	15.54
Slovakia		1,483	1,783	2,857	1,900	2,354	0.17	23.89
Ukraine		1,329	782	1,018	1,304	1,995	0.15	52.99
Northern Europe		142,705	125,773	119,926	116,372	131,123	9.73	12.68
Denmark		16,005	13,205	11,695	7,248	6,905	0.51	-4.73
Finland		5,284	5,081	4,908	5,170	5,111	0.38	-1.14
Iceland		1,468	1,205	1,707	2,159	2,063	0.15	-4.45
Ireland		7,945	5,883	6,450	7,158	6,906	0.51	-3.52
Norway		5,019	3,970	3,923	4,502	4,319	0.32	-4.06
Sweden		11,862	9,782	10,599	8,611	8,068	0.60	-6.31
United Kingdom		95,122	86,647	80,644	81,524	97,751	7.25	19.90
Southern Europe		98,816	83,460	82,209	85,892	93,473	6.94	8.83
Greece		7,000	5,546	4,902	4,830	5,042	0.37	4.39
Italy		45,514	36,223	34,743	36,427	38,310	2.84	5.17
Malta		2,642	2,078	1,906	1,953	2,097	0.16	7.37
Portugal		14,620	13,610	14,380	16,744	17,346	1.29	3.60
Slovenia		2,673	2,531	2,688	1,758	2,667	0.20	51.71
Spain		26,367	23,472	23,590	24,180	28,011	2.08	15.84
Western Europe		824,680	780,844	746,740	802,940	838,195	62.20	4.39
Austria		10,674	11,642	11,656	12,074	12,095	0.90	0.17
Belgium		270,446	249,866	241,942	274,201	270,940	20.11	-1.19
France		170,327	169,769	180,836	195,957	197,756	14.68	0.92

432

LUXEMBOURG

5. Overnight stays of non-resident tourists in hotels and similar establishments, by country of residence

	2008	2009	2010	2011	2012	Market share 2012	% Change 2012-2011
Germany	184,824	172,075	161,798	177,812	196,140	14.56	10.31
Netherlands	154,750	143,938	120,316	112,302	126,476	9.39	12.62
Switzerland	33,659	33,554	30,192	30,594	34,788	2.58	13.71
East Mediterranean Europe	**6,157**	**5,820**	**6,381**	**7,718**	**10,462**	**0.78**	**35.55**
Cyprus	999	1,230	1,013	1,375	1,852	0.14	34.69
Turkey	5,158	4,590	5,368	6,343	8,610	0.64	35.74
Other Europe	**26,332**	**19,010**	**16,633**	**25,206**	**24,905**	**1.85**	**-1.19**
Other countries of Europe	26,332	19,010	16,633	25,206	24,905	1.85	-1.19
NOT SPECIFIED	**6,013**	**4,245**	**3,676**				
Other countries of the World	6,013	4,245	3,676				

Yearbook of Tourism Statistics, Data 2008 – 2012, 2014 Edition

LUXEMBOURG

6. Overnight stays of non-resident tourists in all types of accommodation establishments, by country of residence

	2008	2009	2010	2011	2012	Market share 2012	% Change 2012-2011
TOTAL	2,261,225	2,073,813	1,717,130	2,067,883	2,217,504	100.00	7.24
AFRICA	12,504	8,572	8,071	22,863	29,863	1.35	30.62
Southern Africa	2,974	1,423	2,694	3,382	3,448	0.16	1.95
South Africa	2,974	1,423	2,694	3,382	3,448	0.16	1.95
Other Africa	9,530	7,149	5,377	19,481	26,415	1.19	35.59
Other countries of Africa	9,530	7,149	5,377	19,481	26,415	1.19	35.59
AMERICAS	79,382	63,780	67,259	89,166	81,516	3.68	-8.58
North America	63,649	52,651	53,059	49,346	54,121	2.44	9.68
Canada	13,759	9,891	8,353	8,871	11,207	0.51	26.33
United States of America	49,890	42,760	44,706	40,475	42,914	1.94	6.03
South America	7,978	5,512	5,801	5,504	6,930	0.31	25.91
Brazil	7,978	5,512	5,801	5,504	6,930	0.31	25.91
Other Americas	7,755	5,617	8,399	34,316	20,465	0.92	-40.36
Other countries of the Americas	7,755	5,617	8,399	34,316	20,465	0.92	-40.36
EAST ASIA AND THE PACIFIC	60,972	61,095	63,983	99,446	117,826	5.31	18.48
North-East Asia	29,770	29,513	29,617	44,909	60,396	2.72	34.49
China	19,570	20,679	19,874	33,542	48,408	2.18	44.32
Japan	7,907	6,912	6,092	8,417	9,991	0.45	18.70
Korea, Republic of	2,293	1,922	3,651	2,950	1,997	0.09	-32.31
Australasia	6,271	4,925	4,669	5,386	5,647	0.25	4.85
Australia	6,271	4,925	4,669	5,386	5,647	0.25	4.85
Other East Asia and the Pacific	24,931	26,657	29,697	49,151	51,783	2.34	5.35
Other countries of Asia	24,931	26,657	29,697	49,151	51,783	2.34	5.35
EUROPE	2,100,971	1,933,744	1,573,840	1,856,408	1,988,299	89.66	7.10
Central/Eastern Europe	69,221	57,424	58,302	61,315	76,794	3.46	25.25
Bulgaria	4,372	3,672	3,047	3,023	3,077	0.14	1.79
Czech Republic	8,173	8,570	7,281	5,712	7,688	0.35	34.59
Estonia	1,787	1,140	1,114	1,305	1,199	0.05	-8.12
Hungary	5,347	5,960	5,415	5,219	6,005	0.27	15.06
Latvia	1,037	1,216	1,319	1,772	1,320	0.06	-25.51
Lithuania	2,653	1,592	1,705	1,793	2,592	0.12	44.56
Poland	22,005	13,403	14,089	16,249	25,578	1.15	57.41
Romania	7,361	6,453	7,214	7,563	7,828	0.35	3.50
Russian Federation	13,430	12,260	13,067	14,962	17,008	0.77	13.67
Slovakia	1,700	2,362	3,025	2,348	2,478	0.11	5.54
Ukraine	1,356	796	1,026	1,369	2,021	0.09	47.63
Northern Europe	180,084	157,494	143,376	145,189	153,342	6.92	5.62
Denmark	22,962	18,830	14,415	11,683	10,886	0.49	-6.82
Finland	6,662	6,138	5,457	6,301	5,615	0.25	-10.89
Iceland	1,572	1,347	1,811	2,342	2,084	0.09	-11.02
Ireland	9,169	7,197	7,727	8,179	7,476	0.34	-8.60
Norway	6,148	5,322	4,335	4,995	5,270	0.24	5.51
Sweden	13,441	11,139	11,267	9,951	8,932	0.40	-10.24
United Kingdom	120,130	107,521	98,364	101,738	113,079	5.10	11.15
Southern Europe	108,259	92,853	87,590	95,401	101,699	4.59	6.60
Greece	7,243	5,756	5,111	5,053	5,131	0.23	1.54
Italy	49,021	39,770	36,700	40,025	40,836	1.84	2.03
Malta	2,655	2,082	1,913	1,959	2,111	0.10	7.76
Portugal	16,398	15,692	15,528	19,078	20,729	0.93	8.65
Slovenia	3,350	3,108	3,191	2,099	2,891	0.13	37.73
Spain	29,592	26,445	25,147	27,187	30,001	1.35	10.35
Western Europe	1,709,928	1,600,560	1,261,046	1,515,911	1,620,428	73.07	6.89
Austria	12,097	12,777	12,722	13,064	13,404	0.60	2.60
Belgium	436,058	378,659	331,401	391,328	425,646	19.19	8.77
France	203,103	197,235	202,414	220,967	215,666	9.73	-2.40

434

LUXEMBOURG

6. Overnight stays of non-resident tourists in all types of accommodation establishments, by country of residence

	2008	2009	2010	2011	2012	Market share 2012	% Change 2012-2011
Germany	255,868	239,284	208,162	240,097	262,002	11.82	9.12
Netherlands	766,364	736,007	474,036	616,386	666,322	30.05	8.10
Switzerland	36,438	36,598	32,311	34,069	37,388	1.69	9.74
East Mediterranean Europe	**6,285**	**5,928**	**6,418**	**7,847**	**10,538**	**0.48**	**34.29**
Cyprus	1,003	1,254	1,019	1,380	1,856	0.08	34.49
Turkey	5,282	4,674	5,399	6,467	8,682	0.39	34.25
Other Europe	**27,194**	**19,485**	**17,108**	**30,745**	**25,498**	**1.15**	**-17.07**
Other countries of Europe	27,194	19,485	17,108	30,745	25,498	1.15	-17.07
NOT SPECIFIED	**7,396**	**6,622**	**3,977**				
Other countries of the World	7,396	6,622	3,977				

Yearbook of Tourism Statistics, Data 2008 – 2012, 2014 Edition

MACAO, CHINA

2. Arrivals of non-resident visitors at national borders, by nationality

		2008	2009	2010	2011	2012	Market share 2012	% Change 2012-2011
TOTAL	(*)	22,933,185	21,752,751	24,965,411	28,002,279	28,082,292	100.00	0.29
AFRICA		22,095	16,702	21,736	25,161	27,945	0.10	11.06
East Africa		2,753	2,015	2,932	3,950	4,509	0.02	14.15
Burundi		53	33	31	39	74	0.00	89.74
Ethiopia		81	61	99	101	180	0.00	78.22
Kenya		232	181	263	423	579	0.00	36.88
Madagascar		240	219	339	342	343	0.00	0.29
Malawi		9	4	12	32	22	0.00	-31.25
Mauritius		751	549	705	672	570	0.00	-15.18
Mozambique		254	364	435	321	442	0.00	37.69
Rwanda		18	31	36	97	114	0.00	17.53
Seychelles		206	126	163	164	169	0.00	3.05
Somalia		38	19	17	31	34	0.00	9.68
Uganda		125	84	369	1,156	1,262	0.00	9.17
United Republic of Tanzania		630	247	320	439	504	0.00	14.81
Zambia		38	36	53	54	69	0.00	27.78
Zimbabwe		78	61	90	79	147	0.00	86.08
Central Africa		3,303	2,517	3,138	4,236	5,076	0.02	19.83
Angola		854	1,029	1,329	1,673	1,756	0.01	4.96
Cameroon		672	611	411	330	374	0.00	13.33
Congo		398	189	223	355	490	0.00	38.03
Democratic Republic of the Congo		1,315	636	1,099	1,808	2,378	0.01	31.53
Equatorial Guinea		12	6	11	22	23	0.00	4.55
Gabon		28	30	35	19	31	0.00	63.16
Sao Tome and Principe		24	16	30	29	24	0.00	-17.24
North Africa		1,135	1,177	1,300	1,310	1,639	0.01	25.11
Algeria		180	235	235	203	396	0.00	95.07
Morocco		410	421	482	527	530	0.00	0.57
Sudan		299	136	151	281	377	0.00	34.16
Tunisia		246	385	432	299	336	0.00	12.37
Southern Africa		4,629	4,287	4,675	5,301	4,743	0.02	-10.53
Botswana		32	17	12	39	21	0.00	-46.15
Lesotho		3	7	3	5	10	0.00	100.00
Namibia		34	28	32	60	41	0.00	-31.67
South Africa		4,551	4,231	4,624	5,186	4,663	0.02	-10.08
Swaziland		9	4	4	11	8	0.00	-27.27
West Africa		9,998	6,366	7,544	7,891	8,103	0.03	2.69
Benin		45	47	92	183	184	0.00	0.55
Burkina Faso		122	48	72	80	47	0.00	-41.25
Cape Verde		177	167	221	198	250	0.00	26.26
Côte d'Ivoire		458	159	156	146	218	0.00	49.32
Gambia		188	136	125	159	171	0.00	7.55
Ghana		674	309	453	396	399	0.00	0.76
Guinea		594	385	607	915	1,100	0.00	20.22
Guinea-Bissau		316	265	170	191	160	0.00	-16.23
Liberia		139	58	64	205	136	0.00	-33.66
Mali		4,678	1,969	3,310	3,969	3,427	0.01	-13.66
Mauritania		45	40	38	68	49	0.00	-27.94
Niger		230	212	226	392	603	0.00	53.83
Nigeria		1,514	2,061	1,371	201	224	0.00	11.44
Senegal		467	200	276	374	511	0.00	36.63
Sierra Leone		101	72	49	91	203	0.00	123.08
Togo		250	238	314	323	421	0.00	30.34
Other Africa		277	340	2,147	2,473	3,875	0.01	56.69
Other countries of Africa		277	340	2,147	2,473	3,875	0.01	56.69

436

Yearbook of Tourism Statistics, Data 2008 – 2012, 2014 Edit

MACAO, CHINA

2. Arrivals of non-resident visitors at national borders, by nationality

	2008	2009	2010	2011	2012	Market share 2012	% Change 2012-2011
AMERICAS	312,920	278,788	297,154	310,564	306,528	1.09	-1.30
Caribbean	872	658	855	844	877	0.00	3.91
Antigua and Barbuda	3	6	17	8	5	0.00	-37.50
Bahamas	71	24	15	34	43	0.00	26.47
Barbados	20	20	20	11	22	0.00	100.00
Cuba	89	58	80	51	60	0.00	17.65
Dominican Republic	344	249	321	349	373	0.00	6.88
Haiti	14	12	15	16	15	0.00	-6.25
Jamaica	165	165	189	209	194	0.00	-7.18
Saint Lucia		3	5	9	4	0.00	-55.56
Saint Vincent and the Grenadines	7	7	9	1	2	0.00	100.00
Trinidad and Tobago	159	114	184	156	159	0.00	1.92
Central America	2,585	2,409	2,676	2,755	2,719	0.01	-1.31
Belize	468	427	497	543	542	0.00	-0.18
Costa Rica	963	786	842	869	737	0.00	-15.19
El Salvador	61	56	64	82	49	0.00	-40.24
Guatemala	175	218	197	181	247	0.00	36.46
Honduras	186	150	150	174	226	0.00	29.89
Nicaragua	14	15	28	22	39	0.00	77.27
Panama	718	757	898	884	879	0.00	-0.57
North America	291,350	258,064	272,567	281,199	277,284	0.99	-1.39
Canada	82,261	74,791	79,152	79,816	83,442	0.30	4.54
Mexico	5,649	3,679	5,145	5,368	5,182	0.02	-3.46
United States of America	203,440	179,594	188,270	196,015	188,660	0.67	-3.75
South America	18,088	17,562	20,908	25,594	25,411	0.09	-0.72
Argentina	1,292	1,335	1,675	1,544	1,718	0.01	11.27
Bolivia	236	205	186	204	177	0.00	-13.24
Brazil	8,976	7,525	8,347	10,501	10,288	0.04	-2.03
Chile	1,065	939	1,142	1,329	1,371	0.00	3.16
Colombia	1,742	1,939	2,309	3,567	3,854	0.01	8.05
Ecuador	479	445	605	682	819	0.00	20.09
Guyana	68	103	95	98	87	0.00	-11.22
Paraguay	65	65	81	86	56	0.00	-34.88
Peru	1,201	1,383	1,340	1,379	1,471	0.01	6.67
Suriname	185	152	177	199	186	0.00	-6.53
Uruguay	171	153	217	167	152	0.00	-8.98
Venezuela	2,608	3,318	4,734	5,838	5,232	0.02	-10.38
Other Americas	25	95	148	172	237	0.00	37.79
Other countries of the Americas	25	95	148	172	237	0.00	37.79
EAST ASIA AND THE PACIFIC	22,223,240	21,077,816	24,223,099	27,237,661	27,325,554	97.31	0.32
North-East Asia	20,594,852	19,598,355	22,740,428	25,762,927	25,903,793	92.24	0.55
China	11,613,064	10,988,796	13,228,418	16,161,927	16,900,964	60.18	4.57
Hong Kong, China	7,013,797	6,727,020	7,465,961	7,582,998	7,081,137	25.22	-6.62
Japan	367,146	379,346	413,529	396,050	396,010	1.41	-0.01
Korea, Dem. People's Republic of	1,161	1,038	1,161	1,167	1,318	0.00	12.94
Korea, Republic of	279,883	204,832	331,786	398,832	444,786	1.58	11.52
Mongolia	3,755	4,255	5,183	6,450	7,157	0.03	10.96
Taiwan, Province of China	1,316,046	1,293,068	1,294,390	1,215,503	1,072,421	3.82	-11.77
South-East Asia	1,471,002	1,344,190	1,324,534	1,314,196	1,257,800	4.48	-4.29
Brunei Darussalam	1,711	1,940	1,829	1,816	1,772	0.01	-2.42
Cambodia	4,574	3,854	4,359	4,467	4,367	0.02	-2.24
Indonesia	180,510	191,494	208,468	220,454	209,110	0.74	-5.15
Lao People's Democratic Republic	685	977	843	1,196	1,292	0.00	8.03
Malaysia	428,680	332,551	338,042	324,503	301,788	1.07	-7.00
Myanmar	3,475	4,081	4,920	4,500	4,573	0.02	1.62
Philippines	283,259	247,573	247,803	268,713	283,862	1.01	5.64
Singapore	263,717	256,556	257,213	280,588	205,688	0.73	-26.69

Yearbook of Tourism Statistics, Data 2008 – 2012, 2014 Edition

2. Arrivals of non-resident visitors at national borders, by nationality

	2008	2009	2010	2011	2012	Market share 2012	% Change 2012-2011
Thailand	252,226	242,592	212,441	196,362	231,293	0.82	17.79
Timor-Leste	136	144	151	174	151	0.00	-13.22
Viet Nam	52,029	62,428	48,465	11,423	13,904	0.05	21.72
Australasia	**156,576**	**134,337**	**126,360**	**126,717**	**127,678**	**0.45**	**0.76**
Australia	139,806	120,449	111,777	111,823	113,287	0.40	1.31
New Zealand	16,770	13,888	14,583	14,894	14,391	0.05	-3.38
Melanesia	**413**	**576**	**839**	**809**	**908**	**0.00**	**12.24**
Fiji	203	306	465	366	379	0.00	3.55
Papua New Guinea	80	91	80	101	125	0.00	23.76
Solomon Islands	85	126	186	251	272	0.00	8.37
Vanuatu	45	53	108	91	132	0.00	45.05
Micronesia	**226**	**199**	**149**	**201**	**322**	**0.00**	**60.20**
Marshall Islands	49	46	46	112	240	0.00	114.29
Micronesia, Federated States of	13	1	28	7	4	0.00	-42.86
Nauru	164	152	75	74	74	0.00	0.00
Palau				8	4	0.00	-50.00
Polynesia	**157**	**146**	**182**	**228**	**235**	**0.00**	**3.07**
Samoa	11	9	19	9	24	0.00	166.67
Tonga	146	137	163	219	211	0.00	-3.65
Other East Asia and the Pacific	**14**	**13**	**30,607**	**32,583**	**34,818**	**0.12**	**6.86**
Other countries of Asia	14	13	30,607	32,583	34,818	0.12	6.86
EUROPE	**272,613**	**254,112**	**244,445**	**251,672**	**262,715**	**0.94**	**4.39**
Central/Eastern Europe	**17,792**	**17,877**	**23,171**	**28,045**	**38,029**	**0.14**	**35.60**
Bulgaria	841	779	800	888	1,136	0.00	27.93
Czech Republic/Slovakia	1,625	1,895	1,552	1,946	1,738	0.01	-10.69
Hungary	1,594	1,544	2,141	1,686	1,732	0.01	2.73
Poland	4,570	3,872	4,515	4,847	4,255	0.02	-12.21
Romania	2,028	1,978	2,465	2,167	2,313	0.01	6.74
USSR (former)	7,134	7,809	11,698	16,511	26,855	0.10	62.65
Northern Europe	**100,028**	**84,226**	**80,141**	**81,305**	**79,245**	**0.28**	**-2.53**
Denmark	4,248	3,556	3,434	3,599	3,260	0.01	-9.42
Finland	4,256	4,474	3,807	3,316	3,411	0.01	2.86
Iceland	159	166	167	109	156	0.00	43.12
Ireland	4,407	3,550	3,256	3,359	3,524	0.01	4.91
Norway	2,613	2,285	2,449	2,442	2,491	0.01	2.01
Sweden	7,168	6,698	6,569	6,825	6,915	0.02	1.32
United Kingdom	77,177	63,497	60,459	61,655	59,488	0.21	-3.51
Southern Europe	**35,457**	**33,837**	**36,756**	**36,286**	**37,038**	**0.13**	**2.07**
Albania	111	87	122	90	80	0.00	-11.11
Andorra	17	19	37	34	22	0.00	-35.29
Greece	1,727	1,048	1,028	908	1,094	0.00	20.48
Holy See		9	4	1	2	0.00	100.00
Italy	12,535	12,223	13,459	13,119	13,003	0.05	-0.88
Malta	99	78	64	98	127	0.00	29.59
Portugal	13,100	12,437	13,577	13,339	14,496	0.05	8.67
San Marino	12	10	16	7	16	0.00	128.57
Spain	7,510	7,919	8,449	8,690	8,198	0.03	-5.66
Yugoslavia, SFR (former)	346	7					
Western Europe	**99,319**	**95,369**	**99,079**	**100,433**	**100,777**	**0.36**	**0.34**
Austria	4,310	4,233	4,482	4,095	4,378	0.02	6.91
Belgium	4,620	4,497	4,793	4,681	4,261	0.02	-8.97
France	40,502	39,158	41,420	42,662	42,480	0.15	-0.43
Germany	29,088	28,176	28,820	28,800	29,310	0.10	1.77
Liechtenstein	38	40	41	57	39	0.00	-31.58
Luxembourg	210	203	277	254	239	0.00	-5.91
Monaco	17	19	24	17	32	0.00	88.24

438

MACAO, CHINA

2. Arrivals of non-resident visitors at national borders, by nationality

	2008	2009	2010	2011	2012	Market share 2012	% Change 2012-2011
Netherlands	14,246	12,897	12,667	12,776	12,519	0.04	-2.01
Switzerland	6,288	6,146	6,555	7,091	7,519	0.03	6.04
East Mediterranean Europe	**13,359**	**16,638**					
Cyprus	258	219					
Israel	10,102	14,021					
Turkey	2,999	2,398					
Other Europe	**6,658**	**6,165**	**5,298**	**5,603**	**7,626**	**0.03**	**36.11**
Other countries of Europe	6,658	6,165	5,298	5,603	7,626	0.03	36.11
MIDDLE EAST	**7,537**	**7,364**					
Bahrain	147	123					
Egypt	913	927					
Iraq	238	136					
Jordan	372	453					
Kuwait	660	654					
Lebanon	1,517	1,501					
Libya	517	410					
Oman	89	104					
Qatar	138	149					
Saudi Arabia	1,418	1,405					
Syrian Arab Republic	743	699					
Yemen	257	243					
Other countries of Middle East	528	560					
SOUTH ASIA	**94,723**	**117,933**	**178,977**	**177,221**	**159,550**	**0.57**	**-9.97**
Afghanistan	121	277	162	157	237	0.00	50.96
Bangladesh	2,652	1,673	1,023	272	294	0.00	8.09
Bhutan	113	126	116	205	198	0.00	-3.41
India	82,492	107,575	169,116	169,682	150,838	0.54	-11.11
Iran, Islamic Republic of	925	1,333	3,673	3,208	3,761	0.01	17.24
Maldives	133	130	157	135	111	0.00	-17.78
Nepal	3,979	2,885	2,109	2,019	2,439	0.01	20.80
Pakistan	3,323	3,129	2,042	975	1,052	0.00	7.90
Sri Lanka	985	805	579	568	620	0.00	9.15
NOT SPECIFIED	**57**	**36**					
Other countries of the World	57	36					

Yearbook of Tourism Statistics, Data 2008 – 2012, 2014 Edition

MACAO, CHINA

2. Arrivals of non-resident visitors at national borders, by country of residence

		2008	2009	2010	2011	2012	Market share 2012	% Change 2012-2011
TOTAL	(*)	22,933,185	21,752,751	24,965,411	28,002,279	28,082,292	100.00	0.29
AFRICA		21,894	16,803	22,845	24,864	26,990	0.10	8.55
Southern Africa		4,543	4,228	4,624	5,185	4,667	0.02	-9.99
South Africa		4,543	4,228	4,624	5,185	4,667	0.02	-9.99
Other Africa		17,351	12,575	18,221	19,679	22,323	0.08	13.44
Other countries of Africa		17,351	12,575	18,221	19,679	22,323	0.08	13.44
AMERICAS		312,611	278,661	297,137	310,608	306,521	1.09	-1.32
North America		290,985	257,920	272,547	281,247	277,372	0.99	-1.38
Canada		82,136	74,744	79,148	79,818	83,459	0.30	4.56
Mexico		5,651	3,676	5,145	5,364	5,183	0.02	-3.37
United States of America		203,198	179,500	188,254	196,065	188,730	0.67	-3.74
South America		8,967	7,521	8,346	10,505	10,283	0.04	-2.11
Brazil		8,967	7,521	8,346	10,505	10,283	0.04	-2.11
Other Americas		12,659	13,220	16,244	18,856	18,866	0.07	0.05
Other countries of the Americas		12,659	13,220	16,244	18,856	18,866	0.07	0.05
EAST ASIA AND THE PACIFIC		22,224,494	21,078,253	24,222,137	27,237,930	27,326,633	97.31	0.33
North-East Asia		20,597,144	19,599,207	22,739,551	25,763,275	25,904,934	92.25	0.55
China		11,613,171	10,989,533	13,229,058	16,162,747	16,902,499	60.19	4.58
Hong Kong, China		7,016,479	6,727,822	7,466,139	7,582,923	7,081,153	25.22	-6.62
Japan		366,920	379,241	413,507	396,023	395,989	1.41	-0.01
Korea, Dem. People's Republic of		1,162	1,038	1,160	1,167	1,318	0.00	12.94
Korea, Republic of		279,794	204,767	331,768	398,807	444,773	1.58	11.53
Taiwan, Province of China		1,315,865	1,292,551	1,292,734	1,215,162	1,072,052	3.82	-11.78
Other countries of North-East Asia		3,753	4,255	5,185	6,446	7,150	0.03	10.92
South-East Asia		1,470,175	1,343,831	1,324,445	1,314,107	1,257,757	4.48	-4.29
Indonesia		180,320	191,425	208,440	220,423	209,084	0.74	-5.14
Malaysia		428,608	332,529	338,058	324,509	301,802	1.07	-7.00
Philippines		282,951	247,459	247,770	268,710	283,881	1.01	5.65
Singapore		263,631	256,520	257,196	280,602	205,692	0.73	-26.70
Thailand		252,124	242,514	212,442	196,375	231,295	0.82	17.78
Viet Nam		51,965	62,388	48,437	11,394	13,868	0.05	21.71
Other countries of South-East Asia		10,576	10,996	12,102	12,094	12,135	0.04	0.34
Australasia		156,363	134,275	126,353	126,724	127,694	0.45	0.77
Australia		139,628	120,395	111,771	111,827	113,295	0.40	1.31
New Zealand		16,735	13,880	14,582	14,897	14,399	0.05	-3.34
Other East Asia and the Pacific		812	940	31,788	33,824	36,248	0.13	7.17
Other countries of Asia				30,584	32,565	34,777	0.12	6.79
Other countries of Oceania		812	940	1,204	1,259	1,471	0.01	16.84
EUROPE		272,188	254,002	244,463	251,748	262,692	0.94	4.35
Central/Eastern Europe		7,123	7,806	11,702	16,512	26,844	0.10	62.57
Russian Federation		7,123	7,806	11,702	16,512	26,844	0.10	62.57
Northern Europe		88,463	73,633	70,270	71,835	69,913	0.25	-2.68
Ireland		4,391	3,551	3,257	3,360	3,527	0.01	4.97
Sweden		7,163	6,698	6,574	6,838	6,918	0.02	1.17
United Kingdom		76,909	63,384	60,439	61,637	59,468	0.21	-3.52
Southern Europe		33,103	32,572	35,492	35,151	35,691	0.13	1.54
Italy		12,524	12,229	13,461	13,121	13,004	0.05	-0.89
Portugal		13,081	12,429	13,583	13,339	14,497	0.05	8.68
Spain		7,498	7,914	8,448	8,691	8,190	0.03	-5.76
Western Europe		94,354	90,601	93,925	95,473	96,208	0.34	0.77
Austria		4,304	4,234	4,474	4,096	4,375	0.02	6.81
France		40,499	39,165	41,417	42,710	42,486	0.15	-0.52
Germany		29,067	28,172	28,820	28,811	29,320	0.10	1.77
Netherlands		14,218	12,888	12,664	12,769	12,506	0.04	-2.06

440

MACAO, CHINA

2. Arrivals of non-resident visitors at national borders, by country of residence

	2008	2009	2010	2011	2012	Market share 2012	% Change 2012-2011
Switzerland	6,266	6,142	6,550	7,087	7,521	0.03	6.12
Other Europe	**49,145**	**49,390**	**33,074**	**32,777**	**34,036**	**0.12**	**3.84**
Other countries of Europe	49,145	49,390	33,074	32,777	34,036	0.12	3.84
MIDDLE EAST	**7,536**	**7,334**					
All countries of Middle East	7,536	7,334					
SOUTH ASIA	**94,428**	**117,677**	**178,829**	**177,129**	**159,456**	**0.57**	**-9.98**
Bangladesh	2,606	1,566	905	209	210	0.00	0.48
India	82,369	107,513	169,096	169,660	150,825	0.54	-11.10
Nepal	3,891	2,827	2,102	2,019	2,444	0.01	21.05
Pakistan	3,290	3,103	2,042	976	1,052	0.00	7.79
Other countries of South Asia	2,272	2,668	4,684	4,265	4,925	0.02	15.47
NOT SPECIFIED	**34**	**21**					
Other countries of the World	34	21					

Yearbook of Tourism Statistics, Data 2008 – 2012, 2014 Edition

MACAO, CHINA

3. Arrivals of non-resident tourists in hotels and similar establishments, by country of residence

		2008	2009	2010	2011	2012	Market share 2012	% Change 2012-2011
TOTAL	(*)	6,193,569	6,398,389	7,288,172	8,051,777	8,882,658	100.00	10.32
AMERICAS		98,387	82,845	88,035	84,947	98,348	1.11	15.78
North America		98,387	82,845	88,035	84,947	98,348	1.11	15.78
Canada		28,403	27,450	29,782	26,726	31,463	0.35	17.72
United States of America		69,984	55,395	58,253	58,221	66,885	0.75	14.88
EAST ASIA AND THE PACIFIC		5,839,708	6,031,777	6,872,539	7,641,077	8,450,080	95.13	10.59
North-East Asia		5,212,948	5,431,239	6,278,219	7,055,066	7,869,033	88.59	11.54
China		3,057,142	3,282,433	4,012,193	4,703,663	5,373,103	60.49	14.23
Hong Kong, China		1,588,549	1,600,074	1,620,471	1,632,010	1,703,458	19.18	4.38
Japan		221,044	210,856	228,266	233,069	243,537	2.74	4.49
Korea, Republic of		110,652	79,636	127,455	152,314	186,228	2.10	22.27
Taiwan, Province of China		235,561	258,240	289,834	334,010	362,707	4.08	8.59
South-East Asia		531,416	506,663	495,914	499,169	480,057	5.40	-3.83
Indonesia		69,851	77,325	82,884	84,971	81,536	0.92	-4.04
Malaysia		129,999	114,284	120,180	120,932	117,615	1.32	-2.74
Philippines		78,007	65,964	69,675	72,284	70,193	0.79	-2.89
Singapore		129,613	126,732	115,951	117,212	99,656	1.12	-14.98
Thailand		123,946	122,358	107,224	103,770	111,057	1.25	7.02
Australasia		54,296	46,829	48,207	49,672	57,488	0.65	15.74
Australia		48,194	41,512	42,472	43,167	50,245	0.57	16.40
New Zealand		6,102	5,317	5,735	6,505	7,243	0.08	11.35
Other East Asia and the Pacific		41,048	47,046	50,199	37,170	43,502	0.49	17.04
Other countries of Asia		41,048	47,046	50,199	37,170	43,502	0.49	17.04
EUROPE		91,676	79,823	81,524	93,773	100,608	1.13	7.29
Northern Europe		22,055	19,782	18,633	20,170	21,497	0.24	6.58
United Kingdom		22,055	19,782	18,633	20,170	21,497	0.24	6.58
Southern Europe		15,505	11,563	13,213	15,254	20,215	0.23	32.52
Italy		5,773	4,842	5,681	6,625	6,830	0.08	3.09
Portugal		9,732	6,721	7,532	8,629	13,385	0.15	55.12
Western Europe		20,887	22,312	22,033	24,022	23,881	0.27	-0.59
France		11,697	13,572	12,070	13,897	14,402	0.16	3.63
Germany		9,190	8,740	9,963	10,125	9,479	0.11	-6.38
Other Europe		33,229	26,166	27,645	34,327	35,015	0.39	2.00
Other countries of Europe		33,229	26,166	27,645	34,327	35,015	0.39	2.00
SOUTH ASIA		51,752	78,458	120,737	123,902	106,029	1.19	-14.43
India		51,752	78,458	120,737	123,902	106,029	1.19	-14.43
NOT SPECIFIED		112,046	125,486	125,337	108,078	127,593	1.44	18.06
Other countries of the World		112,046	125,486	125,337	108,078	127,593	1.44	18.06

442

MACAO, CHINA

5. Overnight stays of non-resident tourists in hotels and similar establishments, by country of residence

	2008	2009	2010	2011	2012	Market share 2012	% Change 2012-2011
TOTAL (*)	8,604,636	9,133,979	10,663,207	11,684,464	11,612,042	100.00	-0.62
AMERICAS	239,511	213,020	240,415	241,506	261,449	2.25	8.26
North America	239,511	213,020	240,415	241,506	261,449	2.25	8.26
Canada	54,487	47,649	57,705	54,858	62,286	0.54	13.54
United States of America	185,024	165,371	182,710	186,648	199,163	1.72	6.71
EAST ASIA AND THE PACIFIC	7,726,246	8,003,440	9,352,712	10,361,698	10,249,390	88.27	-1.08
North-East Asia	6,767,229	7,037,836	8,344,807	9,365,089	9,256,245	79.71	-1.16
China	3,891,829	4,062,398	5,083,252	5,989,362	5,947,606	51.22	-0.70
Hong Kong, China	1,937,352	2,023,718	2,132,874	2,145,908	1,994,720	17.18	-7.05
Japan	379,034	378,152	398,449	415,574	427,665	3.68	2.91
Korea, Republic of	175,512	134,561	224,940	230,636	274,323	2.36	18.94
Taiwan, Province of China	383,502	439,007	505,292	583,609	611,931	5.27	4.85
South-East Asia	838,633	851,843	874,810	866,073	847,982	7.30	-2.09
Indonesia	128,671	148,912	165,835	167,433	161,162	1.39	-3.75
Malaysia	184,209	183,356	194,114	181,783	184,498	1.59	1.49
Philippines	130,188	120,162	132,299	131,776	130,308	1.12	-1.11
Singapore	201,240	204,341	199,476	207,728	188,966	1.63	-9.03
Thailand	194,325	195,072	183,086	177,353	183,048	1.58	3.21
Australasia	120,384	113,761	133,095	130,536	145,163	1.25	11.21
Australia	107,986	99,876	115,017	110,536	119,347	1.03	7.97
New Zealand	12,398	13,885	18,078	20,000	25,816	0.22	29.08
EUROPE	208,426	205,509	254,450	244,901	263,327	2.27	7.52
Northern Europe	46,426	49,530	67,347	60,256	56,569	0.49	-6.12
United Kingdom	46,426	49,530	67,347	60,256	56,569	0.49	-6.12
Southern Europe	30,611	28,959	36,835	32,257	51,621	0.44	60.03
Italy	12,631	12,654	17,130	15,321	23,173	0.20	51.25
Portugal	17,980	16,305	19,705	16,936	28,448	0.24	67.97
Western Europe	44,414	47,680	57,986	58,020	64,301	0.55	10.83
France	26,336	29,061	33,194	34,682	37,063	0.32	6.87
Germany	18,078	18,619	24,792	23,338	27,238	0.23	16.71
Other Europe	86,975	79,340	92,282	94,368	90,836	0.78	-3.74
Other countries of Europe	86,975	79,340	92,282	94,368	90,836	0.78	-3.74
SOUTH ASIA	95,473	142,338	208,342	223,133	257,470	2.22	15.39
India	95,473	142,338	208,342	223,133	257,470	2.22	15.39
NOT SPECIFIED	334,980	569,672	607,288	613,226	580,406	5.00	-5.35
Other countries of the World	334,980	569,672	607,288	613,226	580,406	5.00	-5.35

Yearbook of Tourism Statistics, Data 2008 – 2012, 2014 Edition

MADAGASCAR

1. Arrivals of non-resident tourists at national borders, by nationality

	2008	2009	2010	2011	2012	Market share 2012	% Change 2012-2011
TOTAL	375,010	162,687	196,052	225,055	255,942	100.00	13.72
AFRICA	83,802	36,732	40,083	39,176	45,179	17.65	15.32
East Africa	68,622	28,304	29,927	27,847	34,196	13.36	22.80
Comoros	803	348	517	4,468	5,969	2.33	33.59
Kenya	318	103		363	571	0.22	57.30
Mauritius	15,000	6,507	7,845	7,261	8,418	3.29	15.93
Reunion	52,501	21,149	21,565	15,360	18,760	7.33	22.14
Seychelles		197		395	478	0.19	21.01
Southern Africa	10,750	6,507	7,842	7,121	5,967	2.33	-16.21
South Africa	10,750	6,507	7,842	7,121	5,967	2.33	-16.21
Other Africa	4,430	1,921	2,314	4,208	5,016	1.96	19.20
Other countries of Africa	4,430	1,921	2,314	4,208	5,016	1.96	19.20
AMERICAS	11,250	4,881	5,882	9,870	10,071	3.93	2.04
North America	11,250	4,881	5,882	9,193	9,291	3.63	1.07
Canada, United States	11,250	4,881	5,882	9,193	9,291	3.63	1.07
Other Americas				677	780	0.30	15.21
Other countries of the Americas				677	780	0.30	15.21
EAST ASIA AND THE PACIFIC	16,500	5,694	6,861	22,955	23,414	9.15	2.00
North-East Asia	7,500	1,627	1,960	2,925	2,434	0.95	-16.79
Japan	7,500	1,627	1,960	2,925	2,434	0.95	-16.79
Other East Asia and the Pacific	9,000	4,067	4,901	20,030	20,980	8.20	4.74
Other countries of Asia	9,000	4,067	4,901	20,030	20,980	8.20	4.74
EUROPE	261,936	110,869	143,226	153,054	177,278	69.26	15.83
Northern Europe	15,000	3,253	3,920	10,730	11,146	4.35	3.88
United Kingdom	15,000	3,253	3,920	9,213	9,029	3.53	-2.00
Scandinavia				1,517	2,117	0.83	39.55
Southern Europe	15,375	4,881	17,645	9,182	11,302	4.42	23.09
Italy	15,000	4,881	17,645	7,162	8,932	3.49	24.71
Portugal					499	0.19	
Spain	375			2,020	1,871	0.73	-7.38
Western Europe	228,750	101,516	121,153	130,081	151,914	59.35	16.78
Benelux				5,204	4,658	1.82	-10.49
France	210,000	95,985	111,750	114,471	137,578	53.75	20.19
Germany	11,250	3,253	5,882	6,504	6,028	2.36	-7.32
Switzerland	7,500	2,278	3,521	3,902	3,650	1.43	-6.46
Other Europe	2,811	1,219	508	3,061	2,916	1.14	-4.74
Other countries of Europe	2,811	1,219	508	3,061	2,916	1.14	-4.74
NOT SPECIFIED	1,522	4,511					
Other countries of the World	1,522	4,511					

444

MADAGASCAR

5. Overnight stays of non-resident tourists in hotels and similar establishments, by nationality

	2008	2009	2010	2011	2012	Market share 2012	% Change 2012-2011
TOTAL (*)	5,815,169	2,413,073	3,298,025	3,763,549			
AFRICA	682,645	326,804	624,549	615,279			
East Africa	424,585	183,528	420,529	401,949			
Comoros	12,848	5,916	8,789	76,519			
Kenya	1,213	927		4,051			
Mauritius	92,500	45,549	109,830	100,825			
Reunion	313,621	126,336	301,910	214,252			
Seychelles	4,403	4,800		6,302			
Southern Africa	182,750	110,619	164,682	141,785			
South Africa	182,750	110,619	164,682	141,785			
Other Africa	75,310	32,657	39,338	71,545			
Other countries of Africa	75,310	32,657	39,338	71,545			
AMERICAS	191,250	82,977	99,994	167,576			
North America	191,250	82,977	99,994	156,098			
Canada, United States	191,250	82,977	99,994	156,098			
Other Americas				11,478			
Other countries of the Americas				11,478			
EAST ASIA AND THE PACIFIC	280,500	96,798	116,637	390,245			
North-East Asia	127,500	27,659	33,320	49,737			
Japan	127,500	27,659	33,320	49,737			
Other East Asia and the Pacific	153,000	69,139	83,317	340,508			
Other countries of Asia	153,000	69,139	83,317	340,508			
EUROPE	4,634,903	1,888,450	2,456,845	2,590,449			
Northern Europe	255,000	55,301	66,640	191,296			
United Kingdom	255,000	55,301	66,640	153,037			
Scandinavia				38,259			
Southern Europe	276,375	102,501	317,610	163,254			
Italy	270,000	102,501	317,610	128,821			
Spain	6,375			34,433			
Western Europe	4,098,750	1,725,772	2,065,483	2,193,049			
Benelux				62,385			
France	3,780,000	1,631,745	1,899,750	1,947,401			
Germany	191,250	55,301	105,876	117,074			
Switzerland	127,500	38,726	59,857	66,189			
Other Europe	4,778	4,876	7,112	42,850			
Other countries of Europe	4,778	4,876	7,112	42,850			
NOT SPECIFIED	25,871	18,044					
Other countries of the World	25,871	18,044					

Yearbook of Tourism Statistics, Data 2008 – 2012, 2014 Edition

MALAWI

1. Arrivals of non-resident tourists at national borders, by country of residence

	2008	2009	2010	2011	2012	Market share 2012	% Change 2012-2011
TOTAL (*)	742,457	755,031	746,129	767,000			
AFRICA	574,544	574,172	562,379	588,306			
East Africa	458,711	462,612	439,600	449,237			
Mozambique	139,296	188,694	159,580	196,629			
Zambia	76,408	102,956	80,428	95,766			
Zimbabwe	143,363	77,281	128,387	131,756			
Other countries of East Africa	99,644	93,681	71,205	25,086			
Southern Africa	106,724	100,958	102,342	115,051			
All countries of Southern Africa	106,724	100,958	102,342	115,051			
Other Africa	9,109	10,602	20,437	24,018			
Other countries of Africa	9,109	10,602	20,437	24,018			
AMERICAS	44,561	46,120	45,893	44,735			
North America	43,085	43,766	44,572	43,778			
Canada, United States	43,085	43,766	44,572	43,778			
Other Americas	1,476	2,354	1,321	957			
Other countries of the Americas	1,476	2,354	1,321	957			
EAST ASIA AND THE PACIFIC	11,588	12,142	20,456	10,247			
Other East Asia and the Pacific	11,588	12,142	20,456	10,247			
All countries of Asia	11,588	12,142	20,456	10,247			
EUROPE	98,330	105,054	104,779	102,389			
Northern Europe	50,786	54,476	53,897	51,936			
United Kingdom/Ireland	50,786	54,476	53,897	51,936			
Other Europe	47,544	50,578	50,882	50,453			
Other countries of Europe	47,544	50,578	50,882	50,453			
MIDDLE EAST	1,581	1,691	2,310	3,400			
All countries of Middle East	1,581	1,691	2,310	3,400			
SOUTH ASIA	10,194	14,299	8,338	15,894			
All countries of South Asia	10,194	14,299	8,338	15,894			
NOT SPECIFIED	1,659	1,553	1,974	2,029			
Other countries of the World	1,659	1,553	1,974	2,029			

Yearbook of Tourism Statistics, Data 2008 – 2012, 2014 Editic

MALAWI

6. Overnight stays of non-resident tourists in all types of accommodation establishments, by country of residence

	2008	2009	2010	2011	2012	Market share 2012	% Change 2012-2011
TOTAL	5,864,441	5,167,246	6,056,990	5,820,695			
AFRICA	3,806,008	3,252,681	3,818,821	3,566,241			
East Africa	2,728,432	2,347,201	2,689,880	2,508,426			
Mozambique	473,606	622,690	622,362	668,539			
Zambia	443,166	391,233	450,396	497,983			
Zimbabwe	903,187	587,336	893,709	1,040,872			
Other countries of East Africa	908,473	745,942	723,413	301,032			
Southern Africa	955,471	798,276	1,012,063	908,903			
All countries of Southern Africa	955,471	798,276	1,012,063	908,903			
Other Africa	122,105	107,204	116,878	148,912			
Other countries of Africa	122,105	107,204	116,878	148,912			
AMERICAS	557,512	496,825	559,693	549,546			
North America	540,908	477,993	545,796	542,847			
Canada, United States	540,908	477,993	545,796	542,847			
Other Americas	16,604	18,832	13,897	6,699			
Other countries of the Americas	16,604	18,832	13,897	6,699			
EAST ASIA AND THE PACIFIC	137,845	194,272	157,350	336,767			
Other East Asia and the Pacific	137,845	194,272	157,350	336,767			
All countries of Asia	137,845	194,272	157,350	336,767			
EUROPE	1,351,707	1,198,620	1,489,710	1,352,721			
Northern Europe	755,530	629,257	805,066	727,104			
United Kingdom/Ireland	755,530	629,257	805,066	727,104			
Other Europe	596,177	569,363	684,644	625,617			
Other countries of Europe	596,177	569,363	684,644	625,617			
NOT SPECIFIED	11,369	24,848	31,416	15,420			
Other countries of the World	11,369	24,848	31,416	15,420			

Yearbook of Tourism Statistics, Data 2008 – 2012, 2014 Edition

MALAYSIA

1. Arrivals of non-resident tourists at national borders, by country of residence

		2008	2009	2010	2011	2012	Market share 2012	% Change 2012-2011
TOTAL	(*)	22,051,798	23,645,337	24,577,196	24,713,029	25,031,411	100.00	1.29
AFRICA		127,361	84,549	41,615	111,182	98,765	0.39	-11.17
East Africa		46,176	24,322		26,754	25,275	0.10	-5.53
British Indian Ocean Territory		27	19		2	1	0.00	-50.00
Burundi		1,246	28		42	22	0.00	-47.62
Comoros		1,792	48		229	268	0.00	17.03
Djibouti		285	187		213	564	0.00	164.79
Ethiopia		1,231	411		371	184	0.00	-50.40
Kenya		3,485	3,296		3,523	3,702	0.01	5.08
Madagascar		11,604	212		297	309	0.00	4.04
Malawi		952	177		326	289	0.00	-11.35
Mauritius		10,494	11,523		10,850	12,342	0.05	13.75
Mozambique		272	180		264	226	0.00	-14.39
Reunion		277	1		3			
Rwanda		847	53		129	130	0.00	0.78
Seychelles		1,428	899		926	614	0.00	-33.69
Somalia		1,782	1,514		2,381			
Uganda		2,076	1,253		1,998	1,740	0.01	-12.91
United Republic of Tanzania		5,069	2,545		2,254	2,782	0.01	23.43
Zambia		1,045	431		887	807	0.00	-9.02
Zimbabwe		2,264	1,545		2,059	1,295	0.01	-37.11
Central Africa		7,889	791		1,126	1,165	0.00	3.46
Angola		268	75		217	144	0.00	-33.64
Cameroon		523	409		469	549	0.00	17.06
Central African Republic		20	3		5	1	0.00	-80.00
Chad		2,946	140		223	186	0.00	-16.59
Congo		294	76		75	144	0.00	92.00
Democratic Republic of the Congo		3,356			1			
Equatorial Guinea		24	28		56	55	0.00	-1.79
Gabon		401	27		77	85	0.00	10.39
Sao Tome and Principe		57	33		3	1	0.00	-66.67
North Africa		19,689	18,586	15,220	25,422	24,562	0.10	-3.38
Algeria		1,955	2,424		2,718	3,401	0.01	25.13
Morocco		3,254	2,864	2,043	2,881	3,533	0.01	22.63
Sudan		10,693	10,993	10,914	13,703	14,343	0.06	4.67
Tunisia		3,787	2,305	2,263	2,892	3,285	0.01	13.59
Western Sahara					3,228			
Southern Africa		32,116	25,275	26,395	34,584	25,285	0.10	-26.89
Botswana		1,635	1,288		1,424	1,080	0.00	-24.16
Lesotho		266	118		134	113	0.00	-15.67
Namibia		3,663	197		326	334	0.00	2.45
South Africa		25,437	23,556	26,395	31,441	23,635	0.09	-24.83
Swaziland		1,115	116		185	123	0.00	-33.51
Other countries of Southern Africa					1,074			
West Africa		21,491	15,575		23,296	22,478	0.09	-3.51
Benin		171	60		179	83	0.00	-53.63
Burkina Faso		170	61		71	67	0.00	-5.63
Cape Verde		103	20		17	14	0.00	-17.65
Côte d'Ivoire		147	109		179	160	0.00	-10.61
Gambia		204	180		198	168	0.00	-15.15
Ghana		1,031	831		1,197	1,157	0.00	-3.34
Guinea		1,117	706		888	881	0.00	-0.79
Guinea-Bissau		34	30		135	28	0.00	-79.26
Liberia		540	162		108	138	0.00	27.78
Mali		207	213		138	107	0.00	-22.46
Mauritania		321	163		152			

448

MALAYSIA

1. Arrivals of non-resident tourists at national borders, by country of residence

	2008	2009	2010	2011	2012	Market share 2012	% Change 2012-2011
Niger	156	22		59	19	0.00	-67.80
Nigeria	12,720	12,421		18,916	18,792	0.08	-0.66
Saint Helena	360	15		11			
Senegal	3,438	386		676	479	0.00	-29.14
Sierra Leone	235	135		279	321	0.00	15.05
Togo	537	61		93	64	0.00	-31.18
AMERICAS	**345,217**	**345,768**	**342,521**	**339,645**	**362,250**	**1.45**	**6.66**
Caribbean	**7,484**	**1,306**		**2,159**	**2,629**	**0.01**	**21.77**
Anguilla	25			5	1	0.00	-80.00
Antigua and Barbuda	32	9		14	4	0.00	-71.43
Aruba	89	3		56	14	0.00	-75.00
Bahamas	1,027	70		49	39	0.00	-20.41
Barbados	580	73		450	84	0.00	-81.33
Bermuda	83	1					
British Virgin Islands	47			2			
Cayman Islands	96			1			
Cuba	602	161		174	217	0.00	24.71
Dominica	542	15		38			
Dominican Republic	341	107		134	129	0.00	-3.73
Grenada	52	7		9	7	0.00	-22.22
Guadeloupe	54	1		1			
Haiti	160	17		27	30	0.00	11.11
Jamaica	220	168		236	1,160	0.00	391.53
Martinique	42				1	0.00	
Montserrat	27			3	1	0.00	-66.67
Netherlands Antilles	442	60		73			
Puerto Rico	120	17		2			
Saint Kitts and Nevis	74	19		138	143	0.00	3.62
Saint Lucia	220	13		10	14	0.00	40.00
Saint Vincent and the Grenadines	1,245	10		9			
Trinidad and Tobago	1,278	545		723	771	0.00	6.64
Turks and Caicos Islands	54	10		5	14	0.00	180.00
United States Virgin Islands	32						
Central America	**3,904**	**1,370**		**6,825**	**1,814**	**0.01**	**-73.42**
Belize	287	156		134	78	0.00	-41.79
Costa Rica	715	536		641	728	0.00	13.57
El Salvador	373	96		203	180	0.00	-11.33
Guatemala	443	210		362	349	0.00	-3.59
Honduras	140	142		179	169	0.00	-5.59
Nicaragua	1,155	47		5,251	40	0.00	-99.24
Panama	791	183		55	270	0.00	390.91
North America	**306,597**	**321,468**	**328,680**	**302,773**	**333,049**	**1.33**	**10.00**
Canada	77,664	88,080	91,701	86,015	86,931	0.35	1.06
Greenland	240	1		1			
Mexico	5,441	4,816	4,014	2	5,984	0.02	299,100.00
Saint Pierre and Miquelon	3						
United States of America	223,249	228,571	232,965	216,755	240,134	0.96	10.79
South America	**27,232**	**21,624**	**13,841**	**27,888**	**24,758**	**0.10**	**-11.22**
Argentina	5,640	6,098	6,014	8,929	5,430	0.02	-39.19
Bolivia	680	201		198	199	0.00	0.51
Brazil	6,222	7,529	6,072	9,254	9,540	0.04	3.09
Chile	2,216	2,286		3,403	3,379	0.01	-0.71
Colombia	1,482	1,401		1,721	1,861	0.01	8.13
Ecuador	167	5		536	610	0.00	13.81
Falkland Islands, Malvinas	159						
French Guiana	5	2		1			
Guyana	72	46		54	44	0.00	-18.52

Yearbook of Tourism Statistics, Data 2008 – 2012, 2014 Edition

MALAYSIA

1. Arrivals of non-resident tourists at national borders, by country of residence

	2008	2009	2010	2011	2012	Market share 2012	% Change 2012-2011
Paraguay	3,362	99	121	125	98	0.00	-21.60
Peru	1,736	1,105		1,075	1,261	0.01	17.30
Suriname	779	152		110	140	0.00	27.27
Uruguay	355	364		470	430	0.00	-8.51
Venezuela	4,357	2,336	1,634	2,012	1,766	0.01	-12.23
EAST ASIA AND THE PACIFIC	**18,972,997**	**20,830,330**	**21,605,363**	**21,667,502**	**21,945,509**	**87.67**	**1.28**
North-East Asia	**1,849,245**	**1,844,375**	**2,021,337**	**2,138,812**	**2,559,216**	**10.22**	**19.66**
China	943,787	1,015,550	1,130,261	1,245,475	1,557,960	6.22	25.09
Hong Kong, China	6,067	4,199		4,716	794	0.00	-83.16
Japan	433,462	395,746	415,881	386,974	470,008	1.88	21.46
Korea, Dem. People's Republic of	3,091	693		1,013	772	0.00	-23.79
Korea, Republic of	267,461	227,312	264,052	263,428	283,977	1.13	7.80
Macao, China	10	7		345	31	0.00	-91.01
Mongolia	4,388	2,999		3,078	3,155	0.01	2.50
Taiwan, Province of China	190,979	197,869	211,143	233,783	242,519	0.97	3.74
South-East Asia	**16,636,977**	**18,386,363**	**18,937,179**	**18,885,302**	**18,809,736**	**75.14**	**-0.40**
Brunei Darussalam	1,085,115	1,061,357	1,124,406	1,239,404	1,258,070	5.03	1.51
Cambodia	35,464	43,146	48,618	49,472	50,179	0.20	1.43
Indonesia	2,428,605	2,405,360	2,506,509	2,134,381	2,382,606	9.52	11.63
Lao People's Democratic Republic	26,564	36,663	38,111	29,520	38,364	0.15	29.96
Myanmar	43,131	60,338	72,792	81,946	83,473	0.33	1.86
Philippines	397,884	447,470	486,790	362,101	508,744	2.03	40.50
Singapore	11,003,492	12,733,082	13,042,004	13,372,647	13,014,268	51.99	-2.68
Thailand	1,493,789	1,449,262	1,458,678	1,442,048	1,263,024	5.05	-12.41
Viet Nam	122,933	149,685	159,271	173,783	211,008	0.84	21.42
Australasia	**483,193**	**596,386**	**646,847**	**639,798**	**573,674**	**2.29**	**-10.34**
Australia	427,076	533,382	580,695	558,411	507,948	2.03	-9.04
New Zealand	56,117	63,004	66,152	81,387	65,726	0.26	-19.24
Melanesia	**3,098**	**2,797**		**3,043**	**2,743**	**0.01**	**-9.86**
Fiji	1,627	1,130		1,391	1,237	0.00	-11.07
New Caledonia	1	2		1			
Papua New Guinea	1,203	1,466		1,325	1,303	0.01	-1.66
Solomon Islands	186	157		244	194	0.00	-20.49
Vanuatu	81	42		82	9	0.00	-89.02
Micronesia	**196**	**138**		**90**	**64**	**0.00**	**-28.89**
Christmas Island, Australia	1						
Cocos (Keeling) Islands	4						
Guam	1						
Kiribati	55	45		29	30	0.00	3.45
Marshall Islands	25	12		7	2	0.00	-71.43
Micronesia, Federated States of	6	20		12	9	0.00	-25.00
Nauru	73	47		25	12	0.00	-52.00
Palau	30	11		17	11	0.00	-35.29
Other countries of Micronesia	1	3					
Polynesia	**288**	**271**		**254**	**76**	**0.00**	**-70.08**
American Samoa	15	1		20	1	0.00	-95.00
French Polynesia	8	1		1			
Samoa	87	59		87			
Tonga	134	160		120	74	0.00	-38.33
Tuvalu	44	50		26	1	0.00	-96.15
Other East Asia and the Pacific				**203**			
Other countries of Oceania				203			
EUROPE	**1,025,342**	**1,164,953**	**1,133,235**	**1,135,148**	**1,160,008**	**4.63**	**2.19**
Central/Eastern Europe	**76,714**	**79,261**	**68,670**	**111,008**	**123,419**	**0.49**	**11.18**
Armenia	162	152		235	273	0.00	16.17
Azerbaijan	641	544		913	1,024	0.00	12.16

Yearbook of Tourism Statistics, Data 2008 – 2012, 2014 Edition

MALAYSIA

1. Arrivals of non-resident tourists at national borders, by country of residence

	2008	2009	2010	2011	2012	Market share 2012	% Change 2012-2011
Bulgaria	1,919	1,614		2,585	2,694	0.01	4.22
Czech Republic	6,314	6,774	6,753	6,818	7,219	0.03	5.88
Hungary	4,927	4,242		4,385	4,584	0.02	4.54
Kazakhstan	5,337	5,493	10,527	17,462	20,188	0.08	15.61
Kyrgyzstan	925	844		1,677	1,795	0.01	7.04
Lithuania	909	1,100		1,720	1,788	0.01	3.95
Poland	11,745	12,544	12,358	13,055	13,432	0.05	2.89
Romania	3,002	2,844		3,398	3,709	0.01	9.15
Russian Federation	26,308	29,202	32,075	38,918	44,765	0.18	15.02
Slovakia	2,660	2,472		3,112	3,451	0.01	10.89
Tajikistan	321	491		499	489	0.00	-2.00
Turkmenistan	436	626		750	799	0.00	6.53
Ukraine	3,772	3,125		6,229	6,312	0.03	1.33
Uzbekistan	7,336	7,194	6,957	9,252	10,897	0.04	17.78
Northern Europe	**513,292**	**579,898**	**571,079**	**533,492**	**526,748**	**2.10**	**-1.26**
Denmark	23,817	25,916	24,869	22,269	24,408	0.10	9.61
Faeroe Islands	32	2					
Finland	23,112	20,912	21,355	19,969	19,342	0.08	-3.14
Iceland	1,672	633		690	737	0.00	6.81
Ireland	23,720	25,347	23,146	22,593	21,639	0.09	-4.22
Isle of Man	1						
Norway	21,516	22,487	22,773	19,891	19,996	0.08	0.53
Svalbard and Jan Mayen Islands	179			2	1	0.00	-50.00
Sweden	48,649	49,509	48,971	44,138	38,418	0.15	-12.96
United Kingdom	370,591	435,091	429,965	403,940	402,207	1.61	-0.43
Other countries of Northern Europe	3	1					
Southern Europe	**80,363**	**86,932**	**72,770**	**82,101**	**84,588**	**0.34**	**3.03**
Albania	373	292		298	316	0.00	6.04
Andorra	753	36		18	16	0.00	-11.11
Bosnia and Herzegovina	585	482		540	528	0.00	-2.22
Croatia	1,957	1,334		1,728	1,948	0.01	12.73
Greece	3,396	3,105		2,624	3,199	0.01	21.91
Holy See	95	8		12	5	0.00	-58.33
Italy	38,945	46,352	47,068	43,864	44,330	0.18	1.06
Malta	531	410		654	640	0.00	-2.14
Portugal	14,482	11,685	6,264	9,842	9,198	0.04	-6.54
San Marino	187	43		43	10	0.00	-76.74
Serbia and Montenegro	88	259		363	691	0.00	90.36
Spain	17,365	22,771	19,438	22,104	23,594	0.09	6.74
Yugoslavia, SFR (former)	461	155		11	113	0.00	927.27
Other countries of Southern Europe	1,145						
Western Europe	**346,004**	**410,032**	**411,567**	**399,340**	**414,798**	**1.66**	**3.87**
Austria	14,231	14,491	10,891	13,082	13,679	0.05	4.56
Belgium	15,618	16,721	15,275	16,436	17,151	0.07	4.35
France	86,030	110,054	111,175	127,980	136,172	0.54	6.40
Germany	111,525	128,288	130,896	124,670	131,277	0.52	5.30
Liechtenstein	339	54		85	84	0.00	-1.18
Luxembourg	638	732	549	666	629	0.00	-5.56
Monaco	332	30		29	42	0.00	44.83
Netherlands	90,802	111,139	114,887	90,590	88,404	0.35	-2.41
Switzerland	26,489	28,523	27,894	25,802	27,360	0.11	6.04
East Mediterranean Europe	**8,969**	**8,830**	**9,149**	**9,207**	**10,455**	**0.04**	**13.55**
Cyprus	794	558		617	528	0.00	-14.42
Israel	23	7		13	18	0.00	38.46
Turkey	8,152	8,265	9,149	8,577	9,909	0.04	15.53
MIDDLE EAST	**216,351**	**196,854**	**166,636**	**236,987**	**265,603**	**1.06**	**12.07**
Bahrain	7,822	6,114		7,128	5,624	0.02	-21.10

Yearbook of Tourism Statistics, Data 2008 – 2012, 2014 Edition

MALAYSIA

1. Arrivals of non-resident tourists at national borders, by country of residence

	2008	2009	2010	2011	2012	Market share 2012	% Change 2012-2011
Egypt	11,926	11,006	11,709	15,359	16,804	0.07	9.41
Iraq	10,032	8,680		13,568	21,939	0.09	61.70
Jordan	7,087	7,713		9,012	8,529	0.03	-5.36
Kuwait	18,853	20,170	17,632	22,833	22,759	0.09	-0.32
Lebanon	5,532	5,187		4,887	4,503	0.02	-7.86
Libya	4,069	3,187		2,881	6,214	0.02	115.69
Oman	17,472	15,280	16,377	22,062	24,977	0.10	13.21
Qatar	7,808	4,257	3,965	5,727	7,742	0.03	35.18
Saudi Arabia	74,632	77,082	86,771	87,693	102,365	0.41	16.73
Syrian Arab Republic	4,838	5,909	4,537	7,241	9,413	0.04	30.00
United Arab Emirates	34,994	22,108	25,645	24,212	18,233	0.07	-24.69
Yemen	11,286	10,161		14,384	16,501	0.07	14.72
SOUTH ASIA	**826,028**	**929,954**	**997,156**	**1,124,647**	**1,185,201**	**4.73**	**5.38**
Afghanistan	1,210	1,026		757	1,710	0.01	125.89
Bangladesh	49,184	87,443	63,886	65,603	86,465	0.35	31.80
Bhutan	451	417		503	535	0.00	6.36
India	550,738	589,838	690,849	693,056	691,271	2.76	-0.26
Iran, Islamic Republic of	63,165	101,664	116,252	139,617	127,404	0.51	-8.75
Maldives	13,396	11,001		11,702	11,833	0.05	1.12
Nepal	36,572	18,898	2,983	81,791	123,173	0.49	50.59
Pakistan	68,538	69,581	65,101	73,046	79,989	0.32	9.50
Sri Lanka	42,774	50,086	58,085	58,572	62,821	0.25	7.25
NOT SPECIFIED	**538,502**	**92,929**	**290,670**	**97,918**	**14,075**	**0.06**	**-85.63**
Other countries of the World	538,502	92,929	290,670	97,918	14,075	0.06	-85.63

Yearbook of Tourism Statistics, Data 2008 – 2012, 2014 Editic

MALDIVES

1. Arrivals of non-resident tourists at national borders, by nationality

	2008	2009	2010	2011	2012	Market share 2012	% Change 2012-2011
TOTAL (*)	683,012	655,852	791,917	931,333	958,027	100.00	2.87
AFRICA	5,694	5,034	5,628	6,452	7,095	0.74	9.97
East Africa	401	596	643	776	815	0.09	5.03
Comoros	3	1	5	12	16	0.00	33.33
Djibouti	2	2	5		3	0.00	
Eritrea	10	22	11	19	20	0.00	5.26
Ethiopia	39	34	57	35	69	0.01	97.14
Kenya	114	143	168	155	224	0.02	44.52
Madagascar	4	5	5	7	15	0.00	114.29
Malawi	7	6	10	10	7	0.00	-30.00
Mauritius	59	218	185	229	211	0.02	-7.86
Mozambique	15	15	24	62	32	0.00	-48.39
Seychelles	48	47	50	81	38	0.00	-53.09
Somalia	1	3		7	7	0.00	0.00
Uganda	16	10	14	30	14	0.00	-53.33
United Republic of Tanzania	35	43	50	45	63	0.01	40.00
Zambia	9	17	21	21	39	0.00	85.71
Zimbabwe	39	30	38	63	57	0.01	-9.52
Central Africa	44	43	61	61	85	0.01	39.34
Angola	24	21	35	29	46	0.00	58.62
Cameroon	12	15	19	16	27	0.00	68.75
Chad	1			3	1	0.00	-66.67
Congo	7	7	7	13	11	0.00	-15.38
North Africa	936	1,205	1,341	1,579	1,805	0.19	14.31
Algeria	222	252	264	326	364	0.04	11.66
Morocco	381	476	464	552	621	0.06	12.50
Sudan	78	112	139	137	171	0.02	24.82
Tunisia	255	365	474	564	649	0.07	15.07
Southern Africa	3,767	3,014	3,195	3,740	4,020	0.42	7.49
Botswana				12			
Lesotho		1	1		1	0.00	
Namibia	30	34	32	40	33	0.00	-17.50
South Africa	3,732	2,975	3,157	3,684	3,967	0.41	7.68
Swaziland	5	4	5	4	19	0.00	375.00
West Africa	500	159	356	149	301	0.03	102.01
Burkina Faso	1				2	0.00	
Cape Verde	2	5	6	6	8	0.00	33.33
Côte d'Ivoire	8	13	17	34			
Gambia	1	2	4	5	11	0.00	120.00
Ghana	17	18	25	21	31	0.00	47.62
Guinea	5	5	12	8	5	0.00	-37.50
Liberia	1	3	4	9	1	0.00	-88.89
Mali		4	2	5	2	0.00	-60.00
Mauritania	373	3	81	8	1	0.00	-87.50
Nigeria	77	91	186	13	202	0.02	1,453.85
Senegal	12	11	12	33	29	0.00	-12.12
Sierra Leone	1	4	4	7	8	0.00	14.29
Togo	2		3		1	0.00	
Other Africa	46	17	32	147	69	0.01	-53.06
Other countries of Africa	46	17	32	147	69	0.01	-53.06
AMERICAS	14,485	15,159	18,601	23,654	26,774	2.79	13.19
Caribbean	78	69	102	110	186	0.02	69.09
Antigua and Barbuda			3	2	48	0.01	2,300.00
Bahamas		4		7	2	0.00	-71.43
Barbados	8	2	7	7	5	0.00	-28.57

453

Yearbook of Tourism Statistics, Data 2008 – 2012, 2014 Edition

MALDIVES

1. Arrivals of non-resident tourists at national borders, by nationality

	2008	2009	2010	2011	2012	Market share 2012	% Change 2012-2011
Cuba	25	33	21	24	28	0.00	16.67
Dominica	12	8	26	24	25	0.00	4.17
Grenada		2		1	3	0.00	200.00
Haiti	1		1	3	6	0.00	100.00
Jamaica	6	4	10	10	11	0.00	10.00
Saint Lucia	2		6	6	1	0.00	-83.33
Trinidad and Tobago	24	16	28	26	57	0.01	119.23
Central America	**77**	**80**	**88**	**98**	**131**	**0.01**	**33.67**
Belize	7	5	10	4	5	0.00	25.00
Costa Rica	6	16	12	26	42	0.00	61.54
El Salvador	14	7	14	11	16	0.00	45.45
Guatemala	13	9	11	17	4	0.00	-76.47
Honduras	1	1	6	5	9	0.00	80.00
Nicaragua	2	3	5	2	3	0.00	50.00
Panama	34	39	30	33	52	0.01	57.58
North America	**12,344**	**12,986**	**15,850**	**19,925**	**21,959**	**2.29**	**10.21**
Canada	2,966	3,043	3,815	4,690	5,070	0.53	8.10
Mexico	525	505	553	745	840	0.09	12.75
United States of America	8,853	9,438	11,482	14,490	16,049	1.68	10.76
South America	**1,981**	**2,018**	**2,554**	**3,474**	**4,454**	**0.46**	**28.21**
Argentina	245	274	288	457	621	0.06	35.89
Bolivia	8	9	19	20	18	0.00	-10.00
Brazil	1,327	1,304	1,761	2,342	3,061	0.32	30.70
Chile	60	57	72	105	101	0.01	-3.81
Colombia	95	110	151	178	210	0.02	17.98
Ecuador	45	25	34	36	35	0.00	-2.78
Paraguay	12	17	18	30	42	0.00	40.00
Peru	64	55	48	89	92	0.01	3.37
Suriname	1	1		1			
Uruguay	12	31	18	37	55	0.01	48.65
Venezuela	112	135	145	179	219	0.02	22.35
Other Americas	**5**	**6**	**7**	**47**	**44**	**0.00**	**-6.38**
Other countries of the Americas	5	6	7	47	44	0.00	-6.38
EAST ASIA AND THE PACIFIC	**127,151**	**137,946**	**214,026**	**303,018**	**339,183**	**35.40**	**11.93**
North-East Asia	**102,886**	**115,434**	**186,414**	**265,096**	**294,397**	**30.73**	**11.05**
China	41,511	60,666	118,961	198,655	229,551	23.96	15.55
Japan	38,193	36,641	38,791	35,782	36,438	3.80	1.83
Korea, Republic of	20,934	16,135	24,808	25,285	23,933	2.50	-5.35
Mongolia	15	17	23	29			
Taiwan, Province of China	2,233	1,975	3,831	5,305	4,430	0.46	-16.49
Other countries of North-East Asia				40	45	0.00	12.50
South-East Asia	**13,672**	**14,095**	**16,807**	**23,726**	**27,960**	**2.92**	**17.85**
Brunei Darussalam	29	16	34	46			
Cambodia	7	15	14	54			
Indonesia	581	677	818	1,283	1,772	0.18	38.11
Lao People's Democratic Republic	13	24	30	58			
Malaysia	3,137	3,139	3,894	6,055	6,766	0.71	11.74
Myanmar	36	60	76	139			
Philippines	871	979	1,066	1,652	2,265	0.24	37.11
Singapore	4,956	5,214	5,332	7,990	9,625	1.00	20.46
Thailand	3,952	3,813	5,397	6,214	6,896	0.72	10.98
Viet Nam	90	158	146	234			
Other countries of South-East Asia				1	636	0.07	63,500.00
Australasia	**10,552**	**8,383**	**10,725**	**14,168**	**16,787**	**1.75**	**18.49**
Australia	9,368	7,392	9,622	12,778	15,208	1.59	19.02
New Zealand	1,184	991	1,103	1,390	1,579	0.16	13.60
Melanesia	**16**	**11**	**18**	**19**	**19**	**0.00**	**0.00**

454

MALDIVES

1. Arrivals of non-resident tourists at national borders, by nationality

	2008	2009	2010	2011	2012	Market share 2012	% Change 2012-2011
Fiji	16	11	17	19	19	0.00	0.00
Vanuatu			1				
Micronesia		**5**	**3**		**2**	**0.00**	
Kiribati		5	2		2	0.00	
Marshall Islands			1				
Polynesia				**2**	**1**		
Tonga				2	1		
Other East Asia and the Pacific	**25**	**18**	**57**	**8**	**18**	**0.00**	**125.00**
Other countries of Asia	19	13	49				
Other countries of Oceania	6	5	8	8	18	0.00	125.00
EUROPE	**497,560**	**462,192**	**505,421**	**537,769**	**517,809**	**54.05**	**-3.71**
Central/Eastern Europe	**71,400**	**62,374**	**75,378**	**95,247**	**100,097**	**10.45**	**5.09**
Armenia	74	79	134	162	185	0.02	14.20
Azerbaijan	169	244	275	288	486	0.05	68.75
Belarus		812	898	1,161	1,509	0.16	29.97
Bulgaria	965	902	1,051	1,368	1,479	0.15	8.11
Czech Republic	3,811	3,851	5,137	6,471	5,588	0.58	-13.65
Estonia	287	262	205	230	362	0.04	57.39
Georgia	57	60	77	74	114	0.01	54.05
Hungary	2,052	1,848	2,434	2,596	2,408	0.25	-7.24
Kazakhstan	1,656	1,756	1,572	1,731	2,875	0.30	66.09
Kyrgyzstan	47	66	59	83	135	0.01	62.65
Latvia	498	383	406	485	621	0.06	28.04
Lithuania	551	446	623	638	777	0.08	21.79
Poland	3,325	3,357	3,795	4,158	3,918	0.41	-5.77
Republic of Moldova	187	219	266	321	360	0.04	12.15
Romania	1,225	1,247	1,290	1,656	1,879	0.20	13.47
Russian Federation	48,978	40,014	49,111	63,936	66,378	6.93	3.82
Slovakia	1,916	1,970	2,348	2,822	2,636	0.28	-6.59
Tajikistan	14	21	22	43	32	0.00	-25.58
Turkmenistan	17	39	42	28	28	0.00	0.00
Ukraine	5,399	4,643	5,445	6,729	8,044	0.84	19.54
Uzbekistan	172	155	188	233	277	0.03	18.88
Other countries Central/East Europe				34	6	0.00	-82.35
Northern Europe	**128,591**	**116,491**	**126,222**	**119,388**	**107,350**	**11.21**	**-10.08**
Denmark	1,834	1,722	2,422	3,173	3,493	0.36	10.09
Finland	865	1,088	1,281	1,535	1,402	0.15	-8.66
Iceland	49	26	56	57	64	0.01	12.28
Ireland	2,884	2,420	2,514	2,444	2,483	0.26	1.60
Norway	2,596	2,120	2,153	2,775	2,902	0.30	4.58
Sweden	3,542	3,165	3,638	4,896	5,230	0.55	6.82
United Kingdom	116,821	105,950	114,158	104,508	91,776	9.58	-12.18
Southern Europe	**123,487**	**109,297**	**111,109**	**104,072**	**81,287**	**8.48**	**-21.89**
Albania	105	127	119	144	142	0.01	-1.39
Andorra	35	10	31	24	21	0.00	-12.50
Bosnia and Herzegovina	120	101	109	170	239	0.02	40.59
Croatia	641	548	551	626	801	0.08	27.96
Greece	4,926	5,406	4,630	3,009	2,058	0.21	-31.61
Italy	103,673	89,292	89,621	83,088	62,687	6.54	-24.55
Malta	181	130	221	214	252	0.03	17.76
Montenegro		12	24	30	39	0.00	30.00
Portugal	4,150	4,822	4,555	4,434	3,660	0.38	-17.46
Serbia		127	575	723	852	0.09	17.84
Slovenia	1,372	1,324	1,647	1,609	1,295	0.14	-19.52
Spain	8,217	7,279	8,912	9,710	8,824	0.92	-9.12
TFYR of Macedonia	67	119	114	194	203	0.02	4.64
Other countries of Southern Europe				97	214	0.02	120.62
Western Europe	**167,424**	**169,027**	**185,433**	**211,755**	**220,817**	**23.05**	**4.28**

455

MALDIVES

1. Arrivals of non-resident tourists at national borders, by nationality

	2008	2009	2010	2011	2012	Market share 2012	% Change 2012-2011
Austria	13,462	13,274	14,944	16,655	18,164	1.90	9.06
Belgium	3,368	3,437	4,386	5,738	5,141	0.54	-10.40
France	48,100	50,373	54,789	59,694	56,775	5.93	-4.89
Germany	69,240	69,085	77,108	90,517	98,351	10.27	8.65
Liechtenstein	174	148	148	177	140	0.01	-20.90
Luxembourg	464	519	575	725	659	0.07	-9.10
Monaco	38	53	35	52	53	0.01	1.92
Netherlands	5,595	5,355	5,682	5,693	6,077	0.63	6.75
Switzerland	26,983	26,783	27,766	32,504	35,457	3.70	9.09
East Mediterranean Europe	**5,182**	**4,517**	**7,166**	**7,307**	**8,256**	**0.86**	**12.99**
Cyprus	359	379	416	332	271	0.03	-18.37
Israel	1,588	1,380	2,113	2,433	2,569	0.27	5.59
Turkey	3,235	2,758	4,637	4,542	5,416	0.57	19.24
Other Europe	**1,476**	**486**	**113**		**2**	**0.00**	
Other countries of Europe	1,476	486	113		2	0.00	
MIDDLE EAST	**9,205**	**9,525**	**11,629**	**14,570**	**21,843**	**2.28**	**49.92**
Bahrain	435	438	629	612	679	0.07	10.95
Egypt	548	559	689	864	1,168	0.12	35.19
Iraq	156	53	72	113	132	0.01	16.81
Jordan	551	538	577	607	744	0.08	22.57
Kuwait	1,340	1,181	1,409	1,797	2,987	0.31	66.22
Lebanon	1,139	984	1,145	1,346	1,666	0.17	23.77
Libya	113	82	131	32	130	0.01	306.25
Oman	158	321	272	418	727	0.08	73.92
Palestine	74	84	77	121	164	0.02	35.54
Qatar	313	418	595	872	1,521	0.16	74.43
Saudi Arabia	2,747	3,036	4,040	5,005	7,263	0.76	45.11
Syrian Arab Republic	189	191	234	398	447	0.05	12.31
United Arab Emirates	1,394	1,580	1,699	2,292	4,047	0.42	76.57
Yemen	48	60	60	93	168	0.02	80.65
SOUTH ASIA	**28,917**	**25,996**	**36,612**	**45,870**	**45,323**	**4.73**	**-1.19**
Afghanistan	23	30	155	134	57	0.01	-57.46
Bangladesh	455	388	525	1,496	1,221	0.13	-18.38
Bhutan	57	45	47	93	54	0.01	-41.94
India	16,663	15,850	25,756	30,978	31,721	3.31	2.40
Iran, Islamic Republic of	522	637	779	1,321	1,295	0.14	-1.97
Nepal	254	167	222	336	258	0.03	-23.21
Pakistan	1,191	1,046	1,256	1,842	1,857	0.19	0.81
Sri Lanka	9,752	7,833	7,872	9,670	8,860	0.92	-8.38

MALI

1. Arrivals of non-resident tourists at national borders, by nationality

		2008	2009	2010	2011	2012	Market share 2012	% Change 2012-2011
TOTAL	(*)	189,511	160,012	169,305	159,782	101,335	100.00	-36.58
AFRICA		47,418	44,589	47,175	52,467	60,166	59.37	14.67
West Africa		15,276	27,408	29,872	33,983			
All countries of West Africa		15,276	27,408	29,872	33,983			
Other Africa		32,142	17,181	17,303	18,484	60,166	59.37	225.50
Other countries of Africa		32,142	17,181	17,303	18,484			
All countries of Africa						60,166	59.37	
AMERICAS		19,519	26,992	23,692	20,826	5,956	5.88	-71.40
North America		19,519	26,992	23,692	20,826			
Canada		6,940	10,091	6,147	5,644			
United States of America		12,579	16,901	17,545	15,182			
Other Americas						5,956	5.88	
All countries of the Americas						5,956	5.88	
EAST ASIA AND THE PACIFIC		4,672	1,307	2,668	3,148	5,517	5.44	75.25
North-East Asia		4,672	1,307	2,668	3,148			
Japan		4,672	1,307	2,668	3,148			
Other East Asia and the Pacific						5,517	5.44	
All countries East Asia/Pacific						5,517	5.44	
EUROPE		100,819	72,872	82,837	68,752	29,164	28.78	-57.58
Central/Eastern Europe		6,494	3,547	5,596	5,580			
Russian Federation		2,376	737	1,541	1,355			
Other countries Central/East Europe		4,118	2,810	4,055	4,225			
Northern Europe		9,240	5,964	6,297	5,911			
United Kingdom		5,357	4,173	4,422	3,595			
Scandinavia		3,883	1,791	1,875	2,316			
Southern Europe		18,433	9,695	12,392	10,766			
Italy		8,269	5,307	6,878	5,955			
Spain		10,164	4,388	5,514	4,811			
Western Europe		66,652	53,666	58,552	46,495			
Austria		2,638	660	1,906	1,648			
Benelux		8,166	6,642	6,306	6,397			
France		41,778	38,261	42,883	30,207			
Germany		9,033	5,380	4,937	5,428			
Switzerland		5,037	2,723	2,520	2,815			
Other Europe						29,164	28.78	
All countries of Europe						29,164	28.78	
MIDDLE EAST		4,176	2,946	2,948	3,910	529	0.52	-86.47
All countries of Middle East		4,176	2,946	2,948	3,910	529	0.52	-86.47
NOT SPECIFIED		12,907	11,306	9,985	10,679	3	0.00	-99.97
Other countries of the World		12,907	11,306	9,985	10,679	3	0.00	-99.97

457

MALI

3. Arrivals of non-resident tourists in hotels and similar establishments, by nationality

	2008	2009	2010	2011	2012	Market share 2012	% Change 2012-2011
TOTAL					31,620	100.00	
AFRICA					13,302	42.07	
West Africa					9,243	29.23	
All countries of West Africa					9,243	29.23	
Other Africa					4,059	12.84	
Other countries of Africa					4,059	12.84	
AMERICAS					5,581	17.65	
North America					5,581	17.65	
Canada					894	2.83	
United States of America					4,687	14.82	
EAST ASIA AND THE PACIFIC					457	1.45	
North-East Asia					457	1.45	
Japan					457	1.45	
EUROPE					9,159	28.97	
Central/Eastern Europe					526	1.66	
Russian Federation					105	0.33	
Other countries Central/East Europe					421	1.33	
Northern Europe					896	2.83	
United Kingdom					485	1.53	
Scandinavia					411	1.30	
Southern Europe					1,705	5.39	
Italy					819	2.59	
Spain					886	2.80	
Western Europe					6,032	19.08	
Austria					184	0.58	
Benelux					785	2.48	
France					4,006	12.67	
Germany					709	2.24	
Switzerland					348	1.10	
MIDDLE EAST					184	0.58	
All countries of Middle East					184	0.58	
NOT SPECIFIED					2,937	9.29	
Other countries of the World					2,937	9.29	

Yearbook of Tourism Statistics, Data 2008 – 2012, 2014 Editi

MALI

5. Overnight stays of non-resident tourists in hotels and similar establishments, by nationality

	2008	2009	2010	2011	2012	Market share 2012	% Change 2012-2011
TOTAL	464,975	352,801	290,936	283,729	61,187	100.00	-78.43
AFRICA	114,776	107,972	97,038	93,136	26,928	44.01	-71.09
West Africa	72,956	66,435	64,929	59,451	17,593	28.75	-70.41
All countries of West Africa	72,956	66,435	64,929	59,451	17,593	28.75	-70.41
Other Africa	41,820	41,537	32,109	33,685	9,335	15.26	-72.29
Other countries of Africa	41,820	41,537	32,109	33,685	9,335	15.26	-72.29
AMERICAS	46,770	57,747	41,200	30,877	9,608	15.70	-68.88
North America	46,770	57,747	41,200	30,877	9,608	15.70	-68.88
Canada	15,872	20,859	10,326	9,534	1,683	2.75	-82.35
United States of America	30,898	36,888	30,874	21,343	7,925	12.95	-62.87
EAST ASIA AND THE PACIFIC	9,234	1,307	4,448	5,358	1,071	1.75	-80.01
North-East Asia	9,234	1,307	4,448	5,358	1,071	1.75	-80.01
Japan	9,234	1,307	4,448	5,358	1,071	1.75	-80.01
EUROPE	237,700	157,888	123,796	94,768	17,253	28.20	-81.79
Central/Eastern Europe	11,244	8,007	7,380	9,299	903	1.48	-90.29
Russian Federation	3,904	1,947	2,005	3,760	218	0.36	-94.20
Other countries Central/East Europe	7,340	6,060	5,375	5,539	685	1.12	-87.63
Northern Europe	21,173	13,956	9,167	8,078	1,421	2.32	-82.41
United Kingdom	14,846	9,986	6,712	5,028	710	1.16	-85.88
Scandinavia	6,327	3,970	2,455	3,050	711	1.16	-76.69
Southern Europe	34,223	20,471	17,563	15,348	2,947	4.82	-80.80
Italy	15,517	11,081	9,720	7,970	1,330	2.17	-83.31
Spain	18,706	9,390	7,843	7,378	1,617	2.64	-78.08
Western Europe	171,060	115,454	89,686	62,043	11,982	19.58	-80.69
Austria	4,469	1,355	2,898	2,077	503	0.82	-75.78
Benelux	17,640	14,092	9,257	9,984	1,465	2.39	-85.33
France	122,486	81,028	65,721	37,776	7,333	11.98	-80.59
Germany	17,390	12,824	8,094	8,234	2,178	3.56	-73.55
Switzerland	9,075	6,155	3,716	3,972	503	0.82	-87.34
MIDDLE EAST	8,606	6,101	4,409	4,969	435	0.71	-91.25
All countries of Middle East	8,606	6,101	4,409	4,969	435	0.71	-91.25
NOT SPECIFIED	47,889	21,786	20,045	54,621	5,892	9.63	-89.21
Other countries of the World	47,889	21,786	20,045	54,621	5,892	9.63	-89.21

Yearbook of Tourism Statistics, Data 2008 – 2012, 2014 Edition

MALTA

1. Arrivals of non-resident tourists at national borders, by nationality

		2008	2009	2010	2011	2012	Market share 2012	% Change 2012-2011
TOTAL	(*)	1,290,856	1,182,489	1,338,841	1,414,502	1,443,973	100.00	2.08
AMERICAS		18,021	13,943	16,418	16,543	18,596	1.29	12.41
North America		18,021	13,943	16,418	16,543	18,596	1.29	12.41
United States of America		18,021	13,943	16,418	16,543	18,596	1.29	12.41
EUROPE		1,195,405	1,088,750	1,221,398	1,299,274	1,322,412	91.58	1.78
Central/Eastern Europe		65,690	56,944	64,231	72,176	93,703	6.49	29.83
Bulgaria		4,495	4,960	3,189	3,467	4,463	0.31	28.73
Czech Republic		7,381	6,796	5,923	7,473	8,907	0.62	19.19
Estonia		1,010	749	1,510	1,472	1,585	0.11	7.68
Hungary		8,327	7,848	7,747	8,158	7,195	0.50	-11.80
Latvia		896	908	1,170	1,369	1,499	0.10	9.50
Lithuania		3,206	2,168	1,673	2,153	6,862	0.48	218.72
Poland		7,079	7,139	12,070	13,543	20,023	1.39	47.85
Romania		7,721	5,557	4,280	6,281	6,304	0.44	0.37
Russian Federation		23,412	17,239	22,727	24,261	31,726	2.20	30.77
Slovakia		2,163	3,580	3,942	3,999	5,139	0.36	28.51
Northern Europe		570,360	489,582	533,165	558,466	565,183	39.14	1.20
Denmark		23,985	21,268	28,830	33,112	33,938	2.35	2.49
Finland		12,632	9,697	11,922	7,433	7,639	0.53	2.77
Ireland		30,489	24,328	25,185	26,881	27,665	1.92	2.92
Norway		16,489	6,470	15,006	13,498	14,192	0.98	5.14
Sweden		32,409	29,347	37,123	39,856	41,433	2.87	3.96
United Kingdom		454,356	398,472	415,099	437,686	440,316	30.49	0.60
Southern Europe		211,436	223,151	300,681	275,924	273,193	18.92	-0.99
Greece		8,496	7,641	5,880	4,337	2,841	0.20	-34.49
Italy		144,456	161,736	219,663	201,253	201,790	13.97	0.27
Portugal		6,680	4,347	4,320	3,832	4,230	0.29	10.39
Slovenia		2,307	4,129	2,976	3,620	3,943	0.27	8.92
Spain		49,497	45,298	67,842	62,882	60,389	4.18	-3.96
Western Europe		343,215	300,777	313,876	354,533	359,825	24.92	1.49
Austria		19,825	21,217	19,908	19,536	19,779	1.37	1.24
Belgium		29,619	23,746	24,296	31,594	27,360	1.89	-13.40
France		81,152	71,931	86,516	103,332	107,530	7.45	4.06
Germany		150,793	127,374	126,193	133,930	137,214	9.50	2.45
Luxembourg		2,912	2,052	2,016	2,210	2,820	0.20	27.60
Netherlands		36,920	33,418	33,425	38,892	39,351	2.73	1.18
Switzerland		21,994	21,039	21,522	25,039	25,771	1.78	2.92
East Mediterranean Europe		4,704	18,296	9,445	7,344	4,572	0.32	-37.75
Cyprus		4,704	18,296	9,445	7,344	4,572	0.32	-37.75
Other Europe					30,831	25,936	1.80	-15.88
Other countries of Europe					30,831	25,936	1.80	-15.88
MIDDLE EAST		9,403	14,282	15,864	6,337	17,367	1.20	174.06
Libya		9,403	14,282	15,864	6,337	17,367	1.20	174.06
NOT SPECIFIED		68,027	65,514	85,161	92,348	85,598	5.93	-7.31
Other countries of the World		68,027	65,514	85,161	92,348	85,598	5.93	-7.31

Yearbook of Tourism Statistics, Data 2008 – 2012, 2014 Edition

MALTA

4. Arrivals of non-resident tourists in all types of accommodation establishments, by country of residence

		2008	2009	2010	2011	2012	Market share 2012	% Change 2012-2011
TOTAL	(*)	1,290,856	1,182,490	1,338,841	1,414,502	1,443,973	100.00	2.08
AMERICAS		18,021	13,943	16,418	16,543	18,596	1.29	12.41
North America		18,021	13,943	16,418	16,543	18,596	1.29	12.41
United States of America		18,021	13,943	16,418	16,543	18,596	1.29	12.41
EUROPE		1,035,419	1,012,578	1,155,257	1,199,185	1,216,094	84.22	1.41
Central/Eastern Europe		23,412	17,240	22,727	24,261	31,726	2.20	30.77
Russian Federation		23,412	17,240	22,727	24,261	31,726	2.20	30.77
Northern Europe		527,248	489,579	533,165	558,466	565,184	39.14	1.20
Denmark		23,985						
Ireland			24,328	25,185	26,881	27,665	1.92	2.92
Norway		16,498						
Sweden		32,409						
United Kingdom		454,356	398,472	415,099	437,686	440,316	30.49	0.60
Scandinavia			66,779	92,881	93,899	97,203	6.73	3.52
Southern Europe		144,456	207,035	287,505	264,135	262,179	18.16	-0.74
Italy		144,456	161,737	219,663	201,253	201,790	13.97	0.27
Spain			45,298	67,842	62,882	60,389	4.18	-3.96
Western Europe		340,303	298,724	311,860	352,323	357,005	24.72	1.33
Austria		19,825	21,218	19,908	19,536	19,779	1.37	1.24
Belgium		29,619	23,746	24,296	31,594	27,360	1.89	-13.40
France		81,152	71,930	86,516	103,332	107,530	7.45	4.06
Germany		150,793	127,373	126,193	133,930	137,214	9.50	2.45
Netherlands		36,920	33,419	33,425	38,892	39,351	2.73	1.18
Switzerland		21,994	21,038	21,522	25,039	25,771	1.78	2.92
MIDDLE EAST		9,403	14,281	15,864	6,337	17,367	1.20	174.06
Libya		9,403	14,281	15,864	6,337	17,367	1.20	174.06
NOT SPECIFIED		228,013	141,688	151,302	192,437	191,916	13.29	-0.27
Other countries of the World		228,013	141,688	151,302	192,437	191,916	13.29	-0.27

Yearbook of Tourism Statistics, Data 2008 – 2012, 2014 Edition

MALTA

6. Overnight stays of non-resident tourists in all types of accommodation establishments, by country of residence

		2008	2009	2010	2011	2012	Market share 2012	% Change 2012-2011
TOTAL	(*)	10,962,465	9,949,379	11,147,939	11,702,616	12,618,372	100.00	7.83
AMERICAS		146,031	114,541	139,709	123,867	153,620	1.22	24.02
North America		146,031	114,541	139,709	123,867	153,620	1.22	24.02
United States of America		146,031	114,541	139,709	123,867	153,620	1.22	24.02
EUROPE		8,734,789	8,439,908	9,431,500	9,774,876	10,320,220	81.79	5.58
Central/Eastern Europe		272,596	232,977	299,778	314,198	477,291	3.78	51.91
Russian Federation		272,596	232,977	299,778	314,198	477,291	3.78	51.91
Northern Europe		4,752,199	4,325,798	4,730,479	4,915,677	5,034,793	39.90	2.42
Denmark		191,083						
Ireland			185,294	197,767	216,295	222,898	1.77	3.05
Norway		123,871						
Sweden		246,857						
United Kingdom		4,190,388	3,632,459	3,814,894	3,965,934	4,022,836	31.88	1.43
Scandinavia			508,045	717,818	733,448	789,059	6.25	7.58
Southern Europe		985,622	1,410,488	1,841,776	1,698,772	1,755,995	13.92	3.37
Italy		985,622	993,826	1,275,909	1,182,520	1,242,605	9.85	5.08
Spain			416,662	565,867	516,252	513,390	4.07	-0.55
Western Europe		2,724,372	2,470,645	2,559,467	2,846,229	3,052,141	24.19	7.23
Austria		146,381	165,497	150,029	145,110	146,829	1.16	1.18
Belgium		211,820	190,777	181,393	218,706	223,123	1.77	2.02
France		608,425	586,106	669,289	776,653	838,446	6.64	7.96
Germany		1,268,844	1,072,509	1,093,633	1,144,791	1,244,692	9.86	8.73
Netherlands		292,170	272,852	277,998	330,129	360,662	2.86	9.25
Switzerland		196,732	182,904	187,125	230,840	238,389	1.89	3.27
MIDDLE EAST		73,809	103,103	131,773	63,872	142,674	1.13	123.37
Libya		73,809	103,103	131,773	63,872	142,674	1.13	123.37
NOT SPECIFIED		2,007,836	1,291,827	1,444,957	1,740,001	2,001,858	15.86	15.05
Other countries of the World		2,007,836	1,291,827	1,444,957	1,740,001	2,001,858	15.86	15.05

Yearbook of Tourism Statistics, Data 2008 – 2012, 2014 Editi

MARSHALL ISLANDS

1. Arrivals of non-resident tourists at national borders, by nationality

		2008	2009	2010	2011	2012	Market share 2012	% Change 2012-2011
TOTAL	(*)	6,022	5,372	4,563	4,555			
AMERICAS		1,725	1,614	1,712	1,619			
North America		1,627	1,519	1,700	1,594			
Canada		64	44	46	45			
United States of America		1,563	1,475	1,654	1,549			
Other Americas		98	95	12	25			
Other countries of the Americas		98	95	12	25			
EAST ASIA AND THE PACIFIC		4,036	3,501	2,622	2,681			
North-East Asia		2,105	1,909	1,164	1,030			
China		93	129	105	126			
Japan		1,501	1,431	585	464			
Korea, Republic of		88	49	52	57			
Taiwan, Province of China		423	300	422	383			
South-East Asia		285	240	274	232			
Philippines		285	240	274	232			
Australasia		308	307	321	357			
Australia		203	216	202	245			
New Zealand		105	91	119	112			
Melanesia		91	95	116	120			
Fiji		91	95	116	120			
Micronesia		757	505	508	752			
Guam		26	16	14	56			
Kiribati		73	97	69	54			
Micronesia, Federated States of		589	327	338	539			
Nauru		11	6	24	8			
Palau		58	59	63	95			
Polynesia		5	16	14	11			
Tuvalu		5	16	14	11			
Other East Asia and the Pacific		485	429	225	179			
Other countries of Asia		417	369	74	63			
Other countries of Oceania		68	60	151	116			
EUROPE		218	207	211	209			
Northern Europe		28	20	53	63			
United Kingdom		28	20	53	63			
Western Europe		35	31	39	18			
Germany		35	31	39	18			
Other Europe		155	156	119	128			
Other countries of Europe		155	156	119	128			
NOT SPECIFIED		43	50	18	46			
Other countries of the World		43	50	18	46			

Yearbook of Tourism Statistics, Data 2008 – 2012, 2014 Edition

MARSHALL ISLANDS

1. Arrivals of non-resident tourists at national borders, by country of residence

		2008	2009	2010	2011	2012	Market share 2012	% Change 2012-2011
TOTAL	(*)	6,022	5,372	4,563	4,559	4,578	100.00	0.42
AMERICAS		1,480	1,354	1,332	1,322	1,140	24.90	-13.77
North America		1,408	1,297	1,323	1,297	1,126	24.60	-13.18
Canada		57	41	26	26	24	0.52	-7.69
United States of America		1,351	1,256	1,297	1,271	1,102	24.07	-13.30
Other Americas		72	57	9	25	14	0.31	-44.00
Other countries of the Americas		72	57	9	25	14	0.31	-44.00
EAST ASIA AND THE PACIFIC		3,663	3,263	2,934	2,877	3,145	68.70	9.32
North-East Asia		1,933	1,731	1,080	946	960	20.97	1.48
China		61	89	79	83	87	1.90	4.82
Japan		1,427	1,349	557	435	448	9.79	2.99
Korea, Republic of		70	38	40	50	62	1.35	24.00
Taiwan, Province of China		375	255	404	378	363	7.93	-3.97
South-East Asia		236	196	216	194	187	4.08	-3.61
Philippines		236	196	216	194	187	4.08	-3.61
Australasia		275	271	274	313	309	6.75	-1.28
Australia		165	177	164	204	192	4.19	-5.88
New Zealand		110	94	110	109	117	2.56	7.34
Melanesia		123	119	138	152	194	4.24	27.63
Fiji		123	119	138	152	194	4.24	27.63
Micronesia		757	654	861	982	1,243	27.15	26.58
Guam		164	193	325	293	232	5.07	-20.82
Kiribati		56	76	59	48	90	1.97	87.50
Micronesia, Federated States of		474	319	383	536	363	7.93	-32.28
Nauru		9	5	24	10	511	11.16	5,010.00
Palau		54	61	70	95	47	1.03	-50.53
Polynesia		2	8	14	10	17	0.37	70.00
Tuvalu		2	8	14	10	17	0.37	70.00
Other East Asia and the Pacific		337	284	351	280	235	5.13	-16.07
Other countries of Asia		254	207	85	70	52	1.14	-25.71
Other countries of Oceania		83	77	266	210	183	4.00	-12.86
EUROPE		177	153	144	137	115	2.51	-16.06
Northern Europe		13	14	26	37	31	0.68	-16.22
United Kingdom		13	14	26	37	31	0.68	-16.22
Western Europe		36	24	28	10	15	0.33	50.00
Germany		36	24	28	10	15	0.33	50.00
Other Europe		128	115	90	90	69	1.51	-23.33
Other countries of Europe		128	115	90	90	69	1.51	-23.33
NOT SPECIFIED		702	602	153	223	178	3.89	-20.18
Other countries of the World		702	602	153	223	178	3.89	-20.18

Yearbook of Tourism Statistics, Data 2008 – 2012, 2014 Editic

MARSHALL ISLANDS

6. Overnight stays of non-resident tourists in all types of accommodation establishments, by country of residence

	2008	2009	2010	2011	2012	Market share 2012	% Change 2012-2011
TOTAL	24,136	27,648	33,705	34,521			
AMERICAS	8,176	11,408	12,390	13,183			
North America	7,844	10,950	12,301	11,010			
Canada	610	485	452	276			
United States of America	7,234	10,465	11,849	10,734			
Other Americas	332	458	89	2,173			
Other countries of the Americas	332	458	89	2,173			
EAST ASIA AND THE PACIFIC	13,675	12,847	19,563	19,660			
North-East Asia	6,617	5,150	7,079	5,842			
China	297	351	326	473			
Japan	5,141	3,616	3,882	2,860			
Korea, Republic of	214	118	183	423			
Taiwan, Province of China	965	1,065	2,688	2,086			
South-East Asia	977	1,190	1,054	1,199			
Philippines	977	1,190	1,054	1,199			
Australasia	1,901	1,787	2,115	2,755			
Australia	1,240	1,167	1,497	1,839			
New Zealand	661	620	618	916			
Melanesia	717	790	983	1,715			
Fiji	717	790	983	1,715			
Micronesia	2,502	2,708	4,686	5,864			
Guam	656	770	1,614	1,181			
Kiribati	434	458	762	833			
Micronesia, Federated States of	1,165	1,110	1,738	2,972			
Nauru	74	43	158	67			
Palau	173	327	414	811			
Polynesia	9		52	56			
Tuvalu	9		52	56			
Other East Asia and the Pacific	952	1,222	3,594	2,229			
Other countries of Asia	445	885	560	386			
Other countries of Oceania	507	337	3,034	1,843			
EUROPE	1,070	1,850	836	939			
Northern Europe	166	998	227	296			
United Kingdom	166	998	227	296			
Western Europe	219	116	169	37			
Germany	219	116	169	37			
Other Europe	685	736	440	606			
Other countries of Europe	685	736	440	606			
NOT SPECIFIED	1,215	1,543	916	739			
Other countries of the World	1,215	1,543	916	739			

MARTINIQUE

1. Arrivals of non-resident tourists at national borders, by country of residence

		2008	2009	2010	2011	2012	Market share 2012	% Change 2012-2011
TOTAL	(*)	481,224	441,648	478,060	496,538	487,769	100.00	-1.77
AMERICAS		85,831	63,145	85,239	86,363	77,648	15.92	-10.09
Caribbean		64,250	46,624	56,961	57,761	52,464	10.76	-9.17
Barbados		1,337	1,164	2,871	2,842	1,226	0.25	-56.86
Dominica		1,383	1,166	3,648	2,841	1,598	0.33	-43.75
Guadeloupe		54,372	38,094	39,863	42,844	45,556	9.34	6.33
Saint Lucia		6,338	5,601	8,201	3,997	1,856	0.38	-53.57
Other countries of the Caribbean		820	599	2,378	5,237	2,228	0.46	-57.46
North America		10,397	7,582	15,998	15,389	11,558	2.37	-24.89
Canada		3,349	1,292	9,535	9,570	9,154	1.88	-4.35
United States of America		7,048	6,290	6,463	5,819	2,404	0.49	-58.69
South America		11,184	8,939	12,280	13,213	13,626	2.79	3.13
French Guiana		8,572	7,141	9,878	10,368	13,626	2.79	31.42
Venezuela		2,612	1,798	2,402	2,845			
EUROPE		390,644	367,030	389,306	404,670	407,783	83.60	0.77
Northern Europe		2,807	1,606	2,595	2,775	2,708	0.56	-2.41
United Kingdom/Ireland		1,786	938	1,610	1,427	1,549	0.32	8.55
Scandinavia		1,021	668	985	1,348	1,159	0.24	-14.02
Southern Europe		1,998	2,029	2,349	2,497	3,057	0.63	22.43
Italy		1,998	2,029	2,349	2,497	3,057	0.63	22.43
Western Europe		385,099	362,994	383,570	397,285	397,883	81.57	0.15
Benelux		8,548	4,823	5,958	7,222	6,229	1.28	-13.75
France		371,073	354,846	372,426	385,358	384,526	78.83	-0.22
Germany		2,515	1,011	2,480	2,567	3,946	0.81	53.72
Switzerland		2,963	2,314	2,706	2,138	3,182	0.65	48.83
Other Europe		740	401	792	2,113	4,135	0.85	95.69
Other countries of Europe		740	401	792	2,113	4,135	0.85	95.69
NOT SPECIFIED		4,749	11,473	3,515	5,505	2,338	0.48	-57.53
Other countries of the World		4,749	11,473	3,515	5,505	2,338	0.48	-57.53

Yearbook of Tourism Statistics, Data 2008 – 2012, 2014 Editic

MARTINIQUE

3. Arrivals of non-resident tourists in hotels and similar establishments, by nationality

	2008	2009	2010	2011	2012	Market share 2012	% Change 2012-2011
TOTAL	**166,065**	**174,400**	**177,826**	**192,816**	**176,625**	**100.00**	**-8.40**
AMERICAS	**25,815**	**17,003**	**27,085**	**17,954**	**20,870**	**11.82**	**16.24**
Caribbean	**20,390**	**12,393**	**17,774**	**12,230**	**15,158**	**8.58**	**23.94**
All countries of the Caribbean	20,390	12,393	17,774	12,230	15,158	8.58	23.94
North America	**5,425**	**4,610**	**9,311**	**5,724**	**5,712**	**3.23**	**-0.21**
Canada	1,419	463	4,771	3,326	4,504	2.55	35.42
United States of America	4,006	4,147	4,540	2,398	1,208	0.68	-49.62
EUROPE	**137,759**	**153,504**	**149,458**	**172,978**	**155,083**	**87.80**	**-10.35**
Western Europe	**129,578**	**147,766**	**141,923**	**163,720**	**143,705**	**81.36**	**-12.23**
France	129,578	147,766	141,923	163,720	143,705	81.36	-12.23
Other Europe	**8,181**	**5,738**	**7,535**	**9,258**	**11,378**	**6.44**	**22.90**
Other countries of Europe	8,181	5,738	7,535	9,258	11,378	6.44	22.90
NOT SPECIFIED	**2,491**	**3,893**	**1,283**	**1,884**	**672**	**0.38**	**-64.33**
Other countries of the World	2,491	3,893	1,283	1,884	672	0.38	-64.33

Yearbook of Tourism Statistics, Data 2008 – 2012, 2014 Edition

MARTINIQUE

4. Arrivals of non-resident tourists in all types of accommodation establishments, by nationality

	2008	2009	2010	2011	2012	Market share 2012	% Change 2012-2011
TOTAL	481,225	441,648	478,059	496,538	487,768	100.00	-1.77
AMERICAS	85,830	63,146	85,238	86,363	77,648	15.92	-10.09
Caribbean	75,433	55,564	69,240	70,974	66,090	13.55	-6.88
All countries of the Caribbean	75,433	55,564	69,240	70,974	66,090	13.55	-6.88
North America	10,397	7,582	15,998	15,389	11,558	2.37	-24.89
Canada	3,349	1,292	9,535	9,570	9,154	1.88	-4.35
United States of America	7,048	6,290	6,463	5,819	2,404	0.49	-58.69
EUROPE	390,646	367,029	389,306	404,669	407,782	83.60	0.77
Western Europe	371,073	354,846	372,426	385,358	384,526	78.83	-0.22
France	371,073	354,846	372,426	385,358	384,526	78.83	-0.22
Other Europe	19,573	12,183	16,880	19,311	23,256	4.77	20.43
Other countries of Europe	19,573	12,183	16,880	19,311	23,256	4.77	20.43
NOT SPECIFIED	4,749	11,473	3,515	5,506	2,338	0.48	-57.54
Other countries of the World	4,749	11,473	3,515	5,506	2,338	0.48	-57.54

Yearbook of Tourism Statistics, Data 2008 – 2012, 2014 Edition

MARTINIQUE

5. Overnight stays of non-resident tourists in hotels and similar establishments, by country of residence

	2008	2009	2010	2011	2012	Market share 2012	% Change 2012-2011
TOTAL	1,340,701	1,388,809	1,401,434	1,652,360	1,379,000	100.00	-16.54
AMERICAS	144,525	136,376	150,450	209,708	101,492	7.36	-51.60
Caribbean	123,061	120,020	86,951	168,141	83,839	6.08	-50.14
All countries of the Caribbean	123,061	120,020	86,951	168,141	83,839	6.08	-50.14
North America	21,464	16,356	63,499	41,567	17,653	1.28	-57.53
Canada	9,242	3,720	39,177	23,881	13,577	0.98	-43.15
United States of America	12,222	12,636	24,322	17,686	4,076	0.30	-76.95
EUROPE	1,184,787	1,222,866	1,243,668	1,421,020	1,271,315	92.19	-10.54
Western Europe	1,146,547	1,189,611	1,198,467	1,367,728	1,179,920	85.56	-13.73
France	1,146,547	1,189,611	1,198,467	1,367,728	1,179,920	85.56	-13.73
Other Europe	38,240	33,255	45,201	53,292	91,395	6.63	71.50
Other countries of Europe	38,240	33,255	45,201	53,292	91,395	6.63	71.50
NOT SPECIFIED	11,389	29,567	7,316	21,632	6,193	0.45	-71.37
Other countries of the World	11,389	29,567	7,316	21,632	6,193	0.45	-71.37

Yearbook of Tourism Statistics, Data 2008 – 2012, 2014 Edition

MARTINIQUE

6. Overnight stays of non-resident tourists in all types of accommodation establishments, by nationality

	2008	2009	2010	2011	2012	Market share 2012	% Change 2012-2011
TOTAL	6,312,307	5,793,364	6,368,874	6,196,064	6,900,859	100.00	11.37
AMERICAS	680,450	576,397	773,454	786,369	733,498	10.63	-6.72
Caribbean	579,396	508,269	579,527	630,498	667,264	9.67	5.83
All countries of the Caribbean	579,396	508,269	579,527	630,498	667,264	9.67	5.83
North America	101,054	68,128	193,927	155,871	66,234	0.96	-57.51
Canada	43,511	15,495	134,233	89,551	51,167	0.74	-42.86
United States of America	57,543	52,633	59,694	66,320	15,067	0.22	-77.28
EUROPE	5,578,233	5,093,806	5,561,063	5,328,580	6,126,217	88.77	14.97
Western Europe	5,398,191	4,955,283	5,387,193	5,128,744	5,781,703	83.78	12.73
France	5,398,191	4,955,283	5,387,193	5,128,744	5,781,703	83.78	12.73
Other Europe	180,042	138,523	173,870	199,836	344,514	4.99	72.40
Other countries of Europe	180,042	138,523	173,870	199,836	344,514	4.99	72.40
NOT SPECIFIED	53,624	123,161	34,357	81,115	41,144	0.60	-49.28
Other countries of the World	53,624	123,161	34,357	81,115	41,144	0.60	-49.28

Yearbook of Tourism Statistics, Data 2008 – 2012, 2014 Edition

MAURITIUS

1. Arrivals of non-resident tourists at national borders, by country of residence

	2008	2009	2010	2011	2012	Market share 2012	% Change 2012-2011
TOTAL	930,318	871,187	934,678	964,419	965,000	100.00	0.06
AFRICA	213,383	203,846	225,754	230,673	264,786	27.44	14.79
East Africa	124,461	125,773	140,190	139,415	167,787	17.39	20.35
Burundi	43	63	76	80	69	0.01	-13.75
Comoros	655	606	746	969	1,076	0.11	11.04
Djibouti	23	20	26	25	52	0.01	108.00
Eritrea	5	7	11	17	14	0.00	-17.65
Ethiopia	121	128	88	155	160	0.02	3.23
Kenya	1,997	1,386	1,548	1,914	2,705	0.28	41.33
Madagascar	10,905	8,333	9,833	11,449	13,563	1.41	18.46
Malawi	245	150	185	197	279	0.03	41.62
Mozambique	403	377	396	414	637	0.07	53.86
Reunion	96,174	104,946	114,914	113,000	139,169	14.42	23.16
Rwanda	68	62	86	75	98	0.01	30.67
Seychelles	10,604	7,532	10,160	8,485	6,779	0.70	-20.11
Somalia	8	3	1	7	12	0.00	71.43
Uganda	238	174	164	264	429	0.04	62.50
United Republic of Tanzania	541	325	321	481	551	0.06	14.55
Zambia	622	335	431	388	626	0.06	61.34
Zimbabwe	1,809	1,326	1,204	1,495	1,568	0.16	4.88
Central Africa	566	466	519	621	818	0.08	31.72
Angola	185	123	155	208	330	0.03	58.65
Cameroon	148	147	160	183	163	0.02	-10.93
Central African Republic	3	5	10	12	9	0.00	-25.00
Chad	3	4	8	13	9	0.00	-30.77
Congo	150	144	147	155	203	0.02	30.97
Democratic Republic of the Congo	13	3	2				
Equatorial Guinea	2		4	8	7	0.00	-12.50
Gabon	62	38	30	39	92	0.01	135.90
Sao Tome and Principe		2	3	3	5	0.00	66.67
North Africa	1,026	1,024	913	1,091	1,029	0.11	-5.68
Algeria	242	242	223	289	139	0.01	-51.90
Morocco	323	389	328	348	372	0.04	6.90
Sudan	52	55	64	64	101	0.01	57.81
Tunisia	409	338	298	390	417	0.04	6.92
Southern Africa	85,783	75,446	82,944	87,856	91,076	9.44	3.67
Botswana	459	450	487	435	550	0.06	26.44
Lesotho	92	86	107	125	168	0.02	34.40
Namibia	598	615	761	856	1,047	0.11	22.31
South Africa	84,448	74,176	81,458	86,232	89,058	9.23	3.28
Swaziland	186	119	131	208	253	0.03	21.63
West Africa	1,013	1,065	1,186	1,683	1,808	0.19	7.43
Benin	35	42	44	72	66	0.01	-8.33
Burkina Faso	21	36	42	46	53	0.01	15.22
Cape Verde	48	31	53	33	33	0.00	0.00
Côte d'Ivoire	168	152	157	211	200	0.02	-5.21
Gambia	22	16	26	37	64	0.01	72.97
Ghana	218	254	263	299	382	0.04	27.76
Guinea	75	18	16	68	30	0.00	-55.88
Guinea-Bissau	1	5	2	2	14	0.00	600.00
Liberia	7	5	16	13	15	0.00	15.38
Mali	40	34	29	57	28	0.00	-50.88
Mauritania	15	32	16	11	70	0.01	536.36
Niger	2	13	8	19	55	0.01	189.47
Nigeria	203	272	318	481	574	0.06	19.33
Senegal	120	129	152	222	141	0.01	-36.49

471

Yearbook of Tourism Statistics, Data 2008 – 2012, 2014 Edition

MAURITIUS

1. Arrivals of non-resident tourists at national borders, by country of residence

	2008	2009	2010	2011	2012	Market share 2012	% Change 2012-2011
Sierra Leone	17	8	18	42	27	0.00	-35.71
Togo	21	18	26	70	56	0.01	-20.00
Other Africa	**534**	**72**	**2**	**7**	**2,268**	**0.24**	**32,300.00**
Other countries of Africa	534	72	2	7	2,268	0.24	32,300.00
AMERICAS	**13,709**	**13,071**	**13,724**	**14,424**	**16,079**	**1.67**	**11.47**
Caribbean	**176**	**100**	**119**	**159**	**248**	**0.03**	**55.97**
Anguilla	16	1			1	0.00	
Antigua and Barbuda	1		2		8	0.00	
Bahamas	1	1	7	6	18	0.00	200.00
Barbados	10	7	6	4	12	0.00	200.00
Bermuda	7	3			4	0.00	
Cuba	25	17	22	27	11	0.00	-59.26
Dominica	3	5	3	2	9	0.00	350.00
Dominican Republic	6	3	11	17	4	0.00	-76.47
Grenada	5	4	5	2	1	0.00	-50.00
Guadeloupe	11				19	0.00	
Haiti	9	9	13	15	16	0.00	6.67
Jamaica	46	19	23	31	27	0.00	-12.90
Martinique	5	1			65	0.01	
Trinidad and Tobago	31	30	27	55	53	0.01	-3.64
Central America	**48**	**39**	**50**	**38**	**46**	**0.00**	**21.05**
Belize	2	8	1	4	4	0.00	0.00
Costa Rica	10	8	9	15	9	0.00	-40.00
El Salvador	12	4	5	4	7	0.00	75.00
Guatemala	8	6	12	6	7	0.00	16.67
Honduras	11	9	19	9	19	0.00	111.11
Nicaragua	5	4	4				
North America	**10,391**	**10,600**	**11,054**	**10,870**	**11,227**	**1.16**	**3.28**
Canada	3,188	3,532	3,619	3,887	4,736	0.49	21.84
Mexico	114	117	119	113	117	0.01	3.54
United States of America	7,089	6,951	7,316	6,870	6,374	0.66	-7.22
South America	**3,074**	**2,208**	**2,469**	**3,330**	**4,331**	**0.45**	**30.06**
Argentina	592	498	627	657	742	0.08	12.94
Bolivia	7	10	12	7	7	0.00	0.00
Brazil	2,015	1,331	1,459	2,235	3,217	0.33	43.94
Chile	153	124	137	153	137	0.01	-10.46
Colombia	64	64	57	79	52	0.01	-34.18
Ecuador	13	15	28	27	16	0.00	-40.74
Guyana	14	7	5	13	22	0.00	69.23
Paraguay	11	17	14	21	12	0.00	-42.86
Peru	124	73	68	67	48	0.00	-28.36
Suriname	9	17	8	21	4	0.00	-80.95
Uruguay	27	25	15	18	40	0.00	122.22
Venezuela	45	27	39	32	34	0.00	6.25
Other Americas	**20**	**124**	**32**	**27**	**227**	**0.02**	**740.74**
Other countries of the Americas	20	124	32	27	227	0.02	740.74
EAST ASIA AND THE PACIFIC	**39,843**	**26,534**	**30,911**	**45,590**	**54,737**	**5.67**	**20.06**
North-East Asia	**12,901**	**10,109**	**11,486**	**20,197**	**27,852**	**2.89**	**37.90**
China	8,425	6,925	7,609	15,133	20,885	2.16	38.01
Hong Kong, China	641	382	415	593	1,269	0.13	114.00
Japan	1,751	1,351	1,485	1,545	1,641	0.17	6.21
Korea, Republic of	1,253	704	1,067	1,935	2,651	0.27	37.00
Macao, China		1		1	11	0.00	1,000.00
Mongolia	8	16	13	3	9	0.00	200.00
Taiwan, Province of China	823	730	897	987	1,386	0.14	40.43
South-East Asia	**6,771**	**5,227**	**7,138**	**8,605**	**8,464**	**0.88**	**-1.64**

472

MAURITIUS

1. Arrivals of non-resident tourists at national borders, by country of residence

	2008	2009	2010	2011	2012	Market share 2012	% Change 2012-2011
Brunei Darussalam	6	18	5	10	34	0.00	240.00
Cambodia	11	11	66	69	33	0.00	-52.17
Indonesia	1,297	853	1,275	1,615	1,626	0.17	0.68
Lao People's Democratic Republic	1	1	2	2	13	0.00	550.00
Malaysia	1,509	1,164	1,438	1,989	1,967	0.20	-1.11
Myanmar	18	21	14	71	50	0.01	-29.58
Philippines	1,437	1,022	1,773	1,850	1,801	0.19	-2.65
Singapore	1,758	1,657	1,909	2,461	2,078	0.22	-15.56
Thailand	237	187	230	190	286	0.03	50.53
Viet Nam	497	293	426	348	576	0.06	65.52
Australasia	**20,092**	**11,113**	**12,219**	**16,725**	**17,737**	**1.84**	**6.05**
Australia	18,852	10,363	11,493	15,726	17,009	1.76	8.16
New Zealand	1,240	750	726	999	728	0.08	-27.13
Melanesia	**60**	**21**	**22**	**30**	**108**	**0.01**	**260.00**
Fiji	28	13	17	19	33	0.00	73.68
New Caledonia	31				50	0.01	
Papua New Guinea	1	2	2	4	10	0.00	150.00
Solomon Islands				4	7	0.00	75.00
Vanuatu		6	3	3	8	0.00	166.67
Micronesia	**1**	**1**			**4**	**0.00**	
Kiribati					3	0.00	
Nauru	1	1			1	0.00	
Polynesia	**6**	**2**			**521**	**0.05**	
American Samoa		1			508	0.05	
Cook Islands		1			1	0.00	
French Polynesia	6				12	0.00	
Other East Asia and the Pacific	**12**	**61**	**46**	**33**	**51**	**0.01**	**54.55**
Other countries of Asia	2	54	40	27	23	0.00	-14.81
Other countries of Oceania	10	7	6	6	28	0.00	366.67
EUROPE	**608,791**	**579,728**	**605,641**	**609,958**	**560,769**	**58.11**	**-8.06**
Central/Eastern Europe	**23,620**	**19,276**	**19,795**	**26,469**	**34,974**	**3.62**	**32.13**
Armenia	24	24	32	48	60	0.01	25.00
Azerbaijan	66	47	73	78	86	0.01	10.26
Bulgaria	629	511	498	639	613	0.06	-4.07
Czech Republic	4,166	3,487	3,477	4,081	5,247	0.54	28.57
Estonia	561	989	549	288	303	0.03	5.21
Georgia	13	18	34	8	31	0.00	287.50
Hungary	3,045	1,382	1,376	1,231	1,013	0.10	-17.71
Kazakhstan	298	276	282	204	210	0.02	2.94
Latvia	313	268	219	250	297	0.03	18.80
Lithuania	322	309	343	372	369	0.04	-0.81
Poland	3,278	2,880	2,560	2,995	2,862	0.30	-4.44
Republic of Moldova	12	68	59	79	70	0.01	-11.39
Romania	996	814	960	1,055	962	0.10	-8.82
Russian Federation	6,763	5,626	6,615	12,224	19,429	2.01	58.94
Slovakia	1,308	1,172	1,366	1,263	1,488	0.15	17.81
Tajikistan	1	1	4	3	2	0.00	-33.33
Turkmenistan	1	5	3	1	14	0.00	1,300.00
Ukraine	1,615	1,178	1,206	1,485	1,754	0.18	18.11
USSR (former)	181	19		2	19	0.00	850.00
Uzbekistan	28	37	50	24	77	0.01	220.83
Other countries Central/East Europe		165	89	139	68	0.01	-51.08
Northern Europe	**133,209**	**120,206**	**114,926**	**104,004**	**102,320**	**10.60**	**-1.62**
Denmark	3,350	2,770	2,678	2,549	2,453	0.25	-3.77
Faeroe Islands	2	1			16	0.00	
Finland	4,792	3,600	4,026	3,133	2,330	0.24	-25.63
Iceland	75	55	44	38	48	0.00	26.32

Yearbook of Tourism Statistics, Data 2008 – 2012, 2014 Edition

MAURITIUS

1. Arrivals of non-resident tourists at national borders, by country of residence

	2008	2009	2010	2011	2012	Market share 2012	% Change 2012-2011
Ireland	5,002	4,249	3,460	2,717	2,009	0.21	-26.06
Norway	3,764	2,475	2,674	3,060	3,521	0.36	15.07
Sweden	8,305	5,060	4,496	4,325	4,295	0.45	-0.69
United Kingdom	107,919	101,996	97,548	88,182	87,648	9.08	-0.61
Southern Europe	**84,844**	**72,015**	**70,548**	**68,109**	**53,916**	**5.59**	**-20.84**
Albania	45	71	49	73	43	0.00	-41.10
Andorra	28	30	17	20	35	0.00	75.00
Bosnia and Herzegovina	50	37	44	36	44	0.00	22.22
Croatia	267	244	272	368	341	0.04	-7.34
Gibraltar	3				2	0.00	
Greece	2,343	1,766	1,447	1,342	998	0.10	-25.63
Italy	66,432	56,736	56,540	52,747	40,009	4.15	-24.15
Malta	182	206	247	365	221	0.02	-39.45
Portugal	1,863	2,098	2,680	2,426	1,799	0.19	-25.85
San Marino	20	52	115	59	41	0.00	-30.51
Serbia and Montenegro	237	91	20	10	4	0.00	-60.00
Slovenia	1,337	1,106	991	841	885	0.09	5.23
Spain	12,001	9,549	8,096	9,801	9,473	0.98	-3.35
TFYR of Macedonia	36	29	30	21	21	0.00	0.00
Western Europe	**365,358**	**366,947**	**398,851**	**409,702**	**368,139**	**38.15**	**-10.14**
Austria	8,974	8,106	9,255	8,822	8,151	0.84	-7.61
Belgium	11,796	10,254	10,214	12,029	10,967	1.14	-8.83
France	260,054	275,599	302,185	302,004	262,100	27.16	-13.21
Germany	61,484	51,279	52,886	56,331	55,186	5.72	-2.03
Liechtenstein	31	61	80	98	80	0.01	-18.37
Luxembourg	819	591	615	710	943	0.10	32.82
Monaco	112	181	174	167	276	0.03	65.27
Netherlands	6,051	5,527	4,865	5,179	4,434	0.46	-14.39
Switzerland	16,037	15,349	18,577	24,362	26,002	2.69	6.73
East Mediterranean Europe	**1,659**	**1,263**	**1,496**	**1,674**	**1,420**	**0.15**	**-15.17**
Cyprus	436	278	314	291	241	0.02	-17.18
Israel	566	391	425	574	541	0.06	-5.75
Turkey	657	594	757	809	638	0.07	-21.14
Other Europe	**101**	**21**	**25**				
Other countries of Europe	101	21	25				
MIDDLE EAST	**7,158**	**5,702**	**6,012**	**6,448**	**8,902**	**0.92**	**38.06**
Bahrain	102	72	69	52	139	0.01	167.31
Egypt	436	395	402	468	401	0.04	-14.32
Iraq	13	11	26	29	17	0.00	-41.38
Jordan	138	178	156	153	109	0.01	-28.76
Kuwait	239	112	101	199	234	0.02	17.59
Lebanon	546	326	323	360	313	0.03	-13.06
Libya	46	69	53	20	25	0.00	25.00
Oman	112	52	57	78	173	0.02	121.79
Palestine	2	9	22	7	6	0.00	-14.29
Qatar	52	59	49	58	243	0.03	318.97
Saudi Arabia	1,283	1,161	1,197	1,188	1,782	0.18	50.00
Syrian Arab Republic	70	101	64	41	39	0.00	-4.88
United Arab Emirates	4,109	3,141	3,470	3,780	5,403	0.56	42.94
Yemen	10	16	23	15	18	0.00	20.00
SOUTH ASIA	**45,848**	**41,014**	**51,348**	**55,743**	**58,606**	**6.07**	**5.14**
Bangladesh	286	496	207	226	1,264	0.13	459.29
Bhutan	1	1	3	1	3	0.00	200.00
India	43,911	39,252	49,779	53,955	55,197	5.72	2.30
Iran, Islamic Republic of	137	133	149	308	235	0.02	-23.70
Maldives	51	18	28	48	64	0.01	33.33

474

MAURITIUS

1. Arrivals of non-resident tourists at national borders, by country of residence

	2008	2009	2010	2011	2012	Market share 2012	% Change 2012-2011
Nepal	188	80	124	264	211	0.02	-20.08
Pakistan	873	621	771	698	946	0.10	35.53
Sri Lanka	401	413	287	243	686	0.07	182.30
NOT SPECIFIED	**1,586**	**1,292**	**1,288**	**1,583**	**1,121**	**0.12**	**-29.19**
Other countries of the World	1,586	1,292	1,288	1,583	1,121	0.12	-29.19

Yearbook of Tourism Statistics, Data 2008 – 2012, 2014 Edition

MAURITIUS

6. Overnight stays of non-resident tourists in all types of accommodation establishments, by country of residence

	2008	2009	2010	2011	2012	Market share 2012	% Change 2012-2011
TOTAL	9,089,972	8,639,304	9,554,437	10,000,136	10,239,544	100.00	2.39
AFRICA	1,804,791	1,826,343	2,092,001	1,994,346	2,149,733	20.99	7.79
East Africa	1,038,194	1,167,314	1,347,076	1,200,888	1,289,036	12.59	7.34
Comoros	9,503	8,503	11,941	18,014	20,949	0.20	16.29
Kenya	14,309	11,767	11,715	17,600	19,058	0.19	8.28
Madagascar	106,400	96,282	110,826	125,848	136,720	1.34	8.64
Reunion	789,617	969,927	1,110,573	943,649	1,031,174	10.07	9.28
Seychelles	93,713	67,976	90,752	80,522	62,914	0.61	-21.87
Zimbabwe	24,652	12,859	11,269	15,255	18,221	0.18	19.44
Southern Africa	699,641	602,983	680,880	720,138	744,119	7.27	3.33
South Africa	699,641	602,983	680,880	720,138	744,119	7.27	3.33
Other Africa	66,956	56,046	64,045	73,320	116,578	1.14	59.00
Other countries of Africa	66,956	56,046	64,045	73,320	116,578	1.14	59.00
AMERICAS	133,303	131,044	126,661	162,574	194,001	1.89	19.33
North America	108,452	112,498	104,772	135,525	154,435	1.51	13.95
Canada	43,175	58,423	52,631	67,860	98,271	0.96	44.81
United States of America	65,277	54,075	52,141	67,665	56,164	0.55	-17.00
Other Americas	24,851	18,546	21,889	27,049	39,566	0.39	46.28
Other countries of the Americas	24,851	18,546	21,889	27,049	39,566	0.39	46.28
EAST ASIA AND THE PACIFIC	460,181	373,044	479,656	577,234	709,609	6.93	22.93
North-East Asia	120,901	84,888	99,347	180,207	260,807	2.55	44.73
China	105,809	69,196	83,408	162,914	239,924	2.34	47.27
Hong Kong, China	4,469	4,211	4,696	6,533	10,500	0.10	60.72
Japan	10,623	11,481	11,243	10,760	10,383	0.10	-3.50
South-East Asia	22,027	21,884	24,205	26,500	31,248	0.31	17.92
Malaysia	10,108	10,554	11,575	11,695	14,606	0.14	24.89
Singapore	11,919	11,330	12,630	14,805	16,642	0.16	12.41
Australasia	150,220	138,665	169,162	200,337	221,613	2.16	10.62
Australia	150,220	138,665	169,162	200,337	221,613	2.16	10.62
Other East Asia and the Pacific	167,033	127,607	186,942	170,190	195,941	1.91	15.13
Other countries of Asia	155,903	117,511	174,229	158,991	186,807	1.82	17.50
Other countries of Oceania	11,130	10,096	12,713	11,199	9,134	0.09	-18.44
EUROPE	6,283,489	5,917,949	6,431,755	6,546,010	6,340,600	61.92	-3.14
Northern Europe	1,276,932	1,344,549	1,270,462	1,151,836	1,237,852	12.09	7.47
Sweden	93,180	62,581	54,857	50,680	48,931	0.48	-3.45
United Kingdom	1,183,752	1,281,968	1,215,605	1,101,156	1,188,921	11.61	7.97
Southern Europe	669,436	597,089	603,905	578,087	459,091	4.48	-20.58
Italy	582,196	512,033	532,786	501,289	388,185	3.79	-22.56
Spain	87,240	85,056	71,119	76,798	70,906	0.69	-7.67
Western Europe	3,859,076	3,566,833	4,105,440	4,488,216	4,321,695	42.21	-3.71
Austria	99,371	92,209	113,700	104,758	95,882	0.94	-8.47
Belgium	148,043	138,764	139,271	150,952	150,913	1.47	-0.03
France	2,629,452	2,498,920	2,861,874	3,190,400	3,024,054	29.53	-5.21
Germany	731,803	579,531	685,258	686,431	672,933	6.57	-1.97
Netherlands	58,561	59,667	54,328	56,328	50,569	0.49	-10.22
Switzerland	191,846	197,742	251,009	299,347	327,344	3.20	9.35
Other Europe	478,045	409,478	451,948	327,871	321,962	3.14	-1.80
Other countries of Europe	478,045	409,478	451,948	327,871	321,962	3.14	-1.80
SOUTH ASIA	398,835	376,783	409,138	488,810	526,724	5.14	7.76
India	398,835	376,783	409,138	488,810	526,724	5.14	7.76
NOT SPECIFIED	9,373	14,141	15,226	231,162	318,877	3.11	37.95
Other countries of the World	9,373	14,141	15,226	231,162	318,877	3.11	37.95

Yearbook of Tourism Statistics, Data 2008 – 2012, 2014 Editi

MEXICO

1. Arrivals of non-resident tourists at national borders, by nationality

		2008	2009	2010	2011	2012	Market share 2012	% Change 2012-2011
TOTAL		22,930,584	22,346,260	23,289,749	23,403,263	23,402,545	100.00	0.00
AFRICA		13,340	9,884	15,005	14,701	15,578	0.07	5.97
Other Africa		13,340	9,884	15,005	14,701	15,578	0.07	5.97
All countries of Africa		13,340	9,884	15,005	14,701	15,578	0.07	5.97
AMERICAS		19,818,344	20,178,443	20,867,904	21,152,561	21,540,885	92.05	1.84
Caribbean		47,825	40,965	39,249	40,873	44,881	0.19	9.81
Cuba		47,825	40,965	39,249	40,873	44,881	0.19	9.81
Central America		88,461	94,843	103,426	88,837	118,452	0.51	33.34
Costa Rica		44,580	42,107	53,152	44,415	59,361	0.25	33.65
Guatemala		43,881	52,736	50,274	44,422	59,091	0.25	33.02
North America		19,116,815	19,484,056	19,987,581	20,117,762	20,229,713	86.44	0.56
Canada		1,135,001	1,222,410	1,460,418	1,563,146	1,571,543	6.72	0.54
United States of America	(*)	17,981,814	18,261,646	18,527,163	18,554,616	18,658,170	79.73	0.56
South America		412,086	401,457	542,831	688,018	881,324	3.77	28.10
Argentina		126,130	127,107	170,467	200,687	251,221	1.07	25.18
Brazil		76,491	68,211	117,658	196,266	248,899	1.06	26.82
Chile		59,634	54,179	67,661	76,379	88,148	0.38	15.41
Colombia		67,378	68,493	102,177	125,882	163,725	0.70	30.06
Venezuela		82,453	83,467	84,868	88,804	129,331	0.55	45.64
Other Americas		153,157	157,122	194,817	217,071	266,515	1.14	22.78
Other countries of the Americas		153,157	157,122	194,817	217,071	266,515	1.14	22.78
EAST ASIA AND THE PACIFIC		105,412	78,407	101,129	112,642	133,302	0.57	18.34
North-East Asia		105,412	78,407	101,129	112,642	133,302	0.57	18.34
Japan		69,716	52,229	66,164	72,339	85,687	0.37	18.45
Korea, Republic of		35,696	26,178	34,965	40,303	47,615	0.20	18.14
EUROPE		1,501,742	1,188,286	1,417,935	1,509,736	1,619,164	6.92	7.25
Northern Europe		311,113	257,367	295,831	330,071	363,142	1.55	10.02
United Kingdom		311,113	257,367	295,831	330,071	363,142	1.55	10.02
Southern Europe		489,678	350,528	469,085	473,679	474,221	2.03	0.11
Italy		167,415	108,547	133,292	150,690	156,532	0.67	3.88
Portugal		37,751	26,312	48,630	43,459	38,877	0.17	-10.54
Spain		284,512	215,669	287,163	279,530	278,812	1.19	-0.26
Western Europe		508,734	418,570	462,343	479,626	500,107	2.14	4.27
Belgium		36,202	30,173	31,188	30,344	29,924	0.13	-1.38
France		208,284	164,236	170,250	186,778	202,855	0.87	8.61
Germany		158,050	140,754	163,266	165,133	172,841	0.74	4.67
Netherlands		75,864	58,317	68,964	67,821	63,159	0.27	-6.87
Switzerland		30,334	25,090	28,675	29,550	31,328	0.13	6.02
Other Europe		192,217	161,821	190,676	226,360	281,694	1.20	24.45
Other countries of Europe		192,217	161,821	190,676	226,360	281,694	1.20	24.45
NOT SPECIFIED		1,491,746	891,241	887,776	613,623	93,616	0.40	-84.74
Other countries of the World	(*)	1,491,746	891,241	887,776	613,623	93,616	0.40	-84.74

Yearbook of Tourism Statistics, Data 2008 – 2012, 2014 Edition

MEXICO

1. Arrivals of non-resident tourists at national borders, by country of residence

		2008	2009	2010	2011	2012	Market share 2012	% Change 2012-2011
TOTAL	(*)	**22,930,584**	**22,346,261**	**23,289,749**	**23,403,274**	**23,402,545**	**100.00**	**0.00**
AMERICAS		**18,800,933**	**18,874,985**	**19,128,045**	**19,314,307**	**19,397,096**	**82.88**	**0.43**
North America		**18,800,933**	**18,874,985**	**19,128,045**	**19,314,307**	**19,397,096**	**82.88**	**0.43**
Canada		819,119	613,339	600,882	759,691	738,926	3.16	-2.73
United States of America		17,981,814	18,261,646	18,527,163	18,554,616	18,658,170	79.73	0.56
NOT SPECIFIED		**4,129,651**	**3,471,276**	**4,161,704**	**4,088,967**	**4,005,449**	**17.12**	**-2.04**
Other countries of the World		4,129,651	3,471,276	4,161,704	4,088,967	4,005,449	17.12	-2.04

Yearbook of Tourism Statistics, Data 2008 – 2012, 2014 Edit

MONACO

3. Arrivals of non-resident tourists in hotels and similar establishments, by nationality

	2008	2009	2010	2011	2012	Market share 2012	% Change 2012-2011
TOTAL	323,705	264,540	279,166	294,901	292,027	100.00	-0.97
AFRICA	2,832	2,342	2,881	2,836	3,765	1.29	32.76
Other Africa	2,832	2,342	2,881	2,836	3,765	1.29	32.76
All countries of Africa	2,832	2,342	2,881	2,836	3,765	1.29	32.76
AMERICAS	35,368	27,456	30,863	33,143	38,241	13.10	15.38
North America	30,805	22,919	25,373	27,887	32,661	11.18	17.12
Canada	4,438	3,330	3,938	4,652	4,944	1.69	6.28
Mexico	795	602	738	904	1,001	0.34	10.73
United States of America	25,572	18,987	20,697	22,331	26,716	9.15	19.64
South America	2,989	3,221	3,814	3,558	3,963	1.36	11.38
Argentina	698	686	659	611	883	0.30	44.52
Brazil	2,291	2,535	3,155	2,947	3,080	1.05	4.51
Other Americas	1,574	1,316	1,676	1,698	1,617	0.55	-4.77
Other countries of the Americas	1,574	1,316	1,676	1,698	1,617	0.55	-4.77
EAST ASIA AND THE PACIFIC	12,535	10,222	11,783	14,650	15,893	5.44	8.48
North-East Asia	8,271	6,920	7,414	9,308	9,346	3.20	0.41
China	2,254	1,796	2,888	4,311	3,770	1.29	-12.55
Japan	6,017	5,124	4,526	4,997	5,576	1.91	11.59
Australasia	4,264	3,302	4,369	5,342	6,547	2.24	22.56
Australia	4,264	3,302	4,369	5,342	6,547	2.24	22.56
EUROPE	260,856	216,280	223,207	232,827	221,937	76.00	-4.68
Central/Eastern Europe	16,762	13,795	14,899	17,229	14,360	4.92	-16.65
Russian Federation	16,762	13,795	14,899	17,229	14,360	4.92	-16.65
Northern Europe	53,939	36,575	37,524	38,124	37,330	12.78	-2.08
Denmark	1,852	1,602	1,710	1,562	1,360	0.47	-12.93
Norway	1,679	1,549	1,639	2,319	1,702	0.58	-26.61
Sweden	2,727	2,357	2,526	2,892	2,445	0.84	-15.46
United Kingdom	47,681	31,067	31,649	31,351	31,823	10.90	1.51
Southern Europe	72,437	60,052	61,870	60,116	49,385	16.91	-17.85
Italy	65,414	52,951	55,129	53,081	43,614	14.93	-17.84
Portugal	1,151	1,111	1,069	1,232	1,055	0.36	-14.37
Spain	5,872	5,990	5,672	5,803	4,716	1.61	-18.73
Western Europe	98,014	87,640	91,800	99,470	97,949	33.54	-1.53
Austria	2,575	2,125	2,485	2,539	2,354	0.81	-7.29
Belgium	5,665	4,632	4,509	4,821	5,154	1.76	6.91
France	62,043	56,685	61,234	65,659	64,561	22.11	-1.67
Germany	13,230	11,587	11,070	13,002	12,015	4.11	-7.59
Netherlands	5,109	4,741	4,342	4,608	4,292	1.47	-6.86
Switzerland	9,392	7,870	8,160	8,841	9,573	3.28	8.28
East Mediterranean Europe	1,341	1,468	1,269	1,397	1,480	0.51	5.94
Israel	1,341	1,468	1,269	1,397	1,480	0.51	5.94
Other Europe	18,363	16,750	15,845	16,491	21,433	7.34	29.97
Other countries of Europe	18,363	16,750	15,845	16,491	21,433	7.34	29.97
MIDDLE EAST	7,045	4,333	5,039	5,386	5,446	1.86	1.11
All countries of Middle East	7,045	4,333	5,039	5,386	5,446	1.86	1.11
NOT SPECIFIED	5,069	3,907	5,393	6,059	6,745	2.31	11.32
Other countries of the World	5,069	3,907	5,393	6,059	6,745	2.31	11.32

Yearbook of Tourism Statistics, Data 2008 – 2012, 2014 Edition

MONACO

5. Overnight stays of non-resident tourists in hotels and similar establishments, by nationality

	2008	2009	2010	2011	2012	Market share 2012	% Change 2012-2011
TOTAL	943,509	778,451	817,011	852,578	802,434	100.00	-5.88
AFRICA	9,037	7,351	8,773	8,775	10,536	1.31	20.07
Other Africa	9,037	7,351	8,773	8,775	10,536	1.31	20.07
All countries of Africa	9,037	7,351	8,773	8,775	10,536	1.31	20.07
AMERICAS	120,106	92,791	103,292	106,963	113,560	14.15	6.17
North America	104,475	79,625	86,965	91,537	98,492	12.27	7.60
Canada	16,057	10,798	12,561	14,932	14,711	1.83	-1.48
Mexico	2,450	1,638	2,095	2,472	2,484	0.31	0.49
United States of America	85,968	67,189	72,309	74,133	81,297	10.13	9.66
South America	10,490	9,062	10,863	9,962	10,139	1.26	1.78
Argentina	2,781	2,567	2,464	2,089	2,308	0.29	10.48
Brazil	7,709	6,495	8,399	7,873	7,831	0.98	-0.53
Other Americas	5,141	4,104	5,464	5,464	4,929	0.61	-9.79
Other countries of the Americas	5,141	4,104	5,464	5,464	4,929	0.61	-9.79
EAST ASIA AND THE PACIFIC	38,296	29,885	32,747	38,571	36,726	4.58	-4.78
North-East Asia	24,519	19,513	19,485	23,415	21,574	2.69	-7.86
China	5,771	4,118	6,361	9,484	7,611	0.95	-19.75
Japan	18,748	15,395	13,124	13,931	13,963	1.74	0.23
Australasia	13,777	10,372	13,262	15,156	15,152	1.89	-0.03
Australia	13,777	10,372	13,262	15,156	15,152	1.89	-0.03
EUROPE	726,854	619,478	636,189	661,030	600,244	74.80	-9.20
Central/Eastern Europe	77,566	65,409	70,750	78,084	61,707	7.69	-20.97
Russian Federation	77,566	65,409	70,750	78,084	61,707	7.69	-20.97
Northern Europe	155,514	111,182	113,894	114,311	102,779	12.81	-10.09
Denmark	5,764	4,348	4,846	4,394	3,742	0.47	-14.84
Norway	4,781	4,365	4,528	6,397	4,359	0.54	-31.86
Sweden	8,095	8,186	8,395	8,479	6,805	0.85	-19.74
United Kingdom	136,874	94,283	96,125	95,041	87,873	10.95	-7.54
Southern Europe	175,960	151,080	155,649	153,932	121,199	15.10	-21.26
Italy	155,856	131,312	136,767	134,476	103,804	12.94	-22.81
Portugal	3,418	3,486	3,345	3,602	2,610	0.33	-27.54
Spain	16,686	16,282	15,537	15,854	14,785	1.84	-6.74
Western Europe	255,593	234,101	241,745	259,067	241,444	30.09	-6.80
Austria	9,277	8,214	8,926	8,377	7,109	0.89	-15.14
Belgium	18,492	17,023	16,352	16,280	15,188	1.89	-6.71
France	142,395	132,822	143,867	153,985	144,933	18.06	-5.88
Germany	40,176	38,001	35,831	41,176	36,281	4.52	-11.89
Netherlands	14,978	13,919	12,229	13,002	11,026	1.37	-15.20
Switzerland	30,275	24,122	24,540	26,247	26,907	3.35	2.51
East Mediterranean Europe	5,790	5,451	4,642	5,090	4,707	0.59	-7.52
Israel	5,790	5,451	4,642	5,090	4,707	0.59	-7.52
Other Europe	56,431	52,255	49,509	50,546	68,408	8.53	35.34
Other countries of Europe	56,431	52,255	49,509	50,546	68,408	8.53	35.34
MIDDLE EAST	33,272	17,550	20,968	21,529	21,593	2.69	0.30
All countries of Middle East	33,272	17,550	20,968	21,529	21,593	2.69	0.30
NOT SPECIFIED	15,944	11,396	15,042	15,710	19,775	2.46	25.88
Other countries of the World	15,944	11,396	15,042	15,710	19,775	2.46	25.88

MONGOLIA

1. Arrivals of non-resident tourists at national borders, by nationality

	2008	2009	2010	2011	2012	Market share 2012	% Change 2012-2011
TOTAL	446,317	411,497	456,963	460,360	475,892	100.00	3.37
AFRICA	592	434	595				
East Africa	82	85	145				
Burundi			58				
Eritrea		1					
Ethiopia	6	16	16				
Kenya	21	15	13				
Madagascar	1	2	2				
Malawi		3					
Mauritius	7	7	16				
Mozambique	2	3	11				
Reunion	4	3	1				
Rwanda	10	4	1				
Uganda	18	12	8				
United Republic of Tanzania	6	4	6				
Zambia	4	7	3				
Zimbabwe	3	8	10				
Central Africa	48	30	21				
Angola	3	1					
Cameroon	20	16	12				
Central African Republic	8	4	1				
Chad			8				
Congo	15	9					
Equatorial Guinea	2						
North Africa	39	42	73				
Algeria	14	11	17				
Morocco	10	14	35				
Sudan	11	12					
Tunisia	4	5	21				
Southern Africa	286	216	271				
Botswana	2						
Lesotho	1		1				
Namibia	4	1	4				
South Africa	257	197	258				
Swaziland	22	18	8				
West Africa	97	61	85				
Benin	5	1	8				
Burkina Faso		1	4				
Côte d'Ivoire	2						
Gambia		1	1				
Ghana	40	27	24				
Guinea-Bissau			1				
Liberia		4	6				
Mali		1	3				
Mauritania			1				
Niger	7	13	12				
Nigeria	24	9	21				
Senegal	4	3	1				
Sierra Leone	15		2				
Togo		1	1				
Other Africa	40						
Other countries of Africa	40						
AMERICAS	15,805	14,161	16,486	18,596	18,415	3.87	-0.97
Caribbean	38	43	42				
Barbados			1				

481

Yearbook of Tourism Statistics, Data 2008 – 2012, 2014 Edition

MONGOLIA

1. Arrivals of non-resident tourists at national borders, by nationality

	2008	2009	2010	2011	2012	Market share 2012	% Change 2012-2011
Bermuda		2					
Cuba	24	25	26				
Dominica	1	2	2				
Dominican Republic	3						
Haiti		4	4				
Jamaica	7	1	3				
Trinidad and Tobago	3	9	6				
Central America	**70**	**30**	**39**				
Belize			3				
Costa Rica	7	5	6				
El Salvador	2	4	6				
Guatemala	1	6	5				
Honduras	55	9	11				
Nicaragua			1				
Panama	5	6	7				
North America	**15,188**	**13,663**	**15,799**	**18,596**	**18,415**	**3.87**	**-0.97**
Canada	2,645	2,255	2,864	3,173	2,828	0.59	-10.87
Mexico	69	73	127				
United States of America	12,474	11,335	12,808	15,423	15,587	3.28	1.06
South America	**509**	**425**	**606**				
Argentina	74	68	179				
Bolivia	15	2	11				
Brazil	220	159	225				
Chile	105	84	59				
Colombia	28	32	32				
Ecuador	8	11	7				
French Guiana	1						
Guyana		1					
Paraguay	3	4	4				
Peru	18	41	51				
Uruguay	8	10	24				
Venezuela	29	13	14				
EAST ASIA AND THE PACIFIC	**266,582**	**241,097**	**264,401**	**269,352**	**300,975**	**63.24**	**11.74**
North-East Asia	**257,365**	**233,067**	**253,808**	**260,870**	**291,914**	**61.34**	**11.90**
China	196,832	181,523	194,333	200,010	228,547	48.02	14.27
Hong Kong, China	369	434	791	1,878	1,888	0.40	0.53
Japan	14,939	11,399	14,140	14,988	17,119	3.60	14.22
Korea, Dem. People's Republic of	402	342	1,068				
Korea, Republic of	43,396	38,272	42,231	43,994	44,360	9.32	0.83
Macao, China	23	11	10				
Taiwan, Province of China	1,404	1,086	1,235				
South-East Asia	**3,780**	**3,586**	**4,229**	**428**	**607**	**0.13**	**41.82**
Brunei Darussalam	8	7	3				
Cambodia	45	85	34				
Indonesia	226	203	246	428	607	0.13	41.82
Lao People's Democratic Republic	90	92	58				
Malaysia	881	846	926				
Myanmar	5	7	8				
Philippines	510	600	823				
Singapore	932	922	1,170				
Thailand	418	443	546				
Viet Nam	665	381	415				
Australasia	**5,394**	**4,431**	**6,325**	**8,054**	**8,454**	**1.78**	**4.97**
Australia	4,466	3,721	5,443	7,093	7,480	1.57	5.46
New Zealand	928	710	882	961	974	0.20	1.35
Melanesia	**29**	**7**	**29**				
Fiji	18		15				

Yearbook of Tourism Statistics, Data 2008 – 2012, 2014 Edition

MONGOLIA

1. Arrivals of non-resident tourists at national borders, by nationality

	2008	2009	2010	2011	2012	Market share 2012	% Change 2012-2011
Papua New Guinea	10	1	12				
Solomon Islands	1	6	1				
Vanuatu			1				
Micronesia	**3**						
Kiribati	2						
Micronesia, Federated States of	1						
Polynesia	**11**	**6**	**10**				
American Samoa	7		2				
Samoa	1	2	5				
Tonga	3	4	3				
EUROPE	**159,884**	**153,785**	**173,381**	**140,386**	**123,699**	**25.99**	**-11.89**
Central/Eastern Europe	**120,776**	**117,535**	**132,127**	**111,720**	**95,310**	**20.03**	**-14.69**
Armenia	177	120	75				
Azerbaijan	147	75	76				
Belarus	237	188	177				
Bulgaria	103	89	123				
Czech Republic	932	815	841				
Estonia	42	35	91				
Georgia	65	50	69				
Hungary	289	281	330				
Kazakhstan	5,473	5,053	5,757	7,973	10,523	2.21	31.98
Kyrgyzstan	342	205	238				
Latvia	31	28	45				
Lithuania	71	53	79				
Poland	1,338	1,048	1,163				
Republic of Moldova	58	40	40				
Romania	62	84	106				
Russian Federation	109,975	107,911	121,705	102,738	83,707	17.59	-18.52
Slovakia	202	196	184				
Tajikistan	114	112	30				
Turkmenistan	5	2	4				
Ukraine	960	967	818	1,009	1,080	0.23	7.04
Uzbekistan	153	183	176				
Northern Europe	**11,925**	**10,254**	**11,179**	**9,312**	**8,928**	**1.88**	**-4.12**
Denmark	917	660	676	729	717	0.15	-1.65
Finland	832	843	945				
Iceland	32	25	18				
Ireland	682	508	490				
Norway	787	737	816				
Sweden	1,894	1,634	1,625	1,463	1,407	0.30	-3.83
United Kingdom	6,781	5,847	6,609	7,120	6,804	1.43	-4.44
Southern Europe	**3,192**	**4,393**	**4,730**				
Albania	10	4	15				
Andorra	2	3	2				
Bosnia and Herzegovina	57	17	27				
Croatia	73	41	37				
Greece	93	92	126				
Italy	2,454	2,415	2,750				
Malta	2	4	9				
Portugal	260	278	192				
Serbia and Montenegro	39	57	60				
Slovenia	167	154	154				
Spain		1,315	1,340				
TFYR of Macedonia	35	13	18				
Western Europe	**22,660**	**20,457**	**23,420**	**19,354**	**19,461**	**4.09**	**0.55**
Austria	1,219	1,105	1,118				
Belgium	1,005	807	964				
France	6,688	6,702	7,527	7,570	7,553	1.59	-0.22

483

MONGOLIA

1. Arrivals of non-resident tourists at national borders, by nationality

	2008	2009	2010	2011	2012	Market share 2012	% Change 2012-2011
Germany	8,027	6,858	8,095	8,545	8,909	1.87	4.26
Liechtenstein	6	10					
Luxembourg	83	37	78				
Netherlands	3,255	2,775	3,244	3,239	2,999	0.63	-7.41
Switzerland	2,377	2,163	2,394				
East Mediterranean Europe	**1,235**	**1,146**	**1,925**				
Cyprus	15	6	11				
Israel	642	619	757				
Turkey	578	521	1,157				
Other Europe	**96**						
Other countries of Europe	96						
MIDDLE EAST	**610**	**645**	**616**				
Bahrain	2	3	9				
Egypt	43	37	34				
Iraq	13	10	18				
Jordan	13	18	81				
Kuwait	203	107	233				
Lebanon	21	7	3				
Libya	2	20	26				
Oman	5	28	8				
Palestine	3	2					
Qatar	134	223	39				
Saudi Arabia	63	49	34				
Syrian Arab Republic	82	104	102				
United Arab Emirates	10	19	11				
Yemen	16	18	18				
SOUTH ASIA	**1,407**	**1,327**	**1,473**	**1,478**	**1,340**	**0.28**	**-9.34**
Afghanistan	16	31	17				
Bangladesh	65	91	82				
Bhutan	18	9	31				
India	881	941	940	1,478	1,340	0.28	-9.34
Iran, Islamic Republic of	56	63	219				
Maldives	58	7	5				
Nepal	125						
Pakistan	107	115	110				
Sri Lanka	81	70	69				
NOT SPECIFIED	**1,437**	**48**	**11**	**30,548**	**31,463**	**6.61**	**3.00**
Other countries of the World	1,437	48	11	30,548	31,463	6.61	3.00

Yearbook of Tourism Statistics, Data 2008 – 2012, 2014 Editi

MONGOLIA

2. Arrivals of non-resident visitors at national borders, by nationality

	2008	2009	2010	2011	2012	Market share 2012	% Change 2012-2011
TOTAL	468,765	467,989	557,452	627,007	623,839	100.00	-0.51
AFRICA	567	418	597				
East Africa	85	87	148				
Burundi			58				
Eritrea		1					
Ethiopia	6	16	16				
Kenya	21	15	13				
Madagascar	1	2	2				
Malawi	1	3	3				
Mauritius	7	9	16				
Mozambique	2	3	11				
Reunion	4	3	1				
Rwanda	10	4	1				
Uganda	18	12	8				
United Republic of Tanzania	6	4	6				
Zambia	6	7	3				
Zimbabwe	3	8	10				
Central Africa	51	33	25				
Angola	3	1					
Cameroon	20	17	12				
Central African Republic	9	4	1				
Chad	1						
Congo	16	11	8				
Equatorial Guinea	2		4				
North Africa	39	43	73				
Algeria	14	11	17				
Morocco	10	15	35				
Sudan	11	12					
Tunisia	4	5	21				
Southern Africa	291	187	271				
Botswana	2						
Lesotho			1				
Namibia	5	1	4				
South Africa	261	168	258				
Swaziland	23	18	8				
West Africa	101	68	80				
Benin	5	1	8				
Burkina Faso		1					
Gambia		2	1				
Ghana	41	31	24				
Guinea	3	1	1				
Liberia	2	4	6				
Mali		1					
Mauritania			1				
Niger	7	14	13				
Nigeria	24	9	22				
Senegal	4	3	1				
Sierra Leone	15		2				
Togo		1	1				
AMERICAS	16,037	14,202	16,686	20,156	21,077	3.38	4.57
Caribbean	38	44	43				
Barbados			1				
Bermuda		2					
Cuba	24	26	27				
Dominica	1		2				
Dominican Republic	3	2					

485

Yearbook of Tourism Statistics, Data 2008 – 2012, 2014 Edition

MONGOLIA

2. Arrivals of non-resident visitors at national borders, by nationality

	2008	2009	2010	2011	2012	Market share 2012	% Change 2012-2011
Haiti		4	4				
Jamaica	7	1	3				
Trinidad and Tobago	3	9	6				
Central America	**70**	**30**	**38**				
Belize			3				
Costa Rica	7	5	6				
El Salvador	2	4	6				
Guatemala	1	6	5				
Honduras	55	9	11				
Panama	5	6	7				
North America	**15,414**	**13,854**	**15,996**	**20,156**	**21,077**	**3.38**	**4.57**
Canada	2,681	2,273	2,887	3,711	3,714	0.60	0.08
Mexico	70	73	127				
United States of America	12,663	11,508	12,982	16,445	17,363	2.78	5.58
South America	**515**	**274**	**609**				
Argentina	75	68	179				
Bolivia	16	2	11				
Brazil	223		227				
Chile	105	84	59				
Colombia	28	31	32				
Ecuador	8	11	7				
Falkland Islands, Malvinas		9	1				
French Guiana	1						
Paraguay	3	4	4				
Peru	19	42	51				
Uruguay	8	10	24				
Venezuela	29	13	14				
EAST ASIA AND THE PACIFIC	**287,400**	**292,096**	**360,681**	**418,673**	**438,040**	**70.22**	**4.63**
North-East Asia	**278,125**	**283,964**	**350,016**	**409,033**	**426,561**	**68.38**	**4.29**
China	217,127	232,038	290,061	346,984	361,506	57.95	4.19
Hong Kong, China	370	435	793	1,903	1,924	0.31	1.10
Japan	15,036	11,496	14,279	15,336	17,642	2.83	15.04
Korea, Dem. People's Republic of	407	343	1,080				
Korea, Republic of	43,750	38,551	42,551	44,810	45,489	7.29	1.52
Macao, China	23	11	10				
Taiwan, Province of China	1,412	1,090	1,242				
South-East Asia	**3,799**	**3,629**	**4,273**	**600**	**919**	**0.15**	**53.17**
Brunei Darussalam		7	2				
Cambodia	46	85	34				
Indonesia	226	204	198	600	919	0.15	53.17
Lao People's Democratic Republic	93	93	66				
Malaysia	882	853	927				
Myanmar	5	7	8				
Philippines	514	607	828				
Singapore	935	931	1,173				
Thailand	422	447	603				
Viet Nam	676	395	434				
Australasia	**5,432**	**4,457**	**6,353**	**9,040**	**10,560**	**1.69**	**16.81**
Australia	4,491	3,741	5,471	7,981	9,348	1.50	17.13
New Zealand	941	716	882	1,059	1,212	0.19	14.45
Melanesia	**30**	**40**	**29**				
Fiji	18	23	15				
Papua New Guinea	10	11	12				
Solomon Islands	2	6	1				
Vanuatu			1				
Micronesia	**3**						
Kiribati	2						

Yearbook of Tourism Statistics, Data 2008 – 2012, 2014 Edition

MONGOLIA

2. Arrivals of non-resident visitors at national borders, by nationality

	2008	2009	2010	2011	2012	Market share 2012	% Change 2012-2011
Micronesia, Federated States of	1						
Polynesia	**11**	**6**	**10**				
American Samoa	7		2				
Samoa	1	2	5				
Tonga	3	4	3				
EUROPE	**161,031**	**154,374**	**177,256**	**143,555**	**127,949**	**20.51**	**-10.87**
Central/Eastern Europe	**121,809**	**119,072**	**136,065**	**114,145**	**98,485**	**15.79**	**-13.72**
Armenia	178	120	75				
Azerbaijan	147	77	78				
Belarus	237	191	182				
Bulgaria	103	90	124				
Czech Republic	942	826	860				
Estonia	42	36	91				
Georgia	65	50	75				
Hungary	292	289	337				
Kazakhstan	5,493	5,094	5,792	8,140	10,697	1.71	31.41
Kyrgyzstan	345	209	242				
Latvia	32	28	45				
Lithuania	71	10	79				
Poland	1,343	1,058	1,170				
Republic of Moldova	58	42	40				
Romania	63	85	110				
Russian Federation	110,955	109,391	125,543	104,916	86,584	13.88	-17.47
Slovakia	202	199	186				
Tajikistan	114	112	30				
Turkmenistan	5	2	4				
Ukraine	967	978	824	1,089	1,204	0.19	10.56
Uzbekistan	155	185	178				
Northern Europe	**11,961**	**10,365**	**10,818**	**9,669**	**9,560**	**1.53**	**-1.13**
Denmark	918	662	676	734	733	0.12	-0.14
Finland	827	862	949				
Iceland	32	25	18				
Ireland	685	510	492				
Norway	791	744	823				
Sweden	1,900	1,667	1,632	1,499	1,458	0.23	-2.74
United Kingdom	6,808	5,895	6,228	7,436	7,369	1.18	-0.90
Southern Europe	**3,215**	**3,097**	**4,833**				
Albania	10	4	15				
Andorra	2	3	2				
Bosnia and Herzegovina	57	18	28				
Croatia	73	50	69				
Greece	94	95	126				
Italy	2,468	2,417	2,819				
Malta	8	4	9				
Portugal	261	278	192				
Serbia and Montenegro	39	60	60				
Slovenia	167	154	154				
Spain			1,340				
TFYR of Macedonia	36	14	19				
Western Europe	**22,781**	**20,693**	**23,576**	**19,741**	**19,904**	**3.19**	**0.83**
Austria	1,226	1,113	1,122				
Belgium	1,007	826	966				
France	6,714	6,737	7,543	7,708	7,716	1.24	0.10
Germany	8,085	6,995	8,220	8,750	9,150	1.47	4.57
Liechtenstein	6	10					
Luxembourg	83	37	78				
Netherlands	3,267	2,791	3,248	3,283	3,038	0.49	-7.46

487

MONGOLIA

2. Arrivals of non-resident visitors at national borders, by nationality

	2008	2009	2010	2011	2012	Market share 2012	% Change 2012-2011
Switzerland	2,393	2,184	2,399				
East Mediterranean Europe	**1,265**	**1,147**	**1,964**				
Cyprus	15	6	11				
Israel	645	604	759				
Turkey	605	537	1,194				
MIDDLE EAST	**584**	**612**	**619**				
Bahrain	2	3	9				
Egypt	43	37	34				
Iraq	13	10	18				
Jordan	13	20	81				
Kuwait	203	107	233				
Lebanon		20	26				
Libya			3				
Oman			8				
Palestine	3	2	2				
Qatar	134	223	39				
Saudi Arabia	63	49	34				
Syrian Arab Republic	82	104	102				
United Arab Emirates	10	19	11				
Yemen	18	18	19				
SOUTH ASIA	**1,370**	**1,447**	**1,597**	**1,611**	**1,546**	**0.25**	**-4.03**
Afghanistan	18	38	26				
Bangladesh	66	91	84				
Bhutan	18	11	31				
India	893	952	949	1,611	1,546	0.25	-4.03
Iran, Islamic Republic of	57	63	219				
Maldives	2	7	5				
Nepal	126	98	98				
Pakistan	109	117	116				
Sri Lanka	81	70	69				
NOT SPECIFIED	**1,776**	**4,840**	**16**	**43,012**	**35,227**	**5.65**	**-18.10**
Other countries of the World	1,776	4,840	16	43,012	35,227	5.65	-18.10

488

MONTENEGRO

3. Arrivals of non-resident tourists in hotels and similar establishments, by nationality

	2008	2009	2010	2011	2012	Market share 2012	% Change 2012-2011
TOTAL	566,454	467,650	485,780	523,631	557,401	100.00	6.45
AMERICAS	8,525	7,694	8,655	8,158	9,494	1.70	16.38
North America	8,525	7,694	8,655	8,158	9,494	1.70	16.38
Canada	1,317	1,310	1,500	1,709	2,107	0.38	23.29
United States of America	7,208	6,384	7,155	6,449	7,387	1.33	14.54
EAST ASIA AND THE PACIFIC	2,669	2,222	3,946	3,980	4,582	0.82	15.13
North-East Asia	665	510	790	1,200	1,464	0.26	22.00
Japan	665	510	790	1,200	1,464	0.26	22.00
Australasia	2,004	1,712	3,156	2,780	3,118	0.56	12.16
Australia	1,639	1,411	1,626	2,392	2,584	0.46	8.03
New Zealand	365	301	1,530	388	534	0.10	37.63
EUROPE	550,983	452,663	466,751	502,089	529,154	94.93	5.39
Central/Eastern Europe	140,127	108,438	136,046	156,128	180,058	32.30	15.33
Belarus	811	766	889	1,121	2,153	0.39	92.06
Bulgaria	4,185	4,787	4,337	4,489	5,241	0.94	16.75
Czech Republic	18,529	11,309	11,735	14,321	16,390	2.94	14.45
Estonia	413	217	928	204	526	0.09	157.84
Hungary	8,684	7,417	8,548	8,336	8,506	1.53	2.04
Latvia	536	171	551	217	448	0.08	106.45
Lithuania	930	927	1,027	1,080	1,266	0.23	17.22
Poland	7,554	11,003	13,568	18,737	23,230	4.17	23.98
Romania	2,499	5,632	7,722	9,321	10,495	1.88	12.60
Russian Federation	79,137	56,226	73,981	83,055	90,656	16.26	9.15
Slovakia	5,888	4,212	5,049	5,644	5,793	1.04	2.64
Ukraine	10,961	5,771	7,711	9,603	15,354	2.75	59.89
Northern Europe	27,522	26,800	27,746	27,815	27,325	4.90	-1.76
Denmark	1,058	943	1,150	1,076	1,312	0.24	21.93
Finland	1,916	1,632	1,469	1,591	1,399	0.25	-12.07
Iceland	260	179	397	188	256	0.05	36.17
Ireland	3,240	1,404	1,474	1,333	1,528	0.27	14.63
Norway	3,396	3,390	3,462	3,638	3,133	0.56	-13.88
Sweden	5,232	7,128	7,077	6,927	6,003	1.08	-13.34
United Kingdom	12,420	12,124	12,717	13,062	13,694	2.46	4.84
Southern Europe	315,239	245,089	229,371	226,106	224,952	40.36	-0.51
Albania	17,003	16,377	17,205	17,536	17,427	3.13	-0.62
Bosnia and Herzegovina	26,772	24,060	22,885	22,504	21,495	3.86	-4.48
Croatia	11,684	12,103	12,808	12,058	12,851	2.31	6.58
Greece	3,088	2,937	3,346	3,975	3,340	0.60	-15.97
Italy	16,804	18,136	19,695	25,064	23,180	4.16	-7.52
Portugal	512	460	571	883	763	0.14	-13.59
Serbia (*)	208,259	143,198	128,160	121,344	123,197	22.10	1.53
Slovenia	16,935	16,683	15,578	14,048	14,456	2.59	2.90
Spain	1,733	1,497	2,336	2,060	2,039	0.37	-1.02
TFYR of Macedonia	12,449	9,638	6,787	6,634	6,204	1.11	-6.48
Western Europe	59,242	51,040	55,249	60,481	68,675	12.32	13.55
Austria	14,678	6,835	7,125	8,264	9,225	1.66	11.63
Belgium	6,730	5,359	5,584	5,571	5,165	0.93	-7.29
France	17,651	19,060	21,091	23,546	27,266	4.89	15.80
Germany	14,997	14,177	13,853	16,507	19,263	3.46	16.70
Luxembourg	209	708	240	279	523	0.09	87.46
Netherlands	2,221	2,356	2,281	2,521	2,671	0.48	5.95
Switzerland	2,756	2,545	5,075	3,793	4,562	0.82	20.27
East Mediterranean Europe	6,571	13,819	15,979	18,752	23,506	4.22	25.35
Israel	4,448	11,003	9,875	11,013	11,419	2.05	3.69
Turkey	2,123	2,816	6,104	7,739	12,087	2.17	56.18

Yearbook of Tourism Statistics, Data 2008 – 2012, 2014 Edition

MONTENEGRO

3. Arrivals of non-resident tourists in hotels and similar establishments, by nationality

	2008	2009	2010	2011	2012	Market share 2012	% Change 2012-2011
Other Europe	**2,282**	**7,477**	**2,360**	**12,807**	**4,638**	**0.83**	**-63.79**
Other countries of Europe	2,282	7,477	2,360	12,807	4,638	0.83	-63.79
NOT SPECIFIED	**4,277**	**5,071**	**6,428**	**9,404**	**14,171**	**2.54**	**50.69**
Other countries of the World	4,277	5,071	6,428	9,404	14,171	2.54	50.69

Yearbook of Tourism Statistics, Data 2008 – 2012, 2014 Edition

MONTENEGRO

4. Arrivals of non-resident tourists in all types of accommodation establishments, by nationality

	2008	2009	2010	2011	2012	Market share 2012	% Change 2012-2011
TOTAL	1,030,825	1,043,933	1,087,794	1,201,099	1,264,163	100.00	5.25
AMERICAS	9,084	8,255	10,622	12,661	13,136	1.04	3.75
North America	9,084	8,255	10,622	12,661	13,136	1.04	3.75
Canada	1,597	1,557	1,853	2,087	2,912	0.23	39.53
United States of America	7,487	6,698	8,769	10,574	10,224	0.81	-3.31
EAST ASIA AND THE PACIFIC	2,839	2,426	3,241	4,918	6,392	0.51	29.97
North-East Asia	700	515	863	1,431	1,748	0.14	22.15
Japan	700	515	863	1,431	1,748	0.14	22.15
Australasia	2,139	1,911	2,378	3,487	4,644	0.37	33.18
Australia	1,765	1,597	1,909	2,962	4,032	0.32	36.12
New Zealand	374	314	469	525	612	0.05	16.57
EUROPE	1,013,406	1,028,084	1,066,715	1,171,855	1,226,970	97.06	4.70
Central/Eastern Europe	244,677	260,417	293,303	415,839	442,111	34.97	6.32
Belarus	3,448	1,480	6,400	7,706	20,504	1.62	166.08
Bulgaria	4,541	6,163	5,604	5,237	7,181	0.57	37.12
Czech Republic	29,837	25,928	24,085	24,702	26,847	2.12	8.68
Estonia	1,963	276	1,162	414	1,246	0.10	200.97
Hungary	29,559	32,631	28,838	17,264	15,857	1.25	-8.15
Latvia	2,667	1,662	741	500	1,031	0.08	106.20
Lithuania	3,505	2,583	4,261	5,046	5,390	0.43	6.82
Poland	13,054	15,039	25,381	39,544	39,131	3.10	-1.04
Romania	3,133	7,895	14,471	22,923	23,108	1.83	0.81
Russian Federation	117,680	145,557	150,194	244,924	243,647	19.27	-0.52
Slovakia	10,117	8,908	7,699	10,729	9,427	0.75	-12.14
Ukraine	25,173	12,295	24,467	36,850	48,742	3.86	32.27
Northern Europe	34,207	31,626	42,617	49,570	43,142	3.41	-12.97
Denmark	1,387	1,191	1,549	1,531	2,580	0.20	68.52
Finland	2,058	1,710	1,579	2,211	1,916	0.15	-13.34
Iceland	290	192	425	634	423	0.03	-33.28
Ireland	3,262	1,493	3,424	4,204	3,479	0.28	-17.25
Norway	6,347	5,156	6,754	8,657	6,267	0.50	-27.61
Sweden	7,928	7,776	8,390	8,429	9,108	0.72	8.06
United Kingdom	12,935	14,108	20,496	23,904	19,369	1.53	-18.97
Southern Europe	645,213	590,011	567,447	533,952	570,445	45.12	6.83
Albania	30,540	39,252	37,601	27,388	27,428	2.17	0.15
Bosnia and Herzegovina	98,822	101,874	103,025	97,497	95,271	7.54	-2.28
Croatia	18,624	15,677	17,497	20,195	24,015	1.90	18.92
Greece	3,380	2,970	3,487	4,373	3,886	0.31	-11.14
Italy	31,341	42,549	39,987	34,403	36,113	2.86	4.97
Portugal	518	8,466	808	5,504	959	0.08	-82.58
Serbia (*)	412,886	338,893	314,836	299,617	337,245	26.68	12.56
Slovenia	17,890	18,891	22,472	20,027	18,463	1.46	-7.81
Spain	1,776	1,528	3,317	2,343	2,501	0.20	6.74
TFYR of Macedonia	29,436	19,911	24,417	22,605	24,564	1.94	8.67
Western Europe	79,767	79,661	100,388	96,925	103,458	8.18	6.74
Austria	17,864	12,204	12,454	12,994	15,865	1.25	22.09
Belgium	7,172	7,473	8,146	7,201	5,983	0.47	-16.91
France	24,474	33,080	42,099	28,336	33,122	2.62	16.89
Germany	22,297	18,329	25,381	33,427	32,648	2.58	-2.33
Luxembourg	241	1,386	2,469	862	728	0.06	-15.55
Netherlands	4,629	4,225	3,468	6,647	5,669	0.45	-14.71
Switzerland	3,090	2,964	6,371	7,458	9,443	0.75	26.62
East Mediterranean Europe	6,937	14,054	16,841	30,671	25,590	2.02	-16.57
Israel	4,599	11,142	10,595	11,799	12,393	0.98	5.03
Turkey	2,338	2,912	6,246	18,872	13,197	1.04	-30.07

MONTENEGRO

4. Arrivals of non-resident tourists in all types of accommodation establishments, by nationality

	2008	2009	2010	2011	2012	Market share 2012	% Change 2012-2011
Other Europe	**2,605**	**52,315**	**46,119**	**44,898**	**42,224**	**3.34**	**-5.96**
Other countries of Europe	2,605	52,315	46,119	44,898	42,224	3.34	-5.96
NOT SPECIFIED	**5,496**	**5,168**	**7,216**	**11,665**	**17,665**	**1.40**	**51.44**
Other countries of the World	5,496	5,168	7,216	11,665	17,665	1.40	51.44

Yearbook of Tourism Statistics, Data 2008 – 2012, 2014 Edition

MONTENEGRO

5. Overnight stays of non-resident tourists in hotels and similar establishments, by nationality

		2008	2009	2010	2011	2012	Market share 2012	% Change 2012-2011
TOTAL		3,234,096	2,388,133	2,478,239	2,647,592	2,702,819	100.00	2.09
AMERICAS		22,988	23,107	26,188	22,764	25,796	0.95	13.32
North America		22,988	23,107	26,188	22,764	25,796	0.95	13.32
Canada		4,217	3,904	4,474	5,410	5,810	0.21	7.39
United States of America		18,771	19,203	21,714	17,354	19,986	0.74	15.17
EAST ASIA AND THE PACIFIC		6,786	5,650	6,789	8,448	10,371	0.38	22.76
North-East Asia		1,879	1,274	1,570	1,863	2,586	0.10	38.81
Japan		1,879	1,274	1,570	1,863	2,586	0.10	38.81
Australasia		4,907	4,376	5,219	6,585	7,785	0.29	18.22
Australia		4,163	3,688	4,402	5,718	6,645	0.25	16.21
New Zealand		744	688	817	867	1,140	0.04	31.49
EUROPE		3,192,988	2,344,820	2,426,615	2,591,984	2,638,548	97.62	1.80
Central/Eastern Europe		1,016,697	691,409	873,732	1,031,655	1,153,493	42.68	11.81
Belarus		7,482	5,772	5,850	7,975	16,032	0.59	101.03
Bulgaria		13,782	13,126	10,393	14,252	13,792	0.51	-3.23
Czech Republic		165,094	74,237	73,549	93,548	108,887	4.03	16.40
Estonia		1,921	786	6,330	595	1,325	0.05	122.69
Hungary		40,405	31,177	36,354	38,862	34,549	1.28	-11.10
Latvia		2,039	447	1,994	674	1,586	0.06	135.31
Lithuania		2,660	2,852	2,894	3,146	3,710	0.14	17.93
Poland		47,539	42,923	46,968	81,995	94,093	3.48	14.75
Romania		10,506	23,243	39,380	46,193	43,191	1.60	-6.50
Russian Federation		601,557	428,511	571,981	644,972	691,089	25.57	7.15
Slovakia		44,383	27,401	28,877	36,013	41,589	1.54	15.48
Ukraine		79,329	40,934	49,162	63,430	103,650	3.83	63.41
Northern Europe		148,401	135,368	134,194	130,969	122,557	4.53	-6.42
Denmark		3,294	3,011	4,279	3,093	4,210	0.16	36.11
Finland		10,924	7,023	5,410	6,818	5,091	0.19	-25.33
Iceland		877	371	1,599	576	672	0.02	16.67
Ireland		12,138	5,237	5,073	5,483	4,947	0.18	-9.78
Norway		15,817	14,585	15,277	17,258	13,109	0.49	-24.04
Sweden		34,222	39,607	38,576	36,036	28,598	1.06	-20.64
United Kingdom		71,129	65,534	63,980	61,705	65,930	2.44	6.85
Southern Europe		1,680,297	1,221,678	1,097,605	1,057,412	997,660	36.91	-5.65
Albania		48,040	37,464	43,006	42,293	44,324	1.64	4.80
Bosnia and Herzegovina		133,537	122,548	106,738	100,511	96,225	3.56	-4.26
Croatia		31,887	29,637	31,594	27,673	28,831	1.07	4.18
Greece		9,866	5,258	5,981	6,485	6,914	0.26	6.62
Italy		53,432	59,227	62,686	78,588	69,962	2.59	-10.98
Portugal		1,726	1,329	1,877	3,821	2,466	0.09	-35.46
Serbia	(*)	1,279,062	854,589	760,121	722,192	668,541	24.73	-7.43
Slovenia		67,970	68,335	58,540	50,581	57,588	2.13	13.85
Spain		4,831	4,393	5,906	4,887	4,835	0.18	-1.06
TFYR of Macedonia		49,946	38,898	21,156	20,381	17,974	0.67	-11.81
Western Europe		324,339	241,266	226,532	290,992	314,012	11.62	7.91
Austria		79,072	19,655	22,242	27,062	31,152	1.15	15.11
Belgium		45,007	32,337	32,645	33,272	27,627	1.02	-16.97
France		96,379	91,804	100,579	121,896	133,768	4.95	9.74
Germany		85,446	76,936	42,145	87,427	95,736	3.54	9.50
Luxembourg		876	3,732	749	1,037	1,577	0.06	52.07
Netherlands		7,439	7,871	6,028	7,010	8,367	0.31	19.36
Switzerland		10,120	8,931	22,144	13,288	15,785	0.58	18.79
East Mediterranean Europe		13,803	25,003	26,419	31,428	36,671	1.36	16.68
Israel		8,505	19,311	16,509	18,862	19,733	0.73	4.62
Turkey		5,298	5,692	9,910	12,566	16,938	0.63	34.79

MONTENEGRO

5. Overnight stays of non-resident tourists in hotels and similar establishments, by nationality

	2008	2009	2010	2011	2012	Market share 2012	% Change 2012-2011
Other Europe	**9,451**	**30,096**	**68,133**	**49,528**	**14,155**	**0.52**	**-71.42**
Other countries of Europe	9,451	30,096	68,133	49,528	14,155	0.52	-71.42
NOT SPECIFIED	**11,334**	**14,556**	**18,647**	**24,396**	**28,104**	**1.04**	**15.20**
Other countries of the World	11,334	14,556	18,647	24,396	28,104	1.04	15.20

MONTENEGRO

6. Overnight stays of non-resident tourists in all types of accommodation establishments, by nationality

	2008	2009	2010	2011	2012	Market share 2012	% Change 2012-2011
TOTAL	6,964,755	6,694,514	6,977,860	7,818,803	8,143,007	100.00	4.15
AMERICAS	28,072	28,765	41,051	54,025	52,414	0.64	-2.98
North America	28,072	28,765	41,051	54,025	52,414	0.64	-2.98
Canada	6,668	6,120	7,231	8,739	11,079	0.14	26.78
United States of America	21,404	22,645	33,820	45,286	41,335	0.51	-8.72
EAST ASIA AND THE PACIFIC	8,135	7,259	10,266	16,248	23,841	0.29	46.73
North-East Asia	2,149	1,288	2,050	3,025	3,829	0.05	26.58
Japan	2,149	1,288	2,050	3,025	3,829	0.05	26.58
Australasia	5,986	5,971	8,216	13,223	20,012	0.25	51.34
Australia	5,189	5,113	6,675	11,141	18,395	0.23	65.11
New Zealand	797	858	1,541	2,082	1,617	0.02	-22.33
EUROPE	6,909,950	6,642,906	6,901,660	7,706,203	8,016,866	98.45	4.03
Central/Eastern Europe	1,777,405	1,818,803	2,059,195	2,870,291	3,182,304	39.08	10.87
Belarus	27,683	14,187	45,636	52,935	134,914	1.66	154.87
Bulgaria	16,533	23,307	18,967	18,849	25,002	0.31	32.64
Czech Republic	242,167	171,643	165,050	171,107	174,634	2.14	2.06
Estonia	10,382	1,350	8,857	2,641	5,956	0.07	125.52
Hungary	187,694	205,259	183,031	98,577	79,743	0.98	-19.11
Latvia	14,722	11,371	2,966	2,683	4,684	0.06	74.58
Lithuania	21,800	18,088	27,592	32,329	34,139	0.42	5.60
Poland	85,450	123,557	84,053	214,927	196,888	2.42	-8.39
Romania	15,778	38,061	84,838	142,281	118,313	1.45	-16.85
Russian Federation	897,921	1,060,458	1,217,978	1,791,616	1,988,533	24.42	10.99
Slovakia	76,253	61,841	52,353	71,168	65,716	0.81	-7.66
Ukraine	181,022	89,681	167,874	271,178	353,782	4.34	30.46
Northern Europe	223,660	190,487	255,749	302,763	241,045	2.96	-20.38
Denmark	6,986	5,371	7,606	6,717	11,635	0.14	73.22
Finland	12,165	7,777	6,370	10,771	8,382	0.10	-22.18
Iceland	1,150	454	1,795	3,303	1,514	0.02	-54.16
Ireland	12,340	6,150	18,458	26,199	18,397	0.23	-29.78
Norway	60,257	43,620	55,550	66,008	47,487	0.58	-28.06
Sweden	55,418	47,696	50,542	50,219	51,401	0.63	2.35
United Kingdom	75,344	79,419	115,428	139,546	102,229	1.26	-26.74
Southern Europe	4,400,675	3,846,545	3,575,364	3,582,990	3,714,245	45.61	3.66
Albania	154,229	191,826	189,074	162,323	159,811	1.96	-1.55
Bosnia and Herzegovina	805,919	778,439	731,633	750,341	679,317	8.34	-9.47
Croatia	82,365	59,767	66,161	89,876	107,786	1.32	19.93
Greece	12,073	5,498	6,794	9,106	10,753	0.13	18.09
Italy	151,376	225,976	199,617	143,938	151,366	1.86	5.16
Portugal	1,747	42,710	3,381	31,572	3,712	0.05	-88.24
Serbia (*)	2,878,395	2,298,717	2,097,051	2,109,159	2,353,370	28.90	11.58
Slovenia	79,073	84,578	106,016	136,108	82,380	1.01	-39.47
Spain	5,158	4,504	11,676	6,483	7,281	0.09	12.31
TFYR of Macedonia	230,340	154,530	163,961	144,084	158,469	1.95	9.98
Western Europe	478,548	458,024	601,875	507,588	532,595	6.54	4.93
Austria	102,300	57,588	58,785	59,475	71,006	0.87	19.39
Belgium	48,274	46,834	48,063	43,677	31,745	0.39	-27.32
France	143,125	193,983	233,959	152,395	167,215	2.05	9.72
Germany	137,146	109,893	151,843	182,724	184,984	2.27	1.24
Luxembourg	1,128	10,192	13,947	4,180	2,716	0.03	-35.02
Netherlands	33,658	27,647	66,161	31,472	33,371	0.41	6.03
Switzerland	12,917	11,887	29,117	33,665	41,558	0.51	23.45
East Mediterranean Europe	17,155	26,407	30,739	53,884	48,230	0.59	-10.49
Israel	9,313	20,163	19,729	22,815	24,209	0.30	6.11
Turkey	7,842	6,244	11,010	31,069	24,021	0.29	-22.68

Yearbook of Tourism Statistics, Data 2008 – 2012, 2014 Edition

6. Overnight stays of non-resident tourists in all types of accommodation establishments, by nationality

	2008	2009	2010	2011	2012	Market share 2012	% Change 2012-2011
Other Europe	12,507	302,640	378,738	388,687	298,447	3.67	-23.22
Other countries of Europe	12,507	302,640	378,738	388,687	298,447	3.67	-23.22
NOT SPECIFIED	18,598	15,584	24,883	42,327	49,886	0.61	17.86
Other countries of the World	18,598	15,584	24,883	42,327	49,886	0.61	17.86

Yearbook of Tourism Statistics, Data 2008 – 2012, 2014 Editio

MONTSERRAT

1. Arrivals of non-resident tourists at national borders, by country of residence

	2008	2009	2010	2011	2012	Market share 2012	% Change 2012-2011
TOTAL	7,360	6,324	5,981	5,395			
AMERICAS	4,989	4,252	4,353	3,749			
Caribbean	2,658	2,267	2,259	1,881			
All countries of the Caribbean	2,658	2,267	2,259	1,881			
North America	2,317	1,973	2,069	1,846			
Canada	395	367	404	320			
United States of America	1,922	1,606	1,665	1,526			
Other Americas	14	12	25	22			
Other countries of the Americas	14	12	25	22			
EAST ASIA AND THE PACIFIC		3	1	14			
North-East Asia		3	1	14			
Japan		3	1	14			
EUROPE	2,333	2,044	1,573	1,535			
Northern Europe	2,163	1,870	1,385	1,333			
Sweden	11	6	5	4			
United Kingdom	2,152	1,864	1,380	1,329			
Southern Europe	21	31	21	27			
Italy	17	18	11	19			
Spain	4	13	10	8			
Western Europe	116	94	114	117			
Belgium	10	12	13	6			
France	48	47	51	60			
Germany	32	18	30	31			
Netherlands	8	5	1	7			
Switzerland	18	12	19	13			
Other Europe	33	49	53	58			
Other countries of Europe	33	49	53	58			
NOT SPECIFIED	38	25	54	97			
Other countries of the World	38	25	54	97			

Yearbook of Tourism Statistics, Data 2008 – 2012, 2014 Edition

MONTSERRAT

2. Arrivals of non-resident visitors at national borders, by country of residence

	2008	2009	2010	2011	2012	Market share 2012	% Change 2012-2011
TOTAL	**8,319**	**7,335**	**7,707**	**7,392**			
AMERICAS	**5,724**	**5,081**	**5,540**	**5,078**			
Caribbean	**3,239**	**2,950**	**3,119**	**2,778**			
All countries of the Caribbean	3,239	2,950	3,119	2,778			
North America	**2,470**	**2,112**	**2,384**	**2,270**			
Canada	428	378	471	396			
United States of America	2,042	1,734	1,913	1,874			
Other Americas	**15**	**19**	**37**	**30**			
Other countries of the Americas	15	19	37	30			
EUROPE	**2,547**	**2,221**	**2,102**	**2,102**			
Northern Europe	**2,304**	**1,991**	**1,848**	**1,851**			
United Kingdom	2,304	1,991	1,848	1,851			
Other Europe	**243**	**230**	**254**	**251**			
Other countries of Europe	243	230	254	251			
NOT SPECIFIED	**48**	**33**	**65**	**212**			
Other countries of the World	48	33	65	212			

Yearbook of Tourism Statistics, Data 2008 – 2012, 2014 Edition

MOROCCO

1. Arrivals of non-resident tourists at national borders, by nationality

	2008	2009	2010	2011	2012	Market share 2012	% Change 2012-2011
TOTAL	7,878,639	8,341,237	9,288,338	9,342,133	9,375,156	100.00	0.35
AFRICA	213,611	222,879	255,564	298,622	316,252	3.37	5.90
East Africa	4,725	4,046	4,478	6,785	6,465	0.07	-4.72
Burundi	286	137	193	189	314	0.00	66.14
Comoros	242	324	470	411	401	0.00	-2.43
Djibouti	839	381	435	361	452	0.00	25.21
Eritrea	101	90	83	116	121	0.00	4.31
Ethiopia	370	479	502	549	532	0.01	-3.10
Kenya	714	883	874	870	1,067	0.01	22.64
Madagascar	350	348	359	406	396	0.00	-2.46
Malawi	66	122	75	27	77	0.00	185.19
Mauritius	518	540	667	2,527	1,253	0.01	-50.42
Mozambique	39	47	53	101	155	0.00	53.47
Rwanda	155	99	110	250	722	0.01	188.80
Seychelles	130	34	57	60	73	0.00	21.67
Somalia	128	100	77	235	149	0.00	-36.60
Uganda	413	138	153	173	191	0.00	10.40
United Republic of Tanzania	122	131	118	178	200	0.00	12.36
Zambia	104	58	88	192	178	0.00	-7.29
Zimbabwe	148	135	164	140	184	0.00	31.43
Central Africa	17,017	19,587	21,994	34,109	26,257	0.28	-23.02
Angola	834	1,426	2,926	4,231	2,378	0.03	-43.80
Cameroon	3,591	3,703	3,869	3,443	3,175	0.03	-7.78
Central African Republic	393	375	855	937	776	0.01	-17.18
Chad	329	268	413	430	513	0.01	19.30
Congo	5,799	6,905	7,906	10,228	12,210	0.13	19.38
Democratic Republic of the Congo	1,099	990	592	1,043	446	0.00	-57.24
Equatorial Guinea	1,321	1,993	1,937	10,005	2,939	0.03	-70.62
Gabon	3,651	3,927	3,496	3,792	3,820	0.04	0.74
North Africa	92,349	95,241	106,537	124,339	137,198	1.46	10.34
Algeria	58,650	59,512	68,183	80,741	93,195	0.99	15.42
Sudan	1,631	1,916	2,019	2,487	2,353	0.03	-5.39
Tunisia	32,068	33,813	36,335	41,111	41,650	0.44	1.31
Southern Africa	4,231	3,765	4,739	4,117	5,362	0.06	30.24
Botswana	107	76	56	95	111	0.00	16.84
Lesotho	57		1	27	37	0.00	37.04
Namibia	95	90	53	69	88	0.00	27.54
South Africa	3,701	3,585	4,547	3,887	5,089	0.05	30.92
Swaziland	271	14	82	39	37	0.00	-5.13
West Africa	95,289	100,240	117,816	129,272	140,970	1.50	9.05
Benin	1,302	1,237	1,369	1,234	1,265	0.01	2.51
Burkina Faso	1,936	2,434	2,742	2,589	2,870	0.03	10.85
Cape Verde	374	456	139	279	255	0.00	-8.60
Côte d'Ivoire	9,158	9,795	12,315	14,666	14,024	0.15	-4.38
Gambia	898	649	708	959	821	0.01	-14.39
Ghana	784	894	781	871	1,061	0.01	21.81
Guinea	9,796	7,756	14,297	10,005	12,042	0.13	20.36
Guinea-Bissau	2,624	4,176	1,085	3,667	517	0.01	-85.90
Liberia	383	370	398	347	664	0.01	91.35
Mali	9,343	10,483	12,441	15,225	16,436	0.18	7.95
Mauritania	29,076	25,267	30,576	34,528	39,035	0.42	13.05
Niger	4,025	4,854	4,933	5,713	6,465	0.07	13.16
Nigeria	873	1,685	1,592	2,025	1,596	0.02	-21.19
Senegal	23,581	28,878	32,969	36,067	42,785	0.46	18.63
Sierra Leone	350	364	439	323	295	0.00	-8.67
Togo	786	942	1,032	774	839	0.01	8.40

Yearbook of Tourism Statistics, Data 2008 – 2012, 2014 Edition

MOROCCO

1. Arrivals of non-resident tourists at national borders, by nationality

	2008	2009	2010	2011	2012	Market share 2012	% Change 2012-2011
AMERICAS	201,867	214,563	250,874	239,497	257,793	2.75	7.64
Caribbean	1,183	1,673	1,464	2,092	3,552	0.04	69.79
Bahamas	23	47	45	86	89	0.00	3.49
Barbados	14	101	163	793	1,854	0.02	133.80
Bermuda	31	142	10	13	17	0.00	30.77
Cuba	263	410	252	176	187	0.00	6.25
Dominica	104	199	260	207	277	0.00	33.82
Haiti	87	51	296	283	191	0.00	-32.51
Jamaica	421	401	129	124	574	0.01	362.90
Puerto Rico	188	97	231	193	177	0.00	-8.29
Trinidad and Tobago	52	225	78	217	186	0.00	-14.29
Central America	860	1,376	3,620	1,301	1,515	0.02	16.45
Belize	2	194	38	9	307	0.00	3,311.11
Costa Rica	236	271	315	307	346	0.00	12.70
El Salvador	175	231	189	187	170	0.00	-9.09
Guatemala	188	330	278	421	200	0.00	-52.49
Honduras	139	147	2,558	162	280	0.00	72.84
Nicaragua	39	76	72	66	83	0.00	25.76
Panama	81	127	170	149	129	0.00	-13.42
North America	173,371	181,410	210,948	200,420	215,683	2.30	7.62
Canada	56,231	54,789	67,925	63,237	69,206	0.74	9.44
Mexico	6,362	5,477	7,647	6,756	6,432	0.07	-4.80
United States of America	110,778	121,144	135,376	130,427	140,045	1.49	7.37
South America	26,453	30,104	34,842	35,684	37,043	0.40	3.81
Argentina	7,219	8,077	9,615	8,447	10,062	0.11	19.12
Bolivia	202	252	263	287	317	0.00	10.45
Brazil	10,146	10,978	13,049	14,552	15,142	0.16	4.05
Chile	2,846	2,788	3,516	3,611	3,543	0.04	-1.88
Colombia	1,506	2,032	2,473	2,386	2,138	0.02	-10.39
Ecuador	460	622	555	630	515	0.01	-18.25
Guyana				3	5	0.00	66.67
Paraguay	97	155	197	163	191	0.00	17.18
Peru	1,105	1,724	2,164	1,960	1,672	0.02	-14.69
Suriname	77	48	59	250	50	0.00	-80.00
Uruguay	1,081	1,383	1,082	1,323	1,095	0.01	-17.23
Venezuela	1,714	2,045	1,869	2,072	2,313	0.02	11.63
EAST ASIA AND THE PACIFIC	76,127	77,415	98,995	87,370	112,571	1.20	28.84
North-East Asia	34,497	35,762	48,235	37,552	61,121	0.65	62.76
China	4,665	4,129	5,769	5,882	6,899	0.07	17.29
Hong Kong, China	1,794	1,154	1,340	1,066	1,968	0.02	84.62
Japan	15,607	19,149	24,366	22,861	30,306	0.32	32.57
Korea, Dem. People's Republic of	3	620	1	912			
Korea, Republic of	11,972	10,001	15,795	5,882	21,092	0.22	258.59
Taiwan, Province of China	456	709	964	949	856	0.01	-9.80
South-East Asia	16,202	16,452	20,873	21,260	23,459	0.25	10.34
Brunei Darussalam	37	64	50	76	100	0.00	31.58
Cambodia	12	25	76	202	92	0.00	-54.46
Indonesia	2,440	2,572	3,606	3,974	4,618	0.05	16.21
Malaysia	2,417	2,101	2,801	2,302	2,877	0.03	24.98
Myanmar	152	109	107	82	106	0.00	29.27
Philippines	6,317	7,989	10,170	10,697	11,486	0.12	7.38
Singapore	1,299	1,412	1,832	1,662	2,096	0.02	26.11
Thailand	1,967	1,838	1,986	1,951	1,708	0.02	-12.46
Viet Nam	1,561	342	245	314	376	0.00	19.75
Australasia	25,427	25,201	29,879	28,541	27,935	0.30	-2.12
Australia	21,467	20,531	24,690	23,502	22,812	0.24	-2.94
New Zealand	3,960	4,670	5,189	5,039	5,123	0.05	1.67

500

Yearbook of Tourism Statistics, Data 2008 – 2012, 2014 Editi

MOROCCO

1. Arrivals of non-resident tourists at national borders, by nationality

	2008	2009	2010	2011	2012	Market share 2012	% Change 2012-2011
Micronesia	1		8	17	56	0.00	229.41
Kiribati	1		8	17	56	0.00	229.41
EUROPE	3,563,990	3,623,479	4,143,648	4,137,156	4,105,231	43.79	-0.77
Central/Eastern Europe	87,214	91,795	117,094	123,972	120,935	1.29	-2.45
Armenia	87	244	96	279	541	0.01	93.91
Azerbaijan	201	384	334	237	209	0.00	-11.81
Belarus	1,226	264	360	446	477	0.01	6.95
Bulgaria	2,684	4,013	4,419	3,990	4,283	0.05	7.34
Czech Republic	4,708	5,685	5,647	10,435	11,729	0.13	12.40
Estonia	802	1,096	1,970	2,629	2,423	0.03	-7.84
Hungary	4,766	5,175	5,171	4,657	3,950	0.04	-15.18
Kazakhstan	175	218	225	225	300	0.00	33.33
Lithuania	1,926	2,093	2,753	3,644	2,871	0.03	-21.21
Poland	36,596	34,686	42,040	49,933	41,768	0.45	-16.35
Romania	9,372	10,974	11,834	13,172	12,386	0.13	-5.97
Russian Federation	16,220	19,114	32,460	22,620	29,644	0.32	31.05
Slovakia	2,869	3,387	5,026	7,013	5,834	0.06	-16.81
Ukraine	5,186	4,368	4,509	4,562	4,353	0.05	-4.58
Uzbekistan	396	94	250	130	167	0.00	28.46
Northern Europe	352,400	327,176	423,567	452,337	439,724	4.69	-2.79
Denmark	12,281	10,512	14,863	22,153	18,253	0.19	-17.60
Finland	10,727	8,874	6,045	5,263	5,658	0.06	7.51
Iceland	882	1,402	844	981	970	0.01	-1.12
Ireland	15,562	17,974	20,341	15,446	14,242	0.15	-7.79
Norway	11,399	10,934	15,255	21,847	17,469	0.19	-20.04
Sweden	26,787	24,535	28,159	34,506	25,785	0.28	-25.27
United Kingdom	274,762	252,945	338,060	352,141	357,347	3.81	1.48
Southern Europe	820,182	889,934	1,039,311	991,457	996,934	10.63	0.55
Albania	136	584	213	283	504	0.01	78.09
Andorra	647	872	563	676	2,008	0.02	197.04
Bosnia and Herzegovina	278	329	358	267	406	0.00	52.06
Croatia	1,299	1,598	2,141	1,922	1,422	0.02	-26.01
Greece	7,473	7,875	7,844	5,340	5,266	0.06	-1.39
Italy	163,315	177,915	233,224	211,405	196,186	2.09	-7.20
Malta	620	812	792	768	897	0.01	16.80
Portugal	47,055	53,079	63,077	72,995	54,194	0.58	-25.76
San Marino	73	40	59	43	38	0.00	-11.63
Serbia	726	824	1,111	997	1,323	0.01	32.70
Slovenia	2,762	2,897	3,274	3,429	3,614	0.04	5.40
Spain	595,279	642,817	726,540	693,255	730,882	7.80	5.43
TFYR of Macedonia	519	292	115	77	194	0.00	151.95
Western Europe	2,268,543	2,283,962	2,523,278	2,537,790	2,510,551	26.78	-1.07
Austria	15,901	13,581	17,731	13,956	14,758	0.16	5.75
Belgium	173,004	188,108	221,371	258,620	255,290	2.72	-1.29
France	1,707,055	1,699,201	1,827,453	1,775,961	1,769,710	18.88	-0.35
Germany	179,037	174,384	205,417	219,576	199,349	2.13	-9.21
Liechtenstein	202	210	103	112	258	0.00	130.36
Luxembourg	2,786	3,509	4,141	3,991	4,188	0.04	4.94
Monaco	175	294	344	317	297	0.00	-6.31
Netherlands	128,093	139,611	175,078	197,642	204,767	2.18	3.61
Switzerland	62,290	65,064	71,640	67,615	61,934	0.66	-8.40
East Mediterranean Europe	35,651	30,612	40,398	31,600	37,087	0.40	17.36
Cyprus	348	438	481	450	504	0.01	12.00
Israel	19,186	13,466	19,190	8,985	10,819	0.12	20.41
Turkey	16,117	16,708	20,727	22,165	25,764	0.27	16.24
MIDDLE EAST	127,486	134,659	142,091	152,326	198,387	2.12	30.24
Bahrain	2,781	2,956	3,028	2,870	3,188	0.03	11.08

Yearbook of Tourism Statistics, Data 2008 – 2012, 2014 Edition

MOROCCO

1. Arrivals of non-resident tourists at national borders, by nationality

	2008	2009	2010	2011	2012	Market share 2012	% Change 2012-2011
Egypt	16,977	16,614	16,543	13,689	18,417	0.20	34.54
Iraq	1,537	1,486	1,688	2,085	2,571	0.03	23.31
Jordan	4,614	4,907	4,945	4,877	5,338	0.06	9.45
Kuwait	7,562	9,131	9,111	12,649	15,669	0.17	23.88
Lebanon	7,510	6,835	7,332	6,337	6,665	0.07	5.18
Libya	16,026	17,174	20,456	18,037	45,400	0.48	151.70
Oman	4,409	4,076	4,305	3,777	5,718	0.06	51.39
Palestine	1,090	1,321	1,337	1,304	1,549	0.02	18.79
Qatar	2,882	2,732	2,976	3,183	4,190	0.04	31.64
Saudi Arabia	42,924	48,780	51,219	62,887	70,666	0.75	12.37
Syrian Arab Republic	5,309	4,505	4,782	4,342	4,587	0.05	5.64
United Arab Emirates	12,384	12,496	12,659	14,552	12,576	0.13	-13.58
Yemen	1,481	1,646	1,710	1,737	1,853	0.02	6.68
SOUTH ASIA	**11,901**	**11,753**	**12,242**	**12,486**	**14,417**	**0.15**	**15.47**
Afghanistan	150	123	143	330	697	0.01	111.21
Bangladesh	384	547	546	942	744	0.01	-21.02
India	6,363	6,995	7,936	7,640	9,343	0.10	22.29
Iran, Islamic Republic of	1,689	959	519	519	515	0.01	-0.77
Maldives	85	64	58	50	78	0.00	56.00
Nepal	195	212	272	289	353	0.00	22.15
Pakistan	2,068	2,343	2,157	2,172	2,080	0.02	-4.24
Sri Lanka	967	510	611	544	607	0.01	11.58
NOT SPECIFIED	**3,683,657**	**4,056,489**	**4,384,924**	**4,414,676**	**4,370,505**	**46.62**	**-1.00**
Other countries of the World	16,873	8,210	7,021	6,426	7,078	0.08	10.15
Nationals Residing Abroad	3,666,784	4,048,279	4,377,903	4,408,250	4,363,427	46.54	-1.02

Yearbook of Tourism Statistics, Data 2008 – 2012, 2014 Editio

MOROCCO

3. Arrivals of non-resident tourists in hotels and similar establishments, by nationality

		2008	2009	2010	2011	2012	Market share 2012	% Change 2012-2011
TOTAL	(*)	**3,824,214**	**3,669,087**	**4,077,535**	**3,455,696**	**3,569,611**	**100.00**	**3.30**
AFRICA		**99,724**	**101,948**	**117,966**	**133,845**	**140,390**	**3.93**	**4.89**
North Africa		**52,963**	**52,294**	**62,050**	**71,389**	**84,231**	**2.36**	**17.99**
Algeria		36,482	35,543	42,718	50,217	61,055	1.71	21.58
Tunisia		16,481	16,751	19,332	21,172	23,176	0.65	9.47
West Africa		**6,929**	**5,139**	**6,445**	**7,308**	**7,766**	**0.22**	**6.27**
Mauritania		6,929	5,139	6,445	7,308	7,766	0.22	6.27
Other Africa		**39,832**	**44,515**	**49,471**	**55,148**	**48,393**	**1.36**	**-12.25**
Other countries of Africa		39,832	44,515	49,471	55,148	48,393	1.36	-12.25
AMERICAS		**132,633**	**129,806**	**152,223**	**127,013**	**143,707**	**4.03**	**13.14**
North America		**132,633**	**129,806**	**152,223**	**127,013**	**143,707**	**4.03**	**13.14**
Canada		28,182	28,094	32,546	28,629	31,584	0.88	10.32
United States of America		104,451	101,712	119,677	98,384	112,123	3.14	13.96
EAST ASIA AND THE PACIFIC		**47,030**	**44,999**	**60,862**	**54,835**	**77,385**	**2.17**	**41.12**
North-East Asia		**47,030**	**44,999**	**60,862**	**54,835**	**77,385**	**2.17**	**41.12**
Japan		47,030	44,999	60,862	54,835	77,385	2.17	41.12
EUROPE		**3,038,577**	**2,913,714**	**3,164,721**	**2,634,037**	**2,615,669**	**73.28**	**-0.70**
Central/Eastern Europe		**60,619**	**71,921**	**90,785**	**90,224**	**93,733**	**2.63**	**3.89**
Commonwealth Independent States		60,619	71,921	90,785	90,224	93,733	2.63	3.89
Northern Europe		**296,156**	**255,464**	**333,058**	**327,033**	**307,881**	**8.63**	**-5.86**
Denmark		5,873	5,235	7,225	10,321	7,810	0.22	-24.33
Finland		7,006	5,920	2,368	2,487	2,363	0.07	-4.99
Norway		6,932	4,570	6,892	10,833	7,437	0.21	-31.35
Sweden		17,941	15,173	17,089	18,237	11,336	0.32	-37.84
United Kingdom		258,404	224,566	299,484	285,155	278,935	7.81	-2.18
Southern Europe		**622,782**	**655,169**	**692,452**	**489,534**	**492,301**	**13.79**	**0.57**
Italy		204,417	208,211	241,119	156,827	157,405	4.41	0.37
Portugal		40,158	41,877	50,817	44,636	40,401	1.13	-9.49
Spain		378,207	405,081	400,516	288,071	294,495	8.25	2.23
Western Europe		**2,059,020**	**1,931,160**	**2,048,426**	**1,727,246**	**1,721,754**	**48.23**	**-0.32**
Austria		13,234	12,688	15,824	11,588	10,944	0.31	-5.56
Belgium		113,867	111,039	111,056	117,688	110,785	3.10	-5.87
France		1,537,273	1,422,823	1,474,509	1,206,521	1,205,641	33.78	-0.07
Germany		230,740	227,808	270,965	251,097	243,699	6.83	-2.95
Netherlands		115,031	112,334	127,023	102,250	113,327	3.17	10.83
Switzerland		48,875	44,468	49,049	38,102	37,358	1.05	-1.95
MIDDLE EAST		**121,941**	**128,002**	**131,274**	**133,680**	**187,636**	**5.26**	**40.36**
Egypt		11,548	12,114	12,217	11,531	11,952	0.33	3.65
Libya		8,678	10,209	12,517	11,283	29,912	0.84	165.11
Saudi Arabia		38,057	44,932	46,315	52,454	70,328	1.97	34.08
Syrian Arab Republic		2,143	2,023	2,302	2,111	2,366	0.07	12.08
United Arab Emirates		15,804	12,153	11,527	10,259	13,646	0.38	33.01
Other countries of Middle East		45,711	46,571	46,396	46,042	59,432	1.66	29.08
NOT SPECIFIED		**384,309**	**350,618**	**450,489**	**372,286**	**404,824**	**11.34**	**8.74**
Other countries of the World		363,187	332,366	434,523	353,721	389,768	10.92	10.19
Nationals Residing Abroad		21,122	18,252	15,966	18,565	15,056	0.42	-18.90

Yearbook of Tourism Statistics, Data 2008 – 2012, 2014 Edition

MOROCCO

5. Overnight stays of non-resident tourists in hotels and similar establishments, by nationality

	2008	2009	2010	2011	2012	Market share 2012	% Change 2012-2011
TOTAL (*)	13,067,592	12,520,803	13,954,610	12,418,682	12,547,875	100.00	1.04
AFRICA	300,093	291,101	330,275	366,492	409,379	3.26	11.70
North Africa	159,631	155,336	184,025	211,251	251,341	2.00	18.98
Algeria	113,135	106,274	129,270	150,366	182,919	1.46	21.65
Tunisia	46,496	49,062	54,755	60,885	68,422	0.55	12.38
West Africa	20,965	10,940	17,320	17,595	17,772	0.14	1.01
Mauritania	20,965	10,940	17,320	17,595	17,772	0.14	1.01
Other Africa	119,497	124,825	128,930	137,646	140,266	1.12	1.90
Other countries of Africa	119,497	124,825	128,930	137,646	140,266	1.12	1.90
AMERICAS	318,955	319,839	363,015	311,801	346,109	2.76	11.00
North America	318,955	319,839	363,015	311,801	346,109	2.76	11.00
Canada	69,041	73,286	76,900	72,380	76,451	0.61	5.62
United States of America	249,914	246,553	286,115	239,421	269,658	2.15	12.63
EAST ASIA AND THE PACIFIC	75,639	78,306	102,374	89,612	116,451	0.93	29.95
North-East Asia	75,639	78,306	102,374	89,612	116,451	0.93	29.95
Japan	75,639	78,306	102,374	89,612	116,451	0.93	29.95
EUROPE	11,021,660	10,485,295	11,548,134	10,147,295	9,929,159	79.13	-2.15
Central/Eastern Europe	278,658	321,288	438,862	367,048	393,251	3.13	7.14
Commonwealth Independent States	278,658	321,288	438,862	367,048	393,251	3.13	7.14
Northern Europe	1,278,187	1,077,219	1,487,413	1,523,310	1,465,977	11.68	-3.76
Denmark	21,501	14,677	22,978	41,141	27,014	0.22	-34.34
Finland	52,178	35,196	7,021	8,067	7,626	0.06	-5.47
Norway	31,766	15,077	25,524	42,984	26,438	0.21	-38.49
Sweden	98,069	82,299	86,339	91,511	44,350	0.35	-51.54
United Kingdom	1,074,673	929,970	1,345,551	1,339,607	1,360,549	10.84	1.56
Southern Europe	1,484,168	1,592,660	1,734,905	1,318,904	1,175,300	9.37	-10.89
Italy	570,730	571,376	657,142	460,409	368,571	2.94	-19.95
Portugal	96,453	99,294	132,303	152,048	122,346	0.98	-19.53
Spain	816,985	921,990	945,460	706,447	684,383	5.45	-3.12
Western Europe	7,980,647	7,494,128	7,886,954	6,938,033	6,894,631	54.95	-0.63
Austria	32,530	32,857	39,869	29,947	28,915	0.23	-3.45
Belgium	590,868	582,277	589,418	641,405	590,649	4.71	-7.91
France	5,936,414	5,550,236	5,814,996	4,906,723	4,931,278	39.30	0.50
Germany	959,079	895,617	946,323	944,226	909,016	7.24	-3.73
Netherlands	309,259	292,937	340,763	290,086	306,427	2.44	5.63
Switzerland	152,497	140,204	155,585	125,646	128,346	1.02	2.15
MIDDLE EAST	421,778	472,371	436,613	469,267	651,987	5.20	38.94
Egypt	32,259	33,508	35,422	38,504	39,397	0.31	2.32
Libya	22,987	23,995	30,617	28,560	79,585	0.63	178.66
Saudi Arabia	172,676	220,651	183,672	209,654	270,825	2.16	29.18
Syrian Arab Republic	5,793	7,677	7,995	12,888	6,811	0.05	-47.15
United Arab Emirates	39,581	27,607	27,864	26,388	30,531	0.24	15.70
Other countries of Middle East	148,482	158,933	151,043	153,273	224,838	1.79	46.69
NOT SPECIFIED	929,467	873,891	1,174,199	1,034,215	1,094,790	8.72	5.86
Other countries of the World	893,555	843,189	1,145,382	996,625	1,061,635	8.46	6.52
Nationals Residing Abroad	35,912	30,702	28,817	37,590	33,155	0.26	-11.80

504

MOZAMBIQUE

2. Arrivals of non-resident visitors at national borders, by country of residence

		2008	2009	2010	2011	2012	Market share 2012	% Change 2012-2011
TOTAL	(*)	1,438,684	1,711,147	1,836,143	2,012,640	2,205,853	100.00	9.60
AFRICA		1,213,201	1,442,962	1,465,793	1,584,095	1,580,523	71.65	-0.23
East Africa		343,821	408,964	377,152	386,764	468,476	21.24	21.13
Malawi		96,562	114,849	228,092	215,374	264,723	12.00	22.91
Zambia		8,434	10,031		20,126	5,732	0.26	-71.52
Zimbabwe		238,825	284,084	149,060	151,264	198,021	8.98	30.91
Southern Africa		833,448	991,290	985,599	1,091,825	1,035,964	46.96	-5.12
South Africa		675,745	803,720	946,583	950,941	971,868	44.06	2.20
Swaziland		157,703	187,570	39,016	140,884	64,096	2.91	-54.50
Other Africa		35,932	42,708	103,042	105,506	76,083	3.45	-27.89
Other countries of Africa		35,932	42,708	103,042	105,506	76,083	3.45	-27.89
AMERICAS		38,981	46,363	102,041	106,670	135,488	6.14	27.02
North America		21,682	25,788	21,292	36,228	76,603	3.47	111.45
United States of America		21,682	25,788	21,292	36,228	76,603	3.47	111.45
Other Americas		17,299	20,575	80,749	70,442	58,885	2.67	-16.41
Other countries of the Americas		17,299	20,575	80,749	70,442	58,885	2.67	-16.41
EAST ASIA AND THE PACIFIC		18,699	22,240	28,211	33,293	28,661	1.30	-13.91
Other East Asia and the Pacific		18,699	22,240	28,211	33,293	28,661	1.30	-13.91
All countries of Asia		18,699	22,240	28,211	33,293	28,661	1.30	-13.91
EUROPE		161,850	192,502	219,089	272,868	444,506	20.15	62.90
Northern Europe		27,900	33,184	50,420	70,442	57,322	2.60	-18.63
United Kingdom		27,900	33,184	50,420	70,442	57,322	2.60	-18.63
Southern Europe		31,406	37,353	25,810	67,214	86,504	3.92	28.70
Portugal		31,406	37,353	25,810	67,214	86,504	3.92	28.70
Other Europe		102,544	121,965	142,859	135,212	300,680	13.63	122.38
Other countries of Europe		102,544	121,965	142,859	135,212	300,680	13.63	122.38
NOT SPECIFIED		5,953	7,080	21,009	15,714	16,675	0.76	6.12
Other countries of the World		5,953	7,080	21,009	15,714	16,675	0.76	6.12

Yearbook of Tourism Statistics, Data 2008 – 2012, 2014 Edition

MYANMAR

1. Arrivals of non-resident tourists at national borders, by nationality

	2008	2009	2010	2011	2012	Market share 2012	% Change 2012-2011
TOTAL (*)	193,319	243,278	310,688	391,176	593,381	100.00	51.69
AFRICA	539	764	816	993	1,598	0.27	60.93
Other Africa	539	764	816	993	1,598	0.27	60.93
All countries of Africa	539	764	816	993	1,598	0.27	60.93
AMERICAS	16,158	18,662	20,580	27,745	47,609	8.02	71.59
North America	15,229	17,440	18,911	25,365	44,074	7.43	73.76
Canada	2,034	2,387	2,407	3,685	6,485	1.09	75.98
United States of America	13,195	15,053	16,504	21,680	37,589	6.33	73.38
Other Americas	929	1,222	1,669	2,380	3,535	0.60	48.53
Other countries of the Americas	929	1,222	1,669	2,380	3,535	0.60	48.53
EAST ASIA AND THE PACIFIC	124,242	157,092	207,450	254,410	382,449	64.45	50.33
North-East Asia	68,598	78,670	99,624	126,787	180,186	30.37	42.12
China	30,792	36,341	46,141	62,018	70,805	11.93	14.17
Hong Kong, China	2,410	2,747	3,081	3,820	4,826	0.81	26.34
Japan	10,881	13,809	16,186	21,321	47,690	8.04	123.68
Korea, Republic of	12,369	12,508	18,930	22,524	34,805	5.87	54.52
Taiwan, Province of China	11,472	12,276	14,170	15,542	22,060	3.72	41.94
Other countries of North-East Asia	674	989	1,116	1,562			
South-East Asia	49,496	70,333	98,992	115,870	151,137	25.47	30.44
Indonesia	1,904	2,072	2,398	2,968			
Malaysia	8,268	9,668	16,186	23,287	30,499	5.14	30.97
Philippines	1,595	1,888	2,169	2,878			
Singapore	8,599	10,712	12,114	15,391	26,296	4.43	70.85
Thailand	27,311	43,254	59,692	61,696	94,342	15.90	52.91
Viet Nam	1,084	1,864	5,609	7,703			
Other countries of South-East Asia	735	875	824	1,947			
Australasia	6,065	7,993	8,686	11,603	20,603	3.47	77.57
Australia	5,374	7,163	7,693	10,415	18,261	3.08	75.33
New Zealand	691	830	993	1,188	2,342	0.39	97.14
Other East Asia and the Pacific	83	96	148	150	30,523	5.14	20,248.67
Other countries of Asia	69	84	139	131	30,476	5.14	23,164.12
Other countries of Oceania	14	12	9	19	47	0.01	147.37
EUROPE	40,885	53,150	65,935	88,517	139,373	23.49	57.45
Central/Eastern Europe	1,726	4,623	6,117	7,622	9,077	1.53	19.09
Russian Federation	1,726	2,070	2,757	3,496	3,749	0.63	7.24
Other countries Central/East Europe		2,553	3,360	4,126	5,328	0.90	29.13
Northern Europe	6,419	7,770	9,504	13,765	24,296	4.09	76.51
Denmark	461	882	1,247	1,527			
Sweden	561	717	917	1,182			
United Kingdom	5,397	6,171	7,340	11,056	24,296	4.09	119.75
Southern Europe	5,618	10,456	12,981	16,369	17,518	2.95	7.02
Italy	3,030	5,975	7,169	9,710	10,830	1.83	11.53
Spain	2,588	4,481	5,812	6,659	6,688	1.13	0.44
Western Europe	23,792	28,477	35,084	47,800	69,277	11.67	44.93
Austria	1,212	1,447	1,896	1,964	3,489	0.59	77.65
Belgium	1,386	1,848	2,411	3,376	4,627	0.78	37.06
France	8,217	10,458	13,143	19,414	30,064	5.07	54.86
Germany	8,947	9,608	11,082	14,006	23,063	3.89	64.67
Netherlands	1,548	1,887	2,384	3,495			
Switzerland	2,482	3,229	4,168	5,545	8,034	1.35	44.89
Other Europe	3,330	1,824	2,249	2,961	19,205	3.24	548.60
Other countries of Europe	3,330	1,824	2,249	2,961	19,205	3.24	548.60
MIDDLE EAST	1,379	1,564	2,208	2,607	3,747	0.63	43.73
All countries of Middle East	1,379	1,564	2,208	2,607	3,747	0.63	43.73

506

MYANMAR

1. Arrivals of non-resident tourists at national borders, by nationality

	2008	2009	2010	2011	2012	Market share 2012	% Change 2012-2011
SOUTH ASIA	**10,116**	**12,046**	**13,699**	**16,904**	**18,605**	**3.14**	**10.06**
Bangladesh	1,001	1,212	1,441	1,988	1,737	0.29	-12.63
India	7,173	8,609	9,849	12,318	16,868	2.84	36.94
Pakistan		733	794				
Other countries of South Asia	1,942	1,492	1,615	2,598			

Yearbook of Tourism Statistics, Data 2008 – 2012, 2014 Edition

MYANMAR

5. Overnight stays of non-resident tourists in hotels and similar establishments, by nationality

	2008	2009	2010	2011	2012	Market share 2012	% Change 2012-2011
TOTAL	1,739,871	2,067,863	2,485,504	3,129,408	4,013,667	100.00	28.26
AFRICA	4,851	6,494	6,536	7,944	11,186	0.28	40.81
Other Africa	4,851	6,494	6,536	7,944	11,186	0.28	40.81
All countries of Africa	4,851	6,494	6,536	7,944	11,186	0.28	40.81
AMERICAS	145,422	158,628	164,632	221,960	333,263	8.30	50.15
North America	137,061	148,241	151,288	202,920	308,518	7.69	52.04
Canada	18,306	20,290	19,256	29,480	45,395	1.13	53.99
United States of America	118,755	127,951	132,032	173,440	263,123	6.56	51.71
Other Americas	8,361	10,387	13,344	19,040	24,745	0.62	29.96
Other countries of the Americas	8,361	10,387	13,344	19,040	24,745	0.62	29.96
EAST ASIA AND THE PACIFIC	1,118,178	1,335,282	1,659,600	2,035,280	2,537,143	63.21	24.66
North-East Asia	617,382	668,696	796,992	1,014,296	1,121,302	27.94	10.55
China	277,128	308,899	369,128	496,144	495,635	12.35	-0.10
Hong Kong, China	21,690	23,350	24,648	30,560	33,782	0.84	10.54
Japan	97,929	117,377	129,488	170,568	333,830	8.32	95.72
Korea, Republic of	111,321	106,318	151,440	180,192	243,635	6.07	35.21
Taiwan, Province of China	103,248	104,346	113,360	124,336	14,420	0.36	-88.40
Other countries of North-East Asia	6,066	8,406	8,928	12,496			
South-East Asia	445,464	597,830	791,936	926,960	1,057,959	26.36	14.13
Indonesia	17,136	17,613	19,184	23,744			
Malaysia	74,412	82,178	129,488	186,296	213,493	5.32	14.60
Philippines	14,355	16,048	17,352	23,024			
Singapore	77,391	91,053	96,912	123,128	184,072	4.59	49.50
Thailand	245,799	367,660	477,536	493,568	660,394	16.45	33.80
Viet Nam	9,756	15,844	44,872	61,624			
Other countries of South-East Asia	6,615	7,434	6,592	15,576			
Australasia	54,585	67,940	69,488	92,824	144,221	3.59	55.37
Australia	48,366	60,885	61,544	83,320	127,827	3.18	53.42
New Zealand	6,219	7,055	7,944	9,504	16,394	0.41	72.50
Other East Asia and the Pacific	747	816	1,184	1,200	213,661	5.32	17,705.08
Other countries of Asia	621	714	1,112	1,048	213,332	5.32	20,256.11
Other countries of Oceania	126	102	72	152	329	0.01	116.45
EUROPE	367,965	451,774	527,480	708,136	975,611	24.31	37.77
Central/Eastern Europe	15,534	39,295	48,936	60,976	63,539	1.58	4.20
Russian Federation	15,534	17,595	22,056	27,968	26,243	0.65	-6.17
Other countries Central/East Europe		21,700	26,880	33,008	37,296	0.93	12.99
Northern Europe	57,771	66,045	76,032	110,120	170,072	4.24	54.44
Denmark	4,149	7,497	9,976	12,216			
Sweden	5,049	6,095	7,336	9,456			
United Kingdom	48,573	52,453	58,720	88,448	170,072	4.24	92.28
Southern Europe	50,562	88,876	103,848	130,952	122,626	3.06	-6.36
Italy	27,270	50,788	57,352	77,680	75,810	1.89	-2.41
Spain	23,292	38,088	46,496	53,272	46,816	1.17	-12.12
Western Europe	214,128	242,054	280,672	382,400	484,939	12.08	26.81
Austria	10,908	12,300	15,168	15,712	24,423	0.61	55.44
Belgium	12,474	15,708	19,288	27,008	32,389	0.81	19.92
France	73,953	88,893	105,144	155,312	210,448	5.24	35.50
Germany	80,523	81,668	88,656	112,048	161,441	4.02	44.08
Netherlands	13,932	16,039	19,072	27,960			
Switzerland	22,338	27,446	33,344	44,360	56,238	1.40	26.78
Other Europe	29,970	15,504	17,992	23,688	134,435	3.35	467.52
Other countries of Europe	29,970	15,504	17,992	23,688	134,435	3.35	467.52
MIDDLE EAST	12,411	13,294	17,664	20,856	26,229	0.65	25.76
All countries of Middle East	12,411	13,294	17,664	20,856	26,229	0.65	25.76

Yearbook of Tourism Statistics, Data 2008 – 2012, 2014 Edition

MYANMAR

5. Overnight stays of non-resident tourists in hotels and similar establishments, by nationality

	2008	2009	2010	2011	2012	Market share 2012	% Change 2012-2011
SOUTH ASIA	**91,044**	**102,391**	**109,592**	**135,232**	**130,235**	**3.24**	**-3.70**
Bangladesh	9,009	10,302	11,528	15,904	12,159	0.30	-23.55
India	64,557	73,177	78,792	98,544	118,076	2.94	19.82
Pakistan		6,230	6,352				
Other countries of South Asia	17,478	12,682	12,920	20,784			

Yearbook of Tourism Statistics, Data 2008 – 2012, 2014 Edition

NAMIBIA

1. Arrivals of non-resident tourists at national borders, by nationality

	2008	2009	2010	2011	2012	Market share 2012	% Change 2012-2011
TOTAL	931,110	980,178	984,098	1,027,230			
AFRICA	676,444	723,762	714,287	784,580			
East Africa	79,529	86,175	91,896	104,065			
Zambia	29,281	31,842	37,667	42,945			
Zimbabwe	50,248	54,333	54,229	61,120			
Central Africa	310,395	309,127	296,825	361,480			
Angola	310,395	309,127	296,825	361,480			
Southern Africa	269,416	312,697	309,158	301,588			
Botswana	26,378	26,918	31,503	28,658			
South Africa	243,038	285,779	277,655	272,930			
Other Africa	17,104	15,763	16,408	17,447			
Other countries of Africa	17,104	15,763	16,408	17,447			
AMERICAS	29,201	26,657	26,175	24,828			
North America	26,346	24,940	22,793	22,790			
Canada	5,490	4,860	4,967	4,844			
United States of America	20,856	20,080	17,826	17,946			
South America	2,855	1,717	3,382	2,038			
Brazil	2,855	1,717	3,382	2,038			
EAST ASIA AND THE PACIFIC	9,778	11,484	11,294	11,668			
North-East Asia	3,661	5,119	4,228	4,035			
China	3,661	5,119	4,228	4,035			
Australasia	6,117	6,365	7,066	7,633			
Australia	6,117	6,365	7,066	7,633			
EUROPE	204,115	206,496	219,070	194,430			
Central/Eastern Europe	1,935	1,806	1,762	1,898			
Russian Federation	1,935	1,806	1,762	1,898			
Northern Europe	37,617	36,720	36,308	31,699			
United Kingdom	28,111	28,039	25,717	21,584			
Scandinavia	9,506	8,681	10,591	10,115			
Southern Europe	23,960	26,176	27,962	25,650			
Italy	11,836	12,095	10,767	11,207			
Portugal	5,965	8,653	9,124	8,774			
Spain	6,159	5,428	8,071	5,669			
Western Europe	132,947	135,460	147,015	129,415			
Austria	6,664	7,201	7,197	6,016			
Belgium	4,909	5,647	7,024	6,170			
France	14,604	15,044	17,039	13,729			
Germany	81,543	81,974	87,072	79,721			
Netherlands	14,382	14,503	16,078	12,346			
Switzerland	10,845	11,091	12,605	11,433			
Other Europe	7,656	6,334	6,023	5,768			
Other countries of Europe	7,656	6,334	6,023	5,768			
NOT SPECIFIED	11,572	11,779	13,272	11,724			
Other countries of the World	11,572	11,779	13,272	11,724			

Yearbook of Tourism Statistics, Data 2008 – 2012, 2014 Editic

NAMIBIA

2. Arrivals of non-resident visitors at national borders, by nationality

	2008	2009	2010	2011	2012	Market share 2012	% Change 2012-2011
TOTAL			1,114,423	1,163,395			
AFRICA			833,316	909,399			
East Africa			160,981	168,949			
Zambia			38,598	44,976			
Zimbabwe			122,383	123,973			
Central Africa			319,987	393,968			
Angola			319,987	393,968			
Southern Africa			335,507	328,157			
Botswana			36,032	33,008			
South Africa			299,475	295,149			
Other Africa			16,841	18,325			
Other countries of Africa			16,841	18,325			
AMERICAS			28,470	26,427			
North America			24,811	24,225			
Canada			5,233	5,052			
United States of America			19,578	19,173			
South America			3,659	2,202			
Brazil			3,659	2,202			
EAST ASIA AND THE PACIFIC			11,581	11,998			
North-East Asia			4,300	4,085			
China			4,300	4,085			
Australasia			7,281	7,913			
Australia			7,281	7,913			
EUROPE			227,519	202,694			
Central/Eastern Europe			1,762	2,496			
Russian Federation			1,762	2,496			
Northern Europe			38,417	34,077			
United Kingdom			27,460	23,368			
Scandinavia			10,957	10,709			
Southern Europe			30,707	27,558			
Italy			10,866	11,566			
Portugal			11,576	10,039			
Spain			8,265	5,953			
Western Europe			150,422	132,291			
Austria			7,360	6,065			
Belgium			7,176	6,255			
France			17,187	14,115			
Germany			88,950	81,423			
Netherlands			16,954	12,741			
Switzerland			12,795	11,692			
Other Europe			6,211	6,272			
Other countries of Europe			6,211	6,272			
NOT SPECIFIED			13,537	12,877			
Other countries of the World			13,537	12,877			

Yearbook of Tourism Statistics, Data 2008 – 2012, 2014 Edition

NEPAL

1. Arrivals of non-resident tourists at national borders, by nationality

	2008	2009	2010	2011	2012	Market share 2012	% Change 2012-2011
TOTAL	500,277	509,956	602,867	736,215	803,092	100.00	9.08
AFRICA	810	435	461	2,239	1,324	0.16	-40.87
East Africa	204	141	219	349			
Kenya	204	141	219	223			
Mauritius				126			
North Africa	493	252	173	231			
Algeria	416	196	53	131			
Morocco	34	42	92	76			
Tunisia	43	14	28	24			
Southern Africa				1,243	1,324	0.16	6.52
South Africa				1,243	1,324	0.16	6.52
West Africa	113	42	69	416			
Benin				321			
Nigeria	113	42	69	95			
AMERICAS	44,953	45,528	51,508	62,505	67,203	8.37	7.52
Caribbean	159	294	9	53			
Bahamas	159	294	9	53			
Central America	541	297	30	33			
Costa Rica	541	297	30	33			
North America	39,388	41,695	47,437	55,735	63,956	7.96	14.75
Canada	8,132	8,965	9,322	11,404	13,507	1.68	18.44
Mexico	1,180	687	1,690	1,456	1,464	0.18	0.55
United States of America	30,076	32,043	36,425	42,875	48,985	6.10	14.25
South America	4,865	3,242	4,032	6,684	3,247	0.40	-51.42
Argentina	2,204	923	1,102	2,226	1,617	0.20	-27.36
Bolivia	262	201	55	29			
Brazil	1,539	1,167	1,794	1,859	1,630	0.20	-12.32
Chile	276	270	606	493			
Colombia	501	459	392	402			
Peru				129			
Suriname				115			
Uruguay				1,226			
Venezuela	83	222	83	205			
EAST ASIA AND THE PACIFIC	129,829	133,009	152,420	195,914	230,911	28.75	17.86
North-East Asia	77,531	70,912	90,129	120,214	135,335	16.85	12.58
China	35,166	32,272	46,360	61,917	71,861	8.95	16.06
Japan	23,383	22,445	23,332	26,283	28,642	3.57	8.98
Korea, Dem. People's Republic of				196			
Korea, Republic of	18,883	16,145	20,320	24,488	26,004	3.24	6.19
Mongolia	99	50	117	362			
Taiwan, Province of China				6,968	8,828	1.10	26.69
South-East Asia	36,103	44,163	43,460	52,642	69,789	8.69	32.57
Brunei Darussalam	348	401	37	18			
Cambodia	535	319	227	141	862	0.11	511.35
Indonesia	1,120	729	1,075	1,027	1,500	0.19	46.06
Malaysia	5,173	5,527	6,752	7,381	11,780	1.47	59.60
Myanmar	3,634	2,600	1,633	328	9,470	1.18	2,787.20
Philippines	1,749	1,247	2,362	2,399	1,757	0.22	-26.76
Singapore	4,120	5,344	8,937	6,985	5,626	0.70	-19.46
Thailand	18,689	27,397	21,528	33,541	36,618	4.56	9.17
Timor-Leste				112			
Viet Nam	735	599	909	710	2,176	0.27	206.48
Australasia	16,121	17,900	18,767	22,923	25,787	3.21	12.49
Australia	13,846	15,461	16,243	19,824	22,030	2.74	11.13
New Zealand	2,275	2,439	2,524	3,099	3,757	0.47	21.23

512

Yearbook of Tourism Statistics, Data 2008 – 2012, 2014 Editio

NEPAL

1. Arrivals of non-resident tourists at national borders, by nationality

		2008	2009	2010	2011	2012	Market share 2012	% Change 2012-2011
Melanesia		74	34	64	135			
Fiji		74	34	64	26			
Vanuatu					109			
EUROPE		**154,959**	**151,792**	**181,836**	**207,447**	**216,964**	**27.02**	**4.59**
Central/Eastern Europe		**11,198**	**8,553**	**18,875**	**15,426**	**24,672**	**3.07**	**59.94**
Armenia					113			
Azerbaijan					147			
Belarus					249			
Bulgaria		328	326	327	302	1,229	0.15	306.95
Czech Republic		1,738	1,307	2,831	2,121	3,592	0.45	69.35
Estonia		82	90	225	87			
Hungary		918	514	1,895	726			
Kazakhstan		110	148	170	211			
Latvia					224			
Lithuania					282			
Poland		2,722	1,784	3,842	3,152	5,689	0.71	80.49
Romania					501	1,336	0.17	166.67
Russian Federation		3,968	3,262	6,846	5,554	9,673	1.20	74.16
Slovakia		519	426	436	564	1,267	0.16	124.65
Ukraine		813	696	2,303	1,193	1,886	0.23	58.09
Northern Europe		**47,366**	**47,728**	**51,706**	**57,166**	**60,626**	**7.55**	**6.05**
Denmark		3,847	4,464	4,359	6,138	7,118	0.89	15.97
Finland		1,567	1,408	3,284	2,276	2,464	0.31	8.26
Iceland		292	179	76	171			
Ireland		1,736	1,643	3,249	2,168	2,018	0.25	-6.92
Norway		3,960	2,329	2,647	3,240	3,280	0.41	1.23
Sweden		2,306	2,323	3,000	4,082	4,452	0.55	9.06
United Kingdom		33,658	35,382	35,091	39,091	41,294	5.14	5.64
Southern Europe		**24,303**	**23,209**	**29,262**	**33,614**	**31,039**	**3.86**	**-7.66**
Andorra					305			
Croatia		374	585	130	198			
Greece	(*)	1,346	979	2,763	1,068	691	0.09	-35.30
Italy		7,914	7,982	10,226	12,621	14,614	1.82	15.79
Portugal		818	657	2,431	1,281	1,185	0.15	-7.49
Serbia					167			
Slovenia					201			
Spain		13,851	13,006	13,712	16,037	14,549	1.81	-9.28
TFYR of Macedonia					1,736			
Western Europe		**65,228**	**65,905**	**74,588**	**92,602**	**91,788**	**11.43**	**-0.88**
Austria		3,540	3,245	3,389	3,998	3,797	0.47	-5.03
Belgium		4,648	4,832	5,275	6,368	6,286	0.78	-1.29
France		22,402	22,154	24,550	26,720	28,805	3.59	7.80
Germany		18,552	19,246	22,583	27,472	30,409	3.79	10.69
Luxembourg					188			
Netherlands		10,900	11,147	13,471	16,836	15,445	1.92	-8.26
Switzerland		5,186	5,281	5,320	11,020	7,046	0.88	-36.06
East Mediterranean Europe		**6,864**	**6,397**	**7,405**	**8,639**	**8,839**	**1.10**	**2.32**
Israel		5,926	5,879	4,594	6,519	7,151	0.89	9.69
Turkey		938	518	2,811	2,120	1,688	0.21	-20.38
MIDDLE EAST		**954**	**922**	**1,580**	**4,130**	**1,209**	**0.15**	**-70.73**
Bahrain		232	262	224	325			
Egypt		135	182	237	287			
Jordan					200			
Kuwait					139			
Lebanon					793			
Oman					389			
Qatar					259			

513

NEPAL

1. Arrivals of non-resident tourists at national borders, by nationality

	2008	2009	2010	2011	2012	Market share 2012	% Change 2012-2011
Saudi Arabia	356	279	536	743	1,209	0.15	62.72
Syrian Arab Republic				165			
United Arab Emirates	231	199	583	830			
SOUTH ASIA	**157,976**	**152,785**	**193,510**	**235,983**	**261,813**	**32.60**	**10.95**
Afghanistan	1,371	512	442	508	503	0.06	-0.98
Bangladesh	20,067	15,385	16,470	17,563	16,764	2.09	-4.55
Bhutan	2,662	1,849	4,742	3,301	4,183	0.52	26.72
India	91,177	93,884	120,898	149,504	165,815	20.65	10.91
Iran, Islamic Republic of	1,143	570	809	522			
Maldives	491	257	245	318			
Pakistan	3,248	3,966	4,373	4,383	5,072	0.63	15.72
Sri Lanka	37,817	36,362	45,531	59,884	69,476	8.65	16.02
NOT SPECIFIED	**10,796**	**25,485**	**21,552**	**27,997**	**23,668**	**2.95**	**-15.46**
Other countries of the World	10,796	25,485	21,552	27,997	23,668	2.95	-15.46

Yearbook of Tourism Statistics, Data 2008 – 2012, 2014 Editic

NEPAL

1. Arrivals of non-resident tourists at national borders, by country of residence

	2008	2009	2010	2011	2012	Market share 2012	% Change 2012-2011
TOTAL	500,277	509,956	602,867	735,947	803,092	100.00	9.12
AFRICA	493	481	437	3,017	1,321	0.16	-56.21
East Africa	173	183	191	494			
Kenya	173	183	191	494			
Central Africa				966			
Angola				966			
North Africa	257	280	185				
Algeria	201	246	112				
Morocco	16	34	73				
Tunisia	40						
Southern Africa				1,244	1,321	0.16	6.19
South Africa				1,244	1,321	0.16	6.19
West Africa	63	18	61	313			
Benin				313			
Nigeria	63	18	61				
AMERICAS	42,080	42,567	49,637	62,430	65,212	8.12	4.46
Caribbean	167	311	28				
Bahamas	167	311	28				
Central America	550	300	27				
Costa Rica	550	300	27				
North America	36,745	38,772	45,763	54,321	62,180	7.74	14.47
Canada	7,603	7,827	9,024	10,705	12,885	1.60	20.36
Mexico	1,151	657	1,779	1,645	1,383	0.17	-15.93
United States of America	27,991	30,288	34,960	41,971	47,912	5.97	14.16
South America	4,618	3,184	3,819	8,109	3,032	0.38	-62.61
Argentina	1,930	913	1,060	2,898	1,552	0.19	-46.45
Bolivia	277	192	32				
Brazil	1,572	1,150	1,682	2,363	1,480	0.18	-37.37
Chile	269	271	580	638			
Colombia	489	433	367	490			
Uruguay				1,720			
Venezuela	81	225	98				
EAST ASIA AND THE PACIFIC	129,469	135,232	148,074	201,134	227,273	28.30	13.00
North-East Asia	76,588	70,360	85,621	121,506	133,349	16.60	9.75
China	36,172	33,487	44,694	64,115	71,380	8.89	11.33
Japan	22,065	21,066	21,594	25,856	27,993	3.49	8.27
Korea, Republic of	18,249	15,757	19,247	24,202	25,129	3.13	3.83
Mongolia	102	50	86	307			
Taiwan, Province of China				7,026	8,847	1.10	25.92
South-East Asia	38,033	47,791	44,706	56,903	68,185	8.49	19.83
Brunei Darussalam	481	439	73				
Cambodia	616	411	251	270	871	0.11	222.59
Indonesia	1,089	754	891	1,167	1,357	0.17	16.28
Malaysia	4,941	5,157	6,376	7,126	11,932	1.49	67.44
Myanmar	3,631	2,601	1,538	1,678	8,043	1.00	379.32
Philippines	1,688	1,351	2,361	2,384	1,734	0.22	-27.27
Singapore	5,031	6,976	10,345	8,648	7,018	0.87	-18.85
Thailand	19,745	29,388	22,318	34,587	35,315	4.40	2.10
Viet Nam	811	714	553	1,043	1,915	0.24	83.60
Australasia	14,784	17,042	17,687	22,725	25,739	3.20	13.26
Australia	12,978	14,897	15,636	19,949	22,272	2.77	11.64
New Zealand	1,806	2,145	2,051	2,776	3,467	0.43	24.89
Melanesia	64	39	60				
Fiji	64	39	60				
EUROPE	146,590	143,814	169,694	212,461	211,322	26.31	-0.54

515

NEPAL

1. Arrivals of non-resident tourists at national borders, by country of residence

	2008	2009	2010	2011	2012	Market share 2012	% Change 2012-2011
Central/Eastern Europe	10,900	8,290	17,687	22,667	23,560	2.93	3.94
Bulgaria	319	308	457	1,204	1,200	0.15	-0.33
Czech Republic	1,721	1,284	2,540	4,170	3,505	0.44	-15.95
Estonia	82	93	202				
Hungary	884	496	1,775	736			
Kazakhstan	126	152	159	259			
Latvia				273			
Lithuania				271			
Poland	2,593	1,654	3,502	4,196	5,107	0.64	21.71
Romania				939	1,195	0.15	27.26
Russian Federation	3,871	3,204	6,472	7,881	9,486	1.18	20.37
Slovakia	502	412	366	1,028	1,195	0.15	16.25
Ukraine	802	687	2,214	1,710	1,872	0.23	9.47
Northern Europe	42,607	44,076	46,803	55,321	58,933	7.34	6.53
Denmark	3,526	4,198	4,295	5,955	6,852	0.85	15.06
Finland	1,408	1,297	2,890	2,380	2,320	0.29	-2.52
Iceland	281	180	102	399			
Ireland	1,508	1,524	2,806	2,333	1,740	0.22	-25.42
Norway	3,766	2,190	2,492	3,268	3,270	0.41	0.06
Sweden	1,993	2,096	2,758	4,005	4,387	0.55	9.54
United Kingdom	30,125	32,591	31,460	36,981	40,364	5.03	9.15
Southern Europe	23,560	22,668	27,685	33,823	30,351	3.78	-10.27
Andorra				296			
Croatia	377	623	120	229			
Greece (*)	1,348	938	2,593	1,114	643	0.08	-42.28
Italy	7,447	7,632	9,594	12,257	14,191	1.77	15.78
Portugal	784	600	2,168	1,346	1,027	0.13	-23.70
Slovenia				224			
Spain	13,604	12,875	13,210	15,593	14,490	1.80	-7.07
TFYR of Macedonia				2,764			
Western Europe	62,831	62,414	70,505	91,842	89,723	11.17	-2.31
Austria	3,436	3,139	3,146	3,885	3,706	0.46	-4.61
Belgium	4,510	4,653	5,036	6,347	6,429	0.80	1.29
France	21,587	20,907	23,032	26,131	27,684	3.45	5.94
Germany	17,739	17,927	21,146	26,866	29,682	3.70	10.48
Liechtenstein				261			
Luxembourg				237			
Netherlands	10,136	10,377	12,659	16,343	14,727	1.83	-9.89
Switzerland	5,423	5,411	5,486	11,772	7,495	0.93	-36.33
East Mediterranean Europe	6,692	6,366	7,014	8,808	8,755	1.09	-0.60
Israel	5,792	5,863	4,314	6,593	7,087	0.88	7.49
Turkey	900	503	2,700	2,215	1,668	0.21	-24.70
MIDDLE EAST	5,647	4,891	7,524	12,857	1,652	0.21	-87.15
Bahrain	365	518	481	578			
Egypt	76	140	137				
Kuwait				294			
Lebanon				892			
Oman				733			
Qatar				1,692			
Saudi Arabia	527	494	755	1,231	1,652	0.21	34.20
United Arab Emirates	4,679	3,739	6,151	7,437			
SOUTH ASIA	149,959	150,951	177,704	234,599	253,980	31.63	8.26
Afghanistan	1,191	594	483	561	570	0.07	1.60
Bangladesh	20,247	15,746	14,681	18,133	16,970	2.11	-6.41
Bhutan	2,578	1,866	4,413	4,291	3,990	0.50	-7.01
India	84,073	91,994	108,077	147,037	165,139	20.56	12.31

Yearbook of Tourism Statistics, Data 2008 – 2012, 2014 Edition

NEPAL

1. Arrivals of non-resident tourists at national borders, by country of residence

	2008	2009	2010	2011	2012	Market share 2012	% Change 2012-2011
Iran, Islamic Republic of	1,086	536	689	467			
Maldives	488	259	227	310			
Pakistan	2,656	3,637	3,742	4,015	4,891	0.61	21.82
Sri Lanka	37,640	36,319	45,392	59,785	62,420	7.77	4.41
NOT SPECIFIED	**26,039**	**32,020**	**49,797**	**9,449**	**42,332**	**5.27**	**348.01**
Other countries of the World	26,039	32,020	49,797	9,449	42,332	5.27	348.01

Yearbook of Tourism Statistics, Data 2008 – 2012, 2014 Edition

NETHERLANDS

3. Arrivals of non-resident tourists in hotels and similar establishments, by country of residence

	2008	2009	2010	2011	2012	Market share 2012	% Change 2012-2011
TOTAL (*)	8,035,200	7,754,300	8,726,800	9,026,500	9,356,700	100.00	3.66
AFRICA	80,800	81,700	100,300	112,100	110,100	1.18	-1.78
Other Africa	80,800	81,700	100,300	112,100	110,100	1.18	-1.78
All countries of Africa	80,800	81,700	100,300	112,100	110,100	1.18	-1.78
AMERICAS	1,059,400	1,010,100	1,215,400	1,311,300	1,313,800	14.04	0.19
North America	908,900	864,800	1,021,400	1,077,500	1,062,900	11.36	-1.35
Canada	115,400	103,300	127,200	131,500	131,400	1.40	-0.08
United States of America	793,500	761,500	894,200	946,000	931,500	9.96	-1.53
Other Americas	150,500	145,300	194,000	233,800	250,900	2.68	7.31
Other countries of the Americas	150,500	145,300	194,000	233,800	250,900	2.68	7.31
EAST ASIA AND THE PACIFIC	551,200	554,800	627,000	684,800	775,500	8.29	13.24
North-East Asia	265,500	258,400	281,000	316,100	363,600	3.89	15.03
China	112,800	122,500	124,300	155,700	172,800	1.85	10.98
Japan	114,400	99,300	119,000	110,500	136,300	1.46	23.35
Korea, Republic of	22,400	22,900	23,200	25,300	27,800	0.30	9.88
Taiwan, Province of China	15,900	13,700	14,500	24,600	26,700	0.29	8.54
South-East Asia	11,400	13,800	21,200	23,600	32,100	0.34	36.02
Indonesia	11,400	13,800	21,200	23,600	32,100	0.34	36.02
Australasia	98,300	96,700	129,700	142,700	150,400	1.61	5.40
Australia	84,800	84,700	115,600	127,100	134,200	1.43	5.59
New Zealand	13,500	12,000	14,100	15,600	16,200	0.17	3.85
Other East Asia and the Pacific	176,000	185,900	195,100	202,400	229,400	2.45	13.34
Other countries of Asia	166,500	176,100	181,100	190,600	220,200	2.35	15.53
Other countries of Oceania	9,500	9,800	14,000	11,800	9,200	0.10	-22.03
EUROPE	6,293,900	6,058,300	6,720,500	6,850,500	7,080,300	75.67	3.35
Central/Eastern Europe	251,300	223,100	264,700	304,300	329,800	3.52	8.38
Czech Republic	34,200	28,200	32,600	36,100	37,800	0.40	4.71
Hungary	27,900	22,800	26,600	30,300	30,500	0.33	0.66
Poland	77,600	68,200	80,600	88,300	94,000	1.00	6.46
Russian Federation	101,300	95,100	114,800	139,000	153,800	1.64	10.65
Slovakia	10,300	8,800	10,100	10,600	13,700	0.15	29.25
Northern Europe	2,033,600	1,781,000	1,983,000	1,937,700	2,055,800	21.97	6.09
Denmark	130,100	117,500	135,500	122,600	121,600	1.30	-0.82
Finland	51,300	42,900	49,200	62,800	62,200	0.66	-0.96
Iceland	8,200	5,400	7,100	8,000	8,300	0.09	3.75
Ireland	109,500	105,400	109,300	87,300	93,300	1.00	6.87
Norway	88,400	85,900	96,100	104,000	114,800	1.23	10.38
Sweden	104,900	93,700	108,400	119,600	132,200	1.41	10.54
United Kingdom	1,541,200	1,330,200	1,477,400	1,433,400	1,523,400	16.28	6.28
Southern Europe	781,500	776,400	934,500	919,300	892,000	9.53	-2.97
Greece	40,700	45,900	44,800	41,500	36,200	0.39	-12.77
Italy	341,000	343,800	411,600	407,600	405,200	4.33	-0.59
Portugal	47,600	50,900	53,200	60,000	54,700	0.58	-8.83
Spain	352,200	335,800	424,900	410,200	395,900	4.23	-3.49
Western Europe	2,787,400	2,807,500	3,132,100	3,254,400	3,360,300	35.91	3.25
Austria	73,800	63,600	69,000	78,100	75,300	0.80	-3.59
Belgium	692,800	712,500	796,500	808,100	884,600	9.45	9.47
France	498,900	497,900	577,900	584,100	558,700	5.97	-4.35
Germany	1,353,500	1,357,000	1,485,100	1,562,100	1,600,300	17.10	2.45
Luxembourg	32,100	31,400	40,000	38,300	43,900	0.47	14.62
Switzerland	136,300	145,100	163,600	183,700	197,500	2.11	7.51
East Mediterranean Europe	95,600	104,200	121,800	144,700	157,600	1.68	8.91
Israel	55,300	60,600	69,600	86,200	85,700	0.92	-0.58
Turkey	40,300	43,600	52,200	58,500	71,900	0.77	22.91

Yearbook of Tourism Statistics, Data 2008 – 2012, 2014 Editic

NETHERLANDS

3. Arrivals of non-resident tourists in hotels and similar establishments, by country of residence

	2008	2009	2010	2011	2012	Market share 2012	% Change 2012-2011
Other Europe	**344,500**	**366,100**	**284,400**	**290,100**	**284,800**	**3.04**	**-1.83**
Other countries of Europe	344,500	366,100	284,400	290,100	284,800	3.04	-1.83
SOUTH ASIA	**49,900**	**49,400**	**63,600**	**67,800**	**77,000**	**0.82**	**13.57**
India	49,900	49,400	63,600	67,800	77,000	0.82	13.57

Yearbook of Tourism Statistics, Data 2008 – 2012, 2014 Edition

NETHERLANDS

4. Arrivals of non-resident tourists in all types of accommodation establishments, by country of residence

	2008	2009	2010	2011	2012	Market share 2012	% Change 2012-2011
TOTAL	10,104,300	9,920,600	10,883,200	11,299,500	11,679,600	100.00	3.36
AFRICA	83,800	83,600	103,300	114,400	112,000	0.96	-2.10
Other Africa	83,800	83,600	103,300	114,400	112,000	0.96	-2.10
All countries of Africa	83,800	83,600	103,300	114,400	112,000	0.96	-2.10
AMERICAS	1,068,000	1,017,700	1,223,000	1,319,800	1,322,800	11.33	0.23
Other Americas	1,068,000	1,017,700	1,223,000	1,319,800	1,322,800	11.33	0.23
All countries of the Americas	1,068,000	1,017,700	1,223,000	1,319,800	1,322,800	11.33	0.23
EAST ASIA AND THE PACIFIC	667,700	673,400	770,100	849,700	949,300	8.13	11.72
Other East Asia and the Pacific	667,700	673,400	770,100	849,700	949,300	8.13	11.72
All countries of Asia	556,000	563,900	622,800	690,800	786,000	6.73	13.78
All countries of Oceania	111,700	109,500	147,300	158,900	163,300	1.40	2.77
EUROPE	8,284,800	8,145,900	8,786,800	9,015,600	9,295,500	79.59	3.10
Northern Europe	1,899,400	1,644,500	1,819,100	1,770,100	1,887,200	16.16	6.62
Denmark	148,200	135,200	150,200	136,900	135,500	1.16	-1.02
Sweden	112,300	100,600	113,400	124,900	138,100	1.18	10.57
United Kingdom	1,638,900	1,408,700	1,555,500	1,508,300	1,613,600	13.82	6.98
Southern Europe	738,400	719,600	882,700	863,000	840,600	7.20	-2.60
Italy	370,400	368,400	443,000	437,700	434,500	3.72	-0.73
Spain	368,000	351,200	439,700	425,300	406,100	3.48	-4.51
Western Europe	4,503,900	4,654,200	4,954,300	5,191,200	5,330,600	45.64	2.69
Belgium	1,108,500	1,171,800	1,256,800	1,345,000	1,461,800	12.52	8.68
France	574,800	574,300	668,500	666,400	641,700	5.49	-3.71
Germany	2,669,000	2,744,000	2,847,700	2,978,000	3,009,600	25.77	1.06
Switzerland	151,600	164,100	181,300	201,800	217,500	1.86	7.78
Other Europe	1,143,100	1,127,600	1,130,700	1,191,300	1,237,100	10.59	3.84
Other countries of Europe	1,143,100	1,127,600	1,130,700	1,191,300	1,237,100	10.59	3.84

Yearbook of Tourism Statistics, Data 2008 – 2012, 2014 Edition

NETHERLANDS

5. Overnight stays of non-resident tourists in hotels and similar establishments, by country of residence

	2008	2009	2010	2011	2012	Market share 2012	% Change 2012-2011
TOTAL (*)	14,961,300	14,428,600	16,175,000	16,684,900	17,065,600	100.00	2.28
AFRICA	146,900	160,500	194,400	211,600	210,500	1.23	-0.52
Other Africa	146,900	160,500	194,400	211,600	210,500	1.23	-0.52
All countries of Africa	146,900	160,500	194,400	211,600	210,500	1.23	-0.52
AMERICAS	1,910,000	1,825,900	2,185,800	2,282,400	2,299,100	13.47	0.73
North America	1,626,100	1,539,500	1,812,800	1,835,700	1,814,000	10.63	-1.18
Canada	222,100	192,800	240,500	244,900	246,900	1.45	0.82
United States of America	1,404,000	1,346,700	1,572,300	1,590,800	1,567,100	9.18	-1.49
Other Americas	283,900	286,400	373,000	446,700	485,100	2.84	8.60
Other countries of the Americas	283,900	286,400	373,000	446,700	485,100	2.84	8.60
EAST ASIA AND THE PACIFIC	971,600	977,200	1,102,100	1,240,600	1,376,000	8.06	10.91
North-East Asia	439,900	426,200	465,400	541,600	590,600	3.46	9.05
China	175,400	200,500	202,700	253,200	266,500	1.56	5.25
Japan	196,200	162,300	196,800	196,700	228,800	1.34	16.32
Korea, Republic of	41,400	38,000	38,900	45,700	48,200	0.28	5.47
Taiwan, Province of China	26,900	25,400	27,000	46,000	47,100	0.28	2.39
South-East Asia	23,000	28,300	39,000	44,200	61,300	0.36	38.69
Indonesia	23,000	28,300	39,000	44,200	61,300	0.36	38.69
Australasia	190,600	188,200	248,600	281,900	295,500	1.73	4.82
Australia	164,300	164,800	222,800	251,700	264,000	1.55	4.89
New Zealand	26,300	23,400	25,800	30,200	31,500	0.18	4.30
Other East Asia and the Pacific	318,100	334,500	349,100	372,900	428,600	2.51	14.94
Other countries of Asia	300,800	318,600	325,500	349,900	411,600	2.41	17.63
Other countries of Oceania	17,300	15,900	23,600	23,000	17,000	0.10	-26.09
EUROPE	11,834,100	11,368,600	12,563,900	12,813,400	13,037,900	76.40	1.75
Central/Eastern Europe	486,500	427,000	497,100	590,600	632,200	3.70	7.04
Czech Republic	63,200	52,400	61,600	66,400	72,900	0.43	9.79
Hungary	52,400	41,700	49,400	59,000	54,900	0.32	-6.95
Poland	152,800	130,400	146,600	169,500	174,700	1.02	3.07
Russian Federation	198,400	185,200	220,700	275,300	303,900	1.78	10.39
Slovakia	19,700	17,300	18,800	20,400	25,800	0.15	26.47
Northern Europe	3,737,900	3,226,600	3,570,700	3,495,900	3,697,400	21.67	5.76
Denmark	240,900	215,000	256,700	237,600	223,200	1.31	-6.06
Finland	91,100	79,300	90,800	118,500	117,200	0.69	-1.10
Iceland	15,500	9,900	12,300	15,000	15,300	0.09	2.00
Ireland	209,000	197,000	189,000	156,700	164,900	0.97	5.23
Norway	162,800	162,200	176,900	188,600	211,500	1.24	12.14
Sweden	180,200	163,300	189,600	208,500	233,300	1.37	11.89
United Kingdom	2,838,400	2,399,900	2,655,400	2,571,000	2,732,000	16.01	6.26
Southern Europe	1,572,500	1,544,300	1,846,800	1,827,900	1,738,700	10.19	-4.88
Greece	84,000	91,700	87,300	81,600	71,400	0.42	-12.50
Italy	683,000	678,500	822,300	822,100	808,900	4.74	-1.61
Portugal	87,900	95,600	103,300	113,500	105,200	0.62	-7.31
Spain	717,600	678,500	833,900	810,700	753,200	4.41	-7.09
Western Europe	5,187,000	5,259,600	5,862,400	6,066,800	6,131,900	35.93	1.07
Austria	159,500	129,000	130,800	157,600	144,700	0.85	-8.19
Belgium	1,123,600	1,176,500	1,301,100	1,312,700	1,437,900	8.43	9.54
France	851,200	875,400	1,020,300	1,022,500	974,100	5.71	-4.73
Germany	2,738,600	2,752,100	3,029,200	3,149,600	3,125,200	18.31	-0.77
Luxembourg	61,600	60,200	81,000	79,200	81,000	0.47	2.27
Switzerland	252,500	266,400	300,000	345,200	369,000	2.16	6.89
East Mediterranean Europe	185,200	200,000	244,000	281,000	311,500	1.83	10.85
Israel	110,500	121,200	149,900	172,000	178,200	1.04	3.60
Turkey	74,700	78,800	94,100	109,000	133,300	0.78	22.29

521

NETHERLANDS

5. Overnight stays of non-resident tourists in hotels and similar establishments, by country of residence

	2008	2009	2010	2011	2012	Market share 2012	% Change 2012-2011
Other Europe	**665,000**	**711,100**	**542,900**	**551,200**	**526,200**	**3.08**	**-4.54**
Other countries of Europe	665,000	711,100	542,900	551,200	526,200	3.08	-4.54
SOUTH ASIA	**98,700**	**96,400**	**128,800**	**136,900**	**142,100**	**0.83**	**3.80**
India	98,700	96,400	128,800	136,900	142,100	0.83	3.80

Yearbook of Tourism Statistics, Data 2008 – 2012, 2014 Editic

NETHERLANDS

6. Overnight stays of non-resident tourists in all types of accommodation establishments, by country of residence

	2008	2009	2010	2011	2012	Market share 2012	% Change 2012-2011
TOTAL (*)	25,267,300	25,013,600	26,799,600	27,738,900	27,898,500	100.00	0.58
AFRICA	162,600	171,200	209,100	224,200	219,400	0.79	-2.14
Other Africa	162,600	171,200	209,100	224,200	219,400	0.79	-2.14
All countries of Africa	162,600	171,200	209,100	224,200	219,400	0.79	-2.14
AMERICAS	1,950,200	1,861,200	2,222,400	2,319,900	2,339,800	8.39	0.86
Other Americas	1,950,200	1,861,200	2,222,400	2,319,900	2,339,800	8.39	0.86
All countries of the Americas	1,950,200	1,861,200	2,222,400	2,319,900	2,339,800	8.39	0.86
EAST ASIA AND THE PACIFIC	1,233,100	1,237,300	1,434,100	1,602,600	1,746,100	6.26	8.95
Other East Asia and the Pacific	1,233,100	1,237,300	1,434,100	1,602,600	1,746,100	6.26	8.95
All countries of Asia	1,011,600	1,022,800	1,148,800	1,281,800	1,420,300	5.09	10.81
All countries of Oceania	221,500	214,500	285,300	320,800	325,800	1.17	1.56
EUROPE	21,921,400	21,743,900	22,934,000	23,592,200	23,593,200	84.57	0.00
Northern Europe	3,836,000	3,242,200	3,542,800	3,433,900	3,653,000	13.09	6.38
Denmark	313,900	289,400	315,000	298,500	279,500	1.00	-6.37
Sweden	204,800	181,500	204,700	226,700	251,100	0.90	10.76
United Kingdom	3,317,300	2,771,300	3,023,100	2,908,700	3,122,400	11.19	7.35
Southern Europe	1,542,700	1,467,500	1,787,400	1,770,200	1,672,200	5.99	-5.54
Italy	767,300	741,200	901,600	905,400	885,700	3.17	-2.18
Spain	775,400	726,300	885,800	864,800	786,500	2.82	-9.05
Western Europe	14,183,700	14,689,900	15,315,100	15,946,200	15,778,600	56.56	-1.05
Belgium	2,816,800	3,039,200	3,196,000	3,460,700	3,710,100	13.30	7.21
France	1,130,200	1,137,200	1,345,800	1,301,400	1,269,000	4.55	-2.49
Germany	9,922,700	10,172,700	10,403,700	10,759,300	10,354,700	37.12	-3.76
Switzerland	314,000	340,800	369,600	424,800	444,800	1.59	4.71
Other Europe	2,359,000	2,344,300	2,288,700	2,441,900	2,489,400	8.92	1.95
Other countries of Europe	2,359,000	2,344,300	2,288,700	2,441,900	2,489,400	8.92	1.95

NEW CALEDONIA

1. Arrivals of non-resident tourists at national borders, by nationality

	2008	2009	2010	2011	2012	Market share 2012	% Change 2012-2011
TOTAL	103,672	99,379	98,562	111,875			
AFRICA	281	251	234	278			
Other Africa	281	251	234	278			
All countries of Africa	281	251	234	278			
AMERICAS	2,769	2,485	2,830	3,106			
North America	2,533	2,218	2,432	2,745			
Canada	1,592	1,307	1,276	1,266			
United States of America	941	911	1,156	1,479			
South America	26	27	23	21			
Argentina	26	27	23	21			
Other Americas	210	240	375	340			
Other countries of the Americas	210	240	375	340			
EAST ASIA AND THE PACIFIC	48,805	47,310	47,146	48,193			
North-East Asia	21,457	21,288	21,049	21,085			
China	143	141	447	600			
Hong Kong, China	7	6	7	10			
Japan	20,062	18,878	18,498	18,089			
Korea, Republic of	1,245	2,263	2,097	2,386			
Australasia	23,214	21,376	20,454	19,574			
Australia	15,487	15,073	14,292	13,625			
New Zealand	7,727	6,303	6,162	5,949			
Melanesia	2,131	1,957	2,473	2,416			
Vanuatu	2,131	1,957	2,473	2,416			
Other East Asia and the Pacific	2,003	2,689	3,170	5,118			
Other countries of Asia	1,146	1,996	1,821	2,402			
Other countries of Oceania	857	693	1,349	2,716			
EUROPE	51,814	49,320	48,352	60,272			
Northern Europe	1,960	1,787	1,726	1,764			
United Kingdom	1,960	1,787	1,726	1,764			
Southern Europe	750	755	835	669			
Italy	750	755	835	669			
Western Europe	46,966	44,564	43,845	55,651			
France	45,890	43,251	42,737	54,334			
Germany	717	905	728	898			
Switzerland	359	408	380	419			
Other Europe	2,138	2,214	1,946	2,188			
Other countries of Europe	2,138	2,214	1,946	2,188			
NOT SPECIFIED	3	13		26			
Other countries of the World	3	13		26			

Yearbook of Tourism Statistics, Data 2008 – 2012, 2014 Edition

NEW CALEDONIA

1. Arrivals of non-resident tourists at national borders, by country of residence

		2008	2009	2010	2011	2012	Market share 2012	% Change 2012-2011
TOTAL	(*)	103,672	99,379	98,562	111,875	112,204	100.00	0.29
AFRICA		713	1,980	2,238	1,904	1,468	1.31	-22.90
East Africa		450	1,653	1,946	1,566	1,109	0.99	-29.18
Reunion		450	1,653	1,946	1,566	1,109	0.99	-29.18
Other Africa		263	327	292	338	359	0.32	6.21
Other countries of Africa		263	327	292	338	359	0.32	6.21
AMERICAS		2,707	2,518	2,891	2,889	2,956	2.63	2.32
Caribbean		136	229	289	275	210	0.19	-23.64
All countries of the Caribbean	(*)	136	229	289	275	210	0.19	-23.64
North America		2,390	2,045	2,255	2,289	2,466	2.20	7.73
Canada		1,475	1,150	1,182	1,192	1,383	1.23	16.02
United States of America		915	895	1,073	1,097	1,083	0.97	-1.28
South America		16	22	27	18	26	0.02	44.44
Argentina		16	22	27	18	26	0.02	44.44
Other Americas		165	222	320	307	254	0.23	-17.26
Other countries of the Americas		165	222	320	307	254	0.23	-17.26
EAST ASIA AND THE PACIFIC		64,578	63,213	64,573	68,172	64,548	57.53	-5.32
North-East Asia		21,755	21,415	21,165	21,546	20,976	18.69	-2.65
China		206	166	499	649	774	0.69	19.26
Hong Kong, China		138	111	89	98	120	0.11	22.45
Japan		20,225	18,926	18,534	18,455	17,430	15.53	-5.55
Korea, Republic of		1,186	2,212	2,043	2,344	2,652	2.36	13.14
Australasia		26,609	25,218	23,957	23,507	23,971	21.36	1.97
Australia		18,185	18,567	17,551	17,040	17,729	15.80	4.04
New Zealand		8,424	6,651	6,406	6,467	6,242	5.56	-3.48
Melanesia		3,136	2,869	3,652	4,061	3,891	3.47	-4.19
Vanuatu		3,136	2,869	3,652	4,061	3,891	3.47	-4.19
Polynesia		10,682	10,550	11,999	12,998	11,354	10.12	-12.65
French Polynesia		4,455	4,096	4,940	4,935	4,258	3.79	-13.72
Wallis and Futuna Islands		6,227	6,454	7,059	8,063	7,096	6.32	-11.99
Other East Asia and the Pacific		2,396	3,161	3,800	6,060	4,356	3.88	-28.12
Other countries of Asia		1,341	2,274	2,122	2,744	3,021	2.69	10.09
Other countries of Oceania		1,055	887	1,678	3,316	1,335	1.19	-59.74
EUROPE		35,636	31,652	28,859	38,886	43,231	38.53	11.17
Northern Europe		713	495	474	598	567	0.51	-5.18
United Kingdom		713	495	474	598	567	0.51	-5.18
Southern Europe		672	650	736	571	717	0.64	25.57
Italy		672	650	736	571	717	0.64	25.57
Western Europe		32,476	28,606	26,021	35,852	39,999	35.65	11.57
France		31,474	27,335	24,960	34,647	38,746	34.53	11.83
Germany		604	765	584	691	704	0.63	1.88
Switzerland		398	506	477	514	549	0.49	6.81
Other Europe		1,775	1,901	1,628	1,865	1,948	1.74	4.45
Other countries of Europe		1,775	1,901	1,628	1,865	1,948	1.74	4.45
NOT SPECIFIED		38	16	1	24	1	0.00	-95.83
Other countries of the World		38	16	1	24	1	0.00	-95.83

Yearbook of Tourism Statistics, Data 2008 – 2012, 2014 Edition

NEW CALEDONIA

3. Arrivals of non-resident tourists in hotels and similar establishments, by country of residence

		2008	2009	2010	2011	2012	Market share 2012	% Change 2012-2011
TOTAL	(*)	**102,394**	**114,842**	**133,385**	**142,437**	**121,497**	**100.00**	**-14.70**
EAST ASIA AND THE PACIFIC		**65,582**	**63,428**	**73,683**	**65,362**	**56,444**	**46.46**	**-13.64**
North-East Asia		**31,371**	**28,776**	**31,173**	**27,573**	**23,582**	**19.41**	**-14.47**
Japan		31,371	28,776	31,173	27,573	23,582	19.41	-14.47
Australasia		**34,211**	**34,652**	**42,510**	**37,789**	**32,862**	**27.05**	**-13.04**
Australia		24,358	24,115	25,789	26,406	22,923	18.87	-13.19
New Zealand		9,853	10,537	16,721	11,383	9,939	8.18	-12.69
EUROPE		**24,531**	**33,673**	**38,286**	**50,674**	**43,962**	**36.18**	**-13.25**
Western Europe		**24,531**	**33,673**	**38,286**	**50,674**	**43,962**	**36.18**	**-13.25**
France		24,531	33,673	38,286	50,674	43,962	36.18	-13.25
NOT SPECIFIED		**12,281**	**17,741**	**21,416**	**26,401**	**21,091**	**17.36**	**-20.11**
Other countries of the World		12,281	17,741	21,416	26,401	21,091	17.36	-20.11

Yearbook of Tourism Statistics, Data 2008 – 2012, 2014 Editi

NEW CALEDONIA

5. Overnight stays of non-resident tourists in hotels and similar establishments, by country of residence

		2008	2009	2010	2011	2012	Market share 2012	% Change 2012-2011
TOTAL	(*)	**360,233**	**304,274**	**279,406**	**316,228**	**288,020**	**100.00**	**-8.92**
EAST ASIA AND THE PACIFIC		**194,425**	**139,827**	**131,591**	**137,817**	**131,680**	**45.72**	**-4.45**
North-East Asia		**80,825**	**62,322**	**57,168**	**59,367**	**55,867**	**19.40**	**-5.90**
Japan		80,825	62,322	57,168	59,367	55,867	19.40	-5.90
Australasia		**113,600**	**77,505**	**74,423**	**78,450**	**75,813**	**26.32**	**-3.36**
Australia		78,008	52,926	48,810	53,296	50,538	17.55	-5.17
New Zealand		35,592	24,579	25,613	25,154	25,275	8.78	0.48
EUROPE		**114,097**	**113,793**	**97,060**	**122,168**	**110,632**	**38.41**	**-9.44**
Western Europe		**114,097**	**113,793**	**97,060**	**122,168**	**110,632**	**38.41**	**-9.44**
France		114,097	113,793	97,060	122,168	110,632	38.41	-9.44
NOT SPECIFIED		**51,711**	**50,654**	**50,755**	**56,243**	**45,708**	**15.87**	**-18.73**
Other countries of the World		51,711	50,654	50,755	56,243	45,708	15.87	-18.73

Yearbook of Tourism Statistics, Data 2008 – 2012, 2014 Edition

NEW ZEALAND

2. Arrivals of non-resident visitors at national borders, by country of residence

		2008	2009	2010	2011	2012	Market share 2012	% Change 2012-2011
TOTAL	(*)	2,447,235	2,447,532	2,510,759	2,594,196	2,554,784	100.00	-1.52
AFRICA		28,507	22,155	20,396	30,199	18,704	0.73	-38.06
East Africa		1,941	1,776	1,986	2,322	1,840	0.07	-20.76
Comoros					41			
Eritrea		75	18					
Ethiopia		23	68	46	128	80	0.00	-37.50
Kenya		330	385	325	374	384	0.02	2.67
Madagascar		19	70		16	48	0.00	200.00
Malawi		49	21	130	56	80	0.00	42.86
Mauritius		174	204	199	309	192	0.01	-37.86
Mozambique		24		29	62	112	0.00	80.65
Reunion		199	151	341	354	224	0.01	-36.72
Rwanda		20	27			32	0.00	
Seychelles		68	23	100	48	80	0.00	66.67
Uganda		137	116	98	149	64	0.00	-57.05
United Republic of Tanzania		186	182	237	239	96	0.00	-59.83
Zambia		208	72	159	213	128	0.01	-39.91
Zimbabwe		429	439	322	333	320	0.01	-3.90
Central Africa		137	155	144	194	224	0.01	15.46
Angola		73	64	74	66	48	0.00	-27.27
Cameroon		42		24		48	0.00	
Chad			41		25			
Congo			23		16	48	0.00	200.00
Democratic Republic of the Congo					25	16	0.00	-36.00
Equatorial Guinea		22	27		46			
Gabon				46	16	64	0.00	300.00
North Africa		149	220	162	360	144	0.01	-60.00
Algeria			23	22	96	32	0.00	-66.67
Morocco		25	72		48	48	0.00	0.00
Sudan		102	80	120	125	64	0.00	-48.80
Tunisia			45	20	91			
Western Sahara		22						
Southern Africa		25,720	19,535	17,719	26,700	15,984	0.63	-40.13
Botswana		201	93	174	105	96	0.00	-8.57
Lesotho			23					
Namibia		126	155	144	261	176	0.01	-32.57
South Africa		25,346	19,214	17,401	26,286	15,712	0.62	-40.23
Swaziland		47	50		48			
West Africa		560	469	385	623	512	0.02	-17.82
Burkina Faso					46	32	0.00	-30.43
Côte d'Ivoire					16			
Gambia				24	16			
Ghana		163	165	168	196	192	0.01	-2.04
Guinea		52						
Liberia		24	28					
Mali					40			
Mauritania		27		29	57			
Niger			27					
Nigeria		206	249	164	208	176	0.01	-15.38
Saint Helena		19				32	0.00	
Senegal		25				64	0.00	
Sierra Leone		19			20	16	0.00	-20.00
Togo		25			24			
AMERICAS		295,915	275,849	268,358	268,501	253,136	9.91	-5.72
Caribbean		1,740	1,509	1,272	1,513	1,232	0.05	-18.57

Yearbook of Tourism Statistics, Data 2008 – 2012, 2014 Edition

NEW ZEALAND

2. Arrivals of non-resident visitors at national borders, by country of residence

	2008	2009	2010	2011	2012	Market share 2012	% Change 2012-2011
Antigua and Barbuda	22	93		32	16	0.00	-50.00
Aruba					30		
Bahamas	91	119	29	78	64	0.00	-17.95
Barbados	102	123	55	86	32	0.00	-62.79
Bermuda	343	343	282	293	224	0.01	-23.55
British Virgin Islands	66	44	47	46	64	0.00	39.13
Cayman Islands	225	227	202	255	272	0.01	6.67
Cuba	25	18	53	16	16	0.00	0.00
Dominica	50	47	25		16	0.00	
Dominican Republic	25	45		40	112	0.00	180.00
Grenada			29		16	0.00	
Guadeloupe	49	21		16	16	0.00	0.00
Haiti			20				
Jamaica	170	89	176	149	80	0.00	-46.31
Martinique		23					
Netherlands Antilles	52	18	24	66			
Puerto Rico	264	89	178	138	64	0.00	-53.62
Saint Kitts and Nevis				16	16	0.00	0.00
Saint Lucia				32	16	0.00	-50.00
Saint Vincent and the Grenadines				16	16	0.00	0.00
Trinidad and Tobago	172	112	128	163	112	0.00	-31.29
Turks and Caicos Islands	62	98		16	64	0.00	300.00
United States Virgin Islands	22		24	25	16	0.00	-36.00
Central America	**532**	**397**	**588**	**404**	**528**	**0.02**	**30.69**
Belize			25				
Costa Rica	199	114	217	165	192	0.01	16.36
El Salvador	52	23	51	16			
Guatemala	66	95	79	52	128	0.01	146.15
Honduras	47		67				
Nicaragua	27	28		16	32	0.00	100.00
Panama	141	137	149	155	176	0.01	13.55
North America	**268,957**	**249,531**	**241,574**	**236,947**	**227,344**	**8.90**	**-4.05**
Canada	53,267	48,656	48,942	49,154	46,448	1.82	-5.51
Greenland	22	23		36	64	0.00	77.78
Mexico	3,258	3,060	2,923	3,043	3,152	0.12	3.58
United States of America	212,410	197,792	189,709	184,714	177,680	6.95	-3.81
South America	**24,686**	**24,412**	**24,924**	**29,637**	**23,984**	**0.94**	**-19.07**
Argentina	5,479	6,237	5,654	9,695	6,048	0.24	-37.62
Bolivia	64	73	105	32	80	0.00	150.00
Brazil	11,413	11,355	11,796	11,587	10,272	0.40	-11.35
Chile	4,839	4,369	4,938	5,382	4,848	0.19	-9.92
Colombia	843	776	765	1,026	848	0.03	-17.35
Ecuador	190	162	99	181	128	0.01	-29.28
Falkland Islands, Malvinas	76	21	20	68	16	0.00	-76.47
French Guiana		28	22				
Guyana	22						
Paraguay	76	75	95	120	64	0.00	-46.67
Peru	397	325	419	366	432	0.02	18.03
Suriname		23	55		16	0.00	
Uruguay	1,001	716	776	902	976	0.04	8.20
Venezuela	286	252	180	278	256	0.01	-7.91
Other Americas					**48**	**0.00**	
Other countries of the Americas					48	0.00	
EAST ASIA AND THE PACIFIC	**1,508,819**	**1,561,724**	**1,649,581**	**1,695,043**	**1,741,744**	**68.18**	**2.76**
North-East Asia	**335,389**	**274,383**	**323,835**	**311,337**	**367,728**	**14.39**	**18.11**
China	112,398	102,259	122,712	145,524	197,024	7.71	35.39
Hong Kong, China	21,776	23,572	24,287	25,397	26,272	1.03	3.45

Yearbook of Tourism Statistics, Data 2008 – 2012, 2014 Edition

NEW ZEALAND

2. Arrivals of non-resident visitors at national borders, by country of residence

	2008	2009	2010	2011	2012	Market share 2012	% Change 2012-2011
Japan	102,482	78,426	87,735	68,963	72,080	2.82	4.52
Korea, Dem. People's Republic of		23	29				
Korea, Republic of	79,061	52,921	67,309	52,787	52,896	2.07	0.21
Macao, China	326	458	450	504	624	0.02	23.81
Mongolia	97	140	121	187	192	0.01	2.67
Taiwan, Province of China	19,249	16,584	21,192	17,975	18,640	0.73	3.70
South-East Asia	**87,641**	**90,894**	**96,989**	**116,580**	**110,096**	**4.31**	**-5.56**
Brunei Darussalam	1,157	1,340	1,369	1,192	1,072	0.04	-10.07
Cambodia	483	646	586	609	640	0.03	5.09
Indonesia	7,569	9,506	9,787	11,450	12,256	0.48	7.04
Lao People's Democratic Republic	173	248	226	222	240	0.01	8.11
Malaysia	19,608	19,702	21,843	35,011	29,424	1.15	-15.96
Myanmar	29	114	144	178	192	0.01	7.87
Philippines	9,230	7,572	8,240	8,563	9,568	0.37	11.74
Singapore	28,836	29,582	30,300	38,680	36,400	1.42	-5.89
Thailand	18,356	19,728	21,434	17,523	16,944	0.66	-3.30
Timor-Leste	166	89	292	238	144	0.01	-39.50
Viet Nam	2,034	2,367	2,768	2,914	3,216	0.13	10.36
Australasia	**976,200**	**1,082,680**	**1,119,879**	**1,156,426**	**1,155,792**	**45.24**	**-0.05**
Australia	976,200	1,082,680	1,119,879	1,156,426	1,155,792	45.24	-0.05
Melanesia	**43,423**	**46,642**	**45,885**	**47,946**	**48,624**	**1.90**	**1.41**
Fiji	22,512	23,608	20,853	21,619	22,432	0.88	3.76
New Caledonia	12,888	15,217	16,148	16,597	16,752	0.66	0.93
Norfolk Island	1,039	798	931	961	848	0.03	-11.76
Papua New Guinea	1,653	1,764	2,293	2,784	2,368	0.09	-14.94
Solomon Islands	1,030	1,027	1,130	1,341	1,360	0.05	1.42
Vanuatu	4,301	4,228	4,530	4,644	4,864	0.19	4.74
Micronesia	**963**	**1,040**	**874**	**1,024**	**880**	**0.03**	**-14.06**
Guam	119	210	154	162	160	0.01	-1.23
Kiribati	638	549	577	670	512	0.02	-23.58
Marshall Islands	114	121	47	48	64	0.00	33.33
Micronesia, Federated States of	29	94		16	64	0.00	300.00
Nauru	44	66	47	48	32	0.00	-33.33
Northern Mariana Islands				32			
Palau	19		49	48	48	0.00	0.00
Polynesia	**65,203**	**66,085**	**62,094**	**61,698**	**58,624**	**2.29**	**-4.98**
American Samoa	1,667	1,174	1,228	1,109	1,008	0.04	-9.11
Cook Islands	11,346	11,042	10,577	11,309	9,856	0.39	-12.85
French Polynesia	16,868	19,632	19,090	16,785	15,552	0.61	-7.35
Niue	1,960	2,151	1,889	1,959	2,032	0.08	3.73
Pitcairn	23	44		16	16	0.00	0.00
Samoa	18,804	17,678	16,250	16,787	16,192	0.63	-3.54
Tokelau	373	232	291	227	224	0.01	-1.32
Tonga	13,513	13,469	12,167	12,914	13,200	0.52	2.21
Tuvalu	410	381	316	390	320	0.01	-17.95
Wallis and Futuna Islands	239	282	286	202	224	0.01	10.89
Other East Asia and the Pacific				**25**	**32**		
Other countries of Oceania				25	32		
EUROPE	**518,767**	**491,498**	**465,308**	**475,955**	**411,360**	**16.10**	**-13.57**
Central/Eastern Europe	**17,147**	**16,987**	**16,451**	**17,719**	**17,808**	**0.70**	**0.50**
Armenia		73	42		16	0.00	
Azerbaijan	116	119	29	48	96	0.00	100.00
Belarus	22	75	123	98	80	0.00	-18.37
Bulgaria	418	450	303	394	528	0.02	34.01
Czech Republic	3,386	3,811	3,605	3,877	3,712	0.15	-4.26
Estonia	567	421	330	306	288	0.01	-5.88
Georgia	24		26	155			

530

NEW ZEALAND

2. Arrivals of non-resident visitors at national borders, by country of residence

	2008	2009	2010	2011	2012	Market share 2012	% Change 2012-2011
Hungary	1,302	1,157	1,191	1,145	1,072	0.04	-6.38
Kazakhstan	189	203	144	157	208	0.01	32.48
Kyrgyzstan	43		53		16	0.00	
Latvia	265	417	306	189	208	0.01	10.05
Lithuania	306	258	204	143	336	0.01	134.97
Poland	2,693	2,433	2,546	2,759	2,752	0.11	-0.25
Republic of Moldova		69	47	16	48	0.00	200.00
Romania	1,082	862	863	921	800	0.03	-13.14
Russian Federation	4,009	3,952	4,135	5,112	5,024	0.20	-1.72
Slovakia	792	778	789	644	800	0.03	24.22
Tajikistan		27		16	48	0.00	200.00
Turkmenistan		24					
Ukraine	1,859	1,817	1,715	1,677	1,712	0.07	2.09
Uzbekistan	74	41		62	64	0.00	3.23
Northern Europe	**337,494**	**304,697**	**277,185**	**275,942**	**228,800**	**8.96**	**-17.08**
Channel Islands	1,225	1,226	1,245	1,420	1,088	0.04	-23.38
Denmark	10,956	10,172	9,854	9,194	8,256	0.32	-10.20
Faeroe Islands	43	52	121	102	32	0.00	-68.63
Finland	3,700	3,951	3,942	3,817	3,632	0.14	-4.85
Iceland	310	301	225	414	656	0.03	58.45
Ireland	21,153	17,055	13,290	16,302	11,120	0.44	-31.79
Isle of Man	441	475	518	526	400	0.02	-23.95
Norway	3,908	3,861	4,325	4,359	3,968	0.16	-8.97
Sweden	12,330	10,867	11,114	11,438	11,488	0.45	0.44
United Kingdom	283,428	256,737	232,551	228,370	188,160	7.37	-17.61
Southern Europe	**21,034**	**22,536**	**22,749**	**22,396**	**20,688**	**0.81**	**-7.63**
Albania				16	16	0.00	0.00
Andorra	47	18	25	48	32	0.00	-33.33
Bosnia and Herzegovina				16			
Croatia	283	211	311	247	240	0.01	-2.83
Gibraltar	49	41		66	96	0.00	45.45
Greece	721	941	723	787	656	0.03	-16.65
Italy	8,151	8,460	8,617	8,952	8,576	0.34	-4.20
Malta	373	311	352	344	320	0.01	-6.98
Montenegro		24		36	32	0.00	-11.11
Portugal	1,084	1,077	1,072	1,036	848	0.03	-18.15
San Marino		27		16			
Serbia	27	162	134	140	112	0.00	-20.00
Serbia and Montenegro	101						
Slovenia	603	670	748	698	640	0.03	-8.31
Spain	9,502	10,539	10,747	9,946	9,024	0.35	-9.27
TFYR of Macedonia	93	55	20	48	96	0.00	100.00
Western Europe	**135,828**	**139,345**	**140,657**	**153,003**	**138,352**	**5.42**	**-9.58**
Austria	6,747	6,819	6,930	6,909	7,184	0.28	3.98
Belgium	4,935	4,962	5,051	5,198	4,736	0.19	-8.89
France	21,125	23,227	24,579	36,607	24,944	0.98	-31.86
Germany	62,300	64,564	64,648	63,719	63,776	2.50	0.09
Liechtenstein	27	27	54	121	80	0.00	-33.88
Luxembourg	523	353	476	504	368	0.01	-26.98
Monaco	102	96	173	161	144	0.01	-10.56
Netherlands	25,536	24,300	23,378	23,608	21,424	0.84	-9.25
Switzerland	14,533	14,997	15,368	16,176	15,696	0.61	-2.97
East Mediterranean Europe	**7,264**	**7,933**	**8,266**	**6,895**	**5,712**	**0.22**	**-17.16**
Cyprus	369	371	277	284	352	0.01	23.94
Israel	5,926	6,768	6,993	5,592	4,528	0.18	-19.03
Turkey	969	794	996	1,019	832	0.03	-18.35
MIDDLE EAST	**13,268**	**15,234**	**16,097**	**16,246**	**13,264**	**0.52**	**-18.36**

Yearbook of Tourism Statistics, Data 2008 – 2012, 2014 Edition

NEW ZEALAND

2. Arrivals of non-resident visitors at national borders, by country of residence

	2008	2009	2010	2011	2012	Market share 2012	% Change 2012-2011
Bahrain	546	756	668	712	496	0.02	-30.34
Egypt	332	344	382	446	336	0.01	-24.66
Iraq	193	220	213	339	176	0.01	-48.08
Jordan	80	152	111	93	96	0.00	3.23
Kuwait	418	504	444	576	464	0.02	-19.44
Lebanon	46	109	146	89	80	0.00	-10.11
Libya	19	73	53	16			
Oman	698	718	778	623	656	0.03	5.30
Palestine	23		29	16			
Qatar	957	867	1,130	1,138	1,136	0.04	-0.18
Saudi Arabia	3,923	4,292	4,418	4,189	3,088	0.12	-26.28
Syrian Arab Republic	51	88	26	16	32	0.00	100.00
United Arab Emirates	5,960	7,088	7,699	7,977	6,672	0.26	-16.36
Yemen	22	23		16	32	0.00	100.00
SOUTH ASIA	**26,927**	**28,461**	**32,948**	**31,927**	**33,104**	**1.30**	**3.69**
Afghanistan	237	166	252	277	272	0.01	-1.81
Bangladesh	236	380	493	377	384	0.02	1.86
Bhutan	22	23		46	32	0.00	-30.43
India	23,860	25,336	29,486	28,262	29,856	1.17	5.64
Iran, Islamic Republic of	354	341	420	505	352	0.01	-30.30
Maldives	86	198	125	140	112	0.00	-20.00
Nepal	189	220	289	227	240	0.01	5.73
Pakistan	576	674	627	606	528	0.02	-12.87
Sri Lanka	1,367	1,123	1,256	1,487	1,328	0.05	-10.69
NOT SPECIFIED	**55,032**	**52,611**	**58,071**	**76,325**	**83,472**	**3.27**	**9.36**
Other countries of the World	31,236	30,077	37,093	46,587	50,928	1.99	9.32
Nationals Residing Abroad	23,796	22,534	20,978	29,738	32,544	1.27	9.44

Yearbook of Tourism Statistics, Data 2008 – 2012, 2014 Edition

NICARAGUA

1. Arrivals of non-resident tourists at national borders, by nationality

	2008	2009	2010	2011	2012	Market share 2012	% Change 2012-2011
TOTAL	857,901	931,904	1,011,251	1,060,031	1,179,581	100.00	11.28
AFRICA	706	563	605	487	622	0.05	27.72
East Africa	99	89	88	87	91	0.01	4.60
Burundi				1			
Djibouti		9	1	1	3	0.00	200.00
Ethiopia	11	10	22	6	9	0.00	50.00
Kenya	22	12	10	18	12	0.00	-33.33
Madagascar	2	1	2	1	1	0.00	0.00
Malawi	3	2	1	5			
Mauritius	16	8	10		3	0.00	
Mozambique	4	5	6	8	6	0.00	-25.00
Rwanda	2	2	1	6			
Seychelles		6	7				
Somalia		3	4	8	8	0.00	0.00
Uganda	8	11	8	13	13	0.00	0.00
United Republic of Tanzania	14	11	12	14	18	0.00	28.57
Zambia	4	2		3	5	0.00	66.67
Zimbabwe	13	7	4	3	13	0.00	333.33
Central Africa	17	29	22	18	18	0.00	0.00
Angola	9	7	5	5	6	0.00	20.00
Cameroon	6	10	7	3	4	0.00	33.33
Central African Republic		4	7	5	2	0.00	-60.00
Congo	2			3	4	0.00	33.33
Equatorial Guinea		6					
Gabon		2	3	2	2	0.00	0.00
North Africa	35	38	45	42	54	0.00	28.57
Algeria	8	16	13	11	14	0.00	27.27
Morocco	20	19	23	25	31	0.00	24.00
Sudan	1	1	1				
Tunisia	6	2	8	6	9	0.00	50.00
Southern Africa	251	255	282	237	276	0.02	16.46
Botswana		2	3	8	4	0.00	-50.00
Lesotho			6		1	0.00	
Namibia		5		1	4	0.00	300.00
South Africa	251	244	271	223	259	0.02	16.14
Swaziland		4	2	5	8	0.00	60.00
West Africa	58	74	55	49	86	0.01	75.51
Benin	1						
Burkina Faso	5			2	15	0.00	650.00
Cape Verde		9	8		1	0.00	
Côte d'Ivoire		23					
Gambia	7		2	1	3	0.00	200.00
Ghana	13	9	14	22	17	0.00	-22.73
Guinea	9	8	1	1	2	0.00	100.00
Guinea-Bissau	3		1		3	0.00	
Mali	2	2	3	1	1	0.00	0.00
Mauritania	1		1				
Niger		1			3	0.00	
Nigeria	9	11	18	18	32	0.00	77.78
Senegal	7	9	4	4	7	0.00	75.00
Sierra Leone	1	1	3		2	0.00	
Togo		1					
Other Africa	246	78	113	54	97	0.01	79.63
Other countries of Africa	246	78	113	54	97	0.01	79.63
AMERICAS	714,212	769,799	846,897	893,498	999,987	84.77	11.92

Yearbook of Tourism Statistics, Data 2008 – 2012, 2014 Edition

NICARAGUA

1. Arrivals of non-resident tourists at national borders, by nationality

	2008	2009	2010	2011	2012	Market share 2012	% Change 2012-2011
Caribbean	**4,127**	**5,032**	**4,530**	**4,770**	**5,707**	**0.48**	**19.64**
Antigua and Barbuda	6	3	4	2	16	0.00	700.00
Aruba	3	2	1				
Bahamas	32	29	37	59	66	0.01	11.86
Barbados	24	33	27	34	30	0.00	-11.76
Bermuda	14	6	8	11	14	0.00	27.27
Bonaire		2	2	1			
Cayman Islands	114	154	121	88	109	0.01	23.86
Cuba	2,091	2,487	2,383	2,238	2,251	0.19	0.58
Dominica	69	24	11	33	10	0.00	-69.70
Dominican Republic	1,425	1,882	1,618	1,794	2,658	0.23	48.16
Grenada	16	20	3	16	15	0.00	-6.25
Guadeloupe		2	4	1			
Haiti	70	81	51	114	91	0.01	-20.18
Jamaica	104	131	132	122	141	0.01	15.57
Martinique				1	1	0.00	0.00
Montserrat		1					
Netherlands Antilles	1		4	1			
Puerto Rico	20	15	4	5	9	0.00	80.00
Saint Lucia	10	8	9	12	15	0.00	25.00
Saint Vincent and the Grenadines	61	57	23	41	119	0.01	190.24
Trinidad and Tobago	67	87	78	180	142	0.01	-21.11
United States Virgin Islands		8	10	17	20	0.00	17.65
Central America	**460,990**	**494,107**	**573,489**	**611,947**	**682,672**	**57.87**	**11.56**
Belize	502	593	578	537	625	0.05	16.39
Costa Rica	70,733	111,861	125,811	136,466	160,108	13.57	17.32
El Salvador	123,501	121,069	135,455	138,120	152,741	12.95	10.59
Guatemala	68,819	67,317	76,695	83,408	92,877	7.87	11.35
Honduras	182,511	176,120	214,776	230,965	251,804	21.35	9.02
Panama	14,924	17,147	20,174	22,451	24,517	2.08	9.20
North America	**231,271**	**250,232**	**247,857**	**253,431**	**287,523**	**24.38**	**13.45**
Canada	20,233	24,161	23,597	25,676	30,710	2.60	19.61
Mexico	14,436	13,423	13,781	13,769	15,967	1.35	15.96
United States of America	196,602	212,648	210,479	213,986	240,846	20.42	12.55
South America	**17,824**	**20,428**	**21,021**	**23,350**	**24,085**	**2.04**	**3.15**
Argentina	2,842	3,638	3,779	3,771	4,339	0.37	15.06
Bolivia	606	740	752	883	761	0.06	-13.82
Brazil	2,451	2,667	3,226	3,659	3,665	0.31	0.16
Chile	1,578	1,685	1,585	1,920	1,823	0.15	-5.05
Colombia	3,227	4,001	4,204	4,869	4,779	0.41	-1.85
Ecuador	1,164	1,263	1,282	1,509	1,694	0.14	12.26
Guyana	51	53	32	22	48	0.00	118.18
Paraguay	164	142	152	209	210	0.02	0.48
Peru	1,960	2,386	2,347	2,233	2,309	0.20	3.40
Suriname	9	30	11	13	61	0.01	369.23
Uruguay	486	615	596	730	660	0.06	-9.59
Venezuela	3,286	3,208	3,055	3,532	3,736	0.32	5.78
EAST ASIA AND THE PACIFIC	**9,360**	**11,982**	**10,620**	**10,252**	**10,785**	**0.91**	**5.20**
North-East Asia	**4,454**	**5,357**	**5,093**	**5,255**	**5,533**	**0.47**	**5.29**
China	220	641	404	303	354	0.03	16.83
Hong Kong, China	12	17	31	18	15	0.00	-16.67
Japan	1,527	1,542	1,669	1,747	1,984	0.17	13.57
Korea, Republic of	1,827	1,992	2,095	2,316	2,209	0.19	-4.62
Mongolia	1			1	1	0.00	0.00
Taiwan, Province of China	867	1,165	894	870	970	0.08	11.49
South-East Asia	**2,479**	**3,194**	**1,864**	**1,087**	**885**	**0.08**	**-18.58**
Indonesia	95	782	86	124	61	0.01	-50.81

534

NICARAGUA

1. Arrivals of non-resident tourists at national borders, by nationality

	2008	2009	2010	2011	2012	Market share 2012	% Change 2012-2011
Lao People's Democratic Republic	1		2				
Malaysia	38	50	50	50	49	0.00	-2.00
Myanmar	89	140	81	47	20	0.00	-57.45
Philippines	2,075	2,056	1,533	741	558	0.05	-24.70
Singapore	26	43	41	52	55	0.00	5.77
Thailand	138	90	46	59	120	0.01	103.39
Viet Nam	17	33	25	14	22	0.00	57.14
Australasia	**2,422**	**3,412**	**3,645**	**3,901**	**4,353**	**0.37**	**11.59**
Australia	1,944	2,787	3,017	3,255	3,665	0.31	12.60
New Zealand	478	625	628	646	688	0.06	6.50
Melanesia	**3**	**3**	**7**	**3**	**5**	**0.00**	**66.67**
Fiji	2	1	4	2	4	0.00	100.00
Papua New Guinea	1	2	3	1	1	0.00	0.00
Micronesia	**1**	**11**	**11**	**6**	**8**	**0.00**	**33.33**
Kiribati	1						
Micronesia, Federated States of		11	11	6	8	0.00	33.33
Polynesia	**1**	**5**			**1**	**0.00**	
French Polynesia		5					
Tonga	1				1	0.00	
EUROPE	**57,649**	**71,540**	**73,644**	**75,948**	**79,435**	**6.73**	**4.59**
Central/Eastern Europe	**2,141**	**2,788**	**3,112**	**2,934**	**3,319**	**0.28**	**13.12**
Armenia	2		3	3	4	0.00	33.33
Azerbaijan		2	2	2	3	0.00	50.00
Belarus				2	44	0.00	2,100.00
Bulgaria	121	97	106	88	95	0.01	7.95
Czech Republic		453	587	470	566	0.05	20.43
Czech Republic/Slovakia	435	87	120	131	162	0.01	23.66
Estonia	72	51	57	64	29	0.00	-54.69
Georgia	55	55	65	35	38	0.00	8.57
Hungary	125	245	205	157	187	0.02	19.11
Kazakhstan		6	8	8	13	0.00	62.50
Kyrgyzstan			5	1			
Latvia	18	50	18	4	40	0.00	900.00
Lithuania	30	39	35	92	85	0.01	-7.61
Poland	356	489	550	595	595	0.05	0.00
Republic of Moldova		7	4	4	6	0.00	50.00
Romania	227	221	172	208	189	0.02	-9.13
Russian Federation	516	770	1,003	893	1,044	0.09	16.91
Tajikistan		3		2			
Turkmenistan		4	4		1	0.00	
Ukraine	175	206	163	171	216	0.02	26.32
USSR (former)	9						
Uzbekistan		3	5	4	2	0.00	-50.00
Northern Europe	**17,044**	**19,119**	**17,729**	**18,071**	**17,975**	**1.52**	**-0.53**
Denmark	1,922	2,230	2,117	2,101	2,099	0.18	-0.10
Finland	587	784	766	617	718	0.06	16.37
Iceland	90	115	81	101	93	0.01	-7.92
Ireland	937	1,047	1,101	992	1,051	0.09	5.95
Norway	1,375	1,610	1,822	1,757	1,704	0.14	-3.02
Sweden	2,122	2,572	2,318	2,396	2,658	0.23	10.93
United Kingdom	10,011	10,761	9,524	10,107	9,652	0.82	-4.50
Southern Europe	**14,941**	**16,559**	**17,823**	**17,680**	**18,808**	**1.59**	**6.38**
Albania	11	8	5	3	8	0.00	166.67
Andorra	9	9	13	13	8	0.00	-38.46
Bosnia and Herzegovina		2	2	7	9	0.00	28.57
Croatia	82	64	65	50	86	0.01	72.00
Greece	151	215	196	195	175	0.01	-10.26
Holy See		2	1	3	2	0.00	-33.33

Yearbook of Tourism Statistics, Data 2008 – 2012, 2014 Edition

NICARAGUA

1. Arrivals of non-resident tourists at national borders, by nationality

	2008	2009	2010	2011	2012	Market share 2012	% Change 2012-2011
Italy	4,355	5,118	5,613	5,541	5,781	0.49	4.33
Malta	7	9	8	10	20	0.00	100.00
Portugal	321	349	361	349	426	0.04	22.06
San Marino	1				2	0.00	
Serbia		1	22	26	33	0.00	26.92
Serbia and Montenegro		35					
Slovenia	117	125	164	164	198	0.02	20.73
Spain	9,830	10,616	11,338	11,305	12,052	1.02	6.61
TFYR of Macedonia		6	7	9	8	0.00	-11.11
Yugoslavia, SFR (former)	57		28	5			
Western Europe	**22,292**	**31,236**	**33,161**	**35,141**	**36,874**	**3.13**	**4.93**
Austria	1,086	1,388	1,399	1,576	1,653	0.14	4.89
Belgium	1,519	2,542	3,538	3,266	2,822	0.24	-13.59
France	5,009	6,496	7,065	7,131	7,648	0.65	7.25
Germany	7,489	10,834	11,048	12,118	13,255	1.12	9.38
Liechtenstein	2	5	14	6	5	0.00	-16.67
Luxembourg	43	74	75	67	95	0.01	41.79
Monaco		2			3	0.00	
Netherlands	4,633	6,418	6,468	7,178	7,370	0.62	2.67
Switzerland	2,511	3,477	3,554	3,799	4,023	0.34	5.90
East Mediterranean Europe	**1,231**	**1,838**	**1,819**	**2,122**	**2,459**	**0.21**	**15.88**
Cyprus	9	15	22	14	11	0.00	-21.43
Israel	1,064	1,618	1,595	1,895	2,187	0.19	15.41
Turkey	158	205	202	213	261	0.02	22.54
MIDDLE EAST	**127**	**164**	**133**	**143**	**193**	**0.02**	**34.97**
Bahrain	1	1	4				
Egypt	13	11	14	27	26	0.00	-3.70
Iraq	1	1			3	0.00	
Jordan	14	15	24	27	35	0.00	29.63
Kuwait	4	4	2	6	4	0.00	-33.33
Lebanon	23	22	18	10	14	0.00	40.00
Libya	60	61	49	35	38	0.00	8.57
Palestine	8	13	8	19	43	0.00	126.32
Qatar			1	8			
Saudi Arabia	3	4	6	3	20	0.00	566.67
Syrian Arab Republic		4	1	1	4	0.00	300.00
United Arab Emirates		28	4	7	6	0.00	-14.29
Yemen			2				
SOUTH ASIA	**1,775**	**733**	**2,089**	**1,573**	**818**	**0.07**	**-48.00**
Afghanistan	3	2		3			
Bangladesh	12	35	17	14	13	0.00	-7.14
India	1,552	513	1,935	1,410	562	0.05	-60.14
Iran, Islamic Republic of	74	105	105	95	195	0.02	105.26
Maldives				1	1	0.00	0.00
Nepal	22	11	7	7	7	0.00	0.00
Pakistan	86	34	13	10	20	0.00	100.00
Sri Lanka	26	33	12	33	20	0.00	-39.39
NOT SPECIFIED	**74,072**	**77,123**	**77,263**	**78,130**	**87,741**	**7.44**	**12.30**
Other countries of the World	54	2	53	50	36	0.00	-28.00
Nationals Residing Abroad	74,018	77,121	77,210	78,080	87,705	7.44	12.33

Yearbook of Tourism Statistics, Data 2008 – 2012, 2014 Edition

NIGER

1. Arrivals of non-resident tourists at national borders, by nationality

	2008	2009	2010	2011	2012	Market share 2012	% Change 2012-2011
TOTAL	73,154	65,883	74,278	82,370			
AFRICA	46,981	42,312	47,702	52,881			
Other Africa	46,981	42,312	47,702	52,881			
All countries of Africa	46,981	42,312	47,702	52,881			
AMERICAS	4,528	4,078	4,598	5,107			
North America	3,600	3,947	4,450	4,942			
Canada	1,252	1,373	1,548	1,719			
United States of America	2,348	2,574	2,902	3,223			
Other Americas	928	131	148	165			
Other countries of the Americas	928	131	148	165			
EAST ASIA AND THE PACIFIC	3,063	3,158	3,560	3,954			
North-East Asia	1,900	2,259	2,547	2,829			
Japan	1,900	2,259	2,547	2,829			
Other East Asia and the Pacific	1,163	899	1,013	1,125			
Other countries of Asia	1,163	899	1,013	1,125			
EUROPE	18,138	16,335	18,418	20,428			
Southern Europe	775	961	1,085	1,109			
Italy	775	961	1,085	1,109			
Western Europe	16,317	15,255	17,331	19,237			
Benelux	881	1,093	1,232	1,373			
France	14,667	13,209	14,892	16,519			
Germany	769	953	1,207	1,345			
Other Europe	1,046	119	2	82			
Other countries of Europe	1,046	119	2	82			
MIDDLE EAST	444						
All countries of Middle East	444						

Yearbook of Tourism Statistics, Data 2008 – 2012, 2014 Edition

NIGERIA

2. Arrivals of non-resident visitors at national borders, by nationality

		2008	2009	2010	2011	2012	Market share 2012	% Change 2012-2011
TOTAL	(*)	5,820,497	6,053,318	6,113,384	3,765,400	4,673,136	100.00	24.11
AFRICA		4,014,981	4,175,489	4,185,492	872,285	1,091,802	23.36	25.17
East Africa		184,689	192,077	192,803	35,887	114,790	2.46	219.87
Burundi						2,922	0.06	
Djibouti						1,152	0.02	
Eritrea						780	0.02	
Ethiopia		77,827	80,941	81,053	6,307	15,434	0.33	144.71
Kenya		40,262	41,872	41,981	22,720	39,362	0.84	73.25
Madagascar						4,140	0.09	
Malawi						1,776	0.04	
Mozambique		20,836	21,669	21,757		1,674	0.04	
Rwanda		277	288	379	1,520	4,080	0.09	168.42
Somalia		554	576	677		5,460	0.12	
Uganda		3,712	3,860	3,886	2,720	9,410	0.20	245.96
United Republic of Tanzania		16,899	17,575	17,666	1,900	13,074	0.28	588.11
Zambia		2,345	2,439	2,483	720	6,622	0.14	819.72
Zimbabwe		21,977	22,857	22,921		8,904	0.19	
Central Africa		490,230	510,574	511,231	270,151	283,496	6.07	4.94
Angola		12,795	13,385	13,496		24,324	0.52	
Cameroon		223,984	233,274	233,370	205,920	174,544	3.74	-15.24
Central African Republic		15,349	15,984	16,035	2,731	8,472	0.18	210.22
Chad		178,100	185,527	185,633	48,400	12,790	0.27	-73.57
Congo		16,226	16,803	16,852	3,560	34,158	0.73	859.49
Democratic Republic of the Congo		16,128	16,801	16,908	4,720	8,530	0.18	80.72
Equatorial Guinea		1,078	1,123	1,195	2,900	796	0.02	-72.55
Gabon		25,982	27,065	27,114	1,920	18,730	0.40	875.52
Sao Tome and Principe		588	612	628		1,152	0.02	
North Africa		383,431	397,936	398,485	17,030	37,316	0.80	119.12
Algeria		76,647	79,547	79,658		8,178	0.18	
Morocco		120,706	125,272	125,421		6,468	0.14	
South Sudan						5,082	0.11	
Sudan		132,130	137,128	137,288	15,480	11,230	0.24	-27.45
Tunisia		53,948	55,989	56,118	1,550	6,358	0.14	310.19
Southern Africa		81,102	84,346	90,682	42,440	95,474	2.04	124.96
Botswana		13,600	14,129	14,220		10,278	0.22	
Lesotho		13,165	13,706	13,812		2,964	0.06	
Namibia		35,076	36,479	36,556		7,140	0.15	
South Africa		19,261	20,032	26,094	42,440	74,384	1.59	75.27
Swaziland						708	0.02	
West Africa		2,875,529	2,990,556	2,992,291	506,777	560,726	12.00	10.65
Benin		822,695	855,605	855,712	65,760	58,110	1.24	-11.63
Burkina Faso		66,713	69,380	69,459	10,000	11,934	0.26	19.34
Cape Verde		575	598	624	4,280	3,914	0.08	-8.55
Côte d'Ivoire		106,394	110,650	110,839	17,720	17,348	0.37	-2.10
Gambia		37,956	39,475	39,587		15,558	0.33	
Ghana		43,420	45,157	45,406	177,640	169,720	3.63	-4.46
Guinea		41,120	42,764	42,836	38,800	22,272	0.48	-42.60
Guinea-Bissau						20,616	0.44	
Liberia		225,153	234,160	234,254	26,000	14,428	0.31	-44.51
Mali		77,639	80,745	80,793	29,200	29,918	0.64	2.46
Mauritania		2,012	2,093	2,284	5,017	7,740	0.17	54.28
Niger		1,224,399	1,273,378	1,273,550	64,400	93,370	2.00	44.98
Senegal		121,347	126,201	126,464	30,920	35,754	0.77	15.63
Sierra Leone		34,793	36,185	36,257	12,960	14,536	0.31	12.16
Togo		71,313	74,165	74,226	24,080	45,508	0.97	88.99

538

NIGERIA

2. Arrivals of non-resident visitors at national borders, by nationality

	2008	2009	2010	2011	2012	Market share 2012	% Change 2012-2011
AMERICAS	244,455	256,055	257,581	176,880	478,144	10.23	170.32
Caribbean	30,043	31,469	31,841	37,760	28,182	0.60	-25.37
Antigua and Barbuda					588	0.01	
Bahamas					2,496	0.05	
Barbados	3,806	3,987	4,064		1,386	0.03	
Cuba	4,323	4,527	4,609	9,960	2,854	0.06	-71.35
Dominican Republic	1,216	1,274	1,342	800	624	0.01	-22.00
Grenada					3,054	0.07	
Haiti	531	557	574				
Jamaica	9,607	10,063	10,139	16,720	6,482	0.14	-61.23
Trinidad and Tobago	10,560	11,061	11,113	10,280	10,698	0.23	4.07
Central America	1,198	1,231	1,292		2,748	0.06	
Costa Rica	678	697	726				
Honduras					240	0.01	
Nicaragua	520	534	566				
Panama					2,508	0.05	
North America	146,306	153,248	153,707	109,800	393,886	8.43	258.73
Canada	21,550	22,573	22,678	13,320	51,084	1.09	283.51
Mexico	49,014	51,339	51,454		5,892	0.13	
United States of America	75,742	79,336	79,575	96,480	336,910	7.21	249.20
South America	66,908	70,107	70,741	29,320	53,328	1.14	81.88
Argentina	13,261	13,895	14,105		10,110	0.22	
Bolivia	1,264	1,325	1,396		642	0.01	
Brazil	25,251	26,458	26,547	10,080	19,920	0.43	97.62
Chile	12,150	12,731	12,777	19,240	11,358	0.24	-40.97
Colombia	10,083	10,565	10,603		6,078	0.13	
Guyana	638	669	718		630	0.01	
Paraguay	1,719	1,801	1,852		1,740	0.04	
Peru	1,592	1,668	1,697		1,032	0.02	
Uruguay					246	0.01	
Venezuela	950	995	1,046		1,572	0.03	
EAST ASIA AND THE PACIFIC	337,587	351,092	352,351	339,879	415,138	8.88	22.14
North-East Asia	184,491	191,873	192,579	270,940	290,608	6.22	7.26
China	72,984	75,904	76,143	241,280	227,694	4.87	-5.63
Hong Kong, China	35,127	36,532	36,710		5,028	0.11	
Japan	26,087	27,130	27,340	26,300	41,988	0.90	59.65
Korea, Republic of	2,859	2,974	2,859	3,360	13,750	0.29	309.23
Taiwan, Province of China	47,434	49,333	49,527		2,124	0.05	
Other countries of North-East Asia					24	0.00	
South-East Asia	145,433	151,250	151,690	45,659	58,830	1.26	28.85
Brunei Darussalam					822	0.02	
Indonesia	35,747	37,177	37,199	6,440	7,924	0.17	23.04
Malaysia	36,750	38,220	38,291	17,499	15,072	0.32	-13.87
Myanmar	174	181	230				
Philippines	30,250	31,460	31,569	11,120	18,568	0.40	66.98
Singapore	24,520	25,500	25,611	10,600	12,718	0.27	19.98
Thailand	17,992	18,712	18,790		3,726	0.08	
Australasia	7,663	7,969	8,082	23,280	65,460	1.40	181.19
Australia	5,127	5,332	5,404	10,880	32,996	0.71	203.27
New Zealand	2,536	2,637	2,678	12,400	32,464	0.69	161.81
Melanesia					240	0.01	
Fiji					240	0.01	
EUROPE	963,874	1,000,609	1,002,737	448,853	699,122	14.96	55.76
Central/Eastern Europe	187,087	194,019	194,379	56,973	81,552	1.75	43.14
Azerbaijan					1,584	0.03	
Belarus					168	0.00	
Bulgaria	29,615	30,713	30,752	7,920	12,952	0.28	63.54

539

Yearbook of Tourism Statistics, Data 2008 – 2012, 2014 Edition

NIGERIA

2. Arrivals of non-resident visitors at national borders, by nationality

	2008	2009	2010	2011	2012	Market share 2012	% Change 2012-2011
Czech Republic					8,014	0.17	
Czech Republic/Slovakia	23,965	24,853	24,905	7,293			
Estonia					3,186	0.07	
Georgia					4,338	0.09	
Hungary	35,733	37,057	37,096		3,312	0.07	
Poland	26,828	27,822	27,893	18,120	15,164	0.32	-16.31
Romania	45,798	47,457	47,546	5,080	11,498	0.25	126.34
Russian Federation	25,148	26,117	26,187	12,560	14,846	0.32	18.20
Slovakia					1,008	0.02	
Ukraine				6,000	5,482	0.12	-8.63
Northern Europe	**225,549**	**234,341**	**234,791**	**233,301**	**234,072**	**5.01**	**0.33**
Denmark	34,150	35,481	35,550	21,141	14,702	0.31	-30.46
Finland	38,208	39,697	39,775	14,240	15,238	0.33	7.01
Iceland					7,710	0.16	
Ireland	21,494	22,332	22,371	2,240	5,970	0.13	166.52
Norway	26,524	27,558	27,589	5,920	10,922	0.23	84.49
Sweden	24,269	25,215	25,277	480	8,466	0.18	1,663.75
United Kingdom	80,904	84,058	84,229	189,280	171,064	3.66	-9.62
Southern Europe	**204,726**	**212,533**	**213,016**	**48,558**	**109,006**	**2.33**	**124.49**
Bosnia and Herzegovina					354	0.01	
Croatia				530	3,628	0.08	584.53
Greece	4,258	4,420	4,468	5,559	12,848	0.27	131.12
Italy	137,473	142,712	142,813	26,480	45,754	0.98	72.79
Malta					1,590	0.03	
Montenegro					4,686	0.10	
Portugal	16,685	17,321	17,392	9,120	12,958	0.28	42.08
Serbia					4,142	0.09	
Spain	43,668	45,332	45,514	6,869	23,022	0.49	235.16
Yugoslavia, SFR (former)	2,642	2,748	2,829		24	0.00	
Western Europe	**294,367**	**305,584**	**306,161**	**94,541**	**225,452**	**4.82**	**138.47**
Austria	8,836	9,171	9,250	880	16,596	0.36	1,785.91
Belgium	14,335	14,881	14,982	6,320	17,588	0.38	178.29
France	129,668	134,609	134,718	19,200	58,934	1.26	206.95
Germany	126,488	131,309	131,418	47,360	90,950	1.95	92.04
Luxembourg	2,325	2,414	2,485				
Netherlands	11,244	11,673	11,781	16,880	34,164	0.73	102.39
Switzerland	1,471	1,527	1,527	3,901	7,220	0.15	85.08
East Mediterranean Europe	**52,145**	**54,132**	**54,390**	**15,480**	**49,040**	**1.05**	**216.80**
Cyprus	5,956	6,183	6,254				
Israel	31,683	32,890	33,029	13,680	18,482	0.40	35.10
Turkey	14,506	15,059	15,107	1,800	30,558	0.65	1,597.67
MIDDLE EAST	**105,357**	**109,559**	**110,692**	**38,423**	**113,260**	**2.42**	**194.77**
Bahrain					558	0.01	
Egypt	34,304	35,674	35,779	9,223	21,880	0.47	137.23
Iraq	7,947	8,265	8,301		1,938	0.04	
Jordan	4,045	4,201	4,253		660	0.01	
Kuwait	1,538	1,599	1,648		6,144	0.13	
Lebanon	40,004	41,601	41,683	24,840	60,544	1.30	143.74
Libya	10,072	10,474	10,518	1,840	1,440	0.03	-21.74
Oman					980	0.02	
Palestine					4,746	0.10	
Saudi Arabia	4,003	4,163	4,224	1,120	5,148	0.11	359.64
Syrian Arab Republic	1,906	1,983	2,661		3,426	0.07	
United Arab Emirates				1,400	5,562	0.12	297.29
Yemen	1,538	1,599	1,625		234	0.01	
SOUTH ASIA	**137,364**	**142,858**	**143,412**	**212,920**	**220,544**	**4.72**	**3.58**

Yearbook of Tourism Statistics, Data 2008 – 2012, 2014 Edition

NIGERIA

2. Arrivals of non-resident visitors at national borders, by nationality

	2008	2009	2010	2011	2012	Market share 2012	% Change 2012-2011
Afghanistan	837	871	883				
Bangladesh	920	957	1,006		14,262	0.31	
India	54,835	57,028	57,229	202,200	181,144	3.88	-10.41
Iran, Islamic Republic of	20,632	20,871	20,913		1,680	0.04	
Nepal	109	114	158				
Pakistan	57,724	60,617	60,699	10,720	20,944	0.45	95.37
Sri Lanka	2,307	2,400	2,524		2,514	0.05	
NOT SPECIFIED	**16,879**	**17,656**	**61,119**	**1,676,160**	**1,655,126**	**35.42**	**-1.25**
Other countries of the World	16,879	17,656	61,119		2,248	0.05	
Nationals Residing Abroad				1,676,160	1,652,878	35.37	-1.39

Yearbook of Tourism Statistics, Data 2008 – 2012, 2014 Edition

NIUE

1. Arrivals of non-resident tourists at national borders, by country of residence

		2008	2009	2010	2011	2012	Market share 2012	% Change 2012-2011
TOTAL	(*)	**4,748**	**4,662**	**6,214**	**6,094**			
AMERICAS		**315**	**203**	**298**	**1,176**			
North America		**315**	**189**	**290**	**1,165**			
Canada		59	32	60	239			
United States of America		256	157	230	926			
Other Americas			**14**	**8**	**11**			
Other countries of the Americas			14	8	11			
EAST ASIA AND THE PACIFIC		**3,913**	**3,550**	**4,156**	**4,432**			
North-East Asia		**59**	**20**	**35**	**30**			
China		32	6	22	6			
Japan		27	14	13	24			
Australasia		**3,324**	**3,151**	**3,474**	**4,166**			
Australia		546	461	539	611			
New Zealand		2,778	2,690	2,935	3,555			
Other East Asia and the Pacific		**530**	**379**	**647**	**236**			
Other countries of Asia		93	146	445	20			
Other countries of Oceania		437	233	202	216			
EUROPE		**492**	**889**	**1,602**	**402**			
Northern Europe		**113**	**71**	**138**	**108**			
Denmark			24	35				
United Kingdom		113	47	103	108			
Southern Europe			**17**	**13**				
Italy			17	13				
Western Europe		**154**	**682**	**1,255**	**99**			
Austria			38	60				
France		82	101	45	48			
Germany		72	475	1,043	51			
Netherlands			17	27				
Switzerland			51	80				
Other Europe		**225**	**119**	**196**	**195**			
Other countries of Europe		225	119	196	195			
NOT SPECIFIED		**28**	**20**	**158**	**84**			
Other countries of the World		28	20	158	84			

Yearbook of Tourism Statistics, Data 2008 – 2012, 2014 Edition

NORTHERN MARIANA ISLANDS

2. Arrivals of non-resident visitors at national borders, by nationality

	2008	2009	2010	2011	2012	Market share 2012	% Change 2012-2011
TOTAL	397,274	353,956	379,091	340,957			
AMERICAS	31,361	29,555	27,319	24,155			
North America	31,361	29,555	27,319	24,155			
Canada	295	296	193	175			
United States of America	31,066	29,259	27,126	23,980			
EAST ASIA AND THE PACIFIC	356,997	316,064	345,874	310,394			
North-East Asia	351,577	310,475	343,043	306,862			
China	26,407	29,528	41,623	54,186			
Hong Kong, China	471	286	369	2,005			
Japan	213,299	191,111	185,032	142,946			
Korea, Republic of	111,116	89,132	115,811	107,503			
Taiwan, Province of China	284	418	208	222			
South-East Asia	1,862	1,660	772	565			
Philippines	1,780	1,591	703	544			
Thailand	82	69	69	21			
Australasia	2,125	2,584	977	2,037			
Australia	2,125	2,584	977	2,037			
Micronesia	1,433	1,345	1,082	930			
Micronesia, Federated States of	861	911	813	665			
Palau	572	434	269	265			
EUROPE	7,742	7,309	4,961	5,646			
Central/Eastern Europe	6,814	6,222	4,391	5,276			
Russian Federation	6,814	6,222	4,391	5,276			
Other Europe	928	1,087	570	370			
Other countries of Europe	928	1,087	570	370			
NOT SPECIFIED	1,174	1,028	937	762			
Other countries of the World	1,174	1,028	937	762			

Yearbook of Tourism Statistics, Data 2008 – 2012, 2014 Edition

NORWAY

1. Arrivals of non-resident tourists at national borders, by nationality

		2008	2009	2010	2011	2012	Market share 2012	% Change 2012-2011
TOTAL	(*)	4,347,000	4,346,000	4,767,000	4,963,000			
AMERICAS		136,000	132,000	160,000	164,000			
North America		136,000	132,000	160,000	164,000			
United States of America		136,000	132,000	160,000	164,000			
EAST ASIA AND THE PACIFIC		29,000	25,000	28,000	27,000			
North-East Asia		29,000	25,000	28,000	27,000			
Japan		29,000	25,000	28,000	27,000			
EUROPE		3,967,000	3,943,000	4,313,000	4,471,000			
Central/Eastern Europe		266,000	257,000	288,000	303,000			
Poland		202,000	188,000	206,000	195,000			
Russian Federation		64,000	69,000	82,000	108,000			
Northern Europe		2,302,000	2,319,000	2,438,000	2,490,000			
Denmark		571,000	539,000	545,000	538,000			
Finland		260,000	239,000	250,000	294,000			
Sweden		1,130,000	1,239,000	1,336,000	1,339,000			
United Kingdom		341,000	302,000	307,000	319,000			
Southern Europe		137,000	130,000	143,000	156,000			
Italy		60,000	62,000	69,000	85,000			
Spain		77,000	68,000	74,000	71,000			
Western Europe		1,031,000	1,039,000	1,188,000	1,200,000			
Austria		27,000	28,000	31,000	36,000			
Belgium		40,000	37,000	51,000	47,000			
France		127,000	128,000	133,000	134,000			
Germany		603,000	617,000	730,000	719,000			
Netherlands		195,000	188,000	194,000	203,000			
Switzerland		39,000	41,000	49,000	61,000			
Other Europe		231,000	198,000	256,000	322,000			
Other countries of Europe		231,000	198,000	256,000	322,000			
NOT SPECIFIED		215,000	246,000	266,000	301,000			
Other countries of the World		215,000	246,000	266,000	301,000			

544

NORWAY

5. Overnight stays of non-resident tourists in hotels and similar establishments, by nationality

	2008	2009	2010	2011	2012	Market share 2012	% Change 2012-2011
TOTAL (*)	4,893,806	4,426,610	4,798,028	4,898,885	5,050,573	100.00	3.10
AFRICA	33,165	28,469	28,419	40,329	38,472	0.76	-4.60
Southern Africa	7,132	5,031	5,353	6,345	6,649	0.13	4.79
South Africa	7,132	5,031	5,353	6,345	6,649	0.13	4.79
Other Africa	26,033	23,438	23,066	33,984	31,823	0.63	-6.36
Other countries of Africa	26,033	23,438	23,066	33,984	31,823	0.63	-6.36
AMERICAS	347,866	302,991	366,634	375,674	378,381	7.49	0.72
North America	315,065	274,233	328,883	327,916	318,391	6.30	-2.90
Canada	20,002	18,180	20,205	21,913	24,743	0.49	12.91
Mexico	5,119	5,367	6,532	7,249	6,765	0.13	-6.68
United States of America	289,944	250,686	302,146	298,754	286,883	5.68	-3.97
South America	32,801	28,758	37,751	47,758	59,990	1.19	25.61
Brazil	16,914	15,079	21,025	28,757	36,966	0.73	28.55
Other countries of South America	15,887	13,679	16,726	19,001	23,024	0.46	21.17
EAST ASIA AND THE PACIFIC	379,148	330,286	401,483	462,263	522,880	10.35	13.11
North-East Asia	185,381	159,991	199,541	225,682	260,871	5.17	15.59
China	43,606	41,562	63,617	86,179	86,007	1.70	-0.20
Japan	103,796	95,316	100,836	97,875	116,397	2.30	18.92
Korea, Republic of	37,979	23,113	35,088	41,628	58,467	1.16	40.45
Australasia	37,246	28,252	36,583	41,247	45,460	0.90	10.21
Australia	37,246	28,252	36,583	41,247	45,460	0.90	10.21
Other East Asia and the Pacific	156,521	142,043	165,359	195,334	216,549	4.29	10.86
Other countries of Asia	140,697	132,018	154,496	182,245	198,878	3.94	9.13
Other countries of Oceania	15,824	10,025	10,863	13,089	17,671	0.35	35.01
EUROPE	4,133,627	3,764,864	4,001,492	4,020,619	4,110,840	81.39	2.24
Central/Eastern Europe	363,668	301,251	359,614	368,179	384,790	7.62	4.51
Czech Republic	20,965	20,231	22,819	30,770	21,299	0.42	-30.78
Estonia	20,519	11,150	8,710	8,073	12,021	0.24	48.90
Hungary	13,687	9,051	10,338	9,645	13,801	0.27	43.09
Latvia	12,677	9,421	12,242	13,958	13,446	0.27	-3.67
Lithuania	12,739	11,439	18,004	17,536	23,758	0.47	35.48
Poland	139,970	111,350	132,445	122,886	125,272	2.48	1.94
Russian Federation	127,708	111,524	135,869	143,854	152,246	3.01	5.83
Slovakia	4,835	5,796	8,244	7,806	8,445	0.17	8.19
Ukraine	10,568	11,289	10,943	13,651	14,502	0.29	6.23
Northern Europe	1,783,495	1,620,761	1,670,595	1,673,142	1,858,270	36.79	11.06
Denmark	540,630	512,279	519,076	491,279	516,216	10.22	5.08
Finland	67,649	66,825	75,487	76,315	78,871	1.56	3.35
Iceland	13,233	11,722	15,746	16,981	22,048	0.44	29.84
Ireland	20,442	16,587	19,045	23,816	24,101	0.48	1.20
Sweden	579,329	568,062	601,797	610,446	707,737	14.01	15.94
United Kingdom	562,212	445,286	439,444	454,305	509,297	10.08	12.10
Southern Europe	389,687	375,647	403,304	393,948	314,386	6.22	-20.20
Greece	17,546	15,564	14,048	11,979	9,987	0.20	-16.63
Italy	139,001	157,245	168,845	152,965	124,238	2.46	-18.78
Malta	876	836	1,193	1,415	1,714	0.03	21.13
Portugal	15,176	17,567	17,124	16,730	15,040	0.30	-10.10
Slovenia	3,752	2,904	4,758	4,298	4,526	0.09	5.30
Spain	213,336	181,531	197,336	206,561	158,881	3.15	-23.08
Western Europe	1,378,069	1,301,354	1,378,192	1,357,629	1,296,919	25.68	-4.47
Austria	30,808	30,850	37,485	37,609	42,118	0.83	11.99
Belgium	39,736	38,672	49,761	47,412	54,754	1.08	15.49
France	201,231	209,560	219,043	211,972	206,800	4.09	-2.44
Germany	729,381	664,459	708,652	699,776	651,739	12.90	-6.86

Yearbook of Tourism Statistics, Data 2008 – 2012, 2014 Edition

NORWAY

5. Overnight stays of non-resident tourists in hotels and similar establishments, by nationality

	2008	2009	2010	2011	2012	Market share 2012	% Change 2012-2011
Liechtenstein	2,280	1,122	1,595	1,445	2,216	0.04	53.36
Luxembourg	2,370	3,140	2,665	3,156	5,466	0.11	73.19
Netherlands	309,379	291,484	285,860	278,474	254,000	5.03	-8.79
Switzerland	62,884	62,067	73,131	77,785	79,826	1.58	2.62
East Mediterranean Europe	**11,583**	**9,171**	**12,135**	**10,801**	**12,109**	**0.24**	**12.11**
Cyprus	1,902	1,372	1,729	1,334	1,743	0.03	30.66
Turkey	9,681	7,799	10,406	9,467	10,366	0.21	9.50
Other Europe	**207,125**	**156,680**	**177,652**	**216,920**	**244,366**	**4.84**	**12.65**
Other countries of Europe	207,125	156,680	177,652	216,920	244,366	4.84	12.65

Yearbook of Tourism Statistics, Data 2008 – 2012, 2014 Edition

NORWAY

6. Overnight stays of non-resident tourists in all types of accommodation establishments, by nationality

	2008	2009	2010	2011	2012	Market share 2012	% Change 2012-2011
TOTAL	8,146,872	7,525,174	7,903,186	7,844,241	7,940,468	100.00	1.23
AFRICA	36,260	42,319	34,507	44,678	41,114	0.52	-7.98
Southern Africa	8,284	6,012	5,831	6,979	7,283	0.09	4.36
South Africa	8,284	6,012	5,831	6,979	7,283	0.09	4.36
Other Africa	27,976	36,307	28,676	37,699	33,831	0.43	-10.26
Other countries of Africa	27,976	36,307	28,676	37,699	33,831	0.43	-10.26
AMERICAS	370,217	324,554	388,266	400,579	403,177	5.08	0.65
North America	334,615	292,442	346,739	349,229	339,205	4.27	-2.87
Canada	23,678	21,873	24,328	25,876	28,857	0.36	11.52
Mexico	5,753	6,230	6,975	7,977	7,069	0.09	-11.38
United States of America	305,184	264,339	315,436	315,376	303,279	3.82	-3.84
South America	35,602	32,112	41,527	51,350	63,972	0.81	24.58
Brazil	18,339	16,827	22,882	30,862	39,491	0.50	27.96
Other countries of South America	17,263	15,285	18,645	20,488	24,481	0.31	19.49
EAST ASIA AND THE PACIFIC	409,676	365,700	431,898	495,132	560,092	7.05	13.12
North-East Asia	195,502	175,722	210,155	238,111	275,257	3.47	15.60
China	45,861	51,795	68,133	91,715	93,532	1.18	1.98
Japan	107,661	98,607	104,014	101,124	119,558	1.51	18.23
Korea, Republic of	41,980	25,320	38,008	45,272	62,167	0.78	37.32
Australasia	45,119	34,724	43,917	48,411	53,863	0.68	11.26
Australia	45,119	34,724	43,917	48,411	53,863	0.68	11.26
Other East Asia and the Pacific	169,055	155,254	177,826	208,610	230,972	2.91	10.72
Other countries of Asia	151,451	143,214	165,176	194,103	211,918	2.67	9.18
Other countries of Oceania	17,604	12,040	12,650	14,507	19,054	0.24	31.34
EUROPE	7,330,719	6,792,601	7,048,515	6,903,852	6,936,085	87.35	0.47
Central/Eastern Europe	696,035	571,836	668,528	701,684	755,442	9.51	7.66
Czech Republic	83,027	79,855	91,349	95,136	81,629	1.03	-14.20
Estonia	45,821	30,536	25,314	26,867	26,990	0.34	0.46
Hungary	20,259	13,048	14,941	15,276	19,607	0.25	28.35
Latvia	39,371	28,430	34,933	37,113	36,966	0.47	-0.40
Lithuania	53,294	45,764	59,391	71,296	96,856	1.22	35.85
Poland	274,029	203,962	235,939	233,399	255,374	3.22	9.42
Russian Federation	154,739	141,166	172,811	186,401	198,201	2.50	6.33
Slovakia	13,767	15,685	20,566	19,456	22,038	0.28	13.27
Ukraine	11,728	13,390	13,284	16,740	17,781	0.22	6.22
Northern Europe	2,795,579	2,563,567	2,587,196	2,493,677	2,656,497	33.46	6.53
Denmark	1,001,359	949,997	914,053	841,484	865,597	10.90	2.87
Finland	150,672	146,013	148,685	147,471	139,806	1.76	-5.20
Iceland	18,261	16,519	20,834	25,025	29,487	0.37	17.83
Ireland	24,323	20,807	24,358	27,303	28,694	0.36	5.09
Sweden	945,097	905,649	958,838	932,923	1,022,597	12.88	9.61
United Kingdom	655,867	524,582	520,428	519,471	570,316	7.18	9.79
Southern Europe	500,720	481,830	515,286	497,120	400,182	5.04	-19.50
Greece	18,574	17,006	15,604	13,367	11,236	0.14	-15.94
Italy	194,704	211,861	222,540	200,287	166,257	2.09	-16.99
Malta	1,090	1,075	1,289	1,506	1,889	0.02	25.43
Portugal	20,199	21,252	21,368	20,994	18,936	0.24	-9.80
Slovenia	7,608	8,446	8,847	7,359	7,795	0.10	5.92
Spain	258,545	222,190	245,638	253,607	194,069	2.44	-23.48
Western Europe	3,090,586	2,980,764	3,061,582	2,954,387	2,820,996	35.53	-4.52
Austria	69,401	66,930	76,045	75,953	76,320	0.96	0.48
Belgium	71,943	72,873	88,866	84,820	95,455	1.20	12.54
France	288,340	298,526	318,280	309,784	301,197	3.79	-2.77
Germany	1,688,603	1,590,305	1,637,206	1,594,621	1,511,995	19.04	-5.18

Yearbook of Tourism Statistics, Data 2008 – 2012, 2014 Edition

NORWAY

6. Overnight stays of non-resident tourists in all types of accommodation establishments, by nationality

	2008	2009	2010	2011	2012	Market share 2012	% Change 2012-2011
Liechtenstein	3,050	1,614	2,084	1,942	2,811	0.04	44.75
Luxembourg	3,835	7,602	6,427	4,573	7,775	0.10	70.02
Netherlands	845,503	825,603	799,515	742,328	677,831	8.54	-8.69
Switzerland	119,911	117,311	133,159	140,366	147,612	1.86	5.16
East Mediterranean Europe	**12,783**	**10,262**	**13,559**	**11,755**	**13,476**	**0.17**	**14.64**
Cyprus	2,019	1,473	1,789	1,378	2,085	0.03	51.31
Turkey	10,764	8,789	11,770	10,377	11,391	0.14	9.77
Other Europe	**235,016**	**184,342**	**202,364**	**245,229**	**289,492**	**3.65**	**18.05**
Other countries of Europe	235,016	184,342	202,364	245,229	289,492	3.65	18.05

Yearbook of Tourism Statistics, Data 2008 – 2012, 2014 Edition

OMAN

3. Arrivals of non-resident tourists in hotels and similar establishments, by nationality

	2008	2009	2010	2011	2012	Market share 2012	% Change 2012-2011
TOTAL	1,378,078	1,279,683	1,038,107	1,013,784			
AFRICA	19,355	32,187	32,118	28,125			
East Africa	864	1,422	867	689			
United Republic of Tanzania	864	1,422	867	689			
North Africa	9,525	7,860	10,611	11,031			
Morocco	2,987	1,960	2,254	2,344			
Sudan	3,231	3,118	4,688	4,873			
Tunisia	3,307	2,782	3,669	3,814			
Southern Africa	4,973	12,441	5,656	4,496			
South Africa	4,973	12,441	5,656	4,496			
Other Africa	3,993	10,464	14,984	11,909			
Other countries of Africa	3,993	10,464	14,984	11,909			
AMERICAS	57,110	174,810	71,416	56,764			
North America	50,668	158,785	64,139	50,980			
Canada	12,038	44,201	19,151	15,222			
United States of America	38,630	114,584	44,988	35,758			
South America	2,410	2,505	3,844	3,055			
Brazil	2,410	2,505	3,844	3,055			
Other Americas	4,032	13,520	3,433	2,729			
Other countries of the Americas	4,032	13,520	3,433	2,729			
EAST ASIA AND THE PACIFIC	104,046	169,568	84,932	88,070			
North-East Asia	16,718	15,377	10,272	12,011			
China	6,443	6,544	4,295	5,022			
Japan	10,275	8,833	5,977	6,989			
South-East Asia	24,238	24,022	16,094	18,818			
Philippines	24,238	24,022	16,094	18,818			
Australasia	20,351	73,724	24,536	19,502			
Australia	17,288	57,118	19,178	15,243			
New Zealand	3,063	16,606	5,358	4,259			
Other East Asia and the Pacific	42,739	56,445	34,030	37,739			
Other countries of Asia	39,390	34,811	28,552	33,385			
Other countries of Oceania	3,349	21,634	5,478	4,354			
EUROPE	437,137	382,353	385,379	350,790			
Central/Eastern Europe	5,474	6,611	6,917	6,297			
Czech Republic	591	1,212	1,827	1,663			
Russian Federation	4,883	5,399	5,090	4,634			
Northern Europe	165,885	107,667	99,255	90,347			
Denmark	5,743	5,455	4,138	3,767			
Finland	1,003	965	1,358	1,236			
Ireland	4,287	4,777	5,224	4,755			
Norway	1,878	2,594	2,238	2,037			
Sweden	30,251	10,241	6,594	6,002			
United Kingdom	122,723	83,635	79,703	72,550			
Southern Europe	30,888	34,100	34,107	31,046			
Italy	23,544	27,522	27,106	24,673			
Portugal	3,320	1,166	2,106	1,917			
Spain	4,024	5,412	4,895	4,456			
Western Europe	202,060	203,954	213,406	194,251			
Austria	8,775	10,218	9,363	8,522			
Belgium	6,806	7,544	6,033	5,492			
France	39,704	46,439	53,389	48,597			
Germany	101,737	99,500	100,785	91,739			
Netherlands	20,615	20,312	21,693	19,746			
Switzerland	24,423	19,941	22,143	20,155			

Yearbook of Tourism Statistics, Data 2008 – 2012, 2014 Edition

OMAN

3. Arrivals of non-resident tourists in hotels and similar establishments, by nationality

	2008	2009	2010	2011	2012	Market share 2012	% Change 2012-2011
Other Europe	**32,830**	**30,021**	**31,694**	**28,849**			
Other countries of Europe	32,830	30,021	31,694	28,849			
MIDDLE EAST	**242,661**	**288,841**	**241,729**	**235,070**			
Bahrain	13,363	15,759	11,513	10,886			
Egypt	22,648	26,853	26,940	28,005			
Jordan	10,068	13,129	11,422	11,873			
Kuwait	16,102	20,728	16,231	15,346			
Lebanon	12,841	14,313	11,368	11,818			
Qatar	10,281	14,836	10,920	10,325			
Saudi Arabia	24,177	25,312	21,120	19,969			
Syrian Arab Republic	6,311	6,452	6,243	6,489			
United Arab Emirates	112,785	130,487	112,623	106,483			
Other countries of Middle East	14,085	20,972	13,349	13,876			
SOUTH ASIA	**189,469**	**203,528**	**208,544**	**243,846**			
India	156,723	166,535	169,799	198,543			
Iran, Islamic Republic of	5,000	4,646	4,687	5,480			
Pakistan	21,867	23,924	25,815	30,185			
Sri Lanka	5,879	8,423	8,243	9,638			
NOT SPECIFIED	**328,300**	**28,396**	**13,989**	**11,119**			
Other countries of the World	328,300	28,396	13,989	11,119			

Yearbook of Tourism Statistics, Data 2008 – 2012, 2014 Editic

OMAN

5. Overnight stays of non-resident tourists in hotels and similar establishments, by nationality

	2008	2009	2010	2011	2012	Market share 2012	% Change 2012-2011
TOTAL	1,661,164	1,452,207	1,365,296				
AFRICA	24,144	35,759	27,320				
East Africa	808	1,614	1,218				
United Republic of Tanzania	808	1,614	1,218				
North Africa	12,175	9,175	8,828				
Morocco	4,163	2,287	2,579				
Sudan	3,906	3,855	3,007				
Tunisia	4,106	3,033	3,242				
Southern Africa	6,145	13,365	9,672				
South Africa	6,145	13,365	9,672				
Other Africa	5,016	11,605	7,602				
Other countries of Africa	5,016	11,605	7,602				
AMERICAS	78,561	210,061	166,856				
North America	70,698	191,547	149,280				
Canada	14,588	36,574	22,519				
United States of America	56,110	154,973	126,761				
South America	2,861	7,309	10,222				
Brazil	2,861	7,309	10,222				
Other Americas	5,002	11,205	7,354				
Other countries of the Americas	5,002	11,205	7,354				
EAST ASIA AND THE PACIFIC	118,799	168,576	149,787				
North-East Asia	18,773	23,066	20,175				
China	7,742	9,174	8,598				
Japan	11,031	13,892	11,577				
South-East Asia	25,570	18,450	13,195				
Philippines	25,570	18,450	13,195				
Australasia	23,967	52,156	32,741				
Australia	20,414	41,055	27,498				
New Zealand	3,553	11,101	5,243				
Other East Asia and the Pacific	50,489	74,904	83,676				
Other countries of Asia	42,932	53,843	62,162				
Other countries of Oceania	7,557	21,061	21,514				
EUROPE	580,375	441,632	456,149				
Central/Eastern Europe	8,957	5,954	5,343				
Russian Federation	8,957	5,954	5,343				
Northern Europe	232,848	162,485	155,892				
Denmark	7,462	4,193	4,469				
Sweden	46,492	25,841	24,451				
United Kingdom	178,894	132,451	126,972				
Southern Europe	35,314	29,417	30,618				
Italy	30,035	24,364	24,498				
Spain	5,279	5,053	6,120				
Western Europe	249,713	199,378	220,270				
Austria	12,146	8,558	8,848				
Belgium	8,842	7,559	8,053				
France	51,611	39,935	47,585				
Germany	118,351	89,782	100,722				
Netherlands	26,742	24,355	24,194				
Switzerland	32,021	29,189	30,868				
Other Europe	53,543	44,398	44,026				
Other countries of Europe	53,543	44,398	44,026				
MIDDLE EAST	290,847	322,397	281,526				
Bahrain	17,143	20,507	15,243				
Egypt	27,578	31,798	35,111				

Yearbook of Tourism Statistics, Data 2008 – 2012, 2014 Edition

OMAN

5. Overnight stays of non-resident tourists in hotels and similar establishments, by nationality

	2008	2009	2010	2011	2012	Market share 2012	% Change 2012-2011
Jordan	14,765	15,592	20,430				
Kuwait	23,100	27,118	21,150				
Lebanon	17,342	17,003	18,984				
Qatar	13,030	18,835	13,689				
Saudi Arabia	30,713	33,905	27,334				
Syrian Arab Republic	9,077	9,535	10,751				
United Arab Emirates	119,940	126,356	99,708				
Other countries of Middle East	18,159	21,748	19,126				
SOUTH ASIA	**204,428**	**206,567**	**216,706**				
India	168,636	172,793	177,241				
Iran, Islamic Republic of	6,506	6,531	7,617				
Pakistan	23,129	20,566	24,535				
Sri Lanka	6,157	6,677	7,313				
NOT SPECIFIED	**364,010**	**67,215**	**66,952**				
Other countries of the World	364,010	67,215	66,952				

Yearbook of Tourism Statistics, Data 2008 – 2012, 2014 Edition

PAKISTAN

1. Arrivals of non-resident tourists at national borders, by nationality

	2008	2009	2010	2011	2012	Market share 2012	% Change 2012-2011
TOTAL	822,828	854,905	906,818	1,161,254	966,277	100.00	-16.79
AFRICA	15,767	14,659	15,290	24,691	19,853	2.05	-19.59
East Africa	5,294	5,428	5,127	8,471	6,648	0.69	-21.52
Burundi	10	3	2	16	15	0.00	-6.25
Comoros	11	8	11	180	155	0.02	-13.89
Djibouti	90	85	40	220	146	0.02	-33.64
Eritrea	31	15	10	26	9	0.00	-65.38
Ethiopia	330	544	309	304	266	0.03	-12.50
Kenya	1,565	1,489	1,447	2,429	1,605	0.17	-33.92
Madagascar	92	69	88	174	94	0.01	-45.98
Malawi	267	234	263	572	477	0.05	-16.61
Mauritius	664	554	513	1,039	871	0.09	-16.17
Mozambique	563	567	650	1,141	1,044	0.11	-8.50
Reunion				6	5	0.00	-16.67
Rwanda	90	308	18	32	18	0.00	-43.75
Seychelles	24	9	4	18	19	0.00	5.56
Somalia	470	347	335	523	489	0.05	-6.50
Uganda	104	67	63	179	133	0.01	-25.70
United Republic of Tanzania	640	772	913	991	813	0.08	-17.96
Zambia	152	216	288	323	207	0.02	-35.91
Zimbabwe	191	141	173	298	282	0.03	-5.37
Central Africa	130	109	95	216	253	0.03	17.13
Angola	25	26	24	46	29	0.00	-36.96
Cameroon	47	38	41	73	36	0.00	-50.68
Chad	34	31	2	74	155	0.02	109.46
Congo	24	14	26	14	23	0.00	64.29
Gabon			2	9	10	0.00	11.11
North Africa	2,313	2,109	1,929	3,256	2,593	0.27	-20.36
Algeria	170	203	142	360	10	0.00	-97.22
Morocco	291	495	329	518	692	0.07	33.59
Sudan	1,684	1,242	1,250	2,015	1,518	0.16	-24.67
Tunisia	168	169	208	363	373	0.04	2.75
Southern Africa	6,243	6,136	7,282	11,007	8,535	0.88	-22.46
Botswana	45	36	46	58	49	0.01	-15.52
Lesotho	77	80	84	91	81	0.01	-10.99
Namibia	7	123	9	28	35	0.00	25.00
South Africa	6,020	5,846	7,093	10,748	8,291	0.86	-22.86
Swaziland	94	51	50	82	79	0.01	-3.66
West Africa	1,787	877	857	1,741	1,824	0.19	4.77
Benin	16	5	5	5	3	0.00	-40.00
Burkina Faso	5	4	3	3	4	0.00	33.33
Gambia	25	11	5	25	17	0.00	-32.00
Ghana	94	118	108	144	117	0.01	-18.75
Guinea	15	14	14	17	25	0.00	47.06
Guinea-Bissau	2	1	1	4	2	0.00	-50.00
Liberia	50	50	12	22	21	0.00	-4.55
Mali	5	14	19	88	26	0.00	-70.45
Mauritania	6	19	43	20	42	0.00	110.00
Niger	27	41	14	36	38	0.00	5.56
Nigeria	1,462	499	560	1,197	1,430	0.15	19.47
Senegal	39	63	36	120	58	0.01	-51.67
Sierra Leone	35	25	33	43	32	0.00	-25.58
Togo	6	13	4	17	9	0.00	-47.06
AMERICAS	155,870	162,451	168,421	250,740	201,865	20.89	-19.49
Caribbean	229	287	233	286	242	0.03	-15.38

553

Yearbook of Tourism Statistics, Data 2008 – 2012, 2014 Edition

PAKISTAN

1. Arrivals of non-resident tourists at national borders, by nationality

	2008	2009	2010	2011	2012	Market share 2012	% Change 2012-2011
Anguilla	3	2	7	6	5	0.00	-16.67
Antigua and Barbuda	7	9	8	17	13	0.00	-23.53
Cuba	23	16	22	60	21	0.00	-65.00
Dominica	32	23	47	14	6	0.00	-57.14
Grenada	30	27	32	37	26	0.00	-29.73
Haiti	3	2	2	6	1	0.00	-83.33
Jamaica	10	4	8	25	24	0.00	-4.00
Netherlands Antilles	20	56	11	8	10	0.00	25.00
Puerto Rico	3	54	2	2			
Trinidad and Tobago	98	94	94	111	136	0.01	22.52
Central America	**350**	**348**	**341**	**379**	**238**	**0.02**	**-37.20**
Belize	18	27	25	13	39	0.00	200.00
Costa Rica	15	11	28	16	18	0.00	12.50
El Salvador	8	15	8	6	8	0.00	33.33
Guatemala	27	20	18	9	12	0.00	33.33
Honduras	30	61	38	154	27	0.00	-82.47
Nicaragua	10	23	11	9	15	0.00	66.67
Panama	242	191	213	172	119	0.01	-30.81
North America	**154,162**	**160,614**	**166,765**	**248,287**	**199,937**	**20.69**	**-19.47**
Canada	39,875	42,954	46,228	79,941	65,168	6.74	-18.48
Mexico	193	195	168	188	173	0.02	-7.98
United States of America	114,094	117,465	120,369	168,158	134,596	13.93	-19.96
South America	**1,129**	**1,202**	**1,082**	**1,788**	**1,448**	**0.15**	**-19.02**
Argentina	212	177	236	344	250	0.03	-27.33
Bolivia	25	42	30	44	45	0.00	2.27
Brazil	362	271	322	500	467	0.05	-6.60
Chile	203	206	139	292	155	0.02	-46.92
Colombia	110	117	134	220	142	0.01	-35.45
Ecuador	24	125	29	86	116	0.01	34.88
Guyana	15	13	14	21	14	0.00	-33.33
Paraguay	8	9	5	22	12	0.00	-45.45
Peru	86	163	78	128	145	0.02	13.28
Suriname	25	3	2	9	10	0.00	11.11
Uruguay	20	25	22	13	9	0.00	-30.77
Venezuela	39	51	71	109	83	0.01	-23.85
EAST ASIA AND THE PACIFIC	**75,967**	**88,984**	**89,748**	**140,015**	**115,293**	**11.93**	**-17.66**
North-East Asia	**43,862**	**42,813**	**41,745**	**63,472**	**55,712**	**5.77**	**-12.23**
China	30,078	29,996	27,887	42,708	39,017	4.04	-8.64
Hong Kong, China	10	7	9	16	14	0.00	-12.50
Japan	8,294	6,705	7,077	9,918	8,242	0.85	-16.90
Korea, Dem. People's Republic of	130	218	389	248	108	0.01	-56.45
Korea, Republic of	4,495	4,926	5,390	9,359	7,450	0.77	-20.40
Macao, China		1	2	96	143	0.01	48.96
Mongolia	65	33	50	35	58	0.01	65.71
Taiwan, Province of China	790	927	941	1,092	680	0.07	-37.73
South-East Asia	**18,181**	**31,443**	**32,645**	**54,312**	**40,554**	**4.20**	**-25.33**
Brunei Darussalam	111	67	60	104	79	0.01	-24.04
Cambodia	80	81	79	181	110	0.01	-39.23
Indonesia	1,778	3,099	3,314	5,775	4,117	0.43	-28.71
Lao People's Democratic Republic	28	22	28	23	49	0.01	113.04
Malaysia	5,758	5,027	5,420	7,915	5,766	0.60	-27.15
Myanmar	811	2,213	2,546	4,532	3,449	0.36	-23.90
Philippines	3,575	15,603	15,871	27,207	19,940	2.06	-26.71
Singapore	3,243	2,585	2,461	3,549	3,191	0.33	-10.09
Thailand	2,618	2,170	2,269	4,177	3,414	0.35	-18.27
Timor-Leste		1		2			
Viet Nam	179	575	597	847	439	0.05	-48.17

554

Yearbook of Tourism Statistics, Data 2008 – 2012, 2014 Editio

PAKISTAN

1. Arrivals of non-resident tourists at national borders, by nationality

	2008	2009	2010	2011	2012	Market share 2012	% Change 2012-2011
Australasia	13,842	14,597	15,283	22,084	18,878	1.95	-14.52
Australia	12,227	13,223	13,931	20,026	17,257	1.79	-13.83
New Zealand	1,615	1,374	1,352	2,058	1,621	0.17	-21.23
Melanesia	82	131	75	147	149	0.02	1.36
Fiji	63	128	68	139	144	0.01	3.60
Papua New Guinea	19	3	7	8	5	0.00	-37.50
EUROPE	389,207	378,643	395,644	485,182	429,920	44.49	-11.39
Central/Eastern Europe	8,231	12,145	11,850	18,032	13,736	1.42	-23.82
Armenia	16	12	16	17	10	0.00	-41.18
Azerbaijan	475	354	272	448	322	0.03	-28.13
Belarus	116	140	134	133	111	0.01	-16.54
Bulgaria	252	660	653	897	581	0.06	-35.23
Czech Republic	751	1,639	603	640	545	0.06	-14.84
Czech Republic/Slovakia	10		222	278	202	0.02	-27.34
Estonia	47	70	80	118	71	0.01	-39.83
Georgia	72	152	160	246	177	0.02	-28.05
Hungary	443	323	327	429	382	0.04	-10.96
Kazakhstan	625	396	435	713	560	0.06	-21.46
Kyrgyzstan	148	129	215	3	340	0.04	11,233.33
Latvia	70	182	188	389	363	0.04	-6.68
Lithuania	87	174	141	306	251	0.03	-17.97
Poland	1,035	974	980	1,953	1,518	0.16	-22.27
Republic of Moldova	5	11	24	41	41	0.00	0.00
Romania	550	624	736	1,692	1,474	0.15	-12.88
Russian Federation	1,581	2,488	2,623	3,991	3,014	0.31	-24.48
Slovakia	197	198					
Tajikistan	105	133	165	318	250	0.03	-21.38
Turkmenistan	149	85	166	183	136	0.01	-25.68
Ukraine	987	3,048	3,347	4,600	2,960	0.31	-35.65
Uzbekistan	510	353	363	637	428	0.04	-32.81
Northern Europe	314,389	301,404	316,433	373,972	339,050	35.09	-9.34
Denmark	7,203	5,747	6,980	9,063	7,610	0.79	-16.03
Finland	718	525	671	829	719	0.07	-13.27
Iceland	34	1,075	27	44	49	0.01	11.36
Ireland	2,919	2,882	2,938	4,560	4,153	0.43	-8.93
Norway	13,954	12,441	13,744	18,521	16,501	1.71	-10.91
Sweden	3,841	3,383	3,835	4,951	3,958	0.41	-20.06
United Kingdom	285,720	275,351	288,238	336,004	306,060	31.67	-8.91
Southern Europe	9,257	9,287	9,442	14,574	12,479	1.29	-14.37
Albania	54	32	26	51	84	0.01	64.71
Andorra	3	2	2	2	4	0.00	100.00
Bosnia and Herzegovina	123	87	79	3	1	0.00	-66.67
Croatia	153	311	287	673	428	0.04	-36.40
Greece	703	808	701	1,389	966	0.10	-30.45
Italy	4,678	4,385	4,543	6,556	5,524	0.57	-15.74
Malta	48	38	55	40	53	0.01	32.50
Montenegro					6	0.00	
Portugal	622	687	765	1,469	1,370	0.14	-6.74
Serbia					143	0.01	
Serbia and Montenegro	137	89		32	3	0.00	-90.63
Slovenia	121	90	96	148	106	0.01	-28.38
Spain	2,576	2,736	2,862	4,185	3,771	0.39	-9.89
TFYR of Macedonia	39	22	26	26	20	0.00	-23.08
Western Europe	52,157	50,840	52,402	69,652	57,058	5.90	-18.08
Austria	2,383	2,301	2,240	3,088	2,235	0.23	-27.62
Belgium	3,648	4,109	4,376	6,266	5,145	0.53	-17.89
France	10,944	10,685	10,887	14,820	12,665	1.31	-14.54
Germany	22,414	21,493	22,555	30,105	24,381	2.52	-19.01

555

PAKISTAN

1. Arrivals of non-resident tourists at national borders, by nationality

	2008	2009	2010	2011	2012	Market share 2012	% Change 2012-2011
Liechtenstein	8	9	14	12	19	0.00	58.33
Luxembourg	48	83	57	51	62	0.01	21.57
Monaco	19	13	9	6	1	0.00	-83.33
Netherlands	10,287	9,976	10,083	12,288	10,040	1.04	-18.29
Switzerland	2,406	2,171	2,181	3,016	2,510	0.26	-16.78
East Mediterranean Europe	**5,173**	**4,967**	**5,517**	**8,952**	**7,597**	**0.79**	**-15.14**
Cyprus	132	120	84	130	94	0.01	-27.69
Turkey	5,041	4,847	5,433	8,822	7,503	0.78	-14.95
MIDDLE EAST	**28,966**	**27,951**	**28,188**	**40,058**	**34,805**	**3.60**	**-13.11**
Bahrain	3,579	3,774	3,403	4,901	5,491	0.57	12.04
Egypt	2,499	2,305	2,306	3,959	3,997	0.41	0.96
Iraq	388	487	588	723	563	0.06	-22.13
Jordan	1,817	1,493	1,436	2,347	1,756	0.18	-25.18
Kuwait	459	477	564	763	743	0.08	-2.62
Lebanon	924	736	590	905	735	0.08	-18.78
Libya	426	279	277	184	337	0.03	83.15
Oman	7,555	7,311	6,944	12,107	9,798	1.01	-19.07
Palestine	367	259	332	449	213	0.02	-52.56
Qatar	523	436	429	661	644	0.07	-2.57
Saudi Arabia	4,550	4,482	5,433	5,955	5,058	0.52	-15.06
Syrian Arab Republic	570	1,160	1,191	2,083	1,095	0.11	-47.43
United Arab Emirates	4,621	3,997	3,889	4,167	3,522	0.36	-15.48
Yemen	688	755	806	854	853	0.09	-0.12
SOUTH ASIA	**153,117**	**178,242**	**204,136**	**212,351**	**158,164**	**16.37**	**-25.52**
Afghanistan	66,353	96,617	110,922	79,291	33,734	3.49	-57.46
Bangladesh	12,230	6,941	6,333	8,750	5,484	0.57	-37.33
Bhutan	48	38	44	78	85	0.01	8.97
India	54,101	42,694	43,751	84,074	77,232	7.99	-8.14
Iran, Islamic Republic of	14,178	26,557	37,722	30,793	34,084	3.53	10.69
Maldives	224	187	141	301	212	0.02	-29.57
Nepal	2,040	1,569	1,345	2,012	2,283	0.24	13.47
Sri Lanka	3,943	3,639	3,878	7,052	5,050	0.52	-28.39
NOT SPECIFIED	**3,934**	**3,975**	**5,391**	**8,217**	**6,377**	**0.66**	**-22.39**
Other countries of the World	3,934	3,975	5,391	8,217	6,377	0.66	-22.39

Yearbook of Tourism Statistics, Data 2008 – 2012, 2014 Editic

PALAU

1. Arrivals of non-resident tourists at national borders, by country of residence

		2008	2009	2010	2011	2012	Market share 2012	% Change 2012-2011
TOTAL	(*)	79,259	71,887	85,593	109,057	116,754	100.00	8.89
AMERICAS		5,235	5,193	5,809	5,890	6,529	5.50	10.85
North America		5,235	5,193	5,809	5,890	6,529	5.50	10.85
United States of America		5,235	5,193	5,809	5,890	6,529	5.50	10.85
EAST ASIA AND THE PACIFIC		69,927	62,970	75,701	98,658	107,128	90.21	8.59
North-East Asia		64,968	56,843	67,841	93,513	102,695	86.48	9.82
China		439	534	725	1,699	4,471	3.76	163.15
Hong Kong, China		344	334	493	701	756	0.64	7.85
Japan		30,018	26,688	29,318	37,800	39,353	33.14	4.11
Korea, Republic of		14,186	13,009	15,144	15,681	19,465	16.39	24.13
Taiwan, Province of China		19,981	16,278	22,161	37,632	38,650	32.55	2.71
South-East Asia		949	998	1,139	1,123	932	0.78	-17.01
Philippines		949	998	913	913	746	0.63	-18.29
Singapore				226	210	186	0.16	-11.43
Australasia		711	700	1,241	1,134	1,366	1.15	20.46
Australia		711	700	1,241	1,134	1,366	1.15	20.46
Micronesia		3,299	4,429	5,480	2,888	2,135	1.80	-26.07
Guam		2,258	3,374	3,336	1,932	1,230	1.04	-36.34
Micronesia, Federated States of		1,041	1,055	1,487	637	710	0.60	11.46
Northern Mariana Islands				657	319	195	0.16	-38.87
EUROPE		3,151	2,923	3,402	3,535	4,353	3.67	23.14
Central/Eastern Europe		637	295	562	577	664	0.56	15.08
Russian Federation		637	295	562	577	664	0.56	15.08
Northern Europe		335	373	311	260	284	0.24	9.23
United Kingdom		335	373	311	260	284	0.24	9.23
Southern Europe		344	327	384	273	397	0.33	45.42
Italy		344	327	384	273	397	0.33	45.42
Western Europe		808	854	1,123	1,317	1,498	1.26	13.74
France				245	279	269	0.23	-3.58
Germany		621	629	662	749	946	0.80	26.30
Switzerland		187	225	216	289	283	0.24	-2.08
Other Europe		1,027	1,074	1,022	1,108	1,510	1.27	36.28
Other countries of Europe		1,027	1,074	1,022	1,108	1,510	1.27	36.28
NOT SPECIFIED		946	801	681	974	744	0.63	-23.61
Other countries of the World		946	801	681	974	744	0.63	-23.61

Yearbook of Tourism Statistics, Data 2008 – 2012, 2014 Edition

PALESTINE

3. Arrivals of non-resident tourists in hotels and similar establishments, by nationality

		2008	2009	2010	2011	2012	Market share 2012	% Change 2012-2011
TOTAL	(*)	387,143	395,622	521,927	448,500	490,110	100.00	9.28
AFRICA		9,679	11,736	14,126	27,837	24,331	4.96	-12.59
Other Africa		9,679	11,736	14,126	27,837	24,331	4.96	-12.59
All countries of Africa		9,679	11,736	14,126	27,837	24,331	4.96	-12.59
AMERICAS		39,453	62,958	87,721	56,701	53,766	10.97	-5.18
North America		31,685	49,890	72,354	42,813	40,626	8.29	-5.11
Canada, United States		31,685	49,890	72,354	42,813	40,626	8.29	-5.11
Other Americas		7,768	13,068	15,367	13,888	13,140	2.68	-5.39
Other countries of the Americas		7,768	13,068	15,367	13,888	13,140	2.68	-5.39
EAST ASIA AND THE PACIFIC		41,344	41,157	67,218	58,394	51,911	10.59	-11.10
Australasia		3,455	1,580	4,553	4,944	3,761	0.77	-23.93
Australia, New Zealand		3,455	1,580	4,553	4,944	3,761	0.77	-23.93
Other East Asia and the Pacific		37,889	39,577	62,665	53,450	48,150	9.82	-9.92
All countries of Asia		37,889	39,577	62,665	53,450	48,150	9.82	-9.92
EUROPE		293,659	275,694	350,543	300,768	353,349	72.10	17.48
East Mediterranean Europe		25,577	44,195	44,003	44,065	66,518	13.57	50.95
Israel		25,577	44,195	44,003	44,065	66,518	13.57	50.95
Other Europe		268,082	231,499	306,540	256,703	286,831	58.52	11.74
Other countries of Europe		268,082	231,499	306,540	256,703	286,831	58.52	11.74
MIDDLE EAST		3,008	4,077	2,319	4,800	6,753	1.38	40.69
All countries of Middle East		3,008	4,077	2,319	4,800	6,753	1.38	40.69

Yearbook of Tourism Statistics, Data 2008 – 2012, 2014 Edition

PALESTINE

5. Overnight stays of non-resident tourists in hotels and similar establishments, by nationality

		2008	2009	2010	2011	2012	Market share 2012	% Change 2012-2011
TOTAL	(*)	1,012,870	926,312	1,165,519	1,112,523	1,162,530	100.00	4.49
AFRICA		17,170	19,442	27,088	50,363	43,988	3.78	-12.66
Other Africa		17,170	19,442	27,088	50,363	43,988	3.78	-12.66
All countries of Africa		17,170	19,442	27,088	50,363	43,988	3.78	-12.66
AMERICAS		113,427	149,612	190,830	149,938	140,999	12.13	-5.96
North America		89,031	120,508	157,176	110,217	106,283	9.14	-3.57
Canada, United States		89,031	120,508	157,176	110,217	106,283	9.14	-3.57
Other Americas		24,396	29,104	33,654	39,721	34,716	2.99	-12.60
Other countries of the Americas		24,396	29,104	33,654	39,721	34,716	2.99	-12.60
EAST ASIA AND THE PACIFIC		110,181	89,195	150,976	140,001	129,663	11.15	-7.38
Australasia		7,115	3,633	8,705	10,273	9,076	0.78	-11.65
Australia, New Zealand		7,115	3,633	8,705	10,273	9,076	0.78	-11.65
Other East Asia and the Pacific		103,066	85,562	142,271	129,728	120,587	10.37	-7.05
All countries of Asia		103,066	85,562	142,271	129,728	120,587	10.37	-7.05
EUROPE		766,756	660,388	787,729	752,319	819,420	70.49	8.92
East Mediterranean Europe		47,581	80,312	77,191	73,538	112,443	9.67	52.90
Israel		47,581	80,312	77,191	73,538	112,443	9.67	52.90
Other Europe		719,175	580,076	710,538	678,781	706,977	60.81	4.15
Other countries of Europe		719,175	580,076	710,538	678,781	706,977	60.81	4.15
MIDDLE EAST		5,336	7,675	8,896	19,902	28,460	2.45	43.00
All countries of Middle East		5,336	7,675	8,896	19,902	28,460	2.45	43.00

Yearbook of Tourism Statistics, Data 2008 – 2012, 2014 Edition

PANAMA

2. Arrivals of non-resident visitors at national borders, by country of residence

		2008	2009	2010	2011	2012	Market share 2012	% Change 2012-2011
TOTAL	(*)	1,136,079	1,054,663	1,162,713	1,310,292	1,478,282	100.00	12.82
AFRICA		1,071	851	1,000	1,921	1,919	0.13	-0.10
East Africa					337	240	0.02	-28.78
Burundi					9	6	0.00	-33.33
Comoros					10	3	0.00	-70.00
Djibouti					1	2	0.00	100.00
Eritrea					10	3	0.00	-70.00
Ethiopia					40	20	0.00	-50.00
Kenya					57	71	0.00	24.56
Madagascar					11	8	0.00	-27.27
Malawi					7	4	0.00	-42.86
Mauritius					19	28	0.00	47.37
Mozambique					22	14	0.00	-36.36
Reunion					5			
Rwanda					6	3	0.00	-50.00
Seychelles					10	9	0.00	-10.00
Somalia					2	1	0.00	-50.00
Uganda					43	24	0.00	-44.19
United Republic of Tanzania					29	25	0.00	-13.79
Zambia					27	8	0.00	-70.37
Zimbabwe					29	11	0.00	-62.07
Central Africa					329	389	0.03	18.24
Angola					226	304	0.02	34.51
Cameroon					24	31	0.00	29.17
Central African Republic					1	1	0.00	0.00
Chad					4	4	0.00	0.00
Congo					13	15	0.00	15.38
Democratic Republic of the Congo					28	23	0.00	-17.86
Gabon					22	8	0.00	-63.64
Sao Tome and Principe					11	3	0.00	-72.73
North Africa					133	214	0.01	60.90
Algeria					42	34	0.00	-19.05
Morocco					53	52	0.00	-1.89
Sudan					11	4	0.00	-63.64
Tunisia					22	23	0.00	4.55
Western Sahara					5	101	0.01	1,920.00
Southern Africa		340	279	319	726	719	0.05	-0.96
Botswana					3	9	0.00	200.00
Lesotho					10	4	0.00	-60.00
Namibia					32	20	0.00	-37.50
South Africa		340	279	319	668	680	0.05	1.80
Swaziland					13	6	0.00	-53.85
West Africa					396	357	0.02	-9.85
Benin					7	8	0.00	14.29
Burkina Faso					18	6	0.00	-66.67
Cape Verde					24	18	0.00	-25.00
Côte d'Ivoire					12	9	0.00	-25.00
Gambia					13	6	0.00	-53.85
Ghana					82	87	0.01	6.10
Guinea					22	46	0.00	109.09
Guinea-Bissau					13	13	0.00	0.00
Liberia					11	10	0.00	-9.09
Mali					12	10	0.00	-16.67
Mauritania					4	5	0.00	25.00
Niger					15	16	0.00	6.67
Nigeria					114	80	0.01	-29.82

Yearbook of Tourism Statistics, Data 2008 – 2012, 2014 Edition

PANAMA

2. Arrivals of non-resident visitors at national borders, by country of residence

	2008	2009	2010	2011	2012	Market share 2012	% Change 2012-2011
Senegal				26	23	0.00	-11.54
Sierra Leone				4	15	0.00	275.00
Togo				19	5	0.00	-73.68
Other Africa	**731**	**572**	**681**				
Other countries of Africa	731	572	681				
AMERICAS	**983,844**	**916,458**	**1,006,007**	**1,134,147**	**1,284,902**	**86.92**	**13.29**
Caribbean	**78,389**	**28,787**	**30,546**	**32,677**	**36,837**	**2.49**	**12.73**
Anguilla				2	13	0.00	550.00
Antigua and Barbuda				103	136	0.01	32.04
Aruba				53	78	0.01	47.17
Bahamas	991	393	373	626	1,178	0.08	88.18
Barbados	826	421	451	485	629	0.04	29.69
Bermuda	174	194	142	186	283	0.02	52.15
British Virgin Islands				3			
Cayman Islands				115	627	0.04	445.22
Cuba	4,877	5,032	5,025	5,461	5,960	0.40	9.14
Curaçao	1,976	40	106	86	73	0.00	-15.12
Dominica				152	141	0.01	-7.24
Dominican Republic	19,222	9,649	11,704	13,412	15,935	1.08	18.81
Grenada				148	142	0.01	-4.05
Haiti	11,166	5,759	4,462	4,081	2,658	0.18	-34.87
Jamaica	13,682	3,345	2,763	2,857	3,294	0.22	15.30
Martinique				2	6	0.00	200.00
Montserrat				1	3	0.00	200.00
Puerto Rico	20,372	664	1,069	750	798	0.05	6.40
Saint Kitts and Nevis				110	151	0.01	37.27
Saint Lucia				132	165	0.01	25.00
Saint Vincent and the Grenadines				143	140	0.01	-2.10
Trinidad and Tobago				3,718	4,376	0.30	17.70
Turks and Caicos Islands				42	36	0.00	-14.29
United States Virgin Islands				3	10	0.00	233.33
Other countries of the Caribbean	5,103	3,290	4,451	6	5	0.00	-16.67
Central America	**145,418**	**100,477**	**114,080**	**111,545**	**123,702**	**8.37**	**10.90**
Belize	1,454	736	1,070	967	1,051	0.07	8.69
Costa Rica	65,438	37,759	39,524	40,524	42,978	2.91	6.06
El Salvador	20,359	15,569	16,547	16,696	20,820	1.41	24.70
Guatemala	27,629	26,064	32,780	27,107	27,913	1.89	2.97
Honduras	14,542	10,383	12,270	13,921	16,400	1.11	17.81
Nicaragua	15,996	9,966	11,889	12,330	14,540	0.98	17.92
North America	**368,090**	**316,945**	**348,999**	**383,896**	**424,441**	**28.71**	**10.56**
Canada	44,171	37,849	48,029	52,731	62,792	4.25	19.08
Mexico	51,533	44,904	48,132	51,422	57,803	3.91	12.41
United States of America	272,386	234,190	252,837	279,742	303,843	20.55	8.62
Other countries of North America		2	1	1	3	0.00	200.00
South America	**391,947**	**470,249**	**512,382**	**606,029**	**699,922**	**47.35**	**15.49**
Argentina	23,598	41,989	47,216	62,357	66,623	4.51	6.84
Bolivia	6,647	4,942	6,744	9,544	12,327	0.83	29.16
Brazil	18,603	24,338	31,520	47,890	59,687	4.04	24.63
Chile	15,880	13,035	16,232	19,020	21,095	1.43	10.91
Colombia	213,776	177,224	219,250	218,962	244,890	16.57	11.84
Ecuador	50,129	22,172	30,861	43,975	59,782	4.04	35.95
French Guiana				19	17	0.00	-10.53
Guyana				1,001	1,192	0.08	19.08
Paraguay	1,662	821	1,078	1,319	3,955	0.27	199.85
Peru	23,251	11,853	15,431	22,382	30,824	2.09	37.72
Suriname				213	281	0.02	31.92
Uruguay	2,991	10,556	11,400	11,163	11,898	0.80	6.58

561

Yearbook of Tourism Statistics, Data 2008 – 2012, 2014 Edition

PANAMA

2. Arrivals of non-resident visitors at national borders, by country of residence

	2008	2009	2010	2011	2012	Market share 2012	% Change 2012-2011
Venezuela	34,403	162,581	131,608	168,184	187,351	12.67	11.40
Other countries of South America	1,007	738	1,042				
EAST ASIA AND THE PACIFIC	**33,286**	**22,550**	**27,020**	**26,993**	**30,503**	**2.06**	**13.00**
North-East Asia	**8,762**	**4,715**	**5,485**	**16,574**	**18,940**	**1.28**	**14.28**
China				6,661	7,714	0.52	15.81
Hong Kong, China				35	28	0.00	-20.00
Japan	6,475	3,133	3,988	4,525	5,043	0.34	11.45
Korea, Dem. People's Republic of				298	10	0.00	-96.64
Korea, Republic of				3,486	4,511	0.31	29.40
Macao, China				18	9	0.00	-50.00
Mongolia				74	98	0.01	32.43
Taiwan, Province of China	2,287	1,582	1,497	1,477	1,527	0.10	3.39
South-East Asia				**6,502**	**6,694**	**0.45**	**2.95**
Brunei Darussalam				7	2	0.00	-71.43
Cambodia				32	12	0.00	-62.50
Indonesia				519	390	0.03	-24.86
Lao People's Democratic Republic				6	8	0.00	33.33
Malaysia				183	214	0.01	16.94
Myanmar				260	209	0.01	-19.62
Philippines				4,608	5,141	0.35	11.57
Singapore				425	407	0.03	-4.24
Thailand				214	191	0.01	-10.75
Timor-Leste				8			
Viet Nam				240	120	0.01	-50.00
Australasia	**4,451**	**2,925**	**3,243**	**3,791**	**4,709**	**0.32**	**24.22**
Australia	3,471	2,352	2,439	3,139	3,990	0.27	27.11
New Zealand	980	573	804	652	719	0.05	10.28
Melanesia				**16**	**10**	**0.00**	**-37.50**
Fiji				12	4	0.00	-66.67
Papua New Guinea				4	6	0.00	50.00
Micronesia				**11**	**10**	**0.00**	**-9.09**
Guam					1	0.00	
Kiribati				3	5	0.00	66.67
Micronesia, Federated States of				8	4	0.00	-50.00
Polynesia				**33**	**32**	**0.00**	**-3.03**
Cook Islands				13	7	0.00	-46.15
Samoa				15	13	0.00	-13.33
Tuvalu				5	12	0.00	140.00
Other East Asia and the Pacific	**20,073**	**14,910**	**18,292**	**66**	**108**	**0.01**	**63.64**
Other countries of Asia	19,980	14,823	18,214	6	20	0.00	233.33
Other countries of Oceania	93	87	78	60	88	0.01	46.67
EUROPE	**117,812**	**114,729**	**128,595**	**141,728**	**155,213**	**10.50**	**9.51**
Central/Eastern Europe				**10,353**	**10,857**	**0.73**	**4.87**
Armenia				5	12	0.00	140.00
Azerbaijan				8	5	0.00	-37.50
Belarus				85	93	0.01	9.41
Bulgaria				423	494	0.03	16.78
Czech Republic				530	632	0.04	19.25
Czech Republic/Slovakia					174	0.01	
Estonia				221	132	0.01	-40.27
Georgia				108	91	0.01	-15.74
Hungary				352	407	0.03	15.63
Kazakhstan				44	53	0.00	20.45
Kyrgyzstan				6	5	0.00	-16.67
Latvia				356	359	0.02	0.84
Lithuania				238	205	0.01	-13.87
Poland				1,583	1,714	0.12	8.28

Yearbook of Tourism Statistics, Data 2008 – 2012, 2014 Edition

PANAMA

2. Arrivals of non-resident visitors at national borders, by country of residence

	2008	2009	2010	2011	2012	Market share 2012	% Change 2012-2011
Republic of Moldova				28	59	0.00	110.71
Romania				733	1,006	0.07	37.24
Russian Federation				3,284	3,156	0.21	-3.90
Slovakia				207	251	0.02	21.26
Tajikistan				2	1	0.00	-50.00
Turkmenistan				6	6	0.00	0.00
Ukraine				2,125	1,994	0.13	-6.16
Uzbekistan				9	8	0.00	-11.11
Northern Europe	**12,682**	**10,818**	**11,181**	**22,468**	**21,301**	**1.44**	**-5.19**
Denmark				1,917	1,892	0.13	-1.30
Finland				3,236	1,061	0.07	-67.21
Iceland				141	154	0.01	9.22
Ireland				1,203	1,253	0.08	4.16
Norway				1,568	1,670	0.11	6.51
Sweden				2,843	2,858	0.19	0.53
United Kingdom	12,682	10,818	11,181	11,560	12,413	0.84	7.38
Southern Europe	**43,489**	**39,633**	**47,660**	**53,423**	**62,129**	**4.20**	**16.30**
Albania				80	102	0.01	27.50
Andorra				175	200	0.01	14.29
Bosnia and Herzegovina				9	17	0.00	88.89
Croatia				408	478	0.03	17.16
Greece	1,463	1,034	1,001	1,062	982	0.07	-7.53
Holy See				2	9	0.00	350.00
Italy	19,784	13,399	15,814	16,295	17,039	1.15	4.57
Malta				30	28	0.00	-6.67
Portugal				2,668	3,106	0.21	16.42
San Marino				4	8	0.00	100.00
Serbia and Montenegro					15	0.00	
Slovenia				117	198	0.01	69.23
Spain	22,242	25,200	30,845	32,560	39,928	2.70	22.63
TFYR of Macedonia				13	19	0.00	46.15
Western Europe	**37,622**	**33,567**	**36,345**	**46,497**	**51,416**	**3.48**	**10.58**
Austria				1,906	1,973	0.13	3.52
Belgium				3,172	3,292	0.22	3.78
France	15,775	11,166	11,665	12,361	13,731	0.93	11.08
Germany	12,024	9,087	9,742	12,847	14,396	0.97	12.06
Liechtenstein				42	51	0.00	21.43
Luxembourg				75	94	0.01	25.33
Monaco				8	4	0.00	-50.00
Netherlands	4,537	9,610	10,732	11,110	12,181	0.82	9.64
Switzerland	5,286	3,704	4,206	4,976	5,694	0.39	14.43
East Mediterranean Europe	**6,476**	**6,800**	**7,826**	**8,858**	**9,478**	**0.64**	**7.00**
Cyprus				53	65	0.00	22.64
Israel	6,476	6,800	7,826	8,312	8,625	0.58	3.77
Turkey				493	788	0.05	59.84
Other Europe	**17,543**	**23,911**	**25,583**	**129**	**32**	**0.00**	**-75.19**
Other countries of Europe	17,543	23,911	25,583	129	32	0.00	-75.19
MIDDLE EAST	**66**	**75**	**91**	**787**	**955**	**0.06**	**21.35**
Bahrain				4	7	0.00	75.00
Egypt	66	75	91	91	104	0.01	14.29
Iraq				16	17	0.00	6.25
Jordan				106	83	0.01	-21.70
Kuwait				45	19	0.00	-57.78
Lebanon				246	458	0.03	86.18
Libya				9	34	0.00	277.78
Oman				9	10	0.00	11.11
Palestine				97	77	0.01	-20.62

563

Yearbook of Tourism Statistics, Data 2008 – 2012, 2014 Edition

PANAMA

2. Arrivals of non-resident visitors at national borders, by country of residence

	2008	2009	2010	2011	2012	Market share 2012	% Change 2012-2011
Qatar				17	22	0.00	29.41
Saudi Arabia				64	58	0.00	-9.38
Syrian Arab Republic				60	36	0.00	-40.00
United Arab Emirates				16	21	0.00	31.25
Yemen				7	9	0.00	28.57
SOUTH ASIA				**4,716**	**4,790**	**0.32**	**1.57**
Afghanistan				19	2	0.00	-89.47
Bangladesh				68	65	0.00	-4.41
India				4,297	4,393	0.30	2.23
Iran, Islamic Republic of				62	53	0.00	-14.52
Maldives				14	3	0.00	-78.57
Nepal				18	12	0.00	-33.33
Pakistan				152	147	0.01	-3.29
Sri Lanka				86	115	0.01	33.72

Yearbook of Tourism Statistics, Data 2008 – 2012, 2014 Editi

PAPUA NEW GUINEA

1. Arrivals of non-resident tourists at national borders, by country of residence

	2008	2009	2010	2011	2012	Market share 2012	% Change 2012-2011
TOTAL	114,207	125,891	146,350	165,059			
AFRICA	947	877	1,056	1,671			
Other Africa	947	877	1,056	1,671			
All countries of Africa	947	877	1,056	1,671			
AMERICAS	8,197	9,029	10,869	11,715			
North America	7,854	8,567	10,362	11,024			
Canada	1,745	1,937	1,927	2,067			
United States of America	6,109	6,630	8,435	8,957			
South America	46	21	14	8			
Chile	46	21	14	8			
Other Americas	297	441	493	683			
Other countries of the Americas	297	441	493	683			
EAST ASIA AND THE PACIFIC	93,542	102,717	119,610	131,593			
North-East Asia	10,078	10,064	12,220	12,098			
China	5,424	6,492	7,435	7,063			
Japan	3,865	2,767	3,804	3,500			
Korea, Republic of	789	805	981	1,535			
South-East Asia	15,273	15,092	19,072	24,869			
Indonesia	2,007	1,831	2,249	2,377			
Malaysia	4,772	5,017	5,915	6,563			
Philippines	7,661	7,333	9,551	14,292			
Singapore	833	911	1,357	1,637			
Australasia	64,123	72,527	82,398	86,451			
Australia	58,724	66,842	75,355	77,396			
New Zealand	5,399	5,685	7,043	9,055			
Other East Asia and the Pacific	4,068	5,034	5,920	8,175			
Other countries of Asia	1,197	1,270	2,064	3,418			
Other countries of Oceania	2,871	3,764	3,856	4,757			
EUROPE	9,237	9,022	12,065	15,130			
Central/Eastern Europe	514	411	559	575			
Russian Federation	514	411	559	575			
Northern Europe	4,257	4,067	5,445	6,315			
United Kingdom	3,800	3,669	5,102	5,753			
Scandinavia	457	398	343	562			
Southern Europe	331	293	270	453			
Italy	331	293	270	453			
Western Europe	1,923	2,318	3,141	4,495			
France	515	584	830	1,271			
Germany	1,408	1,219	1,680	2,480			
Netherlands		515	631	744			
East Mediterranean Europe	100	144	55	132			
Israel	100	144	55	132			
Other Europe	2,112	1,789	2,595	3,160			
Other countries of Europe	2,112	1,789	2,595	3,160			
SOUTH ASIA	2,284	2,382	2,750	4,950			
India	2,284	2,382	2,750	4,950			
NOT SPECIFIED		1,864					
Other countries of the World		1,864					

Yearbook of Tourism Statistics, Data 2008 – 2012, 2014 Edition

PARAGUAY

1. Arrivals of non-resident tourists at national borders, by nationality

	2008	2009	2010	2011	2012	Market share 2012	% Change 2012-2011
TOTAL (*)	428,215	439,246	465,363	523,740	579,305	100.00	10.61
AFRICA	301	401	386	354	593	0.10	67.51
East Africa	15	103	91	34	63	0.01	85.29
Burundi	1	2	1		2	0.00	
Ethiopia		10	9	3	4	0.00	33.33
Kenya	4	15	18	13	14	0.00	7.69
Madagascar	2	6	3	5	5	0.00	0.00
Malawi		5	4		2	0.00	
Mauritius				1			
Mozambique	6	6	7	4	13	0.00	225.00
Rwanda	1			2	2	0.00	0.00
Somalia		1					
Uganda		4	1	3	5	0.00	66.67
United Republic of Tanzania		14	14	1	10	0.00	900.00
Zambia		8	6	1	6	0.00	500.00
Zimbabwe	1	32	28	1			
Central Africa	25	39	62	58	142	0.02	144.83
Angola	7	28	40	40	115	0.02	187.50
Cameroon	11	3	13	5	5	0.00	0.00
Central African Republic	1			3	4	0.00	33.33
Congo	6	5	6	4	9	0.00	125.00
Equatorial Guinea		3	3	6	9	0.00	50.00
North Africa	39	12	8	6	41	0.01	583.33
Algeria	9	6	4	1	2	0.00	100.00
Morocco	26	4	1	4	33	0.01	725.00
Sudan	2				1	0.00	
Tunisia	2	2	3	1	5	0.00	400.00
Southern Africa	179	185	192	220	286	0.05	30.00
Botswana	2	3	2				
Lesotho		1			1	0.00	
Namibia	2	3	9	3	4	0.00	33.33
South Africa	175	176	181	216	281	0.05	30.09
Swaziland		2		1			
West Africa	43	62	33	33	54	0.01	63.64
Benin	1	3			2	0.00	
Burkina Faso	1	8	4	2	3	0.00	50.00
Cape Verde	5	8	2	8	5	0.00	-37.50
Côte d'Ivoire	3	3	4	1	3	0.00	200.00
Gambia		3	1				
Ghana	5	9	9	1	7	0.00	600.00
Guinea	1	3	1				
Guinea-Bissau				4	2	0.00	-50.00
Liberia	1	2			1	0.00	
Mauritania	2	2			2	0.00	
Nigeria	11	17	9	15	22	0.00	46.67
Senegal	11	3	3	2	7	0.00	250.00
Sierra Leone	1	1					
Togo	1						
Other Africa				3	7	0.00	133.33
Other countries of Africa				3	7	0.00	133.33
AMERICAS	384,216	394,649	432,963	480,529	519,208	89.63	8.05
Caribbean	633	612	316	683	916	0.16	34.11
Anguilla			1	3	2	0.00	-33.33
Antigua and Barbuda		2	1	1	1	0.00	0.00
Bahamas	24	4		5	5	0.00	0.00

566

Yearbook of Tourism Statistics, Data 2008 – 2012, 2014 Edition

PARAGUAY

1. Arrivals of non-resident tourists at national borders, by nationality

	2008	2009	2010	2011	2012	Market share 2012	% Change 2012-2011
Barbados	7	6	2	9	3	0.00	-66.67
Cuba	396	337	190	381	553	0.10	45.14
Dominican Republic	140	113	96	219	274	0.05	25.11
Haiti	22	33	13	29	34	0.01	17.24
Jamaica	27	15	9	14	18	0.00	28.57
Martinique					1	0.00	
Puerto Rico	2	1	1	3	2	0.00	-33.33
Saint Kitts and Nevis	1						
Saint Lucia	3	2		1	1	0.00	0.00
Saint Vincent and the Grenadines		89		1	3	0.00	200.00
Trinidad and Tobago	11	10	3	12	13	0.00	8.33
Other countries of the Caribbean					5	6	0.00	20.00
Central America	**1,537**	**1,546**	**868**	**1,901**	**3,022**	**0.52**	**58.97**
Belize	15	9	1	103	10	0.00	-90.29
Costa Rica	305	346	253	526	816	0.14	55.13
El Salvador	258	250	166	239	361	0.06	51.05
Guatemala	220	361	202	298	593	0.10	98.99
Honduras	204	120	45	134	231	0.04	72.39
Nicaragua	183	144	64	163	254	0.04	55.83
Panama	352	316	137	438	757	0.13	72.83
North America	**17,293**	**18,858**	**13,290**	**15,454**	**23,522**	**4.06**	**52.21**
Canada	2,239	2,669	1,647	1,606	2,292	0.40	42.71
Mexico	1,813	2,177	1,501	2,563	3,950	0.68	54.12
United States of America	13,241	14,012	10,142	11,285	17,280	2.98	53.12
South America	**364,753**	**373,633**	**418,489**	**462,491**	**491,748**	**84.89**	**6.33**
Argentina	195,948	196,149	218,418	222,901	254,328	43.90	14.10
Bolivia	6,905	13,203	11,646	23,256	18,202	3.14	-21.73
Brazil	134,985	131,429	159,280	176,440	171,925	29.68	-2.56
Chile	9,517	11,115	9,829	11,706	11,780	2.03	0.63
Colombia	2,348	3,017	2,482	4,177	7,129	1.23	70.67
Ecuador	856	1,266	779	1,815	2,369	0.41	30.52
Guyana	4	3	4	15	21	0.00	40.00
Peru	3,577	5,044	4,141	6,219	7,909	1.37	27.17
Suriname	60	2		23	26	0.00	13.04
Uruguay	9,327	11,130	11,216	14,154	15,448	2.67	9.14
Venezuela	1,226	1,275	694	1,784	2,611	0.45	46.36
Other countries of South America				1			
EAST ASIA AND THE PACIFIC	**8,390**	**8,478**	**7,177**	**8,037**	**11,971**	**2.07**	**48.95**
North-East Asia	**7,750**	**7,743**	**6,574**	**7,408**	**10,888**	**1.88**	**46.98**
China	146	218	193	363	741	0.13	104.13
Hong Kong, China		1	2	1			
Japan	3,816	3,319	3,134	2,666	3,947	0.68	48.05
Korea, Republic of	3,321	3,672	2,917	3,923	5,571	0.96	42.01
Mongolia	6	2	1		2	0.00	
Taiwan, Province of China	461	531	327	455	627	0.11	37.80
South-East Asia	**169**	**189**	**152**	**138**	**241**	**0.04**	**74.64**
Cambodia	1	2			2	0.00	
Indonesia	74	96	56	29	24	0.00	-17.24
Lao People's Democratic Republic			3	11	2	0.00	-81.82
Malaysia	23	26	40	16	23	0.00	43.75
Myanmar		1			2	0.00	
Philippines	34	43	32	62	105	0.02	69.35
Singapore	8	2	5	7	12	0.00	71.43
Thailand	19	8	11	4	22	0.00	450.00
Viet Nam	10	11	5	9	49	0.01	444.44
Australasia	**466**	**543**	**447**	**472**	**825**	**0.14**	**74.79**
Australia	353	391	319	341	694	0.12	103.52

Yearbook of Tourism Statistics, Data 2008 – 2012, 2014 Edition

PARAGUAY

1. Arrivals of non-resident tourists at national borders, by nationality

	2008	2009	2010	2011	2012	Market share 2012	% Change 2012-2011
New Zealand	113	152	128	131	131	0.02	0.00
Melanesia	**5**	**3**	**3**	**1**	**3**	**0.00**	**200.00**
Fiji	1	3	2				
Papua New Guinea			1		3	0.00	
Solomon Islands	2			1			
Vanuatu	2						
Micronesia				**1**			
Guam				1			
Other East Asia and the Pacific				**18**	**14**	**0.00**	**-22.22**
Other countries of Asia				16	3	0.00	-81.25
Other countries of Oceania				2	11	0.00	450.00
EUROPE	**34,259**	**34,716**	**24,280**	**34,014**	**46,279**	**7.99**	**36.06**
Central/Eastern Europe	**1,075**	**1,040**	**745**	**1,035**	**1,552**	**0.27**	**49.95**
Armenia	2	3	3	7	12	0.00	71.43
Azerbaijan	3	5		4	3	0.00	-25.00
Belarus	3	14	3				
Bulgaria	18	22	20	51	69	0.01	35.29
Czech Republic	156	142	83	160	280	0.05	75.00
Estonia	4	51	48	24	53	0.01	120.83
Georgia	1	1			5	0.00	
Hungary	173	102	18	81	122	0.02	50.62
Kazakhstan	5	2			6	0.00	
Latvia	14	25	11	26	31	0.01	19.23
Lithuania	13	24	11	19	19	0.00	0.00
Poland	223	353	195	292	448	0.08	53.42
Republic of Moldova	1	1		7	19	0.00	171.43
Romania	50	1	2	2	4	0.00	100.00
Russian Federation	311	202	196	265	263	0.05	-0.75
Slovakia	46	51	22	35	74	0.01	111.43
Ukraine	49	41	133	57	133	0.02	133.33
Uzbekistan	3			5	11	0.00	120.00
Northern Europe	**3,747**	**3,666**	**2,456**	**3,668**	**5,086**	**0.88**	**38.66**
Denmark	293	323	213	431	646	0.11	49.88
Finland	123	132	103	137	205	0.04	49.64
Iceland	23	15	15	20	28	0.00	40.00
Ireland	308	307	229	230	261	0.05	13.48
Norway	350	321	218	342	463	0.08	35.38
Sweden	575	518	296	531	1,017	0.18	91.53
United Kingdom	2,075	2,050	1,382	1,977	2,466	0.43	24.73
Southern Europe	**11,571**	**11,416**	**7,772**	**12,138**	**16,974**	**2.93**	**39.84**
Albania	2	1	3	6	8	0.00	33.33
Andorra	3	1	1	11	11	0.00	0.00
Bosnia and Herzegovina	2	4			4	0.00	
Croatia	21	55	10	24	38	0.01	58.33
Greece	351	116	176	101	150	0.03	48.51
Holy See	5	29	4	7	8	0.00	14.29
Italy	3,055	3,270	2,376	3,008	4,185	0.72	39.13
Malta	3	3	3	7	12	0.00	71.43
Portugal	344	336	238	557	720	0.12	29.26
San Marino					1	0.00	
Serbia and Montenegro	7	8	3				
Slovenia	26	32	29	50	34	0.01	-32.00
Spain	7,751	7,557	4,929	8,364	11,801	2.04	41.09
TFYR of Macedonia	1	4		3	2	0.00	-33.33
Western Europe	**17,255**	**18,053**	**12,969**	**16,551**	**21,339**	**3.68**	**28.93**
Austria	591	706	610	702	930	0.16	32.48
Belgium	613	701	436	521	949	0.16	82.15

Yearbook of Tourism Statistics, Data 2008 – 2012, 2014 Edition

PARAGUAY

1. Arrivals of non-resident tourists at national borders, by nationality

	2008	2009	2010	2011	2012	Market share 2012	% Change 2012-2011
France	3,038	3,414	2,568	3,632	4,512	0.78	24.23
Germany	10,467	10,289	7,173	9,057	11,486	1.98	26.82
Liechtenstein	7	5	5	5	6	0.00	20.00
Luxembourg	20	23	19	51	38	0.01	-25.49
Monaco		3			30	0.01	
Netherlands	822	1,065	701	859	1,223	0.21	42.37
Switzerland	1,697	1,847	1,457	1,724	2,165	0.37	25.58
East Mediterranean Europe	**611**	**541**	**332**	**618**	**1,322**	**0.23**	**113.92**
Cyprus	15	22	2	8	22	0.00	175.00
Israel	523	462	298	508	1,030	0.18	102.76
Turkey	73	57	32	102	270	0.05	164.71
Other Europe			**6**	**4**	**6**	**0.00**	**50.00**
Other countries of Europe			6	4	6	0.00	50.00
MIDDLE EAST	**642**	**654**	**348**	**468**	**718**	**0.12**	**53.42**
Egypt	25	22	8	22	32	0.01	45.45
Iraq		8	4	10	6	0.00	-40.00
Jordan	3	6	10	8	29	0.01	262.50
Kuwait	3	1		1	2	0.00	100.00
Lebanon	589	583	316	399	593	0.10	48.62
Libya				1	2	0.00	100.00
Palestine	3	4	3	7	14	0.00	100.00
Qatar		4	1		3	0.00	
Saudi Arabia	5	11	1	2	1	0.00	-50.00
Syrian Arab Republic	8	10	4	7	13	0.00	85.71
United Arab Emirates	6	5	1	11	23	0.00	109.09
SOUTH ASIA	**393**	**348**	**209**	**338**	**536**	**0.09**	**58.58**
Afghanistan		3	2				
Bangladesh	44	24	16	28	92	0.02	228.57
India	300	258	177	281	398	0.07	41.64
Iran, Islamic Republic of	6	26	8	9	8	0.00	-11.11
Maldives		1					
Nepal	6	5	1	1	8	0.00	700.00
Pakistan	27	28	5	18	25	0.00	38.89
Sri Lanka	10	3		1	5	0.00	400.00
NOT SPECIFIED	**14**						
Other countries of the World	14						

Yearbook of Tourism Statistics, Data 2008 – 2012, 2014 Edition

PERU

1. Arrivals of non-resident tourists at national borders, by country of residence

		2008	2009	2010	2011	2012	Market share 2012	% Change 2012-2011
TOTAL	(*)	2,052,323	2,133,621	2,291,871	2,589,587	2,836,756	100.00	9.54
AFRICA		3,511	3,478	3,714	4,247	4,406	0.16	3.74
North Africa		101	136	130	229	225	0.01	-1.75
Morocco		101	136	130	229	225	0.01	-1.75
Southern Africa		2,666	2,444	2,689	2,994	2,943	0.10	-1.70
South Africa		2,666	2,444	2,689	2,994	2,943	0.10	-1.70
Other Africa		744	898	895	1,024	1,238	0.04	20.90
Other countries of Africa		744	898	895	1,024	1,238	0.04	20.90
AMERICAS		1,485,900	1,581,215	1,746,961	1,996,759	2,190,815	77.23	9.72
Caribbean		6,407	9,815	8,574	7,406	6,555	0.23	-11.49
Cuba		3,285	5,139	4,855	4,172	3,755	0.13	-10.00
Dominican Republic		3,122	4,676	3,719	3,234	2,800	0.10	-13.42
Central America		25,564	27,578	31,321	40,229	38,085	1.34	-5.33
Costa Rica		7,630	7,842	8,765	9,302	9,319	0.33	0.18
El Salvador		2,822	2,938	2,663	4,948	5,746	0.20	16.13
Guatemala		3,033	2,971	2,797	3,451	3,486	0.12	1.01
Panama		7,344	8,956	10,718	10,960	12,908	0.46	17.77
Other countries of Central America		4,735	4,871	6,378	11,568	6,626	0.23	-42.72
North America		503,172	509,543	508,284	515,394	559,809	19.73	8.62
Canada		51,975	54,595	52,955	57,454	61,362	2.16	6.80
Mexico		30,589	28,623	38,097	46,005	51,229	1.81	11.36
United States of America		420,608	426,325	417,232	411,935	447,218	15.77	8.57
South America		950,757	1,034,279	1,198,782	1,433,730	1,586,366	55.92	10.65
Argentina		97,478	121,172	127,062	147,403	158,950	5.60	7.83
Bolivia		86,619	93,408	86,181	88,042	101,546	3.58	15.34
Brazil		64,573	82,764	87,674	117,537	126,085	4.44	7.27
Chile		452,705	464,153	595,944	741,717	806,929	28.45	8.79
Colombia		76,559	87,225	98,642	112,816	133,975	4.72	18.76
Ecuador		128,063	136,054	152,445	160,841	176,071	6.21	9.47
Paraguay		2,775	3,914	3,914	4,631	4,756	0.17	2.70
Uruguay		7,962	8,648	8,219	10,303	11,846	0.42	14.98
Venezuela		33,871	36,789	38,469	50,185	65,930	2.32	31.37
Other countries of South America		152	152	232	255	278	0.01	9.02
EAST ASIA AND THE PACIFIC		109,250	103,333	95,966	116,608	138,089	4.87	18.42
North-East Asia		66,727	59,525	53,129	71,190	86,042	3.03	20.86
China		8,043	9,257	9,484	11,896	12,180	0.43	2.39
Hong Kong, China		379	369	615	952	1,027	0.04	7.88
Japan		46,059	40,018	30,604	43,794	56,526	1.99	29.07
Korea, Republic of		9,840	7,824	10,157	12,059	13,318	0.47	10.44
Taiwan, Province of China		2,406	2,057	2,269	2,489	2,991	0.11	20.17
South-East Asia		7,027	5,846	6,360	8,159	8,537	0.30	4.63
Indonesia		1,143	1,114	1,432	1,533	1,584	0.06	3.33
Malaysia		869	748	916	1,246	1,155	0.04	-7.30
Philippines		2,528	2,492	2,268	2,628	2,701	0.10	2.78
Singapore		1,014	661	868	1,348	1,252	0.04	-7.12
Thailand		937	603	647	799	1,023	0.04	28.04
Viet Nam		536	228	229	605	822	0.03	35.87
Australasia		33,844	36,210	35,022	35,570	41,361	1.46	16.28
Australia		28,542	30,947	29,659	30,436	35,745	1.26	17.44
New Zealand		5,302	5,263	5,363	5,134	5,616	0.20	9.39
Other East Asia and the Pacific		1,652	1,752	1,455	1,689	2,149	0.08	27.24
Other countries of Asia		1,559	1,681	1,390	1,635	2,054	0.07	25.63
Other countries of Oceania		93	71	65	54	95	0.00	75.93
EUROPE		448,917	440,091	439,745	466,745	497,269	17.53	6.54

Yearbook of Tourism Statistics, Data 2008 – 2012, 2014 Edition

PERU

1. Arrivals of non-resident tourists at national borders, by country of residence

	2008	2009	2010	2011	2012	Market share 2012	% Change 2012-2011
Central/Eastern Europe	**20,495**	**19,189**	**17,305**	**20,145**	**21,673**	**0.76**	**7.59**
Czech Republic	3,624	3,569	3,052	3,211	3,568	0.13	11.12
Poland	8,169	7,510	6,140	6,268	6,076	0.21	-3.06
Romania	1,398	1,252	1,237	1,511	1,794	0.06	18.73
Russian Federation	5,560	5,373	5,487	7,429	8,469	0.30	14.00
Ukraine	1,744	1,485	1,389	1,726	1,766	0.06	2.32
Northern Europe	**100,960**	**89,125**	**83,751**	**85,130**	**87,140**	**3.07**	**2.36**
Denmark	5,854	5,903	5,760	6,023	5,884	0.21	-2.31
Finland	2,510	2,334	2,451	2,445	2,628	0.09	7.48
Ireland	10,022	7,587	6,346	5,525	5,655	0.20	2.35
Norway	6,188	5,701	5,675	5,827	5,923	0.21	1.65
Sweden	9,931	8,971	9,337	9,895	10,664	0.38	7.77
United Kingdom	66,455	58,629	54,182	55,415	56,386	1.99	1.75
Southern Europe	**127,995**	**134,484**	**142,003**	**154,450**	**162,486**	**5.73**	**5.20**
Italy	39,825	40,426	41,831	45,192	46,845	1.65	3.66
Portugal	3,264	3,344	3,506	4,027	4,600	0.16	14.23
Spain	84,906	90,714	96,666	105,231	111,041	3.91	5.52
Western Europe	**174,676**	**173,585**	**174,407**	**183,740**	**201,669**	**7.11**	**9.76**
Austria	6,025	6,087	6,454	6,791	7,498	0.26	10.41
Belgium	7,775	5,864	4,755	4,534	5,128	0.18	13.10
France	63,920	66,071	66,985	72,900	81,851	2.89	12.28
Germany	52,173	51,864	53,201	56,197	62,051	2.19	10.42
Netherlands	27,031	25,530	24,795	24,486	24,831	0.88	1.41
Switzerland	17,752	18,169	18,217	18,832	20,310	0.72	7.85
East Mediterranean Europe	**13,511**	**14,477**	**13,928**	**14,356**	**14,662**	**0.52**	**2.13**
Israel	12,569	13,657	12,978	12,809	13,082	0.46	2.13
Turkey	942	820	950	1,547	1,580	0.06	2.13
Other Europe	**11,280**	**9,231**	**8,351**	**8,924**	**9,639**	**0.34**	**8.01**
Other countries of Europe	11,280	9,231	8,351	8,924	9,639	0.34	8.01
MIDDLE EAST	**88**	**131**	**141**	**222**	**225**	**0.01**	**1.35**
Egypt	88	131	141	222	225	0.01	1.35
SOUTH ASIA	**3,714**	**4,305**	**4,411**	**4,177**	**4,897**	**0.17**	**17.24**
India	3,046	3,406	3,526	3,471	4,165	0.15	19.99
Pakistan	668	899	885	706	732	0.03	3.68
NOT SPECIFIED	**943**	**1,068**	**933**	**829**	**1,055**	**0.04**	**27.26**
Other countries of the World	943	1,068	933	829	1,055	0.04	27.26

Yearbook of Tourism Statistics, Data 2008 – 2012, 2014 Edition

PERU

3. Arrivals of non-resident tourists in hotels and similar establishments, by nationality

	2008	2009	2010	2011	2012	Market share 2012	% Change 2012-2011
TOTAL	4,464,506	4,059,014	4,340,718	5,487,862	6,778,169	100.00	23.51
AMERICAS	2,182,262	2,021,589	2,234,873	2,863,269	3,633,016	53.60	26.88
North America	1,296,509	1,109,434	1,192,922	1,398,933	1,728,806	25.51	23.58
Canada	170,228	165,713	175,064	213,967	256,844	3.79	20.04
Mexico	83,891	69,120	94,512	130,568	177,944	2.63	36.28
United States of America	1,042,390	874,601	923,346	1,054,398	1,294,018	19.09	22.73
South America	885,753	912,155	1,041,951	1,464,336	1,904,210	28.09	30.04
Argentina	196,249	204,232	227,772	330,773	387,546	5.72	17.16
Bolivia	39,303	41,763	46,548	53,491	67,165	0.99	25.56
Brazil	149,717	199,894	207,583	321,836	379,749	5.60	17.99
Chile	218,883	191,920	242,723	344,057	477,111	7.04	38.67
Colombia	145,496	131,621	163,687	218,674	314,287	4.64	43.72
Ecuador	88,736	95,301	103,247	121,667	148,223	2.19	21.83
Venezuela	47,369	47,424	50,391	73,838	130,129	1.92	76.24
EAST ASIA AND THE PACIFIC	164,690	158,367	113,123	203,285	259,912	3.83	27.86
North-East Asia	164,690	158,367	113,123	203,285	259,912	3.83	27.86
Japan	164,690	158,367	113,123	203,285	259,912	3.83	27.86
EUROPE	914,182	841,389	863,879	1,036,604	1,216,547	17.95	17.36
Southern Europe	399,321	336,865	353,917	428,210	473,493	6.99	10.57
Italy	144,906	107,860	113,499	141,346	150,239	2.22	6.29
Spain	254,415	229,005	240,418	286,864	323,254	4.77	12.69
Western Europe	514,861	504,524	509,962	608,394	743,054	10.96	22.13
France	306,649	326,158	319,081	368,135	450,512	6.65	22.38
Germany	208,212	178,366	190,881	240,259	292,542	4.32	21.76
NOT SPECIFIED	1,203,372	1,037,669	1,128,843	1,384,704	1,668,694	24.62	20.51
Other countries of the World	1,203,372	1,037,669	1,128,843	1,384,704	1,668,694	24.62	20.51

Yearbook of Tourism Statistics, Data 2008 – 2012, 2014 Edit

PERU

5. Overnight stays of non-resident tourists in hotels and similar establishments, by nationality

	2008	2009	2010	2011	2012	Market share 2012	% Change 2012-2011
TOTAL	8,324,682	7,606,573	8,129,518	9,849,154	12,624,778	100.00	28.18
AMERICAS	4,395,022	4,057,047	4,418,979	5,363,016	7,194,670	56.99	34.15
North America	2,474,560	2,124,065	2,222,415	2,499,964	3,153,947	24.98	26.16
Canada	317,413	320,233	325,984	383,356	460,271	3.65	20.06
Mexico	193,098	156,493	220,187	266,182	388,124	3.07	45.81
United States of America	1,964,049	1,647,339	1,676,244	1,850,426	2,305,552	18.26	24.60
South America	1,920,462	1,932,982	2,196,564	2,863,052	4,040,723	32.01	41.13
Argentina	433,713	422,642	461,344	618,098	783,827	6.21	26.81
Bolivia	79,919	77,613	87,737	97,690	126,149	1.00	29.13
Brazil	319,376	423,388	442,942	630,420	789,805	6.26	25.28
Chile	449,064	391,320	493,917	684,989	1,036,714	8.21	51.35
Colombia	334,883	307,110	372,287	422,762	678,296	5.37	60.44
Ecuador	183,250	193,559	211,998	237,792	306,909	2.43	29.07
Venezuela	120,257	117,350	126,339	171,301	319,023	2.53	86.24
EAST ASIA AND THE PACIFIC	241,509	231,348	173,399	334,604	387,621	3.07	15.84
North-East Asia	241,509	231,348	173,399	334,604	387,621	3.07	15.84
Japan	241,509	231,348	173,399	334,604	387,621	3.07	15.84
EUROPE	1,537,368	1,451,432	1,481,319	1,738,830	2,119,813	16.79	21.91
Southern Europe	710,098	601,067	637,829	765,228	914,759	7.25	19.54
Italy	263,150	200,986	199,400	257,435	271,546	2.15	5.48
Spain	446,948	400,081	438,429	507,793	643,213	5.09	26.67
Western Europe	827,270	850,365	843,490	973,602	1,205,054	9.55	23.77
France	469,022	510,473	491,731	555,263	693,357	5.49	24.87
Germany	358,248	339,892	351,759	418,339	511,697	4.05	22.32
NOT SPECIFIED	2,150,783	1,866,746	2,055,821	2,412,704	2,922,674	23.15	21.14
Other countries of the World	2,150,783	1,866,746	2,055,821	2,412,704	2,922,674	23.15	21.14

Yearbook of Tourism Statistics, Data 2008 – 2012, 2014 Edition

PHILIPPINES

1. Arrivals of non-resident tourists at national borders, by country of residence

	2008	2009	2010	2011	2012	Market share 2012	% Change 2012-2011
TOTAL	3,139,422	3,017,099	3,520,472	3,917,454	4,272,811	100.00	9.07
AFRICA	3,317	3,082	3,584	4,193	5,163	0.12	23.13
Southern Africa	2,540	2,311	2,774	3,221	3,691	0.09	14.59
South Africa	2,540	2,311	2,774	3,221	3,691	0.09	14.59
West Africa	777	771	810	972	1,472	0.03	51.44
Nigeria	777	771	810	972	1,472	0.03	51.44
AMERICAS	685,427	686,293	711,356	747,656	783,295	18.33	4.77
North America	681,922	682,696	707,706	743,448	778,162	18.21	4.67
Canada	102,381	99,012	106,345	117,423	123,699	2.90	5.34
Mexico	1,295	1,147	1,195	1,498	1,837	0.04	22.63
United States of America	578,246	582,537	600,166	624,527	652,626	15.27	4.50
South America	3,505	3,597	3,650	4,208	5,133	0.12	21.98
Argentina	594	687	684	786	1,112	0.03	41.48
Brazil	1,594	1,595	1,652	2,078	2,559	0.06	23.15
Colombia	511	573	581	689	754	0.02	9.43
Peru	446	422	403	391	433	0.01	10.74
Venezuela	360	320	330	264	275	0.01	4.17
EAST ASIA AND THE PACIFIC	1,798,719	1,643,595	2,064,400	2,404,758	2,666,888	62.42	10.90
North-East Asia	1,370,059	1,202,995	1,563,013	1,844,942	2,038,987	47.72	10.52
China	163,689	155,019	187,446	243,137	250,883	5.87	3.19
Hong Kong, China	116,653	122,786	133,746	112,106	118,666	2.78	5.85
Japan	359,306	324,980	358,744	375,496	412,474	9.65	9.85
Korea, Republic of	611,629	497,936	740,622	925,204	1,031,155	24.13	11.45
Macao, China				7,261	9,298	0.22	28.05
Taiwan, Province of China	118,782	102,274	142,455	181,738	216,511	5.07	19.13
South-East Asia	254,077	255,586	298,176	331,672	375,190	8.78	13.12
Brunei Darussalam	3,456	3,592	4,072	5,247	5,992	0.14	14.20
Cambodia	1,834	1,942	2,244	2,469	2,661	0.06	7.78
Indonesia	27,830	29,188	31,997	34,542	36,627	0.86	6.04
Lao People's Democratic Republic	814	831	1,079	971	1,088	0.03	12.05
Malaysia	69,676	68,679	79,694	91,752	114,513	2.68	24.81
Myanmar	5,116	5,445	3,983	3,246	4,290	0.10	32.16
Singapore	100,177	98,305	121,083	137,802	148,215	3.47	7.56
Thailand	31,499	34,212	36,713	37,862	40,987	0.96	8.25
Viet Nam	13,675	13,392	17,311	17,781	20,817	0.49	17.07
Australasia	132,186	142,852	158,792	183,518	205,250	4.80	11.84
Australia	121,514	132,330	147,469	170,736	191,150	4.47	11.96
New Zealand	10,672	10,522	11,323	12,782	14,100	0.33	10.31
Melanesia	2,020	2,835	3,475	3,594	4,726	0.11	31.50
Papua New Guinea	2,020	2,835	3,475	3,594	4,726	0.11	31.50
Micronesia	40,377	39,327	40,944	41,032	42,735	1.00	4.15
Guam	40,364	39,323	40,928	41,013	42,695	1.00	4.10
Nauru	13	4	16	19	40	0.00	110.53
EUROPE	322,864	329,840	360,991	402,073	442,686	10.36	10.10
Central/Eastern Europe	16,819	16,522	21,821	27,171	37,916	0.89	39.55
Poland	2,249	2,372	2,917	3,263	4,187	0.10	28.32
Russian Federation	10,959	10,674	14,642	20,185	28,270	0.66	40.05
Other countries Central/East Europe	3,611	3,476	4,262	3,723	5,459	0.13	46.63
Northern Europe	136,260	138,950	150,178	164,205	181,978	4.26	10.82
Denmark	11,890	10,971	11,609	13,004	13,556	0.32	4.24
Finland	2,954	3,331	4,024	4,780	5,399	0.13	12.95
Ireland	5,176	5,475	5,368	6,023	8,362	0.20	38.83
Norway	14,963	14,781	16,742	17,959	19,572	0.46	8.98
Sweden	13,855	13,383	15,510	17,973	21,807	0.51	21.33
United Kingdom	87,422	91,009	96,925	104,466	113,282	2.65	8.44

574

PHILIPPINES

1. Arrivals of non-resident tourists at national borders, by country of residence

	2008	2009	2010	2011	2012	Market share 2012	% Change 2012-2011
Southern Europe	31,229	29,281	32,388	45,781	43,268	1.01	-5.49
Andorra				12,250	7,333	0.17	-40.14
Greece	1,914	1,666	2,104	1,855	1,834	0.04	-1.13
Italy	15,136	15,047	16,350	15,798	16,740	0.39	5.96
Montenegro	26						
Portugal	990	865	1,175	1,230	1,466	0.03	19.19
Serbia	157						
Serbia and Montenegro	60						
Spain	12,946	11,703	12,759	14,648	15,895	0.37	8.51
Western Europe	134,663	138,946	149,193	157,265	170,498	3.99	8.41
Austria	10,120	10,974	11,537	11,603	11,718	0.27	0.99
Belgium	9,143	9,729	10,512	10,959	11,649	0.27	6.30
France	22,891	24,572	27,302	29,591	33,709	0.79	13.92
Germany	55,303	55,912	58,725	61,193	67,023	1.57	9.53
Luxembourg	494	462	666	555	647	0.02	16.58
Netherlands	18,527	18,586	19,227	21,029	22,195	0.52	5.54
Switzerland	18,185	18,711	21,224	22,335	23,557	0.55	5.47
East Mediterranean Europe	3,893	6,141	7,411	7,651	9,026	0.21	17.97
Israel	3,893	4,061	4,525	4,990	5,895	0.14	18.14
Turkey		2,080	2,886	2,661	3,131	0.07	17.66
MIDDLE EAST	36,615	46,811	48,716	55,829	57,275	1.34	2.59
Bahrain	2,928	3,014	3,334	3,304	3,528	0.08	6.78
Egypt	751	1,036	1,135	1,389	1,619	0.04	16.56
Jordan	538	635	691	755	756	0.02	0.13
Kuwait	3,952	9,605	5,230	5,430	4,877	0.11	-10.18
Qatar		2,932	3,378	3,602	3,771	0.09	4.69
Saudi Arabia	17,515	19,101	22,214	27,945	30,040	0.70	7.50
United Arab Emirates	10,931	10,488	12,734	13,404	12,684	0.30	-5.37
SOUTH ASIA	43,662	46,960	50,914	61,259	63,860	1.49	4.25
Bangladesh	1,924	2,107	2,569	2,862	3,188	0.07	11.39
India	31,135	32,817	34,581	42,844	46,395	1.09	8.29
Iran, Islamic Republic of	3,196	4,256	5,516	6,258	5,017	0.12	-19.83
Nepal	1,246	1,411	1,794	1,874	2,107	0.05	12.43
Pakistan	2,405	2,705	2,722	3,344	3,541	0.08	5.89
Sri Lanka	3,756	3,664	3,732	4,077	3,612	0.08	-11.41
NOT SPECIFIED	248,818	260,518	280,511	241,686	253,644	5.94	4.95
Other countries of the World	53,531	62,597	52,066	34,534	37,701	0.88	9.17
Nationals Residing Abroad (*)	195,287	197,921	228,445	207,152	215,943	5.05	4.24

Yearbook of Tourism Statistics, Data 2008 – 2012, 2014 Edition

PHILIPPINES

4. Arrivals of non-resident tourists in all types of accommodation establishments, by country of residence

		2008	2009	2010	2011	2012	Market share 2012	% Change 2012-2011
TOTAL	(*)	3,084,753	2,960,282	3,461,007	3,884,055	4,237,935	100.00	9.11
AFRICA		3,238	2,950	3,466	4,152	5,118	0.12	23.27
Southern Africa		2,462	2,180	2,657	3,181	3,646	0.09	14.62
South Africa		2,462	2,180	2,657	3,181	3,646	0.09	14.62
West Africa		776	770	809	971	1,472	0.03	51.60
Nigeria		776	770	809	971	1,472	0.03	51.60
AMERICAS		683,151	684,028	709,423	745,291	782,046	18.45	4.93
North America		680,000	680,833	706,129	741,124	776,948	18.33	4.83
Canada		102,067	98,563	106,062	117,055	123,412	2.91	5.43
Mexico		1,259	1,095	1,124	1,475	1,814	0.04	22.98
United States of America		576,674	581,175	598,943	622,594	651,722	15.38	4.68
South America		3,151	3,195	3,294	4,167	5,098	0.12	22.34
Argentina		548	665	644	781	1,107	0.03	41.74
Brazil		1,510	1,492	1,565	2,060	2,547	0.06	23.64
Colombia		438	437	505	681	750	0.02	10.13
Peru		303	282	254	383	424	0.01	10.70
Venezuela		352	319	326	262	270	0.01	3.05
EAST ASIA AND THE PACIFIC		1,769,713	1,612,169	2,034,014	2,377,612	2,637,300	62.23	10.92
North-East Asia		1,357,735	1,189,983	1,551,201	1,828,624	2,020,515	47.68	10.49
China		154,840	146,566	180,346	238,126	245,153	5.78	2.95
Hong Kong, China		116,620	122,715	133,721	112,076	118,579	2.80	5.80
Japan		358,743	323,638	357,660	374,128	410,976	9.70	9.85
Korea, Republic of		609,226	496,031	738,258	923,691	1,029,617	24.30	11.47
Taiwan, Province of China		118,306	101,033	141,216	180,603	216,190	5.10	19.70
South-East Asia		238,526	240,037	282,845	321,147	365,207	8.62	13.72
Brunei Darussalam		3,422	3,576	4,052	5,210	5,985	0.14	14.88
Cambodia		1,833	1,940	2,242	2,440	2,660	0.06	9.02
Indonesia		23,106	24,030	27,207	31,640	34,231	0.81	8.19
Lao People's Democratic Republic		814	831	1,078	942	1,088	0.03	15.50
Malaysia		68,621	67,616	78,116	90,133	112,923	2.66	25.28
Myanmar		1,404	1,763	1,693	1,652	1,995	0.05	20.76
Singapore		100,113	98,113	120,961	137,741	147,963	3.49	7.42
Thailand		29,820	32,594	35,359	36,970	40,337	0.95	9.11
Viet Nam		9,393	9,574	12,137	14,419	18,025	0.43	25.01
Australasia		131,068	140,000	155,560	183,221	204,119	4.82	11.41
Australia		120,512	129,608	144,432	170,480	190,080	4.49	11.50
New Zealand		10,556	10,392	11,128	12,741	14,039	0.33	10.19
Melanesia		2,007	2,822	3,464	3,588	4,724	0.11	31.66
Papua New Guinea		2,007	2,822	3,464	3,588	4,724	0.11	31.66
Micronesia		40,377	39,327	40,944	41,032	42,735	1.01	4.15
Guam		40,364	39,323	40,928	41,013	42,695	1.01	4.10
Nauru		13	4	16	19	40	0.00	110.53
EUROPE		297,226	314,335	341,812	384,006	427,235	10.08	11.26
Central/Eastern Europe		3,734	12,593	17,427	25,178	35,237	0.83	39.95
Commonwealth Independent States		1,767	1,792	2,381	2,755	3,864	0.09	40.25
Poland		1,967	1,958	2,403	3,035	3,847	0.09	26.75
Russian Federation			8,843	12,643	19,388	27,526	0.65	41.97
Northern Europe		131,621	134,152	144,198	162,000	179,309	4.23	10.68
Denmark		11,801	10,915	11,541	12,952	13,536	0.32	4.51
Finland		2,943	3,310	4,013	4,780	5,396	0.13	12.89
Ireland		5,127	5,398	5,260	5,997	8,330	0.20	38.90
Norway		14,942	14,758	16,692	17,930	19,527	0.46	8.91
Sweden		13,819	13,345	15,404	17,949	21,725	0.51	21.04
United Kingdom		82,989	86,426	91,288	102,392	110,795	2.61	8.21
Southern Europe		27,176	26,726	29,662	33,283	35,665	0.84	7.16

576

Yearbook of Tourism Statistics, Data 2008 – 2012, 2014 Edition

PHILIPPINES

4. Arrivals of non-resident tourists in all types of accommodation establishments, by country of residence

	2008	2009	2010	2011	2012	Market share 2012	% Change 2012-2011
Greece	1,792	1,583	1,977	1,751	1,760	0.04	0.51
Italy	12,783	13,165	14,118	15,711	16,660	0.39	6.04
Portugal	930	814	1,123	1,217	1,387	0.03	13.97
Serbia and Montenegro	184						
Spain	11,487	11,164	12,444	14,604	15,858	0.37	8.59
Western Europe	**130,805**	**135,031**	**143,440**	**156,012**	**168,159**	**3.97**	**7.79**
Austria	9,926	10,728	11,056	11,550	11,622	0.27	0.62
Belgium	8,773	9,547	10,392	10,917	11,595	0.27	6.21
France	21,185	23,584	26,360	29,540	33,268	0.79	12.62
Germany	54,243	54,007	55,904	60,355	65,551	1.55	8.61
Luxembourg	481	449	655	550	644	0.02	17.09
Netherlands	18,315	18,322	18,858	20,861	22,060	0.52	5.75
Switzerland	17,882	18,394	20,215	22,239	23,419	0.55	5.31
East Mediterranean Europe	**3,890**	**5,833**	**7,085**	**7,533**	**8,865**	**0.21**	**17.68**
Israel	3,890	4,057	4,521	4,990	5,895	0.14	18.14
Turkey		1,776	2,564	2,543	2,970	0.07	16.79
MIDDLE EAST	**36,595**	**46,775**	**48,641**	**55,782**	**57,237**	**1.35**	**2.61**
Bahrain	2,928	3,014	3,334	3,304	3,528	0.08	6.78
Egypt	731	1,001	1,063	1,342	1,581	0.04	17.81
Jordan	538	635	691	755	756	0.02	0.13
Kuwait	3,952	9,605	5,230	5,430	4,877	0.12	-10.18
Qatar		2,932	3,378	3,602	3,771	0.09	4.69
Saudi Arabia	17,515	19,100	22,214	27,945	30,040	0.71	7.50
United Arab Emirates	10,931	10,488	12,731	13,404	12,684	0.30	-5.37
SOUTH ASIA	**39,721**	**41,634**	**45,410**	**57,366**	**60,039**	**1.42**	**4.66**
Bangladesh	1,699	1,923	2,333	2,680	2,978	0.07	11.12
India	28,871	29,293	30,691	40,195	43,578	1.03	8.42
Iran, Islamic Republic of	3,115	4,232	5,513	6,237	5,016	0.12	-19.58
Nepal	1,221	1,389	1,762	1,853	2,092	0.05	12.90
Pakistan	2,354	2,674	2,647	3,272	3,517	0.08	7.49
Sri Lanka	2,461	2,123	2,464	3,129	2,858	0.07	-8.66
NOT SPECIFIED	**255,109**	**258,391**	**278,241**	**259,846**	**268,960**	**6.35**	**3.51**
Other countries of the World	59,822	60,470	49,796	52,694	53,017	1.25	0.61
Nationals Residing Abroad (*)	195,287	197,921	228,445	207,152	215,943	5.10	4.24

Yearbook of Tourism Statistics, Data 2008 – 2012, 2014 Edition

POLAND

2. Arrivals of non-resident visitors at national borders, by nationality

	2008	2009	2010	2011	2012	Market share 2012	% Change 2012-2011
TOTAL (*)	59,935,000	53,839,000	58,340,000	60,745,000	67,390,000	100.00	10.94
AFRICA	15,000	20,000	20,000	15,000	15,000	0.02	0.00
Other Africa	15,000	20,000	20,000	15,000	15,000	0.02	0.00
All countries of Africa	15,000	20,000	20,000	15,000	15,000	0.02	0.00
AMERICAS	380,000	338,000	395,000	400,000	425,000	0.63	6.25
North America	350,000	298,000	340,000	365,000	390,000	0.58	6.85
Canada	80,000	68,000	75,000	80,000	90,000	0.13	12.50
Mexico				15,000			
United States of America	270,000	230,000	265,000	270,000	300,000	0.45	11.11
South America	20,000	10,000	15,000	25,000	25,000	0.04	0.00
Argentina				10,000	10,000	0.01	0.00
Brazil	20,000	10,000	15,000	15,000	15,000	0.02	0.00
Other Americas	10,000	30,000	40,000	10,000	10,000	0.01	0.00
Other countries of the Americas	10,000	30,000	40,000	10,000	10,000	0.01	0.00
EAST ASIA AND THE PACIFIC	220,000	207,000	280,000	300,000	320,000	0.47	6.67
North-East Asia	128,000	100,000	135,000	135,000	135,000	0.20	0.00
China	20,000	25,000	35,000	40,000	40,000	0.06	0.00
Hong Kong, China	3,000	5,000	5,000	5,000	5,000	0.01	0.00
Japan	42,000	35,000	60,000	45,000	40,000	0.06	-11.11
Korea, Republic of	63,000	35,000	35,000	35,000	40,000	0.06	14.29
Taiwan, Province of China				10,000	10,000	0.01	0.00
South-East Asia				30,000	30,000	0.04	0.00
Indonesia				5,000	5,000	0.01	0.00
Malaysia				5,000	5,000	0.01	0.00
Philippines				5,000	5,000	0.01	0.00
Singapore				10,000	10,000	0.01	0.00
Thailand				5,000	5,000	0.01	0.00
Australasia	45,000	37,000	55,000	65,000	85,000	0.13	30.77
Australia	45,000	37,000	55,000	55,000	75,000	0.11	36.36
New Zealand				10,000	10,000	0.01	0.00
Other East Asia and the Pacific	47,000	70,000	90,000	70,000	70,000	0.10	0.00
Other countries East Asia/Pacific	47,000	70,000	90,000	70,000	70,000	0.10	0.00
EUROPE	59,290,000	53,220,000	57,540,000	59,950,000	66,545,000	98.75	11.00
Central/Eastern Europe	21,515,000	24,170,000	28,475,000	31,030,000	36,410,000	54.03	17.34
Armenia				20,000	20,000	0.03	0.00
Belarus	2,130,000	2,360,000	3,090,000	3,450,000	3,920,000	5.82	13.62
Bulgaria	95,000	85,000	80,000	85,000	100,000	0.15	17.65
Czech Republic	7,820,000	8,180,000	9,240,000	10,840,000	12,380,000	18.37	14.21
Estonia	185,000	130,000	115,000	120,000	110,000	0.16	-8.33
Georgia				5,000	5,000	0.01	0.00
Hungary	255,000	225,000	220,000	230,000	235,000	0.35	2.17
Kazakhstan	35,000			40,000	40,000	0.06	0.00
Latvia	540,000	390,000	350,000	360,000	385,000	0.57	6.94
Lithuania	1,930,000	2,640,000	2,690,000	2,420,000	3,010,000	4.47	24.38
Republic of Moldova	55,000			40,000	40,000	0.06	0.00
Romania	120,000	90,000	120,000	120,000	125,000	0.19	4.17
Russian Federation	1,290,000	1,210,000	1,530,000	1,850,000	2,670,000	3.96	44.32
Slovakia	3,740,000	5,040,000	6,010,000	5,620,000	6,630,000	9.84	17.97
Ukraine	3,320,000	3,820,000	5,030,000	5,830,000	6,740,000	10.00	15.61
Northern Europe	1,212,000	1,085,000	1,150,000	1,100,000	1,205,000	1.79	9.55
Denmark	130,000	120,000	125,000	110,000	110,000	0.16	0.00
Finland	80,000	75,000	90,000	95,000	85,000	0.13	-10.53
Iceland	2,000			5,000	5,000	0.01	0.00
Ireland	90,000	80,000	80,000	85,000	120,000	0.18	41.18
Norway	145,000	120,000	120,000	120,000	140,000	0.21	16.67

578

POLAND

2. Arrivals of non-resident visitors at national borders, by nationality

	2008	2009	2010	2011	2012	Market share 2012	% Change 2012-2011
Sweden	210,000	190,000	195,000	185,000	205,000	0.30	10.81
United Kingdom	555,000	500,000	540,000	500,000	540,000	0.80	8.00
Southern Europe	**540,000**	**550,000**	**580,000**	**630,000**	**660,000**	**0.98**	**4.76**
Croatia	35,000	30,000	20,000	20,000	20,000	0.03	0.00
Greece	30,000	45,000	35,000	40,000	50,000	0.07	25.00
Italy	275,000	255,000	285,000	315,000	320,000	0.47	1.59
Portugal	70,000	70,000	75,000	70,000	80,000	0.12	14.29
Serbia				10,000	10,000	0.01	0.00
Slovenia	20,000	20,000	20,000	20,000	20,000	0.03	0.00
Spain	110,000	130,000	145,000	155,000	160,000	0.24	3.23
Western Europe	**35,720,000**	**27,145,000**	**27,030,000**	**26,975,000**	**27,960,000**	**41.49**	**3.65**
Austria	320,000	325,000	345,000	355,000	360,000	0.53	1.41
Belgium	110,000	110,000	125,000	130,000	140,000	0.21	7.69
France	240,000	240,000	260,000	280,000	280,000	0.42	0.00
Germany	34,630,000	26,070,000	25,860,000	25,740,000	26,720,000	39.65	3.81
Luxembourg		5,000	10,000	20,000	10,000	0.01	-50.00
Netherlands	355,000	335,000	370,000	390,000	390,000	0.58	0.00
Switzerland	65,000	60,000	60,000	60,000	60,000	0.09	0.00
East Mediterranean Europe	**120,000**	**120,000**	**145,000**	**175,000**	**200,000**	**0.30**	**14.29**
Cyprus		5,000	5,000		5,000	0.01	
Israel	65,000	60,000	70,000	90,000	90,000	0.13	0.00
Turkey	55,000	55,000	70,000	85,000	105,000	0.16	23.53
Other Europe	**183,000**	**150,000**	**160,000**	**40,000**	**110,000**	**0.16**	**175.00**
Other countries of Europe	183,000	150,000	160,000	40,000	110,000	0.16	175.00
MIDDLE EAST	**10,000**	**15,000**	**15,000**	**15,000**	**15,000**	**0.02**	**0.00**
All countries of Middle East	10,000	15,000	15,000	15,000	15,000	0.02	0.00
SOUTH ASIA	**20,000**	**20,000**	**30,000**	**20,000**	**20,000**	**0.03**	**0.00**
India	15,000	10,000	15,000	15,000	15,000	0.02	0.00
Other countries of South Asia	5,000	10,000	15,000	5,000	5,000	0.01	0.00
NOT SPECIFIED		**19,000**	**60,000**	**45,000**	**50,000**	**0.07**	**11.11**
Other countries of the World		19,000	60,000	45,000	50,000	0.07	11.11

Yearbook of Tourism Statistics, Data 2008 – 2012, 2014 Edition

POLAND

3. Arrivals of non-resident tourists in hotels and similar establishments, by country of residence

	2008	2009	2010	2011	2012	Market share 2012	% Change 2012-2011
TOTAL (*)	3,565,828	3,394,053	3,667,358	3,907,422	4,369,548	100.00	11.83
AFRICA	5,866	8,089	8,370	7,530	12,106	0.28	60.77
East Africa	740	615	1,065	618			
British Indian Ocean Territory	7						
Burundi	59	39	33	42			
Comoros		4	2				
Djibouti	2	23	4	8			
Eritrea	2						
Ethiopia	60	112	205	54			
Kenya	192	153	173	167			
Madagascar	23	5	36	17			
Malawi	2	10	12	4			
Mauritius	35	23	57	33			
Mozambique	12	5	13	21			
Reunion	31	1					
Rwanda	101	14	138	25			
Seychelles	47	18	17	20			
Somalia	15	23	45	52			
Uganda	37	60	98	68			
United Republic of Tanzania	34	34	171	37			
Zambia	57	29	32	14			
Zimbabwe	24	62	29	56			
Central Africa	332	656	822	655			
Angola	116	292	581	402			
Cameroon	55	95	86	80			
Central African Republic	15	36	37	80			
Chad	3	25	3	4			
Congo	94	147	88	71			
Democratic Republic of the Congo	23	43	23	15			
Equatorial Guinea			4	3			
Gabon	21	18					
Sao Tome and Principe	5						
North Africa	1,311	2,402	3,005	2,841			
Algeria	434	962	1,556	1,632			
Morocco	490	533	826	500			
Sudan	26	71	56	116			
Tunisia	357	481	498	574			
Western Sahara	4	355	69	19			
Southern Africa	1,689	2,207	1,755	2,090	2,210	0.05	5.74
Botswana	41	125	60	5			
Lesotho		1	5	5			
Namibia	75	124	26	48			
South Africa	1,413	1,765	1,664	2,032	2,210	0.05	8.76
Swaziland	160	192					
West Africa	1,794	2,209	1,723	1,326			
Benin	39	37	26	15			
Burkina Faso	10	4	15	23			
Cape Verde	22	8	7	14			
Côte d'Ivoire	55	14	138	36			
Gambia	82	17	33	4			
Ghana	35	31	78	65			
Guinea	51	27	5	10			
Guinea-Bissau	4	2		14			
Liberia	15	7	20	12			
Mali	20	19	28	27			
Mauritania	298	46	15	23			

580

Yearbook of Tourism Statistics, Data 2008 – 2012, 2014 Ed.

POLAND

3. Arrivals of non-resident tourists in hotels and similar establishments, by country of residence

	2008	2009	2010	2011	2012	Market share 2012	% Change 2012-2011
Niger	144	364	382	164			
Nigeria	707	945	609	571			
Saint Helena	4	22	24	7			
Senegal	76	409	145	91			
Sierra Leone	218	243	195	232			
Togo	14	14	3	18			
Other Africa					**9,896**	**0.23**	
Other countries of Africa					9,896	0.23	
AMERICAS	**186,723**	**171,859**	**203,579**	**208,953**	**237,449**	**5.43**	**13.64**
Caribbean	**1,124**	**735**	**673**	**1,662**			
Anguilla	2	12					
Antigua and Barbuda	10	9					
Aruba	10	16	11	3			
Bahamas	89	28	100	599			
Barbados	267	120	59	26			
Bermuda	27	23	13	28			
British Virgin Islands	154	1					
Cayman Islands	1	20	20	13			
Cuba	226	224	232	255			
Dominica	11	8	18	31			
Dominican Republic	26	28	54	122			
Grenada	25	2					
Guadeloupe	3	11		1			
Haiti	33	12	16	40			
Jamaica	91	124	48	73			
Martinique	5	2		3			
Netherlands Antilles	6	1					
Puerto Rico	61	80	86	451			
Saint Kitts and Nevis	1	3					
Saint Lucia	10						
Trinidad and Tobago	64	10	16	17			
Turks and Caicos Islands	1	1					
United States Virgin Islands	1						
Central America	**845**	**580**	**665**	**680**			
Belize	70	90	36	65			
Costa Rica	230	192	150	195			
El Salvador	67	57	54	106			
Guatemala	68	49	64	56			
Honduras	57	88	167	173			
Nicaragua	229	33	135	31			
Panama	124	71	59	54			
North America	**171,535**	**158,082**	**186,488**	**190,195**	**209,429**	**4.79**	**10.11**
Canada	19,641	21,468	25,478	26,549	29,459	0.67	10.96
Greenland	1	5	1				
Mexico	3,851	3,355	3,598	5,051			
Saint Pierre and Miquelon	2						
United States of America	148,040	133,254	157,411	158,595	179,970	4.12	13.48
South America	**13,219**	**12,462**	**15,753**	**16,416**	**12,941**	**0.30**	**-21.17**
Argentina	2,141	2,063	2,046	2,967			
Bolivia	53	605	1,041	1,036			
Brazil	7,865	6,955	9,488	9,310	12,941	0.30	39.00
Chile	828	748	887	1,007			
Colombia	506	437	571	719			
Ecuador	116	253	176	125			
Falkland Islands, Malvinas		84	1	7			
French Guiana	15	2	1	4			
Guyana	14	1	3	85			

581

POLAND

3. Arrivals of non-resident tourists in hotels and similar establishments, by country of residence

	2008	2009	2010	2011	2012	Market share 2012	% Change 2012-2011
Paraguay	4	14	61	74			
Peru	273	450	280	270			
Suriname	136	65	33				
Uruguay	177	278	464	463			
Venezuela	1,091	507	701	349			
Other Americas					**15,079**	**0.35**	
Other countries of the Americas					15,079	0.35	
EAST ASIA AND THE PACIFIC	**112,338**	**111,645**	**141,195**	**145,032**	**343,436**	**7.86**	**136.80**
North-East Asia	**88,597**	**86,574**	**109,545**	**103,918**	**86,805**	**1.99**	**-16.47**
China	19,100	18,990	25,421	32,000	38,685	0.89	20.89
Hong Kong, China	1,713	3,403	3,912	4,566			
Japan	35,781	32,860	48,772	37,353	33,855	0.77	-9.36
Korea, Dem. People's Republic of	5,018	11,709	15,859	14,364			
Korea, Republic of	25,678	17,786	13,734	13,291	14,265	0.33	7.33
Macao, China	17	55	62	48			
Mongolia	254	389	490	376			
Taiwan, Province of China	1,036	1,382	1,295	1,920			
South-East Asia	**6,487**	**8,568**	**10,647**	**17,916**			
Brunei Darussalam	6	5	54	12			
Cambodia	36	7	38	11			
Indonesia	1,008	1,013	885	2,522			
Lao People's Democratic Republic	17	17	16	43			
Malaysia	983	952	1,170	2,041			
Myanmar	7	10	2	3			
Philippines	820	991	824	2,317			
Singapore	1,462	2,052	4,004	5,738			
Thailand	1,232	1,651	1,987	3,545			
Timor-Leste	11		1	3			
Viet Nam	905	1,870	1,666	1,681			
Australasia	**16,426**	**16,363**	**20,883**	**23,091**	**22,484**	**0.51**	**-2.63**
Australia	14,893	14,713	18,647	20,988	22,484	0.51	7.13
New Zealand	1,533	1,650	2,236	2,103			
Melanesia	**92**	**94**	**35**	**65**			
Fiji	26	46	8	14			
New Caledonia	18	13	8	35			
Norfolk Island	8	27					
Papua New Guinea	31	8	19	16			
Solomon Islands	9						
Micronesia	**55**	**3**	**2**	**14**			
Guam	2	3	2	8			
Kiribati	19						
Micronesia, Federated States of				6			
Nauru	33						
Palau	1						
Polynesia	**681**	**43**	**83**	**28**			
American Samoa	262	28					
French Polynesia	23	9	36	24			
Niue	52						
Samoa	22	5					
Tokelau	6						
Tonga	8	1	47	4			
Tuvalu	9						
Wallis and Futuna Islands	299						
Other East Asia and the Pacific					**234,147**	**5.36**	
Other countries of Asia					231,392	5.30	
Other countries of Oceania					2,755	0.06	

Yearbook of Tourism Statistics, Data 2008 – 2012, 2014 Editic

POLAND

3. Arrivals of non-resident tourists in hotels and similar establishments, by country of residence

	2008	2009	2010	2011	2012	Market share 2012	% Change 2012-2011
EUROPE	3,202,245	3,063,367	3,260,437	3,494,942	3,730,162	85.37	6.73
Central/Eastern Europe	705,566	639,280	727,434	870,726	948,899	21.72	8.98
Armenia	459	2,376	3,119	3,521			
Azerbaijan	662	915	720	793			
Belarus	59,060	63,213	72,545	93,956			
Bulgaria	8,339	8,450	9,297	9,488	10,416	0.24	9.78
Czech Republic	68,895	66,975	68,726	77,388	84,857	1.94	9.65
Estonia	38,522	31,558	30,510	34,057	34,970	0.80	2.68
Georgia	1,412	1,780	1,979	1,663			
Hungary	41,627	40,192	41,239	44,522	51,620	1.18	15.94
Kazakhstan	2,267	2,369	2,494	3,650			
Kyrgyzstan	169	95	184	288			
Latvia	48,251	34,689	40,106	46,530	53,849	1.23	15.73
Lithuania	94,548	88,702	87,690	91,868	94,756	2.17	3.14
Republic of Moldova	2,579	2,077	2,099	2,349			
Romania	19,491	17,785	23,302	24,693	27,234	0.62	10.29
Russian Federation	184,442	149,529	198,801	255,376	361,642	8.28	41.61
Slovakia	28,446	33,244	36,316	42,123	43,613	1.00	3.54
Tajikistan	85	47	164	60			
Turkmenistan	13	31	26	56			
Ukraine	105,954	94,935	107,365	137,399	185,942	4.26	35.33
Uzbekistan	345	318	752	946			
Northern Europe	741,392	671,581	692,474	698,763	769,810	17.62	10.17
Denmark	84,511	81,265	74,855	78,987	83,707	1.92	5.98
Faeroe Islands	72	4					
Finland	40,794	42,831	52,596	59,813	57,081	1.31	-4.57
Iceland	1,993	1,662	2,531	1,750	2,534	0.06	44.80
Ireland	45,932	37,327	38,081	37,775	49,747	1.14	31.69
Norway	94,679	86,554	96,225	98,166	125,957	2.88	28.31
Svalbard and Jan Mayen Islands	10	11	2				
Sweden	103,159	97,659	93,584	97,968	108,503	2.48	10.75
United Kingdom	370,242	324,268	334,600	324,304	342,281	7.83	5.54
Southern Europe	318,625	323,206	349,942	400,845	388,126	8.88	-3.17
Albania	325	1,384	1,313	1,631			
Andorra	94	122	372	276			
Bosnia and Herzegovina	743	1,167	774	1,131			
Croatia	6,736	6,067	6,570	7,757			
Gibraltar	9	26	38	46			
Greece	11,338	15,014	12,218	14,071	15,978	0.37	13.55
Holy See	10	161	138	108			
Italy	172,632	168,068	181,952	195,474	201,393	4.61	3.03
Malta	787	515	714	1,285	1,260	0.03	-1.95
Montenegro	158	126	153	372			
Portugal	13,924	16,659	18,212	19,771	22,500	0.51	13.80
San Marino	22	116	26	179			
Serbia	1,543	1,793	4,014	3,537			
Slovenia	7,205	8,176	7,869	9,005	9,306	0.21	3.34
Spain	102,595	103,125	114,920	145,465	137,689	3.15	-5.35
TFYR of Macedonia	504	687	659	737			
Western Europe	1,320,710	1,286,299	1,335,250	1,360,478	1,435,632	32.86	5.52
Austria	50,489	50,882	54,543	57,533	58,663	1.34	1.96
Belgium	51,755	50,908	57,511	60,923	57,447	1.31	-5.71
France	164,111	156,874	166,367	177,404	175,231	4.01	-1.22
Germany	925,394	903,444	928,727	928,048	1,002,624	22.95	8.04
Liechtenstein	283	1,122	246	337			
Luxembourg	2,449	2,732	3,271	3,363	3,289	0.08	-2.20
Monaco	231	398	278	207			

Yearbook of Tourism Statistics, Data 2008 – 2012, 2014 Edition

POLAND

3. Arrivals of non-resident tourists in hotels and similar establishments, by country of residence

	2008	2009	2010	2011	2012	Market share 2012	% Change 2012-2011
Netherlands	94,449	89,011	92,260	98,327	99,291	2.27	0.98
Switzerland	31,549	30,928	32,047	34,336	39,087	0.89	13.84
East Mediterranean Europe	**115,952**	**143,001**	**155,337**	**164,130**	**22,842**	**0.52**	**-86.08**
Cyprus	2,465	2,413	2,194	1,976	2,359	0.05	19.38
Israel	101,527	126,974	138,007	143,915			
Turkey	11,960	13,614	15,136	18,239	20,483	0.47	12.30
Other Europe					**164,853**	**3.77**	
Other countries of Europe					164,853	3.77	
MIDDLE EAST	**4,585**	**6,591**	**6,658**	**8,620**			
Bahrain	112	157	213	159			
Egypt	1,153	1,277	1,422	1,546			
Iraq	350	554	421	657			
Jordan	225	274	201	408			
Kuwait	462	519	484	676			
Lebanon	395	836	461	610			
Libya	227	207	281	308			
Oman	24	40	96	26			
Qatar	46	297	285	237			
Saudi Arabia	659	1,022	1,476	2,216			
Syrian Arab Republic	158	290	299	467			
United Arab Emirates	748	1,080	989	1,271			
Yemen	26	38	30	39			
SOUTH ASIA	**12,005**	**12,962**	**14,644**	**16,266**			
Afghanistan	223	1,224	1,219	1,440			
Bangladesh	353	765	784	918			
Bhutan	1,074	262	394	107			
India	7,260	8,231	9,226	10,826			
Iran, Islamic Republic of	2,272	1,567	2,147	1,892			
Maldives	8	8	46	15			
Nepal	199	169	110	85			
Pakistan	533	644	583	806			
Sri Lanka	83	92	135	177			
NOT SPECIFIED	**42,066**	**19,540**	**32,475**	**26,079**	**46,395**	**1.06**	**77.90**
Other countries of the World	42,066	19,540	32,475	26,079	46,395	1.06	77.90

Yearbook of Tourism Statistics, Data 2008 – 2012, 2014 Edition

POLAND

4. Arrivals of non-resident tourists in all types of accommodation establishments, by country of residence

	2008	2009	2010	2011	2012	Market share 2012	% Change 2012-2011
TOTAL	4,046,312	3,861,942	4,134,970	4,409,550	4,979,294	100.00	12.92
AFRICA	6,538	8,783	9,318	9,209	15,090	0.30	63.86
East Africa	824	689	1,231	788			
British Indian Ocean Territory	7						
Burundi	60	45	33	42			
Comoros		4	2				
Djibouti	5	23	4	9			
Eritrea	3						
Ethiopia	72	135	228	78			
Kenya	220	161	218	203			
Madagascar	24	6	38	19			
Malawi	3	10	15	7			
Mauritius	44	24	61	36			
Mozambique	12	5	13	24			
Reunion	31	1					
Rwanda	101	14	147	28			
Seychelles	47	18	17	20			
Somalia	31	24	84	52			
Uganda	41	75	110	102			
United Republic of Tanzania	35	42	178	45			
Zambia	58	32	47	61			
Zimbabwe	30	70	36	62			
Central Africa	435	740	930	711			
Angola	155	295	619	419			
Cameroon	80	114	115	102			
Central African Republic	16	38	46	81			
Chad	3	31	8	4			
Congo	122	167	114	87			
Democratic Republic of the Congo	33	51	24	15			
Equatorial Guinea			4	3			
Gabon	21	44					
Sao Tome and Principe	5						
North Africa	1,495	2,537	3,294	3,162			
Algeria	482	1,022	1,644	1,778			
Morocco	560	560	950	581			
Sudan	29	76	64	137			
Tunisia	420	524	567	647			
Western Sahara	4	355	69	19			
Southern Africa	1,798	2,314	1,892	2,457	2,348	0.05	-4.44
Botswana	42	125	60	5			
Lesotho	4	2	11	5			
Namibia	78	130	26	281			
South Africa	1,500	1,865	1,795	2,166	2,348	0.05	8.40
Swaziland	174	192					
West Africa	1,986	2,503	1,971	2,091			
Benin	46	38	26	16			
Burkina Faso	17	25	15	26			
Cape Verde	22	8	7	14			
Côte d'Ivoire	57	34	142	36			
Gambia	131	23	35	7			
Ghana	45	36	91	89			
Guinea	53	43	17	11			
Guinea-Bissau	4	2		14			
Liberia	15	7	20	13			
Mali	20	20	30	27			
Mauritania	299	48	15	24			

585

Yearbook of Tourism Statistics, Data 2008 – 2012, 2014 Edition

POLAND

4. Arrivals of non-resident tourists in all types of accommodation establishments, by country of residence

	2008	2009	2010	2011	2012	Market share 2012	% Change 2012-2011
Niger	145	377	455	213			
Nigeria	802	1,059	720	1,224			
Saint Helena	4	51	24	7			
Senegal	89	471	175	119			
Sierra Leone	221	243	195	233			
Togo	16	18	4	18			
Other Africa					12,742	0.26	
Other countries of Africa					12,742	0.26	
AMERICAS	**198,941**	**184,464**	**217,610**	**225,130**	**257,697**	**5.18**	**14.47**
Caribbean	**1,418**	**773**	**751**	**1,719**			
Anguilla	4	12					
Antigua and Barbuda	10	9					
Aruba	11	17	11	3			
Bahamas	232	33	108	600			
Barbados	271	132	65	26			
Bermuda	47	25	13	28			
British Virgin Islands	176	1					
Cayman Islands	1	20	20	13			
Cuba	237	231	279	277			
Dominica	14	8	18	31			
Dominican Republic	32	30	56	126			
Grenada	25	2					
Guadeloupe	3	12	3	1			
Haiti	34	13	17	48			
Jamaica	98	126	48	75			
Martinique	5	2		3			
Netherlands Antilles	6	1					
Puerto Rico	115	85	93	457			
Saint Kitts and Nevis	1	3					
Saint Lucia	10						
Trinidad and Tobago	64	10	20	31			
Turks and Caicos Islands	21	1					
United States Virgin Islands	1						
Central America	**868**	**1,516**	**1,437**	**1,294**			
Belize	70	90	41	68			
Costa Rica	243	198	249	220			
El Salvador	70	59	56	111			
Guatemala	72	55	74	65			
Honduras	57	930	777	722			
Nicaragua	229	113	143	45			
Panama	127	71	97	63			
North America	**181,896**	**168,322**	**197,815**	**203,052**	**224,568**	**4.51**	**10.60**
Canada	22,313	24,197	28,135	29,289	33,030	0.66	12.77
Greenland	1	5	2				
Mexico	4,404	3,697	4,082	5,765			
Saint Pierre and Miquelon	3						
United States of America	155,175	140,423	165,596	167,998	191,538	3.85	14.01
South America	**14,759**	**13,853**	**17,607**	**19,065**	**14,870**	**0.30**	**-22.00**
Argentina	2,292	2,265	2,339	3,230			
Bolivia	63	620	1,046	1,047			
Brazil	8,817	7,689	10,467	10,890	14,870	0.30	36.55
Chile	961	882	1,019	1,229			
Colombia	603	498	643	941			
Ecuador	148	306	254	180			
Falkland Islands, Malvinas		84	1	7			
French Guiana	15	2	1	4			
Guyana	14	1	3	89			

586

POLAND

4. Arrivals of non-resident tourists in all types of accommodation establishments, by country of residence

	2008	2009	2010	2011	2012	Market share 2012	% Change 2012-2011
Paraguay	9	17	89	77			
Peru	310	509	386	370			
Suriname	137	69	33				
Uruguay	227	326	517	547			
Venezuela	1,163	585	809	454			
Other Americas					18,259	0.37	
Other countries of the Americas					18,259	0.37	
EAST ASIA AND THE PACIFIC	**121,129**	**120,014**	**151,559**	**156,583**	**364,330**	**7.32**	**132.68**
North-East Asia	**92,364**	**90,107**	**113,881**	**108,818**	**91,580**	**1.84**	**-15.84**
China	20,189	20,033	26,578	33,182	41,233	0.83	24.26
Hong Kong, China	1,808	3,566	4,231	4,958			
Japan	37,175	34,386	50,499	39,202	35,620	0.72	-9.14
Korea, Dem. People's Republic of	5,237	12,022	16,413	15,006			
Korea, Republic of	26,301	17,901	13,943	13,702	14,727	0.30	7.48
Macao, China	17	65	63	52			
Mongolia	344	559	644	591			
Taiwan, Province of China	1,293	1,575	1,510	2,125			
South-East Asia	**7,204**	**9,230**	**11,838**	**18,986**			
Brunei Darussalam	6	5	54	16			
Cambodia	37	7	41	13			
Indonesia	1,124	1,169	980	2,578			
Lao People's Democratic Republic	18	18	17	47			
Malaysia	1,196	1,138	1,403	2,242			
Myanmar	7	10	2	6			
Philippines	861	1,015	1,025	2,489			
Singapore	1,628	2,146	4,243	6,025			
Thailand	1,275	1,712	2,116	3,730			
Timor-Leste	11		1	3			
Viet Nam	1,041	2,010	1,956	1,837			
Australasia	**20,671**	**20,527**	**25,700**	**28,662**	**29,285**	**0.59**	**2.17**
Australia	18,377	18,216	22,902	25,959	29,285	0.59	12.81
New Zealand	2,294	2,311	2,798	2,703			
Melanesia	**107**	**96**	**53**	**71**			
Fiji	39	48	8	19			
New Caledonia	18	13	26	36			
Norfolk Island	8	27					
Papua New Guinea	31	8	19	16			
Solomon Islands	11						
Micronesia	**62**	**5**	**2**	**14**			
Guam	2	3	2	8			
Kiribati	25						
Micronesia, Federated States of				6			
Nauru	34	2					
Palau	1						
Polynesia	**721**	**49**	**85**	**32**			
American Samoa	262	28					
French Polynesia	25	15	38	28			
Niue	52						
Samoa	22	5					
Tokelau	6						
Tonga	8	1	47	4			
Tuvalu	9						
Wallis and Futuna Islands	337						
Other East Asia and the Pacific					243,465	4.89	
Other countries of Asia					239,984	4.82	
Other countries of Oceania					3,481	0.07	

Yearbook of Tourism Statistics, Data 2008 – 2012, 2014 Edition

POLAND

4. Arrivals of non-resident tourists in all types of accommodation establishments, by country of residence

	2008	2009	2010	2011	2012	Market share 2012	% Change 2012-2011
EUROPE	3,659,440	3,507,918	3,696,478	3,966,041	4,294,484	86.25	8.28
Central/Eastern Europe	820,306	743,407	830,132	993,938	1,077,907	21.65	8.45
Armenia	579	2,485	3,203	3,651			
Azerbaijan	723	998	830	903			
Belarus	66,319	71,485	81,928	107,304			
Bulgaria	9,673	9,539	10,203	10,584	12,114	0.24	14.46
Czech Republic	81,213	78,708	79,603	89,567	98,561	1.98	10.04
Estonia	41,789	34,592	32,486	36,152	37,604	0.76	4.02
Georgia	1,662	2,364	2,174	2,032			
Hungary	51,534	48,063	48,153	52,708	59,868	1.20	13.58
Kazakhstan	2,629	2,638	2,815	4,013			
Kyrgyzstan	203	125	237	378			
Latvia	55,895	38,112	43,265	50,691	58,874	1.18	16.14
Lithuania	111,383	101,950	100,255	103,789	106,165	2.13	2.29
Republic of Moldova	3,043	2,625	3,210	2,931			
Romania	22,291	20,552	25,836	27,371	30,421	0.61	11.14
Russian Federation	196,005	161,353	214,544	280,975	397,857	7.99	41.60
Slovakia	36,391	41,627	45,401	50,928	52,972	1.06	4.01
Tajikistan	93	49	196	109			
Turkmenistan	14	37	27	59			
Ukraine	138,433	125,707	134,930	168,738	223,471	4.49	32.44
Uzbekistan	434	398	836	1,055			
Northern Europe	792,417	717,561	744,176	747,170	857,476	17.22	14.76
Denmark	91,126	87,299	79,932	84,630	89,420	1.80	5.66
Faeroe Islands	73	8					
Finland	46,101	47,492	58,511	64,834	61,573	1.24	-5.03
Iceland	2,106	1,785	2,722	1,905	2,676	0.05	40.47
Ireland	49,003	40,525	42,122	41,243	81,685	1.64	98.06
Norway	101,355	91,042	102,124	104,421	133,359	2.68	27.71
Svalbard and Jan Mayen Islands	10	11	2				
Sweden	114,343	108,850	102,784	106,586	118,722	2.38	11.39
United Kingdom	388,300	340,549	355,979	343,551	370,041	7.43	7.71
Southern Europe	343,408	350,611	381,226	435,968	430,698	8.65	-1.21
Albania	381	1,477	1,418	1,702			
Andorra	98	130	373	290			
Bosnia and Herzegovina	860	1,239	852	1,276			
Croatia	7,635	7,090	7,564	8,852			
Gibraltar	16	26	38	46			
Greece	11,863	15,601	12,805	14,702	16,853	0.34	14.63
Holy See	10	204	141	155			
Italy	185,010	180,442	194,892	208,737	219,652	4.41	5.23
Malta	902	584	775	1,373	1,520	0.03	10.71
Montenegro	175	170	188	383			
Portugal	15,553	18,285	20,299	22,181	25,503	0.51	14.98
San Marino	22	118	32	197			
Serbia	2,125	2,374	4,855	4,726			
Slovenia	8,029	9,251	8,866	10,014	10,436	0.21	4.21
Spain	110,094	112,831	126,883	160,397	156,734	3.15	-2.28
TFYR of Macedonia	635	789	1,245	937			
Western Europe	1,583,611	1,550,661	1,582,580	1,621,143	1,709,726	34.34	5.46
Austria	54,601	54,810	59,050	62,469	64,634	1.30	3.47
Belgium	57,647	56,663	63,964	66,987	64,449	1.29	-3.79
France	182,607	174,044	187,267	198,572	197,328	3.96	-0.63
Germany	1,142,337	1,126,573	1,128,378	1,141,632	1,224,852	24.60	7.29
Liechtenstein	310	1,149	267	351			
Luxembourg	2,621	2,838	3,593	3,565	3,577	0.07	0.34
Monaco	251	415	300	219			

Yearbook of Tourism Statistics, Data 2008 – 2012, 2014 Edition

POLAND

4. Arrivals of non-resident tourists in all types of accommodation establishments, by country of residence

	2008	2009	2010	2011	2012	Market share 2012	% Change 2012-2011
Netherlands	109,721	101,006	105,631	110,934	113,111	2.27	1.96
Switzerland	33,516	33,163	34,130	36,414	41,775	0.84	14.72
East Mediterranean Europe	**119,698**	**145,678**	**158,364**	**167,822**	**25,647**	**0.52**	**-84.72**
Cyprus	2,496	2,532	2,255	2,048	2,468	0.05	20.51
Israel	104,120	128,419	139,567	145,572			
Turkey	13,082	14,727	16,542	20,202	23,179	0.47	14.74
Other Europe					**193,030**	**3.88**	
Other countries of Europe					193,030	3.88	
MIDDLE EAST	**5,024**	**7,061**	**7,198**	**9,264**			
Bahrain	112	165	229	159			
Egypt	1,364	1,398	1,565	1,756			
Iraq	384	614	520	767			
Jordan	249	313	228	433			
Kuwait	476	543	498	680			
Lebanon	429	866	500	632			
Libya	245	229	303	347			
Oman	28	42	99	27			
Qatar	49	325	288	265			
Saudi Arabia	677	1,085	1,535	2,304			
Syrian Arab Republic	215	338	328	489			
United Arab Emirates	754	1,105	1,074	1,361			
Yemen	42	38	31	44			
SOUTH ASIA	**12,564**	**14,134**	**18,472**	**17,072**			
Afghanistan	233	1,248	3,757	1,458			
Bangladesh	365	791	859	928			
Bhutan	1,075	263	398	109			
India	7,561	8,943	9,952	11,324			
Iran, Islamic Republic of	2,391	1,648	2,255	2,048			
Maldives	8	9	46	16			
Nepal	234	419	325	121			
Pakistan	585	695	727	878			
Sri Lanka	112	118	153	190			
NOT SPECIFIED	**42,676**	**19,568**	**34,335**	**26,251**	**47,693**	**0.96**	**81.68**
Other countries of the World	42,676	19,568	34,335	26,251	47,693	0.96	81.68

 Yearbook of Tourism Statistics, Data 2008 – 2012, 2014 Edition

POLAND

5. Overnight stays of non-resident tourists in hotels and similar establishments, by country of residence

		2008	2009	2010	2011	2012	Market share 2012	% Change 2012-2011
TOTAL	(*)	7,939,328	7,478,048	8,029,202	8,397,392	9,424,550	100.00	12.23
AFRICA		17,672	20,722	20,737	20,073	29,516	0.31	47.04
East Africa		2,103	1,466	2,180	1,583			
British Indian Ocean Territory		17						
Burundi		84	74	46	74			
Comoros			4	4				
Djibouti		2	52	4	16			
Eritrea		10						
Ethiopia		195	156	365	151			
Kenya		615	517	409	382			
Madagascar		76	7	100	66			
Malawi		2	27	29	21			
Mauritius		90	32	136	83			
Mozambique		17	9	48	58			
Reunion		147	2					
Rwanda		112	30	224	196			
Seychelles		108	33	47	31			
Somalia		21	49	107	93			
Uganda		88	188	298	192			
United Republic of Tanzania		62	39	212	74			
Zambia		363	68	59	43			
Zimbabwe		94	179	92	103			
Central Africa		910	1,421	1,604	1,908			
Angola		274	595	1,212	954			
Cameroon		115	163	124	159			
Central African Republic		23	175	65	553			
Chad		5	93	4	16			
Congo		234	263	165	182			
Democratic Republic of the Congo		178	105	28	37			
Equatorial Guinea				6	7			
Gabon		60	27					
Sao Tome and Principe		21						
North Africa		3,982	5,582	8,007	7,787			
Algeria		1,713	2,144	4,051	4,081			
Morocco		1,281	1,273	2,597	1,644			
Sudan		61	167	144	234			
Tunisia		923	1,396	1,085	1,783			
Western Sahara		4	602	130	45			
Southern Africa		4,382	5,288	4,490	5,498	5,955	0.06	8.31
Botswana		54	132	79	25			
Lesotho			7	13	19			
Namibia		87	233	60	130			
South Africa		4,015	4,628	4,338	5,324	5,955	0.06	11.85
Swaziland		226	288					
West Africa		6,295	6,965	4,456	3,297			
Benin		100	116	94	51			
Burkina Faso		39	4	25	76			
Cape Verde		44	16	14	42			
Côte d'Ivoire		138	38	168	68			
Gambia		238	34	83	5			
Ghana		89	62	183	335			
Guinea		349	118	17	24			
Guinea-Bissau		8	3		14			
Liberia		105	11	56	38			
Mali		66	35	57	92			
Mauritania		364	86	28	28			

Yearbook of Tourism Statistics, Data 2008 – 2012, 2014 Edition

POLAND

5. Overnight stays of non-resident tourists in hotels and similar establishments, by country of residence

	2008	2009	2010	2011	2012	Market share 2012	% Change 2012-2011
Niger	282	651	1,017	365			
Nigeria	3,751	3,737	1,664	1,443			
Saint Helena	8	61	31	8			
Senegal	299	1,376	651	338			
Sierra Leone	371	587	365	350			
Togo	44	30	3	20			
Other Africa					23,561	0.25	
Other countries of Africa					23,561	0.25	
AMERICAS	**431,228**	**388,543**	**450,356**	**463,590**	**529,846**	**5.62**	**14.29**
Caribbean	**3,742**	**1,732**	**1,558**	**4,019**			
Anguilla	4	14					
Antigua and Barbuda	22	18					
Aruba	15	26	15	16			
Bahamas	436	59	195	1,539			
Barbados	622	173	110	73			
Bermuda	38	35	14	116			
British Virgin Islands	353	1					
Cayman Islands	4	50	56	27			
Cuba	787	639	541	669			
Dominica	36	21	59	79			
Dominican Republic	79	235	189	336			
Grenada	93	2					
Guadeloupe	5	17		5			
Haiti	66	19	56	159			
Jamaica	692	248	136	156			
Martinique	15	2		34			
Netherlands Antilles	12	1					
Puerto Rico	116	145	143	738			
Saint Kitts and Nevis	4	6					
Saint Lucia	24						
Trinidad and Tobago	312	19	44	72			
Turks and Caicos Islands	1	2					
United States Virgin Islands	6						
Central America	**1,556**	**1,300**	**1,266**	**1,432**			
Belize	98	131	77	105			
Costa Rica	544	350	273	417			
El Salvador	114	112	88	184			
Guatemala	110	150	119	176			
Honduras	156	334	317	309			
Nicaragua	371	74	257	96			
Panama	163	149	135	145			
North America	**395,657**	**357,942**	**413,234**	**415,694**	**462,891**	**4.91**	**11.35**
Canada	43,760	46,492	55,395	56,280	64,034	0.68	13.78
Greenland	2	19	2				
Mexico	10,951	7,397	8,960	12,902			
Saint Pierre and Miquelon	2						
United States of America	340,942	304,034	348,877	346,512	398,857	4.23	15.11
South America	**30,273**	**27,569**	**34,298**	**42,445**	**32,285**	**0.34**	**-23.94**
Argentina	4,796	4,465	4,458	7,237			
Bolivia	118	1,699	2,309	2,513			
Brazil	18,276	15,431	21,052	25,389	32,285	0.34	27.16
Chile	1,818	1,469	1,807	2,274			
Colombia	1,205	1,359	1,407	1,868			
Ecuador	303	528	400	266			
Falkland Islands, Malvinas		86	2	8			
French Guiana	32	7	1	39			
Guyana	25	3	3	143			

Yearbook of Tourism Statistics, Data 2008 – 2012, 2014 Edition

POLAND

5. Overnight stays of non-resident tourists in hotels and similar establishments, by country of residence

	2008	2009	2010	2011	2012	Market share 2012	% Change 2012-2011
Paraguay	22	30	168	225			
Peru	660	783	607	610			
Suriname	212	93	66				
Uruguay	312	461	802	1,148			
Venezuela	2,494	1,155	1,216	725			
Other Americas					34,670	0.37	
Other countries of the Americas					34,670	0.37	
EAST ASIA AND THE PACIFIC	**255,718**	**221,960**	**292,648**	**280,049**	**674,776**	**7.16**	**140.95**
North-East Asia	**196,557**	**164,718**	**224,414**	**197,875**	**156,963**	**1.67**	**-20.68**
China	45,553	35,840	54,866	62,809	61,416	0.65	-2.22
Hong Kong, China	3,009	6,777	7,856	8,510			
Japan	92,059	70,599	101,297	72,520	71,331	0.76	-1.64
Korea, Dem. People's Republic of	11,233	22,619	30,110	23,309			
Korea, Republic of	41,905	25,273	26,802	25,621	24,216	0.26	-5.48
Macao, China	23	195	102	91			
Mongolia	550	735	850	731			
Taiwan, Province of China	2,225	2,680	2,531	4,284			
South-East Asia	**21,096**	**20,774**	**22,646**	**32,559**			
Brunei Darussalam	46	13	80	18			
Cambodia	54	26	70	67			
Indonesia	3,506	1,971	2,038	4,304			
Lao People's Democratic Republic	44	37	33	51			
Malaysia	6,907	4,976	5,137	4,677			
Myanmar	14	17	5	7			
Philippines	2,651	2,512	1,724	4,362			
Singapore	3,498	4,244	6,770	9,276			
Thailand	2,694	3,420	3,694	6,585			
Timor-Leste	15		1	6			
Viet Nam	1,667	3,558	3,094	3,206			
Australasia	**36,290**	**36,154**	**45,265**	**49,371**	**48,087**	**0.51**	**-2.60**
Australia	32,619	31,439	40,306	44,741	48,087	0.51	7.48
New Zealand	3,671	4,715	4,959	4,630			
Melanesia	**300**	**215**	**109**	**183**			
Fiji	61	93	20	53			
New Caledonia	77	26	13	61			
Norfolk Island	24	84					
Papua New Guinea	117	12	76	69			
Solomon Islands	21						
Micronesia	**151**	**13**	**2**	**22**			
Guam	20	13	2	16			
Kiribati	28						
Micronesia, Federated States of				6			
Nauru	93						
Palau	10						
Polynesia	**1,324**	**86**	**212**	**39**			
American Samoa	519	46					
French Polynesia	46	27	150	25			
Niue	113						
Samoa	51	11					
Tokelau	7						
Tonga	21	2	62	14			
Tuvalu	38						
Wallis and Futuna Islands	529						
Other East Asia and the Pacific					469,726	4.98	
Other countries of Asia					464,061	4.92	
Other countries of Oceania					5,665	0.06	

Yearbook of Tourism Statistics, Data 2008 – 2012, 2014 Edition

POLAND

5. Overnight stays of non-resident tourists in hotels and similar establishments, by country of residence

	2008	2009	2010	2011	2012	Market share 2012	% Change 2012-2011
EUROPE	7,107,836	6,757,450	7,147,489	7,514,760	8,112,135	86.07	7.95
Central/Eastern Europe	1,230,703	1,133,044	1,245,609	1,422,092	1,517,759	16.10	6.73
Armenia	966	6,664	7,830	9,317			
Azerbaijan	1,882	2,364	2,039	2,513			
Belarus	85,000	84,504	100,399	126,589			
Bulgaria	24,087	19,447	17,852	21,385	26,910	0.29	25.84
Czech Republic	129,379	145,521	150,899	153,983	154,324	1.64	0.22
Estonia	45,956	38,970	36,553	42,981	43,990	0.47	2.35
Georgia	4,484	15,936	15,851	4,661			
Hungary	85,278	80,692	84,227	90,651	105,085	1.12	15.92
Kazakhstan	5,105	4,897	5,254	7,445			
Kyrgyzstan	294	232	582	899			
Latvia	58,094	42,741	48,878	57,067	65,900	0.70	15.48
Lithuania	126,848	118,738	116,183	119,978	127,015	1.35	5.87
Republic of Moldova	16,228	10,731	5,771	5,537			
Romania	48,119	43,429	50,647	56,908	58,105	0.62	2.10
Russian Federation	325,423	277,456	313,057	383,731	545,314	5.79	42.11
Slovakia	55,449	64,611	88,294	94,274	87,996	0.93	-6.66
Tajikistan	244	216	440	109			
Turkmenistan	59	67	63	212			
Ukraine	215,390	175,161	199,268	241,771	303,120	3.22	25.37
Uzbekistan	2,418	667	1,522	2,081			
Northern Europe	1,669,463	1,513,900	1,537,774	1,559,441	1,746,135	18.53	11.97
Denmark	203,893	195,061	172,905	178,090	185,650	1.97	4.25
Faeroe Islands	142	4					
Finland	81,920	89,536	106,234	121,936	118,466	1.26	-2.85
Iceland	5,150	3,475	5,545	3,949	5,520	0.06	39.78
Ireland	110,836	91,898	94,366	94,655	118,593	1.26	25.29
Norway	215,500	211,537	240,910	245,009	323,810	3.44	32.16
Svalbard and Jan Mayen Islands	16	23	15				
Sweden	210,072	206,559	195,175	203,457	228,752	2.43	12.43
United Kingdom	841,934	715,807	722,624	712,345	765,344	8.12	7.44
Southern Europe	711,397	703,608	739,941	837,877	828,354	8.79	-1.14
Albania	635	3,213	3,178	3,982			
Andorra	164	193	930	548			
Bosnia and Herzegovina	1,393	2,502	4,599	3,211			
Croatia	16,415	13,765	16,812	17,822			
Gibraltar	16	37	144	103			
Greece	28,109	36,397	26,242	28,691	33,920	0.36	18.23
Holy See	12	374	246	174			
Italy	398,082	374,970	397,485	420,638	441,178	4.68	4.88
Malta	2,641	1,398	2,439	4,021	4,742	0.05	17.93
Montenegro	430	347	336	1,063			
Portugal	33,956	35,512	36,687	44,338	50,841	0.54	14.67
San Marino	38	257	58	305			
Serbia	4,189	4,962	8,466	9,486			
Slovenia	13,960	17,139	15,482	16,692	18,421	0.20	10.36
Spain	210,241	210,777	225,405	285,020	279,252	2.96	-2.02
TFYR of Macedonia	1,116	1,765	1,432	1,783			
Western Europe	3,271,411	3,127,648	3,327,263	3,370,504	3,739,999	39.68	10.96
Austria	96,668	100,498	100,215	107,819	109,842	1.17	1.88
Belgium	101,772	99,348	113,774	118,769	114,189	1.21	-3.86
France	334,525	312,494	324,221	350,702	342,627	3.64	-2.30
Germany	2,489,128	2,377,950	2,540,966	2,533,533	2,896,873	30.74	14.34
Liechtenstein	475	1,497	486	605			
Luxembourg	4,548	4,937	6,836	6,533	6,481	0.07	-0.80
Monaco	412	601	386	337			

Yearbook of Tourism Statistics, Data 2008 – 2012, 2014 Edition

POLAND

5. Overnight stays of non-resident tourists in hotels and similar establishments, by country of residence

	2008	2009	2010	2011	2012	Market share 2012	% Change 2012-2011
Netherlands	182,438	170,440	179,677	187,680	195,957	2.08	4.41
Switzerland	61,445	59,883	60,702	64,526	74,030	0.79	14.73
East Mediterranean Europe	**224,862**	**279,250**	**296,902**	**324,846**	**50,176**	**0.53**	**-84.55**
Cyprus	6,686	6,334	5,928	4,180	5,410	0.06	29.43
Israel	188,868	242,475	258,838	281,377			
Turkey	29,308	30,441	32,136	39,289	44,766	0.47	13.94
Other Europe					**229,712**	**2.44**	
Other countries of Europe					229,712	2.44	
MIDDLE EAST	**11,330**	**17,626**	**20,015**	**25,821**			
Bahrain	254	763	883	865			
Egypt	3,161	3,743	4,493	4,955			
Iraq	847	941	750	2,043			
Jordan	501	530	457	977			
Kuwait	1,104	1,195	1,332	1,898			
Lebanon	807	1,505	1,036	1,233			
Libya	595	397	862	586			
Oman	48	163	635	269			
Qatar	231	1,522	2,765	1,384			
Saudi Arabia	1,742	2,568	3,508	7,264			
Syrian Arab Republic	310	522	520	959			
United Arab Emirates	1,682	3,700	2,730	3,245			
Yemen	48	77	44	143			
SOUTH ASIA	**33,906**	**33,415**	**39,877**	**46,033**			
Afghanistan	447	2,928	4,590	6,255			
Bangladesh	826	1,959	1,628	2,899			
Bhutan	1,074	278	399	212			
India	23,717	22,201	26,395	29,273			
Iran, Islamic Republic of	5,669	4,014	4,990	4,948			
Maldives	27	11	126	34			
Nepal	632	466	204	187			
Pakistan	1,285	1,368	1,212	1,711			
Sri Lanka	229	190	333	514			
NOT SPECIFIED	**81,638**	**38,332**	**58,080**	**47,066**	**78,277**	**0.83**	**66.31**
Other countries of the World	81,638	38,332	58,080	47,066	78,277	0.83	66.31

Yearbook of Tourism Statistics, Data 2008 – 2012, 2014 Edition

POLAND

6. Overnight stays of non-resident tourists in all types of accommodation establishments, by country of residence

	2008	2009	2010	2011	2012	Market share 2012	% Change 2012-2011
TOTAL	10,173,237	9,609,447	10,064,628	10,620,264	11,876,599	100.00	11.83
AFRICA	19,849	23,095	25,862	26,068	52,055	0.44	99.69
East Africa	2,477	1,803	2,958	2,152			
British Indian Ocean Territory	17						
Burundi	93	83	46	74			
Comoros		4	4				
Djibouti	8	52	4	17			
Eritrea	16						
Ethiopia	235	229	527	244			
Kenya	783	538	629	528			
Madagascar	80	15	106	78			
Malawi	5	27	34	24			
Mauritius	107	33	152	89			
Mozambique	17	9	48	61			
Reunion	147	2					
Rwanda	112	30	235	200			
Seychelles	108	33	47	31			
Somalia	40	51	222	93			
Uganda	92	238	343	262			
United Republic of Tanzania	63	65	261	137			
Zambia	365	79	108	144			
Zimbabwe	189	315	192	170			
Central Africa	1,312	1,744	1,957	2,367			
Angola	416	654	1,365	1,074			
Cameroon	220	254	212	467			
Central African Republic	28	187	95	555			
Chad	5	101	9	16			
Congo	295	350	232	211			
Democratic Republic of the Congo	267	118	38	37			
Equatorial Guinea			6	7			
Gabon	60	80					
Sao Tome and Principe	21						
North Africa	4,490	6,064	10,117	9,495			
Algeria	1,840	2,435	4,270	4,726			
Morocco	1,470	1,331	4,174	2,530			
Sudan	65	176	154	277			
Tunisia	1,111	1,520	1,389	1,917			
Western Sahara	4	602	130	45			
Southern Africa	4,658	5,747	4,871	6,472	6,354	0.05	-1.82
Botswana	57	132	79	25			
Lesotho	4	23	19	19			
Namibia	94	240	60	803			
South Africa	4,232	5,064	4,713	5,625	6,354	0.05	12.96
Swaziland	271	288					
West Africa	6,912	7,737	5,959	5,582			
Benin	110	117	94	52			
Burkina Faso	46	75	25	82			
Cape Verde	44	16	14	42			
Côte d'Ivoire	140	130	176	68			
Gambia	522	70	85	10			
Ghana	109	91	215	436			
Guinea	351	140	36	25			
Guinea-Bissau	8	3		14			
Liberia	105	11	56	40			
Mali	66	38	59	92			
Mauritania	365	88	28	33			

595

POLAND

6. Overnight stays of non-resident tourists in all types of accommodation establishments, by country of residence

	2008	2009	2010	2011	2012	Market share 2012	% Change 2012-2011
Niger	285	674	2,057	477			
Nigeria	3,995	4,129	1,939	3,183			
Saint Helena	8	90	31	8			
Senegal	335	1,444	774	649			
Sierra Leone	376	587	365	351			
Togo	47	34	5	20			
Other Africa					45,701	0.38	
Other countries of Africa					45,701	0.38	
AMERICAS	471,598	427,512	493,842	510,862	588,011	4.95	15.10
Caribbean	4,948	1,883	1,761	4,232			
Anguilla	6	14					
Antigua and Barbuda	22	18					
Aruba	17	27	15	16			
Bahamas	834	69	212	1,540			
Barbados	631	239	123	73			
Bermuda	158	41	14	116			
British Virgin Islands	431	1					
Cayman Islands	4	50	56	27			
Cuba	807	685	672	723			
Dominica	61	21	59	79			
Dominican Republic	97	245	191	343			
Grenada	93	2					
Guadeloupe	5	19	4	5			
Haiti	68	20	57	167			
Jamaica	706	252	136	177			
Martinique	15	2		34			
Netherlands Antilles	12	1					
Puerto Rico	454	150	171	843			
Saint Kitts and Nevis	4	6					
Saint Lucia	24						
Trinidad and Tobago	312	19	51	89			
Turks and Caicos Islands	181	2					
United States Virgin Islands	6						
Central America	1,598	3,628	3,300	2,758			
Belize	98	131	82	114			
Costa Rica	570	374	639	481			
El Salvador	118	114	102	192			
Guatemala	114	156	137	192			
Honduras	156	2,438	1,510	1,489			
Nicaragua	371	266	271	132			
Panama	171	149	559	158			
North America	429,124	390,051	448,751	454,374	507,067	4.27	11.60
Canada	52,717	54,822	64,142	64,778	74,755	0.63	15.40
Greenland	2	19	3				
Mexico	13,255	8,251	10,631	15,572			
Saint Pierre and Miquelon	3						
United States of America	363,147	326,959	373,975	374,024	432,312	3.64	15.58
South America	35,928	31,950	40,030	49,498	37,229	0.31	-24.79
Argentina	5,421	5,121	5,381	7,838			
Bolivia	135	1,729	2,318	2,535			
Brazil	22,312	17,624	23,497	29,395	37,229	0.31	26.65
Chile	2,094	1,759	2,195	2,742			
Colombia	1,388	1,522	1,662	2,584			
Ecuador	485	839	841	383			
Falkland Islands, Malvinas		86	2	8			
French Guiana	32	7	1	39			
Guyana	25	3	3	151			

Yearbook of Tourism Statistics, Data 2008 – 2012, 2014 Editi

POLAND

6. Overnight stays of non-resident tourists in all types of accommodation establishments, by country of residence

	2008	2009	2010	2011	2012	Market share 2012	% Change 2012-2011
Paraguay	32	37	280	234			
Peru	735	918	851	812			
Suriname	215	97	66				
Uruguay	388	571	959	1,282			
Venezuela	2,666	1,637	1,974	1,495			
Other Americas					43,715	0.37	
Other countries of the Americas					43,715	0.37	
EAST ASIA AND THE PACIFIC	286,891	243,534	317,019	311,619	736,817	6.20	136.45
North-East Asia	215,066	174,133	234,855	212,601	168,366	1.42	-20.81
China	57,754	39,383	58,167	66,542	66,292	0.56	-0.38
Hong Kong, China	3,245	7,054	8,553	9,866			
Japan	95,559	74,193	105,300	76,584	76,732	0.65	0.19
Korea, Dem. People's Republic of	11,977	23,418	31,279	25,940			
Korea, Republic of	43,057	25,589	27,208	26,483	25,342	0.21	-4.31
Macao, China	23	220	117	96			
Mongolia	744	1,034	1,166	2,309			
Taiwan, Province of China	2,707	3,242	3,065	4,781			
South-East Asia	24,283	23,467	25,495	36,413			
Brunei Darussalam	46	13	80	25			
Cambodia	55	26	75	73			
Indonesia	4,431	3,305	2,279	4,514			
Lao People's Democratic Republic	45	47	34	57			
Malaysia	8,072	5,315	5,601	5,163			
Myanmar	14	17	5	16			
Philippines	2,783	2,613	2,241	5,331			
Singapore	3,824	4,429	7,457	9,858			
Thailand	2,765	3,571	4,004	7,135			
Timor-Leste	15		1	6			
Viet Nam	2,233	4,131	3,718	4,235			
Australasia	45,599	45,594	56,287	62,351	63,156	0.53	1.29
Australia	40,311	39,392	50,090	56,364	63,156	0.53	12.05
New Zealand	5,288	6,202	6,197	5,987			
Melanesia	346	217	166	189			
Fiji	105	95	20	58			
New Caledonia	77	26	70	62			
Norfolk Island	24	84					
Papua New Guinea	117	12	76	69			
Solomon Islands	23						
Micronesia	194	26	2	22			
Guam	20	13	2	16			
Kiribati	70						
Micronesia, Federated States of				6			
Nauru	94	13					
Palau	10						
Polynesia	1,403	97	214	43			
American Samoa	519	46					
French Polynesia	50	38	152	29			
Niue	113						
Samoa	51	11					
Tokelau	7						
Tonga	21	2	62	14			
Tuvalu	38						
Wallis and Futuna Islands	604						
Other East Asia and the Pacific					505,295	4.25	
Other countries of Asia					497,987	4.19	
Other countries of Oceania					7,308	0.06	

Yearbook of Tourism Statistics, Data 2008 – 2012, 2014 Edition

POLAND

6. Overnight stays of non-resident tourists in all types of accommodation establishments, by country of residence

	2008	2009	2010	2011	2012	Market share 2012	% Change 2012-2011
EUROPE	9,260,421	8,802,443	9,083,870	9,644,744	10,418,543	87.72	8.02
Central/Eastern Europe	1,571,415	1,428,204	1,525,689	1,734,920	1,861,308	15.67	7.28
Armenia	1,384	6,982	8,089	9,618			
Azerbaijan	2,121	2,932	2,514	2,902			
Belarus	111,505	110,874	128,721	166,008			
Bulgaria	28,851	24,208	20,935	26,336	39,902	0.34	51.51
Czech Republic	170,684	185,282	182,037	182,488	192,350	1.62	5.40
Estonia	51,125	45,398	39,420	46,080	47,561	0.40	3.21
Georgia	6,337	19,092	16,480	6,384			
Hungary	110,708	98,695	102,314	109,595	125,834	1.06	14.82
Kazakhstan	7,817	6,461	6,955	8,796			
Kyrgyzstan	435	330	696	1,185			
Latvia	67,875	48,525	54,450	64,043	73,942	0.62	15.46
Lithuania	158,702	146,607	139,407	141,070	150,294	1.27	6.54
Republic of Moldova	17,804	12,394	8,453	6,669			
Romania	60,572	55,041	69,533	74,049	75,960	0.64	2.58
Russian Federation	364,182	314,452	356,019	439,405	630,619	5.31	43.52
Slovakia	74,516	87,764	110,548	116,362	124,093	1.04	6.64
Tajikistan	349	222	1,032	1,023			
Turkmenistan	60	95	64	221			
Ukraine	333,110	261,125	275,695	330,374	400,753	3.37	21.30
Uzbekistan	3,278	1,725	2,327	2,312			
Northern Europe	1,811,326	1,646,811	1,678,802	1,690,748	1,940,885	16.34	14.79
Denmark	225,635	215,086	189,395	195,853	204,571	1.72	4.45
Faeroe Islands	148	50					
Finland	93,995	98,262	117,164	132,129	128,704	1.08	-2.59
Iceland	5,428	4,085	5,935	4,246	5,967	0.05	40.53
Ireland	119,170	100,562	106,780	103,997	164,492	1.39	58.17
Norway	230,785	224,005	256,073	261,127	344,083	2.90	31.77
Svalbard and Jan Mayen Islands	16	23	15				
Sweden	245,986	242,071	226,951	233,081	263,735	2.22	13.15
United Kingdom	890,163	762,667	776,489	760,315	829,333	6.98	9.08
Southern Europe	773,145	777,522	826,288	923,809	934,795	7.87	1.19
Albania	792	3,620	3,433	4,200			
Andorra	177	209	938	569			
Bosnia and Herzegovina	2,062	2,852	4,942	3,769			
Croatia	18,668	16,447	19,381	20,682			
Gibraltar	25	37	144	103			
Greece	30,165	38,505	28,300	30,780	37,063	0.31	20.41
Holy See	12	497	252	234			
Italy	427,114	408,730	430,151	454,508	489,062	4.12	7.60
Malta	2,913	1,578	2,756	4,229	5,476	0.05	29.49
Montenegro	473	558	456	1,091			
Portugal	38,471	39,842	41,738	50,117	58,062	0.49	15.85
San Marino	38	271	84	419			
Serbia	6,421	7,610	11,012	12,420			
Slovenia	15,890	20,070	17,862	18,644	22,086	0.19	18.46
Spain	228,102	234,380	252,341	318,698	323,046	2.72	1.36
TFYR of Macedonia	1,822	2,316	12,498	3,346			
Western Europe	4,866,456	4,656,940	4,742,259	4,953,847	5,312,399	44.73	7.24
Austria	107,889	111,382	112,274	119,380	123,185	1.04	3.19
Belgium	117,435	114,459	131,160	133,359	131,884	1.11	-1.11
France	385,550	359,408	380,666	403,854	401,456	3.38	-0.59
Germany	3,960,270	3,797,376	3,828,542	4,002,950	4,337,643	36.52	8.36
Liechtenstein	511	1,528	513	633			
Luxembourg	5,040	5,348	7,763	7,066	7,305	0.06	3.38
Monaco	499	710	500	378			

598

POLAND

6. Overnight stays of non-resident tourists in all types of accommodation establishments, by country of residence

	2008	2009	2010	2011	2012	Market share 2012	% Change 2012-2011
Netherlands	222,707	201,404	214,978	216,947	230,363	1.94	6.18
Switzerland	66,555	65,325	65,863	69,280	80,563	0.68	16.29
East Mediterranean Europe	**238,079**	**292,966**	**310,832**	**341,420**	**63,145**	**0.53**	**-81.51**
Cyprus	6,832	6,839	6,165	4,617	5,814	0.05	25.93
Israel	196,656	252,245	267,809	288,906			
Turkey	34,591	33,882	36,858	47,897	57,331	0.48	19.70
Other Europe					**306,011**	**2.58**	
Other countries of Europe					306,011	2.58	
MIDDLE EAST	**14,129**	**20,722**	**23,400**	**29,779**			
Bahrain	254	782	899	865			
Egypt	5,068	4,807	5,022	6,191			
Iraq	1,086	1,178	1,359	2,533			
Jordan	612	739	579	1,184			
Kuwait	1,236	1,349	1,399	1,919			
Lebanon	887	1,641	1,156	1,275			
Libya	669	582	1,004	786			
Oman	61	169	640	270			
Qatar	236	1,710	2,795	1,719			
Saudi Arabia	1,793	2,798	3,712	7,519			
Syrian Arab Republic	417	720	869	1,192			
United Arab Emirates	1,729	4,170	3,897	4,174			
Yemen	81	77	69	152			
SOUTH ASIA	**37,029**	**53,656**	**58,210**	**49,475**			
Afghanistan	476	2,966	8,622	6,285			
Bangladesh	851	2,495	1,827	2,916			
Bhutan	1,075	280	403	214			
India	25,969	34,300	34,791	31,282			
Iran, Islamic Republic of	6,199	4,397	5,342	5,604			
Maldives	27	13	126	35			
Nepal	724	7,272	4,466	384			
Pakistan	1,435	1,590	2,240	2,220			
Sri Lanka	273	343	393	535			
NOT SPECIFIED	**83,320**	**38,485**	**62,425**	**47,717**	**81,173**	**0.68**	**70.11**
Other countries of the World	83,320	38,485	62,425	47,717	81,173	0.68	70.11

Yearbook of Tourism Statistics, Data 2008 – 2012, 2014 Edition

PORTUGAL

3. Arrivals of non-resident tourists in hotels and similar establishments, by country of residence

	2008	2009	2010	2011	2012	Market share 2012	% Change 2012-2011
TOTAL	6,421,762	5,911,079	6,256,808	6,792,220	7,043,478	100.00	3.70
AFRICA	66,113	72,785	73,519	82,981	95,137	1.35	14.65
Southern Africa	9,484	6,941	8,497	10,208	9,276	0.13	-9.13
South Africa	9,484	6,941	8,497	10,208	9,276	0.13	-9.13
Other Africa	56,629	65,844	65,022	72,773	85,861	1.22	17.98
Other countries of Africa	56,629	65,844	65,022	72,773	85,861	1.22	17.98
AMERICAS	657,972	607,432	743,093	860,255	933,643	13.26	8.53
North America	303,147	285,548	322,548	351,429	384,735	5.46	9.48
Canada	78,859	59,676	69,459	86,492	95,000	1.35	9.84
United States of America	224,288	225,872	253,089	264,937	289,735	4.11	9.36
South America	295,971	260,801	355,226	433,344	472,061	6.70	8.93
Brazil	295,971	260,801	355,226	433,344	472,061	6.70	8.93
Other Americas	58,854	61,083	65,319	75,482	76,847	1.09	1.81
Other countries of the Americas	58,854	61,083	65,319	75,482	76,847	1.09	1.81
EAST ASIA AND THE PACIFIC	190,427	181,740	221,740	253,807	293,323	4.16	15.57
North-East Asia	98,414	88,383	114,810	125,097	150,282	2.13	20.13
China	22,665	21,647	29,089	37,258	51,602	0.73	38.50
Japan	62,471	56,727	60,942	57,857	63,788	0.91	10.25
Korea, Republic of	13,278	10,009	24,779	29,982	34,892	0.50	16.38
Australasia	29,281	25,334	29,481	34,051	35,987	0.51	5.69
Australia	29,281	25,334	29,481	34,051	35,987	0.51	5.69
Other East Asia and the Pacific	62,732	68,023	77,449	94,659	107,054	1.52	13.09
Other countries of Asia	54,283	62,224	71,211	88,336	98,387	1.40	11.38
Other countries of Oceania	8,449	5,799	6,238	6,323	8,667	0.12	37.07
EUROPE	5,507,250	5,049,122	5,218,456	5,595,177	5,721,375	81.23	2.26
Central/Eastern Europe	192,934	171,187	203,747	258,004	288,133	4.09	11.68
Bulgaria	6,018	6,584	7,043	6,842	8,213	0.12	20.04
Hungary	22,485	16,646	16,422	18,165	19,027	0.27	4.75
Poland	76,422	72,596	82,609	102,417	99,158	1.41	-3.18
Romania	25,245	19,942	21,101	22,591	27,020	0.38	19.61
USSR (former)	62,764	55,419	76,572	107,989	134,715	1.91	24.75
Northern Europe	1,732,964	1,386,825	1,431,672	1,535,947	1,610,067	22.86	4.83
Denmark	91,836	76,368	86,693	74,899	78,833	1.12	5.25
Finland	79,068	74,647	75,031	70,353	57,282	0.81	-18.58
Iceland	4,478	2,213	4,135	2,546	4,090	0.06	60.64
Ireland	164,739	146,703	148,647	154,546	174,430	2.48	12.87
Norway	70,756	55,776	58,085	64,889	68,913	0.98	6.20
Sweden	102,277	79,878	86,906	84,460	95,346	1.35	12.89
United Kingdom	1,219,810	951,240	972,175	1,084,254	1,131,173	16.06	4.33
Southern Europe	1,608,775	1,615,501	1,666,233	1,696,479	1,510,420	21.44	-10.97
Greece	17,932	17,570	14,417	18,221	17,852	0.25	-2.03
Italy	355,061	309,075	344,508	363,427	334,539	4.75	-7.95
Spain	1,235,782	1,288,856	1,307,308	1,314,831	1,158,029	16.44	-11.93
Western Europe	1,844,259	1,723,294	1,798,845	1,950,529	2,149,338	30.52	10.19
Austria	67,336	68,680	63,340	67,583	83,285	1.18	23.23
Belgium	147,859	136,618	135,527	146,513	158,116	2.24	7.92
France	532,754	527,501	542,195	619,753	695,242	9.87	12.18
Germany	678,918	636,281	643,359	650,096	714,182	10.14	9.86
Luxembourg	9,604	11,103	10,597	12,887	14,450	0.21	12.13
Netherlands	311,933	287,335	304,404	338,848	355,166	5.04	4.82
Switzerland	95,855	55,776	99,423	114,849	128,897	1.83	12.23
East Mediterranean Europe	7,639	6,618	8,740	11,083	14,390	0.20	29.84
Turkey	7,639	6,618	8,740	11,083	14,390	0.20	29.84
Other Europe	120,679	145,697	109,219	143,135	149,027	2.12	4.12
Other countries of Europe	120,679	145,697	109,219	143,135	149,027	2.12	4.12

PORTUGAL

4. Arrivals of non-resident tourists in all types of accommodation establishments, by country of residence

	2008	2009	2010	2011	2012	Market share 2012	% Change 2012-2011
TOTAL	6,961,707	6,439,022	6,756,354	7,263,644	7,503,252	100.00	3.30
AFRICA	67,619	73,882	75,446	84,319	96,330	1.28	14.24
Southern Africa	9,794	7,163	8,944	10,464	9,522	0.13	-9.00
South Africa	9,794	7,163	8,944	10,464	9,522	0.13	-9.00
Other Africa	57,825	66,719	66,502	73,855	86,808	1.16	17.54
Other countries of Africa	57,825	66,719	66,502	73,855	86,808	1.16	17.54
AMERICAS	676,186	622,683	759,506	874,361	946,990	12.62	8.31
North America	308,875	290,834	328,002	356,165	389,313	5.19	9.31
Canada	81,807	62,058	71,851	88,732	97,289	1.30	9.64
United States of America	227,068	228,776	256,151	267,433	292,024	3.89	9.20
South America	306,228	268,913	363,871	440,787	479,115	6.39	8.70
Brazil	306,228	268,913	363,871	440,787	479,115	6.39	8.70
Other Americas	61,083	62,936	67,633	77,409	78,562	1.05	1.49
Other countries of the Americas	61,083	62,936	67,633	77,409	78,562	1.05	1.49
EAST ASIA AND THE PACIFIC	201,612	190,419	229,173	261,440	301,056	4.01	15.15
North-East Asia	100,573	89,799	116,108	126,292	151,600	2.02	20.04
China	23,152	21,929	29,424	37,587	51,932	0.69	38.16
Japan	63,486	57,641	61,690	58,492	64,578	0.86	10.40
Korea, Republic of	13,935	10,229	24,994	30,213	35,090	0.47	16.14
Australasia	34,783	30,308	33,143	38,225	39,382	0.52	3.03
Australia	34,783	30,308	33,143	38,225	39,382	0.52	3.03
Other East Asia and the Pacific	66,256	70,312	79,922	96,923	110,074	1.47	13.57
Other countries of Asia	55,185	62,887	72,417	89,359	100,100	1.33	12.02
Other countries of Oceania	11,071	7,425	7,505	7,564	9,974	0.13	31.86
EUROPE	6,016,290	5,552,038	5,692,229	6,043,524	6,158,876	82.08	1.91
Central/Eastern Europe	204,304	181,256	212,829	266,584	296,495	3.95	11.22
Bulgaria	6,320	6,941	7,358	7,178	8,473	0.11	18.04
Hungary	23,919	17,694	17,271	18,933	19,655	0.26	3.81
Poland	83,918	79,323	89,095	108,350	104,807	1.40	-3.27
Romania	26,182	20,622	21,885	23,395	27,976	0.37	19.58
USSR (former)	63,965	56,676	77,220	108,728	135,584	1.81	24.70
Northern Europe	1,789,132	1,436,703	1,478,999	1,576,701	1,652,120	22.02	4.78
Denmark	95,927	79,924	89,879	78,116	81,984	1.09	4.95
Finland	80,951	76,455	76,757	72,518	58,842	0.78	-18.86
Iceland	4,516	2,231	4,192	2,566	4,115	0.05	60.37
Ireland	168,705	149,809	151,786	156,990	176,895	2.36	12.68
Norway	72,292	57,199	59,380	66,291	70,229	0.94	5.94
Sweden	104,870	81,962	88,864	86,822	97,579	1.30	12.39
United Kingdom	1,261,871	989,123	1,008,141	1,113,398	1,162,476	15.49	4.41
Southern Europe	1,764,218	1,767,778	1,818,614	1,836,104	1,623,828	21.64	-11.56
Greece	18,620	18,319	14,722	18,657	18,027	0.24	-3.38
Italy	380,226	330,105	364,908	382,711	350,167	4.67	-8.50
Spain	1,365,372	1,419,354	1,438,984	1,434,736	1,255,634	16.73	-12.48
Western Europe	2,121,535	2,006,249	2,057,084	2,203,102	2,415,414	32.19	9.64
Austria	71,867	72,873	67,169	71,523	87,454	1.17	22.27
Belgium	169,913	154,990	152,851	162,325	175,004	2.33	7.81
France	665,737	663,022	666,958	747,153	826,798	11.02	10.66
Germany	736,200	702,542	695,247	701,458	770,115	10.26	9.79
Luxembourg	10,072	11,745	11,078	13,487	15,109	0.20	12.03
Netherlands	363,215	337,349	356,749	384,694	402,891	5.37	4.73
Switzerland	104,531	63,728	107,032	122,462	138,043	1.84	12.72
East Mediterranean Europe	7,830	6,737	8,873	11,347	14,583	0.19	28.52
Turkey	7,830	6,737	8,873	11,347	14,583	0.19	28.52
Other Europe	129,271	153,315	115,830	149,686	156,436	2.08	4.51
Other countries of Europe	129,271	153,315	115,830	149,686	156,436	2.08	4.51

Yearbook of Tourism Statistics, Data 2008 – 2012, 2014 Edition

PORTUGAL

5. Overnight stays of non-resident tourists in hotels and similar establishments, by country of residence

	2008	2009	2010	2011	2012	Market share 2012	% Change 2012-2011
TOTAL	26,204,245	23,214,377	23,608,207	26,003,760	27,256,580	100.00	4.82
AFRICA	235,565	266,501	268,870	292,404	338,084	1.24	15.62
Southern Africa	31,657	23,388	26,925	33,413	25,908	0.10	-22.46
South Africa	31,657	23,388	26,925	33,413	25,908	0.10	-22.46
Other Africa	203,908	243,113	241,945	258,991	312,176	1.15	20.54
Other countries of Africa	203,908	243,113	241,945	258,991	312,176	1.15	20.54
AMERICAS	1,674,192	1,482,342	1,785,586	2,064,495	2,273,438	8.34	10.12
North America	860,174	738,068	800,925	864,745	948,880	3.48	9.73
Canada	292,121	207,890	224,106	252,847	286,008	1.05	13.12
United States of America	568,053	530,178	576,819	611,898	662,872	2.43	8.33
South America	672,970	595,511	828,510	1,015,458	1,139,398	4.18	12.21
Brazil	672,970	595,511	828,510	1,015,458	1,139,398	4.18	12.21
Other Americas	141,048	148,763	156,151	184,292	185,160	0.68	0.47
Other countries of the Americas	141,048	148,763	156,151	184,292	185,160	0.68	0.47
EAST ASIA AND THE PACIFIC	438,573	433,282	484,508	556,593	637,694	2.34	14.57
North-East Asia	190,592	172,618	214,763	231,637	276,771	1.02	19.48
China	48,980	47,124	59,812	74,861	101,363	0.37	35.40
Japan	120,214	108,278	117,721	113,267	127,254	0.47	12.35
Korea, Republic of	21,398	17,216	37,230	43,509	48,154	0.18	10.68
Australasia	76,307	67,630	74,038	87,805	89,244	0.33	1.64
Australia	76,307	67,630	74,038	87,805	89,244	0.33	1.64
Other East Asia and the Pacific	171,674	193,034	195,707	237,151	271,679	1.00	14.56
Other countries of Asia	146,545	172,936	180,177	220,043	239,642	0.88	8.91
Other countries of Oceania	25,129	20,098	15,530	17,108	32,037	0.12	87.26
EUROPE	23,855,915	21,032,252	21,069,243	23,090,268	24,007,364	88.08	3.97
Central/Eastern Europe	807,577	652,778	754,449	994,900	1,098,295	4.03	10.39
Bulgaria	17,652	18,382	19,896	21,726	27,648	0.10	27.26
Hungary	76,216	55,551	57,445	62,971	69,333	0.25	10.10
Poland	353,851	301,687	338,544	429,573	392,070	1.44	-8.73
Romania	104,582	69,866	66,225	84,854	98,843	0.36	16.49
USSR (former)	255,276	207,292	272,339	395,776	510,401	1.87	28.96
Northern Europe	10,099,163	7,989,061	7,857,143	8,574,675	8,916,653	32.71	3.99
Denmark	482,287	388,854	434,122	362,288	397,075	1.46	9.60
Finland	408,340	401,017	393,782	380,438	310,769	1.14	-18.31
Iceland	32,129	16,250	28,494	9,334	26,173	0.10	180.40
Ireland	1,023,505	872,146	826,785	865,949	991,997	3.64	14.56
Norway	335,154	263,453	273,625	290,201	329,975	1.21	13.71
Sweden	515,670	377,660	405,382	407,902	439,122	1.61	7.65
United Kingdom	7,302,078	5,669,681	5,494,953	6,258,563	6,421,542	23.56	2.60
Southern Europe	4,058,436	4,065,206	4,190,547	4,419,837	3,993,159	14.65	-9.65
Greece	59,872	58,225	43,452	56,515	49,496	0.18	-12.42
Italy	929,096	803,211	869,313	918,210	867,038	3.18	-5.57
Spain	3,069,468	3,203,770	3,277,782	3,445,112	3,076,625	11.29	-10.70
Western Europe	8,479,346	7,896,037	7,895,256	8,611,941	9,455,535	34.69	9.80
Austria	294,959	307,855	266,003	289,739	307,531	1.13	6.14
Belgium	585,559	552,940	510,108	567,767	605,980	2.22	6.73
France	1,590,488	1,595,447	1,619,416	1,931,067	2,224,668	8.16	15.20
Germany	3,657,516	3,341,911	3,279,012	3,392,161	3,684,847	13.52	8.63
Luxembourg	43,878	45,284	42,866	48,786	54,617	0.20	11.95
Netherlands	1,974,157	1,789,147	1,843,369	1,992,895	2,137,313	7.84	7.25
Switzerland	332,789	263,453	334,482	389,526	440,579	1.62	13.11
East Mediterranean Europe	20,975	18,114	22,902	29,759	35,903	0.13	20.65
Turkey	20,975	18,114	22,902	29,759	35,903	0.13	20.65
Other Europe	390,418	411,056	348,946	459,156	507,819	1.86	10.60
Other countries of Europe	390,418	411,056	348,946	459,156	507,819	1.86	10.60

Yearbook of Tourism Statistics, Data 2008 – 2012, 2014 Edition

PORTUGAL

6. Overnight stays of non-resident tourists in all types of accommodation establishments, by country of residence

	2008	2009	2010	2011	2012	Market share 2012	% Change 2012-2011
TOTAL	28,126,581	25,024,678	25,386,084	27,860,103	29,033,970	100.00	4.21
AFRICA	240,313	269,905	277,411	296,810	342,420	1.18	15.37
Southern Africa	32,651	23,973	27,914	34,176	26,371	0.09	-22.84
South Africa	32,651	23,973	27,914	34,176	26,371	0.09	-22.84
Other Africa	207,662	245,932	249,497	262,634	316,049	1.09	20.34
Other countries of Africa	207,662	245,932	249,497	262,634	316,049	1.09	20.34
AMERICAS	1,720,215	1,518,453	1,829,088	2,106,853	2,314,958	7.97	9.88
North America	874,578	749,296	813,649	876,451	960,788	3.31	9.62
Canada	299,398	212,555	229,296	258,611	291,668	1.00	12.78
United States of America	575,180	536,741	584,353	617,840	669,120	2.30	8.30
South America	699,127	616,386	854,456	1,041,180	1,164,721	4.01	11.87
Brazil	699,127	616,386	854,456	1,041,180	1,164,721	4.01	11.87
Other Americas	146,510	152,771	160,983	189,222	189,449	0.65	0.12
Other countries of the Americas	146,510	152,771	160,983	189,222	189,449	0.65	0.12
EAST ASIA AND THE PACIFIC	465,042	453,336	502,231	597,457	661,926	2.28	10.79
North-East Asia	194,904	175,146	217,356	233,912	279,314	0.96	19.41
China	49,781	47,693	60,429	75,579	102,173	0.35	35.19
Japan	122,358	109,890	119,251	114,441	128,635	0.44	12.40
Korea, Republic of	22,765	17,563	37,676	43,892	48,506	0.17	10.51
Australasia	90,001	78,953	83,014	111,130	99,660	0.34	-10.32
Australia	90,001	78,953	83,014	111,130	99,660	0.34	-10.32
Other East Asia and the Pacific	180,137	199,237	201,861	252,415	282,952	0.97	12.10
Other countries of Asia	148,643	174,717	183,800	225,945	245,691	0.85	8.74
Other countries of Oceania	31,494	24,520	18,061	26,470	37,261	0.13	40.77
EUROPE	25,701,011	22,782,984	22,777,354	24,858,983	25,714,666	88.57	3.44
Central/Eastern Europe	835,114	677,274	779,780	1,025,421	1,123,240	3.87	9.54
Bulgaria	18,372	19,181	20,720	22,734	28,737	0.10	26.41
Hungary	79,247	57,811	59,376	66,734	71,085	0.24	6.52
Poland	371,085	317,452	354,935	450,480	408,135	1.41	-9.40
Romania	107,311	72,354	70,499	87,232	102,565	0.35	17.58
USSR (former)	259,099	210,476	274,250	398,241	512,718	1.77	28.75
Northern Europe	10,464,028	8,299,604	8,145,104	8,863,685	9,207,166	31.71	3.88
Denmark	499,017	403,189	448,050	376,360	411,428	1.42	9.32
Finland	416,088	409,470	401,517	392,306	319,010	1.10	-18.68
Iceland	32,281	16,275	28,633	9,404	26,244	0.09	179.07
Ireland	1,042,689	889,769	844,271	880,667	1,005,917	3.46	14.22
Norway	348,766	277,630	288,228	303,621	340,562	1.17	12.17
Sweden	530,434	391,407	419,147	424,754	455,496	1.57	7.24
United Kingdom	7,594,753	5,911,864	5,715,258	6,476,573	6,648,509	22.90	2.65
Southern Europe	4,487,148	4,475,777	4,616,274	4,853,777	4,340,144	14.95	-10.58
Greece	61,849	63,374	44,081	57,720	50,042	0.17	-13.30
Italy	990,475	852,761	913,932	970,194	906,315	3.12	-6.58
Spain	3,434,824	3,559,642	3,658,261	3,825,863	3,383,787	11.65	-11.55
Western Europe	9,481,647	8,885,462	8,846,151	9,604,981	10,479,786	36.09	9.11
Austria	306,287	319,275	276,170	301,794	319,237	1.10	5.78
Belgium	657,587	618,754	574,808	632,650	673,453	2.32	6.45
France	1,982,158	1,980,920	1,989,283	2,325,934	2,648,302	9.12	13.86
Germany	3,883,691	3,567,813	3,479,508	3,615,029	3,896,194	13.42	7.78
Luxembourg	45,727	47,388	44,751	52,382	57,716	0.20	10.18
Netherlands	2,250,176	2,066,269	2,125,748	2,261,326	2,415,700	8.32	6.83
Switzerland	356,021	285,043	355,883	415,866	469,184	1.62	12.82
East Mediterranean Europe	21,323	18,360	23,207	30,301	36,432	0.13	20.23
Turkey	21,323	18,360	23,207	30,301	36,432	0.13	20.23
Other Europe	411,751	426,507	366,838	480,818	527,898	1.82	9.79
Other countries of Europe	411,751	426,507	366,838	480,818	527,898	1.82	9.79

Yearbook of Tourism Statistics, Data 2008 – 2012, 2014 Edition

PUERTO RICO

1. Arrivals of non-resident tourists at national borders, by country of residence

		2008	2009	2010	2011	2012	Market share 2012	% Change 2012-2011
TOTAL	(*)	3,716,246	3,183,252	3,185,606	3,047,915	3,069,087	100.00	0.69
AMERICAS		2,911,974	2,704,074	2,639,721	2,593,837	2,587,942	84.32	-0.23
Caribbean		17,154	13,007	8,823	7,231	6,924	0.23	-4.25
United States Virgin Islands		17,154	13,007	8,823	7,231	6,924	0.23	-4.25
North America		2,894,820	2,691,067	2,630,898	2,586,606	2,581,018	84.10	-0.22
United States of America		2,894,820	2,691,067	2,630,898	2,586,606	2,581,018	84.10	-0.22
NOT SPECIFIED		804,272	479,178	545,885	454,078	481,145	15.68	5.96
Other countries of the World		804,272	479,178	545,885	454,078	481,145	15.68	5.96

Yearbook of Tourism Statistics, Data 2008 – 2012, 2014 Edit

PUERTO RICO

3. Arrivals of non-resident tourists in hotels and similar establishments, by country of residence

		2008	2009	2010	2011	2012	Market share 2012	% Change 2012-2011
TOTAL	(*)	1,335,322	1,280,937	1,349,449	1,414,082	1,508,200	100.00	6.66
AFRICA		1,484	1,456	1,327	1,361	1,500	0.10	10.21
Other Africa		1,484	1,456	1,327	1,361	1,500	0.10	10.21
All countries of Africa		1,484	1,456	1,327	1,361	1,500	0.10	10.21
AMERICAS		1,272,899	1,218,956	1,289,492	1,355,330	1,445,131	95.82	6.63
Caribbean		36,531	30,714	30,275	30,905	33,106	2.20	7.12
Cuba		42	25	30	49	44	0.00	-10.20
Dominican Republic		6,129	5,948	6,056	6,123	6,511	0.43	6.34
United States Virgin Islands		2,575			1,804	2,216	0.15	22.84
Other countries of the Caribbean	(*)	27,785	24,741	24,189	22,929	24,335	1.61	6.13
Central America		3,935	3,243	3,272	3,615	4,331	0.29	19.81
Belize		23	19	38	50	52	0.00	4.00
Costa Rica		1,142	690	785	795	1,285	0.09	61.64
El Salvador		125	98	113	175	161	0.01	-8.00
Guatemala		374	422	443	550	543	0.04	-1.27
Honduras		94	91	142	159	166	0.01	4.40
Nicaragua		91	49	45	75	72	0.00	-4.00
Panama		853	788	766	888	986	0.07	11.04
Other countries of Central America		1,233	1,086	940	923	1,066	0.07	15.49
North America		1,219,787	1,173,826	1,244,696	1,308,692	1,393,324	92.38	6.47
Canada		16,690	15,012	19,632	23,290	23,631	1.57	1.46
Mexico		10,856	8,388	8,195	8,057	9,540	0.63	18.41
United States of America		1,192,241	1,150,426	1,216,869	1,277,345	1,360,153	90.18	6.48
South America		12,646	11,173	11,249	12,118	14,370	0.95	18.58
Argentina		1,870	1,961	2,230	2,035	2,537	0.17	24.67
Bolivia		396	450	463	453	467	0.03	3.09
Brazil		2,024	1,882	1,916	2,300	2,667	0.18	15.96
Chile		846	650	637	649	760	0.05	17.10
Colombia		1,996	2,023	2,123	2,501	2,881	0.19	15.19
Ecuador		199	186	159	175	246	0.02	40.57
French Guiana		15	5	3	18	24	0.00	33.33
Guyana		9	15	17	27	12	0.00	-55.56
Paraguay		41	27	64	41	85	0.01	107.32
Peru		451	335	380	418	555	0.04	32.78
Suriname		14	20	30	19	38	0.00	100.00
Uruguay		218	142	193	169	424	0.03	150.89
Venezuela		3,083	2,465	2,403	2,909	3,287	0.22	12.99
Other countries of South America		1,484	1,012	631	404	387	0.03	-4.21
EAST ASIA AND THE PACIFIC		3,472	2,997	3,342	3,926	4,819	0.32	22.75
North-East Asia		1,231	1,194	1,240	1,584	1,874	0.12	18.31
China		429	448	514	636	684	0.05	7.55
Hong Kong, China		139	86	81	91	142	0.01	56.04
Japan		638	642	625	805	984	0.07	22.24
Taiwan, Province of China		25	18	20	52	64	0.00	23.08
South-East Asia		332	199	162	209	211	0.01	0.96
Philippines		256	113	153	186	172	0.01	-7.53
Thailand		76	86	9	23	39	0.00	69.57
Australasia		1,108	861	891	1,261	1,424	0.09	12.93
Australia		1,018	781	813	1,175	1,323	0.09	12.60
New Zealand		90	80	78	86	101	0.01	17.44
Other East Asia and the Pacific		801	743	1,049	872	1,310	0.09	50.23
Other countries of Asia		801	743	1,049	872	1,310	0.09	50.23
EUROPE		29,903	29,951	24,315	26,231	32,093	2.13	22.35
Central/Eastern Europe		1,074	1,431	1,101	1,334	1,661	0.11	24.51

Yearbook of Tourism Statistics, Data 2008 – 2012, 2014 Edition

PUERTO RICO

3. Arrivals of non-resident tourists in hotels and similar establishments, by country of residence

	2008	2009	2010	2011	2012	Market share 2012	% Change 2012-2011
Baltic countries		207	59	80	144	0.01	80.00
Bulgaria	27	16	28	64	11	0.00	-82.81
Czech Republic	61	82	78	113	175	0.01	54.87
Hungary	84	46	48	110	98	0.01	-10.91
Poland	60	161	82	142	190	0.01	33.80
Romania	43	40	33	44	79	0.01	79.55
Russian Federation	799	879	746	771	917	0.06	18.94
Slovakia		207	27	10	47	0.00	370.00
Northern Europe	**6,614**	**5,087**	**6,015**	**6,216**	**6,686**	**0.44**	**7.56**
Denmark	547	656	612	670	679	0.05	1.34
Finland	207	241	369	354	413	0.03	16.67
Iceland	25	11	33	34	26	0.00	-23.53
Ireland	382	313	346	487	452	0.03	-7.19
Norway	406	301	358	348	460	0.03	32.18
Sweden	789	677	762	852	896	0.06	5.16
United Kingdom	4,258	2,888	3,535	3,471	3,760	0.25	8.33
Southern Europe	**9,044**	**9,081**	**6,972**	**6,873**	**7,325**	**0.49**	**6.58**
Albania		38	53	62	67	0.00	8.06
Gibraltar	6	33	3	4	24	0.00	500.00
Greece	156	437	442	407	468	0.03	14.99
Italy	1,371	1,413	1,306	1,404	1,862	0.12	32.62
Malta	22	16	14	7	13	0.00	85.71
Portugal	146	296	146	210	79	0.01	-62.38
San Marino	4	12	6	3	8	0.00	166.67
Spain	7,267	6,754	4,739	4,666	4,666	0.31	0.00
Yugoslavia, SFR (former)	72	82	263	110	138	0.01	25.45
Western Europe	**6,275**	**6,253**	**6,738**	**7,999**	**11,230**	**0.74**	**40.39**
Austria	328	215	265	351	339	0.02	-3.42
Belgium	585	479	636	566	634	0.04	12.01
France	1,243	1,499	1,521	1,933	2,450	0.16	26.75
Germany	2,582	2,676	2,932	3,586	5,488	0.36	53.04
Luxembourg	22	25	29	45	52	0.00	15.56
Netherlands	808	784	808	823	1,366	0.09	65.98
Switzerland	707	575	547	695	901	0.06	29.64
East Mediterranean Europe	**395**	**414**	**431**	**561**	**631**	**0.04**	**12.48**
Israel	332	310	355	480	436	0.03	-9.17
Turkey	63	104	76	81	195	0.01	140.74
Other Europe	**6,501**	**7,685**	**3,058**	**3,248**	**4,560**	**0.30**	**40.39**
Other countries of Europe	6,501	7,685	3,058	3,248	4,560	0.30	40.39
MIDDLE EAST	**82**	**111**	**135**	**38**	**67**	**0.00**	**76.32**
Egypt	23	9	85	3	20	0.00	566.67
Iraq					2	0.00	
Saudi Arabia	59	102	50	35	45	0.00	28.57
SOUTH ASIA	**57**	**210**	**167**	**338**	**348**	**0.02**	**2.96**
India	57	210	167	338	348	0.02	2.96
NOT SPECIFIED	**27,425**	**27,256**	**30,671**	**26,858**	**24,242**	**1.61**	**-9.74**
Other countries of the World (*)	27,425	27,256	30,671	26,858	24,242	1.61	-9.74

606

QATAR

3. Arrivals of non-resident tourists in hotels and similar establishments, by country of residence

		2008	2009	2010	2011	2012	Market share 2012	% Change 2012-2011
TOTAL	(*)	1,404,850	1,658,569	1,518,953	2,527,285	2,461,276	100.00	-2.61
AFRICA				86,118	52,353	138,314	5.62	164.19
Other Africa				86,118	52,353	138,314	5.62	164.19
All countries of Africa				86,118	52,353	138,314	5.62	164.19
EAST ASIA AND THE PACIFIC		216,742	264,550	298,395	567,543	425,912	17.30	-24.96
Other East Asia and the Pacific		216,742	264,550	298,395	567,543	425,912	17.30	-24.96
All countries of Asia		216,742	264,550	298,395	567,543	425,912	17.30	-24.96
EUROPE		329,059	406,725	730,034	1,079,523	619,829	25.18	-42.58
Other Europe		329,059	406,725	730,034	1,079,523	619,829	25.18	-42.58
All countries of Europe	(*)	329,059	406,725	730,034	1,079,523	619,829	25.18	-42.58
MIDDLE EAST		628,440	679,859	404,406	827,866	529,112	21.50	-36.09
Bahrain				23,028	38,500	26,148	1.06	-32.08
Kuwait				29,031	46,307	33,012	1.34	-28.71
Oman				12,573	18,637	47,001	1.91	152.19
Saudi Arabia				100,453	203,871	133,675	5.43	-34.43
United Arab Emirates				62,619	86,380	67,413	2.74	-21.96
Other countries of Middle East				176,702	434,171	221,863	9.01	-48.90
All countries of Middle East		628,440	679,859					
NOT SPECIFIED		230,609	307,435			748,109	30.40	
Other countries of the World		230,609	307,435			748,109	30.40	

Yearbook of Tourism Statistics, Data 2008 – 2012, 2014 Edition

QATAR

5. Overnight stays of non-resident tourists in hotels and similar establishments, by country of residence

		2008	2009	2010	2011	2012	Market share 2012	% Change 2012-2011
TOTAL	(*)	1,992,786	1,535,145	1,467,034	2,358,575	2,815,160	100.00	19.36
AFRICA				81,175	48,245	193,133	6.86	300.32
Other Africa				81,175	48,245	193,133	6.86	300.32
All countries of Africa				81,175	48,245	193,133	6.86	300.32
EAST ASIA AND THE PACIFIC		299,177	283,557	324,222	541,929	555,904	19.75	2.58
Other East Asia and the Pacific		299,177	283,557	324,222	541,929	555,904	19.75	2.58
All countries of Asia		299,177	283,557	324,222	541,929	555,904	19.75	2.58
EUROPE		503,902	377,394	679,776	1,023,782	899,685	31.96	-12.12
Other Europe		503,902	377,394	679,776	1,023,782	899,685	31.96	-12.12
All countries of Europe	(*)	503,902	377,394	679,776	1,023,782	899,685	31.96	-12.12
MIDDLE EAST		809,993	606,729	381,861	744,619	529,981	18.83	-28.83
Bahrain				20,658	34,770	28,664	1.02	-17.56
Kuwait				24,335	37,683	30,911	1.10	-17.97
Oman				12,887	17,905	21,238	0.75	18.61
Saudi Arabia				75,589	157,165	120,580	4.28	-23.28
United Arab Emirates				53,757	71,164	91,776	3.26	28.96
Other countries of Middle East				194,635	425,932	236,812	8.41	-44.40
All countries of Middle East		809,993	606,729					
NOT SPECIFIED		379,714	267,465			636,457	22.61	
Other countries of the World		379,714	267,465			636,457	22.61	

REPUBLIC OF MOLDOVA

2. Arrivals of non-resident visitors at national borders, by nationality

		2008	2009	2010	2011	2012	Market share 2012	% Change 2012-2011
TOTAL	(*)	8,710	9,189	8,956	10,788	12,797	100.00	18.62
AFRICA			2	2	14			
Central Africa					1			
Congo					1			
North Africa				1	2			
Algeria				1	2			
Southern Africa				1	5			
South Africa				1	3			
Swaziland					2			
West Africa			2		6			
Benin			2					
Ghana					5			
Mauritania					1			
AMERICAS		305	232	524	651	593	4.63	-8.91
Caribbean					23			
British Virgin Islands					23			
North America		272	227	490	611	577	4.51	-5.56
Canada		33	33	38	53	40	0.31	-24.53
Mexico				1		3	0.02	
United States of America		239	194	451	558	534	4.17	-4.30
South America		33	5	34	17	16	0.13	-5.88
Argentina			2	1	2			
Bolivia			1			1	0.01	
Brazil		33		29	11	15	0.12	36.36
Colombia			1					
Ecuador			1					
Peru				3	4			
Venezuela			1					
EAST ASIA AND THE PACIFIC		188	107	162	545	375	2.93	-31.19
North-East Asia		169	106	133	487	305	2.38	-37.37
China		19	8	27	166	75	0.59	-54.82
Japan		119	76	93	258	193	1.51	-25.19
Korea, Dem. People's Republic of		17						
Korea, Republic of				12	23	37	0.29	60.87
Mongolia				1				
Taiwan, Province of China		14	22		40			
South-East Asia		11	1	3	34	25	0.20	-26.47
Indonesia		11						
Philippines				1	1			
Singapore			1		2			
Thailand				2	2	8	0.06	300.00
Viet Nam					29	17	0.13	-41.38
Australasia		8		26	24	45	0.35	87.50
Australia		6		25	16	40	0.31	150.00
New Zealand		2		1	8	5	0.04	-37.50
EUROPE		8,209	8,837	8,229	9,559	11,753	91.84	22.95
Central/Eastern Europe		5,280	4,744	4,685	5,459	6,567	51.32	20.30
Armenia		23	49	23	39	21	0.16	-46.15
Azerbaijan		37	76	29	13	41	0.32	215.38
Belarus		145	176	105	44	57	0.45	29.55
Bulgaria		46	380	324	289	401	3.13	38.75
Czech Republic		140	40	24	57	93	0.73	63.16
Estonia		40	42	70	76	58	0.45	-23.68
Georgia		21	53	7	85	19	0.15	-77.65
Hungary		36	31	18	84	79	0.62	-5.95

609

REPUBLIC OF MOLDOVA

2. Arrivals of non-resident visitors at national borders, by nationality

	2008	2009	2010	2011	2012	Market share 2012	% Change 2012-2011
Kazakhstan	23	56	23	16	29	0.23	81.25
Kyrgyzstan	9	15	5	11	19	0.15	72.73
Latvia	95	14	80	40	35	0.27	-12.50
Lithuania	57	34	12	69	88	0.69	27.54
Poland	140	291	204	371	505	3.95	36.12
Romania	1,070	765	1,698	1,600	1,782	13.93	11.38
Russian Federation	1,793	1,713	1,327	1,404	2,204	17.22	56.98
Slovakia	54	11	6	52	130	1.02	150.00
Tajikistan	4	4		3	9	0.07	200.00
Turkmenistan		2		12	2	0.02	-83.33
Ukraine	1,542	979	730	1,189	987	7.71	-16.99
Uzbekistan	5	13		5	8	0.06	60.00
Northern Europe	**652**	**1,032**	**625**	**965**	**1,031**	**8.06**	**6.84**
Denmark	20	100	15	54	26	0.20	-51.85
Finland	56	84	66	128	49	0.38	-61.72
Ireland	35	10	7	12	19	0.15	58.33
Norway	46	35	33	87	66	0.52	-24.14
Sweden	65	59	99	334	207	1.62	-38.02
United Kingdom	430	744	405	350	664	5.19	89.71
Southern Europe	**700**	**612**	**764**	**789**	**920**	**7.19**	**16.60**
Albania	3	3		3	4	0.03	33.33
Bosnia and Herzegovina	6	2	2	52	4	0.03	-92.31
Croatia	47	85	37	12	12	0.09	0.00
Greece	86	118	91	86	78	0.61	-9.30
Italy	440	258	474	445	622	4.86	39.78
Montenegro				3	2	0.02	-33.33
Portugal	32	44	5	14	8	0.06	-42.86
San Marino	1			50			
Serbia			19	16	55	0.43	243.75
Serbia and Montenegro	12	26					
Slovenia	20	8	53	31	55	0.43	77.42
Spain	45	60	79	69	72	0.56	4.35
TFYR of Macedonia	8	8	4	8	8	0.06	0.00
Western Europe	**954**	**1,265**	**1,392**	**1,689**	**2,209**	**17.26**	**30.79**
Austria	115	147	103	95	269	2.10	183.16
Belgium	16	17	103	46	129	1.01	180.43
France	174	196	283	248	155	1.21	-37.50
Germany	502	460	482	1,001	1,275	9.96	27.37
Luxembourg			2	2	1	0.01	-50.00
Netherlands	125	154	311	219	288	2.25	31.51
Switzerland	22	291	108	78	92	0.72	17.95
East Mediterranean Europe	**623**	**1,184**	**763**	**657**	**1,026**	**8.02**	**56.16**
Cyprus	13	26	12	42	44	0.34	4.76
Israel	149	156	225	138	163	1.27	18.12
Turkey	461	1,002	526	477	819	6.40	71.70
MIDDLE EAST	**4**	**5**	**24**	**10**	**45**	**0.35**	**350.00**
Egypt				19	6	0.05	
Iraq	1	1	1		2	0.02	
Jordan	1		1		1	0.01	
Kuwait				1	2	0.02	100.00
Lebanon		1	1		17	0.13	
Syrian Arab Republic		3		3	16	0.13	433.33
United Arab Emirates	2		2	6	1	0.01	-83.33
SOUTH ASIA	**4**	**6**	**15**	**9**	**18**	**0.14**	**100.00**
Afghanistan				12			
Bangladesh					1		

610

REPUBLIC OF MOLDOVA

2. Arrivals of non-resident visitors at national borders, by nationality

	2008	2009	2010	2011	2012	Market share 2012	% Change 2012-2011
India	4	5	2	6	12	0.09	100.00
Iran, Islamic Republic of		1	1	1	5	0.04	400.00
Pakistan				1	1	0.01	0.00
NOT SPECIFIED					**13**	**0.10**	
Other countries of the World					13	0.10	

Yearbook of Tourism Statistics, Data 2008 – 2012, 2014 Edition

REPUBLIC OF MOLDOVA

4. Arrivals of non-resident tourists in all types of accommodation establishments, by nationality

		2008	2009	2010	2011	2012	Market share 2012	% Change 2012-2011
TOTAL	(*)	73,288	59,563	63,593	75,000	88,956	100.00	18.61
AFRICA		54	127	127	300	340	0.38	13.33
Other Africa		54	127	127	300	340	0.38	13.33
All countries of Africa		54	127	127	300	340	0.38	13.33
AMERICAS		3,559	3,703	3,666	5,245	7,146	8.03	36.24
North America		3,452	3,636	3,524	4,960	6,855	7.71	38.21
Canada		393	274	388	495	444	0.50	-10.30
United States of America		3,040	3,328	3,132	4,419	6,338	7.12	43.43
Other countries of North America		19	34	4	46	73	0.08	58.70
South America		100	60	108	201	235	0.26	16.92
All countries of South America		100	60	108	201	235	0.26	16.92
Other Americas		7	7	34	84	56	0.06	-33.33
Other countries of the Americas		7	7	34	84	56	0.06	-33.33
EAST ASIA AND THE PACIFIC		829	806	1,006	1,968	2,068	2.32	5.08
North-East Asia		473	453	525	985	1,122	1.26	13.91
China		143	144	188	518	555	0.62	7.14
Japan		330	309	337	467	567	0.64	21.41
Other East Asia and the Pacific		356	353	481	983	946	1.06	-3.76
Other countries of Asia		248	220	426	837	727	0.82	-13.14
All countries of Oceania		108	133	55	146	219	0.25	50.00
EUROPE		68,846	54,927	58,794	67,487	79,402	89.26	17.66
Central/Eastern Europe		42,743	31,669	36,332	40,749	45,698	51.37	12.15
Armenia		321	252	167	324	313	0.35	-3.40
Azerbaijan		397	451	332	471	611	0.69	29.72
Belarus		1,455	1,379	932	923	1,194	1.34	29.36
Bulgaria		1,431	1,458	1,384	1,163	1,373	1.54	18.06
Czech Republic		923	684	438	1,145	771	0.87	-32.66
Estonia		333	241	504	456	373	0.42	-18.20
Georgia		435	259	433	616	717	0.81	16.40
Hungary		715	450	480	755	552	0.62	-26.89
Kazakhstan		496	362	247	247	453	0.51	83.40
Kyrgyzstan		129	124	510	112	147	0.17	31.25
Latvia		400	178	273	332	249	0.28	-25.00
Lithuania		710	440	400	506	600	0.67	18.58
Poland		2,145	1,639	1,390	1,872	2,295	2.58	22.60
Romania		15,858	8,796	15,403	16,097	17,549	19.73	9.02
Russian Federation		8,428	7,314	6,484	7,840	9,244	10.39	17.91
Slovakia		322	240	198	292	263	0.30	-9.93
Tajikistan		131	117	60	186	377	0.42	102.69
Turkmenistan		45	39	268	30	82	0.09	173.33
Ukraine		7,944	7,115	6,083	7,194	8,216	9.24	14.21
Uzbekistan		125	131	346	188	319	0.36	69.68
Northern Europe		3,913	4,112	4,062	5,215	5,956	6.70	14.21
Denmark		245	367	302	311	383	0.43	23.15
Finland		354	360	764	510	386	0.43	-24.31
Ireland		367	385	172	466	328	0.37	-29.61
Norway		296	377	342	598	461	0.52	-22.91
Sweden		800	781	889	1,432	1,144	1.29	-20.11
United Kingdom		1,851	1,842	1,593	1,898	3,254	3.66	71.44
Southern Europe		7,151	6,157	6,118	7,272	8,197	9.21	12.72
Albania		79	37	139	104	144	0.16	38.46
Bosnia and Herzegovina		80	36	106	162	93	0.10	-42.59
Croatia		158	233	221	247	191	0.21	-22.67
Greece		864	923	598	648	762	0.86	17.59
Italy		4,766	3,777	3,942	4,447	5,001	5.62	12.46

612

REPUBLIC OF MOLDOVA

4. Arrivals of non-resident tourists in all types of accommodation establishments, by nationality

	2008	2009	2010	2011	2012	Market share 2012	% Change 2012-2011
Montenegro				49	60	0.07	22.45
Portugal	146	138	148	347	147	0.17	-57.64
Serbia			148	201	237	0.27	17.91
Serbia and Montenegro	236	157					
Slovenia	287	283	345	388	632	0.71	62.89
Spain	535	573	471	679	930	1.05	36.97
Western Europe	**8,875**	**8,390**	**7,966**	**9,011**	**11,003**	**12.37**	**22.11**
Austria	1,059	927	820	1,003	1,124	1.26	12.06
Belgium	505	388	405	577	678	0.76	17.50
France	1,878	1,805	1,479	2,130	2,103	2.36	-1.27
Germany	4,018	2,959	3,468	3,863	5,520	6.21	42.89
Luxembourg	50	77	22	31	34	0.04	9.68
Netherlands	973	979	1,283	1,036	977	1.10	-5.69
Switzerland	392	1,255	489	371	567	0.64	52.83
East Mediterranean Europe	**5,455**	**3,969**	**3,837**	**4,306**	**7,701**	**8.66**	**78.84**
Cyprus				204	249	0.28	22.06
Israel	1,217	878	1,299	1,321	1,654	1.86	25.21
Turkey	4,238	3,091	2,538	2,781	5,798	6.52	108.49
Other Europe	**709**	**630**	**479**	**934**	**847**	**0.95**	**-9.31**
Other countries of Europe	709	630	479	934	847	0.95	-9.31

Yearbook of Tourism Statistics, Data 2008 – 2012, 2014 Edition

REPUBLIC OF MOLDOVA

6. Overnight stays of non-resident tourists in all types of accommodation establishments, by nationality

		2008	2009	2010	2011	2012	Market share 2012	% Change 2012-2011
TOTAL	(*)	201,624	147,762	162,755	173,893	190,766	100.00	9.70
AFRICA		145	293	401	687	598	0.31	-12.95
Other Africa		145	293	401	687	598	0.31	-12.95
All countries of Africa		145	293	401	687	598	0.31	-12.95
AMERICAS		11,939	11,410	12,780	12,646	13,854	7.26	9.55
North America		11,574	11,185	12,097	10,963	13,382	7.01	22.07
Canada		1,195	1,079	1,500	1,208	1,016	0.53	-15.89
United States of America		10,335	10,032	10,593	9,565	12,195	6.39	27.50
Other countries of North America		44	74	4	190	171	0.09	-10.00
South America		347	207	560	918	395	0.21	-56.97
All countries of South America		347	207	560	918	395	0.21	-56.97
Other Americas		18	18	123	765	77	0.04	-89.93
Other countries of the Americas		18	18	123	765	77	0.04	-89.93
EAST ASIA AND THE PACIFIC		2,168	2,268	2,817	5,481	4,378	2.29	-20.12
North-East Asia		1,329	1,374	1,429	2,978	2,648	1.39	-11.08
China		581	514	569	1,771	1,245	0.65	-29.70
Japan		748	860	860	1,207	1,403	0.74	16.24
Other East Asia and the Pacific		839	894	1,388	2,503	1,730	0.91	-30.88
Other countries of Asia		600	639	1,188	2,181	1,353	0.71	-37.96
All countries of Oceania		239	255	200	322	377	0.20	17.08
EUROPE		187,372	133,791	146,757	155,079	171,936	90.13	10.87
Central/Eastern Europe		106,433	75,438	86,134	93,390	100,362	52.61	7.47
Armenia		1,220	897	641	948	695	0.36	-26.69
Azerbaijan		1,273	1,260	1,074	1,237	1,347	0.71	8.89
Belarus		4,440	6,151	3,092	3,188	3,759	1.97	17.91
Bulgaria		3,866	2,867	2,512	2,815	3,512	1.84	24.76
Czech Republic		2,127	1,297	918	2,288	2,464	1.29	7.69
Estonia		931	604	1,099	1,140	924	0.48	-18.95
Georgia		1,209	821	1,169	1,449	1,442	0.76	-0.48
Hungary		1,867	1,028	1,146	1,497	1,113	0.58	-25.65
Kazakhstan		1,124	962	724	653	963	0.50	47.47
Kyrgyzstan		409	431	1,377	346	441	0.23	27.46
Latvia		1,106	455	799	741	554	0.29	-25.24
Lithuania		1,658	1,089	1,006	1,103	1,227	0.64	11.24
Poland		4,783	3,964	3,084	4,211	4,235	2.22	0.57
Romania		38,226	19,144	37,728	36,487	37,969	19.90	4.06
Russian Federation		23,956	20,114	17,043	20,117	21,615	11.33	7.45
Slovakia		752	491	511	573	570	0.30	-0.52
Tajikistan		487	328	199	458	1,159	0.61	153.06
Turkmenistan		135	324	538	121	183	0.10	51.24
Ukraine		16,457	12,834	10,811	13,596	15,551	8.15	14.38
Uzbekistan		407	377	663	422	639	0.33	51.42
Northern Europe		10,765	10,776	11,016	12,803	12,569	6.59	-1.83
Denmark		725	1,191	712	803	917	0.48	14.20
Finland		747	941	2,102	1,251	719	0.38	-42.53
Ireland		969	945	528	1,345	713	0.37	-46.99
Norway		818	1,103	1,045	1,437	1,105	0.58	-23.10
Sweden		2,210	1,941	2,195	3,177	2,742	1.44	-13.69
United Kingdom		5,296	4,655	4,434	4,790	6,373	3.34	33.05
Southern Europe		17,271	14,161	15,658	17,816	19,743	10.35	10.82
Albania		240	92	309	254	365	0.19	43.70
Bosnia and Herzegovina		224	126	289	340	232	0.12	-31.76
Croatia		436	538	628	611	444	0.23	-27.33
Greece		1,894	2,053	1,556	1,300	1,568	0.82	20.62
Italy		11,628	9,044	10,287	11,274	12,809	6.71	13.62

Yearbook of Tourism Statistics, Data 2008 – 2012, 2014 Editio

REPUBLIC OF MOLDOVA

6. Overnight stays of non-resident tourists in all types of accommodation establishments, by nationality

	2008	2009	2010	2011	2012	Market share 2012	% Change 2012-2011
Montenegro				110	174	0.09	58.18
Portugal	422	284	335	1,004	427	0.22	-57.47
Serbia			374	456	674	0.35	47.81
Serbia and Montenegro	486	356					
Slovenia	619	495	750	859	1,310	0.69	52.50
Spain	1,322	1,173	1,130	1,608	1,740	0.91	8.21
Western Europe	**22,139**	**19,535**	**19,495**	**20,502**	**22,437**	**11.76**	**9.44**
Austria	2,295	1,827	1,819	2,086	2,184	1.14	4.70
Belgium	1,154	949	880	1,140	1,319	0.69	15.70
France	4,365	4,296	3,653	4,675	4,404	2.31	-5.80
Germany	10,847	7,305	8,790	9,112	10,728	5.62	17.73
Luxembourg	97	154	46	43	70	0.04	62.79
Netherlands	2,476	2,381	3,100	2,490	2,553	1.34	2.53
Switzerland	905	2,623	1,207	956	1,179	0.62	23.33
East Mediterranean Europe	**28,859**	**12,341**	**13,151**	**9,212**	**15,583**	**8.17**	**69.16**
Cyprus				554	507	0.27	-8.48
Israel	3,671	2,470	4,472	3,631	4,686	2.46	29.06
Turkey	25,188	9,871	8,679	5,027	10,390	5.45	106.68
Other Europe	**1,905**	**1,540**	**1,303**	**1,356**	**1,242**	**0.65**	**-8.41**
Other countries of Europe	1,905	1,540	1,303	1,356	1,242	0.65	-8.41

Yearbook of Tourism Statistics, Data 2008 – 2012, 2014 Edition

REUNION

1. Arrivals of non-resident tourists at national borders, by country of residence

		2008	2009	2010	2011	2012	Market share 2012	% Change 2012-2011
TOTAL	(*)	**396,400**	**421,900**	**420,200**	**471,300**	**446,500**	**100.00**	**-5.26**
AFRICA		**51,300**	**41,600**	**34,000**	**42,500**	**46,100**	**10.32**	**8.47**
East Africa		**20,800**	**20,300**	**18,400**	**18,200**			
Mauritius		20,800	20,300	18,400	18,200			
Other Africa		**30,500**	**21,300**	**15,600**	**24,300**	**46,100**	**10.32**	**89.71**
Other countries of Africa		30,500	21,300	15,600	24,300			
All countries of Africa						46,100	10.32	
EUROPE		**335,100**	**364,300**	**367,900**	**406,100**	**379,400**	**84.97**	**-6.57**
Western Europe		**311,000**	**344,300**	**346,200**	**381,600**	**355,900**	**79.71**	**-6.73**
France		311,000	344,300	346,200	381,600	355,900	79.71	-6.73
Other Europe		**24,100**	**20,000**	**21,700**	**24,500**	**23,500**	**5.26**	**-4.08**
Other countries of Europe		24,100	20,000	21,700	24,500	23,500	5.26	-4.08
NOT SPECIFIED		**10,000**	**16,000**	**18,300**	**22,700**	**21,000**	**4.70**	**-7.49**
Other countries of the World		10,000	16,000	18,300	22,700	21,000	4.70	-7.49

Yearbook of Tourism Statistics, Data 2008 – 2012, 2014 Edition

ROMANIA

2. Arrivals of non-resident visitors at national borders, by country of residence

	2008	2009	2010	2011	2012	Market share 2012	% Change 2012-2011
TOTAL	8,862,119	7,575,298	7,498,307	7,611,124	7,936,694	100.00	4.28
AFRICA	12,638	12,803	14,464	15,568	16,325	0.21	4.86
East Africa	827	968	1,293	1,469	1,510	0.02	2.79
Burundi	11	6	8	10	17	0.00	70.00
Comoros	3	3	7	1	6	0.00	500.00
Djibouti		1		1			
Eritrea	47	6	6	11	7	0.00	-36.36
Ethiopia	45	36	44	69	65	0.00	-5.80
Kenya	98	100	118	153	155	0.00	1.31
Madagascar	53	84	102	76	73	0.00	-3.95
Mauritius	445	532	695	712	706	0.01	-0.84
Mozambique	4	21	21	14	24	0.00	71.43
Rwanda	8	13	14	14	12	0.00	-14.29
Somalia	7	3	8	9	15	0.00	66.67
Uganda	12	23	31	30	50	0.00	66.67
United Republic of Tanzania	43	75	176	273	230	0.00	-15.75
Zambia	16	18	17	25	39	0.00	56.00
Zimbabwe	35	47	46	71	111	0.00	56.34
Central Africa	690	645	653	789	710	0.01	-10.01
Angola	102	126	97	149	150	0.00	0.67
Cameroon	279	269	316	359	313	0.00	-12.81
Central African Republic	31	26	13	14	16	0.00	14.29
Chad	4	5	8	8	10	0.00	25.00
Congo	228	183	119	130	91	0.00	-30.00
Democratic Republic of the Congo	4	15	43	79	80	0.00	1.27
Equatorial Guinea	2	1	11	7	14	0.00	100.00
Gabon	36	18	45	42	34	0.00	-19.05
Sao Tome and Principe	4	2	1	1	2	0.00	100.00
North Africa	7,319	8,029	9,165	9,492	9,878	0.12	4.07
Algeria	666	761	748	896	957	0.01	6.81
Morocco	2,100	2,197	2,472	2,887	3,302	0.04	14.37
Sudan	416	334	356	296	231	0.00	-21.96
Tunisia	4,137	4,737	5,589	5,413	5,388	0.07	-0.46
Southern Africa	1,761	1,249	1,465	1,834	2,104	0.03	14.72
Botswana	8	8	10	10	17	0.00	70.00
Lesotho	2	1	2	1	4	0.00	300.00
Namibia	11	15	59	51	42	0.00	-17.65
South Africa	1,740	1,225	1,394	1,772	2,041	0.03	15.18
West Africa	2,041	1,912	1,860	1,963	2,091	0.03	6.52
Benin	87	47	34	53	45	0.00	-15.09
Burkina Faso	42	38	21	31	47	0.00	51.61
Cape Verde	117	63	84	69	66	0.00	-4.35
Côte d'Ivoire	140	150	160	192	173	0.00	-9.90
Gambia	17	11	15	6	10	0.00	66.67
Ghana	124	149	143	177	132	0.00	-25.42
Guinea	187	144	69	66	71	0.00	7.58
Guinea-Bissau	23	3	5	9	17	0.00	88.89
Liberia	41	15	11	17	12	0.00	-29.41
Mali	34	20	21	19	30	0.00	57.89
Mauritania	38	49	35	23	12	0.00	-47.83
Niger	24	24	39	28	12	0.00	-57.14
Nigeria	918	911	948	1,023	1,144	0.01	11.83
Senegal	175	249	218	198	237	0.00	19.70
Sierra Leone	32	15	37	30	32	0.00	6.67
Togo	42	24	20	22	51	0.00	131.82

Yearbook of Tourism Statistics, Data 2008 – 2012, 2014 Edition

ROMANIA

2. Arrivals of non-resident visitors at national borders, by country of residence

	2008	2009	2010	2011	2012	Market share 2012	% Change 2012-2011
Other Africa				28	21	32	0.00	52.38
Other countries of Africa				28	21	32	0.00	52.38
AMERICAS	191,709	168,744	170,757	182,169	207,627	2.62	13.97
Caribbean	601	545	542	505	674	0.01	33.47
Cuba	396	390	311	245	354	0.00	44.49
Dominican Republic	136	102	160	186	233	0.00	25.27
Haiti	21	16	21	13	22	0.00	69.23
Jamaica	48	37	50	61	65	0.00	6.56
Central America	744	695	834	918	982	0.01	6.97
Belize	10	1	4	11	9	0.00	-18.18
Costa Rica	224	237	301	272	248	0.00	-8.82
El Salvador	70	55	69	70	68	0.00	-2.86
Guatemala	158	142	172	151	159	0.00	5.30
Honduras	148	132	168	268	338	0.00	26.12
Nicaragua	45	49	45	75	53	0.00	-29.33
Panama	89	79	75	71	107	0.00	50.70
North America	180,257	158,019	158,688	168,589	192,557	2.43	14.22
Canada	39,989	36,592	38,740	41,595	44,964	0.57	8.10
Mexico	2,958	2,293	2,999	3,659	3,853	0.05	5.30
United States of America	137,310	119,134	116,949	123,335	143,740	1.81	16.54
South America	10,107	9,485	10,427	11,949	13,236	0.17	10.77
Argentina	2,093	1,961	1,841	2,193	2,317	0.03	5.65
Bolivia	137	194	181	204	158	0.00	-22.55
Brazil	4,169	3,741	4,331	5,216	5,856	0.07	12.27
Chile	784	681	768	885	1,095	0.01	23.73
Colombia	687	680	787	744	956	0.01	28.49
Ecuador	543	532	538	543	584	0.01	7.55
Guyana	9	6	5	9	9	0.00	0.00
Paraguay	101	89	112	120	132	0.00	10.00
Peru	644	630	792	900	981	0.01	9.00
Suriname	9	5	13	17	39	0.00	129.41
Uruguay	198	205	270	251	332	0.00	32.27
Venezuela	733	761	789	867	777	0.01	-10.38
Other Americas			266	208	178	0.00	-14.42
Other countries of the Americas			266	208	178	0.00	-14.42
EAST ASIA AND THE PACIFIC	97,417	70,145	79,098	92,027	97,728	1.23	6.19
North-East Asia	52,733	41,899	44,748	51,524	55,417	0.70	7.56
China	26,182	19,681	17,796	18,570	19,991	0.25	7.65
Hong Kong, China	977	788	824	1,225	2,230	0.03	82.04
Japan	13,095	10,345	12,333	13,544	14,252	0.18	5.23
Korea, Dem. People's Republic of	174	96	114	114	120	0.00	5.26
Korea, Republic of	11,129	10,109	12,628	16,077	16,370	0.21	1.82
Mongolia	249	233	150	181	180	0.00	-0.55
Taiwan, Province of China	927	647	903	1,813	2,274	0.03	25.43
South-East Asia	28,883	14,662	20,829	25,072	26,324	0.33	4.99
Cambodia	9	25	27	38	48	0.00	26.32
Indonesia	3,288	1,279	2,001	2,405	3,104	0.04	29.06
Lao People's Democratic Republic		6	5		10	0.00	
Malaysia	1,702	1,293	2,078	1,764	1,728	0.02	-2.04
Myanmar	1,191	850	664	1,324	842	0.01	-36.40
Philippines	18,130	7,824	13,372	16,668	17,328	0.22	3.96
Singapore	683	548	593	735	1,014	0.01	37.96
Thailand	2,308	1,159	1,027	984	805	0.01	-18.19
Viet Nam	1,572	1,678	1,062	1,154	1,445	0.02	25.22
Australasia	15,761	13,502	13,323	15,263	15,847	0.20	3.83
Australia	12,927	11,218	11,117	12,976	13,272	0.17	2.28
New Zealand	2,834	2,284	2,206	2,287	2,575	0.03	12.59

618

ROMANIA

2. Arrivals of non-resident visitors at national borders, by country of residence

	2008	2009	2010	2011	2012	Market share 2012	% Change 2012-2011
Melanesia	5	41	23	16			
Fiji	5	41	23	16			
Other East Asia and the Pacific	35	41	175	152	140	0.00	-7.89
Other countries East Asia/Pacific	35	41	175	152	140	0.00	-7.89
EUROPE	8,506,343	7,278,936	7,179,264	7,266,677	7,556,131	95.21	3.98
Central/Eastern Europe	5,913,628	5,065,085	5,008,381	4,955,252	5,157,216	64.98	4.08
Armenia	1,260	1,511	1,836	2,067	2,450	0.03	18.53
Azerbaijan	2,682	2,499	3,191	4,024	5,821	0.07	44.66
Belarus	37,190	42,933	56,757	56,871	95,496	1.20	67.92
Bulgaria	1,114,082	877,287	786,452	797,382	943,501	11.89	18.32
Czech Republic	135,368	100,656	79,709	80,145	96,437	1.22	20.33
Estonia	6,179	3,913	4,471	3,981	3,978	0.05	-0.08
Georgia	4,520	7,573	9,900	16,617	21,684	0.27	30.49
Hungary	1,950,383	1,836,334	1,734,844	1,545,502	1,547,014	19.49	0.10
Kazakhstan	1,053	1,266	1,948	2,226	2,723	0.03	22.33
Kyrgyzstan	208	114	183	288	226	0.00	-21.53
Latvia	4,153	3,760	3,669	4,425	4,239	0.05	-4.20
Lithuania	10,156	10,155	9,153	8,771	10,810	0.14	23.25
Poland	276,525	222,783	237,922	249,731	300,794	3.79	20.45
Republic of Moldova	1,428,559	1,042,871	1,216,140	1,330,322	1,120,272	14.12	-15.79
Russian Federation	62,648	73,203	91,907	119,502	158,983	2.00	33.04
Slovakia	148,444	113,990	97,676	84,310	100,061	1.26	18.68
Tajikistan	21	48	84	94	61	0.00	-35.11
Turkmenistan	148	129	207	348	314	0.00	-9.77
Ukraine	729,758	723,813	672,065	648,394	739,545	9.32	14.06
Uzbekistan	291	242	219	252	233	0.00	-7.54
Other countries Central/East Europe		5	48		2,574	0.03	
Northern Europe	206,636	165,980	154,462	184,131	183,365	2.31	-0.42
Denmark	16,522	13,168	10,827	13,652	14,225	0.18	4.20
Finland	10,110	8,975	8,266	10,549	7,337	0.09	-30.45
Iceland	916	1,075	2,122	1,767	2,015	0.03	14.04
Ireland	14,579	11,071	10,046	13,054	12,533	0.16	-3.99
Norway	11,978	8,714	7,608	10,446	9,372	0.12	-10.28
Sweden	24,381	19,363	23,964	25,559	25,301	0.32	-1.01
United Kingdom	128,150	103,614	91,629	109,104	112,582	1.42	3.19
Southern Europe	909,609	804,001	827,506	879,960	898,597	11.32	2.12
Albania	4,549	4,919	4,720	6,757	7,142	0.09	5.70
Bosnia and Herzegovina	5,006	3,971	3,603	5,952	7,188	0.09	20.77
Croatia	27,398	25,192	20,326	19,362	19,335	0.24	-0.14
Greece	117,901	89,747	70,593	83,083	76,786	0.97	-7.58
Holy See	5	8	9	7	7	0.00	0.00
Italy	433,167	374,702	330,909	352,310	340,138	4.29	-3.45
Malta	902	1,083	1,465	1,603	3,142	0.04	96.01
Montenegro					2,537	0.03	
Portugal	15,671	20,209	47,460	47,234	41,496	0.52	-12.15
San Marino	252	156	217	231	236	0.00	2.16
Serbia					286,291	3.61	
Serbia and Montenegro	183,812	170,025	243,775	250,531			
Slovenia	36,612	34,563	23,224	16,774	19,081	0.24	13.75
Spain	70,969	66,952	63,306	77,101	74,048	0.93	-3.96
TFYR of Macedonia	13,365	12,474	17,899	19,015	21,170	0.27	11.33
Western Europe	1,066,725	901,923	834,887	882,888	961,144	12.11	8.86
Austria	210,143	180,579	177,544	192,814	217,629	2.74	12.87
Belgium	43,878	36,772	42,407	49,856	47,081	0.59	-5.57
France	183,361	150,052	131,050	153,118	149,769	1.89	-2.19
Germany	521,675	442,805	394,387	381,336	439,219	5.53	15.18
Liechtenstein	222	151	214	479	388	0.00	-19.00

Yearbook of Tourism Statistics, Data 2008 – 2012, 2014 Edition

ROMANIA

2. Arrivals of non-resident visitors at national borders, by country of residence

	2008	2009	2010	2011	2012	Market share 2012	% Change 2012-2011
Luxembourg	1,372	980	854	1,329	1,234	0.02	-7.15
Monaco	20	17	27	25	25	0.00	0.00
Netherlands	79,951	66,947	66,157	78,315	76,134	0.96	-2.78
Switzerland	26,103	23,620	22,247	25,616	29,665	0.37	15.81
East Mediterranean Europe	**409,745**	**341,947**	**354,028**	**364,446**	**355,809**	**4.48**	**-2.37**
Cyprus	11,463	8,492	7,955	10,408	8,742	0.11	-16.01
Israel	95,758	75,918	81,179	83,376	79,984	1.01	-4.07
Turkey	302,524	257,537	264,894	270,662	267,083	3.37	-1.32
MIDDLE EAST	**31,793**	**26,520**	**33,482**	**33,500**	**36,608**	**0.46**	**9.28**
Bahrain	60	67	90	101	98	0.00	-2.97
Egypt	5,517	4,405	6,191	6,397	7,036	0.09	9.99
Iraq	1,979	2,300	2,470	2,634	3,005	0.04	14.09
Jordan	2,396	2,385	2,532	2,520	2,228	0.03	-11.59
Kuwait	468	427	421	532	636	0.01	19.55
Lebanon	5,334	5,051	5,267	4,884	5,045	0.06	3.30
Libya	289	220	326	184	555	0.01	201.63
Oman	65	103	121	204	91	0.00	-55.39
Palestine	503	554	587	573	528	0.01	-7.85
Qatar	199	89	77	133	141	0.00	6.02
Saudi Arabia	565	583	563	853	831	0.01	-2.58
Syrian Arab Republic	13,858	9,846	14,193	13,839	15,732	0.20	13.68
United Arab Emirates	444	395	480	473	492	0.01	4.02
Yemen	116	95	164	173	190	0.00	9.83
SOUTH ASIA	**20,500**	**17,083**	**20,825**	**20,710**	**21,832**	**0.28**	**5.42**
Afghanistan	227	185	218	203	243	0.00	19.70
Bangladesh	998	456	274	202	227	0.00	12.38
India	9,364	6,662	8,861	9,040	9,964	0.13	10.22
Iran, Islamic Republic of	7,368	7,416	8,873	8,626	8,602	0.11	-0.28
Maldives	68	53	129	36	21	0.00	-41.67
Nepal	149	65	223	186	138	0.00	-25.81
Pakistan	1,875	1,689	1,770	1,848	2,020	0.03	9.31
Sri Lanka	451	557	477	569	617	0.01	8.44
NOT SPECIFIED	**1,719**	**1,067**	**417**	**473**	**443**	**0.01**	**-6.34**
Other countries of the World	1,719	1,067	417	473	443	0.01	-6.34

620

ROMANIA

3. Arrivals of non-resident tourists in hotels and similar establishments, by country of residence

	2008	2009	2010	2011	2012	Market share 2012	% Change 2012-2011
TOTAL	1,439,231	1,255,703	1,323,585	1,494,024	1,633,162	100.00	9.31
AFRICA	7,730	7,435	8,854	10,279	14,051	0.86	36.70
Other Africa	7,730	7,435	8,854	10,279	14,051	0.86	36.70
All countries of Africa (*)	7,730	7,435	8,854	10,279	14,051	0.86	36.70
AMERICAS	97,239	93,504	105,060	107,766	116,313	7.12	7.93
North America	90,236	88,063	98,014	100,209	106,934	6.55	6.71
Canada	12,984	10,732	12,174	11,991	13,794	0.84	15.04
Mexico	1,459	1,411	1,535	2,429	3,289	0.20	35.41
United States of America	75,793	75,920	84,305	85,789	89,851	5.50	4.73
Other Americas	7,003	5,441	7,046	7,557	9,379	0.57	24.11
Other countries of the Americas	7,003	5,441	7,046	7,557	9,379	0.57	24.11
EAST ASIA AND THE PACIFIC	54,619	47,908	53,586	66,003	75,131	4.60	13.83
North-East Asia	22,865	18,681	19,188	25,447	28,971	1.77	13.85
China	7,622	6,929	5,936	9,046	11,370	0.70	25.69
Japan	15,243	11,752	13,252	16,401	17,601	1.08	7.32
Other East Asia and the Pacific	31,754	29,227	34,398	40,556	46,160	2.83	13.82
Other countries of Asia	23,314	21,944	26,107	30,045	35,984	2.20	19.77
All countries of Oceania	8,440	7,283	8,291	10,511	10,176	0.62	-3.19
EUROPE	1,264,622	1,085,493	1,132,656	1,288,795	1,405,555	86.06	9.06
Central/Eastern Europe	232,238	198,652	191,838	250,097	281,920	17.26	12.72
Bulgaria	26,227	23,764	24,538	31,276	37,203	2.28	18.95
Czech Republic	19,652	18,530	17,070	19,705	21,653	1.33	9.89
Hungary	89,818	75,569	75,056	85,544	88,782	5.44	3.79
Poland	31,497	29,689	35,573	45,672	50,410	3.09	10.37
Republic of Moldova	22,246	19,893	7,455	25,757	28,635	1.75	11.17
Russian Federation	17,101	13,101	14,714	19,261	27,552	1.69	43.05
Slovakia	11,958	7,510	7,724	9,524	10,940	0.67	14.87
Ukraine	13,739	10,596	9,708	13,358	16,745	1.03	25.36
Northern Europe	129,988	115,105	114,469	130,023	151,242	9.26	16.32
Denmark	12,129	11,104	11,091	13,868	20,194	1.24	45.62
Finland	8,020	7,366	6,332	6,046	5,551	0.34	-8.19
Ireland	7,849	6,957	7,684	7,922	8,331	0.51	5.16
Norway	8,928	8,004	7,455	8,628	11,150	0.68	29.23
Sweden	11,513	10,893	10,512	12,811	14,625	0.90	14.16
United Kingdom	81,549	70,781	71,395	80,748	91,391	5.60	13.18
Southern Europe	296,935	252,047	262,369	300,468	317,959	19.47	5.82
Greece	37,530	36,706	35,824	36,773	34,829	2.13	-5.29
Italy	164,017	141,131	144,496	171,537	181,201	11.10	5.63
Montenegro	644	543	422	550	691	0.04	25.64
Portugal	12,567	7,446	8,692	10,391	12,268	0.75	18.06
Serbia	8,486	7,868	6,714	9,103	11,887	0.73	30.58
Slovenia	6,715	5,362	5,640	5,268	6,702	0.41	27.22
Spain	66,976	52,991	60,581	66,846	70,381	4.31	5.29
Western Europe	458,681	404,019	411,095	448,888	491,821	30.11	9.56
Austria	70,109	57,791	61,013	61,722	62,458	3.82	1.19
Belgium	23,508	22,815	23,126	23,986	26,631	1.63	11.03
France	112,813	99,246	97,934	107,839	116,971	7.16	8.47
Germany	203,092	170,994	175,425	196,714	219,704	13.45	11.69
Luxembourg	1,138	1,143	1,047	1,413	1,343	0.08	-4.95
Netherlands	42,956	36,594	36,286	40,402	45,371	2.78	12.30
Switzerland	5,065	15,436	16,264	16,812	19,343	1.18	15.05
East Mediterranean Europe	92,364	74,479	96,460	113,991	115,362	7.06	1.20
Israel	65,906	53,606	71,630	86,647	81,282	4.98	-6.19
Turkey	26,458	20,873	24,830	27,344	34,080	2.09	24.63

Yearbook of Tourism Statistics, Data 2008 – 2012, 2014 Edition

ROMANIA

3. Arrivals of non-resident tourists in hotels and similar establishments, by country of residence

	2008	2009	2010	2011	2012	Market share 2012	% Change 2012-2011
Other Europe	54,416	41,191	56,425	45,328	47,251	2.89	4.24
Other countries of Europe	54,416	41,191	56,425	45,328	47,251	2.89	4.24
NOT SPECIFIED	15,021	21,363	23,429	21,181	22,112	1.35	4.40
Other countries of the World	15,021	21,363	23,429	21,181	22,112	1.35	4.40

622

ROMANIA

4. Arrivals of non-resident tourists in all types of accommodation establishments, by country of residence

		2008	2009	2010	2011	2012	Market share 2012	% Change 2012-2011
TOTAL		1,465,891	1,275,590	1,343,078	1,514,781	1,653,361	100.00	9.15
AFRICA		7,882	7,437	8,875	10,292	14,078	0.85	36.79
Other Africa		7,882	7,437	8,875	10,292	14,078	0.85	36.79
All countries of Africa	(*)	7,882	7,437	8,875	10,292	14,078	0.85	36.79
AMERICAS		97,504	93,625	105,166	107,836	116,410	7.04	7.95
North America		90,436	88,162	98,075	100,277	107,016	6.47	6.72
Canada		13,037	10,780	12,196	12,023	13,813	0.84	14.89
Mexico		1,464	1,411	1,536	2,429	3,289	0.20	35.41
United States of America		75,935	75,971	84,343	85,825	89,914	5.44	4.76
Other Americas		7,068	5,463	7,091	7,559	9,394	0.57	24.28
Other countries of the Americas		7,068	5,463	7,091	7,559	9,394	0.57	24.28
EAST ASIA AND THE PACIFIC		54,970	47,015	53,653	66,077	75,235	4.55	13.86
North-East Asia		22,890	18,714	19,203	25,469	28,995	1.75	13.84
China		7,632	6,946	5,949	9,063	11,390	0.69	25.68
Japan		15,258	11,768	13,254	16,406	17,605	1.06	7.31
Other East Asia and the Pacific		32,080	28,301	34,450	40,608	46,240	2.80	13.87
Other countries of Asia		23,356	20,903	26,119	30,076	36,025	2.18	19.78
All countries of Oceania		8,724	7,398	8,331	10,532	10,215	0.62	-3.01
EUROPE		1,290,414	1,106,150	1,151,955	1,309,395	1,425,522	86.22	8.87
Central/Eastern Europe		237,408	202,823	208,844	249,216	285,852	17.29	14.70
Bulgaria		26,368	23,820	24,605	31,352	37,287	2.26	18.93
Czech Republic		19,902	18,804	17,221	20,086	22,083	1.34	9.94
Hungary		92,178	76,906	75,904	86,489	89,599	5.42	3.60
Poland		32,842	31,579	37,254	47,006	52,154	3.15	10.95
Republic of Moldova		22,818	20,094	21,479	25,952	28,988	1.75	11.70
Russian Federation		17,400	13,402	14,900	19,503	27,893	1.69	43.02
Slovakia		12,057	7,561	7,773	5,357	11,001	0.67	105.36
Ukraine		13,843	10,657	9,708	13,471	16,847	1.02	25.06
Northern Europe		131,774	115,898	115,041	130,403	151,714	9.18	16.34
Denmark		12,369	11,162	11,146	13,901	20,285	1.23	45.92
Finland		8,061	7,409	6,348	6,059	5,567	0.34	-8.12
Ireland		8,162	6,989	7,696	7,950	8,339	0.50	4.89
Norway		9,111	8,037	7,495	8,645	11,160	0.67	29.09
Sweden		11,610	10,944	10,566	12,854	14,669	0.89	14.12
United Kingdom		82,461	71,357	71,790	80,994	91,694	5.55	13.21
Southern Europe		298,573	252,673	263,439	301,519	318,905	19.29	5.77
Greece		37,592	36,735	35,854	36,845	34,877	2.11	-5.34
Italy		165,018	141,568	145,304	172,245	181,812	11.00	5.55
Montenegro		644	543	422	550	691	0.04	25.64
Portugal		12,614	7,456	8,700	10,397	12,299	0.74	18.29
Serbia		8,577	7,881	6,721	9,118	11,903	0.72	30.54
Slovenia		6,809	5,423	5,761	5,357	6,771	0.41	26.40
Spain		67,319	53,067	60,677	67,007	70,552	4.27	5.29
Western Europe		482,986	417,626	424,961	464,196	505,862	30.60	8.98
Austria		70,821	58,401	61,330	62,123	63,143	3.82	1.64
Belgium		24,164	23,197	23,754	24,601	26,911	1.63	9.39
France		115,192	100,330	99,225	109,346	117,929	7.13	7.85
Germany		213,005	181,084	184,626	206,932	229,823	13.90	11.06
Luxembourg		1,142	1,145	1,051	1,417	1,343	0.08	-5.22
Netherlands		44,624	37,713	38,038	42,428	47,058	2.85	10.91
Switzerland		14,038	15,756	16,937	17,349	19,655	1.19	13.29
East Mediterranean Europe		92,725	75,657	96,637	114,066	115,445	6.98	1.21
Israel		66,187	53,649	71,672	86,679	81,324	4.92	-6.18
Turkey		26,538	22,008	24,965	27,387	34,121	2.06	24.59

Yearbook of Tourism Statistics, Data 2008 – 2012, 2014 Edition

4. Arrivals of non-resident tourists in all types of accommodation establishments, by country of residence

	2008	2009	2010	2011	2012	Market share 2012	% Change 2012-2011
Other Europe	**46,948**	**41,473**	**43,033**	**49,995**	**47,744**	**2.89**	**-4.50**
Other countries of Europe	46,948	41,473	43,033	49,995	47,744	2.89	-4.50
NOT SPECIFIED	**15,121**	**21,363**	**23,429**	**21,181**	**22,116**	**1.34**	**4.41**
Other countries of the World	15,121	21,363	23,429	21,181	22,116	1.34	4.41

Yearbook of Tourism Statistics, Data 2008 – 2012, 2014 Edition

ROMANIA

5. Overnight stays of non-resident tourists in hotels and similar establishments, by country of residence

		2008	2009	2010	2011	2012	Market share 2012	% Change 2012-2011
TOTAL		3,251,357	2,581,861	2,673,714	2,978,217	3,214,602	100.00	7.94
AFRICA		18,545	18,184	23,426	23,548	42,644	1.33	81.09
Other Africa		18,545	18,184	23,426	23,548	42,644	1.33	81.09
All countries of Africa	(*)	18,545	18,184	23,426	23,548	42,644	1.33	81.09
AMERICAS		207,921	170,573	198,437	212,257	217,968	6.78	2.69
North America		191,301	159,421	182,902	194,854	197,873	6.16	1.55
Canada		27,894	21,066	25,195	23,647	26,657	0.83	12.73
Mexico		3,587	3,315	3,351	12,705	7,492	0.23	-41.03
United States of America		159,820	135,040	154,356	158,502	163,724	5.09	3.29
Other Americas		16,620	11,152	15,535	17,403	20,095	0.63	15.47
Other countries of the Americas		16,620	11,152	15,535	17,403	20,095	0.63	15.47
EAST ASIA AND THE PACIFIC		148,321	105,115	119,008	132,426	145,330	4.52	9.74
North-East Asia		73,715	41,704	40,429	49,450	56,033	1.74	13.31
China		46,733	21,192	18,050	21,362	22,004	0.68	3.01
Japan		26,982	20,512	22,379	28,088	34,029	1.06	21.15
Other East Asia and the Pacific		74,606	63,411	78,579	82,976	89,297	2.78	7.62
Other countries of Asia		58,459	27,085	62,859	64,569	70,401	2.19	9.03
All countries of Oceania		16,147	36,326	15,720	18,407	18,896	0.59	2.66
EUROPE		2,850,301	2,251,663	2,293,900	2,575,787	2,772,658	86.25	7.64
Central/Eastern Europe		537,153	438,831	417,645	506,898	581,448	18.09	14.71
Bulgaria		60,167	59,893	45,653	55,863	67,707	2.11	21.20
Czech Republic		41,348	33,645	30,738	34,851	38,481	1.20	10.42
Hungary		193,184	162,445	152,770	175,619	181,352	5.64	3.26
Poland		75,371	53,712	66,281	90,101	104,321	3.25	15.78
Republic of Moldova		54,320	54,155	53,905	64,764	79,480	2.47	22.72
Russian Federation		49,685	32,195	33,111	42,216	56,531	1.76	33.91
Slovakia		27,461	19,954	15,307	18,833	22,675	0.71	20.40
Ukraine		35,617	22,832	19,880	24,651	30,901	0.96	25.35
Northern Europe		294,533	228,647	226,188	244,210	284,450	8.85	16.48
Denmark		27,671	24,824	25,093	30,434	40,943	1.27	34.53
Finland		19,488	16,039	13,184	11,879	11,293	0.35	-4.93
Ireland		16,533	14,976	15,214	16,665	18,034	0.56	8.21
Norway		26,974	16,898	14,725	16,700	21,835	0.68	30.75
Sweden		23,934	20,102	20,162	24,074	27,485	0.86	14.17
United Kingdom		179,933	135,808	137,810	144,458	164,860	5.13	14.12
Southern Europe		644,954	506,579	521,502	611,470	624,272	19.42	2.09
Greece		85,745	70,431	72,038	96,135	72,332	2.25	-24.76
Italy		368,545	295,924	296,239	339,604	357,489	11.12	5.27
Montenegro		1,708	804	945	976	1,648	0.05	68.85
Portugal		29,707	16,543	19,879	23,059	24,129	0.75	4.64
Serbia		21,502	16,730	12,938	18,721	23,048	0.72	23.11
Slovenia		13,164	10,267	10,471	9,214	13,946	0.43	51.36
Spain		124,583	95,880	108,992	123,761	131,680	4.10	6.40
Western Europe		998,566	799,412	813,908	870,311	934,094	29.06	7.33
Austria		133,241	97,786	106,036	106,699	111,239	3.46	4.25
Belgium		48,598	43,758	44,393	44,789	47,632	1.48	6.35
France		236,269	190,815	188,030	209,080	216,721	6.74	3.65
Germany		463,073	362,888	372,799	397,893	438,656	13.65	10.24
Luxembourg		2,429	2,184	2,187	3,212	2,776	0.09	-13.57
Netherlands		89,215	74,330	71,755	79,126	83,763	2.61	5.86
Switzerland		25,741	27,651	28,708	29,512	33,307	1.04	12.86
East Mediterranean Europe		240,783	180,799	214,179	243,754	252,057	7.84	3.41
Israel		176,003	135,782	164,384	188,320	186,727	5.81	-0.85
Turkey		64,780	45,017	49,795	55,434	65,330	2.03	17.85

Yearbook of Tourism Statistics, Data 2008 – 2012, 2014 Edition

ROMANIA

5. Overnight stays of non-resident tourists in hotels and similar establishments, by country of residence

	2008	2009	2010	2011	2012	Market share 2012	% Change 2012-2011
Other Europe	134,312	97,395	100,478	99,144	96,337	3.00	-2.83
Other countries of Europe	134,312	97,395	100,478	99,144	96,337	3.00	-2.83
NOT SPECIFIED	26,269	36,326	38,943	34,199	36,002	1.12	5.27
Other countries of the World	26,269	36,326	38,943	34,199	36,002	1.12	5.27

Yearbook of Tourism Statistics, Data 2008 – 2012, 2014 Edition

ROMANIA

6. Overnight stays of non-resident tourists in all types of accommodation establishments, by country of residence

	2008	2009	2010	2011	2012	Market share 2012	% Change 2012-2011
TOTAL	3,359,244	2,667,666	2,755,083	3,062,968	3,291,504	100.00	7.46
AFRICA	18,848	18,189	23,488	23,593	42,679	1.30	80.90
Other Africa	18,848	18,189	23,488	23,593	42,679	1.30	80.90
All countries of Africa (*)	18,848	18,189	23,488	23,593	42,679	1.30	80.90
AMERICAS	208,647	171,091	198,780	212,720	218,254	6.63	2.60
North America	191,708	159,896	183,088	195,296	198,130	6.02	1.45
Canada	27,971	21,247	25,251	23,931	26,744	0.81	11.75
Mexico	3,608	3,315	3,356	12,705	7,492	0.23	-41.03
United States of America	160,129	135,334	154,481	158,660	163,894	4.98	3.30
Other Americas	16,939	11,195	15,692	17,424	20,124	0.61	15.50
Other countries of the Americas	16,939	11,195	15,692	17,424	20,124	0.61	15.50
EAST ASIA AND THE PACIFIC	152,773	105,688	119,133	132,788	145,509	4.42	9.58
North-East Asia	73,764	41,826	40,466	49,513	56,072	1.70	13.25
China	46,761	21,246	18,085	21,385	22,039	0.67	3.06
Japan	27,003	20,580	22,381	28,128	34,033	1.03	20.99
Other East Asia and the Pacific	79,009	63,862	78,667	83,275	89,437	2.72	7.40
Other countries of Asia	62,525	49,779	62,891	64,702	70,471	2.14	8.92
All countries of Oceania	16,484	14,083	15,776	18,573	18,966	0.58	2.12
EUROPE	2,952,565	2,336,372	2,374,739	2,659,668	2,849,023	86.56	7.12
Central/Eastern Europe	552,035	449,444	425,539	514,397	591,141	17.96	14.92
Bulgaria	60,382	60,040	45,746	56,028	67,846	2.06	21.09
Czech Republic	41,807	34,118	31,055	35,150	39,605	1.20	12.67
Hungary	200,550	165,613	155,067	177,625	182,858	5.56	2.95
Poland	77,677	56,975	69,315	92,332	106,646	3.24	15.50
Republic of Moldova	56,112	54,667	54,336	65,273	80,767	2.45	23.74
Russian Federation	51,719	34,968	34,594	44,178	59,499	1.81	34.68
Slovakia	27,769	20,060	15,365	18,892	22,763	0.69	20.49
Ukraine	36,019	23,003	20,061	24,919	31,157	0.95	25.03
Northern Europe	299,389	230,426	227,533	245,061	285,534	8.67	16.52
Denmark	29,109	25,002	25,217	30,499	41,260	1.25	35.28
Finland	19,579	16,142	13,224	11,904	11,318	0.34	-4.92
Ireland	17,325	15,043	15,243	16,770	18,044	0.55	7.60
Norway	27,409	17,060	14,968	16,790	21,855	0.66	30.17
Sweden	24,228	20,206	20,318	24,142	27,548	0.84	14.11
United Kingdom	181,739	136,973	138,563	144,956	165,509	5.03	14.18
Southern Europe	649,454	507,754	523,356	613,190	625,890	19.02	2.07
Greece	85,877	70,512	72,080	96,260	72,438	2.20	-24.75
Italy	370,418	296,735	297,627	340,733	358,352	10.89	5.17
Montenegro	1,708	804	945	976	1,648	0.05	68.85
Portugal	29,785	16,553	19,891	23,075	24,203	0.74	4.89
Serbia	21,748	16,775	12,966	18,756	23,077	0.70	23.04
Slovenia	13,407	10,365	10,718	9,356	14,053	0.43	50.20
Spain	126,511	96,010	109,129	124,034	132,119	4.01	6.52
Western Europe	1,068,081	869,499	881,446	942,590	996,962	30.29	5.77
Austria	135,314	100,275	107,540	107,817	113,203	3.44	5.00
Belgium	49,959	44,527	45,602	45,911	48,089	1.46	4.74
France	240,899	192,790	190,304	211,340	218,216	6.63	3.25
Germany	519,790	424,532	428,587	459,617	494,004	15.01	7.48
Luxembourg	2,455	2,212	2,215	3,224	2,776	0.08	-13.90
Netherlands	92,808	76,684	76,464	83,841	86,357	2.62	3.00
Switzerland	26,856	28,479	30,734	30,840	34,317	1.04	11.27
East Mediterranean Europe	241,423	180,973	214,719	243,914	252,205	7.66	3.40
Israel	176,397	135,837	164,601	188,409	186,799	5.68	-0.85
Turkey	65,026	45,136	50,118	55,505	65,406	1.99	17.84

627

Yearbook of Tourism Statistics, Data 2008 – 2012, 2014 Edition

ROMANIA

6. Overnight stays of non-resident tourists in all types of accommodation establishments, by country of residence

	2008	2009	2010	2011	2012	Market share 2012	% Change 2012-2011
Other Europe	142,183	98,276	102,146	100,516	97,291	2.96	-3.21
Other countries of Europe	142,183	98,276	102,146	100,516	97,291	2.96	-3.21
NOT SPECIFIED	26,411	36,326	38,943	34,199	36,039	1.09	5.38
Other countries of the World	26,411	36,326	38,943	34,199	36,039	1.09	5.38

628

RUSSIAN FEDERATION

2. Arrivals of non-resident visitors at national borders, by nationality

	2008	2009	2010	2011	2012	Market share 2012	% Change 2012-2011
TOTAL	23,676,140	21,338,650	22,281,217	24,932,061	28,176,502	100.00	13.01
AFRICA	35,734	34,649	36,833	2,307	3,149	0.01	36.50
East Africa	4,067	4,871	5,041				
British Indian Ocean Territory	4	28	182				
Burundi	117	120	108				
Comoros	30	51	63				
Djibouti	24	24	72				
Eritrea	50	58	69				
Ethiopia	395	368	420				
Kenya	968	958	1,062				
Madagascar	144	243	198				
Malawi	60	59	53				
Mauritius	480	79	590				
Mozambique	109	1,105	158				
Rwanda	50	34	41				
Seychelles	153	515	200				
Somalia	86	75	116				
Uganda	435	195	403				
United Republic of Tanzania	355	378	502				
Zambia	317	295	444				
Zimbabwe	290	286	360				
Central Africa	2,603	3,531	2,981				
Angola	917	1,033	1,091				
Cameroon	718	806	785				
Central African Republic	18	144	24				
Chad	132	123	121				
Congo	522	551	328				
Democratic Republic of the Congo	33	672	416				
Equatorial Guinea	138	117	132				
Gabon	124	75	71				
Sao Tome and Principe	1	10	13				
North Africa	8,392	9,786	10,090	2,307	3,149	0.01	36.50
Algeria	2,548	3,140	2,564				
Morocco	2,955	3,679	4,146				
Sudan	966	1,157	1,220				
Tunisia	1,923	1,809	2,159	2,307	3,149	0.01	36.50
Western Sahara		1	1				
Southern Africa	11,807	7,830	8,695				
Botswana	57	66	123				
Lesotho	57	16	58				
Namibia	219	232	416				
South Africa	11,428	7,447	8,022				
Swaziland	46	69	76				
West Africa	8,865	8,631	10,026				
Benin	122	150	215				
Burkina Faso	30	32	56				
Cape Verde	280	137	323				
Côte d'Ivoire	274	446	425				
Gambia	31	21	38				
Ghana	744	822	890				
Guinea	201	209	283				
Guinea-Bissau	108	121	749				
Liberia	4,332	3,768	3,746				
Mali	173	169	270				
Mauritania	98	79	131				
Niger	17	51	24				

Yearbook of Tourism Statistics, Data 2008 – 2012, 2014 Edition

RUSSIAN FEDERATION

2. Arrivals of non-resident visitors at national borders, by nationality

	2008	2009	2010	2011	2012	Market share 2012	% Change 2012-2011
Nigeria	2,027	2,244	2,552				
Senegal	173	148	198				
Sierra Leone	179	136	65				
Togo	76	98	61				
AMERICAS	**503,456**	**469,112**	**420,512**	**331,576**	**346,520**	**1.23**	**4.51**
Caribbean	**45,799**	**52,965**	**33,947**	**4,099**	**5,239**	**0.02**	**27.81**
Anguilla	30	7	1,183				
Antigua and Barbuda	8,269	4,860	5,673				
Bahamas	21,028	29,122	18,871				
Barbados	447	670	492				
Bermuda	2,827	9,254	457				
British Virgin Islands	268	11					
Cayman Islands	271	919	267				
Cuba	4,386	4,172	4,053	4,099	5,239	0.02	27.81
Dominica	569	330	213				
Dominican Republic	259	667	690				
Grenada	36	114	45				
Haiti	79	68	66				
Jamaica	1,056	630	447				
Martinique		15					
Netherlands Antilles	652	256					
Puerto Rico	10	15	15				
Saint Kitts and Nevis	846	238	120				
Saint Lucia	51	139	62				
Saint Vincent and the Grenadines	4,555	1,227	999				
Trinidad and Tobago	160	251	294				
Central America	**26,274**	**21,065**	**12,854**				
Belize	1,954	1,199	1,208				
Costa Rica	691	454	710				
El Salvador	120	245	198				
Guatemala	453	1,202	1,002				
Honduras	9,331	5,397	3,022				
Nicaragua	319	455	396				
Panama	13,406	12,113	6,318				
North America	**381,338**	**354,963**	**324,394**	**327,477**	**341,281**	**1.21**	**4.22**
Canada	62,004	59,537	48,559	52,238	54,730	0.19	4.77
Greenland	11	1	8				
Mexico	14,269	10,058	13,767				
United States of America	305,054	285,367	262,060	275,239	286,551	1.02	4.11
South America	**50,045**	**40,119**	**49,317**				
Argentina	7,147	9,598	9,044				
Bolivia	597	354	365				
Brazil	23,522	15,540	21,950				
Chile	3,126	3,207	3,438				
Colombia	3,402	3,794	4,620				
Ecuador	1,053	1,233	1,495				
Falkland Islands, Malvinas	132	57	355				
Guyana	781	60	66				
Paraguay	117	198	185				
Peru	4,908	1,601	3,351				
Suriname	4	8	25				
Uruguay	2,527	813	896				
Venezuela	2,729	3,656	3,527				
EAST ASIA AND THE PACIFIC	**1,477,644**	**1,294,719**	**1,358,186**	**1,179,411**	**1,368,863**	**4.86**	**16.06**
North-East Asia	**1,193,738**	**1,068,706**	**1,121,871**	**1,013,127**	**1,160,716**	**4.12**	**14.57**
China	815,469	718,581	747,640	845,588	978,988	3.47	15.78
Hong Kong, China	5,230	8,169	14,852				

Yearbook of Tourism Statistics, Data 2008 – 2012, 2014 Edition

RUSSIAN FEDERATION

2. Arrivals of non-resident visitors at national borders, by nationality

	2008	2009	2010	2011	2012	Market share 2012	% Change 2012-2011
Japan	86,237	74,159	78,188	76,204	86,806	0.31	13.91
Korea, Dem. People's Republic of	20,739	18,686	21,167				
Korea, Republic of	101,304	84,166	90,622	91,335	94,922	0.34	3.93
Macao, China	73	104	95				
Mongolia	155,101	156,997	157,367				
Taiwan, Province of China	9,585	7,844	11,940				
South-East Asia	**232,735**	**185,855**	**196,816**	**131,416**	**165,042**	**0.59**	**25.59**
Brunei Darussalam	92	211	58				
Cambodia	1,101	416	443				
Indonesia	30,817	24,841	14,448				
Lao People's Democratic Republic	146	114	252				
Malaysia	13,249	11,844	16,508	14,988	15,126	0.05	0.92
Myanmar	6,297	3,467	5,424				
Philippines	92,801	79,365	81,385	99,405	130,541	0.46	31.32
Singapore	12,486	10,226	12,283				
Thailand	16,150	14,562	15,192	17,023	19,375	0.07	13.82
Viet Nam	59,596	40,809	50,823				
Australasia	**43,824**	**36,948**	**36,199**	**34,868**	**43,105**	**0.15**	**23.62**
Australia	37,574	31,931	30,584	34,868	43,105	0.15	23.62
New Zealand	6,250	5,017	5,615				
Melanesia	**168**	**492**	**604**				
Fiji	19	39	43				
New Caledonia	16	3	1				
Papua New Guinea	1	4	44				
Solomon Islands	3	3	434				
Vanuatu	129	443	82				
Micronesia	**7,029**	**2,468**	**2,575**				
Guam	5	1	29				
Kiribati	563	118	347				
Marshall Islands	6,455	2,342	2,189				
Micronesia, Federated States of	3		1				
Nauru	1	6	3				
Northern Mariana Islands			4				
Palau	2	1	2				
Polynesia	**150**	**250**	**121**				
American Samoa	1	1	11				
Pitcairn	86		13				
Samoa	5	27					
Tokelau			1				
Tonga	29	9	12				
Tuvalu	29	212	85				
EUROPE	**21,186,817**	**18,790,566**	**19,568,815**	**5,938,542**	**6,502,565**	**23.08**	**9.50**
Central/Eastern Europe	**17,799,810**	**15,578,448**	**16,370,280**	**2,572,612**	**2,879,635**	**10.22**	**11.93**
Armenia	458,621	379,525	459,040				
Azerbaijan	989,529	892,435	979,778				
Belarus	255,143	286,495	259,191				
Bulgaria	41,053	37,704	38,446	42,031	45,312	0.16	7.81
Czech Republic	44,720	38,356	40,565	46,776	62,980	0.22	34.64
Estonia	662,917	920,497	474,949	519,402	494,282	1.75	-4.84
Georgia	46,362	19,846	24,568				
Hungary	24,014	19,791	20,736	23,241	23,047	0.08	-0.83
Kazakhstan	2,732,118	2,590,688	2,747,358				
Kyrgyzstan	552,715	406,504	552,909				
Latvia	423,050	516,838	569,330	571,374	461,162	1.64	-19.29
Lithuania	680,461	600,785	760,728	622,740	553,896	1.97	-11.06
Poland	779,826	434,529	394,872	704,610	1,190,003	4.22	68.89
Republic of Moldova	1,167,266	884,999	988,084				

Yearbook of Tourism Statistics, Data 2008 – 2012, 2014 Edition

RUSSIAN FEDERATION

2. Arrivals of non-resident visitors at national borders, by nationality

	2008	2009	2010	2011	2012	Market share 2012	% Change 2012-2011
Romania	15,593	14,072	17,884	21,993	24,792	0.09	12.73
Slovakia	20,195	15,863	18,512	20,445	24,161	0.09	18.18
Tajikistan	900,682	674,572	830,160				
Turkmenistan	33,947	27,704	35,017				
Ukraine	6,415,361	5,604,433	5,574,067				
Uzbekistan	1,556,237	1,212,812	1,584,086				
Northern Europe	**1,443,552**	**1,452,439**	**1,371,633**	**1,542,391**	**1,716,299**	**6.09**	**11.28**
Denmark	35,302	30,316	33,121				
Faeroe Islands	14	25	24				
Finland	1,000,238	1,057,575	1,012,621	1,211,519	1,375,614	4.88	13.54
Iceland	1,867	1,627	1,437				
Ireland	15,483	14,078	11,990				
Norway	56,878	49,488	45,340	48,614	50,115	0.18	3.09
Svalbard and Jan Mayen Islands	6	97					
Sweden	59,629	59,438	54,253	60,840	58,900	0.21	-3.19
United Kingdom	274,135	239,795	212,847	221,418	231,670	0.82	4.63
Southern Europe	**536,029**	**470,045**	**479,838**	**396,321**	**368,490**	**1.31**	**-7.02**
Albania	1,209	1,681	1,086				
Andorra	150	107	127				
Bosnia and Herzegovina	8,065	5,669	5,970				
Croatia	13,399	11,954	14,638	15,295	15,990	0.06	4.54
Gibraltar	6,405	4,467	3,711				
Greece	39,704	39,130	33,296	33,569	36,474	0.13	8.65
Italy	224,849	190,862	198,002	207,476	212,411	0.75	2.38
Malta	22,148	21,970	27,204	10,251	2,079	0.01	-79.72
Montenegro	2,843	4,302	4,691				
Portugal	17,969	16,281	18,434				
San Marino	108	179	201				
Serbia	55,332	44,342	47,939				
Slovenia	13,336	10,569	11,160				
Spain	126,646	115,975	110,601	129,730	101,536	0.36	-21.73
TFYR of Macedonia	3,866	2,557	2,778				
Western Europe	**1,082,196**	**1,008,243**	**1,034,731**	**1,048,779**	**1,102,450**	**3.91**	**5.12**
Austria	68,370	69,715	67,606	70,388	71,367	0.25	1.39
Belgium	36,472	32,575	33,571				
France	201,205	185,082	194,218	213,473	225,343	0.80	5.56
Germany	636,347	592,313	611,367	629,391	671,676	2.38	6.72
Liechtenstein	192	244	205				
Luxembourg	3,009	1,993	1,912				
Monaco	144	148	168				
Netherlands	87,866	78,752	80,720	87,549	81,212	0.29	-7.24
Switzerland	48,591	47,421	44,964	47,978	52,852	0.19	10.16
East Mediterranean Europe	**325,230**	**281,391**	**312,333**	**378,439**	**435,691**	**1.55**	**15.13**
Cyprus	15,846	14,961	15,338	14,950	6,288	0.02	-57.94
Israel	70,289	89,098	100,291	114,380	123,974	0.44	8.39
Turkey	239,095	177,332	196,704	249,109	305,429	1.08	22.61
MIDDLE EAST	**38,839**	**38,009**	**41,496**	**15,913**	**18,131**	**0.06**	**13.94**
Bahrain	301	222	494				
Egypt	9,448	9,983	10,273	11,561	13,344	0.05	15.42
Iraq	1,746	1,549	2,760				
Jordan	2,784	2,649	3,024	3,215	3,383	0.01	5.23
Kuwait	336	649	386				
Lebanon	4,236	4,035	4,510				
Libya	1,259	979	1,316				
Oman	421	580	623				
Palestine	822	749	1,200				
Qatar	171	203	369				

632

RUSSIAN FEDERATION

2. Arrivals of non-resident visitors at national borders, by nationality

	2008	2009	2010	2011	2012	Market share 2012	% Change 2012-2011
Saudi Arabia	935	1,151	1,390				
Syrian Arab Republic	14,454	13,188	12,882				
United Arab Emirates	1,001	1,070	1,083	1,137	1,404	0.00	23.48
Yemen	925	1,002	1,186				
SOUTH ASIA	**96,376**	**93,311**	**89,407**				
Afghanistan	7,244	7,258	7,336				
Bangladesh	1,395	1,464	1,580				
Bhutan	21	26	57				
India	62,163	59,815	53,364				
Iran, Islamic Republic of	18,007	18,607	20,576				
Maldives	152	105	122				
Nepal	1,755	1,171	1,237				
Pakistan	4,037	3,347	3,262				
Sri Lanka	1,602	1,518	1,873				
NOT SPECIFIED	**337,274**	**618,284**	**765,968**	**17,464,312**	**19,937,274**	**70.76**	**14.16**
Other countries of the World	337,274	618,284	765,968	17,464,312	19,937,274	70.76	14.16

Yearbook of Tourism Statistics, Data 2008 – 2012, 2014 Edition

RWANDA

2. Arrivals of non-resident visitors at national borders, by nationality

	2008	2009	2010	2011	2012	Market share 2012	% Change 2012-2011
TOTAL	**668,524**	**662,556**	**666,001**	**908,009**	**1,075,789**	**100.00**	**18.48**
AFRICA	**556,943**	**559,668**	**546,904**	**773,841**	**940,921**	**87.46**	**21.59**
East Africa	**261,567**	**241,826**	**287,330**	**370,515**	**445,427**	**41.40**	**20.22**
Burundi	74,686	69,304	72,316	75,824	77,600	7.21	2.34
Comoros	53	42	33	57	50	0.00	-12.28
Djibouti	72	66	255	197	103	0.01	-47.72
Eritrea	407	421	658	677	626	0.06	-7.53
Ethiopia	933	697	948	1,040	1,120	0.10	7.69
Kenya	25,870	30,721	37,193	44,020	60,433	5.62	37.29
Madagascar	211	241	303	436	427	0.04	-2.06
Malawi	346	278	566	422	388	0.04	-8.06
Mauritius	214	101	105	172	263	0.02	52.91
Mozambique	110	161	221	177	254	0.02	43.50
Seychelles	28	16	37	41	54	0.01	31.71
Somalia	107	263	134	169	126	0.01	-25.44
Uganda	113,267	106,622	133,089	191,927	207,090	19.25	7.90
United Republic of Tanzania	44,166	31,784	40,286	53,560	94,912	8.82	77.21
Zambia	349	412	336	637	866	0.08	35.95
Zimbabwe	748	697	850	1,159	1,115	0.10	-3.80
Central Africa	**282,338**	**305,221**	**245,838**	**386,066**	**477,617**	**44.40**	**23.71**
Angola	127	146	268	173	154	0.01	-10.98
Cameroon	828	1,127	1,232	1,323	1,206	0.11	-8.84
Central African Republic	153	131	147	167	178	0.02	6.59
Chad	139	174	318	446	281	0.03	-37.00
Congo	132	121	134	236	133	0.01	-43.64
Democratic Republic of the Congo	280,297	302,786	242,976	383,099	474,634	44.12	23.89
Equatorial Guinea	535	659	722	542	827	0.08	52.58
Gabon	127	77	41	80	204	0.02	155.00
North Africa	**1,108**	**880**	**947**	**1,163**	**1,218**	**0.11**	**4.73**
Algeria	107	197	97	109	133	0.01	22.02
Morocco	56	87	173	189	92	0.01	-51.32
Sudan	724	404	509	507	492	0.05	-2.96
Tunisia	221	192	168	358	501	0.05	39.94
Southern Africa	**6,277**	**6,216**	**6,097**	**8,570**	**8,291**	**0.77**	**-3.26**
Botswana	73	89	98	235	146	0.01	-37.87
Lesotho	48	108	46	55	54	0.01	-1.82
Namibia	72	59	39	62	204	0.02	229.03
South Africa	5,934	5,903	5,839	8,085	7,703	0.72	-4.72
Swaziland	150	57	75	133	184	0.02	38.35
West Africa	**5,653**	**5,522**	**6,690**	**7,479**	**7,946**	**0.74**	**6.24**
Benin	509	542	761	745	615	0.06	-17.45
Burkina Faso	503	573	488	729	543	0.05	-25.51
Côte d'Ivoire	498	612	712	787	754	0.07	-4.19
Gambia	140	147	103	149	146	0.01	-2.01
Ghana	733	692	995	1,098	1,078	0.10	-1.82
Liberia	232	183	243	249	200	0.02	-19.68
Mali	360	366	452	539	669	0.06	24.12
Mauritania	141	140	192	183	122	0.01	-33.33
Niger	109	85	249	247	266	0.02	7.69
Nigeria	1,120	1,027	1,149	1,356	2,130	0.20	57.08
Senegal	768	630	785	820	840	0.08	2.44
Sierra Leone	270	327	372	351	317	0.03	-9.69
Togo	270	198	189	226	266	0.02	17.70
Other Africa		**3**	**2**	**48**	**422**	**0.04**	**779.17**
Other countries of Africa		3	2	48	422	0.04	779.17

634

RWANDA

2. Arrivals of non-resident visitors at national borders, by nationality

	2008	2009	2010	2011	2012	Market share 2012	% Change 2012-2011
AMERICAS	31,043	28,116	33,189	37,919	35,032	3.26	-7.61
Caribbean	361	151	150	180	271	0.03	50.56
Barbados	7	14	26	22	11	0.00	-50.00
Haiti	320	115	96	138	247	0.02	78.99
Jamaica	34	22	28	20	13	0.00	-35.00
Central America	57	101	42	65	214	0.02	229.23
Costa Rica	27	9	6	6	110	0.01	1,733.33
Guatemala	20	77	22	40	56	0.01	40.00
Nicaragua	7	15	5	5	47	0.00	840.00
Panama	3		9	14	1	0.00	-92.86
North America	27,843	25,437	30,700	35,366	31,212	2.90	-11.75
Canada	6,480	5,689	6,991	6,964	6,952	0.65	-0.17
Mexico	112	170	298	321	219	0.02	-31.78
United States of America	21,251	19,578	23,411	28,081	24,041	2.23	-14.39
South America	2,782	2,427	2,297	2,308	3,335	0.31	44.50
Argentina	159	83	79	127	139	0.01	9.45
Brazil	207	193	220	308	299	0.03	-2.92
Chile	36	25	67	36	62	0.01	72.22
Colombia	103	61	68	73	128	0.01	75.34
Guyana	15	10	8	4	5	0.00	25.00
Peru	36	47	115	81	166	0.02	104.94
Uruguay	1,949	1,590	1,231	1,139	2,194	0.20	92.63
Venezuela	20	19	33	35	35	0.00	0.00
Other countries of South America	257	399	476	505	307	0.03	-39.21
EAST ASIA AND THE PACIFIC	7,063	8,059	10,521	12,868	12,481	1.16	-3.01
North-East Asia	3,987	4,467	5,909	6,906	6,758	0.63	-2.14
China	2,507	2,965	4,062	4,533	4,077	0.38	-10.06
Japan	1,046	1,110	1,042	1,195	1,597	0.15	33.64
Korea, Republic of	421	372	775	940	955	0.09	1.60
Taiwan, Province of China	13	20	30	238	129	0.01	-45.80
South-East Asia	486	1,013	1,604	1,181	1,409	0.13	19.31
Indonesia	64	77	64	120	315	0.03	162.50
Malaysia	107	103	196	178	199	0.02	11.80
Philippines	268	588	908	399	582	0.05	45.86
Thailand	31	217	407	455	277	0.03	-39.12
Viet Nam	16	28	29	29	36	0.00	24.14
Australasia	2,544	2,541	2,997	4,446	3,526	0.33	-20.69
Australia	2,159	2,068	2,453	3,863	3,029	0.28	-21.59
New Zealand	385	473	544	583	497	0.05	-14.75
Melanesia	46	38	11	9	21	0.00	133.33
Fiji	46	38	11	9	21	0.00	133.33
Other East Asia and the Pacific				326	767	0.07	135.28
Other countries of Asia				324	755	0.07	133.02
Other countries of Oceania				2	12	0.00	500.00
EUROPE	49,130	46,968	54,253	66,961	66,472	6.18	-0.73
Central/Eastern Europe	2,592	2,339	2,853	2,553	3,309	0.31	29.61
Armenia	27	14	29	29	2	0.00	-93.10
Belarus	44	41	28	23	32	0.00	39.13
Bulgaria	507	72	176	95	153	0.01	61.05
Czech Republic	84	119	302	243	615	0.06	153.09
Estonia	19	18	10	32	37	0.00	15.63
Hungary	41	43	62	82	103	0.01	25.61
Kazakhstan	93	63	68	75	22	0.00	-70.67
Poland	407	466	574	651	602	0.06	-7.53
Republic of Moldova	2	2		14	39	0.00	178.57
Romania	90	170	369	262	186	0.02	-29.01

Yearbook of Tourism Statistics, Data 2008 – 2012, 2014 Edition

RWANDA

2. Arrivals of non-resident visitors at national borders, by nationality

	2008	2009	2010	2011	2012	Market share 2012	% Change 2012-2011
Russian Federation	402	534	960	700	932	0.09	33.14
Ukraine	876	797	275	347	586	0.05	68.88
Northern Europe	**14,044**	**14,650**	**16,154**	**20,485**	**20,865**	**1.94**	**1.86**
Denmark	648	627	745	947	1,140	0.11	20.38
Finland	307	350	435	482	532	0.05	10.37
Norway	802	839	923	985	1,195	0.11	21.32
Sweden	2,049	2,092	1,903	2,393	2,903	0.27	21.31
United Kingdom	10,238	10,295	10,824	13,915	13,355	1.24	-4.02
Other countries of Northern Europe		447	1,324	1,763	1,740	0.16	-1.30
Southern Europe	**5,289**	**5,201**	**5,714**	**6,729**	**7,313**	**0.68**	**8.68**
Bosnia and Herzegovina	104	116	54	137	54	0.01	-60.58
Croatia	134	89	104	119	140	0.01	17.65
Holy See	2		2	4	1	0.00	-75.00
Italy	3,127	3,409	3,456	4,338	4,511	0.42	3.99
Portugal	135	125	298	261	318	0.03	21.84
Serbia	138	67	181	177	65	0.01	-63.28
Slovenia	142	42	79	108	121	0.01	12.04
Spain	1,507	1,353	1,540	1,585	2,103	0.20	32.68
Western Europe	**26,571**	**23,607**	**28,138**	**35,665**	**33,848**	**3.15**	**-5.09**
Austria	441	395	707	949	672	0.06	-29.19
Belgium	11,161	8,166	10,100	11,870	9,192	0.85	-22.56
France	4,165	5,058	5,990	7,090	7,931	0.74	11.86
Germany	5,944	5,652	6,157	7,741	9,180	0.85	18.59
Luxembourg	114	80	136	1,676	120	0.01	-92.84
Netherlands	3,356	2,979	3,376	4,403	4,388	0.41	-0.34
Switzerland	1,390	1,277	1,672	1,936	2,365	0.22	22.16
East Mediterranean Europe	**634**	**1,171**	**1,394**	**1,529**	**1,137**	**0.11**	**-25.64**
Israel	556	467	455	563	520	0.05	-7.64
Turkey	78	704	939	966	617	0.06	-36.13
MIDDLE EAST	**3,366**	**2,104**	**2,784**	**2,308**	**1,989**	**0.18**	**-13.82**
Egypt	316	462	772	642	369	0.03	-42.52
Jordan	83	66	96	84	86	0.01	2.38
Kuwait	7	7	9	4	7	0.00	75.00
Lebanon	710	829	925	831	600	0.06	-27.80
Libya	261	164	398	185	47	0.00	-74.59
Oman	488	495	521	434	640	0.06	47.47
Saudi Arabia	40	42	32	36	79	0.01	119.44
Syrian Arab Republic	18	13	20	32	51	0.00	59.38
United Arab Emirates	1,443	26	11	18	6	0.00	-66.67
Other countries of Middle East				42	104	0.01	147.62
SOUTH ASIA	**19,232**	**16,931**	**17,794**	**13,774**	**16,914**	**1.57**	**22.80**
Bangladesh	148	346	388	343	497	0.05	44.90
India	17,111	13,085	16,178	12,347	14,947	1.39	21.06
Iran, Islamic Republic of	48	65	39	66	167	0.02	153.03
Nepal	134	140	127	100	176	0.02	76.00
Pakistan	1,465	2,961	552	470	731	0.07	55.53
Sri Lanka	326	334	510	403	292	0.03	-27.54
Other countries of South Asia				45	104	0.01	131.11
NOT SPECIFIED	**1,747**	**710**	**556**	**338**	**1,980**	**0.18**	**485.80**
Other countries of the World	1,747	710	556	338	1,980	0.18	485.80

636

SAINT KITTS AND NEVIS

1. Arrivals of non-resident tourists at national borders, by country of residence

		2008	2009	2010	2011	2012	Market share 2012	% Change 2012-2011
TOTAL	(*)	127,705	93,081	98,329	101,701	104,240	100.00	2.50
AMERICAS		113,242	83,233	85,940	89,099	91,378	87.66	2.56
Caribbean		28,982	22,410	21,176	18,893	17,317	16.61	-8.34
All countries of the Caribbean		28,982	22,410	21,176	18,893	17,317	16.61	-8.34
North America		84,260	60,823	64,764	70,206	74,061	71.05	5.49
Canada		7,805	6,413	6,054	5,961	7,073	6.79	18.65
United States of America		76,455	54,410	58,710	64,245	66,988	64.26	4.27
EUROPE		9,970	6,496	8,455	8,047	7,975	7.65	-0.89
Northern Europe		9,970	6,496	8,455	8,047	7,975	7.65	-0.89
United Kingdom		9,970	6,496	8,455	8,047	7,975	7.65	-0.89
NOT SPECIFIED		4,493	3,352	3,934	4,555	4,887	4.69	7.29
Other countries of the World		4,493	3,352	3,934	4,555	4,887	4.69	7.29

Yearbook of Tourism Statistics, Data 2008 – 2012, 2014 Edition

SAINT LUCIA

1. Arrivals of non-resident tourists at national borders, by country of residence

		2008	2009	2010	2011	2012	Market share 2012	% Change 2012-2011
TOTAL	(*)	295,761	278,491	305,937	312,404	306,801	100.00	-1.79
AMERICAS		197,750	189,805	216,734	216,461	208,841	68.07	-3.52
Caribbean		59,757	60,183	53,998	56,929	54,386	17.73	-4.47
Anguilla					120	176	0.06	46.67
Antigua and Barbuda		2,215	2,141	2,126	1,941	2,041	0.67	5.15
Aruba					58	45	0.01	-22.41
Bahamas					179	222	0.07	24.02
Barbados		10,935	9,269	7,201	7,016	6,851	2.23	-2.35
Bermuda					190	172	0.06	-9.47
Bonaire					18	16	0.01	-11.11
British Virgin Islands					270	429	0.14	58.89
Cuba					187	149	0.05	-20.32
Curaçao					123	181	0.06	47.15
Dominica		3,101	2,996	3,070	3,168	2,208	0.72	-30.30
Dominican Republic		179	133	115	109	136	0.04	24.77
Grenada		2,131	1,763	1,489	1,584	1,518	0.49	-4.17
Guadeloupe					2,525	2,020	0.66	-20.00
Haiti		106	127	116	110	255	0.08	131.82
Jamaica		2,682	2,123	1,756	1,804	1,593	0.52	-11.70
Martinique					23,326	19,114	6.23	-18.06
Montserrat					74	66	0.02	-10.81
Netherlands Antilles				654	87	10	0.00	-88.51
Puerto Rico		613	931	829	1,505	559	0.18	-62.86
Saint Kitts and Nevis		807	915	840	677	602	0.20	-11.08
Saint Vincent and the Grenadines		2,400	2,657	2,509	2,438	2,253	0.73	-7.59
Sint Maarten					261	216	0.07	-17.24
Trinidad and Tobago		8,827	9,139	8,788	8,259	12,608	4.11	52.66
Turks and Caicos Islands					30	86	0.03	186.67
United States Virgin Islands		1,034	828	675	675	541	0.18	-19.85
Other countries of the Caribbean		24,727	27,161	23,830	195	319	0.10	63.59
Central America					113	96	0.03	-15.04
Belize					113	96	0.03	-15.04
North America		134,875	127,248	161,239	157,749	152,774	49.80	-3.15
Canada		26,279	28,563	32,154	35,393	37,709	12.29	6.54
United States of America		108,596	98,685	129,085	122,356	115,065	37.50	-5.96
South America		1,584	1,849	1,089	1,670	1,585	0.52	-5.09
Guyana		1,584	1,849	1,089	1,546	1,466	0.48	-5.17
Suriname					124	119	0.04	-4.03
Other Americas		1,534	525	408				
Other countries of the Americas		1,534	525	408				
EAST ASIA AND THE PACIFIC		152	207	183	224	170	0.06	-24.11
North-East Asia		152	207	183	224	170	0.06	-24.11
Japan		152	207	183	224	170	0.06	-24.11
EUROPE		93,601	84,238	85,695	91,759	93,400	30.44	1.79
Northern Europe		84,272	72,374	68,136	73,758	76,449	24.92	3.65
Sweden		579	521	719	699	772	0.25	10.44
United Kingdom		83,693	71,853	67,417	73,059	75,677	24.67	3.58
Southern Europe		1,495	1,229	1,465	1,605	1,195	0.39	-25.55
Italy		1,132	925	1,134	1,239	829	0.27	-33.09
Spain		363	304	331	366	366	0.12	0.00
Western Europe		6,937	8,707	11,843	12,294	10,758	3.51	-12.49
Austria		239	308	579	399	399	0.13	0.00
Belgium		209	241	264	255	257	0.08	0.78
France		4,271	5,356	5,822	7,428	5,467	1.78	-26.40
Germany		1,823	2,416	4,142	3,041	3,165	1.03	4.08
Netherlands				400	320	644	0.21	101.25

SAINT LUCIA

1. Arrivals of non-resident tourists at national borders, by country of residence

	2008	2009	2010	2011	2012	Market share 2012	% Change 2012-2011
Switzerland	395	386	636	851	826	0.27	-2.94
Other Europe	**897**	**1,928**	**4,251**	**4,102**	**4,998**	**1.63**	**21.84**
Other countries of Europe	897	1,928	4,251	4,102	4,998	1.63	21.84
NOT SPECIFIED	**4,258**	**4,241**	**3,325**	**3,960**	**4,390**	**1.43**	**10.86**
Other countries of the World	4,258	4,241	3,325	3,960	4,390	1.43	10.86

Yearbook of Tourism Statistics, Data 2008 – 2012, 2014 Edition

SAINT VINCENT AND THE GRENADINES

1. Arrivals of non-resident tourists at national borders, by country of residence

		2008	2009	2010	2011	2012	Market share 2012	% Change 2012-2011
TOTAL	(*)	84,101	75,446	72,478	73,866	74,364	100.00	0.67
AMERICAS		60,549	55,424	53,933	52,391	52,724	70.90	0.64
Caribbean		28,475	26,835	23,968	23,272	22,768	30.62	-2.17
Antigua and Barbuda		1,078	1,093	921	847	914	1.23	7.91
Barbados		8,993	8,335	7,375	6,562	6,665	8.96	1.57
Grenada		1,374	1,521	1,075	1,007	946	1.27	-6.06
Netherlands Antilles		443	419	294	375	388	0.52	3.47
Saint Lucia		2,197	2,122	1,917	1,937	1,862	2.50	-3.87
Trinidad and Tobago		8,335	7,346	6,709	7,110	7,290	9.80	2.53
Other countries of the Caribbean		6,055	5,999	5,677	5,434	4,703	6.32	-13.45
North America		30,924	26,979	28,759	27,883	28,878	38.83	3.57
Canada		6,882	6,820	7,208	6,719	7,424	9.98	10.49
United States of America		24,042	20,159	21,551	21,164	21,454	28.85	1.37
Other Americas		1,150	1,610	1,206	1,236	1,078	1.45	-12.78
Other countries of the Americas		1,150	1,610	1,206	1,236	1,078	1.45	-12.78
EUROPE		22,302	19,097	17,665	20,549	20,410	27.45	-0.68
Northern Europe		16,276	14,054	12,957	15,650	15,878	21.35	1.46
Ireland		225	209	190	199	194	0.26	-2.51
Norway		149	144	148	165	163	0.22	-1.21
Sweden		460	354	483	391	498	0.67	27.37
United Kingdom		15,442	13,347	12,136	14,895	15,023	20.20	0.86
Southern Europe		1,895	1,591	1,265	1,208	1,108	1.49	-8.28
Italy		1,650	1,429	1,105	1,037	965	1.30	-6.94
Spain		245	162	160	171	143	0.19	-16.37
Western Europe		3,096	2,427	2,468	2,516	2,431	3.27	-3.38
Belgium		222	151	141	171	104	0.14	-39.18
France		1,505	1,113	994	1,051	1,069	1.44	1.71
Germany		861	731	824	744	742	1.00	-0.27
Netherlands		123	67	193	166	98	0.13	-40.96
Switzerland		385	365	316	384	418	0.56	8.85
Other Europe		1,035	1,025	975	1,175	993	1.34	-15.49
Other countries of Europe		1,035	1,025	975	1,175	993	1.34	-15.49
NOT SPECIFIED		1,250	925	880	926	1,230	1.65	32.83
Other countries of the World		1,250	925	880	926	1,230	1.65	32.83

Yearbook of Tourism Statistics, Data 2008 – 2012, 2014 Edition

SAINT VINCENT AND THE GRENADINES

2. Arrivals of non-resident visitors at national borders, by country of residence

		2008	2009	2010	2011	2012	Market share 2012	% Change 2012-2011
TOTAL	(*)	89,882	80,631	77,564	77,807	77,415	100.00	-0.50
AMERICAS		62,779	57,967	56,592	54,516	54,199	70.01	-0.58
Caribbean		29,829	28,507	25,654	24,628	23,656	30.56	-3.95
Antigua and Barbuda		1,113	1,132	971	889	940	1.21	5.74
Barbados		9,560	8,926	8,014	7,507	7,015	9.06	-6.55
Grenada		1,525	1,709	1,204	1,097	969	1.25	-11.67
Netherlands Antilles		440	422	374	386	394	0.51	2.07
Saint Lucia		2,382	2,347	2,139	2,133	1,971	2.55	-7.59
Trinidad and Tobago		8,601	7,754	7,092	7,415	7,446	9.62	0.42
Other countries of the Caribbean		6,208	6,217	5,860	5,201	4,921	6.36	-5.38
North America		31,757	27,812	29,682	28,601	29,419	38.00	2.86
Canada		7,131	7,120	7,565	6,957	7,602	9.82	9.27
United States of America		24,626	20,692	22,117	21,644	21,817	28.18	0.80
Other Americas		1,193	1,648	1,256	1,287	1,124	1.45	-12.67
Other countries of the Americas		1,193	1,648	1,256	1,287	1,124	1.45	-12.67
EUROPE		25,799	21,697	20,041	22,323	21,933	28.33	-1.75
Northern Europe		19,210	16,036	14,715	16,890	17,011	21.97	0.72
Ireland		262	266	225	227	226	0.29	-0.44
Norway		162	146	165	170	164	0.21	-3.53
Sweden		474	381	498	408	511	0.66	25.25
United Kingdom		18,312	15,243	13,827	16,085	16,110	20.81	0.16
Southern Europe		1,985	1,699	1,230	1,261	1,162	1.50	-7.85
Italy		1,735	1,530	1,067	1,079	1,017	1.31	-5.75
Spain		250	169	163	182	145	0.19	-20.33
Western Europe		3,494	2,791	2,832	2,910	2,589	3.34	-11.03
Belgium		237	146	146	178	110	0.14	-38.20
France		1,660	1,213	1,086	1,228	1,110	1.43	-9.61
Germany		1,048	969	1,058	885	816	1.05	-7.80
Netherlands		141	67	196	180	109	0.14	-39.44
Switzerland		408	396	346	439	444	0.57	1.14
Other Europe		1,110	1,171	1,264	1,262	1,171	1.51	-7.21
Other countries of Europe		1,110	1,171	1,264	1,262	1,171	1.51	-7.21
NOT SPECIFIED		1,304	967	931	968	1,283	1.66	32.54
Other countries of the World		1,304	967	931	968	1,283	1.66	32.54

Yearbook of Tourism Statistics, Data 2008 – 2012, 2014 Edition

SAMOA

2. Arrivals of non-resident visitors at national borders, by country of residence

	2008	2009	2010	2011	2012	Market share 2012	% Change 2012-2011
TOTAL	122,163	129,305	129,500	127,603	134,694	100.00	5.56
AMERICAS	8,893	9,794	9,238	7,875	7,948	5.90	0.93
North America	8,893	9,794	9,238	7,875	7,948	5.90	0.93
Canada	428	530	580	450	351	0.26	-22.00
United States of America	8,465	9,264	8,658	7,425	7,597	5.64	2.32
EAST ASIA AND THE PACIFIC	107,580	113,425	115,163	114,798	122,573	91.00	6.77
North-East Asia	1,450	1,794	1,866	2,044	2,359	1.75	15.41
China	720	1,193	1,356	1,512	1,671	1.24	10.52
Japan	730	601	510	532	688	0.51	29.32
Australasia	74,176	79,094	81,252	80,121	87,968	65.31	9.79
Australia	22,643	24,507	23,415	25,197	28,161	20.91	11.76
New Zealand	51,533	54,587	57,837	54,924	59,807	44.40	8.89
Melanesia	2,439	2,538	2,636	2,646	2,876	2.14	8.69
Fiji	2,439	2,538	2,636	2,646	2,876	2.14	8.69
Polynesia	23,672	24,491	23,847	24,787	23,392	17.37	-5.63
American Samoa	23,351	24,298	23,737	24,582	23,180	17.21	-5.70
Cook Islands	321	193	110	205	212	0.16	3.41
Other East Asia and the Pacific	5,843	5,508	5,562	5,200	5,978	4.44	14.96
Other countries of Asia	1,551	1,627	1,927	1,500	2,301	1.71	53.40
Other countries of Oceania	4,292	3,881	3,635	3,700	3,677	2.73	-0.62
EUROPE	5,091	5,547	4,658	4,055	3,487	2.59	-14.01
Northern Europe	2,239	2,392	2,171	1,601	1,351	1.00	-15.62
United Kingdom	1,707	1,719	1,306	1,163	1,031	0.77	-11.35
Scandinavia	532	673	865	438	320	0.24	-26.94
Western Europe	1,457	1,633	1,228	1,291	1,149	0.85	-11.00
Benelux	272	183	139	140	146	0.11	4.29
Germany	1,185	1,450	1,089	1,151	1,003	0.74	-12.86
Other Europe	1,395	1,522	1,259	1,163	987	0.73	-15.13
Other countries of Europe	1,395	1,522	1,259	1,163	987	0.73	-15.13
NOT SPECIFIED	599	539	441	875	686	0.51	-21.60
Other countries of the World	599	539	441	875	686	0.51	-21.60

Yearbook of Tourism Statistics, Data 2008 – 2012, 2014 Edition

SAN MARINO

2. Arrivals of non-resident visitors at national borders, by nationality

	2008	2009	2010	2011	2012	Market share 2012	% Change 2012-2011
TOTAL	2,111,736	2,055,705	1,976,481	2,038,359	1,869,393	100.00	-8.29
AFRICA	188	130	275	206	357	0.02	73.30
East Africa		97	96				
Mozambique			96				
Somalia		97					
Central Africa					100	0.01	
Congo					100	0.01	
North Africa	12		44		138	0.01	
Algeria			29				
Morocco	12		15		51	0.00	
Tunisia					87	0.00	
Southern Africa	176	33	135	206	52	0.00	-74.76
South Africa	176	33	135	206	52	0.00	-74.76
West Africa					67	0.00	
Senegal					67	0.00	
AMERICAS	18,669	12,063	12,142	19,225	17,721	0.95	-7.82
Caribbean	25			71	120	0.01	69.01
Cuba	25			54	50	0.00	-7.41
Puerto Rico				17	70	0.00	311.76
Central America				52	100	0.01	92.31
Costa Rica				52			
Panama					100	0.01	
North America	15,042	10,084	8,188	13,878	10,914	0.58	-21.36
Canada	4,014	3,371	3,115	3,462	3,056	0.16	-11.73
Mexico	278	228	70	140	521	0.03	272.14
United States of America	10,750	6,485	5,003	10,276	7,337	0.39	-28.60
South America	3,602	1,979	3,954	5,224	6,587	0.35	26.09
Argentina	1,267	665	1,514	1,639	1,724	0.09	5.19
Bolivia	130				113	0.01	
Brazil	1,824	1,033	1,904	3,394	4,043	0.22	19.12
Chile	113		221				
Colombia	100		105		265	0.01	
Ecuador		72	33	56			
Paraguay					71	0.00	
Peru					153	0.01	
Uruguay			40		42	0.00	
Venezuela	128	209	60	103	176	0.01	70.87
Other countries of South America	40		77	32			
EAST ASIA AND THE PACIFIC	17,411	18,790	18,386	19,930	21,715	1.16	8.96
North-East Asia	13,426	16,045	14,952	16,731	17,807	0.95	6.43
China	9,665	9,041	10,189	12,206	14,363	0.77	17.67
Hong Kong, China	41				136	0.01	
Japan	3,170	4,998	4,281	3,590	2,933	0.16	-18.30
Korea, Dem. People's Republic of		41					
Korea, Republic of	369	1,965	454	786	358	0.02	-54.45
Taiwan, Province of China	181		28	149	17	0.00	-88.59
South-East Asia	1,037	960	1,327	1,602	1,616	0.09	0.87
Indonesia	25	67	208	209	152	0.01	-27.27
Malaysia	338	246	282	308	696	0.04	125.97
Philippines	601	610	757	699	563	0.03	-19.46
Singapore	37						
Thailand	22	37	80	363	205	0.01	-43.53
Viet Nam	14			23			
Australasia	2,948	1,785	2,107	1,597	2,292	0.12	43.52
Australia	2,884	1,657	2,004	1,483	2,207	0.12	48.82

643

SAN MARINO

2. Arrivals of non-resident visitors at national borders, by nationality

	2008	2009	2010	2011	2012	Market share 2012	% Change 2012-2011
New Zealand	64	128	103	114	85	0.00	-25.44
EUROPE	**2,074,061**	**2,023,438**	**1,944,198**	**1,997,416**	**1,828,558**	**97.82**	**-8.45**
Central/Eastern Europe	**230,300**	**170,000**	**224,078**	**269,567**	**268,902**	**14.38**	**-0.25**
Armenia		63	79		19	0.00	
Belarus	2,267	1,371	1,378	973	1,869	0.10	92.09
Bulgaria	4,792	3,810	2,560	2,991	4,157	0.22	38.98
Czech Republic	14,191	12,363	12,011	10,838	11,621	0.62	7.22
Estonia	4,797	2,387	2,428	3,471	3,819	0.20	10.03
Georgia	71	196	119	27	94	0.01	248.15
Hungary	7,996	6,604	6,784	6,542	4,516	0.24	-30.97
Kazakhstan	50	50	100	23	245	0.01	965.22
Latvia	3,194	1,141	1,116	1,643	1,340	0.07	-18.44
Lithuania	7,812	5,179	5,000	6,266	3,971	0.21	-36.63
Poland	68,382	54,556	57,208	52,725	45,926	2.46	-12.90
Republic of Moldova	505	424	200	91	241	0.01	164.84
Romania	5,839	4,490	4,599	5,004	3,626	0.19	-27.54
Russian Federation	103,983	71,212	123,517	170,781	176,613	9.45	3.41
Slovakia	3,290	1,971	1,994	2,827	3,992	0.21	41.21
Ukraine	2,516	3,733	4,915	5,365	6,288	0.34	17.20
Uzbekistan	50	50	70				
Other countries Central/East Europe	565	400			565	0.03	
Northern Europe	**20,846**	**17,971**	**13,389**	**14,720**	**15,767**	**0.84**	**7.11**
Denmark	1,823	1,901	2,035	1,450	1,824	0.10	25.79
Finland	4,472	3,993	3,852	3,780	3,824	0.20	1.16
Iceland	200		46	276	338	0.02	22.46
Ireland	268	230	305	260	360	0.02	38.46
Norway	2,080	2,837	2,019	1,702	2,686	0.14	57.81
Sweden	4,864	2,742	2,384	3,329	3,207	0.17	-3.66
United Kingdom	6,639	5,868	2,748	3,923	3,528	0.19	-10.07
Other countries of Northern Europe	500	400					
Southern Europe	**1,493,157**	**1,513,729**	**1,415,331**	**1,416,209**	**1,263,728**	**67.60**	**-10.77**
Albania	541	773	379	258	222	0.01	-13.95
Andorra			132		45	0.00	
Bosnia and Herzegovina	1,233	427	1,517	1,819	2,010	0.11	10.50
Croatia	5,547	4,447	4,074	4,060	3,368	0.18	-17.04
Greece	10,282	8,493	6,100	5,848	1,426	0.08	-75.62
Italy	1,454,094	1,483,490	1,381,570	1,385,681	1,238,576	66.26	-10.62
Malta	177	16	88	311	455	0.02	46.30
Portugal	814	629	565	463	481	0.03	3.89
Serbia and Montenegro	9,426	7,467	12,951	9,640	10,043	0.54	4.18
Slovenia	7,649	6,271	5,616	4,693	4,224	0.23	-9.99
Spain	2,848	1,066	2,027	3,344	1,652	0.09	-50.60
TFYR of Macedonia	291	83	238	92	58	0.00	-36.96
Other countries of Southern Europe	255	567	74		1,168	0.06	
Western Europe	**328,084**	**320,268**	**289,484**	**295,388**	**278,389**	**14.89**	**-5.75**
Austria	23,867	23,838	21,544	23,672	20,714	1.11	-12.50
Belgium	22,913	21,684	18,342	18,291	15,766	0.84	-13.80
France	73,404	69,199	62,358	61,498	56,650	3.03	-7.88
Germany	126,049	127,913	110,676	111,885	113,820	6.09	1.73
Liechtenstein	18						
Luxembourg	1,269	1,533	1,989	2,298	2,865	0.15	24.67
Monaco				16			
Netherlands	34,701	33,553	32,035	33,068	26,496	1.42	-19.87
Switzerland	45,863	42,548	42,540	44,660	42,078	2.25	-5.78
East Mediterranean Europe	**1,674**	**1,470**	**1,916**	**1,532**	**1,772**	**0.09**	**15.67**
Cyprus	77	185	81				
Israel	780	979	977	927	832	0.04	-10.25

644

Yearbook of Tourism Statistics, Data 2008 – 2012, 2014 Edition

SAN MARINO

2. Arrivals of non-resident visitors at national borders, by nationality

	2008	2009	2010	2011	2012	Market share 2012	% Change 2012-2011
Turkey	817	306	858	605	940	0.05	55.37
MIDDLE EAST	**272**	**393**	**457**	**469**	**281**	**0.02**	**-40.09**
Egypt			20	166	93	0.00	-43.98
Iraq			12		50	0.00	
Jordan				19	121	0.01	536.84
Lebanon			59	201			
Saudi Arabia	28	38		27	17	0.00	-37.04
Syrian Arab Republic	244	355	366	56			
SOUTH ASIA	**379**	**130**	**364**	**428**	**556**	**0.03**	**29.91**
Bangladesh	379	130	199				
India			105	216	338	0.02	56.48
Iran, Islamic Republic of			60		183	0.01	
Sri Lanka				212	35	0.00	-83.49
NOT SPECIFIED	**756**	**761**	**659**	**685**	**205**	**0.01**	**-70.07**
Other countries of the World	756	761	659	685	205	0.01	-70.07

Yearbook of Tourism Statistics, Data 2008 – 2012, 2014 Edition

SAO TOME AND PRINCIPE

1. Arrivals of non-resident tourists at national borders, by nationality

	2008	2009	2010	2011	2012	Market share 2012	% Change 2012-2011
TOTAL	14,456		7,963	12,221			
AFRICA	2,460		2,123	2,992			
East Africa			24				
Mozambique			24				
Central Africa	1,454		1,484				
Angola	1,141		1,105				
Cameroon	90		71				
Chad			2				
Congo			24				
Equatorial Guinea	53		138				
Gabon	170		144				
North Africa			2				
Morocco			2				
Southern Africa			80				
South Africa			80				
West Africa	470		486				
Benin			9				
Cape Verde	25		251				
Côte d'Ivoire			4				
Ghana			6				
Guinea-Bissau			6				
Mali			5				
Nigeria	445		198				
Senegal			7				
Other Africa	536		47	2,992			
Other countries of Africa	536		47				
All countries of Africa				2,992			
AMERICAS	411		489	980			
Caribbean			1				
Cuba			1				
North America	158		327				
Canada			47				
United States of America	158		280				
South America			139				
Brazil			139				
Other Americas	253		22	980			
Other countries of the Americas	253		22				
All countries of the Americas				980			
EAST ASIA AND THE PACIFIC			85	491			
North-East Asia			79				
China			13				
Japan			23				
Taiwan, Province of China			43				
South-East Asia			6				
Philippines			6				
Other East Asia and the Pacific				491			
All countries East Asia/Pacific				491			
EUROPE	6,348		5,090	6,704			
Northern Europe	138		262				
Denmark			6				
Norway			11				
Sweden			16				
United Kingdom	138		229				
Southern Europe	4,942		3,807				
Italy			80				

Yearbook of Tourism Statistics, Data 2008 – 2012, 2014 Edition

SAO TOME AND PRINCIPE

1. Arrivals of non-resident tourists at national borders, by nationality

	2008	2009	2010	2011	2012	Market share 2012	% Change 2012-2011
Portugal	4,835		3,578				
Spain	107		149				
Western Europe	**593**		**942**				
Austria			23				
Belgium			52				
France	593		514				
Germany			193				
Netherlands			115				
Switzerland			45				
Other Europe	**675**		**79**	**6,704**			
Other countries of Europe	675		79				
All countries of Europe				6,704			
MIDDLE EAST			**27**	**87**			
Lebanon			27				
All countries of Middle East				87			
SOUTH ASIA			**5**	**967**			
India			5				
All countries of South Asia				967			
NOT SPECIFIED	**5,237**		**144**				
Other countries of the World	5,237		144				

Yearbook of Tourism Statistics, Data 2008 – 2012, 2014 Edition

SAUDI ARABIA

1. Arrivals of non-resident tourists at national borders, by nationality

	2008	2009	2010	2011	2012	Market share 2012	% Change 2012-2011
TOTAL	14,757,444	10,896,712	10,850,188	17,497,887	14,276,196	100.00	-18.41
AFRICA	1,033,258	260,717	368,610	790,301	1,138,839	7.98	44.10
East Africa	18,701	12,142	22,313	74,904	118,494	0.83	58.19
Burundi	10	16		85	12	0.00	-85.88
Comoros	65	229	1,051	2,761	4,558	0.03	65.09
Djibouti	557	348	429	1,220	422	0.00	-65.41
Eritrea	5,754	1,282	2,804	14,156	6,851	0.05	-51.60
Ethiopia	4,158	4,086	9,628	38,080	93,479	0.65	145.48
Kenya	4,896	1,858	1,825	6,723	4,776	0.03	-28.96
Madagascar	5	53		171	164	0.00	-4.09
Malawi	30	787		2,015	183	0.00	-90.92
Mauritius	828		1,677	1,414	1,837	0.01	29.92
Mozambique	63	207		1,232	997	0.01	-19.07
Rwanda				59	26	0.00	-55.93
Seychelles	33						
Somalia	1,789	1,623	1,268	3,880	2,320	0.02	-40.21
Uganda	86	229	758	630	405	0.00	-35.71
United Republic of Tanzania	279			1,525	1,468	0.01	-3.74
Zambia	103	72		261	319	0.00	22.22
Zimbabwe	45	739		492	438	0.00	-10.98
Other countries of East Africa		613	2,873	200	239	0.00	19.50
Central Africa	765	5,104	3,888	7,196	171,174	1.20	2,278.74
Angola		13		599	12	0.00	-98.00
Cameroon	108	2,504	1,029	1,357	1,311	0.01	-3.39
Central African Republic	4	36		73	49	0.00	-32.88
Chad	612	2,465	2,686	4,832	3,861	0.03	-20.10
Congo	28	37		221	165,799	1.16	74,922.17
Equatorial Guinea		8		5	1	0.00	-80.00
Gabon	13	41		97	133	0.00	37.11
Other countries of Central Africa			173	12	8	0.00	-33.33
North Africa	951,638	205,734	256,445	581,493	537,483	3.76	-7.57
Algeria	393,609	64,015	96,097	124,163	226,139	1.58	82.13
Morocco	66,838	41,108	60,995	108,339	97,546	0.68	-9.96
Sudan	398,607	88,269	65,352	298,344	159,581	1.12	-46.51
Tunisia	92,584	12,342	34,001	50,647	54,217	0.38	7.05
Southern Africa	24,039	14,144	25,203	41,244	54,861	0.38	33.02
Botswana	42	52		67	97	0.00	44.78
Lesotho	6	29		126	60	0.00	-52.38
Namibia	12	16		80	110	0.00	37.50
South Africa	23,979	14,024	24,996	40,910	54,477	0.38	33.16
Swaziland		23		59	78	0.00	32.20
Other countries of Southern Africa			207	2	39	0.00	1,850.00
West Africa	38,115	23,593	60,761	85,464	256,827	1.80	200.51
Benin	53	234		693	475	0.00	-31.46
Burkina Faso	61	390		1,361	878	0.01	-35.49
Côte d'Ivoire	90	149		512	341	0.00	-33.40
Gambia	32	91		398	226	0.00	-43.22
Ghana	18,870	954	1,568	3,244	1,593	0.01	-50.89
Guinea	98	219		892	654	0.00	-26.68
Guinea-Bissau		6		86	50	0.00	-41.86
Liberia	15	102		103	64	0.00	-37.86
Mali	319	465					
Mauritania	393	1,128	2,354	4,261	3,474	0.02	-18.47
Niger	230	609	1,965	2,905	2,839	0.02	-2.27
Nigeria	10,065	17,759	51,090	66,599	241,868	1.69	263.17
Senegal	1,862	399	1,175	2,232	862	0.01	-61.38

SAUDI ARABIA

1. Arrivals of non-resident tourists at national borders, by nationality

	2008	2009	2010	2011	2012	Market share 2012	% Change 2012-2011
Sierra Leone	24	123		241	462	0.00	91.70
Togo	6,003	120		255	129	0.00	-49.41
Other countries of West Africa		845	2,609	1,682	2,912	0.02	73.13
AMERICAS	**297,143**	**56,841**	**53,432**	**182,105**	**162,863**	**1.14**	**-10.57**
Caribbean	**3,605**	**309**	**1,369**	**1,479**	**1,178**	**0.01**	**-20.35**
Bahamas				26	12	0.00	-53.85
Barbados	13	12		49	39	0.00	-20.41
British Virgin Islands	65	7					
Cuba	8	4	1,092	29	16	0.00	-44.83
Dominica	11			54	62	0.00	14.81
Dominican Republic		6					
Haiti	99	3		15	5	0.00	-66.67
Jamaica	3,077	17	277	82	47	0.00	-42.68
Puerto Rico					366	0.00	
Saint Lucia				5	2	0.00	-60.00
Trinidad and Tobago	332	260		1,219	629	0.00	-48.40
Central America	**118**	**320**		**814**	**846**	**0.01**	**3.93**
Belize	16	15		75	34	0.00	-54.67
Costa Rica	21	33		178	27	0.00	-84.83
El Salvador		33		160	525	0.00	228.13
Guatemala	27	12		41	29	0.00	-29.27
Honduras	36	22		102	145	0.00	42.16
Nicaragua		151		24	14	0.00	-41.67
Panama	18	54		234	72	0.00	-69.23
North America	**289,948**	**53,476**	**50,043**	**169,002**	**97,569**	**0.68**	**-42.27**
Canada	46,568	11,468	11,716	67,877	17,321	0.12	-74.48
Mexico	266	231	550	1,432	245	0.00	-82.89
United States of America	243,114	41,777	37,777	99,693	80,003	0.56	-19.75
South America	**3,321**	**2,736**	**2,020**	**10,810**	**63,175**	**0.44**	**484.41**
Argentina	536	1,468	351	1,294	469	0.00	-63.76
Bolivia	20	17		162	42	0.00	-74.07
Brazil	1,500	735	935	2,154	1,237	0.01	-42.57
Chile	57	37		229	93	0.00	-59.39
Colombia	163	176		2,020	352	0.00	-82.57
Ecuador	72	14		203	95	0.00	-53.20
Paraguay		7		21	7	0.00	-66.67
Peru	33	39		257	65	0.00	-74.71
Suriname	5	1		12	60,166	0.42	501,283.33
Uruguay	13	11		97	56	0.00	-42.27
Venezuela	922	231	734	4,361	593	0.00	-86.40
Other Americas	**151**				**95**	**0.00**	
Other countries of the Americas	151				95	0.00	
EAST ASIA AND THE PACIFIC	**940,928**	**362,500**	**485,534**	**844,723**	**1,016,597**	**7.12**	**20.35**
North-East Asia	**90,738**	**39,022**	**40,655**	**66,644**	**64,020**	**0.45**	**-3.94**
China	55,352	18,298	20,416	24,409	19,436	0.14	-20.37
Hong Kong, China	380	237		30	11,011	0.08	36,603.33
Japan	14,590	6,539	9,210	16,410	11,803	0.08	-28.07
Korea, Republic of	20,400	13,842	10,932	25,738	21,742	0.15	-15.53
Mongolia	16	105		51	24	0.00	-52.94
Other countries of North-East Asia		1	97	6	4	0.00	-33.33
South-East Asia	**831,129**	**320,255**	**436,692**	**734,899**	**934,987**	**6.55**	**27.23**
Brunei Darussalam	1,024	5,134	4,927	2,281	3,613	0.03	58.40
Cambodia	13	48	26	146	86	0.00	-41.10
Indonesia	501,758	205,374	235,636	404,903	676,764	4.74	67.14
Malaysia	141,778	62,749	152,396	110,148	165,086	1.16	49.88
Myanmar	12,231	479	3,149	1,244	1,180	0.01	-5.14

Yearbook of Tourism Statistics, Data 2008 – 2012, 2014 Edition

SAUDI ARABIA

1. Arrivals of non-resident tourists at national borders, by nationality

	2008	2009	2010	2011	2012	Market share 2012	% Change 2012-2011
Philippines	73,981	35,213	28,053	197,463	63,114	0.44	-68.04
Singapore	4,951	4,875	5,935	9,375	20,095	0.14	114.35
Thailand	50,845	5,217	3,425	8,108	4,880	0.03	-39.81
Viet Nam	44,548	1,166	3,145	1,231	169	0.00	-86.27
Australasia	**19,021**	**3,192**	**8,187**	**42,988**	**17,518**	**0.12**	**-59.25**
Australia	17,511	2,794	6,036	37,450	14,568	0.10	-61.10
New Zealand	1,510	398	2,151	5,538	2,950	0.02	-46.73
Melanesia	**40**	**20**		**32**	**15**	**0.00**	**-53.13**
Fiji	40	20		32	15	0.00	-53.13
Micronesia				**131**	**30**	**0.00**	**-77.10**
Kiribati				1	20	0.00	1,900.00
Marshall Islands				130	10	0.00	-92.31
Polynesia		**11**		**12**	**20**	**0.00**	**66.67**
American Samoa		11		1	19	0.00	1,800.00
French Polynesia				5	1	0.00	-80.00
Tonga				6			
Other East Asia and the Pacific				**17**	**7**	**0.00**	**-58.82**
Other countries of Oceania				17	7	0.00	-58.82
EUROPE	**1,185,068**	**444,667**	**367,238**	**722,534**	**982,253**	**6.88**	**35.95**
Central/Eastern Europe	**151,216**	**13,633**	**24,465**	**47,048**	**30,596**	**0.21**	**-34.97**
Armenia	211	42		45	36	0.00	-20.00
Azerbaijan	66,467	552	974	1,762	1,719	0.01	-2.44
Belarus	77	116		434	232	0.00	-46.54
Bulgaria	223	170		756	603	0.00	-20.24
Czech Republic	641	2,233		2,447	725	0.01	-70.37
Estonia	13	39		116	60	0.00	-48.28
Georgia	234	33		197	169	0.00	-14.21
Hungary	385	271		987	740	0.01	-25.03
Kazakhstan	394	176	4,207	2,146	2,750	0.02	28.15
Kyrgyzstan	70				482	0.00	
Latvia	35	80		221	233	0.00	5.43
Lithuania	35	58		138	156	0.00	13.04
Poland	6,768	476	909	2,319	2,157	0.02	-6.99
Republic of Moldova	8	22		60	39	0.00	-35.00
Romania	882	626	1,040	3,504	1,748	0.01	-50.11
Russian Federation	73,645	3,540	3,418	5,894	4,985	0.03	-15.42
Slovakia	145	156		767	387	0.00	-49.54
Tajikistan	135	877		1,045	1,651	0.01	57.99
Turkmenistan	34	174		720	886	0.01	23.06
Ukraine	497	738	1,212	2,560	2,996	0.02	17.03
Uzbekistan	317	2,792	9,084	5,547	7,018	0.05	26.52
Other countries Central/East Europe		462	3,621	15,383	824	0.01	-94.64
Northern Europe	**341,403**	**182,008**	**113,147**	**283,717**	**156,026**	**1.09**	**-45.01**
Denmark	1,280	1,906	4,823	8,446	3,905	0.03	-53.77
Finland	836	669	1,100	2,774	1,868	0.01	-32.66
Iceland	145	69	76	258	256	0.00	-0.78
Ireland	5,804	4,853	4,155	11,757	7,401	0.05	-37.05
Norway	1,037	1,918	1,742	3,564	2,895	0.02	-18.77
Sweden	41,471	2,126	3,107	5,724	4,441	0.03	-22.41
United Kingdom	284,685	170,467	98,144	251,194	135,260	0.95	-46.15
Other countries of Northern Europe	6,145						
Southern Europe	**122,184**	**26,836**	**19,506**	**45,105**	**33,656**	**0.24**	**-25.38**
Albania	70	129	195	332	251	0.00	-24.40
Andorra		1		2	4	0.00	100.00
Bosnia and Herzegovina	202	281	552	885	799	0.01	-9.72
Croatia	379	910	398	1,143	1,292	0.01	13.04
Greece	13,141	1,831	1,677	7,266	3,435	0.02	-52.73

650

SAUDI ARABIA

1. Arrivals of non-resident tourists at national borders, by nationality

	2008	2009	2010	2011	2012	Market share 2012	% Change 2012-2011
Italy	48,909	11,504	9,599	23,743	16,026	0.11	-32.50
Malta	48	61	183	497	190	0.00	-61.77
Portugal	484	856	1,049	2,281	2,161	0.02	-5.26
San Marino		3					
Serbia		12					
Slovenia	41,904	97	137	221	296	0.00	33.94
Spain	16,965	10,999	5,460	8,392	8,788	0.06	4.72
Other countries of Southern Europe	82	152	256	343	414	0.00	20.70
Western Europe	**321,180**	**66,012**	**80,667**	**148,438**	**107,085**	**0.75**	**-27.86**
Austria	23,964	9,954	3,726	5,377	3,601	0.03	-33.03
Belgium	8,414	2,797	5,383	8,240	6,777	0.05	-17.75
France	107,584	20,720	28,802	68,663	37,496	0.26	-45.39
Germany	80,192	22,940	28,818	39,202	30,587	0.21	-21.98
Liechtenstein				4	6	0.00	50.00
Luxembourg	1,036	64		148	109	0.00	-26.35
Netherlands	95,123	5,213	10,412	19,057	15,721	0.11	-17.51
Switzerland	4,867	4,324	3,421	7,747	12,788	0.09	65.07
Other countries of Western Europe			105				
East Mediterranean Europe	**249,085**	**156,178**	**129,453**	**198,226**	**654,890**	**4.59**	**230.38**
Cyprus	585	2,167	526	1,147	758	0.01	-33.91
Turkey	248,500	154,011	128,927	197,079	654,132	4.58	231.91
MIDDLE EAST	**9,333,965**	**8,677,688**	**8,244,721**	**11,098,731**	**8,063,169**	**56.48**	**-27.35**
Bahrain	594,188	624,793	820,132	1,220,651	1,012,397	7.09	-17.06
Egypt	1,853,663	538,287	763,901	1,157,812	1,142,021	8.00	-1.36
Iraq	24,282	64,138	171,913	44,862	165,896	1.16	269.79
Jordan	501,269	517,167	451,099	1,666,814	1,352,257	9.47	-18.87
Kuwait	2,589,988	2,475,318	2,507,813	2,578,541	1,855,774	13.00	-28.03
Lebanon	307,492	58,337	116,129	164,157	111,810	0.78	-31.89
Libya	8,202	27,835	42,976	1,651	86,674	0.61	5,149.79
Oman	125,552	165,875	176,687	373,421	357,811	2.51	-4.18
Palestine	1,997	14,487	26,084	82,814	11,982	0.08	-85.53
Qatar	808,072	1,470,382	843,762	1,058,300	810,336	5.68	-23.43
Syrian Arab Republic	708,034	730,306	254,140	765,908	86,129	0.60	-88.75
United Arab Emirates	1,613,574	1,889,187	1,957,613	1,531,429	861,735	6.04	-43.73
Yemen	197,652	101,576	112,472	452,371	205,657	1.44	-54.54
Other countries of Middle East					2,690	0.02	
SOUTH ASIA	**1,967,082**	**1,094,282**	**1,330,271**	**3,858,203**	**2,902,963**	**20.33**	**-24.76**
Afghanistan	5,562	5,140	8,793	24,403	17,238	0.12	-29.36
Bangladesh	34,187	23,698	188,584	407,697	93,593	0.66	-77.04
Bhutan				1,590	4	0.00	-99.75
India	601,922	247,075	389,116	1,501,308	998,779	7.00	-33.47
Iran, Islamic Republic of	349,848	413,656	220,051	559,690	506,192	3.55	-9.56
Maldives	188	2,456	3,466	1,729	1,942	0.01	12.32
Nepal	126,444	32,694	25,841	57,586	40,342	0.28	-29.94
Pakistan	817,550	336,255	465,571	1,219,287	1,172,470	8.21	-3.84
Sri Lanka	31,381	33,308	28,779	84,913	72,403	0.51	-14.73
Other countries of South Asia			70				
NOT SPECIFIED		**17**	**382**	**1,290**	**9,512**	**0.07**	**637.36**
Other countries of the World		17	382	1,290	9,512	0.07	637.36

651

SENEGAL

1. Arrivals of non-resident tourists at national borders, by nationality

		2008	2009	2010	2011	2012	Market share 2012	% Change 2012-2011
TOTAL	(*)	491,552	458,912	492,261	449,954			
AFRICA		121,286	111,525	114,623	107,990			
North Africa				6,217	5,701			
Morocco				4,427	3,997			
Tunisia				1,790	1,704			
West Africa		60,610	52,803	74,901	65,317			
Burkina Faso				4,902	5,083			
Côte d'Ivoire		10,182	8,659	9,981	8,975			
Gambia				7,301	6,168			
Guinea		15,779	14,114	15,327	13,269			
Guinea-Bissau				4,737	4,051			
Mali		11,746	10,885	11,919	10,746			
Mauritania		8,916	7,847	8,139	6,773			
Nigeria		13,987	11,298	12,595	10,252			
Other Africa		60,676	58,722	33,505	36,972			
Other countries of Africa		60,676	58,722	33,505	36,972			
AMERICAS		17,783	18,942	19,958	18,366			
North America		17,783	18,942	19,958	18,366			
United States of America		17,783	18,942	19,958	18,366			
EUROPE		280,044	263,657	271,324	257,208			
Southern Europe		26,030	25,579	26,106	24,095			
Italy		11,482	11,547	11,603	10,960			
Spain		14,548	14,032	14,503	13,135			
Western Europe		229,567	213,189	229,032	218,168			
Belgium		17,271	14,211	14,400	14,343			
France		212,296	198,978	205,114	194,892			
Germany				6,091	5,683			
Luxembourg				3,427	3,250			
Other Europe		24,447	24,889	16,186	14,945			
Other countries of Europe		24,447	24,889	16,186	14,945			
NOT SPECIFIED		72,439	64,788	86,356	66,390			
Other countries of the World		22,115	16,879	27,477	21,427			
Nationals Residing Abroad		50,324	47,909	58,879	44,963			

652

SENEGAL

1. Arrivals of non-resident tourists at national borders, by country of residence

		2008	2009	2010	2011	2012	Market share 2012	% Change 2012-2011
TOTAL	(*)	**491,552**	**458,912**	**492,261**	**449,954**			
AFRICA		**126,321**	**113,109**	**123,273**	**113,067**			
North Africa		**7,395**	**7,026**	**8,133**	**7,491**			
Morocco		5,514	4,989	5,969	5,524			
Tunisia		1,881	2,037	2,164	1,967			
West Africa		**49,187**	**44,687**	**47,332**	**41,044**			
Gambia		7,351	7,603	7,369	6,254			
Guinea		15,167	13,740	14,841	12,843			
Guinea-Bissau		6,077	4,783	5,005	4,345			
Mali		12,300	11,275	12,494	11,336			
Mauritania		8,292	7,286	7,623	6,266			
Other Africa		**69,739**	**61,396**	**67,808**	**64,532**			
Other countries of Africa		69,739	61,396	67,808	64,532			
AMERICAS		**20,146**	**21,690**	**23,048**	**20,672**			
North America		**20,146**	**21,690**	**23,048**	**20,672**			
United States of America		20,146	21,690	23,048	20,672			
EUROPE		**325,135**	**303,445**	**319,882**	**293,812**			
Southern Europe		**50,277**	**46,215**	**52,207**	**43,556**			
Italy		27,080	25,583	29,996	23,764			
Spain		23,197	20,632	22,211	19,792			
Western Europe		**253,365**	**237,632**	**249,896**	**234,644**			
Belgium		17,812	14,771	14,895	14,744			
France		229,559	216,599	225,214	210,878			
Germany		5,994	6,262	6,178	5,695			
Luxembourg				3,609	3,327			
Other Europe		**21,493**	**19,598**	**17,779**	**15,612**			
Other countries of Europe		21,493	19,598	17,779	15,612			
NOT SPECIFIED		**19,950**	**20,668**	**26,058**	**22,403**			
Other countries of the World		19,950	20,668	26,058	22,403			

Yearbook of Tourism Statistics, Data 2008 – 2012, 2014 Edition

SERBIA

3. Arrivals of non-resident tourists in hotels and similar establishments, by nationality

	2008	2009	2010	2011	2012	Market share 2012	% Change 2012-2011
TOTAL	563,593	569,535	612,989	680,365	707,173	100.00	3.94
AMERICAS	14,209	15,064	17,459	18,005	19,790	2.80	9.91
North America	14,209	15,064	17,459	18,005	19,790	2.80	9.91
Canada	3,687	3,429	4,081	4,177	4,581	0.65	9.67
United States of America	10,522	11,635	13,378	13,828	15,209	2.15	9.99
EAST ASIA AND THE PACIFIC	7,112	6,897	8,798	10,647	12,713	1.80	19.40
North-East Asia	2,228	2,379	2,842	3,846	5,026	0.71	30.68
Japan	2,228	2,379	2,842	3,846	5,026	0.71	30.68
Australasia	4,884	4,518	5,956	6,801	7,687	1.09	13.03
Australia	4,221	4,001	5,329	6,096	6,993	0.99	14.71
New Zealand	663	517	627	705	694	0.10	-1.56
EUROPE	529,384	532,804	566,315	630,597	649,788	91.89	3.04
Central/Eastern Europe	100,836	111,019	114,325	128,645	142,357	20.13	10.66
Bulgaria	19,786	22,472	22,912	25,626	31,767	4.49	23.96
Czech Republic	7,524	8,346	9,147	8,613	9,070	1.28	5.31
Hungary	13,765	14,666	15,050	17,144	18,281	2.59	6.63
Poland	18,858	20,624	18,997	19,810	19,504	2.76	-1.54
Romania	19,298	21,073	22,478	28,292	29,337	4.15	3.69
Russian Federation	15,242	15,712	19,827	22,957	28,478	4.03	24.05
Slovakia	6,363	8,126	5,914	6,203	5,920	0.84	-4.56
Northern Europe	34,720	30,722	34,321	40,246	44,420	6.28	10.37
Denmark	3,093	2,996	3,378	3,634	5,007	0.71	37.78
Finland	1,622	1,533	1,831	2,523	1,963	0.28	-22.20
Iceland	490	321	339	342	518	0.07	51.46
Ireland	1,555	1,452	1,583	1,849	1,855	0.26	0.32
Norway	4,373	3,948	4,881	5,126	6,268	0.89	22.28
Sweden	6,682	6,089	6,637	9,341	11,136	1.57	19.22
United Kingdom	16,905	14,383	15,672	17,431	17,673	2.50	1.39
Southern Europe	274,444	269,557	286,275	310,181	304,853	43.11	-1.72
Bosnia and Herzegovina	58,545	56,705	55,805	56,639	53,980	7.63	-4.69
Croatia	36,698	38,667	43,870	48,073	43,682	6.18	-9.13
Greece	21,672	21,927	23,026	25,128	25,690	3.63	2.24
Italy	29,069	28,847	30,651	36,255	47,551	6.72	31.16
Montenegro	53,506	40,108	38,026	39,096	36,467	5.16	-6.72
Portugal	1,525	1,239	1,414	1,666	1,678	0.24	0.72
Slovenia	42,943	50,156	61,938	68,735	60,027	8.49	-12.67
Spain	4,694	5,048	5,667	6,275	5,679	0.80	-9.50
TFYR of Macedonia	25,792	26,860	25,878	28,314	30,099	4.26	6.30
Western Europe	92,291	93,665	103,716	113,684	116,138	16.42	2.16
Austria	19,201	20,585	22,978	23,948	23,476	3.32	-1.97
Belgium	4,454	4,288	4,929	6,530	6,248	0.88	-4.32
France	15,387	15,073	16,734	16,559	17,896	2.53	8.07
Germany	35,894	37,348	40,739	45,774	46,420	6.56	1.41
Luxembourg	412	249	393	386	467	0.07	20.98
Netherlands	11,163	9,668	10,601	11,173	11,220	1.59	0.42
Switzerland	5,780	6,454	7,342	9,314	10,411	1.47	11.78
East Mediterranean Europe	14,378	16,044	16,562	21,762	21,498	3.04	-1.21
Israel	3,337	2,599	3,009	3,286	3,781	0.53	15.06
Turkey	11,041	13,445	13,553	18,476	17,717	2.51	-4.11
Other Europe	12,715	11,797	11,116	16,079	20,522	2.90	27.63
Other countries of Europe	12,715	11,797	11,116	16,079	20,522	2.90	27.63
NOT SPECIFIED	12,888	14,770	20,417	21,116	24,882	3.52	17.83
Other countries of the World	12,888	14,770	20,417	21,116	24,882	3.52	17.83

654

Yearbook of Tourism Statistics, Data 2008 – 2012, 2014 Edition

SERBIA

4. Arrivals of non-resident tourists in all types of accommodation establishments, by nationality

	2008	2009	2010	2011	2012	Market share 2012	% Change 2012-2011
TOTAL	646,494	645,022	682,681	764,167	809,967	100.00	5.99
AMERICAS	15,002	16,266	18,554	19,180	21,641	2.67	12.83
North America	15,002	16,266	18,554	19,180	21,641	2.67	12.83
Canada	3,886	3,969	4,408	4,542	5,140	0.63	13.17
United States of America	11,116	12,297	14,146	14,638	16,501	2.04	12.73
EAST ASIA AND THE PACIFIC	7,826	8,160	9,903	12,193	14,997	1.85	23.00
North-East Asia	2,342	2,929	3,011	3,988	5,251	0.65	31.67
Japan	2,342	2,929	3,011	3,988	5,251	0.65	31.67
Australasia	5,484	5,231	6,892	8,205	9,746	1.20	18.78
Australia	4,711	4,613	6,137	7,283	8,772	1.08	20.44
New Zealand	773	618	755	922	974	0.12	5.64
EUROPE	610,004	602,599	632,964	710,757	745,959	92.10	4.95
Central/Eastern Europe	108,995	120,985	123,547	139,951	159,172	19.65	13.73
Bulgaria	22,727	24,476	24,582	28,054	35,243	4.35	25.63
Czech Republic	8,022	9,271	9,844	9,278	10,042	1.24	8.23
Hungary	14,870	16,291	16,276	18,660	20,315	2.51	8.87
Poland	19,855	22,304	20,672	21,548	23,323	2.88	8.24
Romania	20,701	22,876	23,907	30,628	32,042	3.96	4.62
Russian Federation	16,092	17,312	21,636	25,236	31,628	3.90	25.33
Slovakia	6,728	8,455	6,630	6,547	6,579	0.81	0.49
Northern Europe	36,573	33,294	38,037	44,250	49,524	6.11	11.92
Denmark	3,404	3,208	3,633	3,872	5,471	0.68	41.30
Finland	1,765	1,728	1,999	2,692	2,223	0.27	-17.42
Iceland	496	337	350	361	539	0.07	49.31
Ireland	1,727	1,665	1,782	2,070	2,049	0.25	-1.01
Norway	4,559	4,203	5,176	5,340	6,765	0.84	26.69
Sweden	6,870	6,531	7,071	9,917	12,186	1.50	22.88
United Kingdom	17,752	15,622	18,026	19,998	20,291	2.51	1.47
Southern Europe	339,499	318,803	331,827	364,725	361,045	44.58	-1.01
Bosnia and Herzegovina	64,729	63,981	63,560	65,960	62,276	7.69	-5.59
Croatia	38,073	40,243	46,367	50,625	47,229	5.83	-6.71
Greece	23,618	24,155	24,726	26,400	26,900	3.32	1.89
Italy	39,919	37,321	34,221	38,105	50,580	6.24	32.74
Montenegro	93,220	61,752	56,888	66,636	64,703	7.99	-2.90
Portugal	1,610	1,425	1,647	1,856	1,967	0.24	5.98
Slovenia	45,661	54,766	66,686	74,674	65,723	8.11	-11.99
Spain	5,043	5,581	6,151	6,850	6,584	0.81	-3.88
TFYR of Macedonia	27,626	29,579	31,581	33,619	35,083	4.33	4.35
Western Europe	96,156	99,672	110,777	121,992	129,206	15.95	5.91
Austria	19,820	21,464	24,075	25,245	25,216	3.11	-0.11
Belgium	4,633	4,529	5,339	7,131	7,090	0.88	-0.57
France	16,324	16,542	18,339	18,191	20,219	2.50	11.15
Germany	37,194	39,497	42,672	48,159	50,896	6.28	5.68
Luxembourg	443	261	415	443	485	0.06	9.48
Netherlands	11,685	10,357	12,082	12,963	14,027	1.73	8.21
Switzerland	6,057	7,022	7,855	9,860	11,273	1.39	14.33
East Mediterranean Europe	15,337	16,701	16,973	22,618	24,822	3.06	9.74
Israel	3,426	2,780	3,131	3,422	3,957	0.49	15.63
Turkey	11,911	13,921	13,842	19,196	20,865	2.58	8.69
Other Europe	13,444	13,144	11,803	17,221	22,190	2.74	28.85
Other countries of Europe	13,444	13,144	11,803	17,221	22,190	2.74	28.85
NOT SPECIFIED	13,662	17,997	21,260	22,037	27,370	3.38	24.20
Other countries of the World	13,662	17,997	21,260	22,037	27,370	3.38	24.20

Yearbook of Tourism Statistics, Data 2008 – 2012, 2014 Edition

SERBIA

5. Overnight stays of non-resident tourists in hotels and similar establishments, by nationality

	2008	2009	2010	2011	2012	Market share 2012	% Change 2012-2011
TOTAL	1,194,593	1,184,154	1,235,654	1,387,148	1,518,577	100.00	9.47
AMERICAS	37,056	40,704	45,661	46,997	52,065	3.43	10.78
North America	37,056	40,704	45,661	46,997	52,065	3.43	10.78
Canada	8,799	9,172	9,917	10,701	10,677	0.70	-0.22
United States of America	28,257	31,532	35,744	36,296	41,388	2.73	14.03
EAST ASIA AND THE PACIFIC	16,015	15,231	19,862	23,426	30,700	2.02	31.05
North-East Asia	4,922	5,744	7,397	8,372	13,241	0.87	58.16
Japan	4,922	5,744	7,397	8,372	13,241	0.87	58.16
Australasia	11,093	9,487	12,465	15,054	17,459	1.15	15.98
Australia	9,445	8,451	11,106	13,694	15,943	1.05	16.42
New Zealand	1,648	1,036	1,359	1,360	1,516	0.10	11.47
EUROPE	1,096,281	1,080,313	1,111,912	1,261,918	1,369,692	90.20	8.54
Central/Eastern Europe	213,082	224,885	218,272	258,003	297,214	19.57	15.20
Bulgaria	40,049	42,260	39,597	48,307	69,132	4.55	43.11
Czech Republic	15,749	16,901	17,994	17,651	18,704	1.23	5.97
Hungary	23,397	25,316	24,745	32,547	34,495	2.27	5.99
Poland	28,235	30,006	28,547	30,972	32,308	2.13	4.31
Romania	40,777	41,141	42,033	53,871	54,673	3.60	1.49
Russian Federation	48,881	46,001	53,578	62,182	75,717	4.99	21.77
Slovakia	15,994	23,260	11,778	12,473	12,185	0.80	-2.31
Northern Europe	90,095	74,015	82,990	103,776	118,183	7.78	13.88
Denmark	7,655	7,018	7,591	9,700	14,361	0.95	48.05
Finland	4,435	3,703	4,294	6,456	4,442	0.29	-31.20
Iceland	1,434	984	984	1,121	1,742	0.11	55.40
Ireland	4,223	3,486	4,945	5,517	4,961	0.33	-10.08
Norway	11,165	9,947	12,146	14,754	20,862	1.37	41.40
Sweden	15,412	13,688	14,196	21,531	26,670	1.76	23.87
United Kingdom	45,771	35,189	38,834	44,697	45,145	2.97	1.00
Southern Europe	545,438	538,648	545,550	594,178	634,472	41.78	6.78
Bosnia and Herzegovina	116,531	120,214	105,503	113,626	110,186	7.26	-3.03
Croatia	67,246	74,597	82,410	85,443	81,838	5.39	-4.22
Greece	47,007	43,540	42,996	46,509	48,737	3.21	4.79
Italy	64,329	67,493	73,909	86,436	138,308	9.11	60.01
Montenegro	113,359	84,625	76,308	81,189	80,002	5.27	-1.46
Portugal	4,146	3,204	3,190	4,774	4,314	0.28	-9.64
Slovenia	74,563	84,333	102,904	110,715	102,682	6.76	-7.26
Spain	11,859	12,199	12,982	16,002	14,082	0.93	-12.00
TFYR of Macedonia	46,398	48,443	45,348	49,484	54,323	3.58	9.78
Western Europe	190,512	187,357	206,361	229,549	239,176	15.75	4.19
Austria	34,479	38,048	41,667	42,618	42,882	2.82	0.62
Belgium	9,413	9,074	9,767	14,165	13,367	0.88	-5.63
France	34,138	31,762	37,555	36,865	40,827	2.69	10.75
Germany	76,168	74,311	78,984	90,227	93,342	6.15	3.45
Luxembourg	868	552	768	922	1,046	0.07	13.45
Netherlands	22,278	18,567	21,740	24,331	24,923	1.64	2.43
Switzerland	13,168	15,043	15,880	20,421	22,789	1.50	11.60
East Mediterranean Europe	26,009	27,302	29,482	39,681	39,397	2.59	-0.72
Israel	8,358	6,092	7,256	8,015	8,613	0.57	7.46
Turkey	17,651	21,210	22,226	31,666	30,784	2.03	-2.79
Other Europe	31,145	28,106	29,257	36,731	41,250	2.72	12.30
Other countries of Europe	31,145	28,106	29,257	36,731	41,250	2.72	12.30
NOT SPECIFIED	45,241	47,906	58,219	54,807	66,120	4.35	20.64
Other countries of the World	45,241	47,906	58,219	54,807	66,120	4.35	20.64

Yearbook of Tourism Statistics, Data 2008 – 2012, 2014 Edition

SERBIA

6. Overnight stays of non-resident tourists in all types of accommodation establishments, by nationality

	2008	2009	2010	2011	2012	Market share 2012	% Change 2012-2011
TOTAL	1,398,887	1,469,102	1,452,156	1,643,054	1,796,217	100.00	9.32
AMERICAS	40,324	49,939	49,310	50,817	57,733	3.21	13.61
North America	40,324	49,939	49,310	50,817	57,733	3.21	13.61
Canada	10,032	14,918	11,072	12,235	12,387	0.69	1.24
United States of America	30,292	35,021	38,238	38,582	45,346	2.52	17.53
EAST ASIA AND THE PACIFIC	19,403	26,500	23,359	27,310	36,330	2.02	33.03
North-East Asia	6,680	12,448	8,805	9,515	14,754	0.82	55.06
Japan	6,680	12,448	8,805	9,515	14,754	0.82	55.06
Australasia	12,723	14,052	14,554	17,795	21,576	1.20	21.25
Australia	10,792	12,543	13,002	16,118	19,717	1.10	22.33
New Zealand	1,931	1,509	1,552	1,677	1,859	0.10	10.85
EUROPE	1,287,470	1,306,508	1,312,069	1,501,808	1,623,215	90.37	8.08
Central/Eastern Europe	239,954	267,327	248,357	300,646	349,377	19.45	16.21
Bulgaria	44,963	46,507	44,448	55,689	76,622	4.27	37.59
Czech Republic	18,349	21,683	20,026	19,436	21,598	1.20	11.12
Hungary	27,360	30,505	27,793	41,005	42,259	2.35	3.06
Poland	32,521	36,123	32,276	35,180	40,350	2.25	14.70
Romania	45,396	47,572	47,068	59,911	62,916	3.50	5.02
Russian Federation	54,035	59,488	62,583	75,308	91,517	5.09	21.52
Slovakia	17,330	25,449	14,163	14,117	14,115	0.79	-0.01
Northern Europe	96,285	87,239	92,626	117,722	131,641	7.33	11.82
Denmark	8,172	7,799	8,354	10,239	15,286	0.85	49.29
Finland	5,083	4,908	4,734	6,900	5,262	0.29	-23.74
Iceland	1,442	1,008	1,034	1,235	1,782	0.10	44.29
Ireland	4,751	5,158	5,382	6,194	5,362	0.30	-13.43
Norway	11,704	10,937	13,165	15,533	22,515	1.25	44.95
Sweden	16,380	16,133	15,729	23,388	29,443	1.64	25.89
United Kingdom	48,753	41,296	44,228	54,233	51,991	2.89	-4.13
Southern Europe	682,213	671,078	679,677	744,260	779,817	43.41	4.78
Bosnia and Herzegovina	152,939	157,106	147,569	165,538	148,784	8.28	-10.12
Croatia	71,787	79,955	89,693	93,339	91,645	5.10	-1.81
Greece	49,961	48,503	46,284	50,318	52,509	2.92	4.35
Italy	80,092	82,382	80,980	91,039	148,147	8.25	62.73
Montenegro	174,857	127,404	120,774	129,455	132,083	7.35	2.03
Portugal	4,877	4,891	4,614	5,732	5,509	0.31	-3.89
Slovenia	80,703	96,332	114,471	124,517	115,718	6.44	-7.07
Spain	14,089	17,308	15,541	19,103	17,335	0.97	-9.26
TFYR of Macedonia	52,908	57,197	59,751	65,219	68,087	3.79	4.40
Western Europe	205,228	211,359	226,895	255,112	270,834	15.08	6.16
Austria	37,682	42,388	45,998	48,472	47,900	2.67	-1.18
Belgium	10,242	9,935	10,799	15,551	15,146	0.84	-2.60
France	37,330	38,735	42,194	41,277	45,698	2.54	10.71
Germany	80,819	81,926	84,203	96,875	103,325	5.75	6.66
Luxembourg	941	617	821	1,121	1,096	0.06	-2.23
Netherlands	24,043	20,419	25,510	29,778	32,315	1.80	8.52
Switzerland	14,171	17,339	17,370	22,038	25,354	1.41	15.05
East Mediterranean Europe	28,418	31,717	31,222	42,316	44,909	2.50	6.13
Israel	8,630	7,268	7,691	8,473	9,070	0.50	7.05
Turkey	19,788	24,449	23,531	33,843	35,839	2.00	5.90
Other Europe	35,372	37,788	33,292	41,752	46,637	2.60	11.70
Other countries of Europe	35,372	37,788	33,292	41,752	46,637	2.60	11.70
NOT SPECIFIED	51,690	86,155	67,418	63,119	78,939	4.39	25.06
Other countries of the World	51,690	86,155	67,418	63,119	78,939	4.39	25.06

Yearbook of Tourism Statistics, Data 2008 – 2012, 2014 Edition

SEYCHELLES

1. Arrivals of non-resident tourists at national borders, by country of residence

	2008	2009	2010	2011	2012	Market share 2012	% Change 2012-2011
TOTAL	**158,849**	**157,485**	**174,429**	**194,348**	**207,831**	**100.00**	**6.94**
AFRICA	**19,117**	**18,499**	**22,163**	**24,422**	**25,435**	**12.24**	**4.15**
East Africa	**9,454**	**8,936**	**10,402**	**11,905**	**10,927**	**5.26**	**-8.22**
Burundi	58	25	22	18	31	0.01	72.22
Comoros	27	28	63	264	58	0.03	-78.03
Djibouti	66	91	48	62	52	0.03	-16.13
Ethiopia	78	77	46	79	683	0.33	764.56
Kenya	940	870	1,018	1,163	1,645	0.79	41.44
Madagascar	687	316	349	590	289	0.14	-51.02
Malawi	27	15	21	36	65	0.03	80.56
Mauritius	4,086	3,476	3,631	3,867	2,868	1.38	-25.83
Mozambique	72	62	52	131	141	0.07	7.63
Reunion	2,834	3,389	4,483	4,789	4,115	1.98	-14.07
Rwanda	25	59	45	20	74	0.04	270.00
Somalia	4		6	28	26	0.01	-7.14
Uganda	136	154	136	185	261	0.13	41.08
United Republic of Tanzania	191	136	229	274	227	0.11	-17.15
Zambia	118	94	92	146	180	0.09	23.29
Zimbabwe	105	144	161	253	212	0.10	-16.21
Central Africa	**102**	**164**	**135**	**168**	**305**	**0.15**	**81.55**
Angola	44	76	52	94	86	0.04	-8.51
Cameroon	30	38	11	12	71	0.03	491.67
Democratic Republic of the Congo	24	39	59	56	113	0.05	101.79
Gabon	4	11	13	6	35	0.02	483.33
North Africa	**330**	**291**	**359**	**522**	**564**	**0.27**	**8.05**
Algeria	27	32	40	126	47	0.02	-62.70
Morocco	100	131	101	166	182	0.09	9.64
South Sudan					37	0.02	
Sudan	58	50	55	68	108	0.05	58.82
Tunisia	145	78	163	162	190	0.09	17.28
Southern Africa	**8,425**	**8,446**	**10,797**	**10,958**	**12,710**	**6.12**	**15.99**
Botswana	75	86	162	185	143	0.07	-22.70
Lesotho	25	13	20	14	14	0.01	0.00
Namibia	77	116	126	127	170	0.08	33.86
South Africa	8,219	8,208	10,425	10,559	12,351	5.94	16.97
Swaziland	29	23	64	73	32	0.02	-56.16
West Africa	**385**	**468**	**294**	**366**	**661**	**0.32**	**80.60**
Côte d'Ivoire	23	22	21	24	50	0.02	108.33
Ghana	52	73	43	105	87	0.04	-17.14
Nigeria	286	346	206	206	497	0.24	141.26
Senegal	24	27	24	31	27	0.01	-12.90
Other Africa	**421**	**194**	**176**	**503**	**268**	**0.13**	**-46.72**
Other countries of Africa	421	194	176	503	268	0.13	-46.72
AMERICAS	**4,163**	**4,541**	**3,960**	**4,730**	**5,590**	**2.69**	**18.18**
North America	**3,774**	**4,139**	**3,488**	**3,956**	**4,710**	**2.27**	**19.06**
Canada	601	493	640	666	720	0.35	8.11
Mexico	57	73	59	79	67	0.03	-15.19
United States of America	3,116	3,573	2,789	3,211	3,923	1.89	22.17
South America	**263**	**254**	**286**	**556**	**613**	**0.29**	**10.25**
Argentina	140	115	126	208	252	0.12	21.15
Brazil	123	139	160	348	361	0.17	3.74
Other Americas	**126**	**148**	**186**	**218**	**267**	**0.13**	**22.48**
Other countries of the Americas	126	148	186	218	267	0.13	22.48
EAST ASIA AND THE PACIFIC	**3,486**	**3,523**	**4,179**	**5,664**	**8,969**	**4.32**	**58.35**
North-East Asia	**1,484**	**1,512**	**1,738**	**3,302**	**6,515**	**3.13**	**97.30**

658

SEYCHELLES

1. Arrivals of non-resident tourists at national borders, by country of residence

	2008	2009	2010	2011	2012	Market share 2012	% Change 2012-2011
China	843	919	1,078	2,124	4,484	2.16	111.11
Hong Kong, China	91	73	98	129	198	0.10	53.49
Japan	392	378	299	541	962	0.46	77.82
Korea, Republic of	91	84	214	472	748	0.36	58.47
Taiwan, Province of China	67	58	49	36	123	0.06	241.67
South-East Asia	**1,154**	**1,131**	**1,324**	**1,214**	**1,093**	**0.53**	**-9.97**
Indonesia	105	96	125	174	169	0.08	-2.87
Malaysia	207	159	147	175	163	0.08	-6.86
Philippines	177	216	226	213	298	0.14	39.91
Singapore	523	511	625	526	321	0.15	-38.97
Thailand	142	149	201	126	142	0.07	12.70
Australasia	**809**	**796**	**1,049**	**1,091**	**1,219**	**0.59**	**11.73**
Australia	697	675	928	980	1,083	0.52	10.51
New Zealand	112	121	121	111	136	0.07	22.52
Other East Asia and the Pacific	**39**	**84**	**68**	**57**	**142**	**0.07**	**149.12**
Other countries East Asia/Pacific	10	35	24	28	121	0.06	332.14
Other countries of Oceania	29	49	44	29	21	0.01	-27.59
EUROPE	**124,725**	**122,266**	**132,154**	**144,016**	**146,289**	**70.39**	**1.58**
Central/Eastern Europe	**12,262**	**13,154**	**14,311**	**15,834**	**22,490**	**10.82**	**42.04**
Armenia					35	0.02	
Azerbaijan					98	0.05	
Bulgaria	212	218	220	352	569	0.27	61.65
Czech Republic	1,409	1,392	1,303	1,849	2,058	0.99	11.30
Estonia	63	68	66	96	188	0.09	95.83
Hungary	927	695	632	677	894	0.43	32.05
Kazakhstan	342	153	182	212	402	0.19	89.62
Kyrgyzstan					9	0.00	
Latvia	172	108	119	127	169	0.08	33.07
Lithuania			107	70	148	0.07	111.43
Poland	898	824	961	1,005	1,289	0.62	28.26
Romania	337	272	333	445	567	0.27	27.42
Russian Federation	6,569	8,098	8,942	8,840	13,494	6.49	52.65
Slovakia	382	223	384	592	654	0.31	10.47
Tajikistan					2	0.00	
Turkmenistan					8	0.00	
Ukraine	765	915	890	1,343	1,821	0.88	35.59
Uzbekistan					16	0.01	
Other countries Central/East Europe	186	188	172	226	69	0.03	-69.47
Northern Europe	**17,186**	**13,846**	**15,936**	**17,096**	**15,606**	**7.51**	**-8.72**
Denmark	1,158	737	727	814	1,185	0.57	45.58
Finland	557	518	694	619	542	0.26	-12.44
Iceland	45	3	5	26	9	0.00	-65.38
Ireland	61	58	450	362	365	0.18	0.83
Norway	658	482	755	856	741	0.36	-13.43
Sweden	952	756	983	1,084	1,511	0.73	39.39
United Kingdom	13,755	11,292	12,322	13,335	11,253	5.41	-15.61
Southern Europe	**27,908**	**30,346**	**29,841**	**30,194**	**27,471**	**13.22**	**-9.02**
Albania	6	3					
Bosnia and Herzegovina	5	12	11	7	18	0.01	157.14
Croatia	111	93	65	119	190	0.09	59.66
Greece	679	695	598	561	394	0.19	-29.77
Italy	23,818	26,114	25,602	25,674	23,401	11.26	-8.85
Portugal	356	403	552	587	333	0.16	-43.27
Serbia	118	107	56	125	173	0.08	38.40
Slovenia	288	311	317	322	351	0.17	9.01
Spain	2,495	2,599	2,627	2,769	2,580	1.24	-6.83
Yugoslavia, SFR (former)	32	9	13	30	31	0.01	3.33

659

SEYCHELLES

1. Arrivals of non-resident tourists at national borders, by country of residence

	2008	2009	2010	2011	2012	Market share 2012	% Change 2012-2011
Western Europe	64,969	63,462	70,570	79,328	78,604	37.82	-0.91
Austria	3,070	2,852	3,446	3,745	4,771	2.30	27.40
Belgium	2,225	2,185	2,247	2,512	2,372	1.14	-5.57
France	31,386	31,341	35,026	39,370	32,248	15.52	-18.09
Germany	21,222	19,736	21,314	23,706	28,163	13.55	18.80
Luxembourg	295	301	431	446	424	0.20	-4.93
Monaco	126	153	148	158	194	0.09	22.78
Netherlands	1,377	1,297	1,435	1,747	1,850	0.89	5.90
Switzerland	5,268	5,597	6,523	7,644	8,582	4.13	12.27
East Mediterranean Europe	1,845	899	1,359	1,374	1,862	0.90	35.52
Cyprus	174	177	116	176	126	0.06	-28.41
Israel	1,397	436	665	661	1,145	0.55	73.22
Turkey	274	286	578	537	591	0.28	10.06
Other Europe	555	559	137	190	256	0.12	34.74
Other countries of Europe	555	559	137	190	256	0.12	34.74
MIDDLE EAST	5,489	6,422	8,332	12,176	18,183	8.75	49.33
Bahrain	239	360	280	264	364	0.18	37.88
Egypt	88	92	149	138	234	0.11	69.57
Iraq	1	5	7	13	22	0.01	69.23
Jordan	32	40	57	51	99	0.05	94.12
Kuwait	149	141	182	204	357	0.17	75.00
Lebanon	146	155	211	266	355	0.17	33.46
Libya	23	44	41	20	19	0.01	-5.00
Oman	86	68	60	95	108	0.05	13.68
Qatar	729	1,033	1,121	1,390	2,124	1.02	52.81
Saudi Arabia	410	603	785	1,212	1,585	0.76	30.78
Syrian Arab Republic	17	26	41	29	15	0.01	-48.28
United Arab Emirates	3,553	3,842	5,387	8,488	12,880	6.20	51.74
Yemen	14	10	5	5	18	0.01	260.00
Other countries of Middle East	2	3	6	1	3	0.00	200.00
SOUTH ASIA	1,869	2,234	3,641	3,340	3,365	1.62	0.75
Bangladesh	24	87	340	43	41	0.02	-4.65
India	1,241	1,616	2,671	2,380	2,546	1.23	6.97
Iran, Islamic Republic of	46	84	122	188	162	0.08	-13.83
Maldives	96	83	68	205	56	0.03	-72.68
Pakistan	120	93	117	212	218	0.10	2.83
Sri Lanka	302	232	208	257	253	0.12	-1.56
Other countries of South Asia	40	39	115	55	89	0.04	61.82

Yearbook of Tourism Statistics, Data 2008 – 2012, 2014 Editi

SIERRA LEONE

1. Arrivals of non-resident tourists at national borders, by country of residence

		2008	2009	2010	2011	2012	Market share 2012	% Change 2012-2011
TOTAL	(*)	35,670	36,775	38,614	52,431	59,709	100.00	13.88
AFRICA		11,915	12,614	10,806	15,885	16,349	27.38	2.92
East Africa				663	2,553	1,632	2.73	-36.08
Burundi				12	46	7	0.01	-84.78
Comoros				24	1			
Djibouti						7	0.01	
Eritrea				9	15			
Ethiopia						41	0.07	
Kenya				251	448	504	0.84	12.50
Madagascar						10	0.02	
Malawi				27	167	133	0.22	-20.36
Mozambique				2	148	22	0.04	-85.14
Rwanda				46	145	52	0.09	-64.14
Seychelles				21	199	6	0.01	-96.98
Somalia				26		3	0.01	
Uganda				34	406	169	0.28	-58.37
United Republic of Tanzania				52	366	168	0.28	-54.10
Zambia				53	300	257	0.43	-14.33
Zimbabwe				106	312	253	0.42	-18.91
Central Africa				198	636	311	0.52	-51.10
Angola				14	46	74	0.12	60.87
Cameroon				139	193	96	0.16	-50.26
Central African Republic				1	3			
Chad				7	40			
Congo				14	308	104	0.17	-66.23
Equatorial Guinea				7				
Gabon				4	40	3	0.01	-92.50
Sao Tome and Principe				12	6	34	0.06	466.67
North Africa				207	411	104	0.17	-74.70
Algeria				22	52	21	0.04	-59.62
Morocco				92	158	32	0.05	-79.75
Sudan				49	186	43	0.07	-76.88
Tunisia				44	15	8	0.01	-46.67
Southern Africa				1,018	998	1,857	3.11	86.07
Botswana				21	47	13	0.02	-72.34
Lesotho				13	22			
Namibia				37	66	34	0.06	-48.48
South Africa				891	852	1,797	3.01	110.92
Swaziland				56	11	13	0.02	18.18
West Africa				6,846	11,054	12,445	20.84	12.58
Benin				17	123	59	0.10	-52.03
Burkina Faso				90	121	96	0.16	-20.66
Cape Verde				8	17	54	0.09	217.65
Côte d'Ivoire				162	205	508	0.85	147.80
Gambia				509	672	946	1.58	40.77
Ghana				1,594	3,580	3,171	5.31	-11.42
Guinea				297	642	1,304	2.18	103.12
Guinea-Bissau				18	18	82	0.14	355.56
Liberia				270	647	819	1.37	26.58
Mali				129	136	203	0.34	49.26
Mauritania				17	34	34	0.06	0.00
Niger				4	16	29	0.05	81.25
Nigeria				3,480	4,003	4,348	7.28	8.62
Senegal				218	689	711	1.19	3.19
Togo				33	151	81	0.14	-46.36

Yearbook of Tourism Statistics, Data 2008 – 2012, 2014 Edition

SIERRA LEONE

1. Arrivals of non-resident tourists at national borders, by country of residence

	2008	2009	2010	2011	2012	Market share 2012	% Change 2012-2011
Other Africa	11,915	12,614	1,874	233			
Other countries of Africa			1,874	233			
All countries of Africa	11,915	12,614					
AMERICAS	6,684	7,238	7,406	10,707	10,574	17.71	-1.24
Caribbean			278	347	59	0.10	-83.00
Haiti			4	3	3	0.01	0.00
Jamaica			165	227	40	0.07	-82.38
Trinidad and Tobago			109	117	16	0.03	-86.32
Central America			13	2	34	0.06	1,600.00
Costa Rica			12	2	32	0.05	1,500.00
El Salvador					2	0.00	
Guatemala			1				
North America			5,023	9,911	10,211	17.10	3.03
Canada			920	3,592	2,240	3.75	-37.64
Mexico			62	249	152	0.25	-38.96
United States of America			4,041	6,070	7,819	13.10	28.81
South America			530	214	234	0.39	9.35
Argentina			338	33	99	0.17	200.00
Brazil			168	127	96	0.16	-24.41
Chile			14		25	0.04	
Paraguay			5	2	3	0.01	50.00
Uruguay			2		1	0.00	
Venezuela			3	52	10	0.02	-80.77
Other Americas	6,684	7,238	1,562	233	36	0.06	-84.55
Other countries of the Americas			1,562	233	36	0.06	-84.55
All countries of the Americas	6,684	7,238					
EAST ASIA AND THE PACIFIC	3,142	4,068	6,261	9,024	7,817	13.09	-13.38
North-East Asia			953	4,957	3,177	5.32	-35.91
China			826	4,179	2,257	3.78	-45.99
Japan			89	589	423	0.71	-28.18
Korea, Dem. People's Republic of			22	87	192	0.32	120.69
Korea, Republic of			15	101	302	0.51	199.01
Mongolia			1	1	3	0.01	200.00
South-East Asia			267	403	350	0.59	-13.15
Cambodia			18	10	1	0.00	-90.00
Indonesia			8	37	57	0.10	54.05
Malaysia			16	54	63	0.11	16.67
Philippines			192	257	175	0.29	-31.91
Singapore			8	12	13	0.02	8.33
Thailand			5	12	32	0.05	166.67
Timor-Leste			6				
Viet Nam			14	21	9	0.02	-57.14
Australasia			3,030	3,664	4,272	7.15	16.59
Australia			2,653	3,364	4,162	6.97	23.72
New Zealand			377	300	110	0.18	-63.33
Melanesia					18	0.03	
Papua New Guinea					18	0.03	
Other East Asia and the Pacific	3,142	4,068	2,011				
Other countries of Asia			1,116				
All countries of Asia	3,142	4,068					
Other countries of Oceania			895				
EUROPE	12,713	10,574	10,294	13,796	15,935	26.69	15.50
Central/Eastern Europe			498	618	772	1.29	24.92
Azerbaijan			7		13	0.02	
Bulgaria			11	18	34	0.06	88.89
Czech Republic			21	33	28	0.05	-15.15

Yearbook of Tourism Statistics, Data 2008 – 2012, 2014 Edition

SIERRA LEONE

1. Arrivals of non-resident tourists at national borders, by country of residence

	2008	2009	2010	2011	2012	Market share 2012	% Change 2012-2011
Estonia					3	0.01	
Georgia					14	0.02	
Hungary			38	59	42	0.07	-28.81
Kazakhstan			24		11	0.02	
Kyrgyzstan			13		10	0.02	
Latvia			165	35	41	0.07	17.14
Lithuania			9	23	25	0.04	8.70
Poland			12	82	76	0.13	-7.32
Republic of Moldova					4	0.01	
Romania			22	154	197	0.33	27.92
Russian Federation			70	149	187	0.31	25.50
Slovakia			7	24	30	0.05	25.00
Tajikistan			24	2	1	0.00	-50.00
Ukraine			75	39	56	0.09	43.59
Northern Europe			**5,478**	**8,202**	**11,173**	**18.71**	**36.22**
Denmark			60	233	288	0.48	23.61
Finland			231	94	106	0.18	12.77
Iceland					10	0.02	
Ireland			1,204	773	638	1.07	-17.46
Norway			81	268	461	0.77	72.01
Sweden			51	243	215	0.36	-11.52
United Kingdom			3,851	6,591	9,455	15.84	43.45
Southern Europe			**1,459**	**1,168**	**955**	**1.60**	**-18.24**
Albania			7		15	0.03	
Andorra					2	0.00	
Bosnia and Herzegovina			9		3	0.01	
Croatia			14	51	44	0.07	-13.73
Greece			19	30	33	0.06	10.00
Holy See					8	0.01	
Italy			480	578	498	0.83	-13.84
Malta					4	0.01	
Montenegro			6		2	0.00	
Portugal			133	53	97	0.16	83.02
Serbia			2	6	12	0.02	100.00
Spain			789	450	221	0.37	-50.89
TFYR of Macedonia					16	0.03	
Western Europe			**1,983**	**3,630**	**2,699**	**4.52**	**-25.65**
Austria			18	54	57	0.10	5.56
Belgium			109	334	383	0.64	14.67
France			514	1,730	680	1.14	-60.69
Germany			537	1,033	629	1.05	-39.11
Luxembourg			5	12	8	0.01	-33.33
Monaco					3	0.01	
Netherlands			767	387	727	1.22	87.86
Switzerland			33	80	212	0.36	165.00
East Mediterranean Europe			**267**	**178**	**336**	**0.56**	**88.76**
Cyprus			25	9			
Israel			211	128	269	0.45	110.16
Turkey			31	41	67	0.11	63.41
Other Europe	**12,713**	**10,574**	**609**				
Other countries of Europe			609				
All countries of Europe	12,713	10,574					
MIDDLE EAST	**888**	**1,750**	**2,667**	**1,562**	**5,711**	**9.56**	**265.62**
Egypt			24	66	1,842	3.08	2,690.91
Iraq			61	28	429	0.72	1,432.14
Jordan			22	8	8	0.01	0.00
Kuwait			4	16	34	0.06	112.50

663

Yearbook of Tourism Statistics, Data 2008 – 2012, 2014 Edition

SIERRA LEONE

1. Arrivals of non-resident tourists at national borders, by country of residence

	2008	2009	2010	2011	2012	Market share 2012	% Change 2012-2011
Lebanon			1,074	1,343	1,740	2.91	29.56
Libya			15	28	506	0.85	1,707.14
Oman					23	0.04	
Palestine			88	12	3	0.01	-75.00
Qatar					41	0.07	
Saudi Arabia			138	13	118	0.20	807.69
Syrian Arab Republic			51	29	871	1.46	2,903.45
United Arab Emirates			17	16	66	0.11	312.50
Yemen			56	3	30	0.05	900.00
Other countries of Middle East			1,117				
All countries of Middle East	888	1,750					
SOUTH ASIA			**1,180**	**1,457**	**3,323**	**5.57**	**128.07**
Afghanistan			4	7			
Bangladesh			13	65	112	0.19	72.31
India			1,014	1,148	2,182	3.65	90.07
Iran, Islamic Republic of			49	48	483	0.81	906.25
Nepal			16	22	32	0.05	45.45
Pakistan			61	122	486	0.81	298.36
Sri Lanka			23	45	28	0.05	-37.78
NOT SPECIFIED	**328**	**531**					
Other countries of the World	328	531					

Yearbook of Tourism Statistics, Data 2008 – 2012, 2014 Edition

SIERRA LEONE

5. Overnight stays of non-resident tourists in hotels and similar establishments, by country of residence

	2008	2009	2010	2011	2012	Market share 2012	% Change 2012-2011
TOTAL	249,690	257,425	270,305	367,094	418,110	100.00	13.90
AFRICA	83,108	81,459	75,142	109,564	130,879	31.30	19.45
Other Africa	83,108	81,459	75,142	109,564	130,879	31.30	19.45
All countries of Africa	83,108	81,459	75,142	109,564	130,879	31.30	19.45
AMERICAS	46,788	51,436	52,066	73,318	74,004	17.70	0.94
Other Americas	46,788	51,436	52,066	73,318	74,004	17.70	0.94
All countries of the Americas	46,788	51,436	52,066	73,318	74,004	17.70	0.94
EAST ASIA AND THE PACIFIC	26,586	28,189	52,256	63,168	74,753	17.88	18.34
Other East Asia and the Pacific	26,586	28,189	52,256	63,168	74,753	17.88	18.34
All countries of Asia	24,290	24,605	24,723	37,520	44,723	10.70	19.20
All countries of Oceania	2,296	3,584	27,533	25,648	30,030	7.18	17.09
EUROPE	86,992	89,705	72,088	96,649	109,669	26.23	13.47
Other Europe	86,992	89,705	72,088	96,649	109,669	26.23	13.47
All countries of Europe	86,992	89,705	72,088	96,649	109,669	26.23	13.47
MIDDLE EAST	6,216	6,636	18,753	24,395	28,805	6.89	18.08
All countries of Middle East	6,216	6,636	18,753	24,395	28,805	6.89	18.08

Yearbook of Tourism Statistics, Data 2008 – 2012, 2014 Edition

SINGAPORE

2. Arrivals of non-resident visitors at national borders, by nationality

		2008	2009	2010	2011	2012	Market share 2012	% Change 2012-2011
TOTAL	(*)	10,116,054	9,682,690	11,641,701	13,171,303	14,496,091	100.00	10.06
AFRICA		85,142	72,110	71,190	73,345	69,407	0.48	-5.37
East Africa		9,451	9,401	10,190	9,147	9,489	0.07	3.74
Mauritius		9,451	9,401	10,190	9,147	9,489	0.07	3.74
Southern Africa		41,375	36,740	34,330	36,714	36,972	0.26	0.70
South Africa		41,375	36,740	34,330	36,714	36,972	0.26	0.70
Other Africa		34,316	25,969	26,670	27,484	22,946	0.16	-16.51
Other countries of Africa		34,316	25,969	26,670	27,484	22,946	0.16	-16.51
AMERICAS		572,115	538,229	610,959	666,791	713,767	4.92	7.05
Caribbean		3,701	4,081	4,449	4,632	3,491	0.02	-24.63
All countries of the Caribbean		3,701	4,081	4,449	4,632	3,491	0.02	-24.63
Central America		2,270	2,122	2,793	2,849	2,937	0.02	3.09
All countries of Central America		2,270	2,122	2,793	2,849	2,937	0.02	3.09
North America		543,333	508,493	575,831	622,995	662,829	4.57	6.39
Canada		111,067	101,463	112,059	123,672	129,418	0.89	4.65
Mexico		9,095	6,904	8,641	9,768	11,566	0.08	18.41
United States of America		423,171	400,126	455,131	489,555	521,845	3.60	6.60
South America		22,811	23,533	27,886	36,315	44,510	0.31	22.57
Argentina		3,286	3,420	4,557	5,430	7,163	0.05	31.92
Brazil		10,135	9,985	12,715	17,828	21,005	0.14	17.82
Chile		2,019	2,698	2,493	3,438	4,271	0.03	24.23
Colombia		2,673	2,712	3,111	4,104	5,509	0.04	34.23
Uruguay		250	311	311	555	668	0.00	20.36
Venezuela		2,266	2,061	2,069	2,304	2,641	0.02	14.63
Other countries of South America		2,182	2,346	2,630	2,656	3,253	0.02	22.48
EAST ASIA AND THE PACIFIC		6,759,583	6,487,570	8,126,315	9,502,765	10,590,764	73.06	11.45
North-East Asia		2,439,057	2,065,296	2,564,646	3,270,413	3,927,354	27.09	20.09
China		1,053,659	913,067	1,150,027	1,554,480	2,198,157	15.16	41.41
Hong Kong, China		152,737	177,199	252,993	312,856	138,849	0.96	-55.62
Japan		608,111	521,688	569,676	701,753	816,448	5.63	16.34
Korea, Dem. People's Republic of		559	463	136	140	690	0.00	392.86
Korea, Republic of		435,732	284,586	379,294	437,155	469,212	3.24	7.33
Macao, China		3,794	4,172	10,915	11,706	4,258	0.03	-63.63
Mongolia		7,722	5,466	6,431	8,824	10,225	0.07	15.88
Taiwan, Province of China		176,743	158,655	195,174	243,499	289,515	2.00	18.90
South-East Asia		3,412,988	3,539,836	4,624,705	5,202,921	5,555,835	38.33	6.78
Brunei Darussalam		39,856	41,951	46,319	46,562	56,918	0.39	22.24
Cambodia		27,491	26,771	32,759	35,782	35,310	0.24	-1.32
Indonesia		1,772,487	1,756,577	2,346,790	2,628,294	2,872,425	19.82	9.29
Lao People's Democratic Republic		3,300	3,385	5,024	5,336	7,334	0.05	37.44
Malaysia		527,416	648,597	832,685	919,061	989,931	6.83	7.71
Myanmar		85,263	72,390	81,082	97,476	96,354	0.66	-1.15
Philippines		435,098	449,968	570,889	711,063	698,878	4.82	-1.71
Thailand		299,311	286,938	398,503	439,378	443,116	3.06	0.85
Viet Nam		222,766	253,259	310,654	319,969	355,569	2.45	11.13
Australasia		899,502	874,752	929,568	1,021,281	1,098,442	7.58	7.56
Australia		779,776	769,549	819,953	888,817	961,774	6.63	8.21
New Zealand		119,726	105,203	109,615	132,464	136,668	0.94	3.17
Melanesia		5,991	6,244	5,923	6,783	7,831	0.05	15.45
Fiji		2,466	2,197	1,811	1,892	2,208	0.02	16.70
New Caledonia		44	63	53	94	79	0.00	-15.96
Papua New Guinea		3,481	3,984	4,059	4,797	5,544	0.04	15.57
Micronesia		189	192	157	143	91	0.00	-36.36
Guam		19	29	31	26	12	0.00	-53.85
Nauru		170	163	126	117	79	0.00	-32.48

Yearbook of Tourism Statistics, Data 2008 – 2012, 2014 Edition

SINGAPORE

2. Arrivals of non-resident visitors at national borders, by nationality

	2008	2009	2010	2011	2012	Market share 2012	% Change 2012-2011
Other East Asia and the Pacific	**1,856**	**1,250**	**1,316**	**1,224**	**1,211**	**0.01**	**-1.06**
Other countries of Oceania	1,856	1,250	1,316	1,224	1,211	0.01	-1.06
EUROPE	**1,544,644**	**1,515,203**	**1,609,141**	**1,656,961**	**1,812,580**	**12.50**	**9.39**
Central/Eastern Europe	**97,604**	**93,511**	**101,752**	**112,706**	**133,667**	**0.92**	**18.60**
Commonwealth Independent States	74,081	68,990	75,276	82,323	96,012	0.66	16.63
Czech Republic	5,391	6,480	6,330	6,789	7,705	0.05	13.49
Hungary	4,478	4,351	5,373	5,490	6,296	0.04	14.68
Poland	13,654	13,690	14,773	18,104	23,654	0.16	30.66
Northern Europe	**770,512**	**723,371**	**730,863**	**726,956**	**763,152**	**5.26**	**4.98**
Denmark	38,212	35,651	35,158	32,992	37,760	0.26	14.45
Finland	16,361	18,959	18,659	27,058	36,977	0.26	36.66
Ireland	37,648	31,987	30,806	29,547	31,264	0.22	5.81
Norway	34,547	31,936	33,108	33,854	38,142	0.26	12.67
Sweden	40,001	36,453	40,336	43,042	48,848	0.34	13.49
United Kingdom	603,743	568,385	572,796	560,463	570,161	3.93	1.73
Southern Europe	**99,253**	**106,346**	**117,726**	**124,246**	**143,201**	**0.99**	**15.26**
Greece	9,514	9,875	8,907	8,162	9,280	0.06	13.70
Italy	50,071	54,198	59,902	63,808	77,427	0.53	21.34
Portugal	8,516	10,072	12,944	14,670	14,762	0.10	0.63
Serbia and Montenegro	2,100	1,913	1,960	2,182	2,072	0.01	-5.04
Spain	29,052	30,288	34,013	35,424	39,660	0.27	11.96
Western Europe	**522,573**	**539,217**	**599,370**	**633,599**	**699,216**	**4.82**	**10.36**
Austria	19,228	19,797	22,693	22,741	26,473	0.18	16.41
Belgium	20,522	20,722	23,787	23,735	25,723	0.18	8.38
France	138,940	147,540	165,255	177,136	198,009	1.37	11.78
Germany	197,412	203,858	231,070	244,815	276,262	1.91	12.85
Luxembourg	1,206	1,138	1,466	1,503	1,610	0.01	7.12
Netherlands	89,252	91,445	92,941	98,021	100,161	0.69	2.18
Switzerland	56,013	54,717	62,158	65,648	70,978	0.49	8.12
East Mediterranean Europe	**28,548**	**25,184**	**30,943**	**28,680**	**33,609**	**0.23**	**17.19**
Israel	11,814	11,283	13,124	12,407	14,062	0.10	13.34
Turkey	16,734	13,901	17,819	16,273	19,547	0.13	20.12
Other Europe	**26,154**	**27,574**	**28,487**	**30,774**	**39,735**	**0.27**	**29.12**
Other countries of Europe	26,154	27,574	28,487	30,774	39,735	0.27	29.12
MIDDLE EAST	**38,347**	**35,875**	**44,730**	**48,960**	**51,920**	**0.36**	**6.05**
Bahrain	2,066	1,708	1,834	1,907	1,884	0.01	-1.21
Egypt	4,079	3,813	4,637	4,255	4,272	0.03	0.40
Jordan	1,170	1,057	1,292	1,770	1,489	0.01	-15.88
Kuwait	3,618	4,119	6,090	6,182	5,554	0.04	-10.16
Lebanon	1,184	1,091	1,310	1,462	1,563	0.01	6.91
Libya	227	293	606	207	329	0.00	58.94
Saudi Arabia	6,919	7,373	8,251	11,740	13,184	0.09	12.30
United Arab Emirates	12,254	10,464	13,194	12,716	13,592	0.09	6.89
Other countries of Middle East	6,830	5,957	7,516	8,721	10,053	0.07	15.27
SOUTH ASIA	**1,109,267**	**1,033,118**	**1,178,866**	**1,221,983**	**1,255,834**	**8.66**	**2.77**
Afghanistan	358	499	370	284	319	0.00	12.32
Bangladesh	95,150	86,459	92,410	95,896	110,648	0.76	15.38
India	848,683	792,245	907,350	949,698	980,479	6.76	3.24
Iran, Islamic Republic of	20,600	25,756	40,385	35,963	21,832	0.15	-39.29
Nepal	23,201	18,441	18,101	16,429	17,490	0.12	6.46
Pakistan	25,962	25,088	25,236	24,815	26,011	0.18	4.82
Sri Lanka	85,223	75,610	85,241	90,175	90,513	0.62	0.37
Other countries of South Asia	10,090	9,020	9,773	8,723	8,542	0.06	-2.07
NOT SPECIFIED	**6,956**	**585**	**500**	**498**	**1,819**	**0.01**	**265.26**
Other countries of the World	6,956	585	500	498	1,819	0.01	265.26

Yearbook of Tourism Statistics, Data 2008 – 2012, 2014 Edition

SINGAPORE

2. Arrivals of non-resident visitors at national borders, by country of residence

	2008	2009	2010	2011	2012	Market share 2012	% Change 2012-2011
TOTAL (*)	**10,116,054**	**9,682,690**	**11,641,701**	**13,171,303**	**14,496,091**	**100.00**	**10.06**
AFRICA	**86,023**	**72,348**	**70,436**	**69,452**	**64,183**	**0.44**	**-7.59**
East Africa	**11,430**	**11,418**	**11,617**	**10,527**	**9,857**	**0.07**	**-6.36**
Mauritius	11,430	11,418	11,617	10,527	9,857	0.07	-6.36
Southern Africa	**40,083**	**34,451**	**32,430**	**33,506**	**32,739**	**0.23**	**-2.29**
South Africa	40,083	34,451	32,430	33,506	32,739	0.23	-2.29
Other Africa	**34,510**	**26,479**	**26,389**	**25,419**	**21,587**	**0.15**	**-15.08**
Other countries of Africa	34,510	26,479	26,389	25,419	21,587	0.15	-15.08
AMERICAS	**505,411**	**467,723**	**524,846**	**563,742**	**616,400**	**4.25**	**9.34**
Caribbean	**2,809**	**2,747**	**3,082**	**2,961**	**3,048**	**0.02**	**2.94**
All countries of the Caribbean	2,809	2,747	3,082	2,961	3,048	0.02	2.94
Central America	**1,638**	**1,441**	**1,947**	**1,895**	**2,060**	**0.01**	**8.71**
All countries of Central America	1,638	1,441	1,947	1,895	2,060	0.01	8.71
North America	**484,026**	**445,816**	**498,803**	**531,073**	**574,353**	**3.96**	**8.15**
Canada	80,044	70,034	75,142	82,932	87,795	0.61	5.86
Mexico	7,351	5,078	6,466	7,565	9,345	0.06	23.53
United States of America	396,631	370,704	417,195	440,576	477,213	3.29	8.32
South America	**16,445**	**17,258**	**20,190**	**27,141**	**36,287**	**0.25**	**33.70**
Argentina	2,405	2,569	3,550	4,234	5,926	0.04	39.96
Brazil	7,843	7,713	9,802	14,209	18,860	0.13	32.73
Chile	1,596	2,287	2,117	2,853	3,400	0.02	19.17
Colombia	1,625	1,570	1,781	2,284	3,544	0.02	55.17
Uruguay	248	295	310	635	697	0.00	9.76
Venezuela	1,369	1,259	1,082	1,374	1,731	0.01	25.98
Other countries of South America	1,359	1,565	1,548	1,552	2,129	0.01	37.18
Other Americas	**493**	**461**	**824**	**672**	**652**	**0.00**	**-2.98**
Other countries of the Americas	493	461	824	672	652	0.00	-2.98
EAST ASIA AND THE PACIFIC	**7,070,353**	**6,785,096**	**8,474,870**	**9,887,028**	**10,987,490**	**75.80**	**11.13**
North-East Asia	**2,541,938**	**2,163,701**	**2,664,002**	**3,379,363**	**4,018,736**	**27.72**	**18.92**
China	1,078,742	936,747	1,171,493	1,577,522	2,034,177	14.03	28.95
Hong Kong, China	278,115	294,420	387,579	464,375	472,167	3.26	1.68
Japan	571,040	489,987	528,951	656,417	757,116	5.22	15.34
Korea, Dem. People's Republic of	714	844	809	899	1,521	0.01	69.19
Korea, Republic of	423,018	271,987	360,703	414,879	445,184	3.07	7.30
Macao, China	6,888	7,713	16,933	18,159	16,274	0.11	-10.38
Mongolia	7,497	5,242	6,348	8,624	10,094	0.07	17.05
Taiwan, Province of China	175,924	156,761	191,186	238,488	282,203	1.95	18.33
South-East Asia	**3,571,408**	**3,684,848**	**4,821,753**	**5,414,250**	**5,779,607**	**39.87**	**6.75**
Brunei Darussalam	54,285	56,531	62,157	62,243	71,755	0.49	15.28
Cambodia	29,917	29,425	34,934	36,520	37,382	0.26	2.36
Indonesia	1,765,429	1,745,330	2,306,243	2,592,222	2,837,537	19.57	9.46
Lao People's Democratic Republic	3,573	3,590	5,196	5,484	7,509	0.05	36.93
Malaysia	647,480	764,309	1,037,489	1,140,935	1,231,686	8.50	7.95
Myanmar	78,582	70,272	78,338	94,184	93,046	0.64	-1.21
Philippines	418,938	432,072	544,449	677,723	656,804	4.53	-3.09
Thailand	333,905	317,905	430,067	472,708	477,654	3.30	1.05
Viet Nam	239,299	265,414	322,880	332,231	366,234	2.53	10.23
Australasia	**943,928**	**924,133**	**976,348**	**1,079,034**	**1,174,074**	**8.10**	**8.81**
Australia	833,156	830,299	880,558	956,039	1,050,373	7.25	9.87
New Zealand	110,772	93,834	95,790	122,995	123,701	0.85	0.57
Melanesia	**10,060**	**9,489**	**9,455**	**10,668**	**11,239**	**0.08**	**5.35**
Fiji	2,039	1,826	1,421	1,567	1,528	0.01	-2.49
New Caledonia	1,818	1,484	1,514	1,498	1,274	0.01	-14.95
Papua New Guinea	6,203	6,179	6,520	7,603	8,437	0.06	10.97
Micronesia	**1,090**	**1,163**	**1,279**	**1,651**	**1,553**	**0.01**	**-5.94**
Guam	998	1,062	1,215	1,604	1,487	0.01	-7.29

668

SINGAPORE

2. Arrivals of non-resident visitors at national borders, by country of residence

	2008	2009	2010	2011	2012	Market share 2012	% Change 2012-2011
Nauru	92	101	64	47	66	0.00	40.43
Other East Asia and the Pacific	**1,929**	**1,762**	**2,033**	**2,062**	**2,281**	**0.02**	**10.62**
Other countries of Oceania	1,929	1,762	2,033	2,062	2,281	0.02	10.62
EUROPE	**1,333,652**	**1,318,260**	**1,386,361**	**1,413,639**	**1,550,934**	**10.70**	**9.71**
Central/Eastern Europe	**93,788**	**88,442**	**95,423**	**104,641**	**123,559**	**0.85**	**18.08**
Commonwealth Independent States	72,480	66,654	72,058	78,130	90,587	0.62	15.94
Czech Republic	5,023	6,141	6,098	6,372	7,178	0.05	12.65
Hungary	4,786	4,447	5,673	6,044	6,889	0.05	13.98
Poland	11,499	11,200	11,594	14,095	18,905	0.13	34.13
Northern Europe	**634,644**	**601,360**	**594,301**	**582,100**	**610,325**	**4.21**	**4.85**
Denmark	32,316	30,571	29,635	27,201	31,479	0.22	15.73
Finland	13,380	16,035	15,611	23,905	33,333	0.23	39.44
Ireland	28,036	22,720	20,437	18,565	18,965	0.13	2.15
Norway	32,816	30,354	31,765	32,450	36,803	0.25	13.41
Sweden	35,163	31,924	35,084	37,368	43,248	0.30	15.74
United Kingdom	492,933	469,756	461,769	442,611	446,497	3.08	0.88
Southern Europe	**89,101**	**95,021**	**101,531**	**105,549**	**121,450**	**0.84**	**15.07**
Greece	9,045	9,250	8,006	7,130	8,137	0.06	14.12
Italy	43,035	46,770	51,086	53,520	65,557	0.45	22.49
Portugal	5,273	6,600	7,115	8,268	8,429	0.06	1.95
Serbia and Montenegro	1,782	1,530	1,559	1,654	1,549	0.01	-6.35
Spain	29,966	30,871	33,765	34,977	37,778	0.26	8.01
Western Europe	**462,245**	**482,467**	**535,112**	**565,232**	**626,904**	**4.32**	**10.91**
Austria	16,649	17,505	20,093	19,889	23,264	0.16	16.97
Belgium	18,937	19,267	21,848	22,048	23,831	0.16	8.09
France	111,198	119,728	130,461	140,299	158,923	1.10	13.27
Germany	175,280	183,681	209,263	219,952	252,433	1.74	14.77
Luxembourg	2,163	2,098	2,551	2,931	2,993	0.02	2.12
Netherlands	73,230	76,359	76,520	81,090	81,603	0.56	0.63
Switzerland	64,788	63,829	74,376	79,023	83,857	0.58	6.12
East Mediterranean Europe	**27,212**	**23,684**	**29,237**	**26,868**	**31,629**	**0.22**	**17.72**
Israel	11,402	10,884	12,833	12,137	13,600	0.09	12.05
Turkey	15,810	12,800	16,404	14,731	18,029	0.12	22.39
Other Europe	**26,662**	**27,286**	**30,757**	**29,249**	**37,067**	**0.26**	**26.73**
Other countries of Europe	26,662	27,286	30,757	29,249	37,067	0.26	26.73
MIDDLE EAST	**87,690**	**85,709**	**101,461**	**113,287**	**117,950**	**0.81**	**4.12**
Bahrain	3,661	3,152	3,536	3,605	3,379	0.02	-6.27
Egypt	4,453	3,861	4,746	3,829	3,630	0.03	-5.20
Jordan	762	684	769	1,054	954	0.01	-9.49
Kuwait	4,838	5,750	8,368	8,278	7,621	0.05	-7.94
Lebanon	767	784	866	1,187	1,047	0.01	-11.79
Libya	155	184	358	109	181	0.00	66.06
Saudi Arabia	10,096	10,815	12,633	17,041	17,969	0.12	5.45
United Arab Emirates	51,170	49,529	56,476	62,736	65,552	0.45	4.49
Other countries of Middle East	11,788	10,950	13,709	15,448	17,617	0.12	14.04
SOUTH ASIA	**1,026,576**	**953,364**	**1,083,673**	**1,124,022**	**1,151,365**	**7.94**	**2.43**
Afghanistan	370	544	434	373	347	0.00	-6.97
Bangladesh	95,818	86,637	92,312	95,531	110,673	0.76	15.85
India	778,303	725,624	828,994	868,991	894,993	6.17	2.99
Iran, Islamic Republic of	19,083	23,917	36,932	32,434	18,553	0.13	-42.80
Nepal	19,752	15,183	14,303	12,757	13,425	0.09	5.24
Pakistan	22,998	22,280	21,927	20,928	21,206	0.15	1.33
Sri Lanka	79,818	70,010	78,973	83,991	83,359	0.58	-0.75
Other countries of South Asia	10,434	9,169	9,798	9,017	8,809	0.06	-2.31
NOT SPECIFIED	**6,349**	**190**	**54**	**133**	**7,769**	**0.05**	**5,741.35**
Other countries of the World	6,349	190	54	133	7,769	0.05	5,741.35

Yearbook of Tourism Statistics, Data 2008 – 2012, 2014 Edition

SINT MAARTEN

1. Arrivals of non-resident tourists at national borders, by nationality

		2008	2009	2010	2011	2012	Market share 2012	% Change 2012-2011
TOTAL	(*)	**475,410**	**440,185**	**443,136**	**424,340**	**456,710**	**100.00**	**7.63**
AMERICAS		**336,013**	**309,659**	**307,871**	**291,734**	**318,833**	**69.81**	**9.29**
Caribbean		**31,152**	**25,266**	**23,780**	**23,314**	**24,236**	**5.31**	**3.95**
All countries of the Caribbean		31,152	25,266	23,780	23,314	24,236	5.31	3.95
North America		**291,967**	**272,708**	**269,877**	**252,460**	**278,964**	**61.08**	**10.50**
Canada		34,055	32,277	33,498	33,256	40,426	8.85	21.56
United States of America		257,912	240,431	236,379	219,204	238,538	52.23	8.82
South America		**3,394**	**3,194**	**2,853**	**2,836**	**3,415**	**0.75**	**20.42**
Venezuela		3,394	3,194	2,853	2,836	3,415	0.75	20.42
Other Americas		**9,500**	**8,491**	**11,361**	**13,124**	**12,218**	**2.68**	**-6.90**
Other countries of the Americas		9,500	8,491	11,361	13,124	12,218	2.68	-6.90
EUROPE		**102,713**	**98,341**	**101,118**	**101,712**	**105,196**	**23.03**	**3.43**
Western Europe		**85,491**	**81,393**	**84,330**	**16,607**	**16,414**	**3.59**	**-1.16**
France	(*)	67,209	66,177	67,833				
Netherlands		18,282	15,216	16,497	16,607	16,414	3.59	-1.16
Other Europe		**17,222**	**16,948**	**16,788**	**85,105**	**88,782**	**19.44**	**4.32**
Other countries of Europe		17,222	16,948	16,788	85,105	88,782	19.44	4.32
NOT SPECIFIED		**36,684**	**32,185**	**34,147**	**30,894**	**32,681**	**7.16**	**5.78**
Other countries of the World		36,684	32,185	34,147	30,894	32,681	7.16	5.78

Yearbook of Tourism Statistics, Data 2008 – 2012, 2014 Edition

SLOVAKIA

4. Arrivals of non-resident tourists in all types of accommodation establishments, by nationality

	2008	2009	2010	2011	2012	Market share 2012	% Change 2012-2011
TOTAL	1,766,529	1,298,075	1,326,639	1,460,361	1,527,500	100.00	4.60
AFRICA	3,318	1,946	2,684	2,926	5,183	0.34	77.14
East Africa	74	51	78	73	139	0.01	90.41
Kenya	74	51	78	73	139	0.01	90.41
North Africa	127	92	105	99	261	0.02	163.64
Tunisia	127	92	105	99	261	0.02	163.64
Southern Africa	973	490	845	624	1,202	0.08	92.63
South Africa	973	490	845	624	1,202	0.08	92.63
Other Africa	2,144	1,313	1,656	2,130	3,581	0.23	68.12
Other countries of Africa	2,144	1,313	1,656	2,130	3,581	0.23	68.12
AMERICAS	41,456	30,137	36,198	43,172	46,250	3.03	7.13
Caribbean	20	28	45	24	38	0.00	58.33
Dominican Republic	20	28	45	24	38	0.00	58.33
North America	36,603	25,897	29,513	34,935	38,388	2.51	9.88
Canada	6,762	4,177	4,861	6,762	6,571	0.43	-2.82
Mexico	1,102	905	2,601	1,691	1,689	0.11	-0.12
United States of America	28,739	20,815	22,051	26,482	30,128	1.97	13.77
South America	2,620	2,084	2,751	3,870	4,446	0.29	14.88
Argentina	497	400	592	561	998	0.07	77.90
Brazil	2,123	1,684	2,159	3,309	3,448	0.23	4.20
Other Americas	2,213	2,128	3,889	4,343	3,378	0.22	-22.22
Other countries of the Americas	2,213	2,128	3,889	4,343	3,378	0.22	-22.22
EAST ASIA AND THE PACIFIC	70,755	53,748	65,064	72,073	80,037	5.24	11.05
North-East Asia	45,063	35,471	43,279	47,898	53,892	3.53	12.51
China	7,675	6,540	8,337	11,857	16,317	1.07	37.61
Japan	13,743	11,351	11,523	8,865	10,117	0.66	14.12
Korea, Republic of	23,645	17,580	23,419	27,176	27,458	1.80	1.04
South-East Asia	1,235	1,164	954	1,160	1,388	0.09	19.66
Thailand	1,235	1,164	954	1,160	1,388	0.09	19.66
Australasia	6,507	4,656	5,535	5,190	6,272	0.41	20.85
Australia	5,669	4,014	4,881	4,545	5,413	0.35	19.10
New Zealand	838	642	654	645	859	0.06	33.18
Other East Asia and the Pacific	17,950	12,457	15,296	17,825	18,485	1.21	3.70
Other countries of Asia	17,950	12,457	15,296	17,825	18,485	1.21	3.70
EUROPE	1,647,872	1,209,816	1,219,740	1,336,504	1,389,146	90.94	3.94
Central/Eastern Europe	1,055,794	737,179	743,991	834,124	855,721	56.02	2.59
Belarus	4,099	2,967	3,506	4,319	5,841	0.38	35.24
Bulgaria	6,891	5,626	5,416	6,517	8,037	0.53	23.32
Czech Republic	537,180	425,414	433,321	477,159	491,136	32.15	2.93
Estonia	5,242	3,250	3,209	2,952	3,918	0.26	32.72
Hungary	90,123	56,111	51,324	59,000	59,885	3.92	1.50
Latvia	8,335	4,472	4,734	5,460	5,843	0.38	7.01
Lithuania	19,698	12,602	13,182	15,046	15,062	0.99	0.11
Poland	308,437	164,712	161,851	172,001	163,754	10.72	-4.79
Republic of Moldova	264	512	440	381	485	0.03	27.30
Romania	20,685	17,513	18,381	20,551	21,485	1.41	4.54
Russian Federation	25,982	23,382	26,968	35,122	40,817	2.67	16.21
Ukraine	28,858	20,618	21,659	35,616	39,458	2.58	10.79
Northern Europe	118,769	77,934	79,581	82,524	90,579	5.93	9.76
Denmark	10,794	7,810	7,153	7,774	9,343	0.61	20.18
Finland	10,295	7,941	7,537	11,982	8,362	0.55	-30.21
Iceland	523	180	293	239	433	0.03	81.17
Ireland	9,613	4,898	6,829	6,853	6,814	0.45	-0.57
Norway	5,153	4,174	5,054	6,224	7,823	0.51	25.69
Sweden	15,763	10,616	11,754	9,976	11,163	0.73	11.90

671

SLOVAKIA

4. Arrivals of non-resident tourists in all types of accommodation establishments, by nationality

	2008	2009	2010	2011	2012	Market share 2012	% Change 2012-2011
United Kingdom	66,628	42,315	40,961	39,476	46,641	3.05	18.15
Southern Europe	**121,764**	**107,455**	**110,470**	**117,591**	**117,423**	**7.69**	**-0.14**
Albania	699	228	240	380	410	0.03	7.89
Bosnia and Herzegovina	1,404	1,281	989	1,390	1,606	0.11	15.54
Croatia	19,545	13,360	12,283	13,487	12,518	0.82	-7.18
Greece	4,591	3,748	3,815	5,130	4,617	0.30	-10.00
Italy	54,722	50,982	54,439	51,957	50,377	3.30	-3.04
Malta	569	1,227	994	231	418	0.03	80.95
Montenegro	219	112	300	372	511	0.03	37.37
Portugal	2,814	2,243	2,732	3,323	3,189	0.21	-4.03
Serbia	4,647	3,301	4,891	7,972	9,738	0.64	22.15
Slovenia	14,338	12,614	11,953	12,901	14,145	0.93	9.64
Spain	17,693	17,549	16,926	19,635	17,969	1.18	-8.48
TFYR of Macedonia	523	810	908	813	1,925	0.13	136.78
Western Europe	**322,068**	**264,350**	**260,562**	**275,390**	**288,024**	**18.86**	**4.59**
Austria	62,052	50,065	51,678	58,983	65,621	4.30	11.25
Belgium	16,036	14,671	14,460	15,242	16,292	1.07	6.89
France	43,958	34,045	32,967	35,931	35,347	2.31	-1.63
Germany	164,694	133,989	131,674	133,431	135,897	8.90	1.85
Liechtenstein	106	121	148	163	234	0.02	43.56
Luxembourg	560	548	489	419	623	0.04	48.69
Netherlands	24,113	20,759	18,776	18,499	20,759	1.36	12.22
Switzerland	10,549	10,152	10,370	12,722	13,251	0.87	4.16
East Mediterranean Europe	**15,739**	**12,471**	**14,394**	**16,450**	**20,666**	**1.35**	**25.63**
Cyprus	1,395	1,371	1,358	1,686	1,884	0.12	11.74
Israel	11,171	8,232	9,690	10,281	13,016	0.85	26.60
Turkey	3,173	2,868	3,346	4,483	5,766	0.38	28.62
Other Europe	**13,738**	**10,427**	**10,742**	**10,425**	**16,733**	**1.10**	**60.51**
Other countries of Europe	13,738	10,427	10,742	10,425	16,733	1.10	60.51
MIDDLE EAST	**533**	**516**	**551**	**579**	**1,182**	**0.08**	**104.15**
Egypt	533	516	551	579	1,182	0.08	104.15
SOUTH ASIA	**1,380**	**1,290**	**1,495**	**2,537**	**2,892**	**0.19**	**13.99**
India	1,380	1,290	1,495	2,537	2,892	0.19	13.99
NOT SPECIFIED	**1,215**	**622**	**907**	**2,570**	**2,810**	**0.18**	**9.34**
Other countries of the World	1,215	622	907	2,570	2,810	0.18	9.34

Yearbook of Tourism Statistics, Data 2008 – 2012, 2014 Edition

SLOVAKIA

6. Overnight stays of non-resident tourists in all types of accommodation establishments, by nationality

	2008	2009	2010	2011	2012	Market share 2012	% Change 2012-2011
TOTAL	5,261,476	3,769,136	3,806,609	4,038,635	4,101,201	100.00	1.55
AFRICA	13,205	8,178	9,637	8,557	20,333	0.50	137.62
East Africa	239	167	162	165	395	0.01	139.39
Kenya	239	167	162	165	395	0.01	139.39
North Africa	523	204	399	323	925	0.02	186.38
Tunisia	523	204	399	323	925	0.02	186.38
Southern Africa	1,972	1,402	2,752	1,543	3,252	0.08	110.76
South Africa	1,972	1,402	2,752	1,543	3,252	0.08	110.76
Other Africa	10,471	6,405	6,324	6,526	15,761	0.38	141.51
Other countries of Africa	10,471	6,405	6,324	6,526	15,761	0.38	141.51
AMERICAS	95,738	72,794	86,304	101,260	102,521	2.50	1.25
Caribbean	58	47	140	29	190	0.00	555.17
Dominican Republic	58	47	140	29	190	0.00	555.17
North America	83,207	62,510	70,966	82,879	86,145	2.10	3.94
Canada	16,915	10,473	12,824	18,237	15,348	0.37	-15.84
Mexico	2,585	2,053	4,139	4,585	4,409	0.11	-3.84
United States of America	63,707	49,984	54,003	60,057	66,388	1.62	10.54
South America	6,594	5,395	6,365	9,710	9,440	0.23	-2.78
Argentina	1,238	780	1,141	1,140	1,978	0.05	73.51
Brazil	5,356	4,615	5,224	8,570	7,462	0.18	-12.93
Other Americas	5,879	4,842	8,833	8,642	6,746	0.16	-21.94
Other countries of the Americas	5,879	4,842	8,833	8,642	6,746	0.16	-21.94
EAST ASIA AND THE PACIFIC	156,578	135,461	174,993	194,358	205,150	5.00	5.55
North-East Asia	72,431	68,548	87,571	103,510	104,367	2.54	0.83
China	12,120	10,441	16,839	19,519	23,643	0.58	21.13
Japan	26,460	18,995	20,187	16,443	16,404	0.40	-0.24
Korea, Republic of	33,851	39,112	50,545	67,548	64,320	1.57	-4.78
South-East Asia	2,735	5,433	4,200	2,092	2,581	0.06	23.37
Thailand	2,735	5,433	4,200	2,092	2,581	0.06	23.37
Australasia	16,430	5,204	13,723	13,716	16,887	0.41	23.12
Australia	14,614	4,014	12,383	12,517	15,057	0.37	20.29
New Zealand	1,816	1,190	1,340	1,199	1,830	0.04	52.63
Other East Asia and the Pacific	64,982	56,276	69,499	75,040	81,315	1.98	8.36
Other countries of Asia	64,982	56,276	69,499	75,040	81,315	1.98	8.36
EUROPE	4,986,808	3,540,645	3,527,429	3,719,751	3,758,567	91.65	1.04
Central/Eastern Europe	3,281,910	2,201,102	2,210,346	2,399,523	2,396,826	58.44	-0.11
Belarus	17,499	10,701	10,369	12,490	17,053	0.42	36.53
Bulgaria	18,348	13,292	10,488	12,871	16,967	0.41	31.82
Czech Republic	1,704,632	1,300,870	1,350,234	1,422,506	1,412,870	34.45	-0.68
Estonia	15,664	9,243	7,744	8,026	9,623	0.23	19.90
Hungary	225,271	136,921	120,304	143,575	131,570	3.21	-8.36
Latvia	21,236	10,649	11,618	11,776	13,099	0.32	11.23
Lithuania	41,007	27,824	26,889	31,117	32,295	0.79	3.79
Poland	941,975	479,774	453,067	471,178	441,447	10.76	-6.31
Republic of Moldova	659	1,650	1,405	1,049	1,325	0.03	26.31
Romania	64,441	45,619	49,722	57,218	53,860	1.31	-5.87
Russian Federation	111,132	88,213	94,325	125,636	151,838	3.70	20.86
Ukraine	120,046	76,346	74,181	102,081	114,879	2.80	12.54
Northern Europe	271,605	178,415	188,546	192,381	203,464	4.96	5.76
Denmark	30,532	20,702	19,167	21,984	25,018	0.61	13.80
Finland	24,732	18,751	19,126	32,776	18,042	0.44	-44.95
Iceland	1,205	390	932	532	1,154	0.03	116.92
Ireland	20,657	10,460	15,453	15,614	15,042	0.37	-3.66
Norway	11,567	10,295	11,717	14,223	20,424	0.50	43.60
Sweden	34,202	22,633	26,935	22,444	23,717	0.58	5.67

673

SLOVAKIA

6. Overnight stays of non-resident tourists in all types of accommodation establishments, by nationality

	2008	2009	2010	2011	2012	Market share 2012	% Change 2012-2011
United Kingdom	148,710	95,184	95,216	84,808	100,067	2.44	17.99
Southern Europe	**258,614**	**238,003**	**238,555**	**243,681**	**254,649**	**6.21**	**4.50**
Albania	1,710	485	656	966	824	0.02	-14.70
Bosnia and Herzegovina	4,266	3,713	2,774	2,773	3,549	0.09	27.98
Croatia	40,929	29,444	26,330	26,782	25,870	0.63	-3.41
Greece	10,525	8,195	8,997	11,311	9,998	0.24	-11.61
Italy	115,502	110,885	118,579	110,966	107,401	2.62	-3.21
Malta	1,732	5,767	2,196	625	1,143	0.03	82.88
Montenegro	611	408	704	641	2,049	0.05	219.66
Portugal	6,312	5,643	6,216	7,246	7,648	0.19	5.55
Serbia	14,718	10,923	14,662	18,483	23,774	0.58	28.63
Slovenia	25,379	23,050	23,067	24,194	30,648	0.75	26.68
Spain	35,725	37,781	32,577	37,978	36,995	0.90	-2.59
TFYR of Macedonia	1,205	1,709	1,797	1,716	4,750	0.12	176.81
Western Europe	**1,059,508**	**837,451**	**786,851**	**774,616**	**766,711**	**18.69**	**-1.02**
Austria	158,594	122,449	120,900	125,499	135,907	3.31	8.29
Belgium	39,143	35,435	35,022	35,093	36,404	0.89	3.74
France	95,660	75,680	69,368	79,757	74,902	1.83	-6.09
Germany	682,274	527,821	490,780	462,503	443,663	10.82	-4.07
Liechtenstein	670	519	399	323	383	0.01	18.58
Luxembourg	1,203	1,312	1,337	902	1,209	0.03	34.04
Netherlands	58,756	53,063	46,894	42,861	47,626	1.16	11.12
Switzerland	23,208	21,172	22,151	27,678	26,617	0.65	-3.83
East Mediterranean Europe	**80,890**	**65,988**	**79,283**	**87,033**	**106,567**	**2.60**	**22.44**
Cyprus	7,962	6,892	7,618	7,884	6,405	0.16	-18.76
Israel	65,095	52,570	64,270	69,636	86,818	2.12	24.67
Turkey	7,833	6,526	7,395	9,513	13,344	0.33	40.27
Other Europe	**34,281**	**19,686**	**23,848**	**22,517**	**30,350**	**0.74**	**34.79**
Other countries of Europe	34,281	19,686	23,848	22,517	30,350	0.74	34.79
MIDDLE EAST	**2,013**	**2,051**	**2,754**	**3,127**	**4,138**	**0.10**	**32.33**
Egypt	2,013	2,051	2,754	3,127	4,138	0.10	32.33
SOUTH ASIA	**4,822**	**3,207**	**4,063**	**6,628**	**6,348**	**0.15**	**-4.22**
India	4,822	3,207	4,063	6,628	6,348	0.15	-4.22
NOT SPECIFIED	**2,312**	**6,800**	**1,429**	**4,954**	**4,144**	**0.10**	**-16.35**
Other countries of the World	2,312	6,800	1,429	4,954	4,144	0.10	-16.35

Yearbook of Tourism Statistics, Data 2008 – 2012, 2014 Edition

SLOVENIA

3. Arrivals of non-resident tourists in hotels and similar establishments, by nationality

		2008	2009	2010	2011	2012	Market share 2012	% Change 2012-2011
TOTAL	(*)	1,532,418	1,411,352	1,422,382	1,528,057	1,592,858	100.00	4.24
AFRICA		3,411	2,518	2,779	3,642	3,982	0.25	9.34
Southern Africa		808	780	956	1,419	1,868	0.12	31.64
South Africa		808	780	956	1,419	1,868	0.12	31.64
Other Africa		2,603	1,738	1,823	2,223	2,114	0.13	-4.90
Other countries of Africa		2,603	1,738	1,823	2,223	2,114	0.13	-4.90
AMERICAS		59,551	49,459	52,235	56,002	62,145	3.90	10.97
North America		53,403	42,694	45,032	46,660	51,635	3.24	10.66
Canada		8,036	7,124	7,435	8,050	8,634	0.54	7.25
United States of America		42,776	33,327	35,487	38,455	42,986	2.70	11.78
Other countries of North America		2,591	2,243	2,110	155	15	0.00	-90.32
South America		2,360	2,776	3,057	3,772	5,185	0.33	37.46
Brazil		2,360	2,776	3,057	3,772	5,185	0.33	37.46
Other Americas		3,788	3,989	4,146	5,570	5,325	0.33	-4.40
Other countries of the Americas		3,788	3,989	4,146	5,570	5,325	0.33	-4.40
EAST ASIA AND THE PACIFIC		79,664	84,457	84,888	95,273	119,400	7.50	25.32
North-East Asia		49,853	57,894	53,090	55,091	68,952	4.33	25.16
China		4,625	5,319	7,613	10,078	13,860	0.87	37.53
Japan		39,078	47,641	39,502	34,187	39,764	2.50	16.31
Korea, Republic of		6,150	4,934	5,975	10,826	15,328	0.96	41.59
Australasia		19,110	14,477	15,551	15,423	14,923	0.94	-3.24
Australia		16,687	12,325	13,035	13,604	13,095	0.82	-3.74
New Zealand		2,423	2,152	2,516	1,819	1,828	0.11	0.49
Other East Asia and the Pacific		10,701	12,086	16,247	24,759	35,525	2.23	43.48
Other countries of Asia		10,023	11,226	15,706	24,040	34,727	2.18	44.46
Other countries of Oceania		678	860	541	719	798	0.05	10.99
EUROPE		1,389,792	1,274,918	1,282,480	1,373,140	1,407,331	88.35	2.49
Central/Eastern Europe		192,227	168,285	178,106	209,763	228,112	14.32	8.75
Bulgaria		17,772	16,135	15,654	18,147	17,087	1.07	-5.84
Czech Republic		27,936	25,225	24,702	27,897	28,336	1.78	1.57
Estonia		2,096	1,438	1,568	1,860	1,775	0.11	-4.57
Hungary		41,195	38,814	36,844	42,088	42,320	2.66	0.55
Latvia		5,405	2,670	3,041	2,444	2,346	0.15	-4.01
Lithuania		3,685	1,979	1,787	2,127	2,104	0.13	-1.08
Poland		26,159	21,556	20,924	23,729	26,813	1.68	13.00
Romania		15,233	15,453	16,204	17,944	18,056	1.13	0.62
Russian Federation		28,803	25,045	30,414	38,019	47,054	2.95	23.76
Slovakia		12,689	11,363	12,093	13,181	14,114	0.89	7.08
Ukraine		11,254	8,607	14,875	22,327	28,107	1.76	25.89
Northern Europe		131,213	103,143	91,464	95,261	91,268	5.73	-4.19
Denmark		9,243	8,058	9,277	10,139	9,103	0.57	-10.22
Finland		19,116	14,071	11,953	12,559	11,387	0.71	-9.33
Iceland		1,583	1,179	659	1,482	1,469	0.09	-0.88
Ireland		8,053	7,481	5,127	5,132	4,190	0.26	-18.36
Norway		7,717	5,759	5,637	5,343	5,561	0.35	4.08
Sweden		16,255	11,959	10,844	11,759	12,771	0.80	8.61
United Kingdom		69,246	54,636	47,967	48,847	46,787	2.94	-4.22
Southern Europe		574,074	556,443	578,563	589,086	572,097	35.92	-2.88
Bosnia and Herzegovina		27,578	23,432	23,899	25,224	24,855	1.56	-1.46
Croatia		99,011	82,404	82,584	87,602	88,298	5.54	0.79
Greece		6,201	6,651	6,050	6,150	6,419	0.40	4.37
Italy		346,020	352,163	348,103	348,128	340,350	21.37	-2.23
Malta		1,497	2,183	2,195	2,664	2,348	0.15	-11.86
Montenegro		3,605	3,871	6,543	6,214	6,278	0.39	1.03
Portugal		6,963	6,091	5,763	5,821	4,786	0.30	-17.78

675

SLOVENIA

3. Arrivals of non-resident tourists in hotels and similar establishments, by nationality

	2008	2009	2010	2011	2012	Market share 2012	% Change 2012-2011
Serbia	46,858	46,489	67,104	70,350	67,054	4.21	-4.69
Spain	25,366	23,390	23,114	24,444	20,989	1.32	-14.13
TFYR of Macedonia	10,975	9,769	13,208	12,489	10,720	0.67	-14.16
Western Europe	**445,176**	**405,634**	**391,862**	**432,070**	**460,389**	**28.90**	**6.55**
Austria	172,717	169,240	164,237	181,515	198,388	12.45	9.30
Belgium	28,014	22,617	22,394	28,400	29,122	1.83	2.54
France	44,457	39,921	37,258	39,326	38,208	2.40	-2.84
Germany	148,042	125,269	123,041	134,573	142,568	8.95	5.94
Luxembourg	2,296	1,107	968	1,066	1,297	0.08	21.67
Netherlands	26,707	25,355	23,309	24,294	26,297	1.65	8.24
Switzerland	22,943	22,125	20,655	22,896	24,509	1.54	7.04
East Mediterranean Europe	**39,086**	**31,931**	**32,817**	**35,791**	**42,414**	**2.66**	**18.50**
Cyprus	1,294	587	713	570	852	0.05	49.47
Israel	26,500	23,770	21,848	22,298	28,989	1.82	30.01
Turkey	11,292	7,574	10,256	12,923	12,573	0.79	-2.71
Other Europe	**8,016**	**9,482**	**9,668**	**11,169**	**13,051**	**0.82**	**16.85**
Other countries of Europe	8,016	9,482	9,668	11,169	13,051	0.82	16.85

Yearbook of Tourism Statistics, Data 2008 – 2012, 2014 Editic

SLOVENIA

4. Arrivals of non-resident tourists in all types of accommodation establishments, by nationality

		2008	2009	2010	2011	2012	Market share 2012	% Change 2012-2011
TOTAL	(*)	1,957,691	1,823,931	1,869,106	2,036,652	2,155,612	100.00	5.84
AFRICA		3,760	2,911	3,396	4,437	4,919	0.23	10.86
Southern Africa		899	898	1,132	1,773	2,258	0.10	27.35
South Africa		899	898	1,132	1,773	2,258	0.10	27.35
Other Africa		2,861	2,013	2,264	2,664	2,661	0.12	-0.11
Other countries of Africa		2,861	2,013	2,264	2,664	2,661	0.12	-0.11
AMERICAS		65,701	55,336	61,941	67,613	75,923	3.52	12.29
North America		58,866	47,777	53,368	56,627	63,037	2.92	11.32
Canada		9,372	8,410	9,598	10,583	11,251	0.52	6.31
United States of America		46,783	37,050	41,566	45,796	51,754	2.40	13.01
Other countries of North America		2,711	2,317	2,204	248	32	0.00	-87.10
South America		2,549	2,998	3,591	4,290	6,075	0.28	41.61
Brazil		2,549	2,998	3,591	4,290	6,075	0.28	41.61
Other Americas		4,286	4,561	4,982	6,696	6,811	0.32	1.72
Other countries of the Americas		4,286	4,561	4,982	6,696	6,811	0.32	1.72
EAST ASIA AND THE PACIFIC		85,552	90,168	94,653	106,067	133,006	6.17	25.40
North-East Asia		51,030	58,958	55,314	57,934	73,089	3.39	26.16
China		4,911	5,638	8,234	11,050	15,294	0.71	38.41
Japan		39,733	48,182	40,455	35,321	41,398	1.92	17.21
Korea, Republic of		6,386	5,138	6,625	11,563	16,397	0.76	41.81
Australasia		23,048	18,379	21,318	21,524	21,407	0.99	-0.54
Australia		19,709	15,308	17,695	18,461	18,216	0.85	-1.33
New Zealand		3,339	3,071	3,623	3,063	3,191	0.15	4.18
Other East Asia and the Pacific		11,474	12,831	18,021	26,609	38,510	1.79	44.73
Other countries of Asia		10,624	11,793	17,071	25,631	37,361	1.73	45.76
Other countries of Oceania		850	1,038	950	978	1,149	0.05	17.48
EUROPE		1,802,678	1,675,516	1,709,116	1,858,535	1,941,764	90.08	4.48
Central/Eastern Europe		267,746	240,190	255,552	299,936	326,586	15.15	8.89
Bulgaria		20,716	19,507	18,833	21,800	20,937	0.97	-3.96
Czech Republic		54,957	52,417	53,205	58,817	63,077	2.93	7.24
Estonia		2,842	1,958	2,072	2,525	2,593	0.12	2.69
Hungary		59,606	55,370	55,325	63,096	62,856	2.92	-0.38
Latvia		6,980	3,339	3,997	3,274	3,385	0.16	3.39
Lithuania		4,938	3,045	2,821	3,386	3,356	0.16	-0.89
Poland		38,539	32,607	33,320	39,626	43,583	2.02	9.99
Romania		18,274	18,660	19,462	21,799	22,298	1.03	2.29
Russian Federation		30,585	26,842	32,690	41,360	52,476	2.43	26.88
Slovakia		17,230	16,329	17,427	19,720	21,258	0.99	7.80
Ukraine		13,079	10,116	16,400	24,533	30,767	1.43	25.41
Northern Europe		164,427	132,595	128,875	134,236	132,008	6.12	-1.66
Denmark		14,974	13,723	15,255	16,576	16,120	0.75	-2.75
Finland		21,828	16,549	15,082	15,629	14,412	0.67	-7.79
Iceland		1,758	1,436	882	1,785	1,817	0.08	1.79
Ireland		10,008	9,354	7,715	7,719	6,667	0.31	-13.63
Norway		9,270	7,150	7,448	6,876	7,314	0.34	6.37
Sweden		19,686	14,955	14,028	14,986	16,614	0.77	10.86
United Kingdom		86,903	69,428	68,465	70,665	69,064	3.20	-2.27
Southern Europe		678,121	663,976	691,750	715,444	705,766	32.74	-1.35
Bosnia and Herzegovina		31,058	26,881	27,299	29,356	30,372	1.41	3.46
Croatia		123,087	104,045	103,134	110,377	113,647	5.27	2.96
Greece		6,756	7,434	6,822	6,885	7,580	0.35	10.09
Italy		406,662	417,771	412,137	420,247	414,041	19.21	-1.48
Malta		1,726	2,389	2,401	2,926	2,637	0.12	-9.88
Montenegro		4,039	4,188	7,277	6,801	7,126	0.33	4.78
Portugal		8,107	7,330	7,422	7,644	6,586	0.31	-13.84

677

SLOVENIA

4. Arrivals of non-resident tourists in all types of accommodation establishments, by nationality

	2008	2009	2010	2011	2012	Market share 2012	% Change 2012-2011
Serbia	50,560	51,388	76,156	80,995	78,207	3.63	-3.44
Spain	33,568	31,409	33,670	35,687	32,563	1.51	-8.75
TFYR of Macedonia	12,558	11,141	15,432	14,526	13,007	0.60	-10.46
Western Europe	**638,392**	**590,074**	**581,231**	**651,247**	**707,735**	**32.83**	**8.67**
Austria	210,229	207,366	201,756	222,192	240,113	11.14	8.07
Belgium	41,920	33,845	35,209	45,312	48,817	2.26	7.74
France	66,233	60,527	62,104	67,019	67,619	3.14	0.90
Germany	222,218	195,240	194,386	218,894	238,352	11.06	8.89
Luxembourg	2,640	1,381	1,253	1,495	1,713	0.08	14.58
Netherlands	66,556	63,803	58,941	65,548	78,049	3.62	19.07
Switzerland	28,596	27,912	27,582	30,787	33,072	1.53	7.42
East Mediterranean Europe	**44,645**	**37,774**	**40,442**	**44,562**	**54,427**	**2.52**	**22.14**
Cyprus	1,390	616	778	685	1,069	0.05	56.06
Israel	31,625	29,110	28,713	30,153	39,595	1.84	31.31
Turkey	11,630	8,048	10,951	13,724	13,763	0.64	0.28
Other Europe	**9,347**	**10,907**	**11,266**	**13,110**	**15,242**	**0.71**	**16.26**
Other countries of Europe	9,347	10,907	11,266	13,110	15,242	0.71	16.26

Yearbook of Tourism Statistics, Data 2008 – 2012, 2014 Edition

SLOVENIA

5. Overnight stays of non-resident tourists in hotels and similar establishments, by nationality

	2008	2009	2010	2011	2012	Market share 2012	% Change 2012-2011
TOTAL (*)	4,051,014	3,684,005	3,715,473	4,005,927	4,150,042	100.00	3.60
AFRICA	12,204	6,896	8,440	13,187	13,143	0.32	-0.33
Southern Africa	2,223	2,157	2,662	3,784	5,124	0.12	35.41
South Africa	2,223	2,157	2,662	3,784	5,124	0.12	35.41
Other Africa	9,981	4,739	5,778	9,403	8,019	0.19	-14.72
Other countries of Africa	9,981	4,739	5,778	9,403	8,019	0.19	-14.72
AMERICAS	139,873	111,159	119,261	126,276	143,875	3.47	13.94
North America	125,127	96,441	104,688	106,094	121,353	2.92	14.38
Canada	18,238	16,506	17,617	18,867	19,196	0.46	1.74
United States of America	101,538	74,623	82,616	86,927	102,127	2.46	17.49
Other countries of North America	5,351	5,312	4,455	300	30	0.00	-90.00
South America	5,496	5,939	5,967	7,542	10,763	0.26	42.71
Brazil	5,496	5,939	5,967	7,542	10,763	0.26	42.71
Other Americas	9,250	8,779	8,606	12,640	11,759	0.28	-6.97
Other countries of the Americas	9,250	8,779	8,606	12,640	11,759	0.28	-6.97
EAST ASIA AND THE PACIFIC	132,767	136,049	137,284	162,107	188,119	4.53	16.05
North-East Asia	72,348	80,420	73,738	81,305	95,921	2.31	17.98
China	9,150	10,300	14,152	19,411	20,377	0.49	4.98
Japan	55,316	63,160	51,986	48,299	56,741	1.37	17.48
Korea, Republic of	7,882	6,960	7,600	13,595	18,803	0.45	38.31
Australasia	36,508	28,017	31,344	32,339	30,266	0.73	-6.41
Australia	31,908	23,856	26,066	27,807	26,759	0.64	-3.77
New Zealand	4,600	4,161	5,278	4,532	3,507	0.08	-22.62
Other East Asia and the Pacific	23,911	27,612	32,202	48,463	61,932	1.49	27.79
Other countries of Asia	22,441	25,755	31,073	46,973	60,264	1.45	28.29
Other countries of Oceania	1,470	1,857	1,129	1,490	1,668	0.04	11.95
EUROPE	3,766,170	3,429,901	3,450,488	3,704,357	3,804,905	91.68	2.71
Central/Eastern Europe	550,356	496,286	539,062	638,430	743,398	17.91	16.44
Bulgaria	32,573	27,247	26,025	29,260	26,532	0.64	-9.32
Czech Republic	64,691	58,710	60,630	69,988	73,604	1.77	5.17
Estonia	5,258	4,092	3,802	4,942	4,690	0.11	-5.10
Hungary	104,475	98,547	93,131	107,350	105,551	2.54	-1.68
Latvia	10,462	5,345	6,042	5,633	5,299	0.13	-5.93
Lithuania	7,622	5,019	4,566	5,043	4,970	0.12	-1.45
Poland	61,163	50,074	45,255	48,668	60,238	1.45	23.77
Romania	33,432	34,094	32,495	37,521	36,902	0.89	-1.65
Russian Federation	157,800	156,770	198,832	243,471	327,339	7.89	34.45
Slovakia	30,865	27,064	30,401	33,652	33,925	0.82	0.81
Ukraine	42,015	29,324	37,883	52,902	64,348	1.55	21.64
Northern Europe	420,308	321,163	291,261	294,406	277,083	6.68	-5.88
Denmark	25,460	23,222	20,128	23,411	20,694	0.50	-11.61
Finland	54,235	38,173	32,708	32,683	29,691	0.72	-9.15
Iceland	4,167	2,148	2,046	3,757	4,511	0.11	20.07
Ireland	26,504	23,926	15,968	16,274	12,474	0.30	-23.35
Norway	19,727	14,950	14,217	12,896	13,423	0.32	4.09
Sweden	42,085	31,747	27,130	28,353	32,974	0.79	16.30
United Kingdom	248,130	186,997	179,064	177,032	163,316	3.94	-7.75
Southern Europe	1,405,898	1,341,168	1,393,598	1,405,182	1,339,865	32.29	-4.65
Bosnia and Herzegovina	84,183	59,005	55,120	56,482	55,459	1.34	-1.81
Croatia	260,519	215,855	209,972	216,121	220,376	5.31	1.97
Greece	13,473	14,491	12,672	13,431	11,814	0.28	-12.04
Italy	830,070	839,009	828,083	825,344	777,204	18.73	-5.83
Malta	5,143	10,988	11,251	13,778	11,774	0.28	-14.54
Montenegro	10,033	9,530	15,855	14,695	14,705	0.35	0.07
Portugal	14,299	11,893	11,596	10,464	10,264	0.25	-1.91

679

SLOVENIA

5. Overnight stays of non-resident tourists in hotels and similar establishments, by nationality

	2008	2009	2010	2011	2012	Market share 2012	% Change 2012-2011
Serbia	114,278	114,736	177,041	180,134	172,199	4.15	-4.41
Spain	49,864	45,173	46,002	49,827	45,061	1.09	-9.57
TFYR of Macedonia	24,036	20,488	26,006	24,906	21,009	0.51	-15.65
Western Europe	**1,269,039**	**1,157,061**	**1,114,777**	**1,235,962**	**1,282,037**	**30.89**	**3.73**
Austria	528,755	519,130	499,393	545,235	568,879	13.71	4.34
Belgium	92,978	75,620	79,154	102,023	102,642	2.47	0.61
France	89,420	80,481	73,371	81,216	77,458	1.87	-4.63
Germany	426,318	361,572	354,612	392,345	407,787	9.83	3.94
Luxembourg	6,083	3,291	2,322	2,583	3,061	0.07	18.51
Netherlands	68,307	63,999	61,056	62,746	69,393	1.67	10.59
Switzerland	57,178	52,968	44,869	49,814	52,817	1.27	6.03
East Mediterranean Europe	**98,100**	**86,554**	**87,128**	**97,138**	**119,742**	**2.89**	**23.27**
Cyprus	3,657	1,990	2,148	1,609	2,047	0.05	27.22
Israel	75,466	67,898	67,081	70,864	93,654	2.26	32.16
Turkey	18,977	16,666	17,899	24,665	24,041	0.58	-2.53
Other Europe	**22,469**	**27,669**	**24,662**	**33,239**	**42,780**	**1.03**	**28.70**
Other countries of Europe	22,469	27,669	24,662	33,239	42,780	1.03	28.70

SLOVENIA

6. Overnight stays of non-resident tourists in all types of accommodation establishments, by nationality

		2008	2009	2010	2011	2012	Market share 2012	% Change 2012-2011
TOTAL	(*)	5,351,282	4,936,293	4,997,031	5,463,931	5,777,204	100.00	5.73
AFRICA		13,376	8,185	11,340	15,500	16,912	0.29	9.11
Southern Africa		2,428	2,452	3,162	4,768	6,663	0.12	39.74
South Africa		2,428	2,452	3,162	4,768	6,663	0.12	39.74
Other Africa		10,948	5,733	8,178	10,732	10,249	0.18	-4.50
Other countries of Africa		10,948	5,733	8,178	10,732	10,249	0.18	-4.50
AMERICAS		156,707	127,357	141,414	153,840	176,654	3.06	14.83
North America		139,565	109,694	124,012	129,885	147,823	2.56	13.81
Canada		22,148	20,102	22,772	24,894	25,175	0.44	1.13
United States of America		111,717	84,076	96,648	104,503	122,580	2.12	17.30
Other countries of North America		5,700	5,516	4,592	488	68	0.00	-86.07
South America		6,315	6,580	6,971	8,565	12,728	0.22	48.60
Brazil		6,315	6,580	6,971	8,565	12,728	0.22	48.60
Other Americas		10,827	11,083	10,431	15,390	16,103	0.28	4.63
Other countries of the Americas		10,827	11,083	10,431	15,390	16,103	0.28	4.63
EAST ASIA AND THE PACIFIC		150,821	154,321	161,964	186,139	221,794	3.84	19.16
North-East Asia		75,625	83,401	77,954	87,599	104,552	1.81	19.35
China		10,159	11,263	15,477	21,785	23,530	0.41	8.01
Japan		57,093	64,712	53,761	50,840	60,278	1.04	18.56
Korea, Republic of		8,373	7,426	8,716	14,974	20,744	0.36	38.53
Australasia		45,767	36,915	44,098	45,274	44,093	0.76	-2.61
Australia		39,289	30,786	36,419	38,064	37,793	0.65	-0.71
New Zealand		6,478	6,129	7,679	7,210	6,300	0.11	-12.62
Other East Asia and the Pacific		29,429	34,005	39,912	53,266	73,149	1.27	37.33
Other countries of Asia		27,313	31,538	36,743	51,129	70,597	1.22	38.08
Other countries of Oceania		2,116	2,467	3,169	2,137	2,552	0.04	19.42
EUROPE		5,030,378	4,646,430	4,682,313	5,108,452	5,361,844	92.81	4.96
Central/Eastern Europe		758,278	691,285	742,046	874,432	1,004,619	17.39	14.89
Bulgaria		38,851	33,699	32,426	36,436	33,521	0.58	-8.00
Czech Republic		127,998	124,415	127,165	141,937	157,175	2.72	10.74
Estonia		7,005	5,246	4,874	6,442	6,451	0.11	0.14
Hungary		160,308	147,338	144,215	165,059	161,233	2.79	-2.32
Latvia		14,178	7,630	8,222	7,941	8,095	0.14	1.94
Lithuania		10,573	7,550	6,706	7,964	7,717	0.13	-3.10
Poland		96,042	80,495	82,639	93,128	108,312	1.87	16.30
Romania		41,777	44,590	40,959	48,216	48,736	0.84	1.08
Russian Federation		166,119	163,903	208,341	257,173	350,319	6.06	36.22
Slovakia		43,914	39,935	43,376	50,424	49,830	0.86	-1.18
Ukraine		51,513	36,484	43,123	59,712	73,230	1.27	22.64
Northern Europe		518,767	409,201	396,526	409,066	394,226	6.82	-3.63
Denmark		46,782	42,790	40,059	47,605	46,625	0.81	-2.06
Finland		62,015	44,915	39,947	41,012	37,625	0.65	-8.26
Iceland		4,650	3,139	2,531	4,804	5,314	0.09	10.62
Ireland		31,601	28,984	22,053	22,536	18,716	0.32	-16.95
Norway		23,806	18,504	18,876	16,561	17,735	0.31	7.09
Sweden		50,364	39,039	34,592	35,819	42,096	0.73	17.52
United Kingdom		299,549	231,830	238,468	240,729	226,115	3.91	-6.07
Southern Europe		1,698,778	1,643,436	1,688,496	1,740,156	1,687,064	29.20	-3.05
Bosnia and Herzegovina		101,078	77,281	66,611	70,478	72,080	1.25	2.27
Croatia		335,403	288,170	274,380	291,186	297,647	5.15	2.22
Greece		15,137	16,911	14,435	15,312	14,717	0.25	-3.89
Italy		987,617	1,004,783	987,268	1,005,222	957,027	16.57	-4.79
Malta		5,761	11,637	11,921	14,529	12,551	0.22	-13.61
Montenegro		11,178	10,410	17,759	16,446	17,497	0.30	6.39
Portugal		17,038	15,055	15,071	14,146	14,262	0.25	0.82

Yearbook of Tourism Statistics, Data 2008 – 2012, 2014 Edition

SLOVENIA

6. Overnight stays of non-resident tourists in all types of accommodation establishments, by nationality

	2008	2009	2010	2011	2012	Market share 2012	% Change 2012-2011
Serbia	125,410	131,177	201,683	209,971	203,807	3.53	-2.94
Spain	70,341	62,432	67,276	71,737	69,396	1.20	-3.26
TFYR of Macedonia	29,815	25,580	32,092	31,129	28,080	0.49	-9.79
Western Europe	**1,915,405**	**1,767,215**	**1,718,709**	**1,923,304**	**2,074,958**	**35.92**	**7.89**
Austria	655,565	642,242	619,259	674,194	695,555	12.04	3.17
Belgium	135,155	111,140	117,980	152,612	168,219	2.91	10.23
France	142,651	130,752	130,968	143,478	145,968	2.53	1.74
Germany	658,714	577,961	578,262	646,696	692,648	11.99	7.11
Luxembourg	6,924	4,116	2,922	3,619	4,087	0.07	12.93
Netherlands	244,645	233,539	208,654	234,390	295,679	5.12	26.15
Switzerland	71,751	67,465	60,664	68,315	72,802	1.26	6.57
East Mediterranean Europe	**112,723**	**102,913**	**106,872**	**122,855**	**152,195**	**2.63**	**23.88**
Cyprus	3,873	2,042	2,292	1,880	2,486	0.04	32.23
Israel	88,498	82,258	84,657	93,915	122,174	2.11	30.09
Turkey	20,352	18,613	19,923	27,060	27,535	0.48	1.76
Other Europe	**26,427**	**32,380**	**29,664**	**38,639**	**48,782**	**0.84**	**26.25**
Other countries of Europe	26,427	32,380	29,664	38,639	48,782	0.84	26.25

682

SOLOMON ISLANDS

1. Arrivals of non-resident tourists at national borders, by country of residence

	2008	2009	2010	2011	2012	Market share 2012	% Change 2012-2011
TOTAL	16,264	18,308	20,521	22,941			
AMERICAS	1,220	1,122	975	1,232			
North America	1,220	1,122	975	1,232			
Canada	115	88	113	192			
United States of America	1,105	1,034	862	1,040			
EAST ASIA AND THE PACIFIC	13,772	15,886	18,255	20,480			
North-East Asia	646	938	627	771			
Hong Kong, China	57	65	38	130			
Japan	589	873	589	641			
Australasia	8,510	10,266	12,461	13,116			
Australia	7,413	8,902	10,751	11,392			
New Zealand	1,097	1,364	1,710	1,724			
Melanesia	2,211	2,323	2,757	3,774			
Fiji	787	917	991	1,204			
Papua New Guinea	906	1,098	1,361	2,057			
Vanuatu	518	308	405	513			
Other East Asia and the Pacific	2,405	2,359	2,410	2,819			
Other countries of Asia	1,249	1,409	1,825	2,056			
Other countries of Oceania	1,156	950	585	763			
EUROPE	1,132	1,091	1,014	941			
Northern Europe	457	419	432	380			
United Kingdom	457	419	432	380			
Southern Europe	37	66	39	80			
Italy	37	66	39	80			
Western Europe	252	232	236	235			
France	91	81	82	60			
Germany	124	100	101	111			
Netherlands	37	51	53	64			
Other Europe	386	374	307	246			
Other countries of Europe	386	374	307	246			
NOT SPECIFIED	140	209	277	288			
Other countries of the World	140	209	277	288			

Yearbook of Tourism Statistics, Data 2008 – 2012, 2014 Edition

SOUTH AFRICA

1. Arrivals of non-resident tourists at national borders, by country of residence

		2008	2009	2010	2011	2012	Market share 2012	% Change 2012-2011
TOTAL	(*)	9,564,207	7,011,416	8,072,979	8,338,689	9,187,703	100.00	10.18
AFRICA		7,343,765	5,083,145	5,733,499	6,129,606	6,648,201	72.36	8.46
East Africa		2,884,396	2,587,771	2,950,813	3,036,469	3,389,016	36.89	11.61
Burundi			960	891	1,010	1,472	0.02	45.74
Comoros			155	209	198	276	0.00	39.39
Djibouti			78	79	97	92	0.00	-5.15
Eritrea			579	602	666	904	0.01	35.74
Ethiopia			10,651	9,397	9,125	7,862	0.09	-13.84
Kenya		26,939	25,581	29,089	30,279	32,992	0.36	8.96
Madagascar			2,623	3,075	2,962	4,813	0.05	62.49
Malawi		163,328	139,605	126,120	135,577	142,063	1.55	4.78
Mauritius		16,214	13,625	16,329	16,545	18,233	0.20	10.20
Mozambique		1,226,989	983,739	1,051,502	1,076,753	1,104,404	12.02	2.57
Reunion		830	596	348	3			
Rwanda			2,841	2,931	2,838	3,429	0.04	20.82
Seychelles		2,480	2,166	2,861	3,182	3,292	0.04	3.46
Somalia			2,863	2,706	829	206	0.00	-75.15
Uganda		12,900	12,257	13,627	14,450	15,522	0.17	7.42
United Republic of Tanzania		15,682	14,732	19,641	28,645	35,928	0.39	25.43
Zambia		192,041	147,089	157,692	160,302	169,555	1.85	5.77
Zimbabwe		1,226,993	1,227,631	1,513,714	1,553,008	1,847,973	20.11	18.99
Central Africa		67,678	85,071	87,644	87,613	99,185	1.08	13.21
Angola		35,993	37,254	38,543	39,217	47,714	0.52	21.67
Cameroon			4,531	6,461	5,357	6,234	0.07	16.37
Central African Republic			120	170	143	191	0.00	33.57
Chad			251	252	339	414	0.00	22.12
Congo			6,347	4,437	3,337	3,868	0.04	15.91
Democratic Republic of the Congo		31,685	30,982	31,285	32,582	32,956	0.36	1.15
Equatorial Guinea			343	311	319	406	0.00	27.27
Gabon			5,077	6,052	6,199	7,168	0.08	15.63
Sao Tome and Principe			166	133	120	234	0.00	95.00
North Africa			5,270	8,479	5,745	6,018	0.07	4.75
Algeria			1,210	3,529	1,259	1,539	0.02	22.24
Morocco			933	1,563	1,364	1,611	0.02	18.11
Sudan			2,087	2,080	1,891	1,665	0.02	-11.95
Tunisia			1,027	1,212	1,221	1,182	0.01	-3.19
Western Sahara			13	95	10	21	0.00	110.00
Southern Africa		4,278,101	2,338,784	2,606,273	2,902,488	3,039,950	33.09	4.74
Botswana		804,701	484,258	507,042	477,937	452,159	4.92	-5.39
Lesotho		2,163,372	1,048,550	1,275,838	1,526,597	1,618,222	17.61	6.00
Namibia		221,995	177,863	190,903	197,835	200,841	2.19	1.52
Swaziland		1,088,033	628,113	632,490	700,119	768,728	8.37	9.80
West Africa		56,721	66,220	80,226	97,291	114,027	1.24	17.20
Benin			1,293	1,234	1,299	1,553	0.02	19.55
Burkina Faso			588	628	697	816	0.01	17.07
Cape Verde			602	554	534	635	0.01	18.91
Côte d'Ivoire			2,182	2,716	1,781	2,415	0.03	35.60
Gambia			631	748	805	1,142	0.01	41.86
Ghana		13,232	11,395	18,435	18,538	22,953	0.25	23.82
Guinea			1,334	1,931	2,127	2,990	0.03	40.57
Guinea-Bissau			174	230	198	212	0.00	7.07
Liberia			498	545	586	708	0.01	20.82
Mali			792	1,190	1,192	1,268	0.01	6.38
Mauritania			118	271	269	241	0.00	-10.41
Niger			244	293	296	369	0.00	24.66
Nigeria		43,489	42,651	46,853	64,402	73,282	0.80	13.79

Yearbook of Tourism Statistics, Data 2008 – 2012, 2014 Editio

SOUTH AFRICA

1. Arrivals of non-resident tourists at national borders, by country of residence

	2008	2009	2010	2011	2012	Market share 2012	% Change 2012-2011
Saint Helena		143	119	80	52	0.00	-35.00
Senegal		2,333	3,005	2,965	3,600	0.04	21.42
Sierra Leone		766	955	930	991	0.01	6.56
Togo		476	519	592	800	0.01	35.14
Other Africa	**56,869**	**29**	**64**		**5**	**0.00**	
Other countries of Africa	56,869	29	64		5	0.00	
AMERICAS	**407,408**	**333,528**	**458,249**	**433,135**	**513,610**	**5.59**	**18.58**
Caribbean		**2,062**	**3,479**	**3,275**	**4,169**	**0.05**	**27.30**
Antigua and Barbuda		28	96	83	51	0.00	-38.55
Bahamas		78	142	137	153	0.00	11.68
Barbados		126	207	174	168	0.00	-3.45
Bermuda		65	73	58	45	0.00	-22.41
British Virgin Islands		26	4		3	0.00	
Cuba		577	1,247	1,139	1,801	0.02	58.12
Dominica		55	116	109	173	0.00	58.72
Grenada		20	33	37	31	0.00	-16.22
Haiti		179	192	98	98	0.00	0.00
Jamaica		497	695	663	743	0.01	12.07
Puerto Rico		6	4	3	3	0.00	0.00
Saint Lucia		38	41	43	36	0.00	-16.28
Saint Vincent and the Grenadines		18	43	36	21	0.00	-41.67
Trinidad and Tobago		347	585	693	839	0.01	21.07
Turks and Caicos Islands		1	1	2	4	0.00	100.00
United States Virgin Islands		1					
Central America		**966**	**3,736**	**1,262**	**1,498**	**0.02**	**18.70**
Belize		66	59	57	78	0.00	36.84
Costa Rica		284	921	401	372	0.00	-7.23
El Salvador		113	391	93	146	0.00	56.99
Guatemala		182	569	181	278	0.00	53.59
Honduras		102	1,330	188	284	0.00	51.06
Nicaragua		57	88	80	80	0.00	0.00
Panama		162	378	262	260	0.00	-0.76
North America	**348,345**	**278,360**	**353,572**	**348,627**	**396,923**	**4.32**	**13.85**
Canada	56,904	45,330	55,263	57,767	66,802	0.73	15.64
Greenland	78	32	9				
Mexico	3,925	2,674	15,923	3,246	3,477	0.04	7.12
United States of America	287,438	230,324	282,377	287,614	326,644	3.56	13.57
South America	**49,391**	**51,752**	**97,172**	**79,864**	**110,920**	**1.21**	**38.89**
Argentina	8,704	9,787	21,701	13,817	17,514	0.19	26.76
Bolivia		549	722	690	1,371	0.01	98.70
Brazil	35,649	32,256	53,756	54,183	78,376	0.85	44.65
Chile	3,269	2,581	7,260	3,210	3,507	0.04	9.25
Colombia		1,582	3,146	1,831	2,627	0.03	43.47
Ecuador		418	1,004	626	750	0.01	19.81
Falkland Islands, Malvinas		5	2				
French Guiana		67	38		4	0.00	
Guyana		293	273	246	254	0.00	3.25
Paraguay		384	1,170	530	692	0.01	30.57
Peru		1,577	2,731	2,185	2,944	0.03	34.74
Suriname		64	95	91	69	0.00	-24.18
Uruguay		944	2,683	1,162	1,370	0.01	17.90
Venezuela	1,769	1,245	2,591	1,293	1,442	0.02	11.52
Other Americas	**9,672**	**388**	**290**	**107**	**100**	**0.00**	**-6.54**
Other countries of the Americas	9,672	388	290	107	100	0.00	-6.54
EAST ASIA AND THE PACIFIC	**243,036**	**216,051**	**293,141**	**304,704**	**401,353**	**4.37**	**31.72**
North-East Asia	**71,459**	**87,140**	**123,223**	**138,377**	**197,840**	**2.15**	**42.97**

Yearbook of Tourism Statistics, Data 2008 – 2012, 2014 Edition

SOUTH AFRICA

1. Arrivals of non-resident tourists at national borders, by country of residence

	2008	2009	2010	2011	2012	Market share 2012	% Change 2012-2011
China	40,320	34,561	65,920	84,862	132,327	1.44	55.93
Hong Kong, China		7,522	2,389	21	7	0.00	-66.67
Japan		20,513	27,577	26,284	34,415	0.37	30.94
Korea, Dem. People's Republic of		125	420	254	402	0.00	58.27
Korea, Republic of	20,285	14,311	17,489	18,290	19,817	0.22	8.35
Macao, China		122	74	1	6	0.00	500.00
Mongolia		89	191	141	180	0.00	27.66
Taiwan, Province of China	10,854	9,897	9,163	8,524	10,686	0.12	25.36
South-East Asia	**31,606**	**27,405**	**41,759**	**43,542**	**60,563**	**0.66**	**39.09**
Brunei Darussalam		59	58	26	37	0.00	42.31
Cambodia		90	173	91	93	0.00	2.20
Indonesia	3,949	3,361	5,158	4,279	6,113	0.07	42.86
Lao People's Democratic Republic		19	72	74	107	0.00	44.59
Malaysia	8,535	7,025	9,175	10,337	10,044	0.11	-2.83
Myanmar		232	401	339	459	0.00	35.40
Philippines	4,510	3,359	9,553	9,203	16,238	0.18	76.44
Singapore	7,486	6,663	6,660	7,874	8,896	0.10	12.98
Thailand	7,126	5,300	7,174	7,468	8,693	0.09	16.40
Timor-Leste		17	17	3	1	0.00	-66.67
Viet Nam		1,280	3,318	3,848	9,882	0.11	156.81
Australasia	**120,078**	**100,795**	**127,706**	**122,365**	**142,524**	**1.55**	**16.47**
Australia	100,133	82,753	107,905	103,506	120,315	1.31	16.24
New Zealand	19,945	18,042	19,801	18,859	22,209	0.24	17.76
Melanesia		**229**	**217**	**281**	**270**	**0.00**	**-3.91**
Fiji		157	119	151	182	0.00	20.53
New Caledonia		4		2			
Norfolk Island		4		1			
Papua New Guinea		46	71	91	62	0.00	-31.87
Solomon Islands		12	12	29	13	0.00	-55.17
Vanuatu		6	15	7	13	0.00	85.71
Micronesia		**132**	**75**	**46**	**40**	**0.00**	**-13.04**
Christmas Island, Australia		18	3				
Cocos (Keeling) Islands		16	27	1	3	0.00	200.00
Guam		24	6	2			
Kiribati		4	11	12	14	0.00	16.67
Marshall Islands		7	2	9	7	0.00	-22.22
Micronesia, Federated States of		12	8	4	3	0.00	-25.00
Nauru		13	2	14	6	0.00	-57.14
Northern Mariana Islands		29	15	1	6	0.00	500.00
Palau		9	1	3	1	0.00	-66.67
Polynesia		**270**	**134**	**87**	**105**	**0.00**	**20.69**
Cook Islands		4			1	0.00	
French Polynesia		140	55	4	3	0.00	-25.00
Pitcairn		4	2				
Samoa		97	46	48	53	0.00	10.42
Tokelau		6	7	2	3	0.00	50.00
Tonga		18	20	24	27	0.00	12.50
Tuvalu		1	4	9	18	0.00	100.00
Other East Asia and the Pacific	**19,893**	**80**	**27**	**6**	**11**	**0.00**	**83.33**
Other countries of Asia	19,042	27	10	1	1	0.00	0.00
Other countries of Oceania	851	53	17	5	10	0.00	100.00
EUROPE	**1,433,586**	**1,248,018**	**1,354,006**	**1,306,129**	**1,433,512**	**15.60**	**9.75**
Central/Eastern Europe	**25,027**	**38,459**	**47,003**	**42,705**	**52,101**	**0.57**	**22.00**
Armenia		58	133	100	163	0.00	63.00
Azerbaijan		136	280	160	237	0.00	48.13
Bulgaria		1,927	2,515	2,233	2,838	0.03	27.09
Czech Republic		5,889	6,058	6,169	6,922	0.08	12.21

686

SOUTH AFRICA

1. Arrivals of non-resident tourists at national borders, by country of residence

	2008	2009	2010	2011	2012	Market share 2012	% Change 2012-2011
Estonia		754	959	676	776	0.01	14.79
Georgia		160	251	194	171	0.00	-11.86
Hungary	3,041	2,480	3,115	2,882	3,253	0.04	12.87
Kazakhstan		517	743	619	590	0.01	-4.68
Kyrgyzstan		105	37	7			
Latvia		693	646	608	704	0.01	15.79
Lithuania		859	785	773	1,057	0.01	36.74
Poland	10,041	9,257	9,970	9,962	11,722	0.13	17.67
Republic of Moldova		114	181	149	205	0.00	37.58
Romania		2,221	2,309	2,188	2,937	0.03	34.23
Russian Federation	11,945	8,893	11,551	10,487	13,350	0.15	27.30
Slovakia		1,964	3,730	2,093	2,619	0.03	25.13
Tajikistan		31	44	53	49	0.00	-7.55
Turkmenistan		28	31	18	48	0.00	166.67
Ukraine		2,233	3,469	3,142	4,276	0.05	36.09
Uzbekistan		140	196	192	184	0.00	-4.17
Northern Europe	**628,424**	**568,656**	**579,063**	**542,563**	**566,984**	**6.17**	**4.50**
Channel Islands		7	6		2	0.00	
Denmark	26,747	22,540	24,212	22,970	25,149	0.27	9.49
Faeroe Islands		46	23				
Finland	9,909	9,404	10,511	10,090	10,203	0.11	1.12
Iceland		492	694	598	733	0.01	22.58
Ireland	42,015	35,166	30,518	29,098	28,862	0.31	-0.81
Isle of Man		45	50	13			
Norway	20,537	18,140	19,330	20,556	23,156	0.25	12.65
Sweden	44,050	36,335	40,662	38,754	40,856	0.44	5.42
United Kingdom	485,166	446,481	453,057	420,484	438,023	4.77	4.17
Southern Europe	**130,438**	**114,372**	**140,473**	**131,426**	**149,220**	**1.62**	**13.54**
Albania		175	223	115	110	0.00	-4.35
Andorra		66	62	32	52	0.00	62.50
Bosnia and Herzegovina		173	267	267	254	0.00	-4.87
Croatia		1,103	1,266	1,159	1,672	0.02	44.26
Gibraltar		14	6		1	0.00	
Greece	9,248	7,296	8,172	5,822	6,157	0.07	5.75
Holy See		13	8	10	27	0.00	170.00
Italy	55,545	50,305	54,645	54,628	61,318	0.67	12.25
Malta		473	568	550	567	0.01	3.09
Portugal	31,762	26,895	40,677	40,302	48,213	0.52	19.63
San Marino		36	25	41	38	0.00	-7.32
Serbia and Montenegro		1,138	441	254	235	0.00	-7.48
Slovenia		958	2,211	1,037	1,178	0.01	13.60
Spain	33,883	25,727	31,902	27,209	29,398	0.32	8.05
Western Europe	**594,146**	**502,348**	**556,227**	**559,664**	**629,451**	**6.85**	**12.47**
Austria	20,904	17,210	20,389	21,841	25,179	0.27	15.28
Belgium	42,276	36,720	39,304	40,478	44,125	0.48	9.01
France	127,956	103,985	115,401	105,420	122,244	1.33	15.96
Germany	238,306	196,643	215,800	235,774	266,333	2.90	12.96
Liechtenstein		237	200	213	271	0.00	27.23
Luxembourg		1,309	1,259	1,271	1,488	0.02	17.07
Monaco		94	61	93	68	0.00	-26.88
Netherlands	128,097	114,431	124,088	113,846	117,936	1.28	3.59
Switzerland	36,607	31,719	39,725	40,728	51,807	0.56	27.20
East Mediterranean Europe	**27,236**	**24,183**	**31,240**	**29,771**	**35,756**	**0.39**	**20.10**
Cyprus		1,585	1,972	1,672	1,659	0.02	-0.78
Israel	18,291	14,950	19,353	17,751	20,640	0.22	16.28
Turkey	8,945	7,648	9,915	10,348	13,457	0.15	30.04
Other Europe	**28,315**						

687

SOUTH AFRICA

1. Arrivals of non-resident tourists at national borders, by country of residence

	2008	2009	2010	2011	2012	Market share 2012	% Change 2012-2011
Other countries of Europe	28,315						
MIDDLE EAST	**23,412**	**19,262**	**21,151**	**20,168**	**22,869**	**0.25**	**13.39**
Bahrain		174	294	177	194	0.00	9.60
Egypt	4,862	4,999	5,967	6,251	7,308	0.08	16.91
Iraq		310	333	285	296	0.00	3.86
Jordan		1,509	1,938	1,696	1,818	0.02	7.19
Kuwait		550	651	632	650	0.01	2.85
Lebanon		1,933	3,183	2,720	3,252	0.04	19.56
Libya		1,181	1,711	977	951	0.01	-2.66
Oman		298	433	349	426	0.00	22.06
Palestine		147	305	245	241	0.00	-1.63
Qatar		399	361	231	303	0.00	31.17
Saudi Arabia	5,539	5,328	3,570	4,733	5,305	0.06	12.09
Syrian Arab Republic		420	707	498	573	0.01	15.06
United Arab Emirates	2,454	1,728	1,332	1,072	1,180	0.01	10.07
Yemen		286	366	302	372	0.00	23.18
Other countries of Middle East	10,557						
SOUTH ASIA	**51,929**	**74,938**	**97,552**	**119,147**	**142,010**	**1.55**	**19.19**
Afghanistan		998	675	206	184	0.00	-10.68
Bangladesh		2,943	3,829	3,900	5,480	0.06	40.51
Bhutan		9	35	27	36	0.00	33.33
India	51,929	55,203	71,587	90,367	106,774	1.16	18.16
Iran, Islamic Republic of		4,037	4,566	4,773	3,806	0.04	-20.26
Maldives		38	86	36	35	0.00	-2.78
Nepal		309	543	490	456	0.00	-6.94
Pakistan		9,596	13,359	16,221	20,799	0.23	28.22
Sri Lanka		1,805	2,872	3,127	4,440	0.05	41.99
NOT SPECIFIED	**61,071**	**36,474**	**115,381**	**25,800**	**26,148**	**0.28**	**1.35**
Other countries of the World	61,071	36,474	115,381	25,800	26,148	0.28	1.35

Yearbook of Tourism Statistics, Data 2008 – 2012, 2014 Edition

SOUTH AFRICA

2. Arrivals of non-resident visitors at national borders, by country of residence

		2008	2009	2010	2011	2012	Market share 2012	% Change 2012-2011
TOTAL	(*)	9,728,860	9,531,615	11,303,087	12,097,490	13,069,034	100.00	8.03
AFRICA		7,388,995	7,406,780	8,725,042	9,654,943	10,305,075	78.85	6.73
East Africa		2,936,250	3,259,300	3,837,056	4,115,170	4,725,255	36.16	14.83
Burundi		1,289	1,041	952	1,049	1,535	0.01	46.33
Comoros		211	164	237	228	286	0.00	25.44
Djibouti		81	81	86	102	94	0.00	-7.84
Eritrea		570	617	645	718	950	0.01	32.31
Ethiopia		9,953	10,971	9,857	9,618	8,459	0.06	-12.05
Kenya		29,218	27,734	32,081	33,651	36,354	0.28	8.03
Madagascar		3,777	2,756	3,208	3,099	4,978	0.04	60.63
Malawi		164,248	149,524	137,023	146,432	151,553	1.16	3.50
Mauritius		16,550	15,525	19,743	19,893	20,525	0.16	3.18
Mozambique		1,228,979	1,324,445	1,328,731	1,389,253	1,502,618	11.50	8.16
Reunion		835	632	370	3			
Rwanda		3,375	3,103	3,076	3,014	3,604	0.03	19.58
Seychelles		2,497	2,367	3,115	3,588	3,571	0.03	-0.47
Somalia		3,080	2,876	2,714	836	223	0.00	-73.33
Uganda		13,684	13,675	15,597	17,024	17,625	0.13	3.53
United Republic of Tanzania		16,183	16,238	21,827	32,059	39,645	0.30	23.66
Zambia		193,677	160,995	172,215	174,782	181,206	1.39	3.68
Zimbabwe		1,248,043	1,526,556	2,085,579	2,279,821	2,752,029	21.06	20.71
Central Africa		85,467	87,973	90,143	90,087	102,181	0.78	13.42
Angola		36,917	38,814	39,535	39,952	48,608	0.37	21.67
Cameroon		5,529	4,731	6,737	5,610	6,585	0.05	17.38
Central African Republic		130	125	175	144	200	0.00	38.89
Chad		299	260	262	355	432	0.00	21.69
Congo		4,939	6,654	4,623	3,393	3,945	0.03	16.27
Democratic Republic of the Congo		32,692	31,569	32,077	33,811	34,348	0.26	1.59
Equatorial Guinea		364	430	347	351	441	0.00	25.64
Gabon		4,433	5,218	6,244	6,346	7,379	0.06	16.28
Sao Tome and Principe		164	172	143	125	243	0.00	94.40
North Africa		6,438	5,653	8,855	6,115	6,245	0.05	2.13
Algeria		1,868	1,359	3,586	1,346	1,623	0.01	20.58
Morocco		1,046	963	1,642	1,444	1,686	0.01	16.76
Sudan		2,131	2,198	2,216	2,043	1,709	0.01	-16.35
Tunisia		1,382	1,119	1,316	1,270	1,206	0.01	-5.04
Western Sahara		11	14	95	12	21	0.00	75.00
Southern Africa		4,285,670	3,983,336	4,703,731	5,340,433	5,351,099	40.94	0.20
Botswana		807,292	822,305	829,518	782,223	717,813	5.49	-8.23
Lesotho		2,165,505	1,890,976	2,610,507	3,160,694	3,122,796	23.89	-1.20
Namibia		222,817	212,098	226,541	235,780	234,205	1.79	-0.67
Swaziland		1,090,056	1,057,957	1,037,165	1,161,736	1,276,285	9.77	9.86
West Africa		75,170	70,372	85,174	103,137	120,289	0.92	16.63
Benin		1,460	1,363	1,334	1,387	1,628	0.01	17.38
Burkina Faso		648	637	643	732	834	0.01	13.93
Cape Verde		739	679	636	603	713	0.01	18.24
Côte d'Ivoire		2,494	2,303	2,789	1,839	2,498	0.02	35.83
Gambia		730	722	801	845	1,187	0.01	40.47
Ghana		14,112	12,419	19,948	20,134	24,857	0.19	23.46
Guinea		1,725	1,478	2,023	2,239	3,131	0.02	39.84
Guinea-Bissau		231	205	260	216	230	0.00	6.48
Liberia		579	540	578	639	737	0.01	15.34
Mali		1,013	832	1,259	1,266	1,298	0.01	2.53
Mauritania		204	126	280	278	245	0.00	-11.87
Niger		262	273	299	307	380	0.00	23.78
Nigeria		46,364	44,817	49,418	67,769	76,787	0.59	13.31

689

SOUTH AFRICA

2. Arrivals of non-resident visitors at national borders, by country of residence

	2008	2009	2010	2011	2012	Market share 2012	% Change 2012-2011
Saint Helena	134	182	131	81	53	0.00	-34.57
Senegal	3,075	2,408	3,115	3,068	3,713	0.03	21.02
Sierra Leone	828	884	1,126	1,115	1,165	0.01	4.48
Togo	572	504	534	619	833	0.01	34.57
Other Africa		146	83	1	6	**0.00**	**500.00**
Other countries of Africa		146	83	1	6	0.00	500.00
AMERICAS	416,581	376,485	505,235	488,018	566,842	4.34	16.15
Caribbean	2,781	2,386	3,873	3,707	4,733	0.04	27.68
Antigua and Barbuda	39	33	112	98	67	0.00	-31.63
Bahamas	125	95	143	148	186	0.00	25.68
Barbados	164	141	221	185	192	0.00	3.78
Bermuda	133	116	97	62	47	0.00	-24.19
British Virgin Islands	23				3	0.00	
Cuba	941	707	1,362	1,301	2,001	0.02	53.80
Dominica	58	56	132	120	218	0.00	81.67
Grenada	33	21	34	38	31	0.00	-18.42
Haiti	225	206	202	120	109	0.00	-9.17
Jamaica	513	578	851	785	875	0.01	11.46
Puerto Rico	15	6	5	6	3	0.00	-50.00
Saint Lucia	51	39	41	54	41	0.00	-24.07
Saint Vincent and the Grenadines	30	20	46	40	23	0.00	-42.50
Trinidad and Tobago	429	366	623	748	932	0.01	24.60
Turks and Caicos Islands	2	2	4	2	5	0.00	150.00
Central America	1,250	1,113	3,945	1,535	1,676	0.01	9.19
Belize	90	83	65	62	84	0.00	35.48
Costa Rica	422	335	984	490	489	0.00	-0.20
El Salvador	154	123	406	99	151	0.00	52.53
Guatemala	226	207	597	194	292	0.00	50.52
Honduras	109	132	1,343	202	306	0.00	51.49
Nicaragua	56	62	97	85	83	0.00	-2.35
Panama	193	171	453	403	271	0.00	-32.75
North America	355,172	314,769	392,007	392,937	440,472	3.37	12.10
Canada	58,195	51,233	61,522	64,857	73,620	0.56	13.51
Greenland	38	34	11				
Mexico	4,055	2,903	16,447	3,556	3,895	0.03	9.53
United States of America	292,884	260,599	314,027	324,524	362,957	2.78	11.84
South America	56,806	57,797	105,091	89,726	119,852	0.92	33.58
Argentina	8,873	10,656	22,715	14,622	18,204	0.14	24.50
Bolivia	499	615	789	774	1,516	0.01	95.87
Brazil	36,436	36,722	59,838	62,083	85,454	0.65	37.64
Chile	3,381	2,911	7,562	3,493	3,733	0.03	6.87
Colombia	1,653	1,656	3,273	1,962	2,729	0.02	39.09
Ecuador	352	433	1,047	673	793	0.01	17.83
Falkland Islands, Malvinas	10	5	2				
French Guiana	64	73	40	1	4	0.00	300.00
Guyana	453	12	5	295	325	0.00	10.17
Paraguay	373	457	1,250	584	748	0.01	28.08
Peru	1,615	1,852	3,030	2,452	3,281	0.03	33.81
Suriname	205	67	99	91	71	0.00	-21.98
Uruguay	1,080	981	2,738	1,259	1,436	0.01	14.06
Venezuela	1,812	1,357	2,703	1,437	1,558	0.01	8.42
Other Americas	572	420	319	113	109	0.00	-3.54
Other countries of the Americas	572	420	319	113	109	0.00	-3.54
EAST ASIA AND THE PACIFIC	274,188	238,400	322,335	337,159	432,223	3.31	28.20
North-East Asia	110,149	95,720	135,436	152,123	211,263	1.62	38.88
China	40,275	36,480	71,921	92,587	140,607	1.08	51.86

690

Yearbook of Tourism Statistics, Data 2008 – 2012, 2014 Edition

SOUTH AFRICA

2. Arrivals of non-resident visitors at national borders, by country of residence

	2008	2009	2010	2011	2012	Market share 2012	% Change 2012-2011
Hong Kong, China	6,623	7,821	2,523	25	8	0.00	-68.00
Japan	29,124	24,424	30,936	29,558	37,097	0.28	25.51
Korea, Dem. People's Republic of	124	137	457	292	437	0.00	49.66
Korea, Republic of	20,914	15,714	18,690	19,639	21,126	0.16	7.57
Macao, China	101	132	83	1	6	0.00	500.00
Mongolia	109	92	200	141	190	0.00	34.75
Taiwan, Province of China	12,879	10,920	10,626	9,880	11,792	0.09	19.35
South-East Asia	**41,649**	**29,776**	**45,485**	**48,418**	**65,455**	**0.50**	**35.19**
Brunei Darussalam	56	65	63	26	37	0.00	42.31
Cambodia	134	95	185	105	93	0.00	-11.43
Indonesia	5,467	3,537	5,370	4,506	6,468	0.05	43.54
Lao People's Democratic Republic	51	23	88	101	128	0.00	26.73
Malaysia	8,848	7,767	9,841	11,192	10,743	0.08	-4.01
Myanmar	585	271	456	413	510	0.00	23.49
Philippines	9,287	4,103	11,406	11,925	19,134	0.15	60.45
Singapore	7,737	7,079	7,175	8,504	9,480	0.07	11.48
Thailand	8,173	5,487	7,480	7,733	8,897	0.07	15.05
Timor-Leste	22	18	17		1	0.00	
Viet Nam	1,289	1,331	3,404	3,913	9,964	0.08	154.64
Australasia	**121,481**	**111,609**	**140,935**	**136,187**	**155,053**	**1.19**	**13.85**
Australia	101,322	91,951	119,455	115,699	131,209	1.00	13.41
New Zealand	20,159	19,658	21,480	20,488	23,844	0.18	16.38
Melanesia	**265**	**224**	**219**	**285**	**279**	**0.00**	**-2.11**
Fiji	147	164	124	154	187	0.00	21.43
New Caledonia	8	6		2			
Norfolk Island	5	4	1	1			
Papua New Guinea	73	32	67	92	62	0.00	-32.61
Solomon Islands	28	12	12	29	13	0.00	-55.17
Vanuatu	4	6	15	7	17	0.00	142.86
Micronesia	**290**	**142**	**79**	**46**	**50**	**0.00**	**8.70**
Christmas Island, Australia	24	19	4				
Cocos (Keeling) Islands	41	17	28	1	3	0.00	200.00
Guam	50	27	6	2			
Kiribati	48	4	12	12	20	0.00	66.67
Marshall Islands	9	7	2	9	7	0.00	-22.22
Micronesia, Federated States of	29	13	8	4	3	0.00	-25.00
Nauru	15	13	3	14	6	0.00	-57.14
Northern Mariana Islands	68	33	15	1	10	0.00	900.00
Palau	6	9	1	3	1	0.00	-66.67
Polynesia	**286**	**304**	**148**	**90**	**110**	**0.00**	**22.22**
Cook Islands	3	4	1		1	0.00	
French Polynesia	151	171	64	4	3	0.00	-25.00
Pitcairn	8	4	2				
Samoa	73	100	50	51	55	0.00	7.84
Tokelau	24	6	7	2	3	0.00	50.00
Tonga	15	18	20	24	30	0.00	25.00
Tuvalu	12	1	4	9	18	0.00	100.00
Other East Asia and the Pacific	**68**	**625**	**33**	**10**	**13**	**0.00**	**30.00**
Other countries of Asia	14	551	10	5	1	0.00	-80.00
Other countries of Oceania	54	74	23	5	12	0.00	140.00
EUROPE	**1,469,765**	**1,367,291**	**1,473,071**	**1,431,337**	**1,552,241**	**11.88**	**8.45**
Central/Eastern Europe	**52,295**	**42,380**	**51,606**	**47,630**	**57,627**	**0.44**	**20.99**
Armenia	65	59	146	103	172	0.00	66.99
Azerbaijan	125	140	287	165	241	0.00	46.06
Belarus	681	493	584	707	687	0.01	-2.83
Bulgaria	2,517	2,091	2,684	2,414	3,219	0.02	33.35
Czech Republic	6,947	6,333	6,520	6,662	7,388	0.06	10.90

Yearbook of Tourism Statistics, Data 2008 – 2012, 2014 Edition

SOUTH AFRICA

2. Arrivals of non-resident visitors at national borders, by country of residence

	2008	2009	2010	2011	2012	Market share 2012	% Change 2012-2011
Estonia	802	779	1,050	732	849	0.01	15.98
Georgia	208	168	258	210	198	0.00	-5.71
Hungary	3,155	2,743	3,418	3,072	3,479	0.03	13.25
Kazakhstan	535		780	670	636	0.00	-5.07
Kyrgyzstan	73	140	73	10	1	0.00	-90.00
Latvia	1,194	749	678	648	766	0.01	18.21
Lithuania	1,480	1,094	852	829	1,104	0.01	33.17
Poland	10,819	10,106	10,897	11,220	12,883	0.10	14.82
Republic of Moldova	140	124	189	158	209	0.00	32.28
Romania	2,447	2,433	2,453	2,318	3,237	0.02	39.65
Russian Federation	13,664	10,097	12,751	11,756	14,835	0.11	26.19
Slovakia	2,264	2,101	3,971	2,319	2,819	0.02	21.56
Tajikistan	61	31	45	55	49	0.00	-10.91
Turkmenistan	27	30	32	19	50	0.00	163.16
Ukraine	4,968	2,525	3,733	3,365	4,620	0.04	37.30
Uzbekistan	123	144	205	198	185	0.00	-6.57
Northern Europe	**640,591**	**614,635**	**626,504**	**589,965**	**609,428**	**4.66**	**3.30**
Channel Islands	12	7	8		2	0.00	
Denmark	27,367	24,535	26,093	25,016	26,897	0.21	7.52
Faeroe Islands	29	50	24				
Finland	10,187	10,140	11,527	10,960	11,105	0.08	1.32
Iceland	788	587	759	684	780	0.01	14.04
Ireland	42,564	38,280	33,935	31,935	31,358	0.24	-1.81
Isle of Man	83	45	53	13	1	0.00	-92.31
Norway	21,017	19,631	20,909	22,425	24,686	0.19	10.08
Sweden	45,129	38,581	43,125	41,155	43,118	0.33	4.77
United Kingdom	493,415	482,779	490,071	457,777	471,481	3.61	2.99
Southern Europe	**138,388**	**138,097**	**165,831**	**161,435**	**179,267**	**1.37**	**11.05**
Albania	219	198	243	128	113	0.00	-11.72
Andorra	69	79	76	46	54	0.00	17.39
Bosnia and Herzegovina	172	178	274	268	265	0.00	-1.12
Croatia	1,678	1,177	1,326	1,213	1,799	0.01	48.31
Gibraltar	10	16	6		1	0.00	
Greece	9,667	8,576	9,086	6,672	6,805	0.05	1.99
Holy See	17						
Italy	56,471	59,599	63,255	63,917	69,018	0.53	7.98
Malta	401	506	614	593	630	0.00	6.24
Portugal	32,293	35,428	51,785	54,770	65,583	0.50	19.74
San Marino	51	43	27	47	42	0.00	-10.64
Serbia and Montenegro	1,881						
Slovenia	976	1,020	2,255	1,113	1,272	0.01	14.29
Spain	34,483	31,277	36,884	32,668	33,685	0.26	3.11
Western Europe	**608,479**	**544,140**	**595,169**	**599,472**	**667,128**	**5.10**	**11.29**
Austria	21,201	18,508	21,697	23,294	26,622	0.20	14.29
Belgium	43,208	40,555	43,000	44,432	47,622	0.36	7.18
France	131,512	117,523	127,804	116,873	133,526	1.02	14.25
Germany	243,578	209,644	227,514	248,400	278,539	2.13	12.13
Liechtenstein	232	265	220	226	290	0.00	28.32
Luxembourg	1,429	1,465	1,333	1,343	1,544	0.01	14.97
Monaco	92	113	76	113	71	0.00	-37.17
Netherlands	130,083	121,274	130,668	120,523	123,888	0.95	2.79
Switzerland	37,144	34,793	42,857	44,268	55,026	0.42	24.30
East Mediterranean Europe	**30,012**	**26,536**	**33,388**	**32,549**	**38,510**	**0.29**	**18.31**
Cyprus	1,694	1,726	2,113	1,821	1,770	0.01	-2.80
Israel	18,872	16,368	20,594	19,489	22,332	0.17	14.59
Turkey	9,446	8,442	10,681	11,239	14,408	0.11	28.20
Other Europe		**1,503**	**573**	**286**	**281**	**0.00**	**-1.75**

692

SOUTH AFRICA

2. Arrivals of non-resident visitors at national borders, by country of residence

	2008	2009	2010	2011	2012	Market share 2012	% Change 2012-2011
Other countries of Europe		1,503	573	286	281	0.00	-1.75
MIDDLE EAST	**21,662**	**20,189**	**22,401**	**21,192**	**23,867**	**0.18**	**12.62**
Bahrain	256	180	299	178	198	0.00	11.24
Egypt	5,305	5,227	6,222	6,536	7,674	0.06	17.41
Iraq	306	332	340	288	305	0.00	5.90
Jordan	1,636	1,604	2,103	1,776	2,108	0.02	18.69
Kuwait	865	561	680	636	675	0.01	6.13
Lebanon	2,452	2,148	3,456	2,938	3,396	0.03	15.59
Libya	961	1,351	2,078	1,297	1,024	0.01	-21.05
Oman	382	299	444	354	433	0.00	22.32
Palestine	214	165	345	282	255	0.00	-9.57
Qatar	317	406	362	237	303	0.00	27.85
Saudi Arabia	5,617	5,415	3,621	4,761	5,327	0.04	11.89
Syrian Arab Republic	620	438	722	512	578	0.00	12.89
United Arab Emirates	2,495	1,771	1,358	1,092	1,214	0.01	11.17
Yemen	236	292	371	305	377	0.00	23.61
SOUTH ASIA	**80,379**	**82,043**	**109,526**	**134,941**	**159,023**	**1.22**	**17.85**
Afghanistan	1,272	1,238	882	220	203	0.00	-7.73
Bangladesh	3,293	3,463	4,821	5,096	6,970	0.05	36.77
Bhutan	7	9	37	27	39	0.00	44.44
India	59,186	59,878	79,529	101,255	117,904	0.90	16.44
Iran, Islamic Republic of	3,486	4,111	4,637	4,856	3,865	0.03	-20.41
Maldives	73	47	88	39	41	0.00	5.13
Nepal	479	345	574	490	464	0.00	-5.31
Pakistan	10,339	10,792	15,428	19,009	24,147	0.18	27.03
Sri Lanka	2,244	2,160	3,530	3,949	5,390	0.04	36.49
NOT SPECIFIED	**77,290**	**40,427**	**145,477**	**29,900**	**29,763**	**0.23**	**-0.46**
Other countries of the World	77,290	40,427	145,477	29,900	29,763	0.23	-0.46

Yearbook of Tourism Statistics, Data 2008 – 2012, 2014 Edition

SPAIN

1. Arrivals of non-resident tourists at national borders, by country of residence

		2008	2009	2010	2011	2012	Market share 2012	% Change 2012-2011
TOTAL	(*)	57,192,015	52,177,640	52,676,972	56,176,886	57,700,711	100.00	2.71
AFRICA			267,458	302,420	508,832	514,640	0.89	1.14
Other Africa			267,458	302,420	508,832	514,640	0.89	1.14
All countries of Africa			267,458	302,420	508,832	514,640	0.89	1.14
AMERICAS		2,397,782	2,573,760	2,617,572	2,886,793	3,130,868	5.43	8.45
North America		1,436,763	1,532,615	1,509,219	1,612,374	1,777,417	3.08	10.24
Canada		151,467	182,604	189,452	216,048	262,323	0.45	21.42
Mexico		160,803	216,300	185,740	259,028	274,276	0.48	5.89
United States of America		1,124,493	1,133,711	1,134,027	1,137,298	1,240,818	2.15	9.10
South America		622,077	536,466	586,557	823,699	968,585	1.68	17.59
Argentina		212,547	257,463	276,408	306,759	346,100	0.60	12.82
Brazil		226,111	227,731	241,214	369,909	408,875	0.71	10.53
Chile		69,600	24,222	17,706	37,671	41,071	0.07	9.03
Venezuela		113,819	27,050	51,229	109,360	172,539	0.30	57.77
Other Americas		338,942	504,679	521,796	450,720	384,866	0.67	-14.61
Other countries of the Americas		338,942	504,679	521,796	450,720	384,866	0.67	-14.61
EAST ASIA AND THE PACIFIC		237,493	504,634	961,998	1,176,192	1,355,001	2.35	15.20
North-East Asia		237,493	229,856	332,930	342,979	362,081	0.63	5.57
Japan		237,493	229,856	332,930	342,979	362,081	0.63	5.57
Other East Asia and the Pacific			274,778	629,068	833,213	992,920	1.72	19.17
Other countries East Asia/Pacific			274,778	629,068	833,213	992,920	1.72	19.17
EUROPE		53,512,149	48,204,400	48,290,225	51,420,001	52,438,020	90.88	1.98
Central/Eastern Europe		509,032	421,993	605,276	862,841	1,206,227	2.09	39.80
Russian Federation		509,032	421,993	605,276	862,841	1,206,227	2.09	39.80
Northern Europe		21,027,772	18,094,666	17,191,654	18,797,582	19,008,528	32.94	1.12
Denmark		956,546	960,009	937,726	909,515	932,539	1.62	2.53
Finland		509,103	517,203	507,161	574,039	581,347	1.01	1.27
Ireland		1,658,899	1,463,913	1,177,253	1,284,168	1,189,523	2.06	-7.37
Norway		952,720	886,830	1,016,339	1,120,269	1,249,926	2.17	11.57
Sweden		1,175,260	969,949	1,112,935	1,294,206	1,401,330	2.43	8.28
United Kingdom		15,775,244	13,296,762	12,440,240	13,615,385	13,653,863	23.66	0.28
Southern Europe		5,661,308	5,331,450	5,534,807	5,760,483	5,522,376	9.57	-4.13
Greece		82,753	81,787	148,881	117,578	89,624	0.16	-23.77
Italy		3,354,251	3,188,147	3,490,352	3,764,818	3,571,659	6.19	-5.13
Portugal		2,224,304	2,061,516	1,895,574	1,878,087	1,861,093	3.23	-0.90
Western Europe		24,294,507	22,326,428	22,655,560	23,958,616	24,693,851	42.80	3.07
Austria		546,060	506,161	561,190	579,430	564,954	0.98	-2.50
Belgium		1,636,636	1,599,004	1,623,375	1,756,695	1,706,354	2.96	-2.87
France		8,149,265	7,955,104	8,125,354	8,375,035	8,969,009	15.54	7.09
Germany		10,062,629	8,935,147	8,814,070	8,975,236	9,335,870	16.18	4.02
Luxembourg		133,264	113,782	97,693	133,654	120,066	0.21	-10.17
Netherlands		2,479,928	2,089,048	2,276,393	2,771,903	2,548,657	4.42	-8.05
Switzerland		1,286,725	1,128,182	1,157,485	1,366,663	1,448,941	2.51	6.02
Other Europe		2,019,530	2,029,863	2,302,928	2,040,479	2,007,038	3.48	-1.64
Other countries of Europe		2,019,530	2,029,863	2,302,928	2,040,479	2,007,038	3.48	-1.64
MIDDLE EAST				68,276	110,027	170,602	0.30	55.05
All countries of Middle East				68,276	110,027	170,602	0.30	55.05
SOUTH ASIA				29,615	73,842	91,580	0.16	24.02
All countries of South Asia				29,615	73,842	91,580	0.16	24.02
NOT SPECIFIED		1,044,591	627,388	406,866	1,199			
Other countries of the World		1,044,591	627,388	406,866	1,199			

Yearbook of Tourism Statistics, Data 2008 – 2012, 2014 Edition

SPAIN

3. Arrivals of non-resident tourists in hotels and similar establishments, by country of residence

		2008	2009	2010	2011	2012	Market share 2012	% Change 2012-2011
TOTAL	(*)	35,757,721	32,002,230	35,655,543	39,542,091	39,936,727	100.00	1.00
AFRICA		353,200	327,060	387,765	421,398	456,897	1.14	8.42
Southern Africa		45,326	38,478	41,754	55,232	64,979	0.16	17.65
South Africa		45,326	38,478	41,754	55,232	64,979	0.16	17.65
Other Africa		307,874	288,582	346,011	366,166	391,918	0.98	7.03
Other countries of Africa		307,874	288,582	346,011	366,166	391,918	0.98	7.03
AMERICAS		3,258,171	3,198,470	3,835,945	4,345,144	4,195,711	10.51	-3.44
North America		2,056,972	2,061,419	2,515,894	2,804,083	2,718,880	6.81	-3.04
Canada		246,717	259,147	396,790	480,827	470,431	1.18	-2.16
United States of America		1,518,108	1,532,535	1,813,566	1,994,258	1,958,383	4.90	-1.80
Other countries of North America		292,147	269,737	305,538	328,998	290,066	0.73	-11.83
South America		322,800	297,077	416,112	510,197	445,046	1.11	-12.77
Brazil		322,800	297,077	416,112	510,197	445,046	1.11	-12.77
Other Americas		878,399	839,974	903,939	1,030,864	1,031,785	2.58	0.09
Other countries of the Americas		878,399	839,974	903,939	1,030,864	1,031,785	2.58	0.09
EAST ASIA AND THE PACIFIC		1,299,055	1,188,417	1,568,090	1,836,473	2,023,202	5.07	10.17
North-East Asia		845,791	751,444	989,141	1,081,627	1,163,941	2.91	7.61
China		146,517	151,439	206,930	284,511	343,168	0.86	20.62
Japan		572,147	511,770	611,531	607,371	626,086	1.57	3.08
Korea, Republic of		127,127	88,235	170,680	189,745	194,687	0.49	2.60
Australasia		169,782	153,006	198,063	244,783	252,789	0.63	3.27
Australia		169,782	153,006	198,063	244,783	252,789	0.63	3.27
Other East Asia and the Pacific		283,482	283,967	380,886	510,063	606,472	1.52	18.90
Other countries of Asia		246,049	251,016	343,701	473,985	572,714	1.43	20.83
Other countries of Oceania		37,433	32,951	37,185	36,078	33,758	0.08	-6.43
EUROPE		30,047,133	26,584,436	29,075,912	32,181,824	32,527,822	81.45	1.08
Central/Eastern Europe		1,521,848	1,358,788	1,744,666	2,331,130	2,607,080	6.53	11.84
Bulgaria		57,409	53,999	63,675	70,231	69,501	0.17	-1.04
Czech Republic		176,759	165,205	163,097	197,668	196,883	0.49	-0.40
Estonia		35,186	29,096	29,435	33,386	34,821	0.09	4.30
Hungary		92,973	83,954	99,470	104,459	107,748	0.27	3.15
Latvia		31,230	24,899	33,872	35,176	35,594	0.09	1.19
Lithuania		39,706	36,858	40,081	48,818	51,441	0.13	5.37
Poland		307,582	311,680	396,108	512,299	484,494	1.21	-5.43
Romania		160,528	149,479	191,711	221,971	203,600	0.51	-8.28
Russian Federation		546,916	430,772	630,965	979,383	1,273,622	3.19	30.04
Slovakia		38,515	36,015	44,422	50,017	54,259	0.14	8.48
Ukraine		35,044	36,831	51,830	77,722	95,117	0.24	22.38
Northern Europe		9,908,008	8,486,289	9,031,576	9,804,697	10,515,445	26.33	7.25
Denmark		404,835	366,740	407,404	463,109	466,046	1.17	0.63
Finland		242,647	235,041	248,601	275,427	287,816	0.72	4.50
Iceland		48,064	33,424	32,175	37,859	39,502	0.10	4.34
Ireland		621,753	550,697	522,505	546,755	564,870	1.41	3.31
Norway		375,971	319,183	388,160	445,760	523,915	1.31	17.53
Sweden		612,616	557,479	645,936	742,767	823,935	2.06	10.93
United Kingdom		7,602,122	6,423,725	6,786,795	7,293,020	7,809,361	19.55	7.08
Southern Europe		4,041,460	3,553,376	4,031,634	4,259,081	3,657,274	9.16	-14.13
Greece		141,641	129,427	175,801	146,534	102,738	0.26	-29.89
Italy		2,528,966	2,237,467	2,543,005	2,833,011	2,420,081	6.06	-14.58
Malta		39,112	26,942	25,416	25,337	26,228	0.07	3.52
Portugal		1,297,037	1,125,591	1,250,973	1,214,535	1,070,205	2.68	-11.88
Slovenia		34,704	33,949	36,439	39,664	38,022	0.10	-4.14
Western Europe		13,983,529	12,675,716	13,628,825	15,042,738	15,043,814	37.67	0.01
Austria		317,003	278,619	337,736	386,465	394,850	0.99	2.17
Belgium		983,607	950,963	949,796	1,044,485	1,075,231	2.69	2.94

695

SPAIN

3. Arrivals of non-resident tourists in hotels and similar establishments, by country of residence

	2008	2009	2010	2011	2012	Market share 2012	% Change 2012-2011
France	3,579,311	3,494,385	3,864,873	4,227,160	4,259,794	10.67	0.77
Germany	7,074,680	6,089,490	6,491,508	7,122,227	7,019,583	17.58	-1.44
Luxembourg	71,592	63,940	67,048	76,209	67,925	0.17	-10.87
Netherlands	1,378,110	1,272,294	1,323,332	1,485,998	1,494,511	3.74	0.57
Switzerland	579,226	526,025	594,532	700,194	731,920	1.83	4.53
East Mediterranean Europe	**122,452**	**105,216**	**148,736**	**163,239**	**171,639**	**0.43**	**5.15**
Cyprus	19,286	15,059	22,236	24,881	22,813	0.06	-8.31
Turkey	103,166	90,157	126,500	138,358	148,826	0.37	7.57
Other Europe	**469,836**	**405,051**	**490,475**	**580,939**	**532,570**	**1.33**	**-8.33**
Other countries of Europe	469,836	405,051	490,475	580,939	532,570	1.33	-8.33
NOT SPECIFIED	**800,162**	**703,847**	**787,831**	**757,252**	**733,095**	**1.84**	**-3.19**
Other countries of the World	800,162	703,847	787,831	757,252	733,095	1.84	-3.19

Yearbook of Tourism Statistics, Data 2008 – 2012, 2014 Edition

SPAIN

4. Arrivals of non-resident tourists in all types of accommodation establishments, by country of residence

		2008	2009	2010	2011	2012	Market share 2012	% Change 2012-2011
TOTAL	(*)	43,727,361	39,204,144	43,182,773	47,652,541	48,100,648	100.00	0.94
AFRICA		370,806	347,353	410,199	448,878	491,493	1.02	9.49
Southern Africa		47,524	40,740	44,085	58,672	69,900	0.15	19.14
South Africa		47,524	40,740	44,085	58,672	69,900	0.15	19.14
Other Africa		323,282	306,613	366,114	390,206	421,593	0.88	8.04
Other countries of Africa		323,282	306,613	366,114	390,206	421,593	0.88	8.04
AMERICAS		3,387,390	3,320,307	3,988,405	4,513,180	4,387,499	9.12	-2.78
North America		2,143,628	2,140,165	2,605,944	2,908,123	2,840,456	5.91	-2.33
Canada		256,453	268,611	409,078	493,819	484,791	1.01	-1.83
United States of America		1,586,628	1,593,206	1,878,192	2,072,053	2,050,747	4.26	-1.03
Other countries of North America		300,547	278,348	318,674	342,251	304,918	0.63	-10.91
South America		328,580	302,882	424,492	518,838	454,602	0.95	-12.38
Brazil		328,580	302,882	424,492	518,838	454,602	0.95	-12.38
Other Americas		915,182	877,260	957,969	1,086,219	1,092,441	2.27	0.57
Other countries of the Americas		915,182	877,260	957,969	1,086,219	1,092,441	2.27	0.57
EAST ASIA AND THE PACIFIC		1,359,418	1,261,815	1,662,979	1,942,206	2,161,202	4.49	11.28
North-East Asia		881,815	793,987	1,045,961	1,140,985	1,241,938	2.58	8.85
China		152,480	159,503	218,795	299,961	365,318	0.76	21.79
Japan		597,039	541,064	647,000	641,263	669,354	1.39	4.38
Korea, Republic of		132,296	93,420	180,166	199,761	207,266	0.43	3.76
Australasia		177,447	162,328	210,097	258,774	269,101	0.56	3.99
Australia		177,447	162,328	210,097	258,774	269,101	0.56	3.99
Other East Asia and the Pacific		300,156	305,500	406,921	542,447	650,163	1.35	19.86
Other countries of Asia		256,774	265,680	363,575	499,833	609,682	1.27	21.98
Other countries of Oceania		43,382	39,820	43,346	42,614	40,481	0.08	-5.01
EUROPE		37,779,376	33,534,133	36,291,222	39,953,668	40,284,522	83.75	0.83
Central/Eastern Europe		1,763,668	1,566,685	1,978,565	2,615,786	2,917,027	6.06	11.52
Bulgaria		68,861	64,505	73,704	80,598	79,975	0.17	-0.77
Czech Republic		222,625	199,679	199,577	232,256	227,613	0.47	-2.00
Estonia		42,525	34,454	34,017	38,243	40,067	0.08	4.77
Hungary		113,620	101,457	116,380	120,713	123,983	0.26	2.71
Latvia		37,689	29,976	39,416	40,405	40,956	0.09	1.36
Lithuania		47,936	44,398	46,529	56,253	59,191	0.12	5.22
Poland		358,555	360,792	451,680	577,957	547,845	1.14	-5.21
Romania		196,592	180,764	224,675	255,990	234,254	0.49	-8.49
Russian Federation		589,099	466,056	682,985	1,070,095	1,396,309	2.90	30.48
Slovakia		46,967	43,699	52,547	58,023	62,436	0.13	7.61
Ukraine		39,199	40,905	57,055	85,253	104,398	0.22	22.46
Northern Europe		13,722,717	11,786,510	12,380,638	13,497,146	14,181,960	29.48	5.07
Denmark		613,519	542,596	582,027	639,841	652,255	1.36	1.94
Finland		403,164	383,557	393,710	436,993	446,778	0.93	2.24
Iceland		53,662	37,265	35,152	41,432	43,358	0.09	4.65
Ireland		1,004,662	859,181	805,687	841,266	850,728	1.77	1.12
Norway		601,199	529,197	595,560	692,752	779,100	1.62	12.46
Sweden		936,312	855,881	940,231	1,072,577	1,160,643	2.41	8.21
United Kingdom		10,110,199	8,578,833	9,028,271	9,772,285	10,249,098	21.31	4.88
Southern Europe		4,481,980	3,929,014	4,489,711	4,724,264	4,089,018	8.50	-13.45
Greece		156,631	138,404	187,438	154,658	109,110	0.23	-29.45
Italy		2,797,530	2,472,479	2,843,261	3,156,911	2,725,480	5.67	-13.67
Malta		47,505	32,232	29,521	29,125	30,181	0.06	3.63
Portugal		1,438,225	1,244,957	1,386,989	1,337,852	1,180,495	2.45	-11.76
Slovenia		42,089	40,942	42,502	45,718	43,752	0.09	-4.30
Western Europe		17,148,704	15,682,976	16,741,389	18,299,528	18,322,356	38.09	0.12
Austria		361,103	317,951	376,581	430,405	434,467	0.90	0.94
Belgium		1,153,602	1,116,593	1,122,324	1,226,717	1,265,693	2.63	3.18

697

SPAIN

4. Arrivals of non-resident tourists in all types of accommodation establishments, by country of residence

	2008	2009	2010	2011	2012	Market share 2012	% Change 2012-2011
France	4,415,557	4,358,571	4,754,050	5,187,844	5,239,738	10.89	1.00
Germany	8,367,405	7,242,350	7,662,337	8,311,039	8,177,033	17.00	-1.61
Luxembourg	90,332	77,733	78,491	90,899	81,060	0.17	-10.82
Netherlands	2,091,916	1,965,074	2,064,753	2,253,468	2,285,060	4.75	1.40
Switzerland	668,789	604,704	682,853	799,156	839,305	1.74	5.02
East Mediterranean Europe	**138,638**	**117,873**	**164,211**	**180,283**	**189,597**	**0.39**	**5.17**
Cyprus	23,529	18,136	26,143	28,715	26,250	0.05	-8.58
Turkey	115,109	99,737	138,068	151,568	163,347	0.34	7.77
Other Europe	**523,669**	**451,075**	**536,708**	**636,661**	**584,564**	**1.22**	**-8.18**
Other countries of Europe	523,669	451,075	536,708	636,661	584,564	1.22	-8.18
NOT SPECIFIED	**830,371**	**740,536**	**829,968**	**794,609**	**775,932**	**1.61**	**-2.35**
Other countries of the World	830,371	740,536	829,968	794,609	775,932	1.61	-2.35

Yearbook of Tourism Statistics, Data 2008 – 2012, 2014 Edition

SPAIN

5. Overnight stays of non-resident tourists in hotels and similar establishments, by country of residence

	2008	2009	2010	2011	2012	Market share 2012	% Change 2012-2011
TOTAL (*)	155,363,549	141,227,941	153,927,193	175,236,929	178,558,302	100.00	1.90
AFRICA	772,602	733,420	949,106	930,591	1,009,190	0.57	8.45
Southern Africa	101,306	89,509	96,034	125,044	139,306	0.08	11.41
South Africa	101,306	89,509	96,034	125,044	139,306	0.08	11.41
Other Africa	671,296	643,911	853,072	805,547	869,884	0.49	7.99
Other countries of Africa	671,296	643,911	853,072	805,547	869,884	0.49	7.99
AMERICAS	7,078,229	7,146,183	8,498,825	9,759,858	9,503,513	5.32	-2.63
North America	4,464,971	4,637,580	5,591,062	6,283,469	6,170,493	3.46	-1.80
Canada	626,508	670,029	953,720	1,142,309	1,154,293	0.65	1.05
United States of America	3,183,458	3,350,590	3,947,861	4,384,027	4,344,385	2.43	-0.90
Other countries of North America	655,005	616,961	689,481	757,133	671,815	0.38	-11.27
South America	754,503	738,504	991,426	1,213,339	1,069,431	0.60	-11.86
Brazil	754,503	738,504	991,426	1,213,339	1,069,431	0.60	-11.86
Other Americas	1,858,755	1,770,099	1,916,337	2,263,050	2,263,589	1.27	0.02
Other countries of the Americas	1,858,755	1,770,099	1,916,337	2,263,050	2,263,589	1.27	0.02
EAST ASIA AND THE PACIFIC	2,362,127	2,261,203	2,917,847	3,571,095	3,960,859	2.22	10.91
North-East Asia	1,348,835	1,245,174	1,604,230	1,788,744	1,932,045	1.08	8.01
China	262,209	270,323	373,936	499,863	602,425	0.34	20.52
Japan	907,220	845,591	987,041	1,020,401	1,050,969	0.59	3.00
Korea, Republic of	179,406	129,260	243,253	268,480	278,651	0.16	3.79
Australasia	372,823	337,522	443,068	567,365	600,989	0.34	5.93
Australia	372,823	337,522	443,068	567,365	600,989	0.34	5.93
Other East Asia and the Pacific	640,469	678,507	870,549	1,214,986	1,427,825	0.80	17.52
Other countries of Asia	572,739	614,125	796,765	1,136,989	1,355,978	0.76	19.26
Other countries of Oceania	67,730	64,382	73,784	77,997	71,847	0.04	-7.88
EUROPE	143,304,627	129,335,156	139,555,580	158,865,426	162,108,857	90.79	2.04
Central/Eastern Europe	6,947,823	6,127,120	8,149,947	11,568,617	13,237,285	7.41	14.42
Bulgaria	147,368	150,467	183,842	229,228	200,735	0.11	-12.43
Czech Republic	904,100	852,714	833,430	1,015,423	967,335	0.54	-4.74
Estonia	140,391	112,131	115,554	127,685	128,215	0.07	0.42
Hungary	348,847	288,085	361,184	384,310	361,400	0.20	-5.96
Latvia	100,365	89,487	104,699	133,056	135,509	0.08	1.84
Lithuania	142,851	145,506	149,572	189,459	193,822	0.11	2.30
Poland	1,366,410	1,446,449	1,770,454	2,454,487	2,358,614	1.32	-3.91
Romania	485,943	437,149	606,685	746,507	636,270	0.36	-14.77
Russian Federation	3,043,365	2,320,571	3,584,505	5,721,742	7,605,640	4.26	32.93
Slovakia	147,674	158,274	208,431	235,878	261,702	0.15	10.95
Ukraine	120,509	126,287	231,591	330,842	388,043	0.22	17.29
Northern Europe	52,178,073	46,823,037	49,576,077	54,944,372	59,394,591	33.26	8.10
Denmark	1,830,986	1,718,683	1,941,915	2,523,244	2,458,862	1.38	-2.55
Finland	1,007,298	1,052,385	1,138,286	1,314,827	1,408,843	0.79	7.15
Iceland	284,808	168,506	184,026	222,853	222,089	0.12	-0.34
Ireland	2,691,464	2,473,845	2,235,348	2,444,829	2,599,832	1.46	6.34
Norway	1,824,763	1,738,795	2,018,901	2,338,035	2,939,936	1.65	25.74
Sweden	3,079,740	3,013,007	3,280,840	3,905,603	4,492,215	2.52	15.02
United Kingdom	41,459,014	36,657,816	38,776,761	42,194,981	45,272,814	25.35	7.29
Southern Europe	12,473,022	10,775,541	12,169,405	13,174,074	11,206,385	6.28	-14.94
Greece	350,133	345,572	515,089	434,151	291,313	0.16	-32.90
Italy	8,385,107	7,216,770	8,151,620	9,378,102	8,005,524	4.48	-14.64
Malta	129,957	93,297	79,914	76,587	75,728	0.04	-1.12
Portugal	3,494,131	3,015,623	3,311,143	3,136,338	2,694,631	1.51	-14.08
Slovenia	113,694	104,279	111,639	148,896	139,189	0.08	-6.52
Western Europe	70,025,850	64,157,947	67,855,105	76,975,346	76,204,852	42.68	-1.00
Austria	1,387,503	1,205,537	1,462,259	1,771,063	1,843,562	1.03	4.09
Belgium	5,038,399	5,022,613	4,931,948	5,439,535	5,543,961	3.10	1.92

Yearbook of Tourism Statistics, Data 2008 – 2012, 2014 Edition

SPAIN

5. Overnight stays of non-resident tourists in hotels and similar establishments, by country of residence

	2008	2009	2010	2011	2012	Market share 2012	% Change 2012-2011
France	9,821,088	9,619,625	10,527,172	12,141,416	12,229,112	6.85	0.72
Germany	44,646,808	39,731,293	41,959,464	47,000,767	45,838,457	25.67	-2.47
Luxembourg	350,666	350,637	383,246	446,311	375,713	0.21	-15.82
Netherlands	6,310,868	5,889,819	6,029,492	7,029,259	7,124,152	3.99	1.35
Switzerland	2,470,518	2,338,423	2,561,524	3,146,995	3,249,895	1.82	3.27
East Mediterranean Europe	**265,518**	**238,353**	**345,569**	**404,789**	**421,251**	**0.24**	**4.07**
Cyprus	47,067	39,711	62,822	80,333	66,610	0.04	-17.08
Turkey	218,451	198,642	282,747	324,456	354,641	0.20	9.30
Other Europe	**1,414,341**	**1,213,158**	**1,459,477**	**1,798,228**	**1,644,493**	**0.92**	**-8.55**
Other countries of Europe	1,414,341	1,213,158	1,459,477	1,798,228	1,644,493	0.92	-8.55
NOT SPECIFIED	**1,845,964**	**1,751,979**	**2,005,835**	**2,109,959**	**1,975,883**	**1.11**	**-6.35**
Other countries of the World	1,845,964	1,751,979	2,005,835	2,109,959	1,975,883	1.11	-6.35

Yearbook of Tourism Statistics, Data 2008 – 2012, 2014 Edition

SPAIN

6. Overnight stays of non-resident tourists in all types of accommodation establishments, by country of residence

	2008	2009	2010	2011	2012	Market share 2012	% Change 2012-2011
TOTAL (*)	223,772,578	200,551,732	213,365,670	239,387,398	243,389,007	100.00	1.67
AFRICA	894,621	859,319	1,095,462	1,122,861	1,236,992	0.51	10.16
Southern Africa	116,452	104,043	109,534	148,813	170,751	0.07	14.74
South Africa	116,452	104,043	109,534	148,813	170,751	0.07	14.74
Other Africa	778,169	755,276	985,928	974,048	1,066,241	0.44	9.46
Other countries of Africa	778,169	755,276	985,928	974,048	1,066,241	0.44	9.46
AMERICAS	7,975,641	7,868,261	9,328,295	10,703,558	10,488,130	4.31	-2.01
North America	5,030,678	5,065,453	6,025,212	6,791,522	6,704,684	2.75	-1.28
Canada	700,642	737,643	1,037,280	1,236,127	1,253,006	0.51	1.37
United States of America	3,626,403	3,667,681	4,237,949	4,733,642	4,711,065	1.94	-0.48
Other countries of North America	703,633	660,129	749,983	821,753	740,613	0.30	-9.87
South America	798,849	777,815	1,044,060	1,271,518	1,129,705	0.46	-11.15
Brazil	798,849	777,815	1,044,060	1,271,518	1,129,705	0.46	-11.15
Other Americas	2,146,114	2,024,993	2,259,023	2,640,518	2,653,741	1.09	0.50
Other countries of the Americas	2,146,114	2,024,993	2,259,023	2,640,518	2,653,741	1.09	0.50
EAST ASIA AND THE PACIFIC	2,659,559	2,568,167	3,287,927	4,002,207	4,562,148	1.87	13.99
North-East Asia	1,507,462	1,403,007	1,798,522	1,997,308	2,219,576	0.91	11.13
China	291,691	303,340	419,353	557,460	690,309	0.28	23.83
Japan	1,016,082	953,799	1,106,837	1,140,843	1,209,915	0.50	6.05
Korea, Republic of	199,689	145,868	272,332	299,005	319,352	0.13	6.80
Australasia	417,511	381,097	497,831	632,237	688,679	0.28	8.93
Australia	417,511	381,097	497,831	632,237	688,679	0.28	8.93
Other East Asia and the Pacific	734,586	784,063	991,574	1,372,662	1,653,893	0.68	20.49
Other countries of Asia	640,831	693,770	894,655	1,267,649	1,553,878	0.64	22.58
Other countries of Oceania	93,755	90,293	96,919	105,013	100,015	0.04	-4.76
EUROPE	210,197,784	187,295,365	197,413,969	221,224,296	224,854,775	92.38	1.64
Central/Eastern Europe	8,780,317	7,585,061	9,677,280	13,469,486	15,394,925	6.33	14.29
Bulgaria	220,155	211,471	237,372	291,118	255,474	0.10	-12.24
Czech Republic	1,215,778	1,077,379	1,049,358	1,229,957	1,164,490	0.48	-5.32
Estonia	211,473	158,262	150,113	162,919	163,173	0.07	0.16
Hungary	528,997	405,747	470,963	487,171	459,934	0.19	-5.59
Latvia	152,873	126,069	135,873	170,166	172,445	0.07	1.34
Lithuania	217,108	204,908	193,735	240,894	246,669	0.10	2.40
Poland	1,715,916	1,774,022	2,089,974	2,869,174	2,779,394	1.14	-3.13
Romania	730,787	613,919	787,577	946,853	809,676	0.33	-14.49
Russian Federation	3,408,975	2,632,296	4,014,664	6,381,181	8,546,313	3.51	33.93
Slovakia	221,626	222,021	271,056	297,323	333,077	0.14	12.03
Ukraine	156,629	158,967	276,595	392,730	464,280	0.19	18.22
Northern Europe	87,132,194	76,003,707	78,183,507	85,951,164	90,430,234	37.15	5.21
Denmark	3,653,317	3,255,430	3,406,994	4,020,160	4,071,655	1.67	1.28
Finland	2,454,111	2,371,404	2,393,517	2,697,213	2,771,719	1.14	2.76
Iceland	373,833	215,399	224,600	269,255	265,731	0.11	-1.31
Ireland	6,145,024	5,068,140	4,436,198	4,714,176	4,921,387	2.02	4.40
Norway	4,130,414	3,945,740	4,119,934	4,760,661	5,591,788	2.30	17.46
Sweden	5,874,738	5,691,244	5,892,123	6,763,657	7,413,587	3.05	9.61
United Kingdom	64,500,757	55,456,350	57,710,141	62,726,042	65,394,367	26.87	4.25
Southern Europe	14,892,697	12,657,316	14,381,746	15,460,472	13,410,809	5.51	-13.26
Greece	470,456	402,901	576,043	482,437	323,535	0.13	-32.94
Italy	9,845,628	8,435,329	9,667,736	11,041,379	9,656,938	3.97	-12.54
Malta	197,558	131,634	104,342	97,762	96,380	0.04	-1.41
Portugal	4,205,150	3,540,535	3,889,037	3,650,401	3,156,812	1.30	-13.52
Slovenia	173,905	146,917	144,588	188,493	177,144	0.07	-6.02
Western Europe	97,203,489	89,180,373	92,992,328	103,685,146	103,142,076	42.38	-0.52
Austria	1,736,144	1,511,202	1,753,595	2,110,051	2,154,338	0.89	2.10
Belgium	6,405,534	6,358,928	6,328,795	6,954,129	7,143,548	2.94	2.72

Yearbook of Tourism Statistics, Data 2008 – 2012, 2014 Edition

SPAIN

6. Overnight stays of non-resident tourists in all types of accommodation establishments, by country of residence

	2008	2009	2010	2011	2012	Market share 2012	% Change 2012-2011
France	14,707,391	14,649,330	15,660,542	17,938,395	18,113,925	7.44	0.98
Germany	57,676,108	51,053,217	52,986,209	58,302,711	56,834,642	23.35	-2.52
Luxembourg	486,125	449,023	453,613	545,132	482,364	0.20	-11.51
Netherlands	13,041,044	12,250,266	12,646,078	14,008,577	14,433,571	5.93	3.03
Switzerland	3,151,143	2,908,407	3,163,496	3,826,151	3,979,688	1.64	4.01
East Mediterranean Europe	**358,199**	**311,405**	**425,169**	**495,850**	**509,072**	**0.21**	**2.67**
Cyprus	72,476	55,704	82,365	102,883	84,767	0.03	-17.61
Turkey	285,723	255,701	342,804	392,967	424,305	0.17	7.97
Other Europe	**1,830,888**	**1,557,503**	**1,753,939**	**2,162,178**	**1,967,659**	**0.81**	**-9.00**
Other countries of Europe	1,830,888	1,557,503	1,753,939	2,162,178	1,967,659	0.81	-9.00
NOT SPECIFIED	**2,044,973**	**1,960,620**	**2,240,017**	**2,334,476**	**2,246,962**	**0.92**	**-3.75**
Other countries of the World	2,044,973	1,960,620	2,240,017	2,334,476	2,246,962	0.92	-3.75

Yearbook of Tourism Statistics, Data 2008 – 2012, 2014 Edition

SRI LANKA

1. Arrivals of non-resident tourists at national borders, by nationality

		2008	2009	2010	2011	2012	Market share 2012	% Change 2012-2011
TOTAL	(*)	438,475	447,890	654,476	855,975	1,005,605	100.00	17.48
AFRICA		2,354	1,591	2,249	6,736	6,912	0.69	2.61
Other Africa		2,354	1,591	2,249	6,736	6,912	0.69	2.61
All countries of Africa		2,354	1,591	2,249	6,736	6,912	0.69	2.61
AMERICAS		26,924	25,710	41,146	54,825	57,695	5.74	5.23
North America		23,203	25,044	40,552	53,658	56,694	5.64	5.66
Canada		9,745	10,785	21,231	26,090	28,786	2.86	10.33
United States of America		13,458	14,259	19,321	27,568	27,908	2.78	1.23
Other Americas		3,721	666	594	1,167	1,001	0.10	-14.22
Other countries of the Americas		3,721	666	594	1,167	1,001	0.10	-14.22
EAST ASIA AND THE PACIFIC		67,199	75,503	110,816	141,751	175,910	17.49	24.10
North-East Asia		27,104	27,136	36,569	50,996	58,678	5.84	15.06
China		10,015	8,574	10,410	16,573	20,323	2.02	22.63
Hong Kong, China		421	1,325	1,824	440	897	0.09	103.86
Japan		10,578	10,931	14,998	20,951	23,421	2.33	11.79
Korea, Republic of		4,102	3,595	4,318	5,965	6,133	0.61	2.82
Taiwan, Province of China		1,988	2,711	5,019	7,067	7,904	0.79	11.84
South-East Asia		17,011	20,512	31,978	36,389	63,438	6.31	74.33
Indonesia		1,258	1,039	1,281	2,011	2,812	0.28	39.83
Malaysia		5,021	6,878	13,101	15,915	29,181	2.90	83.36
Philippines		1,520	1,421	1,369	2,394	4,761	0.47	98.87
Singapore		5,702	7,976	12,514	10,666	15,453	1.54	44.88
Thailand		3,510	3,198	3,713	5,403	11,231	1.12	107.87
Australasia		21,293	25,872	36,813	48,912	48,147	4.79	-1.56
Australia		19,145	23,249	33,512	43,737	42,310	4.21	-3.26
New Zealand		2,148	2,623	3,301	5,175	5,837	0.58	12.79
Other East Asia and the Pacific		1,791	1,983	5,456	5,454	5,647	0.56	3.54
Other countries of Asia		1,706	1,832	5,244	2,955	3,755	0.37	27.07
Other countries of Oceania		85	151	212	2,499	1,892	0.19	-24.29
EUROPE		195,174	196,363	290,802	372,353	448,310	44.58	20.40
Central/Eastern Europe		29,352	26,177	35,630	51,922	70,437	7.00	35.66
Russian Federation		15,831	11,390	13,312	21,291	30,156	3.00	41.64
Other countries Central/East Europe		13,521	14,787	22,318	30,631	40,281	4.01	31.50
Northern Europe		87,404	88,977	123,222	134,204	152,069	15.12	13.31
Denmark		1,336	1,306	4,301	6,640	9,753	0.97	46.88
Finland		489	742	1,971	3,819	6,230	0.62	63.13
Norway		1,620	1,669	3,884	5,135	9,093	0.90	77.08
Sweden		3,745	3,578	7,128	11,715	15,165	1.51	29.45
United Kingdom		80,214	81,682	105,938	106,895	111,828	11.12	4.61
Southern Europe		11,388	9,597	16,001	20,061	27,370	2.72	36.43
Italy		9,137	7,214	11,512	14,182	17,661	1.76	24.53
Spain		2,251	2,383	4,489	5,879	9,709	0.97	65.15
Western Europe		64,376	68,437	113,576	161,717	191,947	19.09	18.69
Austria		2,684	2,411	3,963	6,185	6,601	0.66	6.73
Belgium		2,394	2,613	5,371	10,853	13,013	1.29	19.90
France		10,703	16,205	31,119	50,175	55,473	5.52	10.56
Germany		30,154	29,664	45,981	55,339	69,652	6.93	25.86
Netherlands		13,180	11,297	17,628	26,004	25,564	2.54	-1.69
Switzerland		5,261	6,247	9,514	13,161	21,644	2.15	64.46
Other Europe		2,654	3,175	2,373	4,449	6,487	0.65	45.81
Other countries of Europe		2,654	3,175	2,373	4,449	6,487	0.65	45.81
MIDDLE EAST		16,701	23,821	37,501	36,376	58,901	5.86	61.92
All countries of Middle East		16,701	23,821	37,501	36,376	58,901	5.86	61.92

 Yearbook of Tourism Statistics, Data 2008 – 2012, 2014 Edition

SRI LANKA

1. Arrivals of non-resident tourists at national borders, by nationality

	2008	2009	2010	2011	2012	Market share 2012	% Change 2012-2011
SOUTH ASIA	**130,123**	**124,902**	**171,962**	**243,934**	**257,877**	**25.64**	**5.72**
Bangladesh	1,438	1,295	1,846	4,934	5,748	0.57	16.50
India	88,628	83,650	125,112	178,359	191,281	19.02	7.24
Maldives	31,458	31,890	35,401	43,926	45,321	4.51	3.18
Nepal	897	679	602	858	984	0.10	14.69
Pakistan	7,702	7,388	9,001	15,857	14,543	1.45	-8.29

Yearbook of Tourism Statistics, Data 2008 – 2012, 2014 Edition

SRI LANKA

1. Arrivals of non-resident tourists at national borders, by country of residence

		2008	2009	2010	2011	2012	Market share 2012	% Change 2012-2011
TOTAL	(*)	438,475	447,820	654,476	855,975	1,005,605	100.00	17.48
AFRICA		2,141	1,479	2,308	3,614	5,045	0.50	39.60
East Africa		711	397	539	621	929	0.09	49.60
Kenya		540	229	297	394	645	0.06	63.71
Mauritius		93	117	179	160	284	0.03	77.50
Zambia		78	51	63	67			
North Africa		120	69	71	64			
Algeria		120	69	71	64			
Southern Africa		756	779	1,415	1,962	3,048	0.30	55.35
South Africa		756	779	1,415	1,962	3,048	0.30	55.35
West Africa		99	131	212	378	684	0.07	80.95
Nigeria		99	131	212	378	684	0.07	80.95
Other Africa		455	103	71	589	384	0.04	-34.80
Other countries of Africa		455	103	71	589	384	0.04	-34.80
AMERICAS		28,050	25,565	40,836	50,093	60,862	6.05	21.50
North America		24,311	24,948	40,216	49,057	59,236	5.89	20.75
Canada		10,258	10,707	21,123	24,671	29,329	2.92	18.88
United States of America		14,053	14,241	19,093	24,386	29,907	2.97	22.64
South America		1,649	500	512	541	1,092	0.11	101.85
Argentina		352	75	133	148	387	0.04	161.49
Bolivia		291	39	76	23	229	0.02	895.65
Brazil		258	157	217	362	476	0.05	31.49
French Guiana		748	229	86	8			
Other Americas		2,090	117	108	495	534	0.05	7.88
Other countries of the Americas		2,090	117	108	495	534	0.05	7.88
EAST ASIA AND THE PACIFIC		66,783	74,397	105,720	142,661	190,506	18.94	33.54
North-East Asia		26,631	27,216	35,715	51,785	74,253	7.38	43.39
China		9,812	8,550	10,430	16,308	25,781	2.56	58.09
Hong Kong, China		537	1,330	1,230	2,199	1,535	0.15	-30.20
Japan		10,075	10,926	14,352	20,586	26,085	2.59	26.71
Korea, Republic of		4,300	3,695	4,426	5,485	7,838	0.78	42.90
Macao, China					197	311	0.03	57.87
Taiwan, Province of China		1,907	2,715	5,277	7,010	12,703	1.26	81.21
South-East Asia		17,969	20,813	32,362	43,672	57,537	5.72	31.75
Indonesia		1,157	1,040	1,343	2,049	2,890	0.29	41.04
Malaysia		5,188	6,850	13,367	16,094	21,776	2.17	35.31
Myanmar		376	262	262	914	1,108	0.11	21.23
Philippines		1,693	1,421	1,391	2,047	5,687	0.57	177.82
Singapore		5,802	7,808	11,875	15,953	17,273	1.72	8.27
Thailand		3,583	3,208	3,684	5,880	7,897	0.79	34.30
Viet Nam		170	224	440	735	906	0.09	23.27
Australasia		21,776	25,911	36,943	45,940	57,255	5.69	24.63
Australia		19,536	23,239	33,456	41,728	51,614	5.13	23.69
New Zealand		2,240	2,672	3,487	4,212	5,641	0.56	33.93
Other East Asia and the Pacific		407	457	700	1,264	1,461	0.15	15.59
Other countries of Asia		344	300	353	737	940	0.09	27.54
Other countries of Oceania		63	157	347	527	521	0.05	-1.14
EUROPE		199,601	198,897	296,961	371,794	452,676	45.02	21.75
Central/Eastern Europe		29,440	26,310	35,517	49,249	70,941	7.05	44.05
Bulgaria		242	207	703	375	789	0.08	110.40
Czech Republic		2,555	2,814	4,204	5,548	5,877	0.58	5.93
Hungary		582	418	836	911	1,418	0.14	55.65
Kazakhstan					240	996	0.10	315.00
Lithuania		459	546	636	673	1,078	0.11	60.18
Poland		4,960	5,138	6,613	5,817	5,806	0.58	-0.19

705

Yearbook of Tourism Statistics, Data 2008 – 2012, 2014 Edition

SRI LANKA

1. Arrivals of non-resident tourists at national borders, by country of residence

	2008	2009	2010	2011	2012	Market share 2012	% Change 2012-2011
Romania	305	272	710	726	1,029	0.10	41.74
Russian Federation	15,797	11,834	13,278	21,385	28,402	2.82	32.81
Slovakia	704	1,164	1,716	1,314	2,040	0.20	55.25
Ukraine	952	2,577	5,703	9,967	22,348	2.22	124.22
Other countries Central/East Europe	2,884	1,340	1,118	2,293	1,158	0.12	-49.50
Northern Europe	**90,090**	**90,286**	**124,648**	**133,679**	**150,810**	**15.00**	**12.82**
Denmark	1,320	1,362	4,393	6,582	8,323	0.83	26.45
Finland	468	738	1,950	3,649	4,840	0.48	32.64
Ireland	1,647	1,366	1,758	1,452	1,951	0.19	34.37
Norway	1,613	1,666	3,955	4,977	7,703	0.77	54.77
Sweden	3,711	3,560	7,096	10,937	13,775	1.37	25.95
United Kingdom	81,331	81,594	105,496	106,082	114,218	11.36	7.67
Southern Europe	**12,212**	**11,372**	**18,333**	**21,685**	**26,889**	**2.67**	**24.00**
Greece	395	906	1,599	1,240	1,415	0.14	14.11
Italy	9,126	7,514	11,423	13,527	15,871	1.58	17.33
Portugal	409	565	850	1,032	1,284	0.13	24.42
Spain	2,282	2,387	4,461	5,886	8,319	0.83	41.34
Western Europe	**64,604**	**68,188**	**113,623**	**159,037**	**194,627**	**19.35**	**22.38**
Austria	2,651	2,409	3,925	6,262	7,991	0.79	27.61
Belgium	2,378	2,617	5,398	10,122	11,323	1.13	11.87
France	10,594	15,886	31,285	48,695	56,863	5.65	16.77
Germany	30,625	29,654	45,727	55,882	71,642	7.12	28.20
Netherlands	13,030	11,291	17,861	23,966	26,754	2.66	11.63
Switzerland	5,326	6,331	9,427	14,110	20,054	1.99	42.13
East Mediterranean Europe	**2,974**	**2,464**	**4,583**	**7,335**	**8,672**	**0.86**	**18.23**
Israel	2,596	1,901	3,919	6,164	7,212	0.72	17.00
Turkey	378	563	664	1,171	1,460	0.15	24.68
Other Europe	**281**	**277**	**257**	**809**	**737**	**0.07**	**-8.90**
Other countries of Europe	281	277	257	809	737	0.07	-8.90
MIDDLE EAST	**11,672**	**20,007**	**31,057**	**47,943**	**47,142**	**4.69**	**-1.67**
Bahrain	805	943	1,459	1,819	2,016	0.20	10.83
Egypt	417	510	849	767	800	0.08	4.30
Jordan	1,398	1,108	1,708	1,478	1,852	0.18	25.30
Kuwait	1,011	1,123	2,303	2,812	3,245	0.32	15.40
Lebanon	759	940	1,816	1,960	2,116	0.21	7.96
Oman	499	727	1,359	2,177	2,602	0.26	19.52
Qatar	312	1,158	1,574	2,788	2,271	0.23	-18.54
Saudi Arabia	3,456	6,685	9,301	15,081	19,423	1.93	28.79
United Arab Emirates	2,469	5,974	9,825	17,664	11,083	1.10	-37.26
Other countries of Middle East	546	839	863	1,397	1,734	0.17	24.12
SOUTH ASIA	**130,228**	**127,475**	**177,594**	**239,870**	**249,374**	**24.80**	**3.96**
Afghanistan	168	200	176	363	649	0.06	78.79
Bangladesh	1,599	1,294	1,954	4,726	4,646	0.46	-1.69
Bhutan	498	668	530	824	831	0.08	0.85
India	85,238	83,634	126,882	171,374	176,340	17.54	2.90
Iran, Islamic Republic of	2,130	1,270	1,900	2,223	1,815	0.18	-18.35
Maldives	31,564	31,916	35,791	44,018	47,572	4.73	8.07
Nepal	888	676	753	826	1,038	0.10	25.67
Pakistan	7,885	7,373	9,148	14,724	16,056	1.60	9.05
Other countries of South Asia	258	444	460	792	427	0.04	-46.09

Yearbook of Tourism Statistics, Data 2008 – 2012, 2014 Edition

SRI LANKA

6. Overnight stays of non-resident tourists in all types of accommodation establishments, by nationality

	2008	2009	2010	2011	2012	Market share 2012	% Change 2012-2011
TOTAL	4,165,511	4,075,799	6,544,760	8,559,753	10,056,053	100.00	17.48
AFRICA	21,421	12,569	22,265	64,666	65,940	0.66	1.97
Other Africa	21,421	12,569	22,265	64,666	65,940	0.66	1.97
All countries of Africa	21,421	12,569	22,265	64,666	65,940	0.66	1.97
AMERICAS	308,219	272,480	430,627	570,943	598,547	5.95	4.83
North America	271,753	265,887	424,628	559,471	588,677	5.85	5.22
Canada	134,481	121,871	231,418	280,207	305,132	3.03	8.90
United States of America	137,272	144,016	193,210	279,264	283,545	2.82	1.53
Other Americas	36,466	6,593	5,999	11,472	9,870	0.10	-13.96
Other countries of the Americas	36,466	6,593	5,999	11,472	9,870	0.10	-13.96
EAST ASIA AND THE PACIFIC	662,603	692,400	1,137,681	1,497,005	1,827,563	18.17	22.08
North-East Asia	224,791	213,271	345,705	488,344	562,966	5.60	15.28
China	76,114	68,592	103,059	161,421	198,352	1.97	22.88
Hong Kong, China	2,989	9,540	17,328	4,092	8,190	0.08	100.15
Japan	81,451	83,076	137,982	201,130	224,842	2.24	11.79
Korea, Republic of	36,508	30,917	40,157	54,282	56,178	0.56	3.49
Taiwan, Province of China	27,729	21,146	47,179	67,419	75,404	0.75	11.84
South-East Asia	121,421	155,091	295,878	342,837	599,645	5.96	74.91
Indonesia	9,435	7,585	11,785	18,903	25,870	0.26	36.86
Malaysia	41,172	53,648	125,770	154,853	284,223	2.83	83.54
Philippines	12,768	11,652	12,184	21,642	43,135	0.43	99.31
Singapore	43,335	59,820	110,123	95,354	138,150	1.37	44.88
Thailand	14,711	22,386	36,016	52,085	108,267	1.08	107.87
Australasia	283,356	292,992	419,388	550,005	537,028	5.34	-2.36
Australia	260,372	266,500	385,388	495,978	475,564	4.73	-4.12
New Zealand	22,984	26,492	34,000	54,027	61,464	0.61	13.77
Other East Asia and the Pacific	33,035	31,046	76,710	115,819	127,924	1.27	10.45
Other countries of Asia	32,178	29,687	74,612	90,685	108,436	1.08	19.57
Other countries of Oceania	857	1,359	2,098	25,134	19,488	0.19	-22.46
EUROPE	1,972,437	1,914,137	3,049,358	3,901,289	4,700,719	46.75	20.49
Central/Eastern Europe	232,574	200,674	365,657	525,555	715,140	7.11	36.07
Russian Federation	129,814	96,815	135,782	218,020	304,274	3.03	39.56
Other countries Central/East Europe	102,760	103,859	229,875	307,535	410,866	4.09	33.60
Northern Europe	927,461	905,446	1,316,932	1,418,104	1,615,543	16.07	13.92
Denmark	14,162	13,321	43,010	67,861	99,676	0.99	46.88
Finland	4,694	6,826	20,104	38,343	62,612	0.62	63.29
Norway	19,440	18,025	40,782	53,404	95,113	0.95	78.10
Sweden	43,068	37,569	74,844	121,133	157,109	1.56	29.70
United Kingdom	846,097	829,705	1,138,192	1,137,363	1,201,033	11.94	5.60
Southern Europe	112,953	95,004	159,308	199,126	272,931	2.71	37.06
Italy	89,543	70,697	113,969	138,984	173,608	1.73	24.91
Spain	23,410	24,307	45,339	60,142	99,323	0.99	65.15
Western Europe	676,226	683,803	1,184,917	1,712,260	2,032,624	20.21	18.71
Austria	25,766	22,422	37,649	59,623	63,634	0.63	6.73
Belgium	25,616	27,175	54,247	110,049	132,342	1.32	20.26
France	101,679	155,568	326,750	548,915	604,656	6.01	10.15
Germany	331,644	302,573	491,997	588,807	741,794	7.38	25.98
Netherlands	135,754	112,970	176,280	266,281	262,287	2.61	-1.50
Switzerland	55,767	63,095	97,994	138,585	227,911	2.27	64.46
Other Europe	23,223	29,210	22,544	46,244	64,481	0.64	39.44
Other countries of Europe	23,223	29,210	22,544	46,244	64,481	0.64	39.44
MIDDLE EAST	126,928	178,658	382,510	371,035	591,366	5.88	59.38
All countries of Middle East	126,928	178,658	382,510	371,035	591,366	5.88	59.38

Yearbook of Tourism Statistics, Data 2008 – 2012, 2014 Edition

SRI LANKA

6. Overnight stays of non-resident tourists in all types of accommodation establishments, by nationality

	2008	2009	2010	2011	2012	Market share 2012	% Change 2012-2011
SOUTH ASIA	**1,073,903**	**1,005,555**	**1,522,319**	**2,154,815**	**2,271,918**	**22.59**	**5.43**
India	718,122	657,835	1,105,900	1,558,858	1,671,796	16.62	7.24
Maldives	295,705	292,310	336,310	454,195	469,526	4.67	3.38
Pakistan	60,076	55,410	80,109	141,762	130,596	1.30	-7.88

Yearbook of Tourism Statistics, Data 2008 – 2012, 2014 Editio

SUDAN

1. Arrivals of non-resident tourists at national borders, by nationality

		2008	2009	2010	2011	2012	Market share 2012	% Change 2012-2011
TOTAL	(*)	439,661	420,370	495,158	536,400			
AFRICA		65,949	59,802	49,516	53,640			
Other Africa		65,949	59,802	49,516	53,640			
All countries of Africa		65,949	59,802	49,516	53,640			
AMERICAS		15,388	21,000	19,806	21,456			
Other Americas		15,388	21,000	19,806	21,456			
All countries of the Americas		15,388	21,000	19,806	21,456			
EAST ASIA AND THE PACIFIC		298,969	239,920	29,709	32,184			
Other East Asia and the Pacific		298,969	239,920	29,709	32,184			
All countries of Asia		298,969	239,920	29,709	32,184			
EUROPE		57,156	99,648	74,274	80,460			
Other Europe		57,156	99,648	74,274	80,460			
All countries of Europe		57,156	99,648	74,274	80,460			
MIDDLE EAST				272,338	295,020			
All countries of Middle East				272,338	295,020			
SOUTH ASIA				39,612	42,912			
All countries of South Asia				39,612	42,912			
NOT SPECIFIED		2,199		9,903	10,728			
Other countries of the World		2,199		9,903	10,728			

Yearbook of Tourism Statistics, Data 2008 – 2012, 2014 Edition

SURINAME

1. Arrivals of non-resident tourists at national borders, by country of residence

	2008	2009	2010	2011	2012	Market share 2012	% Change 2012-2011
TOTAL	150,711	150,628	204,519	220,475	240,041	100.00	8.87
AFRICA	183	171	246	290	525	0.22	81.03
Other Africa	183	171	246	290	525	0.22	81.03
All countries of Africa	183	171	246	290	525	0.22	81.03
AMERICAS	51,386	59,175	88,680	103,709	123,731	51.55	19.31
Caribbean	8,845	10,497	13,417	14,448	14,329	5.97	-0.82
Dominican Republic	38	77	71	48	76	0.03	58.33
Haiti	101	127	202	216	272	0.11	25.93
Trinidad and Tobago	2,374	2,567	3,972	4,862	4,370	1.82	-10.12
Other countries of the Caribbean	6,332	7,726	9,172	9,322	9,611	4.00	3.10
Central America	489	397	504	568	472	0.20	-16.90
All countries of Central America	489	397	504	568	472	0.20	-16.90
North America	6,166	6,284	8,320	9,726	10,380	4.32	6.72
Canada	1,193	1,320	1,720	1,972	2,206	0.92	11.87
United States of America	4,973	4,964	6,600	7,754	8,174	3.41	5.42
South America	35,886	41,997	66,439	78,967	98,550	41.06	24.80
Brazil	7,488	7,840	11,158	14,427	19,452	8.10	34.83
Colombia	223	178	173	286	290	0.12	1.40
Guyana	13,445	18,753	30,446	33,010	43,846	18.27	32.83
Venezuela	326	287	430	474	435	0.18	-8.23
Other countries of South America	14,404	14,939	24,232	30,770	34,527	14.38	12.21
EAST ASIA AND THE PACIFIC	2,732	1,940	3,382	4,838	4,714	1.96	-2.56
North-East Asia	1,879	1,241	2,220	2,713	2,681	1.12	-1.18
China	1,737	1,069	1,980	2,470	2,491	1.04	0.85
Japan	99	124	206	214	154	0.06	-28.04
Korea, Republic of	43	48	34	29	36	0.01	24.14
South-East Asia	198	144	252	526	262	0.11	-50.19
Indonesia	198	144	252	526	262	0.11	-50.19
Other East Asia and the Pacific	655	555	910	1,599	1,771	0.74	10.76
Other countries of Asia	647	542	824	1,441	1,530	0.64	6.18
All countries of Oceania	8	13	86	158	241	0.10	52.53
EUROPE	95,299	87,817	110,255	108,188	107,655	44.85	-0.49
Northern Europe	508	471	775	1,010	1,487	0.62	47.23
United Kingdom	508	471	775	1,010	1,487	0.62	47.23
Western Europe	93,774	86,344	108,106	105,479	104,639	43.59	-0.80
Belgium	985	1,013	1,464	1,640	2,009	0.84	22.50
France	3,976	3,794	4,455	5,222	6,983	2.91	33.72
Germany	433	420	609	563	556	0.23	-1.24
Netherlands	88,380	81,117	101,578	98,054	95,091	39.61	-3.02
Other Europe	1,017	1,002	1,374	1,699	1,529	0.64	-10.01
Other countries of Europe	1,017	1,002	1,374	1,699	1,529	0.64	-10.01
MIDDLE EAST	30	19	47	42	56	0.02	33.33
All countries of Middle East	30	19	47	42	56	0.02	33.33
SOUTH ASIA	551	454	556	585	504	0.21	-13.85
India	551	454	556	585	504	0.21	-13.85
NOT SPECIFIED	530	1,052	1,353	2,823	2,856	1.19	1.17
Other countries of the World	530	1,052	1,353	2,823	2,856	1.19	1.17

Yearbook of Tourism Statistics, Data 2008 – 2012, 2014 Edition

SWAZILAND

2. Arrivals of non-resident visitors at national borders, by country of residence

	2008	2009	2010	2011	2012	Market share 2012	% Change 2012-2011
TOTAL	1,185,998	1,343,967	1,342,531	1,328,363	1,278,528	100.00	-3.75
AFRICA	1,041,211	1,191,259	1,218,054	1,225,220	1,165,225	91.14	-4.90
East Africa	237,915	302,780	283,808	280,437	272,268	21.30	-2.91
Kenya	2,111	2,343	2,709	2,069	2,072	0.16	0.14
Malawi	2,846	3,109	3,017	3,183	3,313	0.26	4.08
Mozambique	209,139	266,560	241,334	236,507	222,989	17.44	-5.72
United Republic of Tanzania	3,575	4,802	4,677	5,522	6,242	0.49	13.04
Zambia	5,682	6,086	7,128	6,915	7,004	0.55	1.29
Zimbabwe	14,562	19,880	24,943	26,241	30,648	2.40	16.79
Southern Africa	790,672	875,379	920,153	931,624	880,095	68.84	-5.53
Botswana	4,331	3,931	4,053	3,710	4,328	0.34	16.66
Lesotho	5,168	4,864	4,906	3,348	4,308	0.34	28.67
South Africa	781,173	866,584	911,194	924,566	871,459	68.16	-5.74
West Africa	3,424	3,202	2,744	2,768	2,785	0.22	0.61
Nigeria	3,424	3,202	2,744	2,768	2,785	0.22	0.61
Other Africa	9,200	9,898	11,349	10,391	10,077	0.79	-3.02
Other countries of Africa	9,200	9,898	11,349	10,391	10,077	0.79	-3.02
AMERICAS	19,607	20,187	20,499	18,826	20,259	1.58	7.61
North America	17,780	18,242	18,333	16,914	18,161	1.42	7.37
Canada	3,359	3,317	3,192	2,696	3,489	0.27	29.41
United States of America	14,421	14,925	15,141	14,218	14,672	1.15	3.19
South America	1,065	1,234	1,085	1,041	1,076	0.08	3.36
Brazil	1,065	1,234	1,085	1,041	1,076	0.08	3.36
Other Americas	762	711	1,081	871	1,022	0.08	17.34
Other countries of the Americas	762	711	1,081	871	1,022	0.08	17.34
EAST ASIA AND THE PACIFIC	11,779	10,945	11,061	9,826	11,263	0.88	14.62
North-East Asia	4,946	4,656	4,299	4,674	4,670	0.37	-0.09
China	2,738	2,137	1,980	2,344	2,531	0.20	7.98
Korea, Republic of	800	1,133	1,137	1,260	988	0.08	-21.59
Taiwan, Province of China	1,408	1,386	1,182	1,070	1,151	0.09	7.57
South-East Asia	669	569	497	339	455	0.04	34.22
Philippines	669	569	497	339	455	0.04	34.22
Australasia	3,142	2,810	2,874	2,191	2,777	0.22	26.75
Australia	3,142	2,810	2,874	2,191	2,777	0.22	26.75
Other East Asia and the Pacific	3,022	2,910	3,391	2,622	3,361	0.26	28.18
Other countries of Asia	3,022	2,910	3,391	2,622	3,361	0.26	28.18
EUROPE	107,712	114,047	85,195	66,930	73,807	5.77	10.27
Northern Europe	25,393	28,050	24,729	18,355	17,390	1.36	-5.26
Norway	894	1,056	891	725	774	0.06	6.76
Sweden	2,918	2,894	2,107	1,271	1,334	0.10	4.96
United Kingdom	21,581	24,100	21,731	16,359	15,282	1.20	-6.58
Southern Europe	10,395	11,647	11,398	9,140	10,157	0.79	11.13
Italy	3,595	3,478	3,104	2,225	2,858	0.22	28.45
Portugal	6,800	8,169	8,294	6,915	7,299	0.57	5.55
Western Europe	61,375	62,334	39,797	31,494	38,903	3.04	23.53
Belgium	5,573	7,892	3,205	3,015	3,158	0.25	4.74
France	16,619	16,638	12,737	8,273	9,776	0.76	18.17
Germany	19,111	15,639	11,294	10,406	14,911	1.17	43.29
Netherlands	17,554	19,604	10,788	8,161	9,011	0.70	10.42
Switzerland	2,518	2,561	1,773	1,639	2,047	0.16	24.89
East Mediterranean Europe	705	877	713	1,058	682	0.05	-35.54
Israel	705	877	713	1,058	682	0.05	-35.54
Other Europe	9,844	11,139	8,558	6,883	6,675	0.52	-3.02
Other countries of Europe	9,844	11,139	8,558	6,883	6,675	0.52	-3.02

Yearbook of Tourism Statistics, Data 2008 – 2012, 2014 Edition

SWAZILAND

2. Arrivals of non-resident visitors at national borders, by country of residence

	2008	2009	2010	2011	2012	Market share 2012	% Change 2012-2011
MIDDLE EAST		218	213	91	143	0.01	57.14
Kuwait		122	63	21	32	0.00	52.38
Saudi Arabia		18	4	13	2	0.00	-84.62
United Arab Emirates		11	30	6	3	0.00	-50.00
Other countries of Middle East		67	116	51	106	0.01	107.84
SOUTH ASIA	5,689	7,311	7,509	7,470	7,831	0.61	4.83
India	3,252	4,339	3,970	4,103	3,972	0.31	-3.19
Iran, Islamic Republic of		43	46	67	84	0.01	25.37
Pakistan	2,437	2,929	3,493	3,300	3,775	0.30	14.39

Yearbook of Tourism Statistics, Data 2008 – 2012, 2014 Edition

SWAZILAND

3. Arrivals of non-resident tourists in hotels and similar establishments, by country of residence

	2008	2009	2010	2011	2012	Market share 2012	% Change 2012-2011
TOTAL	323,538	334,391	338,032	308,389	304,594	100.00	-1.23
AFRICA	186,884	201,585	257,997	235,377	232,231	76.24	-1.34
East Africa	12,177	9,613	15,326	14,000	13,835	4.54	-1.18
Mozambique	12,177	9,613	15,326	14,000	13,835	4.54	-1.18
Southern Africa	150,814	170,468	230,768	219,269	216,298	71.01	-1.35
South Africa	147,639	167,520	227,986	207,981	205,059	67.32	-1.40
Other countries of Southern Africa	3,175	2,948	2,782	11,288	11,239	3.69	-0.43
Other Africa	23,893	21,504	11,903	2,108	2,098	0.69	-0.47
Other countries of Africa	23,893	21,504	11,903	2,108	2,098	0.69	-0.47
AMERICAS	21,503	14,105	19,557	17,114	16,974	5.57	-0.82
Other Americas	21,503	14,105	19,557	17,114	16,974	5.57	-0.82
All countries of the Americas	21,503	14,105	19,557	17,114	16,974	5.57	-0.82
EAST ASIA AND THE PACIFIC	12,035	13,196	6,158	5,618	5,800	1.90	3.24
Australasia	2,197	2,423	1,717	1,566	1,560	0.51	-0.38
Australia	2,197	2,423	1,717	1,566	1,560	0.51	-0.38
Other East Asia and the Pacific	9,838	10,773	4,441	4,052	4,240	1.39	4.64
Other countries of Asia	9,838	10,773	4,441	4,052	4,240	1.39	4.64
EUROPE	103,116	105,505	54,320	49,553	49,589	16.28	0.07
Northern Europe	9,300	13,351	10,780	9,834	10,794	3.54	9.76
United Kingdom	9,300	13,351	10,780	9,834	10,794	3.54	9.76
Other Europe	93,816	92,154	43,540	39,719	38,795	12.74	-2.33
Other countries of Europe	93,816	92,154	43,540	39,719	38,795	12.74	-2.33
NOT SPECIFIED				727			
Other countries of the World				727			

Yearbook of Tourism Statistics, Data 2008 – 2012, 2014 Edition

SWEDEN

2. Arrivals of non-resident visitors at national borders, by country of residence

	2008	2009	2010	2011	2012	Market share 2012	% Change 2012-2011
TOTAL (*)				15,380,588	15,981,098	100.00	3.90
AFRICA				40,973	36,580	0.23	-10.72
Other Africa				40,973	36,580	0.23	-10.72
All countries of Africa				40,973	36,580	0.23	-10.72
AMERICAS				656,081	668,164	4.18	1.84
North America				555,725	576,227	3.61	3.69
Canada				67,752	87,215	0.55	28.73
United States of America				487,973	489,012	3.06	0.21
Other Americas				100,356	91,937	0.58	-8.39
Other countries of the Americas				100,356	91,937	0.58	-8.39
EAST ASIA AND THE PACIFIC				327,122	317,676	1.99	-2.89
Other East Asia and the Pacific				327,122	317,676	1.99	-2.89
All countries of Asia				220,731	195,206	1.22	-11.56
All countries of Oceania				106,391	122,470	0.77	15.11
EUROPE				14,235,830	14,834,089	92.82	4.20
Central/Eastern Europe				2,347,511	2,447,923	15.32	4.28
All countries Central/East Europe				2,347,511	2,447,923	15.32	4.28
Northern Europe				9,443,185	9,528,914	59.63	0.91
Denmark				3,657,248	3,492,246	21.85	-4.51
Finland				2,379,028	2,579,911	16.14	8.44
Norway				2,772,580	2,659,875	16.64	-4.06
United Kingdom				634,329	796,882	4.99	25.63
Western Europe				2,336,046	2,744,506	17.17	17.49
France				262,483	301,476	1.89	14.86
Germany				1,715,400	1,948,516	12.19	13.59
Netherlands				358,163	494,514	3.09	38.07
Other Europe				109,088	112,746	0.71	3.35
Other countries of Europe				109,088	112,746	0.71	3.35
MIDDLE EAST				73,214	77,402	0.48	5.72
All countries of Middle East				73,214	77,402	0.48	5.72
SOUTH ASIA				45,663	40,084	0.25	-12.22
All countries of South Asia				45,663	40,084	0.25	-12.22
NOT SPECIFIED				1,705	7,103	0.04	316.60
Other countries of the World				1,705	7,103	0.04	316.60

Yearbook of Tourism Statistics, Data 2008 – 2012, 2014 Edition

SWEDEN

3. Arrivals of non-resident tourists in hotels and similar establishments, by country of residence

	2008	2009	2010	2011	2012	Market share 2012	% Change 2012-2011
TOTAL	2,944,161	3,044,347	3,284,613	3,370,310	3,360,128	100.00	-0.30
AMERICAS	226,141	200,876	244,812	259,294	267,831	7.97	3.29
North America	207,880	183,915	220,526	227,311	235,453	7.01	3.58
Canada	20,716	16,853	20,347	21,399	21,128	0.63	-1.27
United States of America	187,164	167,062	200,179	205,912	214,325	6.38	4.09
Other Americas	18,261	16,961	24,286	31,983	32,378	0.96	1.24
Other countries of the Americas	18,261	16,961	24,286	31,983	32,378	0.96	1.24
EAST ASIA AND THE PACIFIC	196,598	163,802	198,254	237,675	270,517	8.05	13.82
North-East Asia	102,046	93,959	109,934	126,528	135,876	4.04	7.39
China	45,343	42,739	52,201	69,226	74,199	2.21	7.18
Japan	47,731	43,039	46,286	44,416	48,507	1.44	9.21
Korea, Republic of	8,972	8,181	11,447	12,886	13,170	0.39	2.20
Australasia	21,838	18,456	21,944	22,941	24,902	0.74	8.55
Australia	18,747	16,332	19,878	20,763	22,650	0.67	9.09
New Zealand	3,091	2,124	2,066	2,178	2,252	0.07	3.40
Other East Asia and the Pacific	72,714	51,387	66,376	88,206	109,739	3.27	24.41
Other countries of Asia	72,714	51,387	66,376	88,206	109,739	3.27	24.41
EUROPE	2,288,461	2,421,540	2,521,029	2,459,976	2,426,006	72.20	-1.38
Central/Eastern Europe	183,208	189,146	179,559	179,833	204,649	6.09	13.80
Czech Republic	10,560	9,897	11,314	11,618	13,688	0.41	17.82
Estonia	9,224	9,608	11,969	11,271	12,602	0.38	11.81
Hungary	8,317	9,582	8,274	9,811	9,582	0.29	-2.33
Latvia	6,618	10,574	6,877	7,468	9,469	0.28	26.79
Lithuania	5,804	13,456	7,677	8,140	10,820	0.32	32.92
Poland	42,881	51,701	36,894	43,873	53,778	1.60	22.58
Russian Federation	96,148	77,655	92,395	83,604	90,456	2.69	8.20
Slovakia	3,656	6,673	4,159	4,048	4,254	0.13	5.09
Northern Europe	1,165,610	1,263,558	1,308,856	1,254,600	1,281,551	38.14	2.15
Denmark	214,057	285,185	273,437	247,121	230,969	6.87	-6.54
Finland	159,670	173,405	185,440	171,935	182,661	5.44	6.24
Iceland	7,686	6,060	7,923	7,159	8,401	0.25	17.35
Ireland	15,881	13,488	11,918	14,563	16,144	0.48	10.86
Norway	480,897	528,083	566,916	552,421	587,487	17.48	6.35
United Kingdom	287,419	257,337	263,222	261,401	255,889	7.62	-2.11
Southern Europe	198,200	225,569	228,353	215,510	171,376	5.10	-20.48
Greece	12,121	12,230	11,389	10,352	8,437	0.25	-18.50
Italy	105,344	130,668	127,241	120,853	95,269	2.84	-21.17
Portugal	10,778	9,134	9,627	9,555	8,779	0.26	-8.12
Spain	69,957	73,537	80,096	74,750	58,891	1.75	-21.22
Western Europe	662,997	684,771	755,932	758,930	717,336	21.35	-5.48
Austria	27,238	31,219	35,835	42,322	31,159	0.93	-26.38
Belgium	33,274	35,719	40,554	42,877	42,873	1.28	-0.01
France	94,479	97,857	107,588	104,211	99,650	2.97	-4.38
Germany	367,632	373,038	407,418	404,026	385,735	11.48	-4.53
Luxembourg	3,308	3,346	3,496	3,675	3,191	0.09	-13.17
Netherlands	86,463	87,303	95,210	95,055	85,969	2.56	-9.56
Switzerland	50,603	56,289	65,831	66,764	68,759	2.05	2.99
East Mediterranean Europe	9,888	7,938	9,599	10,081	11,590	0.34	14.97
Turkey	9,888	7,938	9,599	10,081	11,590	0.34	14.97
Other Europe	68,558	50,558	38,730	41,022	39,504	1.18	-3.70
Other countries of Europe	68,558	50,558	38,730	41,022	39,504	1.18	-3.70
NOT SPECIFIED	232,961	258,129	320,518	413,365	395,774	11.78	-4.26
Other countries of the World	232,961	258,129	320,518	413,365	395,774	11.78	-4.26

Yearbook of Tourism Statistics, Data 2008 – 2012, 2014 Edition

SWEDEN

4. Arrivals of non-resident tourists in all types of accommodation establishments, by country of residence

	2008	2009	2010	2011	2012	Market share 2012	% Change 2012-2011
TOTAL	4,554,936	4,678,402	4,951,122	5,005,825	4,943,808	100.00	-1.24
AMERICAS	239,202	212,567	257,437	272,807	250,884	5.07	-8.04
North America	218,089	193,153	230,018	236,819	218,332	4.42	-7.81
Canada	23,059	18,882	22,581	23,374	21,309	0.43	-8.83
United States of America	195,030	174,271	207,437	213,445	197,023	3.99	-7.69
Other Americas	21,113	19,414	27,419	35,988	32,552	0.66	-9.55
Other countries of the Americas	21,113	19,414	27,419	35,988	32,552	0.66	-9.55
EAST ASIA AND THE PACIFIC	216,443	182,862	216,885	257,236	263,800	5.34	2.55
North-East Asia	109,151	101,555	116,496	133,713	129,936	2.63	-2.82
China	49,229	47,011	55,548	73,331	71,333	1.44	-2.72
Japan	50,020	45,549	48,377	46,718	45,723	0.92	-2.13
Korea, Republic of	9,902	8,995	12,571	13,664	12,880	0.26	-5.74
Australasia	26,838	22,368	26,372	27,080	28,512	0.58	5.29
Australia	23,038	19,703	23,771	24,434	25,943	0.52	6.18
New Zealand	3,800	2,665	2,601	2,646	2,569	0.05	-2.91
Other East Asia and the Pacific	80,454	58,939	74,017	96,443	105,352	2.13	9.24
Other countries of Asia	80,454	58,939	74,017	96,443	105,352	2.13	9.24
EUROPE	3,847,867	4,005,127	4,143,159	4,048,017	4,072,481	82.38	0.60
Central/Eastern Europe	237,691	241,560	232,753	245,017	271,559	5.49	10.83
Czech Republic	16,260	14,404	15,711	17,056	18,055	0.37	5.86
Estonia	12,902	12,320	17,151	17,041	17,558	0.36	3.03
Hungary	10,608	11,296	9,849	11,052	10,875	0.22	-1.60
Latvia	9,716	13,359	11,791	11,947	15,161	0.31	26.90
Lithuania	8,751	16,400	12,863	14,763	16,967	0.34	14.93
Poland	72,469	80,607	59,875	76,542	97,390	1.97	27.24
Russian Federation	101,863	82,499	99,613	91,120	90,379	1.83	-0.81
Slovakia	5,122	10,675	5,900	5,496	5,174	0.10	-5.86
Northern Europe	2,000,824	2,161,939	2,264,641	2,174,404	2,265,337	45.82	4.18
Denmark	418,369	519,792	488,207	412,303	396,631	8.02	-3.80
Finland	198,775	213,152	225,682	211,278	208,396	4.22	-1.36
Iceland	8,403	6,636	8,817	7,897	8,090	0.16	2.44
Ireland	17,755	14,776	15,220	18,106	17,053	0.34	-5.82
Norway	1,042,636	1,128,207	1,238,771	1,238,971	1,385,191	28.02	11.80
United Kingdom	314,886	279,376	287,944	285,849	249,976	5.06	-12.55
Southern Europe	232,966	254,502	256,180	242,983	177,114	3.58	-27.11
Greece	12,748	12,852	12,041	11,072	8,150	0.16	-26.39
Italy	123,977	148,798	143,673	136,170	98,737	2.00	-27.49
Portugal	15,995	11,039	11,513	11,421	9,236	0.19	-19.13
Spain	80,246	81,813	88,953	84,320	60,991	1.23	-27.67
Western Europe	1,261,002	1,254,487	1,325,184	1,318,307	1,285,156	26.00	-2.51
Austria	32,291	36,883	46,735	53,520	38,309	0.77	-28.42
Belgium	36,467	39,181	50,599	52,145	48,621	0.98	-6.76
France	123,584	126,640	136,683	135,116	122,780	2.48	-9.13
Germany	738,470	727,792	749,480	752,248	756,097	15.29	0.51
Luxembourg	3,629	3,491	3,941	4,106	3,179	0.06	-22.58
Netherlands	249,630	236,199	239,601	219,626	213,833	4.33	-2.64
Switzerland	76,931	84,301	98,145	101,546	102,337	2.07	0.78
East Mediterranean Europe	10,684	8,836	10,538	10,799	11,233	0.23	4.02
Turkey	10,684	8,836	10,538	10,799	11,233	0.23	4.02
Other Europe	104,700	83,803	53,863	56,507	62,082	1.26	9.87
Other countries of Europe	104,700	83,803	53,863	56,507	62,082	1.26	9.87
NOT SPECIFIED	251,424	277,846	333,641	427,765	356,643	7.21	-16.63
Other countries of the World	251,424	277,846	333,641	427,765	356,643	7.21	-16.63

Yearbook of Tourism Statistics, Data 2008 – 2012, 2014 Edition

SWEDEN

5. Overnight stays of non-resident tourists in hotels and similar establishments, by country of residence

	2008	2009	2010	2011	2012	Market share 2012	% Change 2012-2011
TOTAL	5,830,414	6,087,096	6,363,074	6,532,078	6,650,445	100.00	1.81
AMERICAS	447,436	401,648	474,260	502,542	530,098	7.97	5.48
North America	411,192	367,735	427,211	440,556	466,014	7.01	5.78
Canada	41,111	33,698	39,417	41,474	41,817	0.63	0.83
United States of America	370,081	334,037	387,794	399,082	424,197	6.38	6.29
South America	12,362	13,730	22,459	26,386	34,796	0.52	31.87
Brazil	12,362	13,730	22,459	26,386	34,796	0.52	31.87
Other Americas	23,882	20,183	24,590	35,600	29,288	0.44	-17.73
Other countries of the Americas	23,882	20,183	24,590	35,600	29,288	0.44	-17.73
EAST ASIA AND THE PACIFIC	349,226	290,423	339,085	460,646	535,415	8.05	16.23
North-East Asia	201,999	187,869	212,967	245,228	268,929	4.04	9.66
China	89,731	85,456	101,125	134,169	146,856	2.21	9.46
Japan	94,545	86,055	89,667	86,084	96,006	1.44	11.53
Korea, Republic of	17,723	16,358	22,175	24,975	26,067	0.39	4.37
Australasia	43,219	36,902	42,512	44,464	49,287	0.74	10.85
Australia	37,064	32,656	38,509	40,242	44,830	0.67	11.40
New Zealand	6,155	4,246	4,003	4,222	4,457	0.07	5.57
Other East Asia and the Pacific	104,008	65,652	83,606	170,954	217,199	3.27	27.05
Other countries of Asia	104,008	65,652	83,606	170,954	217,199	3.27	27.05
EUROPE	4,531,093	4,841,808	4,883,830	4,766,504	4,802,840	72.22	0.76
Central/Eastern Europe	372,865	389,877	363,460	365,352	428,825	6.45	17.37
Bulgaria	2,848	3,657	4,496	3,570	4,803	0.07	34.54
Czech Republic	20,996	19,788	21,918	22,518	27,092	0.41	20.31
Estonia	18,298	19,210	23,186	21,844	24,942	0.38	14.18
Hungary	16,521	19,159	16,029	19,015	18,964	0.29	-0.27
Latvia	13,178	21,143	13,323	14,474	18,742	0.28	29.49
Lithuania	11,503	26,905	14,872	15,777	21,416	0.32	35.74
Poland	85,165	103,375	71,472	85,031	106,438	1.60	25.18
Romania	6,251	8,029	11,116	13,242	18,975	0.29	43.29
Russian Federation	190,837	155,269	178,991	162,035	179,033	2.69	10.49
Slovakia	7,268	13,342	8,057	7,846	8,420	0.13	7.32
Northern Europe	2,308,336	2,526,451	2,535,563	2,431,572	2,536,474	38.14	4.31
Denmark	424,351	570,220	529,712	478,952	457,140	6.87	-4.55
Finland	316,162	346,719	359,242	333,232	361,526	5.44	8.49
Iceland	15,319	12,116	15,348	13,875	16,627	0.25	19.83
Ireland	31,555	26,969	23,088	28,225	31,952	0.48	13.20
Norway	950,086	1,055,889	1,098,250	1,070,661	1,162,768	17.48	8.60
United Kingdom	570,863	514,538	509,923	506,627	506,461	7.62	-0.03
Southern Europe	395,396	458,961	447,732	423,750	345,213	5.19	-18.53
Greece	24,001	24,454	22,064	20,063	16,698	0.25	-16.77
Italy	208,562	261,268	246,496	234,228	188,559	2.84	-19.50
Malta	651	1,937	1,650	2,151	2,288	0.03	6.37
Portugal	21,338	18,264	18,650	18,518	17,375	0.26	-6.17
Slovenia	2,206	6,003	3,708	3,916	3,735	0.06	-4.62
Spain	138,638	147,035	155,164	144,874	116,558	1.75	-19.55
Western Europe	1,310,833	1,369,182	1,464,420	1,470,899	1,419,769	21.35	-3.48
Austria	53,881	62,421	69,421	82,025	61,671	0.93	-24.81
Belgium	65,974	71,419	78,563	83,101	84,856	1.28	2.11
France	187,169	195,663	208,424	201,973	197,230	2.97	-2.35
Germany	725,778	745,879	789,265	783,052	763,455	11.48	-2.50
Luxembourg	6,593	6,691	6,773	7,122	6,316	0.09	-11.32
Netherlands	171,240	174,560	184,444	184,229	170,152	2.56	-7.64
Switzerland	100,198	112,549	127,530	129,397	136,089	2.05	5.17
East Mediterranean Europe	21,071	17,829	20,051	21,968	25,394	0.38	15.60
Cyprus	1,387	1,958	1,455	2,430	2,454	0.04	0.99

SWEDEN

5. Overnight stays of non-resident tourists in hotels and similar establishments, by country of residence

	2008	2009	2010	2011	2012	Market share 2012	% Change 2012-2011
Turkey	19,684	15,871	18,596	19,538	22,940	0.34	17.41
Other Europe	**122,592**	**79,508**	**52,604**	**52,963**	**47,165**	**0.71**	**-10.95**
Other countries of Europe	122,592	79,508	52,604	52,963	47,165	0.71	-10.95
SOUTH ASIA	**40,376**	**37,095**	**44,981**	**64,082**	**97,794**	**1.47**	**52.61**
India	40,376	37,095	44,981	64,082	97,794	1.47	52.61
NOT SPECIFIED	**462,283**	**516,122**	**620,918**	**738,304**	**684,298**	**10.29**	**-7.31**
Other countries of the World	462,283	516,122	620,918	738,304	684,298	10.29	-7.31

Yearbook of Tourism Statistics, Data 2008 – 2012, 2014 Editio

SWEDEN

6. Overnight stays of non-resident tourists in all types of accommodation establishments, by country of residence

	2008	2009	2010	2011	2012	Market share 2012	% Change 2012-2011
TOTAL	12,495,002	12,872,513	12,802,832	12,880,617	12,774,599	100.00	-0.82
AMERICAS	484,970	436,557	512,699	544,031	575,365	4.50	5.76
North America	440,770	395,329	456,360	470,110	500,964	3.92	6.56
Canada	47,617	39,725	46,579	47,351	48,828	0.38	3.12
United States of America	393,153	355,604	409,781	422,759	452,136	3.54	6.95
South America			27,746	33,833	39,907	0.31	17.95
Brazil			27,746	33,833	39,907	0.31	17.95
Other Americas	44,200	41,228	28,593	40,088	34,494	0.27	-13.95
Other countries of the Americas	44,200	41,228	28,593	40,088	34,494	0.27	-13.95
EAST ASIA AND THE PACIFIC	445,370	383,393	380,880	442,123	495,873	3.88	12.16
North-East Asia	222,226	210,077	232,317	266,589	297,339	2.33	11.53
China	100,819	97,950	111,126	146,432	163,377	1.28	11.57
Japan	100,991	93,433	95,764	92,891	104,519	0.82	12.52
Korea, Republic of	20,416	18,694	25,427	27,266	29,443	0.23	7.98
Australasia	57,408	48,667	55,499	56,929	65,450	0.51	14.97
Australia	49,295	42,869	49,947	51,331	59,509	0.47	15.93
New Zealand	8,113	5,798	5,552	5,598	5,941	0.05	6.13
Other East Asia and the Pacific	165,736	124,649	93,064	118,605	133,084	1.04	12.21
Other countries of Asia	165,736	124,649	93,064	118,605	133,084	1.04	12.21
EUROPE	10,927,210	11,466,606	11,182,645	10,966,570	10,775,192	84.35	-1.75
Central/Eastern Europe	524,965	595,374	588,742	630,186	727,419	5.69	15.43
Bulgaria			6,482	7,159	6,189	0.05	-13.55
Czech Republic	37,009	34,183	37,528	42,163	46,817	0.37	11.04
Estonia	28,661	46,760	54,609	49,506	55,452	0.43	12.01
Hungary	22,931	24,722	20,781	22,844	24,913	0.20	9.06
Latvia	21,843	36,179	33,086	31,672	35,928	0.28	13.44
Lithuania	19,828	34,227	31,226	36,952	38,906	0.30	5.29
Poland	176,921	202,070	151,466	201,409	239,854	1.88	19.09
Romania			15,455	19,015	33,203	0.26	74.61
Russian Federation	206,394	192,284	225,015	207,306	232,565	1.82	12.18
Slovakia	11,378	24,949	13,094	12,160	13,592	0.11	11.78
Northern Europe	5,610,662	6,119,642	5,896,321	5,654,279	5,651,356	44.24	-0.05
Denmark	1,348,399	1,620,559	1,538,968	1,279,661	1,187,530	9.30	-7.20
Finland	475,634	521,606	527,349	502,313	523,312	4.10	4.18
Iceland	17,675	14,005	18,225	16,302	18,664	0.15	14.49
Ireland	36,709	30,917	32,862	39,009	39,302	0.31	0.75
Norway	3,084,018	3,332,729	3,176,610	3,219,249	3,294,129	25.79	2.33
United Kingdom	648,227	599,826	602,307	597,745	588,419	4.61	-1.56
Southern Europe	491,745	537,056	533,667	511,463	415,250	3.25	-18.81
Greece	25,778	26,338	24,035	22,218	18,637	0.15	-16.12
Italy	262,240	315,110	296,578	282,609	227,832	1.78	-19.38
Malta			1,879	2,681	2,583	0.02	-3.66
Portugal	36,112	23,838	24,132	24,009	21,202	0.17	-11.69
Slovenia			4,915	5,848	4,925	0.04	-15.78
Spain	167,615	171,770	182,128	174,098	140,071	1.10	-19.54
Western Europe	4,040,355	3,990,862	4,050,886	4,057,515	3,859,749	30.21	-4.87
Austria	68,266	85,106	106,959	121,685	94,745	0.74	-22.14
Belgium	74,894	84,331	113,525	116,752	115,644	0.91	-0.95
France	270,828	281,848	297,748	296,988	283,738	2.22	-4.46
Germany	2,690,148	2,619,562	2,598,505	2,649,661	2,553,629	19.99	-3.62
Luxembourg	7,689	7,755	8,441	8,538	7,725	0.06	-9.52
Netherlands	750,975	704,576	685,834	619,614	551,697	4.32	-10.96
Switzerland	177,555	207,684	239,874	244,277	252,571	1.98	3.40
East Mediterranean Europe	21,790	18,447	22,923	24,181	28,223	0.22	16.72
Cyprus			1,610	2,529	2,523	0.02	-0.24

719

SWEDEN

6. Overnight stays of non-resident tourists in all types of accommodation establishments, by country of residence

	2008	2009	2010	2011	2012	Market share 2012	% Change 2012-2011
Turkey	21,790	18,447	21,313	21,652	25,700	0.20	18.70
Other Europe	**237,693**	**205,225**	**90,106**	**88,946**	**93,195**	**0.73**	**4.78**
Other countries of Europe	237,693	205,225	90,106	88,946	93,195	0.73	4.78
SOUTH ASIA			**57,789**	**76,993**	**107,801**	**0.84**	**40.01**
India			57,789	76,993	107,801	0.84	40.01
NOT SPECIFIED	**637,452**	**585,957**	**668,819**	**850,900**	**820,368**	**6.42**	**-3.59**
Other countries of the World	637,452	585,957	668,819	850,900	820,368	6.42	-3.59

Yearbook of Tourism Statistics, Data 2008 – 2012, 2014 Edition

SWITZERLAND

3. Arrivals of non-resident tourists in hotels and similar establishments, by country of residence

		2008	2009	2010	2011	2012	Market share 2012	% Change 2012-2011
TOTAL	(*)	8,608,337	8,293,918	8,628,284	8,534,305	8,566,037	100.00	0.37
AFRICA		88,625	79,919	77,745	74,107	81,655	0.95	10.19
North Africa		19,755	17,881	15,931	15,931	20,176	0.24	26.65
All countries of North Africa	(*)	19,755	17,881	15,931	15,931	20,176	0.24	26.65
Southern Africa		26,897	20,263	22,695	23,457	23,028	0.27	-1.83
South Africa		26,897	20,263	22,695	23,457	23,028	0.27	-1.83
Other Africa		41,973	41,775	39,119	34,719	38,451	0.45	10.75
Other countries of Africa		41,973	41,775	39,119	34,719	38,451	0.45	10.75
AMERICAS		878,356	820,495	916,493	924,383	952,018	11.11	2.99
North America		746,720	701,100	778,988	787,365	808,271	9.44	2.66
Canada		94,844	91,222	98,772	99,509	101,350	1.18	1.85
Mexico					18,895	19,879	0.23	5.21
United States of America		651,876	609,878	680,216	668,961	687,042	8.02	2.70
South America		96,715	91,213	105,286	120,704	127,156	1.48	5.35
Argentina		10,962	11,359	12,957	14,634	15,313	0.18	4.64
Brazil		59,662	55,991	66,845	79,080	84,167	0.98	6.43
Chile		4,530	4,299	4,655	5,472	5,660	0.07	3.44
Other countries of South America		21,561	19,564	20,829	21,518	22,016	0.26	2.31
Other Americas		34,921	28,182	32,219	16,314	16,591	0.19	1.70
Other countries of the Americas		34,921	28,182	32,219	16,314	16,591	0.19	1.70
EAST ASIA AND THE PACIFIC		841,465	873,877	1,073,702	1,300,226	1,490,662	17.40	14.65
North-East Asia		558,075	600,652	761,743	951,757	1,107,025	12.92	16.31
China		129,176	187,138	286,420	452,724	575,326	6.72	27.08
Hong Kong, China		26,676	37,125	46,051	50,610	59,683	0.70	17.93
Japan		277,657	275,505	297,562	275,923	295,991	3.46	7.27
Korea, Republic of		91,973	71,517	94,110	115,733	122,772	1.43	6.08
Taiwan, Province of China		32,593	29,367	37,600	56,767	53,253	0.62	-6.19
South-East Asia		168,583	173,649	196,967	226,663	253,071	2.95	11.65
Indonesia		11,049	15,930	19,660	30,691	35,695	0.42	16.30
Malaysia		15,793	15,429	21,618	25,557	29,278	0.34	14.56
Philippines		3,825	4,736	6,214	7,499	8,172	0.10	8.97
Singapore		42,268	52,171	51,431	55,310	70,565	0.82	27.58
Thailand		44,879	44,680	51,907	56,919	60,107	0.70	5.60
Other countries of South-East Asia		50,769	40,703	46,137	50,687	49,254	0.57	-2.83
Australasia				98,374	106,439	113,783	1.33	6.90
Australia				98,374	106,439	113,783	1.33	6.90
Other East Asia and the Pacific		114,807	99,576	16,618	15,367	16,783	0.20	9.21
Other countries of Oceania				16,618	15,367	16,783	0.20	9.21
All countries of Oceania		114,807	99,576					
EUROPE		6,520,802	6,249,760	6,237,359	5,867,915	5,612,190	65.52	-4.36
Central/Eastern Europe		372,432	367,959	389,001	412,380	434,806	5.08	5.44
Baltic countries		21,370	16,603					
Belarus		4,480	5,236	6,254	5,932	5,476	0.06	-7.69
Bulgaria		17,530	15,632	14,970	14,449	13,820	0.16	-4.35
Czech Republic		42,045	40,060	42,106	42,803	43,291	0.51	1.14
Estonia				7,568	7,185	7,503	0.09	4.43
Hungary		32,475	34,351	35,030	33,746	33,219	0.39	-1.56
Latvia				4,053	5,726	5,338	0.06	-6.78
Lithuania				5,382	6,072	6,272	0.07	3.29
Poland		50,325	46,920	51,020	49,148	48,060	0.56	-2.21
Romania		40,596	30,153	30,561	30,523	30,079	0.35	-1.45
Russian Federation		130,853	145,751	157,085	179,168	201,488	2.35	12.46
Slovakia		12,658	12,128	11,634	12,323	12,549	0.15	1.83
Ukraine		20,100	21,125	23,338	25,305	27,711	0.32	9.51

721

SWITZERLAND

3. Arrivals of non-resident tourists in hotels and similar establishments, by country of residence

	2008	2009	2010	2011	2012	Market share 2012	% Change 2012-2011
Northern Europe	1,105,124	950,924	997,306	942,073	907,705	10.60	-3.65
Denmark	62,708	59,504	59,916	57,611	52,815	0.62	-8.32
Finland	38,243	38,736	40,149	38,342	36,353	0.42	-5.19
Iceland	7,210	5,531	4,689	5,020	4,940	0.06	-1.59
Ireland	38,772	32,018	30,499	28,805	29,064	0.34	0.90
Norway	41,250	39,427	44,873	43,975	43,638	0.51	-0.77
Sweden	91,222	84,299	85,130	86,203	81,605	0.95	-5.33
United Kingdom	825,719	691,409	732,050	682,117	659,290	7.70	-3.35
Southern Europe	904,821	885,438	867,142	840,908	819,444	9.57	-2.55
Croatia	11,772	11,183	10,369	9,717	10,714	0.13	10.26
Greece	49,724	51,162	44,591	41,097	33,426	0.39	-18.67
Italy	552,953	546,564	520,542	489,182	482,940	5.64	-1.28
Malta			3,266	3,395	2,875	0.03	-15.32
Portugal	53,075	43,061	44,723	46,284	46,765	0.55	1.04
Serbia			10,179	11,025	12,656	0.15	14.79
Serbia and Montenegro	11,006	9,944					
Slovenia	10,926	10,902	12,161	11,105	10,524	0.12	-5.23
Spain	215,365	212,622	221,311	229,103	219,544	2.56	-4.17
Western Europe	3,917,745	3,861,998	3,815,056	3,515,558	3,284,685	38.35	-6.57
Austria	189,159	187,528	195,190	190,153	187,368	2.19	-1.46
Belgium	246,741	241,830	240,784	215,240	203,768	2.38	-5.33
France	670,663	685,842	700,578	680,932	669,344	7.81	-1.70
Germany	2,344,337	2,294,411	2,237,941	2,038,680	1,871,498	21.85	-8.20
Liechtenstein	12,942	12,180	13,044	12,398	12,278	0.14	-0.97
Luxembourg	41,344	43,254	44,480	40,563	37,875	0.44	-6.63
Netherlands	412,559	396,953	383,039	337,592	302,554	3.53	-10.38
East Mediterranean Europe	101,987	93,046	100,333	104,291	109,951	1.28	5.43
Cyprus			3,322	3,342	3,791	0.04	13.44
Israel	64,099	61,915	61,183	64,756	68,474	0.80	5.74
Turkey	37,888	31,131	35,828	36,193	37,686	0.44	4.13
Other Europe	118,693	90,395	68,521	52,705	55,599	0.65	5.49
Other countries of Europe	118,693	90,395	68,521	52,705	55,599	0.65	5.49
MIDDLE EAST	146,982	133,545	156,986	167,050	211,649	2.47	26.70
Bahrain				5,044	7,281	0.08	44.35
Egypt	12,074	11,548	11,430	11,423	11,851	0.14	3.75
Kuwait				15,368	17,779	0.21	15.69
Oman				3,815	7,436	0.09	94.91
Qatar				13,876	17,238	0.20	24.23
Saudi Arabia				47,672	65,472	0.76	37.34
United Arab Emirates				47,267	59,998	0.70	26.93
Other countries of Middle East	134,908	121,997	145,556	22,585	24,594	0.29	8.90
SOUTH ASIA	132,107	136,322	165,999	200,624	217,863	2.54	8.59
India	132,107	136,322	165,999	200,624	217,863	2.54	8.59

Yearbook of Tourism Statistics, Data 2008 – 2012, 2014 Edition

SWITZERLAND

5. Overnight stays of non-resident tourists in hotels and similar establishments, by country of residence

		2008	2009	2010	2011	2012	Market share 2012	% Change 2012-2011
TOTAL	(*)	21,508,296	20,164,425	20,442,508	19,733,889	19,076,238	100.00	-3.33
AFRICA		260,608	232,588	228,776	243,150	265,533	1.39	9.21
North Africa		64,927	52,474	46,627	51,124	66,259	0.35	29.60
All countries of North Africa	(*)	64,927	52,474	46,627	51,124	66,259	0.35	29.60
Southern Africa		80,286	60,549	63,678	67,438	69,934	0.37	3.70
South Africa		80,286	60,549	63,678	67,438	69,934	0.37	3.70
Other Africa		115,395	119,565	118,471	124,588	129,340	0.68	3.81
Other countries of Africa		115,395	119,565	118,471	124,588	129,340	0.68	3.81
AMERICAS		2,081,131	1,908,158	2,086,735	2,115,099	2,159,916	11.32	2.12
North America		1,731,779	1,590,209	1,731,575	1,765,488	1,805,045	9.46	2.24
Canada		213,403	207,353	225,140	228,137	231,642	1.21	1.54
Mexico					45,220	48,225	0.25	6.65
United States of America		1,518,376	1,382,856	1,506,435	1,492,131	1,525,178	8.00	2.21
South America		259,360	240,950	269,240	305,527	310,449	1.63	1.61
Argentina		31,129	31,573	33,417	37,851	37,274	0.20	-1.52
Brazil		159,058	144,977	168,771	194,492	201,298	1.06	3.50
Chile		12,333	12,063	11,737	13,898	14,472	0.08	4.13
Other countries of South America		56,840	52,337	55,315	59,286	57,405	0.30	-3.17
Other Americas		89,992	76,999	85,920	44,084	44,422	0.23	0.77
Other countries of the Americas		89,992	76,999	85,920	44,084	44,422	0.23	0.77
EAST ASIA AND THE PACIFIC		1,554,044	1,535,073	1,824,939	2,115,976	2,359,424	12.37	11.51
North-East Asia		944,841	958,220	1,174,915	1,399,029	1,589,737	8.33	13.63
China		214,349	271,717	404,218	595,264	743,656	3.90	24.93
Hong Kong, China		51,077	61,506	73,207	81,956	92,043	0.48	12.31
Japan		493,901	474,720	507,138	479,743	509,757	2.67	6.26
Korea, Republic of		137,376	106,700	135,377	167,866	172,467	0.90	2.74
Taiwan, Province of China		48,138	43,577	54,975	74,200	71,814	0.38	-3.22
South-East Asia		353,537	359,533	396,998	446,297	484,977	2.54	8.67
Indonesia		25,779	32,546	38,327	55,797	64,347	0.34	15.32
Malaysia		40,708	35,348	44,590	50,573	57,018	0.30	12.74
Philippines		14,065	14,877	17,138	18,651	20,508	0.11	9.96
Singapore		88,382	106,260	104,563	109,974	129,970	0.68	18.18
Thailand		76,200	73,278	85,851	93,402	101,281	0.53	8.44
Other countries of South-East Asia		108,403	97,224	106,529	117,900	111,853	0.59	-5.13
Australasia				217,688	235,603	247,930	1.30	5.23
Australia				217,688	235,603	247,930	1.30	5.23
Other East Asia and the Pacific		255,666	217,320	35,338	35,047	36,780	0.19	4.94
Other countries of Oceania				35,338	35,047	36,780	0.19	4.94
All countries of Oceania		255,666	217,320					
EUROPE		16,782,796	15,694,888	15,381,336	14,272,892	13,189,024	69.14	-7.59
Central/Eastern Europe		1,098,062	1,046,029	1,077,998	1,148,374	1,191,385	6.25	3.75
Baltic countries		53,289	43,645					
Belarus		12,861	14,978	17,161	15,010	15,101	0.08	0.61
Bulgaria		41,434	37,741	38,124	38,356	39,422	0.21	2.78
Czech Republic		102,449	101,882	104,170	105,436	107,324	0.56	1.79
Estonia				20,244	16,349	17,046	0.09	4.26
Hungary		81,665	82,413	83,597	84,364	86,876	0.46	2.98
Latvia				11,585	15,057	14,633	0.08	-2.82
Lithuania				12,736	14,275	15,748	0.08	10.32
Poland		134,238	134,546	143,288	150,097	140,502	0.74	-6.39
Romania		114,351	78,822	83,536	86,785	80,182	0.42	-7.61
Russian Federation		456,995	454,525	467,884	513,754	561,490	2.94	9.29
Slovakia		33,634	33,433	29,822	36,284	35,498	0.19	-2.17
Ukraine		67,146	64,044	65,851	72,607	77,563	0.41	6.83

723

SWITZERLAND

5. Overnight stays of non-resident tourists in hotels and similar establishments, by country of residence

	2008	2009	2010	2011	2012	Market share 2012	% Change 2012-2011
Northern Europe	**2,958,265**	**2,480,438**	**2,480,756**	**2,313,644**	**2,114,638**	**11.09**	**-8.60**
Denmark	142,897	134,697	137,162	133,762	120,158	0.63	-10.17
Finland	93,304	96,478	97,015	95,284	85,410	0.45	-10.36
Iceland	16,386	11,983	10,966	11,494	10,504	0.06	-8.61
Ireland	97,271	82,296	72,489	65,265	63,722	0.33	-2.36
Norway	100,788	93,270	108,990	104,576	102,690	0.54	-1.80
Sweden	225,918	205,494	200,577	203,516	187,918	0.99	-7.66
United Kingdom	2,281,701	1,856,220	1,853,557	1,699,747	1,544,236	8.10	-9.15
Southern Europe	**1,961,676**	**1,893,828**	**1,836,482**	**1,760,959**	**1,692,792**	**8.87**	**-3.87**
Croatia	31,633	29,599	26,664	26,760	30,219	0.16	12.93
Greece	128,565	125,956	115,528	101,562	81,523	0.43	-19.73
Italy	1,157,902	1,137,588	1,074,447	1,007,519	971,776	5.09	-3.55
Malta			11,521	10,228	7,784	0.04	-23.90
Portugal	127,719	104,800	107,642	110,019	109,833	0.58	-0.17
Serbia			24,706	27,696	29,059	0.15	4.92
Serbia and Montenegro	28,508	24,387					
Slovenia	25,217	24,317	26,150	25,712	27,929	0.15	8.62
Spain	462,132	447,181	449,824	451,463	434,669	2.28	-3.72
Western Europe	**10,235,755**	**9,830,381**	**9,571,896**	**8,669,586**	**7,794,023**	**40.86**	**-10.10**
Austria	412,777	403,871	413,575	400,266	378,277	1.98	-5.49
Belgium	829,194	775,090	742,277	678,517	620,658	3.25	-8.53
France	1,439,158	1,433,452	1,449,278	1,394,166	1,318,460	6.91	-5.43
Germany	6,313,240	6,031,325	5,816,520	5,207,892	4,625,384	24.25	-11.19
Liechtenstein	29,954	26,092	26,379	26,286	24,638	0.13	-6.27
Luxembourg	130,592	134,243	134,324	115,021	99,970	0.52	-13.09
Netherlands	1,080,840	1,026,308	989,543	847,438	726,636	3.81	-14.25
East Mediterranean Europe	**270,814**	**238,768**	**254,090**	**262,197**	**272,681**	**1.43**	**4.00**
Cyprus			9,622	9,234	9,493	0.05	2.80
Israel	170,456	161,799	155,512	163,041	168,392	0.88	3.28
Turkey	100,358	76,969	88,956	89,922	94,796	0.50	5.42
Other Europe	**258,224**	**205,444**	**160,114**	**118,132**	**123,505**	**0.65**	**4.55**
Other countries of Europe	258,224	205,444	160,114	118,132	123,505	0.65	4.55
MIDDLE EAST	**502,417**	**469,438**	**527,870**	**526,332**	**627,459**	**3.29**	**19.21**
Bahrain				13,510	25,253	0.13	86.92
Egypt	40,529	37,958	38,801	37,097	38,001	0.20	2.44
Kuwait				47,769	50,219	0.26	5.13
Oman				12,631	19,625	0.10	55.37
Qatar				40,154	53,952	0.28	34.36
Saudi Arabia				163,968	201,061	1.05	22.62
United Arab Emirates				140,577	168,732	0.88	20.03
Other countries of Middle East	461,888	431,480	489,069	70,626	70,616	0.37	-0.01
SOUTH ASIA	**327,300**	**324,280**	**392,852**	**460,440**	**474,882**	**2.49**	**3.14**
India	327,300	324,280	392,852	460,440	474,882	2.49	3.14

Yearbook of Tourism Statistics, Data 2008 – 2012, 2014 Edition

SYRIAN ARAB REPUBLIC

2. Arrivals of non-resident visitors at national borders, by nationality

		2008	2009	2010	2011	2012	Market share 2012	% Change 2012-2011
TOTAL	(*)	6,950,852	7,720,795	10,969,682	6,476,408			
AFRICA		85,242	76,245	89,670	46,654			
North Africa		85,242	76,245	89,670	46,654			
Algeria		35,231	31,238	37,664	22,463			
Morocco		9,257	8,610	10,009	5,385			
Sudan		21,989	20,378	23,636	9,359			
Tunisia		18,765	16,019	18,361	9,447			
AMERICAS		75,375	84,293	96,601	36,817			
North America		62,773	71,523	81,839	28,909			
Canada		20,236	22,869	26,068	10,972			
United States of America		42,537	48,654	55,771	17,937			
South America		12,602	12,770	14,762	7,908			
Argentina		1,215	1,419	2,149	544			
Brazil		3,368	3,518	4,979	1,715			
Venezuela		8,019	7,833	7,634	5,649			
EAST ASIA AND THE PACIFIC		52,913	60,349	78,102	31,442			
North-East Asia		14,661	17,203	25,887	9,254			
China		6,336	8,296	12,526	6,080			
Japan		8,325	8,907	13,361	3,174			
South-East Asia		22,709	24,511	29,723	14,201			
Indonesia		18,800	19,134	21,802	10,227			
Malaysia		3,909	5,377	7,921	3,974			
Australasia		15,543	18,635	22,492	7,987			
Australia		13,896	16,867	20,349	7,378			
New Zealand		1,647	1,768	2,143	609			
EUROPE		904,726	1,141,584	1,959,035	1,467,615			
Central/Eastern Europe		81,105	94,001	99,657	41,753			
Bulgaria		4,919	4,611	5,090	2,571			
Czech Republic/Slovakia		4,348	4,476	5,190	1,639			
Hungary		4,800	4,204	4,237	2,159			
Poland		3,540	8,123	8,736	2,196			
Romania		5,328	5,469	6,131	2,945			
Ukraine		4,701	4,720	6,201	3,713			
USSR (former)		53,469	62,398	64,072	26,530			
Northern Europe		70,282	86,172	105,065	46,033			
Denmark		12,289	14,489	17,899	7,331			
Norway		4,556	5,513	7,709	3,952			
Sweden		21,807	27,137	31,412	13,538			
United Kingdom		31,630	39,033	48,045	21,212			
Southern Europe		56,465	67,943	83,529	19,153			
Greece		7,195	8,091	7,415	2,696			
Italy		24,871	33,331	44,608	9,393			
Spain		18,625	21,661	25,763	4,866			
Yugoslavia, SFR (former)		5,774	4,860	5,743	2,198			
Western Europe		125,384	150,393	201,223	67,112			
Austria		6,494	7,878	10,970	4,379			
Belgium		6,818	8,440	10,621	3,489			
France		40,487	51,086	68,515	19,697			
Germany		53,301	60,146	80,804	29,303			
Netherlands		12,627	15,936	21,206	7,794			
Switzerland		5,657	6,907	9,107	2,450			
East Mediterranean Europe		571,490	743,075	1,469,561	1,293,564			
Cyprus		8,658	9,943	9,981	3,194			
Turkey		562,832	733,132	1,459,580	1,290,370			

Yearbook of Tourism Statistics, Data 2008 – 2012, 2014 Edition

SYRIAN ARAB REPUBLIC

2. Arrivals of non-resident visitors at national borders, by nationality

		2008	2009	2010	2011	2012	Market share 2012	% Change 2012-2011
MIDDLE EAST		**4,390,535**	**4,711,686**	**6,191,855**	**3,112,533**			
Bahrain		65,808	75,695	80,382	23,215			
Egypt		45,060	49,092	56,771	22,643			
Iraq	(*)	889,463	894,477	1,006,434	1,000,895			
Jordan		1,044,564	1,062,990	1,949,551	560,132			
Kuwait		126,977	146,724	134,255	33,161			
Lebanon		1,587,115	1,815,003	2,291,802	1,262,398			
Libya		31,749	30,433	35,967	8,133			
Oman		13,650	11,592	13,822	3,009			
Palestine		92,751	51,687	35,520	37,360			
Qatar		18,001	19,267	17,357	3,901			
Saudi Arabia		403,140	476,346	484,087	134,397			
United Arab Emirates		45,187	52,536	57,064	11,077			
Yemen		22,519	21,747	24,570	10,206			
Other countries of Middle East		4,551	4,097	4,273	2,006			
SOUTH ASIA		**388,819**	**499,183**	**961,342**	**700,723**			
Afghanistan		1,090	1,432	4,229	15,928			
India		14,619	20,984	31,056	30,343			
Iran, Islamic Republic of		361,605	455,012	891,807	614,529			
Pakistan		11,505	21,755	34,250	39,923			
NOT SPECIFIED		**1,053,242**	**1,147,455**	**1,593,077**	**1,080,624**			
Other countries of the World		94,504	82,518	80,017	37,412			
Nationals Residing Abroad		958,738	1,064,937	1,513,060	1,043,212			

Yearbook of Tourism Statistics, Data 2008 – 2012, 2014 Edition

SYRIAN ARAB REPUBLIC

3. Arrivals of non-resident tourists in hotels and similar establishments, by nationality

		2008	2009	2010	2011	2012	Market share 2012	% Change 2012-2011
TOTAL	(*)	1,868,654	2,068,935	2,756,635	1,503,766			
AFRICA		47,414	42,409	50,167	17,913			
North Africa		47,414	42,409	50,167	17,913			
Algeria		25,244	21,762	24,108	6,073			
Morocco		3,734	3,822	5,619	2,577			
Sudan		8,316	8,132	10,575	4,187			
Tunisia		10,120	8,693	9,865	5,076			
AMERICAS		33,401	38,723	50,849	18,671			
North America		23,381	28,790	41,994	14,594			
Canada		10,523	11,516	10,960	4,613			
United States of America		12,858	17,274	31,034	9,981			
South America		10,020	9,933	8,855	4,077			
Argentina		1,008	1,150	1,335	314			
Brazil		2,998	3,002	3,219	1,021			
Venezuela		6,014	5,781	4,301	2,742			
EAST ASIA AND THE PACIFIC		38,274	43,456	49,473	19,421			
North-East Asia		12,045	13,669	17,535	6,281			
China		4,693	6,243	8,521	4,140			
Japan		7,352	7,426	9,014	2,141			
South-East Asia		18,311	19,451	18,180	8,254			
Indonesia		15,416	15,451	13,182	5,619			
Malaysia		2,895	4,000	4,998	2,635			
Australasia		7,918	10,336	13,758	4,886			
Australia		6,815	9,132	12,413	4,501			
New Zealand		1,103	1,204	1,345	385			
EUROPE		330,815	397,613	538,926	301,682			
Central/Eastern Europe		51,880	66,636	68,407	22,226			
Bulgaria		3,689	3,481	3,416	1,562			
Czech Republic/Slovakia		3,913	3,870	3,613	1,092			
Hungary		3,696	3,185	2,757	973			
Poland		2,478	5,869	6,049	1,521			
Romania		3,197	3,509	4,393	1,721			
Ukraine		3,526	3,560	4,148	2,098			
USSR (former)		31,381	43,162	44,031	13,259			
Northern Europe		48,482	57,772	58,553	25,660			
Denmark		9,217	10,555	9,996	4,094			
Norway		3,645	4,204	4,336	2,223			
Sweden		13,520	16,884	17,155	7,393			
United Kingdom		22,100	26,129	27,066	11,950			
Southern Europe		44,676	49,893	51,478	11,568			
Greece		4,596	5,116	4,160	1,512			
Italy		20,146	24,160	27,686	5,830			
Spain		15,373	16,807	15,572	2,941			
Yugoslavia, SFR (former)		4,561	3,810	4,060	1,285			
Western Europe		83,417	95,504	105,312	35,334			
Austria		5,130	5,931	5,981	2,387			
Belgium		5,480	6,449	5,986	2,133			
France		24,481	29,605	34,637	9,958			
Germany		36,901	39,253	41,968	15,219			
Netherlands		7,182	9,318	11,516	4,232			
Switzerland		4,243	4,948	5,224	1,405			
East Mediterranean Europe		102,360	127,808	255,176	206,894			
Cyprus		4,329	5,343	5,623	1,800			
Turkey		98,031	122,465	249,553	205,094			

Yearbook of Tourism Statistics, Data 2008 – 2012, 2014 Edition

SYRIAN ARAB REPUBLIC

3. Arrivals of non-resident tourists in hotels and similar establishments, by nationality

		2008	2009	2010	2011	2012	Market share 2012	% Change 2012-2011
MIDDLE EAST		1,092,522	1,101,986	1,164,219	539,598			
Bahrain		16,556	19,640	22,376	6,462			
Egypt		17,644	21,591	30,980	12,356			
Iraq	(*)	238,627	239,075	253,496	211,843			
Jordan		391,314	375,338	461,406	132,568			
Kuwait		18,326	22,378	25,827	6,379			
Lebanon		254,643	265,905	235,194	129,552			
Libya		18,752	17,106	16,734	3,784			
Oman		3,959	3,453	4,185	911			
Palestine		21,333	11,171	5,475	5,759			
Qatar		3,420	3,756	3,651	821			
Saudi Arabia		87,094	100,407	83,027	23,051			
United Arab Emirates		11,071	12,517	11,541	2,240			
Yemen		8,782	8,514	8,548	3,551			
Other countries of Middle East		1,001	1,135	1,779	321			
SOUTH ASIA		223,819	343,596	781,743	522,090			
Afghanistan		872	1,127	2,799	9,324			
India		6,428	10,018	16,326	15,951			
Iran, Islamic Republic of		210,287	321,725	748,986	480,925			
Pakistan		6,232	10,726	13,632	15,890			
NOT SPECIFIED		102,409	101,152	121,258	84,391			
Other countries of the World		52,079	45,247	41,828	19,557			
Nationals Residing Abroad		50,330	55,905	79,430	64,834			

728

SYRIAN ARAB REPUBLIC

4. Arrivals of non-resident tourists in all types of accommodation establishments, by nationality

		2008	2009	2010	2011	2012	Market share 2012	% Change 2012-2011
TOTAL	(*)	5,430,182	6,091,889	8,545,848	5,070,380			
AFRICA		75,953	68,159	79,745	41,519			
North Africa		75,953	68,159	79,745	41,519			
Algeria		32,784	28,882	34,149	20,367			
Morocco		8,486	7,742	8,756	4,711			
Sudan		19,800	18,486	21,206	8,397			
Tunisia		14,883	13,049	15,634	8,044			
AMERICAS		69,575	77,621	84,195	32,019			
North America		56,973	64,851	71,382	25,166			
Canada		20,236	22,380	22,235	9,359			
United States of America		36,737	42,471	49,147	15,807			
South America		12,602	12,770	12,813	6,853			
Argentina		1,215	1,419	1,841	466			
Brazil		3,368	3,518	4,380	1,509			
Venezuela		8,019	7,833	6,592	4,878			
EAST ASIA AND THE PACIFIC		49,521	56,937	66,696	26,800			
North-East Asia		14,048	16,517	22,560	8,076			
China		5,723	7,753	10,960	5,320			
Japan		8,325	8,764	11,600	2,756			
South-East Asia		22,709	24,449	24,896	11,896			
Indonesia		18,800	19,072	18,254	8,563			
Malaysia		3,909	5,377	6,642	3,333			
Australasia		12,764	15,971	19,240	6,828			
Australia		11,117	14,203	17,357	6,293			
New Zealand		1,647	1,768	1,883	535			
EUROPE		618,272	772,031	1,305,301	920,736			
Central/Eastern Europe		79,323	91,604	86,936	36,413			
Bulgaria		4,919	4,611	4,437	2,241			
Czech Republic/Slovakia		4,348	4,476	4,692	1,482			
Hungary		4,800	4,204	3,789	1,931			
Poland		3,540	8,123	7,633	1,919			
Romania		5,328	5,469	5,379	2,584			
Ukraine		4,701	4,720	5,387	3,226			
USSR (former)		51,687	60,001	55,619	23,030			
Northern Europe		66,568	82,233	92,455	40,516			
Denmark		12,289	14,489	15,805	6,473			
Norway		4,556	5,513	6,855	3,514			
Sweden		21,807	27,137	27,122	11,689			
United Kingdom		27,916	35,094	42,673	18,840			
Southern Europe		56,465	65,310	74,688	17,152			
Greece		7,195	8,040	6,575	2,391			
Italy		24,871	31,115	40,302	8,486			
Spain		18,625	21,295	22,538	4,257			
Yugoslavia, SFR (former)		5,774	4,860	5,273	2,018			
Western Europe		118,931	141,264	177,343	59,101			
Austria		6,494	7,878	9,455	3,774			
Belgium		6,818	8,440	9,464	3,109			
France		37,662	46,906	60,527	17,401			
Germany		51,251	56,690	71,430	25,903			
Netherlands		11,049	14,443	18,207	6,692			
Switzerland		5,657	6,907	8,260	2,222			
East Mediterranean Europe		296,985	391,620	873,879	767,554			
Cyprus		8,658	9,943	8,891	2,845			
Turkey		288,327	381,677	864,988	764,709			

Yearbook of Tourism Statistics, Data 2008 – 2012, 2014 Edition

SYRIAN ARAB REPUBLIC

4. Arrivals of non-resident tourists in all types of accommodation establishments, by nationality

		2008	2009	2010	2011	2012	Market share 2012	% Change 2012-2011
MIDDLE EAST		3,235,057	3,522,115	4,574,783	2,352,504			
Bahrain		65,302	75,059	70,169	20,265			
Egypt		41,032	45,154	50,171	20,011			
Iraq	(*)	795,424	806,118	897,975	893,033			
Jordan		869,586	882,750	1,363,644	391,793			
Kuwait		122,176	140,716	120,977	29,881			
Lebanon		727,553	921,762	1,467,701	808,457			
Libya		29,765	28,337	31,841	7,200			
Oman		13,650	11,592	12,299	2,677			
Palestine		85,331	47,943	32,502	34,185			
Qatar		18,001	19,053	15,173	3,410			
Saudi Arabia		395,884	467,095	435,663	120,953			
United Arab Emirates		44,283	50,794	51,521	10,001			
Yemen		22,519	21,747	21,585	8,966			
Other countries of Middle East		4,551	3,995	3,562	1,672			
SOUTH ASIA		355,431	467,012	853,065	621,327			
Afghanistan		1,090	1,432	3,719	14,008			
India		10,964	16,980	27,346	26,719			
Iran, Islamic Republic of		333,789	430,880	792,258	545,932			
Pakistan		9,588	17,720	29,742	34,668			
NOT SPECIFIED		1,026,373	1,128,014	1,582,063	1,075,475			
Other countries of the World		67,635	63,077	69,003	32,263			
Nationals Residing Abroad		958,738	1,064,937	1,513,060	1,043,212			

Yearbook of Tourism Statistics, Data 2008 – 2012, 2014 Edition

SYRIAN ARAB REPUBLIC

5. Overnight stays of non-resident tourists in hotels and similar establishments, by nationality

		2008	2009	2010	2011	2012	Market share 2012	% Change 2012-2011
TOTAL	(*)	10,686,192	11,530,321	12,869,132	5,471,525			
AFRICA		359,048	315,672	346,318	50,546			
North Africa		359,048	315,672	346,318	50,546			
Algeria		156,098	135,173	151,845	11,826			
Morocco		41,070	35,182	32,670	7,731			
Sudan		98,130	88,349	90,271	13,818			
Tunisia		63,750	56,968	71,532	17,171			
AMERICAS		257,556	286,050	312,612	59,267			
North America		210,424	238,008	265,883	47,135			
Canada		94,704	92,379	43,059	13,535			
United States of America		115,720	145,629	222,824	33,600			
South America		47,132	48,042	46,729	12,132			
Argentina		8,068	8,743	7,509	1,142			
Brazil		8,993	9,923	14,486	2,311			
Venezuela		30,071	29,376	24,734	8,679			
EAST ASIA AND THE PACIFIC		239,241	282,720	354,791	76,983			
North-East Asia		81,517	95,368	120,549	30,843			
China		44,757	55,557	64,974	25,420			
Japan		36,760	39,811	55,575	5,423			
South-East Asia		84,546	96,500	129,471	34,352			
Indonesia		61,664	66,469	96,982	23,531			
Malaysia		22,882	30,031	32,489	10,821			
Australasia		73,178	90,852	104,771	11,788			
Australia		70,419	86,229	94,345	10,858			
New Zealand		2,759	4,623	10,426	930			
EUROPE		2,087,088	2,517,393	2,876,047	805,497			
Central/Eastern Europe		478,204	646,934	615,671	74,727			
Bulgaria		29,514	27,628	26,477	3,866			
Czech Republic/Slovakia		35,219	33,660	27,999	2,899			
Hungary		25,872	23,256	22,283	2,691			
Poland		42,126	83,739	40,831	2,797			
Romania		38,362	37,246	27,821	5,941			
Ukraine		24,680	25,506	32,148	5,590			
USSR (former)		282,431	415,899	438,112	50,943			
Northern Europe		464,645	511,639	380,203	82,120			
Denmark		101,384	108,567	64,977	13,892			
Norway		25,514	29,040	28,184	7,261			
Sweden		94,642	116,687	111,507	27,644			
United Kingdom		243,105	257,345	175,535	33,323			
Southern Europe		280,149	325,657	379,635	33,167			
Greece		30,154	32,048	24,257	4,351			
Italy		130,389	163,353	212,372	16,585			
Spain		92,237	105,440	111,541	8,806			
Yugoslavia, SFR (former)		27,369	24,816	31,465	3,425			
Western Europe		570,676	653,571	706,883	97,710			
Austria		30,334	35,758	38,874	6,445			
Belgium		32,881	39,312	38,908	5,825			
France		215,986	249,341	242,494	26,523			
Germany		221,404	239,813	277,798	43,492			
Netherlands		50,271	63,965	74,852	11,042			
Switzerland		19,800	25,382	33,957	4,383			
East Mediterranean Europe		293,414	379,592	793,655	517,773			
Cyprus		21,645	29,380	36,552	5,606			
Turkey		271,769	350,212	757,103	512,167			

Yearbook of Tourism Statistics, Data 2008 – 2012, 2014 Edition

SYRIAN ARAB REPUBLIC

5. Overnight stays of non-resident tourists in hotels and similar establishments, by nationality

		2008	2009	2010	2011	2012	Market share 2012	% Change 2012-2011
MIDDLE EAST		5,778,506	5,454,032	3,593,764	1,932,302			
Bahrain		198,667	217,890	134,933	42,640			
Egypt		123,506	148,474	205,331	45,209			
Iraq	(*)	1,431,763	1,310,543	807,296	805,003			
Jordan		1,956,570	1,714,380	1,178,750	461,740			
Kuwait		109,958	129,934	128,760	32,497			
Lebanon		763,930	754,041	491,109	349,792			
Libya		143,824	130,139	123,616	12,487			
Oman		27,710	23,098	22,039	3,871			
Palestine		71,998	40,969	29,105	18,726			
Qatar		37,622	37,625	19,318	4,078			
Saudi Arabia		696,756	742,792	334,917	133,248			
United Arab Emirates		91,588	97,896	53,787	11,558			
Yemen		118,607	99,200	53,183	10,652			
Other countries of Middle East		6,007	7,051	11,620	801			
SOUTH ASIA		1,368,759	2,067,934	4,621,581	2,155,678			
Afghanistan		3,488	5,259	18,192	42,957			
India		57,848	83,094	114,183	72,230			
Iran, Islamic Republic of		1,261,723	1,903,989	4,362,885	1,971,794			
Pakistan		45,700	75,592	126,321	68,697			
NOT SPECIFIED		595,994	606,520	764,019	391,252			
Other countries of the World		253,891	226,522	224,119	55,355			
Nationals Residing Abroad		342,103	379,998	539,900	335,897			

732

SYRIAN ARAB REPUBLIC

6. Overnight stays of non-resident tourists in all types of accommodation establishments, by nationality

		2008	2009	2010	2011	2012	Market share 2012	% Change 2012-2011
TOTAL	(*)	73,492,019	77,128,427	84,775,969	47,618,777			
AFRICA		644,317	557,453	577,805	272,681			
North Africa		644,317	557,453	577,805	272,681			
Algeria		217,297	190,135	223,172	158,999			
Morocco		82,904	66,572	61,037	25,975			
Sudan		230,424	203,132	183,835	50,866			
Tunisia		113,692	97,614	109,761	36,841			
AMERICAS		553,725	641,010	638,403	184,279			
North America		493,507	575,466	568,469	156,127			
Canada		160,674	175,687	160,662	63,033			
United States of America		332,833	399,779	407,807	93,094			
South America		60,218	65,544	69,934	28,152			
Argentina		8,561	13,800	12,210	2,579			
Brazil		10,643	12,056	20,453	4,950			
Venezuela		41,014	39,688	37,271	20,623			
EAST ASIA AND THE PACIFIC		289,479	349,445	515,698	137,930			
North-East Asia		89,557	106,821	156,687	41,305			
China		49,392	61,829	92,175	33,759			
Japan		40,165	44,992	64,512	7,546			
South-East Asia		95,276	111,654	205,733	67,648			
Indonesia		67,116	74,117	154,240	52,063			
Malaysia		28,160	37,537	51,493	15,585			
Australasia		104,646	130,970	153,278	28,977			
Australia		100,619	124,211	138,104	26,723			
New Zealand		4,027	6,759	15,174	2,254			
EUROPE		5,822,270	6,552,963	7,841,108	4,535,014			
Central/Eastern Europe		753,618	963,078	969,868	360,228			
Bulgaria		32,711	32,391	39,959	12,759			
Czech Republic/Slovakia		36,088	36,962	42,256	8,065			
Hungary		27,749	26,616	33,438	13,249			
Poland		43,424	86,897	45,414	3,949			
Romania		45,288	44,728	42,070	18,047			
Ukraine		31,262	32,901	48,518	20,457			
USSR (former)		537,096	702,583	718,213	283,702			
Northern Europe		701,100	806,310	709,244	226,514			
Denmark		106,095	120,931	110,995	32,740			
Norway		30,164	37,046	48,144	17,494			
Sweden		238,132	278,004	190,479	61,680			
United Kingdom		326,709	370,329	359,626	114,600			
Southern Europe		370,093	452,260	558,428	79,054			
Greece		36,299	45,860	46,090	12,290			
Italy		207,287	250,671	289,004	32,722			
Spain		97,776	126,951	175,846	20,952			
Yugoslavia, SFR (former)		28,731	28,778	47,488	13,090			
Western Europe		1,045,810	1,192,710	1,339,266	302,988			
Austria		36,374	46,847	66,406	17,435			
Belgium		43,903	55,571	66,464	13,960			
France		356,290	423,885	524,644	107,636			
Germany		504,634	527,104	495,880	122,578			
Netherlands		80,213	104,078	127,865	30,526			
Switzerland		24,396	35,225	58,007	10,853			
East Mediterranean Europe		2,951,649	3,138,605	4,264,302	3,566,230			
Cyprus		71,789	79,000	62,440	13,890			
Turkey		2,879,860	3,059,605	4,201,862	3,552,340			

733

SYRIAN ARAB REPUBLIC

6. Overnight stays of non-resident tourists in all types of accommodation establishments, by nationality

		2008	2009	2010	2011	2012	Market share 2012	% Change 2012-2011
MIDDLE EAST		36,780,745	35,915,459	26,497,001	15,369,581			
Bahrain		842,723	938,829	636,653	187,541			
Egypt		833,358	763,315	343,228	100,209			
Iraq	(*)	12,790,415	11,669,785	7,200,257	7,793,504			
Jordan		6,565,378	6,054,940	5,873,743	1,810,674			
Kuwait		2,036,666	2,221,736	1,064,245	263,561			
Lebanon		6,535,025	6,935,404	6,430,478	3,621,387			
Libya		264,203	250,733	253,144	41,776			
Oman		135,943	111,914	77,069	15,851			
Palestine		873,807	497,498	328,655	333,794			
Qatar		300,077	296,611	114,806	25,539			
Saudi Arabia		4,527,367	5,105,003	3,485,226	1,007,868			
United Arab Emirates		591,103	665,615	493,833	96,977			
Yemen		378,026	324,652	165,983	57,508			
Other countries of Middle East		106,654	79,424	29,681	13,392			
SOUTH ASIA		1,816,380	2,517,819	5,209,221	2,957,846			
Afghanistan		3,815	6,158	27,330	86,080			
India		80,690	123,582	352,138	304,722			
Iran, Islamic Republic of		1,668,246	2,273,867	4,624,482	2,406,320			
Pakistan		63,629	114,212	205,271	160,724			
NOT SPECIFIED		27,585,103	30,594,278	43,496,733	24,161,446			
Other countries of the World		316,515	305,159	462,049	166,598			
Nationals Residing Abroad		27,268,588	30,289,119	43,034,684	23,994,848			

Yearbook of Tourism Statistics, Data 2008 – 2012, 2014 Edition

TAIWAN, PROVINCE OF CHINA

2. Arrivals of non-resident visitors at national borders, by country of residence

	2008	2009	2010	2011	2012	Market share 2012	% Change 2012-2011
TOTAL	3,845,187	4,395,004	5,567,277	6,087,484	7,311,470	100.00	20.11
AFRICA	8,499	7,735	8,254	8,938	8,865	0.12	-0.82
Southern Africa	4,904	4,009	4,066	4,709	4,222	0.06	-10.34
South Africa	4,904	4,009	4,066	4,709	4,222	0.06	-10.34
Other Africa	3,595	3,726	4,188	4,229	4,643	0.06	9.79
Other countries of Africa	3,595	3,726	4,188	4,229	4,643	0.06	9.79
AMERICAS	461,269	442,036	474,709	495,136	497,597	6.81	0.50
North America	449,656	431,183	462,610	482,172	484,353	6.62	0.45
Canada	60,236	60,138	64,739	67,545	70,614	0.97	4.54
Mexico	2,223	1,787	2,142	2,010	2,323	0.03	15.57
United States of America	387,197	369,258	395,729	412,617	411,416	5.63	-0.29
South America	5,066	4,491	5,090	5,163	5,142	0.07	-0.41
Argentina	884	873	984	968	1,045	0.01	7.95
Brazil	4,182	3,618	4,106	4,195	4,097	0.06	-2.34
Other Americas	6,547	6,362	7,009	7,801	8,102	0.11	3.86
Other countries of the Americas	6,547	6,362	7,009	7,801	8,102	0.11	3.86
EAST ASIA AND THE PACIFIC	3,121,838	3,690,485	4,817,622	5,297,032	6,512,815	89.08	22.95
North-East Asia	2,286,828	2,859,231	3,722,151	4,139,789	5,294,188	72.41	27.89
China	329,204	972,123	1,630,735	1,784,185	2,586,428	35.37	44.96
Hong Kong, China	618,667	718,806	794,362	817,944	1,016,356	13.90	24.26
Japan	1,086,691	1,000,661	1,080,153	1,294,758	1,432,315	19.59	10.62
Korea, Republic of	252,266	167,641	216,901	242,902	259,089	3.54	6.66
South-East Asia	725,751	689,027	911,174	1,071,975	1,132,592	15.49	5.65
Indonesia	110,420	106,612	123,834	156,281	163,598	2.24	4.68
Malaysia	155,783	166,987	285,734	307,898	341,032	4.66	10.76
Philippines	87,936	77,206	87,944	101,539	105,130	1.44	3.54
Singapore	205,449	194,523	241,334	299,599	327,253	4.48	9.23
Thailand	84,586	78,405	92,949	102,902	97,712	1.34	-5.04
Viet Nam					89,354	1.22	
Other countries of South-East Asia	81,577	65,294	79,379	103,756	8,513	0.12	-91.80
Australasia	67,310	65,158	70,898	69,503	74,331	1.02	6.95
Australia	58,199	57,147	62,254	60,067	63,597	0.87	5.88
New Zealand	9,111	8,011	8,644	9,436	10,734	0.15	13.76
Other East Asia and the Pacific	41,949	77,069	113,399	15,765	11,704	0.16	-25.76
Other countries of Asia	40,704	76,054	112,344	14,728	10,621	0.15	-27.89
Other countries of Oceania	1,245	1,015	1,055	1,037	1,083	0.01	4.44
EUROPE	200,914	197,070	203,301	212,148	218,045	2.98	2.78
Central/Eastern Europe			5,457	6,667	7,066	0.10	5.98
Russian Federation			5,457	6,667	7,066	0.10	5.98
Northern Europe	54,854	50,822	50,949	50,402	49,904	0.68	-0.99
Sweden	6,463	6,007	6,519	6,983	7,128	0.10	2.08
United Kingdom	48,391	44,815	44,430	43,419	42,776	0.59	-1.48
Southern Europe	19,524	19,237	19,274	19,732	20,287	0.28	2.81
Greece	1,358	1,348	1,258	1,129	1,192	0.02	5.58
Italy	12,752	12,237	12,246	12,407	12,932	0.18	4.23
Spain	5,414	5,652	5,770	6,196	6,163	0.08	-0.53
Western Europe	92,222	91,917	98,894	105,801	110,262	1.51	4.22
Austria	5,161	4,968	5,806	6,368	5,609	0.08	-11.92
Belgium	4,166	4,492	4,435	4,348	4,781	0.07	9.96
France	24,164	25,245	26,455	29,082	31,452	0.43	8.15
Germany	40,309	39,533	42,446	44,644	45,054	0.62	0.92
Netherlands	12,126	11,230	13,158	14,401	15,797	0.22	9.69
Switzerland	6,296	6,449	6,594	6,958	7,569	0.10	8.78

Yearbook of Tourism Statistics, Data 2008 – 2012, 2014 Edition

TAIWAN, PROVINCE OF CHINA

2. Arrivals of non-resident visitors at national borders, by country of residence

	2008	2009	2010	2011	2012	Market share 2012	% Change 2012-2011
Other Europe	**34,314**	**35,094**	**28,727**	**29,546**	**30,526**	**0.42**	**3.32**
Other countries of Europe	34,314	35,094	28,727	29,546	30,526	0.42	3.32
MIDDLE EAST	**12,524**	**12,217**	**13,542**	**13,791**	**13,032**	**0.18**	**-5.50**
All countries of Middle East	12,524	12,217	13,542	13,791	13,032	0.18	-5.50
SOUTH ASIA	**19,976**	**18,555**	**23,849**	**23,927**	**23,251**	**0.32**	**-2.83**
India	19,976	18,555	23,849	23,927	23,251	0.32	-2.83
NOT SPECIFIED	**20,167**	**26,906**	**26,000**	**36,512**	**37,865**	**0.52**	**3.71**
Other countries of the World	20,167	26,906	26,000	36,512	37,865	0.52	3.71

Yearbook of Tourism Statistics, Data 2008 – 2012, 2014 Edition

TAIWAN, PROVINCE OF CHINA

4. Arrivals of non-resident tourists in all types of accommodation establishments, by country of residence

	2008	2009	2010	2011	2012	Market share 2012	% Change 2012-2011
TOTAL	3,368,990	3,899,831	5,061,513	5,519,231	6,735,639	100.00	22.04
AFRICA	6,860	6,277	6,645	6,634	6,932	0.10	4.49
Southern Africa	3,668	3,086	3,066	3,246	3,079	0.05	-5.14
South Africa	3,668	3,086	3,066	3,246	3,079	0.05	-5.14
Other Africa	3,192	3,191	3,579	3,388	3,853	0.06	13.72
Other countries of Africa	3,192	3,191	3,579	3,388	3,853	0.06	13.72
AMERICAS	426,806	403,374	435,573	447,827	458,296	6.80	2.34
North America	417,105	394,748	425,735	437,624	447,409	6.64	2.24
Canada	53,174	52,611	57,285	60,033	64,840	0.96	8.01
Mexico	1,899	1,291	1,816	1,716	2,032	0.03	18.41
United States of America	362,032	340,846	366,634	375,875	380,537	5.65	1.24
South America	4,479	3,696	4,337	4,542	4,645	0.07	2.27
Argentina	810	728	814	836	875	0.01	4.67
Brazil	3,669	2,968	3,523	3,706	3,770	0.06	1.73
Other Americas	5,222	4,930	5,501	5,661	6,242	0.09	10.26
Other countries of the Americas	5,222	4,930	5,501	5,661	6,242	0.09	10.26
EAST ASIA AND THE PACIFIC	2,716,482	3,270,919	4,389,655	4,819,702	6,018,906	89.36	24.88
North-East Asia	1,900,934	2,684,917	3,577,379	3,929,895	5,084,050	75.48	29.37
China		860,075	1,548,139	1,666,562	2,456,742	36.47	47.41
Hong Kong, China	590,820	690,933	768,217	789,520	988,231	14.67	25.17
Japan	1,065,467	975,832	1,052,541	1,242,652	1,392,557	20.67	12.06
Korea, Republic of	244,647	158,077	208,482	231,161	246,520	3.66	6.64
South-East Asia	485,498	488,637	689,941	783,390	858,359	12.74	9.57
Indonesia	42,264	43,472	54,229	70,444	75,161	1.12	6.70
Malaysia	144,345	153,344	271,956	287,318	317,937	4.72	10.66
Philippines	35,849	36,422	42,704	47,245	52,852	0.78	11.87
Singapore	200,519	189,115	235,754	290,029	317,568	4.71	9.50
Thailand	38,670	42,156	53,751	53,794	55,561	0.82	3.28
Other countries of South-East Asia	23,851	24,128	31,547	34,560	39,280	0.58	13.66
Australasia	57,267	55,994	60,684	60,783	66,770	0.99	9.85
Australia	49,050	48,726	52,864	52,483	57,007	0.85	8.62
New Zealand	8,217	7,268	7,820	8,300	9,763	0.14	17.63
Other East Asia and the Pacific	272,783	41,371	61,651	45,634	9,727	0.14	-78.68
Other countries of Asia	271,616	40,441	60,728	44,716	8,788	0.13	-80.35
Other countries of Oceania	1,167	930	923	918	939	0.01	2.29
EUROPE	179,001	170,053	179,090	186,429	194,470	2.89	4.31
Central/Eastern Europe			4,479	5,700	6,212	0.09	8.98
Russian Federation			4,479	5,700	6,212	0.09	8.98
Northern Europe	48,217	43,004	44,231	44,541	45,263	0.67	1.62
Sweden	6,013	5,705	6,046	6,405	6,643	0.10	3.72
United Kingdom	42,204	37,299	38,185	38,136	38,620	0.57	1.27
Southern Europe	16,864	15,884	17,500	18,043	18,567	0.28	2.90
Greece	1,156	1,056	985	886	930	0.01	4.97
Italy	10,861	10,231	11,270	11,602	12,045	0.18	3.82
Spain	4,847	4,597	5,245	5,555	5,592	0.08	0.67
Western Europe	83,982	80,401	87,815	92,622	97,975	1.45	5.78
Austria	4,552	4,145	4,733	5,269	4,879	0.07	-7.40
Belgium	3,684	3,870	3,850	3,916	4,326	0.06	10.47
France	22,197	22,332	23,716	25,644	28,070	0.42	9.46
Germany	36,654	34,231	38,358	39,566	40,360	0.60	2.01
Netherlands	11,133	9,966	11,044	11,853	13,316	0.20	12.34
Switzerland	5,762	5,857	6,114	6,374	7,024	0.10	10.20
Other Europe	29,938	30,764	25,065	25,523	26,453	0.39	3.64
Other countries of Europe	29,938	30,764	25,065	25,523	26,453	0.39	3.64

Yearbook of Tourism Statistics, Data 2008 – 2012, 2014 Edition

TAIWAN, PROVINCE OF CHINA

4. Arrivals of non-resident tourists in all types of accommodation establishments, by country of residence

	2008	2009	2010	2011	2012	Market share 2012	% Change 2012-2011
MIDDLE EAST	**11,851**	**11,349**	**12,630**	**12,709**	**12,021**	**0.18**	**-5.41**
All countries of Middle East	11,851	11,349	12,630	12,709	12,021	0.18	-5.41
SOUTH ASIA	**17,233**	**15,841**	**19,702**	**20,192**	**19,560**	**0.29**	**-3.13**
India	17,233	15,841	19,702	20,192	19,560	0.29	-3.13
NOT SPECIFIED	**10,757**	**22,018**	**18,218**	**25,738**	**25,454**	**0.38**	**-1.10**
Other countries of the World	10,757	22,018	18,218	25,738	25,454	0.38	-1.10

Yearbook of Tourism Statistics, Data 2008 – 2012, 2014 Edition

TAIWAN, PROVINCE OF CHINA

6. Overnight stays of non-resident tourists in all types of accommodation establishments, by country of residence

	2008	2009	2010	2011	2012	Market share 2012	% Change 2012-2011
TOTAL	24,607,223	27,948,655	35,754,330	38,934,884	46,297,554	100.00	18.91
AFRICA	94,415	75,930	78,195	80,527	88,656	0.19	10.09
Southern Africa	59,750	43,869	38,613	43,382	44,400	0.10	2.35
South Africa	59,750	43,869	38,613	43,382	44,400	0.10	2.35
Other Africa	34,665	32,061	39,582	37,145	44,256	0.10	19.14
Other countries of Africa	34,665	32,061	39,582	37,145	44,256	0.10	19.14
AMERICAS	4,708,755	4,434,211	4,585,544	4,751,009	4,980,712	10.76	4.83
North America	4,585,583	4,323,272	4,468,060	4,624,435	4,837,156	10.45	4.60
Canada	556,732	521,194	536,943	604,594	692,612	1.50	14.56
Mexico	17,536	12,617	17,031	17,611	19,101	0.04	8.46
United States of America	4,011,315	3,789,461	3,914,086	4,002,230	4,125,443	8.91	3.08
South America	53,344	43,478	47,356	51,043	55,637	0.12	9.00
Argentina	11,462	10,396	11,430	13,021	12,097	0.03	-7.10
Brazil	41,882	33,082	35,926	38,022	43,540	0.09	14.51
Other Americas	69,828	67,461	70,128	75,531	87,919	0.19	16.40
Other countries of the Americas	69,828	67,461	70,128	75,531	87,919	0.19	16.40
EAST ASIA AND THE PACIFIC	17,910,005	21,552,207	29,053,026	31,740,080	38,555,010	83.28	21.47
North-East Asia	9,162,728	15,570,102	21,360,551	23,423,166	30,553,443	65.99	30.44
China		6,832,027	11,902,626	13,162,258	18,477,125	39.91	40.38
Hong Kong, China	2,638,293	2,995,864	3,305,994	3,463,681	4,329,675	9.35	25.00
Japan	5,427,141	4,925,098	5,178,283	5,751,580	6,566,496	14.18	14.17
Korea, Republic of	1,097,294	817,113	973,648	1,045,647	1,180,147	2.55	12.86
South-East Asia	4,720,651	4,480,228	5,703,915	6,425,003	7,239,102	15.64	12.67
Indonesia	666,059	640,284	691,853	823,093	864,958	1.87	5.09
Malaysia	1,145,073	1,173,741	1,896,448	2,045,601	2,367,082	5.11	15.72
Philippines	489,967	433,040	449,484	475,826	563,575	1.22	18.44
Singapore	1,384,341	1,320,923	1,592,265	1,877,456	2,077,679	4.49	10.66
Thailand	451,356	411,026	469,501	511,492	528,641	1.14	3.35
Other countries of South-East Asia	583,855	501,214	604,364	691,535	837,167	1.81	21.06
Australasia	439,250	442,571	490,904	540,125	604,918	1.31	12.00
Australia	359,070	365,122	402,031	433,424	479,424	1.04	10.61
New Zealand	80,180	77,449	88,873	106,701	125,494	0.27	17.61
Other East Asia and the Pacific	3,587,376	1,059,306	1,497,656	1,351,786	157,547	0.34	-88.35
Other countries of Asia	3,576,031	1,049,739	1,487,441	1,340,780	145,243	0.31	-89.17
Other countries of Oceania	11,345	9,567	10,215	11,006	12,304	0.03	11.79
EUROPE	1,556,794	1,548,243	1,572,059	1,773,600	2,020,577	4.36	13.93
Central/Eastern Europe			53,825	63,643	68,612	0.15	7.81
Russian Federation			53,825	63,643	68,612	0.15	7.81
Northern Europe	374,340	355,294	362,450	397,677	439,223	0.95	10.45
Sweden	58,801	55,755	56,026	62,597	72,393	0.16	15.65
United Kingdom	315,539	299,539	306,424	335,080	366,830	0.79	9.48
Southern Europe	125,834	124,658	140,488	149,958	176,970	0.38	18.01
Greece	7,331	7,611	5,489	5,596	6,806	0.01	21.62
Italy	76,026	75,003	85,206	90,127	103,344	0.22	14.66
Spain	42,477	42,044	49,793	54,235	66,820	0.14	23.20
Western Europe	816,867	801,080	809,994	925,038	1,070,040	2.31	15.68
Austria	44,248	44,478	44,963	52,033	55,001	0.12	5.70
Belgium	28,783	34,721	32,004	34,896	41,753	0.09	19.65
France	241,823	245,079	247,128	293,062	357,413	0.77	21.96
Germany	358,131	336,545	344,795	375,832	405,408	0.88	7.87
Netherlands	88,835	85,530	86,415	109,376	137,816	0.30	26.00
Switzerland	55,047	54,727	54,689	59,839	72,649	0.16	21.41
Other Europe	239,753	267,211	205,302	237,284	265,732	0.57	11.99
Other countries of Europe	239,753	267,211	205,302	237,284	265,732	0.57	11.99

Yearbook of Tourism Statistics, Data 2008 – 2012, 2014 Edition

TAIWAN, PROVINCE OF CHINA

6. Overnight stays of non-resident tourists in all types of accommodation establishments, by country of residence

	2008	2009	2010	2011	2012	Market share 2012	% Change 2012-2011
MIDDLE EAST	87,149	85,839	92,117	101,194	90,554	0.20	-10.51
All countries of Middle East	87,149	85,839	92,117	101,194	90,554	0.20	-10.51
SOUTH ASIA	189,068	165,749	189,515	199,597	234,762	0.51	17.62
India	189,068	165,749	189,515	199,597	234,762	0.51	17.62
NOT SPECIFIED	61,037	86,476	183,874	288,877	327,283	0.71	13.29
Other countries of the World	61,037	86,476	183,874	288,877	327,283	0.71	13.29

Yearbook of Tourism Statistics, Data 2008 – 2012, 2014 Edition

TAJIKISTAN

2. Arrivals of non-resident visitors at national borders, by country of residence

	2008	2009	2010	2011	2012	Market share 2012	% Change 2012-2011
TOTAL	325,420	207,439	159,680	183,154	244,275	100.00	33.37
AFRICA	27	129	188		32	0.01	
East Africa					7	0.00	
Kenya					7	0.00	
Central Africa	1						
Cameroon	1						
North Africa					9	0.00	
Algeria					9	0.00	
Southern Africa	26	129	188		16	0.01	
South Africa	26	129	188		16	0.01	
AMERICAS	1,265	1,334	1,465	587	1,085	0.44	84.84
North America	1,263	1,321	1,415	573	1,047	0.43	82.72
Canada	190	203	221	161	178	0.07	10.56
Mexico	3	4	6		21	0.01	
United States of America	1,070	1,114	1,188	412	848	0.35	105.83
South America	2	13	50	14	38	0.02	171.43
Argentina		13	24	13	13	0.01	0.00
Brazil				1	15	0.01	1,400.00
Colombia	2		26		10	0.00	
EAST ASIA AND THE PACIFIC	2,919	3,384	3,546	4,280	4,616	1.89	7.85
North-East Asia	2,674	3,130	3,208	4,196	4,411	1.81	5.12
China	1,522	2,437	2,694	3,788	4,105	1.68	8.37
Japan	716	369	294	90	109	0.04	21.11
Korea, Dem. People's Republic of	434	311	200	318	182	0.07	-42.77
Mongolia		13	20		15	0.01	
Taiwan, Province of China	2						
South-East Asia	80	84	128	43	51	0.02	18.60
Indonesia	14	21	36	31	9	0.00	-70.97
Malaysia	11	19	33	3	24	0.01	700.00
Philippines	20	12	8		9	0.00	
Singapore		5	8	5	4	0.00	-20.00
Thailand	1	27	43	4			
Viet Nam	34				5	0.00	
Australasia	165	170	210	41	154	0.06	275.61
Australia	152	136	128	36	130	0.05	261.11
New Zealand	13	34	82	5	24	0.01	380.00
EUROPE	309,659	188,760	139,902	167,069	222,816	91.22	33.37
Central/Eastern Europe	303,215	182,883	134,795	164,184	217,578	89.07	32.52
Armenia	213	283	328	343	345	0.14	0.58
Azerbaijan	349	328	315	708	698	0.29	-1.41
Belarus	70	342	796	785	1,675	0.69	113.38
Bulgaria	29	17	23	5	13	0.01	160.00
Czech Republic	83	70	74	77	109	0.04	41.56
Estonia	19	30	39	58	3	0.00	-94.83
Georgia	91	136	184	669	444	0.18	-33.63
Hungary	15	35	46	1	36	0.01	3,500.00
Kazakhstan	4,394	3,956	3,464	3,694	5,792	2.37	56.79
Kyrgyzstan	33,328	29,675	24,079	7,799	53,437	21.88	585.18
Latvia	19	103	138	112	83	0.03	-25.89
Lithuania	161	55			48	0.02	
Poland	106	137	152	154	87	0.04	-43.51
Republic of Moldova	184	176	171	971	1,644	0.67	69.31
Romania	3	14	17	22	41	0.02	86.36
Russian Federation	22,103	22,556	21,138	18,490	38,461	15.74	108.01
Slovakia	46	49	52	36	32	0.01	-11.11

Yearbook of Tourism Statistics, Data 2008 – 2012, 2014 Edition

TAJIKISTAN

2. Arrivals of non-resident visitors at national borders, by country of residence

	2008	2009	2010	2011	2012	Market share 2012	% Change 2012-2011
Turkmenistan	1,288	832	756	727	497	0.20	-31.64
Ukraine	477	607	773	3,035	5,968	2.44	96.64
Uzbekistan	240,237	123,482	82,250	126,498	108,165	44.28	-14.49
Northern Europe	**649**	**847**	**955**	**513**	**1,208**	**0.49**	**135.48**
Denmark	7	76	99	55	40	0.02	-27.27
Finland	35	57	65	22	28	0.01	27.27
Iceland					20	0.01	
Ireland	89	70	57	22	2	0.00	-90.91
Norway	15	47	53	27	29	0.01	7.41
Sweden	168	235	300	60	31	0.01	-48.33
United Kingdom	335	362	381	327	1,058	0.43	223.55
Southern Europe	**489**	**515**	**551**	**246**	**364**	**0.15**	**47.97**
Bosnia and Herzegovina					25	0.01	
Croatia	2		3		11	0.00	
Greece	22	13			20	0.01	
Holy See	1						
Italy	301	346	372	189	124	0.05	-34.39
Portugal	6	5			9	0.00	
Serbia	77	41	28	2	10	0.00	400.00
Slovenia					1	0.00	
Spain	78	95	111	43	164	0.07	281.40
TFYR of Macedonia	2	15	37	12			
Western Europe	**3,182**	**2,582**	**2,117**	**1,465**	**2,009**	**0.82**	**37.13**
Austria	124	103	120	135	79	0.03	-41.48
Belgium	135	179	234	76	149	0.06	96.05
France	1,674	1,067	542	448	409	0.17	-8.71
Germany	1,012	985	975	570	1,067	0.44	87.19
Luxembourg	2						
Netherlands	77	107	118	95	71	0.03	-25.26
Switzerland	158	141	128	141	234	0.10	65.96
East Mediterranean Europe	**2,124**	**1,933**	**1,484**	**661**	**1,657**	**0.68**	**150.68**
Israel	102	76	43	41	84	0.03	104.88
Turkey	2,022	1,857	1,441	620	1,573	0.64	153.71
MIDDLE EAST	**225**	**202**	**170**	**56**	**1,001**	**0.41**	**1,687.50**
Egypt	105	63	27		35	0.01	
Iraq	90	36			16	0.01	
Jordan		8	19				
Lebanon	1	13	22		1	0.00	
Saudi Arabia	3	30	19	17	893	0.37	5,152.94
Syrian Arab Republic	3	16	24	10	55	0.02	450.00
United Arab Emirates	23	36	59	29			
Yemen					1	0.00	
SOUTH ASIA	**11,325**	**13,630**	**14,409**	**11,162**	**14,725**	**6.03**	**31.92**
Afghanistan	8,010	10,536	11,456	5,790	8,476	3.47	46.39
Bangladesh		27	48	1	18	0.01	1,700.00
India	495	227	254	121	128	0.05	5.79
Iran, Islamic Republic of	2,462	2,437	2,387	5,199	5,853	2.40	12.58
Nepal	2	18	40	3	3	0.00	0.00
Pakistan	356	385	224	46	245	0.10	432.61
Sri Lanka				2	2	0.00	0.00

Yearbook of Tourism Statistics, Data 2008 – 2012, 2014 Edition

THAILAND

1. Arrivals of non-resident tourists at national borders, by nationality

	2008	2009	2010	2011	2012	Market share 2012	% Change 2012-2011
TOTAL	14,584,220	14,149,841	15,936,400	19,230,470	22,353,903	100.00	16.24
AFRICA	119,000	112,403	127,930	137,907	155,544	0.70	12.79
Southern Africa	48,566	43,277	57,100	68,496	76,326	0.34	11.43
South Africa	48,566	43,277	57,100	68,496	76,326	0.34	11.43
Other Africa	70,434	69,126	70,830	69,411	79,218	0.35	14.13
Other countries of Africa	70,434	69,126	70,830	69,411	79,218	0.35	14.13
AMERICAS	909,017	853,380	844,644	952,519	1,083,433	4.85	13.74
North America	849,997	796,556	780,185	876,104	987,992	4.42	12.77
Canada	180,900	169,482	168,393	194,356	219,354	0.98	12.86
United States of America	669,097	627,074	611,792	681,748	768,638	3.44	12.75
South America	23,937	25,108	30,682	37,530	48,240	0.22	28.54
Argentina	7,132	7,458	10,292	12,970	17,853	0.08	37.65
Brazil	16,805	17,650	20,390	24,560	30,387	0.14	23.73
Other Americas	35,083	31,716	33,777	38,885	47,201	0.21	21.39
Other countries of the Americas	35,083	31,716	33,777	38,885	47,201	0.21	21.39
EAST ASIA AND THE PACIFIC	8,395,969	7,813,650	8,956,796	11,279,400	13,571,969	60.71	20.33
North-East Asia	3,600,741	3,081,733	3,607,034	4,714,867	6,192,086	27.70	31.33
China	826,660	777,508	1,122,219	1,721,247	2,786,860	12.47	61.91
Hong Kong, China	337,827	318,762	316,476	411,834	473,666	2.12	15.01
Japan	1,153,868	1,004,453	993,674	1,127,893	1,373,716	6.15	21.79
Korea, Republic of	889,210	618,227	805,445	1,006,283	1,163,619	5.21	15.64
Taiwan, Province of China	393,176	362,783	369,220	447,610	394,225	1.76	-11.93
South-East Asia	3,971,429	3,968,579	4,534,235	5,594,577	6,281,153	28.10	12.27
Brunei Darussalam	9,055	8,353	7,073	7,471	10,459	0.05	39.99
Cambodia	85,790	96,586	146,274	265,903	423,642	1.90	59.32
Indonesia	247,930	227,205	286,072	370,795	447,820	2.00	20.77
Lao People's Democratic Republic	621,564	655,034	715,345	891,950	975,999	4.37	9.42
Malaysia	1,805,332	1,757,813	2,058,956	2,500,280	2,554,397	11.43	2.16
Myanmar	71,902	79,279	90,179	110,671	129,385	0.58	16.91
Philippines	221,506	217,705	246,430	268,375	289,566	1.30	7.90
Singapore	570,047	563,575	603,538	682,364	831,215	3.72	21.81
Viet Nam	338,303	363,029	380,368	496,768	618,670	2.77	24.54
Australasia	792,367	735,103	787,410	930,947	1,044,112	4.67	12.16
Australia	694,473	646,705	698,046	829,855	930,241	4.16	12.10
New Zealand	97,894	88,398	89,364	101,092	113,871	0.51	12.64
Other East Asia and the Pacific	31,432	28,235	28,117	39,009	54,618	0.24	40.01
Other countries of Asia	29,468	25,878	25,895	36,422	51,975	0.23	42.70
Other countries of Oceania	1,964	2,357	2,222	2,587	2,643	0.01	2.16
EUROPE	4,092,889	4,170,872	4,558,425	5,226,499	5,780,170	25.86	10.59
Central/Eastern Europe	488,149	518,212	856,350	1,295,073	1,597,540	7.15	23.36
Russian Federation	324,120	336,965	644,678	1,054,187	1,316,564	5.89	24.89
Other countries Central/East Europe	164,029	181,247	211,672	240,886	280,976	1.26	16.64
Northern Europe	1,721,603	1,680,183	1,654,908	1,735,846	1,769,253	7.91	1.92
Denmark	149,683	144,834	152,398	164,096	167,499	0.75	2.07
Finland	155,143	156,000	146,946	157,046	154,919	0.69	-1.35
Ireland	73,380	65,530	57,515	58,945	60,305	0.27	2.31
Norway	124,600	121,575	132,108	136,931	148,796	0.67	8.66
Sweden	392,274	350,819	355,214	373,856	364,681	1.63	-2.45
United Kingdom	826,523	841,425	810,727	844,972	873,053	3.91	3.32
Southern Europe	239,882	245,467	235,445	281,252	313,844	1.40	11.59
Italy	159,513	170,105	168,203	185,869	200,703	0.90	7.98
Spain	80,369	75,362	67,242	95,383	113,141	0.51	18.62
Western Europe	1,434,432	1,520,427	1,591,325	1,675,492	1,847,357	8.26	10.26
Austria	80,561	85,786	90,026	89,242	94,667	0.42	6.08

743

THAILAND

1. Arrivals of non-resident tourists at national borders, by nationality

	2008	2009	2010	2011	2012	Market share 2012	% Change 2012-2011
Belgium	76,132	80,420	80,000	82,610	94,896	0.42	14.87
France	398,407	427,067	461,670	515,572	576,106	2.58	11.74
Germany	542,726	573,473	606,874	619,133	682,419	3.05	10.22
Netherlands	193,541	205,412	196,994	198,891	208,122	0.93	4.64
Switzerland	143,065	148,269	155,761	170,044	191,147	0.86	12.41
East Mediterranean Europe	**108,275**	**110,884**	**116,050**	**125,093**	**129,551**	**0.58**	**3.56**
Israel	108,275	110,884	116,050	125,093	129,551	0.58	3.56
Other Europe	**100,548**	**95,699**	**104,347**	**113,743**	**122,625**	**0.55**	**7.81**
Other countries of Europe	100,548	95,699	104,347	113,743	122,625	0.55	7.81
MIDDLE EAST	**356,055**	**373,099**	**453,284**	**476,053**	**475,926**	**2.13**	**-0.03**
Egypt	14,122	15,733	16,729	16,703	19,918	0.09	19.25
Kuwait	32,130	44,500	41,224	55,788	64,611	0.29	15.82
Saudi Arabia	16,489	10,911	8,463	12,521	17,084	0.08	36.44
United Arab Emirates	95,490	83,625	105,162	108,608	113,547	0.51	4.55
Other countries of Middle East	197,824	218,330	281,706	282,433	260,766	1.17	-7.67
SOUTH ASIA	**711,290**	**826,437**	**995,321**	**1,158,092**	**1,286,861**	**5.76**	**11.12**
Bangladesh	46,682	53,420	68,081	65,150	72,657	0.33	11.52
India	536,964	614,566	760,371	914,971	1,013,308	4.53	10.75
Nepal	20,589	25,499	28,621	25,382	26,277	0.12	3.53
Pakistan	49,169	63,260	65,171	73,727	71,982	0.32	-2.37
Sri Lanka	38,993	47,138	49,738	53,636	73,346	0.33	36.75
Other countries of South Asia	18,893	22,554	23,339	25,226	29,291	0.13	16.11

Yearbook of Tourism Statistics, Data 2008 – 2012, 2014 Edition

THAILAND

1. Arrivals of non-resident tourists at national borders, by country of residence

	2008	2009	2010	2011	2012	Market share 2012	% Change 2012-2011
TOTAL	14,581,990	14,146,394	15,931,223	19,224,433	22,353,903	100.00	16.28
AFRICA	108,890	107,837	121,816	141,255	157,309	0.70	11.37
East Africa	28,972	35,140	36,599	42,447			
Burundi	75	152	127	142			
Comoros	20	49	188	470			
Djibouti	56	151	164	192			
Eritrea	30	47	79	124			
Ethiopia	4,025	5,204	5,875	6,234			
Kenya	4,537	6,303	5,860	6,134			
Madagascar	5,239	5,362	5,229	5,622			
Malawi	213	399	284	315			
Mauritius	2,889	3,689	3,938	4,752			
Mozambique	624	824	1,018	1,182			
Reunion	370	3,446	4,054	6,955			
Rwanda	165	136	211	243			
Seychelles	2,903	1,323	1,570	1,597			
Somalia	295	149	223	309			
Uganda	2,046	2,168	2,160	2,474			
United Republic of Tanzania	3,294	3,623	3,460	3,434			
Zambia	1,678	1,611	1,624	1,521			
Zimbabwe	513	504	535	747			
Central Africa	6,324	5,930	4,575	5,617			
Angola	2,536	2,445	1,669	1,941			
Cameroon	2,283	2,048	1,436	1,866			
Central African Republic	121	73	41	31			
Chad	22	22	36	70			
Congo	1,058	1,185	1,117	1,022			
Democratic Republic of the Congo	181	20		277			
Equatorial Guinea	13	5	33	45			
Gabon	70	114	219	327			
Sao Tome and Principe	40	18	24	38			
North Africa	8,473	8,226	7,802	9,379			
Algeria	1,574	1,592	1,383	1,433			
Morocco	4,072	3,443	3,075	4,039			
Sudan	1,458	1,910	2,034	2,645			
Tunisia	1,183	1,281	1,310	1,262			
Western Sahara	186						
Southern Africa	47,406	41,937	56,985	68,275	73,530	0.33	7.70
Botswana	546	589	649	681			
Lesotho	116	476	215	101			
Namibia	309	331	506	626			
South Africa	46,271	40,465	55,467	66,705	73,530	0.33	10.23
Swaziland	164	76	148	162			
West Africa	17,585	16,104	15,319	15,184			
Benin	512	477	497	531			
Burkina Faso	142	202	305	250			
Cape Verde	416	59	46	134			
Côte d'Ivoire	544	695	816	693			
Gambia	466	368	366	361			
Ghana	2,672	2,303	1,877	2,378			
Guinea	2,835	2,739	2,592	2,417			
Liberia	1,171	1,371	1,019	793			
Mali	2,075	2,027	1,734	1,995			
Mauritania	429	487	275	151			
Niger	253	74	150	215			
Nigeria	2,407	3,099	3,334	3,606			

745

THAILAND

1. Arrivals of non-resident tourists at national borders, by country of residence

	2008	2009	2010	2011	2012	Market share 2012	% Change 2012-2011
Senegal	1,585	1,486	1,648	931			
Sierra Leone	1,453	182	198	229			
Togo	625	535	462	500			
Other Africa	**130**	**500**	**536**	**353**	**83,779**	**0.37**	**23,633.43**
Other countries of Africa	130	500	536	353	83,779	0.37	23,633.43
AMERICAS	**853,348**	**795,110**	**792,190**	**885,598**	**1,006,911**	**4.50**	**13.70**
Caribbean	**2,370**	**1,645**	**2,160**	**2,392**			
Antigua and Barbuda	75	24	21	19			
Bahamas	733	60	115	131			
Barbados	270	141	166	154			
Bermuda	57	95	164	235			
Cayman Islands		22	67	60			
Cuba	269	181	222	239			
Curaçao	3	4	36	74			
Dominica	42	41	40	91			
Dominican Republic	187	255	210	200			
Grenada	8	15	8	17			
Guadeloupe	9	8	29	79			
Haiti	75	20	52	67			
Jamaica	196	158	229	284			
Martinique	12	80	75	86			
Puerto Rico	123	86	153	119			
Saint Kitts and Nevis	17	19	52	56			
Saint Lucia	15	10	37	27			
Saint Vincent and the Grenadines	4	13	20	21			
Trinidad and Tobago	272	405	448	421			
United States Virgin Islands	3	8	16	12			
Central America	**2,222**	**2,204**	**2,507**	**2,773**			
Belize	267	58	134	100			
Costa Rica	645	731	915	952			
El Salvador	191	121	115	176			
Guatemala	321	644	439	437			
Honduras	223	211	343	417			
Nicaragua	200	85	109	117			
Panama	375	354	452	574			
North America	**813,722**	**755,664**	**744,744**	**826,817**	**919,092**	**4.11**	**11.16**
Canada	153,420	147,191	148,287	170,981	192,602	0.86	12.65
Greenland	24	66	188	274			
Mexico	11,579	8,932	9,761	10,835			
United States of America	648,699	599,475	586,508	644,727	726,490	3.25	12.68
South America	**34,995**	**35,096**	**41,591**	**52,636**	**43,892**	**0.20**	**-16.61**
Argentina	6,198	6,452	9,336	12,005	16,895	0.08	40.73
Bolivia	335	269	254	317			
Brazil	14,524	13,890	16,753	21,231	26,997	0.12	27.16
Chile	4,973	5,607	5,989	7,748			
Colombia	3,784	3,922	3,838	4,601			
Ecuador	472	550	529	966			
Guyana	40	46	56	77			
Paraguay	252	93	150	158			
Peru	1,804	1,671	2,058	2,314			
Suriname	168	95	137	172			
Uruguay	676	689	1,025	1,311			
Venezuela	1,769	1,812	1,466	1,736			
Other Americas	**39**	**501**	**1,188**	**980**	**43,927**	**0.20**	**4,382.35**
Other countries of the Americas	39	501	1,188	980	43,927	0.20	4,382.35
EAST ASIA AND THE PACIFIC	**8,626,039**	**7,994,238**	**9,091,305**	**11,480,750**	**13,810,993**	**61.78**	**20.30**

Yearbook of Tourism Statistics, Data 2008 – 2012, 2014 Edition

THAILAND

1. Arrivals of non-resident tourists at national borders, by country of residence

	2008	2009	2010	2011	2012	Market share 2012	% Change 2012-2011
North-East Asia	3,710,434	3,189,936	3,706,326	4,829,983	6,312,354	28.24	30.69
China	937,358	815,708	1,132,267	1,704,800	2,761,213	12.35	61.97
Hong Kong, China	343,896	378,948	391,067	531,192	604,900	2.71	13.88
Japan	1,110,729	982,607	980,424	1,103,073	1,341,063	6.00	21.58
Korea, Republic of	897,918	620,700	805,179	1,001,105	1,153,457	5.16	15.22
Macao, China	13,843	21,077	21,457	32,889			
Mongolia	3,893	4,179	4,647	6,347			
Taiwan, Province of China	402,797	366,717	371,285	449,346	393,335	1.76	-12.47
Other countries of North-East Asia				1,231	58,386	0.26	4,642.97
South-East Asia	4,125,527	4,075,459	4,596,750	5,718,982	6,462,647	28.91	13.00
Brunei Darussalam	12,357	10,517	8,906	10,142	13,319	0.06	31.33
Cambodia	93,301	103,168	150,011	271,265	430,538	1.93	58.71
Indonesia	259,284	226,506	285,666	370,681	449,360	2.01	21.23
Lao People's Democratic Republic	624,645	657,658	718,377	895,359	981,081	4.39	9.57
Malaysia	1,828,324	1,748,341	2,047,175	2,492,034	2,546,072	11.39	2.17
Myanmar	75,667	80,068	91,111	111,545	129,714	0.58	16.29
Philippines	223,968	215,150	242,859	262,839	280,585	1.26	6.75
Singapore	651,978	651,454	654,342	789,339	994,631	4.45	26.01
Timor-Leste	337	791	857	977			
Viet Nam	355,666	381,806	397,446	514,801	637,347	2.85	23.80
Australasia	785,436	723,791	782,581	925,152	1,029,393	4.60	11.27
Australia	694,439	645,534	702,921	835,719	929,962	4.16	11.28
New Zealand	90,997	78,257	79,660	89,433	99,431	0.44	11.18
Melanesia	1,970	3,307	4,223	5,104			
Fiji	514	801	794	876			
New Caledonia	1,009	1,391	2,071	2,442			
Papua New Guinea	323	914	1,041	1,027			
Solomon Islands	64	84	113	371			
Vanuatu	60	117	204	388			
Micronesia	478	688	660	672			
Guam	106	316	341	382			
Kiribati	23	40	40	38			
Marshall Islands	4	9	44	33			
Micronesia, Federated States of	27	19	15	31			
Nauru	200	266	174	143			
Northern Mariana Islands	48	23	10	4			
Palau	70	15	36	41			
Polynesia	343	600	740	816			
Cook Islands	7	37	41	43			
French Polynesia	133	202	448	557			
Samoa	56	99	115	89			
Tonga	108	92	131	116			
Tuvalu	39	170	5	11			
Other East Asia and the Pacific	1,851	457	25	41	6,599	0.03	15,995.12
Other countries of Asia	1,851	442					
Other countries of Oceania		15	25	41	6,599	0.03	15,995.12
EUROPE	3,961,096	4,027,809	4,440,367	5,052,546	5,580,160	24.96	10.44
Central/Eastern Europe	466,419	498,593	839,410	1,272,043	1,578,057	7.06	24.06
Armenia	909	551	819	933			
Azerbaijan	653	695	906	1,230			
Bulgaria	3,289	2,809	3,419	4,339			
Czech Republic	18,264	25,507	27,370	28,764			
Estonia	7,893	6,811	8,357	9,448			
Georgia	200	460	631	530			
Hungary	15,771	14,374	16,757	16,163			
Kazakhstan	26,966	24,994	28,922	35,345			
Kyrgyzstan	1,009	938	1,243	1,491			

747

Yearbook of Tourism Statistics, Data 2008 – 2012, 2014 Edition

THAILAND

1. Arrivals of non-resident tourists at national borders, by country of residence

	2008	2009	2010	2011	2012	Market share 2012	% Change 2012-2011
Latvia	4,126	3,278	4,233	5,079			
Lithuania	3,922	4,867	5,298	6,215			
Poland	24,409	30,074	34,832	36,546			
Republic of Moldova	356	425	660	799			
Romania	5,012	5,624	6,670	8,400			
Russian Federation	319,587	334,915	643,839	1,052,361	1,311,358	5.87	24.61
Slovakia	5,577	7,544	8,426	9,124			
Tajikistan	352	175	295	299			
Turkmenistan	777	2,207	3,811	4,808			
Ukraine	22,179	28,005	36,886	41,233			
Uzbekistan	3,608	3,971	5,858	8,720			
Other countries Central/East Europe	1,560	369	178	216	266,699	1.19	123,371.76
Northern Europe	**1,663,558**	**1,603,566**	**1,595,573**	**1,649,950**	**1,619,090**	**7.24**	**-1.87**
Denmark	151,903	143,326	150,300	159,620	162,022	0.72	1.50
Finland	158,480	155,574	145,510	154,002	151,516	0.68	-1.61
Iceland	3,334	2,549	3,276	3,614			
Ireland	73,220	63,755	54,733	55,038			
Norway	128,380	120,668	132,865	137,066	148,689	0.67	8.48
Sweden	389,665	340,381	348,640	369,144	356,791	1.60	-3.35
United Kingdom	758,576	777,313	760,249	771,466	800,072	3.58	3.71
Southern Europe	**274,107**	**287,075**	**276,659**	**320,211**	**301,430**	**1.35**	**-5.87**
Albania	320	291	289	316			
Andorra	201	200	227	231			
Bosnia and Herzegovina	333	314	381	597			
Croatia	2,747	2,807	2,828	3,437			
Greece	19,218	18,483	17,529	15,231			
Italy	147,541	164,341	161,086	174,902	187,552	0.84	7.23
Malta	1,012	1,243	1,565	1,926			
Montenegro		69	164	226			
Portugal	16,823	13,418	14,463	16,259			
San Marino	269	119	174	209			
Serbia	554	2,441	2,628	3,224			
Slovenia	4,535	5,863	5,732	6,062			
Spain	80,287	77,160	69,223	97,149	113,878	0.51	17.22
TFYR of Macedonia	267	326	370	442			
Western Europe	**1,418,077**	**1,492,771**	**1,567,854**	**1,635,111**	**1,789,101**	**8.00**	**9.42**
Austria	76,563	87,469	88,788	86,987	92,550	0.41	6.40
Belgium	75,254	81,514	80,246	82,699	94,134	0.42	13.83
France	384,342	401,293	439,773	484,602	538,327	2.41	11.09
Germany	531,241	556,852	596,960	603,979	663,611	2.97	9.87
Liechtenstein	424	514	610	676			
Luxembourg	3,357	4,011	4,713	4,962			
Monaco	405	526	643	759			
Netherlands	193,740	203,675	190,539	189,727	197,721	0.88	4.21
Switzerland	152,751	156,917	165,582	180,720	202,758	0.91	12.19
East Mediterranean Europe	**138,899**	**145,281**	**159,373**	**173,969**	**125,666**	**0.56**	**-27.77**
Cyprus	3,979	3,426	3,472	3,704			
Israel	100,947	111,243	115,961	125,149	125,666	0.56	0.41
Turkey	33,973	30,612	39,940	45,116			
Other Europe	**36**	**523**	**1,498**	**1,262**	**166,816**	**0.75**	**13,118.38**
Other countries of Europe	36	523	1,498	1,262	166,816	0.75	13,118.38
MIDDLE EAST	**282,878**	**298,079**	**331,253**	**379,382**	**273,752**	**1.22**	**-27.84**
Bahrain	14,237	18,545	20,527	23,167			
Egypt	13,048	13,394	15,215	15,094	17,918	0.08	18.71
Iraq	1,656	1,973	2,173	2,096			
Jordan	8,070	8,913	7,459	8,348			
Kuwait	31,890	47,115	45,223	60,425	69,223	0.31	14.56

748

THAILAND

1. Arrivals of non-resident tourists at national borders, by country of residence

	2008	2009	2010	2011	2012	Market share 2012	% Change 2012-2011
Lebanon	5,457	6,036	5,666	6,494			
Libya	957	1,439	2,164	866			
Oman	49,328	42,451	47,787	57,876			
Palestine	861	718	1,037	1,427			
Qatar	15,138	15,913	22,341	27,788			
Saudi Arabia	18,328	14,636	13,031	17,535	23,007	0.10	31.21
Syrian Arab Republic	3,775	4,503	4,315	4,850			
United Arab Emirates	116,664	119,450	140,884	149,873	163,604	0.73	9.16
Yemen	3,469	2,993	3,431	3,543			
SOUTH ASIA	**749,739**	**923,321**	**1,152,890**	**1,284,902**	**1,260,263**	**5.64**	**-1.92**
Afghanistan	855	1,533	1,511	2,127			
Bangladesh	46,839	55,818	70,598	68,024	75,354	0.34	10.78
Bhutan	10,710	12,993	13,664	15,227			
India	497,022	596,529	746,214	891,748	985,883	4.41	10.56
Iran, Islamic Republic of	79,687	114,021	167,792	147,381			
Maldives	7,332	7,784	9,197	8,672			
Nepal	21,079	26,683	29,994	26,237	26,326	0.12	0.34
Pakistan	46,978	62,517	64,091	71,704	69,419	0.31	-3.19
Sri Lanka	39,233	45,443	49,827	53,782	73,249	0.33	36.20
Other countries of South Asia	4		2		30,032	0.13	
NOT SPECIFIED			**1,402**		**264,515**	**1.18**	
Other countries of the World			1,402		264,515	1.18	

Yearbook of Tourism Statistics, Data 2008 – 2012, 2014 Edition

THAILAND

3. Arrivals of non-resident tourists in hotels and similar establishments, by country of residence

	2008	2009	2010	2011	2012	Market share 2012	% Change 2012-2011
TOTAL	12,814,543	11,809,657	13,394,911	16,678,985			
AFRICA	99,074	94,090	107,364	125,341			
Southern Africa	41,198	35,708	49,161	59,381			
South Africa	41,198	35,708	49,161	59,381			
Other Africa	57,876	58,382	58,203	65,960			
Other countries of Africa	57,876	58,382	58,203	65,960			
AMERICAS	691,712	600,320	593,219	678,010			
North America	645,223	560,343	545,037	617,599			
Canada	131,855	113,047	112,121	139,435			
United States of America	513,368	447,296	432,916	478,164			
South America	18,295	16,908	21,998	28,796			
Argentina	4,836	4,989	7,727	10,203			
Brazil	13,459	11,919	14,271	18,593			
Other Americas	28,194	23,069	26,184	31,615			
Other countries of the Americas	28,194	23,069	26,184	31,615			
EAST ASIA AND THE PACIFIC	7,564,208	6,812,307	7,703,950	10,072,456			
North-East Asia	3,481,648	2,811,051	3,290,272	4,359,712			
China	901,524	737,552	1,034,585	1,585,394			
Hong Kong, China	328,299	354,285	366,216	504,231			
Japan	1,021,194	834,661	823,694	928,510			
Korea, Republic of	856,005	558,166	742,905	940,368			
Taiwan, Province of China	374,626	326,387	322,872	401,209			
South-East Asia	3,393,988	3,365,480	3,741,320	4,885,978			
Brunei Darussalam	11,729	9,413	7,899	9,327			
Cambodia	75,856	82,425	114,203	213,047			
Indonesia	233,530	200,466	255,480	343,688			
Lao People's Democratic Republic	315,492	439,080	448,412	599,791			
Malaysia	1,607,078	1,514,040	1,771,632	2,278,863			
Myanmar	56,902	56,665	63,434	80,684			
Philippines	179,295	165,915	180,341	206,581			
Singapore	591,827	569,176	564,058	698,750			
Viet Nam	322,279	328,300	335,861	455,247			
Australasia	686,139	607,971	641,929	782,190			
Australia	606,949	545,001	577,413	706,856			
New Zealand	79,190	62,970	64,516	75,334			
Other East Asia and the Pacific	2,433	27,805	30,429	44,576			
Other countries of Asia		24,018	25,663	38,944			
Other countries of Oceania	2,433	3,787	4,766	5,632			
EUROPE	3,487,501	3,192,749	3,629,839	4,258,422			
Central/Eastern Europe	452,143	442,463	775,368	1,191,791			
Russian Federation	309,786	300,739	599,780	988,463			
Other countries Central/East Europe	142,357	141,724	175,588	203,328			
Northern Europe	1,352,024	1,185,544	1,181,229	1,230,800			
Denmark	133,901	113,462	122,325	132,702			
Finland	144,073	126,718	115,461	121,881			
Norway	104,565	88,528	95,734	99,739			
Sweden	334,820	264,074	267,304	281,746			
United Kingdom	634,665	592,762	580,405	594,732			
Southern Europe	206,888	198,624	192,329	235,630			
Italy	131,954	134,454	133,869	150,302			
Spain	74,934	64,170	58,460	85,328			
Western Europe	1,229,012	1,148,975	1,249,964	1,344,446			
Austria	68,368	70,104	73,136	74,001			
Belgium	64,113	60,572	62,511	66,966			
France	334,728	302,883	350,595	403,593			

750

THAILAND

3. Arrivals of non-resident tourists in hotels and similar establishments, by country of residence

	2008	2009	2010	2011	2012	Market share 2012	% Change 2012-2011
Germany	463,527	435,050	478,332	494,598			
Netherlands	167,535	158,499	151,030	154,122			
Switzerland	130,741	121,867	134,360	151,166			
East Mediterranean Europe	**95,489**	**92,728**	**103,208**	**117,430**			
Israel	95,489	92,728	103,208	117,430			
Other Europe	**151,945**	**124,415**	**127,741**	**138,325**			
Other countries of Europe	151,945	124,415	127,741	138,325			
MIDDLE EAST	**347,786**	**381,935**	**466,625**	**494,620**			
Egypt	12,837	12,305	14,032	14,007			
Kuwait	31,344	43,408	43,172	57,806			
Saudi Arabia	16,972	13,139	11,297	15,914			
United Arab Emirates	110,634	108,940	130,195	138,852			
Other countries of Middle East	175,999	204,143	267,929	268,041			
SOUTH ASIA	**624,262**	**728,256**	**893,914**	**1,050,136**			
Bangladesh	43,117	50,269	63,891	61,921			
India	465,617	540,141	682,264	829,328			
Nepal	18,778	23,021	25,049	22,324			
Pakistan	43,566	55,805	57,605	66,422			
Sri Lanka	36,543	40,771	46,102	49,926			
Other countries of South Asia	16,641	18,249	19,003	20,215			

Yearbook of Tourism Statistics, Data 2008 – 2012, 2014 Edition

THE FORMER YUGOSLAV REPUBLIC OF MACEDONIA

3. Arrivals of non-resident tourists in hotels and similar establishments, by nationality

	2008	2009	2010	2011	2012	Market share 2012	% Change 2012-2011
TOTAL	213,829	219,803	231,485	301,304	324,372	100.00	7.66
AFRICA			214	390	314	0.10	-19.49
Southern Africa			31	48	52	0.02	8.33
South Africa			31	48	52	0.02	8.33
Other Africa			183	342	262	0.08	-23.39
Other countries of Africa			183	342	262	0.08	-23.39
AMERICAS	8,443	8,165	9,014	10,150	9,930	3.06	-2.17
North America	8,443	8,165	8,657	9,554	8,920	2.75	-6.64
Canada	975	1,132	1,155	1,268	1,319	0.41	4.02
United States of America	7,468	7,033	7,056	7,655	7,319	2.26	-4.39
Other countries of North America			446	631	282	0.09	-55.31
South America			132	236	395	0.12	67.37
Brazil			132	236	395	0.12	67.37
Other Americas			225	360	615	0.19	70.83
Other countries of the Americas			225	360	615	0.19	70.83
EAST ASIA AND THE PACIFIC	4,121	3,755	9,612	11,637	14,512	4.47	24.71
North-East Asia	1,084	1,152	3,034	4,823	6,321	1.95	31.06
China			818	1,616	2,754	0.85	70.42
Japan	1,084	1,152	1,538	2,142	2,396	0.74	11.86
Korea, Republic of			678	1,065	1,171	0.36	9.95
Australasia	3,037	2,603	3,677	3,852	5,137	1.58	33.36
Australia	2,808	2,446	3,524	3,642	4,955	1.53	36.05
New Zealand	229	157	153	210	182	0.06	-13.33
Other East Asia and the Pacific			2,901	2,962	3,054	0.94	3.11
Other countries of Asia			1,941	2,723	2,640	0.81	-3.05
Other countries of Oceania			960	239	414	0.13	73.22
EUROPE	197,173	202,839	212,645	279,127	299,616	92.37	7.34
Central/Eastern Europe	29,300	34,262	31,731	37,943	40,798	12.58	7.52
Belarus	238	156	86	1,146	225	0.07	-80.37
Bulgaria	18,036	19,479	13,109	16,163	17,419	5.37	7.77
Czech Republic	1,911	1,984	1,986	2,390	2,212	0.68	-7.45
Estonia			144	248	339	0.10	36.69
Hungary	2,041	3,014	3,100	3,083	2,459	0.76	-20.24
Latvia			219	246	556	0.17	126.02
Lithuania			201	257	541	0.17	110.51
Poland	2,018	4,445	5,736	5,895	6,516	2.01	10.53
Romania	1,770	2,143	3,007	3,559	4,493	1.39	26.24
Russian Federation	1,841	1,605	2,493	3,131	3,327	1.03	6.26
Slovakia	623	867	889	887	1,104	0.34	24.46
Ukraine	822	569	761	938	1,607	0.50	71.32
Northern Europe	14,016	11,083	12,142	15,204	13,975	4.31	-8.08
Denmark	1,608	1,178	1,188	1,198	1,233	0.38	2.92
Finland	943	1,048	1,137	3,083	2,302	0.71	-25.33
Iceland	200	147	154	122	96	0.03	-21.31
Ireland	714	521	694	1,424	675	0.21	-52.60
Norway	1,751	1,473	1,423	1,127	1,405	0.43	24.67
Sweden	2,035	2,089	2,300	2,496	2,469	0.76	-1.08
United Kingdom	6,765	4,627	5,246	5,754	5,795	1.79	0.71
Southern Europe	103,735	103,318	114,626	136,034	135,466	41.76	-0.42
Albania	14,223	16,232	14,226	11,022	10,798	3.33	-2.03
Bosnia and Herzegovina	3,799	3,961	4,856	4,308	4,350	1.34	0.97
Croatia	10,821	11,285	11,715	12,724	13,058	4.03	2.62
Greece	18,551	19,379	24,109	44,007	42,652	13.15	-3.08
Italy	4,910	4,899	5,650	6,522	7,293	2.25	11.82
Malta			21	57	271	0.08	375.44

752

THE FORMER YUGOSLAV REPUBLIC OF MACEDONIA

3. Arrivals of non-resident tourists in hotels and similar establishments, by nationality

	2008	2009	2010	2011	2012	Market share 2012	% Change 2012-2011
Montenegro	2,221	2,205	3,407	3,149	2,923	0.90	-7.18
Portugal	518	482	622	593	733	0.23	23.61
Serbia	35,956	30,671	29,324	30,587	31,240	9.63	2.13
Slovenia	11,184	12,375	11,511	13,169	12,347	3.81	-6.24
Spain	1,552	1,829	1,547	1,641	1,668	0.51	1.65
Other countries of Southern Europe			7,638	8,255	8,133	2.51	-1.48
Western Europe	**24,887**	**25,873**	**28,481**	**45,457**	**53,804**	**16.59**	**18.36**
Austria	4,837	5,758	5,723	5,347	5,781	1.78	8.12
Belgium	1,497	1,596	1,643	2,335	3,513	1.08	50.45
France	3,736	4,344	4,573	4,627	5,279	1.63	14.09
Germany	8,407	8,326	8,700	9,070	10,331	3.18	13.90
Luxembourg			52	74	68	0.02	-8.11
Netherlands	4,634	4,275	5,867	21,553	26,160	8.06	21.38
Switzerland	1,776	1,574	1,923	2,451	2,672	0.82	9.02
East Mediterranean Europe	**20,497**	**21,796**	**21,872**	**41,867**	**53,274**	**16.42**	**27.25**
Cyprus			193	631	543	0.17	-13.95
Israel	6,424	5,928	2,799	3,212	3,215	0.99	0.09
Turkey	14,073	15,868	18,880	38,024	49,516	15.27	30.22
Other Europe	**4,738**	**6,507**	**3,793**	**2,622**	**2,299**	**0.71**	**-12.32**
Other countries of Europe	4,738	6,507	3,793	2,622	2,299	0.71	-12.32
NOT SPECIFIED	**4,092**	**5,044**					
Other countries of the World	4,092	5,044					

Yearbook of Tourism Statistics, Data 2008 – 2012, 2014 Edition

THE FORMER YUGOSLAV REPUBLIC OF MACEDONIA

4. Arrivals of non-resident tourists in all types of accommodation establishments, by nationality

	2008	2009	2010	2011	2012	Market share 2012	% Change 2012-2011
TOTAL	254,957	259,204	261,696	327,471	351,359	100.00	7.29
AFRICA			228	408	333	0.09	-18.38
Southern Africa			32	52	61	0.02	17.31
South Africa			32	52	61	0.02	17.31
Other Africa			196	356	272	0.08	-23.60
Other countries of Africa			196	356	272	0.08	-23.60
AMERICAS	9,632	9,083	9,724	10,744	10,612	3.02	-1.23
North America	9,632	9,083	9,353	10,084	9,525	2.71	-5.54
Canada	1,160	1,257	1,247	1,366	1,465	0.42	7.25
United States of America	8,472	7,826	7,655	8,082	7,773	2.21	-3.82
Other countries of North America			451	636	287	0.08	-54.87
South America			142	252	411	0.12	63.10
Brazil			142	252	411	0.12	63.10
Other Americas			229	408	676	0.19	65.69
Other countries of the Americas			229	408	676	0.19	65.69
EAST ASIA AND THE PACIFIC	4,674	4,255	10,331	12,153	15,531	4.42	27.80
North-East Asia	1,236	1,268	3,160	4,928	6,495	1.85	31.80
China			853	1,664	2,828	0.80	69.95
Japan	1,236	1,268	1,621	2,194	2,488	0.71	13.40
Korea, Republic of			686	1,070	1,179	0.34	10.19
Australasia	3,438	2,987	4,174	4,227	5,941	1.69	40.55
Australia	3,165	2,784	3,967	3,974	5,668	1.61	42.63
New Zealand	273	203	207	253	273	0.08	7.91
Other East Asia and the Pacific			2,997	2,998	3,095	0.88	3.24
Other countries of Asia			2,015	2,755	2,676	0.76	-2.87
Other countries of Oceania			982	243	419	0.12	72.43
EUROPE	236,122	240,333	241,413	304,166	324,883	92.46	6.81
Central/Eastern Europe	36,483	42,033	36,639	42,903	46,552	13.25	8.51
Belarus	253	178	101	1,151	329	0.09	-71.42
Bulgaria	21,922	23,619	15,513	18,541	19,815	5.64	6.87
Czech Republic	2,406	2,583	2,423	2,695	2,830	0.81	5.01
Estonia			176	260	390	0.11	50.00
Hungary	3,254	3,365	3,492	3,342	2,829	0.81	-15.35
Latvia			239	308	587	0.17	90.58
Lithuania			251	280	729	0.21	160.36
Poland	2,434	5,827	6,182	6,758	7,490	2.13	10.83
Romania	2,240	2,677	3,351	3,882	4,964	1.41	27.87
Russian Federation	2,091	1,872	2,848	3,545	3,613	1.03	1.92
Slovakia	811	1,140	1,082	1,099	1,277	0.36	16.20
Ukraine	1,072	772	981	1,042	1,699	0.48	63.05
Northern Europe	15,779	12,611	13,095	16,373	14,931	4.25	-8.81
Denmark	1,748	1,338	1,273	1,251	1,307	0.37	4.48
Finland	1,088	1,220	1,233	3,432	2,379	0.68	-30.68
Iceland	230	161	164	137	99	0.03	-27.74
Ireland	792	610	745	1,500	715	0.20	-52.33
Norway	1,920	1,618	1,503	1,212	1,499	0.43	23.68
Sweden	2,311	2,355	2,530	2,702	2,654	0.76	-1.78
United Kingdom	7,690	5,309	5,647	6,139	6,278	1.79	2.26
Southern Europe	126,109	123,310	133,039	150,726	149,495	42.55	-0.82
Albania	19,314	19,757	17,110	13,614	13,412	3.82	-1.48
Bosnia and Herzegovina	4,443	4,672	5,619	4,959	4,740	1.35	-4.42
Croatia	12,302	12,519	12,791	13,885	13,939	3.97	0.39
Greece	21,060	22,253	26,843	45,509	43,976	12.52	-3.37
Italy	5,674	6,050	6,181	7,140	7,926	2.26	11.01
Malta			23	60	274	0.08	356.67

Yearbook of Tourism Statistics, Data 2008 – 2012, 2014 Edition

THE FORMER YUGOSLAV REPUBLIC OF MACEDONIA

4. Arrivals of non-resident tourists in all types of accommodation establishments, by nationality

	2008	2009	2010	2011	2012	Market share 2012	% Change 2012-2011
Montenegro	2,761	2,653	4,180	3,522	3,197	0.91	-9.23
Portugal	552	601	655	727	835	0.24	14.86
Serbia	45,134	38,744	35,840	35,692	36,530	10.40	2.35
Slovenia	13,159	13,970	12,606	14,063	13,252	3.77	-5.77
Spain	1,710	2,091	1,711	1,726	1,801	0.51	4.35
Other countries of Southern Europe			9,480	9,829	9,613	2.74	-2.20
Western Europe	**28,613**	**29,821**	**31,240**	**47,982**	**57,193**	**16.28**	**19.20**
Austria	5,315	6,437	6,143	5,681	6,275	1.79	10.46
Belgium	1,711	1,839	1,848	2,519	3,716	1.06	47.52
France	4,278	4,914	4,858	4,901	5,663	1.61	15.55
Germany	9,655	9,795	9,573	9,822	11,306	3.22	15.11
Luxembourg			53	107	71	0.02	-33.64
Netherlands	5,606	4,988	6,612	22,219	27,121	7.72	22.06
Switzerland	2,048	1,848	2,153	2,733	3,041	0.87	11.27
East Mediterranean Europe	**22,093**	**23,072**	**23,126**	**43,235**	**54,254**	**15.44**	**25.49**
Cyprus			194	675	570	0.16	-15.56
Israel	6,532	6,110	2,885	3,309	3,278	0.93	-0.94
Turkey	15,561	16,962	20,047	39,251	50,406	14.35	28.42
Other Europe	**7,045**	**9,486**	**4,274**	**2,947**	**2,458**	**0.70**	**-16.59**
Other countries of Europe	7,045	9,486	4,274	2,947	2,458	0.70	-16.59
NOT SPECIFIED	**4,529**	**5,533**					
Other countries of the World	4,529	5,533					

Yearbook of Tourism Statistics, Data 2008 – 2012, 2014 Edition

THE FORMER YUGOSLAV REPUBLIC OF MACEDONIA

5. Overnight stays of non-resident tourists in hotels and similar establishments, by nationality

	2008	2009	2010	2011	2012	Market share 2012	% Change 2012-2011
TOTAL	474,577	468,706	468,822	667,430	727,246	100.00	8.96
AFRICA			537	1,114	835	0.11	-25.04
Southern Africa			72	238	136	0.02	-42.86
South Africa			72	238	136	0.02	-42.86
Other Africa			465	876	699	0.10	-20.21
Other countries of Africa			465	876	699	0.10	-20.21
AMERICAS	22,109	21,647	23,864	24,948	22,447	3.09	-10.02
North America	22,109	21,647	23,185	23,799	20,782	2.86	-12.68
Canada	2,326	2,592	2,274	3,171	2,632	0.36	-17.00
United States of America	19,783	19,055	19,939	19,309	17,518	2.41	-9.28
Other countries of North America			972	1,319	632	0.09	-52.08
South America			268	472	679	0.09	43.86
Brazil			268	472	679	0.09	43.86
Other Americas			411	677	986	0.14	45.64
Other countries of the Americas			411	677	986	0.14	45.64
EAST ASIA AND THE PACIFIC	8,345	7,036	18,719	22,222	25,816	3.55	16.17
North-East Asia	1,840	2,057	5,354	8,279	9,116	1.25	10.11
China			1,735	3,929	4,325	0.59	10.08
Japan	1,840	2,057	2,776	3,114	3,460	0.48	11.11
Korea, Republic of			843	1,236	1,331	0.18	7.69
Australasia	6,505	4,979	7,293	8,252	11,050	1.52	33.91
Australia	6,039	4,745	7,060	7,836	10,747	1.48	37.15
New Zealand	466	234	233	416	303	0.04	-27.16
Other East Asia and the Pacific			6,072	5,691	5,650	0.78	-0.72
Other countries of Asia			4,117	5,031	4,648	0.64	-7.61
Other countries of Oceania			1,955	660	1,002	0.14	51.82
EUROPE	433,527	427,495	425,702	619,146	678,148	93.25	9.53
Central/Eastern Europe	62,056	71,841	65,681	78,318	89,593	12.32	14.40
Belarus	832	379	216	2,702	730	0.10	-72.98
Bulgaria	34,558	37,823	23,573	29,903	32,798	4.51	9.68
Czech Republic	3,906	4,034	3,921	5,006	4,844	0.67	-3.24
Estonia			350	902	693	0.10	-23.17
Hungary	3,924	5,227	5,333	5,694	4,743	0.65	-16.70
Latvia			541	718	1,174	0.16	63.51
Lithuania			503	960	1,676	0.23	74.58
Poland	5,077	10,998	12,008	11,397	15,132	2.08	32.77
Romania	4,405	4,780	6,888	7,622	9,841	1.35	29.11
Russian Federation	5,425	4,543	7,963	8,952	10,807	1.49	20.72
Slovakia	1,342	2,301	2,279	2,083	2,642	0.36	26.84
Ukraine	2,587	1,756	2,106	2,379	4,513	0.62	89.70
Northern Europe	34,560	26,012	28,839	38,442	36,418	5.01	-5.27
Denmark	4,054	2,638	2,412	2,766	3,072	0.42	11.06
Finland	2,009	2,093	2,398	9,731	7,765	1.07	-20.20
Iceland	588	483	293	217	215	0.03	-0.92
Ireland	1,952	1,246	1,992	3,523	1,765	0.24	-49.90
Norway	5,211	3,793	3,399	2,418	3,687	0.51	52.48
Sweden	5,329	4,850	5,010	5,780	5,766	0.79	-0.24
United Kingdom	15,417	10,909	13,335	14,007	14,148	1.95	1.01
Southern Europe	212,022	205,111	219,982	259,689	255,928	35.19	-1.45
Albania	26,814	28,698	25,716	19,508	18,039	2.48	-7.53
Bosnia and Herzegovina	8,382	8,947	11,813	9,638	10,284	1.41	6.70
Croatia	21,795	23,104	23,116	25,051	25,976	3.57	3.69
Greece	34,805	32,158	38,845	74,697	70,442	9.69	-5.70
Italy	10,505	10,939	12,042	15,081	15,578	2.14	3.30
Malta			62	148	1,027	0.14	593.92

Yearbook of Tourism Statistics, Data 2008 – 2012, 2014 Edition

THE FORMER YUGOSLAV REPUBLIC OF MACEDONIA

5. Overnight stays of non-resident tourists in hotels and similar establishments, by nationality

	2008	2009	2010	2011	2012	Market share 2012	% Change 2012-2011
Montenegro	4,533	4,492	6,413	6,448	6,274	0.86	-2.70
Portugal	1,146	1,233	1,332	1,770	1,621	0.22	-8.42
Serbia	78,112	66,906	59,971	60,243	60,469	8.31	0.38
Slovenia	21,503	24,720	23,654	28,343	27,292	3.75	-3.71
Spain	4,427	3,914	3,413	3,278	4,315	0.59	31.64
Other countries of Southern Europe			13,605	15,484	14,611	2.01	-5.64
Western Europe	**60,111**	**56,660**	**62,120**	**162,044**	**204,922**	**28.18**	**26.46**
Austria	9,673	10,945	10,196	9,959	10,430	1.43	4.73
Belgium	3,310	3,662	3,401	6,923	13,131	1.81	89.67
France	8,027	8,346	9,183	8,849	9,595	1.32	8.43
Germany	19,256	20,011	20,334	19,980	23,621	3.25	18.22
Luxembourg			152	271	145	0.02	-46.49
Netherlands	16,176	10,434	15,117	110,061	142,707	19.62	29.66
Switzerland	3,669	3,262	3,737	6,001	5,293	0.73	-11.80
East Mediterranean Europe	**55,352**	**53,603**	**40,935**	**72,794**	**85,788**	**11.80**	**17.85**
Cyprus			305	1,426	1,138	0.16	-20.20
Israel	26,727	22,440	7,645	10,252	6,749	0.93	-34.17
Turkey	28,625	31,163	32,985	61,116	77,901	10.71	27.46
Other Europe	**9,426**	**14,268**	**8,145**	**7,859**	**5,499**	**0.76**	**-30.03**
Other countries of Europe	9,426	14,268	8,145	7,859	5,499	0.76	-30.03
NOT SPECIFIED	**10,596**	**12,528**					
Other countries of the World	10,596	12,528					

Yearbook of Tourism Statistics, Data 2008 – 2012, 2014 Edition

THE FORMER YUGOSLAV REPUBLIC OF MACEDONIA

6. Overnight stays of non-resident tourists in all types of accommodation establishments, by nationality

	2008	2009	2010	2011	2012	Market share 2012	% Change 2012-2011
TOTAL	587,447	583,796	559,032	755,166	811,746	100.00	7.49
AFRICA			589	1,219	906	0.11	-25.68
Southern Africa			74	251	165	0.02	-34.26
South Africa			74	251	165	0.02	-34.26
Other Africa			515	968	741	0.09	-23.45
Other countries of Africa			515	968	741	0.09	-23.45
AMERICAS	25,877	24,564	25,614	27,078	24,290	2.99	-10.30
North America	25,877	24,564	24,899	25,588	22,308	2.75	-12.82
Canada	2,913	2,889	2,458	3,630	2,968	0.37	-18.24
United States of America	22,964	21,675	21,456	20,632	18,700	2.30	-9.36
Other countries of North America			985	1,326	640	0.08	-51.73
South America			292	520	741	0.09	42.50
Brazil			292	520	741	0.09	42.50
Other Americas			423	970	1,241	0.15	27.94
Other countries of the Americas			423	970	1,241	0.15	27.94
EAST ASIA AND THE PACIFIC	9,576	8,070	20,978	24,252	28,187	3.47	16.23
North-East Asia	2,228	2,274	5,630	8,467	9,500	1.17	12.20
China			1,842	4,027	4,478	0.55	11.20
Japan	2,228	2,274	2,905	3,196	3,634	0.45	13.70
Korea, Republic of			883	1,244	1,388	0.17	11.58
Australasia	7,348	5,796	8,835	9,908	12,885	1.59	30.05
Australia	6,793	5,488	8,523	9,397	12,434	1.53	32.32
New Zealand	555	308	312	511	451	0.06	-11.74
Other East Asia and the Pacific			6,513	5,877	5,802	0.71	-1.28
Other countries of Asia			4,472	5,213	4,788	0.59	-8.15
Other countries of Oceania			2,041	664	1,014	0.12	52.71
EUROPE	539,964	536,748	511,851	702,617	758,363	93.42	7.93
Central/Eastern Europe	77,913	90,111	77,966	92,372	106,248	13.09	15.02
Belarus	882	466	290	2,715	1,185	0.15	-56.35
Bulgaria	42,246	46,656	29,098	35,152	38,551	4.75	9.67
Czech Republic	5,111	5,074	4,978	5,807	6,421	0.79	10.57
Estonia			517	938	859	0.11	-8.42
Hungary	5,840	6,310	6,333	6,458	5,837	0.72	-9.62
Latvia			663	982	1,328	0.16	35.23
Lithuania			743	1,051	2,526	0.31	140.34
Poland	6,243	14,099	13,140	13,730	18,119	2.23	31.97
Romania	5,846	6,393	7,940	8,757	11,490	1.42	31.21
Russian Federation	6,514	6,001	9,035	11,082	11,987	1.48	8.17
Slovakia	1,769	2,836	2,794	2,783	2,995	0.37	7.62
Ukraine	3,462	2,276	2,435	2,917	4,950	0.61	69.69
Northern Europe	38,943	29,787	31,608	41,819	39,141	4.82	-6.40
Denmark	4,482	3,088	2,680	2,899	3,254	0.40	12.25
Finland	2,397	2,391	2,710	10,459	8,099	1.00	-22.56
Iceland	714	522	321	257	220	0.03	-14.40
Ireland	2,148	1,488	2,109	3,771	1,861	0.23	-50.65
Norway	5,729	4,056	3,596	2,717	3,935	0.48	44.83
Sweden	5,879	5,442	5,786	6,488	6,314	0.78	-2.68
United Kingdom	17,594	12,800	14,406	15,228	15,458	1.90	1.51
Southern Europe	271,971	266,210	278,647	313,521	303,394	37.38	-3.23
Albania	48,086	47,711	43,269	35,916	34,707	4.28	-3.37
Bosnia and Herzegovina	10,316	10,861	13,985	14,317	11,625	1.43	-18.80
Croatia	25,034	26,061	26,111	28,531	28,574	3.52	0.15
Greece	38,918	37,478	43,043	77,651	73,018	9.00	-5.97
Italy	12,493	15,233	13,381	16,509	17,295	2.13	4.76
Malta			68	156	1,045	0.13	569.87

758

Yearbook of Tourism Statistics, Data 2008 – 2012, 2014 Edition

6. Overnight stays of non-resident tourists in all types of accommodation establishments, by nationality

	2008	2009	2010	2011	2012	Market share 2012	% Change 2012-2011
Montenegro	5,720	5,412	7,825	7,366	6,943	0.86	-5.74
Portugal	1,273	1,619	1,385	2,038	1,960	0.24	-3.83
Serbia	99,985	88,882	74,959	72,601	71,153	8.77	-1.99
Slovenia	25,274	28,048	26,200	30,681	29,595	3.65	-3.54
Spain	4,872	4,905	3,905	3,490	4,752	0.59	36.16
Other countries of Southern Europe			24,516	24,265	22,727	2.80	-6.34
Western Europe	**69,010**	**66,682**	**70,459**	**169,672**	**214,599**	**26.44**	**26.48**
Austria	10,835	12,253	11,506	10,754	11,976	1.48	11.36
Belgium	4,000	4,353	4,097	7,418	13,907	1.71	87.48
France	9,215	9,963	9,909	9,665	10,627	1.31	9.95
Germany	22,465	23,845	22,767	22,222	26,120	3.22	17.54
Luxembourg			165	472	149	0.02	-68.43
Netherlands	18,313	12,502	17,417	112,309	145,280	17.90	29.36
Switzerland	4,182	3,766	4,598	6,832	6,540	0.81	-4.27
East Mediterranean Europe	**58,702**	**56,036**	**44,142**	**76,523**	**89,065**	**10.97**	**16.39**
Cyprus			306	1,597	1,167	0.14	-26.93
Israel	26,996	22,823	7,821	10,459	6,907	0.85	-33.96
Turkey	31,706	33,213	36,015	64,467	80,991	9.98	25.63
Other Europe	**23,425**	**27,922**	**9,029**	**8,710**	**5,916**	**0.73**	**-32.08**
Other countries of Europe	23,425	27,922	9,029	8,710	5,916	0.73	-32.08
NOT SPECIFIED	**12,030**	**14,414**					
Other countries of the World	12,030	14,414					

Yearbook of Tourism Statistics, Data 2008 – 2012, 2014 Edition

TIMOR-LESTE

1. Arrivals of non-resident tourists at national borders, by country of residence

		2008	2009	2010	2011	2012	Market share 2012	% Change 2012-2011
TOTAL	(*)	35,999	44,131	39,825	50,590	57,517	100.00	13.69
AMERICAS		2,879	3,402	2,523	3,185	3,933	6.84	23.49
Caribbean		292	279					
Cuba		292	279					
North America		1,765	2,274	1,720	2,207	2,211	3.84	0.18
Canada		470	472					
United States of America		1,295	1,802	1,720	2,207	2,211	3.84	0.18
South America		822	849	803	978	1,722	2.99	76.07
Brazil		822	849	803	978	1,722	2.99	76.07
EAST ASIA AND THE PACIFIC		20,707	26,269	28,101	34,766	41,606	72.34	19.67
North-East Asia		2,806	3,739	3,867	4,696	6,183	10.75	31.67
China		976	1,991	2,659	3,464	4,972	8.64	43.53
Japan		967	1,106	1,208	1,232	1,211	2.11	-1.70
Korea, Republic of		863	642					
South-East Asia		8,101	10,501	12,172	16,940	22,470	39.07	32.64
Indonesia		4,212	5,443	6,744	11,179	15,303	26.61	36.89
Malaysia		1,232	1,956	1,756	1,829	1,944	3.38	6.29
Philippines		1,566	1,709	2,177	2,413	3,842	6.68	59.22
Singapore		1,091	1,393	1,495	1,519	1,381	2.40	-9.08
Australasia		9,800	12,029	12,062	13,130	12,953	22.52	-1.35
Australia		8,948	11,207	11,262	12,419	12,138	21.10	-2.26
New Zealand		852	822	800	711	815	1.42	14.63
EUROPE		5,117	6,066	1,925	6,918	7,045	12.25	1.84
Northern Europe		722	806	929	1,002	915	1.59	-8.68
United Kingdom		722	806	929	1,002	915	1.59	-8.68
Southern Europe		3,929	4,795	996	5,916	6,130	10.66	3.62
Italy		204	294					
Portugal		3,725	4,501	996	5,916	6,130	10.66	3.62
Western Europe		466	465					
Germany		466	465					
SOUTH ASIA		834	2,351	2,426	1,900	1,175	2.04	-38.16
Bangladesh		434	459					
India		400	1,464	2,027	1,451	862	1.50	-40.59
Pakistan			428	399	449	313	0.54	-30.29
NOT SPECIFIED		6,462	6,043	4,850	3,821	3,758	6.53	-1.65
Other countries of the World		6,462	6,043	4,850	3,821	3,758	6.53	-1.65

Yearbook of Tourism Statistics, Data 2008 – 2012, 2014 Edition

TOGO

3. Arrivals of non-resident tourists in hotels and similar establishments, by country of residence

		2008	2009	2010	2011	2012	Market share 2012	% Change 2012-2011
TOTAL		73,982	149,945	202,044	300,479	234,762	100.00	-21.87
AFRICA		38,792	76,496	110,821	135,683	127,254	54.21	-6.21
West Africa		19,274	40,231	48,737	65,158	51,350	21.87	-21.19
Benin		5,465	12,520	13,788	16,850	14,627	6.23	-13.19
Burkina Faso	(*)	5,104	10,258	13,618	18,620	13,818	5.89	-25.79
Côte d'Ivoire		3,607	6,780	8,933	11,624	7,219	3.08	-37.90
Ghana		1,795	3,800	4,553	7,961	6,521	2.78	-18.09
Nigeria		3,303	6,873	7,845	10,103	9,165	3.90	-9.28
Other Africa		19,518	36,265	62,084	70,525	75,904	32.33	7.63
Other countries of Africa		19,518	36,265	62,084	70,525	75,904	32.33	7.63
AMERICAS		2,405	5,727	5,921	7,959	7,679	3.27	-3.52
North America		1,904	5,448	5,571	6,764	7,265	3.09	7.41
Canada		424	946	1,111	1,039	1,028	0.44	-1.06
United States of America		1,480	4,502	4,460	5,725	6,237	2.66	8.94
Other Americas		501	279	350	1,195	414	0.18	-65.36
Other countries of the Americas		501	279	350	1,195	414	0.18	-65.36
EAST ASIA AND THE PACIFIC		3,269	6,002	9,578	11,075	10,942	4.66	-1.20
North-East Asia		49	326	714	860	1,298	0.55	50.93
Japan		49	326	714	860	1,298	0.55	50.93
Other East Asia and the Pacific		3,220	5,676	8,864	10,215	9,644	4.11	-5.59
Other countries of Asia		3,220	5,676	8,864	10,215	9,644	4.11	-5.59
EUROPE		29,376	61,385	75,136	144,043	87,536	37.29	-39.23
Central/Eastern Europe		3	19	458	3,562	245	0.10	-93.12
Russian Federation		3	19	458	3,562	245	0.10	-93.12
Northern Europe		761	1,145	2,528	1,138	1,566	0.67	37.61
United Kingdom		747	1,073	1,545	1,032	1,073	0.46	3.97
Scandinavia		14	72	983	106	493	0.21	365.09
Southern Europe		723	2,286	2,655	2,779	3,705	1.58	33.32
Italy		723	2,286	2,655	2,779	3,705	1.58	33.32
Western Europe		15,729	33,456	44,504	50,710	49,762	21.20	-1.87
Benelux		708	1,515	2,696	2,219	2,106	0.90	-5.09
France		13,480	28,229	37,911	44,552	42,502	18.10	-4.60
Germany		1,305	3,034	3,029	3,009	4,076	1.74	35.46
Switzerland		236	678	868	930	1,078	0.46	15.91
Other Europe		12,160	24,479	24,991	85,854	32,258	13.74	-62.43
Other countries of Europe		12,160	24,479	24,991	85,854	32,258	13.74	-62.43
MIDDLE EAST		66	166	374	1,224	1,084	0.46	-11.44
All countries of Middle East		66	166	374	1,224	1,084	0.46	-11.44
NOT SPECIFIED		74	169	214	495	267	0.11	-46.06
Other countries of the World		74	169	214	495	267	0.11	-46.06

Yearbook of Tourism Statistics, Data 2008 – 2012, 2014 Edition

TOGO

5. Overnight stays of non-resident tourists in hotels and similar establishments, by country of residence

		2008	2009	2010	2011	2012	Market share 2012	% Change 2012-2011
TOTAL		**208,827**	**317,644**	**420,516**	**673,219**	**515,248**	**100.00**	**-23.47**
AFRICA		**97,331**	**170,482**	**197,335**	**275,346**	**243,559**	**47.27**	**-11.54**
West Africa		**46,601**	**103,801**	**85,287**	**129,699**	**101,551**	**19.71**	**-21.70**
Benin		11,242	21,532	16,050	25,044	20,171	3.91	-19.46
Burkina Faso	(*)	12,946	38,443	28,904	42,353	34,506	6.70	-18.53
Côte d'Ivoire		9,738	17,984	18,902	29,564	17,974	3.49	-39.20
Ghana		5,070	6,892	6,851	12,620	9,423	1.83	-25.33
Nigeria		7,605	18,950	14,580	20,118	19,477	3.78	-3.19
Other Africa		**50,730**	**66,681**	**112,048**	**145,647**	**142,008**	**27.56**	**-2.50**
Other countries of Africa		50,730	66,681	112,048	145,647	142,008	27.56	-2.50
AMERICAS		**7,101**	**13,198**	**18,045**	**25,940**	**28,498**	**5.53**	**9.86**
North America		**6,848**	**12,852**	**17,424**	**22,425**	**27,062**	**5.25**	**20.68**
Canada		1,140	1,562	2,322	4,085	3,432	0.67	-15.99
United States of America		5,708	11,290	15,102	18,340	23,630	4.59	28.84
Other Americas		**253**	**346**	**621**	**3,515**	**1,436**	**0.28**	**-59.15**
Other countries of the Americas		253	346	621	3,515	1,436	0.28	-59.15
EAST ASIA AND THE PACIFIC		**8,510**	**15,840**	**17,561**	**27,840**	**21,998**	**4.27**	**-20.98**
North-East Asia		**155**	**481**	**912**	**2,421**	**4,615**	**0.90**	**90.62**
Japan		155	481	912	2,421	4,615	0.90	90.62
Other East Asia and the Pacific		**8,355**	**15,359**	**16,649**	**25,419**	**17,383**	**3.37**	**-31.61**
Other countries of Asia		8,355	15,359	16,649	25,419	17,383	3.37	-31.61
EUROPE		**95,644**	**117,244**	**186,984**	**340,344**	**219,202**	**42.54**	**-35.59**
Central/Eastern Europe		**54**	**14**	**649**	**1,523**	**255**	**0.05**	**-83.26**
Russian Federation		54	14	649	1,523	255	0.05	-83.26
Northern Europe		**2,221**	**1,907**	**6,377**	**2,040**	**4,800**	**0.93**	**135.29**
United Kingdom		2,109	1,831	5,230	1,921	4,237	0.82	120.56
Scandinavia		112	76	1,147	119	563	0.11	373.11
Southern Europe		**1,748**	**3,290**	**4,742**	**4,414**	**14,989**	**2.91**	**239.58**
Italy		1,748	3,290	4,742	4,414	14,989	2.91	239.58
Western Europe		**54,146**	**62,041**	**85,197**	**100,562**	**123,318**	**23.93**	**22.63**
Benelux		2,141	2,796	4,646	6,034	5,465	1.06	-9.43
France		48,328	51,546	72,725	86,397	102,953	19.98	19.16
Germany		3,013	6,465	4,626	6,447	12,460	2.42	93.27
Switzerland		664	1,234	3,200	1,684	2,440	0.47	44.89
Other Europe		**37,475**	**49,992**	**90,019**	**231,805**	**75,840**	**14.72**	**-67.28**
Other countries of Europe		37,475	49,992	90,019	231,805	75,840	14.72	-67.28
MIDDLE EAST		**86**	**343**	**350**	**3,130**	**1,647**	**0.32**	**-47.38**
All countries of Middle East		86	343	350	3,130	1,647	0.32	-47.38
NOT SPECIFIED		**155**	**537**	**241**	**619**	**344**	**0.07**	**-44.43**
Other countries of the World		155	537	241	619	344	0.07	-44.43

762

TONGA

1. Arrivals of non-resident tourists at national borders, by country of residence

		2008	2009	2010	2011	2012	Market share 2012	% Change 2012-2011
TOTAL	(*)	50,462	45,711	47,081	46,005	49,000	100.00	6.51
AFRICA		113	203	50	42			
Other Africa		113	203	50	42			
All countries of Africa		113	203	50	42			
AMERICAS		6,444	6,137	6,837	5,942	5,000	10.20	-15.85
North America		6,259	5,884	6,766	5,779			
Canada		576	459	394	271			
United States of America		5,683	5,425	6,372	5,508			
Other Americas		185	253	71	163	5,000	10.20	2,967.48
Other countries of the Americas		185	253	71	163			
All countries of the Americas						5,000	10.20	
EAST ASIA AND THE PACIFIC		30,807	28,887	36,810	36,814	34,000	69.39	-7.64
North-East Asia		1,506	1,659	1,558	1,380			
China		762	807	850	671			
Japan		636	709	607	541			
Korea, Republic of		108	143	101	168			
Australasia		25,589	24,420	32,022	32,573			
Australia		9,735	9,370	10,392	10,320			
New Zealand		15,854	15,050	21,630	22,253			
Melanesia		1,939	1,497	1,502	1,535			
Fiji		1,939	1,497	1,502	1,535			
Polynesia		511	369	648	416			
American Samoa		24	33	213	130			
Samoa		487	336	435	286			
Other East Asia and the Pacific		1,262	942	1,080	910	34,000	69.39	3,636.26
Other countries of Asia		545	538	396	356			
All countries East Asia/Pacific						34,000	69.39	
Other countries of Oceania		717	404	684	554			
EUROPE		5,713	4,844	3,325	3,176	4,000	8.16	25.94
Northern Europe		2,033	1,705	819	696			
United Kingdom		2,033	1,705	819	696			
Southern Europe		334	282	187	175			
Italy		334	282	187	175			
Western Europe		1,687	1,494	1,085	1,085			
France		587	553	300	305			
Germany		1,100	941	785	780			
Other Europe		1,659	1,363	1,234	1,220	4,000	8.16	227.87
Other countries of Europe		1,659	1,363	1,234	1,220			
All countries of Europe						4,000	8.16	
SOUTH ASIA		106	90	33	31			
India		106	90	33	31			
NOT SPECIFIED		7,279	5,550	26		6,000	12.24	
Other countries of the World		7,279	5,550	26		6,000	12.24	

Yearbook of Tourism Statistics, Data 2008 – 2012, 2014 Edition

TRINIDAD AND TOBAGO

1. Arrivals of non-resident tourists at national borders, by country of residence

		2008	2009	2010	2011	2012	Market share 2012	% Change 2012-2011
TOTAL	(*)	437,272	418,863	385,506				
AFRICA		1,349	1,823	1,159				
East Africa		195	415	122				
British Indian Ocean Territory		4	3	4				
Burundi		1						
Comoros				1				
Eritrea		1						
Ethiopia		4	6	5				
Kenya		63	114	35				
Madagascar		2		1				
Malawi		10	28	2				
Mauritius		16	23	10				
Mozambique		2	9					
Reunion			3	2				
Rwanda		1	12	5				
Seychelles		7	6	5				
Uganda		53	74	11				
United Republic of Tanzania		15	89	13				
Zambia		10	35	13				
Zimbabwe		6	13	15				
Central Africa		50	52	52				
Angola		28	1	31				
Cameroon		4	41	6				
Central African Republic		3		4				
Chad		5		5				
Congo		1	5	3				
Democratic Republic of the Congo			4					
Equatorial Guinea		7		2				
Gabon		2	1	1				
North Africa		56	23	14				
Algeria		17	3	2				
Morocco		19	2	1				
Sudan		8	4	2				
Tunisia		12	14	9				
Southern Africa		482	555	469				
Botswana		79	130	89				
Lesotho		3	4					
Namibia		4	4	4				
South Africa		366	406	370				
Swaziland		30	11	6				
West Africa		566	778	502				
Benin		4	3	1				
Burkina Faso		1	1					
Côte d'Ivoire		3	6					
Gambia		4	11	4				
Ghana		190	94	123				
Guinea		2	7	3				
Guinea-Bissau		2						
Liberia		3	5	7				
Mali		1	1	1				
Mauritania		2	6	1				
Niger			3					
Nigeria		332	612	348				
Saint Helena		1						
Senegal		5	6	5				
Sierra Leone		16	22	9				

764

TRINIDAD AND TOBAGO

1. Arrivals of non-resident tourists at national borders, by country of residence

	2008	2009	2010	2011	2012	Market share 2012	% Change 2012-2011
Togo		1					
AMERICAS	364,524	351,216	325,384				
Caribbean	69,132	58,752	54,713				
Anguilla	334	245	228				
Antigua and Barbuda	3,138	2,283	2,158				
Aruba	395	355	351				
Bahamas	1,328	1,244	1,076				
Barbados	19,350	15,672	13,576				
Bermuda	708	694	556				
British Virgin Islands	806	646	579				
Cayman Islands	731	579	538				
Cuba	369	439	467				
Curaçao	772	730	692				
Dominica	1,453	1,239	1,154				
Dominican Republic	1,134	1,115	1,196				
Grenada	9,162	7,339	7,269				
Guadeloupe	628	451	525				
Haiti	267	188	216				
Jamaica	8,658	7,776	7,548				
Martinique	1,016	912	950				
Montserrat	161	147	134				
Netherlands Antilles	586	495	522				
Puerto Rico	1,992	1,824	1,809				
Saint Kitts and Nevis	1,255	1,132	936				
Saint Lucia	5,071	4,429	4,187				
Saint Vincent and the Grenadines	8,064	7,421	6,726				
Turks and Caicos Islands	179	138	94				
United States Virgin Islands	1,575	1,259	1,226				
Central America	3,226	4,034	3,206				
Belize	408	508	442				
Costa Rica	820	1,091	859				
El Salvador	248	245	134				
Guatemala	356	390	400				
Honduras	239	521	173				
Nicaragua	43	65	64				
Panama	1,112	1,214	1,134				
North America	245,240	246,531	230,910				
Canada	54,205	49,514	46,390				
Mexico	1,480	1,573	1,347				
Saint Pierre and Miquelon	2	6	2				
United States of America	189,553	195,438	183,171				
South America	46,926	41,899	36,555				
Argentina	909	1,106	730				
Bolivia	65	117	90				
Brazil	1,761	1,481	1,524				
Chile	326	511	351				
Colombia	2,305	2,431	2,313				
Ecuador	222	220	219				
Falkland Islands, Malvinas	1	1	3				
French Guiana	176	220	289				
Guyana	25,097	20,679	18,339				
Paraguay	13	40	19				
Peru	325	349	290				
Suriname	3,370	3,085	2,791				
Uruguay	104	138	54				
Venezuela	12,252	11,521	9,543				
EAST ASIA AND THE PACIFIC	5,190	5,394	4,582				

Yearbook of Tourism Statistics, Data 2008 – 2012, 2014 Edition

TRINIDAD AND TOBAGO

1. Arrivals of non-resident tourists at national borders, by country of residence

	2008	2009	2010	2011	2012	Market share 2012	% Change 2012-2011
North-East Asia	2,895	3,039	2,452				
China	1,936	2,057	1,548				
Hong Kong, China	86	109	125				
Japan	446	372	374				
Korea, Dem. People's Republic of	205	272	266				
Korea, Republic of	156	189	75				
Macao, China			4				
Mongolia	2	2					
Taiwan, Province of China	64	38	60				
South-East Asia	1,151	1,140	1,100				
Brunei Darussalam		13	4				
Cambodia	3	3	1				
Indonesia	50	55	39				
Malaysia	346	338	369				
Myanmar	24	12	12				
Philippines	586	431	474				
Singapore	99	209	139				
Thailand	36	70	55				
Viet Nam	7	9	7				
Australasia	1,103	1,130	1,004				
Australia	910	950	819				
New Zealand	193	180	185				
Melanesia	14	46	14				
Fiji	6	5	9				
New Caledonia		1	1				
Papua New Guinea	1	26	1				
Solomon Islands	5	6	2				
Vanuatu	2	8	1				
Micronesia	17	11	2				
Guam	5						
Marshall Islands	3	1					
Micronesia, Federated States of	4	1					
Nauru	3	2					
Northern Mariana Islands	2	7	1				
Wake Island			1				
Polynesia	10	28	10				
American Samoa		1					
Cook Islands	1	4					
French Polynesia	2	4	3				
Niue	2						
Pitcairn			1				
Samoa	4	9	1				
Tonga	1	5	5				
Tuvalu		4					
Wallis and Futuna Islands		1					
EUROPE	63,231	57,666	52,360				
Central/Eastern Europe	892	893	916				
Armenia	1						
Azerbaijan	9	25	13				
Bulgaria	49	32	23				
Czech Republic	103	105	111				
Estonia	49	28	78				
Georgia	2		1				
Hungary	54	72	71				
Kazakhstan	17	13	8				
Kyrgyzstan			1				
Latvia	41	47	63				
Lithuania	17	35	19				

Yearbook of Tourism Statistics, Data 2008 – 2012, 2014 Edition

TRINIDAD AND TOBAGO

1. Arrivals of non-resident tourists at national borders, by country of residence

	2008	2009	2010	2011	2012	Market share 2012	% Change 2012-2011
Poland	277	256	256				
Republic of Moldova	1		1				
Romania	91	115	88				
Russian Federation	81	84	79				
Slovakia	30	35	39				
Tajikistan	2	4	2				
Turkmenistan	1						
Ukraine	49	32	60				
Uzbekistan	18	10	3				
Northern Europe	**47,968**	**42,965**	**38,264**				
Denmark	1,018	1,193	963				
Faeroe Islands	4	1	3				
Finland	234	226	206				
Iceland	10	17	20				
Ireland	999	722	783				
Isle of Man	16	13	8				
Norway	1,268	1,107	993				
Sweden	1,495	1,286	1,109				
United Kingdom	42,924	38,400	34,179				
Southern Europe	**2,015**	**2,226**	**2,335**				
Albania	4	4	1				
Andorra	5	10	7				
Bosnia and Herzegovina	13	7	8				
Croatia	77	29	67				
Gibraltar	4	6	7				
Greece	73	108	135				
Holy See		1					
Italy	920	1,062	966				
Malta	24	36	28				
Montenegro			2				
Portugal	91	98	188				
San Marino	1	1					
Serbia and Montenegro	18	8	6				
Slovenia	40	48	41				
Spain	745	808	879				
Western Europe	**12,102**	**11,288**	**10,567**				
Austria	469	437	533				
Belgium	487	453	409				
France	2,277	2,177	1,829				
Germany	4,876	4,895	4,657				
Luxembourg	13	14	15				
Monaco	5	4	2				
Netherlands	3,141	2,409	2,202				
Switzerland	834	899	920				
East Mediterranean Europe	**254**	**294**	**278**				
Cyprus	14	33	20				
Israel	141	203	168				
Turkey	99	58	90				
MIDDLE EAST	**462**	**468**	**390**				
Bahrain	12	4	21				
Egypt	79	70	63				
Iraq	6	2	4				
Jordan		2	1				
Kuwait	13	14	12				
Lebanon	28	31	14				
Libya	3	2	8				
Oman	11	9	6				

Yearbook of Tourism Statistics, Data 2008 – 2012, 2014 Edition

TRINIDAD AND TOBAGO

1. Arrivals of non-resident tourists at national borders, by country of residence

	2008	2009	2010	2011	2012	Market share 2012	% Change 2012-2011
Qatar	43	32	40				
Saudi Arabia	31	82	63				
Syrian Arab Republic	65	29	25				
United Arab Emirates	171	188	133				
Yemen		3					
SOUTH ASIA	**2,329**	**2,267**	**1,620**				
Afghanistan	47	96	40				
Bangladesh	70	134	72				
India	2,017	1,894	1,344				
Iran, Islamic Republic of	4	7	2				
Nepal	8	10	14				
Pakistan	110	76	115				
Sri Lanka	73	50	33				
NOT SPECIFIED	**187**	**29**	**11**				
Other countries of the World	187	29	11				

Yearbook of Tourism Statistics, Data 2008 – 2012, 2014 Edition

TUNISIA

1. Arrivals of non-resident tourists at national borders, by nationality

	2008	2009	2010	2011	2012	Market share 2012	% Change 2012-2011
TOTAL (*)	**7,050,434**	**6,901,406**	**6,902,749**	**4,785,119**	**5,950,464**	**100.00**	**24.35**
AFRICA	**1,043,121**	**1,036,070**	**1,136,066**	**829,254**	**996,044**	**16.74**	**20.11**
North Africa	**1,001,987**	**991,827**	**1,090,339**	**746,276**	**937,598**	**15.76**	**25.64**
Algeria	968,499	961,343	1,060,043	693,732	901,677	15.15	29.97
Morocco	32,430	29,458	29,104	34,748	34,875	0.59	0.37
Sudan	1,058	1,026	1,192	17,796	1,046	0.02	-94.12
West Africa	**12,049**	**13,063**	**13,279**	**13,100**	**18,977**	**0.32**	**44.86**
Mauritania	12,049	13,063	13,279	13,100	18,977	0.32	44.86
Other Africa	**29,085**	**31,180**	**32,448**	**69,878**	**39,469**	**0.66**	**-43.52**
Other countries of Africa	29,085	31,180	32,448	69,878	39,469	0.66	-43.52
AMERICAS	**38,877**	**39,369**	**39,195**	**24,098**	**30,711**	**0.52**	**27.44**
North America	**36,275**	**36,275**	**36,203**	**22,722**	**28,540**	**0.48**	**25.61**
Canada	17,109	16,969	16,910	8,385	11,237	0.19	34.01
United States of America	19,166	19,306	19,293	14,337	17,303	0.29	20.69
South America	**2,602**	**3,094**	**2,992**	**1,376**	**2,171**	**0.04**	**57.78**
Brazil	2,602	3,094	2,992	1,376	2,171	0.04	57.78
EAST ASIA AND THE PACIFIC	**16,472**	**17,016**	**20,997**	**16,344**	**13,415**	**0.23**	**-17.92**
North-East Asia	**13,954**	**14,582**	**17,997**	**14,992**	**11,773**	**0.20**	**-21.47**
China	2,748	3,509	4,612	11,872	3,771	0.06	-68.24
Japan	11,206	11,073	13,385	3,120	8,002	0.13	156.47
Australasia	**2,518**	**2,434**	**3,000**	**1,352**	**1,642**	**0.03**	**21.45**
Australia	2,518	2,434	3,000	1,352	1,642	0.03	21.45
EUROPE	**4,106,676**	**3,743,509**	**3,814,402**	**2,133,916**	**2,965,111**	**49.83**	**38.95**
Central/Eastern Europe	**630,144**	**480,784**	**494,435**	**359,697**	**503,758**	**8.47**	**40.05**
Bulgaria	6,965	6,125	6,720	1,334	2,613	0.04	95.88
Czech Republic	125,573	92,713	76,678	67,362	84,895	1.43	26.03
Hungary	54,734	30,148	30,331	17,233	21,028	0.35	22.02
Poland	207,531	175,319	151,372	97,457	109,554	1.84	12.41
Romania	31,490	14,256	10,494	4,893	8,634	0.15	76.46
Russian Federation	160,518	126,516	188,261	151,911	250,732	4.21	65.05
Slovakia	43,333	35,707	30,579	19,507	26,302	0.44	34.83
Northern Europe	**387,445**	**397,519**	**499,754**	**254,258**	**386,544**	**6.50**	**52.03**
Denmark	26,543	23,386	31,565	6,453	14,575	0.24	125.86
Finland	21,691	15,992	15,822	2,165	7,420	0.12	242.73
Ireland	17,564	17,250	14,821	4,479	6,620	0.11	47.80
Norway	18,036	18,636	21,467	4,397	6,749	0.11	53.49
Sweden	48,689	46,603	62,797	9,267	21,561	0.36	132.66
United Kingdom	254,922	275,652	353,282	227,497	329,619	5.54	44.89
Southern Europe	**632,361**	**545,042**	**507,857**	**162,784**	**282,908**	**4.75**	**73.79**
Greece	12,085	7,887	5,436	1,966	2,771	0.05	40.95
Italy	444,541	383,851	354,127	120,933	216,633	3.64	79.13
Malta	5,127	2,985	2,962	1,897	1,998	0.03	5.32
Portugal	41,697	36,567	40,097	9,786	15,990	0.27	63.40
Serbia	24,129	23,522	21,364	9,635	14,711	0.25	52.68
Spain	104,782	90,230	83,871	18,567	30,805	0.52	65.91
Western Europe	**2,366,553**	**2,247,450**	**2,238,370**	**1,316,123**	**1,726,666**	**29.02**	**31.19**
Austria	72,866	60,654	53,558	23,946	35,132	0.59	46.71
Belgium	169,061	168,108	163,124	138,426	168,532	2.83	21.75
France	1,395,255	1,344,697	1,385,293	808,548	985,217	16.56	21.85
Germany	521,513	484,154	458,631	270,668	411,828	6.92	52.15
Luxembourg	6,823	7,111	6,201	3,484	5,201	0.09	49.28
Netherlands	95,307	82,904	75,244	28,571	61,178	1.03	114.13
Switzerland	105,728	99,822	96,319	42,480	59,578	1.00	40.25
East Mediterranean Europe	**13,874**	**14,438**	**18,252**	**10,716**	**14,525**	**0.24**	**35.54**

Yearbook of Tourism Statistics, Data 2008 – 2012, 2014 Edition

TUNISIA

1. Arrivals of non-resident tourists at national borders, by nationality

	2008	2009	2010	2011	2012	Market share 2012	% Change 2012-2011
Turkey	13,874	14,438	18,252	10,716	14,525	0.24	35.54
Other Europe	**76,299**	**58,276**	**55,734**	**30,338**	**50,710**	**0.85**	**67.15**
Other countries of Europe	76,299	58,276	55,734	30,338	50,710	0.85	67.15
MIDDLE EAST	**1,809,090**	**2,034,494**	**1,862,630**	**1,730,832**	**1,925,760**	**32.36**	**11.26**
Bahrain	944	663	823	376	657	0.01	74.73
Egypt	10,240	11,151	9,135	67,282	10,999	0.18	-83.65
Iraq	2,765	1,180	1,598	2,022	1,833	0.03	-9.35
Jordan	2,753	2,571	2,546	2,226	3,190	0.05	43.31
Kuwait	1,859	1,689	1,825	801	1,602	0.03	100.00
Lebanon	4,950	5,097	4,539	3,399	4,342	0.07	27.74
Libya	1,766,881	1,995,236	1,825,542	1,642,620	1,887,740	31.72	14.92
Oman	1,375	1,074	1,072	514	1,095	0.02	113.04
Palestine	1,922	1,624	1,691	1,591	2,235	0.04	40.48
Qatar	1,212	1,051	897	992	1,255	0.02	26.51
Saudi Arabia	7,193	6,633	6,550	3,068	6,259	0.11	104.01
Syrian Arab Republic	3,960	3,819	3,597	3,448	2,323	0.04	-32.63
United Arab Emirates	1,966	1,980	1,692	2,093	1,319	0.02	-36.98
Yemen	1,070	726	1,123	400	911	0.02	127.75
NOT SPECIFIED	**36,198**	**30,948**	**29,459**	**50,675**	**19,423**	**0.33**	**-61.67**
Other countries of the World	36,198	30,948	29,459	50,675	19,423	0.33	-61.67

Yearbook of Tourism Statistics, Data 2008 – 2012, 2014 Edition

TUNISIA

3. Arrivals of non-resident tourists in hotels and similar establishments, by nationality

	2008	2009	2010	2011	2012	Market share 2012	% Change 2012-2011
TOTAL	5,602,579	5,041,840	5,149,048	2,622,578	4,086,320	100.00	55.81
AFRICA	314,940	338,012	394,026	185,406	294,949	7.22	59.08
North Africa	279,252	301,877	353,215	155,381	258,711	6.33	66.50
Algeria	262,432	288,109	336,768	143,672	240,715	5.89	67.54
Morocco	16,820	13,768	16,447	11,709	17,996	0.44	53.69
Other Africa	35,688	36,135	40,811	30,025	36,238	0.89	20.69
Other countries of Africa	35,688	36,135	40,811	30,025	36,238	0.89	20.69
AMERICAS	74,255	80,719	80,270	26,169	36,594	0.90	39.84
North America	72,922	79,105	78,396	23,965	34,986	0.86	45.99
Canada	41,855	40,469	45,927	9,588	18,958	0.46	97.73
United States of America	31,067	38,636	32,469	14,377	16,028	0.39	11.48
South America	1,333	1,614	1,874	2,204	1,608	0.04	-27.04
Brazil	1,333	1,614	1,874	2,204	1,608	0.04	-27.04
EAST ASIA AND THE PACIFIC	49,397	50,943	66,817	15,593	52,868	1.29	239.05
North-East Asia	47,001	48,187	63,181	14,055	51,075	1.25	263.39
China	2,670	4,663	9,572	4,556	12,427	0.30	172.76
Japan	44,331	43,524	53,609	9,499	38,648	0.95	306.86
Australasia	2,396	2,756	3,636	1,538	1,793	0.04	16.58
Australia	2,396	2,756	3,636	1,538	1,793	0.04	16.58
EUROPE	4,781,705	4,217,298	4,191,497	1,967,865	3,104,373	75.97	57.75
Central/Eastern Europe	780,813	545,389	552,134	394,668	579,020	14.17	46.71
Bulgaria	5,228	5,729	4,562	1,197	3,042	0.07	154.14
Czech Republic	154,085	101,953	89,086	71,565	85,215	2.09	19.07
Hungary	58,547	36,764	33,347	18,011	22,938	0.56	27.36
Poland	245,517	188,509	165,150	95,955	117,023	2.86	21.96
Romania	33,823	12,916	9,723	2,089	5,971	0.15	185.83
Russian Federation	236,167	166,387	220,557	189,567	323,048	7.91	70.41
Slovakia	47,446	33,131	29,709	16,284	21,783	0.53	33.77
Northern Europe	437,021	459,474	549,488	258,974	402,506	9.85	55.42
Ireland	7,330	9,039	8,108	2,077	3,319	0.08	59.80
United Kingdom	310,971	327,631	412,581	235,960	353,557	8.65	49.84
Scandinavia	118,720	122,804	128,799	20,937	45,630	1.12	117.94
Southern Europe	878,416	785,824	658,807	142,768	319,289	7.81	123.64
Greece	27,706	17,857	12,445	2,732	5,198	0.13	90.26
Italy	491,740	473,022	360,571	93,501	204,486	5.00	118.70
Malta	4,633	2,741	2,782	1,625	2,360	0.06	45.23
Portugal	30,477	23,660	28,146	5,301	10,026	0.25	89.13
Serbia	23,389	16,082	13,856	5,604	14,215	0.35	153.66
Spain	300,471	252,462	241,007	34,005	83,004	2.03	144.09
Western Europe	2,608,635	2,357,807	2,365,398	1,136,539	1,740,339	42.59	53.13
Austria	47,576	41,549	39,925	15,605	23,669	0.58	51.68
Belgium	197,523	181,458	178,201	116,848	170,043	4.16	45.52
France	1,520,655	1,374,242	1,418,234	653,082	906,432	22.18	38.79
Germany	633,250	563,536	552,683	286,146	507,057	12.41	77.20
Luxembourg	34,533	35,473	31,955	14,011	26,145	0.64	86.60
Netherlands	84,841	78,014	68,384	22,361	63,097	1.54	182.17
Switzerland	90,257	83,535	76,016	28,486	43,896	1.07	54.10
East Mediterranean Europe	12,239	11,576	12,315	6,476	11,048	0.27	70.60
Turkey	12,239	11,576	12,315	6,476	11,048	0.27	70.60
Other Europe	64,581	57,228	53,355	28,440	52,171	1.28	83.44
Other countries of Europe	64,581	57,228	53,355	28,440	52,171	1.28	83.44
MIDDLE EAST	210,560	207,645	242,515	320,080	428,953	10.50	34.01
Libya	165,979	169,741	202,987	299,904	394,510	9.65	31.55
Other countries of Middle East	44,581	37,904	39,528	20,176	34,443	0.84	70.71

Yearbook of Tourism Statistics, Data 2008 – 2012, 2014 Edition

TUNISIA

3. Arrivals of non-resident tourists in hotels and similar establishments, by nationality

	2008	2009	2010	2011	2012	Market share 2012	% Change 2012-2011
NOT SPECIFIED	171,722	147,223	173,923	107,465	168,583	4.13	56.87
Other countries of the World	150,644	128,640	150,146	88,536	130,300	3.19	47.17
Nationals Residing Abroad	21,078	18,583	23,777	18,929	38,283	0.94	102.25

Yearbook of Tourism Statistics, Data 2008 – 2012, 2014 Edition

TUNISIA

5. Overnight stays of non-resident tourists in hotels and similar establishments, by nationality

	2008	2009	2010	2011	2012	Market share 2012	% Change 2012-2011
TOTAL	35,048,653	31,556,910	32,136,191	17,207,634	25,920,529	100.00	50.63
AFRICA	929,143	997,642	1,144,741	551,477	858,629	3.31	55.70
North Africa	805,222	868,249	996,312	437,051	725,473	2.80	65.99
Algeria	758,517	821,824	945,553	401,765	673,684	2.60	67.68
Morocco	46,705	46,425	50,759	35,286	51,789	0.20	46.77
Other Africa	123,921	129,393	148,429	114,426	133,156	0.51	16.37
Other countries of Africa	123,921	129,393	148,429	114,426	133,156	0.51	16.37
AMERICAS	277,757	259,458	251,585	129,607	131,850	0.51	1.73
North America	275,156	255,228	248,579	127,224	126,906	0.49	-0.25
Canada	173,274	164,801	169,754	47,236	71,940	0.28	52.30
United States of America	101,882	90,427	78,825	79,988	54,966	0.21	-31.28
South America	2,601	4,230	3,006	2,383	4,944	0.02	107.47
Brazil	2,601	4,230	3,006	2,383	4,944	0.02	107.47
EAST ASIA AND THE PACIFIC	77,312	84,053	115,008	35,930	92,719	0.36	158.05
North-East Asia	71,161	76,334	103,356	32,061	86,920	0.34	171.11
China	7,036	8,272	18,017	14,093	28,558	0.11	102.64
Japan	64,125	68,062	85,339	17,968	58,362	0.23	224.81
Australasia	6,151	7,719	11,652	3,869	5,799	0.02	49.88
Australia	6,151	7,719	11,652	3,869	5,799	0.02	49.88
EUROPE	32,598,397	29,157,852	29,403,758	15,125,247	23,171,488	89.39	53.20
Central/Eastern Europe	5,713,625	4,311,470	4,493,330	3,210,712	4,508,393	17.39	40.42
Bulgaria	26,039	29,170	26,384	10,880	20,605	0.08	89.38
Czech Republic	1,203,841	831,093	763,478	576,037	703,075	2.71	22.05
Hungary	391,006	218,581	199,423	118,187	156,333	0.60	32.28
Poland	1,749,104	1,508,855	1,328,247	800,813	910,827	3.51	13.74
Romania	171,743	71,180	44,902	6,324	28,948	0.11	357.75
Russian Federation	1,830,231	1,407,781	1,902,077	1,582,276	2,532,645	9.77	60.06
Slovakia	341,661	244,810	228,819	116,195	155,960	0.60	34.22
Northern Europe	3,417,099	3,606,448	4,281,921	2,132,066	3,302,101	12.74	54.88
Denmark	166,173	151,044	148,373	29,615	45,298	0.17	52.96
Finland	174,593	154,063	160,627	21,551	54,291	0.21	151.92
Ireland	54,597	69,280	57,959	11,708	16,440	0.06	40.42
Norway	95,297	87,975	101,930	19,557	30,438	0.12	55.64
Sweden	397,561	414,058	454,243	66,640	159,706	0.62	139.65
United Kingdom	2,528,878	2,730,028	3,358,789	1,982,995	2,995,928	11.56	51.08
Southern Europe	4,231,389	3,410,170	3,194,606	693,436	1,694,428	6.54	144.35
Greece	65,890	43,179	27,182	11,524	18,641	0.07	61.76
Italy	3,009,982	2,397,247	2,216,105	472,386	1,226,047	4.73	159.54
Malta	25,185	14,314	16,759	6,832	12,110	0.05	77.25
Portugal	141,280	113,910	155,792	31,663	55,623	0.21	75.67
Serbia	165,057	122,718	109,028	52,534	120,511	0.46	129.40
Spain	823,995	718,802	669,740	118,497	261,496	1.01	120.68
Western Europe	18,805,249	17,435,009	17,089,975	8,914,555	13,328,996	51.42	49.52
Austria	358,411	317,173	288,858	124,451	191,709	0.74	54.04
Belgium	1,624,706	1,553,429	1,503,313	1,084,538	1,482,931	5.72	36.73
France	9,158,374	8,451,002	8,700,649	4,417,827	5,887,340	22.71	33.26
Germany	6,099,223	5,655,768	5,336,495	2,768,191	4,780,952	18.44	72.71
Luxembourg	274,462	304,744	268,263	124,703	230,824	0.89	85.10
Netherlands	646,217	541,781	491,312	192,260	454,052	1.75	136.17
Switzerland	643,856	611,112	501,085	202,585	301,188	1.16	48.67
East Mediterranean Europe	46,596	50,222	45,659	20,129	39,732	0.15	97.39
Turkey	46,596	50,222	45,659	20,129	39,732	0.15	97.39
Other Europe	384,439	344,533	298,267	154,349	297,838	1.15	92.96
Other countries of Europe	384,439	344,533	298,267	154,349	297,838	1.15	92.96

773

TUNISIA

5. Overnight stays of non-resident tourists in hotels and similar establishments, by nationality

	2008	2009	2010	2011	2012	Market share 2012	% Change 2012-2011
MIDDLE EAST	511,706	512,952	566,020	958,383	1,089,323	4.20	13.66
Libya	340,058	371,985	427,399	881,939	976,670	3.77	10.74
Other countries of Middle East	171,648	140,967	138,621	76,444	112,653	0.43	47.37
NOT SPECIFIED	654,338	544,953	655,079	406,990	576,520	2.22	41.65
Other countries of the World	581,354	498,141	593,672	354,203	477,636	1.84	34.85
Nationals Residing Abroad	72,984	46,812	61,407	52,787	98,884	0.38	87.33

Yearbook of Tourism Statistics, Data 2008 – 2012, 2014 Edition

TURKEY

1. Arrivals of non-resident tourists at national borders, by nationality

		2008	2009	2010	2011	2012	Market share 2012	% Change 2012-2011
TOTAL	(*)	29,792,105	30,186,614	31,364,004	34,653,876	35,697,900	100.00	3.01
AFRICA		203,772	286,493	246,790	300,712	371,997	1.04	23.71
North Africa		157,548	222,205	186,653	220,419	271,526	0.76	23.19
Algeria		62,085	89,776	66,089	82,615	102,358	0.29	23.90
Morocco		43,710	65,398	56,838	67,660	75,966	0.21	12.28
Sudan		8,984	10,578	6,621	7,441	8,158	0.02	9.64
Tunisia		42,769	56,453	57,105	62,703	85,044	0.24	35.63
Southern Africa		16,852	19,982	23,097	27,851	33,445	0.09	20.09
South Africa		16,852	19,982	23,097	27,851	33,445	0.09	20.09
Other Africa		29,372	44,306	37,040	52,442	67,026	0.19	27.81
Other countries of Africa		29,372	44,306	37,040	52,442	67,026	0.19	27.81
AMERICAS		560,904	559,017	550,380	660,300	713,981	2.00	8.13
Central America		6,203	6,649	6,396	8,788	8,983	0.03	2.22
All countries of Central America		6,203	6,649	6,396	8,788	8,983	0.03	2.22
North America		490,939	477,577	457,112	545,698	587,152	1.64	7.60
Canada		77,858	81,976	79,427	94,723	97,916	0.27	3.37
Mexico		15,252	10,253	11,175	12,584	15,221	0.04	20.96
United States of America		397,829	385,348	366,510	438,391	474,015	1.33	8.13
South America		63,762	74,791	86,872	105,814	117,846	0.33	11.37
Argentina		12,601	12,776	14,943	16,358	18,245	0.05	11.54
Brazil		29,419	39,368	51,545	63,974	70,204	0.20	9.74
Chile		5,830	4,875	4,931	6,609	7,085	0.02	7.20
Colombia		3,652	3,859	4,430	5,444	8,070	0.02	48.24
Venezuela		5,792	5,462	4,061	4,811	5,131	0.01	6.65
Other countries of South America		6,468	8,451	6,962	8,618	9,111	0.03	5.72
EAST ASIA AND THE PACIFIC		554,227	544,858	627,896	720,949	784,130	2.20	8.76
North-East Asia		316,657	292,109	379,789	412,616	457,080	1.28	10.78
China		58,526	67,471	74,763	92,820	109,533	0.31	18.01
Japan		141,865	137,843	184,410	173,672	191,318	0.54	10.16
Korea, Republic of		116,266	86,795	120,616	146,124	156,229	0.44	6.92
South-East Asia		91,007	100,165	104,438	124,598	151,130	0.42	21.29
Indonesia		14,540	18,765	22,404	33,199	47,538	0.13	43.19
Malaysia		25,941	28,778	31,381	34,453	39,053	0.11	13.35
Philippines		22,493	23,330	24,416	27,149	32,399	0.09	19.34
Singapore		18,212	19,656	17,759	19,402	20,661	0.06	6.49
Thailand		9,821	9,636	8,478	10,395	11,479	0.03	10.43
Australasia		114,890	122,030	110,802	127,623	131,497	0.37	3.04
Australia		97,499	104,927	93,106	108,779	111,683	0.31	2.67
New Zealand		17,391	17,103	17,696	18,844	19,814	0.06	5.15
Other East Asia and the Pacific		31,673	30,554	32,867	56,112	44,423	0.12	-20.83
Other countries of Asia		31,504	30,413	30,031	55,788	42,581	0.12	-23.67
Other countries of Oceania		169	141	2,836	324	1,842	0.01	468.52
EUROPE		21,197,868	21,142,283	21,665,925	23,500,920	24,166,936	67.70	2.83
Central/Eastern Europe		8,254,913	8,086,131	8,735,805	9,582,745	10,052,939	28.16	4.91
Armenia		63,845	64,899	69,268	72,349	70,835	0.20	-2.09
Azerbaijan		457,581	422,606	484,850	576,187	591,727	1.66	2.70
Belarus		151,384	141,197	152,176	123,334	137,607	0.39	11.57
Bulgaria		1,252,718	1,402,195	1,432,416	1,488,384	1,488,398	4.17	0.00
Czech Republic		150,946	156,420	168,434	215,323	215,608	0.60	0.13
Estonia		33,391	36,044	34,855	34,512	35,028	0.10	1.50
Georgia		828,264	992,886	1,109,614	1,149,360	1,402,018	3.93	21.98
Hungary		88,137	79,082	88,100	100,362	89,347	0.25	-10.98
Kazakhstan		212,905	219,060	247,690	315,644	379,650	1.06	20.28
Kyrgyzstan		47,712	40,879	35,618	41,186	42,800	0.12	3.92

Yearbook of Tourism Statistics, Data 2008 – 2012, 2014 Edition

TURKEY

1. Arrivals of non-resident tourists at national borders, by nationality

	2008	2009	2010	2011	2012	Market share 2012	% Change 2012-2011
Latvia	58,064	40,451	38,079	43,918	45,041	0.13	2.56
Lithuania	92,405	76,018	71,255	73,629	67,426	0.19	-8.42
Poland	387,422	408,137	419,094	469,314	413,888	1.16	-11.81
Republic of Moldova	141,370	115,948	96,047	100,852	107,771	0.30	6.86
Romania	444,589	362,830	350,679	383,837	378,560	1.06	-1.37
Russian Federation	2,865,814	2,682,332	3,091,930	3,446,907	3,579,957	10.03	3.86
Slovakia	66,433	78,109	90,032	120,029	124,899	0.35	4.06
Tajikistan	36,262	19,814	17,737	16,820	22,823	0.06	35.69
Turkmenistan	88,897	112,356	114,388	137,472	135,165	0.38	-1.68
Ukraine	717,820	561,055	555,477	588,364	618,453	1.73	5.11
Uzbekistan	68,954	73,813	68,066	84,962	105,938	0.30	24.69
Northern Europe	**3,114,823**	**3,403,380**	**3,706,888**	**3,841,929**	**3,818,163**	**10.70**	**-0.62**
Denmark	271,196	289,496	308,927	361,299	381,767	1.07	5.67
Finland	98,727	129,052	137,607	174,865	187,931	0.53	7.47
Iceland	8,314	7,353	6,250	5,905	5,562	0.02	-5.81
Ireland	109,063	110,050	103,930	106,602	99,188	0.28	-6.95
Norway	242,314	251,191	288,044	359,437	388,886	1.09	8.19
Sweden	396,492	389,773	435,634	555,061	599,536	1.68	8.01
United Kingdom	1,988,717	2,226,465	2,426,496	2,278,760	2,155,293	6.04	-5.42
Southern Europe	**1,697,344**	**1,630,674**	**1,682,132**	**1,770,299**	**1,790,102**	**5.01**	**1.12**
Albania	62,234	58,961	49,075	51,499	58,033	0.16	12.69
Bosnia and Herzegovina	58,784	52,021	47,107	56,068	61,213	0.17	9.18
Croatia	29,740	28,328	30,567	38,072	43,121	0.12	13.26
Greece	514,314	560,998	633,458	644,566	627,160	1.76	-2.70
Italy	439,941	373,674	376,559	415,378	421,216	1.18	1.41
Malta	2,504	2,819	2,603	2,977	3,214	0.01	7.96
Montenegro		11,705	11,051	13,427	15,916	0.04	18.54
Portugal	29,353	36,408	43,519	42,614	36,761	0.10	-13.73
Serbia	169,718	101,529	112,548	136,749	155,858	0.44	13.97
Slovenia	37,615	32,975	34,378	37,825	35,630	0.10	-5.80
Spain	246,539	263,942	225,769	200,718	194,609	0.55	-3.04
TFYR of Macedonia	106,602	107,314	115,498	130,406	137,371	0.38	5.34
Western Europe	**7,582,955**	**7,692,064**	**7,377,379**	**8,162,679**	**8,345,617**	**23.38**	**2.24**
Austria	506,370	530,703	479,501	503,118	476,732	1.34	-5.24
Belgium	582,836	575,876	528,108	565,196	585,711	1.64	3.63
France	834,388	862,382	858,503	1,033,647	940,106	2.63	-9.05
Germany	4,301,054	4,354,164	4,207,162	4,568,619	4,773,423	13.37	4.48
Luxembourg	7,557	8,335	10,386	11,658	12,734	0.04	9.23
Netherlands	1,108,276	1,094,332	1,042,712	1,180,504	1,233,678	3.46	4.50
Switzerland	242,474	266,272	251,007	299,937	323,233	0.91	7.77
East Mediterranean Europe	**545,812**	**299,407**	**115,430**	**84,527**	**87,636**	**0.25**	**3.68**
Cyprus	8,480	9,637	10,441	9,196	8,110	0.02	-11.81
Israel	537,332	289,770	104,989	75,331	79,526	0.22	5.57
Other Europe	**2,021**	**30,627**	**48,291**	**58,741**	**72,479**	**0.20**	**23.39**
Other countries of Europe	2,021	30,627	48,291	58,741	72,479	0.20	23.39
MIDDLE EAST	**1,205,650**	**1,424,470**	**1,895,836**	**2,133,169**	**2,376,988**	**6.66**	**11.43**
Bahrain	7,998	9,034	9,294	9,571	13,083	0.04	36.69
Egypt	57,410	65,733	60,452	77,570	109,526	0.31	41.20
Iraq	250,116	285,203	280,317	368,974	533,096	1.49	44.48
Jordan	74,289	87,285	96,454	94,530	101,912	0.29	7.81
Kuwait	21,989	26,730	27,207	41,328	64,854	0.18	56.93
Lebanon	53,561	70,839	133,725	135,608	139,011	0.39	2.51
Libya	43,779	64,702	60,892	53,560	213,651	0.60	298.90
Oman	5,877	5,185	5,394	5,973	7,899	0.02	32.25
Qatar	4,855	4,845	6,024	7,600	13,820	0.04	81.84
Saudi Arabia	55,443	66,625	84,549	116,051	174,981	0.49	50.78
Syrian Arab Republic	405,726	508,385	898,123	970,147	727,319	2.04	-25.03

776

TURKEY

1. Arrivals of non-resident tourists at national borders, by nationality

	2008	2009	2010	2011	2012	Market share 2012	% Change 2012-2011
United Arab Emirates	19,615	21,965	30,432	35,492	47,962	0.13	35.13
Yemen	4,971	6,174	6,343	8,065	11,825	0.03	46.62
Other countries of Middle East	200,021	201,765	196,630	208,700	218,049	0.61	4.48
SOUTH ASIA	**1,212,330**	**1,461,908**	**1,967,804**	**1,973,643**	**1,300,052**	**3.64**	**-34.13**
Bangladesh	2,948	3,573	2,172	4,786	6,542	0.02	36.69
India	52,185	51,369	58,367	63,613	79,799	0.22	25.44
Iran, Islamic Republic of	1,134,826	1,383,057	1,884,897	1,879,033	1,185,864	3.32	-36.89
Pakistan	22,371	23,909	22,368	26,211	27,847	0.08	6.24
NOT SPECIFIED	**4,857,354**	**4,767,585**	**4,409,373**	**5,364,183**	**5,983,816**	**16.76**	**11.55**
Other countries of the World	59,256	86,755	45,178	53,503	55,302	0.15	3.36
Nationals Residing Abroad	4,798,098	4,680,830	4,364,195	5,310,680	5,928,514	16.61	11.63

Yearbook of Tourism Statistics, Data 2008 – 2012, 2014 Edition

TURKEY

2. Arrivals of non-resident visitors at national borders, by nationality

		2008	2009	2010	2011	2012	Market share 2012	% Change 2012-2011
TOTAL	(*)	31,137,774	31,759,816	32,997,308	36,769,039	37,715,225	100.00	2.57
AFRICA		210,323	294,486	254,823	312,260	387,484	1.03	24.09
East Africa		3,627	4,991	4,319	4,541	5,510	0.01	21.34
Kenya		3,627	4,991	4,319	4,541	5,510	0.01	21.34
North Africa		159,754	224,385	189,890	224,123	277,129	0.73	23.65
Algeria		63,904	91,222	67,954	84,844	104,489	0.28	23.15
Morocco		44,023	65,875	57,447	68,645	77,884	0.21	13.46
Sudan		8,987	10,581	6,634	7,458	8,161	0.02	9.43
Tunisia		42,840	56,707	57,855	63,176	86,595	0.23	37.07
Southern Africa		20,774	24,402	27,177	34,394	40,771	0.11	18.54
South Africa		20,774	24,402	27,177	34,394	40,771	0.11	18.54
West Africa		10,208	13,497	13,927	20,143	25,547	0.07	26.83
Nigeria		7,237	9,420	9,172	14,564	19,897	0.05	36.62
Senegal		2,971	4,077	4,755	5,579	5,650	0.01	1.27
Other Africa		15,960	27,211	19,510	29,059	38,527	0.10	32.58
Other countries of Africa		15,960	27,211	19,510	29,059	38,527	0.10	32.58
AMERICAS		958,053	964,103	946,114	1,151,666	1,165,693	3.09	1.22
Caribbean		948	913	1,467	2,924	2,073	0.01	-29.10
Dominican Republic		948	913	1,467	2,924	2,073	0.01	-29.10
Central America		5,055	6,399	4,289	7,121	7,654	0.02	7.48
Panama		732	1,398	776	1,347	1,529	0.00	13.51
Other countries of Central America		4,323	5,001	3,513	5,774	6,125	0.02	6.08
North America		854,073	844,341	818,232	978,652	985,665	2.61	0.72
Canada		147,631	155,270	152,556	191,903	182,252	0.48	-5.03
Mexico		26,997	21,912	22,908	29,606	31,576	0.08	6.65
United States of America		679,445	667,159	642,768	757,143	771,837	2.05	1.94
South America		93,347	107,331	117,636	157,862	164,491	0.44	4.20
Argentina		18,599	20,578	22,255	27,136	28,559	0.08	5.24
Brazil		43,647	53,574	65,246	89,442	88,903	0.24	-0.60
Chile		8,580	7,612	8,183	11,964	12,765	0.03	6.70
Colombia		6,070	7,248	7,129	9,853	12,987	0.03	31.81
Ecuador		2,308	2,478	2,704	3,892	4,433	0.01	13.90
Paraguay		323	385	431	586	700	0.00	19.45
Peru		1,735	1,926	2,016	2,697	2,952	0.01	9.45
Uruguay		2,481	4,246	2,903	3,735	3,592	0.01	-3.83
Venezuela		9,604	9,284	6,769	8,557	9,600	0.03	12.19
Other Americas		4,630	5,119	4,490	5,107	5,810	0.02	13.77
Other countries of the Americas		4,630	5,119	4,490	5,107	5,810	0.02	13.77
EAST ASIA AND THE PACIFIC		613,852	612,084	705,357	839,723	921,152	2.44	9.70
North-East Asia		337,688	312,685	402,303	445,622	490,396	1.30	10.05
China		61,882	69,336	77,142	96,701	114,582	0.30	18.49
Hong Kong, China		6,575	6,560	6,442	10,666	13,138	0.03	23.18
Japan		149,731	147,641	195,404	188,312	203,592	0.54	8.11
Korea, Republic of		119,500	89,148	123,315	149,943	159,084	0.42	6.10
South-East Asia		99,992	119,175	116,741	160,138	196,971	0.52	23.00
Indonesia		15,627	23,361	24,349	40,282	56,113	0.15	39.30
Malaysia		26,881	29,557	32,458	36,222	41,169	0.11	13.66
Philippines		28,222	35,814	31,658	51,610	65,272	0.17	26.47
Singapore		19,121	20,451	18,994	20,957	22,206	0.06	5.96
Thailand		10,141	9,992	9,282	11,067	12,211	0.03	10.34
Australasia		147,866	153,540	156,321	182,718	193,177	0.51	5.72
Australia		124,400	129,642	131,685	156,009	164,899	0.44	5.70
New Zealand		23,466	23,898	24,636	26,709	28,278	0.07	5.87
Other East Asia and the Pacific		28,306	26,684	29,992	51,245	40,608	0.11	-20.76

Yearbook of Tourism Statistics, Data 2008 – 2012, 2014 Edition

TURKEY

2. Arrivals of non-resident visitors at national borders, by nationality

	2008	2009	2010	2011	2012	Market share 2012	% Change 2012-2011
Other countries of Asia	28,053	26,493	27,116	50,886	35,918	0.10	-29.41
Other countries of Oceania	253	191	2,876	359	4,690	0.01	1,206.41
EUROPE	**22,070,327**	**22,222,671**	**22,807,259**	**24,970,083**	**25,550,426**	**67.75**	**2.32**
Central/Eastern Europe	**8,322,215**	**8,155,350**	**8,796,238**	**9,669,035**	**10,138,223**	**26.88**	**4.85**
Armenia	63,855	64,982	69,323	72,393	70,956	0.19	-1.98
Azerbaijan	459,593	424,155	486,381	578,685	593,238	1.57	2.51
Belarus	152,961	142,422	152,421	123,607	138,007	0.37	11.65
Bulgaria	1,255,343	1,406,604	1,433,970	1,491,561	1,492,073	3.96	0.03
Czech Republic	158,858	164,733	174,426	223,369	223,986	0.59	0.28
Estonia	33,752	36,413	35,136	34,921	35,459	0.09	1.54
Georgia	830,184	995,381	1,112,193	1,152,661	1,404,882	3.72	21.88
Hungary	95,414	82,684	90,944	103,918	94,409	0.25	-9.15
Kazakhstan	213,072	219,445	247,784	315,907	380,046	1.01	20.30
Kyrgyzstan	47,730	40,882	35,665	41,197	42,866	0.11	4.05
Latvia	58,460	40,686	39,102	45,074	45,725	0.12	1.44
Lithuania	92,939	76,730	71,992	76,036	69,520	0.18	-8.57
Poland	397,682	419,475	428,275	486,319	428,440	1.14	-11.90
Republic of Moldova	141,514	117,856	96,196	101,124	108,032	0.29	6.83
Romania	447,419	366,698	355,144	390,248	385,055	1.02	-1.33
Russian Federation	2,879,278	2,694,733	3,107,043	3,468,214	3,599,925	9.55	3.80
Slovakia	69,168	80,687	91,765	122,088	126,974	0.34	4.00
Tajikistan	36,262	19,816	17,737	16,822	22,823	0.06	35.67
Turkmenistan	88,915	112,358	114,390	137,476	135,168	0.36	-1.68
Ukraine	730,689	574,700	568,227	602,404	634,663	1.68	5.36
Uzbekistan	69,127	73,910	68,124	85,011	105,976	0.28	24.66
Northern Europe	**3,328,924**	**3,648,575**	**3,995,471**	**4,210,678**	**4,184,264**	**11.09**	**-0.63**
Denmark	276,805	296,085	314,446	369,867	391,312	1.04	5.80
Finland	102,883	136,489	143,204	186,562	195,083	0.52	4.57
Iceland	9,374	7,838	6,476	6,156	5,797	0.02	-5.83
Ireland	115,388	117,360	111,065	118,620	110,863	0.29	-6.54
Norway	250,458	262,314	299,405	375,502	406,879	1.08	8.36
Sweden	404,092	401,740	447,270	571,917	617,811	1.64	8.02
United Kingdom	2,169,924	2,426,749	2,673,605	2,582,054	2,456,519	6.51	-4.86
Southern Europe	**2,026,553**	**2,081,304**	**2,129,507**	**2,288,499**	**2,235,196**	**5.93**	**-2.33**
Albania	63,146	59,958	49,954	53,141	59,565	0.16	12.09
Bosnia and Herzegovina	58,910	52,271	47,361	56,522	61,851	0.16	9.43
Croatia	31,186	31,407	33,563	41,959	47,144	0.12	12.36
Greece	572,212	616,489	670,297	702,017	669,823	1.78	-4.59
Italy	600,261	634,886	671,060	752,238	714,041	1.89	-5.08
Malta	3,412	3,616	3,361	5,974	6,397	0.02	7.08
Montenegro		11,837	11,610	13,793	16,559	0.04	20.05
Portugal	36,977	46,900	53,373	52,319	46,606	0.12	-10.92
Serbia	170,399	102,202	113,465	137,934	157,568	0.42	14.23
Slovenia	41,301	38,134	38,597	41,870	39,899	0.11	-4.71
Spain	342,104	376,215	321,325	300,084	278,164	0.74	-7.30
TFYR of Macedonia	106,645	107,389	115,541	130,648	137,579	0.36	5.31
Western Europe	**7,822,664**	**7,981,251**	**7,712,428**	**8,646,534**	**8,817,029**	**23.38**	**1.97**
Austria	520,334	548,117	500,321	528,966	505,560	1.34	-4.42
Belgium	596,442	592,078	543,003	585,860	608,071	1.61	3.79
France	885,006	932,809	928,376	1,140,459	1,032,565	2.74	-9.46
Germany	4,415,525	4,488,350	4,385,263	4,826,315	5,028,745	13.33	4.19
Luxembourg	10,852	9,687	11,262	13,286	14,034	0.04	5.63
Netherlands	1,141,580	1,127,150	1,073,064	1,222,823	1,273,593	3.38	4.15
Switzerland	252,925	283,060	271,139	328,825	354,461	0.94	7.80
East Mediterranean Europe	**567,800**	**325,156**	**124,980**	**95,889**	**102,664**	**0.27**	**7.07**
Cyprus	9,617	13,574	15,421	16,749	18,924	0.05	12.99
Israel	558,183	311,582	109,559	79,140	83,740	0.22	5.81

Yearbook of Tourism Statistics, Data 2008 – 2012, 2014 Edition

TURKEY

2. Arrivals of non-resident visitors at national borders, by nationality

	2008	2009	2010	2011	2012	Market share 2012	% Change 2012-2011
Other Europe	2,171	31,035	48,635	59,448	73,050	0.19	22.88
Other countries of Europe	2,171	31,035	48,635	59,448	73,050	0.19	22.88
MIDDLE EAST	1,208,379	1,430,016	1,899,958	2,142,401	2,389,706	6.34	11.54
Bahrain	8,081	9,090	9,375	9,712	13,342	0.04	37.38
Egypt	57,994	66,912	61,560	79,665	112,025	0.30	40.62
Iraq	250,130	285,229	280,328	369,033	533,149	1.41	44.47
Jordan	74,340	87,694	96,562	94,914	102,154	0.27	7.63
Kuwait	22,084	26,801	27,281	41,617	65,167	0.17	56.59
Lebanon	53,948	71,771	134,554	137,110	144,491	0.38	5.38
Libya	43,779	64,721	60,917	53,562	213,890	0.57	299.33
Oman	5,904	5,203	5,408	5,998	7,959	0.02	32.69
Palestine	4,130	5,402	4,685	5,447	6,327	0.02	16.16
Qatar	4,862	4,902	6,043	7,661	13,971	0.04	82.37
Saudi Arabia	55,636	66,938	84,934	116,711	175,467	0.47	50.34
Syrian Arab Republic	406,935	509,679	899,494	974,054	730,039	1.94	-25.05
United Arab Emirates	19,676	22,051	30,480	35,579	48,071	0.13	35.11
Yemen	4,971	6,181	6,344	8,066	11,826	0.03	46.62
Other countries of Middle East	195,909	197,442	191,993	203,272	211,828	0.56	4.21
SOUTH ASIA	1,229,818	1,490,181	1,987,969	2,005,224	1,331,712	3.53	-33.59
Afghanistan	11,473	21,508	12,511	16,395	15,373	0.04	-6.23
Bangladesh	2,950	3,599	2,190	6,168	6,652	0.02	7.85
India	55,798	55,114	63,406	73,731	90,934	0.24	23.33
Iran, Islamic Republic of	1,134,965	1,383,261	1,885,097	1,879,304	1,186,343	3.15	-36.87
Pakistan	22,473	24,004	22,540	26,735	28,394	0.08	6.21
Other countries of South Asia	2,159	2,695	2,225	2,891	4,016	0.01	38.91
NOT SPECIFIED	4,847,022	4,746,275	4,395,828	5,347,682	5,969,052	15.83	11.62
Other countries of the World	45,925	63,573	30,724	34,719	36,659	0.10	5.59
Nationals Residing Abroad	4,801,097	4,682,702	4,365,104	5,312,963	5,932,393	15.73	11.66

Yearbook of Tourism Statistics, Data 2008 – 2012, 2014 Edition

TURKEY

3. Arrivals of non-resident tourists in hotels and similar establishments, by nationality

		2008	2009	2010	2011	2012	Market share 2012	% Change 2012-2011
TOTAL	(*)	13,627,758	14,362,491	17,111,736	18,790,691	19,998,885	100.00	6.43
AFRICA		68,472	85,379	180,168	148,587	168,576	0.84	13.45
North Africa		39,804	58,173	71,638	96,698	119,978	0.60	24.07
Algeria		11,086	16,313	18,905	31,313	41,310	0.21	31.93
Morocco		10,524	21,335	23,619	35,449	33,488	0.17	-5.53
Sudan		1,914	3,531	3,148	5,549	4,885	0.02	-11.97
Tunisia		16,280	16,994	25,966	24,387	40,295	0.20	65.23
Southern Africa		11,405	14,036	17,922	25,245	24,165	0.12	-4.28
South Africa		11,405	14,036	17,922	25,245	24,165	0.12	-4.28
Other Africa		17,263	13,170	90,608	26,644	24,433	0.12	-8.30
Other countries of Africa		17,263	13,170	90,608	26,644	24,433	0.12	-8.30
AMERICAS		551,911	529,404	639,657	809,563	858,352	4.29	6.03
Central America		2,411	4,375	6,916	5,555	7,473	0.04	34.53
All countries of Central America		2,411	4,375	6,916	5,555	7,473	0.04	34.53
North America		498,370	457,673	536,910	670,600	692,027	3.46	3.20
Canada		49,807	44,492	57,509	87,039	90,718	0.45	4.23
Mexico		13,338	10,925	9,150	11,136	14,288	0.07	28.30
United States of America		435,225	402,239	470,243	572,421	587,003	2.94	2.55
Other countries of North America			17	8	4	18	0.00	350.00
South America		51,130	67,356	95,831	133,408	158,852	0.79	19.07
Argentina		15,882	13,636	21,966	33,439	33,299	0.17	-0.42
Brazil		22,051	40,846	60,742	79,711	100,218	0.50	25.73
Chile		3,050	5,261	3,357	4,680	6,177	0.03	31.99
Colombia		1,978	1,937	3,513	4,750	6,955	0.03	46.42
Venezuela		4,992	2,174	2,659	2,723	6,250	0.03	129.53
Other countries of South America		3,177	3,502	3,594	8,105	5,953	0.03	-26.55
EAST ASIA AND THE PACIFIC		894,082	802,853	887,307	1,121,244	1,237,605	6.19	10.38
North-East Asia		702,507	580,121	631,461	786,304	875,912	4.38	11.40
China		52,365	47,714	63,560	113,444	161,373	0.81	42.25
Japan		466,642	430,706	413,508	412,388	418,867	2.09	1.57
Korea, Republic of		183,500	101,701	154,393	260,472	295,672	1.48	13.51
South-East Asia		59,751	85,475	90,876	113,794	143,066	0.72	25.72
Indonesia		7,187	8,262	10,453	19,078	36,367	0.18	90.62
Malaysia		19,913	31,342	37,088	38,070	41,496	0.21	9.00
Philippines		4,461	5,178	4,902	6,977	8,606	0.04	23.35
Singapore		20,769	31,465	31,110	34,571	41,594	0.21	20.31
Thailand		7,421	9,228	7,323	15,098	15,003	0.08	-0.63
Australasia		102,682	108,056	127,068	145,178	157,556	0.79	8.53
Australia		94,064	99,164	112,065	132,395	143,288	0.72	8.23
New Zealand		8,618	8,892	15,003	12,783	14,268	0.07	11.62
Other East Asia and the Pacific		29,142	29,201	37,902	75,968	61,071	0.31	-19.61
Other countries of Asia		27,800	28,122	34,404	65,351	58,591	0.29	-10.34
All countries of Oceania		1,342	1,079	3,498	10,617	2,480	0.01	-76.64
EUROPE		11,305,798	11,921,431	14,066,151	15,267,394	15,804,091	79.02	3.52
Central/Eastern Europe		3,440,207	3,541,263	4,006,528	4,450,274	4,665,072	23.33	4.83
Armenia		12,792	21,262	16,943	14,062	18,217	0.09	29.55
Azerbaijan		59,824	78,758	85,532	111,442	128,488	0.64	15.30
Belarus		38,665	39,249	44,619	47,161	47,591	0.24	0.91
Bulgaria		119,402	128,412	149,420	135,651	158,414	0.79	16.78
Czech Republic		87,623	114,066	122,884	174,899	159,878	0.80	-8.59
Estonia		12,839	17,329	26,186	24,236	26,865	0.13	10.85
Georgia		35,888	45,051	47,867	43,623	37,023	0.19	-15.13
Hungary		56,705	49,441	64,320	59,323	70,772	0.35	19.30
Kazakhstan		97,295	127,596	145,637	172,148	255,009	1.28	48.13

   Yearbook of Tourism Statistics, Data 2008 – 2012, 2014 Edition

TURKEY

3. Arrivals of non-resident tourists in hotels and similar establishments, by nationality

	2008	2009	2010	2011	2012	Market share 2012	% Change 2012-2011
Kyrgyzstan	10,847	10,911	10,986	14,035	12,820	0.06	-8.66
Latvia	17,441	12,708	18,928	20,352	30,049	0.15	47.65
Lithuania	69,628	45,666	53,493	57,214	67,075	0.34	17.24
Poland	187,632	212,989	270,327	311,361	260,920	1.30	-16.20
Republic of Moldova	28,368	32,863	39,444	44,427	75,507	0.38	69.96
Romania	215,599	201,619	212,955	208,741	205,289	1.03	-1.65
Russian Federation	2,054,253	2,045,159	2,344,193	2,549,215	2,619,041	13.10	2.74
Slovakia	24,491	42,780	59,553	86,327	81,564	0.41	-5.52
Tajikistan	7,592	4,721	3,985	13,571	8,352	0.04	-38.46
Turkmenistan	13,094	15,740	21,820	22,525	28,236	0.14	25.35
Ukraine	272,630	275,305	247,723	314,751	343,289	1.72	9.07
Uzbekistan	17,599	19,638	19,713	25,210	30,673	0.15	21.67
Northern Europe	**1,269,219**	**1,650,995**	**2,109,166**	**2,314,032**	**2,271,219**	**11.36**	**-1.85**
Denmark	84,734	82,964	94,358	135,164	160,823	0.80	18.98
Finland	43,670	61,242	71,357	82,751	103,601	0.52	25.20
Iceland	7,772	5,779	6,392	5,210	7,559	0.04	45.09
Ireland	48,213	70,886	65,476	85,486	72,368	0.36	-15.35
Norway	76,366	97,334	149,087	229,215	248,002	1.24	8.20
Sweden	141,365	153,068	234,312	348,455	352,684	1.76	1.21
United Kingdom	867,099	1,179,722	1,488,184	1,427,751	1,326,182	6.63	-7.11
Southern Europe	**1,029,591**	**1,226,180**	**1,199,618**	**1,141,344**	**1,159,624**	**5.80**	**1.60**
Albania	26,625	30,505	28,890	23,609	28,204	0.14	19.46
Bosnia and Herzegovina	23,868	24,575	27,783	34,192	38,140	0.19	11.55
Croatia	16,526	17,028	19,966	35,698	43,764	0.22	22.60
Greece	190,748	201,220	243,232	224,117	197,278	0.99	-11.98
Italy	307,395	428,935	349,605	411,653	413,106	2.07	0.35
Malta	1,429	1,562	1,579	1,533	1,521	0.01	-0.78
Montenegro		8	72	158	119	0.00	-24.68
Portugal	32,962	50,946	64,667	38,971	37,030	0.19	-4.98
Serbia	43,321	46,711	57,816	59,110	74,032	0.37	25.24
Slovenia	16,599	18,365	20,687	45,273	31,673	0.16	-30.04
Spain	346,081	376,837	353,195	236,552	260,952	1.30	10.31
TFYR of Macedonia	24,037	29,488	32,126	30,478	33,805	0.17	10.92
Western Europe	**5,263,009**	**5,265,506**	**6,642,861**	**7,265,100**	**7,637,822**	**38.19**	**5.13**
Austria	176,613	263,973	246,480	271,668	243,563	1.22	-10.35
Belgium	435,457	474,758	454,774	466,602	479,148	2.40	2.69
France	518,838	627,269	762,928	935,719	751,436	3.76	-19.69
Germany	3,413,529	3,142,293	4,328,235	4,571,741	4,996,223	24.98	9.28
Luxembourg	10,770	11,556	13,214	17,148	16,167	0.08	-5.72
Netherlands	599,390	607,770	681,948	795,739	912,816	4.56	14.71
Switzerland	108,412	137,887	155,282	206,483	238,469	1.19	15.49
East Mediterranean Europe	**300,960**	**230,906**	**101,681**	**89,048**	**61,242**	**0.31**	**-31.23**
Cyprus	4,648	4,902	13,706	38,809	14,180	0.07	-63.46
Israel	296,312	226,004	87,975	50,239	47,062	0.24	-6.32
Other Europe	**2,812**	**6,581**	**6,297**	**7,596**	**9,112**	**0.05**	**19.96**
Other countries of Europe	2,812	6,581	6,297	7,596	9,112	0.05	19.96
MIDDLE EAST	**503,298**	**613,018**	**768,447**	**829,125**	**1,282,483**	**6.41**	**54.68**
Bahrain	6,542	7,353	7,386	9,844	13,168	0.07	33.77
Egypt	37,860	43,559	51,039	63,762	92,981	0.46	45.83
Iraq	71,837	105,817	129,815	165,889	273,072	1.37	64.61
Jordan	54,343	76,663	57,835	55,580	81,253	0.41	46.19
Kuwait	18,763	23,081	26,914	38,991	62,819	0.31	61.11
Lebanon	35,940	47,729	84,934	81,192	101,375	0.51	24.86
Libya	12,334	16,832	26,834	32,433	193,411	0.97	496.34
Oman	3,101	3,258	4,103	3,328	4,964	0.02	49.16
Qatar	5,778	3,968	6,524	7,015	17,111	0.09	143.92
Saudi Arabia	77,807	89,463	134,463	172,789	241,411	1.21	39.71

Yearbook of Tourism Statistics, Data 2008 – 2012, 2014 Edition

TURKEY

3. Arrivals of non-resident tourists in hotels and similar establishments, by nationality

	2008	2009	2010	2011	2012	Market share 2012	% Change 2012-2011
Syrian Arab Republic	59,446	76,370	121,355	71,777	64,491	0.32	-10.15
United Arab Emirates	30,866	37,402	47,509	49,101	65,285	0.33	32.96
Yemen	1,902	3,631	4,532	4,572	7,744	0.04	69.38
Other countries of Middle East	86,779	77,892	65,204	72,852	63,398	0.32	-12.98
SOUTH ASIA	**238,856**	**312,878**	**447,938**	**501,883**	**529,692**	**2.65**	**5.54**
Bangladesh	1,085	1,709	1,545	2,941	2,867	0.01	-2.52
India	34,703	36,212	45,516	67,084	78,240	0.39	16.63
Iran, Islamic Republic of	188,382	259,500	383,312	410,040	431,827	2.16	5.31
Pakistan	14,686	15,457	17,565	21,818	16,758	0.08	-23.19
NOT SPECIFIED	**65,341**	**97,528**	**122,068**	**112,895**	**118,086**	**0.59**	**4.60**
Other countries of the World	65,341	97,528	122,068	112,895	118,086	0.59	4.60

Yearbook of Tourism Statistics, Data 2008 – 2012, 2014 Edition

TURKEY

4. Arrivals of non-resident tourists in all types of accommodation establishments, by nationality

		2008	2009	2010	2011	2012	Market share 2012	% Change 2012-2011
TOTAL	(*)	13,647,606	14,388,998	17,415,364	19,264,058	20,481,308	100.00	6.32
AFRICA		68,483	85,583	180,409	149,448	170,236	0.83	13.91
North Africa		39,808	58,263	71,793	97,213	120,365	0.59	23.82
Algeria		11,086	16,326	18,917	31,404	41,446	0.20	31.98
Morocco		10,524	21,367	23,668	35,569	33,598	0.16	-5.54
Sudan		1,914	3,534	3,166	5,750	4,910	0.02	-14.61
Tunisia		16,284	17,036	26,042	24,490	40,411	0.20	65.01
Southern Africa		11,408	14,039	17,942	25,342	25,247	0.12	-0.37
South Africa		11,408	14,039	17,942	25,342	25,247	0.12	-0.37
Other Africa		17,267	13,281	90,674	26,893	24,624	0.12	-8.44
Other countries of Africa		17,267	13,281	90,674	26,893	24,624	0.12	-8.44
AMERICAS		552,102	530,008	663,999	842,432	893,752	4.36	6.09
Central America		2,411	4,387	6,984	5,583	7,505	0.04	34.43
All countries of Central America		2,411	4,387	6,984	5,583	7,505	0.04	34.43
North America		498,561	458,238	558,090	699,486	724,579	3.54	3.59
Canada		49,930	44,561	58,176	88,394	93,401	0.46	5.66
Mexico		13,338	10,951	9,267	11,348	14,601	0.07	28.67
United States of America		435,293	402,709	490,639	599,740	616,559	3.01	2.80
Other countries of North America			17	8	4	18	0.00	350.00
South America		51,130	67,383	98,925	137,363	161,668	0.79	17.69
Argentina		15,882	13,645	22,528	33,586	33,565	0.16	-0.06
Brazil		22,051	40,856	62,961	83,153	102,455	0.50	23.21
Chile		3,050	5,261	3,390	4,691	6,257	0.03	33.38
Colombia		1,978	1,937	3,514	4,818	7,016	0.03	45.62
Venezuela		4,992	2,174	2,659	2,727	6,300	0.03	131.02
Other countries of South America		3,177	3,510	3,873	8,388	6,075	0.03	-27.58
EAST ASIA AND THE PACIFIC		894,332	803,739	996,822	1,241,879	1,430,342	6.98	15.18
North-East Asia		702,531	580,691	735,566	897,382	1,049,413	5.12	16.94
China		52,371	47,941	68,569	124,986	179,495	0.88	43.61
Japan		466,658	430,985	500,873	489,160	530,552	2.59	8.46
Korea, Republic of		183,502	101,765	166,124	283,236	339,366	1.66	19.82
South-East Asia		59,751	85,530	92,499	115,425	155,827	0.76	35.00
Indonesia		7,187	8,276	10,780	19,487	37,198	0.18	90.89
Malaysia		19,913	31,362	37,383	38,406	50,171	0.24	30.63
Philippines		4,461	5,194	4,972	7,052	8,765	0.04	24.29
Singapore		20,769	31,469	31,772	35,283	43,915	0.21	24.47
Thailand		7,421	9,229	7,592	15,197	15,778	0.08	3.82
Australasia		102,908	108,308	128,324	147,307	159,838	0.78	8.51
Australia		94,233	99,393	113,310	134,433	145,308	0.71	8.09
New Zealand		8,675	8,915	15,014	12,874	14,530	0.07	12.86
Other East Asia and the Pacific		29,142	29,210	40,433	81,765	65,264	0.32	-20.18
Other countries of Asia		27,800	28,128	36,904	71,120	62,780	0.31	-11.73
All countries of Oceania		1,342	1,082	3,529	10,645	2,484	0.01	-76.67
EUROPE		11,323,454	11,936,444	14,217,939	15,565,736	16,027,373	78.25	2.97
Central/Eastern Europe		3,444,310	3,544,735	4,021,775	4,481,312	4,698,290	22.94	4.84
Armenia		12,792	21,267	16,949	14,062	18,267	0.09	29.90
Azerbaijan		59,842	78,953	85,829	111,835	129,481	0.63	15.78
Belarus		38,667	39,279	44,640	47,253	48,473	0.24	2.58
Bulgaria		119,599	128,594	150,170	137,663	159,310	0.78	15.72
Czech Republic		89,050	114,182	124,979	190,104	161,877	0.79	-14.85
Estonia		12,839	17,335	26,358	24,429	27,144	0.13	11.11
Georgia		35,888	45,165	47,941	43,752	37,592	0.18	-14.08
Hungary		56,863	49,443	64,920	60,151	75,610	0.37	25.70
Kazakhstan		97,295	127,748	145,863	172,460	255,250	1.25	48.01

Yearbook of Tourism Statistics, Data 2008 – 2012, 2014 Edition

TURKEY

4. Arrivals of non-resident tourists in all types of accommodation establishments, by nationality

	2008	2009	2010	2011	2012	Market share 2012	% Change 2012-2011
Kyrgyzstan	10,851	11,000	10,994	14,056	12,873	0.06	-8.42
Latvia	17,441	12,710	18,928	20,352	30,070	0.15	47.75
Lithuania	69,628	45,666	53,722	57,496	67,390	0.33	17.21
Poland	188,783	213,249	270,892	312,286	263,565	1.29	-15.60
Republic of Moldova	28,378	33,204	39,453	44,565	75,572	0.37	69.58
Romania	215,671	201,822	213,907	209,220	208,273	1.02	-0.45
Russian Federation	2,055,205	2,046,457	2,352,400	2,557,505	2,629,697	12.84	2.82
Slovakia	24,519	42,780	60,252	87,070	82,560	0.40	-5.18
Tajikistan	7,592	4,759	4,014	13,635	8,457	0.04	-37.98
Turkmenistan	13,094	15,850	21,931	22,712	28,760	0.14	26.63
Ukraine	272,683	275,492	247,900	315,441	346,737	1.69	9.92
Uzbekistan	17,630	19,780	19,733	25,265	31,332	0.15	24.01
Northern Europe	**1,270,182**	**1,655,058**	**2,119,469**	**2,331,365**	**2,293,194**	**11.20**	**-1.64**
Denmark	84,960	83,047	94,696	135,755	161,906	0.79	19.26
Finland	43,671	61,270	71,602	83,417	104,517	0.51	25.29
Iceland	7,781	5,886	6,457	5,260	7,575	0.04	44.01
Ireland	48,236	70,933	65,570	86,098	72,734	0.36	-15.52
Norway	76,366	99,946	151,991	234,798	255,330	1.25	8.74
Sweden	141,393	153,257	235,140	349,825	357,358	1.74	2.15
United Kingdom	867,775	1,180,719	1,494,013	1,436,212	1,333,774	6.51	-7.13
Southern Europe	**1,029,889**	**1,228,386**	**1,245,370**	**1,197,890**	**1,203,053**	**5.87**	**0.43**
Albania	26,625	30,541	28,896	23,654	28,274	0.14	19.53
Bosnia and Herzegovina	23,877	24,600	27,818	34,256	38,351	0.19	11.95
Croatia	16,528	17,028	19,968	35,837	45,012	0.22	25.60
Greece	190,853	202,289	245,473	230,514	200,760	0.98	-12.91
Italy	307,467	429,688	360,830	429,276	425,727	2.08	-0.83
Malta	1,429	1,562	1,586	1,541	1,574	0.01	2.14
Montenegro		8	72	158	119	0.00	-24.68
Portugal	32,962	50,971	69,908	44,329	41,391	0.20	-6.63
Serbia	43,349	46,752	57,869	59,185	74,315	0.36	25.56
Slovenia	16,630	18,373	20,707	45,463	32,669	0.16	-28.14
Spain	346,130	377,053	380,081	263,132	280,697	1.37	6.68
TFYR of Macedonia	24,039	29,521	32,162	30,545	34,164	0.17	11.85
Western Europe	**5,275,280**	**5,270,735**	**6,723,216**	**7,457,986**	**7,762,255**	**37.90**	**4.08**
Austria	176,803	264,163	248,559	274,668	244,726	1.19	-10.90
Belgium	435,495	474,845	455,798	468,468	480,482	2.35	2.56
France	519,670	627,822	786,450	995,943	783,252	3.82	-21.36
Germany	3,418,321	3,145,853	4,379,380	4,694,645	5,078,937	24.80	8.19
Luxembourg	10,773	11,556	13,217	17,202	16,220	0.08	-5.71
Netherlands	605,597	608,528	684,089	799,403	917,541	4.48	14.78
Switzerland	108,621	137,968	155,723	207,657	241,097	1.18	16.10
East Mediterranean Europe	**300,979**	**230,946**	**101,806**	**89,581**	**61,438**	**0.30**	**-31.42**
Cyprus	4,648	4,904	13,721	39,061	14,217	0.07	-63.60
Israel	296,331	226,042	88,085	50,520	47,221	0.23	-6.53
Other Europe	**2,814**	**6,584**	**6,303**	**7,602**	**9,143**	**0.04**	**20.27**
Other countries of Europe	2,814	6,584	6,303	7,602	9,143	0.04	20.27
MIDDLE EAST	**503,316**	**616,430**	**784,240**	**845,149**	**1,307,598**	**6.38**	**54.72**
Bahrain	6,542	7,358	8,632	9,921	13,311	0.06	34.17
Egypt	37,862	43,586	51,100	64,019	93,328	0.46	45.78
Iraq	71,842	106,061	130,081	166,398	274,159	1.34	64.76
Jordan	54,344	76,667	58,040	58,109	81,658	0.40	40.53
Kuwait	18,763	23,097	27,492	39,552	63,763	0.31	61.21
Lebanon	35,941	47,736	85,888	81,600	102,309	0.50	25.38
Libya	12,334	16,847	26,896	32,537	203,845	1.00	526.50
Oman	3,101	3,259	4,151	3,386	5,005	0.02	47.81
Qatar	5,778	3,968	6,703	7,196	17,591	0.09	144.46
Saudi Arabia	77,807	89,621	136,810	175,356	248,060	1.21	41.46

Yearbook of Tourism Statistics, Data 2008 – 2012, 2014 Edition

TURKEY

4. Arrivals of non-resident tourists in all types of accommodation establishments, by nationality

	2008	2009	2010	2011	2012	Market share 2012	% Change 2012-2011
Syrian Arab Republic	59,447	79,091	129,205	75,187	65,476	0.32	-12.92
United Arab Emirates	30,868	37,417	48,331	49,604	67,210	0.33	35.49
Yemen	1,902	3,631	4,582	4,638	7,863	0.04	69.53
Other countries of Middle East	86,785	78,091	66,329	77,646	64,020	0.31	-17.55
SOUTH ASIA	**238,882**	**313,101**	**448,820**	**504,456**	**532,763**	**2.60**	**5.61**
Bangladesh	1,085	1,709	1,560	2,949	2,887	0.01	-2.10
India	34,707	36,221	45,942	67,901	79,516	0.39	17.11
Iran, Islamic Republic of	188,399	259,698	383,660	411,647	433,254	2.12	5.25
Pakistan	14,691	15,473	17,658	21,959	17,106	0.08	-22.10
NOT SPECIFIED	**67,037**	**103,693**	**123,135**	**114,958**	**119,244**	**0.58**	**3.73**
Other countries of the World	67,037	103,693	123,135	114,958	119,244	0.58	3.73

Yearbook of Tourism Statistics, Data 2008 – 2012, 2014 Edition

TURKEY

5. Overnight stays of non-resident tourists in hotels and similar establishments, by nationality

		2008	2009	2010	2011	2012	Market share 2012	% Change 2012-2011
TOTAL	(*)	56,864,692	59,873,570	73,924,293	78,257,238	90,099,501	100.00	15.13
AFRICA		206,583	239,091	759,662	442,085	523,204	0.58	18.35
North Africa		114,879	166,387	224,150	296,287	393,359	0.44	32.76
Algeria		32,860	46,119	62,174	110,427	148,363	0.16	34.35
Morocco		28,766	62,616	73,780	103,892	107,133	0.12	3.12
Sudan		7,043	8,051	9,222	12,713	13,035	0.01	2.53
Tunisia		46,210	49,601	78,974	69,255	124,828	0.14	80.24
Southern Africa		24,809	30,543	38,231	58,995	63,911	0.07	8.33
South Africa		24,809	30,543	38,231	58,995	63,911	0.07	8.33
Other Africa		66,895	42,161	497,281	86,803	65,934	0.07	-24.04
Other countries of Africa		66,895	42,161	497,281	86,803	65,934	0.07	-24.04
AMERICAS		1,185,163	1,140,453	1,387,177	2,070,670	1,997,060	2.22	-3.55
Central America		6,088	8,768	12,558	14,543	26,965	0.03	85.42
All countries of Central America		6,088	8,768	12,558	14,543	26,965	0.03	85.42
North America		1,072,071	978,686	1,152,195	1,776,364	1,622,288	1.80	-8.67
Canada		102,214	95,639	122,030	186,418	203,599	0.23	9.22
Mexico		25,625	21,517	19,464	26,532	31,258	0.03	17.81
United States of America		944,232	861,460	1,010,691	1,563,398	1,387,292	1.54	-11.26
Other countries of North America			70	10	16	139	0.00	768.75
South America		107,004	152,999	222,424	279,763	347,807	0.39	24.32
Argentina		33,220	27,761	60,839	75,402	76,671	0.09	1.68
Brazil		45,164	78,374	129,608	162,069	206,356	0.23	27.33
Chile		7,229	24,487	8,400	10,447	13,971	0.02	33.73
Colombia		4,366	4,612	7,585	10,440	14,686	0.02	40.67
Venezuela		9,627	4,953	6,255	6,397	21,023	0.02	228.64
Other countries of South America		7,398	12,812	9,737	15,008	15,100	0.02	0.61
EAST ASIA AND THE PACIFIC		1,383,405	1,316,967	1,439,411	1,844,814	2,047,741	2.27	11.00
North-East Asia		982,885	805,105	922,909	1,150,270	1,350,641	1.50	17.42
China		122,117	94,634	129,901	206,148	357,812	0.40	73.57
Japan		617,505	564,617	576,610	606,808	598,066	0.66	-1.44
Korea, Republic of		243,263	145,854	216,398	337,314	394,763	0.44	17.03
South-East Asia		96,916	140,536	146,608	194,652	225,014	0.25	15.60
Indonesia		13,167	14,728	18,875	31,949	55,064	0.06	72.35
Malaysia		31,262	51,739	53,519	64,074	70,426	0.08	9.91
Philippines		9,677	11,796	11,190	15,257	15,648	0.02	2.56
Singapore		31,398	48,392	49,965	62,071	60,148	0.07	-3.10
Thailand		11,412	13,881	13,059	21,301	23,728	0.03	11.39
Australasia		248,701	324,915	285,884	341,457	364,640	0.40	6.79
Australia		233,700	306,865	256,750	317,065	336,415	0.37	6.10
New Zealand		15,001	18,050	29,134	24,392	28,225	0.03	15.71
Other East Asia and the Pacific		54,903	46,411	84,010	158,435	107,446	0.12	-32.18
Other countries of Asia		51,707	42,522	74,509	108,904	92,077	0.10	-15.45
All countries of Oceania		3,196	3,889	9,501	49,531	15,369	0.02	-68.97
EUROPE		51,957,616	54,630,674	66,808,767	69,892,338	79,858,154	88.63	14.26
Central/Eastern Europe		16,721,563	17,032,704	19,153,341	20,207,385	24,166,205	26.82	19.59
Armenia		41,262	72,281	59,401	47,101	68,248	0.08	44.90
Azerbaijan		182,512	265,305	304,033	351,877	467,013	0.52	32.72
Belarus		153,280	240,075	252,010	243,280	311,987	0.35	28.24
Bulgaria		342,777	387,122	428,868	373,211	438,180	0.49	17.41
Czech Republic		477,314	579,391	614,268	713,512	762,373	0.85	6.85
Estonia		61,849	93,731	143,767	127,224	141,307	0.16	11.07
Georgia		79,914	131,301	119,365	105,320	96,510	0.11	-8.36
Hungary		247,120	209,527	316,227	281,164	316,914	0.35	12.71
Kazakhstan		427,211	598,343	725,185	820,144	1,184,056	1.31	44.37

787

Yearbook of Tourism Statistics, Data 2008 – 2012, 2014 Edition

TURKEY

5. Overnight stays of non-resident tourists in hotels and similar establishments, by nationality

	2008	2009	2010	2011	2012	Market share 2012	% Change 2012-2011
Kyrgyzstan	27,401	25,808	26,851	31,893	37,149	0.04	16.48
Latvia	96,940	68,539	99,093	101,856	135,535	0.15	33.07
Lithuania	306,539	205,498	275,576	268,688	337,597	0.37	25.65
Poland	940,900	1,023,017	1,455,787	1,353,244	1,272,024	1.41	-6.00
Republic of Moldova	115,346	140,742	181,778	181,468	324,501	0.36	78.82
Romania	762,459	754,973	900,166	818,250	774,939	0.86	-5.29
Russian Federation	10,854,943	10,594,606	11,540,679	12,504,898	15,118,830	16.78	20.90
Slovakia	144,168	239,148	390,416	373,526	490,913	0.54	31.43
Tajikistan	16,208	11,945	11,700	53,889	23,036	0.03	-57.25
Turkmenistan	32,450	35,781	44,390	56,145	69,127	0.08	23.12
Ukraine	1,368,080	1,277,169	1,176,919	1,313,844	1,680,827	1.87	27.93
Uzbekistan	42,890	78,402	86,862	86,851	115,139	0.13	32.57
Northern Europe	**6,234,781**	**7,915,450**	**10,295,216**	**11,162,624**	**11,889,279**	**13.20**	**6.51**
Denmark	406,882	424,949	447,875	667,373	723,148	0.80	8.36
Finland	233,855	314,509	335,372	410,695	520,382	0.58	26.71
Iceland	28,489	30,956	21,417	22,497	28,391	0.03	26.20
Ireland	184,431	324,930	296,304	392,913	332,447	0.37	-15.39
Norway	431,989	480,635	821,156	924,423	1,161,686	1.29	25.67
Sweden	682,238	712,347	1,017,083	1,516,503	1,699,339	1.89	12.06
United Kingdom	4,266,897	5,627,124	7,356,009	7,228,220	7,423,886	8.24	2.71
Southern Europe	**2,549,004**	**2,888,676**	**3,071,508**	**2,899,345**	**2,981,748**	**3.31**	**2.84**
Albania	107,854	126,948	118,909	73,730	94,732	0.11	28.49
Bosnia and Herzegovina	82,282	76,943	113,457	109,308	127,652	0.14	16.78
Croatia	52,956	45,973	55,183	96,854	110,188	0.12	13.77
Greece	416,755	434,905	549,864	479,398	416,931	0.46	-13.03
Italy	742,672	946,224	851,921	1,038,782	1,010,674	1.12	-2.71
Malta	3,404	4,293	3,696	4,148	4,088	0.00	-1.45
Montenegro		65	125	288	485	0.00	68.40
Portugal	65,846	111,211	155,417	113,688	93,284	0.10	-17.95
Serbia	192,139	169,436	227,249	241,089	325,689	0.36	35.09
Slovenia	67,387	77,364	87,120	122,562	80,575	0.09	-34.26
Spain	742,275	800,952	809,997	532,169	614,288	0.68	15.43
TFYR of Macedonia	75,434	94,362	98,570	87,329	103,162	0.11	18.13
Western Europe	**25,491,651**	**26,160,413**	**33,951,969**	**35,318,089**	**40,582,077**	**45.04**	**14.90**
Austria	850,868	1,235,296	1,272,529	1,411,417	1,175,934	1.31	-16.68
Belgium	2,252,590	2,426,030	2,458,136	2,253,374	2,338,358	2.60	3.77
France	1,817,726	2,155,145	2,511,518	3,139,182	2,557,436	2.84	-18.53
Germany	16,904,892	16,453,952	23,116,350	23,516,104	28,477,289	31.61	21.10
Luxembourg	59,998	60,958	76,375	92,191	82,035	0.09	-11.02
Netherlands	3,107,529	3,172,840	3,721,425	3,964,994	4,731,613	5.25	19.33
Switzerland	498,048	656,192	795,636	940,827	1,219,412	1.35	29.61
East Mediterranean Europe	**947,923**	**597,791**	**312,128**	**266,773**	**193,132**	**0.21**	**-27.60**
Cyprus	21,543	12,308	59,973	119,138	47,673	0.05	-59.99
Israel	926,380	585,483	252,155	147,635	145,459	0.16	-1.47
Other Europe	**12,694**	**35,640**	**24,605**	**38,122**	**45,713**	**0.05**	**19.91**
Other countries of Europe	12,694	35,640	24,605	38,122	45,713	0.05	19.91
MIDDLE EAST	**1,254,659**	**1,439,671**	**1,940,036**	**2,213,042**	**3,711,264**	**4.12**	**67.70**
Bahrain	18,186	17,920	20,936	28,564	33,825	0.04	18.42
Egypt	92,889	111,004	139,242	183,168	308,476	0.34	68.41
Iraq	190,520	257,193	310,869	404,696	622,974	0.69	53.94
Jordan	131,721	167,641	156,654	146,505	230,708	0.26	57.47
Kuwait	47,754	61,374	78,473	117,581	205,394	0.23	74.68
Lebanon	100,518	121,396	210,549	228,156	316,418	0.35	38.68
Libya	34,098	43,935	75,073	94,077	749,816	0.83	697.02
Oman	11,368	7,795	14,970	9,306	14,108	0.02	51.60
Qatar	15,575	10,375	20,850	25,705	62,989	0.07	145.05
Saudi Arabia	212,345	216,813	358,747	495,531	686,311	0.76	38.50

788

TURKEY

5. Overnight stays of non-resident tourists in hotels and similar establishments, by nationality

	2008	2009	2010	2011	2012	Market share 2012	% Change 2012-2011
Syrian Arab Republic	138,304	170,987	254,731	181,053	150,662	0.17	-16.79
United Arab Emirates	86,449	92,732	134,156	136,530	175,760	0.20	28.73
Yemen	5,083	9,433	12,789	12,062	21,761	0.02	80.41
Other countries of Middle East	169,849	151,073	151,997	150,108	132,062	0.15	-12.02
SOUTH ASIA	**712,863**	**912,636**	**1,311,944**	**1,544,555**	**1,683,261**	**1.87**	**8.98**
Bangladesh	2,381	3,859	3,642	6,977	10,375	0.01	48.70
India	98,248	96,602	120,979	171,817	180,415	0.20	5.00
Iran, Islamic Republic of	573,839	776,692	1,147,783	1,311,620	1,446,438	1.61	10.28
Pakistan	38,395	35,483	39,540	54,141	46,033	0.05	-14.98
NOT SPECIFIED	**164,403**	**194,078**	**277,296**	**249,734**	**278,817**	**0.31**	**11.65**
Other countries of the World	164,403	194,078	277,296	249,734	278,817	0.31	11.65

Yearbook of Tourism Statistics, Data 2008 – 2012, 2014 Edition

TURKEY

6. Overnight stays of non-resident tourists in all types of accommodation establishments, by nationality

	2008	2009	2010	2011	2012	Market share 2012	% Change 2012-2011
TOTAL (*)	56,918,298	59,986,967	74,325,670	78,888,865	90,779,045	100.00	15.07
AFRICA	206,594	239,633	760,093	443,980	526,070	0.58	18.49
North Africa	114,883	166,561	224,407	297,229	394,547	0.43	32.74
Algeria	32,860	46,132	62,203	110,634	148,818	0.16	34.51
Morocco	28,766	62,684	73,843	104,165	107,420	0.12	3.12
Sudan	7,043	8,057	9,259	13,017	13,129	0.01	0.86
Tunisia	46,214	49,688	79,102	69,413	125,180	0.14	80.34
Southern Africa	24,812	30,546	38,263	59,221	65,300	0.07	10.26
South Africa	24,812	30,546	38,263	59,221	65,300	0.07	10.26
Other Africa	66,899	42,526	497,423	87,530	66,223	0.07	-24.34
Other countries of Africa	66,899	42,526	497,423	87,530	66,223	0.07	-24.34
AMERICAS	1,186,274	1,142,026	1,414,045	2,115,535	2,043,964	2.25	-3.38
Central America	6,088	8,840	12,790	14,609	27,031	0.03	85.03
All countries of Central America	6,088	8,840	12,790	14,609	27,031	0.03	85.03
North America	1,073,182	980,116	1,175,575	1,815,595	1,664,858	1.83	-8.30
Canada	103,218	95,749	122,855	189,000	207,221	0.23	9.64
Mexico	25,625	21,562	19,603	26,919	31,694	0.03	17.74
United States of America	944,339	862,735	1,033,107	1,599,660	1,425,804	1.57	-10.87
Other countries of North America		70	10	16	139	0.00	768.75
South America	107,004	153,070	225,680	285,331	352,075	0.39	23.39
Argentina	33,220	27,794	61,457	75,697	77,347	0.09	2.18
Brazil	45,164	78,404	131,872	166,922	209,392	0.23	25.44
Chile	7,229	24,487	8,478	10,464	14,094	0.02	34.69
Colombia	4,366	4,612	7,587	10,535	14,794	0.02	40.43
Venezuela	9,627	4,953	6,255	6,401	21,108	0.02	229.76
Other countries of South America	7,398	12,820	10,031	15,312	15,340	0.02	0.18
EAST ASIA AND THE PACIFIC	1,384,184	1,318,491	1,550,223	1,972,048	2,252,974	2.48	14.25
North-East Asia	982,940	805,975	1,027,664	1,265,824	1,533,970	1.69	21.18
China	122,135	94,980	135,052	218,223	376,978	0.42	72.75
Japan	617,539	565,034	664,353	687,219	715,696	0.79	4.14
Korea, Republic of	243,266	145,961	228,259	360,382	441,296	0.49	22.45
South-East Asia	96,916	140,633	148,551	196,761	238,425	0.26	21.17
Indonesia	13,167	14,742	19,254	32,410	56,010	0.06	72.82
Malaysia	31,262	51,763	53,832	64,520	79,228	0.09	22.80
Philippines	9,677	11,847	11,319	15,432	15,858	0.02	2.76
Singapore	31,398	48,399	50,776	62,867	62,821	0.07	-0.07
Thailand	11,412	13,882	13,370	21,532	24,508	0.03	13.82
Australasia	249,425	325,427	287,429	344,527	368,874	0.41	7.07
Australia	234,203	307,350	258,263	319,914	340,141	0.37	6.32
New Zealand	15,222	18,077	29,166	24,613	28,733	0.03	16.74
Other East Asia and the Pacific	54,903	46,456	86,579	164,936	111,705	0.12	-32.27
Other countries of Asia	51,707	42,534	77,016	115,235	96,327	0.11	-16.41
All countries of Oceania	3,196	3,922	9,563	49,701	15,378	0.02	-69.06
EUROPE	52,001,411	54,713,782	67,033,714	70,304,422	80,214,603	88.36	14.10
Central/Eastern Europe	16,730,880	17,040,896	19,173,876	20,246,957	24,213,329	26.67	19.59
Armenia	41,262	72,293	59,414	47,101	68,367	0.08	45.15
Azerbaijan	182,544	265,804	305,304	352,927	470,471	0.52	33.31
Belarus	153,282	240,163	252,067	243,420	312,918	0.34	28.55
Bulgaria	343,122	387,482	430,122	377,536	440,043	0.48	16.56
Czech Republic	480,893	579,646	616,487	728,868	764,873	0.84	4.94
Estonia	61,849	93,746	143,955	127,423	141,682	0.16	11.19
Georgia	79,914	131,573	119,497	105,533	97,154	0.11	-7.94
Hungary	248,286	209,529	316,898	282,251	321,982	0.35	14.08
Kazakhstan	427,211	598,700	725,788	820,855	1,184,750	1.31	44.33

790

Yearbook of Tourism Statistics, Data 2008 – 2012, 2014 Edition

TURKEY

6. Overnight stays of non-resident tourists in all types of accommodation establishments, by nationality

	2008	2009	2010	2011	2012	Market share 2012	% Change 2012-2011
Kyrgyzstan	27,474	26,026	26,876	31,934	37,262	0.04	16.68
Latvia	96,940	68,541	99,093	101,856	135,595	0.15	33.12
Lithuania	306,539	205,498	275,826	269,068	338,058	0.37	25.64
Poland	942,312	1,023,361	1,456,762	1,354,592	1,275,603	1.41	-5.83
Republic of Moldova	115,356	141,392	181,791	181,809	324,600	0.36	78.54
Romania	762,662	755,333	901,401	819,130	779,020	0.86	-4.90
Russian Federation	10,856,861	10,598,132	11,550,617	12,515,472	15,134,166	16.67	20.92
Slovakia	144,443	239,148	391,174	374,352	492,048	0.54	31.44
Tajikistan	16,208	12,020	11,757	54,066	23,282	0.03	-56.94
Turkmenistan	32,450	36,025	44,769	56,623	70,354	0.08	24.25
Ukraine	1,368,310	1,277,592	1,177,377	1,315,090	1,684,909	1.86	28.12
Uzbekistan	42,962	78,892	86,901	87,051	116,192	0.13	33.48
Northern Europe	**6,237,875**	**7,955,652**	**10,339,025**	**11,208,792**	**11,949,571**	**13.16**	**6.61**
Denmark	407,386	425,480	448,974	669,073	725,377	0.80	8.42
Finland	233,856	314,622	335,723	412,142	521,388	0.57	26.51
Iceland	28,510	31,322	21,513	22,558	28,439	0.03	26.07
Ireland	184,463	324,981	296,520	394,576	333,287	0.37	-15.53
Norway	431,989	515,450	853,600	949,040	1,198,009	1.32	26.23
Sweden	682,291	713,702	1,019,359	1,519,418	1,707,740	1.88	12.39
United Kingdom	4,269,380	5,630,095	7,363,336	7,241,985	7,435,331	8.19	2.67
Southern Europe	**2,550,310**	**2,894,934**	**3,121,575**	**2,969,147**	**3,042,900**	**3.35**	**2.48**
Albania	107,854	127,080	118,962	73,836	94,918	0.10	28.55
Bosnia and Herzegovina	82,293	77,093	113,581	109,389	128,086	0.14	17.09
Croatia	52,958	45,973	55,188	97,129	111,516	0.12	14.81
Greece	417,243	437,943	554,235	491,098	426,466	0.47	-13.16
Italy	742,887	948,587	864,644	1,061,724	1,030,235	1.13	-2.97
Malta	3,404	4,293	3,743	4,161	4,153	0.00	-0.19
Montenegro		65	125	288	485	0.00	68.40
Portugal	65,846	111,281	160,730	119,441	98,105	0.11	-17.86
Serbia	192,277	169,505	227,354	241,192	326,434	0.36	35.34
Slovenia	67,677	77,378	87,171	123,011	81,636	0.09	-33.64
Spain	742,435	801,320	837,163	560,413	636,069	0.70	13.50
TFYR of Macedonia	75,436	94,416	98,679	87,465	104,797	0.12	19.82
Western Europe	**25,521,694**	**26,188,754**	**34,062,125**	**35,573,689**	**40,812,445**	**44.96**	**14.73**
Austria	851,266	1,235,901	1,275,012	1,415,987	1,178,126	1.30	-16.80
Belgium	2,252,679	2,426,247	2,459,627	2,256,942	2,341,267	2.58	3.74
France	1,819,184	2,156,631	2,538,021	3,207,763	2,596,094	2.86	-19.07
Germany	16,913,407	16,474,891	23,190,309	23,684,650	28,642,258	31.55	20.93
Luxembourg	60,001	60,958	76,382	92,348	82,149	0.09	-11.04
Netherlands	3,126,114	3,177,548	3,725,732	3,971,501	4,748,224	5.23	19.56
Switzerland	499,043	656,578	797,042	944,498	1,224,327	1.35	29.63
East Mediterranean Europe	**947,956**	**597,892**	**312,470**	**267,708**	**150,576**	**0.17**	**-43.75**
Cyprus	21,543	12,334	60,021	119,618	4,772	0.01	-96.01
Israel	926,413	585,558	252,449	148,090	145,804	0.16	-1.54
Other Europe	**12,696**	**35,654**	**24,643**	**38,129**	**45,782**	**0.05**	**20.07**
Other countries of Europe	12,696	35,654	24,643	38,129	45,782	0.05	20.07
MIDDLE EAST	**1,254,689**	**1,446,457**	**1,974,936**	**2,241,479**	**3,769,049**	**4.15**	**68.15**
Bahrain	18,186	17,927	24,651	28,687	34,239	0.04	19.35
Egypt	92,892	111,058	139,471	183,601	309,317	0.34	68.47
Iraq	190,526	257,647	311,566	405,828	625,683	0.69	54.17
Jordan	131,722	167,654	157,164	149,990	231,975	0.26	54.66
Kuwait	47,754	61,421	80,875	119,202	207,534	0.23	74.10
Lebanon	100,519	121,410	212,176	228,863	318,748	0.35	39.27
Libya	34,098	43,980	75,222	94,236	771,593	0.85	718.79
Oman	11,368	7,796	15,091	9,406	14,203	0.02	51.00
Qatar	15,575	10,375	21,305	26,124	64,142	0.07	145.53
Saudi Arabia	212,345	217,118	364,700	502,198	701,846	0.77	39.75

Yearbook of Tourism Statistics, Data 2008 – 2012, 2014 Edition

TURKEY

6. Overnight stays of non-resident tourists in all types of accommodation establishments, by nationality

	2008	2009	2010	2011	2012	Market share 2012	% Change 2012-2011
Syrian Arab Republic	138,305	176,097	267,585	186,472	153,280	0.17	-17.80
United Arab Emirates	86,457	92,767	136,902	137,733	180,469	0.20	31.03
Yemen	5,083	9,433	12,890	12,219	22,015	0.02	80.17
Other countries of Middle East	169,859	151,774	155,338	156,920	134,005	0.15	-14.60
SOUTH ASIA	**712,890**	**913,204**	**1,313,594**	**1,550,249**	**1,690,618**	**1.86**	**9.05**
Bangladesh	2,381	3,859	3,685	7,001	10,413	0.01	48.74
India	98,252	96,618	121,560	173,954	183,170	0.20	5.30
Iran, Islamic Republic of	573,857	777,220	1,148,675	1,314,890	1,450,417	1.60	10.31
Pakistan	38,400	35,507	39,674	54,404	46,618	0.05	-14.31
NOT SPECIFIED	**172,256**	**213,374**	**279,065**	**261,152**	**281,767**	**0.31**	**7.89**
Other countries of the World	172,256	213,374	279,065	261,152	281,767	0.31	7.89

Yearbook of Tourism Statistics, Data 2008 – 2012, 2014 Edition

TURKS AND CAICOS ISLANDS

1. Arrivals of non-resident tourists at national borders, by country of residence

	2008	2009	2010	2011	2012	Market share 2012	% Change 2012-2011
TOTAL				354,223	298,936	100.00	-15.61
AMERICAS				344,337	264,830	88.59	-23.09
Caribbean				39,913			
All countries of the Caribbean				39,913			
North America				304,424	264,830	88.59	-13.01
Canada				42,282	35,253	11.79	-16.62
United States of America				262,142	229,577	76.80	-12.42
EUROPE				6,902			
Other Europe				6,902			
All countries of Europe				6,902			
NOT SPECIFIED				2,984	34,106	11.41	1,042.96
Other countries of the World				2,984	34,106	11.41	1,042.96

Yearbook of Tourism Statistics, Data 2008 – 2012, 2014 Edition

TUVALU

1. Arrivals of non-resident tourists at national borders, by nationality

	2008	2009	2010	2011	2012	Market share 2012	% Change 2012-2011
TOTAL	1,651	1,580	1,657	1,232			
AMERICAS	79	83	97	94			
North America	79	83	97	94			
Canada	12	13	26	9			
United States of America	67	70	71	85			
EAST ASIA AND THE PACIFIC	1,320	1,267	1,288	909			
North-East Asia	432	471	418	190			
China	20	74	41	9			
Japan	412	397	377	150			
Taiwan, Province of China				31			
Australasia	345	382	350	249			
Australia	205	194	166	116			
New Zealand	140	188	184	133			
Melanesia	324	251	285	311			
Fiji	324	251	285	311			
Micronesia	23	51	34	22			
Kiribati	23	51	34	22			
Other East Asia and the Pacific	196	112	201	137			
Other countries of Asia	124	54	133	48			
All countries of Oceania	72	58	68	89			
EUROPE	136	143	134	81			
Northern Europe	44	54	42	22			
United Kingdom	44	54	42	22			
Western Europe	30	45	45	24			
France	12	15	17	8			
Germany	18	30	28	16			
Other Europe	62	44	47	35			
Other countries of Europe	62	44	47	35			
NOT SPECIFIED	116	87	138	148			
Other countries of the World	116	87	138	148			

Yearbook of Tourism Statistics, Data 2008 – 2012, 2014 Edition

UGANDA

1. Arrivals of non-resident tourists at national borders, by country of residence

	2008	2009	2010	2011	2012	Market share 2012	% Change 2012-2011
TOTAL	843,864	806,655	945,899	1,151,356	1,196,765	100.00	3.94
AFRICA	624,352	630,014	675,931	873,348	929,569	77.67	6.44
East Africa	484,720	515,714	520,159	675,592	735,532	61.46	8.87
Ethiopia	8,319	5,907	6,657	6,148	6,364	0.53	3.51
Kenya	249,786	261,329	294,170	344,210	393,369	32.87	14.28
Rwanda	181,339	199,530	177,043	266,221	256,004	21.39	-3.84
United Republic of Tanzania	45,276	48,948	42,289	59,013	79,795	6.67	35.22
Central Africa	12,495	11,664	20,306	42,147	42,604	3.56	1.08
Democratic Republic of the Congo	12,495	11,664	20,306	42,147	42,604	3.56	1.08
North Africa	16,169	15,088	22,909	39,333	2,397	0.20	-93.91
Sudan	16,169	15,088	22,909	39,333	2,397	0.20	-93.91
Southern Africa	13,940	14,034	15,115	16,152	19,292	1.61	19.44
South Africa	13,940	14,034	15,115	16,152	19,292	1.61	19.44
Other Africa	97,028	73,514	97,442	100,124	129,744	10.84	29.58
Other countries of Africa	97,028	73,514	97,442	100,124	129,744	10.84	29.58
AMERICAS	53,950	47,065	65,175	59,477	70,749	5.91	18.95
North America	51,604	44,970	54,209	56,419	66,098	5.52	17.16
Canada	9,186	6,999	8,353	8,550	10,186	0.85	19.13
United States of America	42,418	37,971	45,856	47,869	55,912	4.67	16.80
Other Americas	2,346	2,095	10,966	3,058	4,651	0.39	52.09
Other countries of the Americas	2,346	2,095	10,966	3,058	4,651	0.39	52.09
EAST ASIA AND THE PACIFIC	14,687	19,357	28,163	29,899	34,081	2.85	13.99
North-East Asia	8,037	6,814	8,002	10,633	12,831	1.07	20.67
China	6,088	4,629	5,692	6,971	8,645	0.72	24.01
Japan	1,949	2,185	2,310	3,662	4,186	0.35	14.31
Australasia	6,264	4,638	5,534	5,250	7,855	0.66	49.62
Australia	5,342	4,087	4,870	4,827	7,165	0.60	48.44
New Zealand	922	551	664	423	690	0.06	63.12
Other East Asia and the Pacific	386	7,905	14,627	14,016	13,395	1.12	-4.43
Other countries of Asia	386	7,905	14,300	12,778	11,031	0.92	-13.67
Other countries of Oceania			327	1,238	2,364	0.20	90.95
EUROPE	106,020	79,710	112,870	154,542	108,707	9.08	-29.66
Central/Eastern Europe	1,221	1,038	1,104	5,018	4,633	0.39	-7.67
Czech Republic/Slovakia	505	425	371	483	383	0.03	-20.70
Russian Federation	716	613	733	4,535	4,250	0.36	-6.28
Northern Europe	66,504	47,827	52,374	50,222	58,025	4.85	15.54
Denmark	3,389	3,000	3,145	4,159	3,890	0.33	-6.47
Finland	585	730	577	513	642	0.05	25.15
Ireland	2,615	1,820	2,143	1,663	2,414	0.20	45.16
Norway	3,528	2,827	2,874	1,877	2,705	0.23	44.11
Sweden	4,575	3,734	4,464	4,308	5,866	0.49	36.17
United Kingdom	51,812	35,716	39,171	37,702	42,508	3.55	12.75
Southern Europe	5,142	4,595	5,622	5,348	7,101	0.59	32.78
Italy	5,063	4,567	5,505	5,335	6,732	0.56	26.19
Serbia and Montenegro	79	28	117	13	369	0.03	2,738.46
Western Europe	26,916	21,669	46,203	81,809	34,502	2.88	-57.83
Austria	1,331	897	20,304	53,820	2,132	0.18	-96.04
Belgium	4,422	2,787	3,629	5,156	5,094	0.43	-1.20
France	3,958	3,467	3,893	4,437	4,938	0.41	11.29
Germany	8,083	6,778	8,650	8,960	11,701	0.98	30.59
Netherlands	7,136	6,017	7,651	8,380	8,275	0.69	-1.25
Switzerland	1,986	1,723	2,076	1,056	2,362	0.20	123.67
Other Europe	6,237	4,581	7,567	12,145	4,446	0.37	-63.39
Other countries of Europe	6,237	4,581	7,567	12,145	4,446	0.37	-63.39

795

UGANDA

1. Arrivals of non-resident tourists at national borders, by country of residence

	2008	2009	2010	2011	2012	Market share 2012	% Change 2012-2011
MIDDLE EAST	**9,720**	**8,942**	**15,538**	**8,652**	**8,105**	**0.68**	**-6.32**
Egypt	1,725	1,244	1,843	1,409	2,080	0.17	47.62
Other countries of Middle East	7,995	7,698	13,695	7,243	6,025	0.50	-16.82
SOUTH ASIA	**18,845**	**14,937**	**18,898**	**21,755**	**27,799**	**2.32**	**27.78**
India	16,236	12,946	16,747	19,419	24,849	2.08	27.96
Pakistan	2,609	1,991	2,151	2,336	2,950	0.25	26.28
NOT SPECIFIED	**16,290**	**6,630**	**29,324**	**3,683**	**17,755**	**1.48**	**382.08**
Other countries of the World	16,290	6,630	29,324	3,683	17,755	1.48	382.08

Yearbook of Tourism Statistics, Data 2008 – 2012, 2014 Edition

UKRAINE

1. Arrivals of non-resident tourists at national borders, by country of residence

	2008	2009	2010	2011	2012	Market share 2012	% Change 2012-2011
TOTAL	22,042,014	17,813,670	18,145,304	18,771,308	19,921,043	100.00	6.12
AFRICA	9,789	10,252	12,219	14,977	14,769	0.07	-1.39
East Africa	1,611	748	1,052	1,730	1,315	0.01	-23.99
British Indian Ocean Territory				21	20	0.00	-4.76
Burundi			4	4	7	0.00	75.00
Comoros			4	21	23	0.00	9.52
Djibouti			8	3	6	0.00	100.00
Eritrea			19	24	29	0.00	20.83
Ethiopia	168	128	104	207	163	0.00	-21.26
Kenya	212	244	223	320	230	0.00	-28.13
Madagascar			20	35	28	0.00	-20.00
Malawi			14	5	8	0.00	60.00
Mauritius			87	90	118	0.00	31.11
Mozambique			21	39	40	0.00	2.56
Rwanda	244		48	158	48	0.00	-69.62
Seychelles			5	9	12	0.00	33.33
Somalia	156	110	119	84	53	0.00	-36.90
Uganda	831	126	125	73	116	0.00	58.90
United Republic of Tanzania		140	126	490	178	0.00	-63.67
Zambia			44	62	99	0.00	59.68
Zimbabwe			81	85	137	0.00	61.18
Central Africa	445	863	1,213	1,381	1,414	0.01	2.39
Angola		151	160	293	340	0.00	16.04
Cameroon	254	417	504	457	435	0.00	-4.81
Central African Republic			4	36	3	0.00	-91.67
Chad			22	17	30	0.00	76.47
Congo	191	155	286	343	439	0.00	27.99
Democratic Republic of the Congo		140	176	170	29	0.00	-82.94
Equatorial Guinea			19	26	124	0.00	376.92
Gabon			42	30	11	0.00	-63.33
Sao Tome and Principe				9	3	0.00	-66.67
North Africa	4,199	4,720	4,771	5,269	5,908	0.03	12.13
Algeria	631	675	677	837	989	0.00	18.16
Morocco	1,592	1,956	1,925	2,297	2,767	0.01	20.46
Sudan	453	538	758	719	690	0.00	-4.03
Tunisia	1,523	1,551	1,411	1,416	1,462	0.01	3.25
Southern Africa	1,184	1,085	1,345	2,099	1,628	0.01	-22.44
Botswana			13	8	45	0.00	462.50
Lesotho			3	828	27	0.00	-96.74
Namibia			29	61	218	0.00	257.38
South Africa	1,184	1,085	1,297	1,196	1,330	0.01	11.20
Swaziland			3	6	8	0.00	33.33
West Africa	2,350	2,836	3,838	4,498	4,504	0.02	0.13
Benin			14	54	15	0.00	-72.22
Burkina Faso			46	17	22	0.00	29.41
Cape Verde			12	12	69	0.00	475.00
Côte d'Ivoire			77	82	73	0.00	-10.98
Gambia			2	2	3	0.00	50.00
Ghana	231	261	312	417	582	0.00	39.57
Guinea	231	160	99	97	77	0.00	-20.62
Guinea-Bissau			3	11	4	0.00	-63.64
Liberia			48	68	16	0.00	-76.47
Mali			46	60	52	0.00	-13.33
Mauritania			16	11	21	0.00	90.91
Niger			15	20	27	0.00	35.00
Nigeria	1,888	2,415	2,997	3,518	3,338	0.02	-5.12

797

UKRAINE

1. Arrivals of non-resident tourists at national borders, by country of residence

	2008	2009	2010	2011	2012	Market share 2012	% Change 2012-2011
Senegal			109	72	121	0.00	68.06
Sierra Leone			20	31	53	0.00	70.97
Togo			22	26	31	0.00	19.23
AMERICAS	**163,371**	**161,412**	**162,853**	**165,068**	**176,315**	**0.89**	**6.81**
Caribbean	**829**	**786**	**842**	**745**	**830**	**0.00**	**11.41**
Anguilla			10	7	4	0.00	-42.86
Antigua and Barbuda			9				
Bahamas			11	18	4	0.00	-77.78
Barbados			5	27	11	0.00	-59.26
Bermuda			4		2	0.00	
British Virgin Islands			5	3	9	0.00	200.00
Cayman Islands					1	0.00	
Cuba	679	786	702	564	599	0.00	6.21
Dominica			1	12	23	0.00	91.67
Dominican Republic			34	43	35	0.00	-18.60
Grenada			3	2	2	0.00	0.00
Guadeloupe					1	0.00	
Haiti			1	5	11	0.00	120.00
Jamaica			12	21	77	0.00	266.67
Montserrat			10	4			
Netherlands Antilles			2	1			
Puerto Rico			1	1			
Saint Kitts and Nevis			7	14	29	0.00	107.14
Saint Lucia			1	1			
Saint Vincent and the Grenadines			2		3	0.00	
Trinidad and Tobago			20	21	16	0.00	-23.81
Turks and Caicos Islands					1	0.00	
United States Virgin Islands	150		2	1	2	0.00	100.00
Central America		**135**	**277**	**400**	**241**	**0.00**	**-39.75**
Belize			14	4	3	0.00	-25.00
Costa Rica			74	70	87	0.00	24.29
El Salvador			11	237	37	0.00	-84.39
Guatemala			56	16	35	0.00	118.75
Honduras		135	28	10	16	0.00	60.00
Nicaragua			21	19	20	0.00	5.26
Panama			73	44	43	0.00	-2.27
North America	**158,197**	**155,488**	**155,539**	**157,462**	**166,755**	**0.84**	**5.90**
Canada	28,855	31,372	28,349	28,409	30,945	0.16	8.93
Greenland				2	1	0.00	-50.00
Mexico	1,220	1,115	1,337	1,127	1,681	0.01	49.16
United States of America	128,122	123,001	125,853	127,924	134,128	0.67	4.85
South America	**4,345**	**5,003**	**6,195**	**6,461**	**8,489**	**0.04**	**31.39**
Argentina	1,319	1,465	1,716	1,710	1,986	0.01	16.14
Bolivia			173	151	74	0.00	-50.99
Brazil	1,845	2,290	2,427	2,740	4,494	0.02	64.01
Chile	264	211	382	255	347	0.00	36.08
Colombia	151	217	278	224	244	0.00	8.93
Ecuador	211	235	270	264	411	0.00	55.68
French Guiana				20	3	0.00	-85.00
Guyana			3		3	0.00	
Paraguay			29	30	57	0.00	90.00
Peru	335	384	397	350	420	0.00	20.00
Suriname			2	7	8	0.00	14.29
Uruguay			84	108	111	0.00	2.78
Venezuela	220	201	434	579	300	0.00	-48.19
Other countries of South America				23	31	0.00	34.78

Yearbook of Tourism Statistics, Data 2008 – 2012, 2014 Edition

UKRAINE

1. Arrivals of non-resident tourists at national borders, by country of residence

	2008	2009	2010	2011	2012	Market share 2012	% Change 2012-2011
EAST ASIA AND THE PACIFIC	45,648	43,750	45,652	49,785	52,537	0.26	5.53
North-East Asia	31,114	28,839	30,111	34,830	37,518	0.19	7.72
China	16,574	16,137	16,794	19,057	19,718	0.10	3.47
Hong Kong, China			134	240	432	0.00	80.00
Japan	6,437	5,439	6,206	7,585	8,528	0.04	12.43
Korea, Dem. People's Republic of	577	333	299	220	502	0.00	128.18
Korea, Republic of	5,985	5,374	5,645	6,322	6,912	0.03	9.33
Macao, China			4	2	1	0.00	-50.00
Mongolia	997	483	651	858	1,053	0.01	22.73
Taiwan, Province of China	544	1,073	378	546	372	0.00	-31.87
South-East Asia	8,250	8,817	8,759	8,305	8,228	0.04	-0.93
Brunei Darussalam			24	3	15	0.00	400.00
Cambodia			14	48	28	0.00	-41.67
Indonesia	273	612	583	569	659	0.00	15.82
Lao People's Democratic Republic			22	36	27	0.00	-25.00
Malaysia	2,166	2,452	1,651	1,106	736	0.00	-33.45
Myanmar			167	12	23	0.00	91.67
Philippines	288	1,371	1,236	480	486	0.00	1.25
Singapore	419	208	357	1,159	733	0.00	-36.76
Thailand	348	480	354	447	665	0.00	48.77
Viet Nam	4,756	3,694	4,351	4,445	4,856	0.02	9.25
Australasia	6,284	6,094	6,742	6,638	6,774	0.03	2.05
Australia	5,277	5,224	5,769	5,706	5,880	0.03	3.05
New Zealand	1,007	870	973	932	894	0.00	-4.08
Melanesia			7	8	8	0.00	0.00
Fiji			1	4	4	0.00	0.00
New Caledonia			2	3	4	0.00	33.33
Solomon Islands			3				
Vanuatu			1	1			
Micronesia			30		3	0.00	
Guam					1	0.00	
Kiribati			12		2	0.00	
Marshall Islands			17				
Palau			1				
Polynesia			3	1	6	0.00	500.00
American Samoa			2	1	4	0.00	300.00
Samoa					2	0.00	
Tonga			1				
Other East Asia and the Pacific					3		
Other countries East Asia/Pacific					3		
EUROPE	21,756,811	17,529,722	17,853,192	18,473,971	19,614,224	98.46	6.17
Central/Eastern Europe	20,961,308	16,799,330	17,072,489	17,599,665	18,550,742	93.12	5.40
Armenia	56,050	53,373	52,492	53,627	68,087	0.34	26.96
Azerbaijan	80,350	66,996	77,123	85,482	101,229	0.51	18.42
Bulgaria	24,588	25,102	27,099	31,661	45,964	0.23	45.18
Czech Republic	43,959	46,646	46,461	51,858	51,955	0.26	0.19
Estonia	21,094	16,016	16,712	17,867	19,812	0.10	10.89
Georgia	53,544	40,544	36,039	35,861	40,799	0.20	13.77
Hungary	1,033,376	814,790	944,777	862,051	742,445	3.73	-13.87
Kazakhstan	48,565	43,524	50,787	61,826	70,784	0.36	14.49
Kyrgyzstan	9,859	10,520	18,102	21,501	19,441	0.10	-9.58
Latvia	44,737	35,555	36,602	36,936	39,840	0.20	7.86
Lithuania	56,991	48,314	48,907	48,677	54,636	0.27	12.24
Poland	5,242,980	2,546,132	2,089,647	1,720,104	1,404,086	7.05	-18.37
Republic of Moldova	4,418,821	4,339,138	4,063,459	4,071,785	4,849,115	24.34	19.09
Romania	1,440,466	1,077,299	910,450	735,233	791,281	3.97	7.62
Russian Federation	7,638,222	6,964,435	7,900,436	9,018,487	9,526,695	47.82	5.64

799

UKRAINE

1. Arrivals of non-resident tourists at national borders, by country of residence

	2008	2009	2010	2011	2012	Market share 2012	% Change 2012-2011
Slovakia	644,918	537,511	609,994	564,337	476,574	2.39	-15.55
Tajikistan	19,875	29,463	27,851	27,149	42,834	0.22	57.77
Turkmenistan	6,039	7,631	10,082	14,060	19,647	0.10	39.74
Uzbekistan	76,874	96,341	105,469	141,163	185,518	0.93	31.42
Northern Europe	**119,490**	**119,819**	**117,530**	**127,844**	**173,805**	**0.87**	**35.95**
Denmark	10,996	12,697	12,051	12,601	20,498	0.10	62.67
Faeroe Islands				.	1	0.00	
Finland	8,298	7,992	8,020	9,764	10,832	0.05	10.94
Iceland	512	566	532	674	708	0.00	5.04
Ireland	5,091	4,951	4,945	6,117	6,318	0.03	3.29
Isle of Man					1	0.00	
Norway	8,892	10,712	10,848	12,022	13,486	0.07	12.18
Sweden	16,992	16,050	16,544	19,491	40,777	0.20	109.21
United Kingdom	68,709	66,851	64,590	67,175	81,183	0.41	20.85
Other countries of Northern Europe					1	0.00	
Southern Europe	**132,175**	**128,763**	**137,629**	**155,643**	**203,988**	**1.02**	**31.06**
Albania	468	567	427	493	528	0.00	7.10
Andorra			23	39	30	0.00	-23.08
Bosnia and Herzegovina	1,924	999	997	1,014	2,976	0.01	193.49
Croatia	4,078	3,172	3,575	3,432	4,957	0.02	44.43
Greece	18,156	16,377	16,926	17,364	22,760	0.11	31.08
Holy See			14	21	22	0.00	4.76
Italy	70,625	73,737	79,174	86,964	89,081	0.45	2.43
Malta	418	408	447	479	599	0.00	25.05
Montenegro	1,999	1,643	2,037	1,239	1,197	0.01	-3.39
Portugal	3,959	3,909	4,857	6,783	18,883	0.09	178.39
San Marino			61	64	94	0.00	46.88
Serbia	5,203	5,065	6,340	12,135	29,607	0.15	143.98
Slovenia	7,570	5,499	5,885	6,980	9,160	0.05	31.23
Spain	14,135	13,453	14,021	16,441	20,628	0.10	25.47
TFYR of Macedonia	3,640	3,934	2,845	2,195	3,466	0.02	57.90
Western Europe	**369,986**	**349,953**	**373,552**	**389,847**	**457,404**	**2.30**	**17.33**
Austria	30,044	27,218	27,512	28,094	30,032	0.15	6.90
Belgium	12,913	13,455	13,796	14,998	16,407	0.08	9.39
France	50,403	49,810	56,268	62,088	64,804	0.33	4.37
Germany	231,632	213,995	227,725	231,718	274,073	1.38	18.28
Liechtenstein			92	91	107	0.00	17.58
Luxembourg	811	661	865	825	858	0.00	4.00
Monaco			26	15	29	0.00	93.33
Netherlands	30,305	31,548	31,965	33,216	52,417	0.26	57.81
Switzerland	13,878	13,266	15,303	18,802	18,677	0.09	-0.66
East Mediterranean Europe	**173,852**	**131,857**	**151,992**	**200,972**	**228,285**	**1.15**	**13.59**
Cyprus	4,061	3,476	3,913	4,428	3,992	0.02	-9.85
Israel	90,353	68,303	81,969	120,181	107,141	0.54	-10.85
Turkey	79,438	60,078	66,110	76,363	117,152	0.59	53.41
MIDDLE EAST	**23,253**	**27,856**	**29,059**	**28,572**	**28,794**	**0.14**	**0.78**
Bahrain	353	563	425	364	313	0.00	-14.01
Egypt	2,534	2,684	2,572	2,649	3,015	0.02	13.82
Iraq	1,596	2,633	4,337	5,201	5,266	0.03	1.25
Jordan	3,613	5,221	5,243	5,728	5,254	0.03	-8.28
Kuwait	517	1,188	928	978	946	0.00	-3.27
Lebanon	3,806	4,693	4,730	4,696	4,180	0.02	-10.99
Libya	2,970	3,198	2,924	998	2,085	0.01	108.92
Oman			87	125	153	0.00	22.40
Palestine	574	753	668	591	1,596	0.01	170.05
Qatar			171	174	183	0.00	5.17
Saudi Arabia	713	792	1,140	1,362	1,375	0.01	0.95

800

UKRAINE

1. Arrivals of non-resident tourists at national borders, by country of residence

	2008	2009	2010	2011	2012	Market share 2012	% Change 2012-2011
Syrian Arab Republic	6,084	5,290	4,919	4,333	3,528	0.02	-18.58
United Arab Emirates	306	573	681	1,169	689	0.00	-41.06
Yemen	187	268	234	204	211	0.00	3.43
SOUTH ASIA	**17,389**	**19,871**	**23,012**	**21,819**	**20,037**	**0.10**	**-8.17**
Afghanistan	798	943	991	1,056	953	0.00	-9.75
Bangladesh	211	184	245	342	352	0.00	2.92
Bhutan				6	13	0.00	116.67
India	7,262	8,183	10,152	9,254	10,264	0.05	10.91
Iran, Islamic Republic of	7,698	8,863	9,677	8,289	6,816	0.03	-17.77
Maldives			36	45	55	0.00	22.22
Nepal		172	183	1,180	159	0.00	-86.53
Pakistan	1,224	1,227	1,297	1,230	1,103	0.01	-10.33
Sri Lanka	196	299	431	417	322	0.00	-22.78
NOT SPECIFIED	**25,753**	**20,807**	**19,317**	**17,116**	**14,367**	**0.07**	**-16.06**
Other countries of the World	25,753	20,807	19,317	17,116	14,367	0.07	-16.06

Yearbook of Tourism Statistics, Data 2008 – 2012, 2014 Edition

UNITED KINGDOM

2. Arrivals of non-resident visitors at national borders, by country of residence

	2008	2009	2010	2011	2012	Market share 2012	% Change 2012-2011
TOTAL	31,888,118	29,889,075	29,803,000	30,797,000	31,084,000	100.00	0.93
AFRICA	644,718	596,415	571,000	527,000	571,200	1.84	8.39
East Africa	20,474	11,451	8,000	6,000	58,400	0.19	873.33
Kenya					32,000	0.10	
Mauritius					19,500	0.06	
Zimbabwe	20,474	11,451	8,000	6,000	6,900	0.02	15.00
North Africa					25,900	0.08	
Morocco					25,900	0.08	
Southern Africa	273,595	244,544	208,000	193,000	210,700	0.68	9.17
South Africa	273,595	244,544	208,000	193,000	210,700	0.68	9.17
West Africa	150,023	145,113	168,000	142,000	175,000	0.56	23.24
Ghana					21,000	0.07	
Nigeria	150,023	145,113	168,000	142,000	154,000	0.50	8.45
Other Africa	200,626	195,307	187,000	186,000	101,200	0.33	-45.59
Other countries of Africa	200,626	195,307	187,000	186,000	101,200	0.33	-45.59
AMERICAS	4,211,749	4,020,126	3,839,000	4,177,000	4,134,200	13.30	-1.02
Caribbean	73,088	89,784	71,000	76,000	59,500	0.19	-21.71
All countries of the Caribbean	73,088	89,784	71,000	76,000	59,500	0.19	-21.71
North America	3,871,154	3,644,923	3,464,000	3,664,000	3,627,500	11.67	-1.00
Canada	856,652	686,872	686,000	740,000	704,000	2.26	-4.86
Mexico	64,694	80,839	67,000	78,000	83,700	0.27	7.31
United States of America	2,949,808	2,877,212	2,711,000	2,846,000	2,839,800	9.14	-0.22
South America	248,295	250,724	275,000	411,000	417,700	1.34	1.63
Argentina	35,616	69,113	63,000	80,000	103,500	0.33	29.38
Brazil	178,734	151,087	177,000	276,000	259,500	0.83	-5.98
Chile	19,688	13,688	13,000	23,000	26,400	0.08	14.78
Colombia	6,248	6,845	18,000	13,000	14,200	0.05	9.23
Venezuela	8,009	9,991	4,000	19,000	14,100	0.05	-25.79
Other Americas	19,212	34,695	29,000	26,000	29,500	0.09	13.46
Other countries of the Americas	19,212	34,695	29,000	26,000	29,500	0.09	13.46
EAST ASIA AND THE PACIFIC	2,146,669	2,065,639	2,202,000	2,433,000	2,339,300	7.53	-3.85
North-East Asia	632,894	581,599	609,000	708,000	751,300	2.42	6.12
China	107,860	89,187	109,000	149,000	178,700	0.57	19.93
Hong Kong, China	129,957	143,472	131,000	149,000	135,200	0.43	-9.26
Japan	238,910	235,471	223,000	237,000	242,700	0.78	2.41
Korea, Republic of	128,346	74,635	115,000	140,000	158,300	0.51	13.07
Taiwan, Province of China	27,821	38,834	31,000	33,000	36,400	0.12	10.30
South-East Asia	244,412	301,288	323,000	329,000	395,300	1.27	20.15
Indonesia					27,300	0.09	
Malaysia	75,626	120,970	133,000	130,000	115,600	0.37	-11.08
Philippines					23,700	0.08	
Singapore	118,475	111,108	123,000	134,000	153,700	0.49	14.70
Thailand	50,311	69,210	67,000	65,000	75,000	0.24	15.38
Australasia	1,164,306	1,099,471	1,173,000	1,281,000	1,168,400	3.76	-8.79
Australia	955,487	912,259	986,000	1,093,000	993,000	3.19	-9.15
New Zealand	208,819	187,212	187,000	188,000	175,400	0.56	-6.70
Other East Asia and the Pacific	105,057	83,281	97,000	115,000	24,300	0.08	-78.87
Other countries of Asia	105,057	83,281	97,000	115,000	22,300	0.07	-80.61
Other countries of Oceania					2,000	0.01	
EUROPE	23,826,127	22,241,150	22,203,000	22,604,000	22,934,100	73.78	1.46
Central/Eastern Europe	3,346,728	2,594,122	2,547,000	2,645,000	2,942,200	9.47	11.24
Bulgaria					138,200	0.44	
Czech Republic	434,929	389,074	278,000	287,000	325,400	1.05	13.38
Estonia					35,700	0.11	
Hungary	299,636	260,340	214,000	211,000	261,600	0.84	23.98

802

UNITED KINGDOM

2. Arrivals of non-resident visitors at national borders, by country of residence

	2008	2009	2010	2011	2012	Market share 2012	% Change 2012-2011
Kazakhstan					21,600	0.07	
Latvia					74,500	0.24	
Lithuania					171,300	0.55	
Poland	1,491,797	1,040,553	1,101,000	1,058,000	1,222,500	3.93	15.55
Romania					267,100	0.86	
Russian Federation	207,740	137,287	170,000	211,000	227,400	0.73	7.77
Slovakia					120,400	0.39	
Ukraine					38,200	0.12	
Other countries Central/East Europe	912,626	766,868	784,000	878,000	38,300	0.12	-95.64
Northern Europe	**5,311,367**	**4,949,677**	**4,798,000**	**5,004,000**	**4,896,000**	**15.75**	**-2.16**
Denmark	561,410	618,804	558,000	622,000	639,100	2.06	2.75
Finland	179,054	167,331	170,000	233,000	208,100	0.67	-10.69
Iceland	70,241	38,500	34,000	41,000	47,300	0.15	15.37
Ireland	3,069,999	2,947,552	2,629,000	2,574,000	2,452,900	7.89	-4.70
Norway	688,161	573,163	649,000	739,000	771,300	2.48	4.37
Sweden	742,502	604,327	758,000	795,000	777,300	2.50	-2.23
Southern Europe	**4,364,109**	**4,077,714**	**3,981,000**	**4,078,000**	**3,906,100**	**12.57**	**-4.22**
Croatia					39,800	0.13	
Gibraltar	25,721	28,207	27,000	28,000	28,700	0.09	2.50
Greece	203,657	192,529	174,000	225,000	159,000	0.51	-29.33
Italy	1,639,316	1,220,907	1,472,000	1,526,000	1,520,500	4.89	-0.36
Malta	84,595	74,990	66,000	64,000	65,200	0.21	1.88
Portugal	274,519	255,096	316,000	283,000	291,700	0.94	3.07
Serbia					31,900	0.10	
Slovenia					53,300	0.17	
Spain	1,974,004	2,163,809	1,809,000	1,836,000	1,716,000	5.52	-6.54
Yugoslavia, SFR (former)	162,297	142,176	117,000	116,000			
Western Europe	**10,374,648**	**10,230,223**	**10,480,000**	**10,464,000**	**10,784,200**	**34.69**	**3.06**
Austria	285,664	286,148	288,000	271,000	267,700	0.86	-1.22
Belgium	970,262	903,127	1,136,000	984,000	1,112,600	3.58	13.07
France	3,636,332	3,784,473	3,618,000	3,633,000	3,786,900	12.18	4.24
Germany	2,899,571	2,779,754	3,004,000	2,947,000	2,967,200	9.55	0.69
Luxembourg	62,149	60,171	53,000	73,000	82,800	0.27	13.42
Netherlands	1,818,249	1,715,460	1,758,000	1,788,000	1,734,900	5.58	-2.97
Switzerland	702,421	701,090	623,000	768,000	832,100	2.68	8.35
East Mediterranean Europe	**429,275**	**389,414**	**397,000**	**413,000**	**387,300**	**1.25**	**-6.22**
Cyprus	138,817	133,704	110,000	124,000	103,900	0.33	-16.21
Israel	160,212	157,994	158,000	164,000	137,900	0.44	-15.91
Turkey	130,246	97,716	129,000	125,000	145,500	0.47	16.40
Other Europe					**18,300**	**0.06**	
Other countries of Europe					18,300	0.06	
MIDDLE EAST	**537,585**	**596,237**	**529,000**	**589,000**	**630,100**	**2.03**	**6.98**
Bahrain					30,400	0.10	
Egypt	41,535	47,936	42,000	41,000	50,000	0.16	21.95
Jordan					15,300	0.05	
Kuwait					66,400	0.21	
Lebanon					24,400	0.08	
Oman					20,200	0.06	
Qatar					45,700	0.15	
Saudi Arabia	93,914	88,605	79,000	105,000	110,600	0.36	5.33
United Arab Emirates	231,735	246,260	213,000	241,000	256,400	0.82	6.39
Other countries of Middle East	170,401	213,436	195,000	202,000	10,700	0.03	-94.70
SOUTH ASIA	**521,270**	**369,508**	**456,000**	**467,000**	**475,100**	**1.53**	**1.73**
Bangladesh	21,550	10,365	13,000	19,000	13,500	0.04	-28.95
India	359,237	272,754	371,000	356,000	339,400	1.09	-4.66
Iran, Islamic Republic of	38,006	25,958	15,000	27,000	16,800	0.05	-37.78

Yearbook of Tourism Statistics, Data 2008 – 2012, 2014 Edition

UNITED KINGDOM

2. Arrivals of non-resident visitors at national borders, by country of residence

	2008	2009	2010	2011	2012	Market share 2012	% Change 2012-2011
Pakistan	102,477	60,431	57,000	65,000	72,500	0.23	11.54
Sri Lanka					20,000	0.06	
Other countries of South Asia					12,900	0.04	
NOT SPECIFIED			**3,000**				
Other countries of the World			3,000				

Yearbook of Tourism Statistics, Data 2008 – 2012, 2014 Edition

UNITED KINGDOM

6. Overnight stays of non-resident tourists in all types of accommodation establishments, by country of residence

	2008	2009	2010	2011	2012	Market share 2012	% Change 2012-2011
TOTAL	245,774,778	229,387,112	227,846,000	235,196,000	230,190,600	100.00	-2.13
AFRICA	11,674,895	10,982,197	8,343,000	8,754,000	8,485,000	3.69	-3.07
East Africa	590,844	208,776	269,000	134,000	958,800	0.42	615.52
Kenya					483,700	0.21	
Mauritius					357,300	0.16	
Zimbabwe	590,844	208,776	269,000	134,000	117,800	0.05	-12.09
North Africa					243,800	0.11	
Morocco					243,800	0.11	
Southern Africa	3,941,943	4,745,254	2,564,000	2,316,000	2,633,200	1.14	13.70
South Africa	3,941,943	4,745,254	2,564,000	2,316,000	2,633,200	1.14	13.70
West Africa	2,495,533	2,216,268	2,428,000	2,292,000	2,802,800	1.22	22.29
Ghana					363,200	0.16	
Nigeria	2,495,533	2,216,268	2,428,000	2,292,000	2,439,600	1.06	6.44
Other Africa	4,646,575	3,811,899	3,082,000	4,012,000	1,846,400	0.80	-53.98
Other countries of Africa	4,646,575	3,811,899	3,082,000	4,012,000	1,846,400	0.80	-53.98
AMERICAS	38,621,607	36,647,738	35,589,000	36,452,000	36,604,900	15.90	0.42
Caribbean	1,239,674	1,533,973	1,108,000	1,022,000	1,092,800	0.47	6.93
All countries of the Caribbean	1,239,674	1,533,973	1,108,000	1,022,000	1,092,800	0.47	6.93
North America	33,395,225	31,362,700	30,659,000	31,088,000	31,153,500	13.53	0.21
Canada	8,114,689	6,802,042	7,413,000	7,061,000	7,035,800	3.06	-0.36
Mexico	538,365	789,409	507,000	694,000	549,400	0.24	-20.84
United States of America	24,742,171	23,771,249	22,739,000	23,333,000	23,568,300	10.24	1.01
South America	3,744,915	3,300,866	3,368,000	4,033,000	3,900,000	1.69	-3.30
Argentina	433,444	676,202	649,000	580,000	1,065,500	0.46	83.71
Brazil	2,489,983	2,248,968	1,764,000	2,652,000	2,400,500	1.04	-9.48
Chile	536,774	96,517	215,000	252,000	184,200	0.08	-26.90
Colombia	197,587	181,067	627,000	430,000	147,600	0.06	-65.67
Venezuela	87,127	98,112	113,000	119,000	102,200	0.04	-14.12
Other Americas	241,793	450,199	454,000	309,000	458,600	0.20	48.41
Other countries of the Americas	241,793	450,199	454,000	309,000	458,600	0.20	48.41
EAST ASIA AND THE PACIFIC	29,457,116	30,005,010	32,306,000	32,601,000	32,576,400	14.15	-0.08
North-East Asia	7,652,950	6,817,481	8,395,000	8,137,000	10,056,800	4.37	23.59
China	2,312,391	1,166,119	2,303,000	2,906,000	4,000,000	1.74	37.65
Hong Kong, China	1,147,778	1,648,135	1,497,000	1,759,000	1,325,900	0.58	-24.62
Japan	2,175,191	2,591,520	1,905,000	1,949,000	2,806,200	1.22	43.98
Korea, Republic of	1,377,692	1,028,912	1,853,000	1,262,000	1,302,400	0.57	3.20
Taiwan, Province of China	639,898	382,795	837,000	261,000	622,300	0.27	138.43
South-East Asia	3,018,492	4,605,929	4,683,000	4,491,000	5,941,800	2.58	32.30
Indonesia					872,800	0.38	
Malaysia	1,325,864	2,415,213	1,899,000	2,073,000	1,536,900	0.67	-25.86
Philippines					574,100	0.25	
Singapore	928,629	1,053,611	1,226,000	1,255,000	1,555,800	0.68	23.97
Thailand	763,999	1,137,105	1,558,000	1,163,000	1,402,200	0.61	20.57
Australasia	16,497,552	16,534,306	16,788,000	17,132,000	16,209,200	7.04	-5.39
Australia	13,198,603	13,309,858	13,929,000	13,601,000	13,365,700	5.81	-1.73
New Zealand	3,298,949	3,224,448	2,859,000	3,531,000	2,843,500	1.24	-19.47
Other East Asia and the Pacific	2,288,122	2,047,294	2,440,000	2,841,000	368,600	0.16	-87.03
Other countries of Asia	2,288,122	2,047,294	2,440,000	2,841,000	361,200	0.16	-87.29
Other countries of Oceania					7,400	0.00	
EUROPE	145,851,141	132,954,907	132,140,000	137,466,000	132,911,800	57.74	-3.31
Central/Eastern Europe	35,025,681	26,355,757	23,997,000	26,444,000	26,581,500	11.55	0.52
Bulgaria					1,289,300	0.56	
Czech Republic	2,817,728	2,301,997	1,831,000	1,865,000	2,296,800	1.00	23.15
Estonia					336,200	0.15	
Hungary	1,799,713	1,909,268	1,536,000	1,762,000	1,493,500	0.65	-15.24

Yearbook of Tourism Statistics, Data 2008 – 2012, 2014 Edition

UNITED KINGDOM

6. Overnight stays of non-resident tourists in all types of accommodation establishments, by country of residence

	2008	2009	2010	2011	2012	Market share 2012	% Change 2012-2011
Kazakhstan					281,500	0.12	
Latvia					712,700	0.31	
Lithuania					2,286,500	0.99	
Poland	17,308,004	12,028,477	10,731,000	10,141,000	11,751,500	5.11	15.88
Romania					2,481,100	1.08	
Russian Federation	1,671,433	1,307,573	1,683,000	2,240,000	2,055,700	0.89	-8.23
Slovakia					831,100	0.36	
Ukraine					303,300	0.13	
Other countries Central/East Europe	11,428,803	8,808,442	8,216,000	10,436,000	462,300	0.20	-95.57
Northern Europe	**21,489,366**	**19,615,071**	**19,935,000**	**22,383,000**	**20,348,700**	**8.84**	**-9.09**
Denmark	2,602,988	2,943,301	2,923,000	2,864,000	2,835,400	1.23	-1.00
Finland	1,267,448	775,290	805,000	1,262,000	1,254,700	0.55	-0.58
Iceland	264,032	170,247	138,000	272,000	183,500	0.08	-32.54
Ireland	10,394,784	9,874,615	9,519,000	10,225,000	9,030,100	3.92	-11.69
Norway	3,397,167	2,573,138	2,807,000	3,442,000	3,392,900	1.47	-1.43
Sweden	3,562,947	3,278,480	3,743,000	4,318,000	3,652,100	1.59	-15.42
Southern Europe	**30,081,349**	**29,826,772**	**29,334,000**	**28,838,000**	**29,323,100**	**12.74**	**1.68**
Croatia					239,300	0.10	
Gibraltar				150,000	144,700	0.06	-3.53
Greece	1,752,489	2,041,851	1,408,000	1,566,000	1,326,700	0.58	-15.28
Italy	11,189,106	8,293,632	10,330,000	9,676,000	10,020,600	4.35	3.56
Malta				583,000	667,400	0.29	14.48
Portugal	2,126,826	1,575,699	2,353,000	1,917,000	2,567,500	1.12	33.93
Serbia					422,000	0.18	
Slovenia					253,700	0.11	
Spain	13,874,348	17,115,037	14,367,000	13,719,000	13,681,200	5.94	-0.28
Yugoslavia, SFR (former)	1,138,580	800,553	876,000	1,227,000			
Western Europe	**54,432,937**	**52,250,184**	**54,143,000**	**55,437,000**	**52,406,400**	**22.77**	**-5.47**
Austria	1,825,065	1,643,383	1,569,000	1,759,000	1,659,300	0.72	-5.67
Belgium	2,929,099	2,925,268	4,002,000	3,101,000	3,551,000	1.54	14.51
France	20,178,582	19,007,830	18,614,000	18,705,000	18,876,500	8.20	0.92
Germany	17,374,318	17,300,078	18,143,000	18,822,000	16,306,100	7.08	-13.37
Luxembourg	267,530	177,002	259,000	319,000	325,600	0.14	2.07
Netherlands	8,482,702	7,255,632	7,870,000	8,413,000	7,593,800	3.30	-9.74
Switzerland	3,375,641	3,940,991	3,686,000	4,318,000	4,094,100	1.78	-5.19
East Mediterranean Europe	**2,338,805**	**2,464,037**	**2,525,000**	**4,364,000**	**3,876,500**	**1.68**	**-11.17**
Cyprus				1,368,000	1,206,100	0.52	-11.83
Israel	996,383	1,067,238	1,155,000	1,160,000	935,800	0.41	-19.33
Turkey	1,342,422	1,396,799	1,370,000	1,836,000	1,734,600	0.75	-5.52
Other Europe	**2,483,003**	**2,443,086**	**2,206,000**		**375,600**	**0.16**	
Other countries of Europe	2,483,003	2,443,086	2,206,000		375,600	0.16	
MIDDLE EAST	**7,243,536**	**8,701,807**	**7,217,000**	**8,263,000**	**7,715,100**	**3.35**	**-6.63**
Bahrain					259,500	0.11	
Egypt	450,364	734,685	559,000	472,000	616,500	0.27	30.61
Jordan					155,100	0.07	
Kuwait					955,200	0.41	
Lebanon					178,300	0.08	
Oman					364,700	0.16	
Qatar					479,500	0.21	
Saudi Arabia	1,650,536	1,549,915	923,000	1,890,000	1,462,500	0.64	-22.62
United Arab Emirates	2,400,399	2,862,588	2,872,000	2,831,000	2,897,200	1.26	2.34
Other countries of Middle East	2,742,237	3,554,619	2,863,000	3,070,000	346,600	0.15	-88.71
SOUTH ASIA	**12,926,483**	**10,095,453**	**12,251,000**	**11,660,000**	**11,897,400**	**5.17**	**2.04**
Bangladesh	639,027	343,966	391,000	399,000	644,200	0.28	61.45
India	7,643,815	7,293,377	9,720,000	8,341,000	7,381,300	3.21	-11.51
Iran, Islamic Republic of	847,881	487,212	492,000	515,000	598,300	0.26	16.17

Yearbook of Tourism Statistics, Data 2008 – 2012, 2014 Edition

UNITED KINGDOM

6. Overnight stays of non-resident tourists in all types of accommodation establishments, by country of residence

	2008	2009	2010	2011	2012	Market share 2012	% Change 2012-2011
Pakistan	3,795,760	1,970,898	1,648,000	2,405,000	2,520,000	1.09	4.78
Sri Lanka					423,300	0.18	
Other countries of South Asia					330,300	0.14	

                                              Yearbook of Tourism Statistics, Data 2008 – 2012, 2014 Edition

UNITED REPUBLIC OF TANZANIA

2. Arrivals of non-resident visitors at national borders, by country of residence

	2008	2009	2010	2011	2012	Market share 2012	% Change 2012-2011
TOTAL	770,469	714,367	782,699	867,994	1,078,178	100.00	24.21
AFRICA	373,053	348,765	392,137	445,750	489,864	45.43	9.90
East Africa	321,282	304,856	334,986	354,635	411,065	38.13	15.91
Burundi	11,721	14,581	17,440	34,341	43,194	4.01	25.78
Comoros	3,864	3,206	2,657	3,835	1,634	0.15	-57.39
Djibouti	282	40	193	413	881	0.08	113.32
Eritrea	54	90	113	137	365	0.03	166.42
Ethiopia	1,734	1,349	1,575	1,675	2,983	0.28	78.09
Kenya	184,269	177,929	193,474	171,473	183,269	17.00	6.88
Madagascar	70	78	222	211	4,064	0.38	1,826.07
Malawi	21,459	19,851	22,233	6,523	14,715	1.36	125.59
Mauritius	403	366	292	475	484	0.04	1.89
Mozambique	3,706	6,253	6,151	11,301	16,292	1.51	44.16
Rwanda	14,394	14,331	14,754	17,676	25,199	2.34	42.56
Seychelles	1,234	171	180	375	292	0.03	-22.13
Somalia	947	784	1,326	8,569	1,139	0.11	-86.71
Uganda	31,682	32,826	31,869	32,634	36,583	3.39	12.10
Zambia	37,682	26,999	34,983	47,898	51,880	4.81	8.31
Zimbabwe	7,781	6,002	7,524	17,099	28,091	2.61	64.28
Central Africa	9,390	7,968	14,465	22,511	18,824	1.75	-16.38
Angola	377	270	517	656	609	0.06	-7.16
Cameroon	739	817	710	593	1,634	0.15	175.55
Central African Republic	202	219	186	701	135	0.01	-80.74
Chad	26	36	48	94	83	0.01	-11.70
Congo	271	605	416	146	728	0.07	398.63
Democratic Republic of the Congo	7,638	5,879	11,836	19,043	10,264	0.95	-46.10
Equatorial Guinea					1,120	0.10	
Gabon	112	133	664	1,149	4,232	0.39	268.32
Sao Tome and Principe	25	9	88	129	19	0.00	-85.27
North Africa	1,133	1,907	3,899	3,886	2,462	0.23	-36.64
Algeria	118	86	105	249	390	0.04	56.63
Morocco	184	118	3,039	465	279	0.03	-40.00
Sudan	719	1,574	612	328	1,383	0.13	321.65
Tunisia	112	129	143	2,844	410	0.04	-85.58
Southern Africa	30,795	27,510	32,442	39,069	35,716	3.31	-8.58
Botswana	879	639	741	944	1,107	0.10	17.27
Lesotho	296	296	261	493	395	0.04	-19.88
Namibia	597	663	895	1,210	924	0.09	-23.64
South Africa	28,721	25,586	29,823	33,543	32,701	3.03	-2.51
Swaziland	302	326	722	2,879	589	0.05	-79.54
West Africa	10,453	6,524	6,345	25,649	21,797	2.02	-15.02
Benin	164	155	143	125	244	0.02	95.20
Burkina Faso	220	508	179	345	338	0.03	-2.03
Cape Verde	43	21	52	716	1,916	0.18	167.60
Côte d'Ivoire	4,922	189	414	9,630	5,530	0.51	-42.58
Gambia	317	221	222	427	483	0.04	13.11
Ghana	1,186	1,340	1,750	4,242	7,127	0.66	68.01
Guinea	554	586	304	110	386	0.04	250.91
Guinea-Bissau	4	8	59	1,082	13	0.00	-98.80
Liberia	109	82	165	182	293	0.03	60.99
Mali	181	148	97	2,065	383	0.04	-81.45
Mauritania	291	147	254	304	446	0.04	46.71
Niger	33	108	147	165	169	0.02	2.42
Nigeria	1,819	2,397	1,982	5,027	3,390	0.31	-32.56
Senegal	257	364	267	389	553	0.05	42.16
Sierra Leone	233	150	156	665	281	0.03	-57.74

Yearbook of Tourism Statistics, Data 2008 – 2012, 2014 Edition

UNITED REPUBLIC OF TANZANIA

2. Arrivals of non-resident visitors at national borders, by country of residence

	2008	2009	2010	2011	2012	Market share 2012	% Change 2012-2011
Togo	120	100	154	175	245	0.02	40.00
AMERICAS	**87,835**	**68,289**	**70,558**	**95,503**	**100,982**	**9.37**	**5.74**
Caribbean	**1,039**	**1,168**	**1,667**	**2,226**	**3,923**	**0.36**	**76.24**
Antigua and Barbuda	131	206	64	408	81	0.01	-80.15
Bahamas	17	22	12	27	31	0.00	14.81
Barbados	102	55	21	11	14	0.00	27.27
Bermuda	30	14	12	873	9	0.00	-98.97
Cuba	61	59	74	123	99	0.01	-19.51
Dominica	109	266	713	102	598	0.06	486.27
Grenada	2	7	15	21	18	0.00	-14.29
Haiti	23	12	24	24	21	0.00	-12.50
Jamaica	146	199	155	152	403	0.04	165.13
Saint Kitts and Nevis	9	4	4	7	7	0.00	0.00
Saint Lucia	3	8	17	5	6	0.00	20.00
Saint Vincent and the Grenadines	4	1	104	14	6	0.00	-57.14
Trinidad and Tobago	102	55	93	196	149	0.01	-23.98
Other countries of the Caribbean	300	260	359	263	2,481	0.23	843.35
Central America	**473**	**204**	**600**	**696**	**4,944**	**0.46**	**610.34**
Belize	265	5	3	314	4	0.00	-98.73
Costa Rica	84	36	411	195	3,349	0.31	1,617.44
El Salvador	27	33	20	20	264	0.02	1,220.00
Guatemala	35	59	46	68	62	0.01	-8.82
Honduras	5	24	46	31	394	0.04	1,170.97
Nicaragua	11	17	50	21	787	0.07	3,647.62
Panama	46	30	24	47	84	0.01	78.72
North America	**84,151**	**63,179**	**64,800**	**65,426**	**84,639**	**7.85**	**29.37**
Canada	16,482	14,642	14,819	16,839	18,777	1.74	11.51
Mexico	716	594	766	821	752	0.07	-8.40
United States of America	66,953	47,943	49,215	47,766	65,110	6.04	36.31
South America	**2,172**	**3,738**	**3,491**	**27,155**	**7,476**	**0.69**	**-72.47**
Argentina	263	293	331	588	653	0.06	11.05
Bolivia	84	102	70	131	108	0.01	-17.56
Brazil	666	1,138	1,482	1,308	2,400	0.22	83.49
Chile	309	660	312	873	1,262	0.12	44.56
Colombia	444	411	337	376	973	0.09	158.78
Ecuador	42	44	398	1,216	339	0.03	-72.12
Guyana	17	18	56	19	73	0.01	284.21
Paraguay	45	88	36	122	108	0.01	-11.48
Peru	137	148	125	1,102	103	0.01	-90.65
Suriname	10	4	37	4,620	110	0.01	-97.62
Uruguay	36	698	189	16,609	1,115	0.10	-93.29
Venezuela	119	134	118	191	232	0.02	21.47
EAST ASIA AND THE PACIFIC	**32,442**	**31,013**	**42,520**	**39,619**	**79,179**	**7.34**	**99.85**
North-East Asia	**16,016**	**15,437**	**19,915**	**16,683**	**33,280**	**3.09**	**99.48**
China	8,982	7,883	10,997	9,018	13,760	1.28	52.58
Hong Kong, China	138	92	46	233	250	0.02	7.30
Japan	3,890	4,168	4,130	3,984	5,522	0.51	38.60
Korea, Dem. People's Republic of	425	197	115	251	10,717	0.99	4,169.72
Korea, Republic of	2,389	2,687	4,309	3,025	2,649	0.25	-12.43
Mongolia	15	40	41	37	15	0.00	-59.46
Taiwan, Province of China	177	370	277	135	367	0.03	171.85
South-East Asia	**3,099**	**2,982**	**8,601**	**5,548**	**19,742**	**1.83**	**255.84**
Brunei Darussalam	10	11	312	905	3,776	0.35	317.24
Cambodia	28	45	24	354	485	0.04	37.01
Indonesia	405	321	614	792	8,556	0.79	980.30
Malaysia	611	540	4,531	844	3,177	0.29	276.42
Myanmar	56	94	334	456	927	0.09	103.29

Yearbook of Tourism Statistics, Data 2008 – 2012, 2014 Edition

UNITED REPUBLIC OF TANZANIA

2. Arrivals of non-resident visitors at national borders, by country of residence

	2008	2009	2010	2011	2012	Market share 2012	% Change 2012-2011
Philippines	965	912	1,470	1,226	921	0.09	-24.88
Singapore	347	307	441	400	1,212	0.11	203.00
Thailand	528	672	721	433	547	0.05	26.33
Viet Nam	149	80	154	138	141	0.01	2.17
Australasia	**13,168**	**12,443**	**13,694**	**15,704**	**25,751**	**2.39**	**63.98**
Australia	10,941	10,389	11,644	13,394	15,838	1.47	18.25
New Zealand	2,227	2,054	2,050	2,310	9,913	0.92	329.13
Melanesia	**159**	**146**	**310**	**1,681**	**406**	**0.04**	**-75.85**
Fiji	149	83	252	157	270	0.03	71.97
Papua New Guinea	10	18	5	5	68	0.01	1,260.00
Solomon Islands		45	53	1,519	68	0.01	-95.52
Polynesia		**5**		**3**			
Samoa		5		3			
EUROPE	**245,873**	**233,559**	**242,828**	**249,910**	**330,207**	**30.63**	**32.13**
Central/Eastern Europe	**10,160**	**12,819**	**17,616**	**12,881**	**40,834**	**3.79**	**217.01**
Armenia	27	573	80	49	282	0.03	475.51
Azerbaijan	13	173	54	249	69	0.01	-72.29
Belarus	98	86	44	750	244	0.02	-67.47
Bulgaria	200	532	470	256	567	0.05	121.48
Czech Republic	1,548	1,942	1,639	780	3,674	0.34	371.03
Estonia	194	129	191	210	306	0.03	45.71
Hungary	1,685	1,262	933	605	3,241	0.30	435.70
Kazakhstan	41	119	417	299	6,430	0.60	2,050.50
Latvia	134	125	102	172	206	0.02	19.77
Lithuania	136	131	102	211	279	0.03	32.23
Poland	2,250	2,241	2,206	2,933	4,863	0.45	65.80
Republic of Moldova	39	24	47	53	126	0.01	137.74
Romania	556	1,708	1,176	2,123	1,208	0.11	-43.10
Russian Federation	2,224	2,794	5,204	2,585	4,021	0.37	55.55
Slovakia	263	307	251	449	713	0.07	58.80
Tajikistan	3	18	14	19	98	0.01	415.79
Ukraine	380	369	4,263	377	3,974	0.37	954.11
Uzbekistan	12	13	93	533	4,935	0.46	825.89
Other countries Central/East Europe	357	273	330	228	5,598	0.52	2,355.26
Northern Europe	**91,589**	**80,369**	**78,224**	**81,832**	**108,496**	**10.06**	**32.58**
Denmark	7,196	5,856	7,898	2,178	7,909	0.73	263.13
Finland	3,493	2,594	2,719	2,625	3,601	0.33	37.18
Iceland	157	229	410	549	1,160	0.11	111.29
Ireland	4,271	3,322	3,096	5,642	4,422	0.41	-21.62
Norway	7,411	5,818	6,492	5,915	9,380	0.87	58.58
Sweden	10,816	8,797	9,022	6,554	12,344	1.14	88.34
United Kingdom	58,245	53,753	48,587	58,369	69,680	6.46	19.38
Southern Europe	**57,399**	**59,899**	**71,553**	**59,234**	**71,443**	**6.63**	**20.61**
Albania	23	29	25	38	132	0.01	247.37
Andorra	21	19	18	54	14	0.00	-74.07
Bosnia and Herzegovina	39	36	42	29	102	0.01	251.72
Croatia	242	233	244	445	1,586	0.15	256.40
Greece	614	798	710	583	1,173	0.11	101.20
Italy	45,950	47,804	59,603	45,590	50,187	4.65	10.08
Malta	64	57	177	102	202	0.02	98.04
Montenegro	28	1		791	26	0.00	-96.71
Portugal	1,259	1,201	1,239	1,022	2,450	0.23	139.73
San Marino	35	67	248	2,143	680	0.06	-68.27
Serbia	163	158	156	1,153	2,372	0.22	105.72
Serbia and Montenegro	35	40	83				
Slovenia	428	334	496	236	1,366	0.13	478.81
Spain	8,470	9,053	8,478	6,826	10,650	0.99	56.02

Yearbook of Tourism Statistics, Data 2008 – 2012, 2014 Edition

UNITED REPUBLIC OF TANZANIA

2. Arrivals of non-resident visitors at national borders, by country of residence

	2008	2009	2010	2011	2012	Market share 2012	% Change 2012-2011
TFYR of Macedonia	28	69	34	222	503	0.05	126.58
Western Europe	**81,846**	**76,937**	**70,558**	**91,304**	**101,891**	**9.45**	**11.60**
Austria	3,445	2,735	3,809	4,126	7,195	0.67	74.38
Belgium	7,229	5,799	5,510	7,323	7,057	0.65	-3.63
France	19,598	20,127	15,650	21,919	28,003	2.60	27.76
Germany	27,100	25,508	25,246	36,010	36,626	3.40	1.71
Liechtenstein	7	13	32	16	86	0.01	437.50
Luxembourg	156	170	206	276	355	0.03	28.62
Monaco	8	29	59	19	10	0.00	-47.37
Netherlands	16,945	16,507	14,598	15,500	12,203	1.13	-21.27
Switzerland	7,358	6,049	5,448	6,115	10,356	0.96	69.35
East Mediterranean Europe	**4,879**	**3,535**	**4,877**	**4,659**	**7,543**	**0.70**	**61.90**
Cyprus	113	182	221	182	231	0.02	26.92
Israel	3,980	2,334	2,805	3,007	4,635	0.43	54.14
Turkey	786	1,019	1,851	1,470	2,677	0.25	82.11
MIDDLE EAST	**10,377**	**11,121**	**10,521**	**15,281**	**21,348**	**1.98**	**39.70**
Bahrain	38	43	56	64	75	0.01	17.19
Egypt	889	1,170	1,186	1,138	1,715	0.16	50.70
Iraq	34	86	61	118	316	0.03	167.80
Jordan	215	285	295	1,799	2,587	0.24	43.80
Kuwait	57	71	57	103	599	0.06	481.55
Lebanon	428	381	303	281	437	0.04	55.52
Libya	289	238	220	139	147	0.01	5.76
Oman	5,747	5,520	5,440	3,288	9,371	0.87	185.01
Palestine	41	63	32	98	893	0.08	811.22
Qatar	64	57	190	1,416	152	0.01	-89.27
Saudi Arabia	288	356	299	284	584	0.05	105.63
Syrian Arab Republic	123	157	189	897	536	0.05	-40.25
United Arab Emirates	1,433	1,917	1,199	4,931	2,970	0.28	-39.77
Yemen	731	777	994	725	966	0.09	33.24
SOUTH ASIA	**20,889**	**21,620**	**24,135**	**21,931**	**56,598**	**5.25**	**158.07**
Afghanistan	32	32	17	36	100	0.01	177.78
Bangladesh	479	661	397	725	597	0.06	-17.66
Bhutan	1	6	5	4	4	0.00	0.00
India	17,530	17,002	19,101	17,731	22,862	2.12	28.94
Iran, Islamic Republic of	475	503	636	524	1,054	0.10	101.15
Nepal	184	288	504	1,792	804	0.07	-55.13
Pakistan	1,732	2,657	2,659	471	4,189	0.39	789.38
Sri Lanka	456	471	816	648	26,988	2.50	4,064.81

Yearbook of Tourism Statistics, Data 2008 – 2012, 2014 Edition

UNITED STATES OF AMERICA

1. Arrivals of non-resident tourists at national borders, by country of residence

	2008	2009	2010	2011	2012	Market share 2012	% Change 2012-2011
TOTAL	57,936,689	54,956,420	59,788,923	62,703,447	66,959,707	100.00	6.79
AFRICA	311,136	290,861	311,205	325,989	371,016	0.55	13.81
East Africa	51,772	49,707	50,749	51,634	58,761	0.09	13.80
Burundi	501	479	671	677	846	0.00	24.96
Comoros	22	30	19	21	23	0.00	9.52
Djibouti	224	354	363	340	319	0.00	-6.18
Eritrea	245	248	263	231	244	0.00	5.63
Ethiopia	8,713	8,629	8,630	9,979	11,189	0.02	12.13
Kenya	17,296	15,833	15,173	13,422	14,954	0.02	11.41
Madagascar	880	780	703	729	787	0.00	7.96
Malawi	1,304	1,210	1,331	1,347	1,519	0.00	12.77
Mauritius	1,776	2,005	2,523	2,669	3,133	0.00	17.38
Mozambique	949	1,151	1,132	1,210	1,473	0.00	21.74
Reunion	437	513	533	566	742	0.00	31.10
Rwanda	1,752	1,649	1,840	2,139	2,691	0.00	25.81
Seychelles	213	186	217	186	185	0.00	-0.54
Somalia	55	72	98	107	42	0.00	-60.75
Uganda	5,891	5,404	5,115	5,611	6,645	0.01	18.43
United Republic of Tanzania	4,765	5,000	4,986	5,013	5,589	0.01	11.49
Zambia	2,489	2,310	2,994	3,052	3,541	0.01	16.02
Zimbabwe	4,260	3,854	4,158	4,335	4,839	0.01	11.63
Central Africa	15,933	17,008	18,213	19,352	22,206	0.03	14.75
Angola	5,633	6,446	6,610	7,726	9,964	0.01	28.97
Cameroon	5,222	5,072	5,517	5,359	5,064	0.01	-5.50
Central African Republic	230	166	234	225	205	0.00	-8.89
Chad	275	424	265	245	258	0.00	5.31
Congo	1,587	1,841	2,077	2,310	2,689	0.00	16.41
Democratic Republic of the Congo	888	1,058	1,189	920	1,316	0.00	43.04
Equatorial Guinea	303	397	368	460	509	0.00	10.65
Gabon	1,762	1,584	1,793	1,927	2,095	0.00	8.72
Sao Tome and Principe	33	20	160	180	106	0.00	-41.11
North Africa	26,545	27,770	30,428	33,578	35,260	0.05	5.01
Algeria	4,274	4,592	4,116	5,054	5,339	0.01	5.64
Morocco	16,426	16,919	18,657	20,230	21,135	0.03	4.47
Sudan	1,395	1,547	2,006	2,499	1,909	0.00	-23.61
Tunisia	4,448	4,711	5,622	5,654	6,786	0.01	20.02
Western Sahara	2	1	27	141	91	0.00	-35.46
Southern Africa	98,331	83,243	85,019	92,020	100,923	0.15	9.68
Botswana	2,572	2,300	2,279	2,163	2,186	0.00	1.06
Lesotho	246	259	298	339	367	0.00	8.26
Namibia	1,246	1,251	1,430	1,732	1,878	0.00	8.43
South Africa	93,692	78,934	80,174	86,597	95,086	0.14	9.80
Swaziland	575	499	838	1,189	1,406	0.00	18.25
West Africa	118,555	113,133	126,796	129,405	153,866	0.23	18.90
Benin	1,715	1,582	1,876	1,804	1,852	0.00	2.66
Burkina Faso	1,651	1,882	1,771	1,934	2,237	0.00	15.67
Cape Verde	2,180	2,708	2,517	1,773	1,695	0.00	-4.40
Côte d'Ivoire	2,583	2,892	2,422	1,584	2,166	0.00	36.74
Gambia	1,381	1,859	2,341	2,288	1,807	0.00	-21.02
Ghana	18,507	17,069	18,554	19,127	20,775	0.03	8.62
Guinea	2,348	1,827	1,536	1,604	1,795	0.00	11.91
Guinea-Bissau	25	24	37	45	31	0.00	-31.11
Liberia	1,345	1,086	1,543	1,877	2,984	0.00	58.98
Mali	3,273	3,115	3,106	2,832	2,188	0.00	-22.74
Mauritania	473	496	636	525	562	0.00	7.05
Niger	1,084	1,039	978	894	1,046	0.00	17.00

812

UNITED STATES OF AMERICA

1. Arrivals of non-resident tourists at national borders, by country of residence

		2008	2009	2010	2011	2012	Market share 2012	% Change 2012-2011
Nigeria		72,669	68,505	79,427	82,945	104,682	0.16	26.21
Senegal		6,623	6,536	7,176	6,967	6,821	0.01	-2.10
Sierra Leone		1,517	1,474	1,734	1,929	1,954	0.00	1.30
Togo		1,181	1,039	1,142	1,277	1,271	0.00	-0.47
AMERICAS		**37,133,338**	**35,911,508**	**38,644,479**	**40,423,276**	**43,558,611**	**65.05**	**7.76**
Caribbean		**1,201,149**	**1,206,068**	**1,200,740**	**1,091,419**	**1,131,480**	**1.69**	**3.67**
Anguilla		6,280	5,020	3,362	2,518	2,075	0.00	-17.59
Antigua and Barbuda		19,713	17,213	16,719	15,639	14,893	0.02	-4.77
Aruba			22,368	16,074	14,752	17,324	0.03	17.43
Bahamas		180,914	224,812	243,204	222,741	224,997	0.34	1.01
Barbados		54,891	52,010	54,486	51,323	50,944	0.08	-0.74
Bermuda		23,445	20,743	17,378	10,822	14,559	0.02	34.53
British Virgin Islands		22,195	23,961	20,262	15,113	14,873	0.02	-1.59
Cayman Islands		51,078	51,085	46,558	42,402	43,456	0.06	2.49
Cuba		22,395	32,666	37,871	36,964	36,655	0.05	-0.84
Dominica		6,635	6,857	7,379	5,911	6,329	0.01	7.07
Dominican Republic		226,184	227,948	239,972	230,188	244,417	0.37	6.18
Grenada		8,673	8,202	8,507	7,928	7,627	0.01	-3.80
Guadeloupe		9,750	9,964	8,205	6,221	6,116	0.01	-1.69
Haiti		91,748	80,572	87,334	79,461	83,312	0.12	4.85
Jamaica		204,982	185,526	178,791	159,235	166,984	0.25	4.87
Martinique		8,175	8,014	7,706	7,015	6,245	0.01	-10.98
Montserrat		726	593	344	191	207	0.00	8.38
Netherlands Antilles		65,516	43,114	26,615	10,755	9,044	0.01	-15.91
Saint Kitts and Nevis		11,045	10,222	10,328	9,496	8,646	0.01	-8.95
Saint Lucia		13,814	13,397	15,072	13,111	11,811	0.02	-9.92
Saint Vincent and the Grenadines		6,043	6,002	6,221	6,057	5,693	0.01	-6.01
Trinidad and Tobago		147,613	141,406	136,628	132,931	144,535	0.22	8.73
Turks and Caicos Islands		19,334	14,373	11,724	10,645	10,738	0.02	0.87
Central America		**775,590**	**757,905**	**760,441**	**747,168**	**802,956**	**1.20**	**7.47**
Belize		20,757	20,227	18,641	17,319	18,672	0.03	7.81
Costa Rica		165,257	157,471	165,594	168,722	179,755	0.27	6.54
El Salvador		136,494	123,185	112,346	97,967	100,978	0.15	3.07
Guatemala		188,177	189,455	188,218	183,671	194,373	0.29	5.83
Honduras		116,902	115,405	115,616	119,671	130,386	0.19	8.95
Nicaragua		45,171	42,194	41,050	40,276	45,524	0.07	13.03
Panama		102,832	109,968	118,976	119,542	133,268	0.20	11.48
North America		**32,601,000**	**31,206,000**	**33,433,000**	**34,828,000**	**37,208,000**	**55.57**	**6.83**
Canada	(*)	18,915,000	17,977,000	19,964,000	21,337,000	22,699,000	33.90	6.38
Mexico	(*)	13,686,000	13,229,000	13,469,000	13,491,000	14,509,000	21.67	7.55
South America		**2,555,599**	**2,741,535**	**3,250,298**	**3,756,689**	**4,416,175**	**6.60**	**17.55**
Argentina		318,144	356,428	436,192	512,258	614,504	0.92	19.96
Bolivia		29,942	31,966	32,504	34,467	35,732	0.05	3.67
Brazil		769,232	892,611	1,197,866	1,508,279	1,791,103	2.67	18.75
Chile		130,813	126,609	146,736	171,459	187,603	0.28	9.42
Colombia		419,268	424,526	494,739	496,814	602,338	0.90	21.24
Ecuador		152,112	168,432	195,546	210,910	209,828	0.31	-0.51
Falkland Islands, Malvinas		130	110	51	60	78	0.00	30.00
French Guiana		314	536	612	760	1,063	0.00	39.87
Guyana		12,974	14,774	15,601	16,427	24,222	0.04	47.45
Paraguay		12,062	12,564	14,657	16,567	19,354	0.03	16.82
Peru		162,883	160,474	173,269	171,870	190,205	0.28	10.67
Suriname		7,022	8,630	8,941	9,043	10,711	0.02	18.45
Uruguay		33,550	36,690	41,980	46,695	54,680	0.08	17.10
Venezuela		507,153	507,185	491,604	561,080	674,754	1.01	20.26
EAST ASIA AND THE PACIFIC		**6,343,399**	**5,905,954**	**7,369,149**	**7,728,449**	**8,796,667**	**13.14**	**13.82**
North-East Asia		**4,939,772**	**4,545,697**	**5,721,747**	**5,906,523**	**6,851,051**	**10.23**	**15.99**

Yearbook of Tourism Statistics, Data 2008 – 2012, 2014 Edition

UNITED STATES OF AMERICA

1. Arrivals of non-resident tourists at national borders, by country of residence

	2008	2009	2010	2011	2012	Market share 2012	% Change 2012-2011
China	492,958	524,817	801,738	1,089,405	1,474,408	2.20	35.34
Hong Kong, China	139,359	116,023	131,712	128,512	133,104	0.20	3.57
Japan	3,249,578	2,918,268	3,386,076	3,249,569	3,698,073	5.52	13.80
Korea, Dem. People's Republic of	17	27	127	132	160	0.00	21.21
Korea, Republic of	759,394	743,846	1,107,518	1,145,216	1,251,432	1.87	9.27
Macao, China	3,573	3,171	3,469	3,376	3,711	0.01	9.92
Taiwan, Province of China	294,893	239,545	291,107	290,313	290,163	0.43	-0.05
South-East Asia	**552,008**	**488,275**	**552,150**	**578,493**	**623,715**	**0.93**	**7.82**
Brunei Darussalam	1,210	1,080	1,095	1,332	1,420	0.00	6.61
Cambodia	2,664	2,314	2,611	2,380	2,906	0.00	22.10
Indonesia	49,348	50,243	54,539	66,069	73,579	0.11	11.37
Lao People's Democratic Republic	1,503	1,103	808	685	857	0.00	25.11
Malaysia	54,262	43,292	54,080	59,857	67,464	0.10	12.71
Myanmar	1,174	1,536	1,960	1,891	2,285	0.00	20.84
Philippines	179,820	171,680	177,525	166,829	176,218	0.26	5.63
Singapore	141,474	107,400	139,319	159,302	162,077	0.24	1.74
Thailand	76,820	69,204	74,293	73,318	81,802	0.12	11.57
Timor-Leste			6	4	6	0.00	50.00
Viet Nam	43,733	40,423	45,914	46,826	55,101	0.08	17.67
Australasia	**835,252**	**854,588**	**1,078,866**	**1,226,826**	**1,307,886**	**1.95**	**6.61**
Australia	689,927	723,576	904,247	1,037,852	1,122,180	1.68	8.13
New Zealand	145,325	131,012	174,619	188,974	185,706	0.28	-1.73
Melanesia	**7,733**	**7,152**	**8,140**	**8,233**	**8,412**	**0.01**	**2.17**
Fiji	5,133	4,588	6,456	6,888	7,027	0.01	2.02
New Caledonia	1,605	1,459	782	481	453	0.00	-5.82
Papua New Guinea	638	778	649	599	620	0.00	3.51
Solomon Islands	132	138	88	106	117	0.00	10.38
Vanuatu	225	189	165	159	195	0.00	22.64
Micronesia	**256**	**308**	**349**	**393**	**322**	**0.00**	**-18.07**
Christmas Island, Australia		5	7	12	2	0.00	-83.33
Cocos (Keeling) Islands	11	6	4	10	7	0.00	-30.00
Kiribati	233	282	258	279	228	0.00	-18.28
Nauru	12	15	80	92	85	0.00	-7.61
Polynesia	**8,378**	**9,934**	**7,897**	**7,981**	**5,281**	**0.01**	**-33.83**
Cook Islands	311	227	66	45	38	0.00	-15.56
French Polynesia	5,181	7,027	5,237	5,677	3,189	0.00	-43.83
Niue	3	7	6	17	7	0.00	-58.82
Pitcairn		1	2	5	11	0.00	120.00
Samoa	1,339	1,264	1,192	1,020	888	0.00	-12.94
Tonga	1,459	1,353	1,316	1,133	1,072	0.00	-5.38
Tuvalu	18	15	57	72	11	0.00	-84.72
Wallis and Futuna Islands	67	40	21	12	65	0.00	441.67
EUROPE	**13,244,056**	**11,972,630**	**12,429,952**	**13,107,614**	**12,944,525**	**19.33**	**-1.24**
Central/Eastern Europe	**588,312**	**576,043**	**613,418**	**681,844**	**738,565**	**1.10**	**8.32**
Armenia	3,713	3,546	3,183	3,032	4,451	0.01	46.80
Azerbaijan	3,236	3,121	3,518	3,841	4,799	0.01	24.94
Bulgaria	23,771	20,000	20,200	20,444	20,570	0.03	0.62
Czech Republic	49,485	65,060	63,909	75,618	76,317	0.11	0.92
Czech Republic/Slovakia	7,287	7,397	4,206	1,935	2,000	0.00	3.36
Estonia	11,686	15,677	10,753	11,997	13,989	0.02	16.60
Georgia	2,987	2,966	3,496	3,492	3,985	0.01	14.12
Hungary	42,209	48,806	51,333	58,313	57,416	0.09	-1.54
Kazakhstan	9,133	8,459	10,852	12,836	15,384	0.02	19.85
Kyrgyzstan	1,252	1,279	1,716	1,851	1,963	0.00	6.05
Latvia	10,240	11,270	11,529	12,568	14,929	0.02	18.79
Lithuania	11,355	14,264	8,846	4,081	3,746	0.01	-8.21
Poland	146,887	115,327	114,702	111,158	111,157	0.17	0.00

Yearbook of Tourism Statistics, Data 2008 – 2012, 2014 Edition

UNITED STATES OF AMERICA

1. Arrivals of non-resident tourists at national borders, by country of residence

	2008	2009	2010	2011	2012	Market share 2012	% Change 2012-2011
Republic of Moldova	3,795	3,976	4,828	5,220	6,345	0.01	21.55
Romania	49,968	41,411	45,444	45,776	47,753	0.07	4.32
Russian Federation	142,998	142,650	174,511	221,888	259,699	0.39	17.04
Slovakia	19,297	27,711	30,911	33,540	33,655	0.05	0.34
Tajikistan	1,440	1,010	1,047	1,246	1,292	0.00	3.69
Turkmenistan	300	504	596	560	678	0.00	21.07
Ukraine	43,348	37,157	42,591	47,417	51,986	0.08	9.64
USSR (former)	261	265	289	300	298	0.00	-0.67
Uzbekistan	3,664	4,187	4,958	4,731	6,153	0.01	30.06
Northern Europe	**6,123,300**	**5,216,618**	**5,214,135**	**5,315,486**	**5,243,001**	**7.83**	**-1.36**
Denmark	256,604	245,623	258,788	274,420	271,363	0.41	-1.11
Finland	118,448	114,364	111,840	121,059	125,475	0.19	3.65
Iceland	41,155	28,526	39,153	49,689	46,097	0.07	-7.23
Ireland	531,198	411,203	360,492	346,879	331,850	0.50	-4.33
Norway	213,983	193,318	221,145	249,167	262,822	0.39	5.48
Sweden	397,017	324,417	371,853	438,972	442,013	0.66	0.69
United Kingdom	4,564,895	3,899,167	3,850,864	3,835,300	3,763,381	5.62	-1.88
Southern Europe	**1,654,200**	**1,538,052**	**1,693,265**	**1,807,548**	**1,645,745**	**2.46**	**-8.95**
Albania	6,317	5,230	5,480	4,775	4,847	0.01	1.51
Andorra	1,791	1,449	1,453	1,266	1,184	0.00	-6.48
Bosnia and Herzegovina	4,370	3,897	4,233	4,386	4,523	0.01	3.12
Croatia	17,270	15,407	15,105	15,241	14,484	0.02	-4.97
Gibraltar	2,058	1,656	1,304	984	1,131	0.00	14.94
Greece	63,760	56,748	64,581	62,948	58,212	0.09	-7.52
Holy See	19	15	32	59	53	0.00	-10.17
Italy	779,463	753,310	838,225	891,571	831,343	1.24	-6.76
Malta	5,063	4,902	5,380	4,961	5,277	0.01	6.37
Portugal	89,158	74,457	93,584	96,434	93,346	0.14	-3.20
San Marino	700	694	674	767	598	0.00	-22.03
Serbia and Montenegro	1,457	723	656	271	146	0.00	-46.13
Slovenia	20,637	19,213	18,845	19,307	18,608	0.03	-3.62
Spain	658,333	596,766	639,654	700,183	607,273	0.91	-13.27
TFYR of Macedonia	3,804	3,585	4,059	4,395	4,720	0.01	7.39
Western Europe	**4,426,898**	**4,229,228**	**4,476,847**	**4,868,536**	**4,867,319**	**7.27**	**-0.02**
Austria	158,764	162,569	168,403	179,482	183,276	0.27	2.11
Belgium	265,383	245,710	254,892	259,490	260,267	0.39	0.30
France	1,243,942	1,204,490	1,342,207	1,504,182	1,455,720	2.17	-3.22
Germany	1,782,299	1,686,825	1,726,193	1,823,797	1,875,952	2.80	2.86
Liechtenstein	1,661	1,877	1,909	2,273	2,145	0.00	-5.63
Luxembourg	18,712	18,084	17,748	17,856	17,457	0.03	-2.23
Monaco	6,380	6,156	4,725	3,941	4,119	0.01	4.52
Netherlands	607,802	547,790	570,179	601,013	591,746	0.88	-1.54
Switzerland	341,955	355,727	390,591	476,502	476,637	0.71	0.03
East Mediterranean Europe	**451,346**	**412,689**	**432,287**	**434,200**	**449,895**	**0.67**	**3.61**
Cyprus	11,517	10,174	10,136	9,505	8,904	0.01	-6.32
Israel	332,257	308,213	306,914	302,673	303,629	0.45	0.32
Turkey	107,572	94,302	115,237	122,022	137,362	0.21	12.57
MIDDLE EAST	**227,629**	**246,018**	**296,242**	**363,024**	**463,230**	**0.69**	**27.60**
Bahrain	7,517	6,566	7,733	7,299	8,702	0.01	19.22
Egypt	34,855	36,044	41,949	46,346	62,342	0.09	34.51
Iraq	872	1,263	2,207	3,786	6,504	0.01	71.79
Jordan	15,712	15,559	16,459	17,246	19,450	0.03	12.78
Kuwait	28,258	29,888	33,296	39,420	46,872	0.07	18.90
Lebanon	18,253	17,969	18,847	20,346	23,055	0.03	13.31
Libya	4,099	2,904	4,440	1,095	2,425	0.00	121.46
Oman	4,771	4,727	4,812	5,629	7,567	0.01	34.43
Qatar	10,759	11,523	14,931	19,101	24,043	0.04	25.87

Yearbook of Tourism Statistics, Data 2008 – 2012, 2014 Edition

UNITED STATES OF AMERICA

1. Arrivals of non-resident tourists at national borders, by country of residence

	2008	2009	2010	2011	2012	Market share 2012	% Change 2012-2011
Saudi Arabia	48,590	62,030	89,409	132,920	182,225	0.27	37.09
Syrian Arab Republic	4,643	5,105	5,625	5,509	5,823	0.01	5.70
United Arab Emirates	48,564	51,472	55,425	63,415	72,949	0.11	15.03
Yemen	718	936	1,072	857	1,206	0.00	40.72
Other countries of Middle East	18	32	37	55	67	0.00	21.82
SOUTH ASIA	**677,131**	**629,449**	**737,896**	**755,095**	**825,658**	**1.23**	**9.34**
Afghanistan	714	1,138	1,261	1,722	1,371	0.00	-20.38
Bangladesh	8,741	10,175	11,561	12,596	15,794	0.02	25.39
Bhutan	368	230	210	225	228	0.00	1.33
India	598,971	549,474	650,935	663,465	724,433	1.08	9.19
Iran, Islamic Republic of	6,098	10,139	11,460	14,559	14,698	0.02	0.95
Maldives	243	181	149	158	184	0.00	16.46
Nepal	14,706	11,908	12,513	12,089	12,311	0.02	1.84
Pakistan	35,738	36,426	38,954	38,156	43,976	0.07	15.25
Sri Lanka	11,552	9,778	10,853	12,125	12,663	0.02	4.44

Yearbook of Tourism Statistics, Data 2008 – 2012, 2014 Edition

UNITED STATES VIRGIN ISLANDS

3. Arrivals of non-resident tourists in hotels and similar establishments, by nationality

	2008	2009	2010	2011	2012	Market share 2012	% Change 2012-2011
TOTAL	740,020	787,153	748,996	680,324	650,834	100.00	-4.33
AFRICA	73	69	62	229	98	0.02	-57.21
Other Africa	73	69	62	229	98	0.02	-57.21
All countries of Africa	73	69	62	229	98	0.02	-57.21
AMERICAS	720,276	766,929	731,749	653,065	617,419	94.87	-5.46
Caribbean	28,851	30,069	27,030	27,739	27,024	4.15	-2.58
Bahamas	196	250	66	146	169	0.03	15.75
Barbados	272	222	130	203	532	0.08	162.07
British Virgin Islands	5,963	7,859	6,792	6,136	5,679	0.87	-7.45
Dominican Republic	50	41	45	82	63	0.01	-23.17
Jamaica	230	503	230	258	219	0.03	-15.12
Puerto Rico	21,319	19,776	19,019	18,855	19,083	2.93	1.21
Trinidad and Tobago	108	115	68	146	237	0.04	62.33
Other countries of the Caribbean	713	1,303	680	1,913	1,042	0.16	-45.53
Central America	338	146	169	274	378	0.06	37.96
Costa Rica	164	63	51	60	103	0.02	71.67
El Salvador	6	2	2		1	0.00	
Guatemala	5	6	1	20	20	0.00	0.00
Honduras	13	6	35	8	7	0.00	-12.50
Nicaragua		7	3	5			
Panama	18	56	75	177	247	0.04	39.55
Other countries of Central America	132	6	2	4			
North America	689,939	735,717	703,643	623,336	587,393	90.25	-5.77
Canada	9,112	10,412	6,601	6,899	7,316	1.12	6.04
Mexico	262	395	154	306	387	0.06	26.47
United States of America	680,565	724,910	696,888	616,131	579,690	89.07	-5.91
South America	1,148	997	907	1,716	2,624	0.40	52.91
Argentina	320	219	229	493	648	0.10	31.44
Bolivia	49	22	59	55	1	0.00	-98.18
Brazil	309	257	244	338	492	0.08	45.56
Chile	153	347	216	450	548	0.08	21.78
Colombia	55	70	20	86	299	0.05	247.67
Ecuador	1	7	4	2	7	0.00	250.00
Guyana		1	6				
Paraguay				1			
Peru	27	1	20	115	22	0.00	-80.87
Uruguay	10	2					
Venezuela	197	70	89	118	528	0.08	347.46
Other countries of South America	27	1	20	58	79	0.01	36.21
EAST ASIA AND THE PACIFIC	377	318	367	458	540	0.08	17.90
North-East Asia	105	118	137	93	122	0.02	31.18
Japan	101	118	136	92	122	0.02	32.61
Taiwan, Province of China	4		1	1			
Australasia	272	200	230	365	418	0.06	14.52
Australia	251	188	213	298	348	0.05	16.78
New Zealand	21	12	17	67	70	0.01	4.48
EUROPE	15,798	16,434	14,393	22,560	30,865	4.74	36.81
Northern Europe	9,839	11,040	9,841	17,245	26,072	4.01	51.19
Denmark	7,077	9,012	8,191	15,390	24,292	3.73	57.84
Finland	145	53	41	57	60	0.01	5.26
Norway	284	405	174	341	283	0.04	-17.01
Sweden	41	133	179	274	320	0.05	16.79
United Kingdom	2,292	1,437	1,256	1,183	1,117	0.17	-5.58
Southern Europe	3,484	3,275	2,569	2,072	1,856	0.29	-10.42

Yearbook of Tourism Statistics, Data 2008 – 2012, 2014 Edition

UNITED STATES VIRGIN ISLANDS

3. Arrivals of non-resident tourists in hotels and similar establishments, by nationality

	2008	2009	2010	2011	2012	Market share 2012	% Change 2012-2011
Greece	112	112	89	388	16	0.00	-95.88
Italy	3,330	2,861	1,908	1,306	1,607	0.25	23.05
Portugal	27	1	20	13	27	0.00	107.69
Spain	15	301	552	365	206	0.03	-43.56
Western Europe	**1,615**	**1,484**	**1,360**	**2,345**	**1,816**	**0.28**	**-22.56**
Austria	162	119	48	120	110	0.02	-8.33
France	433	317	280	308	439	0.07	42.53
Germany	567	477	724	1,134	835	0.13	-26.37
Netherlands	320	241	159	329	260	0.04	-20.97
Switzerland	133	330	149	454	172	0.03	-62.11
Other Europe	**860**	**635**	**623**	**898**	**1,121**	**0.17**	**24.83**
Other countries of Europe	860	635	623	898	1,121	0.17	24.83
NOT SPECIFIED	**3,496**	**3,403**	**2,425**	**4,012**	**1,912**	**0.29**	**-52.34**
Other countries of the World	3,496	3,403	2,425	4,012	1,912	0.29	-52.34

Yearbook of Tourism Statistics, Data 2008 – 2012, 2014 Edition

URUGUAY

2. Arrivals of non-resident visitors at national borders, by nationality

	2008	2009	2010	2011	2012	Market share 2012	% Change 2012-2011
TOTAL (*)	1,997,884	2,098,780	2,407,676	2,960,155	2,845,989	100.00	-3.86
AMERICAS	1,544,086	1,643,319	1,888,374	2,401,187	2,416,628	84.91	0.64
North America	93,123	90,660	87,010	87,264	80,912	2.84	-7.28
Canada	9,976	10,411	10,212	10,361	9,589	0.34	-7.45
Mexico	14,778	13,026	14,370	16,327	13,771	0.48	-15.66
United States of America	68,369	67,223	62,428	60,576	57,552	2.02	-4.99
South America	1,418,597	1,515,944	1,759,347	2,286,025	2,289,651	80.45	0.16
Argentina	1,025,574	1,150,492	1,261,516	1,723,005	1,763,518	61.97	2.35
Bolivia	2,737	3,209	3,959	4,468	4,635	0.16	3.74
Brazil	300,791	263,414	376,894	426,315	396,828	13.94	-6.92
Chile	39,236	41,106	53,194	57,283	53,385	1.88	-6.80
Paraguay	27,708	34,347	36,672	42,980	39,321	1.38	-8.51
Peru	12,396	11,722	13,673	15,623	13,806	0.49	-11.63
Venezuela	10,155	11,654	13,439	16,351	18,158	0.64	11.05
Other Americas	32,366	36,715	42,017	27,898	46,065	1.62	65.12
Other countries of the Americas	32,366	36,715	42,017	27,898	46,065	1.62	65.12
EAST ASIA AND THE PACIFIC	14,374	17,193	17,327	18,516	19,223	0.68	3.82
North-East Asia	5,779	5,359	6,482	7,100	8,093	0.28	13.99
Japan	2,663	2,673	3,046	3,177	3,232	0.11	1.73
Other countries of North-East Asia	3,116	2,686	3,436	3,923	4,861	0.17	23.91
Australasia	7,770	10,985	10,077	9,593	9,340	0.33	-2.64
Australia	5,958	8,198	7,512	7,571	7,466	0.26	-1.39
New Zealand	1,812	2,787	2,565	2,022	1,874	0.07	-7.32
Other East Asia and the Pacific	825	849	768	1,823	1,790	0.06	-1.81
Other countries East Asia/Pacific	825	849	768	1,823	1,790	0.06	-1.81
EUROPE	139,282	140,398	146,774	151,049	130,004	4.57	-13.93
Northern Europe	28,482	26,709	28,064	30,854	27,677	0.97	-10.30
Denmark	1,832	1,742	1,893	2,187	2,021	0.07	-7.59
Finland	2,366	1,767	1,757	2,270	3,305	0.12	45.59
Ireland	3,320	2,489	2,374	2,136	1,897	0.07	-11.19
Norway	2,180	1,998	2,429	2,158	2,117	0.07	-1.90
Sweden	4,387	3,750	3,874	4,683	4,582	0.16	-2.16
United Kingdom	14,397	14,963	15,737	17,420	13,755	0.48	-21.04
Southern Europe	53,966	50,683	52,529	53,889	40,446	1.42	-24.95
Greece	1,471	1,033	1,362	912	723	0.03	-20.72
Italy	17,267	16,098	16,603	17,518	15,423	0.54	-11.96
Portugal	2,896	2,470	3,033	3,152	3,116	0.11	-1.14
Spain	32,332	31,082	31,531	32,307	21,184	0.74	-34.43
Western Europe	45,569	51,563	53,632	56,045	52,711	1.85	-5.95
Austria	1,994	2,511	2,867	2,794	2,878	0.10	3.01
Belgium	2,353	2,461	2,190	2,742	2,713	0.10	-1.06
France	15,430	17,573	18,505	19,250	17,606	0.62	-8.54
Germany	16,499	18,450	19,102	20,267	18,017	0.63	-11.10
Luxembourg	78	56	103	78	84	0.00	7.69
Netherlands	4,827	5,296	5,018	4,834	5,060	0.18	4.68
Switzerland	4,388	5,216	5,847	6,080	6,353	0.22	4.49
East Mediterranean Europe	3,438	3,601	3,680	3,601	2,376	0.08	-34.02
Israel	3,438	3,601	3,680	3,601	2,376	0.08	-34.02
Other Europe	7,827	7,842	8,869	6,660	6,794	0.24	2.01
Other countries of Europe	7,827	7,842	8,869	6,660	6,794	0.24	2.01
MIDDLE EAST	261	226	567	349	304	0.01	-12.89
All countries of Middle East	261	226	567	349	304	0.01	-12.89
NOT SPECIFIED	299,881	297,644	354,634	389,054	279,830	9.83	-28.07
Other countries of the World	26,100	769	1,656	50,705	2,006	0.07	-96.04
Nationals Residing Abroad	273,781	296,875	352,978	338,349	277,824	9.76	-17.89

Yearbook of Tourism Statistics, Data 2008 – 2012, 2014 Edition

UZBEKISTAN

1. Arrivals of non-resident tourists at national borders, by country of residence

	2008	2009	2010	2011	2012	Market share 2012	% Change 2012-2011
TOTAL	1,069,300	1,214,700	974,573				
AFRICA	2,500	100	35				
Other Africa	2,500	100	35				
All countries of Africa	2,500	100	35				
AMERICAS	8,000	6,500	1,189				
Other Americas	8,000	6,500	1,189				
All countries of the Americas	8,000	6,500	1,189				
EAST ASIA AND THE PACIFIC	578,600	649,300	768,160				
Other East Asia and the Pacific	578,600	649,300	768,160				
All countries of Asia	578,600	649,300	768,160				
EUROPE	385,200	333,200	156,766				
Other Europe	385,200	333,200	156,766				
All countries of Europe	385,200	333,200	156,766				
MIDDLE EAST	55,000	66,800	36,839				
All countries of Middle East	55,000	66,800	36,839				
SOUTH ASIA	40,000	158,800	11,584				
All countries of South Asia	40,000	158,800	11,584				

Yearbook of Tourism Statistics, Data 2008 – 2012, 2014 Edition

VANUATU

1. Arrivals of non-resident tourists at national borders, by country of residence

	2008	2009	2010	2011	2012	Market share 2012	% Change 2012-2011
TOTAL	90,656	100,675	97,180	93,960	108,158	100.00	15.11
AMERICAS	2,578	2,549	2,395	1,922	2,094	1.94	8.95
North America	2,578	2,549	2,395	1,922	2,094	1.94	8.95
All countries of North America	2,578	2,549	2,395	1,922	2,094	1.94	8.95
EAST ASIA AND THE PACIFIC	81,162	91,021	87,333	84,645	97,988	90.60	15.76
North-East Asia	589	643	517	630	705	0.65	11.90
Japan	589	643	517	630	705	0.65	11.90
Australasia	67,167	77,515	70,687	69,242	79,832	73.81	15.29
Australia	53,251	64,909	58,760	57,843	65,402	60.47	13.07
New Zealand	13,916	12,606	11,927	11,399	14,430	13.34	26.59
Melanesia	9,648	9,155	11,410	11,376	13,138	12.15	15.49
New Caledonia	9,648	9,155	11,410	11,376	13,138	12.15	15.49
Other East Asia and the Pacific	3,758	3,708	4,719	3,397	4,313	3.99	26.96
Other countries of Oceania	3,758	3,708	4,719	3,397	4,313	3.99	26.96
EUROPE	4,886	4,889	4,888	5,265	5,491	5.08	4.29
Other Europe	4,886	4,889	4,888	5,265	5,491	5.08	4.29
All countries of Europe	4,886	4,889	4,888	5,265	5,491	5.08	4.29
NOT SPECIFIED	2,030	2,216	2,564	2,128	2,585	2.39	21.48
Other countries of the World	2,030	2,216	2,564	2,128	2,585	2.39	21.48

Yearbook of Tourism Statistics, Data 2008 – 2012, 2014 Edition

VENEZUELA

1. Arrivals of non-resident tourists at national borders, by nationality

	2008	2009	2010	2011	2012	Market share 2012	% Change 2012-2011
TOTAL	744,709	615,188	526,255	594,681	709,585	100.00	19.32
AFRICA	721	736	311	711	1,514	0.21	112.94
North Africa			23	117	887	0.13	658.12
Algeria			5	1	62	0.01	6,100.00
Morocco			18	116	825	0.12	611.21
Southern Africa	452	456	198	365	335	0.05	-8.22
South Africa	452	456	198	365	335	0.05	-8.22
West Africa	269	280	90	229	292	0.04	27.51
Nigeria	269	280	90	229	292	0.04	27.51
AMERICAS	408,219	339,636	313,029	373,176	527,786	74.38	41.43
Caribbean	39,480	33,110	36,257	40,424	35,636	5.02	-11.84
Barbados	671	488	227	431	302	0.04	-29.93
Cuba	12,175	10,259	8,318	8,344	9,308	1.31	11.55
Dominica			110	47	61	0.01	29.79
Dominican Republic	9,604	7,983	7,038	8,413	6,302	0.89	-25.09
Grenada	655	498	123	300	232	0.03	-22.67
Haiti	660	831	269	651	931	0.13	43.01
Jamaica	303	292	244	255	184	0.03	-27.84
Puerto Rico	169	164	159	143	157	0.02	9.79
Saint Lucia	373	372	312	504	262	0.04	-48.02
Saint Vincent and the Grenadines			78	34	72	0.01	111.76
Trinidad and Tobago	14,870	12,223	19,379	21,302	17,825	2.51	-16.32
Central America	11,377	10,760	8,119	9,505	8,645	1.22	-9.05
Costa Rica	3,426	2,880	2,300	2,633	1,905	0.27	-27.65
El Salvador	678	751	255	692	573	0.08	-17.20
Guatemala	1,221	1,515	1,160	1,287	1,159	0.16	-9.95
Honduras	621	747	608	546	777	0.11	42.31
Nicaragua	743	916	777	876	729	0.10	-16.78
Panama	4,688	3,951	3,019	3,471	3,502	0.49	0.89
North America	130,257	109,848	97,249	106,197	75,228	10.60	-29.16
Canada	25,870	18,165	21,151	24,712	13,196	1.86	-46.60
Mexico	17,405	15,624	12,934	13,636	11,553	1.63	-15.28
United States of America	86,982	76,059	63,164	67,849	50,479	7.11	-25.60
South America	227,105	185,918	171,404	217,050	408,277	57.54	88.10
Argentina	26,055	24,601	24,585	35,286	32,243	4.54	-8.62
Bolivia	2,522	1,844	1,554	2,083	1,790	0.25	-14.07
Brazil	58,539	42,813	48,099	58,550	54,088	7.62	-7.62
Chile	15,424	13,175	10,656	10,645	10,761	1.52	1.09
Colombia	77,417	61,659	52,599	74,989	270,691	38.15	260.97
Ecuador	14,661	12,636	10,319	12,707	15,104	2.13	18.86
Guyana	460	616	327	643	518	0.07	-19.44
Paraguay	795	616	558	602	645	0.09	7.14
Peru	26,720	24,069	19,545	18,413	18,862	2.66	2.44
Uruguay	4,512	3,889	3,162	3,132	3,575	0.50	14.14
EAST ASIA AND THE PACIFIC	19,451	14,897	11,145	12,541	18,706	2.64	49.16
North-East Asia	14,494	13,086	10,381	10,954	17,127	2.41	56.35
China	8,733	7,415	6,006	6,271	13,151	1.85	109.71
Japan	4,378	3,840	3,258	3,278	2,564	0.36	-21.78
Korea, Dem. People's Republic of	293	280	229	227	131	0.02	-42.29
Korea, Republic of	720	1,092	733	849	1,079	0.15	27.09
Taiwan, Province of China	370	459	155	329	202	0.03	-38.60
South-East Asia			21	45	490	0.07	988.89
Philippines			21	45	490	0.07	988.89
Australasia	4,957	1,811	743	1,542	1,089	0.15	-29.38
Australia	4,546	1,419	608	1,249	866	0.12	-30.66

Yearbook of Tourism Statistics, Data 2008 – 2012, 2014 Edition

VENEZUELA

1. Arrivals of non-resident tourists at national borders, by nationality

	2008	2009	2010	2011	2012	Market share 2012	% Change 2012-2011
New Zealand	411	392	135	293	223	0.03	-23.89
EUROPE	**301,579**	**241,431**	**193,584**	**194,289**	**146,383**	**20.63**	**-24.66**
Central/Eastern Europe	**14,475**	**9,828**	**8,694**	**11,913**	**10,306**	**1.45**	**-13.49**
Belarus			1	10	564	0.08	5,540.00
Bulgaria	445	375	309	301	205	0.03	-31.89
Czech Republic	4,496	2,878	3,588	3,568	1,823	0.26	-48.91
Estonia			156	211	41	0.01	-80.57
Hungary	681	699	251	465	433	0.06	-6.88
Kazakhstan			9	1	4	0.00	300.00
Latvia			104	24	77	0.01	220.83
Lithuania	949	397	214	320	235	0.03	-26.56
Poland	4,991	2,802	2,177	4,426	2,952	0.42	-33.30
Romania	929	846	363	662	654	0.09	-1.21
Russian Federation	1,731	1,627	1,308	1,591	2,698	0.38	69.58
Slovakia			83	117	217	0.03	85.47
Ukraine	253	204	131	217	403	0.06	85.71
Northern Europe	**53,816**	**33,436**	**18,807**	**20,392**	**11,335**	**1.60**	**-44.41**
Denmark	7,480	4,012	2,354	2,376	1,154	0.16	-51.43
Finland	4,342	2,462	240	682	329	0.05	-51.76
Ireland	831	636	221	474	301	0.04	-36.50
Norway	2,977	2,080	373	1,254	626	0.09	-50.08
Sweden	11,006	7,127	4,138	3,775	2,163	0.30	-42.70
United Kingdom	27,180	17,119	11,481	11,831	6,762	0.95	-42.85
Southern Europe	**139,129**	**127,215**	**99,672**	**95,673**	**82,876**	**11.68**	**-13.38**
Bosnia and Herzegovina			2	1	4	0.00	300.00
Croatia	268	231	171	180	201	0.03	11.67
Greece	615	942	310	736	782	0.11	6.25
Italy	52,131	45,926	37,382	36,384	31,057	4.38	-14.64
Portugal	19,466	17,268	13,906	13,347	13,660	1.93	2.35
Slovenia			61	34	98	0.01	188.24
Spain	66,649	62,848	47,840	44,991	37,074	5.22	-17.60
Western Europe	**91,936**	**68,943**	**65,604**	**64,832**	**40,363**	**5.69**	**-37.74**
Austria	3,079	3,545	3,058	2,850	1,663	0.23	-41.65
Belgium	3,708	2,573	2,055	2,014	1,299	0.18	-35.50
France	23,026	19,739	22,600	22,645	13,068	1.84	-42.29
Germany	37,719	27,040	21,985	18,488	9,408	1.33	-49.11
Luxembourg			34	10	22	0.00	120.00
Netherlands	17,651	10,528	10,889	14,269	11,888	1.68	-16.69
Switzerland	6,753	5,518	4,983	4,556	3,015	0.42	-33.82
East Mediterranean Europe	**2,223**	**2,009**	**807**	**1,479**	**1,503**	**0.21**	**1.62**
Israel	1,902	1,639	484	1,135	893	0.13	-21.32
Turkey	321	370	323	344	610	0.09	77.33
MIDDLE EAST	**10,389**	**8,970**	**6,946**	**7,657**	**8,134**	**1.15**	**6.23**
Egypt	289	304	114	234	281	0.04	20.09
Jordan	511	497	86	353	337	0.05	-4.53
Lebanon	5,293	4,474	3,657	3,698	4,453	0.63	20.42
Libya	329	331	285	284	94	0.01	-66.90
Saudi Arabia			1	3	46	0.01	1,433.33
Syrian Arab Republic	3,967	3,364	2,803	3,085	2,923	0.41	-5.25
SOUTH ASIA	**1,418**	**1,698**	**620**	**1,307**	**2,036**	**0.29**	**55.78**
India	858	1,131	150	809	870	0.12	7.54
Iran, Islamic Republic of	560	567	470	498	1,166	0.16	134.14
NOT SPECIFIED	**2,932**	**7,820**	**620**	**5,000**	**5,026**	**0.71**	**0.52**
Other countries of the World	2,932	7,820	620	5,000	5,026	0.71	0.52

823

VIET NAM

2. Arrivals of non-resident visitors at national borders, by country of residence

	2008	2009	2010	2011	2012	Market share 2012	% Change 2012-2011
TOTAL	4,235,800	3,747,400	5,049,800	6,014,000	6,847,680	100.00	13.86
AMERICAS	501,600	487,600	533,200	546,300	557,389	8.14	2.03
North America	501,600	487,600	533,200	546,300	557,389	8.14	2.03
Canada	86,800	84,600	102,200	106,400	113,563	1.66	6.73
United States of America	414,800	403,000	431,000	439,900	443,826	6.48	0.89
EAST ASIA AND THE PACIFIC	2,790,800	2,422,300	3,497,700	4,383,600	4,809,027	70.23	9.70
North-East Asia	1,788,600	1,505,700	2,177,400	2,795,800	3,128,764	45.69	11.91
China	643,300	518,900	905,400	1,416,800	1,428,693	20.86	0.84
Hong Kong, China					13,383	0.20	
Japan	393,100	356,700	442,100	481,500	576,386	8.42	19.71
Korea, Republic of	449,000	360,100	495,900	536,400	700,917	10.24	30.67
Taiwan, Province of China	303,200	270,000	334,000	361,100	409,385	5.98	13.37
South-East Asia	746,700	681,000	1,017,500	1,271,500	1,363,798	19.92	7.26
Cambodia	129,700	118,300	254,600	423,400	331,939	4.85	-21.60
Indonesia	24,900	27,300	51,500	55,400	60,857	0.89	9.85
Lao People's Democratic Republic	30,900	26,100	37,400	118,500	150,678	2.20	27.15
Malaysia	174,500	165,600	211,300	233,100	299,041	4.37	28.29
Philippines	45,800	45,700	69,200	86,800	99,192	1.45	14.28
Singapore	158,500	138,400	170,700	172,500	196,225	2.87	13.75
Thailand	182,400	159,600	222,800	181,800	225,866	3.30	24.24
Australasia	255,500	235,600	302,800	316,300	316,465	4.62	0.05
Australia	234,700	217,200	278,200	289,800	289,844	4.23	0.02
New Zealand	20,800	18,400	24,600	26,500	26,621	0.39	0.46
EUROPE	623,500	617,900	757,000	811,600	926,957	13.54	14.21
Central/Eastern Europe	49,000	55,200	82,800	101,600	174,287	2.55	71.54
Russian Federation	49,000	55,200	82,800	101,600	174,287	2.55	71.54
Northern Europe	171,800	176,500	207,900	231,500	270,183	3.95	16.71
Denmark	20,400	19,600	24,400	25,700	27,970	0.41	8.83
Finland					16,204	0.24	
Norway	15,200	13,300	16,800	19,500	19,928	0.29	2.19
Sweden	29,100	28,100	27,500	30,000	35,735	0.52	19.12
United Kingdom	107,100	115,500	139,200	156,300	170,346	2.49	8.99
Southern Europe	45,700	41,100	54,300	60,800	62,642	0.91	3.03
Italy	21,100	20,000	24,700	28,300	31,337	0.46	10.73
Spain	24,600	21,100	29,600	32,500	31,305	0.46	-3.68
Western Europe	357,000	345,100	412,000	417,700	419,845	6.13	0.51
Belgium	17,000	16,000	20,400	21,900	18,914	0.28	-13.63
France	182,100	173,000	199,400	211,400	219,721	3.21	3.94
Germany	102,800	101,800	123,200	113,900	106,608	1.56	-6.40
Netherlands	35,400	34,700	43,700	45,000	45,862	0.67	1.92
Switzerland	19,700	19,600	25,300	25,500	28,740	0.42	12.71
NOT SPECIFIED	319,900	219,600	261,900	272,500	554,307	8.09	103.42
Other countries of the World	319,900	219,600	261,900	272,500	554,307	8.09	103.42

Yearbook of Tourism Statistics, Data 2008 – 2012, 2014 Edition

YEMEN

1. Arrivals of non-resident tourists at national borders, by nationality

		2008	2009	2010	2011	2012	Market share 2012	% Change 2012-2011
TOTAL	(*)	1,022,737	1,028,127	1,024,762	829,190	1,173,975	100.00	41.58
AFRICA		17,715	23,587	33,387	27,835	19,210	1.64	-30.99
East Africa		13,720	18,920	26,961	24,138	17,627	1.50	-26.97
Comoros					3,715			
Djibouti		4,242	7,169	8,636	3,852			
Eritrea			2,487	5,361	4,182	2,413	0.21	-42.30
Ethiopia		4,624	6,711	9,359	8,134	11,927	1.02	46.63
Kenya		996	1,382	1,998	1,634	2,202	0.19	34.76
Somalia		3,001			1,697			
United Republic of Tanzania		857	1,171	1,607	924	1,085	0.09	17.42
North Africa		3,507	3,190	4,494	2,852			
Algeria		458						
Morocco		334						
Sudan		2,275	3,190	4,494	2,852			
Tunisia		440						
Southern Africa		402	425	391	182	221	0.02	21.43
South Africa		402	425	391	182	221	0.02	21.43
West Africa		86						
Mauritania		86						
Other Africa			1,052	1,541	663	1,362	0.12	105.43
Other countries of Africa			1,052	1,541	663	1,362	0.12	105.43
AMERICAS		18,118	25,493	28,006	18,275	27,894	2.38	52.63
North America		16,172	23,441	25,784	16,968	24,235	2.06	42.83
Canada		3,301	3,914	3,321	1,434	1,664	0.14	16.04
United States of America		12,871	19,527	22,463	15,534	22,571	1.92	45.30
Other Americas		1,946	2,052	2,222	1,307	3,659	0.31	179.95
Other countries of the Americas		1,946	2,052	2,222	1,307	3,659	0.31	179.95
EAST ASIA AND THE PACIFIC		20,466	26,004	26,222	13,306	15,713	1.34	18.09
North-East Asia		7,622	8,331	7,261	2,638	2,277	0.19	-13.68
China		4,695	5,843	5,331	1,824	1,831	0.16	0.38
Japan		1,874	1,465	987	343	205	0.02	-40.23
Korea, Republic of		1,053	1,023	943	316	241	0.02	-23.73
Taiwan, Province of China					155			
South-East Asia		8,250	12,192	12,553	8,981	8,690	0.74	-3.24
Indonesia		4,647	6,799	6,832	5,389	5,140	0.44	-4.62
Malaysia		1,295	2,560	2,427	1,657	1,998	0.17	20.58
Philippines		1,875	2,833	3,294	1,340	1,552	0.13	15.82
Singapore					126			
Thailand		433			202			
Viet Nam					267			
Australasia		1,147	1,440	1,296	425	567	0.05	33.41
Australia		1,147	1,440	1,296	425	567	0.05	33.41
Other East Asia and the Pacific		3,447	4,041	5,112	1,262	4,179	0.36	231.14
Other countries of Asia		3,447	4,041	5,112	1,262	4,179	0.36	231.14
EUROPE		36,099	43,493	37,730	18,507	22,113	1.88	19.48
Central/Eastern Europe		1,700	1,615	1,501	770	880	0.07	14.29
Bulgaria		147						
Poland		236						
Romania		222						
Russian Federation		1,095	1,615	1,501	770	880	0.07	14.29
Northern Europe		9,128	13,844	10,949	5,174	7,331	0.62	41.69
Denmark					91			
Ireland					99			
Norway					104			

Yearbook of Tourism Statistics, Data 2008 – 2012, 2014 Edition

YEMEN

1. Arrivals of non-resident tourists at national borders, by nationality

	2008	2009	2010	2011	2012	Market share 2012	% Change 2012-2011
Sweden				176			
United Kingdom	9,128	13,844	10,949	4,704	7,331	0.62	55.85
Southern Europe	**3,497**	**2,749**	**2,003**	**1,017**	**562**	**0.05**	**-44.74**
Greece	191						
Italy	2,937	2,749	2,003	791	562	0.05	-28.95
Spain	369			226			
Western Europe	**13,733**	**13,555**	**12,412**	**4,963**	**4,805**	**0.41**	**-3.18**
Austria	561	532	331	164	100	0.01	-39.02
Belgium	418			129			
France	5,123	6,141	5,567	2,724	2,024	0.17	-25.70
Germany	5,477	4,257	4,559	1,235	1,509	0.13	22.19
Netherlands	1,591	2,058	1,565	532	931	0.08	75.00
Switzerland	563	567	390	179	241	0.02	34.64
East Mediterranean Europe	**4,160**	**4,619**	**5,673**	**5,127**	**5,759**	**0.49**	**12.33**
Turkey	4,160	4,619	5,673	5,127	5,759	0.49	12.33
Other Europe	**3,881**	**7,111**	**5,192**	**1,456**	**2,776**	**0.24**	**90.66**
Other countries of Europe	3,881	7,111	5,192	1,456	2,776	0.24	90.66
MIDDLE EAST	**293,275**	**289,737**	**376,882**	**289,515**	**348,939**	**29.72**	**20.53**
Bahrain	2,307	4,205	4,568	2,255	5,861	0.50	159.91
Egypt	10,263	14,293	18,204	8,855	10,029	0.85	13.26
Iraq	2,283	3,447	3,271	2,669	2,361	0.20	-11.54
Jordan	6,604	7,880	9,069	7,600	4,972	0.42	-34.58
Kuwait	1,249		1,518	527			
Lebanon	2,221	3,142	2,795	1,243	1,631	0.14	31.21
Libya	241						
Oman	50,232	46,098	49,559	38,497	49,587	4.22	28.81
Palestine	2,609		3,228	2,228			
Qatar	2,899	4,964	3,643	1,713	3,457	0.29	101.81
Saudi Arabia	176,305	163,000	235,412	198,823	217,291	18.51	9.29
Syrian Arab Republic	8,436	10,792	14,668	12,876	17,656	1.50	37.12
United Arab Emirates	20,942	22,438	21,681	10,904	17,983	1.53	64.92
Other countries of Middle East	6,684	9,478	9,266	1,325	18,111	1.54	1,266.87
SOUTH ASIA	**18,824**	**25,607**	**33,793**	**20,060**	**25,460**	**2.17**	**26.92**
Bangladesh				680			
India	13,867	19,608	26,112	13,251	16,407	1.40	23.82
Nepal				432			
Pakistan	4,957	5,999	7,681	5,350	9,053	0.77	69.21
Sri Lanka				347			
NOT SPECIFIED	**618,240**	**594,206**	**488,742**	**441,692**	**714,646**	**60.87**	**61.80**
Nationals Residing Abroad	618,240	594,206	488,742	441,692	714,646	60.87	61.80

Yearbook of Tourism Statistics, Data 2008 – 2012, 2014 Edition

YEMEN

5. Overnight stays of non-resident tourists in hotels and similar establishments, by nationality

	2008	2009	2010	2011	2012	Market share 2012	% Change 2012-2011
TOTAL (*)	11,891,336	11,790,252	16,506,710	9,283,672	13,679,676	100.00	47.35
AFRICA	127,248	188,696	267,096	222,680	153,680	1.12	-30.99
East Africa	85,752	151,360	215,688	193,104	141,016	1.03	-26.97
Comoros				29,720			
Djibouti	33,936	57,352	69,088	30,816			
Eritrea		19,896	42,888	33,456	19,304	0.14	-42.30
Ethiopia	36,992	53,688	74,872	65,072	95,416	0.70	46.63
Kenya	7,968	11,056	15,984	13,072	17,616	0.13	34.76
Somalia				13,576			
United Republic of Tanzania	6,856	9,368	12,856	7,392	8,680	0.06	17.42
North Africa	25,384	25,520	35,952	22,816			
Algeria	3,664						
Sudan	18,200	25,520	35,952	22,816			
Tunisia	3,520						
Southern Africa		3,400	3,128	1,456	1,768	0.01	21.43
South Africa		3,400	3,128	1,456	1,768	0.01	21.43
Other Africa	16,112	8,416	12,328	5,304	10,896	0.08	105.43
Other countries of Africa	16,112	8,416	12,328	5,304	10,896	0.08	105.43
AMERICAS	144,944	203,944	224,048	146,200	223,152	1.63	52.63
North America	129,376	187,528	206,272	135,744	193,880	1.42	42.83
Canada	26,408	31,312	26,568	11,472	13,312	0.10	16.04
United States of America	102,968	156,216	179,704	124,272	180,568	1.32	45.30
Other Americas	15,568	16,416	17,776	10,456	29,272	0.21	179.95
Other countries of the Americas	15,568	16,416	17,776	10,456	29,272	0.21	179.95
EAST ASIA AND THE PACIFIC	150,344	208,032	208,976	106,448	125,704	0.92	18.09
North-East Asia	60,976	66,656	57,288	21,104	18,216	0.13	-13.68
China	37,560	46,752	42,648	14,592	14,648	0.11	0.38
Japan	14,992	11,720	7,896	2,744	1,640	0.01	-40.23
Korea, Republic of	8,424	8,184	6,744	2,528	1,928	0.01	-23.73
Taiwan, Province of China				1,240			
South-East Asia	66,000	97,536	100,424	71,848	69,520	0.51	-3.24
Indonesia	37,176	54,392	54,656	43,112	41,120	0.30	-4.62
Malaysia	10,360	20,480	19,416	13,256	15,984	0.12	20.58
Philippines	15,000	22,664	26,352	10,720	12,416	0.09	15.82
Singapore				1,008			
Thailand	3,464			1,616			
Viet Nam				2,136			
Australasia	9,176	11,520	10,368	3,400	4,536	0.03	33.41
Australia	9,176	11,520	10,368	3,400	4,536	0.03	33.41
Other East Asia and the Pacific	14,192	32,320	40,896	10,096	33,432	0.24	231.14
Other countries of Asia	14,192	32,320	40,896	10,096	33,432	0.24	231.14
EUROPE	279,928	347,944	301,840	148,056	176,904	1.29	19.48
Central/Eastern Europe	8,760	12,920	12,008	6,160	7,040	0.05	14.29
Russian Federation	8,760	12,920	12,008	6,160	7,040	0.05	14.29
Northern Europe	73,024	110,752	87,592	41,392	58,648	0.43	41.69
Denmark				728			
Ireland				792			
Norway				832			
Sweden				1,408			
United Kingdom	73,024	110,752	87,592	37,632	58,648	0.43	55.85
Southern Europe	26,920	21,992	16,024	8,136	4,496	0.03	-44.74
Italy	23,496	21,992	16,024	6,328	4,496	0.03	-28.95
Spain	3,424			1,808			
Western Europe	110,008	108,440	99,296	39,704	38,440	0.28	-3.18

 Yearbook of Tourism Statistics, Data 2008 – 2012, 2014 Edition

YEMEN

5. Overnight stays of non-resident tourists in hotels and similar establishments, by nationality

	2008	2009	2010	2011	2012	Market share 2012	% Change 2012-2011
Austria	4,488	4,256	2,648	1,312	800	0.01	-39.02
Belgium	3,488			1,032			
France	40,984	49,128	44,536	21,792	16,192	0.12	-25.70
Germany	43,816	34,056	36,472	9,880	12,072	0.09	22.19
Netherlands	12,728	16,464	12,520	4,256	7,448	0.05	75.00
Switzerland	4,504	4,536	3,120	1,432	1,928	0.01	34.64
East Mediterranean Europe	**33,280**	**36,952**	**45,384**	**41,016**	**46,072**	**0.34**	**12.33**
Turkey	33,280	36,952	45,384	41,016	46,072	0.34	12.33
Other Europe	**27,936**	**56,888**	**41,536**	**11,648**	**22,208**	**0.16**	**90.66**
Other countries of Europe	27,936	56,888	41,536	11,648	22,208	0.16	90.66
MIDDLE EAST	**2,324,448**	**2,317,896**	**3,015,856**	**2,316,120**	**2,791,512**	**20.41**	**20.53**
Bahrain	18,456	33,640	36,544	18,040	46,888	0.34	159.91
Egypt	82,104	114,344	145,632	70,840	80,232	0.59	13.26
Iraq	18,264	27,576	26,168	21,352	18,888	0.14	-11.54
Jordan	52,832	63,040	72,552	60,800	39,776	0.29	-34.58
Kuwait	9,992			4,216			
Lebanon	17,768	25,136	22,360	9,944	13,048	0.10	31.21
Oman	401,856	368,784	397,272	307,976	396,696	2.90	28.81
Palestine	20,872			17,824			
Qatar	23,192	39,712	29,144	13,704	27,656	0.20	101.81
Saudi Arabia	1,410,440	1,304,000	1,883,296	1,590,584	1,738,328	12.71	9.29
Syrian Arab Republic	67,488	86,336	117,344	103,008	141,248	1.03	37.12
United Arab Emirates	167,536	179,504	173,448	87,232	143,864	1.05	64.92
Other countries of Middle East	33,648	75,824	112,096	10,600	144,888	1.06	1,266.87
SOUTH ASIA	**150,592**	**204,856**	**270,344**	**160,480**	**203,680**	**1.49**	**26.92**
Bangladesh				5,440			
India	110,936	156,864	208,896	106,008	131,256	0.96	23.82
Nepal				3,456			
Pakistan	39,656	47,992	61,448	42,800	72,424	0.53	69.21
Sri Lanka				2,776			
NOT SPECIFIED	**8,713,832**	**8,318,884**	**12,218,550**	**6,183,688**	**10,005,044**	**73.14**	**61.80**
Other countries of the World	58,472						
Nationals Residing Abroad	8,655,360	8,318,884	12,218,550	6,183,688	10,005,044	73.14	61.80

Yearbook of Tourism Statistics, Data 2008 – 2012, 2014 Edition

ZAMBIA

1. Arrivals of non-resident tourists at national borders, by country of residence

	2008	2009	2010	2011	2012	Market share 2012	% Change 2012-2011
TOTAL	811,775	709,948	815,164	920,299	859,088	100.00	-6.65
AFRICA	606,641	467,045	583,377	652,276	654,114	76.14	0.28
East Africa	362,500	276,338	316,600	378,072	368,660	42.91	-2.49
Kenya	12,331	10,378	12,785	14,698	10,643	1.24	-27.59
United Republic of Tanzania	106,284	81,288	121,275	116,280	214,820	25.01	84.74
Zimbabwe	226,428	171,232	171,806	227,733	119,100	13.86	-47.70
Other countries of East Africa	17,457	13,440	10,734	19,361	24,097	2.80	24.46
Central Africa	80,674	57,955	80,314	71,332	65,194	7.59	-8.60
All countries of Central Africa	80,674	57,955	80,314	71,332	65,194	7.59	-8.60
North Africa	4,859	1,397	2,671	2,817	1,474	0.17	-47.67
All countries of North Africa	4,859	1,397	2,671	2,817	1,474	0.17	-47.67
Southern Africa	154,511	125,604	178,643	194,607	209,232	24.36	7.52
South Africa	95,415	84,413	144,980	134,556	134,602	15.67	0.03
Other countries of Southern Africa	59,096	41,191	33,663	60,051	74,630	8.69	24.28
West Africa	4,097	5,751	5,149	5,448	9,554	1.11	75.37
All countries of West Africa	4,097	5,751	5,149	5,448	9,554	1.11	75.37
AMERICAS	47,360	63,089	41,703	51,668	31,559	3.67	-38.92
North America	43,053	58,939	36,899	45,537	29,344	3.42	-35.56
Canada	9,183	9,488	7,378	10,441	5,517	0.64	-47.16
United States of America	33,870	49,451	29,521	35,096	23,827	2.77	-32.11
Other Americas	4,307	4,150	4,804	6,131	2,215	0.26	-63.87
Other countries of the Americas	4,307	4,150	4,804	6,131	2,215	0.26	-63.87
EAST ASIA AND THE PACIFIC	34,658	38,542	64,271	80,429	92,256	10.74	14.70
North-East Asia	4,241	5,373	26,660	41,422	67,427	7.85	62.78
China			18,319	30,076	63,892	7.44	112.44
Japan	4,241	5,373	8,341	11,346	3,535	0.41	-68.84
Australasia	17,873	20,308	13,880	27,982	12,397	1.44	-55.70
Australia	14,517	16,316	10,430	12,599	10,814	1.26	-14.17
New Zealand	3,356	3,992	3,450	15,383	1,583	0.18	-89.71
Other East Asia and the Pacific	12,544	12,861	23,731	11,025	12,432	1.45	12.76
Other countries of Asia	12,544	12,861	23,731	11,025	12,432	1.45	12.76
EUROPE	109,182	128,340	104,399	113,831	65,826	7.66	-42.17
Northern Europe	60,591	72,190	65,405	71,268	36,636	4.26	-48.59
Denmark	3,982	2,665	3,752	2,377	1,861	0.22	-21.71
Sweden	3,301	3,166	3,640	3,625	2,057	0.24	-43.26
United Kingdom	46,516	53,370	50,958	59,084	25,446	2.96	-56.93
Scandinavia	6,792	12,989	7,055	6,182	7,272	0.85	17.63
Southern Europe	5,190	8,238	5,515	6,883	2,972	0.35	-56.82
Italy	5,190	8,238	5,515	6,883	2,972	0.35	-56.82
Western Europe	21,363	19,368	16,189	16,360	9,642	1.12	-41.06
France	9,264	6,701	6,418	6,049	3,023	0.35	-50.02
Germany	12,099	12,667	9,771	10,311	6,619	0.77	-35.81
Other Europe	22,038	28,544	17,290	19,320	16,576	1.93	-14.20
Other countries of Europe	22,038	28,544	17,290	19,320	16,576	1.93	-14.20
SOUTH ASIA	13,934	12,932	21,414	22,095	15,333	1.78	-30.60
India	13,934	12,932	21,414	22,095	15,333	1.78	-30.60

Yearbook of Tourism Statistics, Data 2008 – 2012, 2014 Edition

ZIMBABWE

2. Arrivals of non-resident visitors at national borders, by country of residence

	2008	2009	2010	2011	2012	Market share 2012	% Change 2012-2011
TOTAL	1,955,597	2,017,264	2,239,165	2,423,280	1,794,230	100.00	-25.96
AFRICA	1,731,528	1,678,884	1,951,330	2,041,291	1,562,194	87.07	-23.47
East Africa	565,295	493,791	389,022	508,728	696,592	38.82	36.93
Kenya	21,459	25,808	8,509	6,514	7,273	0.41	11.65
Malawi	63,597	108,103	67,291	138,676	241,344	13.45	74.03
Mauritius	875	967	1,066	2,779	1,191	0.07	-57.14
Mozambique	118,117	110,058	131,653	148,857	146,922	8.19	-1.30
Seychelles	280	360	434	1,321	2,352	0.13	78.05
Uganda	4,387	6,906	2,893	11,555	3,914	0.22	-66.13
United Republic of Tanzania	10,236	11,391	8,454	14,038	14,740	0.82	5.00
Zambia	346,344	230,198	168,722	184,988	278,856	15.54	50.74
Central Africa	30,476	27,580	18,036	17,137	25,021	1.39	46.01
Angola	10,439	8,131	2,285	3,297	1,437	0.08	-56.41
Democratic Republic of the Congo	20,037	19,449	15,751	13,840	23,584	1.31	70.40
Southern Africa	1,115,218	1,137,761	1,522,208	1,471,791	825,439	46.01	-43.92
Botswana	147,780	183,212	114,718	119,098	64,926	3.62	-45.49
Lesotho	4,551	5,367	4,957	6,655	20,051	1.12	201.29
Namibia	19,860	33,806	19,917	23,322	11,487	0.64	-50.75
South Africa	936,727	912,244	1,368,238	1,309,463	719,637	40.11	-45.04
Swaziland	6,300	3,132	14,378	13,253	9,338	0.52	-29.54
West Africa	5,395	4,656	3,290	5,126	2,135	0.12	-58.35
Ghana	1,619	1,258	1,428	3,857	1,274	0.07	-66.97
Nigeria	3,776	3,398	1,862	1,269	861	0.05	-32.15
Other Africa	15,144	15,096	18,774	38,509	13,007	0.72	-66.22
Other countries of Africa	15,144	15,096	18,774	38,509	13,007	0.72	-66.22
AMERICAS	43,412	57,842	69,008	89,756	58,873	3.28	-34.41
Caribbean	1,935	2,513	804	892	450	0.03	-49.55
All countries of the Caribbean	1,935	2,513	804	892	450	0.03	-49.55
North America	38,172	49,355	63,343	80,596	54,960	3.06	-31.81
Canada	5,480	5,538	4,098	6,999	3,890	0.22	-44.42
Mexico	418	546	2,829	992	1,010	0.06	1.81
United States of America	32,274	43,271	56,416	72,605	50,060	2.79	-31.05
South America	1,700	2,643	2,986	5,778	2,819	0.16	-51.21
Argentina	655	1,058	1,027	1,682	858	0.05	-48.99
Brazil	1,045	1,585	1,959	4,096	1,961	0.11	-52.12
Other Americas	1,605	3,331	1,875	2,490	644	0.04	-74.14
Other countries of the Americas	1,605	3,331	1,875	2,490	644	0.04	-74.14
EAST ASIA AND THE PACIFIC	63,194	104,366	84,092	125,257	55,560	3.10	-55.64
North-East Asia	37,181	61,534	37,385	75,591	30,765	1.71	-59.30
Hong Kong, China	14,169	30,102	12,343	30,549	4,937	0.28	-83.84
Japan	14,803	18,389	18,593	32,784	18,032	1.00	-45.00
Korea, Republic of	8,209	13,043	6,449	12,258	7,796	0.43	-36.40
South-East Asia	2,326	4,016	5,537	7,114	2,722	0.15	-61.74
Malaysia	1,770	2,416	3,497	3,452	1,115	0.06	-67.70
Singapore	556	1,600	2,040	3,662	1,607	0.09	-56.12
Australasia	20,201	33,041	37,708	38,841	20,966	1.17	-46.02
Australia	13,866	22,612	25,240	26,833	13,355	0.74	-50.23
New Zealand	6,335	10,429	12,468	12,008	7,611	0.42	-36.62
Other East Asia and the Pacific	3,486	5,775	3,462	3,711	1,107	0.06	-70.17
Other countries of Asia	2,143	2,363	2,155	1,333	580	0.03	-56.49
Other countries of Oceania	1,343	3,412	1,307	2,378	527	0.03	-77.84

Yearbook of Tourism Statistics, Data 2008 – 2012, 2014 Edition

ZIMBABWE

2. Arrivals of non-resident visitors at national borders, by country of residence

	2008	2009	2010	2011	2012	Market share 2012	% Change 2012-2011
EUROPE	**111,121**	**160,316**	**128,082**	**158,141**	**113,956**	**6.35**	**-27.94**
Northern Europe	**30,558**	**42,165**	**35,169**	**47,627**	**38,503**	**2.15**	**-19.16**
United Kingdom	22,778	27,580	24,192	35,913	27,587	1.54	-23.18
Scandinavia	7,780	14,585	10,977	11,714	10,916	0.61	-6.81
Southern Europe	**20,118**	**29,446**	**23,342**	**27,432**	**20,220**	**1.13**	**-26.29**
Italy	7,655	14,161	9,221	13,806	9,127	0.51	-33.89
Portugal	8,461	9,883	4,951	5,482	3,791	0.21	-30.85
Spain	4,002	5,402	9,170	8,144	7,302	0.41	-10.34
Western Europe	**50,453**	**77,430**	**57,997**	**69,629**	**47,365**	**2.64**	**-31.98**
Austria	3,247	5,520	6,475	6,245	4,228	0.24	-32.30
France	15,134	27,193	13,687	16,232	11,149	0.62	-31.31
Germany	14,929	22,936	16,910	24,300	17,126	0.95	-29.52
Netherlands	14,722	16,967	14,088	15,927	9,362	0.52	-41.22
Switzerland	2,421	4,814	6,837	6,925	5,500	0.31	-20.58
East Mediterranean Europe	**2,960**	**4,451**	**2,851**	**3,838**	**2,427**	**0.14**	**-36.76**
Israel	2,960	4,451	2,851	3,838	2,427	0.14	-36.76
Other Europe	**7,032**	**6,824**	**8,723**	**9,615**	**5,441**	**0.30**	**-43.41**
Other countries of Europe	7,032	6,824	8,723	9,615	5,441	0.30	-43.41
MIDDLE EAST	**928**	**5,456**	**1,758**	**2,863**	**1,160**	**0.06**	**-59.48**
Egypt	639	1,198	641	728	428	0.02	-41.21
Saudi Arabia	92	116	62	60	12	0.00	-80.00
United Arab Emirates	197	208	101	503	120	0.01	-76.14
Other countries of Middle East		3,934	954	1,572	600	0.03	-61.83
SOUTH ASIA	**5,414**	**10,400**	**4,895**	**5,972**	**2,487**	**0.14**	**-58.36**
India	3,911	5,446	3,571	3,499	1,809	0.10	-48.30
Iran, Islamic Republic of	215	1,368	758	1,228	55	0.00	-95.52
Pakistan	1,288	3,586	566	1,245	623	0.03	-49.96

Yearbook of Tourism Statistics, Data 2008 – 2012, 2014 Edition

NOTES 2008 - 2012

1. Arrivals of non-resident tourists at national borders, by nationality

Belarus	**Total**	Organized tourism.
Bhutan	**Total**	Total arrivals 2010: 40,873; 2011: 65,756; 2012: 105,407. The huge margin of difference in 2010, 2011 and 2012 as compared to the previous years is because starting from 2010 the regional high end tourists are included in the total figures.
Bolivia	**Total**	Preliminary data.
Brunei Darussalam	**Total**	Air arrivals.
Burundi	**Total**	Including nationals residing abroad. From 2010: break in the series due to implementation of improved methodology for distinguishing visitors (tourists) from other travellers.
Central African Republic	**Total**	Arrivals by air to Bangui only.
Chile	**Total**	Including nationals residing abroad.
Comoros	**Total**	Air arrivals.
Democratic Republic of the Congo	**Total**	2008-2010: arrival by air only; 2011: the arrivals data relate only to three border posts (N'Djili airport in Kinshasa, the Luano airport in Lubumbashi, and the land border-crossing of Kasumbalesa in Katanga province).
Gambia	**Total**	Charter tourists only.
Honduras	**Total**	Excluding tourists arrivals by sea.
Iceland	**Total**	Source: Icelandic Tourist Board. 2012: arrivals at Keflavik airport only.
India	**Total**	Excluding nationals residing abroad.
Italy	**Total**	Seasonal and border workers are excluded.
Kiribati	**Total**	Air arrivals. Tarawa and Christmas Island.
Lebanon	**Total**	Excluding nationals residing abroad, Syrian nationals, Palestinians and students.
Maldives	**Total**	Arrivals by air.
Mali	**Total**	2012: arrivals by air only.
Malta	**Total**	Data based on departures by air and by sea.
Marshall Islands	**Total**	Air arrivals. 2009: air and sea arrivals.
Mexico	**United States of America**	Includes tourists arriving by air and land, border tourists and domestic tourists residing in the United States of America.
	Other countries of the World	Includes border tourists from the southern zone.
Myanmar	**Total**	Including tourist arrivals through border entry points to Yangon.
Nepal	**Greece**	Including Cyprus.
Norway	**Total**	2008-2011: figures are based on "The Guest survey" carried out by "Institute of Transport Economics". The survey has been discontinued since 2012.
Paraguay	**Total**	Excluding nationals residing abroad and crew members. E/d cards in the "Silvio Petirossi" airport and passenger counts at the national border crossings - National Police and SENATUR.
Senegal	**Total**	Arrivals by air at "Léopold Sédar Senghor (LSS)" only. Including the nationals residing abroad. Country estimated totals: 2008: 866,700 2009: 810,000 2010: 900,000 2011: 1,001,000
Sint Maarten	**Total**	Arrivals at Princess Juliana International Airport. Including visitors to St. Maarten (the French side of the island).
	France	Including residents of the French West Indies.

833

NOTES 2008 - 2012

1. Arrivals of non-resident tourists at national borders, by nationality

Sri Lanka	**Total**	Excluding nationals residing abroad.
Sudan	**Total**	Including nationals residing abroad.
Tunisia	**Total**	Excluding nationals residing abroad.
Turkey	**Total**	Turkish citizens resident abroad are included.
Yemen	**Total**	Including nationals residing abroad.

NOTES 2008 - 2012

1. Arrivals of non-resident tourists at national borders, by country of residence

Andorra	Total	In 2009 and 2011 there were changes in the methodology for calculating the number of visitors of the country. In this regard, it is not possible to have comparability for data obtained using different methodologies because the variations reflect not only the variation in the number of visitors but also variations caused by the methodological changes.
Anguilla	Total	Excluding nationals residing abroad.
Antigua and Barbuda	Total	Air arrivals. Excluding nationals residing abroad.
Bermuda	Total	Air arrivals.
Canada	Total	Source: Canadian Tourism Commission and Statistics Canada
	Other countries of Africa	Including Chagos Archipelago, Ascension Island and Tristan da Cunha.
	Panama	Including Panama Canal Zone.
	Other countries of Oceania	Including Bismark Archipelago, Marquesas Island, Pitcairn Island and Tuamotu Islands.
Cayman Islands	Total	Air arrivals.
Colombia	Total	Source: Administrative Department of Security (DAS) / "Migración Colombia". Provisional data. Excluding cruise passengers. 2010-2012: arrivals of non-resident tourists by immigration checkpoints. 2011-2012: including nationals residing abroad. 2008-2009: data by nationality.
Cook Islands	Total	Air and sea arrivals.
Curaçao	Total	Arrivals by air.
Dominican Republic	Total	Arrivals by air.
Ethiopia	Total	2008: arrivals to Bole airport only. 2009-2012: arrivals through all ports of entry.
Fiji	Total	Excluding nationals residing abroad.
France	Total	Source: "Dgcis", "Banque de France". Non resident visitor survey ("EVE") - results 2010 and 2011 revised, results 2012 provisional.
	All countries of North Africa	Algeria, Egypt, Libya, Morocco and Tunisia.
	China	Including Hong Kong, China and Macao, China.
	Switzerland	Including Liechtenstein.
French Polynesia	Total	Air arrivals. Excluding nationals residing abroad.
	Samoa	Including American Samoa.
Greece	Total	From 2008, the information is based on the border survey conducted by the Bank of Greece.
	Egypt	Including Sudan.
	Lebanon	Including Syria.
Guadeloupe	Total	Arrivals by air.
Guyana	Total	Arrivals to Timehri Airport only.
Haiti	Total	Air arrivals. Including nationals residing abroad.
Ireland	United Kingdom	Including Northern Ireland resident arrivals. Change in methodology in estimating Northern Ireland tourists in 2010; as a result figures prior to 2010 not directly comparable.
Israel	Total	Excluding nationals residing abroad.

NOTES 2008 - 2012

1. Arrivals of non-resident tourists at national borders, by country of residence

Jamaica	**Total**	Air arrivals. Including nationals residing abroad.
Malawi	**Total**	Departures.
Malaysia	**Total**	Includes Singapore residents crossing the frontier by road through Johore Causeway.
Marshall Islands	**Total**	Air arrivals. 2009: air and sea arrivals.
Martinique	**Total**	Including French overseas departments and territories.
Mexico	**Total**	Including nationals residing abroad.
Nepal	**Greece**	Including Cyprus.
New Caledonia	**Total**	Including nationals residing abroad.
	All countries of the Caribbean	Martinique, Guadeloupe and Guyana.
Niue	**Total**	Including Niuans residing usually in New Zealand.
Palau	**Total**	Air arrivals (Palau International Airport).
Peru	**Total**	Including nationals residing abroad. Preliminary data.
Philippines	**Nationals Residing Abroad**	Philippine passport holders permanently residing abroad; excludes overseas Filipino workers.
Puerto Rico	**Total**	Arrivals by air. Fiscal year July to June. Source: "Junta de Planificación de Puerto Rico".
Reunion	**Total**	Source: INSEE: Survey on Tourism Flows
Saint Kitts and Nevis	**Total**	Air arrivals.
Saint Lucia	**Total**	Excluding nationals residing abroad.
Saint Vincent and the Grenadines	**Total**	Arrivals by air.
Senegal	**Total**	Arrivals by air at "Léopold Sédar Senghor (LSS)" only. Including the nationals residing abroad. Country estimated totals: 2008: 866,700 2009: 810,000 2010: 900,000 2011: 1,001,000
Sierra Leone	**Total**	Arrivals by air.
South Africa	**Total**	2008: excluding arrivals for work and contract workers. Since 2009 a new methodology has been applied and therefore, the information is not comparable to previous years.
Spain	**Total**	2012: provisional data.
Sri Lanka	**Total**	Excluding nationals residing abroad.
Timor-Leste	**Total**	Arrivals by air at Dili Airport.
Tonga	**Total**	Arrivals by air.
Trinidad and Tobago	**Total**	Arrivals by air.
United States of America	**Canada**	Historical data may reflect revisions made by "Statistics Canada".
	Mexico	Historical data may reflect revisions made by "Banco de México".

836

NOTES 2008 - 2012

2. Arrivals of non-resident visitors at national borders, by nationality

Albania	**Total**	Excluding nationals residing abroad.
	Other countries of Southern Europe	Arrivals from Kosovo.
Algeria	**Total**	Including nationals residing abroad.
Bahrain	**Total**	Excluding nationals residing abroad.
Belize	**Total**	Including transit passengers and border permits.
Ecuador	**Total**	Excluding nationals residing abroad. 2012: provisional data.
Egypt	**Total**	Excluding nationals residing abroad.
Guatemala	**Total**	2009-2012: data compiled by country of residence.
Italy	**Total**	Border survey. Seasonal and border workers are excluded.
Japan	**Total**	Excluding nationals residing abroad.
Korea, Republic of	**Total**	Including nationals residing abroad and crew members.
Macao, China	**Total**	Source of data: Public Security Police
Nigeria	**Total**	Source: Nigerian Tourism Development Corporation (NTDC)
Poland	**Total**	Since Poland joined the Schengen area, precise counting of incoming traffic is not possible. Data presented here are based on surveys by the Institute of Tourism. Only approximate results for main countries can be given.
Republic of Moldova	**Total**	Visitors who have benefited from tourism servies provided by the tourism agencies and tour operators (titulars of tourism licences). Excluding the left side of the river Nistru and the municipality of Bender.
Singapore	**Total**	Excluding Malaysian citizens arriving by land.
Syrian Arab Republic	**Total**	Survey of the incoming tourism.
	Iraq	The Iraqi nationals are included from 2008 only and they have been excluded in the previous years (from the beginning of 2008, they have to require a visa to enter Syria; if they arrived previously to this date, it is considered that they staid for a period longer than a year, becoming residents).
Turkey	**Total**	Turkish citizens resident abroad are included.
Uruguay	**Total**	Excluding cruise passengers arrivals.

NOTES 2008 - 2012

2. Arrivals of non-resident visitors at national borders, by country of residence

Australia	**Total**	Excluding nationals residing abroad and crew members. Source: Australian Bureau of Statistics
Canada	**Total**	Source: Canadian Tourism Commission and Statistics Canada
	China	Including Mongolia and Tibet.
	Estonia	Including Latvia and Lithuania.
	Hungary	Including Slovenia, Bulgaria and Romania.
	Denmark	Including Faeroe Islands.
	United Kingdom	Including Gibraltar.
	Italy	Including San Marino, the Holy See and Malta.
	Yugoslavia, SFR (former)	Including Croatia, Bosnia and Herzegovina, The Former Yugoslav Republic of Macedonia and Albania.
	France	Including Andorra and Monaco.
	Switzerland	Including Liechtenstein.
Congo	**Total**	Source: "Direction Générale de l'Industrie Touristique", surveys 2011 and 2012
Finland	**Total**	Border survey.
Hong Kong, China	**United States of America**	Including Guam.
	New Zealand	Including Cook Islands.
	France	Including New Caledonia and French Polynesia.
Israel	**Total**	Excluding nationals residing abroad.
Latvia	**Total**	Non-resident departures. Survey of persons crossing the state border.
Macao, China	**Total**	Source of data: Public Security Police
Mozambique	**Total**	Note 2008: Change of methodology. Until 2007 the data correspond only to 12 border posts. From 2008, the data of all the border posts of the country are used.
New Zealand	**Total**	Data regarding to short term movements are compiled from a random sample of passenger declarations. Including nationals residing abroad. Source: Statistics New Zealand (International Travel and Migration).
Panama	**Total**	Total number of visitors broken down by permanent residence who arrived in Panama at Tocumen International Airport.
Saint Vincent and the Grenadines	**Total**	Arrivals by air.
Singapore	**Total**	Excluding Malaysian citizens arriving by land.
South Africa	**Total**	2008: Excluding nationals residing abroad. Including arrivals by purpose of holiday, business, study, work, transit, border traffic and contract workers. Since 2009 a new methodology has been applied and therefore, the information is not comparable to previous years.
Sweden	**Total**	Data for 2011 and 2012 according to new national border survey (IBIS, Incoming Visitors to Sweden). No data collected during 2008 to 2010. The new border survey (IBIS) started in 2011. Source: Swedish Agency for Economic and Regional Growth.

Yearbook of Tourism Statistics, Data 2008 – 2012, 2014 Edition

3. Arrivals of non-resident tourists in hotels and similar establishments, by nationality

Bolivia	**Total**	Preliminary data. Hotel arrivals in the regional capitals.
Chad	**Total**	2010: Partial data.
Italy	**Total**	Arrivals at hotels only.
Montenegro	**Serbia**	Including arrivals from Kosovo.
Morocco	**Total**	Arrivals in classified hotels, holiday villages, tourist residences and Riad.
Palestine	**Total**	Source: Palestinian Central Bureau of Statistics, 2013. Hotel Activity Survey 2012. Ramallah - Palestine.
Slovenia	**Total**	2008: New methodology of accommodation statistics survey.
Syrian Arab Republic	**Total**	Survey of the incoming tourism.
	Iraq	The Iraqi nationals are included from 2008 only and they have been excluded in the previous years (from the beginning of 2008, they have to require a visa to enter Syria; if they arrived previously to this date, it is considered that they staid for a period longer than a year, becoming residents).
Turkey	**Total**	Arrivals at licensed establishments including: hotels, motels, boarding houses, inns, apartment hotels, holiday villages and special hotels. Results of a monthly survey carried out among accommodation establishments licensed by the Ministry of Tourism.

NOTES 2008 - 2012

3. Arrivals of non-resident tourists in hotels and similar establishments, by country of residence

Austria	**Total**	Hotels only.
Cape Verde	**Belgium**	Including Netherlands.
Congo	**Total**	Source: "Direction Générale de l'Industrie Touristique", surveys 2008 to 2012
Croatia	**Total**	According to the Regulation on Classification, Minimum Standards and Categorization of Accommodation Facilities, data for hotels and similar establishments do not include Inns and Bed and breakfast since 2006.
Curaçao	**Total**	Large and small hotels, guest houses, apartments and bungalows.
Denmark	**Total**	Hotels only. 2011: change of methodology.
France	**Total**	Source: "Insee", "Dgcis", regional partners. Hotel occupancy survey ("EFH").
Germany	**China**	Including Hong Kong, China.
	Other countries East Asia/Pacific	Including India.
Israel	**Total**	Arrivals at tourist hotels and not yet listed hotels.
	All countries of South America	Including Central America.
Luxembourg	**Total**	NACE Rev2 55.100
Macao, China	**Total**	Source of data: Monthly Survey of Travel Agencies
Netherlands	**Total**	Hotels and boarding houses.
New Caledonia	**Total**	It refers to hotels in Noumea.
Poland	**Total**	Excluding hostels.
Puerto Rico	**Total**	Fiscal year July to June. Hotels registered by the "Compañía de Turismo de Puerto Rico".
	Other countries of the Caribbean	Aggregated data of tourists coming from minor Antilles who did not specify their country of origin are included.
	Other countries of the World	Including crew members.
Qatar	**Total**	Arrivals at hotels only. 2008,2009: including domestic tourism.
	All countries of Europe	2010-2011: Europe and Americas.
Romania	**All countries of Africa**	Including Egypt and Libya.
Spain	**Total**	Arrivals at hotels and "hostales" (accommodation establishments providing limited services).
Switzerland	**Total**	Including health establishments.
	All countries of North Africa	Algeria, Libya, Morocco and Tunisia.
Togo	**Burkina Faso**	Including Mali and Niger.

Yearbook of Tourism Statistics, Data 2008 – 2012, 2014 Edition

NOTES 2008 - 2012

4. Arrivals of non-resident tourists in all types of accommodation establishments, by nationality

Hungary	**Total**	Collective accommodation establishments.
Montenegro	**Serbia**	Including arrivals from Kosovo.
Republic of Moldova	**Total**	Excluding the left side of the river Nistru and the municipality of Bender.
Slovenia	**Total**	2008: New methodology of accommodation statistics survey.
Syrian Arab Republic	**Total**	Excluding private accommodation. Survey of the incoming tourism.
	Iraq	The Iraqi nationals are included from 2008 only and they have been excluded in the previous years (from the beginning of 2008, they have to require a visa to enter Syria; if they arrived previously to this date, it is considered that they staid for a period longer than a year, becoming residents).
Turkey	**Total**	Results of a monthly survey carried out among accommodation establishments licensed by the Ministry of Tourism.

NOTES 2008 - 2012

4. Arrivals of non-resident tourists in all types of accommodation establishments, by country of residence

Austria	**Total**	Only paid accommodation; excluding stays at friends and relatives and second homes.
Belgium	**Total**	Hotel establishments, campings, holiday centres, holiday villages and specific categories of accommodation. From 2012 including bed and breakfast.
Croatia	**Total**	Excluding arrivals in ports of nautical tourism.
Denmark	**Total**	Including non-commercial tourism. 2011: change of methodology.
Germany	**China**	Including Hong Kong, China.
	Other countries East Asia/Pacific	Including India.
Malta	**Total**	Data based on departures by air and by sea. Source: National Statistics Office.
Philippines	**Total**	Air arrivals.
	Nationals Residing Abroad	Philippine passport holders permanently residing abroad; excludes overseas Filipino workers.
Romania	**All countries of Africa**	Including Egypt and Libya.
Spain	**Total**	Arrivals at hotels, "hostales", camping, tourism apartments and rural dwellings.

5. Overnight stays of non-resident tourists in hotels and similar establishments, by nationality

Bolivia	**Total**	Preliminary data. Hotel nights in the regional capitals.
Chad	**Total**	2010: Partial data.
Italy	**Total**	Nights in hotels only.
Madagascar	**Total**	All star-establishments (registered and non-registered).
Montenegro	**Serbia**	Including arrivals from Kosovo.
Morocco	**Total**	Overnight stays in classified hotels, holiday villages, tourist residences and Riad.
Norway	**Total**	Nights in registered establishments. Figures relate to establishments with 20 or more beds.
Palestine	**Total**	Source: Palestinian Central Bureau of Statistics, 2013. Hotel Activity Survey 2012. Ramallah - Palestine.
Slovenia	**Total**	2008: New methodology of accommodation statistics survey.
Syrian Arab Republic	**Total**	Survey of the incoming tourism.
	Iraq	The Iraqi nationals are included from 2008 only and they have been excluded in the previous years (from the beginning of 2008, they have to require a visa to enter Syria; if they arrived previously to this date, it is considered that they staid for a period longer than a year, becoming residents).
Turkey	**Total**	Classified hotels, motels, boarding houses, inns, apartment hotels, holiday villages and special hotels. Results of a monthly survey carried out among accommodation establishments licensed by the Ministry of Tourism.
Yemen	**Total**	Including nationals residing abroad.

NOTES 2008 - 2012

5. Overnight stays of non-resident tourists in hotels and similar establishments, by country of residence

Austria	**Total**	Hotels only.
Cape Verde	**Belgium**	Including Netherlands.
Congo	**Total**	Source: "Direction Générale de l'Industrie Touristique", surveys 2008 to 2012
Croatia	**Total**	According to the Regulation on Classification, Minimum Standards and Categorization of Accommodation Facilities, data for hotels and similar establishments do not include Inns and Bed and breakfast since 2006.
Denmark	**Total**	Hotels only. 2011: change of methodology.
France	**Total**	Source: "Insee", "Dgcis", regional partners. Hotel occupancy survey ("EFH").
Germany	**China**	Including Hong Kong, China.
	Other countries East Asia/Pacific	Including India.
Israel	**Total**	Nights in tourist hotels and apartment hotels.
	All countries of South America	Including Central America.
Luxembourg	**Total**	NACE Rev2 55.100
Macao, China	**Total**	Source of data: Monthly Survey of Hotels and Similar Establishments
Netherlands	**Total**	Hotels and boarding houses.
New Caledonia	**Total**	It refers to hotels in Noumea.
Poland	**Total**	Excluding hostels.
Qatar	**Total**	Nights in hotels only. 2008,2009: including domestic tourism.
	All countries of Europe	2010-2011: Europe and Americas.
Romania	**All countries of Africa**	Including Egypt and Libya.
Spain	**Total**	Nights in hotels and "hostales" (accommodation establishments providing limited services).
Switzerland	**Total**	Including health establishments.
	All countries of North Africa	Algeria, Libya, Morocco and Tunisia.
Togo	**Burkina Faso**	Including Mali and Niger.

6. Overnight stays of non-resident tourists in all types of accommodation establishments, by nationality

Hungary	**Total**	Collective accommodation establishments.
Montenegro	**Serbia**	Including arrivals from Kosovo.
Republic of Moldova	**Total**	Excluding the left side of the river Nistru and the municipality of Bender.
Slovenia	**Total**	2008: New methodology of accommodation statistics survey.
Syrian Arab Republic	**Total**	Survey of the incoming tourism.
	Iraq	The Iraqi nationals are included from 2008 only and they have been excluded in the previous years (from the beginning of 2008, they have to require a visa to enter Syria; if they arrived previously to this date, it is considered that they staid for a period longer than a year, becoming residents).
Turkey	**Total**	Results of a monthly survey carried out among accommodation establishments licensed by the Ministry of Tourism.

NOTES 2008 - 2012

6. Overnight stays of non-resident tourists in all types of accommodation establishments, by country of residence

Austria	**Total**	Only paid accommodation; excluding stays at friends and relatives and second homes.
Bahamas	**Total**	Nights in all forms of commercial accommodation.
Belgium	**Total**	Hotel establishments, campings, holiday centres, holiday villages and specific categories of accommodation. From 2012 including bed and breakfast.
Canada	**Total**	Source: Canadian Tourism Commission and Statistics Canada
	China	Including Mongolia and Tibet.
	Estonia	Including Latvia and Lithuania.
	Hungary	Including Slovenia, Bulgaria and Romania.
	Denmark	Including Faeroe Islands.
	United Kingdom	Including Gibraltar.
	Italy	Including San Marino, the Holy See and Malta.
	Yugoslavia, SFR (former)	Including Croatia, Bosnia and Herzegovina, The Former Yugoslav Republic of Macedonia and Albania.
	France	Including Andorra and Monaco.
	Switzerland	Including Liechtenstein.
Croatia	**Total**	Excluding overnight stays at ports of nautical tourism.
Denmark	**Total**	Including non-commercial tourism. 2011: change of methodology.
France	**Total**	Source: "Dgcis", "Banque de France". Non resident visitor survey ("EVE") - results 2010 and 2011 revised, results 2012 provisional.
	All countries of North Africa	Algeria, Egypt, Libya, Morocco and Tunisia.
	China	Including Hong Kong, China and Macao, China.
	Switzerland	Including Liechtenstein.
Germany	**China**	Including Hong Kong, China.
	Other countries East Asia/Pacific	Including India.
Ireland	**Total**	Including nights spent in private homes and holiday homes where no payment is made.
	United Kingdom	Including Northern Ireland residents.
Jamaica	**Total**	Information obtained by multiplying the average length of stay by the number of stop-overs of each country origin. Excluding nationals residing abroad.
	Other countries of the Americas	Latin America.
	All countries of Europe	United Kingdom and rest of Europe.
Malta	**Total**	Data based on departures by air and by sea. Source: National Statistics Office.
Netherlands	**Total**	Excluding overnight stays at fixed pitches (hired on a yearly or seasonal basis).
Romania	**All countries of Africa**	Including Egypt and Libya.
Spain	**Total**	Nights in hotels, "hostales", camping, tourism apartments and rural dwellings.

1. Arrivées de touristes non résidents aux frontières nationales, par nationalité

Bélarus	**Total**	Tourisme organisé.
Bhoutan	**Total**	Total des arrivées 2010: 40.873; 2011: 65.756; 2012: 105.407. L'écart important que l'on peut observer en 2010, 2011 et 2012 par rapport aux années précédentes tient au fait que l'on a inclus les touristes régionaux haut de gamme dans les totaux à partir de 2010.
Bolivie	**Total**	Données préliminaires.
Brunéi Darussalam	**Total**	Arrivées par voie aérienne.
Burundi	**Total**	Y compris les nationaux résidant à l'étranger. A partir de 2010: rupture de série due à la mise en œuvre d'une méthodologie améliorée qui distingue les visiteurs (touristes) des autres voyageurs.
Chili	**Total**	Y compris les nationaux résidant à l'étranger.
Comores	**Total**	Arrivées par voie aérienne.
Gambie	**Total**	Arrivées en vols à la demande seulement.
Honduras	**Total**	Sont exclus les arrivées de touristes par voie maritime.
Inde	**Total**	À l'exclusion des nationaux résidant à l'étranger.
Islande	**Total**	Source: "Icelandic Tourist Board". 2012: arrivées à l'aéroport Keflavik seulement.
Îles Marshall	**Total**	Arrivées par voie aérienne. 2009: arrivées par voies aérienne et maritime.
Italie	**Total**	À l'exclusion des travailleurs saisonniers et frontaliers.
Kiribati	**Total**	Arrivées par voie aérienne. Tarawa et Île Christmas.
Liban	**Total**	À l'exclusion des nationaux résidant à l'étranger, Syriens, Palestiniens et étudiants.
Maldives	**Total**	Arrivées par voie aérienne.
Mali	**Total**	2012: arrivées par voie aérienne uniquement.
Malte	**Total**	Données tirées des départs par voies aérienne et maritime.
Mexique	**États-Unis d'Amérique**	Comprend les touristes d'entrée arrivant par voie aérienne et terrestre, les touristes frontaliers et les touristes nationaux résidant aux États-Unis d'Amérique.
	Autres pays du monde	Comprend les touristes frontaliers de la zone méridionale.
Myanmar	**Total**	Comprenant les arrivées de touristes aux postes-frontières de Yangon.
Népal	**Grèce**	Y compris Chypre.
Norvège	**Total**	2008-2011 : les chiffres se fondent sur l'enquête auprès de la clientèle de l'Institut d'économie des transports. À partir de 2012, l'enquête a été interrompue.
Paraguay	**Total**	À l'exclusion des nationaux résidant à l'étranger et des membres des équipages. Cartes d'embarquement et de débarquement à l'aéroport Silvio Petirossi et comptages des passagers lors du franchissement des frontières nationales – Police nationale et SENATUR.
République centrafricaine	**Total**	Arrivées par voie aérienne à Bangui uniquement.
République démocratique du Congo	**Total**	2008-2010 : arrivées par voie aérienne uniquement ; 2011 : les données des entrées ne concernent que 3 postes frontaliers (aéroport de N'Djili à Kinshasa ; aéroport de la Luano à Lubumbashi et le poste terrestre de Kasumbalesa de la province du Katanga).
Saint-Martin	**Total**	Arrivées à l'aéroport international "Princess Juliana". Y compris les visiteurs à St. Martin (partie française de l'île).
	France	Y compris les résidents des Antilles françaises.

1. Arrivées de touristes non résidents aux frontières nationales, par nationalité

Sénégal	**Total**	Arrivées par voie aérienne à l'aéroport Léopold Sédar Senghor (LSS) seulement. Y compris les nationaux résidant à l'étranger. Totaux estimés par le pays: 2008: 866.700 2009: 810.000 2010: 900.000 2011: 1.001.000
Soudan	**Total**	Y compris les nationaux résidant à l'étranger.
Sri Lanka	**Total**	À l'exclusion des nationaux résidant à l'étranger.
Tunisie	**Total**	À l'exclusion des nationaux résidant à l'étranger.
Turquie	**Total**	Y compris les citoyens turcs résidant à l'étranger.
Yémen	**Total**	Y compris les nationaux résidant à l'étranger.

Yearbook of Tourism Statistics, Data 2008 – 2012, 2014 Edition

NOTES 2008 - 2012

1. Arrivées de touristes non résidents aux frontières nationales, par pays de résidence

Afrique du Sud	**Total**	2008: à l'exclusion des arrivées pour travail et les travailleurs contractuels. À partir de 2009, une nouvelle méthodologie a été appliquée. L'information n'est donc pas comparable à celle des années précédentes.
Andorre	**Total**	En 2009 et 2011, des changements ont été apportés à la méthodologie de calcul du nombre de visiteurs du pays. De ce fait, la comparabilité des données obtenues à l'aide des différentes méthodologies n'est pas possible, car les variations reflètent les variations du nombre de visiteurs mais également les variations induites par les changements méthodologiques.
Anguilla	**Total**	À l'exclusion des nationaux résidant à l'étranger.
Antigua-et-Barbuda	**Total**	Arrivées par voie aérienne. À l'exclusion des nationaux résidant à l'étranger.
Bermudes	**Total**	Arrivées par voie aérienne.
Canada	**Total**	Source: "Canadian Tourism Commission" et "Statistics Canada"
	Autres pays d'Afrique	Y compris "Chagos Archipelago", "Ascension Islands" et "Tristan da Cunha".
	Panama	Y compris Panama Canal Zone.
	Autres pays d'Océanie	Y compris "Bismark Archipelago", "Marquesas Island", "Pitcairn Island" et "Tuamotu Islands".
Colombie	**Total**	Source : Département administratif de sécurité (DAS) / « Migración Colombia ». Données provisoires. Sont exclus les passagers en croisière. 2010-2012 : arrivées de touristes non-résidents par des contrôles d'immigration. 2011-2012 : y compris les nationaux résidant à l'étranger. 2008-2009: données par nationalité.
Curaçao	**Total**	Arrivées par voie aérienne.
Espagne	**Total**	2012: données provisoires.
États-Unis d'Amérique	**Canada**	Les données historiques peuvent refléter les révisions apportées par "Statistics Canada".
	Mexique	Les données historiques peuvent refléter les révisions apportées par "Banco de México".
Éthiopie	**Total**	2008: arrivées à l'aéroport de Bole seulement. 2009-2012: arrivées à travers tous les ports d'entrée.
Fidji	**Total**	À l'exclusion des nationaux résidant à l'étranger.
France	**Total**	Source: Dgcis, Banque de France. Enquête auprès des visiteurs venant de l'étranger (EVE) – résultats 2010 et 2011 révisés, résultats 2012 provisoires.
	Toutes pays Afrique du Nord	Algérie, Égypte, Libye, Maroc et Tunisie.
	Chine	Y compris Hong-Kong (Chine) et Macao (Chine).
	Suisse	Y compris Liechtenstein.
Grèce	**Total**	A partir de 2008, l'information est basée sur l'enquête aux frontières réalisée par la Banque de Grèce.
	Égypte	Y compris le Soudan.
	Liban	Y compris la Syrie.
Guadeloupe	**Total**	Arrivées par voie aérienne.
Guyane	**Total**	Arrivées à l'aéroport de Timehri seulement.
Haïti	**Total**	Arrivées par voie aérienne. Les nationaux résidant à l'étranger sont inclus.
Îles Caïmanes	**Total**	Arrivées par voie aérienne.
Îles Cook	**Total**	Arrivées par voies aérienne et maritime.

849

NOTES 2008 - 2012

1. Arrivées de touristes non résidents aux frontières nationales, par pays de résidence

Îles Marshall	**Total**	Arrivées par voie aérienne. 2009: arrivées par voies aérienne et maritime.
Irlande	**Royaume-Uni**	Y compris les arrivées des résidents de l'Irlande du nord. Changement de méthodologie de l'estimation des touristes d'Irlande du Nord en 2010; par conséquent les chiffres antérieurs à 2010 ne sont pas directement comparables.
Israël	**Total**	À l'exclusion des nationaux résidant à l'étranger.
Jamaïque	**Total**	Arrivées par voie aérienne. Y compris les nationaux résidants à l'étranger.
Malaisie	**Total**	Y compris les résidents de Singapour traversant la frontière par voie terrestre à travers le Johore Causeway.
Malawi	**Total**	Départs.
Martinique	**Total**	Y compris les départements et territoires français d'outremer.
Mexique	**Total**	Y compris les nationaux résidant à l'étranger.
Népal	**Grèce**	Y compris Chypre.
Nioué	**Total**	Y compris les nationaux de Niue résidant habituellement en Nouvelle-Zélande.
Nouvelle-Calédonie	**Total**	Y compris les nationaux résidant à l'étranger.
	Toutes pays Caraïbes	Martinique, Guadeloupe et Guyane.
Palaos	**Total**	Arrivées par voie aérienne (aéroport international de Palaos).
Pérou	**Total**	Y compris les nationaux résidant à l'étranger. Données préliminaires.
Philippines	**Nationaux résidents à l'étranger**	Titulaires d'un passeport philippin résidant en permanence à l'étranger; travailleurs philippins exclus.
Polynésie française	**Total**	Arrivées par voie aérienne. À l'exclusion des nationaux résidant à l'étranger.
	Samoa	Y compris les Samoa américaines.
Porto Rico	**Total**	Arrivées par voie aérienne. Année fiscale de juillet à juin. Source: "Junta de Planificación de Puerto Rico".
République dominicaine	**Total**	Arrivées par voie aérienne.
Réunion	**Total**	Source: INSEE - Enquête flux touristiques.
Saint-Kitts-et-Nevis	**Total**	Arrivées par voie aérienne.
Saint-Vincent-et-les Grenadines	**Total**	Arrivées par voie aérienne.
Sainte-Lucie	**Total**	À l'exclusion des nationaux résidant à l'étranger.
Sénégal	**Total**	Arrivées par voie aérienne à l'aéroport Léopold Sédar Senghor (LSS) seulement. Y compris les nationaux résidant à l'étranger. Totaux estimés par le pays: 2008: 866.700 2009: 810.000 2010: 900.000 2011: 1.001.000
Sierra Leone	**Total**	Arrivées par voie aérienne.
Sri Lanka	**Total**	À l'exclusion des nationaux résidant à l'étranger.
Timor-Leste	**Total**	Arrivées par voie aérienne à l'aéroport de Dili.
Tonga	**Total**	Arrivées par voie aérienne.
Trinité-et-Tobago	**Total**	Arrivées par voie aérienne.

NOTES 2008 - 2012

2. Arrivées de visiteurs non résidents aux frontières nationales, par nationalité

Albanie	**Total**	À l'exclusion des nationaux résidant à l'étranger.
	Autres pays Europe du Sud	Arrivées en provenance du Kosovo.
Algérie	**Total**	Y compris les nationaux résidant à l'étranger.
Bahreïn	**Total**	À l'exclusion des nationaux résidant à l'étranger.
Belize	**Total**	Y compris passagers en transit et passagers à la frontière.
Corée (République de)	**Total**	Y compris les nationaux résidant à l'étranger et les membres des équipages.
Égypte	**Total**	À l'exclusion des nationaux résidant à l'étranger.
Équateur	**Total**	À l'exclusion des nationaux résidant à l'étranger. 2012: données provisoires.
Guatemala	**Total**	2009-2012: données compilées par pays de résidence.
Italie	**Total**	Enquête aux frontières. À l'exclusion des travailleurs saisonniers et frontaliers.
Japon	**Total**	À l'exclusion des nationaux résidant à l'étranger.
Macao (Chine)	**Total**	Source des données: Force de sécurité publique
Nigéria	**Total**	Source: "Nigerian Tourism Development Corporation (NTDC)"
Pologne	**Total**	Depuis que la Pologne est entrée dans l'espace Schengen, le comptage précis du trafic entrant n'est pas possible. Les données présentées ici sont basées sur les enquêtes de l'Institut du Tourisme. Seuls des résultats approximatifs des principaux pays peuvent être fournis.
République arabe syrienne	**Total**	Enquête du tourisme récepteur.
	Iraq	Les citoyens de l'Iraq sont inclus uniquement à partir de 2008 et ont été exclus des années précédentes (depuis le début de l'année 2008, ils doivent demander un visa pour entrer en Syrie ; s'ils sont entrés avant 2008, il est considéré que leur séjour est maintenant supérieur à un an et qu'ils sont de ce fait devenus des résidents).
République de Moldova	**Total**	Visiteurs qui ont bénéficié des services touristiques des agences de tourisme et des voyagistes (titulaires d'une licence touristique). À l'exception de la rive gauche de la rivière Nistru et de la municipalité de Bender.
Singapour	**Total**	À l'exclusion des arrivées de Malaisiens par voie terrestre.
Turquie	**Total**	Y compris les citoyens turcs résidant à l'étranger.
Uruguay	**Total**	À l'exclusion des arrivées de passagers en croisière.

NOTES 2008 - 2012

2. Arrivées de visiteurs non résidents aux frontières nationales, par pays de résidence

Afrique du Sud	**Total**	2008: À l'exclusion des nationaux résidant à l'étranger. Y compris les arrivées pour motif de vacances, affaires, études, travail, transit, trafic frontalier et travailleurs contractuels. À partir de 2009, une nouvelle méthodologie a été apliquée. L'information n'est donc pas comparable à celle des années précédentes.
Australie	**Total**	À l'exclusion des nationaux résidant à l'étranger et les membres des équipages. Source: "Australian Bureau of Statistics"
Canada	**Total**	Source: "Canadian Tourism Commission" et "Statistics Canada"
	Chine	Y compris la Mongolie et le Tibet.
	Estonie	Y compris la Lettonie et la Lituanie.
	Hongrie	Y compris Slovénie, Bulgarie et Roumanie.
	Danemark	Y compris les Îles Féroé.
	Royaume-Uni	Y compris Gibraltar.
	Italie	Y compris Saint-Marin, le Saint Siège et Malte.
	Yougoslavie, SFR (ancienne)	Y compris Croatie, Bosnie-Herzégovine, Ex-République yougoslave de Macédoine et Albanie.
	France	Y compris Andorre et Monaco.
	Suisse	Y compris le Liechtenstein.
Congo	**Total**	Source: Direction Générale de l'Industrie Touristique, enquêtes 2011 et 2012
Finlande	**Total**	Enquête aux frontières.
Hong-Kong (Chine)	**États-Unis d'Amérique**	Y compris Guam.
	Nouvelle-Zélande	Y compris les Îles Cook.
	France	Y compris la Nouvelle-Calédonie et la Polynésie française.
Israël	**Total**	À l'exclusion des nationaux résidant à l'étranger.
Lettonie	**Total**	Départs des non-résidents. Enquête auprès des personnes qui traversent les frontières du pays.
Macao (Chine)	**Total**	Source des données: Force de sécurité publique
Mozambique	**Total**	Note 2008: Changement de méthodologie. Jusqu'en 2007, les données correspondent seulement à 12 postes frontaliers. A partir de 2008, les données de tous les postes frontaliers du pays sont utilisées.
Nouvelle-Zélande	**Total**	Les données relatives aux mouvements de courte durée sont obtenues à partir d'un échantillon aléatoire de déclarations des passagers. Y compris les nationaux résidant à l'étranger. Source: Statistiques de la Nouvelle Zélande ("International Travel and Migration").
Panama	**Total**	Nombre total de visiteurs arrivés au Panama par l'aéroport international de Tocumen, classés selon leur résidence permanente.
Saint-Vincent-et-les Grenadines	**Total**	Arrivées par voie aérienne.
Singapour	**Total**	À l'exclusion des arrivées de Malaisiens par voie terrestre.
Suède	**Total**	Données pour 2011 et 2012 d'après la nouvelle enquête aux frontières nationales (IBIS, visiteurs entrant en Suède). Pas de données recueillies entre 2008 et 2010. La nouvelle enquête à la frontière (IBIS) a commencé en 2011. Source : Agence suédoise pour la croissance économique et régionale.

Yearbook of Tourism Statistics, Data 2008 – 2012, 2014 Edition

NOTES 2008 - 2012

3. Arrivées de touristes non résidents dans les hôtels et établissements assimilés, par nationalité

Bolivie	**Total**	Données préliminaires. Mouvement hôtelier dans les capitales de département.
Italie	**Total**	Arrivées dans les hôtels uniquement.
Maroc	**Total**	Arrivées dans les hôtels homologués, villages de vacances, résidences touristiques et Riad.
Monténégro	**Serbie**	Comprenant les arrivées en provenance du Kosovo.
Palestine	**Total**	Source: "Palestinian Central Bureau of Statistics, 2013. Hotel Activity Survey 2012. Ramallah - Palestine"
République arabe syrienne	**Total**	Enquête du tourisme récepteur.
	Iraq	Les citoyens de l'Iraq sont inclus uniquement à partir de 2008 et ont été exclus des années précédentes (depuis le début de l'année 2008, ils doivent demander un visa pour entrer en Syrie ; s'ils sont entrés avant 2008, il est considéré que leur séjour est maintenant supérieur à un an et qu'ils sont de ce fait devenus des résidents).
Slovénie	**Total**	2008: Nouvelle méthodologie de l'enquête sur l'hébergement.
Tchad	**Total**	2010: Données partielles.
Turquie	**Total**	Arrivées dans les établissements homologues y compris: hôtels, motels, pensions, auberges, hôtels-appartements, villages de vacances et hôtels spéciaux. Résultats de l'enquête mensuelle réalisée auprès des établissements d'hébergement classés par le Ministère du Tourisme.

NOTES 2008 - 2012

3. Arrivées de touristes non résidents dans les hôtels et établissements assimilés, par pays de résidence

Allemagne	**Chine**	Y compris Hong-Kong, Chine.
	Autres pays Asie Est/Pacifique	Y compris l'Inde.
Autriche	**Total**	Hôtels uniquement.
Cap-Vert	**Belgique**	Y compris les Pays-Bas.
Congo	**Total**	Source: Direction Générale de l'Industrie Touristique, enquêtes 2008 à 2012
Croatie	**Total**	Conformément au Règlement sur la classification, les normes minimales et la catégorisation des structures d'hébergement, les données relatives aux hôtels et établissements assimilés ne comprennent pas les auberges et chambres d'hôtes depuis 2006.
Curaçao	**Total**	Grands et petits hôtels, pensions de famille, appartements et bungalows.
Danemark	**Total**	Hôtels uniquement. 2011: changement de méthodologie.
Espagne	**Total**	Arrivées dans les hôtels et les "hostales" (établissements d'hébergement offrant des services limités).
France	**Total**	Source: Insee, Dgcis, partenaires régionaux. Enquête de fréquentation hôtelière (EFH).
Israël	**Total**	Arrivées dans les hôtels de tourisme et les hôtels non encore enregistrés.
	Toutes pays Amérique du Sud	Y compris l'Amérique centrale.
Luxembourg	**Total**	NACE Rev2 55.100
Macao (Chine)	**Total**	Source des données: Enquête mensuelle auprès des agences de voyage
Nouvelle-Calédonie	**Total**	Il s'agit des hôtels de Nouméa.
Pays-Bas	**Total**	Hôtels et pensions.
Pologne	**Total**	À l'exclusion des hôtelleries.
Porto Rico	**Total**	Année fiscale de juillet à juin. Hôtels enregistrés par la "Compañía de Turismo de Puerto Rico".
	Autres pays Caraïbes	Les données agrégées des touristes en provenance des petites Antilles qui n'ont pas spécifié leur pays d'origine sont incluses.
	Autres pays du monde	Y compris les membres des équipages.
Qatar	**Total**	Arrivées dans les hôtels uniquement. 2008,2009: y compris le tourisme interne.
	Toutes pays d'Europe	2010-2011: Europe et Amériques.
Roumanie	**Toutes les pays d'Afrique**	Y compris l'Égypte et la Libye.
Suisse	**Total**	Y compris les établissements de cure.
	Toutes pays Afrique du Nord	Algérie, Libye, Maroc et Tunisie.
Togo	**Burkina Faso**	Y compris le Mali et le Niger.

NOTES 2008 - 2012

4. Arrivées de touristes non résidents dans tous les types d'établissements d'hébergement, par nationalité

Hongrie	**Total**	Établissements d'hébergement collectif.
Monténégro	**Serbie**	Comprenant les arrivées en provenance du Kosovo.
République arabe syrienne	**Total**	À l'exclusion de l'hébergement chez des particuliers. Enquête du tourisme récepteur.
	Iraq	Les citoyens de l'Iraq sont inclus uniquement à partir de 2008 et ont été exclus des années précédentes (depuis le début de l'année 2008, ils doivent demander un visa pour entrer en Syrie ; s'ils sont entrés avant 2008, il est considéré que leur séjour est maintenant supérieur à un an et qu'ils sont de ce fait devenus des résidents).
République de Moldova	**Total**	À l'exception de la rive gauche de la rivière Nistru et de la municipalité de Bender.
Slovénie	**Total**	2008: Nouvelle méthodologie de l'enquête sur l'hébergement.
Turquie	**Total**	Résultats de l'enquête mensuelle réalisée auprès des établissements d'hébergement classés par le Ministère du Tourisme.

NOTES 2008 - 2012

4. Arrivées de touristes non résidents dans tous les types d'établissements d'hébergement, par pays de résidence

Allemagne	**Chine**	Y compris Hong-Kong, Chine.
	Autres pays Asie Est/Pacifique	Y compris l'Inde.
Autriche	**Total**	Seulement logement payé; sont exclus les séjours chez des amis et membres de la famille et des résidences secondaires.
Belgique	**Total**	Établissements hôteliers, terrains de camping, centres de vacances, villages de vacances et catégories spécifiques d'hébergement. À partir de 2012 les chambres d'hôtes sont incluses.
Croatie	**Total**	À l'exclusion des arrivées dans des ports à tourisme nautique.
Danemark	**Total**	Y compris le tourisme non commercial. 2011: changement de méthodologie.
Espagne	**Total**	Arrivées dans hôtels, "hostales", camping, appartements touristiques et logements ruraux.
Malte	**Total**	Données tirées des départs par voies aérienne et maritime. Source: "National Statistics Office".
Philippines	**Total**	Arrivées par voie aérienne.
	Nationaux résidents à l'étranger	Titulaires d'un passeport philippin résidant en permanence à l'étranger; travailleurs philippins exclus.
Roumanie	**Toutes les pays d'Afrique**	Y compris l'Égypte et la Libye.

Yearbook of Tourism Statistics, Data 2008 – 2012, 2014 Edition

NOTES 2008 - 2012

5. Nuitées de touristes non résidents dans les hôtels et établissements assimilés, par nationalité

Bolivie	**Total**	Données préliminaires. Nuitées dans les capitales de département.
Italie	**Total**	Nuitées dans les hôtels uniquement.
Madagascar	**Total**	Établissements de classe étoile (classés et non classés).
Maroc	**Total**	Nuitées dans les hôtels homologués, villages de vacances, résidences touristiques et Riad.
Monténégro	**Serbie**	Comprenant les arrivées en provenance du Kosovo.
Norvège	**Total**	Nuitées dans les établissements homologués. Les données ne couvrent que les établissements avec une capacité d'au moins 20 lits.
Palestine	**Total**	Source: "Palestinian Central Bureau of Statistics, 2013. Hotel Activity Survey 2012. Ramallah - Palestine"
République arabe syrienne	**Total**	Enquête du tourisme récepteur.
	Iraq	Les citoyens de l'Iraq sont inclus uniquement à partir de 2008 et ont été exclus des années précédentes (depuis le début de l'année 2008, ils doivent demander un visa pour entrer en Syrie ; s'ils sont entrés avant 2008, il est considéré que leur séjour est maintenant supérieur à un an et qu'ils sont de ce fait devenus des résidents).
Slovénie	**Total**	2008: Nouvelle méthodologie de l'enquête sur l'hébergement.
Tchad	**Total**	2010: Données partielles.
Turquie	**Total**	Hôtels classés, motels, pensions de familles, auberges, aparthôtels, villages de vacances et hôtels spéciaux. Résultats de l'enquête mensuelle réalisée auprès des établissements d'hébergement classés par le Ministère du Tourisme.
Yémen	**Total**	Y compris les nationaux résidant à l'étranger.

NOTES 2008 - 2012

5. Nuitées de touristes non résidents dans les hôtels et établissements assimilés, par pays de résidence

Allemagne	**Chine**	Y compris Hong-Kong, Chine.
	Autres pays Asie Est/Pacifique	Y compris l'Inde.
Autriche	**Total**	Hôtels uniquement.
Cap-Vert	**Belgique**	Y compris les Pays-Bas.
Congo	**Total**	Source: Direction Générale de l'Industrie Touristique, enquêtes 2008 à 2012
Croatie	**Total**	Conformément au Règlement sur la classification, les normes minimales et la catégorisation des structures d'hébergement, les données relatives aux hôtels et établissements assimilés ne comprennent pas les auberges et chambres d'hôtes depuis 2006.
Danemark	**Total**	Hôtels uniquement. 2011: changement de méthodologie.
Espagne	**Total**	Nuitées dans les hôtels et les "hostales" (établissements d'hébergement offrant des services limités).
France	**Total**	Source: Insee, Dgcis, partenaires régionaux. Enquête de fréquentation hôtelière (EFH).
Israël	**Total**	Nuitées dans les hôtels de tourisme et aparthôtels.
	Toutes pays Amérique du Sud	Y compris l'Amérique centrale.
Luxembourg	**Total**	NACE Rev2 55.100
Macao (Chine)	**Total**	Source des données: Enquête mensuelle auprès des hôtels et établissements comparables
Nouvelle-Calédonie	**Total**	Il s'agit des hôtels de Nouméa.
Pays-Bas	**Total**	Hôtels et pensions.
Pologne	**Total**	À l'exclusion des hôtelleries.
Qatar	**Total**	Nuitées dans les hôtels uniquement. 2008,2009: y compris le tourisme interne.
	Toutes pays d'Europe	2010-2011: Europe et Amériques.
Roumanie	**Toutes les pays d'Afrique**	Y compris l'Égypte et la Libye.
Suisse	**Total**	Y compris les établissements de cure.
	Toutes pays Afrique du Nord	Algérie, Libye, Maroc et Tunisie.
Togo	**Burkina Faso**	Y compris le Mali et le Niger.

NOTES 2008 - 2012

6. Nuitées de touristes non résidents dans tous les types d'établissements d'hébergement, par nationalité

Hongrie	**Total**	Établissements d'hébergement collectif.
Monténégro	**Serbie**	Comprenant les arrivées en provenance du Kosovo.
République arabe syrienne	**Total**	Enquête du tourisme récepteur.
	Iraq	Les citoyens de l'Iraq sont inclus uniquement à partir de 2008 et ont été exclus des années précédentes (depuis le début de l'année 2008, ils doivent demander un visa pour entrer en Syrie ; s'ils sont entrés avant 2008, il est considéré que leur séjour est maintenant supérieur à un an et qu'ils sont de ce fait devenus des résidents).
République de Moldova	**Total**	À l'exception de la rive gauche de la rivière Nistru et de la municipalité de Bender.
Slovénie	**Total**	2008: Nouvelle méthodologie de l'enquête sur l'hébergement.
Turquie	**Total**	Résultats de l'enquête mensuelle réalisée auprès des établissements d'hébergement classés par le Ministère du Tourisme.

NOTES 2008 - 2012

6. Nuitées de touristes non résidents dans tous les types d'établissements d'hébergement, par pays de résidence

Allemagne	**Chine**	Y compris Hong-Kong, Chine.
	Autres pays Asie Est/Pacifique	Y compris l'Inde.
Autriche	**Total**	Seulement logement payé; sont exclus les séjours chez des amis et membres de la famille et des résidences secondaires.
Bahamas	**Total**	Nuitées dans tout moyen d'hébergement commercial.
Belgique	**Total**	Établissements hôteliers, terrains de camping, centres de vacances, villages de vacances et catégories spécifiques d'hébergement. À partir de 2012 les chambres d'hôtes sont incluses.
Canada	**Total**	Source: "Canadian Tourism Commission" et "Statistics Canada"
	Chine	Y compris la Mongolie et le Tibet.
	Estonie	Y compris la Lettonie et la Lituanie.
	Hongrie	Y compris Slovénie, Bulgarie et Roumanie.
	Danemark	Y compris les Îles Féroé.
	Royaume-Uni	Y compris Gibraltar.
	Italie	Y compris Saint-Marin, le Saint Siège et Malte.
	Yougoslavie, SFR (ancienne)	Y compris Croatie, Bosnie-Herzégovine, Ex-République yougoslave de Macédoine et Albanie.
	France	Y compris Andorre et Monaco.
	Suisse	Y compris le Liechtenstein.
Croatie	**Total**	À l'exclusion des nuitées dans des ports à tourisme nautique.
Danemark	**Total**	Y compris le tourisme non commercial. 2011: changement de méthodologie.
Espagne	**Total**	Nuitées dans hôtels, "hostales", camping, appartements touristiques et logements ruraux.
France	**Total**	Source: Dgcis, Banque de France. Enquête auprès des visiteurs venant de l'étranger (EVE) – résultats 2010 et 2011 révisés, résultats 2012 provisoires.
	Toutes pays Afrique du Nord	Algérie, Égypte, Libye, Maroc et Tunisie.
	Chine	Y compris Hong-Kong (Chine) et Macao (Chine).
	Suisse	Y compris Liechtenstein.
Irlande	**Total**	Y compris nuitées dans hébergement privé non payant (maisons privées et maisons de vacances).
	Royaume-Uni	Y compris les résidents de l'Irlande du Nord.
Jamaïque	**Total**	L'information à été obtenue en multipliant la durée moyenne de séjour par le nombre de touristes (stop-over) provenant de chaque pays d'origine. À l'exclusion des nationaux résidant à l'étranger.
	Autres pays Amériques	Amérique latine.
	Toutes pays d'Europe	Royaume-Uni et le reste de l'Europe.
Malte	**Total**	Données tirées des départs par voies aérienne et maritime. Source: "National Statistics Office".
Pays-Bas	**Total**	À l'exclusion des nuitées dans des installations fixes (louées sur une base annuelle ou saisonnière).
Roumanie	**Toutes les pays d'Afrique**	Y compris l'Égypte et la Libye.

Yearbook of Tourism Statistics, Data 2008 – 2012, 2014 Edition

NOTAS 2008 - 2012

1. Llegadas de turistas no residentes en las fronteras nacionales, por nacionalidad

Belarús	**Total**	Turismo organizado.
Bhután	**Total**	Total de llegadas 2010: 40.873; 2011: 65.756; 2012: 105.407. El gran margen de diferencia en 2010, 2011 y 2012 en comparación con los años anteriores se debe a que a partir de 2010 se incluyen en las cifras totales los turistas regionales de alto nivel de renta.
Bolivia	**Total**	Datos preliminares.
Brunei Darussalam	**Total**	Llegadas por vía aérea.
Burundi	**Total**	Incluidos los nacionales residentes en el extranjero. A partir de 2010: ruptura en la serie debido a la implementación de una mejora en la metodología que distingue a los visitantes (turistas) de otros viajeros.
Chile	**Total**	Incluidos los nacionales residentes en el extranjero.
Comoras	**Total**	Llegadas por vía aérea.
Gambia	**Total**	Llegadas en vuelos fletados únicamente.
Honduras	**Total**	Excluidas las llegadas de turistas por vía marítima.
India	**Total**	Excluidos los nacionales residentes en el extranjero.
Islandia	**Total**	Fuente: "Icelandic Tourist Board". 2012: llegadas al aeropuerto Keflavik únicamente.
Islas Marshall	**Total**	Llegadas por vía aérea. 2009: llegadas por vías aérea y marítima.
Italia	**Total**	Excluidos los trabajadores estacionales y fronterizos.
Kiribati	**Total**	Llegadas por vía aérea. Tarawa e Isla Christmas.
Líbano	**Total**	Excluidos los nacionales residentes en el extranjero, nacionales de Siria, Palestina y estudiantes.
Maldivas	**Total**	Llegadas por vía aérea.
Malí	**Total**	2012: llegadas por vía aérea únicamente.
Malta	**Total**	Datos procedentes de las salidas por vías aérea y marítima.
México	**Estados Unidos de América**	Incluye turistas de internación vía aérea y terrestre, turistas fronterizos y turistas nacionales residentes en los Estados Unidos de Américas.
	Otros países del Mundo	Incluye turistas fronterizos de la zona sur.
Myanmar	**Total**	Incluidas las llegadas de turistas a través de los puntos de entrada fronterizos a Yangon.
Nepal	**Grecia**	Incluido Chipre.
Noruega	**Total**	2008-2011: las cifras se basan en "The Guest Survey", un estudio realizado por el "Institute of Transport Economics". A partir de 2012 la encuesta ha sido suspendida.
Paraguay	**Total**	Excluidos los nacionales residentes en el extranjero y los miembros de tripulaciones. Tarjetas E/D en el aeropuerto Silvio Petirossi y planillas de pasajeros en los puestos terrestres - Policía Nacional y SENATUR.
República Centroafricana	**Total**	Llegadas por vía aérea a Bangui únicamente.
República Democrática del Congo	**Total**	2008-2010: llegadas por vía aérea únicamente; 2011: los datos de entradas se refieren sólo a 3 puestos fronterizos (aeropuerto de N'Djili, en Kinshasa; aeropuerto de Luano, en Lubumbashi, y puesto terrestre de Kasumbalesa, en la provincia de Katanga).
San Martín	**Total**	Llegadas al aeropuerto internacional "Princess Juliana". Incluidos los visitantes a San Martín (parte francesa de la isla).
	Francia	Incluidos los residentes de las Antillas Francesas.

Yearbook of Tourism Statistics, Data 2008 – 2012, 2014 Edition

NOTAS 2008 - 2012

1. Llegadas de turistas no residentes en las fronteras nacionales, por nacionalidad

Senegal	Total	Llegadas por vía aérea al aeropuerto "Léopold Sédar Senghor (LSS)" únicamente. Incluidos los nacionales residentes en el extranjero. Totales estimados por el país: 2008: 866.700 2009: 810.000 2010: 900.000 2011: 1.001.000
Sri Lanka	Total	Excluidos los nacionales residentes en el extranjero.
Sudán	Total	Incluidos los nacionales residentes en el extranjero.
Túnez	Total	Excluidos los nacionales residentes en el extranjero.
Turquía	Total	Incluidos los ciudadanos turcos residentes en el extranjero.
Yemen	Total	Incluidos los nacionales residentes en el extranjero.

NOTAS 2008 - 2012

1. Llegadas de turistas no residentes en las fronteras nacionales, por país de residencia

Andorra	Total	En 2009 y 2011 se produjeron cambios en la metodología de cálculo del número de visitantes del país. En éste sentido, la comparabilidad de los datos obtenidos con diferentes metodologías no es posible porque las variaciones recogen la variación del número de visitantes, pero también las variaciones motivadas por los cambios metodológicos.
Anguila	Total	Excluidos los nacionales residentes en el extranjero.
Antigua y Barbuda	Total	Llegadas por vía aérea. Excluidos los nacionales residentes en el extranjero.
Bermuda	Total	Llegadas por vía aérea.
Canadá	Total	Fuente: "Canadian Tourism Commission" y "Statistics Canada"
	Otros países de África	Incluido "Chagos Archipelago", "Ascension Islands" y "Tristan da Cunha".
	Panamá	Incluida la Zona del Canal de Panamá.
	Otros países de Oceanía	Incluido "Bismark Archipelago", "Marquesas Island", "Pitcairn Island" y "Tuamotu Islands".
Colombia	Total	Fuente: Departamento Administrativo de Seguridad (DAS) / Migración Colombia. Datos provisionales. Excluidos los pasajeros en crucero. 2010-2012: llegadas de turistas no residentes por puntos de control migratorio. 2011-2012: incluidos los nacionales residentes en el extranjero. 2008-2009: datos por nacionalidad.
Curaçao	Total	Llegadas por vía aérea.
España	Total	2012: datos provisionales.
Estados Unidos de América	Canadá	Los datos históricos pueden reflejar revisiones hechas por "Statistics Canada".
	México	Los datos históricos pueden reflejar revisiones hechas por "Banco de México".
Etiopía	Total	2008: llegadas al aeropuerto de Bole únicamente. 2009-2012: llegadas a todos los puestos fronterizos.
Fiji	Total	Excluidos los nacionales residentes en el extranjero.
Filipinas	Nacionales residentes en el extranjero	Titulares de pasaportes filipinos que residen permanentemente en el extranjero; están excluidos los trabajadores filipinos.
Francia	Total	Fuente: "Dgcis", "Banque de France". Encuesta a los visitantes que vienen del extranjero ("EVE") - resultados 2010 y 2011 revisados, resultados 2012 provisionales
	Todos los países de África del Norte	Argelia, Egipto, Libia, Marruecos y Túnez.
	China	Incluye Hong-Kong (China) y Macao (China).
	Suiza	Incluye Liechtentein.
Grecia	Total	A partir de 2008, la información se basa en la encuesta en fronteras realizada por el Banco de Grecia.
	Egipto	Incluido Sudán.
	Líbano	Incluido Siria.
Guadalupe	Total	Llegadas por vía aérea.
Guyana	Total	Llegadas al aeropuerto de Timehri únicamente.
Haití	Total	Llegadas por vía aérea. Se incluye a los nacionales residentes en el extranjero.
Irlanda	Reino Unido	Incluidas las llegadas de los residentes de Irlanda del Norte. Cambio en la metodología de estimación de turistas del norte de Irlanda en 2010; como resultado las cifras anteriores a 2010 no son directamente comparables.

NOTAS 2008 - 2012

1. Llegadas de turistas no residentes en las fronteras nacionales, por país de residencia

Islas Caimán	Total	Llegadas por vía aérea.
Islas Cook	Total	Llegadas por vías aérea y marítima.
Islas Marshall	Total	Llegadas por vía aérea. 2009: llegadas por vías aérea y marítima.
Israel	Total	Excluidos los nacionales residentes en el extranjero.
Jamaica	Total	Llegadas por vía aérea. Incluidos los nacionales residentes en el extranjero.
Malasia	Total	Incluidos residentes de Singapur que atraviesan la frontera por vía terrestre a través de Johore Causeway.
Malawi	Total	Salidas.
Martinica	Total	Incluidos los departamentos y territorios franceses de ultramar.
México	Total	Incluidos los nacionales residentes en el extranjero.
Nepal	Grecia	Incluido Chipre.
Niue	Total	Incluidos los nacionales de Niue que residen habitualmente en Nueva Zelandia.
Nueva Caledonia	Total	Incluidos los nacionales residentes en el extranjero.
	Todos los países del Caribe	Martinica, Guadalupe y Guyana.
Palau	Total	Llegadas por vía aérea (aeropuerto internacional de Palau).
Perú	Total	Incluidos los nacionales residentes en el extranjero. Datos preliminares.
Polinesia Francesa	Total	Llegadas por vía aérea. Excluidos los nacionales residentes en el extranjero.
	Samoa	Incluida Samoa americana.
Puerto Rico	Total	Llegadas por vía aérea. Año fiscal de julio a junio. Fuente: Junta de Planificación de Puerto Rico.
República Dominicana	Total	Llegadas por vía aérea.
Reunión	Total	Fuente: INSEE, encuesta de flujos turísticos
Saint Kitts y Nevis	Total	Llegadas por vía aérea.
San Vicente y las Granadinas	Total	Llegadas por vía aérea.
Santa Lucía	Total	Excluidos los nacionales residentes en el extranjero.
Senegal	Total	Llegadas por vía aérea al aeropuerto "Léopold Sédar Senghor (LSS)" únicamente. Incluidos los nacionales residentes en el extranjero. Totales estimados por el país: 2008: 866.700 2009: 810.000 2010: 900.000 2011: 1.001.000
Sierra Leona	Total	Llegadas por vía aérea.
Sri Lanka	Total	Excluidos los nacionales residentes en el extranjero.
Sudáfrica	Total	2008: excluidas las llegadas por trabajo y los trabajadores con contrato. A partir de 2009 se aplicó una nueva metodología y por lo tanto la información no es comparable con años anteriores.
Timor-Leste	Total	Llegadas por vía aérea al aeropuerto de Dili.
Tonga	Total	Llegadas por vía aérea.
Trinidad y Tabago	Total	Llegadas por vía aérea.

Yearbook of Tourism Statistics, Data 2008 – 2012, 2014 Edition

NOTAS 2008 - 2012

2. Llegadas de visitantes no residentes en las fronteras nacionales, por nacionalidad

Albania	**Total**	Excluidos los nacionales residentes en el extranjero.
	Otros países de Europa meridional	Llegadas de Kosovo.
Argelia	**Total**	Incluidos los nacionales residentes en el extranjero.
Bahrein	**Total**	Excluidos los nacionales residentes en el extranjero.
Belice	**Total**	Incluidos pasajeros en tránsito y cruce de fronteras.
Corea (República de)	**Total**	Incluidos los nacionales residentes en el extranjero y los miembros de las tripulaciones.
Ecuador	**Total**	Excluidos los nacionales residentes en el extranjero. 2012: datos provisionales.
Egipto	**Total**	Excluidos los nacionales residentes en el extranjero.
Guatemala	**Total**	2009-2012: datos compilados por país de residencia.
Italia	**Total**	Encuesta en fronteras. Excluidos los trabajadores estacionales y fronterizos.
Japón	**Total**	Excluidos los nacionales residentes en el extranjero.
Macao (China)	**Total**	Fuente de los datos: Fuerza de seguridad pública
Nigeria	**Total**	Fuente: "Nigerian Tourism Development Corporation (NTDC)"
Polonia	**Total**	Dado que Polonia se unió al espacio Schengen, el recuento preciso de tráfico entrante no es posible. Los datos presentados aquí se basan en encuestas realizadas por el Instituto de Turismo. Únicamente se cuenta con resultados aproximados de los principales países.
República Árabe Siria	**Total**	Encuesta del turismo receptor.
	Iraq	Los nacionales de Iraq se incluyen únicamente a partir de 2008 y se han excluido en los años anteriores (desde principios de 2008, tienen que pedir un visado para entrar en Siria; si entraron anteriormente a esa fecha, se considera que han permanecido por un periodo superior a un año, convirtiéndose en residentes).
República de Moldova	**Total**	Visitantes que se beneficiaron de los servicios turísticos de las agencias de turismo y operadores turísticos (titulares de licencias turísticas). Excluido el margen izquierdo del río Nistru y la municipalidad de Bender.
Singapur	**Total**	Excluidas llegadas de los malasios por vía terrestre.
Turquía	**Total**	Incluidos los ciudadanos turcos residentes en el extranjero.
Uruguay	**Total**	Excluidas las llegadas de pasajeros en crucero.

NOTAS 2008 - 2012

2. Llegadas de visitantes no residentes en las fronteras nacionales, por país de residencia

Australia	**Total**	Excluidos los nacionales residentes en el extranjero y los miembros de tripulaciones. Fuente: "Australian Bureau of Statistics"
Canadá	**Total**	Fuente: "Canadian Tourism Commission" y "Statistics Canada"
	China	Incluido Mongolia y Tibet.
	Estonia	Incluido Letonia y Lituania.
	Hungría	Incluido Eslovenia, Bulgaria y Rumania.
	Dinamarca	Incluido las Islas Feroe.
	Reino Unido	Incluido Gibraltar.
	Italia	Incluido San Marino, la Santa Sede y Malta.
	Yugoslavia, RSF (antigua)	Incluido Croacia, Bosnia y Herzegovina, Ex República Yugoslava de Macedonia y Albania.
	Francia	Incluido Andorra y Mónaco.
	Suiza	Incluido Liechtenstein.
Congo	**Total**	Fuente: "Direction Générale de l'Industrie Touristique", encuestas 2011 y 2012
Finlandia	**Total**	Encuesta en las fronteras.
Hong Kong (China)	**Estados Unidos de América**	Incluido Guam.
	Nueva Zelandia	Incluidas las Islas Cook.
	Francia	Incluidas Nueva Caledonia y la Polinesia Francesa.
Israel	**Total**	Excluidos los nacionales residentes en el extranjero.
Letonia	**Total**	Salidas de no residentes. Encuesta realizada en los puestos fronterizos del país.
Macao (China)	**Total**	Fuente de los datos: Fuerza de seguridad pública
Mozambique	**Total**	Nota 2008: Cambio de metodología. Hasta 2007 los datos corresponden únicamente a 12 puestos fronterizos. A partir de 2008 se utilizan los datos de todos los puestos fronterizos del país.
Nueva Zelandia	**Total**	Los datos relativos a los movimientos de corta duración se obtienen de una muestra aleatoria de declaraciones de los pasajeros. Incluidos los nacionales residentes en el extranjero. Fuente: Estadísticas Nueva Zelanda ("International Travel and Migration").
Panamá	**Total**	Total de visitantes ingresados a Panamá por el aeropuerto internacional de Tocumen según domicilio permanente.
San Vicente y las Granadinas	**Total**	Llegadas por vía aérea.
Singapur	**Total**	Excluidas llegadas de los malasios por vía terrestre.
Sudáfrica	**Total**	2008: Excluidos los nacionales residentes en el extranjero. Incluidas las llegadas por motivo de vacaciones, negocios, estudios, trabajo, tránsito, tráfico fronterizo y trabajadores con contrato. A partir de 2009 se aplicó una nueva metodología y por lo tanto la información no es comparable con años anteriores.
Suecia	**Total**	Datos para 2011 y 2012 según una nueva encuesta nacional de fronteras (IBIS, visitantes que entran en Suecia). De 2008 a 2010 no se recopilaron datos. La nueva encuesta de fronteras (IBIS) se empezó a realizar en 2011. Fuente: Agencia Sueca de Crecimiento Económico y Regional.

Yearbook of Tourism Statistics, Data 2008 – 2012, 2014 Edition

NOTAS 2008 - 2012

3. Llegadas de turistas no residentes a los hoteles y establecimientos asimilados, por nacionalidad

Bolivia	**Total**	Datos preliminares. Movimiento hotelero en las capitales de departamento.
Chad	**Total**	2010: Datos parciales.
Eslovenia	**Total**	2008: Nueva metodología de la encuesta de alojamiento.
Italia	**Total**	Llegadas a los hoteles únicamente.
Marruecos	**Total**	Llegadas en hoteles homologados, ciudades de vacaciones, residencias turísticas y Riad.
Montenegro	**Serbia**	Incluidas las llegadas de Kosovo.
Palestina	**Total**	Fuente: "Palestinian Central Bureau of Statistics, 2013. Hotel Activity Survey 2012. Ramallah - Palestine"
República Árabe Siria	**Total**	Encuesta del turismo receptor.
	Iraq	Los nacionales de Iraq se incluyen únicamente a partir de 2008 y se han excluido en los años anteriores (desde principios de 2008, tienen que pedir un visado para entrar en Siria; si entraron anteriormente a esa fecha, se considera que han permanecido por un periodo superior a un año, convirtiéndose en residentes).
Turquía	**Total**	Llegadas a los establecimientos homologados incluidos: hoteles, moteles, pensiones, albergues, apartahoteles, ciudades de vacaciones y hoteles especiales. Resultados de la encuesta mensual realizada en ciertos establecimientos de alojamiento clasificados por el Ministerio de Turismo.

NOTAS 2008 - 2012

3. Llegadas de turistas no residentes a los hoteles y establecimientos asimilados, por país de residencia

Alemania	**China**	Incluido Hong Kong, China.
	Otros países Asia Oriental/Pacífico	Incluido la India.
Austria	**Total**	Hoteles únicamente.
Cabo Verde	**Bélgica**	Incluido los Países Bajos.
Congo	**Total**	Fuente: "Direction Générale de l'Industrie Touristique", encuestas 2008 a 2012
Croacia	**Total**	Según el Reglamento sobre clasificación, normas mínimas y categorización de las instalaciones de alojamiento, los datos para los hoteles y establecimientos asimilados no incluyen hostales ni habitaciones con desayuno desde 2006.
Curaçao	**Total**	Grandes y pequeños hoteles, casas de huéspedes, apartamentos y bungalows.
Dinamarca	**Total**	Hoteles únicamente. 2011: cambio de metodología.
España	**Total**	Llegadas a hoteles y hostales.
Francia	**Total**	Fuente: "Insee", "Dgcis", socios regionales. Encuesta de ocupación hotelera ("EFH").
Israel	**Total**	Llegadas a los hoteles de turismo en aquellos aun no homologados.
	Todos los países de América del Sur	Incluida América Central.
Luxemburgo	**Total**	NACE Rev2 55.100
Macao (China)	**Total**	Fuente de los datos: Encuesta mensual de agencias de viajes
Nueva Caledonia	**Total**	Corresponde a los hoteles de Noumea.
Países Bajos	**Total**	Hoteles y pensiones.
Polonia	**Total**	Excluidos los hostales.
Puerto Rico	**Total**	Año fiscal de julio a junio. Hoteles endosados por la Compañía de Turismo de Puerto Rico.
	Otros países del Caribe	Se incluyen cifras agregadas de los turistas procedentes de las Antillas menores que no especificaron su país de procedencia.
	Otros países del Mundo	Incluye a los miembros de las tripulaciones.
Qatar	**Total**	Llegadas a los hoteles únicamente. 2008,2009: incluido el turismo interno.
	Todos los países de Europa	2010-2011: Europa y Américas
Rumania	**Todos los países de África**	Incluido Egipto y Libia.
Suiza	**Total**	Incluye los establecimientos de cura.
	Todos los países de África del Norte	Argelia, Libia, Marruecos y Túnez.
Togo	**Burkina Faso**	Incluidos Malí y Níger.

NOTAS 2008 - 2012

4. Llegadas de turistas no residentes en todo tipo de establecimientos de alojamiento, por nacionalidad

Eslovenia	**Total**	2008: Nueva metodología de la encuesta de alojamiento.
Hungría	**Total**	Establecimientos de alojamiento colectivo.
Montenegro	**Serbia**	Incluidas las llegadas de Kosovo.
República Árabe Siria	**Total**	Se excluye el alojamiento privado. Encuesta del turismo receptor.
	Iraq	Los nacionales de Iraq se incluyen únicamente a partir de 2008 y se han excluido en los años anteriores (desde principios de 2008, tienen que pedir un visado para entrar en Siria; si entraron anteriormente a esa fecha, se considera que han permanecido por un periodo superior a un año, convirtiéndose en residentes).
República de Moldova	**Total**	Excluido el margen izquierdo del río Nistru y la municipalidad de Bender.
Turquía	**Total**	Resultados de la encuesta mensual realizada en ciertos establecimientos de alojamiento clasificados por el Ministerio de Turismo.

4. Llegadas de turistas no residentes en todo tipo de establecimientos de alojamiento, por país de residencia

Alemania	**China**	Incluido Hong Kong, China.
	Otros países Asia Oriental/Pacífico	Incluido la India.
Austria	**Total**	Únicamente alojamiento de pago; excluidas las estancias con amigos y familiares y las viviendas secundarias.
Bélgica	**Total**	Establecimientos hoteleros, terrenos de camping, centros vacacionales, ciudades de vacaciones y categorías específicas de alojamiento. A partir de 2012 se incluye "bed and breakfast".
Croacia	**Total**	Excluidas las llegadas a puertos de turismo náutico.
Dinamarca	**Total**	Incluye el turismo no comercial. 2011: cambio de metodología.
España	**Total**	Llegadas en hoteles, hostales, camping, apartamentos turísticos y alojamientos/casas rurales.
Filipinas	**Total**	Llegadas por vía aérea.
	Nacionales residentes en el extranjero	Titulares de pasaportes filipinos que residen permanentemente en el extranjero; están excluidos los trabajadores filipinos.
Malta	**Total**	Datos procedentes de las salidas por vías aérea y marítima. Fuente: "National Statistics Office".
Rumania	**Todos los países de África**	Incluido Egipto y Libia.

5. Pernoctaciones de turistas no residentes en hoteles y establecimientos asimilados, por nacionalidad

Bolivia	**Total**	Datos preliminares. Pernoctaciones en las capitales de departamento.
Chad	**Total**	2010: Datos parciales.
Eslovenia	**Total**	2008: Nueva metodología de la encuesta de alojamiento.
Italia	**Total**	Pernoctaciones en los hoteles únicamente.
Madagascar	**Total**	Todos los establecimientos categorizados por estrellas (homologados y no homologados).
Marruecos	**Total**	Pernoctaciones en hoteles homologados, ciudades de vacaciones, residencias turísticas y Riad.
Montenegro	**Serbia**	Incluidas las llegadas de Kosovo.
Noruega	**Total**	Pernoctaciones en los establecimientos homologados. Los datos cubren solamente los establecimientos con una capacidad de 20 o más camas.
Palestina	**Total**	Fuente: "Palestinian Central Bureau of Statistics, 2013. Hotel Activity Survey 2012. Ramallah - Palestine"
República Árabe Siria	**Total**	Encuesta del turismo receptor.
	Iraq	Los nacionales de Iraq se incluyen únicamente a partir de 2008 y se han excluido en los años anteriores (desde principios de 2008, tienen que pedir un visado para entrar en Siria; si entraron anteriormente a esa fecha, se considera que han permanecido por un periodo superior a un año, convirtiéndose en residentes).
Turquía	**Total**	Hoteles homologados, moteles, pensiones, albergues, apartahoteles, ciudades de vacaciones y hoteles especiales. Resultados de la encuesta mensual realizada en ciertos establecimientos de alojamiento clasificados por el Ministerio de Turismo.
Yemen	**Total**	Incluidos los nacionales residentes en el extranjero.

NOTAS 2008 - 2012

5. Pernoctaciones de turistas no residentes en hoteles y establecimientos asimilados, por país de residencia

Alemania	**China**	Incluido Hong Kong, China.
	Otros países Asia Oriental/Pacífico	Incluido la India.
Austria	**Total**	Hoteles únicamente.
Cabo Verde	**Bélgica**	Incluido los Países Bajos.
Congo	**Total**	Fuente: "Direction Générale de l'Industrie Touristique", encuestas 2008 a 2012
Croacia	**Total**	Según el Reglamento sobre clasificación, normas mínimas y categorización de las instalaciones de alojamiento, los datos para los hoteles y establecimientos asimilados no incluyen hostales ni habitaciones con desayuno desde 2006.
Dinamarca	**Total**	Hoteles únicamente. 2011: cambio de metodología.
España	**Total**	Pernoctaciones en hoteles y hostales.
Francia	**Total**	Fuente: "Insee", "Dgcis", socios regionales. Encuesta de ocupación hotelera ("EFH").
Israel	**Total**	Pernoctaciones en hoteles de turismo y apartahoteles.
	Todos los países de América del Sur	Incluida América Central.
Luxemburgo	**Total**	NACE Rev2 55.100
Macao (China)	**Total**	Fuente de los datos: Encuesta mensual de hoteles y establecimientos asimilados
Nueva Caledonia	**Total**	Corresponde a los hoteles de Noumea.
Países Bajos	**Total**	Hoteles y pensiones.
Polonia	**Total**	Excluidos los hostales.
Qatar	**Total**	Pernoctaciones en los hoteles únicamente. 2008,2009: incluido el turismo interno.
	Todos los países de Europa	2010-2011: Europa y Américas
Rumania	**Todos los países de África**	Incluido Egipto y Libia.
Suiza	**Total**	Incluye los establecimientos de cura.
	Todos los países de África del Norte	Argelia, Libia, Marruecos y Túnez.
Togo	**Burkina Faso**	Incluidos Malí y Níger.

Yearbook of Tourism Statistics, Data 2008 – 2012, 2014 Edition

NOTAS 2008 - 2012

6. Pernoctaciones de turistas no residentes en todo tipo de establecimientos de alojamiento, por nacionalidad

Eslovenia	**Total**	2008: Nueva metodología de la encuesta de alojamiento.
Hungría	**Total**	Establecimientos de alojamiento colectivo.
Montenegro	**Serbia**	Incluidas las llegadas de Kosovo.
República Árabe Siria	**Total**	Encuesta del turismo receptor.
	Iraq	Los nacionales de Iraq se incluyen únicamente a partir de 2008 y se han excluido en los años anteriores (desde principios de 2008, tienen que pedir un visado para entrar en Siria; si entraron anteriormente a esa fecha, se considera que han permanecido por un periodo superior a un año, convirtiéndose en residentes).
República de Moldova	**Total**	Excluido el margen izquierdo del río Nistru y la municipalidad de Bender.
Turquía	**Total**	Resultados de la encuesta mensual realizada en ciertos establecimientos de alojamiento clasificados por el Ministerio de Turismo.

6. Pernoctaciones de turistas no residentes en todo tipo de establecimientos de alojamiento, por país de residencia

Alemania	**China**	Incluido Hong Kong, China.
	Otros países Asia Oriental/Pacífico	Incluido la India.
Austria	**Total**	Únicamente alojamiento de pago; excluidas las estancias con amigos y familiares y las viviendas secundarias.
Bahamas	**Total**	Pernoctaciones en todo tipo de alojamiento comercial.
Bélgica	**Total**	Establecimientos hoteleros, terrenos de camping, centros vacacionales, ciudades de vacaciones y categorías específicas de alojamiento. A partir de 2012 se incluye "bed and breakfast".
Canadá	**Total**	Fuente: "Canadian Tourism Commission" y "Statistics Canada"
	China	Incluido Mongolia y Tibet.
	Estonia	Incluido Letonia y Lituania.
	Hungría	Incluido Eslovenia, Bulgaria y Rumania.
	Dinamarca	Incluido las Islas Feroe.
	Reino Unido	Incluido Gibraltar.
	Italia	Incluido San Marino, la Santa Sede y Malta.
	Yugoslavia, RSF (antigua)	Incluido Croacia, Bosnia y Herzegovina, Ex República Yugoslava de Macedonia y Albania.
	Francia	Incluido Andorra y Mónaco.
	Suiza	Incluido Liechtenstein.
Croacia	**Total**	Excluidas las pernoctaciones en puertos de turismo náutico.
Dinamarca	**Total**	Incluye el turismo no comercial. 2011: cambio de metodología.
España	**Total**	Pernoctaciones en hoteles, hostales, camping, apartamentos turísticos y alojamientos/casas rurales.
Francia	**Total**	Fuente: "Dgcis", "Banque de France". Encuesta a los visitantes que vienen del extranjero ("EVE") - resultados 2010 y 2011 revisados, resultados 2012 provisionales
	Todos los países de África del Norte	Argelia, Egipto, Libia, Marruecos y Túnez.
	China	Incluye Hong-Kong (China) y Macao (China).
	Suiza	Incluye Liechtentein.
Irlanda	**Total**	Incluidas pernoctaciones en alojamiento privado gratuito (casas de huéspedes y casas particulares).
	Reino Unido	Incluidos los residentes de Irlanda del Norte.
Jamaica	**Total**	Se ha obtenido la información multiplicando la duración media de estancia por el numero de turistas (stop-overs) procedentes de cada país de origen. Excluidos los nacionales residentes en el extranjero.
	Otros países de las Américas	América Latina.
	Todos los países de Europa	Reino unido y resto de Europa.
Malta	**Total**	Datos procedentes de las salidas por vías aérea y marítima. Fuente: "National Statistics Office".
Países Bajos	**Total**	Excluidas las pernoctaciones en instalaciones fijas (alquiladas anualmente o por temporada).
Rumania	**Todos los países de África**	Incluido Egipto y Libia.

DATA SOURCES

Albania	Institute of Statistics – INSTAT
	http://www.instat.gov.al/
Algeria	Ministère de l'Aménagement du Territoire, de l'Environnement et du Tourisme and Office National des Statistiques
	http://www.mta.gov.dz
American Samoa	Department of Commerce - Statistics Division
	http://www.spc.int/prism/americansamoa/
Andorra	Ministerio de Turismo y Medio Ambiente and Ministerio de Finanzas
	http://www.estadistica.ad/serveiestudis/web/index.asp?lang=2
Angola	Ministério de Hotelaria e Turismo - Gabinete de Estudos, Planeamento e Estatística
Anguilla	Anguilla Statistics Department - Ministry of Finance, Economic Development, Investment, Commerce and Tourism
	http://www.gov.ai/statistics/cab_external.htm
Antigua and Barbuda	Ministry of Tourism
	http://www.visitantiguabarbuda.com/
Argentina	Dirección de Estudios de Mercado y Estadística - Secretaría de Turismo de la Nación
	http://www.turismo.gov.ar/ http://desarrolloturistico.gob.ar/estadistica/ultimas-cifras
Armenia	Tourism Department - Ministry of Economy of the Republic of Armenia
	http://www.armstat.am/en/
Aruba	Aruba Tourism Authority
	http://www.cbs.aw/index.php/statistics
Australia	Australian Bureau of Statistics
	http://www.abs.gov.au/
Austria	Statistics Austria
	http://www.statistik.at/web_en/statistics/tourism/accommodation/index.html
Azerbaijan	Ministry of Culture and Tourism and Statistical Committee
	http://www.stat.gov.az
Bahamas	Bahamas Ministry of Tourism
	http://www.tourismtoday.com/home/statistics/
Bahrain	Tourism Sector - Ministry of Culture and Information
Barbados	Barbados Tourism Authority
	http://www.tourism.gov.bb/tourism-publications.html
Belarus	State Committee of Frontier Troops and Ministry of Statistics and Analysis
Belgium	Institut National de Statistique
Belize	Belize Tourist Board
Benin	Direction du développement et de promotion touristiques - Ministère de la culture, de l'alphabétisation, de l'artisanat et du tourisme
Bermuda	Bermuda Department of Tourism
	http://www.gov.bm/portal/server.pt?space=CommunityPage&control=SetCommunity&CommunityID=227
Bhutan	Department of Tourism - Royal Government of Bhutan
	http://www.nsb.gov.bt/index.php?id=13
Bolivia	Instituto Nacional de Estadística
	http://www.ine.gov.bo/default.aspx
Bosnia and Herzegovina	Agency for Statistics of Bosnia and Herzegovina
	http://www.bhas.ba
Brazil	Ministério do Turismo
	http://www.dadosefatos.turismo.gov.br/dadosefatos/home.html
British Virgin Islands	The Development Planning Unit - Ministry of Finance
	http://dpu.gov.vg
Brunei Darussalam	Brunei Tourism - Ministry of Industry and Primary Resources

DATA SOURCES

Bulgaria	Ministry of Economy, Energy and Tourism and National Statistical Institute, Bulgarian National Bank
	http://www.nsi.bg/otrasalen.php?otr=57
Burkina Faso	Service de l'analyse statistique et de la Coopération touristique - Ministère de la Culture, des Arts et du Tourisme
	http://www.insd.bf/
Burundi	Office National du Tourisme
Cambodia	Ministry of Tourism
	http://www.tourismcambodia.org/mot/index.php?view=statistic_report#comp
Canada	Canadian Tourism Commission and Statistics Canada
	http://en-corporate.canada.travel/research/statistics-figures
Cape Verde	Instituto Nacional de Estatística Ministério da Economia, Crescimento e Competitividade
	http://www.ine.cv/dadostats/dados.aspx?d=2
Cayman Islands	Cayman Islands Department of Tourism
	http://www.caymanislands.ky/statistics/ http://www.eso.ky
Central African Republic	Ministère du Développement du Tourisme et de l'Artisanat
Chad	Ministère du Tourisme et de l'Artisanat - Direction de la Planification et des Études Prospectives
Chile	Servicio Nacional de Turismo - SERNATUR
	http://www.sernatur.cl/institucional/htm_instit/estadisticas.html
China	National Tourism Administration
	http://en.cnta.gov.cn/
Colombia	Departamento Administrativo de Seguridad (DAS) / Migración Colombia / Puertos Marítimos Ministerio de Comercio, Industria y Turismo
	http://www.mincomercio.gov.co
Comoros	Direction Nationale de la Promotion du Tourisme et de l'Hôtellerie - Ministère du Transport, Tourisme, Postes et Télécommunications Banque centrale des Comores
Congo	Direction Générale de l'Industrie Touristique - Ministère du tourisme et de l'environnement
Cook Islands	Cook Islands Tourism Corporation Cook Islands Statistics Office
Costa Rica	Banco Central de Costa Rica (BCCR) Instituto Costarricense de Turismo (ICT) Instituto Nacional de Estadística y Censos (INEC)
	http://www.visitcostarica.com/ict/paginas/modEst/estudios_demanda_turistica.asp?ididioma=1
Croatia	Central Bureau of Statistics
	http://www.dzs.hr/default_e.htm http://www.mint.hr/default.aspx?id=363
Cuba	Oficina Nacional de Estadísticas
	http://www.one.cu/sitioone2006.asp
Curaçao	Curaçao Tourist Board
	http://www.curacao.com/Corporate/Statistics
Cyprus	Statistical Service of Cyprus Cyprus Tourism Organization
	http://www.mof.gov.cy/mof/cystat/statistics.nsf/index_en/index_en?OpenDocument
Czech Republic	Czech Statistical Office, TSA Ministry for Regional Development
	http://www.czso.cz/eng/redakce.nsf/i/home
Democratic Republic of the Congo	Office National du Tourisme
Denmark	VisitDenmark
	http://www.dst.dk/HomeUK.aspx
Dominica	Discover Dominica Authority
	http://tourism.gov.dm/statistics

Yearbook of Tourism Statistics, Data 2008 – 2012, 2014 Edition

DATA SOURCES

Dominican Republic	Secretaría de Estado de Turismo
	http://www.bancentral.gov.do/estadisticas.asp?a=Sector_Turismo
Ecuador	Ministerio de Turismo
	http://servicios.turismo.gob.ec/index.php/?option=com_content&view=article&id=30#comp-i
Egypt	Ministry of Tourism
El Salvador	Corporación Salvadoreña de Turismo (CORSATUR) - Ministerio de Turismo
	http://www.elsalvador.travel/category/estadisticas/
Eritrea	Ministry of Tourism
Estonia	Estonian Tourist Board / Enterprise Estonia
	http://pub.stat.ee/px-web.2001/I_Databas/Economy/databasetree.asp
	http://visitestonia.com/en/additional-navigation/press-room/eas-views-on-tourism/estonian-tourism-statistics
Ethiopia	Ministry of Culture and Tourism
Fiji	Fiji Islands Bureau of Statistics
	http://www.statsfiji.gov.fj/
Finland	Tourism Statistics - Statistics Finland
	http://www.mek.fi/w5/mekfi/index.nsf/(pages)/Tutkimukset_ja_tilastot
France	DGCIS (Direction Générale de la Compétitivité, de l'Industrie et des Services) INSEE (Institut national de la statistique et des études économiques)
	http://www.dgcis.gouv.fr/etudes-et-statistiques/statistiques-du-tourisme/accueil http://www.insee.fr/fr/default.asp
French Polynesia	Service du Tourisme
	http://www.ispf.pf/Home.aspx http://www.servicedutourisme.gov.pf http://www.tahiti-tourisme.com/Partners/
Gambia	Gambia Tourism Authority
	http://www.visitthegambia.gm
Georgia	Georgian National Tourism Agency - Ministry of Economy and Sustainable Development National Statistics Office of Georgia
	http://www.gnta.ge/?61/statistics/&lan=en
Germany	Statistiches Bundesamt
	http://www.destatis.de
Greece	Hellenic Statistical Authority (EL STAT.)
	http://www.statistics.gr/portal/page/portal/ESYE
Grenada	Grenada Board of Tourism
Guadeloupe	Comité du Tourisme des Îles de la Guadeloupe
Guam	Guam Visitors Bureau
	http://www.bsp.guam.gov http://www.visitguam.org
Guatemala	Instituto Guatemalteco de Turismo - INGUAT
	http://www.inguat.gob.gt/estadisticas.html
Guyana	Guyana Tourism Authority
Haiti	Ministère du Tourisme
Honduras	Instituto Hondureño de Turismo
	http://www.iht.hn
Hong Kong, China	Hong Kong Tourism Board
	http://partnernet.hktb.com/en/research_statistics/index.html http://www.censtatd.gov.hk/hong_kong_statistics/index.jsp
Hungary	Hungarian Central statistical Office
	http://www.ksh.hu/tourism_catering
Iceland	Hagstofa Íslands Statistics Iceland
	http://www.statice.is/Statistics/Tourism,-transport-and-informati

DATA SOURCES

India	Ministry of Tourism - Government of India
	http://tourism.gov.in/
Indonesia	Ministry of Tourism and Creative Economy
	BPS Statistics Indonesia
	http://www.bps.go.id/eng/menutab.php?tabel=1&kat=2&id_subyek=16
	http://www.budpar.go.id/asp/index.asp
Iran, Islamic Republic of	Iran Cultural Heritage and Tourism Organization (ICHTO)
Iraq	Iraqi Tourism Board
Ireland	Fáilte Ireland
	http://www.failteireland.ie/Home
Israel	Ministry of Tourism
	http://www1.cbs.gov.il/reader/?MIval=cw_usr_view_SHTML&ID=432
Italy	Banca d'Italia
	Istituto Nazionale di Statistica (ISTAT)
	http://www.bancaditalia.it
	http://www.istat.it
Jamaica	Jamaica Tourist Board
	http://www.jtbonline.org/statistics/Annual%20Travel/Forms/AllItems.aspx
Japan	Japan Tourism Agency
	Japan National Tourism Organization
	http://www.mlit.go.jp/kankocho/en/siryou/toukei/index.html
	http://www.tourism.jp/english/statistics/index.php
Jordan	Ministry of Tourism and Antiquities
	http://www.tourism.jo
Kazakhstan	Agency of Statistics of the Republic of Kazakhstan
	http://www.eng.stat.kz/digital/Tourism/Pages/default.aspx
Kenya	Kenya Tourist Board
Kiribati	Kiribati National Tourism Office, Ministry of Communication, Transport and Tourism Development and PATA
Korea, Republic of	Ministry of Culture and Tourism
	http://kto.visitkorea.or.kr/eng/tourismStatics/keyFacts/visitorArrivals.kto
Kuwait	Central Statistical Bureau
	http://www.csb.gov.kw/Socan_Statistic_EN.aspx?ID=19
Kyrgyzstan	National Statistical Committee
Lao People's Democratic Republic	Lao National Tourism Administration
	Ministry of Information, Culture and Tourism - Tourism Development Department
	http://www.tourismlaos.org/show.php?Cont_ID=43
Latvia	Transport and Tourism Statistics Section - Central Statistical Bureau
	http://www.csb.gov.lv/en/statistikas-temas/tourism-key-indicators-30715.html
Lebanon	Ministère du Tourisme
Lesotho	Lesotho Tourism Development Corporation
	http://www.ltdc.org.ls/researchArrivalStats.php
Liechtenstein	Office of Statistics Liechtenstein. Tourism Statistics
	http://www.llv.li/amtsstellen/llv-as-tourismus.htm
Lithuania	Lithuanian State Department of Tourism
	http://www.stat.gov.lt/
Luxembourg	STATEC
	http://www.statistiques.public.lu
Macao, China	Statistics and Census Service
	Macau Government Tourist Office
	http://www.dsec.gov.mo/Statistic/TourismAndServices/VisitorArrivals.aspx
	http://industry.macautourism.gov.mo/en/index.php
Madagascar	Ministère des Transports et du Tourisme
Malawi	Ministry of Tourism, Wildlife and Culture

878

DATA SOURCES

Malaysia	Department of Statistics Malaysia Tourism Malaysia http://corporate.tourism.gov.my/research.asp?page=facts_figures
Maldives	Ministry of Tourism http://www.tourism.gov.mv
Mali	Office malien du tourisme et de l'hôtellerie (O.MA.T.HO)
Malta	Malta Tourism Authority National Statistics Office http://www.mta.com.mt/research http://www.nso.gov.mt
Marshall Islands	Marshall Islands Visitors Authority
Martinique	Comité Martiniquais du Tourisme
Mauritius	Ministry of Tourism and Leisure http://www.gov.mu/portal/site/cso/menuitem.dee225f644ffe2aa338852f8a0208a0c/?content_id=52160fa6727 8c010VgnVCM1000000a04a8c0RCRD
Mexico	Secretaría de Turismo de México (SECTUR) Instituto Nacional de Estadística y Geografía (INEGI) http://datatur.sectur.gob.mx/wb/datatur/publicaciones http://www.inegi.org.mx
Monaco	Direction du Tourisme et des Congrès http://www.gouv.mc/Action-Gouvernementale/L-Economie/Analyses-et-Statistiques/Publications
Mongolia	National Tourism Center - Ministry of Nature, Environment and Tourism
Montenegro	Ministry of Sustainable Development and Tourism http://www.monstat.org/eng/page.php?id=43&pageid=43
Montserrat	Statistics Department Montserrat
Morocco	Ministère du tourisme http://www.tourisme.gov.ma/
Mozambique	Ministry of Tourism Instituto Nacional de Estatística http://www.ine.gov.mz
Myanmar	Ministry of Hotels and Tourism http://www.myanmartourism.org/tourismstatistics.htm
Namibia	Ministry of Environment and Tourism Namibian Tourism Board http://www.namibiatourism.com.na/research-center/
Nepal	Nepal Tourism Board Ministry of Culture, Tourism and Civil Aviation http://www.tourism.gov.np
Netherlands	Statistics Netherlands http://www.cbs.nl/en-GB/menu/themas/vrije-tijd-cultuur/nieuws/default.htm
New Caledonia	Institut de la Statistique et des Études Économiques (ISEE) http://www.isee.nc/
New Zealand	Statistics New Zealand (SNZ) Ministry of Business, Innovation & Employment (MBIE) http://www.stats.govt.nz/ http://www.med.govt.nz/sectors-industries/tourism/tourism-research-data
Nicaragua	Instituto Nicaragüense de Turismo (INTUR) http://www.intur.gob.ni/index.php?option=com_content&view=article&id=27&Itemid=14
Niger	Ministère du Tourisme et de l'Artisanat Institut National de la Statistique http://www.stat-niger.org/statistique/
Nigeria	Nigerian Tourism Development Corporation
Niue	Statistics Niue
Northern Mariana Islands	Marianas Visitors Authority

DATA SOURCES

Norway	Statistics Norway Institute of Transport Economics http://www.ssb.no/english/subjects/
Oman	Ministry of Tourism Ministry of National Economy http://www.omantourism.gov.om
Pakistan	Pakistan Tourism Development Corporation - Ministry of Tourism
Palau	Office of Planning and Statistics, Bureau of Budget and Planning - Ministry of Finance Palau Visitors Authority http://www.visit-palau.com/publication/index.cfm
Palestine	Palestinian Central Bureau of Statistics http://www.pcbs.gov.ps
Panama	Autoridad de Turismo de Panamá http://www.atp.gob.pa
Papua New Guinea	Papua New Guinea Tourism Promotion Authority http://www.tpa.papuanewguinea.travel/
Paraguay	Secretaría Nacional de Turismo - SENATUR http://www.senatur.gov.py/index.php?option=com_docman&Itemid=91
Peru	Superintendencia Nacional de Migraciones (Ex DIGEMIN) Ministerio de Comercio Exterior y Turismo (MINCETUR) http://www.mincetur.gob.pe/newweb/Default.aspx?tabid=141
Philippines	Department of Tourism http://www.tourism.gov.ph/Pages/TourismResearch.aspx
Poland	Institute of Tourism http://www.intur.com.pl/itenglish/institute_en.htm
Portugal	Turismo de Portugal, I.P. http://www.ine.pt/xportal/xmain?xpid=INE&xpgid=ine_main
Puerto Rico	Junta de Planificación de Puerto Rico Compañía de Turismo de Puerto Rico http://www.jp.gobierno.pr/
Qatar	Qatar Statistics Authority http://www.qsa.gov.qa
Republic of Moldova	National Bureau of Statistics http://www.statistica.md/category.php?l=en&idc=293&
Reunion	Institut National de la Statistique et des Études Économique - INSEE Comité du Tourisme de la Réunion http://www.insee.fr/fr/themes/theme.asp?theme=13&nivgeo=24
Romania	National Institute of Statistics https://statistici.insse.ro/shop/index.jsp?page=tempo2&lang=en&context=63
Russian Federation	Russian Federal Agency for Tourism
Rwanda	Rwanda Development Board http://www.rdb.rw/welcome-to-rwanda/tourism-research-and-statistics.html
Saint Kitts and Nevis	Eastern Caribbean Central Bank http://www.eccb-centralbank.org/Statistics/index.asp#tourismdata
Saint Lucia	Saint Lucia Tourist Board http://investstlucia.com/sectors/view/tourism.html
Saint Vincent and the Grenadines	St. Vincent and the Grenadines Tourism Authority http://www.discoversvg.com/index.php/es/about-svg/tourism-statistics
Samoa	Samoa Tourism Authority Statistical Services Division (Ministry of Finance) http://www.sbs.gov.ws/ http://www.mof.gov.ws
San Marino	Segreteria di Stato per il Turismo ed i Rapporti con l'AASS http://www.statistica.sm/on-line/home/dati-statistici/attivita-economiche-e-turismo.html

Yearbook of Tourism Statistics, Data 2008 – 2012, 2014 Edition

DATA SOURCES

Sao Tome and Principe	Direcçao do Turismo e Hotelaria
Saudi Arabia	The Saudi Commission for Tourism and Antiquities (SCTA)
	http://www.mas.gov.sa/
Senegal	Ministère du Tourisme et des Transports Aériens
Serbia	Statistical Office of the Republic of Serbia National Bank of Serbia
	http://webrzs.stat.gov.rs/WebSite/
Seychelles	National Bureau of Statistics Seychelles Tourism Board
	http://www.nbs.gov.sc/
Sierra Leone	National Tourist Board Statistics Sierra Leone
	http://www.statistics.sl/
Singapore	Singapore Tourism Board
	http://www.singstat.gov.sg https://app.stb.gov.sg/asp/tou/tou02.asp#VS
Sint Maarten	St. Maarten Tourist Bureau
Slovakia	Statistical Office of the Slovak Republic National Bank of Slovakia
	www.statistics.sk www.nbs.sk www.mindop.sk
Slovenia	Statistical Office - Tourism Statistics, Structual Business Statistics, Statistical register of employment Bank of Slovenia
	http://www.stat.si/eng/tema_ekonomsko_turizem.asp
Solomon Islands	Solomon Islands National Statistics Office
South Africa	Statistics South Africa South African Tourism
	http://www.statssa.gov.za/default.asp
Spain	Instituto de Estudios Turísticos Instituto Nacional de Estadística
	http://www.iet.tourspain.es/paginas/home.aspx?idioma=es-ES http://www.ine.es/inebmenu/mnu_hosteleria.htm
Sri Lanka	Sri Lanka Tourist Board
	http://www.sltda.lk/statistics
Sudan	Ministry of Tourism and Wildlife
Suriname	Suriname Tourism Foundation
Swaziland	Swaziland Tourism Authority Ministry of Tourism, Environment and Communications
	http://www.thekingdomofswaziland.com/pages/content/index.asp?PageID=57
Sweden	Swedish Agency for Economic and Regional Growth - Tillväxtverket
	http://www.tillvaxtverket.se/english http://www.scb.se/Pages/Product____11830.aspx
Switzerland	Swiss Federal Statistical Office
	http://www.bfs.admin.ch/bfs/portal/fr/index/themen/10.html
Syrian Arab Republic	Ministry of Tourism - Survey of the incoming tourism
Taiwan (Province of China)	Planning Division Tourism Bureau - Ministry of Transportation and Communication
	http://admin.taiwan.net.tw/statistics/release_en.aspx?no=7
Tajikistan	Committee of Youth Affairs, Sports and Tourism under the Government of the Republic of Tajikistan
Thailand	Ministry of Tourism and Sports
	http://www.tourism.go.th/cover.php
The Former Yugoslav Republic of Macedonia	State Statistical Office
	http://www.stat.gov.mk/OblastOpsto_en.aspx?id=25

Yearbook of Tourism Statistics, Data 2008 – 2012, 2014 Edition

DATA SOURCES

Timor-Leste	Direcçao Nacional de Estatística
	http://dne.mof.gov.tl/publications/index.htm
Togo	Ministère du Tourisme
Tonga	Ministry of Commerce, Tourism and Labour
Trinidad and Tobago	Tourism Development Company Limited
	http://www.tdc.co.tt/stopover_statistics.htm
Tunisia	Ministère du Tourisme - Office National du Tourisme Institut National de la Statistique
	http://www.ins.nat.tn/indexfr.php
Turkey	Ministry of Culture and Tourism
	http://sgb.kulturturizm.gov.tr/belge/1-90750/turizm-istatistikleri.html http://www.turkstat.gov.tr/PreTablo.do?tb_id=51&ust_id=14
Turks and Caicos Islands	Turks and Caicos Tourist Board
Tuvalu	Ministry of Foreign Affairs, Trade, Tourism, Environment and Labour
	http://www.spc.int/prism/tuvalu/index.php/migration-and-tourism
Uganda	Ministry of Tourism, Trade and Industry Uganda Bureau of Statistics
	http://www.ubos.org/?st=pagerelations2&id=19&p=related%20pages%202:Migration%20and%20Tourism%20Statistics
Ukraine	State Statistics Committee of Ukraine
	http://www.ukrstat.gov.ua/operativ/operativ2007/tyr/tyr_e/arh_vig_e.html
United Kingdom	VisitBritain Office for National Statistics
	http://www.visitbritain.org/insightsandstatistics/ http://www.ons.gov.uk/ons/index.html
United Republic of Tanzania	Tourism Division - Ministry of Natural Resources and Tourism National Bureau of Statistics
United States of America	Office of Travel and Tourism Industries (OTTI)
	http://tinet.ita.doc.gov/ http://www.ahla.com/content.aspx?id=3448
United States Virgin Islands	Bureau of Economic Research
	http://www.usviber.org/publications.htm
Uruguay	Ministerio de Turismo y Deporte
	http://www.mintur.gub.uy
Uzbekistan	National Company "Uzbektourism"
Vanuatu	Vanuatu National Statistics Office
	http://www.vnso.gov.vu/
Venezuela	Ministerio del Poder Popular para el Turismo
	http://www.mintur.gob.ve/estadisticasTur.php
Viet Nam	Viet Nam National Administration of Tourism General Statistics Office
	http://www.vietnamtourism.com/e_pages/news/index.asp?loai=1&chucnang=07 http://www.gso.gov.vn/default_en.aspx?tabid=491
Yemen	Ministry of Tourism Central Statistical Organization
	http://www.yementourism.com/statistics/ http://www.cso-yemen.org/content.php?lng=english&pcat=131
Zambia	Ministry of Tourism and Arts
Zimbabwe	Zimbabwe Tourism Authority – ZTA
	http://www.zimbabwetourism.net/directory/index.php/downloads/category/tourism-trends

Yearbook of Tourism Statistics, Data 2008 – 2012, 2014 Edition

Other UNWTO publications of interest!

**Compendium
of Tourism Statistics
Data 2008–2012
2014 Edition**

trilingual version

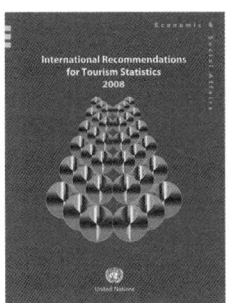

**International
Recommendations for
Tourism Statistics 2008**

published in
English, Spanish, French, Russian
Arabic and Chinese

**Tourism Satellite Account –
Recommended
Methodological Framework
2008**

published in
English, Spanish, French, Russian
Arabic and Chinese

**UNWTO
World Tourism Barometer**

Six numbers per year
published in English, Spanish,
French and Russian

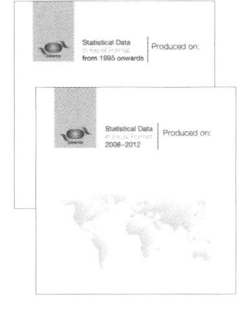

**Statistical Data in Excel™
Format**
  **– Data from 2008 – 2012
  – Data from 1995 onwards**

Seperate country tables
in Excel™ format,
updated three times per year

**Statistics and TSA
Issue Paper Series** (2013)

– Governance for the Tourism
  Sector and its Measurement

– Regional Tourism Satellite
  Account

– The Economic Impact
  of Tourism – Overview and
  Examples of Macroeconomic
  Analysis

**Sources and Methods: Labour
Statistics – Employment in the
Tourism Industries
(Special Edition)**

published in English

For UNWTO publications in printed version visit the UNWTO Infoshop: www.unwto.org/infoshop …
… and for the electronic versions visit the UNWTO Elibrary: www.e-unwto.org